Contemporary Advertising

The **Irwin/McGraw-Hill** Series in **Marketing**

Contemporary

Advertising

7th Edition

William F. Arens

Irwin
McGraw-Hill

Boston   Burr Ridge, IL   Dubuque, IA   Madison, WI   New York   San Francisco   St. Louis
Bangkok   Bogotá   Caracas   Lisbon   London   Madrid
Mexico City   Milan   New Delhi   Seoul   Singapore   Sydney   Taipei   Toronto

Irwin/McGraw-Hill

*A Division of The **McGraw·Hill** Companies*

CONTEMPORARY ADVERTISING

international   1 2 3 4 5 6 7 8 9 0 VNH/VNH 9 3 2 1 0 9 8

domestic   1 2 3 4 5 6 7 8 9 0 VNH/VNH 9 3 2 1 0 9 8

ISBN 0-256-26253-5

Vice president and editorial director: *Michael W. Junior*
Publisher: *Gary Burke*
Executive editor: *Stephen M. Patterson*
Senior developmental editor: *Diane E. Beausoleil*
Senior marketing manager: *Colleen J. Suljic*
Senior project manager: *Susan Trentacosti*
Production supervisor: *Scott M. Hamilton*
Designer: *Michael Warrell*
Cover illustrator: *Wendy Grossman*
Senior photo research coordinator: *Keri Johnson*
Photo research: *Michael J. Hruby and Associates*
Supplement coordinator: *Becky Szura*
Compositor: *Precision Graphics/H&S Graphics*
Typeface: *10/12 Garamond Light*
Printer: *Von Hoffmann Press, Inc.*

Library of Congress Cataloging-in-Publication Data

Arens, William F.
    Contemporary advertising / William F. Arens. — 7th ed.
        p.   cm.
    Includes bibliographical references and index.
    ISBN 0-256-26253-5
    1. Advertising.   I. Title.
HF5821.B62   1999
659.1--dc21   98-8632

INTERNATIONAL EDITION
Copyright © 1999. Exclusive rights by The McGraw-Hill Companies, Inc. for manufacture and export.
This book cannot be re-exported from the country to which it is consigned by McGraw-Hill. The International Edition is not available in North America.

When ordering the title, use ISBN 0-07-115652-6

http://www.mhhe.com

To John O'Toole,
a gentleman amongst men.
Thanks for the **memories.**

The **Preface**

Everyone living and working in the modern world today is influenced by advertising. In fact, at some time in their lives, most people become creators of advertising—whether they design a flier for a school car wash, write classified ads for a garage sale, or develop a whole campaign for a business, charity, or political endeavor.

While advertising may have been viewed as a particularly American institution in the first half of the 20th century, that is certainly no longer the case. In fact, as early as 1917, British novelist Norman Douglas affirmed the global significance of advertising when he remarked, "You can tell the ideals of a nation by its advertisements." That was before radio and television. Today, our voices are no longer limited by the scope of 20th-century media. Thanks to the Internet and a variety of online database services, people and organizations can now send advertising messages to millions of people around the world instantly. Advertising is undergoing a transformation of historic proportions—from a monopolistic corporate monolog to a totally democratic dialog. Suddenly everybody has a voice.

www.mhhe.com/arens That makes the study of advertising more important today than ever before, not only for students of business or journalism (who may be contemplating a career in the field) but also for students of sociology, psychology, political science, economics, history, language, science, or the arts. Most of these people will become users of advertising; all will be lifetime consumers of it.

The study of advertising gives students, regardless of their major, many valuable tools to use in any subsequent profession. For example, it helps them learn to:

- Plan and think strategically.
- Gather and analyze primary and secondary research data.
- Compute and evaluate the potential of alternative courses of action.
- Cooperate with a team in developing creative solutions to a problem.
- Analyze competitive proposals.
- Understand why people behave the way they do.
- Express themselves and their ideas with clarity and simplicity.
- Persuade others to their point of view.
- Appreciate and assess the quality of different creative endeavors.
- Use data to speak with knowledge, confidence, and conviction.

In addition, students of business and journalism gain several specific benefits from studying advertising. For example, it can help them:

- Discern the real economic, social, and cultural roles of advertising and, conversely, the impact of a society's values on advertising.
- Understand how advertising supports the profession of journalism and relates to the whole field of communications.
- Appreciate the important global effect of marketing and advertising on business, industry, and national economies.
- Comprehend the strategic function of advertising within the broader context of business and marketing.
- Evaluate and appreciate the impressive artistic creativity and technical expertise advertising requires.
- Discover what people in advertising and related disciplines do, how they do it, and the expanding career opportunities these fields now offer.

Student-Oriented Features for the 21st Century

In previous editions of *Contemporary Advertising,* our mission was to present advertising as it is actually practiced—to put flesh on the bones of academic theory—with clarity and verve. As we enter the 21st century, our purpose remains the same. Advertising should be taught as it really is: as a business, a marketing tool, a creative process, and a dynamic, hybrid discipline that employs various elements of the arts and sciences. We also believe advertising should be taught in an intelligible manner and lively style relevant to today's student.

For these reasons, *Contemporary Advertising* provides a number of exclusive student-oriented features.

Award-Winning Graphic Design

Contemporary Advertising has always been distinguished by its elegant, coffee-table-book feel and award-winning graphic design—an important feature for a book that has the responsibility of teaching students about the importance of quality in advertising art and production. The open, airy look (reinforced by the book's high-quality, non-see-through, clay-coated paper stock) contributes to learning by making the text material colorful, inviting, and accessible to the widest range of students. In the Seventh Edition, the elegance of this design is further enhanced with a completely new cover design, a striking new interior color palette, beautiful new part and chapter openers, and a redesign of all the technical illustrations for greater clarity and simplicity. The text material is made reader-friendly with part and chapter overviews, chapter learning objectives, and key terms printed in boldface.

Chapter-Opening Vignettes

To capture and hold student interest, each chapter begins not with a case but with a story. Written in a warm, narrative style, each vignette depicts an actual situation that illustrates a basic concept in the study of advertising. Wherever possible, the opening story is then woven through the chapter to demonstrate how textbook concepts actually come to life in real-world situations. For example, throughout Chapter 1, we use the history of the world's first branded commodity—Sunkist—to trace the development and growth of modern advertising and to demonstrate its marketing and economic functions. In Chapter 6, we use the charming story of Healthtex baby clothes to illustrate the depth and complexity of marketing and advertising research. And in Chapter 9, we wrapped the whole subject of creativity and the creative process around the story of how the VitroRobertson agency developed its magnificent, award-winning campaign for Taylor Guitars.

Extensive Illustration Program

The best way to teach is to set a good example. So each of the 17 chapters features beautiful full-color illustrations of currently running, award-winning ads, commercials, and campaigns that demonstrate the best in the business from the last three years. In fact, *Contemporary Advertising* is one of the most heavily illustrated textbooks on the market, with all the major media—print, electronic, outdoor—represented in a balanced manner. We carefully selected the examples and illustrations for both their quality and their relevance to students.

Furthermore, we feature a mix of local, national, and international ads from both business-to-business and consumer campaigns. In-depth captions tell the stories behind many of the ads and explain how the ads demonstrate the concepts discussed in the text.

The book is liberally illustrated with models, charts, graphs, and tables. Some of these encapsulate useful information on advertising concepts or the advertising industry. Others depict the processes employed in account management, research, account planning, media planning, and production.

Full-Color Portfolios

In addition to the individual print ads and actual frames from TV commercials, the book contains several multipage portfolios of outstanding creative work. These include Strategic Use of the Creative Mix, Award-Winning

Magazine Advertising, Hot Web Sites, Corporate Advertising, and others. Accompanying captions and questions tie the ads to topics germane to the chapter in which they appear.

Creative Department The Creative Department is a special section in Chapter 13 that describes how an interesting print ad and TV commercial were produced from beginning to end. A full-color print ad for the 1998 Toyota 4Runner sports utility vehicle features an actual acetate color key (called a *transvision*)—a first in advertising texts. And the TV commercial for the 4Runner created by Saatchi & Saatchi Los Angeles illustrates an extraordinary combination of artistry, sensitivity, and subtle humor as a harried New York executive experiences a personal epiphany.

Ad Labs Active participation enhances learning, so Ad Labs play a significant role in every chapter. These unique sidebars to the world of advertising introduce students to topics of current interest or controversy and then involve them in the subject by posing questions that stimulate critical thinking. Among the many topics presented in Ad Labs are government regulation, bottom-up marketing, creativity, the psychological impact of color, advertising on the Internet, "green" marketing, sales promotion, and direct-response advertising.

Ethical Issues in Advertising Today's students will be 21st-century practitioners. They will face new and challenging ethical issues, and they will need to exercise even greater sensitivity than their 20th-century counterparts. Therefore, in *every* chapter of the book, we introduce a current Ethical Issue in advertising—to focus attention on the most critical social questions facing advertisers today. These include the debate over puffery, advertising to children, comparative advertising, the targeting of ethnic minorities, privacy, negative political advertising, visual and statistical manipulation, and other issues.

Practical Checklists Advertising is a broad subject encompassing many disciplines, and one dilemma both advertising students and practitioners face is how to handle and organize large volumes of information and then creatively convert these data into effective advertising. For this reason, students truly appreciate the numerous, handy Checklists that appear regularly throughout the text. The Checklists can stimulate memory, organize thinking, and reinforce important concepts. They include a Checklist for Writing Effective Copy, Checklist for International Media Planning, Checklist for Creating Effective TV Commercials, and Checklist for Writing News Releases, to mention just a few. In the years that follow, students will find the Checklists an invaluable, practical career resource for developing marketing and advertising plans, writing and designing effective ads and commercials, selecting and scheduling media, evaluating advertising proposals, and making advertising decisions.

Reference Library In keeping with our desire to build long-term value into the book (without adding text length), we introduced the Reference Library as a new feature in the Sixth Edition. Located at the end of the book immediately following Epilogue: The Complete Campaign, the Reference Library contains a wealth of supplementary exhibits, checklists, tables, and models for students or professors who seek additional information or greater detail on a subject of interest. The exhibits in the Reference Library are numbered to correspond to relevant chapters. Professors can assign this material or not, depending on their course objectives. But students will find the Reference Library a valuable, long-term handbook for their future careers and lives. Exhibits in the Reference Library include Advertising Regulations in Western Europe; Using Marketing Research for New Product Development; Checklist of Product Marketing Facts for Creatives; Detailed Explanation of Duncan's IMC Model; Trade-Show Budgeting Checklist; and many, many others.

Additional Learning Aids Each chapter concludes with a summary followed by questions for review and discussion. These pedagogical aids are designed to help students review chapter contents and assimilate what they have learned. Throughout the text, key ideas and terms are highlighted with boldface type and defined when introduced. The definitions of all these terms are collected at the end of the book in a thorough and extensive Glossary.

NEW Internet Exercises The Internet is the fastest-growing medium in the history of advertising, so it is important for students to become familiar and comfortable with the Net and to understand the resources it offers. In the new Seventh Edition, each chapter features exercises that require students to access the World Wide Web and research questions relevant to the chapter topic.

For the **Professor:** The Seventh Edition Has Been **Extensively Revised** Our continuing goal has been to bring clarity to the often murky subject of advertising. Our method has been to personally involve students as much as possible in the practical experiences of advertising while simultaneously giving them a clear understanding of advertising's dynamic role in both marketing management and the human communication process. In the pursuit of this objective, we have made numerous modifications and improvements in the Seventh Edition of *Contemporary Advertising*.

Because of the growing importance of integrated marketing communications (IMC) and the changing role of advertising in the marketing mix, we have restructured the sequence of some chapters and included a significant amount of new material in them. For instance, to illustrate early on how marketers integrate advertising with other marketing communications tools, we have introduced in Chapter 1 new material on direct marketing, personal selling, sales promotion, public relations, events and sponsorships, and corporate advertising, and then devoted all of Part Three to these topics, before our discussion of advertising creativity. New material, and even new chapters, on the economics of advertising, relationship marketing and IMC, the new digital interactive media, and global/international advertising will help keep *Contemporary Advertising* both current and comprehensive.

Current and Concise In this edition, our first effort was to update all statistics and tables and to document the most recent academic and professional source material to give *Contemporary Advertising* the most current and relevant compendium of academic and trade citations in the field. We've referenced important recent research on topics ranging from the effects of advertising and sales promotion on brand-building to relationship marketing, integrated communications, and Internet advertising. And we've introduced or redesigned the building-block models that facilitate student comprehension of the often complex processes involved in human communication, consumer behavior, marketing research, and IMC.

Second, thanks to recommendations from our academic reviewers, we have attempted to bring a clearer theoretical structure to the book. For example, in Part One, we introduce the principles of free enterprise economics. Then, throughout the part, we show how these principles have affected the evolution of modern advertising from a 19th century American phenomenon to an accepted global practice in the 21st century. This framework creates the underpinning for our discussion of the social and regulatory aspects of advertising as well as our examination of how the business of advertising has evolved from local to national to global. In the next two parts, contemporary theories of marketing and communication create the framework for our discussion of advertising's role in marketing and integrated marketing communications. This then evolves to a theory of creative excellence in Part Four. In Part Five, all these theories come together as advertisers search for the most economically efficient communications media to create effective marketing relationships with customers and other stakeholders.

Third, we have prudently governed the length of the text material. While integrating new material on the economic aspects of advertising, personal selling, sponsorships, and digital interactive media, we maintained a manageable length. The main body of text still measures only 350 pages. The remaining 300 pages are devoted to illustrations, graphics, sidebar information, and design, all of which keep the text open, airy, and inviting while sharpening *clarity*—the hallmark of *Contemporary Advertising*.

Compared to the true length of other comprehensive course books, some of which have masked almost 25 percent more body text by the clever compression of type, *Contemporary Advertising* is actually one of the most concise texts in the field.

Fresh, Contemporary, Relevant Examples

We added many new, real-world examples, selected for their currency and their relevance to students. Likewise, many of the chapter-opening stories are new, such as the advertising success stories of Healthtex, Windows 95, IMGIS, Toyota, and the "Got milk?" campaign. Others document marketing or communications misfires by companies like Prodigy and Intel, and even advertising controversies such as Calvin Klein's. All of the full-color portfolios have been updated, expanded, or replaced with more recent examples and all of the Ad Labs, Checklists, and Ethical Issues have been updated and edited for currency and accuracy.

Global Orientation Integrated Throughout

In light of the increasing globalization of business, we've introduced the subject of global advertising early in the book in a revised Chapter 3: "The Scope of Advertising: From Local to Global." We've also added more examples of international advertising throughout the book. All the international data have been extensively revised and updated to reflect the increased importance of advertising in the new economic and marketing realities of Europe. Throughout the text, a new global icon denotes international examples or data.

NEW Tech Talk Boxes

In recent years, the technology of advertising has changed dramatically. For example, in just the last decade, the computer has revolutionized the way advertising is planned, designed, produced, and scheduled. And the introduction of the new digital interactive media is sparking another creative revolution in advertising. To highlight the integration of technology and advertising, we developed an all-new feature for the Seventh Edition: Tech Talk boxes. We've included one in every chapter. Cutting-edge topics include wireless communications, presentation technology, electronic prepress technology, high-definition TV, media planning software, direct marketing technology, and others. In all cases, we explain the new technology, how it works, and its use in or effect on advertising.

Focus on Integrated Marketing Communications

One result of this exploding technology—and consequent market fragmentation—has been the growing realization by major advertisers and agencies of the importance of relationship marketing and integrated marketing communications. In response to this, we have woven the IMC perspective throughout the text. We first introduce the concept of IMC in Chapter 1. Next, in Part Two, we explain its impact on marketing, advertising, and media planning. Then we focus all of Part Three on how companies build relationships by integrating their advertising with other marketing communications tools. Finally, in Part Five, we show how each of the major media contributes to the IMC process. Throughout, we cite the most recent important research on all these topics.

NEW Epilogue: The Complete Campaign

So that students can see how many of the principles taught in the text come together in the real world, we have included an Epilogue, immediately following Chapter 17, on the complete story behind the currently running, highly successful "Everyday" branding campaign for Toyota created by Saatchi & Saatchi Los Angeles. We are indebted to both Saatchi & Saatchi and Toyota for authorizing us to share the details of this interesting, student-relevant campaign.

Local and Business-to-Business Advertising Coverage

Throughout the book, *Contemporary Advertising* addresses the needs of both small and large consumer and business-to-business advertisers with its many examples, case histories, Ad Labs, Checklists, and advertisements. Moreover, this is one of the few texts to devote adequate attention to the needs of the small retail advertiser by discussing how local advertisers can integrate their marketing communications.

Highlights of This Revision

While all the chapters have been edited and updated, other specific highlights of the Seventh Edition include the following:

Chapter 1: The Dimensions of Advertising. We begin the book by offering a slightly modified definition of advertising—as *composed* and *structured* communication. Immediately following the definition, we present the communication process, along with a new diagram of Stern's advertising communication model. We have moved the introductory marketing material up from Chapter 4, since that's what actually defines advertising's role in business. This discussion also enables us to present the concept of IMC and to differentiate advertising from other marketing communications tools. The chapter then introduces the economic framework and uses it to illustrate the evolution of advertising. We also augment the history section with a thorough discussion of the impact of new technology, which lays the groundwork for the creative revolution on the horizon. The Ethical Issue in this chapter focuses on puffery.

Chapter 2: The Economic, Social, and Regulatory Aspects of Advertising. This chapter has been retitled and opens with a new story—the highly controversial campaign for Calvin Klein Jeans. This sets the stage for a detailed discussion of advertising's proper role in our economic system and our society. By using the economic framework set up in Chapter 1 for our discussion of advertising controversies, we have a basis for understanding how advertising may contribute to or detract from the basic goal of free enterprise: "the most good for the most people." In the section on the social impact of advertising, we classify the criticisms of advertising into two groups: short-term manipulative arguments and long-term macro arguments. The chapter offers a more balanced presentation of what's right and wrong about advertising, acknowledging the profession's shortcomings—for instance, in the area of deception with the widespread use of puffery, and in the area of sexual and ethnic stereotyping. The discussion of deception in advertising has been updated, referencing the recent work by Ivan Preston. We treat the subject of ethics in advertising in the text, and we modified our model explaining the levels of ethical responsibility. Further, the Ethical Issue in this chapter explains the difference between an ethical dilemma and an ethical lapse.

Chapter 3: The Scope of Advertising: From Local to Global. This chapter has also been retitled and extensively reorganized. The chapter discusses the organizations involved in the advertising business. Beginning with the advertisers, the chapter classifies them by their scope of business: local, regional, national, and transnational. Much of the material from the Local Advertising chapter in the Sixth Edition was moved to this chapter, enabling us to eliminate that chapter entirely from the Seventh Edition. The agency section demonstrates what agency people do and how they work. We expanded the material on account planning as well as the material on the media and suppliers in order to present a balanced view of all the participants in the advertising industry.

Chapter 4: Marketing and Consumer Behavior: The Foundations of Advertising. The marketing misfire of Prodigy's online service introduces this chapter and demonstrates the important role marketing plays in advertising success. The chapter discusses the main participants in the marketing process and then focuses on the consumer, pointing out that consumer behavior is the key to advertising success. In the section on learning and persuasion, we introduce Petty, Cacioppo, and Schumann's Elaboration Likelihood Model and compare the central route to the peripheral route to persuasion. Then, in the section on needs and motives, the chapter explains Rossiter and Percy's classification system of informational and transformational purchase and usage motives. The Ethical Issue analyzes the line between marketing and exploitation.

Chapter 5: Market Segmentation and the Marketing Mix: Determinants of Advertising Strategy. We retitled this chapter to more clearly define the topics discussed. The chapter briefly discusses how marketing strategies have evolved and explains the challenge of finding profitable market niches as segments become smaller and smaller. While we expanded the coverage of international information, such as segmenting methods used in Europe, and focused more attention on the role of branding, we also succeeded in cutting the chapter's overall length. We describe the elements of the marketing mix as product, price, distribution, and communication, referring to the 4Ps as a convenient mnemonic device for remembering these elements. The Ethical Issue deals with the morality of targeting ethnic markets.

Chapter 6: Information Gathering: Inputs to Advertising Planning. Here again, we retitled the chapter to indicate a slight change of focus. The chapter is now more advertising specific. The successful, award-winning campaign for Healthtex children's wear is recounted in the chapter-opening story and then used throughout the chapter to demonstrate the basic steps in the research process. We reorganized the chapter substantially. The Seventh Edition presents all the qualitative material first and then keeps all the quantitative material together following that. We also expanded the international material substantially. The Ethical Issue looks at the uses and misuses of research statistics.

Chapter 7: Marketing and Advertising Planning: Top-Down, Bottom-Up, and IMC. This chapter has been extensively revised. We present the three models for marketing planning in use today: top-down, bottom-up, and integrated marketing communications (IMC). The Saturn story, highlighted with many illustrations and specific examples, demonstrates the importance of IMC and serves as an apt case for introducing this popular new concept and process. We moved the IMC material, previously in Chapter 15, up to this chapter to reflect the growing importance of IMC planning. The section on advertising planning now includes a discussion of SWOT analysis. We also show how the accepted concept of advertising effects is changing in light of new research. In the section on the creative mix, we expanded our discussion of the new Kim-Lord Grid, an improvement over the old FCB Grid, to further clarify the product concept element for students. The Ethical Issue considers the comparative advertising wars.

Chapter 8: Planning Media Strategy: Finding Links to the Market. Chapter 8 features a new opening story—the incredibly successful launch of Windows 95. We discuss the growing importance of media planning in light of the proliferation of media options and the interest in IMC. We also expanded our discussion of message distribution objectives and completely reorganized the section for greater clarity and depth of understanding. The Ethical Issue in this chapter deals with negative political advertising.

Chapter 9: Relationship Building: Direct Marketing, Personal Selling, and Sales Promotion. This chapter begins a new unit in the book, Part Three: Integrating Advertising with Other Elements of the Communications Mix. Some of the material for this chapter came from the old Chapter 15, but the focus and much of the topical material are completely new to the Seventh Edition. For instance, we moved previous material on direct mail to its rightful place within the media unit (now Chapter 16). That material has been replaced with a completely new section on personal selling. This chapter, and indeed this whole part, focuses on the philosophy that, while advertising can create an image for a company, a reputation must be earned. In other words, *everything* a company does (and doesn't do, for that matter) sends a message to its various stakeholders. Advertising, along with sales promotion, personal selling, and other marketing communications tools, just happens to be one of the *planned* messages that companies employ. While the integration of marketing with other company functions is beyond the scope of this book, it is important for advertising people to be aware of these other communications tools, and they need to recognize (at the planning stage) that some of them are better suited for solving certain marketing problems than advertising is. Still, they must all be integrated with everything else a company does to truly realize the firm's reputation potential. We've enhanced the section on direct marketing with substantial new material about database marketing and management, including Bob Stone's RFM formula. We've also focused on the importance of direct marketing to IMC programs. Personal selling is presented as the "human" medium, and again our focus is on its use in IMC. The sales promotion section leads off with a fun new story about the introduction of Snapple's Mango Madness—a big media and sales promotion idea from Kirshenbaum Bond & Partners in New York. We've clarified the distinction between push and pull strategies, and we've added a section on the importance of sales promotion to IMC. The Ethical Issue discusses the ethical cost of gifts and commissions.

Chapter 10: Relationship Building: Public Relations, Sponsorship, and Corporate Advertising. Continuing the same themes, the second chapter in this new part was Chapter 16 in the Sixth Edition. We've added a stronger IMC focus to the chapter and broadened the material with a completely new section on events and sponsorships. We lead that segment off with the story of how Bennett Gibbs turned his $200,000-a-year local bike shop into a $3 million enterprise through the effective use of event sponsorship. The section explains the various types of sponsorships companies use and discusses topics like sports marketing and ambush marketing. The Ethical Issue debates the controversy surrounding advertorials.

Chapter 11: Creative Strategy and the Creative Process. Formerly Chapter 9, this chapter was new to the Sixth Edition and received kudos from our academic reviewers. In the Seventh Edition we have enhanced the chapter by leading off with a theory of advertising excellence based on two dimensions of greatness: audience resonance and strategic relevance. The chapter examines the nature of creativity, styles of thinking, and the role of the agency creative team. It also explains the importance of creativity, showing how creativity puts the "boom" factor in advertising. We retained the chapter-opening story—VitroRobertson's highly creative campaign for Taylor Guitars—and the Ethical Issue from the last edition on the controversy surrounding the use of sex appeal in advertising. We've also added a section dealing with the development of message strategies for international audiences.

Chapter 12: Creative Execution: Art and Copy. We retained the elegant Timberland story to introduce this chapter since it is a stunning example of the best in advertising copywriting and art direction. We added a section on principles of design, explaining which design formats work best. We've included a completely new illustration program in this chapter, and the art director's portfolio contains current, student-relevant ads to enliven the text matter. The Ethical Issue in this chapter discusses plagiarism and shows how close borrowing can come to stealing.

Chapter 13: Producing Ads for Print, Electronic, and Digital Media. This chapter begins with a completely new opening story about the development of the currently running print ad for the 1998 Toyota 4Runner sports utility vehicle, and we weave this story throughout the chapter. In the television section, for instance, we explain the development of the 4Runner TV commercial, which is a completely different execution of the same strategic idea. Then we revisit the story in the Creative Department: From Concept through Production of a Magazine Ad and TV Commercial. The chapter was carefully edited throughout to ensure that students gain the most practical information possible on how to manage the production of quality print, broadcast, and digital media materials. An updated Ethical Issue focuses on the morality of using high-tech methods to make changes in other people's artistic work.

Chapter 14: Using Print Media. The well-known "milk mustache" campaign from the National Fluid Milk Processor Promotion Board provides a fresh opening for the magazine section of this chapter, and we retained the amusing story about the irreverent campaign for the *Village Voice* for the newspaper section. Following the chapter-opening story, we've added a brief discussion of the role of the media buyer. The section on using magazines in the creative mix has been reorganized, and we reduced the section on Print Media and New Technologies, moving much of that material to the new Chapter 16. We carefully edited the chapter for currency, efficiency, and clarity. The Ethical Issue discusses employee medical problems that may arise in the absence of ethical decisions about the workplace environment.

Chapter 15: Using Electronic Media: Television and Radio. Since we used the milk mustache story in Chapter 14, we decided to start Chapter 15 with the other side of the coin: the highly popular, award-winning "Got milk?" television campaign from the California Milk Processor Board. We've added a section on the use of TV in IMC, and we've edited and updated the material on measuring TV audiences. Similarly, in the radio section, we've added a discussion of how to use radio in an IMC program. The material on digital interactive media has been moved to the new Chapter 16. The Ethical Issue in this chapter focuses on advertising to and through children.

Chapter 16: Using Digital Interactive Media and Direct Mail. This is a completely new chapter in the Seventh Edition, created in response to the realities of our changing advertising world. The chapter-opening story concerns the success of IMGIS—the technological leader in the management and targeting of Internet advertising founded by two savvy brothers in their mid-twenties. The chapter discusses the history of the Internet, the growth of online services and the World Wide Web, the different types of digital interactive advertising available, some of the problems with Internet advertising, and the use of these new media in IMC. The last part of the chapter deals with direct mail as a medium and explains its use in IMC programs as well. The Ethical Issue in this chapter discusses privacy—the individual's rights versus the rights of the public.

Chapter 17: Using Out-of-Home, Exhibitive, and Supplementary Media. We added an overview section on out-of-home media to the beginning of this chapter. In the outdoor advertising portion, we added a discussion of the new technologies, such as global positioning systems, that companies are using to produce and sell outdoor. We updated and streamlined the information on outdoor and transit advertising. From the *exhibitive media* section (media designed to bring customers eyeball-to-eyeball with the product) we removed point of purchase and moved it to the Sales Promotion chapter. The supplementary media section features an expanded discussion of product placement in movies. The Ethical Issue discusses the effect of spillover media on unintended audiences, such as children.

Epilogue: The Complete Campaign: "Toyota/Everyday." The fascinating, new branding campaign for Toyota developed by Saatchi & Saatchi Los Angeles shows in detail how all the concepts taught in the book come together in real life. A video supplement to the text includes commercials from the campaign.

Reference Library. We've completely redesigned the Reference Library to make it easier to find and use. Many of the most popular elements from the Sixth Edition have been retained, and we've added others we believe professors and students will find helpful.

Appendix C: Integrated Marketing Communications Plan Outline. Complementing the Top-Down Marketing and Advertising Plan Outlines in Appendixes A and B, we've added an IMC Plan Outline as Appendix C. This IMC plan was developed by Brannon Wait at Saatchi & Saatchi Los Angeles. We appreciate his permission to use it, and we hope students find the plan useful in their future endeavors.

Appendix D: Career Planning in Advertising. This section has been completely updated with many helpful hints for students about to launch their careers. It includes salary figures for entry-level employees in a variety of advertising-related positions.

Appendix E: Industry Resources. This appendix organizes a great deal of practical information students can use to perform further research in areas of interest or to advance their careers by joining an organization focused on their specialty.

Supplementary Materials

While the text itself is a complete introduction to the field of advertising, it is accompanied by a number of valuable supplemental materials designed to assist the instructor.

Instructor's Manual

With the assistance of Jack Whidden, to whom we are truly indebted, we expanded the Instructor's Manual to include a wealth of new material and suggestions for classroom lectures and discussions. It includes a lecture outline for each chapter, answers to all discussion questions, including the end-of-chapter Internet exercises, suggested workshops, projects, and debates, and additional material for reading or project assignments.

Video Supplements

To illustrate how the principles discussed in the text have actually been applied in business, the book is supplemented by two special video programs and a video instructor's guide. One video was produced exclusively for *Contemporary Advertising* by the author for instructor use in the classroom. It includes a wide variety of domestic and international commercials specially referenced with voiceover introductions to specific chapters. Not only is this video text-specific in subject matter, but it also includes many of the commercials discussed in the text—such as the Toyota campaign from the Epilogue, the Got milk? campaign discussed in Chapter 15, and the Saturn campaign from Chapter 7, to mention just a few.

The second video was produced by the Advertising Educational Foundation, to whom we express our deep gratitude and appreciation. It includes a behind-the-scenes look at advertising research at work. The video, entitled "Good-bye Guesswork: How Research Guides Today's Advertisers," includes case studies for V8 Juice, Maidenform, and AT&T's toll-free service, and shows how research is used to develop new ads, refine ad campaigns, decide the best place to advertise, and evaluate current ads.

Offered at no charge to adopters of *Contemporary Advertising,* these video supplements are designed to help the instructor teach real-world decision making and demonstrate some of the best current examples of television advertising from around the world.

Color Transparencies

Also available to instructors is a high-quality selection of overhead transparencies. These include important models and graphs presented in the text and over 70 ads from the text, all produced in full color.

PowerPoint Presentation Materials

In addition, Irwin/McGraw-Hill offers adopters of *Contemporary Advertising* a complete PowerPoint presentation created by Jack Whidden for use in class. This includes some 100 full-color slides of the key points made in each chapter as well as most of the tables and models employed—a real boon to the classroom lecture.

NEW Internet Web Site Complementing the Seventh Edition is a new Internet Web site (www.mhhe.com/arens). Our hope is that both professors and students will find the supplemental material on this site (such as our semiannual newletter and hot links to other interesting Web sites) both useful and enjoyable, and we welcome your feedback.

Testing Systems An extensive bank of objective test questions prepared by Tom Pritchett and Betty Pritchett of Kennesaw State University was carefully designed to provide a fair, structured program of evaluation.

- Diploma—a microcomputer testing system that provides convenient and flexible retrieval from an extensive bank of questions to use as is or with additional questions of your own.

Presentation CD-ROM This instructor's CD-ROM contains all the supplements in an electronic format, as well as selected video clips.

Uses for This **Text** *Contemporary Advertising* was written for undergraduate students in liberal arts, journalism, and business schools. However, because of its practical, hands-on approach, depth of coverage, and marketing management emphasis, it is also widely used in independent schools, university extension courses, and courses on advertising management. The wealth of award-winning advertisements also makes it a resource guide to the best work in the field for students in art and graphic design courses and for professionals in the field.

Many of the stories, materials, and techniques included in this text come from the author's personal experience as a full-time marketing communications executive and adjunct professor at San Diego State University and the University of California at San Diego. Others come from the experiences of friends and colleagues in the business. We believe this book will be a valuable resource guide, not only in the study of advertising but later in the practice of it as well. In all cases, we hope readers will experience the feel and the humanness of the advertising world—whether they intend to become professionals in the business, to work with practitioners, or simply to become more sophisticated consumers.

William F. Arens

Our **Thanks**

Writing a textbook on any subject is a mammoth undertaking. An advertising textbook, though, would be virtually impossible without the assistance and cooperation of a legion of individuals on the professional side. I am therefore deeply indebted to many individuals in advertising and related fields for their personal encouragement and professional assistance. These include, but are certainly not limited to, Joyce Harrington and Burtch Drake at the American Association of Advertising Agencies; Paula Alex and Linda McCreight at the Advertising Educational Foundation; Shawn O'Neill at IMGIS; Bob Pritikin at the Mansion, San Francisco; Vonda LePage, Stephen McGinniss, and Lynne Collins at FCB/Leber Katz; Phillippe Krakowski at BBDO; Peter Farago at Farago & Partners; Larry Jones and Nicoletta Poloynis at Foote Cone & Belding, Los Angeles, and Tom Robbins at FCB, San Francisco; Russ Hanlin and Gene Sass at Sunkist Growers; Jackie Rigoni at Publicis/Hal Riney & Partners; Vicki Holman and Steve Shannon at Saturn Corporation; Jo Muse at Muse Cordero Chen; Gerry Rubin at Rubin Postaer; Cindy Becker and Alan Bonine at VitroRobertson, San Diego; John Martin at Healthtex and Beth Rilee-Kelley at the Martin Agency, Richmond; Michael Gerard at Snow Valley Ski Resort; Maureen Sweeney at Sweeney Media; Diana Adachi at ViewZ; John Garrett, SRI International; Brandy Constantino, Sean Hardwick, and Duncan Milner at TBWA/Chiat Day, Los Angeles; Raphaële at Raphaële Digital Transparencies; Jon Bond at Kirshenbaum, Bond & Partners; and Paula Veale at the Ad Council.

Also I extend heartfelt thanks to everybody at Saatchi & Saatchi Los Angeles and Toyota Motor Sales U.S.A. for their invaluable assistance, openness, and cooperation in providing the material for our chapter on advertising production and the complete campaign in the Epilogue. These include Michael Bevan and David Pelliccioni at Toyota and Scott Gilbert, Joe McDonagh, Sally Reinman, Bill Gordon, Emily Weiss, Kim Edward, Kim Wright, Mike Whitlow, Doug Van Andel, Damon Webster, Charlene Washburn, Alicia Perez, Dean Van Eimeren, and Brannon Wait at Saatchi & Saatchi.

For their warm, open, and gracious contributions of time, counsel, and materials, I extend my appreciation, *avec tous mes remerciements,* to all our Canadian friends, especially Joe Mullie at the Association des Agences de Publicité du Quebec; Chuck McDonald and Robert West at Schering Canada; François Duffar, Daniel Rabinowicz, Pierre Delagrave, Nicole Lapierre, Normand Chiasson, Ian Saville, Jocelyn Laverdure, and Manon Caza at Cossette Communication-Marketing; Marcel Barthe at Optimum; François Descarie at Impact Research; Yves Gougoux at Publicis/BCP Stratégie Créativité; Andre Morrow at Marketel; Patrick Pierra at *InfoPress;* Paul Lavoie at Taxi; Normand Grenier at Communications Grenier; Nathalie Lévesque of Saint-Jacques Vallée Young & Rubicam; and Elisabeth Cohen at the Place des Arts, Montreal.

For helping us navigate the international legal waters, I greatly appreciate the generous contributions of Eric Gross of Gowling and Henderson, Toronto; Bryan Fraser of Hooey-Remus, Toronto; Robert Legault of Legault & Joly, Montreal, and Margit Capus-LeClerc, Luxembourg. And for great support and assistance, I am indebted to the Canadian Consulate General in Los Angeles, especially Pamela Johnson and Rosalind Wolfe.

Special thanks go to several longtime friends in the business whose contributions, continuous support, and wise counsel I value and appreciate immeasurably: Al Ries at Ries & Ries; Susan Irwin at McCann-Erickson; Victoria Horstmann, formerly at Ketchum Advertising; Jan Sneed, formerly at Wells, Rich, Green/BDDP; Rance Crain at *Advertising Age;* Gary Corolis at MacLaren LINTAS/ Toronto; Jack

Trout at Trout and Partners; Jorge Gutierrez Orvañanos at MerchanDesign, Guadalajara, Mexico; Alistair Gillett at M/B Interactive; and Brad Lynch, formerly of the Ad Council.

In addition, I appreciate the moral support, encouragement, and generous assistance of numerous friends and colleagues: Tom and Dena Michael, Carlos and Yolanda Cortez, Bob and Demmie Divine, Bob and Sally Bosler, Rudy and Martha Gonzales, Sid and Iris Stein, Professor E. L. Deckinger, Rob Settle and Pam Alreck, Bruce Henderson, Jann Pasler, Jack Savidge, Mary Beth McCabe, Barnard and Sylvia Thompson, Don and Ann Ritchey, Susan Harding, Randy Schroeder, Jim and LeAnna Zevely, Fred and Brenda Bern, Bill and Olivia Werner, and Alan and Rita Moller. Special thanks for generous assistance and encouragement to John Nauman, and—for giving so much to so many for so long—Stanley D. Woodworth, Sid Bernstein, and John O'Toole, gone from our midst but never forgotten.

Deadlines impinge on family life the worst. For their incredible understanding and patience, I thank my sons, William and Christian, my parents, John and Ruth Arens, and my partner in life, Olivia, for her blind love, good humor, and unwavering support.

I very much appreciate the assistance of former students and friends from San Diego State University and the University of California–San Diego. Kristie Linn, Raquel de la Cruz, Anita Lyall, Debbie Lumayag, Dan Santero, Maria Garza, Nicole Russo, and Linda McAleer gave so much of their time and help for so little in return. Lisa Kaplan and Monica Spears demonstrated their artistic skills by assisting in ad selection. And I am especially grateful to Greg Armstrong for his work on the Windows 95 story and for so many little details he helped pull together.

A special thank-you to Alex Thiesen for his expert editorial assistance and incredible good humor, positive attitude, and loyalty during the toughest of months. Thanks also to Cassie Divine and Mary Zimmer for able assistance on some of the most tedious editorial tasks. Likewise, great appreciation to Brannon Wait for his incredibly thorough work on the Internet exercises and to Jim and Diana Priddy, Brent Manuel, Scott Puckett, and Lisa Kaplan (again) for timely editorial help and for being there when we needed them most. I also thank Tom and Betty Pritchett of Kennesaw State University, who worked against incredible deadlines to prepare the Manual of Tests. We are particularly thankful for the skill and expertise of our video mavens, Kelly and Jake Seagraves. Finally, special recognition goes to Jack Whidden for his excellent editorial and design collaboration on the Instructor's Manual and his unswerving devotion to quality and clarity.

I have always appreciated the skill and dedication of our publishing team at Irwin. This edition we were blessed with a new association with McGraw-Hill, and the publishing commitment has only gotten stronger. Thank you Jeff Sund, John Black, Jerry Saykes, and Gary Burke. For several editions, now, I have been fortunate enough to have the best editor in the business. I cannot thank Steve Patterson enough for hanging in there when the motivation got tough and the days very long. Unfortunately for us, he has decided to take some time for a well-earned, extended sabbatical. Thanks, Steve. We'll miss you. The McGraw-Hill/Irwin A-team also included Diane Beausoleil, Michael Warrell, Susan Trentacosti, Mike Hruby, Harriet Stockanes, Keri Johnson, Colleen Suljic, and Scott Hamilton. A major thank-you to all of you for again finding the way to do the impossible. I appreciate your patience, your dedication to excellence, and your friendship more than you can possibly know.

I also want to recognize and thank the American Academy of Advertising, the American Association for Education in Journalism and Mass Communications, and the American Marketing Association, three organizations whose publications and meetings provide valuable forums for the exchange of ideas and for professional growth.

I am deeply grateful to the many instructors, professors, academic reviewers, and friends in academia who do the real heavy lifting through their ongoing research, writing, and teaching. Their creative ideas and critical insights were invaluable in the preparation of this edition. If you like the changes and additions to this edition, the credit belongs to them for their wise counsel and intelligent suggestions. If not, the responsibility is entirely mine. These people include, but are certainly not limited to, the following individuals: Kak Yoon, Washington State University; Janice Bukovac, Michigan State University; Wayne Hilinski, Penn State University; Ivan L. Preston, University of Wisconsin, Madison; Shay Sayre, California State University, Fullerton; Patricia Rose, Florida International University; Richard L. Roth, University of Kentucky; Marilyn Kern-Foxworth, Texas A&M University; Joel Dubow, St. Joseph's University; Tom Duncan and Sandra Moriarty, University of Colorado, Boulder; Keith Johnson, Texas Tech University; Johan Yssel, University of Southern Mississippi; Richard M. Lei, Northern Arizona University; Glen Riecken, East Tennessee State University; Beth Barnes, Syracuse University; Marla Stafford, University of North Texas; Jan Slater, Ohio University; John Murphy, University of Texas; Eric Haley, University of Tennessee; Charles Frazer, University of Oregon; Michael Dotson, Appalachian State Univeristy; Henry S. Cole, Northeast Louisiana University; Ed Petkus, Boise State University; Pekka Kess at the University of Oulu, Finland; Joseph Ha, Ramapo College of New Jersey; Joe Kilpatrick, California State University at Sacramento; and Mike Weigold, University of Florida. Finally, a special thank-you to Hugh Cannon of Wayne State University, a good and generous friend whose personal contributions to this edition were extensive and inestimable.

To all of you, thank you. Without you, it would be an impossible task.

W. F. A.

Contents in **Brief**

Detailed **Contents**

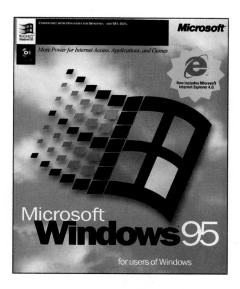

Part **Five**
Using Advertising Media

16   *Using Digital Interactive Media and Direct Mail, 502*

Contemporary
Advertising

Part One

Advertising Perspectives

There are many ways to look at advertising—as a business, a creative communication process, a social phenomenon, and a fundamental ingredient of the free enterprise system. The first part of this text defines advertising, examines the most important dimensions of the field, considers how changing economics has influenced the evolution of the profession, outlines advertising's functions and scope, considers its social and legal ramifications, and looks at the major participants in the advertising business, not just in North America but around the world. ●

chapter 1 *The Dimensions of Advertising* gives an overview of the profession. It defines advertising, examines its role in the communication process, and discusses its various functions and classifications. The chapter focuses on how economics has affected the evolution of advertising and discusses advertising's effects on society.

chapter 2 *The Economic, Social, and Regulatory Aspects of Advertising* discusses the impact of advertising on the economy and society, considers some common criticisms of advertising, and debates the ethical and social responsibilities of companies that advertise. It describes the roles played by government, industry, and consumer groups in regulating advertising. Finally, it compares important laws governing the practice of advertising in the United States and Canada with those in foreign countries.

chapter 3 *The Scope of Advertising: From Local to Global* shows how people and groups organize themselves—as advertisers, agencies, media, and suppliers—around the world to create, produce, and manage advertising. The chapter describes the role of each of these organizations and discusses critical factors that affect the client/agency relationship and the management of advertising in different cultural, economic, and social environments.

Chapter **One**

The Dimensions of Advertising

Objective   To define advertising and introduce the profession. You'll learn the fundamental role of advertising in the communication process; how it works as an element of the marketing process; the basic terminology it uses; the functions and effects of advertising in business; the influence of economics on the evolution of advertising; and advertising's overall impact on the society in which it operates. These basics set the framework for the more detailed study to follow.

After studying this chapter, you will be able to:

- Define advertising and differentiate it from other forms of marketing communications.

- Explain how advertising communication differs from basic human communication.

- Understand and describe advertising's role in the marketing communication process.

- Discuss milestones in the evolution of advertising.

- Explore the impact of advertising on society.

When the worried band of small, independent orange growers from Southern California gathered at the Chamber of Commerce building in downtown Los Angeles, they had no idea that the little organization they were starting would one day become a billion-dollar business, marketing one of the best-known and respected brands in the world. The date was August 29, 1893. • Farmers across the United States had difficult times that year. California's citrus farmers' problems were made even worse by the distance that separated them from their Eastern markets. The growers were at the mercy of often unscrupulous commission agents who took their fruit on consignment and paid them only if and when it sold. • Led by T. H. B. Chamblin, an earnest, persuasive, 60-year-old Ohioan, the growers formed a nonprofit farmers' cooperative, the Southern California Fruit Exchange, to manage and control the packing and marketing of high-quality fresh citrus products from Southern California. • So desperate were the region's farmers and so persuasive were Chamblin's arguments that growers signed up in droves. In its first season, the Exchange represented 80 percent of the citrus growers of Southern California. It shipped 6,000 of the state's 7,000 total carloads. (Three hundred boxes of

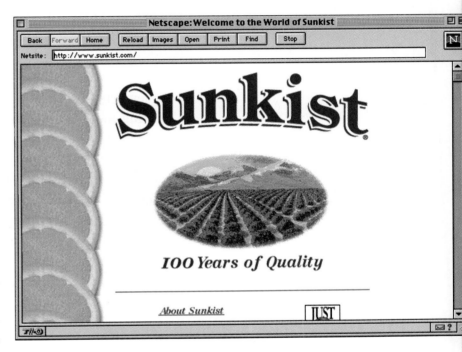

fruit constituted a carload.) By regulating shipments, the Exchange enabled the farmers to net about $1 per box—four times what they would have gotten from commission agents. • Rocky times lay ahead, but the Exchange weathered them all and eventually added lemons and grapefruit to its product line. In 1904 the Exchange expanded and began to actively convince retailers and wholesalers to handle its fruit exclusively. In 1905 it invited northern growers to participate and changed its name to the California Fruit Growers Exchange. • By 1907 orange shipments increased fivefold, to nearly 30,000 carloads. But this increase brought other problems, namely oversaturation of the market for this "luxury" product. Management realized it had to promote greater consumer consumption. With some trepidation, the board budgeted $10,000 for the Exchange's first advertising effort. That turned out to be the best investment it ever made. It was also the first time a perishable product had ever been advertised. • With the assistance of the Lord & Thomas advertising agency (now Foote, Cone & Belding), the Exchange developed a three-color newspaper ad to promote its oranges. The campaign, launched in the *Des Moines Register,* declared the first week in March "Orange Week in Iowa." The ad announced that Des Moines would receive "direct from the beautiful groves of California hundreds of carloads of the choicest oranges in the world." The Southern Pacific Railroad co-funded the campaign to promote tickets to California and posted billboards throughout Iowa with slogans such as "Oranges for Health, California for Wealth." This is one of the earliest known cases of *co-marketing* and of what is now called *integrated marketing communications (IMC).* ● The Exchange directors were so amazed by the results—a stunning 50 percent increase in sales—that they increased the budget to $25,000. In the fall of 1908, they pasted 6 million stickers on the Exchange's shipping boxes proudly proclaiming the Exchange's new trademark: Sunkist, the name by which it would be known around the world forevermore.[1] ● Today Sunkist Growers, Inc., is a 100-year-old not-for-profit cooperative marketing organization owned and operated by over 6,000 citrus growers in California and Arizona. Membership is voluntary. Sunkist provides income to its members by marketing their fresh citrus around the globe and by licensing the Sunkist brand to related products that use its extract. ● Though not large by national standards, Sunkist is still a major international advertiser. It spends millions of dollars every year to stimulate demand for its brand and to support the retailers who carry it. Foote, Cone & Belding has also fared well. Working with clients such as Mattel and RJR Nabisco, it is one of the world's oldest and largest advertising agencies. The agency's association with Sunkist is one of the oldest and most successful client/agency partnerships in the world. Spanning more than 90 years, their relationship not only parallels the history of modern advertising but has literally *made* advertising history. ●

What Is **Advertising**?

To initiate and maintain contact with their customers and prospects, organizations use a wide variety of communication tools. Solicitation letters, newspaper ads, event sponsorships, publicity, telemarketing sales calls, statement stuffers, coupons, and sweepstakes are just a few. As consumers, we are all exposed to hundreds and maybe even thousands of these commercial messages every day. Many people simply refer to all of them as "advertising," but in fact, collectively these various tools are correctly called **marketing communications.** And advertising is just one of these tools.

So what is advertising?

At the beginning of the 20th century, Albert Lasker, generally regarded as the father of modern advertising, was the owner of Sunkist's advertising agency, Lord & Thomas (the predecessor of Foote, Cone & Belding). He defined advertising as "salesmanship in print, driven by a reason why."[2] But that was long before the advent of radio, television, or the Internet. The nature and scope of the business world, and advertising, were quite limited. A century later, our planet is a far different place. The nature and needs of business have changed, and so have the concept and practice of advertising.

Tying in with the Girl Scouts during their peak cookie selling season is a great marketing and advertising idea for the California Milk Processor Board (www.got-milk.com/mainmenu.shtml).

Today, definitions of advertising abound. Journalists, for example, might define it as a communication, public relations, or persuasion process; businesspeople see it as a marketing process; economists and sociologists tend to focus on its economic, societal, or ethical significance. And some consumers might define it simply as a nuisance. Each of these dimensions is important to consider, but for now we'll use the following functional definition:

Advertising is the structured and composed nonpersonal communication of information, usually paid for and usually persuasive in nature, about products (goods, services, and ideas) by identified sponsors through various media.

Let's take this definition apart and analyze its components. Advertising is, first of all, a type of *communication*. It is a very *structured* form of applied communication, employing both verbal and nonverbal elements that are *composed* to fill predetermined space and time formats that are controlled by the sponsor.

Second, advertising is typically directed to groups of people rather than to individuals. It is therefore *nonpersonal,* or *mass,* communication. These groups might be consumers, such as people who buy fresh oranges at the store; or they might be the businesspeople who own and manage those stores and buy oranges directly from Sunkist for resale.

Most advertising is *paid for* by sponsors. GM, Kmart, Coca-Cola, and your local fitness salon pay the newspaper or the radio or TV station to carry the ads you read, see, and hear. But some sponsors don't have to pay for their ads. The American Red Cross, United Way, and American Cancer Society are among the many national organizations whose public service messages are carried at no charge. Likewise, a poster on a school bulletin board promoting a dance is not paid for, but it is still an ad, a structured, nonpersonal, persuasive communication.

Of course, most advertising is intended to be *persuasive*—to win converts to a product, service, or idea. Some ads, such as legal announcements, are intended merely to inform, not to persuade. But they are still ads because they satisfy all the other requirements of the definition.

In addition to promoting tangible **goods** such as oranges, oatmeal, and olive oil, advertising helps publicize the intangible **services** of bankers, beauticians, bike repair shops, and bill collectors. Increasingly, advertising is used to advocate a wide variety of **ideas,** whether economic, political, religious, or social. In this book the term **product** encompasses goods, services, and ideas. Ad Lab 1–A lists some classic advertising slogans that have helped promote a variety of products over the years.

An ad *identifies* its sponsor. This seems obvious. The sponsor wants to be identified, or why pay to advertise? One of the basic differences between advertising and *public relations,* though, is that many PR activities (for example, publicity) aren't openly sponsored. We'll discuss the differences between advertising and other forms of marketing communications later in this chapter.

Advertising reaches us through a channel of communication referred to as a **medium.** An advertising medium is any paid means used to present an ad to its target audience. Thus, we have radio advertising, television advertising, newspaper ads, and so on. *Word-of-mouth,* while it is a communication medium, *is not* an advertising medium. Historically, advertisers have used the traditional mass **media** (the plural of *medium*)—radio, TV, newspapers, magazines, and billboards—to send their messages. But today technology enables advertising to reach us efficiently through a variety of *addressable media* (for example, direct mail) and *interactive media* (like the World Wide Web and kiosks). Advertisers also use an increasing variety of other *nontraditional media* such as shopping carts, blimps, and videocassettes to find their audience. The planning, scheduling, and buying of media space and time are so important to advertising effectiveness that we devote five full chapters to the subject, one in Part Two and four in Part Five.

This is a good working definition of advertising. But to get a full sense of what it really is today, we need to understand where it has come from, how and why it grew to be so large, and what the forces are that drive it. In this chapter, therefore, we'll briefly examine some of the important dimensions of advertising. We'll look at the *communication dimension* first to better understand how advertising is actually a form of structured, literary communication. Then the *marketing dimension* will explain the role advertising plays in business. The *economic dimension* will show us how and why advertising evolved the way it did. And finally, the *social and ethical dimension* will enable us to understand people's attitudes about advertising and to consider what the future holds in store. Examining the diverse dimensions of advertising here in Chapter 1 should lead us toward a deeper understanding of contemporary advertising as it is currently practiced.

The next two chapters of Part I will then deal in greater depth with the economic, social, and regulatory aspects of advertising as well as the broad scope of the field.

Communication: What Makes Advertising Unique

First and foremost, advertising is communication—a special kind of communication. McCann-Erickson, the ad agency for Coca-Cola, says that advertising is "Truth well told." This means that ethical advertisers, and the agencies they employ, work as a team to discover and use the best methods possible to tell their story truthfully but creatively to the marketplace. To succeed, they must understand the elements of the advertising communication process, which is derived from the basic human communication process.

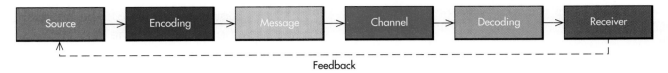

Feedback

Exhibit 1–1
The human communication process.

The Human Communication Process

From our first cry at birth, our survival depends on our ability to inform others or persuade them to take some action. As we develop, we learn to listen and respond to others' messages. The traditional model in Exhibit 1–1 summarizes the series of events that take place when people share ideas in informal oral communication. The process begins when one party, called the **source,** formulates an idea, **encodes** it as a **message,** and sends it via some **channel** to another party, called the **receiver.** The receiver must **decode** the message in order to understand it. To respond, the receiver formulates a new idea, encodes it, and then sends the new message back through some channel, or medium. A message that acknowledges or responds to the original message constitutes **feedback,** which also affects the encoding of a new message.[3]

Applying this model to advertising, we could say that the source is the sponsor, the message is the ad, the channel is the medium, and the receiver is the consumer or prospect. But this model oversimplifies the process that occurs in advertising or other sponsored marketing communications. It doesn't take into account either the structure or the creativity inherent in composing the advertising message. We need to consider some of the many complexities involved, especially with the advent of *interactive media,* which let consumers participate in the communication by extracting the information they need, manipulating what they see on their computer or TV screens in real time, and responding in real time.

Applying the Communication Process to Advertising

Barbara Stern at Rutgers University sees advertising as a form of structured, literary text, rather different from the spontaneous, word-of-mouth communication of oral speech. She proposes a more sophisticated communication model, derived from the traditional oral one but applied specifically to advertising as *composed commercial text* rather than informal speech. The Stern model recognizes that in advertising, the source, the message, and the receiver all have multiple dimensions (see Exhibit 1–2 on page 10). Some of these dimensions exist in the real world; others exist on a different level of reality—a virtual world within the text of the advertising message itself.

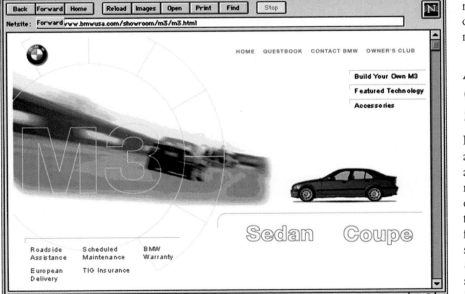

The World Wide Web is the fastest-growing media for advertisers, topping an estimated $1 billion in expenditures in 1998. BMW (www.bmwusa.com) uses its interactive site to provide detailed information to the consumer and promote customer feedback, a feat that could not easily be accomplished under the constraints of normal print, radio, or television ads.

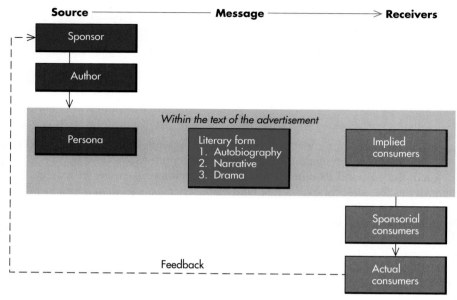

Exhibit 1–2
The advertising communication process.

Source Dimensions: The Sponsor, the Author, and the Persona

In oral communication, the source is typically one person talking to another person or a group. But in advertising, who is really the source of the communication? The sponsor named in the ad? Certainly the real-world **sponsor** is legally responsible for the communication and has a message to communicate to actual consumers. But as the model shows, the path from sponsor to actual consumer is a long and circuitous one. To begin with, the sponsor does not usually produce the message. That is the typically role of the sponsor's ad agency or other specialists. So the **author** of the communication is actually a copywriter, an art director, or, most often, a creative group at the agency. Commissioned by the sponsor to create the advertising message, these people exist in the real world but are completely invisible to the reader or viewer, even though they play a key role in composing the text and the tenor of the message.

At the same time, *within the text* of the ad resides some real or imaginary spokesperson (a **persona**) who lends some voice or tone to the ad or commercial. To the consumer, this persona, who represents the sponsor, is the source of the within-text message. But the persona's discourse is composed and crafted by the ad's authors solely for the purposes of the text; it is not a part of real life. It exists only in the virtual world of the ad. (See Ad Lab 1–B: Advertising as a Literary Form.)

Message Dimensions: Autobiography, Narrative, and Drama

The types of messages typically communicated in advertising may also be multidimensional. As artful imitations of life, advertising messages typically use one or a blend of three literary forms: autobiography, narrative, or drama. In **autobiographical messages,** "I" tell a story about myself to "you," the imaginary audience eavesdropping on my private personal experience. Other ads use **narrative messages** in which a third-person persona tells a story about others to an imagined audience. Finally, in the **drama message,** the characters act out events directly in front of an imagined empathetic audience.

Thus, among the most important decisions the authors of advertising messages make are what kind of persona and which literary form to use to express the sales message. Considering the emotions, attitudes, and motives that drive particular customers in their target audience, the creative team develops the persona and message, along with any images and text that will act as communication symbols or triggers. Then they place these words and visuals in the structured format most suitable to the medium selected for delivering the message. The format may be a dramatic 30-second TV commercial; an autobiographical, full-page, black-and-white magazine ad; a colorful, narrative brochure; or a multipage Internet website that employs a variety of message styles. In all cases, though, the message exists only within the text of the ad. To do all this effectively requires great skill, but it's this creativity that truly distinguishes advertising from other forms of communication. For that reason, we'll devote Part Four of this text exclusively to the subject of advertising creativity.

Advertising as a Literary Form

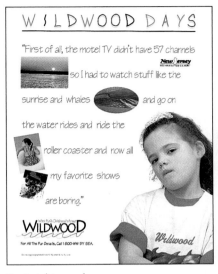

1. Autobiography.

2. Narrative.

3. Drama.

The message content in advertising typically involves three literary forms: autobiography, narrative, and drama (examples 1 through 3 above).

Autobiography uses the voice of the first-person "I" to express the speaker's point of view. The narrative form uses a third-person voice that often exudes a well-informed, respectable quality. The drama form presents a series of events whose information and sequencing combine to imply a message and require the viewer to connect the sequences, thereby experiencing the message rather than having to be told.

Two other key elements are the persona that usually represents the advertiser and the implied consumer. The persona may appear as a character such as the Pillsbury Doughboy or Bob Vila, the Sears spokesperson. A logo is also a form of persona. The implied consumer may be represented by a character, such as the girl in example 1 or the unseen owner of the car in example 2.

Ads like the one in example 3 may employ a number of these literary forms simultaneously.

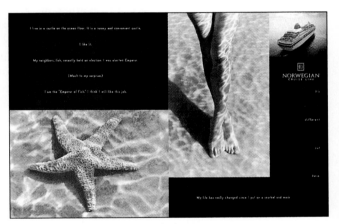

4. Mixture of literary forms and elements.

Laboratory Application

Can you identify which two literary forms appear in example 4? Does it have a persona and/or an implied consumer? If so, describe their use.

Receiver Dimensions: Implied, Sponsorial, and Actual Consumers

The receivers of advertising are also multidimensional. First, within the text, every ad or commercial presumes some audience is there. These **implied consumers,** who are addressed by the ad's persona, are not real. They are imagined by the ad's creators to be ideal consumers who acquiesce in whatever beliefs the text requires. They are, in effect, part of the drama of the ad.

When we move outside the text of the ad, though, the first audience is, in fact, a group of decision makers at the sponsor's company or organization. These **sponsorial consumers** are the gatekeepers who decide if the ad will run or not. So, before an ad ever gets a chance to persuade a real consumer, the ad's authors must first persuade the sponsor's executives and managers who have the responsibility for approving the campaign and funding it.

The **actual consumers**—equivalent to the receiver in oral communications—are people in the real world who comprise the ad's target audience. They are the people to whom the sponsor's message is ultimately directed, but they will get to see, hear, or read it only with the sponsor's approval.[4]

Actual consumers do not usually think or behave the same as the implied consumer, or even the sponsorial consumer. Thus, the advertiser (and the creative team) must be concerned about how the actual consumer will decode, or interpret, the message. The last thing an advertiser wants is to be misunderstood. Unfortunately, message interpretation is only partially determined by the words and symbols in the ad. The medium used may have an effect as well. As Marshall McLuhan said, "The medium is the message." However, Stern's model does not directly address the fact that advertisers communicate their messages through a wide variety of mass, addressable, and interactive media. With today's advances in technology, the boundaries between the print and electronic media are now blurring. We read text on a computer screen, and soon the average person will be able to print whatever appears on a TV screen. How will this affect the way people receive and interpret advertising messages? Stern acknowledges the need for additional study in this area.

Further, the unique characteristics of the receivers themselves are also very important, and the sponsor may know little or nothing about them. As we shall see in Chapter 4, attitudes, perceptions, personality, self-concept, and culture are just some of the many important influences that affect the way people receive and respond to messages and how they behave as consumers in the marketplace.

Complicating this problem is the fact that the sponsor's advertising message must compete with hundreds of other commercial and noncommercial messages every day. This is referred to as **noise.** So the sender doesn't know *how* the message is received, or even *if* it's received, until a consumer acknowledges it.

Feedback and Interactivity

That's why **feedback** is so important. It completes the cycle, verifying that the message was received. Feedback employs a sender–message–receiver pattern, except that it is directed from the receiver back to the source.

In advertising, feedback can take many forms: redeemed coupons, phone inquiries, visits to a store, requests for more information, increased sales, or responses to a survey. Dramatically low responses to an ad indicate a break in the communication process. Questions arise: Is the product wrong for the market? Is the message unclear? Are we using the right media? Without feedback, these questions cannot be answered.

In the past, the consumer's feedback rarely used the same channels as the original message. But now, thanks again to technology, the audiences of advertising are no longer just passive receivers of impersonal mass messages. They are now active decision makers who can control what communications they receive and choose the information they want about a particular product. With the growth of interactive media, they can give instantaneous, real-time feedback on the same channel used by the original message sender.

This offers advertisers the chance for a more in-depth relationship with their customers, one that will be more fruitful for both sponsors and consumers.

Marketing: Determining the Type of Advertising to Use

Now that we have some understanding of advertising's communication dimension, let's consider the marketing dimension, because that's what defines advertising's role in business. Every business organization performs a number of diverse activities. Management typically classifies these activities into three broad functional divisions:

- Operations (produ................).
- Administration/finance.
- Marketing.

Students who major in business study a variety of subjects related to one or all of these general functions. Courses in purchasing and manufacturing relate to the operations function. Courses in accounting and industrial relations relate to the administration/finance area. While many students study advertising in a school of journalism or communications, advertising is actually a specialty area within the broad domain of marketing. Other disciplines in marketing include market research, distribution, and selling.

Marketing is the one business function whose primary role is to attract revenues. Without revenue, of course, a company cannot recover its initial investment, pay its employees' salaries, grow, or earn a profit. So marketing is very important.

What Is Marketing?

Over the years, the concept of marketing has evolved based on the supply of and demand for products. Because we need to understand marketing as it relates to *advertising,* we define the term as follows:

Marketing is the process of planning and executing the conception, pricing, distribution, and promotion of ideas, goods, and services to create exchanges that satisfy the perceived needs, wants, and objectives of individuals and organizations.[5]

We'll devote all of Part Two to the subject of developing marketing and advertising strategies. The important element to understand in this definition now is that marketing is a strategic **process**—a planned series of actions or methods that take place sequentially. This process includes developing products, pricing them strategically, making them available to customers through a distribution network, and promoting them through sales and advertising activities. The ultimate goal of the marketing process is to earn a profit for the firm by consummating the exchange of products or services with those customers who need or want them. And the role of advertising is to inform, persuade, and remind groups of customers, or markets, about the need-satisfying value of the company's goods and services. Today even many nonprofit organizations now use the marketing process to develop and promote services that will satisfy their constituents' needs.

Advertising and the Marketing Process

Advertising helps the organization achieve its marketing goals. So do market research, sales, and distribution. And these other marketing specialties all have an impact on the kind of advertising a company employs. An effective advertising specialist must have a broad understanding of the whole marketing process in order to know what type of advertising to use in a given situation.

Companies and organizations use many different types of advertising, depending on their particular marketing strategy. The strategy determines who the targets of advertising should be, in what locales the advertising should run, what media should be used, and what purposes the advertising should accomplish (see Exhibit 1–3 on page 14). These various criteria also determine what advertising skills are required.

Identifying Target Markets and Target Audiences

A firm's marketing activities are always aimed at a particular segment of the population—its **target market.** Likewise, advertising is aimed at a particular group called the **target audience.** When we see an ad that doesn't appeal to us, it may be because the ad is not aimed at any of the groups we belong to. For example, a TV commercial for denture cream isn't meant to appeal to youngsters. They're not part of either the target market or the target audience. There are two main types of target audiences, *consumers* and *businesses.*

Exhibit 1–3
The classifications of advertising

By target audience	By geographic area	By purpose
Consumer advertising: Aimed at people who buy the product for their own or someone else's use.	*Local (retail) advertising:* Advertising by businesses whose customers come from only one city or local trading area.	*Product advertising:* Promotes the sale of products and services.
Business advertising: Aimed at people who buy or specify products and services for use in business.	*Regional advertising:* Advertising for products sold in one area or region, but not the entire country.	*Nonproduct (corporate or institutional) advertising:* Promotes the organiztion's mission or philosophy rather than a specific product.
• *Trade:* Aimed at middlemen (wholesalers and retailers) of products and services who buy for resale to their cusotmers.	*National advertising:* Advertising aimed at customers in several regions of the country.	*Commercial advertising:* Promotes products, services, or ideas with the expectation of making a profit.
• *Professional:* Aimed at people licensed under a code of ethics or set of professional standards.	*International advertising:* Advertising directed at foreign markets.	*Noncommerical advertising:* Sponsored by or for a charitable or nonprofit institution, civic group, or religious or political organization.
• *Agricultural:* Aimed at people in farming or agribusiness.	**By medium**	*Action advertising:* Attempts to stimulate immediate action by the reader.
	Print advertising: Newspapers, magazines.	*Awareness advertising:* Attempts to build the image of a product or familiarity with the product's name and package.
	Broadcast (electronic) advertising: Radio, TV.	
	Out-of-home advertising: Outdoor, transit.	
	Direct-mail advertising: Advertising sent through the mail.	

Consumer Markets

Much of the advertising we see daily in the mass media—TV, radio, newspapers, and magazines—falls under the broad category of **consumer advertising.** Usually sponsored by the producer (or manufacturer) of the product or service, these ads are typically directed at **consumers,** people who buy the product for their own or someone else's personal use. This includes **retail advertising,** advertising sponsored by retail stores and businesses. Consumer advertising also includes noncommercial *public service announcements* (PSAs) from the American Cancer Society or the Partnership for a Drug-Free America.

In the end, customers are people. So advertising professionals must understand how people act and think—and why they buy what they buy. This requires great skill. In fact, this area of study is the province of another specialty in marketing, *consumer behavior*—a topic we'll discuss in Chapter 4. The better advertisers understand the buying behavior of people, the better they can bring their products into the collective consciousness of prospective customers.

Industrial/Business Markets

Companies use **business advertising** to reach people who buy or specify goods and services for business use. It tends to appear in specialized business publications or professional journals, in direct-mail pieces sent to businesses, or in trade shows. Since business advertising (also

Defining the target audience is a necessary step in creating any advertisement. Northrop Grumman (www.northgrum.com), a defense contractor for the U.S. military, uses this corporate advertisement to promote itself to prospective employees as well as the financial community, namely high-end investors.

YOU NEED OPTIONS.

At Mannington Commercial, we want the environment you're creating to be as grand. Intimate. Elegant. Austere. Spare. Or as spectacular as you do. Which is why we provide you with more than 1200 flooring options. No single source in the flooring industry gives you as many color, texture, design and styling options as Mannington Commercial. And all have been specifically designed to work together and complement each other.

And no single source provides you with as wide a range of service options, from the planning stages, through installation, and beyond.

Flooring options. Design options. Service options. All these options make Mannington Commercial your best option.

To find out what your Mannington options are, call 1-800-241-2262.

A 65,000 SQUARE FOOT FLOOR IN A NEO-CLASSIC TURN-OF-THE CENTURY LANDMARK. CONVERT THIS HISTORICALLY CERTIFIED SPACE FOR THE CITY'S HOT AD AGENCY. FROM DESIGN TO MOVE-IN: EIGHT MONTHS.

MANNINGTON. COMMERCIAL

Trade advertising is not aimed at consumers, but at people who buy—or influence the purchase of—products and services used in various business situations. This ad for Mannington Commercial (www.mannington.com) is targeted toward architects, flooring retailers, and contractors—other businesses—who could use Mannington's flooring services.

called **business-to-business, or BTB, advertising**) rarely uses consumer mass media, it is typically invisible to consumers. However, some business-to-business ads, by computer manufacturers and firms like FedEx, do appear on prime-time TV and in consumer magazines.

There are three types of business advertising: trade, professional, and agricultural. Companies aim **trade advertising** at resellers (wholesalers, dealers, and retailers) to obtain greater distribution of their products. For example, the objective of Sunkist's trade advertising in publications such as *California Grocer* is to develop more grocery outlets or to increase sales to existing outlets.

Advertising aimed at teachers, accountants, doctors, dentists, architects, engineers, lawyers, and the like is called **professional advertising** and typically appears in official publications of professional societies (such as the *Archives of Ophthalmology,* published by the American Medical Association). Professional advertising has three objectives: to convince professional people (people with specialized training who work under a code of ethics) to recommend or prescribe a specific product or service to their clients, to buy particular brands of equipment and supplies for use in their work, or to use the product personally.

Companies use **agricultural** (or **farm**) **advertising** to promote products and services used in agriculture to farm families and to individuals employed in agribusiness. FMC Corp., for example, might advertise its plant nutrition products in *California Farmer* magazine to growers of Sunkist oranges. Agricultural advertising typically shows farmers how the advertised product will increase efficiency, reduce risks, and widen profit margins.

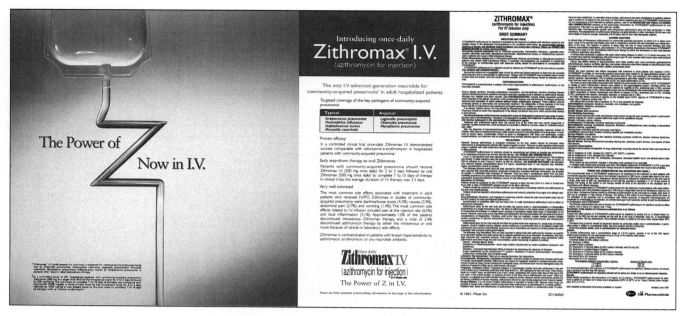

Professional advertising encompasses the fields of education, accounting, medicine, dentistry, engineering, and the law, just to name a few. In this instance, Pfizer provides pharmaceutical information to consumers about Zithromax (www.KidsEars.com), but, in so doing, actually promotes the brand to family physicians. Thus, this could be viewed as both a consumer ad and a professional ad.

Business customers are often very knowledgeable, sophisticated buyers, and they may require extensive technical information before making the purchase decision. So people who work in business-to-business advertising need more specialized product knowledge and experience than their consumer advertising colleagues, who may spend their time promoting one fast-food hamburger over another.

Implementing Marketing Strategy

Once the organization determines the target market for its products, it designs a strategy for serving that market profitably. As we'll discuss in Chapter 5, marketing strategy is the particular blend, or *mix,* of strategic elements over which the marketer has control: product concept, pricing, distribution, and communication. Each of these elements affects the type of advertising used.

The Product Element

For example, for mass-merchandised grocery brands like Tide laundry detergent, companies use a type of advertising called *consumer packaged-goods advertising.* An insurance company or tax preparation firm is likely to use *service advertising.* Manufacturers of scientific and technical products use *high-tech advertising.* In other words, for virtually every product category, specialists in that area use a specific type of advertising.

The Price Element

A firm's pricing strategy also affects advertising style. Companies that don't compete on price typically use **image advertising** to create a particular perception of the company or personality for the brand. Or they may use **regular price-line advertising,** in which the price of a product is not shown, or at least not highlighted. More price-competitive companies use *sale advertising, clearance advertising,* or *loss-leader advertising* to either increase store traffic or create an impression of everyday low prices.

Global companies must advertise not only in their home country but also overseas to cover the distribution element of their marketing strategies. To promote its snow tires, Goodyear (www.goodyear.com) targets German consumers in their native language by suggesting that its tires offer protection "against risks and side effects."

The Distribution Element

The third element of marketing strategy, distribution, also affects the type of advertising used. Global marketers like Coca-Cola, IBM, and Kodak may use **global advertising,** in which messages are consistent in ads placed around the world. Other firms may promote their products in foreign markets with **international advertising,** which may contain different messages and even be created locally in each geographic market. The field of international marketing has become so important that we discuss global advertising issues wherever applicable in every chapter of this book.

Companies that market in several regions of the United States and use the major mass media are called national advertisers, and their promotion is called **national advertising.** Some companies sell only in one part of the country or in two or three states. They use **regional advertising,** placing their ads in local media or regional editions of national media. Finally, businesses and retailers that sell within one small trading area typically use **local advertising** placed in local media or direct mail. We'll explore this topic further in Chapter 3, "The Scope of Advertising."

The Communication Element

The final element of marketing strategy is communication. As we mentioned at the beginning of this chapter, advertising is just one of the tools in the marketing communications tool kit. **Marketing communications** (often called *marcom*) typically refers to all the *planned messages* that companies and organizations create and disseminate to support their marketing objectives and strategies. In addition to advertising, major marketing communication tools include *personal selling, sales promotion, public relations activities,* and *collateral materials.* The extent to which an organization uses any or all of these tools again depends on its marketing needs, objectives, and strategy.

Each marketing communication tool offers particular opportunities and benefits to the marketer. **Personal selling,** for example, in which salespeople deal directly with customers either face-to-face or via telemarketing, offers the flexibility possible only through human interaction. Personal selling is thus an excellent tool for conveying information, for giving demonstrations, and particularly for consummating the sale (or exchange) especially on high-ticket items like cars, real estate, and furniture as well as most business-to-business products. The drawback to personal selling is its high cost, so companies that emphasize personal selling in their marketing mix often spend a lower percentage of sales on advertising than other firms. We'll discuss personal selling in greater detail in Chapter 9.

As a marketing communications tool, **advertising** enables marketers to reach more prospects at lower cost than a salesperson could ever do. Further, the creativity inherent in advertising allows the marketer to conjure an image or personality, full of symbolic meaning and benefits, for the company's brand. No salesperson can do this. In fact, of all the marketing communication tools, only advertising has this ability. However, advertising does suffer from credibility gaps, a topic we'll discuss in Chapter 2. For creating brand awareness, familiarity, and image, as well as for reinforcing prior purchase decisions, advertising is usually the marcom tool of choice.

Advertising can be used to satisfy a variety of sponsor objectives. Some advertising is meant to help generate profits for the advertiser; some is sponsored by nonprofit groups. Some ads try to spur the target audience to immediate action, others to create awareness or understanding of the advertiser's offering.

For example, to promote their goods and services, companies use **product advertising.** To sell ideas, though, organizations use **nonproduct advertising.** A Citgo ad for its gasoline is a product ad. So are ads for banking, insurance, or legal services. But a Citgo ad promoting the company's mission or philosophy (how the company protects the environment while drilling for oil) is called *nonproduct, corporate,* or *institutional advertising.* Corporate advertising is so important that we'll focus on it in Chapter 10.

Similarly, while commercial advertising seeks profits, **noncommercial advertising** is used around the world by governments and nonprofit organizations to seek donations, volunteer support, or a change in consumer behavior.

Some ads are intended to bring about immediate action by the reader; others have a longer-term goal. The objectives of **awareness advertising,** for example, are to create interest in, and an image for, a product and to influence readers or viewers to select a specific brand the next time they shop.

A direct-mail ad, on the other hand, exemplifies **action** (or **direct-response**) **advertising** because it seeks an immediate, direct response from the reader. Most ads on TV and radio are awareness ads, but some are a mixture of awareness and action. For example, a 60-second TV commercial may devote the first 50 seconds to image building and the last 10 to a local phone number for immediate information.

As we'll discuss in Chapter 9, **sales promotion** is a communication tool that offers special incentives to motivate people to act right away. The incentives may be coupons, free samples, contests, or rebates on the purchase price. By offering added value, sales promotion accelerates sales. So it is a very effective tool. It is often used in conjunction with advertising—to promote the promotion. However, like personal selling, it is very expensive; it suffers from other drawbacks as well. While ad agencies create and place media advertising, most sales promotion programs are created by firms that specialize in that field.

Public relations (PR) is an umbrella process—much like marketing—responsible for managing the firm's relationships with its various *publics.* These publics may include customers but are certainly not limited to them. Public relations is also concerned with employees, stockholders, vendors and suppliers, government regulators, and the press. So PR is much larger than just a tool of marketing communications. However, as part of their marketing mix, marketers use a number of **public relations activities** because they are so good at creating awareness and credibility for the firm at low cost. These activities (often referred to as **marketing PR**) include publicity, press agentry, sponsorships, special events, and a special kind of advertising called **public relations advertising,** which uses the structured, sponsored format of media advertising to accomplish public relations goals. While PR is closely aligned with advertising, it requires very different skills and is usually performed by professionals in PR firms rather than ad agency people. However, advertising people need to understand how important PR activities are, so we'll discuss the topic in some detail in Chapter 10.

Companies use a wide variety of promotional tools in nonpaid media to communicate information about themselves and their brands. These **collateral materials** include fliers, brochures, catalogs, posters, sales kits, product specification sheets, instruction booklets, and so on. These materials may be very inexpensive or frightfully costly. But because they contribute so much information to customers and prospects, they are very important to both closing sales and reinforcing prior sales decisions. The people who produce collateral materials may work for the company's advertising agency, but often they work for outside graphic design firms, packaging specialists, and independent film and video producers.

Integrating Marketing Communications

In recent years, as new media have proliferated and the cost of competition has intensified, sophisticated marketers have searched for new ways to get more bang (and accountability) from their marketing communications buck. The result has been a growing understanding on the part of corporate management that (1) the efficiencies of mass media advertising are not what they used to be; (2) consumers are more sophisticated, cynical, and distrusting than ever before; (3) tremendous gaps exist between what companies say in their advertising and what they actually do; and (4) in the long run, nourishing good customer relationships is far more important than making simple exchanges.[6] As a result, there is now a growing movement toward integrating all the messages created by an advertiser's various communication agencies and sent out by various departments within the company to achieve consistency. This process, called *integrated marketing communications (IMC),* is an important marketing trend that we will discuss further in the next section and throughout the book.

Economics: The Growing Need for Advertising

By looking at the communication dimension, we've gotten a sense of what advertising is. The marketing dimension has shown us the many possible roles advertising can play in helping a business succeed. Now we'll turn our attention to a broader dimension—economics, which has driven the growth of advertising since its earliest beginnings and has made it one of the hallmarks of the free enterprise system. As English historian Raymond Williams said, advertising is "nothing other than the official art of capitalism."[7]

Today, business and advertising are undergoing the most dramatic changes in history. To understand the nature of these changes and why they're taking place, we need to look at how the industry has evolved. In this chapter, we'll explain how the changing economic environment has influenced the evolution of advertising. In Chapter 2, we'll take a closer look at how advertising itself influences the economy and society.

Principles of Free-Market Economics

In Economics 101 we learn that, while there is no such thing as *pure competition,* there are four fundamental assumptions of free-market economics that, to a greater or lesser extent, all market-driven societies believe in and/or strive to achieve:

1. *Self-interest.* People and organizations tend to act in their own self-interest. By their very nature, people are acquisitive. They always want more—for less. Therefore, open competition between self-interested sellers advertising to self-interested buyers naturally leads to greater product availability at more competitive prices.

2. *Perfect information.* Access by buyers and sellers to all information at all times about what products are available, at what quality, and at what prices leads to greater competition and lower prices for all. (This is why attorneys are now allowed to advertise, so that people can know what services are available at what prices.)

3. *Many buyers and sellers.* Having a wide range of options is usually preferable to dealing with monopolies because the competitive marketplace rather than a single, self-interested entity controls the supply of and demand for products. (This is why we have antitrust laws and why the few monopolies we do have are closely regulated by the government.)

4. *Absence of externalities (social costs).* Sometimes the sale or consumption of products may benefit (for example, by crime prevention) or harm (for example, with pollution) other people who are not involved in the transaction and didn't pay for the product. In these cases, the government may use taxation and/or regulation to compensate for or eliminate the externalities (as with tobacco advertising).

Now, given these basic assumptions, let's see how advertising fits into the scheme of a free-market economy.

Functions and Effects of Advertising in a Free Economy

For any business, advertising may perform a variety of functions, and its effects may be dramatic. To see how this works, let's go back to the beginnings of Sunkist.

The new Sunkist logo introduced in 1995.

When the California citrus growers came up with the idea of the "Sunkist" brand, they decided to write the product's new name in a distinctive way. They even had the name and style of lettering trademarked with the U.S. Patent Office to reserve use of the Sunkist name and logo solely for the advertising and packaging of the California Fruit Growers Exchange. This demonstrates one of the most basic marketing functions of **branding** and advertising: *to identify products and their source and differentiate them from others.* (The functions and effects discussed here are listed in Exhibit 1–4.) Once the growers named the product, they ran ads to promote the oranges and to tell people where could they could get them. Here is another basic function of advertising: *to communicate information about the product, its features, and its place of sale.*

Prior to World War I, there was an enormous overproduction of oranges and no place to sell them. The market was saturated. So the marketing department of Sunkist, working with Lord & Thomas, came up with a remarkable notion: to educate consumers about a new idea—orange *juice.* Sunkist manufactured millions of glass reamers and ran ads telling people how they could "Drink an Orange" by making fresh juice in their homes. The campaign changed the whole demand pattern for oranges and demonstrated another reason for advertising: *to induce consumers to try new products and get users to repurchase them.*[8]

As more people tried the oranges, liked them, and requested them, more grocery stores stocked the brand. Today, Sunkist citrus fruits are distributed around the world. In fact, Sunkist introduced the first lemons to Japan. *Stimulating the distribution of a product* is yet another function of advertising.

In the 1920s and 30s, the benefits of vitamin C became evident, but not everybody knew how to get the nutrient. One of the many purposes of advertising, though, is *to increase product use.* Sunkist introduced the word "vitamin" to the public in a campaign that told the world that oranges contain vitamin C.[9]

continued on page 25

Exhibit 1–4
Functions and effects of advertising as a marketing tool.

- To identify products and differentiate them from others.
- To communicate information about the product, its features, and its place of sale.
- To induce consumers to try new products and to suggest reuse.
- To stimulate the distribution of a product.
- To increase product use.
- To build value, brand preference, and loyalty.
- To lower the overall cost of sales.

In **1893,** 60 orange growers met to organize a farmers' co-operative that became the California Fruit Growers Exchange. Their objective was to gain a stronger voice in the marketplace and to help coordinate distribution. In 1907, they hired the Lord & Thomas advertising agency (now Foote, Cone & Belding), which helped them create the Sunkist brand name.

The client-agency relationship remains to this day one of the longest associations in advertising history. Sunkist Growers, Inc., is the largest citrus cooperative in the world, with total yearly sales of over $800 million. By national standards, though, it only spends a small amount on media advertising annually.

● *Study the array of historical Sunkist ads in this portfolio and consider how well each illustrates the contemporary definition of advertising presented in the text. Next, select one ad from the portfolio and analyze the multiple dimensions of the communication process as they apply to that ad. Finally, select a different ad from the portfolio and determine which of the six functions of advertising described in the text are applicable to the ad.*

The first Exchange advertisement ran in the Des Moines Register *on March 2, 1908. Surprisingly, the ad ran in three colors (orange, green, and black), an unheard-of accomplishment at that time. The campaign celebrated "Orange Week" with fruit shipped via rail from California to Iowa—another unheard-of feat in those days.*

Early Sunkist ads offered recipes and suggestions for additional citrus uses. By 1915, the Exchange's advertising budget totaled $250,000 per year, up from $25,000 in 1908.

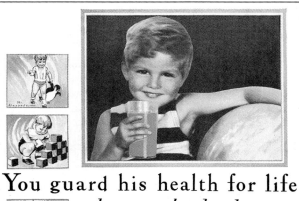

In 1930, the reality of scurvy was still vivid to Americans who were not as educated as we are today about the cause of the disease and its link to diet. So in the early part of the century, Sunkist capitalized on this with ads that touted vitamin C and other health benefits of orange juice.

Creation of the Sunkist name represented the first branding of a commodity. Early on, the decision was made to select only the finest oranges and lemons and to wrap them in tissue printed with the Sunkist label. Thus, the Sunkist name rapidly became more than just a trademark; it also became a grade mark that stood for superior quality. Until 1916, oranges were only eaten as a fruit, but sales quadrupled after Sunkist introduced its "Drink an Orange" ads. The following year, Sunkist introduced juice extractors to restaurants and soda fountains and later to consumers for home use. Over time, Sunkist used advertising to broaden the many uses of its products. For instance, it marketed lemons as a marvelous way for women to increase the softness and luster of their hair.

Just One 100% Daily 'C'

Decades later, Sunkist continues to emphasize the vitamin C benefits of oranges. By now, since most people are educated about the health qualities of citrus fruit, Sunkist simply uses this tantalizing ad as a reminder of these benefits—and the brand name that means quality.

In television, the task was to show brand differentiation in a memorable, engaging, entertaining, and informative manner. To find the best orange, the commercials said, some customers squeeze, shake, or study every orange. But all they really need to do is "twist the wrist" and "always read the label."

Have you ever watched people at the market? They all think they know how to pick the best orange.	They squeeze . . . They tap . . . They shake . . . I have no idea what she's doing.	But all they have to do is twist the wrist. If it says Sunkist . . . you pick it. Hey, always read the label.

THE SHAPE of THINGS to COME.

Advertising to the trade: Sunkist aims messages at its customers in the supermarket trade—produce buyers. Using seasonal specialty citrus fruit, Sunkist builds on its brand name with the added value of labels that indicate individual subvarieties.

Sweet, Smart & Sassy.

Consumers of oranges want the juiciest and best-tasting oranges available. The photography in this ad vividly shows the product to its best and juiciest advantage. The clever alliteration of the headline copy emphasizes the tangy qualities of the fruit. Everything else that needs to be said is implicit in the Sunkist name at the base of the ad.

concluded from page 20

As with any popular product, imitators with confusingly similar names soon appeared. The company has battled competitors ever since. However, another function of advertising is *to build value, brand preference, and loyalty.* Sunkist's ongoing, consistent promotional campaign has helped accomplish this.

For more than 100 years, Sunkist has used a variety of media, from prime-time TV to billboards, to communicate advertising messages to mass audiences. Why? To achieve the most important function of advertising: *lowering the cost of sales.* For what it would cost to reach just one customer through personal selling, Sunkist can reach thousands of people through mass media advertising. According to a Cahners Advertising Research Report, the average cost to make a face-to-face, field sales call in the mid-90s was $292—and growing.[10] Multiply $292 by the more than 10 million people who watch a top-rated prime-time show, and the cost comes to a mind-boggling $2.9 *billion.* However, for only $120,000, Sunkist can buy 30-second TV commercials during "Ally McBeal" and reach the same 10 million people. In fact, through television, advertisers can talk to a *thousand* prospects for only $7.50 total, or about 3 percent of what it costs to talk to *one* prospect through personal selling.

Now, considering this brief synopsis of Sunkist history, how does Sunkist's advertising fit with the basic assumptions of a free-market economy? Has Sunkist's advertising helped make more citrus products available to more people at less cost? Has it contributed important information to people? Has the freedom to advertise contributed to the competitive environment? What if any externalities (or social costs) has Sunkist's advertising created?

Perhaps you can see from this one example how advertising contributes to a free economy. But, then why is advertising such a 20th-century phenomenon? Why wasn't it developed and used for the first few thousand years of recorded history?

The answer is simple: again, economics.

The Evolution of Advertising as an Economic Tool

Thousands of years ago, most people were engaged in hunting, herding, farming, or handicrafts. To make products, they used primitive hand tools. Most human effort was devoted to meeting basic survival needs: food, clothing, shelter. They lived in small, isolated communities where artisans and farmers bartered products and services among themselves. Distribution was limited to how far vendors could walk and "advertising" to how loud they could shout. Because goods weren't produced in great quantity, there was no need for advertising to stimulate mass purchases. There were also no mass media available for possible advertisers to use.

The Preindustrial Age

As the marketplace grew larger and became more complex, the demand for products increased, and the need for advertising slowly developed. At first, merchants hung carved signs in front of their shops so passersby could see what products were being offered. Most people couldn't read, so the signs often used symbols, such as a boot for a cobbler. This period was called the **preindustrial age,** and, for Western civilization, it extended from the beginning of recorded history to roughly the start of the 19th century.[11] (For a synopsis of advertising's role throughout the economic ages, see RL 1–1 in the Reference Library at the back of your book.)

During the preindustrial age, several important developments enabled the eventual birth of modern advertising. The Chinese invented paper and Europe had its first paper mill by 1275. In the 1440s, Johannes Gutenberg invented the printing press in Germany. The press was not only the most important development in the history of advertising; it also revolutionized the way people lived and worked.

Before the printing press, most people were illiterate. Only monks and scholars could read and write; the average person had to memorize important information

An early form of advertising. Until the advent of public schooling, most people couldn't read—so signs featured symbols of the goods or services for sale, such as the jerkin on this tailor's sign in Williamsburg, Virginia.

It wasn't until 1729 that Ben Franklin, innovator of advertising art, made ads more readable by using larger headlines and adding art. This 1746 ad announces the availability of the brigantine Elizabeth *to carry goods and passengers to Antigua.*

and communicate orally. Since oral communication could not be substantiated, people lived without documentable facts. And because dialects varied from region to region, most news never traveled more than 50 miles.

The introduction of printing allowed facts to be established, substantiated, recorded, and transported. People no longer had to rely on their memories. Movable letters provided the flexibility to print in local dialects. The slow hand transcription of the monks gave way to more rapid, volume printing by a less select group. Some entrepreneurs bought printing presses, mounted them in wagons, and traveled from town to town selling printing. This new technology made possible the first formats of advertising—posters, handbills, and signs—and the first mass medium—the newspaper. In effect, the cry of the vendor could now be multiplied many times and heard beyond the immediate neighborhood.

In 1472, the first ad in English appeared: a handbill tacked on church doors in London announcing a prayer book for sale. Two hundred years later the first newspaper ad was published, offering a reward for the return of 12 stolen horses. Soon newspapers carried ads for coffee, chocolate, tea, real estate, medicines, and even personal ads. These early ads were still directed to a very limited number of people: the customers of the coffeehouses where most newspapers were read.

By the early 1700s, the world's population had grown to about 600 million people, and some major cities were big enough to support larger volumes of advertising. In fact, the greater volume caused a shift in advertising strategy. Samuel Johnson, the famous English literary figure, observed in 1758 that advertisements were now so numerous that they were "negligently perused" and that it had become necessary to gain attention "by magnificence of promise." This was the beginning of *puffery* in advertising. (See the Ethical Issue on fluffing and puffing.)

In the American colonies, the *Boston Newsletter* began carrying ads in 1704. About 25 years later, Benjamin Franklin, the father of advertising art, made ads more readable by using large headlines and considerable white space. In fact, Franklin was the first American known to use illustrations in ads.

The Industrializing Age

In the mid-1700s, the Industrial Revolution began in England and by the early 1800s it had reached North America. Machinery began to replace animal power. By using these machines to mass-produce goods with uniform quality, large companies increased their productivity. For the first time, it cost people less to buy a product than to make it themselves. As people left the farm to work in the city, mass urban markets began to emerge. This further fueled market development and the growth of advertising.

Now producers needed mass consumption to match the high levels of manufactured goods. Fortunately, breakthroughs in bulk transportation, namely the railroad

This full-page of advertising from an 1894 Scientific American *(www.scientificamerican.com) is historically telling in that nearly all the ads have yet to develop any brand identity, but merely sell unbranded commodities like soap, paper, paint, or services.*

and steamship, facilitated sales beyond their local markets. By the mid-1800s, the world's population had doubled to 1.2 billion. The need for and the use of advertising and mass marketing techniques also began to grow.

During this **industrializing age,** which lasted roughly until the end of World War I, manufacturers were principally concerned with production. The primary burden of marketing fell on the wholesalers, who knew the sources of supply, the sources of transportation, the market requirements, and how to arrange for product shipments to the appropriate locations. They used advertising primarily as an information vehicle, placing announcements in publications called *price currents* to let retailer customers know about the sources of supply and shipping schedules for the basic, unbranded commodities they carried. Advertising to consumers was the job of the local retailer and the large mail-order catalog companies like Montgomery Ward and Sears Roebuck. Only a few innovative manufacturers (mostly of patent medicines, soaps, tobacco products, and canned foods) foresaw the usefulness of mass media advertising to stimulate consumer demand for their products beyond their immediate market areas.

For Americans, the *profession* of advertising began when Volney B. Palmer set up business in Philadelphia in 1841. He contracted with newspapers for large volumes of advertising space at discount rates and then resold the space to advertisers at a higher rate. The advertisers usually prepared the ads themselves.

In 1869, America's oldest existing advertising agency was formed in Philadelphia by Francis Ayer, who named the business after his father. N. W. Ayer & Sons was the first agency to charge a commission based on the "net cost of space" and the first to conduct a formal market survey. In 1890, Ayer became the first ad agency to operate as they do today—planning, creating, and executing complete ad campaigns in exchange for media-paid commissions or fees from advertisers. In 1892, Ayer set up a copy department and hired the first full-time agency copywriter.

The technological advances of the Industrial Revolution enabled the greatest changes in advertising since the 1400s. Photography, introduced in 1839, added credibility and a new world of creativity. Now ads could show products, people, and places as they really were, rather than how an artist visualized them.

In the 1840s, some manufacturers began using magazine ads to reach the mass market and stimulate mass consumption. Magazines became an ideal medium because they provided national advertising and offered the best quality of reproduction.

The telegraph, telephone, typewriter, phonograph, and later, motion pictures, all let people communicate as never before. With the development of the nationwide railroad system, the United States entered a period of spectacular economic growth. In 1896, when the federal government inaugurated rural free

In 1890, N. W. Ayer & Sons became the first agency to operate as agencies do today, planning, creating, and executing complete ad campaigns for advertisers. This 1899 Ayer ad for Uneeda biscuits (catch the play on words!) was one of a series of popular ads of the times.

Truth in Advertising: Fluffing and Puffing

Perhaps nothing characterizes advertising in the minds of most people more than the term *puffery*. In advertising, puffery means exaggerated commendation, or hype. The term comes from the Old English word *pyffan,* meaning "to blow in short gusts" or "to inflate; make proud or conceited." Puffery surely predates recorded history.

The Nature of Puffery

Regardless of its long heritage and current widespread use, we should question puffery's role in advertising. Inherently, puffery erodes advertising's credibility as a trustworthy messenger by first lowering the public's belief in the advertising they see. People begin to question those who support and create such advertising—the advertisers, ad professionals, and ultimately the media that run such ads. A slogan like "Quality worth your trust" is immediately deemed false when used in an ad for a product that's generally perceived as inferior. Soon people begin joking that the agency is out of touch or lying or "should be shot."

Puffery often employs literary devices such as metonymy, metaphor, irony, and absurdity. *Metonymy* is a verbal expression that associates similar entities. A king, for example, may be represented by "the Crown," a term that implies broader notions (royal heritage, the royal family, power and wealth, and so on). To claim, for example, that a TV antenna is a "miracle" implies that the antenna has wondrous and heavenly characteristics. In fact, this metonym sparked a lawsuit in which the advertiser failed to prove the antenna had miraculous qualities.

The *metaphor,* a close relative of the metonym, often uses the terms associated with one entity to describe another. The concepts "cash flow, liquid assets, pouring money into" use terms allied with water to portray financial activities. An ad proclaiming "Smartcard" in the headline and picturing a credit card with a huge computer chip employs the human characteristic of "smart" to metaphorically imply that the nonhuman card also has excellent reasoning powers. Obviously the card is not really smart, but few people would consider this metaphor unethical. They'd more likely be thankful for the way it simplifies a complex set of issues.

Irony relies on a double meaning and typically appears as a statement in a straightforward or colloquial language that cloaks a second meaning. Advertisers gravitate to irony for the shock value derived from the difference between the two meanings. An Allstate ad against drunk driving reads "It's amazing how much scrap metal you can get from a few cans of beer" and pictures a totaled car. Irony can be easily misunderstood by young or less-educated audiences and has resulted in court cases leading to disclaimers in advertising such as "do not try this at home."

Absurdity, like irony, relies on the juxtaposition of ideas, but in a seemingly irrational or unrelated manner. *M* magazine created an ad with the headline "An antique pocket watch held by a man in clothes from Cerruti atop an autographed baseball and balanced on a very dry martini with a French goose in the early stages of foie gras" and art portraying all the objects with tags. The visual's caption stated: "If you don't see the connection, you don't read *M*." Attention-getting absurdity? Yes. Puffery? Probably—but to understand better, we need to look at the law.

Defining Puffery

Regardless of the criticisms, puffery remains legal. And in the United States, it's relatively well-defined by law.

In 1906, as part of the Uniform Sales Act (now called the Uniform Commercial Code), a seller's opinion (an element of puffery) cannot constitute the sole basis of a warranty to the customer; more information is required. In 1916, the law stipulated puffery is acceptable if it is "mere exaggeration" but illegal if it invents advantages and then "falsely asserts their existence." The buyer's state of mind entered the definiton in 1941: "'Sales talk', or 'puffing',... is considered to be offered and understood as an expression of the seller's opinion only, which is to be discounted as such by the buyer, and on which no reasonable man would rely." The Federal Trade Commission joined the dialog in the late 1950s, confirming, "Puffery does not embrace misstatements of material facts."

---

mail delivery, direct-mail advertising and mail-order selling flourished. Manufacturers now had an ever-increasing variety of products to sell and a new way to deliver their advertisements and products to the public.

With the advent of public schooling, the nation reached an unparalleled 90 percent literacy rate. Manufacturers gained a large reading public that could understand print ads. The United States thus entered the 20th century as a great industrial state with a national marketing system propelled by advertising. With the end of World War I, the modern period in advertising emerged (for a timeline of advertising history, see Exhibit 1–5 on page 30).

The Industrial Age

The **industrial age** started around the turn of the century and lasted well into the 1970s. It was a period marked by tremendous growth and maturation of the country's industrial base. As U.S. industry met the basic needs of most of the population, commodity markets became saturated. Fresh mass markets then developed for the new, inexpensive brands of consumer luxury and convenience goods we referred to earlier as *consumer packaged goods.*

As you can see, puffery's legal definition establishes that the characteristics puffed must, in fact, actually exist. The challenge is defining where puffing crosses over from exaggeration to falsehood and then to deception. Falsehood is often the starting point of exaggeration, but falsehood is not necessarily harmful or injurious—in fact, it may be playful and creative. Deception, however, is interpreted as being injurious to consumers and is therefore illegal. Thus, puffery exists where exaggeration is not injurious or deceptive.

The Use of Puffery

Common usage portrays puffery as praise for the item to be sold using subjective opinions, superlatives, exaggerations, and vagueness, and generally stating no specific facts. Ivan Preston, the leading scholar on the issue of puffery, has established six levels of puffery:

- "Best" (strongest claim): "Nestlé's makes the very best chocolate."
- Best possible": "Nothing cleans stains better than Clorox bleach" or "Visa—it's everywhere you want to be."
- "Better": "Advil just works better."
- "Especially good": "Extraordinary elegance." (Coty)
- "Good": "M'm, m'm good." (Campbell's soup)
- "Subjective qualities" (weakest claim): "There's a smile in every Hershey bar."

Puffery often takes the form of "nonproduct facts," information not specifically about the product and therefore not directly ascertainable as being truths, falsehoods, or deceptions specific to the product. Nonproduct facts are typically about consumers: their personalities, lifestyles, fears, anxieties. An example is the Army's positioning message, "Be all that you can be in the Army." The claim relies on the potential for what can happen to the ad's readers while they're in the Army. It doesn't actually promise any specific benefits such as improved physical fitness or more education. Thus, regardless of what actually happens to readers who join up, the claim is neither true nor false about the Army.

Puffery can also be "artful display," the visual presentation of a product. Although not well defined by law, visual exaggeration is ever-present in ads to enhance moods, excite viewers, and more. The existence of professional models, for example, suggests that some individuals are more visually attractive than others. This factor makes them appealing (see the Ethical Issue in Chapter 11, "Does Sex Appeal?"). But does their appearance in an ad imply that owning the product will make the buyer more physically attractive? Although most prospective purchasers don't expect the product to improve their physical appearance, they might well become disappointed if the product failed to live up to the implied promise—the puffery—that it can improve their psychological self-image.

Judging Puffery

We live in exciting times. Populations are more literate, satellites and the Internet keep the world informed instantly, and modern technology speeds up the way we live and play. And part of the glitz of our modern life is puffery, adding pizzazz and stimulating our dreams.

But who should protect consumers from their love/hate relationship with puffery, especially when puffery crosses the line and becomes injurious? Who should evaluate puffery's ethics? The courts may, but only when a consumer challenges an advertiser. The actions and attitudes of the advertising profession can make a huge difference. If the First Amendment doesn't curtail them, the media can also affect the use and abuse of puffery.

Sources: John R. Rossiter and Larry Percy, *Advertising Communications & Promotion Management,* 2nd ed. (New York: The McGraw-Hill Companies, 1997), pp. 192–99; Barbara Stern, "Crafty Advertisers: Literary versus Literal Deceptiveness." *Journal of Public Policy & Marketing* 11 (April 1, 1992), p. 72; Barbara Stern, "Crafty Advertisers"; Alexander Simonson and Morris Holbrook, "Permissible Puffery versus Actionable Warranty in. . . ." *Journal of Public Policy & Marketing* 12 (September 1993), pp. 216; Ivan Preston, *Journal of Public Policy & Marketing* 16 (September 1997).

During the industrializing age of the 19th century, wholesalers controlled the marketing process as they distributed the manufacturers' unbranded commodity products. When those markets became saturated though, the wholesalers started playing one manufacturer off against another. This hurt manufacturers' profits dramatically, so they started looking for ways to wrest back control. The manufacturers changed their focus from a *production* orientation to a *sales* orientation. They dedicated themselves to new product development, strengthened their own sales forces, packaged and branded their products, and engaged in heavy national brand advertising. Early brands of this era included Wrigley's spearmint gum, Coca-Cola, Jell-O, Kellogg's corn flakes, and Campbell's soup.

In the 1920s, the United States was rich and powerful. As the war machine returned to peacetime production, society became consumption driven. The era of salesmanship had arrived and its bible was *Scientific Advertising,* written by the legendary copywriter Claude Hopkins at Lord & Thomas. Published in 1923, it became a classic and was republished in 1950 and 1980. "Advertising has reached the status of a science," Hopkins proclaimed. "It is based on fixed principles." His principles outlawed humor, style, literary flair, and anything that might detract from his basic copy strategy of a preemptive product claim repeated loudly and often.[12]

Exhibit 1–5
Timetable of advertising history.

3000 BC–1 AD	500–1599 AD	1600–1799	1800–1899
3000 BC. Written advertisement offering "Whole gold coin" for runaway slave "Shem." **500 BC.** Political and trade graffiti on Pompeii walls. **1 AD.** First upper-case lettering appears on Greek buildings.	**1455.** First printed Bible. **1472.** First printed ad in English tacked on London church doors. **1544.** Claude Garamond, first "typefounder," perfects a roman typeface that bears his name and is still used today.	**1650.** First newspaper ad offers reward for stolen horses. **1662.** *London Gazette* offers first advertising supplement. **1704.** First Ads in America published in the Boston Newsletter. **1729.** Ben Franklin is first to use "white space" and illustration in ads. **1785.** Widespread use of advertising and long print runs become possible.	**1841.** Volney B. Palmer becomes first "newspaper agent" (advertising agent) in America. **1844.** First magazine ad runs. **1869.** Francis W. Ayer founds ad agency bearing his father's name, N. W. Ayer & Sons, in Philadelphia. He initiates first "for commission" ad contract (1876), first market survey for an ad (1879), and first on-staff creative services (art in 1890, copywriting in 1892). **1888.** *Printers' Ink* is first U.S. publication for ad profession.

1900–1919	1920–1939	1940–1959	1960–1969
1900. Psychologists study the attention-getting and persuasive qualities of advertising. **1900.** Northwestern University is first to offer advertising as a discipline. **1903.** Scripps-McRae League of Newspapers appoints ad censor, rejects $500,000 in ads in first year. **1905.** First national ad plan is for the "Gillette Safety Razor." **1911.** First "truth in advertising" codes are established by what is now called the American Advertising Federation (AAF).	**1920s.** Albert Lasker, father of modern advertising, calls advertising "salesmanship in print." First ad testimonials by movie stars appear. Full-color printing is available in magazines. **1922.** First radio ad solves radio's need for financing. **1924.** N. W. Ayer produces first sponsored radio broadcast, the "Eveready Hour." **1930.** *Advertising Age* magazine is founded. **1938.** Wheeler-Lea amendments to FTC Act of 1938 grant FTC further power to curb false ad practices.	**1947.** Lanham Trademark Act protects brand names and slogans. **1946.** America has 12 TV stations broadcasting to the public. **1948.** 46 TV stations are operating and 300 others are awaiting FCC approval. **1950.** First political ads are used on TV by Gov. Dewey of New York. **1950s.** David Ogilvy's "Hathaway man" and "Commander Whitehead" become popular ad personae.	**1960s.** Doyle Dane Bernbach's "Think small" ad for American Volkswagen becomes one of the most famous ads of the decade, establishing a strong market position for the smallest European import. The agency's slogan for Avis, "We're only No. 2, so we try harder" is also very successful. New York's Madison Avenue becomes known worldwide as the center of the advertising world and features the best in advertising creativity.

1970–1979	1980–1989	1990–2000	
1971. Armed services begin first advertising for the new "all-volunteer" military ("Be all that you can be in the Army"). **1972.** The *Ad Age* article "Positioning: The Battle for Your Mind" by Al Ries and Jack Trout details the strategy of positioning that dominates the 70s. **1973.** Oil shortages begin period of "demarketing," ads aimed at slowing demand. **1970s (late).** Growth in self-indulgence, signified by popularity of self-fulfillment activities, spurs some agencies into making infomercials.	**1980s.** The "me" decade begins (baby-boomers are indulgent but want social accountability). Ad agency megamergers take place worldwide. **1982.** First edition of *Contemporary Advertising* is published. **1984.** The Internet (government controlled since 1973) is turned over to the private sector. **1986.** *Marketing Warfare* by Al Ries and Jack Trout portrays marketing in terms of classic warfare manual written by General Clausewitz in 1831.	**1990s.** Early part of decade experiences recession. Marketers shift funds from advertising to sales promotion, leaving major agencies to fail or merge. **1994.** Media glut leads to market fragmentation; network TV is no longer sole medium for reaching total marketplace. Ad professions adopt integrated marketing communications (IMC) as the new strategy to build market relationships. **2000.** The Internet is the fastest-growing new ad medium since TV, with 400 million users.	

This 1907 ad for Coca-Cola (www.coca-cola.com) reflects the styles of the period—not just in clothing but also in the use of language.

Radio was born at about the same time and rapidly became the nation's primary means of mass communication and a powerful new advertising medium with great immediacy. World and national news now arrived direct from the scene, and a whole new array of family entertainment—music, drama, and sports—became possible. Suddenly, national advertisers could quickly reach huge audiences. In fact, the first radio shows were produced by their sponsors' ad agencies.

On October 29, 1929, the stock market crashed, the Great Depression began, and advertising expenditures plummeted. In the face of consumer sales resistance and corporate budget cutting, the advertising industry needed to improve its effectiveness. It turned to research. Daniel Starch, A. C. Nielsen, and George Gallup had founded research groups to study consumer attitudes and preferences. By providing information on public opinion, the performance of ad messages, and sales of advertised products, these companies started a whole new business: the marketing research industry.

During this period, each brand sought to sell the public on its own special qualities. Wheaties became the "Breakfast of Champions" not because of its ingredients but because of its advertising. Manufacturers followed this strategy of *product differentiation* vigorously, seeking to portray their brands as different from and better than the competition by offering consumers quality, variety, and convenience.

But the greatest expansion of any medium occurred with the introduction of television in 1941. After World War II, TV advertising grew rapidly, and in time achieved its current status as the largest advertising medium in terms of advertising revenues.

During the postwar prosperity of the late 1940s and early 50s, consumers tried to climb the social ladder by buying more and more modern products. Advertising entered its golden era. A creative revolution ensued in which ads focused on product features that implied social acceptance, style, luxury, and success. Giants in the field emerged—people like Leo Burnett, David Ogilvy, and Bill Bernbach, who built their agencies from scratch and forever changed the way advertising was planned and created.[13] (RL 1–2 in the Reference Library profiles outstanding professionals from advertising's history.)

Rosser Reeves of the Ted Bates Agency introduced the idea that every ad must point out the product's *USP (unique selling proposition)*—features that differentiate it from competitive products. The USP was a logical extension of the Lasser and Hopkins "reason why" credo. But as the USP was used over and over, consumers started finding it difficult to see what was unique anymore.

Finally, as more and more imitative products showed up in the marketplace, all offering quality, variety, and convenience, the effectiveness of this strategy wore out. Companies turned to a new mantra: *market segmentation,* a process by which marketers searched for unique groups of people whose needs could be addressed through more specialized products. The image era of the 1960s was thus the natural culmination of the creative revolution. Advertising's emphasis shifted from product features to brand image or personality as advertisers sought to align their brands with particularly profitable market segments. Cadillac became the worldwide image of luxury, the consummate symbol of success, surpassed only by the aristocratic snootiness of Rolls-Royce.

But just as me-too product features killed the product differentiation era, me-too images eventually killed the market segmentation era. With increased competition, a new kind of advertising strategy evolved in the 1970s, where competitors' strengths became just as important as the advertiser's. Jack Trout and Al Ries trumpeted the arrival of the *positioning era.* They acknowledged the importance of

Think small.

Our little car isn't so much of a novelty any more.
A couple of dozen college kids don't try to squeeze inside it.
The guy at the gas station doesn't ask where the gas goes.
Nobody even stares at our shape.
In fact, some people who drive our little

flivver don't even think that about 27 miles to the gallon is going any great guns.
Or using five pints of oil instead of five quarts.
Or never needing anti-freeze.
Or racking up about 40,000 miles on a set of tires.
That's because once you get used to

some of our economies, you don't even think about them any more.
Except when you squeeze into a small parking spot.
Or renew your small insurance. Or pay a small repair bill. Or trade in your old VW for a new one.
Think it over.

Hailed by Jack Trout and Al Ries as "the most famous ad of the 60s," this Volkswagen ad co-opted the "small" position in consumers' minds, giving VW a leadership rank for many years.

product features and image, but they insisted that what really mattered was how the brand ranked against the competition in the consumer's mind—how it was positioned.

Positioning strategy proved to be an effective way to separate a particular brand from its competitors by associating that brand with a particular set of customer needs that ranked high on the consumer's priority list. Thus, it became a more effective way to use product differentiation and market segmentation. The most famous American ads of the positioning era were Volkswagen ("Think small"), Avis ("We're only no. 2"), and 7UP ("The uncola"). Other manufacturers tried the approach with great success. And product failures of the period, like Life Savers gum and RCA computers, were blamed on flawed positioning. Product differentiation, market segmentation, and positioning are all very important strategies to understand, so we will discuss them further in Chapter 5.

While this was all going on in the United States, across the Atlantic a new generation of advertising professionals had graduated from the training grounds of Procter & Gamble (P&G) and Colgate-Palmolive and were now teaching their clients the secrets of mass marketing. Lagging somewhat behind their U.S. counterparts due to the economic ravages of World War II, European marketers discovered the USP and the one-page strategic brief that P&G had popularized to bring focus to ad campaigns. Immediately following the war, French advertising pioneer Marcel Bleustein-Blanchet waged a frustrating battle to introduce U.S. research techniques to his country; a decade or two later, in-depth attitude and behavioral research was all the rage.[14] Since commercial TV was not as big as in the United States, European advertisers divided their media money between newspapers and outdoor media, along with a healthy dose of cinema advertising. Germany, the Netherlands, and Scandinavia wouldn't get commercial TV for another decade.[15]

In the 70s, though, the European Common Market already offered untapped opportunities. Following the American example, agencies and clients began to think multinationally to gain economies of scale. But it was not easy. While physically close, the countries of Europe were separated by a chasm of cultural diversity, making the use of single Europe-wide campaigns nearly impossible.[16]

The Postindustrial Age

Beginning around 1980, the **postindustrial age** has been a period of cataclysmic change. For the first time, people became truly aware of the sensitive environment in which we live and frightened by our dependence on vital natural resources. During the acute energy shortages of the 70s and 80s, a new marketing term, *demarketing,* appeared. Producers of energy and energy-consuming goods started using advertising to slow the demand for their products. Ads asked people to refrain from operating washers and dryers during the day when the demand for electricity peaked. In time, demarketing became a more aggressive strategic tool for advertisers to use against competitors, political opponents, and social problems. The California Department of Health Services, for example, is one of many organizations today that actively seek to demarket tobacco.

Then, following a period of unprecedented boom in the West and bust in the East, the Berlin Wall and the Iron Curtain came tumbling down. This finally ended the Cold War and with it the need for a defense-driven economy. Ogling the huge, new, untapped markets in the former Warsaw Pact states, Western financiers and marketers rubbed their hands in glee. To expand their power globally, big multi-

With the wave of new antismoking legislation came a raft of demarketing ads across the United States. In this American Lung Association ad, a man casually puffs on a cigarette while the vultures patiently wait for their next meal—him. This is a powerful way to reinforce the negative effects of smoking and to reduce demand for cigarettes (www.lungusa.org).

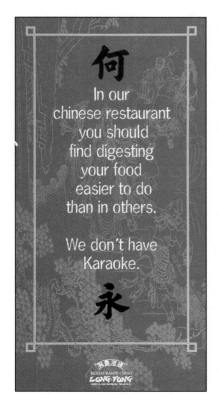

The United States isn't the only country to produce advertisements with zing. The U.K., France, and Spain are just as well-known for the panache and humor in their ads, such as this one made in Barcelona for Long-Fong Chinese restaurant.

national companies and their advertising agencies went on a binge, buying other big companies and creating a new word in the financial lexicon: *megamerger.*

By now European and Asian advertising had caught up with the United States. TV was suddenly the hot medium, and agencies focused on growth, acquisitions, and superior creative executions. For several years, Young & Rubicam in New York and Dentsu in Japan alternated as the largest advertising agency in the world. Then two brothers in London, Charles and Maurice Saatchi, started acquiring agencies globally. In rapid succession, a number of high-profile U.S. agencies disappeared under the Saatchi & Saatchi umbrella—big companies like Ted Bates Worldwide and Dancer, Fitzgerald, Sample. Saatchi & Saatchi was suddenly the largest agency in the world. Then followed more buyouts as the big agencies from Europe, the United States, and Japan emulated the merger mania of their huge multinational clients. Names of agency founders disappeared from the doors, replaced by initials and acronyms: WPP Group, RSCG, TBWA, FCA, DDB Needham, and FCB/Publicis, to mention just a few.[17]

The European agencies fueled their growth by establishing huge bulk-media-buying conglomerates, although their now-sophisticated clients stopped looking to the agencies for research and marketing advice. Rather, they expected extraordinary creative executions to give their brands an edge, and the agencies delivered. Awards at the Cannes film festival disclosed the blossoming of creative advertising from Spain and confirmed the creative leadership of the British, who were only slightly ahead of the French.[18]

Unfortunately, the euphoria of this period was short-lived. Sparked by unprecedented layoffs in the defense industries, the United States—indeed, most of the world—fell into the deepest and longest recession since the Great Depression. The effects lasted from the late 80s well into the 90s. The mergers stopped, the business world sucked in its collective belt, and management turned to new theories of total quality management (TQM), reengineering, and downsizing. The goal was to cut costs and increase efficiency, all in the name of better customer service. But to many employees, they were simply euphemisms for "you're fired." All too often the struggle to maintain profits actually led to reduced customer service.

Technology and Advertising

Today, high technology surrounds us—at work, at home, and where we play. It's so pervasive we often take it for granted and even refer to some sophisticated devices as "tools" or "toys." However, technology also shapes our daily lives profoundly in subtle ways we rarely realize.

Obviously advances in communications—the press, the telephone, radio, and television—enormously affect the way we think and act. But while we're happy with our new abilities to communicate faster and more conveniently, this new ease comes at a cost. Suddenly, for example, we find our planned schedules interrupted as people call day and night.

So what are the dynamics of technological change and how will new technologies impact our future?

Marshall McLuhan, the famous scholar of informational technologies, described the broad effects of technology on modern civilization in his classic series of articles and books. Today everyone is familiar with his concept of the "global village," where space satellites have eliminated geographic barriers, enabling news to spread worldwide as quickly as gossip in a small tribe.

According to McLuhan, human inventions are merely enhancements or extensions of ourselves. For example, a car enhances our capability to travel farther and faster than before. But curiously, the technologies that allow us to do a task more quickly, create a sort of reversal in thinking. Instead of saving us from more work, these devices allow people to do their own work. "What the nineteenth century had delegated to servants and housemaids we now do for ourselves," he explains.

McLuhan made this statement 30 years before the desktop computer let small businesspeople tackle projects that were once too costly. We can apply these theories to today's marketing and advertising in the form of database marketing and the production of promotional materials. This work was formerly subcontracted to larger, specialized firms that could afford mainframe computers and typesetting equipment.

This relatively sudden change affects advertising quite profoundly. According to McLuhan, "[In] the new electric Age of Information and programmed production, commodities themselves assume more and more the character of information." Now individuals take the responsibility for judging the quality and safety of products. Consumers take the tasks of the trusted butcher, baker, and candlestick maker and carefully evaluate comparative advertising, brand history, label data, magazine reviews, and Web site data before purchasing products.

So to increase awareness of recent and relevant technology in advertising, there's a Tech Talk box for each chapter. The goal is to introduce technologies in a manner that portrays their nature, characteristics, and probable effects on advertising. These are:

Chapter	Tech Talk Subjects(s)
2	Wireless communications
3	PDAs (personal digital assistant)
4	DVDs (digital video disk)
5	Market segmentation technologies
6	Database management software
7	Project planning software
8	Media planning software
9	Direct marketing software
10	Presentation technology
11	Web page design and editing
12	TV commercial computer story boards
13	Graphic productions technologies
14	Electric prepress technology
15	Media buying technologies
16	Multimedia and the Internet
17	Outdoor technology

Source: Marhsall McLuhan, *Understanding Media: The Extensions of Man* (New York: McGraw-Hill Paperbacks, 1965), p. 37.

Two related economic factors characterize the marketing world of this period: (1) the aging of traditional products, with a corresponding growth in competition, and (2) the growing affluence and sophistication of the consuming public, led by the huge baby-boomer generation.[19]

The most important factor was competition, intensified by lower trade barriers and growing international trade. As high profits lured imitators into the marketplace, each offering the most attractive product features at less expense, consumers became the beneficiaries of more choices, higher quality, and lower prices. The priests of positioning, Al Ries and Jack Trout, foresaw this competitive struggle in the mid-80s. They published *Marketing Warfare,* which portrayed marketing as a *war* that businesses must be prepared to wage. Ries and Trout outlined four strategic positions in the marketplace: *defensive, offensive, flanking,* and *guerrilla.* Companies had to operate from one of these strategic positions, they said, based on their relative strengths and weaknesses.

On the demand side, newly affluent consumers concerned themselves more with the quality of their lives. With their basic commodity needs already met, the baby boomers were now interested in saving time and money to spend on more leisure-time activities or on products, services, and social causes that represented the kind of people they aspired to be.

In highly competitive industries, a company may benefit by going head-to-head against the competition through marketing warfare. In this ad, for instance, Pepsico (www.pepsiworld.com) attempts to distinguish its brand from Coca-Cola by parodying a Coke delivery driver trying a can of Pepsi.

"Diner" :60

(Open on a diner with a Pepsi truck and a Coca-Cola truck parked outside in the snow. The camera moves into the diner and the waitress serves the Coca-Cola driver.)

WAITRESS: Here we go.

COCA-COLA DRIVER: Thanks, Darlene.

(A Pepsi driver walks in and sits down at the counter, a seat or two away from the Coca-Cola driver.)

PEPSI DRIVER: Aaah, blueberry pie and a Pepsi.

WAITRESS: You got it.

PEPSI DRIVER: Thanks.

SFX: Jukebox starts playing a song. (The waitress puts a Pepsi in front of the Pepsi driver.)

PEPSI DRIVER: Good song.

COCA-COLA DRIVER: Great song.

PEPSI DRIVER: Working late on the holidays?

COCA-COLA DRIVER: Yeah, it's hard on the kids.

(The two move in closer to each other and start exchanging photographs, stories, both are laughing and having a good time. The Coca-Cola driver

pushes over his can of soda and the Pepsi driver takes a sip. The Pepsi driver does the same to the Coca-Cola driver and he takes a sip. The Pepsi driver reaches over to get his can of Pepsi back.)

COCA-COLA DRIVER: Naah, naah, naah.

(The Coca-Cola driver refuses. The camera cuts to the outside of the diner, and a chair goes flying through the window.)

SUPER: Nothing else is a Pepsi.

By the mid-1980s, an avalanche of ads—especially in the toiletry and cosmetics industries—was aimed at the "me" generation ("L'Oreal. Because I'm worth it."). At the same time, the nation's largest industrial concerns spent millions of dollars on corporate advertising to extol their social consciousness and good citizenship for cleaning up after themselves and protecting the environment.

As the U.S. economy slowed, many companies were chasing too few consumer dollars. Clients trimmed their ad budgets, and many turned to more cost-effective sales promotion alternatives, such as coupons, direct mail, and direct marketing. By 1990, advertising had lost 25 percent of its share of the marketing budget to other forms of marketing communications.[20]

As the 90s unfolded, this recession deepened. The traditional advertising industry found itself threatened on all sides and suffering from overpopulation.[21] Clients demanded better results from their promotional dollars; small, imaginative, upstart agencies competed for (and won) some big accounts that had never been available to them; TV viewers appeared immune to conventional commercials; and a plethora of new media options based on new technologies promised to reinvent the very process of advertising. In three short years, the advertising agency business lost over 13,500 jobs. Major clients like Coca-Cola defected from Madison Avenue, giving

The recession of the early 90s slammed the advertising industry with over 13,500 layoffs. However, specialists in small, regional creative shops were able to snatch away some large accounts during this period and produce ads for established corporations. This Coca-Cola ad came from the clever minds at Creative Artists Agency in Hollywood (a talent agency!).

New technology has meant new media in the 90s, manifested largely in the Internet.
This has opened new avenues of exposure for advertisers. This Web site for the
Discovery Channel (www.discovery.com) promotes the cable TV network's programs
and, at the same time, features ad banners for other companies, too.

various portions of their business to specialists in small, regional creative shops and media-buying services. But the setback went far beyond the agency business. Throughout the media world, newspapers, magazines, and TV networks all lost advertising dollars. About 40 magazines went out of business during the two-year slump.[22]

At the same time, a five-year study by the Ayer agency found consumers and marketers moving in opposite directions. Corporate management felt pressure to simplify and consolidate operations, but consumer markets were becoming increasingly diverse and fragmented. Armed with remote controls, VCRs, 50-plus channels, and pockets full of competitors' coupons, consumers had become too sophisticated, too quick, and too fickle for slow-moving, traditional marketers who were disarmed by shrinking budgets. To counter this, Fred Posner, Ayer's director of research, urged marketers to redefine and reembrace the concept of branding (a subject we discuss in chapters 5 and 9).[23]

Other industry leaders echoed the need to get back to basics. Hank Seiden, former chair of Ketchum Advertising, denounced the glut of irrelevant and costly product commercials that were "99 percent show biz and 1 percent advertising." In an era when most sales are conquest sales (won at the expense of a competitor), he maintained that a "mean, lean sales point the advertiser believes in should come wrapped in a commercial without a trace of fat on it."[24]

But more and more, industry spokespeople viewed the problems as systemic. Keith Reinhard, CEO of DDB Needham Worldwide, acknowledged, "This isn't [just] a recession we're in, and we're not going to go back to the good old days."

In 1992 and 1993, U.S. marketers began shifting dollars back from sales promotion to advertising to build their brands. In 1994, ad budgets surged by 8.1 percent to $150 billion nationally. But hardly anybody thought the problems were over.[25] Technology, evolving lifestyles, and the rising cost of reaching consumers had already changed the advertising business forever. With the explosion of interest in the Internet and the World Wide Web, we were on the threshold of a new electronic frontier, entering what Tom Cuniff, VP/creative director at Lord, Dentsu & Partners, calls "the second creative revolution."[26] The future would not be business as usual.

The Global Interactive Age: Looking toward the 21st Century

In the last 15 years, expenditures by foreign advertisers increased more rapidly than either U.S. or Canadian expenditures, thanks to improved economic conditions and a desire for expansion. Recent estimates of worldwide advertising expenditures outside the United States exceed $193 billion per year.[27] The importance of advertising in individual countries depends on the nation's level of development and national attitude toward promotion. Typically, advertising expenditures are higher in countries with higher personal incomes. As Exhibit 1–6 shows, the top 10 worldwide advertisers are based in many different countries.

While the Communist countries once condemned advertising as an evil of capitalism, Eastern European countries now encourage private enterprise and realize the benefits of advertising. Even China appears to have inherited the capitalist sensibility of Hong Kong.[28]

The explosion of new technologies in the last decade has affected advertising considerably. With cable TV and satellite receivers, viewers can watch channels devoted to single types of programming, such as straight news, home shopping, sports, or comedy. This shift transformed television from the most widespread of mass media to a more specialized, "narrowcasting" medium.[29] Now small companies and product marketers that appeal to a limited clientele can use TV to reach audiences with select interests.

A concurrent change is the growing presence of VCRs and remote controls, which allow viewers to avoid commercials altogether by channel surfing during breaks or simply zipping through them when watching a previously recorded show. Advertisers have tried placing commercials on rented videos, but the trend has yet to take hold, perhaps because viewers can still zap them.

Computer technology has also had a huge impact. Personal computers, modems, e-mail, and electronic bulletin boards give advertisers new media for reaching potential customers. Now even the smallest companies can maintain computer databases of customers' names to integrate their marketing campaigns.

But what's in store is even more dynamic—the global information highway, and with it an interactive revolution. Advertising is evolving into a two-way medium where consumers with PCs, modems, CD-ROMs, and cable TV can choose the information they access and then spend time researching the product information they desire.[30] With interactivity, rather than zipping or zapping commercials, people actually seek them out. As we discuss in Chapter 16, this is a revolutionary way for advertisers to reach consumers. Agencies now have the opportunity to prove once again that advertising creativity is not about winning awards but about helping marketers *sell* things.[31]

Exhibit 1–6
Top 10 international advertisers.

Rank	Advertiser (parent company)	Headquarters	Primary business	Countries in which spending was reported
1	Procter & Gamble	Cincinnati	Soaps	Australia, Austria, Britain, Canada, France, Germany, Greece, India, Italy, Japan, Malaysia, Mexico, Netherlands, Pan Arabia, Puerto Rico, Taiwan, Thailand, Turkey, U.S.
2	Unilever	Rotterdam/London	Soaps	Argentina, Australia, Brazil, Britain, Canada, Denmark, France, Germany, Greece, India, Italy, Japan, Malaysia, Mexico, Netherlands, Pan Arabia, Portugal, Puerto Rico, South Africa, Spain, Switzerland, Taiwan, Thailand, Turkey, U.S.
3	Nestlé SA	Vevey, Switzerland	Food	Argentina, Australia, Austria, Brazil, Britain, France, Germany, India, Japan, Malaysia, Mexico, Netherlands, Pan Arabia, Portugal, Puerto Rico, Spain, Switzerland, Taiwan, Thailand, Turkey, U.S.
4	Toyota Motor Corp	Toyota City, Japan	Automotive	Canada, Finland, Japan, Norway, Taiwan, Thailand, U.S.
5	PSA Peugeot-Citroen SA	Paris	Automotive	Argentina, Austria, Britain, Denmark, France, Germany, Netherlands, Pan Arabia, Portugal, Spain, Switzerland, Thailand, U.S.
6	Volkswagen AG	Wolfsburg, Germany	Automotive	Brazil, Britain, France, Germany, Mexico, South Africa, Spain, Sweden, Switzerland, Thailand, U.S.
7	Nissan Motor Co.	Tokyo, Japan	Automotive	Australia, Britain, Germany, Japan, Mexico, Pan Arabia, Switzerland, Thailand, U.S.
8	Coca-Cola Co.	Atlanta	Soft drinks	Argentina, Belgium, Brazil, Canada, Chile, Czech Republic, Greece, Hungary, Mexico, Peru, Romania, Slovak Republic, Turkey, U.S., Vietnam
9	Philip Morris Cos.	New York	Food	Argentina, Australia, Austria, Brazil, Britain, Canada, Denmark, France, Germany, Hong Kong, Japan, Malaysia, Mexico, Netherlands, Pan Arabia, Spain, Taiwan, Thailand, U.S.
10	General Motors	Detroit	Automotive	Brazil, Canada, Switzerland, U.K., U.S.

Advertising has come a long way from the simple sign on the bootmaker's shop. Today it is a powerful device that announces the availability and location of products, describes their quality and value, imbues brands with personality, and simultaneously defines the personalities of the people who buy them. More than a reflection of society and its desires, advertising can start and end fads, trends, and credos—sometimes all by itself.[32]

In turn, advertising is shaped by the very technology used to convey its message. In the past it was always a monolog. But today it's evolving into a dialog. The medium and the message have become virtually inseparable.

The endless search for competitive advantage and efficiency has made advertising's journey in the last 100 years fascinating. Now companies are realizing that their most important asset is not capital equipment, or research capability, or their line of products. In the heated competition of the global marketplace, their most important asset is their customer and the relationship they have with that person or organization. Protecting that asset has become the new marketing imperative for the 21st century. In an effort to do a better job of *relationship marketing,* companies are now learning that they must be consistent in both what they say and what they do. It's not enough to produce outstanding advertising anymore. They must integrate all their marketing communications with everything else they do, too. That's what *integrated marketing communications* really means. And that will present exciting new challenges to advertising professionals in the years ahead.

Society and Ethics:
The Effects of Advertising

As a social force, advertising has been a major factor in improving the standard of living in the United States and around the world. By publicizing the material, social, and cultural opportunities of a free enterprise society, advertising has encouraged increased productivity by both management and labor.

With just a small amount of money, for instance, you can buy a car today. It may be secondhand, but from advertising you know it's available. If you earn more money, you can buy a new car or one with more luxury features. You can also make a statement about yourself as an individual with the vehicle you purchase. As with many products, advertising has created a personality for each automobile make and model on the market. You, as a free individual, have the opportunity to select the product that best matches your functional or social needs and aspirations.

Advertising serves other social needs besides simply stimulating sales. Newspapers, magazines, radio, and television all receive their primary income from advertising. This facilitates freedom of the press. Public services by a number of advertising organizations also foster growth and understanding of important social issues and causes. The Red Cross, Community Chest, United Way, and other noncommercial organizations receive continuous financial support and volunteer assistance due in large part to the power of advertising.

However, advertising is certainly not without its shortcomings. Since its beginnings, the profession has had to struggle with issues of honesty and ethics. In fact, in the early 1900s, the advertising profession was forced to mend its ethical ways. Consumers suffered for years from unsubstantiated product claims, especially for patent medicines and health devices. The simmering resentment finally boiled over into a full-blown consumer movement, which led to government regulation and ultimately to industry efforts at self-regulation.

In 1906, Congress responded to public outrage by passing the Pure Food and Drug Act to protect the public's health and control drug advertising. In 1914, it passed the Federal Trade Commission Act to protect the public from unfair business practices, including misleading and deceptive advertising.

Advertising practitioners themselves formed groups to improve advertising effectiveness and promote professionalism and started vigilance committees to safeguard

Like any business, the Boy Scouts of America (www.bsa.scouting.org) needs public exposure for support. But to get it, it uses noncommercial advertising. These ads are considered public service announcements because they provide a social service to the community without a profit motive.

the integrity of the industry. The Association of National Advertisers (ANA), the American Advertising Federation (AAF), and the Better Business Bureau (BBB) are today's outgrowths of those early groups.

But in times of economic crisis, false and misleading advertising would invariably reappear, perhaps out of advertisers' desperation. During the Depression years, several best-selling books exposed the advertising industry as an unscrupulous exploiter of consumers, giving birth to a new consumer movement and further government regulation.

In the 1970s, a new American consumer movement grew out of the widespread disillusionment following the Kennedy assassination, the Vietnam War, the Watergate scandals, and the sudden shortage of vital natural resources—all communicated instantly to the world via new satellite technology. These issues fostered cynicism and distrust of the establishment and tradition, and gave rise to a new twist in moral consciousness. On the one hand, people justified their personal irresponsibility and self-indulgence in the name of self-fulfillment. On the other, they attacked corporate America's quest for self-fulfillment (profits) in the name of social accountability.

Today, corporate America has generally cleaned up the major inequities in advertising. But now attention has shifted to more subtle problems of puffery, advertising to children, the advertising of legal but unhealthful products, and advertising ethics. We believe ethics in advertising is such an important issue that we have included a feature on this topic in every chapter (see Exhibit 1–7).

Exhibit 1–7

Ethical issues discussed in this text.

Chapter/ethical issue	Issue discussed
1. Truth in Advertising: Fluffing and Puffing	How exaggeration spans acceptable limits to illegality
2. Ethical Dilemma or Ethical Lapse?	Ignoring ethical issues and being confused about them
3. Accounting for Account Reviews	Etiquette between agencies and prospective clients
4. Is It Marketing or Is It Exploitation?	Taking advantage of markets in a crisis
5. Brand Niching May Cause Brand Switching	Targeting markets can lead to ethical problems
6. Research Statistics Can Be Friends or Foes	How statistics can be misunderstood and/or misrepresented
7. The Winds of Ad Wars	Comparative advertising must be done with care
8. Political Advertising: Positively Negative?	Pointing out individual failures is legal but not necessarily ethical
9. The Ethical Cost of Gifts and Commissions	Influence and the appearance of it can be illegal
10. When Is Advertising Not Really Advertising?	Editorials promoting products can be misleading
11. Does Sex Appeal?	Sexual inferences can lead to real consequences
12. Imitation, Plagiarism, or Flattery?	It's a close call between borrowing and stealing
13. Manipulating Morphing's Magic	Artistic changes may create new meaning and violate rights
14. Ethics, Ergonomics, and Economics	Ethical decision or indecision may create medical problems
15. Children's Advertising: Child's Play?	Protecting the innocent from calculated sales pitches
16. Is Privacy Going Public?	The individual's rights versus the public's rights
17. Does Spillover Need Mopping Up?	Messages designed for one audience may hurt others

In short, advertising has had a pronounced effect on society as well as the economy. It has also fostered a host of social attitudes and laws that have dramatically affected advertising itself. We'll take a closer look at these issues in Chapter 2.

Chapter **Summary**

As a tool of marketing communications, advertising is the structured and composed, nonpersonal communication of information. It is usually paid for and usually persuasive, about products, services, or ideas, by identified sponsors through various media. Looking at four important dimensions of advertising (communication, marketing, economic, and social) can help us better understand what advertising is and how it has evolved.

Since advertising is first and foremost communication, advertisers cannot afford to take the communication process for granted. The basic human communication process begins when one party (the source) formulates an idea, encodes it as a message, and sends it via some channel or medium to another party (the receiver). The receiver must decode the message in order to understand it. To respond, the receiver formulates a new idea, encodes that concept, and then sends a new message back through some channel. A message that acknowledges or responds to the original message is feedback, and it affects the encoding of a new message. In advertising, the communication process is complex because of the multidimensional nature of the source, the message, and the recipient. Traditionally, advertising has been principally a one-way process, but with today's new Internet technology consumers can give feedback to advertising messages in real time using the same channels as the sender.

Marketing is the one business function whose primary role is to attract revenues, so advertising is an important marketing tool. The targets of a firm's marketing will determine the targets of its advertising. There are two major types of audiences marketers address with their advertising: consumers and businesses. Within each of these categories, though, are special forms of advertising, such as retail, trade, professional, and agricultural.

Similarly, a firm's marketing mix—or strategy—will establish the type of advertising needed and the skills required to implement it. The marketing mix includes those elements over which the marketer has control: product, price, distribution, and communication. Depending on the product marketed, the advertiser may use packaged-goods advertising, professional services advertising, or some other type such as high-tech advertising. Likewise, the firm's pricing strategy will determine if it should use sale advertising, loss-leader advertising, or regular price-line advertising.

The distribution strategy dictates the firm's use of local, regional, national, or international advertising. The communication element determines the mix of marketing communications tools to be used.

These include advertising, personal selling, sales promotion, public relations activities, and collateral materials.

To achieve consistency in all the organization's messages, sophisticated companies seek to integrate their marketing communications with all other corporate activities through a process called integrated marketing communications.

In economic theory, there are four fundamental assumptions of free-market economics: self-interest, perfect information, many buyers and sellers, and absence of externalities. Given these principles, there are a number of functions and effects of advertising in a free economy. It identifies and differentiates products; communicates information about them; induces nonusers to try products and users to repurchase them; stimulates products' distribution; increases product use; builds value, brand preference, and loyalty; and lowers the overall cost of sales.

The greatest impact on the evolution of advertising has been economic. In ancient times when most people could not read or write, there was little need for advertising. Marketers used symbols on signs to advertise their products. As the world expanded, urban populations soared, and manufacturing and communication technologies developed, as did advertising. Printing was the first major technology to affect advertising; cable TV and computers are the most recent.

With changing economies and increased competition, advertising has evolved from the preindustrial age through the industrializing and industrial ages to the postindustrial age. Since World War II, advertisers have used a variety of strategies, such as product differentiation, market segmentation, and positioning, to set their products apart. Recently the advertising industry experienced a period of retrenchment and reevaluation, but the future offers new opportunities for advertisers and agencies that can harness the interactive revolution and develop deep relationships with their customers.

As a social force, advertising has helped improve the standard of living in the United States and around the world. Advertising makes us aware of the availability of products, imbues products with personality, and enables us to communicate information about ourselves through the products we buy. Through its financial support, advertising also fosters the free press and the growth of many nonprofit organizations.

However, advertising has also been severely criticized over the years for its lack of honesty and ethics. This has given rise to numerous consumer movements and a plethora of laws that now regulate the practice of advertising.

Important **Terms**

action advertising, *18*
actual consumers, *12*
advertising, *7, 18*
agricultural advertising, *15*
author, *10*

autobiographical messages, *10*
awareness advertising, *18*
branding, *20*
business advertising, *14*
business-to-business advertising, *15*

channel, *9*
collateral materials, *19*
consumer advertising, *14*
consumers, *14*
decode, *9*

direct-response advertising *18*

drama messages, *10*

encoding, *9*

farm advertising, *15*

feedback, *9*

global advertising, *17*

goods, *7*

ideas, *7*

image advertising, *16*

implied consumers, *11*

industrial age, *28*

industrializing age, *27*

international advertising, *17*

local advertising, *17*

marketing, *13*

marketing communications, *6, 17*

marketing PR, *18*

media, *8*

medium, *7*

message, *9*

narrative messages, *10*

national advertising, *17*

noise, *12*

noncommercial advertising, *18*

nonproduct advertising, *18*

persona, *10*

personal selling, *17*

postindustrial age, *32*

preindustrial age, *25*

process, *13*

product, *7*

product advertising, *18*

professional advertising, *15*

public relations (PR), *18*

public relations activities, *18*

public relations advertising, *18*

receiver, *9*

regional advertising, *17*

regular price-line advertising, *16*

retail advertising, *14*

sales promotion, *18*

services, *7*

source, *9*

sponsor, *10*

sponsorial consumers, *11*

target audience, *13*

target market, *13*

trade advertising, *15*

Review **Questions**

1. How does advertising for the American Cancer Society compare with the standard definition of advertising?

2. How does advertising differ from public relations activities?

3. In the marketing communication process, what are the various dimensions of the source, the message, and the receiver?

4. How does marketing strategy affect the type of advertising used?

5. How would you differentiate the advertising used in the industrializing age and the industrial age?

6. What has been the most important influence on advertising in the postindustrial age?

7. What are three examples of companies or organizations that use a demarketing strategy?

8. What companies can you think of that are engaged in marketing warfare?

9. As a consumer, are you likely to save money buying at a store that doesn't advertise? Explain.

10. What effects do you believe advertising has had on society in general? Explain.

Exploring the **Internet**

The Internet exercises here address the two core areas of advertising covered in Chapter 1: advertising as communication (Exercise 1) and as a marketing tool (Exercise 2).

1. The Communication Process

    If you have not done so already, go online and surf the Net for a while. Then anwer the following questions:

    a. What are the various means available to advertisers for encoding and sending a message in cyberspace?

    b. What are some potential sources of noise when marketers send a message via the Internet and/or online services?

    c. What types of feedback are available to marketers that can help determine message delivery/comprehension?

    d. Choose one website or advertising banner as an example and identify the following communication elements: source, author, message, channel, receiver, feedback, and potential noise.

2. Role of Advertising

    In Chapter 1, you learned about the standard definition of advertising and the various roles and forms that advertising can take. Browse through the following websites and discuss what type of advertising each uses and what the purpose of the advertising is:

    a. American Cancer Society **www.cancer.org**

    b. Tobacco BBS **www.tobacco.org**

    c. Nike **www.nike.com**

    d. Ford **www.ford.com**

    e. McDonald's **www.mcdonalds.com**

    f. F.A.O. Schwartz
        www.faoschwartz.com/shopping/index.html

    g. United Parcel Service **www.ups.com**

Chapter **Two**

The Economic, Social, and Regulatory Aspects of Advertising

Objective   To identify and explain the economic, social, ethical, and legal issues advertisers must consider. The basic economic principles that guided the evolution of advertising have social and legal effects. When they are violated, social issues arise and the government may take corrective measures. Society determines what is offensive, excessive, and irresponsible; government bodies determine what is deceptive and unfair. To be law-abiding, ethical, and socially responsible, as well as economically effective, advertisers must understand these issues.

After studying this chapter, you will be able to:

- **Debate** advertising's role in a variety of economic issues.
- **Categorize** the two main types of social criticisms of advertising.
- **Apply** an economic model to advertising's effect on society.
- **Discuss** the difference between social responsibility and ethics in advertising.
- **Understand** how governments regulate advertising here and abroad.
- **Discuss** recent court rulings that affect advertisers' freedom of speech.
- **Explain** how federal agencies regulate advertising to protect both consumers and competitors.
- **Describe** the roles state and local governments play in advertising regulation.
- **Evaluate** the effectiveness of nongovernment organizations in regulating advertising.

On rare occasions, an advertiser will produce an ad or campaign that is so arresting, so eye-catching, so sensational, that print and broadcast journalists devote millions of dollars worth of free time and space to show it and discuss it. Like Apple Computer's famous "1984" commercial and Wendy's "Where's the beef?" series, these campaigns often become part of advertising folklore as they create huge sales for their sponsors and industry kudos for the agencies that produce them. • Not always, though. • In 1995, one campaign created such a stir that not only the press talked about it. So did a wide variety of industry and consumer groups and even the FBI, which decided to investigate the advertiser for possible violations of child pornography laws. • Of course we're talking about Calvin Klein. • Calvin Klein had always pushed the sexual envelope in his ads for perfume, underwear, and jeans. This time, though, people said he went too far. In fact, ad critic Bob Garfield wrote that as often as Calvin Klein had crossed the line beyond taste and decency over the past 15 years, this time he went utterly beyond the pale: "He has gone beyond gratuitousness, beyond titillation, beyond vulgarity to the very core of our moral sensibilities." • The campaign in question was for CK Jeans and depicted young men and women trying out for a commercial or movie role. The actors, who actually looked like young teenagers, posed in various provocative states of undress as an older man asked leering questions off-camera. While there was no nudity, in some shots the models' underwear showed, and the style and setting of both the commercials and print ads

were reminiscent of low-budget, basement pornography flicks of the 70s. • Immediately dubbed the kiddie-porn campaign, it drew complaints from every quarter. Various church and family groups threatened to picket department stores carrying the Calvin Klein line. One New York City councilman even called for a boycott of all the designer's products. Executives in the media debated whether to accept the ads; industry experts criticized the campaign roundly; and Klein's own retailers begged the company to pull the campaign. • Very few people stood up for Calvin Klein's freedom of speech. The American Booksellers Association did, as did Larry Flynt, the publisher of *Hustler* magazine. They were very concerned about the far-reaching consequences of any attempt to expand the child pornography laws. Maya Stowe of the *College Hill Independent* pointed out that while lots of campaigns employ suggestive sex, Calvin Klein's ads are far more honest. She saw the campaign as a sophisticated quasi-joke that laughed at the cult of objectification, and she lamented the fact that

"Americans just didn't get it." ● "People weren't supposed to buy the jeans because they wanted to look like the models in the ads," she said. "They were supposed to buy the jeans because the ads were unique, racy, and cool in some complex way."[1] ● Perhaps this is what Calvin Klein meant when he hastily removed the campaign and contritely proclaimed that he was "taken aback," that his campaign had been "misunderstood," and that the ads "weren't conveying the message we had hoped."[2] ● Critics were more cynical. Carolyn Christenson of *The Bucknellian* wrote that Klein knows his ads are controversial and shocking. "He has learned that if you make a small amount of the right kind of noise, the media will deliver millions of dollars' worth of free publicity. The whole arc of the campaign—the ads, the controversy, the contrite reaction—was a win-win proposition for Klein."[3] ● Maya Stowe agreed, but she was impressed with the creative way Klein instigated the scandal: "His ads are simultaneously straightforward and ironic; they define aesthetics while questioning the role of media in all our lives." ● "After all," she said, "if you're Calvin Klein, you can probably afford to make people a little uncomfortable every now and then." ●

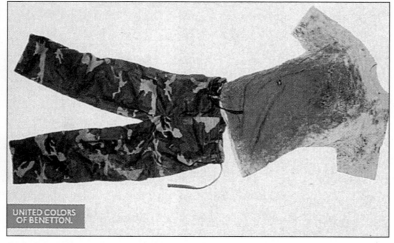

Views of offensiveness do not always revolve around the sexual content of ads. In 1994, the fashion designer Benetton began its campaign for peace. The blood-stained T-shirt and trousers belonging to Marinko Gagro, who was killed during the war in the Balkans, became a symbol for peace in Oliviero Toscani's famous photo. While the ad became quite controversial, many peace associations expressed solidarity with Benetton, and the Art Director's Club of New York awarded Benetton a medal for raising social awareness through its advertising campaigns. Spend some time on Benetton's Web site (www.benetton.com) and see how the company uses its themeline, the United Colors of Benetton, to promote racial tolerance and peace among nations.

The Many **Controversies** about Advertising

Advertising is one of the most visible activities of business. By inviting people to try their products, companies risk public criticism and attack if their advertising displeases or offends the audience or if their products don't measure up to the advertised promise. Proponents of advertising say it's therefore safer to buy advertised products because, when a company's name and reputation are on the line, it tries harder to fulfill its promises (especially when it lists product benefits).

Advertising is both applauded and criticized not only for its role in selling products but also for its influence on the economy and on society. For years, critics have denigrated advertising for a wide range of sins—some real, some imagined.

John O'Toole, the late chair of Foote, Cone & Belding and president of the American Association of Advertising Agencies, pointed out that many critics attack advertising because it *isn't something else.* Advertising isn't journalism, education, or entertainment—although it often performs the tasks of all three. To go back to Albert Lasker's original definition, advertising is salesmanship in print (or in today's parlance, *in the paid space and time of mass media*). As a means of communication, advertising shares certain traits of journalism, education, and entertainment, but it shouldn't be judged by those standards. Sponsors advertise because they hope it will help them sell some product, service, or idea.[4]

Notwithstanding O'Toole's articulate defense, many controversies still swirl around the whole field of advertising. Some of them focus on advertising's economic role. For example, how does advertising affect the value of products? Does it cause higher or lower prices? Does it promote competition or discourage it? How does advertising affect overall consumer demand? What effect does it have on consumer choice and on the overall business cycle?

Other controversies focus on the societal effects of advertising. For instance, does advertising make us more materialistic? Does it force us to buy things we don't need? Does it reach us subliminally in ways we can't control? How does it affect the art and culture of our society? Does advertising debase our language?

From these economic and social controversies, new questions arise regarding the responsibility for and control of advertising. What is the proper role for participants in the marketing process? How much latitude should marketers have in the kinds of products they promote and how they advertise them? And what about consumers? Don't they have some responsibility in the process? Finally, what is the proper role of government? What laws should we have to protect consumers? And what laws go too far and violate the marketer's freedom of speech?

These are important questions, and there are no simple answers. But debate is healthy. This chapter addresses some of the major questions and criticisms about advertising, both the pros and the cons, and delves into the regulatory methods used to remedy abuses of the system.

Recall from Chapter 1 the underlying principle of free-market economics—that a society is best served by empowering people to make their own decisions and act as free agents, within a system characterized by four fundamental assumptions: *self-interest, many buyers and sellers, perfect information,* and *absence of externalities* (social costs).

This fundamentally utilitarian framework, derived from the goal of society to promote behaviors that foster the greatest good for the most people, offers a system of economic activity—free enterprise—that has accomplished that goal better than any other economic system in history. This is why societies around the world are increasingly adopting free-enterprise economics.

By using this framework for our discussion of advertising controversies, we have a basis for understanding how advertising may contribute to, or detract from, the basic goal of free enterprise: "the most good for the most people."

The **Economic Impact** of Advertising

Advertising accounts for approximately 2.3 percent of the U.S. gross domestic product (GDP). In relation to the total U.S. economy, this percentage is small, but it's higher than in most countries. As Marcel Bleustein-Blanchet, the father of modern French advertising, pointed out that it's no coincidence that the level of advertising investment in a country is directly proportional to its standard of living.[5] (Exhibit 2–1 on page 46 shows the level of advertising expenditure in countries around the world.)

The economic effect of advertising is like the break shot in billiards. The moment a company begins to advertise, it sets off a chain reaction of economic events as shown in Exhibit 2–2 on page 47. The result of the chain reaction, although hard to predict, is related to the force of the shot and the economic environment in which it occurred. Let's consider the economic questions we asked earlier.

Effect on the Value of Products

Why do most people prefer Coca-Cola to some other cola? Why do some people prefer Calvin Klein underwear to some other unadvertised brand? Are the advertised products functionally better? Not necessarily. But advertising *can* add value to a product in the consumer's mind.

Exhibit 2–1
Level of advertising expenditures around the world (by GDP).

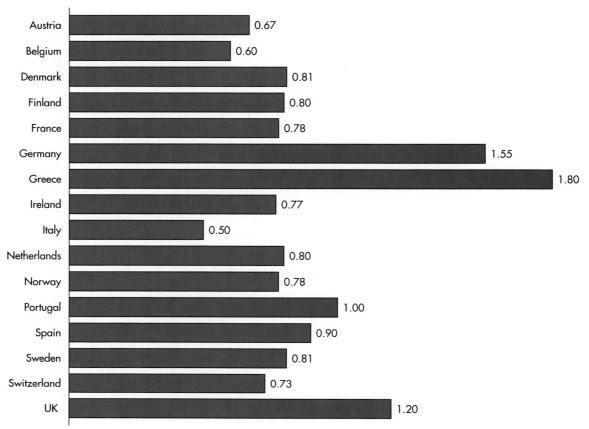

In the mid-1960s, Ernest Dichter, a psychologist known as the father of *motivational research,* asserted that a product's image, created in part by advertising and promotion, is an inherent feature of the product itself.[6] Subsequent studies showed that while an ad may not speak directly about a product's quality, the positive image conveyed by advertising may imply quality, make the product more desirable to the consumer, and thereby add value to the product.[7] That's why people pay more for Bufferin than for an unadvertised brand displayed right next to it—even though by law all buffered aspirin is functionally the same.[8]

Advertising also creates added value by educating customers about new uses for a product. Kleenex was originally advertised as a makeup remover, later as a disposable handkerchief. Sunkist first promoted oranges as a food and later as a drink.

One advantage of the free-market system is that consumers can choose the values they want in the products they buy. If low price is important, for example, they can buy an inexpensive economy car. If status and luxury are important, they can buy a fancy sedan or racy sports car. Many of our wants are emotional, social, or psychological rather than functional. One way we communicate who we are (or want to be) is through the products we purchase and display. By associating the product with some desirable image, advertising offers people the opportunity to satisfy those psychic or symbolic wants and needs.

In terms of our economic framework, by adding value to products, advertising contributes to self-interest—for both the consumer and the advertiser. It also contributes to the number of sellers. That increases competition, which also serves the consumer's self-interest.

Effect on Prices If advertising adds value to products, it follows that advertising also adds cost, right? And if companies stopped all that expensive advertising, products would cost less, right?

Wrong.

Some advertised products do cost more than unadvertised products, but the opposite is also true. Both the Federal Trade Commission and the Supreme Court have ruled that, by encouraging competition, advertising has the effect of keeping prices down. That again serves the consumer's self-interest. And that is why professionals such as attorneys and physicians are now allowed to advertise.

Sweeping statements about advertising's positive or negative effect on prices are likely to be too simplistic. We can make some important points, though.

- As one of the many costs of doing business, advertising is indeed paid for by the consumer who buys the product. In most product categories, though, the amount spent on advertising is usually very small compared to the total cost of the product.

- Advertising is one element of the mass-distribution system that enables many manufacturers to engage in mass production, which in turn lowers the unit cost of products. These savings can then be passed on to consumers in the form of lower prices. In this indirect way, advertising helps lower prices.

- In industries subject to government price regulation (agriculture, utilities), advertising has historically had no effect on prices. In the 1980s, though, the government deregulated many of these industries in an effort to restore free-market pressures on prices. In these cases, advertising has affected price— often downward, but sometimes upward.

- In retailing, price is a prominent element in many ads, so advertising tends to hold prices down. On the other hand, manufacturing firms use advertising to stress features that make their products better; in these cases advertising tends to support higher prices.

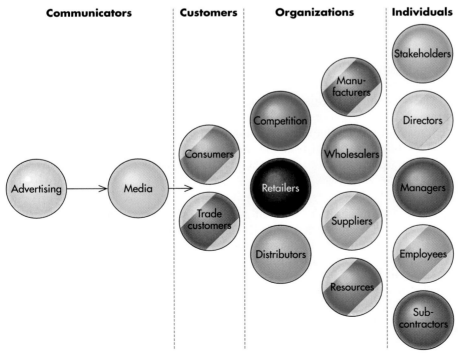

Communicators   **Customers**   **Organizations**   **Individuals**

Exhibit 2–2
The economic effect of advertising is like the opening break shot in billiards.

Effect on Competition

Some observers believe advertising actually restricts competition because small companies or industry newcomers can't compete with the immense advertising budgets of large firms.

It's true that intense competition does tend to reduce the number of businesses in an industry. However some of the firms eliminated by competition may be those that served customers least effectively. In other cases, competition is reduced because of mergers and acquisitions (big companies working in their own self-interest).

High costs may inhibit the entry of new competitors in industries that spend heavily on advertising. In some markets, the original brands probably benefit greatly from this barrier. However, the investments needed for plants, machinery, and labor are of far greater significance. These are typically the real barriers to entry, not advertising.

*This Nike (www.nike.com) ad from Weiden &
Kennedy/Portland exhibits company and product
image.The ad features Olympian Jackie Joyner-Kersee
gearing up to jump from the top of one bluff to the next,
thereby implying that Nike can be the best shoe to
overcome any obstacle.*

Advertising by big companies often has only a limited effect on
small businesses because a single advertiser is rarely large enough to
dominate the whole country. Regional oil companies, for example,
compete very successfully with national oil companies on the local
level. In fact, the right to advertise encourages more sellers to enter
the market. And we've all seen nonadvertised store brands of food
that compete very effectively with nationally advertised brands on the
same shelves.

Effect on Consumer Demand

The question of advertising's effect on total consumer demand is extremely complex. Numerous studies show that promotional activity
does affect aggregate consumption, but disagree as to the extent.
Many social and economic forces, including technological advances,
the population's educational level, increases in population and income, and revolutionary changes in lifestyle, are more significant. For
example, the demand for CD players, cellular phones, and personal
computers expanded at a tremendous rate, thanks in part to advertising but more to favorable market conditions. At the same time, advertising hasn't reversed declining sales of such items as hats, fur coats,
and manual typewriters.

Advertising can help get new products off the ground by giving
more people more "perfect information," thereby stimulating demand
for a product class. But in declining markets, when the only information people want is price information, advertising can only slow the
rate of decline. In growing markets, advertisers generally compete for
shares of that growth. In mature, static, or declining markets, they
compete for each other's shares—*conquest sales.*

Effect on Consumer Choice

For manufacturers, the best way to beat the competition is to make
their product different. For example, look at the long list of car models, sizes, colors, and features used to attract different buyers. And grocery shelves may carry 15
to 20 different brands of breakfast cereals—something for everybody.

The freedom to advertise encourages businesses to create new brands and improve old ones. When one brand reaches market dominance, smaller brands may
disappear for a time. But the moment a better product comes along and is advertised skillfully, the dominant brand loses out to the newer, better product. Once
again, the right to advertise promotes the existence of more sellers, and that gives
consumers wider choices.

Effect on the Business Cycle

The relationship between advertising and gross domestic product has
long been debated. John Kenneth Galbraith, a perennial critic of advertising, concedes that, by helping to maintain the flow of consumer demand (encouraging more buyers), advertising helps sustain employment and income. But he
maintains that, despite declines in the value of the dollar, the U.S. trade deficit persists because advertising and marketing activities create consumer preference for
certain foreign products.[9]

Historically, when business cycles dip, companies cut advertising expenditures. That may help short-term profits, but studies prove that businesses that continue to invest in advertising during a recession are better able to protect, and
sometimes build, market shares.[10] However, no study has shown that if everybody

A CPA CAN MAKE
THE DIFFERENCE BETWEEN
BEING RIGHT ON TARGET
OR BECOMING ONE.

In business, it's critical to stay ahead of the curve. With a wide-ranging expertise in strategic planning, turn-around consulting, risk management and more, your CPA can help you make all the right moves at the right time. And stay right on target. You see numbers. We see opportunities. (CPA)

The ad industry saw a proliferation of ads from professional fields after the Supreme Court passed a ruling that allowed these businesses to advertise. Today, attorneys, physicians, accountants, and others advertise their services much as any other business. This ad promotes the professionalism of accounting by touting the skills of certified public accountants.

keeps advertising, the recessionary cycle will turn around. We conclude that when business cycles are up, advertising contributes to the increase. When business cycles are down, advertising may act as a stabilizing force by encouraging more buyers to buy.

The Abundance Principle: The Economic Impact of Advertising in Perspective

To individual businesses like Calvin Klein, the local car dealer, and the convenience store on the corner, advertising pays back more than it costs. If advertising didn't pay, no one would use it. And the various news and entertainment media that depend on advertising for financial support would go out of business.

Advertising costs less for the consumer than most people think. The cost of a bottle of Coke includes about a penny for advertising. And the $15,000 price tag on a new car usually includes a manufacturer's advertising cost of less than $300.

To the economy as a whole, the importance of advertising may best be demonstrated by the *abundance principle*. This states that in an economy that produces more goods and services than can be consumed, advertising serves two important purposes: It keeps consumers informed of their alternatives (*perfect information*), and it allows companies to compete more effectively for consumer dollars (*self-interest*). In North America alone, the U.S. and Canadian economies produce an enormous selection of products. Most supermarkets carry more than 15,000 different items. Each carmaker markets dozens of models. And many suppliers compete for the consumer dollar. This competition generally results in more and better products at similar or lower prices.

Advertising stimulates competition (*many buyers and sellers*). In countries where consumers have more income to spend after their physical needs are satisfied, advertising also stimulates innovation and new products. However, no amount of advertising can achieve long-term acceptance for products that do not meet consumer approval. Despite massive advertising expenditures, fewer than a dozen of the 50 best-known cars developed in the 20th century are still sold today.

Advertising stimulates a healthy economy. It also helps create financially healthy consumers who are more informed, better educated, and more demanding. As a result, consumers now demand that manufacturers be held accountable for their advertising. This has led to an unprecedented level of social criticism and legal regulation, the subject of our next sections.

The **Social Impact** of Advertising

Because it's so visible, advertising gets criticized frequently, for both what it is and what it isn't. Many of the criticisms focus on the style of advertising; they say it's deceptive or manipulative. Collectively we might refer to these as **short-term manipulative arguments.** Other criticisms focus on the social or environmental impact of advertising. These are **long-term macro arguments.**[11]

In our discussion of the economic impact of advertising, we focused primarily on the first two principles of free-market economics: self-interest and many buyers and sellers. The social aspect of advertising typically involves the last two principles: perfect information and absence of externalities. In fact, social issue debates can be seen as instances where advertising tends to violate one or more of these

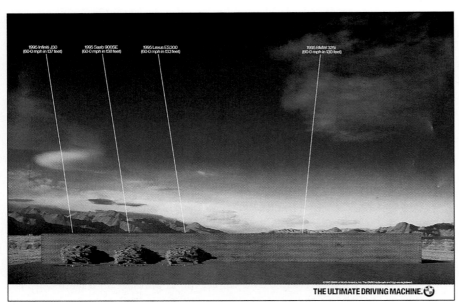

This BMW (www.bmw.com) ad developed by Keith Weinman demonstrates the braking power of the BMW 325i over its competitors by showing the cars in action, supplemented with valid statisitics.

basic economic principles. We can examine many issues from these two perspectives. Some of the most important are deception and manipulation in advertising, the effect of advertising on our value system, commercial clutter, stereotypes, and offensiveness. Let's look at some of these common criticisms of advertising, debunk some misconceptions, and examine the problems that do exist.

Deception in Advertising

One of the most common short-term arguments about advertising is that it is so frequently deceptive. Professor Ivan Preston notes that the essence of a marketplace lies in the willingness of buyers and sellers to enter commercial transactions. Anything that detracts from the satisfaction of the transaction produces a loss of activity that is unfortunate for both parties.[12] If a product does not live up to its ads, dissatisfaction occurs—and that is ultimately as harmful to the advertiser as to the buyer.

For advertising to be effective, consumers must have confidence in it. So any kind of deception not only detracts from the "perfect information" principle of free enterprise but also risks being self-defeating. Even meaningless (but legal) puffery might be taken literally and therefore become deceptive. As you learned in Chapter 1, **puffery** refers to exaggerated, subjective claims that can't be proven true or false, such as "the best," "premier," or "the only way to fly."

Under current advertising law, the only product claims—explicit or implied— that are considered deceptive are those that are *factually false* or convey a false impression and therefore have the potential to deceive or mislead reasonable people.[13] But puffery is excluded from this requirement because regulators maintain that reasonable people don't believe it anyway. Preston points out that since advertisers regularly use puffery and nonproduct facts to enhance the image of their products, they must think consumers *do* believe it. **Nonproduct facts** are not about the brand but about the consumer or the social context in which the consumer uses the brand. An example is "Pepsi. The choice of a new generation."

The fact is that advertising, by its very nature, is *not* "perfect information." It is biased in favor of the advertiser and the brand. People expect that and don't usually mind it. When advertisers cross the line between simply giving their point of view and creating false expectations, people begin to object. One problem is the difficulty to see this line, which may be drawn differently by different people. Preston's goal is to encourage marketers to improve the kind of information they give in their advertising. He would require advertisers to have a reasonable basis for any claims they make, whether those claims are facts about the product, nonfacts such as "Coke is it," or nonproduct facts.[14] This, he believes, would improve our free-market system. Ad Lab 2–A lists some common deceptive practices.

The Subliminal Advertising Myth

Wilson Bryan Key promotes the notion that, to seduce consumers, advertisers intentionally create ads with sexual messages hidden in the illustrations just below the threshold of perception. He calls this **subliminal advertising.** His premise is

---

The most beautiful thing that ever happened to horsepower

It steals the show wherever you go—the long, clean, powerful 1958 Edsel

1958 EDSEL

Of all medium-priced cars, the one that's really new is the lowest-priced, too!

Despite extensive advertising efforts, some products, like the Edsel automobile, will fail simply because they do not meet the expectations of customers at that particular time. Many of the best-known cars developed in the 20th century are no longer sold today. Ironically, the Edsel has since become a pricy collector's item for automobile afficionados.

Unfair and Deceptive Practices in Advertising

The courts have held that these acts constitute unfair or deceptive trade practices and are therefore illegal.

False Promises

Making an advertising promise that cannot be kept, such as "restores youth" or "prevents cancer." When Listerine claimed to prevent or reduce the impact of colds and sore throats, the FTC banned the campaign and required the company to run millions of dollars' worth of corrective ads.

Incomplete Description

Stating some but not all of a product's contents, such as advertising a "solid oak" desk without mentioning that only the top is solid oak and the rest is pine.

False and Misleading Comparisons

Making false comparisons, either explicitly or by implication, such as "Like Tylenol, Advil doesn't upset my stomach." That implies that Advil is equal in avoiding stomach upset, though in truth Tylenol is better. To some people, Advil's claim might even suggest that Tylenol upsets the stomach, which is also false.

Bait-and-Switch Offers

Advertising an item at an unusually low price to bring people into the store and then "switching" them to a higher-priced model by claiming that the advertised product is out of stock or poorly made.

Visual Distortions and False Demonstrations

Using trick photography or computer manipulation to enhance a product's appearance—for example, a TV commercial for a "giant steak" dinner special showing the steak on a miniature plate that makes it look extra large. In one classic case, General Motors and its window supplier, Libby Owens-Ford, rigged a demonstration to show how clear their windows were. The GM cars were photographed with the windows down, the competitor's car with the windows up—and Vaseline smeared on them.

False Testimonials

Implying that a product has the endorsement of a celebrity or an authority who is not a bona-fide user, or implying that endorsers have a certain expertise that in fact they don't.

Partial Disclosure

Stating certain facts about the advertised product but omitting other material information. An example is claiming, "Kraft's Singles processed cheese slices are made from five ounces of milk," which give Singles more calcium than the imitators' without mentioning that processing loses about two ounces of the milk.

Small-Print Qualifications

Making a statement in large print, such as Beneficial's "Instant Tax Refund," only to qualify or retract it in obscure, small, or unreadable type elsewhere in the ad: "If you qualify for one of our loans." To the FTC, if readers don't see the qualification, it's not there.

Laboratory Applications

1. Describe some examples of deception you have seen in advertising.
2. Do you think the rules that apply to commercial speech should also apply to political advertising?

that by embedding dirty words in ice cubes in a liquor ad, for instance, advertisers can somehow make us want to buy the product. Over the years, many academic studies have completely debunked this theory.[15] In fact, to date, no study has proved that such embedding exists or that it would have any effect. Unfortunately, by promulgating this fiction, Key has been able to sell many thousands of books; worse, he has propagated a generation of consumers who believe in the poppycock of subliminal advertising.[16]

The chord that Key managed to touch, though, is important to discuss. That is the widespread fear that advertisers are messing with our heads—manipulating us psychologically into buying things we don't want or need and without our consent. This gets to the heart of the "perfect information" principle because it suggests that advertising does not give proper information on which to base rational decisions but instead manipulates us through brainwashing. Consumers are, therefore, completely powerless against the forces of the almighty advertiser.

If this were true, it would be cause for a congressional investigation (of course, all the congressmen on the committee would have been elected by means of the same manipulative advertising). But if we stop to think about it, we all know it's *not* true. Marketers introduce thousands of new products to the marketplace every year. And every year, the vast majority of them fail—despite massive advertising expenditures. Why? Because of competition. Many sellers compete fiercely for the patronage of the same customers.

If you think about the products you buy, how many involve a choice between different brands and different styles? And how many involve a decision based on price or convenience? Probably most. So how many of your purchases can you trace to having been helplessly manipulated? Probably none. You receive information from

SHIRT.   BULLSHIRT.

Men's, women's & children's fashion & designer clothing 40-75% off, every day. Located in New York City; Manhasset, NY; Paramus, Elizabeth, East Hanover and Wayne, NJ; Philadelphia; Potomac Mills Mall, Virginia. **DAFFY'S**

Daffy's (www.daffys.com) uses tongue-in-cheek humor to take a stand against advertising puffery—inflated promises and claims often accompanied by inflated prices. Daffy's beckons smart consumers to shop where they can find the same quality goods with "no bull" price tags.

many different sources: friends and relatives, store displays, ads, packaging, and retail store clerks. At some point, you make a decision. In many cases, your decision is not to buy at all—to wait for either more information or more money. As always, the customer, acting in his or her own self-interest, is king.

The Effect of Advertising on Our Value System

A related long-term argument, often voiced by professional critics—academics, journalists, consumer advocates, and government regulators—is that advertising degrades people's value systems by promoting a hedonistic, materialistic way of life. Advertising, they say, encourages us to buy more cars, more CDs, more clothing, and more junk we don't need. It is destroying the essence of our "citizen democracy," replacing it with a self-oriented consumer democracy.[17]

Critics claim advertising manipulates us into buying things by playing on our emotions and promising greater status, social acceptance, and sex appeal. It causes people to take up harmful habits, makes poor kids buy $170 sneakers, and tempts ordinary people to buy useless products in the vain attempt to emulate celebrity endorsers.[18] Again, they claim advertising is so powerful consumers are helpless to defend themselves against it.

Once again, advertising's powers have been greatly exaggerated. In fact, Americans in particular are highly skeptical of it. Studies show that only 17 percent of U.S. consumers see advertising as a source of information to help them decide what to buy.[19] Perhaps that's why more advertised products fail than succeed in the marketplace.

Still, this may be the most damning criticism of advertising because there's no question that advertisers do indeed spend millions trying to convince people their products will make them sexier, healthier, and more successful. The very amount of advertising we witness every day seems to suggest that every problem we have can be solved by the purchase of some product.

Even if we assume that most people can willingly accept or reject an advertising message, they are still not getting the whole picture. After all, advertising is supported by marketers who want to sell their products, but nobody markets the opposite stance of why we don't need to or shouldn't buy a particular product at all. In this sense, consumers don't have "perfect information," so our advocacy system has failed. This is an important issue of "externalities," where the aggregate activities of the nation's advertisers affect many people outside the immediate marketing transaction and create an unexpected cost to society.

The Proliferation of Advertising

One of the most common long-term complaints about advertising is that there's just too much of it. In the United States alone, the average person may be exposed to 500 to 1,000 commercial messages a day. With so many products competing for attention (over 15,000 in the average supermarket), advertisers themselves worry about the negative impact of excessive advertising. A recent study by the Association of National Advertisers and the American Association of Advertising Agencies showed that TV networks added to the problem of ad clutter by jamming every possible second with promotions for their shows. Too much advertising creates an externality not only for consumers (a nuisance), but for the advertisers themselves; the more commercials that hit the consumer's brain, the less effective paid advertising is. The cable channels used to be a haven for the weary, but now they are even worse. Some run as much as 17 minutes per hour of non-programming material, not to mention those that run continuous infomercials.[20]

Status comes in many forms. For some, it means vacationing at the most prestigious, upscale resorts. For others, status is gained by avoiding such places. In this ad Copper Mountain ski resort (www.ski-copper.com) takes a humorous pot shot at its neighbor Vail by appealing to the anti-status seekers, beckoning hardcore skiers and snowboarders to its hill.

Clutter is not so evident in other countries. In France, for example, government-owned stations can carry no more than 12 minutes of commercials per hour. During movies there is only one four-minute commercial break (although the government is considering changing that rule to allow two breaks).[21]

In North America we should be so lucky. During political campaigns, the clutter problem gets worse, seriously devaluing an advertiser's commercial. The Association of Canadian Advertisers, in fact, called on its members one year to renegotiate the prices they had been charged for air time after an overwhelming number of political ads ran during the fall election season.[22]

While this problem is irksome to viewers and advertisers alike, most people tolerate it as the price for free TV, freedom of the press, and a high standard of living. However, with the proliferation of new media choices, this externality is likely to get worse. As a result, the FCC is again considering reinstating commercial time limits on television.[23]

The Use of Stereotypes in Advertising

Advertising has long been criticized for insensitivity to minorities, women, immigrants, the disabled, and a myriad of other groups—that is, for not being "politically correct."[24] This long-term argument also addresses externalities because the very presence of advertising affects the nature of our culture and environment, even when we do not want it. This is ironic, because marketing and advertising practitioners are supposed to be professional students of consumer behavior (a subject we cover in Chapter 4) and the communication process. But, in fact, they sometimes lose touch with the very people they're trying to reach. This is one reason the discipline of *account planning* (discussed in Chapter 3) is growing so rapidly.

Since the 80s, national advertisers have become more sensitive to the concerns of minorities and women. Latinos, African-Americans, Asians, Native Americans, and others are now usually portrayed favorably in ads, not only because of pressure from watchdog groups, but also because it's just good business; these consumers represent sizable target markets. Marilyn Kern-Foxworth, a Texas A&M professor and an expert on minorities in advertising, points out that positive role portrayal in some mainstream ads has had a positive effect on the self-esteem of African-American youth.[25] As we'll see in Chapter 3, this positive trend

The song above was written by Schumann as an expression of love for his wife, Clara.

The song below was written by Brahms as an expression of love for Schumann's wife, Clara.

(Above) According to Clara's notation in the top right hand corner, Brahms gave her this ornately decorated copy of "To a Violet" on her birthday. (Top) Schumann's not-so-fancy draft of "The Shepherd's Farewell."

hough it's never been proven, there's a lot of speculation that music wasn't the only thing for which Robert Schumann and Johannes Brahms shared a love.

The setting was Germany. 1853. Schumann and his wife Clara were, by most accounts, a happily married couple. In fact, during just one year of marriage, Schumann wrote 150 songs out of love for his Clara.

Enter Johannes Brahms. A handsome, young musical prodigy who managed to make quite an impact on the Schumanns. The three became very close.

Brahms moved in. And, for a while, all three made beautiful music together – Brahms taking instruction from Schumann and Clara supporting everyone by playing the piano in concerts.

After awhile, Schumann had a mental breakdown and in 1856 died in an asylum.

Clara Wieck Schumann. The object of her husband's affections. And perhaps those of Brahms as well?

For the next 40 years, Brahms and Clara occasionally lived in the same building together. Often performed in concert together. And, until their deaths, which occurred within just a few months of each other, the two remained "very close friends".

Exactly what Clara and Brahms meant to each other, no one will ever know. But here is something that can't be disputed: Now through July 13, two original artifacts of this unusual relationship, Brahms' "To a Violet" and Schumann's

"The Shepherd's Farewell," will be on display at the Library of Congress.

They're here on loan as part of an exhibition from the Saxon State

An institution in Dresden's long musical history was the performing troupe, the Hofkapelle. Here, a long procession of men dressed as women.

Library in Dresden, Germany.

Along with them, you can see Martin Luther's original New Testament, responsible for adding hundreds of denominations to the Christian faith. Grimace over the details of 16th century equestrian dental procedures. And find out why Germany's most famed musical

troupe from 400 years ago, the Hofkapelle, today would give *Mrs. Doubtfire* a run for its money.

These Saxon State Library treasures have survived the Dark Ages, the devastation of World War II, and for the last 50 years they were all but inaccessible to most Americans, locked away behind the Iron Curtain.

They're here for the first time. And it's uncertain when, or if, they'll ever be here again.

The exhibition is on display in the Great Hall of the Library of

Congress, open Monday through Saturday, from 10 a.m. to 5:30 p.m. For any additional information, call (202) 707-8000.

THE LIBRARY OF CONGRESS

Dresden: Treasures from the Saxon State Library

Some advertising reflects the interest of the public at-large in the form of government ads, such as this public service announcement from the Library of Congress. Check out its Web site (http://lcweb.loc.gov).

The 1997 LeSabre.
The comfort and safety of home...
on the road.

Its comfort will put you at ease. Its arsenal of safety features will give you a sense of inner peace. Make you feel almost invulnerable. That's why those who want to feel at home on the road drive the 1997 Buick LeSabre. For your peace of mind, drive LeSabre. For more details, visit our Web site at http://www.buick.com or call 1-800-4A-BUICK.

LeSABRE
PEACE OF MIND

BUICK

With tightening markets, advertisers must double their efforts to maintain or expand market share. One way is to cater to minority communities, which have enormous buying power and comprise a significant amount of market share. (www.buick.com)

has accelerated with the emergence of many ad agencies owned and staffed by minorities that specialize in reaching minority markets.

In national advertising, the image of women is also changing from their historic depiction as either subservient housewives or sex objects (see the Ethical Issue: "Does Sex Appeal?" in Chapter 11). Recent research indicates that since the early 80s, these traditional depictions of women have decreased and "equality" portrayals are on the rise.[26] More than 59.3 percent of all women now work outside the home, and more than 38 million of them are in professional, managerial, technical, sales, or administrative careers.[27] Advertisers want to reach, not offend, this sizable market of upwardly mobile consumers. Some agencies now retain feminist consultants to review ads that may risk offending women.[28]

However, problems still exist, especially in local and regional advertising and in certain product categories like beer and sports promotions. Many advertisers are just not aware of the externalities that their ads can create, and they may perpetuate male and female stereotypes without even realizing it.[29] Other advertisers resort to stereotypes for convenience. All too often, women are still not represented accurately. And the minimal use of minorities in mainstream ads, both local and national, still smacks of tokenism. Observers hope that with increasing numbers of women and minorities joining the ranks of marketing and advertising professionals, and with continuing academic studies of minority and sex-role stereotyping, greater attention will be focused on these issues.

Offensiveness in Advertising

Offensiveness is another short-term style argument that also speaks to externalities. Many parents, for instance, were incensed at Calvin Klein's ads because they perceived them as pornographic, thereby causing a social cost that extended well beyond the limited scope of merely selling clothes. People don't want their children exposed to messages that they deem immoral, offensive, or strictly adult-oriented.

Taste, of course, is highly subjective: What is bad taste to some is perfectly acceptable to others. And tastes change. What is considered offensive today may not be so tomorrow. People were outraged when the first ad for underarm deodorant appeared in a 1927 *Ladies Home Journal;* today no one questions such ads. Yet, even with the AIDS scare, all the broadcast networks except Fox still restrict condom ads to local stations, and all forbid any talk of contraception.[30]

Taste is also geographic. A shockingly bloody ad for a small surfwear company in Sydney, Australia, showed a gutted shark lying on a dock. Protruding from its cut-open belly were a human skeleton and an intact pair of surfer shorts. The tagline: "Tough clothes by Kadu—Triple stitched. Strongest materials available. Homegrown and sewn."

While we might consider that ad quite offensive in North America, it won the Grand Prix at the International Advertising Festival in Cannes, France. In Australia it received wide media coverage, since two surfers were killed by sharks while it was running. Rather than pulling the ad out of respect, the company reveled in its timeliness, and the local surfer set responded very favorably.[31]

Today, grooming, fashion, and personal hygiene products often use nudity in their ads. Where nudity is relevant to the product, people are less likely to regard it as obscene or offensive. In many international markets, nudity in commercials is commonplace. Some industry observers predict that nudity in U.S. advertising will increase in the 21st century, but there will be fewer overtly sexual scenes of the Calvin Klein style.[32]

Some consumers get so offended by both advertising and TV programming that they boycott sponsors' products.[33] Of course, they also have the option to just change the channel. Both of these are effective strategies for consumers because, ultimately, the marketplace has veto power. As Calvin Klein showed, if ads don't attract the target audience, the campaign will falter and die.

Tastes of consumers—and advertisers— may differ geographically, as shown in this award-winning Australian surfwear ad. Local Sydney surfers responded quite favorably to the ad.

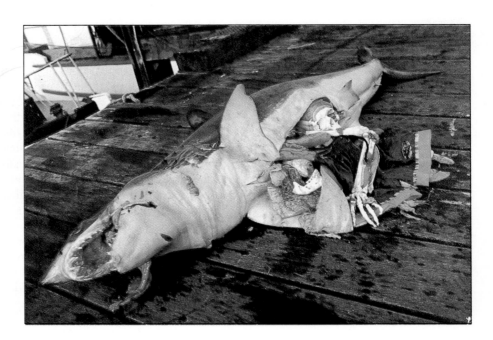

The Social Impact of Advertising in Perspective

Critics often forget (or choose to ignore) that advertising benefits society greatly. Advertising encourages the development and speeds the acceptance of new products and technologies. It fosters employment. It gives consumers and business customers a wider variety of choices. It helps keep prices down by encouraging mass production. And it stimulates healthy competition among producers, which benefits all buyers.[34] Advertising also promotes a higher standard of living; it pays for most of our news media and subsidizes the arts; it supports freedom of the press; and it provides a means to disseminate public information about important health and social issues.

We can conclude that while advertising may legitimately be criticized for offering less than perfect information and, in some instances, for creating unwanted externalities, it should also be praised if it contributes to the principles of free-enterprise economics. In most cases, by being a rich (if not perfect) information source, advertising contributes to the existence of many buyers and sellers and, therefore, to the self-interest of both consumers and marketers.

Social **Responsibility** and Advertising **Ethics**

When advertising violates one of the basic economic assumptions we've described, some corrective action is needed. As we'll discuss in the next section, numerous laws determine what advertisers can and cannot do, but they also allow a significant amount of leeway. That's where ethics and social responsibility come into play. An advertiser can act unethically or irresponsibly without breaking any laws. Beer and tobacco companies can sponsor rock concerts for college students, and a shoe company can market a basketball sneaker to urban youth as the "Run 'N Gun" brand. As Ivan Preston says, ethics begin where the law ends.[35]

Ethical advertising means doing what the advertiser and the advertiser's peers believe is morally right in a given situation. **Social responsibility** means doing what society views as best for the welfare of people in general or for a specific community of people. Together, ethics and social responsibility can be seen as the moral obligation of advertisers not to violate our basic economic assumptions, even when there is no legal obligation.

Advertisers' Social Responsibility

The foundation of any human society is the amicable relationship among its members. Without harmony, a society will collapse. So all the institutions within a society have some responsibility for helping to maintain social harmony through proper stewardship of families and companies, exercise of honesty and integrity in all relationships, adherence to accepted ethical standards, willingness to assist various segments of the society, and the courtesy to respect the privacy of others.

Advertising plays an important role in developed countries. It influences a society's stability and growth. It helps secure large armies, creates entertainment events attracting hundreds of thousands of fans, and often affects the outcome of political elections. Such power places a burden of responsibility on those who sponsor, buy, create, produce, and sell advertising to maintain ethical standards that support the society and contribute to the economic system.

In the United States, for example, the advertising industry is part of a large business community. Like any good neighbor, it has responsibilities: to keep its property clean, participate in civic events, support local enterprises, and improve the community. U.S. advertising professionals have met these challenges by forming local advertising clubs, the American Advertising Federation (AAF), the American Association of Advertising Agencies (AAAA), and the Ad Council. These

Without advertising, public service organizations, like the Friends of Education, would be unable to reach a mass audience to educate people about important health and social issues.

Today's consumer is more sophisticated than ever about social issues like environmentalism. Marketers must adjust accordingly and exhibit their corporate responsibility, which has given rise to projects like Chevron's famous "People Do" campaign (www.chevron.com).

organizations provide thousands of hours and millions of dollars' worth of *pro bono* (free) work to charitable organizations and public agencies. They also provide scholarships and internships, contributions that serve the whole society. As we discuss later, they even regulate themselves fairly effectively.

Many advertisers, including Chevron, Mobil, General Electric, and even local quick-lube shops, have demonstrated their social responsibility by reformulating their products and packaging to be more environmentally responsible and by launching major "green" advertising campaigns. Similarly, many retailers have jumped on the green bandwagon, advertising environmentally friendly merchandise in their communities.[36] Advertisers like AT&T, IBM, and Honda commit significant dollars to supporting the arts, education, and various charitable causes as well as their local Better Business Bureaus and Chambers of Commerce.

Still, advertisers are regularly chided when they fail the social responsibility litmus test. Concerned citizens, consumer advocates, and special-interest groups pressure advertisers when they perceive the public's welfare is at risk—thus the furor over tobacco advertising in recent years. Advertisers also receive criticism when they sponsor programming with content that offends particular interest groups. The Southern Baptist Church, for instance, urged its members in 1997 to boycott Disney theme parks and movies because of its perception that Disney had strayed from its tradition of promoting family values.

Ethics of Advertising

Philosophies of ethics span the centuries since Socrates at least. We can hardly do them justice here. But for practical purposes, let's consider three levels of ethical responsibility and apply them to advertising.

On one level, ethics comprise two interrelated components: the traditional actions taken by people in a society or community and the philosophical rules that society establishes to justify such past actions and decree future actions. These components create the primary rules of ethical behavior in the society and enable us to measure how far an individual or company (or advertiser) strays from the norm. Here, the individual's rights are subject to the standards of what is customary (and therefore proper) for the group (see Exhibit 2–3).

Every individual also faces a second set of ethical issues: the attitudes, feelings, and beliefs that add up to a personal value system. When these two systems conflict, should the individual act on personal beliefs or on the obligation to serve the group and its policies? For example, nonsmoking ad agency people may create ads for a tobacco client. At the first, societal level of ethics there is some conflict: smoking has been a custom in the United States for centuries and is not illegal today. However, the U.S. Surgeon General has declared that smoking is a national health problem (harmful to the group). This conflict at the first ethical level passes the responsibility for decision making to the second, individual level. Since the penalty may be the loss of income, nonsmokers may decide to produce the ads while keeping their own work area smoke-free. The ethical issue is at least temporarily and partially resolved, or at least rationalized, at the second ethical level.

When the group or individuals cannot resolve an ethical dilemma, they must redefine the issue in dispute. Thus, the third level of ethics concerns singular ethical concepts such as good, bad, right, wrong, duty, integrity, and truth. Are these concepts absolute, universal, and binding? Or are they relative, dependent on situations and consequences? A person's moral and ethical philosophy, influenced by religion, society, and individual values, will determine their answer.

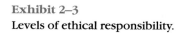
Exhibit 2–3
Levels of ethical responsibility.

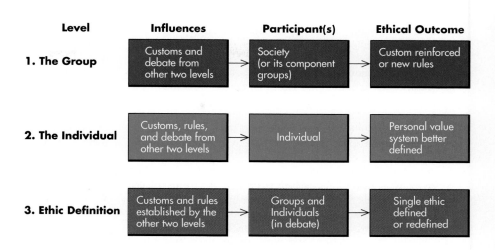

Let's say, for example, the copywriter for a cigarette ad is a smoker, and he writes copy that implies that smoking is a favorable behavior. But the ad's art director, a nonsmoker, complains that the ad is unethical because the copy conflicts with the truth, since smoking is actually an unsafe behavior. At this point they reach the third ethical level, and a more senior person, such as the creative director, may step in and lead a discussion aimed at defining the agency's ethical policy on smoking.

As we mentioned before, ethics is such an important topic that we address those issues that pertain to advertising in Ethical Issue sidebars in each chapter. The Ethical Issue here considers the difference between an ethical dilemma and an ethical lapse.

Most advertisers today strive to maintain fair ethical standards and practice socially responsible advertising. Ad agencies rarely force employees to work on accounts they morally oppose. Once a free-swinging, unchecked business, advertising is today a closely scrutinized and heavily regulated profession. Advertising's past shortcomings have created layer upon layer of laws, regulations, and regulatory bodies. Consumer groups, governments, special-interest groups, and even other advertisers now review, control, and modify advertising in order to create more "perfect information" and reduce the impact of unwanted externalities.

How **Government** **Regulates** Advertising

One of the characteristics of the American political scene is our tripartite system of checks and balances. There are many laws that govern what advertisers can and cannot do. These laws are passed by legislatures, enforced by the executive branch, and interpreted by the judiciary. This system is repeated at the state and local levels.

On the national level, the president, cabinet departments, and various federal commissions are responsible for executing the laws passed by Congress. On the state level, the governor, attorney general, and state departments administer state laws. Locally, mayors, city managers, city attorneys, and police chiefs enforce the laws passed by city councils.

Similarly, local laws are interpreted by municipal courts, while the superior courts and state Supreme Courts interpret state laws. Federal laws are interpreted by federal district courts and the U.S. Supreme Court. Every day, advertisers from the local copy shop to international soft-drink marketers have to deal with the actions and decisions of all these branches of government. We'll discuss shortly some of the most important issues that concern U.S. regulators.

Government **Restraints** on **International** Advertisers

Now that advertising has become more global, many campaigns use similar themes and even the same ads across frontiers. But foreign governments often regulate advertising considerably more than either the United States or Canada. And while Europe has moved toward uniformity

Ethical Dilemma or Ethical Lapse?

False and misleading advertising—and all the damage they can create—begin with unethical judgments. Hence, it pays to understand the differences between ethical dilemmas and ethical lapses.

An *ethical dilemma* arises from an unresolved interpretation of an ethical issue. To begin, there is a distinction between "having a right" and "the right thing to do." For example, should advertisers attempt to persuade poor, inner-city youths to buy sneakers priced at more than $170 a pair? There's no law against it, but the responsible action (both socially and morally) may be to refrain. And so we have an ethical dilemma.

How are such ethical dilemmas resolved? According to University of Wisconsin professor Ivan L. Preston, it appears advertising professionals find ethics largely synonymous with legality. Many believe that advertising $170 sneakers to all markets, including to those who should not buy them, is "acceptable" ethical behavior. But as Preston says, "You can be ethical only when you have the option of being unethical. You can't choose to be ethical when you can't choose at all, so ethics begins only where the law ends."

The prospect of a serious protest from watchdog groups, civic leaders, and clergy generally eliminates an advertiser's hesitancy to resolve an ethical dilemma. For small companies, a hostile public reaction can even lead to bankruptcy. In contrast, a strong market leader may have the goodwill and deep pockets to survive an ethically borderline advertising campaign—and go forward to stimulate greater name awareness from the ensuing publicity. Calvin Klein's jeans campaign, for example, depicted models who looked 15, were dressed skimpily, and posed suggestively. The huge outcry against those "kiddie porn" ads that emerged from all sectors, including trade publications and the national press, prompted Klein to discontinue the campaign. However, the press continued carrying the story for weeks. Some people outside the target group thought Calvin Klein had effectively stimulated a *positive* dialogue about the moral issues involved in advertising to young people. With minimal advertising, Klein established huge name awareness.

Ivan Preston notes that ethical dilemmas can occur because advertisers typically sell brands, not just products. Since each brand must be presented as being different from other brands—even though functionally it may not be—advertisers are tempted to create false differences. Incomplete information is another breeding ground for ethical dilemmas. Advertisers tend to highlight the

in marketing activities, the laws governing advertising remain largely national.[37] So advertisers need to keep up with the changing legal environments of the countries in which they advertise.

Foreign governments are frequently more authoritarian, and many do not have a system of checks and balances like ours. Some governments not only regulate what ads say, show, or do; they often prohibit advertising altogether.

Throughout Europe, broadcast advertising for tobacco products is prohibited, and liquor ads are sharply restricted. In fact, in 1994 a British parliamentary committee demanded a ban on tobacco-sponsored sporting events—even though these events earned the government millions every year in ad revenues.[38]

Many countries prohibit puffery superlatives. In Germany, for example, advertisers may use only scientifically provable superlatives. McCann-Erickson once had to retranslate the old Coca-Cola slogan, "Refreshes you best," because it implied a leadership position that was unprovable. The agency substituted "Refreshes you right" in Germany (in Austria, however, which typically follows Germany's lead in advertising law, the original line would be permissible).[39]

Many European countries also ban coupons, premiums, free tie-in offers, and the like. Companies may advertise price cuts only during "official sales periods," and advertisers often need government approval before publishing a sale ad. Across Europe, TV ads must be clearly recognizable and kept separate from other programming. Paid *product placements* in programs, therefore, are typically prohibited.[40] To see some of the regulations that various Western European countries impose on advertisers, look at RL 2–1 in the Reference Library.

In Singapore, the state-owned broadcasting company yanked a Qantas Airline spot after the Ministry of Information and the Arts criticized the ad's "harmful values." The spot had used the line "last of the big spenders," which the ministry felt encouraged reckless spending by consumers (see Ad Lab 2–B).[41]

Costa Rica has more than 250 laws regulating advertising. Recently, government officials agreed to consider an industry proposal that would overturn the particularly onerous law mandating preclearance of all advertising.[42]

Regulators are cracking down in China as well. A new comprehensive advertising law targets false, "unscientific, and superstitious" claims and requires preclearance of all advertising in all media. However, China now allows Taiwanese advertising on mainland billboards—after preclearance, of course.[43]

good things about their brands and omit the neutral and bad. Nothing that's said is false, yet the ad does not tell the whole truth. The use of technology to distort images to portray the product most favorably can create new ethical dilemmas. Models, for example, can be made to appear slimmer than they really are, with the possible social consequence of a rise in eating disorders in young women.

In contrast, *ethical lapse* is typically a clear case of illegal behavior. In 1997, three subsidiaries of Quaker State Corp., for example, were sued by the Federal Trade Commission. Eleven claims promising or suggesting that Quaker State's highly respected Slick 50 Engine Treatment could reduce wear in engines during cold startup, increase engine life, lower toxic emissions, increase horsepower, and more, could not be proven by the research presented by the companies. The company was assessed at least $10 million in class-action redress moneys. The fact that Quaker State could not prove many major claims strongly suggests a significant lapse in ethical judgment and an intent to mislead the public.

A myriad of federal, state, and local laws govern what is legal in advertising, but laws ultimately reflect ethical judgments. As for self-regulation, the creative code of the American Association of Advertising Agencies also reflects legalities rather than philoso-phies. However, the eternal question remains: when, how, and by whom, are these laws to be enforced in resolving ethical dilemmas and lapses?

Exploring the Internet

Along with consumer and government organizations, the advertising industry is itself concerned about ethics in advertising. One of the industry's most prestigious organizations, the American Advertising Federation (AAF), gives its Donald W. Davis Award for Ethics in Advertising each year to an advertising practitioner or academic who has made a significant contribution to ethics in advertising. Visit the AAF's website and learn more about this award and its contribution to ethical advertising. (www.aaf.org/davisaward.html)

Sources: Ivan Preston, *The Tangled Web They Weave: Truth, Falsity and Advertisers* (Madison, WI: University of Wisconsin Press, 1994); "Calvin Klein Ad Rekindles Debate as It Runs in Youth's Magazine," *The Wall Street Journal,* July 10, 1995; "Quaker State Subsidiaries Settle FTC Charges against Slick 50," news release from the Bureau of Consumer Protection of the Federal Trade Commission, July 23, 1997; James V. Pokrywczynski, Kevin L. Keenan, and Bridget Boyle, "Kodak Moments for Marketers," presented at the Association for Education in Journalism and Mass Communication Conference, August 1996.

In international advertising, the only solution to this morass of potential legal problems is to retain a good local lawyer who specializes in advertising law.

Recent **Court Rulings** Affecting U.S. Advertisers

In recent years, both federal and state courts have made a number of significant rulings pertaining to advertising issues, including First Amendment rights, privacy rights, and comparative advertising.

E-mail: ivo.sahkolampo@ivo.fi   IVO

SE MUKAVAMPI TAPA. SÄHKÖLÄMPÖ.
☎ 0800-411411

Despite the constraints of stricter advertising laws overseas, ads can still be very effective and creative. The copy for this cute ad from IVO, Finland's power company, reads: "The more pleasant way. Electrical heating." The ad is certainly appropriate given that country's somewhat chilly climate.

First Amendment Rights

The Supreme Court historically distinguishes between "speech" and "commercial speech" (speech that promotes a commercial transaction). But decisions over the last two decades suggest that truthful commercial speech is also entitled to significant, if not full, protection under the First Amendment.

The trend started in 1976 when the Supreme Court held in *Virginia State Board of Pharmacy v. Virginia Citizens Consumer Council* that ads enjoy protection under the First Amendment as commercial speech.[44] The next year the Court declared that the ban by state bar associations on attorney advertising also violated the First Amendment. Now a third of all lawyers advertise, and a few states even permit client testimonials. One Wisconsin lawyer said his firm gained 200 new clients after a $25,000 local TV ad campaign featuring client testimonials.[45] To help guard against deceptive and misleading legal ads, the American Bar Association issues guidelines for attorneys.

To Regulate or Not to Regulate

The dispute over government intervention in our lives rages on as vigorously as ever, and with the advertising industry the case is no different. But the majority of consumer advocates, regardless of political bent, argue fiercely that some measure of government regulation is necessary. Most advertising enhances market performance by providing useful information to consumers. But deceptive or fraudulent advertising offers imperfect information that undermines the consumers' ability to exercise purchasing choices. This is where the government steps in.

The Federal Trade Commission (FTC) is the government agency that monitors advertising and investigates allegations of fraud or deception in the industry. The FTC uses an "unfairness policy," which consists of five questions, to examine questionable advertisements. Is the ad moral? Is it unethical? Is it oppressive? Is it unscrupulous? Will the ad cause substantial injury to consumers or competitors? After evaluating these five questions, the FTC will pursue the matter in court or discontinue its investigation.

In 1994 the FTC persuaded Congress to approve a bill that legally defines advertising unfairness as "acts or practices that cause or are likely to cause substantial injury to consumers, which is not reasonably avoidable by consumers themselves and not outweighed by contervailing benefits to consumers or competition."

Fraud and deception are not the only forms of unfairness regulated by the FTC. Advertising can also run into problems with word usage in vague phrases like "highest performance" and "light," as in the case of Texaco.

The FTC investigated Texaco after its $40 million advertising campaign for a new gasoline, CleanSystem[3]. Chevron challenged Texaco's campaign after its own tests proved that Texaco's claims were false. CleanSystem[3] gasoline did clean car engines, boost mileage, and reduce polluting emissions. But Texaco could not prove that it was the *best* gasoline. In the end, Texaco agreed to rephrase the ads to say, "a breakthrough in Texaco technology" and changed "highest performance" to "higher performance."

Consumers look to advertisers for input on all types of information, from the cleanest gasoline to the healthiest foods. But ads that don't communicate effectively risk conveying potentially bad information. That's why in 1994 the FTC created guidelines for labeling food products. Now foods that use the words "reduced," "light," and "fat-free" must meet Food and Drug Administration guidelines: they must contain less that 0.5 gram of fat per serving.

Food, gasoline, and many other products are regulated for their contents, but what about the accuracy of claims such as "made in USA"? The FTC recently proposed regulations for the label because many products claiming to be "made in USA" are actually manufactured outside the country.

The process began after the FTC filed charges against New Balance Athletic Footwear because the outer soles of its shoes were produced in China. According to New Balance CEO Jim Davis, "We do import the outer sole from China, primarily because we cannot find it in the U.S." Under these circumstances, the company felt that it was accurate to say its product is "made in USA."

The FTC has proposed these guidelines for a product to merit the "made in USA" label:

- A product must be significantly made in the United States.
- A product will be considered substantially all made in the United States if:
  1. U.S. manufacturing costs are at least 75 percent of manufacturing costs and the product was last substantially transformed in the United States, or
  2. The product was last substantially transformed in the United States and all significant parts or components of the product were last substantially transformed in the United States.

Government regulation is often viewed as unnecessary, but it can be more than helpful for consumers. For further information on government regulations for advertising, look up the Federal Trade Commission on the Internet at www.ftc.gov.

Laboratory Applications

Where do you draw the line on the government's involvement in regulating advertising? Answer the following questions and provide data to support your answers.

1. Since many people in North America criticize advertising for being offensive, to what degree should the United States adopt a code of standards requiring ads to promote traditional family values?

2. At what point should the U.S. government use the threat of intervention to curb false and misleading political advertising?

Source: Mary L. Azcuenaga, FTC Commissioner, "The Role of Advertising and Advertising Regulation in the Free Market," April 8, 1997; Christy Fisher, "How Congress Broke Unfair Ad Impasse," *Advertising Age*, August 22, 1994, p. 34; Caleb Soloman, "Gasoline Ads Canceled; Lack of Truth Cited," *The Wall Street Journal*, July 21, 1994, p. B1; Steven W. Colford, "FTC's Rules for Food Ads Win Healthy Reaction," *Advertising Age*, May 16, 1994, p. 2; "FTC to Look at 'Made-in-the-USA' Policy," *Morning Edition* (NPR), March 28, 1996; "FTC: FTC Proposes New Standard for 'Made in USA' claims," *M2 PressWIRE*, May 5, 1997.

In 1980 the Court used *Central Hudson Gas v. Public Service Commission* to test whether specific examples of commercial speech can be regulated.[46] The four-pronged *Central Hudson* test includes the following parts:

1. *Does the commercial speech at issue concern a lawful activity?* The ad in question must be for a legal product and must be free of misleading claims.

2. *Will the restriction of commercial speech serve the asserted government interest substantially?* The government must prove that the absence of regulation would have a substantial negative effect.

3. *Does the regulation directly advance the government interest asserted?* The government must be able to establish conclusively that cessation of the advertising would be effective in furthering the government's interest.

When looking to advertise overseas, companies must be very cautious about the do's and don'ts of other countries. Typically, they retain the services of attorneys familiar with local laws. Many international law firms have Web pages that can be quickly located on the Internet, such as this site by the Australian firm of Gilbert & Tobin (www.gtlaw.com.au).

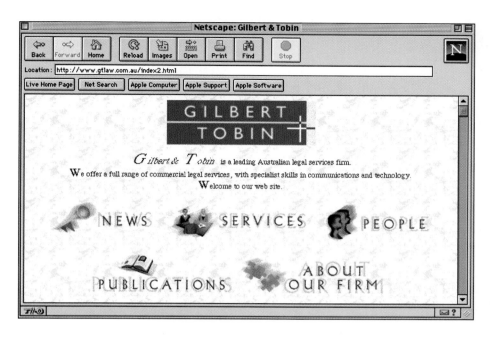

4. *Is the restriction no more than necessary to further the interest asserted?* The government would have to establish that there are no other means to accomplish the same end without restricting free speech.[47]

In 1982, the Supreme Court upheld an FTC order allowing physicians and dentists to advertise. Since then, their advertising has exploded.

In 1993, the Supreme Court gave the advertising industry the biggest win in years. It said the Cincinnati City Council violated the First Amendment when it banned racks of advertising brochures from city streets for "aesthetic and safety reasons" while permitting newspaper vending machines.[48]

The issue of freedom of commercial speech is far from settled. Allowing greater freedom of commercial speech enhances the "government interests" of many buyers and sellers and perfect information. But the additional interest of reducing externalities means the heated controversies surrounding issues like tobacco advertising and advertising to children will likely continue for years to come.

Privacy Rights

Most advertisers know it's illegal to use a person's likeness in an ad without the individual's permission, but since a 1987 court ruling, even using a celebrity lookalike (or soundalike) can violate that person's rights. Other courts have ruled that **privacy rights** continue even after a person's death.

The privacy issue is coming up again now with the increased use of computers and fax machines for advertising directly to prospects. As we shall see in Chapter 13, privacy is an ethical as well as a legal issue. It's also a practical one; prospective customers who find advertising faxes and telemarketing calls annoying aren't likely to buy the offending company's products.

Comparative Advertising

Advertisers use **comparative advertising** to claim superiority to competitors in some aspect. In the United States, such ads are legal (and encouraged) so long as the comparison is truthful.

The 1988 Trademark Law Revision Act closed a loophole in the Lanham Act, which governed comparison ads but did not mention misrepresenting another company's product. Under current law, any advertiser that misrepresents its own or another firm's goods, services, or activities is vulnerable to a civil action.

In addition to being truthful, comparative ads must compare some objectively measurable characteristic. Wilkinson Sword encountered a million-dollar problem when it claimed its Ultra-Glide razor blade's lubricant strip was six times smoother than Gillette's and preferred by more men. Gillette sued and won.[49]

Federal Regulation of Advertising in the United States

The U.S. government imposes strict controls on advertisers through laws, regulations, and judicial interpretations. Among the many federal agencies and departments that regulate advertising are the Federal Trade Commission, the Food and Drug Administration, the Federal Communications Commission, the Patent and Trademark Office, and the Library of Congress. Because their jurisdictions often overlap, advertisers may sometimes have difficulty complying with their regulations. (See RL 2–2 in the Reference Library).

Canada has a similar maze of federal regulators. But the Canadian legal situation is considerably more complex than the United States' due to the separate (but often concurrent) jurisdictions of paternalistic federal and provincial governments, the broad powers of government regulators, the vast array of self-regulatory codes, and the very nature of a bilingual and bicultural society. One simple example of this is the fact that all packages and labels must be printed in both English and French throughout Canada.[50]

The U.S. Federal Trade Commission

In the United States, the **Federal Trade Commission (FTC)** is the major regulator of advertising for products sold in interstate commerce. Established by an act of Congress, the FTC has a mission of ensuring "that the nation's markets function competitively, and are vigorous, efficient, and free of undue restrictions."[51] The commission enforces a variety of federal antitrust and consumer protection laws and works to enhance the operation of the marketplace by eliminating acts or practices that are deceptive or unfair. In other words, it is the FTC's responsibility to maintain the existence of *many sellers* in the marketplace, strive to provide more *perfect information* to consumers, and keep the marketing process as free of *externalities* as possible.

The FTC's job is complicated by the fact that the definitions of deceptive and unfair are controversial.

Defining Deception

The FTC defines **deceptive advertising** as any ad that contains a misrepresentation, omission, or other practice that can mislead a significant number of reasonable consumers to their detriment. Proof that consumers were deceived is not required, and the representation may be either expressed or implied. The issue is whether the ad conveys a false impression—even if it is literally true.[52]

Take the case of the FTC against the weight-loss industry. Weight Watchers, Jenny Craig, Nutri System, and others used print and broadcast ads featuring customer testimonials. Jenny Craig even offered consumers the chance to "lose all the weight you want" for a fixed price. The FTC filed a complaint against the firms alleging false and deceptive advertising. Why? Because the ads *implied* (but gave no substantiation) that their customers are successful at losing weight and maintaining weight loss. The FTC additionally accused Jenny Craig of falsely representing that the advertised prices were the only costs associated with the programs and of failing to adequately disclose additional mandatory expenses.[53]

The FTC signed consent orders with several of the firms requiring them to disclose in their ads how many customers lose weight, report how much they lose over how long a time, and provide a warning that most dieters eventually regain lost weight. But Jenny Craig decided to fight the charges as a matter of principle, claiming that the company had never misled the public and the FTC requirements would place an unfair burden on it.[54]

Our delivery truck.

Their delivery truck.

Dy•Dee Wash
Cloth Diaper Service

The purpose of comparative ads is to demonstrate the superiority of one product over the another. Dy•Dee Wash takes the au natural marketing approach, with a cloth diaper service that is more environmentally friendly than the use of disposable diapers.

In Canada, all packages and labels must be printed in both English and French, and most major companies also run their ads in both languages. Here we see both the French and English versions of a service ad for General Motors, and the company's Web site is bilingual, too. Check it out (www.gmcanada.com).

Many FTC critics agreed with Jenny Craig's position. To comply with the FTC demands, firms making a weight-loss claim would have to provide a table listing the average weight loss by past participants and its duration. The companies would have to collect large amounts of data, often covering two years or more, involving all customers who had stayed in the program for more than two weeks. If a seller made a comparative claim, the data acquisition problem would increase exponentially. One former FTC staffer asserts that the requirements are little more than disguised prohibitions. Effectively comparative ads are banned, as are simple benefit claims.[55] Nonetheless, four years later, without admitting any wrongdoing, Jenny Craig settled with the FTC and agreed to sign the consent decree.[56]

Regardless of the criticisms leveled at it, the FTC remains a powerful regulator. The commission cracked down on Exxon and ordered a groundbreaking educational campaign to inform consumers that the right octane for most cars is regular octane, not the more expensive premium grade.[57] The FTC also looks at environmental claims such as biodegradable, degradable, photodegradable, and recyclable. To avoid confusing terminology, the FTC and the Environmental Protection Agency (EPA) worked jointly with attorneys general from many states to develop uniform national guidelines for environmental marketing claims.[58]

Defining Unfairness

According to FTC policy, some ads that are not deceptive may still be considered unfair to consumers. **Unfair advertising** occurs when a consumer is "unjustifiably injured" or there is a "violation of public policy" (such as other government statutes). In other words, unfair advertising is due to the inadequacy of *perfect information* or some other *externality*. For example, practices considered unfair are claims made without prior substantiation, claims that exploit vulnerable groups such as children and the elderly, and cases where the consumer cannot make a valid choice because the advertiser omits important information about the product or about competing products mentioned in the ad.[59]

In one case, the FTC found that an automaker's failure to warn of a safety problem was not deceptive but was unfair. Advertising organizations have argued that the word unfair is so vague it can mean whatever any given individual wants it to. They have lobbied Congress to eliminate the FTC's power to prosecute on unfairness grounds, and Congress did pass a compromise bill requiring the FTC to show that (1) an alleged unfair practice involves substantial, unavoidable injury to consumers; (2) the injury is not reasonably avoidable by consumers themselves; and (3) the injury is not outweighed by benefits to consumers or competition.[60] This legislation suggests that in the future the FTC will have to balance on a far narrower beam in its effort to regulate unfairness.[61]

Investigating Suspected Violations

If it receives complaints from consumers, competitors, or its own staff members who monitor ads in various media, the FTC may decide to investigate an advertiser. The agency has broad powers to pursue suspected violators and demand information from them. Typically, the FTC looks for three kinds of information: *substantiation, endorsements,* and *affirmative disclosures.*

If a suspected violator cites survey findings or scientific studies, the FTC may ask for **substantiation.** Advertisers are expected to have supporting data before running an ad, although the FTC sometimes allows postclaim evidence. The FTC does not solicit substantiation for ads it is not investigating.

The FTC also scrutinizes ads that contain questionable **endorsements** or **testimonials.** If a noncelebrity endorser is paid, the ad must disclose this on-screen.[62] The endorsers may not make claims the advertiser can't substantiate. Further, celebrity endorsers must actually use the product or service (if portrayed), and they can be held personally liable if they misrepresent it.[63]

Advertisers must make **affirmative disclosure** of their product's limitations or deficiencies: for example, EPA mileage ratings for cars, pesticide warnings, and statements that saccharin may be hazardous to one's health.

Le Clerc wants its customers to help protect the environment from "plastic bag pollution." So, in a beautifully produced campaign, it tells them, "No, Le Clerc does not really want to be seen everywhere." Other ads in the series say, "There are some places we don't want to see our name," and "Some advertising we'll pass up willingly."

Remedies for Unfair or Deceptive Advertising

When the FTC determines that an ad is deceptive or unfair, it may take three courses of action: negotiate with the advertiser for a consent decree, issue a cease-and-desist order, and/or require corrective advertising.

A **consent decree** is a document the advertiser signs agreeing to stop the objectionable advertising without admitting any wrongdoing. Before signing, the advertiser can negotiate specific directives with the FTC that will govern future advertising claims.

If an advertiser won't sign a consent decree, the FTC may issue a **cease-and-desist order** prohibiting further use of the ad. Before the order is final, it is heard by an administrative law judge (RL 2–3 in the Reference Library shows a flowchart of the FTC complaint procedure). Most advertisers sign the consent decree after the hearing and agree, without admitting guilt, to halt the advertising. Advertisers who violate either a consent decree or a cease-and-desist order can be fined up to $11,000 per showing of the offending ad.

The FTC may also require **corrective advertising** for some period of time to explain and correct offending ads. In the Exxon case mentioned earlier, the FTC required the company to spend millions—enough to reach 75 percent of the target audience (adults 18–49 years old) in 18 U.S. cities an average of nearly four times per person.[64] To help advertisers avoid such expense, the FTC will review advertising before it runs and give "advance clearance" in an advisory opinion. It also publishes *Industry Guides and Trade Regulation Rules,* which gives advertisers, agencies, and the media ongoing information about FTC regulations.

In Canada, the laws are even tougher and the consequences stiffer. It's an offense for any public promotion to be "false or misleading in a material respect." It is not necessary that anyone be misled by the representation, only that it be false. An *offense* is a crime. If convicted, an advertiser or agency executive could go to jail for up to five years, pay a fine, or both.[65]

To provide consumers with more perfect information, the U.S. Food and Drug Administration regulates the content of pharmaceutical ads, requiring advertisers to include all information from the product package insert, which necessitated lengthy commercials or miniscule copy. In 1997 the rule was changed, allowing pharmaceutical companies to advertise on TV and radio as long as they mentioned any important possible side effects and directed consumers to other resources for further information such as their magazine advertising or Internet sites. In 1997 Novartis (www.novartis.com) introduced Transderm Scop motion sickness patches with a series of magazine ads.

The Food and Drug Administration (FDA)

A division of the Department of Health and Human Services, the **Food and Drug Administration (FDA)** regulates over $1 trillion worth of products, which account for 25 cents of every dollar spent annually by American consumers.[66] It's the FDA's job to see that the food we eat is safe, the cosmetics we use won't hurt us, and the medicines and therapeutic devices we buy are safe and effective. With authority over the labeling, packaging, and branding of packaged foods and therapeutic devices, the FDA strives to give consumers *perfect information* by ensuring that products are labeled truthfully with the information people need to use them properly. The FDA requires manufacturers to disclose all ingredients on product labels, in in-store product advertising, and in product literature. The label must accurately state the weight or volume of the contents. Labels on therapeutic devices must give clear instructions for use. The FDA can require warning statements on packages of hazardous products. It regulates "cents off" and other promotions on package labels and has jurisdiction over the use of words such as *giant* or *family* to describe package sizes.

When consumer-oriented drug ads became common in the mid-80s, the FDA ruled that any ad for a brand-name drug must include all the information in the package insert.[67] That meant advertisers had to run lengthy commercials or use minuscule type in print ads. In 1997, the FDA changed that rule, allowing pharmaceutical companies to advertise their drugs on broadcast media as long as they mentioned any important possible side effects and directed people to their print ads, their Internet sites, or consumers' own doctors for more information.[68] With that ruling, prescription drug advertising instantly soared on television and radio.

The **Nutritional Labeling and Education Act (NLEA),** which went into effect in 1994, gave the FDA additional muscle by setting stringent legal definitions for terms such as *fresh, light, low fat,* and *reduced calories.* It also sets standard serving sizes and requires labels to show food value for one serving alongside the total recommended daily value as established by the National Research Council.[69]

The first time the FDA took severe action against a prominent marketer over a labeling dispute, it seized 2,400 cases of Procter & Gamble's Citrus Hill Fresh Choice orange juice. Fresh Choice was made from concentrate, not fresh-squeezed juice as P&G claimed.[70] Due to increased FDA scrutiny, many advertisers are now more cautious about their health and nutritional claims.

Wireless Communications

Imagine the future of wireless communications: videoconferencing with your legal department from your car, or being able to show production and postproduction samples of ads or spots to your clients through cellular and digital technology. To quote the AT&T ads, "You will. . ."

"Wireless communications" is the newest species on the technological evolution chart. Wireless market penetration in the United States is currently around 16 percent and expected to reach 48 percent by 2006. The analog phones of yesteryear are rapidly being replaced with the wireless communications of the future.

While systems for analog and digital cellular telephony, radio paging, and cordless telephones are now commonplace, the recent breakthrough of code division multiple access (CDMA) technology has brought a new generation of "digital" phones from companies like Qualcomm, PCSI, and Nokia. These phones offer a number of options that the analog phones do not. Standard features now include answering machine, pager, caller ID, call waiting, conference calling, call forwarding, and 911 emergency. They give advertising

account executives a secure way to communicate with clients almost anywhere—the digital phone circuits are encrypted to protect the conversation and number of the caller.

Another up-and-coming form of wireless communications is the satellite mobile telephone system, which will give the advertising industry access to clients virtually anywhere in the world. The phone works by transmitting a signal from the hand-held unit to a satellite. The signal is then transmitted back to earth, where it enters the company's receiver and routes through an analog land line to the destination dialed. The process is reversed for incoming calls.

Next-generation systems promise enhanced communication services, such as data, e-mail, satellite telephony, high-resolution digital video, and even multimedia communication. In the forefront of this new technology is Motorola with its new wireless Internet service, based on the CDMA technology. This allows cellular users to retrieve e-mail, weather forecasts, stock prices, and sports scores on their hand-held unit. It's a brave new world.

Sources: John Markoff (New York Time News Service), *San Diego Union-Tribune* (Computer Link), April 8, 1997, pp. 8–9; "Cyber Cellular Phones," *PC Magazine On-line*, May 28, 1996, retrieved from http://www8.zdnet.com.

The Federal Communications Commission (FCC)

The seven-member **Federal Communications Commission (FCC)** is an independent federal agency with jurisdiction over the radio, television, telephone, satellite, the Internet, and cable TV industries. The FCC is responsible for protecting the public interest and encouraging competition. Its control over broadcast advertising is actually *indirect,* stemming from its authority to license broadcasters (or take away their licenses). The FCC stringently controls the airing of obscenity and profanity, and it can restrict both the products advertised and the content of ads. For example, the FCC required stations to run commercials about the harmful effects of smoking even before Congress banned cigarette advertising on TV and radio.

In the 1980s, the FCC decided there were enough buyers and sellers that marketplace forces could adequately control broadcast media, so it deregulated both radio and TV stations. The FCC no longer limits commercial time or requires stations to maintain detailed program and commercial logs. However, stations still keep records of commercial broadcasts to assure advertisers they ran.

The 1992 Cable Television Consumer Protection and Competition Act gave the FCC additional teeth. It placed new controls on the cable TV industry to encourage a more service-oriented attitude and to improve the balance between rates and escalating ad revenues.[71] The FCC can set subscriber rates for cable TV, so subscription revenues should slow while advertising rates rise.

Studies show violence on TV is linked to violent behavior (a public health issue). Congress responded by enacting the 1992 Television Violence Act, exempting network and cable companies from antitrust laws if they agree to self-regulate violence. Because network and cable companies deny that violence on TV is related to violence in life, government intervention is a possibility.[72]

The Patent and Trademark Office and the Library of Congress

A basic role of government is to promote and protect the economic well-being (*self-interest*) of its citizens. One way the U.S government does this is by promoting "the progress of science and useful arts, by securing for limited times to authors and inventors the exclusive right to their respective writings and discoveries"; in other words, by registering and protecting their **intellectual property.**[73]

A trademark like Coca-Cola or Levi's is a valuable asset. According to the Lanham Trade-Mark Act (1947), a **trademark** is "any word, name, symbol, or device or any combination thereof adopted and used by a manufacturer or merchant to identify

Coca-Cola's trademark varies from country to country. But the overall look is retained through use of similar letterforms and style, even with different alphabets.

1. Arabic
2. French
3. Japanese
4. Thai
5. Spanish
6. Chinese
7. Hebrew
8. Polish

his goods and distinguish them from those manufactured or sold by others."

Through the issuance of **patents,** the government provides incentives to invent, invest in, and disclose new technology worldwide. By registering trademarks and copyrights, the government helps businesses protect their investments, promote their goods and services, and safeguard consumers against confusion and deception in the marketplace (*perfect information*).

Patents and trademarks are registered with and protected by the **U.S. Patent and Trademark Office,** a bureau of the Department of Commerce. Ownership of a trademark may be designated in advertising or on a label, package, or letterhead by the word *Registered,* the symbol ®, or the symbol ™. If someone persists in using a trademark owned by another, the trademark owner can ask for a court order and sue for trademark infringement.

The Library of Congress protects all copyrighted material, including advertising, in the United States. A **copyright** is a form of protection provided to the authors of "original works of authorship," including literary, dramatic, musical, artistic, and certain other "intellectual works."[74] A copyright issued to an advertiser grants the exclusive right to print, publish, or reproduce the protected ad for the life of the copyright owner plus 50 years. An ad can be copyrighted only if it contains original copy or illustrations. An idea cannot be copyrighted; nor can slogans, short phrases, and familiar symbols and designs (although the latter may be trademarkable).

Copyright is indicated by the word *Copyright,* the abbreviation *Copr.,* or the symbol © followed by the year of first publication and the name of the advertiser or copyright owner. (For more on trademarks and copyrights, see RL 2–4 in the Reference Library).

State and Local Regulation

Advertisers are also subject to state or local laws. Since the U.S. federal deregulation trend of the 1980s, state and local governments have taken a far more active role.

Regulation by State Governments

State legislation governing advertising is often based on the truth-in-advertising model statute developed in 1911 by *Printer's Ink,* for many years the major trade publication of the industry. The statute holds that any maker of an ad found to contain "untrue, deceptive, or misleading" material is guilty of a misdemeanor. Today 46 states (all except Arkansas, Delaware, Mississippi, and New Mexico) enforce laws patterned after this statute.

All states also have "little FTC acts," consumer protection laws that govern unfair and deceptive business practices. States themselves can investigate and prosecute cases, and individual consumers can bring civil suits against businesses. To increase their clout, some states team up on legal actions—for example, to challenge deceptive ad promotions in the airline, rental-car, and food-making industries. As one observer pointed out, "Many of the food manufacturers could litigate some of the smaller states into the ground, but they might not be willing to fight it out against 10 states simultaneously."[75]

Different states have different regulations governing what can be advertised. Some states prohibit advertising for certain types of wine and liquor, and most states restrict the use of federal and state flags in advertising.

This can present a major problem to national marketers. And in some cases, it actually hurts consumers. For example, many companies trying to conduct environmentally responsible marketing programs feel stymied by the different state laws governing packaging materials and recycling.[76]

Regulation by Local Governments

Many cities and counties also have consumer protection agencies to enforce laws regulating local advertising practices. The chief function of these agencies is to protect local consumers against unfair and misleading practices by area merchants.

In one year alone, the Orange County, California, district attorney's office received over 1,200 complaint letters from consumers about everything from dishonest mechanics and phony sale ads to a taco stand that skimped on the beef in its "macho" burrito.[77] In a case against Montgomery Ward, the DA collected $310,000 in civil penalties to settle a false advertising suit. The company was charged with a variety of deceptions, including increasing retail prices before applying sale discounts and advertising that sales were of limited duration when in fact they were ongoing. It was the third time in a decade that the company was ordered to halt misleading advertising.[78]

Nongovernment Regulation

Nongovernment organizations also issue advertising guidelines (see Exhibit 2–4). In fact, advertisers face considerable regulation by business-monitoring organizations, related trade associations, the media, consumer groups, and advertising agencies themselves.

The Better Business Bureau (BBB)

The largest of the U.S. business-monitoring organizations is the **Better Business Bureau (BBB),** established in 1916. Funded by dues from over 100,000 member companies, it operates primarily at the local level to protect consumers against fraudulent and deceptive advertising and sales practices. When local bureaus contact violators and ask them to revise their advertising, most comply.

Exhibit 2–4
American Association of Advertising Agencies policy statement and guidelines for comparative advertising.

The Board of Directors of the American Association of Advertising Agencies recognizes that when used truthfully and fairly, comparative advertising provides the consumer with needed and useful information.

However, extreme caution should be exercised. The use of comparative advertising, by its very nature, can distort facts and, by implication, convey to the consumer information that misrepresents the truth.

Therefore, the Board believes that comparative advertising should follow certain guidelines:

1. The intent and connotation of the ad should be to inform and never to discredit or unfairly attack competitors, competing products, or services.
2. When a competitive product is named, it should be one that exists in the marketplace as significant competition.
3. The competition should be fairly and properly identified but never in a manner or tone of voice that degrades the competitive product or service.
4. The advertising should compare related or similar properties or ingredients of the product, dimension to dimension, feature to feature.
5. The identification should be for honest comparison purposes and not simply to upgrade by association.
6. If a competitive test is conducted, it should be done by an objective testing source, preferably an independent one, so that there will be no doubt as to the veracity of the test.
7. In all cases the test should be supportive of all claims made in the advertising that are based on the test.
8. The advertising should never use partial results or stress insignificant differences to cause the consumer to draw an improper conclusion.
9. The property being compared should be significant in terms of value or usefulness of the product to the consumer.
10. Comparatives delivered through the use of testimonials should not imply that the testimonial is more than one individual's thought unless that individual represents a sample of the majority viewpoint.

The BBB's files on violators are open to the public. Records of violators who do not comply are sent to appropriate government agencies for further action. The BBB often works with local law enforcement agencies to prosecute advertisers guilty of fraud and misrepresentation. Each year, the BBB investigates thousands of ads for possible violations of truth and accuracy.

The Council of Better Business Bureaus is the parent organization of the Better Business Bureau and a sponsoring member of the National Advertising Review Council. One of its functions is to help new industries develop standards for ethical and responsible advertising. The Code of Advertising of the Council of Better Business Bureaus (the BBB Code) has been called the most important self-regulation of advertising.[79] The BBB Code is only a few pages long, but it is supplemented by a monthly publication called *Do's and Don'ts in Advertising Copy,* which provides on-going information about advertising regulations and recent court and administrative rulings that affect advertising.[80] Since 1983, the National Advertising Division of the Council of Better Business Bureaus has published guidelines for advertising to children, a particularly sensitive area.

The National Advertising Review Council (NARC)

The **National Advertising Review Council (NARC)** was established in 1971 by the Council of Better Business Bureaus, the American Association of Advertising Agencies, the American Advertising Federation, and the Association of National Advertisers. Its primary purpose is to promote and enforce standards of truth, accuracy, taste, morality, and social responsibility in advertising.

NARC is one of the most comprehensive and effective mechanisms for regulating American advertising. A U.S. district court judge noted in a 1985 case that its "speed, informality, and modest cost," as well as its expertise, give NARC special advantages over the court system in resolving advertising disputes.[81]

NARC Operating Arms

The NARC has two operating arms: the **National Advertising Division (NAD)** of the Council of Better Business Bureaus and the **National Advertising Review Board (NARB).** The NAD monitors advertising practices and reviews complaints about advertising from consumers and consumer groups, brand competitors, local Better Business Bureaus, trade associations, and others. The appeals board for NAD decisions is the NARB, which consists of a chairperson and 70 volunteer members (39 national advertisers, 21 agency representatives, and 10 laypeople).

The NAD/NARB Review Process

To encourage consumers to register complaints, the NAD itself runs ads that include a complaint form. Most target untruthfulness or inaccuracy.

When the NAD finds a valid complaint, it contacts the advertiser, specifying any claims to be substantiated. If substantiation is inadequate, the NAD requests modification or discontinuance of the claims.

The Texaco–Chevron dispute shows how well the NAD process works. In 1994, Texaco introduced a new gasoline, CleanSystem[3], amid much hoopla. It claimed the product represented a new generation of fuel and would provide the "*highest* performance" and the "*best* mileage." Chevron protested to the NAD that its gas was just as good as Texaco's. The NAD pored over 1,500 pages of test data and eventually sided with Chevron. Texaco agreed to alter its ads to say "a breakthrough in Texaco technology" and "higher performance" instead of "highest performance."[82]

If the NAD and an advertiser reach an impasse, either party has the right to a review by a five-member NARB panel (consisting of three advertisers, one agency representative, and one layperson). The panel's decision is binding. If an advertiser refuses to comply with the panel's decision (which has never yet occurred), the NARB will refer the matter to an appropriate government body and so indicates in its public record. (For a flowchart of the NAD/NARB review process, see RL 2–5 in the Reference Library.) Of 3,000 NAD investigations conducted between 1971 and 1990, only 70 were disputed and referred to the NARB for resolution.[83]

Regulation by the Media

Almost all media review ads and reject material they regard as objectionable, even if it isn't deceptive. Many people think the media are more effective regulators than the government.

Television

Of all media, the TV networks conduct the strictest review. Advertisers must submit all commercials intended for a network or affiliated station to its broadcast standards department. Many commercials (in script or storyboard form) are returned with suggestions for changes or greater substantiation. Some ads are rejected outright if they violate network policies. (See Ad Lab 2–C.)

The three major U.S. broadcast networks base their policies on the original National Association of Broadcasters Television Code. But network policies vary enough that it's difficult to prepare universally acceptable commercials. Cable networks and local stations tend to be much less stringent, as demonstrated by their acceptance of condom ads.

Radio

The 19 U.S. radio networks, unlike TV networks, supply only a small percentage of their affiliates' programming, so they have little or no say in what their affiliates advertise. A radio station is also less likely to return a script or tape for changes. Some stations, like KLBJ in Austin, Texas, look mainly at whether the advertising is illegal, unethical, or immoral.[84] They don't want spots to offend listeners or detract from the rest of the programming.

Every radio station typically has its own unwritten guidelines. KDWB, a Minneapolis/St. Paul station with a large teenage audience, turned down a psychic who wanted to buy advertising time but did allow condom and other contraceptive ads.[85] KSDO in San Diego, a station with a business and information format, won't air commercials for X-rated movies or topless bars.[86]

Magazines

National magazines monitor all advertising, especially by new advertisers and for new products. Newer publications eager to sell space may not be so vigilant, but established magazines, like *Time* and *Newsweek*, are highly scrupulous. Many magazines will not accept advertising for certain types of products. The *New Yorker* won't run discount retail store advertising or ads for feminine hygiene or self-medication products. *Reader's Digest* won't accept tobacco ads.

Some magazines test every product before accepting the advertising. *Good Housekeeping* rejects ads if its tests don't substantiate the advertiser's claims. Products that pass are allowed to feature the Good Housekeeping seal of approval.

Newspapers

Newspapers also monitor and review advertising. Larger newspapers have clearance staffs who read every ad submitted; most smaller newspapers rely on the advertising manager, sales personnel, or proofreaders.

The advertising policies set forth in *Newspaper Rates & Data* specify, "No objectionable medical, personal, matrimonial, clairvoyant, or palmistry advertising accepted; no stock promotion or financial advertising, other than those securities of known value." Another rule prohibits ads that might easily be mistaken for regular reading material unless they feature the word *advertisement* or *advt.*

Editorial and Advertorial: It's Adversarial

Pick up a glossy magazine like *Vogue, Esquire,* or *Sports Illustrated* and you'll find it loaded with ads for cars, liquor, and cigarettes. Advertising agencies like buying space in these upscale publications as long as nothing in the publication directly offends their clients. Agencies are very protective of their clients, so they're careful about where their ads are placed. If an ad runs alongside a story that might reflect badly on the client's product or, even worse, might offend the client's customers, the ad agency will either pull the ad or request that the article be dropped. Moreover, agencies and their clients want to be warned ahead of time when a controversial story will appear. Increasingly, this is becoming a sore point with magazine editors and is creating an ethical stir in the industry. Editors see it as an assault on their independence and integrity. Advertisers see it as their responsibility to sponsor content suitable for, and not offensive to, their customers.

On the other hand, a survey sponsored by the Newspaper Advertising Association and the American Society of Magazine Editors discovered that newspaper ads actually meet consumer expectations better than the quality of news coverage. Consumers told the survey they believe newspaper ads are useful and relevant, saving them both time and money by allowing them to comparison shop at home. As a result, newspaper editors are now looking at expanding their partnership with advertisers.

"I think we need to have advertising and editorial work more closely together to produce a paper, especially since advertising has this solid local franchise," said *Washington Post* research chief Sharon P. Warden.

In the world of print media, publishers are the business people who worry about the bottom line and editors worry about editorial content and journalistic integrity. Often their interests collide. To interest more advertisers, magazine publishers now create whole sections, sometime entire issues devoted to *advertorials*—pages of commercial copy dressed up as news stories. Often it's difficult to differentiate between actual editorial copy and advertising text. *Sports Illustrated (SI)* publishes an annual special issue called *Golf Plus,* figuring that the 500,000-plus copies will generate higher interest from advertisers such as Foot Joy and Titlist golf balls.

Maxim Publications is one of a few remaining publications that separate the editorial and business sides of publications. Even so, advertisers with Maxim exert influence over the content that surrounds their ads by reminding editors of revenue loss if certain material is published. *Ms* magazine solved the conflict by going ad-free in 1990.

Print is not the only medium that falls under editorial scrutiny. Radio and TV are also constantly monitored for content. Some advertisers buying time on radio stations that air syndicated personalities like Rush Limbaugh and Howard Stern specify "NO RUSH" and "NO HOWARD." Because of the shows' controversial content, they simply refuse to allow their ads to be placed there. Except for the news, television is taped in advance. Many advertisers can review episodes prior to airing and decide to pull the ads if necessary. (See Chapters 12 through 14 for more information on media buying.)

One Michigan homemaker was angered by sexual innuendoes on Fox's TV sitcom, "Married . . . with Children." So she persuaded Procter & Gamble and other leading advertisers not to buy time on the show. Similarly, many blue-chip advertisers shunned the police drama "NYPD Blue" on ABC because of scenes with partial nudity and blunt language—until it did too well in the ratings for them to ignore. During the coming-out episode of "Ellen" in 1997, many advertisers like Chrysler pulled their spots. The spots, however, were quickly replaced by sponsors eager to be part of a show that was expected to reach an unusually large audience.

"With TV, it's a case of supply and demand, and right now the demand for commercial time exceeds the supply," said Kevin Goldman, a former advertising columnist for *The Wall Street Journal.*

However, the case is not the same for magazines. "Magazines are different because there's a finite number of advertisers that want in on a particular book. If Chrysler pulls out of an issue, the pool of advertisers that might take its place is shallow," explained Goldman.

Moreover, magazines (especially new specialty magazines) increasingly tailor their editorial focus to reach niche audiences or a particular demographic. This narrows their options for ad dollars to those marketers targeting the same groups—in effect, giving greater influence to fewer advertisers.

Years ago, the American Society of Magazine Editors drew up guidelines on how magazines should distinguish advertorials from regular editorial pages. In October 1996, The ASME released a three-paragraph "Standard for Editorial Independence" following a few episodes in which editors left magazines as a result of apparent interference from their corporate employers. The standard states, "Editors need the maximum possible protection from untoward commercial or extra-journalistic pressures. The chief editor of any magazine must have final authority over the editorial content, words and pictures, that appear in the publication."

Laboratory Applications

When is it okay for an advertiser to give its "editorial" view in a publication or on a show? Provide data to support your answers to the following questions.

1. To what degree, if any, should an advertiser have editorial control over placement of its ads or content of the publication?
2. What effect, if any, could advertorials have on national problems such as age discrimination, racism, sexism, and teenage pregnancy? Be specific.

Sources: "Corporations, Magazines, and Advertising," *All Things Considered* (National Public Radio), May 20, 1997; Mark Fitzgerald, "Ads More Relevant than News?" *Editor & Publisher,* May 17, 1997, p. 19; "Pressured to Please: Advertisers' Concerns about Story Content Are Having an Impact on Magazine Editors," *Newsday,* June 28, 1997.

Freshness Counts!

Fresh bread...   *Fresh tea...*

Fresh flowers...   *Fresh fruit...*

Fresh air...   *Fresh batteries...*

We guarantee ours.

Fresh batteries make things run better and longer. We sell millions of our top-rated alkalines every week, stocking new ones daily. So you can always be sure they're fresh. We're so confident you'll agree, that we back every one with a guarantee.*

RadioShack alkalines
have earned the
Good Housekeeping Seal.

*If you're not satisfied, return your RadioShack alkaline purchase within 30 days for a one-time replacement or refund. You can't find a better, longer-lasting battery. **GUARANTEED.**

RadioShack.
You've got questions.
We've got answers.

To help consumers make informed decisions, Good Housekeeping *magazine tests the products in their ads and provides a seal of approval to those advertisers, like Radio Shack (www.radioshack.com), who substantiate their claims. This gives the consumer a more authoritative voice to listen to when trying to decide on purchases.*

In addition, most papers have their own acceptability guidelines, ranging from one page for small local papers to more than 50 pages for large dailies such as the *Los Angeles Times.* Some codes are quite specific. The *Detroit Free Press* won't accept classified ads containing such words as "affair" or "swinger." Some newspapers require advertisers who claim "the lowest price in town" to include a promise to meet or beat any price readers find elsewhere within 30 days.

One problem advertisers face is that newspapers' codes are far from uniform. Handgun ads may be prohibited by one newspaper, accepted by another if the guns are antique, and permitted by a third so long as the guns aren't automatic. And newspapers do revise their policies from time to time.

Regulation by Consumer Groups

Of all the regulatory forces governing advertising, consumer protection organizations have shown the greatest growth. Starting in the 1960s, the consumer movement became increasingly active in fighting fraudulent and deceptive advertising. Consumers demanded that products perform as advertised and that more product information be provided for people to compare and make better buying decisions. The consumer movement gave rise to **consumerism,** social action to dramatize the rights of the buying public. It is clear now that the U.S. consumer has the power to influence advertising practices dramatically.

Today, advertisers and agencies pay more attention to product claims, especially those related to energy use (such as the estimated miles per gallon of a new car) and the nutritional value of processed foods. Consumerism fostered the growth of consumer advocacy groups and regulatory agencies and promoted more consumer research by advertisers, agencies, and the media in an effort to learn what consumers want—and how to provide it. Investment in public goodwill pays off in improved consumer relations and sales.

Consumer Information Networks

Organizations like the Consumer Federation of America (CFA), the National Council of Senior Citizens, the National Consumer League, and the National Stigma Clearinghouse exchange and disseminate information among members. These **consumer information networks** help develop state, regional, and local consumer organizations and work with national, regional, county, and municipal consumer groups.

Consumer interests also are served by private, nonprofit testing organizations such as Consumers Union, Consumers' Research, and Underwriters Laboratories.

Consumer Advocates

Consumer advocate groups investigate advertising complaints received from the public and those that grow out of their own research. If a complaint is warranted, they ask the advertiser to halt the objectionable ad or practice. If the advertiser does not comply, they release publicity or criticism about the offense to the media and submit complaints with substantiating evidence to appropriate government agencies for further action. In some instances, they file a lawsuit to obtain a cease-and-desist order, a fine, or other penalty against the violator.

Today, with so many special-interest advocacy groups, even the most sensitive advertisers feel challenged. To attract attention, advertising must be creative and stand out from competing noise. Yet advertisers fear attention from politically correct activists (the "PC police"). Calvin Klein ads were attacked by the Boycott Anorexic Marketing group. A Nike ad starring Porky Pig was protested by the National Stuttering Project in San Francisco. An animated public service spot from Aetna Insurance even drew curses from a witches' rights group.[87]

When the protests start flying, the ads usually get pulled. Steve Hayden, chair of BBDO Los Angeles, believes it would be possible to get any spot pulled with "about five letters that appear on the right stationery."[88] As Shelly Garcia noted in *Adweek*, "The way things are these days, nothing motivates middle managers like the need to avoid attention." She lamented the fact that "there are fewer and fewer opportunities to have any fun in advertising."[89]

Self-Regulation by Advertisers

Advertisers also regulate themselves. They have to. In today's competitive marketplace, consumer confidence is essential. Most large advertisers gather strong data to substantiate their claims. They maintain careful systems of advertising review to ensure that ads meet both their own standards and industry, media, and legal requirements. Many advertisers try to promote their social responsibility by tying in with a local charity or educational organization.

Many industries maintain advertising codes that companies agree to follow. These codes also establish a basis for complaints. However, industry advertising codes are only as effective as the enforcement powers of the individual trade associations. And since enforcement may conflict with antitrust laws, trade associations usually use peer pressure rather than hearings or penalties.

Self-Regulation by Ad Agencies and Associations

Most ad agencies monitor their own practices. Professional advertising associations also oversee members' activities to prevent problems that might trigger government intervention. Advertising publications report issues and court actions to educate agencies and advertisers and warn them about possible legal infractions.

Advertising Agencies

Although advertisers supply information about their product or service to their agencies, the agencies must research and verify product claims and comparative product data before using them in advertising. The media may require such documentation before accepting the advertising, and substantiation may be needed if government or consumer agencies challenge the claims.

Agencies can be held legally liable for fraudulent or misleading advertising claims. (See the Chapter 7 Ethical Issue, When Advertisers Dare to Compare.) For this reason, most major advertising agencies have in-house legal counsel and regularly submit their ads for review. If any aspect of the advertising is challenged, the agency asks its client to review the advertising and either confirm claims as truthful or replace unverified material.

Advertising Associations

Several associations monitor industrywide advertising practices. The **American Association of Advertising Agencies (AAAA),** an association of the largest advertising agencies throughout the United States, controls agency practices by denying membership to any agency judged unethical. The AAAA *Standards of Practice and Creative Code* set advertising principles for member agencies.

The **American Advertising Federation (AAF)** helped to establish the FTC, and its early vigilance committees were the forerunners of the Better Business Bureau. The AAF *Advertising Principles of American Business,* adopted in 1984, define standards for truthful and responsible advertising (see Exhibit 2–5 on page 77). Since most local advertising clubs belong to the AAF, it is instrumental in influencing agencies and advertisers to abide by these principles.

In the aftermath of the vicious political advertising for the November 1994 elections, Ketchum Advertising published this ad in The Wall Street Journal *calling on the broadcasting and publishing community to hold political advertising to the same standards as consumer advertising.*

Don't call it advertising.

A distraught woman is persuaded to appear in a commercial where she accuses the Governor of New York of being responsible for the murder of her son.

A gubernatorial candidate is forced to do a commercial denying the charges that his recent divorce was a result of his beating his wife.

In a local race for Comptroller, a commercial was created that opened with white letters against a black screen asking "KILL THE JEWS?"

This is filth.

Political filth that is not advertising and shouldn't be dignified by being called advertising.

Whether you are a Democrat, Republican, Conservative or Liberal, if you are a decent, thinking human being you must be appalled at the political communication that came into your home during this dirty election.

Once again let us reiterate: This is not advertising.

The practitioners of the bulk of this trash are those so-called "political consultants" who might have been part of a "dirty tricks" team in the 1970s. Now, in 1994, they publish and broadcast their "dirty tricks" and they claim that it's advertising.

If a reputable corporation produced advertising with the same exaggerated claims and promises for their products and then failed to deliver on these claims, their executives would be fined or led off to jail in handcuffs. And, standing on the sidelines, shouting, "How dare they not deliver on what they promised!" would be those politicians who have condoned this year's group of political lies and exaggerations.

We say it must stop.

And it must stop now.

Let it start with this advertisement.

Let it start today, November 9, 1994, the day after one of the dirtiest elections in the history of this country.

Let those of us in advertising, broadcasting, publishing and business stand up together and say, "Stop."

Stop the character assassination.

Stop the lies.

Stop the ugliness.

And, above all, stop calling what you're doing advertising.

Advertising enhances a product. What you do tears it down.

Advertising that is effective is built on truth.

What you are doing is built on lies.

We at Ketchum Advertising are calling on the broadcasting and publishing community to hold political advertising to the same standards you hold consumer advertising.

We're calling on you to set up a bi-partisan group, to screen all future political advertising.

A group made up of broadcasting executives, publishing executives, and bona fide advertising executives.

We are calling on you to hold political advertisers to the same rules of disparagement you hold other advertisers.

But most of all, we're calling on you and every concerned citizen to get involved.

Now at this point you might be asking how you and your company can make a contribution towards bringing about this change.

Our answer is we don't want your money, we want your name.

If you want to register your vote for a change in the nature and tone of political advertising in the United States, write to:

Ketchum Advertising
527 Madison Avenue
New York, NY 10022
Or fax: (212) 907-9332

We promise your voice will be heard.

This advertisement was developed from an idea by Dianne Snedaker who heads up the San Francisco office of Ketchum Advertising. Art direction by Bruce Campbell, Creative Director, Ketchum/S.F. The body copy was written by Jerry Della Femina in New York. The sentiments are those of the 1,200 employees of Ketchum Communications.

Exhibit 2–5
Advertising Principles of American
Business of the American Advertising
Federation (AAF).

1. *Truth.* Advertising shall reveal the truth, and shall reveal significant facts, the omission of which would mislead the public.
2. *Substantiation.* Advertising claims shall be substantiated by evidence in possession of the advertiser and the advertising agency prior to making such claims.
3. *Comparisons.* Advertising shall refrain from making false, misleading, or unsubstantiated statements or claims about a competitor or his products or service.
4. *Bait advertising.* Advertising shall not offer products or services for sale unless such offer constitutes a bona fide effort to sell the advertised products or services and is not a device to switch consumers to other goods or services, usually higher priced.
5. *Guarantees and warranties.* Advertising of guarantees and warranties shall be explicit, with sufficient information to apprise consumers of their principal terms and limitations or, when space or time restrictions preclude such disclosures, the advertisement shall clearly reveal where the full text of the guarantee or warranty can be examined before purchase.
6. *Price claims.* Advertising shall avoid price claims that are false or misleading, or savings claims that do not offer provable savings.
7. *Testimonials.* Advertising containing testimonials shall be limited to those of competent witnesses who are reflecting a real and honest opinion or experience.
8. *Taste and decency.* Advertising shall be free of statements, illustrations, or implications that are offensive to good taste or public decency.

The **Association of National Advertisers (ANA)** comprises 400 major manufacturing and service companies that are clients of member agencies of the AAAA. These companies, pledged to uphold the ANA code of advertising ethics, work with the ANA through a joint Committee for Improvement of Advertising Content.

The **Ethical** and **Legal Aspects** of Advertising in Perspective

Unquestionably, advertising offers considerable benefits to marketers and consumers alike. However, there's also no disputing that advertising has been and still is too often misused. As *Adweek* editor Andrew Jaffe says, the industry should do all it can to "raise its standards and try to drive out that which is misleading, untruthful, or downright tasteless and irresponsible." Otherwise, he warns, the pressure to regulate even more will become overwhelming.[90]

Advertising apologists point out that of all the advertising reviewed by the Federal Trade Commission in a typical year, 97 percent is found to be satisfactory.[91] In the end, advertisers and consumers need to work together to ensure that advertising is used intelligently, ethically, and responsibly for the benefit of all.

Chapter **Summary**

As one of the most visible activities of business, advertising is both lauded and criticized for the role it plays in selling products and influencing society. Some controversy surrounds advertising's role in the economy. To debate advertising's economic effects, we employ the four basic assumptions of free-enterprise economics: self-interest, many buyers and sellers, perfect information, and absence of externalities.

The economic impact of advertising can be likened to the opening shot in billiards—a chain reaction that affects the company as well as its competitors, customers, and the business community. On a broader scale, advertising is often considered the trigger on a country's mass-distribution system, enabling manufacturers to produce the products people want in high volume, at low prices, with standardized quality. People may argue though, about how advertising adds value to products, affects prices, encourages or discourages competition, promotes consumer demand, narrows or widens consumer choice, and affects business cycles.

Although controversy surrounds some of these economic issues, few dispute the abundance principle: in an economy that produces more goods and services than can be consumed, advertising gives consumers more perfect information about the choices available to them, encourages more sellers to compete more effectively, and thereby serves the self-interest of both consumers and marketers.

Social criticisms of advertising may be short-term manipulative arguments or long-term macro arguments. While the economic aspect of advertising focuses on the free-enterprise principles of self-interest and many buyers and sellers, the social aspect typically involves the concepts of perfect information and externalities.

Critics say advertising is deceptive; it manipulates people into buying unneeded products; it makes our society too materialistic; and there's just too much of it. Further, they say, advertising perpetuates stereotypes, and all too frequently, it is offensive and in bad taste.

Proponents admit that advertising is sometimes misused. However, they point out that despite its problems, advertising offers many social benefits. It encourages the development of new products and speeds their acceptance. It fosters employment, gives consumers and businesses a wider variety of product choices, and helps keep prices down by encouraging mass production. It stimulates healthy competition among companies and raises the overall standard of living. Moreover, sophisticated marketers know the best way to sell their products is to appeal to genuine consumer needs and be honest in their advertising claims.

In short, while advertising can be criticized for giving less than perfect information and for creating some unwanted externalities, it also contributes to the free enterprise system by encouraging many buyers and sellers to participate in the process, thereby serving the self-interest of all.

Under growing pressure from consumers, special-interest groups, and government regulation, advertisers developed higher standards of ethical conduct and social responsibility. Advertisers confront three levels of ethical consideration: the primary rules of ethical behavior in society, their personal value system, and their personal philosophy of singular ethical concepts.

The federal and state courts are involved in several advertising issues, including First Amendment protection of commercial speech, professionals' right to advertise, infringements of the right to privacy, and lawsuits over comparative advertising. Advertising is regulated by federal, state, and local government agencies, business-monitoring organizations, the media, consumer groups, and the advertising industry itself. All of these groups encourage advertisers to give more perfect information to consumers and eliminate any externalities in the process.

The Federal Trade Commission, the major federal regulator of advertising in the United States, is responsible for protecting consumers and competitors from deceptive and unfair business practices. If the FTC finds an ad deceptive or unfair, it may issue a cease-and-desist order or require corrective advertising.

The Food and Drug Administration (FDA) monitors advertising for food and drugs and regulates product labels and packaging. The Federal Communications Commission (FCC) has jurisdiction over the radio and TV industries, although deregulation severely limited its control over advertising in these media. The Patent and Trademark Office governs ownership of U.S. trademarks, trade names, house marks, and similar distinctive features of companies and brands. The Library of Congress registers and protects copyrighted materials.

State and local governments also enact consumer protection laws that regulate advertising.

Nongovernment regulators include the Council of Better Business Bureaus and its National Advertising Division. The NAD, the most effective U.S. nongovernment regulatory body, investigates complaints from consumers, brand competitors, or local Better Business Bureaus and suggests corrective measures. Advertisers that refuse to comply are referred to the National Advertising Review Board (NARB), which may uphold, modify, or reverse the NAD's findings.

Other sources of regulation include the codes and policies of the print media and broadcast media. Consumer organizations and advocates also control advertising by investigating and filing complaints against advertisers and by providing information to consumers. Finally, advertisers and agencies regulate themselves.

Important **Terms**

affirmative disclosure, *66*
American Advertising Federation (AAF), *75*
American Association of Advertising Agencies (AAAA), *75*
Association of National Advertisers (ANA), *77*
Better Business Bureau (BBB), *70*
cease-and-desist order, *66*
comparative advertising, *63*
consent decree, *66*
consumer advocates, *74*
consumer information networks, *74*
consumerism, *74*
copyright, *69*
corrective advertising, *67*

deceptive advertising, *64*
endorsements, *66*
ethical advertising, *57*
Federal Communications Commission (FCC), *68*
Federal Trade Commission (FTC), *64*
Food and Drug Administration (FDA), *67*
intellectual property, *68*
long-term macro arguments, *49*
National Advertising Division (NAD), *71*
National Advertising Review Board (NARD), *71*
National Advertising Review Council (NARC), *71*

nonproduct facts, *50*
Nutritional Labeling and Education Act, *67*
patent, *69*
privacy rights, *63*
puffery, *50*
short-term manipulative arguments, *49*
social responsibility, *57*
subliminal advertising, *50*
substantiation, *66*
testimonials, *66*
trademark, *68*
unfair advertising, *65*
U.S. Patent and Trademark Office, *69*

Review **Questions**

1. What role does advertising play in our economic system?
2. What are the two types of social criticisms of advertising?
3. What is puffery? Give some examples. Do you ever feel deceived by puffery in advertising?
4. Does advertising affect our value system? In what ways?
5. What is the difference between an advertiser's ethics and its social responsibility?
6. How does government regulation of advertising in the United States differ from regulation in many foreign countries?
7. How does commercial speech differ from political speech? Do you think advertisers should have the same First Amendment rights as everyone else? Explain.
8. What is the role of the FTC in advertising? Do you think this role should be expanded or restricted?
9. How do regional and local governments affect advertisers?
10. How well do advertisers regulate themselves? In what areas do you think advertisers have done well, and where should they clean up their act?

Exploring the **Internet**

The Internet exercises for Chapter 2 address two of the four areas of advertising covered in the chapter: advertising law and the regulation of advertising.

1. Advertising Law

   As you learned in this chapter, advertisers and their agencies are held accountable for the work they produce and must know the law(s) governing their communication. Understanding the legal ramifications behind a piece of communication is critical to any advertiser.

   Therefore, finding ways to keep abreast of the latest cases/issues relating to advertising law and the implications thereof is of the utmost importance to advertising practitioners. Visit advertising law firm Lewis Rose's Advertising Law Internet site (**www.webcom.com/lewrose/**) and the Advertising Law Resource Center (**www.lawpublish.com**), then discuss the following.

   a. Review the documents/articles at these sites and discuss the fundamental principles behind advertising law, including substantiation, deception, and unfairness.
   b. Choose one article/discussion or one case study in Lewis Rose's archives and illustrate its importance to advertisers and their agencies.
   c. Discuss the value these websites provide the advertising community, with special emphasis on local advertisers.

2. Regulation of Advertising

   The FTC's Division of Advertising Practices protects consumers from deceptive and unsubstantiated advertising. Apply what you have learned by visiting the division's Web site (**www.ftc.gov**) and answering the following questions. (You may want to review the policies and guides found at **http://www.ftc.gov/bcp/guides/guides.htm.**)

   a. Give a general description of what the FTC considers to be deceptive and unfair advertising.
   b. Describe the requirements for substantiating advertising and the process advertisers and their agencies must undergo to do so.
   c. Choose a fourth topic covered on the site and discuss its relevance and importance to the advertising industry.

   Be sure to surf the following sites that are also related to regulation of the advertising industry:

   - Council of Better Business Bureaus' National Advertising Division (NAD) **www.bbb.org/advertising**
   - National Advertising Review Board **www.bbb.org/advertising/narb.html**
   - European Commission for Advertising/Consumer Law **europa.eu.int/en/comm/spc/spc.html**

Chapter Three

The Scope of Advertising: From Local to Global

Objective   To introduce the people and groups who create, produce, and run advertising here and abroad. Advertising people may serve in a variety of roles. This chapter discusses the basic tasks of both the client and the agency, the roles of suppliers and the media, the way agencies acquire clients and are compensated, and the overall relationship between the agency and the client.

After studying this chapter, you will be able to:

- **Describe** the various groups in the advertising business and explain their relationship to one another.
- **Explain** how advertisers organize themselves to manage their advertising both here and abroad.
- **Define** the main types of advertising agencies.
- **Explain** the range of work people do in an ad agency and an advertising department.
- **Discuss** how agencies get new clients and how they make money.
- **Debate** the pros and cons of an in-house advertising agency.
- **Discuss** factors that affect the client/agency relationship.
- **Explain** how suppliers and the media help advertisers and agencies.

When Mike Whitlow first got the project assignment, it was anything but exciting. As a creative director at Muse Cordero Chen, he was accustomed to getting the juicy jobs for the agency's plum accounts: Nike, Honda, Snapple. Those were the projects you could win awards for, the kind of jobs that made other creatives envious. • But with this one—well, he could already imagine the grumblings from his art directors and copywriters. Lisa Wright, the account executive on Honda, had just handed him the creative brief for the project. They needed some ideas for a dealer kit: a package, usually in the form of a binder, containing information and sample ads that the car dealers could use to plan and create their local advertising. Typically not Emmy award–winning stuff. • Lisa sensed his ambivalence. "Look, Mike," she said. "I really want something spectacular, something that will get these dealers to sit up and take notice of our market. • "Oh, and Mike, there's no budget on this." • Mike smiled. Lisa was good. She not only worked with clients well, she knew how to challenge the creatives, dangling just the right amount of bait to pique their interest and get their creative juices flowing. • The market she referred to was the 31-million-strong African-American market. This group spends $15 billion on vehicle purchases every year, so it's an important market to Honda. Muse Cordero Chen is a full-service advertising agency that specializes in multicultural communications. Founded in 1986, the Los Angeles–based

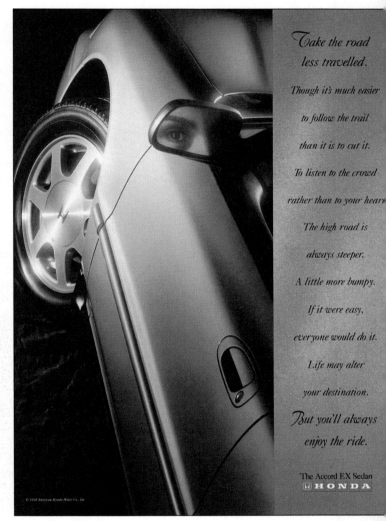

Take the road
less travelled.

Though it's much easier

to follow the trail

than it is to cut it.

To listen to the crowd

rather than to your heart.

The high road is

always steeper.

A little more bumpy.

If it were easy,

everyone would do it.

Life may alter

your destination.

But you'll always

enjoy the ride.

The Accord EX Sedan
HONDA

shop is one of the fastest-growing ethnic agencies in the country. Its 29 employees speak a total of 19 languages. Over the years, the agency has worked very closely with Rubin/Postaer, Honda's general-market agency of record, to make sure the work it produces for the African-American market reflects the overall Honda strategy. In the process, MCC has won numerous awards for outstanding national ads. Lisa wanted the dealer kits to be conceived with the same pride. • Mike assembled his creative team of art directors and copywriters and gave them the same challenge. "Remember, you guys, there are no bad assignments," he said, "just bad work. Let's do something out of the ordinary and have some fun with this, OK?" • They did, as we shall see. •

The Advertising **Industry**

The range of work performed by advertising people goes far beyond what we see daily on TV. In fact, that's barely the tip of the iceberg. Moreover, many people and organizations besides those usually thought of as advertising folks are involved in the advertising business. That's because every successful company needs to advertise.

The Organizations in Advertising

The advertising business has evolved into four distinct groups. The two main ones are the *advertisers* and the *agencies.* The advertisers (or clients) are the companies—like Honda, Coca-Cola, or the local shoe store—that sponsor advertising for themselves and their products. Advertisers range in size from small independent businesses to huge multinational firms, and in type from service organizations to industrial manufacturers to local charities and political action committees. The second group, *advertising agencies,* assist the advertisers to plan, create, and prepare ad campaigns and other promotional materials.

A third group, the *suppliers,* includes the photographers, illustrators, printers, digital service bureaus, color film separators, video production houses, Internet web developers, and others who assist both advertisers and agencies in preparing advertising materials. Suppliers also include consultants, research firms, and professional services that work with both advertisers and agencies. The fourth group, the *media,* sell time (in electronic media) and space (in print and digital media) to carry the advertiser's message to the target audience.

The People in Advertising

When most people think of advertising, they imagine the copywriters and art directors who work for ad agencies. But the majority of people in advertising are actually employed by the advertisers. Most companies have an advertising department, even if it's just one person.

In addition, many other people work for the suppliers and the media. They're in advertising, too. The fact is, advertising is a very broad field that employs a wide variety of people in sales, research, management, accounting, computer science, and law, as well as specialists in the various communication arts—artists, writers, photographers, musicians, performers, and cinematographers.

In this chapter, we'll see what all these people do at the various venues where they work. In the process, we'll get a good working understanding of how the business operates both in the United States and abroad.

The **Advertisers** (The **Clients**)

While every company has some sort of advertising department, its importance depends on the size of the company, the type of industry it operates in, the size of the advertising program, the advertising role in the company's marketing mix, and most of all, the involvement of top management.

To get a sense of the diversity of companies that advertise, we'll look first at local advertisers to see how they operate. Then, we'll examine the regional and national advertisers. Finally we'll look at the companies that market their products abroad.

Local Advertising: Where the Action Is

Not long after graduating from San Diego State, Ralph Rubio opened his first Mexican restaurant. He offered an unusual specialty: fish tacos—lightly battered and fried whitefish served in soft-shelled corn tortillas with white sauce, salsa, cabbage, and a wedge of lime. At the time, very few other Mexican eateries offered fish tacos, and none featured them. So Rubio found fish tacos hard to sell, even with his secret batter recipe (which he'd gotten from a street vendor in San Felipe, Mexico). The first month's sales at the restaurant averaged only $163 a day.

Rubio started using small newspaper ads with coupons to lure courageous customers. It worked. As business picked up, he expanded his advertising to radio and TV, targeting his market further with ads on Hispanic stations (whose listeners

Local advertisers such as Rubio's Fish Tacos must find ways to differentiate their products from the competition—and then create awareness through advertising. This tabletop point-of-purchase card invites customers already in the restaurant to try Rubio's legendary fish taco.

knew what fish tacos were). And he went after younger, venturesome customers ages 18 to 34 by advertising at local movie theaters. Business picked up some more. Rubio soon opened another restaurant, and another.

With each new opening, Rubio distributed direct-mail flyers in the area and took free samples to nearby stores. Working with an artist, he created a cartoon character named Pesky Pescado out of the fish taco. He purchased a 15-foot inflatable Pesky to display at his restaurants. Employee T-shirts sported Pesky's picture, and Rubio sold Pesky T-shirts and sweatshirts to enthusiastic patrons. He also ordered bumper stickers and antenna balls to add some fun to his promotions. To further integrate his activities, Rubio took an active part in community affairs, including tie-ins with a blood bank, a literacy program, and fundraising activities for both a Tijuana medical clinic and a local university's athletic program.

As the popularity of the fish taco grew, so did Rubio's revenues, doubling every year for the first five years. After 10 years, Rubio had 17 restaurants in three counties serving over 25,000 fish tacos a day and doing over $12 million in annual sales. He trademarked the phrase "Rubio's, home of the fish taco." A local restaurant critic called it "the food San Diegans would miss the most."[1]

Every year, advertisers spend billions of dollars in the United States. Almost half of that is spent on **local advertising** by local businesses in a particular city or county targeting customers in their geographic area.

Local advertising is sometimes called *retail advertising* because so much is placed by retail stores. But retail advertising isn't always local; Sears and JCPenney advertise nationally. And many businesses besides retail stores use local advertising: banks, real estate developers, movie theaters, auto mechanics, plumbers, radio and TV stations, funeral homes, museums, and local politicians, to name a few.

Local advertising is critically important because most consumer sales are made (or lost) locally. An auto manufacturer may spend millions advertising new cars nationwide, but if its dealers don't make a strong effort locally, the dollars will be wasted. When it comes to making the sale and dealing with customers, local advertising is where the action is—where relationships often start and truly develop.

Types of Local Advertisers

There are four main types of local advertisers.

- Dealers or local franchisees of national companies that specialize in one main product line or service (Honda, Wendy's, Mailboxes Etc., Kinko's, H&R Block).
- Stores that sell a variety of branded merchandise, usually on a nonexclusive basis (convenience, grocery, and department stores).
- Specialty businesses and services (banks, insurance brokers, restaurants, music stores, shoe-repair shops, remodeling contractors, florists, hair salons, travel agencies, attorneys, accountants).

Almost half the U.S. advertising dollars every year are spent on local advertising like this ad for the Embarcadero Center in San Francisco.

- Governmental, quasigovernmental, and nonprofit organizations (municipalities, utility companies, charities, arts organizations, political candidates).

A small, local business—say, a hardware, clothing, or electronics store—may have just one person in charge of advertising. That person, the advertising manager, performs all the administrative, planning, budgeting, and coordinating functions. He or she may lay out ads, write ad copy, and select the media. A manager with some artistic talent may even design the actual ads and produce them on a desktop computer.

Chain stores often maintain a completely staffed advertising department to handle production, media placement, and marketing support services. The department needs artists, copywriters, and production specialists. The department head usually reports to a vice president or marketing manager, as shown in Exhibit 3–1.

Types of Local Advertising

Most of the ads placed in local media are either product, institutional, or classified advertising. Each type serves a different purpose.

Product advertising   **Product advertising** promotes a specific product or service and stimulates short-term action while building awareness of the business. Three major types of product ads are used by local advertisers: regular price-line, sale, and clearance. **Regular price-line advertising** informs consumers about services or merchandise offered at regular prices. An accounting firm might use regular price-line advertising to promote its accounting and tax services.

To stimulate sales of particular merchandise or increase store traffic, local merchants occasionally use **sale advertising,** placing items on sale and offering two-for-one specials or reduced prices. Local advertisers use **clearance advertising** (a special form of sale advertising) to make room for new product lines or new models and to get rid of slow-moving lines, floor samples, broken or distressed merchandise, or out-of-season items. Companies going out of business also use clearance advertising.

Institutional advertising   **Institutional advertising** attempts to create a favorable long-term perception of the business as a whole, not just of a particular product or service. Many types of businesses (stores, restaurants, banks, professional firms, hospitals) use institutional advertising to promote an *idea* about the company and build long-term goodwill. It makes the public aware of what the business stands for and attempts to build reputation and image. An institutional ad might focus on convenient hours, a new credit policy, store expansion, or company philosophy.

Although readership is often lower, effective institutional ads build a favorable image for the business, attract new customers, and encourage customer loyalty.

Classified advertising   Advertisers use **classified advertising** in the newspaper for a variety of reasons: to locate and recruit new employees, offer services (such as those of an employment agency or business opportunity broker), or sell or lease new and used merchandise (such as cars, real estate, and office equipment).

Local Advertisers: The Original Integrators

When Ralph Rubio built his restaurant business, his promotional activities involved a lot more than just running ads in the media. In fact, he did everything he could to develop a *relationship* with his customers and to promote good word-of-mouth. That meant using

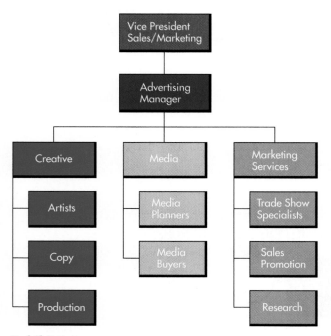

Exhibit 3–1
Typical department structure for small advertisers with high volumes of work, such as grocery store chains.

A business that sells locally promotes its company's identity in a variety of ways—such as this distinctly urban poster from Bronx Bagel Bar, a cafe in Nashville, Tennessee.

publicity, sales promotion, and direct response, as well as media advertising—all integrated with consistently good food, reasonable prices, and excellent service. That is what is meant by **integrated marketing communications (IMC).** Thanks to IMC, Rubio's fish taco became a local staple.

Local advertisers and the local agencies that serve them are not stuck with the traditional national view that advertising means "ads placed in the media." By necessity, local advertisers wear many hats every day. They tend the cash register, deal with customers, prepare mailers, write and place ads, evaluate suppliers' trade promotions, answer phone inquiries, spruce up the office, talk to newspaper editors, coordinate the graphics on premiums for a seasonal promotion. By successfully combining personal selling with media advertising, direct marketing, sales promotion, and public relations, the local advertiser can be the consummate integrator of marketing communications.[2]

Creating Local Advertising

Cal Worthington first pitched his car dealership on Los Angeles TV stations in 1951 and 47 years later, he's still at it. He sponsors third-rate movies on late-night and Saturday afternoon TV. In his zany ads, he often appears in cowboy garb with a variety of domesticated wild animals, all introduced as "my dog Spot." Some low-budget, do-it-yourself advertisers like Worthington are so successful they engender a near-cult following. Others who try the same approach fail miserably.

In print advertising, many local advertisers achieve remarkable success with what professionals would call a *schlock* approach—heavy bold type, items crowded into ad space, loud headlines, and unsophisticated graphic design. If the message is honest, consistent, and effective and meets the advertiser's objectives, that may be all that matters.

To direct and control the creative aspects of their ads and commercials and ensure consistency, local advertisers should develop a checklist of creative do's and don'ts. (See the Checklist for Creating Local Advertising on page 86.)

Finding big ideas for local ad campaigns can be extremely difficult. Some advertisers look to the merchandise for ideas; others look to the customer. An important goal for local advertisers is to achieve a consistent, distinctive look that makes their ads both appealing and identifiable. We discuss the creative process in depth in Part Four.

Local advertisers can turn to a number of sources for creative help, including reps from the local media, local ad agencies, freelancers and consultants, creative boutiques, syndicated art services, and the *cooperative advertising programs* of wholesalers, manufacturers, and trade associations.

Cooperative Advertising

As a service to their distributors and dealers, and to assure proper reproduction of their products, wholesalers and manufacturers as well as some trade associations often provide local advertisers with ready-made advertising materials and cooperative advertising programs where the costs are shared.

There are two key purposes for **cooperative (co-op) advertising:** to build the manufacturer's brand image and to help its distributors, dealers, or retailers make more sales.[3] Every year, national manufacturers give their local retailers more than $20 billion for co-op projects. Newspapers, network and cable TV, and radio are the favored media of co-op spending, with newspapers claiming 55 percent of co-op dollars.[4] Intel alone spends over $250 million annually to help PC marketers who display the "Intel Inside" logo.[5]

Creating Local Advertising

_____ **Stand out from the competition.** Make your ads easily recognizable. Ads with unusual art, layout, and typefaces have higher readership. Make the ads distinctive but keep their appearance consistent.

_____ **Use a simple layout.** The layout should carry the reader's eye through the message easily and in proper sequence from headline to illustration to explanatory copy to price to store name. Avoid using too many typefaces.

_____ **Use a dominant element.** A large picture or headline ensures quick visibility. Photos of real people and action pictures win more readership, as do photos of local people or places. Color attracts more readers.

_____ **Stress the benefits.** Present the emotional reason to buy or the tangible performance element customers seek.

_____ **Make the headline count.** Use a compelling headline to feature the main benefit.

_____ **Watch your language.** Make your writing style active, lively, and involving. Make the readers feel they already own the product. Avoid negativism and profanity.

_____ **Let white space work for you.** White space focuses the reader's attention and makes the headline and illustration stand out.

_____ **Make the copy complete.** Emphasize the benefits most appealing to customers.

_____ **Make your visual powerful and eye-catching. Make sure it demonstrates your message.** The main visual is often more important than the headline. Photos work better than artwork.

_____ **State price or range of prices.** Dollar figures have good attention value, and readers often overestimate omitted prices. Spell out credit and layaway plans.

_____ **Specify branded merchandise.** If the item is a known brand, say so.

_____ **Include related items.** Make two sales instead of one by offering related items along with a featured one.

_____ **Urge readers to buy now.** Ask for the sale. Stimulate prompt action by using "limited supply" or "this week only."

_____ **Don't forget the store name and address.** Check every ad to be certain the store name, address, phone number, and hours are included.

_____ **Don't be too clever.** Many people distrust or misunderstand cleverness.

_____ **Don't use unusual or difficult words.** Everyone understands simple language. Use it.

_____ **Don't generalize.** Be specific. Shoppers want all the facts before they buy.

_____ **Don't make excessive claims.** Advertisers lose customers when they make claims they can't back up.

_____ **Plan ad size carefully.** Attention increases with size.

_____ **Consider your target customers.** People notice ads more if they are directed at their own gender or age group.

_____ **Use tie-ins** with local or special news events.

Exhibit 3–2

The importance of co-op advertising dollars.

Store	Co-op dollars as a percentage of total ad budget
Appliance dealers	80%
Clothing stores	35
Department stores	50
Discount stores	20
Drugstores	70
Food stores	75
Furniture stores	30
Household goods	30
Jewelers	30
Shoe stores	50

In **vertical cooperative advertising,** the manufacturer provides the complete ad and shares the cost of the advertising time or space. The local newspaper sets the name and address of the local advertiser, or the radio station adds a tagline with the advertiser's name, address, and phone number. Exhibit 3–2 lists typical co-op advertising allowances. (See Ad Lab 3–A for the pros and cons of co-op advertising.)

With **horizontal cooperative advertising,** firms in the same business (real estate agents, insurance agents, pharmacies, car dealers, or travel agents) or in the same part of town advertise jointly. Competing auto dealers, for example, might pool their dollars to advertise their common retail area as the "Mile of Cars."

Regional and National Advertisers

Some companies operate in one part of the country—in one of several states—and market exclusively within that region. These are referred to as **regional advertisers.** Typical examples include regional grocery and department store chains, governmental bodies (such as state lotteries), franchise groups (such as the Southern California Toyota dealers), telephone companies (such as NYNEX), and statewide or multistate banks (Bank of America).

Other companies sell in several regions or throughout the country and are called **national advertisers.** These include the consumer packaged-goods manufacturers (like Procter & Gamble and RJR Nabisco), national airlines (United, American), media and entertainment companies (Disney, Time Warner), electronics manufacturers (Apple, Hewlett-Packard), and all the auto companies. These firms also make up the membership of the **Association of National Advertisers (ANA)** and comprise the largest advertisers in the country (see Exhibit 3–3).

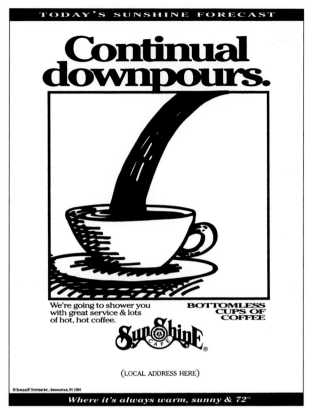

Cooperative advertising reduces the burden on distributors, dealers, or retailers. Wholesalers, manufacturers, and franchisors often provide ready-made ads which only require that a local address be inserted, such as in this case with Sunshine Cafe.

Exhibit 3–3
Top advertisers in the United States in 1996 by total U.S. ad spending ($ millions rounded).

1.	Procter & Gamble (Cincinnati)	$2,622.7
2.	General Motors (Detroit)	2,373.4
3.	Philip Morris (New York)	2,278.9
4.	Chrysler (Highland Park, MI)	1,419.7
5.	Time Warner (New York)	1,409.9
6.	Sears, Roebuck (Chicago)	1,317.1
7.	Walt Disney Co. (Burbank, CA)	1,288.8
8.	PepsiCo (Purchase, NY)	1,268.8
9.	Grand Metropolitan (London, UK)	1,257.4
10.	Ford Motor (Dearborn, MI)	1,179.2
11.	Warner-Lambert (Morris Plains, NJ)	1,086.2
12.	McDonald's (Oak Brook, IL)	1,074.6
13.	AT&T (New York)	1,058.6
14.	Johnson & Johnson (New Brunswick, NJ)	1,052.8
15.	Unilever NV (London/Rotterdam)	948.5

Source: Reprinted with permission from the September 29, 1997 issue of *Advertising Age.* Copyright, Crain Communications, Inc. 1997.

How National and Local Advertisers Differ

The basic principles of advertising are the same in both local and national advertising. However, local advertisers have special challenges stemming from the day-to-day realities of running a small business. As a result, local and national advertisers differ in terms of focus, time orientation, and resources (see Exhibit 3–4).

Focus   National companies are concerned about building their brands, so their advertising tends to focus on the competitive features of one brand over another, especially in conquest sales situations. Local merchants or dealers often carry hundreds of different brands or numerous models of an exclusive brand, so they focus on attracting customers to a particular **point**—their place of business. That's why local car dealers typically advertise their dealerships rather than the make of car. And local grocers often promote only those brands for which they receive co-op advertising or trade allowances from the national manufacturer.

In every product category, big companies battle for market share against a few competitors, and every share point is worth millions of dollars. Local advertisers compete with many companies, so their focus is on gross sales or volume: 60 cars a month, 5 new insurance policies a week, 55 oil changes a day.

National advertisers plan *strategically* to launch, build, and sustain brands. Local advertisers think *tactically*. Will a new $15,000 sign bring more people into the store? Should we stay open Labor Day? Can we attract more lunchtime customers by offering free refills on soft drinks?

The relationship with the customer may be the greatest difference between national and local advertisers. National advertisers' marketing executives rarely see retail customers; instead, they traditionally think in terms of large groups of people—segments, niches, target markets—with various geographic, demographic, or psychographic descriptions. They design their strategies and campaigns to appeal to these large groups.

But local advertisers deal with individual customers every day. They (and their families) also interact with their customers in nonbusiness ways; they may be neighbors, friends, or schoolmates. The local advertiser gets feedback every day—on the company's advertising, prices, product performance, employee service, store decor, and the new sign out front. The national marketer gets occasional feedback—from surveys and from customer complaint lines.

Time orientation   Due to differences in their focus and perspective, national and local advertisers also have a different time orientation. National companies think long term. They develop five-year strategic plans and budget for annual advertising campaigns. Local advertisers worry that this week's ad in the *Pennysaver* didn't *pull* as well as last week's (a term rarely used by national marketers). A New York advertiser may have months to develop a network TV campaign; the little market on Main Street may have to churn out a new newspaper ad every week to reach its local customers.

Resources   Finally, national advertisers have more resources available—both money and people. A local advertiser that spends $100,000 a year has a relatively large budget. A national advertiser needs to spend at least $5 million a year just to get started. (Walt Disney, by the way, spends $1.2 *billion!*)

Ad Lab 3–A

The Co-op Marriage

On the surface, cooperative advertising seems like a great arrangement for retailers. A manufacturer supplies advertising materials (saving the retailer production costs) and pays a percentage of the media cost. The retailer drops in the store's logo, arranges for the ad to run, and collects the co-op dollars from the manufacturer. The small retail business can stretch its ad budget and associate its business with a nationally advertised product. The retailer receives professionally prepared ads and acquires greater leverage with the local media that carry the co-op ads.

But as with any marriage, there is give and take.

A retailer may have to sell a lot of merchandise to qualify for significant co-op funds. More often, the retailer and manufacturer have different advertising objectives and different ideas about how the ads should be executed.

The manufacturer often wants total control. The manufacturer expects co-op ads to tie in with its national advertising promotions. It wants the right product advertised at the right time. Manufacturers prepare guideline pamphlets specifying when and where the ads should appear, what form they should take, and what uses of the name and logo are not allowed.

Retailers have their own ideas about which products to advertise when. They're more concerned with daily volume and with projecting an image of value and variety. An appliance store might prefer to advertise inexpensive TVs even though the manufacturer wants to emphasize its top-of-the-line models.

Manufacturers worry that retailers will place the product in a cluttered, ugly ad or next to inferior products, that the ad will run in inappropriate publications, and that it will not run at the best time. Retailers counter that they know the local market better. In short, manufacturers think they don't have enough control; retailers think they have too much.

A retailer contemplating co-op funds should consider the following questions:

- What advertising qualifies in terms of products and special requirements?
- What percentage is paid by each party?
- When can ads be run?
- What media can be used?
- Are there special provisions for message content?
- What documentation is required for reimbursement?
- How does each party benefit?
- Do cooperative ads obscure the retailer's image?

Laboratory Applications

1. Look through today's edition of a daily paper in your city. Identify two ads that can qualify as co-op. Do the ads fit both the store's image and the manufacturer's image? Explain.

2. A store may develop its own ad and drop in the manufacturer's logo or it may take an ad created by the manufacturer and simply add the store's location. Which do your two ads do?

The national advertiser has an army of specialists dedicated to the successful marketing of its brands. The local advertiser may have a small staff or just one person—the owner—to market the business. So the local entrepreneur has to know more about every facet of marketing communications.

How Large Companies Manage Their Advertising

In large companies, many people are involved in the advertising function. Company owners and top corporate executives make key advertising decisions; sales and marketing personnel often assist in the creative process, help choose the ad agency, and evaluate proposed ad programs; artists and writers produce ads, brochures, and other materials; product engineers and designers give input to the creative process and provide information about competitive products; administrators evaluate the cost of ad campaigns and help plan budgets; and clerical staff coordinate various promotional activities, including advertising.

A large company's advertising department may employ many people and be headed by an advertising manager who reports to a marketing director or marketing services manager (see Exhibit 3–5). The exact department structure depends on many variables. Most large advertisers tend to use some mix of two basic management structures: *centralized* and *decentralized*.

Centralized Organization Companies are concerned with cost efficiency and continuity in their communications programs. So many embrace the **centralized advertising department** because it gives the greatest control and offers both efficiency and continuity across divisional boundaries. In centralized departments, an advertising manager typically reports to a marketing vice president. But beyond this one feature, companies may organize the department in any of five ways:

Exhibit 3-4

Differences between local and national advertisers.

	National	Local
Focus	Brand	Point
	Market share	Volume, gross sales
	Strategies	Tactics
	Markets	Customers
Time	Long-term campaigns	Short-term ads
Resources	$5–$10 million+	Less than $1 million
	Many specialists	A few generalists

Source: Reprinted with permission from the September 29, 1997 issue of *Advertising Age.* Copyright, Crain Communications, Inc. 1997.

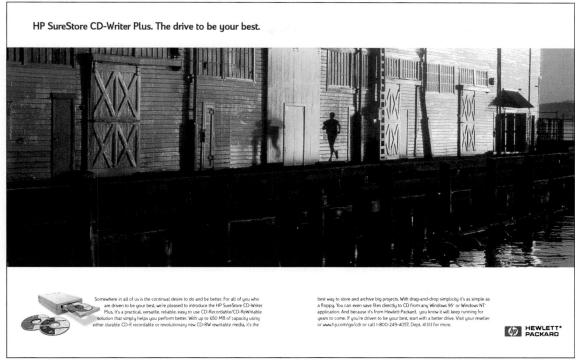

Companies that sell their products or services throughout the country are called national advertisers. Unlike their local counterparts, national advertisers plan strategically to launch, build, and sustain brands. While a local advertiser may run ads that announce an annual sale for localized consumers, national advertisers like Hewlett-Packard (www.hp.com) target large demographic groups and are concerned with issues of market share and brand equity.

- By product or brand.
- By subfunction of advertising (copy, art, print production, media buying).
- By end user (consumer advertising, trade advertising).
- By media (radio, TV, newspapers, outdoor).
- By geography (western advertising, eastern advertising, European advertising).

The cereal giant General Mills, for example, is one of the nation's largest advertisers. It operates a vast advertising and marketing services department with some 350 employees. It spends close to $500 million annually in media advertising and other promotional activities.[6]

General Mills' Marketing Services is really many departments within a department. Its centralized structure enables it to administer, plan, and coordinate the promotion of more than 60 brands. It also supervises nine outside ad agencies and operates its own in-house agency for new or smaller brands.[7]

Organized around functional specialties (market research, media, graphics), Marketing Services helps General Mills' brand managers consolidate many of their expenditures for maximum efficiency. The media department, for example, prepares all media plans for the marketing divisions. The production and art department designs the packages for all brands and the graphics for the company's in-house agency. From one spot, Marketing Services handles a wide variety of brands efficiently and effectively (see Exhibit 3–6).

Decentralized organization   As some companies become larger, diversify their product line, acquire subsidiaries, and establish divisions in different regions

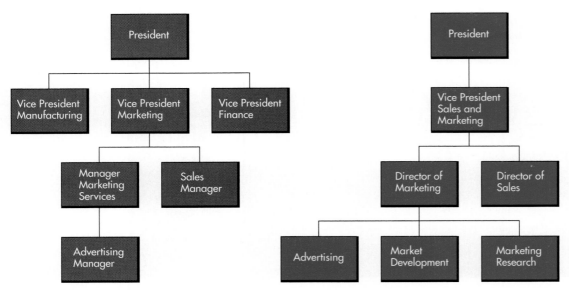

Exhibit 3–5
Many large companies have a separate advertising department able to perform a wide variety of functions. Small departments generally subcontract for creative and camera services; larger departments handle the majority of work on site.

or even different countries, a centralized advertising department often becomes impractical.

In a **decentralized system,** the company sets up separate ad departments for different divisions, subsidiaries, regions, brands, or other categories that suit the company's needs. The general manager of each division or brand is responsible for that group's advertising.

For large companies with many divisions, decentralized advertising is more flexible. Campaigns and media schedules can be adjusted faster. New approaches and creative ideas can be introduced more easily, and sales results can be measured independently of other divisions. In effect, each division is its own marketing department, with the advertising manager reporting to the division head (see Exhibit 3–7).

A drawback, though, is that decentralized departments often concentrate on their own budgets, problems, and promotions rather than the good of the whole company. Across divisions, ads typically lack uniformity, diminishing the power of repetitive corporate advertising. Rivalry among brand managers may even escalate into unhealthy competition or deteriorate into secrecy and jealousy.

Transnational Advertisers Companies advertising abroad typically face markets with different value systems, environments, and languages. Their customers have different purchasing abilities, habits, and motivations. Media customary to U.S. and Canadian advertisers may be unavailable or ineffective. The companies will therefore likely need different advertising strategies. But they face a more basic problem: How to manage and produce the advertising? Should their U.S. agency or in-house advertising department do it? Should they use a foreign agency or set up a local advertising department?

As advertisers break into new international markets, they may start by simply exporting their existing products. At first, the home office controls all foreign marketing and advertising. Everything is centralized. Then, as companies get more involved in foreign markets, they may form joint ventures or invest in foreign sales offices, warehouses, plants, and other facilities. Advertisers typically view such operations as foreign marketing divisions and use a decentralized **international**

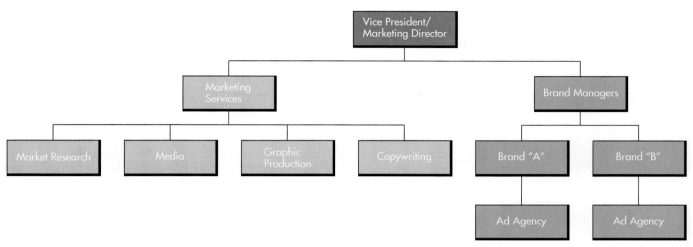

Exhibit 3–6
General Mills has a centralized advertising department like the model here.

structure, in which the divisions are responsible for their own product lines, marketing operations, and profits, and create customized advertising for each market.[8]

Procter & Gamble, for example, is a 160-year-old, $36 billion company. It sells over 2,300 consumer brands internationally in 41 different product categories. These brands include such market leaders as Tide laundry detergent, Ivory soap, Pampers diapers, Duncan Hines cake mixes, Crisco oils, and Crest toothpaste.[9]

P&G is one of the biggest and most influential consumer advertisers in the world; its expenditures in the United States alone exceed $2.5 billion annually. But more than half its sales come from abroad.[10] Each overseas division is set up almost like a separate company with its own research and development department, manufacturing plant, advertising department, sales force, and finance and accounting staff. Every brand within a division has a **brand manager** who oversees a brand group and directs his or her own ad agency to create the brand's media advertising. Brand managers work under a marketing manager, who reports to a *category manager.*[11]

Each division also has an advertising department to help coordinate sales promotion and merchandising programs across brands. The corporate advertising department provides statistical information and guidance.

While the brand manager's primary goal is to use advertising and promotion to build market share, the category manager focuses on sharpening overall strategy and building profits.[12] In recent years, P&G has streamlined the system by eliminating extra layers of management and redundant facilities. This commits to each brand the single-minded

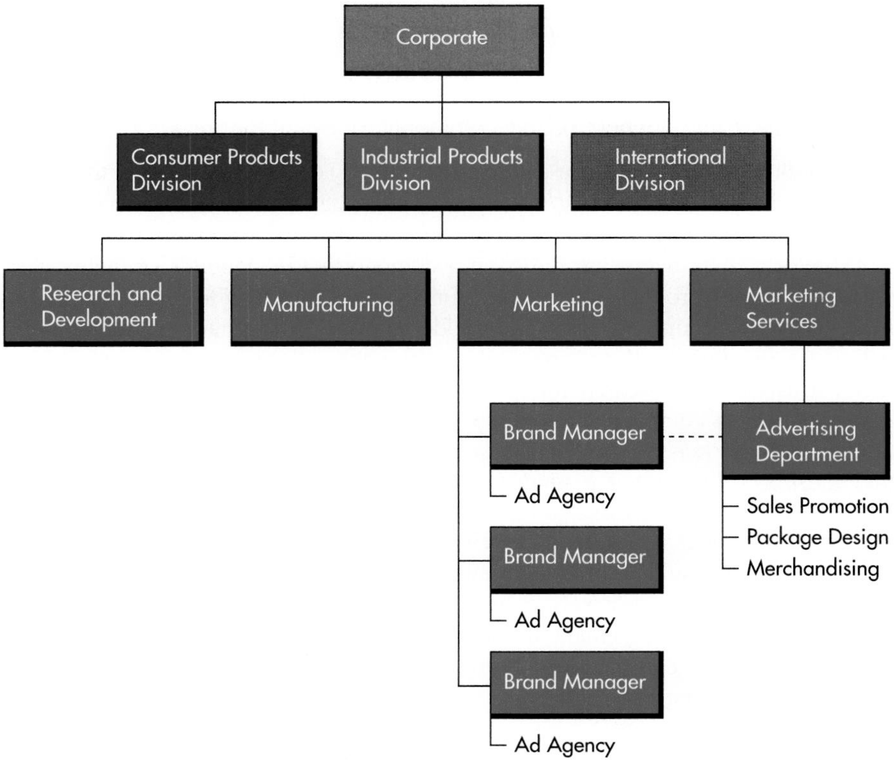

Exhibit 3–7
In a decentralized department, each division is its own marketing department.

With an international structure, advertisers' local divisions are responsible for their own product lines and create customized ads for each market. This Pepsi Slam (www.pepsi.com) ad was created by Abbott Mead Vickers-BBDO, London, and ran only in the United Kingdom.

drive needed for success and gives more authority to the individual responsible for the brand.[13]

As companies continue to grow and prosper around the world, they may invest directly in many countries. True **multinational corporations** strive for full, integrated participation in world markets.[14] Foreign sales often grow faster than domestic sales. Multinationals like Exxon and IBM earn about 50 percent of their sales abroad; Kodak and Xerox, about 25 percent. Typically, the top 25 U.S. multinational corporations earn more than 40 percent of their revenues and two-thirds of their profits overseas.[15]

A multinational usually exerts strong centralized control over all its marketing activities. Multinational firms like Kodak get strong direction and coordination from headquarters and have a standardized product line and marketing structure. Exhibit 3–8 shows the largest advertisers in various countries.

Multinationals that use a *standardized approach* to marketing and advertising in all countries are **global marketers,** and they create global brands. Their assumption is that the way the product is used and the needs it satisfies are universal.[16] Max Factor, for example, markets and advertises its cosmetics globally with a campaign that makes the brand relevant through the use of strong, contemporary, self-confident women. The campaign has drawn favorable reactions from women worldwide.[17] Other global advertisers include Coca-Cola, British Airways, British Petroleum, TGI Friday's, FedEx, and Chiclets.[18]

Companies must research extensively before attempting a global advertising strategy. So much depends on the product and where they try to sell it. A "no" answer to any of the following questions means the attempt will probably fail.

1. *Has each country's market for the product developed in the same way?* A Ford is a Ford in most markets. On the other hand, many Europeans use clotheslines, so they don't need fabric softeners for dryers.

2. *Are the targets similar in different nations?* Japanese consumers like jeans, running shoes, and rock and roll. The same is true in Europe and the United States. But it might not be true for certain foods or fashions.

3. *Do consumers share the same wants and needs?* Breakfast in Brazil is usually a cup of coffee. Kellogg's corn flakes won't be served the same way there as in the United States, where people commonly eat cereal for breakfast.[19]

According to the worldwide creative director of J. Walter Thompson, the secret to success in global advertising is knowing how to tap into basic human emotions and uncover universal appeals that don't depend solely on language.[20]

Ultimately, the advertising direction a company takes depends on many variables: breadth of product line, quality of management, ability to repeat marketing strategies across countries, costs, and the decision to operate internationally, multinationally, or globally. Every organization operates in a slightly different environment. This alters the search for an *ideal structure* into a search for a *suitable structure.*[21] Most companies blend aspects of centralized and decentralized structures to fit their own needs. And when an existing structure shows signs of decay, they must be willing to test new ideas and make changes.

The Advertising **Agency**

Why does a company like Honda hire an advertising agency in the first place? Couldn't it save money by hiring its own staff and creating its own ads? How does Muse Cordero Chen win such a large account? Must an agency's accounts be that big for it to make money? This section sheds some light on these issues and gives a clearer understanding of what agencies do and why so many advertisers use agencies.

The Role of the Advertising Agency

The American Association of Advertising Agencies (AAAA) defines an **advertising agency** as an independent organization of creative people and businesspeople who specialize in developing and preparing marketing and

Exhibit 3–8
Top 15 global marketers by ad spending outside the United States. Figures are in millions of U.S. dollars.

Rank Advertiser 1996	Headquarters	Non-U.S. Ad Spending 1996	Non-U.S. Ad Spending 1995	95–96 Percent Change
1. Procter & Gamble Co.	Cincinnati	$2,479.1	$2,567.7	−3.4
2. Unilever	Rotterdam/London	2,355.3	2,430.3	−3.1
3. Nestlé SA	Vevey, Switzerland	1,574.7	1,478.4	+6.5
4. Toyota Motor Corp.	Toyota City, Japan	988.6	951.4	+3.9
5. PSA Peugeot-Citroen SA*	Paris	958.6	887.3	+8.0
6. Volkswagen AG	Wolfsburg, Germany	933.2	832.5	+12.1
7. Nissan Motor Co.	Tokyo	855.2	862.5	−0.9
8. Coca-Cola Co.	Atlanta	832.2	771.8	+7.8
9. Philip Morris Cos.	New York	813.0	881.9	−7.8
10. General Motors Corp.	Detroit	773.1	814.4	−5.1
11. Ford Motor Co.	Dearborn, MI	741.0	730.6	+1.4
12. Mars Inc.	McLean, VA	731.2	767.7	−4.8
13. Renault SA*	Paris	664.1	584.3	+13.7
14. Kao Corp.*	Tokyo	628.4	681.7	−7.8
15. Fiat SpA*	Turin, Italy	606.3	589.9	+2.8

*Indicates U.S. spending includes measured media only as reported by Competitive Media Reporting. All other U.S. ad spending figures are *Advertising Age* estimates and include nonmedia forms of advertising as reported in "100 Leading National Advertisers" (*Advertising Age,* September 29, 1997).
Notes: Figures are in millions of U.S. dollars. 1995 ranking reflects data compiled in 1997.
Source: Reprinted with permission from the November 10, 1997 issue of *Advertising Age.* Copyright, Crain Communications, Inc. 1997.

Advertising agencies, like any other profession, have to get the word out that they're open for business. Many are capitalizing on new media like the World Wide Web, as shown in this photo of Fallon McElligott's (www.fallon.com) home page.

advertising plans, advertisements, and other promotional tools. The agency purchases advertising space and time in various media on behalf of different advertisers, or sellers (its clients) to find customers for their goods and services.[22]

This definition offers clues to why so many advertisers hire ad agencies. First, an agency like Muse Cordero Chen is *independent.* The agency isn't owned by the advertiser, the media, or the suppliers, so it can bring an outside, objective viewpoint to the advertiser's business—a state the advertiser can never attain.

Second, like all agencies, MCC employs a combination of *businesspeople* and *creative people,* including administrators, accountants, marketing executives, researchers, market and media analysts, writers, and artists. They have day-to-day contact with outside professional suppliers who create illustrations, take photos, retouch art, shoot commercials, record sound, and print brochures.

The agency provides yet another service by researching, negotiating, arranging, and contracting for commercial space and time with the various print, electronic, and digital media. Because of its *media expertise,* Muse Cordero Chen saves its clients time and money.

Agencies don't work for the media or the suppliers. Their moral, ethical, financial, and legal obligation is to their clients. Just as a well-run business seeks professional help from attorneys, accountants, bankers, or management specialists, advertisers use agencies out of *self-interest,* because the agencies can create more effective advertising and select more effective media than the advertisers can themselves. Today, almost all sizable advertisers rely on an ad agency for expert, objective counsel and unique creative skills—to be the "guardian of their brands."[23]

Finally, a good agency serves its clients' needs because of its daily exposure to a broad spectrum of marketing situations and problems both here and abroad. As technology has enabled companies to work across borders with relative ease, the advertising business has boomed worldwide. All the large U.S. agencies, for example, maintain offices in many foreign countries. Ad Lab 3–B describes the global ad industry.

Types of Agencies

Advertising agencies are normally classified by their geographic scope, the range of services they offer, and the type of business they handle.

Local Agencies

Every community of any size has reputable small ad agencies that offer expert assistance to local advertisers. A competent **local agency** can help:

- Analyze the local advertiser's business and the product or service being sold.
- Evaluate the markets for the business, including channels of distribution.
- Evaluate the advertiser's competitive position and offer strategic options.
- Evaluate media alternatives and offer rational recommendations.
- Devise an integrated communications plan and implement it with consistency and creativity.
- Save the advertiser valuable time by taking over media interviewing, analysis, checking, billing, and bookkeeping.
- Assist in other aspects of advertising and promotion by implementing sales contests, publicity, grand openings, and other activities.

Unfortunately, local advertisers use ad agencies less extensively than national advertisers. Many advertisers simply don't spend enough money on advertising to warrant hiring an agency. And some large agencies don't accept local advertisers because their budgets are too low to support the agency's overhead.

Regional and National Agencies

Every major city has numerous agencies that can produce and place the quality of advertising suitable for national campaigns. **Regional** and **national agencies** typically participate in either the 4As (American Association of Advertising Agencies) or some similar trade group such as the Western States Advertising Agency Association (WSAAA). The *Standard Directory of Advertising Agencies* (the Red Book) lists these agencies geographically, so they're easy to find.

International Agencies

The largest national agencies are also **international agencies.** That is, they have offices or affiliates in major communications centers around the world and can help their clients market internationally or globally as the case may be. Likewise, many foreign-based agencies have offices and affiliates in the United States. For example, the largest advertising agency organization in the world today, WPP Group, is based in London. But it owns several of the top agencies in the United States, such as Ogilvy & Mather and J. Walter Thompson.

Ad Lab 3–B

How Big Is the Agency Business?

Advertising today is a worldwide business. In 1994, New York (with $26.5 billion in billings) regained the lead from Tokyo (with $25.4 billion) as the world's advertising capital. London and Paris were third and fourth, respectively. Leading advertising centers in North America are New York, Los Angeles, Chicago, Toronto, and Montreal.

All U.S. and Canadian cities with at least 100,000 people have ad agencies. So do many smaller cities and towns. Of over 10,000 U.S. agencies, the top 500 represent about $65.1 billion in domestic billing (the amount of client money the agency spends on media and equivalent activities)—almost half of all U.S. advertising expenditures.

Interestingly, the top 10 U.S. agencies handle over half the total volume of business done by the top 500 agencies, and that's just their U.S. billing. Their overseas operations often equal or exceed their U.S. billings.

The top 500 domestic ad agencies employ about 70,000 people. Agencies need fewer people than businesses in many other industries: five or six people can easily handle $1 million in annual billings. In agencies that bill $20 million or more a year, the ratio is even lower.

Basic information about advertisers and agencies can be found in the *Standard Directory of Advertising Agencies* (the "Red Book"), which lists agencies; a related volume, the *Standard Directory of Advertisers,* which lists U.S. companies that advertise; and magazines such as *Advertising Age, Adweek,* and *Marketing* (Canada).

Laboratory Application

From your library, obtain a copy of the agency Red Book. How many agencies in your town are listed? If none, what town nearest you has agency listings? How many?

Top 10 advertising organizations		
Rank	**Organization**	**Income**
1.	WPP Group	$3,419.9
2.	Omnicom Group	3,035.5
3.	Interpublic Group of Cos.	2,751.2
4.	Dentsu	1,929.9
5.	Young & Rubicam	1,356.4
6.	Cordiant	1,169.3
7.	Grey Advertising	987.8
8.	Havas Advertising	974.3
9.	Hakuhodo	897.7
10.	True North Communications	889.5

Note: Income is 1996 worldwide gross income ($ millions).

Top 10 U.S.-based consolidated agencies		
Rank	**Agency**	**Income**
1.	McCann-Erickson Worldwide	$1,386.1
2.	BBDO Worldwide	1,280.2
3.	Young & Rubicam	1,271.2
4.	DDB Needham Worldwide	1,266.1
5.	J. Walter Thompson Co.	1,119.1
6.	Ogilvy & Mather Worldwide	986.5
7.	Grey Advertising	935.5
8.	Leo Burnett Co.	866.3
9.	Foote, Cone & Belding	798.9
10.	Ammirati Puris Lintas	775.4

Note: Income is 1996 worldwide gross income ($ millions).

Top 10 U.S. agency brands		
Rank	**Agency brand**	**Income**
1.	Leo Burnett Co.	$393.7
2.	J. Walter Thompson Co.	375.2
3.	Grey Advertising	352.2
4.	McCann-Erickson Worldwide	329.6
5.	Foote, Cone & Belding	299.9
6.	BBDO Worldwide	289.3
7.	Saatchi & Saatchi Advertising	274.1
8.	DDB Needham Worldwide	271.9
9.	Y&R Advertising	241.9
10.	Ogilvy & Mather Worldwide	233.3

Note: Income is 1996 U.S. gross income ($ millions).

Table source: Reprinted with permission from the April 21, 1997 issue of *Advertising Age.* Copyright, Crain Communications, Inc., 1997.

Full-Service Agencies

The modern **full-service advertising agency** supplies both advertising and non-advertising services in all areas of communications and promotion. *Advertising services* include planning, creating, and producing ads; performing research; and selecting media. *Nonadvertising functions* run the gamut from packaging to public relations to producing sales promotion materials, annual reports, and trade-show exhibits. With the trend toward IMC, many of the largest agencies today are in the forefront of the emerging *interactive media.*[24]

Full-service agencies may specialize in certain kinds of clients. Most, though, can be classified as either *general consumer agencies* or *business-to-business agencies.*

General consumer agencies A **general consumer agency** represents the widest variety of accounts, but it concentrates on *consumer accounts*—companies that make goods purchased chiefly by consumers (soaps, cereals, cars, pet foods, toiletries). Most of the ads are placed in consumer media (TV, radio, magazines, and so on) that pay a *commission* to the agency. General agencies often derive much of their income from these commissions.

General agencies include the international superagency groups headquartered in communication capitals like New York, London, Paris, and Tokyo, as well as many other large firms in New York, Chicago, Los Angeles, Minneapolis, Montreal, and Toronto. A few of the better-known names in North America are the Interpublic Group; Saatchi & Saatchi; Ogilvy & Mather; Foote, Cone & Belding; BBDO; Cossette Communications-Marketing (Canada); and Young & Rubicam. But general agencies also include the thousands of smaller *entrepreneurial agencies* located in every major city across the country (Martin Agency, Richmond, Virginia; Rubin/Postaer, Los Angeles; Ruhr/Paragon, Minneapolis; Wieden & Kennedy, Portland, Oregon).

Profit margins in entrepreneurial agencies are often slimmer, but these shops are typically more responsive to the smaller clients they serve. They offer the hands-on involvement of the firm's principals, and their work is frequently startling in its creativity. For these very reasons, many large agencies are spinning off smaller subsidiaries.[25] Some entrepreneurial agencies, like Muse Cordero Chen, carve a niche for themselves by serving particular market segments.

Business-to-business agencies   A **business-to-business** (or *high-tech*) **agency** represents clients that market products to other businesses. Examples are electronic components for computer manufacturers, equipment used in oil and gas refineries, and MRI equipment for radiology. High-tech advertising requires some technical knowledge and the ability to translate that knowledge into precise, persuasive communications.

When high-tech businesses advertise, their agencies must have a firm grasp of the relevant technical details and be able to communicate this information clearly. Moreover, high-tech agencies also have to know which media to use. A trade publication, like PC World (www.pcworld.com), is typical of the many media whose audiences are largely composed of the business readers likely to purchase high-tech products and services.

Most business-to-business advertising is placed in trade magazines or other business publications. These media are commissionable, but because their circulation is smaller, their rates are far lower than those of consumer media. Since commissions usually don't cover the cost of the agency's services, business agencies typically charge their clients service fees. They can be expensive, especially for small advertisers, but failure to obtain a business agency's expertise may carry an even higher price in lost marketing opportunities.

Business and industrial agencies may be large international firms like MacLaren/Lintas in Toronto or HCM/New York, or smaller firms experienced in areas of recruitment, biomedical, or electronics advertising.

Specialized Service Agencies

Many small agencies assist their clients with a variety of limited services. In the early 90s the trend toward specialization blossomed, giving impetus to many of the small agency-type groups called *creative boutiques* and other specialty businesses such as *media-buying services* and *interactive agencies.*

Creative boutiques   Some talented artists—like graphic designers and copywriters—set up their own creative services, or **creative boutiques.** They work for advertisers and occasionally subcontract to ad agencies. Their mission is to develop exciting creative concepts and produce fresh, distinctive advertising messages. Creative Artists Agency (CAA), a Hollywood talent agency, caused a stir on Madison Avenue (the collective term for New York agencies) by taking on the role of a creative boutique, using its pool of actors, directors, and cinematographers to create a series of commercials for Coca-Cola. McCann-Erickson Worldwide remained Coke's *agency of record,* but the majority of the creative work came from CAA and several other, smaller agencies.[26]

Advertising effectiveness depends on originality in concept, design, and writing. However, while boutiques may be economical, they usually don't provide the research, marketing, sales expertise, or deep customer service that full-service agencies offer. So boutiques tend to be limited to the role of creative suppliers.

Media-buying services   Some experienced media specialists set up organizations to purchase and package radio and TV time. In the United States, the largest of these **media-buying services** is Western International Media in Los Angeles, which places over $1.6 billion worth of advertising annually for clients such as Walt Disney, Atlantic Richfield (Arco), US Airways, and Times-Mirror.[27]

Radio and TV time is perishable. A 60-second radio spot at 8 PM can't be sold later. So radio and TV stations presell as much time as possible and discount their rates for large buys. The media-buying service negotiates a special discount with the stations and then sells the time to agencies or advertisers.

Media-buying firms provide customers (both clients and agencies) with a detailed analysis of the media buy. Once the media package is sold, the buying service orders spots, verifies performance, sees that stations "make good" for any missed spots, and even pays the media bills. Compensation methods vary. Some services charge a set fee; others get a percentage of what they save the client.

Interactive agencies   With the stunning growth of the Internet and the heightened interest in integrated marketing communications comes a new breed of specialist, the **interactive agency.** MB Interactive (owned by Mezzina Brown) and Poppe Tyson Interactive (owned by Bozell Jacobs) are just two of the many innovative firms with specialized experience in designing World Wide Web pages and creating fun, involving, information-rich Internet advertising.

Other specialists, such as *direct-response* and *sales promotion agencies,* are also growing in response to client demands for greater expertise and accountability.

Because of the technical expertise needed for interactive media, some small agencies have made a big name for themselves in this new specialty. Agencies like Eagle River Interactive (www.eriver.com) are similar to the creative boutiques that produce print, television, or radio advertising.

What People in an Agency Do

The American Association of Advertising Agencies (4As) is the national organization of the advertising agency business. Its diverse base of 650 agency members handle almost 75 percent of all national advertising contracted to agencies in the United States.[28]

The AAAA Service Standards explain that an agency's purpose is to interpret to the public, or to desired segments of the public, information about a legally marketed product or service. How does an agency do this? First, it studies the client's product to determine its strengths and weaknesses. Next, it analyzes the product's present and potential market. Then, using its knowledge of the channels of distribution and available media, the agency formulates a plan to carry the advertiser's message to consumers, wholesalers, dealers, or contractors. Finally the agency writes, designs, and produces ads; contracts for media space and time; verifies media insertions; and bills for services and media used.

The agency also works with the client's marketing staff to enhance the advertising's effect through package design, sales research and training, and production of sales literature and displays.[29] To understand these functions, consider the people who were involved—directly or indirectly—in the creation, production, and supervision of the Honda dealer kits created by Muse Cordero Chen.

Account Management

Muse Cordero Chen's **account executives (AEs)** are the liaison between the agency and the client. Large agencies typically have many account executives, who report to **management** (or **account**) **supervisors.** They in turn report to the agency's director of account (or client) services.

The account executive is often caught in the middle of the fray, as they are responsible for formulating and executing advertising plans (discussed in Chapter 7), mustering the agency's services, and representing the client's point of view to the agency. As one observer commented, to succeed today, an AE like Lisa Wright needs to be more of a strategist than an advocate. She must be well-versed in an extraordinary range of media and demonstrate how her agency's creative work satisfies both her client's marketing needs and the market's product needs. That means she must be enterprising and courageous, demanding yet tactful, artistic and articulate, meticulous, forgiving, perceptive, persuasive, ethical, and discreet—all at once. And she must always deliver the work on time and within budget.[30]

To grow, agencies require a steady flow of new projects. Sometimes agencies get new assignments when their existing clients develop new products or enter new markets. Sometimes clients seek out agencies whose work they are familiar with. Thanks to its reputation, Muse Cordero Chen receives 10 to 15 new-business calls a week.

Research and Account Planning

Clients and agencies must give their creatives (artists and copywriters) a wealth of product, market, and competitive information because, at its core, advertising is based on information. Before creating any advertising, agencies research the uses and advantages of the product, analyze current and potential customers, and try to determine what will influence them to buy. After the ads are placed, agencies use more research to investigate how the campaign fared. Chapter 6 discusses some of the many types of research ad agencies conduct.

When Goodby, Berlin & Silverstein won the Porsche Cars North America account, *Adweek* commented: "In the end, what distinguished GBS was the sophistication of its *account planning*."[31] **Account planning** is a hybrid discipline that uses research to bridge the gap between account management and creatives. The

The Personal Digital Assistant:
The Gen X Bible

The latest innovation for the professional businessperson or student on the go is the personal digital assistant. At first glance the PDA looks like a glorified digital address book, but in fact it is much more.

The first PDA was introduced by Apple Computer in 1993. The Newton Message Pad weighed about a pound and was used primarily in the medical field, replacing patient index cards, reference books, drug databases, and more.

Today, Apple's fourth generation of Message Pads is competing with other companies' versions. The new PDAs offer many new features—for example, handwriting recognition. The user writes notes or messages with a stylus and the PDA will convert the handwritten image into computer text.

In the age of digital awareness, competition to be number one is fast and fierce. This chart shows some of the PDAs that are available and what they have to offer.

The advantage of the PDA is mobility. It can go anywhere in a briefcase, purse, or even a coat pocket.

"I've come to rely on my Cassiopeia to keep track of my appointments, contacts, and tasks, of course," says Paul Hulse of Warner Bros. Studios in Burbank, CA.

PDAs come in both Macintosh and PC Windows formats and are available at most office supply and retail computer stores.

Sources: *Florida Family Physician*, January 1996, 46, no. 1; "Letters from the Editor," *Mobile Worker Magazine*, http://microsoft.com/windowsce/hpc/mobile/letters.htm.

	Newton Message Pad 2000	U.S. Robotics Pilot	Microsoft Windows CE Palmtops
Memory	5 MB	Under 1 MB	2 MB or 4 MB
Fax	—	—	—
E-mail	—		—
Handwriting recognition	—	—	—
Software	Newton Works, Quick Figure Pro, Net strategy, EnRoute, i-net email, WWW browser, etc.	Graffiti, Date Book, Address, mail	Windows 95, Pocket Word, Pocket Excel, Microsoft Office, Contacts, Pocket Internet Explorer, etc.
Platform	Macintosh	Macintosh/PC	PC
Dimensions (L × W × H)	4.7 × 8.3 in.	4.7 × 3.2 × .7 in.	7 × 4 × 1 in.
Weight	1.4 lbs.	5.7 oz.	12 oz.

account planner defends the consumer's point of view and the creative strategy in the debate between the agency's creative team and the client.

Account planners study consumer needs and desires through phone surveys and focus groups, but primarily through personal interviews. They help the creative team translate their findings into imaginative, successful campaigns. Not attached to either account management or creative, the account planner balances both elements to make sure the research is reflected in the ads.[32]

Working on the Nike account, Berni Neal, an account planner at Muse Cordero Chen, spent many afternoons in L.A. just talking to young people to understand their attitudes, feelings, language, and habits. Then she represented their views in agency meetings with Nike. The result was the discovery of a new market segment for Nike: *urban youth*—defined not by ethnicity but by a cultural attitude, shaped by inner-city life, that crossed demographic lines to foster the market's core values: irreverence, fitness, athleticism, and discipline.

By putting the consumer, instead of the advertiser, at the center of the process, account planning changes the task from simply creating an advertisement to nurturing a relationship between consumer and brand. That requires tremendous understanding, intuition, and insight. But when performed properly, planning provides that mystical leap into the future—the brilliant, simplifying insight that lights the client's and the creative's way. Interestingly, the U.S. agencies that have adopted account planning in the last decade are the very ones now considered to be the hottest shops. They're performing the best work, getting the biggest accounts, and winning all the awards.[33]

Creative Concepts

Most ads rely heavily on **copy,** the words that make up the headline and message. The people who create these words, called **copywriters,** must condense all that can be said about a product into a few pertinent, succinct points.

Ads also use *nonverbal communication*. That is the purview of the **art directors,** graphic designers, and production artists, who determine how the ad's verbal and visual symbols will fit together. (The creative process is discussed in Chapters 11–13.) The agency's copywriters and artists work as a creative team under a **creative director.** Each team is usually assigned a particular client's business.

In the case of the Honda dealer kits, Mike Whitlow brought two copywriters, Ed Mun and Chase Connerly, together with two art directors, Alfonso ("Fons") Covarrubias and Wilky Lau. The team immediately discarded the traditional binder format as too pedestrian. They wanted to develop an overall *concept* for the kit, not just a nice package of materials. They thought of several ideas: a magic kit ("pulling sales out of a hat"); a cookbook ("the recipe for greater sales"); a tourbook ("your guide to the African-American market").

Eventually they hit on the big idea: a model car—in a kit—complete with instructions on "how to put together a model sales year." That was the concept, but developing it was not easy. They wanted the box to look like a real model kit you might buy at the store. Then they had to find an actual model of a current Honda to put in the kit. Next they had to design a book of advertising plans that would fit into the box. They had to create the ads and commercials the local dealers would use for a variety of local media, which meant the box would have to be designed to hold an audiotape and a videotape. Finally, to meet the client's deadline for the new model year, the kit had to get into production fast.

Advertising Production: Print and Broadcast

Once an ad (or a kit) is designed, written, and approved by the client, it is turned over to the agency's print production manager or broadcast producers.

For print ads, the production department buys type, photos, illustrations, and other components and works with printers, reproduction service bureaus, and suppliers. For a broadcast commercial, production people work from an approved script or storyboard. They use actors, camera operators, and production specialists (studios, directors, editors) to produce a commercial on audiotape (for radio) or on film or videotape (for TV).

But as the Honda case shows, production work is not limited to just ads and commercials. MCC's print production manager had to find suppliers to create and print the box. Inside the box was a spiral-bound book, designed with heavy pages similar to the cardboard of the box. Covarrubias even designed a system of interlocking trays in the box to hold the tapes and the book at the bottom and keep the model at the top, safe from damage. Meanwhile Christine Sloan, the

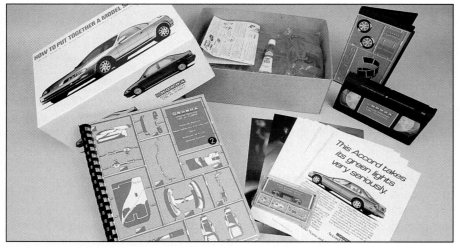

Items in the Honda dealer promotion kit included an $8\frac{1}{2} \times 11$-inch spiral-bound notebook with three color magazine ad slicks, five black-and-white newspaper ad slicks, and marketing and media information; a 25-second "I Am Me" video commercial; an audiocassette with three 55-second radio commercials; and a model kit of the Honda Prelude for the dealer to assemble.

broadcast production manager, supervised all the commercial production and the duplication and packaging of the audio and videotapes.

Media Planning and Buying

Ad agencies perform a variety of media services for their clients: research, negotiating, scheduling, buying, and verifying. Media planning is critical, because the only way advertisers can communicate is through some medium. We discuss the media extensively in Chapters 8 and 14–17, but for now it's important to understand the changes over the last decade that have made the media function so important.

With an unprecedented fragmentation of audiences from the explosion of new media options, media planning and buying is no longer a simple task. Today, many more media vehicles are available for advertisers to consider, as the traditional major media offer smaller audiences than before—at higher prices. Add to this the trend toward IMC and relationship marketing, and the whole media task takes on added significance. This fueled the growth of media specialty companies and simultaneously recast agency media directors as the new rising stars in the business.

Tight budgets demand ingenious thinking, tough negotiating, and careful attention to details. In this age of specialization, what advertisers really need are exceptional generalists who understand how advertising works in coordination with other marketing communication tools and can come up with creative media solutions to tough marketing problems. Today, many products, such as Snapple, owe their success more to creative media buying than to clever ads.

Traffic Management

One of the greatest sins in an ad agency is a missed deadline. If Muse Cordero Chen missed the deadline for a monthly magazine read by Nike's youthful customers, the agency would have to wait another month to run the ad—much to Nike's displeasure. And if the Honda dealer kits didn't arrive on time for the new model year, that could mean lost sales around the country.

The agency traffic department coordinates all phases of production and makes sure everything is completed before client and/or media deadlines. Traffic is often the first stop for entry-level college graduates and an excellent place to learn about agency operations. (See Appendix D for information on careers in advertising.)

Additional Services

The growth of IMC has caused some agencies to employ specialists who provide services besides advertising. While Muse Cordero Chen uses its regular creative department for both advertising and nonadvertising services, larger agencies may have a fully staffed **sales promotion department** to produce dealer ads, window posters, point-of-purchase displays, and dealer sales material. Or, depending on the nature and needs of their clients, they may employ public relations people and direct-marketing specialists, web page designers, home economics experts, or package designers.

Agency Administration

In small agencies, administrative functions may be handled by the firm's principals. Large agencies often have departments for accounting, human resources, data processing, purchasing, financial analysis, legal issues, and insurance.

How Agencies Are Structured

An ad agency organizes its functions, operations, and personnel according to the types of accounts it serves, its size, and its geographic scope.

In small agencies (annual billings of less than $15 million), each employee may wear many hats. The owner usually supervises daily business operations, client

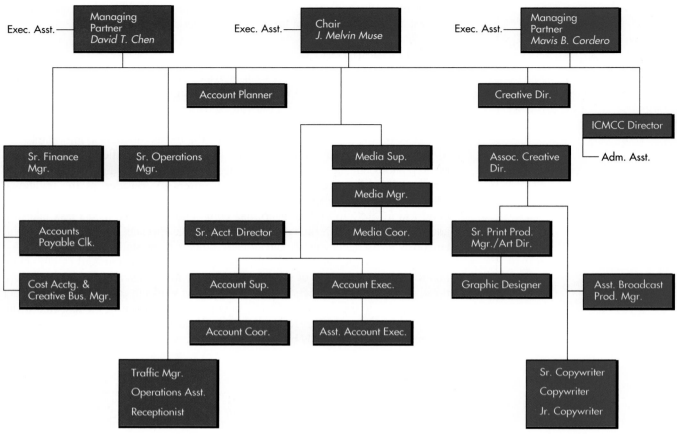

Exhibit 3–9
Muse Cordero Chen organization.

services, and new-business development. Account executives generally handle day-to-day client contact. AEs may also do some creative work, such as writing copy. Artwork may be produced by an art director or purchased from an independent studio or freelance designer. Most small agencies have production and traffic departments or an employee who fulfills these functions. They may have a media buyer, but in very small agencies account executives also purchase media time and space. Exhibit 3–9 shows how Muse Cordero Chen is organized.

Medium and large agencies are usually structured in a *departmental* or *group system*. In the **departmental system,** the agency organizes its various functions—account services, creative services, marketing services, and administration—into separate departments (see RL 3–1 in the Reference Library).

In the **group system,** the agency is divided into a number of "little" agencies or groups (see RL 3–2 in the Reference Library). Each group may serve one large account or, in some cases, three or four smaller ones. An account supervisor heads each group's staff of account executives, copywriters, art directors, a media director, and any other necessary specialists. A very large agency may have dozens of groups with separate production and traffic units.

To deal with the economic pressures of the 90s, many agencies have looked for ways to reorganize. TBWA Chiat/Day in Venice, California, invented a high-tech "virtual office" that frees employees from a regular desk, allowing them to roam around with their notebook computers and sit wherever the needs of the moment dictate.[34] In Chicago, Leo Burnett, which was traditionally highly centralized, has restructured itself into numerous client-oriented mini-agencies, each meant to function as an agency within an agency.[35] And in France, Young & Rubicam encourages

Thanks to modern telecommunications, clients and agencies can locate themselves almost anywhere. Today, virtual manufacturers work out of seaside resorts and their agencies can operate the same way—tied to their researchers, creatives, media departments, and suppliers by wireless phones, fax machines, personal digital assistants, and high-speed modems.

employees to spend more time out of the office with clients and to work from home while linked to the agency via laptop.[36]

How Agencies Are Compensated

To survive, agencies must make a profit. But recent trends in the business—mergers of superagencies, shifts in emphasis from advertising to sales promotion and direct marketing, increased production costs, and the fragmentation of media vehicles—have all cut into agency profits.[37] Moreover, different clients demand different services, forcing agencies to develop various compensation methods. Still, there are really only three ways for agencies to make money: *media commissions, markups,* and *fees* or *retainers.*

Media Commissions

As we saw in Chapter 1, when ad agencies first came on the scene over a hundred years ago, it was as space brokers, or reps, for the newspapers. Since they saved the media much of the expense of sales and collections, the media allowed the agencies to retain a 15 percent **media commission** on the space or time they purchased on behalf of their clients. That started a tradition that endures to this day, although it is now changing rapidly. Let's see how it works.

Say a national rate-card price for a full-page color ad is $100,000. The magazine bills the agency, and the agency in turn bills the client for the $100,000. The client pays that amount to the agency, and the agency sends $85,000 to the magazine, keeping its 15 percent commission ($15,000). For large accounts, the agency typically provides extensive services (creative, media, accounting, and account management) for this commission. With dwindling profits, though, many agencies now charge for services that used to be free.[38]

Markups

In the process of creating an ad, the agency normally buys a variety of services or materials from outside suppliers—for example, photos and illustrations. The agency pays the supplier's charge and then adds a **markup** to the client's bill, typically 17.65 percent of the invoice (which becomes 15 percent of the new total).

For example, a markup of 17.65 percent on an $8,500 photography bill yields a $1,500 profit. When billing the client, the agency adds the $1,500 to the $8,500 for a new total of $10,000. When the client pays the bill, the agency keeps the $1,500 (15 percent of the total)—which, not coincidentally, is the standard agency commission.

$$\$8,500 \times 17.65\% = \$1,500$$

$$\$8,500 + \$1,500 = \$10,000$$

$$\$10,000 \times 15\% = \$1,500$$

Some media—local newspapers, for example—allow a commission on the higher rates they charge national advertisers but not the lower rates they charge local advertisers. So, to get their commission, the agencies have to use the markup formula.

Today many agencies find that the markup doesn't cover their costs of handling the work, so they're increasing their markups to 20 or 25 percent. While this helps, agency profits are still under pressure, forcing many agencies to a fee system in place of, or in addition to, commissions and markups.

Fees

Clients today expect agencies to solve problems rather than just place ads, so fees are becoming more common. In fact, one study shows that only about one-third of national advertisers still rely on the 15 percent commission system. An equal number now use some fee-based system. The rest use some reduced commission or incentive system.[39]

There are two pricing methods in the fee system. With the **fee-commission combination,** the agency charges a basic monthly fee for all its services to the client and retains any media commissions earned. In the **straight-fee** or **retainer method,** agencies charge for all their services, either by the hour or by the month, and credit any media commissions earned to the client.

Accountability is a major issue in client/agency relationships. With a new type of agency compensation, the **incentive system,** the agency earns more if the campaign attains specific, agreed-on goals. DDB Needham, for example, offers its clients a "guaranteed results" program. If a campaign wins, the agency earns more; if it loses, the agency earns less. Kraft General Foods rewards its agencies based on their performance. An A grade gets an extra 3 percent commission; C grades are put on review.[40] To avoid these costs altogether, some advertisers create their own in-house advertising agencies.

The In-House Agency

Some companies set up a wholly owned **in-house agency** (or *house agency*) to save money and tighten control over their advertising. The in-house agency may do all the work of an independent full-service agency, including creative tasks, production, media placement, publicity, and sales promotion.

Advertisers with in-house agencies hope to save money by cutting overhead, keeping the media commission, and avoiding markups on outside purchases. Small, local advertisers in particular seek this goal.

Advertisers also expect more attention from their house agencies, which know the company's products and markets better and can focus all their resources to meet its deadlines. Management is often more involved in the advertising when it's done by company people, especially in "single-business" companies. And some in-house advertising is outstanding, especially in the fashion field. But usually companies sacrifice more than they gain. In-house flexibility is often won at the expense of creativity. Outside agencies typically offer greater experience, versatility, and talent. In-house agencies have difficulty attracting and keeping the best creative people, who tend to prefer the variety and challenge offered by independent agencies. In fact, in Italy, Benetton's stock fell 6 percent in one day when Oliviero Toscani, the company's celebrated in-house ad director, threatened to resign over the issue of creative control.[41]

The biggest problem for in-house agencies is loss of objectivity. In the shadow of internal politics, linear-thinking policy makers, and

Some companies like Benetton (www.benetton.com) prefer to create ads using their own in-house agency. Advertisers hope to save money and gain more attention to their needs by using their house agency, but they can lose the greater experience, objectivity, and talent of an outside agency.

harangues from management, ads may become insipid contemplations of corporate navels rather than relevant messages to customers. In advertising, that's the kiss of death.

The Client/Agency **Relationship**

Many factors affect the success of a company's advertising program, but one of the most important is the relationship between the advertiser and its agency.

How Agencies Get Clients

To succeed, ad agencies need clients. New clients come from personal contact with top management, referrals from satisfied clients or advertising consultants, publicity on recent successful campaigns, trade advertising, direct-mail solicitation, or the agency's general reputation.[42] The three most successful ways to develop new business are having clients who strongly champion the agency, having superior presentation skills, and cultivating a personal relationship with a network of top executives.

Referrals

Most good agencies get clients by referral—from existing clients, friends, advertising consultants, or even other agencies. The head of one company asks another who's doing her ads, and the next week the agency gets a call. If a prospective client presents a conflict of interest with an existing client, the agency may decline the business and refer the prospect to another agency.[43]

Independent *advertising consultants* often help arrange marriages between agencies and clients. In fact, independent advisers were involved in most of the important recent account shuffles on Madison Avenue: Sears, IBM, BMW, Burger King, and MasterCard, to name a few.[44]

Sales reps for media and suppliers frequently refer local advertisers to an agency they know. So it's important for agencies to maintain cordial relations with the media, suppliers, other agencies, and, of course, their existing clients.

Presentations

An advertiser may ask an agency to make a presentation—anything from a simple discussion of the agency's philosophy, experience, personnel, and track record to a full-blown audiovisual presentation of a proposed campaign. Successful agencies, therefore, need excellent presentation skills.

Some advertisers ask for or imply that they want a **speculative presentation,** meaning they want to see what the agency will do before they sign on. But most agencies prefer to build their presentations around the work they've already done, to demonstrate their capabilities without giving away ideas for a new campaign. Invariably, the larger the client, the bigger the presentation. Some agencies now spend upwards of $500,000 to stage a new-business presentation.

The presentation process also allows the agency and the advertiser to get to know each other before they agree to work together. Advertising is a people business, so human qualities—mutual regard, trust, and communication—play an important role (see the Ethical Issue: Accounting for Account Reviews).

Networking and Community Relations

Agencies frequently find that the best source of new business is people their employees know socially in the community. Some agencies work pro bono (for free) for charities or nonprofit organizations such as the American Indian College Fund. Jo Muse at Muse Cordero Chen contributes time to the Rebuild L.A. campaign, which started after the civil disorders of 1992.

Agencies may help local politicians (a controversial practice in some areas) or contribute to the arts, education, religion, or the community. Some agencies

Accounting for Account Reviews

Clients periodically review the effectiveness of their advertising agency and invite presentations from other agencies. Typically, clients are excited by the prospect of seeing new creative work, while prospective agencies worry that they'll lose the contest after spending big bucks to prepare a killer presentation. Meanwhile, the incumbent agency must continue providing all advertising currently planned, prepare a new dynamite presentation portraying the winning creative direction for the future, and smooth over any past difficulties.

Ethically, advertisers are expected to show some allegiance to their current agency, unless the agency has shown poor performance or the program has proven ineffective. *Advertising Age* reports, "Ad agency executives are decrying an alarming trend: advertisers are changing course on a review in midstream and appointing agencies not involved originally." The article says in August 1997, Citibank was secretly negotiating the compensation details for a final contract with Young and Rubicam for up to $800 million in global business while prospective agencies were scheduled to make costly presentations for another six weeks!

"Tension comes from the fact that the whole business of advertising has had to become more accountable in recent years due to corporate restructuring," states Nancy Salz, president of Nancy L.

Salz Consulting, a firm that advises advertisers and agencies how to improve their relationships.

Advertisers are also tempted to conduct reviews for other reasons. To begin with, advertisers usually don't mind a little attention from a new agency. Second, the advertiser has no finanical or legal commitment to pay agencies for a presentation (although ethically, one would think it should). Third, some advertisers succumb to the lure of free creative work. They review several presentations, incorporate and plagiarize elements from each, redesign the art and script elements, and refuse to reimburse the agencies for the cost of research and creative ideas.

To keep costs low, some advertisers put their agencies on the defensive by threatening to choose other creative sources. "Advertisers have gotten smarter over the years," says James Desrosier, vice president of marketing and product management at Maestro USA, a subsidiary of MasterCard International. "And they have led the charge that has created the erosion of traditional agency revenue streams. First it was the strategic consultant. Then it was the independent media-buying service. Now it's the external creative resource." This third situation is exemplified by Coca-Cola's use of Creative Artists Agency, a talent agency that has traditionally served as a temporary agency for actors, writers, and filmmakers but has turned to contracting its creative resources to create and produce advertising like an ad agency.

The agency review process is hard on incumbents. An informal survey by *Adweek* revealed that only one incumbent agency out of

---

sponsor seminars; others assist ad clubs or other professional organizations. All these activities help an agency become known and respected in its community.

Soliciting and Advertising for New Business

The use of creative collateral material is often an effective way to get the attention of prospective customers, as demonstrated by the Honda dealer kit shown earlier. Fallon McElligott (www.fallon.com) solicits new business in a similar manner, by mailing prospects an empty box with their phone number inside, along with a quarter to place the call.

Lesser-known agencies must take a more aggressive approach. An agency may solicit new business by advertising, writing letters, making cold calls, or following up leads from sources in the business. An agency principal usually solicits new business, but staffers help prepare presentations.

Today, more agencies are advertising themselves. The Ad Store, a small agency in New York, even advertises on television to reach small, first-time advertisers.[45] Many agencies submit their best ads to competitions around the world to win awards and gain publicity and professional respect for their creative excellence.[46] (Most of the ads in this book are award winners.)

Stages in the Client/Agency Relationship

Just as people and products have life cycles, so do relationships. In the advertising business, the life cycle of the agency/

dozens actually survives a review. "Ninety percent of client/agency breakups happen because the relationship goes bad. If the relationship is bad, nothing will save the advertising," says Ed Vick, president/CEO of Young & Rubicam.

Although many advertising professionals insist the process must be changed, there are no financial reasons for advertisers to initiate reform, only ethical ones. In 1994, the CD-i Division of Philips Interactive Media of America initiated an agency review that led to the selection of Cohen/Johnson (Los Angeles) and Woolworth & Partners (San Francisco) as two of three finalists for its $10 million CD-i account. Suddenly the review process was put on hold when Philips Interactive appointed a new senior vice president of sales and marketing who decided to "rethink" the list of solicited agencies. Woolworth & Partners and Cohen/Johnson responded with a lawsuit demanding $20,000 reimbursement for incurred costs and claiming that "Philips has not stood by its good faith commitment." Philips settled out of court, offering each agency $10,000.

Evidently, ethical reform in the agency selection process will come only from actions like those of Woolworth and Cohen/Johnson, a bottom-line accounting created by the advertising industry. As Desrosier says, "The advertising industry wants to be taken more seriously. But so far it has been incapable of conducting itself in the way it wants to be perceived. The only way out of this situation is through change. But rather than playing catch-up, the industry would change the game it plays."

Questions

1. Many advertisers complain that their agencies are not truly customer focused. What can an ad agency do to change this perception and thus keep its clients from changing agencies?

2. It seems clear that the agency review process is here to stay. What guidelines might advertisers and agencies establish to make the process more equitable and ethical for all parties?

Sources: Mercedes M. Cardona, "Agencies Irked by Surprises in Reviews," *Advertising Age,* August 18, 1997, p. 3; James Desrosier, "How to Repair the Agency/Client Rift," *Adweek,* January 31, 1994, p. 52; Noreen O'Leary, "Against All Odds," *Adweek,* August 8, 1994, p. 19; Kevin Goldman, "Philips Infomercial Does Its Thing in Popular TV-Watching Hours," *The Wall Street Journal,* September 22, 1993, p. B6; Patrick M. Reilly, "Philips Media Plans Reorganization to Consolidate Its Global Properties," *The Wall Street Journal,* August 16, 1993, p. B4; "Ad Notes: Philips Consumer Electronics Fires DMB&B," *The Wall Street Journal,* July 19, 1994, p. B6; Kathy Tyler, "Broken Promise," *Adweek,* March 21, 1994, pp. 1, 9; Kathy Tyler, "Philips Interactive Media Nears Decision among Three Finalists," *Adweek,* February 28, 1994, p. 4; Kathy Tyler, "Philips Interactive Meets with Four Shops," *Adweek,* February 7, 1994, p. 5; Kathy Tyler, "RPA Hooks Up with Philips after a Rocky Review," *Adweek,* April 25, 1994, p. 3; Kathy Tyler and Shelly Garcia, "Philips Reopens Talks on CD-i Biz," *Adweek,* March 28, 1994, p. 3; Tom Weisand, "Riney Out of Philips Review," *Adweek,* February 14, 1994, p. 3.

client relationship has four distinct stages: *prerelationship, development, maintenance,* and *termination.*[47]

The Prerelationship Stage

The **prerelationship stage** occurs before an agency and client officially do business. They may know each other by reputation, by previous ads, or through social contact. Initial perceptions usually determine whether an agency is invited to pitch the account. Through the presentation process, the agency tries to give the best impression it can, because it is selling and the client is buying (the Checklist for Agency Review offers guidelines for selecting an agency).

The Development Stage

Once the agency is appointed, the **development stage** begins. During this honeymoon period, the agency and the client are at the peak of their optimism and eager to develop a mutually profitable relationship. Expectations are at their highest, and both sides are most forgiving. During development, the rules of the relationship are established. The respective roles get set quickly, the true personalities of all the players come out, and the agency creates its first work. At this point, the agency's output is eagerly awaited and then judged very thoroughly. The agency also discovers how receptive the client is to new ideas, how easy the client's staff is to work with, and how well the client pays its bills. During the development stage the first problems in the relationship also occur.

The Maintenance Stage

The year-in, year-out, day-to-day working relationship is called the **maintenance stage.** When successful, it may go on for many years. Sunkist has used the same agency, Foote, Cone & Belding, for close to 100 years. Other long-lasting relationships include Unilever/J. Walter Thompson, Exxon/McCann-Erickson, and Hammermill Papers/BBDO Worldwide, all more than 80 years. Unfortunately, the average client/agency relationship is much shorter—usually seven or eight years.

The Termination Stage

At some point, an irreconcilable difference may occur, and the relationship reaches the **termination stage.** Perhaps the agency has acquired a competing account, or the agency's creative work doesn't seem to be working. Or perhaps one party or the other simply decides it is time to move on.

During the nervous 90s, several long-standing client/agency relationships were terminated. After 75 years, AT&T replaced Ayer as the company's lead agency on its $200 million consumer long-distance account, giving the business to FCB/Leber Katz in New York. Ayer retained AT&T's $100 million corporate image business.[48] Seagram fired DDB Needham from its $40 million Chivas Regal account after a 32-year marriage. And Anheuser-Busch dropped a bombshell on D'Arcy Masius Benton & Bowles when it pulled the Budweiser account after 79 years.[49]

The way a termination is handled will affect both sides for a long time and is an important factor in whether the two ever get back together. After losing the Apple Computer account in 1986, TBWA Chiat/Day gave Madison Avenue a lesson in class by placing an ad that thanked Apple for their many years together. In 1997, the account came back.[50]

Factors Affecting the Client/Agency Relationship

Many forces influence the client/agency relationship. Generally they can be grouped into the four Cs: *chemistry, communication, conduct,* and *changes.*

The most critical factor is the personal *chemistry* between the client's and the agency's staff.[51] Agencies are very conscious of this factor and wine and dine their clients in hopes of improving it. Smart clients do the same.

Poor *communication,* a problem often cited by both agencies and advertisers, leads to misunderstandings about objectives, strategies, roles, and expectations—and to poor advertising. Constant, open communication and an explicit agreement on mutual contribution for mutual gain are key to a good relationship.[52]

Dissatisfaction with agency *conduct,* or performance, is the most commonly cited reason for agency switches in every country.[53] Services, like products, move through life cycles. The service the agency marketed two years ago may not be perceived by the client in the same way today.[54] Or perhaps the agency doesn't understand the client's marketing problems. And clients change, too. Does the client give the agency timely, accurate information? Does it appreciate good work, or does it treat the agency like a vendor?[55] (For more on how clients hold up their end of the relationship, see the Checklist for Ways to Be a Better Client.)

Changes occur in every relationship. Unfortunately, some of them damage the agency/client partnership. The client's market position or policies may change, or new management may arrive. Agencies may lose key staff people. Client conflicts may arise if one agency buys another that handles competing accounts. Legally, an ad agency cannot represent a client's competition without the client's consent.[56] Saatchi & Saatchi was forced to resign Helene Curtis under pressure from Saatchi's biggest client, Procter & Gamble.[57]

Perhaps the best way to improve understanding between clients and agencies would be to have staff members change places for a while. A Foote, Cone & Belding account executive did just that with great success, filling in temporarily as marketing manager at Levi's Jeans for Women. It gave her a whole new perspective on her agency job and the daily challenges faced by her client.[58]

To help understand the challenges faced by the client, a Foote, Cone & Belding account executive made the unusual move of temporarily filling in as a marketing manger for Levi's Jeans for Women. The experiment provided a whole new perspective on her agency job and offered great insight on the needs and demands of her client.

Ways to Be a Better Client

Relationships

____ **Cultivate honesty.** Be truthful in your meetings and in your ads.

____ **Be enthusiastic.** When you like the ads, let the agency know.

____ **Be frank when you don't like the advertising.** Always cite a reason when turning down an idea.

____ **Be human.** React like a person, not a corporation. Laugh at funny ads even if they don't work.

____ **Be willing to admit you're unsure.** Don't be pressured. Let your agency know when you need time.

____ **Allow the agency to feel responsible.** Tell the agency what you feel is wrong, not how to fix it.

____ **Care about being a client.** Creative people work best for clients they like.

Management

____ **Don't insulate your top people from creative people.** Agency creative people work best when objectives come from the top, not filtered through layers.

____ **Set objectives.** For timely and quality service from your agency, establish and openly share your marketing objectives.

____ **Switch people, not agencies.** When problems arise, agencies often prefer to bring in fresh talent rather than lose you as a client.

____ **Be sure the agency makes a profit on your account.** Demanding more services from your agency than fees or commissions can cover hurts relationships.

Production

____ **Avoid nitpicking last-minute changes.** Perfection is important, but waiting until the last moment to make minor changes can damage the client/agency relationship. Agencies see such behavior as indecisive and/or arrogant and lose respect for the client.

____ **Be aware of the cost of changes (both time and money).** The costs of making major changes at the production stage may be five times greater than in the earlier stages.

____ **Don't change concepts during the production stage.** Late concept changes can inadvertently change product positioning and personality.

Media

____ **Understand the economics (and economies) of media.** Be prepared to deal with costs per thousand (CPMs), costs per ratings point (CPP), and other key elements of media planning and buying so that you can evaluate and appreciate your agency's media strategy.

____ **Understand the importance of lead time.** Early buys can eliminate late fees, earn discounts, make you eligible for special promotions, strengthen your agency's buying position, and reduce anxiety.

____ **Avoid interfering with the agency's media relationship.** The stronger your agency's buying position, the greater the discounts available to you. Refrain from cutting deals with media reps directly and plan media well in advance.

____ **Avoid media arrogance ("they need us").** Some media will deal with clients, and some won't. Misinterpret this relationship and you may either pay more than you should or be too late to get into a medium you need.

____ **Avoid insularity.** Be wiling to let your mind travel beyond your immediate environment and lifestyle.

____ **Suggest work sessions.** Set up informal give-and-take sessions with creatives and strategists.

____ **Keep the creative people involved in your business.** Agency creatives do their best work for you when they're in tune with the ups and downs of your business.

Research

____ **Share information.** Pool information to create new and bigger opportunities.

____ **Involve the agency in research projects.** An agency's creative talent gets its best ideas from knowledge of your environment.

Creative

____ **Learn the fine art of conducting the creative meeting.** Deal with the important issues first: strategy, consumer benefits, and reasons why.

____ **Look for the big idea.** Concentrate on positioning strategy and brand personality. Don't allow a single ad—no matter how brilliant—to change the positioning or personality of the product.

____ **Insist on creative discipline.** The creative process stimulates concepts and actions. Discipline helps keep focus on those that count the most.

____ **Don't be afraid to ask for great advertising.** Agencies prefer the high road, but as the client you must be willing to accompany them. If the agency slips, be strong and ask it to try again.

The **Suppliers** in Advertising The people and organizations that provide specialized services to the advertising business are called **suppliers.** Without their services it would be impossible to produce the billions of dollars' worth of advertising placed every year.

Although we can't mention them all, important suppliers include *art studios and web design houses, printers, film and video production houses,* and *research companies.*

Art Studios and Web Designers

Art studios design and produce artwork and illustrations for advertisements. They may supplement the work of an agency or even take its place for small agencies. Art studios are usually small organizations with as few as three or four employees. Some, though, are large enough to employ several art directors, graphic designers, layout artists, production artists, and sales reps.

Most studios are owned and managed by a graphic designer or illustrator, who calls on agencies and advertising managers to sell the studio's services, takes projects back to the office to be produced, and then delivers them for the client's approval. The work is very time-consuming and requires a talent for organization and management as well as a core competency in art direction and computer graphics.

Similar to art studios, **Web design houses** employ specialists who understand the intricacies of HTML and Java programming languages and can design ads and Internet Web pages that are both effective and cost efficient.

Printers and Related Specialists

The printers who produce brochures, stationery, business cards, sales promotion materials, and point-of-purchase displays are vital to the advertising business. Ranging from small instant-print shops to large offset operations, **printers** employ or contract with highly trained specialists who prepare artwork for reproduction, operate digital scanning machines to make color separations and plates, operate presses and collating machines, and run binderies.

As we discuss in Chapter 11, printers may specialize in offset lithography, rotogravure, letterpress, engraving, or other techniques. Their sales reps must be highly skilled, and often earn very large commissions.

Film and Video Houses

Few agencies have in-house TV production capabilities. Small agencies often work with local TV stations to produce commercials. But the large agencies normally work with **independent production houses** that specialize in film or video production or both.

Research Companies

Advertisers are concerned about the attitudes of their customers, the size of potential markets, and the acceptability of their products. Agencies want to know what advertising approaches to use, which concepts communicate most efficiently, and how effective past campaigns have been.

The media are concerned with the reading and viewing habits of their audiences, the desired markets of their advertiser-customers, and public perceptions toward their own particular medium.

Research, therefore, is closely allied to advertising and an important tool of marketing professionals. But most firms do not maintain a fully staffed research department. Instead, they use **independent research companies** or consultants. Research firms come in all sizes and specialties, and they employ statisticians, field interviewers, and computer programmers, as well as analysts with degrees in psychology, sociology, and marketing. We discuss research in Chapter 6.

The Media of Advertising

The *medium* that carries the advertiser's message is the vital connection between the company that manufactures a product or offers a service and the customer who may wish to buy it. Although the plural term **media** commonly describes channels of mass communication such as television, radio, newspapers, and magazines, it also refers to other communications vehicles such as direct mail, out-of-home media (transit, billboards, etc.), specialized media (aerial/blimps, inflatables), specialty advertising items (imprinted coffee mugs, balloons), and new communication technologies such as interactive TV, fax, and satellite networks. (Exhibit 3–10 on page 113 shows the largest U.S. media companies.)

It's important to understand the various media, their role in the advertising business, and the significance of current media trends. For a person seeking a career in advertising, the media may offer the first door to employment, and for many they have provided great financial rewards.

We classify advertising media into six major categories: *print, electronic, digital interactive, out-of-home, direct mail,* and *other media.* Due to recent media trends, there is some overlap. We shall mention these in passing, along with a brief description of each major category.

Print Media

The term **print media** refers to any commercially published, printed medium—such as newspapers and magazines—that sells advertising space to a variety of advertisers. In the United States today, there are 1,520 daily newspapers and over 10,000 weekly newspapers and shoppers guides.[59] Most are local. However, some national newspapers such as *USA Today, The Wall Street Journal, Barron's,* and trade publications like *Electronic News* and *Supermarket News* have become quite successful. Once strictly a local newspaper, *The New York Times* is now distributed to more than a million readers nationwide.[60]

Magazines, on the other hand, have long been national, and some periodicals, like *Elle,* publish editions in many countries. For over a decade, though, the trend has been toward localization and specialization.

There are nearly 11,000 different magazines published in the United States alone.[61] These include national consumer publications like *Time* and *TV Guide;* national trade publications like *Progressive Grocer* and *Marketing News;* local city magazines like *Palm Springs Life* and *Chicago;* regional consumer magazines like *Sunset;* and local or regional trade or farm publications such as *California Farmer.*

Print media also include directories such as the Yellow Pages; school or church newspapers and yearbooks; and programs used at sporting events and theatrical performances. As we shall see in Chapter 14, "Using Print Media," the vast array of newspapers and magazines makes it possible for both consumer and business advertisers to pinpoint the delivery of their messages to highly select target markets in a variety of fields or geographic locations.

Electronic Media

The **electronic media** of radio and television used to be called the broadcast media. But with the advent of cable TV, many programs are now transmitted electronically through wires rather than broadcast through the air.

The United States alone has more than 1,000 local commercial TV stations and nearly 10,000 local radio stations as well as major TV and radio networks, including ABC, CBS, NBC, Fox, Westinghouse, and Mutual. More than 11,000 local cable systems blanket the country, serving more than 57 million subscribers.[62] Major cable networks like USA, A&E, and CNN serve these systems. Cable also provides channels with specialized offerings, such as QVC, which offers products that can be purchased by phone; Cinemax, which features recently released films; and American Movie Classics (AMC), which features vintage films. We discuss electronic media in Chapter 15, "Using Electronic Media."

Digital Interactive Media

The advent of the information superhighway has brought a new media form. **Digital interactive media** allow the audience to participate actively and immediately. They are changing the way advertisers and agencies do business.

The traditional advertising media are, of course, print, television, and radio. We recognize these ads in our local paper, during our favorite television show, or on a syndicated radio program. However, some ads are much more clever, like this example from Citibank (www.citibank.com). The advertisement is read as travelers walk up the steps of the train terminal in Pittsburgh.

Exhibit 3–10
Top U.S. media companies by category in 1996 ($ millions rounded)

Newspapers			Television		
1.	Gannett Co.	$3,335.2	1.	NBC TV (General Electric Co.)	$4,940.0
2.	Knight-Ridder	2,851.9	2.	Walt Disney Co.	4,005.0
3.	New York Times Co.	2,335.3	3.	CBS Corp.	3,390.0
4.	Advance Publications	2,209.0	4.	News Corp.	2,500.0
5.	Times Mirror Co.	2,080.2	5.	Tribune Co.	681.0
Magazines			**Cable TV**		
1.	Time Warner	$2,764.1	1.	Time Warner	$9,000.0
2.	Reed Elsevier	1,308.4	2.	Tele-Communications Inc.	5,954.0
3.	Hearst Corp.	1,303.0	3.	Viacom	2,013.7
4.	Advance Publications	1,176.0	4.	Comcast Corp.	1,878.1
5.	Thomson Corp.	941.7	5.	US West Media Group	1,726.0

Note: Time Warner includes two full years of Turner Broadcasting Systems.
Source: Reprinted with permission from the August 18, 1997 issue of *Advertising Age.* Copyright, Crain Communications, Inc. 1997.

As we shall see in Chapters 13 and 16, this presents a challenge to advertisers and agencies to learn new forms of creativity. They have to deal with a whole new environment for their ads. It's an environment where customers may spend 20 minutes or more, not just 30 seconds, and where advertising is a dialog, not a monolog. And on the Internet, advertisers risk getting "flamed" (receiving harsh criticism by e-mail) if the techies don't like their ads.[63]

Technology and competition for viewers have led to tremendous audience fragmentation. Running a spot on network TV used to cover the majority of a market. Now ad budgets must be bigger to encompass many media. Wherever elusive customers hide, new media forms emerge to seek them out. But for the big, mass-market advertiser, this represents an enormous financial burden.

Out-of-Home Media

The major categories of out-of-home media are *outdoor advertising* and *transit advertising.* In the United States, most **outdoor advertising** (billboard) companies are local firms, but most of their revenue comes from national advertisers such as tobacco, liquor, and airline companies. **Transit advertising** (bus, taxi, and subway advertising) is an effective and inexpensive medium to reach the public while they're in the retail neighborhood. Out-of-home media also include posters in bus shelters and train stations, billboards in airport terminals, stadium scoreboards, flying banners and lights, skywriting, and kiosk posters.

Out-of-home media is frequently used to reach a large consumer audience and to avoid the clutter of ads in the traditional media. Ads on buses, posters in train stations, and outdoor billboards, such as this one from Sunglass Hut International (www.sunglasshut.com), are some of the more popular forms of this type of advertising.

Direct Mail

When companies mail their advertising directly to prospective customers without using one of the commercial media forms, it's called **direct-mail advertising.** The ad may be a simple sales letter, or it may be a complex package with coupons, brochures, samples, or other devices designed to stimulate a response. Direct mail is the most expensive medium on a cost-per-exposure basis, but it is also the most effective because marketers can target customers directly without competition from other advertisers. We discuss direct mail in Chapter 16.

Other Media   Technology has spawned a host of new advertising media that can confound even the most knowledgeable media planner and buyer. Advertising appears on videocassettes and computer disks. Computers dial telephones and deliver messages by simulating speech or playing a prerecorded message. Computers can also put callers on hold and play prerecorded sales messages until a customer sevice rep answers. Business presentations are created on computer and copied to disks that are mailed to prospective customers. As progress continues, so will the proliferation of new media and the opportunities for those seeking careers (or fortunes) in the media.

Media around the World   Many U.S. advertising people get used to foreign styles of advertising faster than they get used to foreign media. In the United States, if you want to promote a soft drink as a youthful, fun refresher, you use TV. In some parts of Europe, Asia, South America, and Africa you may not be able to. Around the world, most broadcast media are owned and controlled by the government, and many governments do not allow commercial advertising on radio or television. In Egypt, the current hot medium used by Coca-Cola and others is the fleet of boats plying the Nile with corporate logos emblazoned on their sails.[64]

Where countries do allow TV advertising, TV ownership is high, cutting across the spectrum of income groups. In less-developed countries, though, TV sets may be found only among upper-income groups. This means advertisers may need a different media mix in foreign markets.

Virtually every country has access to radio, television, newspapers, magazines, outdoor media, and direct mail. However, the legalities of different media forms vary from country to country. Generally, the media available to the international advertiser can be categorized as either *international* or *foreign media,* depending on the audience they serve.

Many of IBM's (www.ibm.com) advertising campaigns use international media. That is to say their campaigns generally remain the same between countries and regions and are typically written in English. The ads are targeted to highly educated, upper-income customers and prospects.

International Media

In the past, **international media**—which serve several countries, usually without any change in content—have been limited to newspapers and magazines. Several large American publishers like Time, McGraw-Hill, and Scientific American circulate international editions of their magazines abroad. Usually written in English, they tend to be read by well-educated, upper-income consumers and are therefore good vehicles for advertising high-end, brand-name products. *Reader's Digest,* on the other hand, is distributed to 126 foreign countries and printed in the local language of each. Today, television is also a viable international medium. And we are beginning to see the emergence of commercial *global media,* like CNN.

Foreign Media

Advertisers use **foreign media**—the local media of each country—for large campaigns targeted to consumers or businesses within a single country. Since foreign media cater to their own national audience, advertisers must produce their ads in the language of each country. In countries like Belgium and Switzerland, with more than one official language, ads are produced in each language.

Unlike the United States, most countries have strong national newspapers that are a good medium for national campaigns. Advertisers also get broad penetration of lower-income markets through radio, which enjoys almost universal ownership. And cinema advertising is a viable alternative to TV in markets with low TV penetration or restricted use of commercial TV.

Chapter **Summary**

The advertising business comprises four main groups: advertisers (clients), agencies, suppliers, and media. It employs a wide range of artists and businesspeople, sales reps and engineers, top executives, and clerical personnel.

There are four main categories of advertisers based on their geographic activities: local, regional, national, and transnational. Local advertising is placed by businesses in a particular city or county and aimed at customers in the same geographic area. It is important because most sales are made or lost in the local arena.

There are three types of local advertising: product, institutional, and classified. Product advertising can be further divided into regular price-line advertising, sale advertising, and clearance advertising. Institutional advertising creates a long-term perception of the business as a whole by positioning it within the competitive framework. Classified advertising is used to recruit new employees, offer services, and sell or lease new or used merchandise.

Local advertisers are the consummate integrators of marketing communications. Successful local advertisers wear many hats every day, and many of their daily activities help "advertise" the business. Building relationships is a key element.

Local advertisers can get creative assistance from local ad agencies, media, freelancers and consultants, creative boutiques, syndicated art services, and desktop publishers. Wholesalers, manufacturers, and trade groups often help with cooperative advertising.

Regional advertisers operate in one or several states and market exclusively within that region. National advertisers operate in several regions or throughout the country and comprise the largest advertisers.

Local and national advertisers differ in focus, time orientation, and resources. National advertisers focus on brand building, share of market, grand strategies, and market groups. Local advertisers focus on daily traffic, gross sales or volume, tactical solutions, and the individual customers they see every day. National advertisers have a long-term perspective, local advertisers a short-term one. National advertisers also have more money and more employees.

A large company's advertising department may be centralized or decentralized. Each structure has advantages and disadvantages. The centralized organization is the most typical and may be structured by product, subfunction of advertising, end user, or geography. Decentralized departments are typical of large, far-flung organizations with numerous divisions, subsidiaries, products, countries, regions, and/or brands.

Transnational advertisers face unique challenges. Their markets have a different value system, environment, and language with customers of different purchasing abilities, habits, and motivations. Media customary in the United States may be unavailable or ineffective. Companies therefore often need different advertising strategies. To manage their advertising, transnational advertisers use either an international, multinational, or global marketing structure.

Ad agencies are independent organizations of creative people and businesspeople who specialize in developing and preparing advertising plans, ads, and other promotional tools on behalf of clients.

Like their clients, ad agencies may be either local, regional, national, or international in scope. Agencies can be classified by the range of services they offer and the types of business they handle. The two basic types are full-service agencies and specialized-service agencies, such as creative boutiques, media-buying services, and interactive agencies. Agencies may specialize in either consumer or business-to-business accounts. The people who work in agencies may be involved in account management, research, account planning, creative services, production, traffic, media, new business, administration, or a host of other activities.

Agencies may be organized into departments of functional specialties or into groups that work as teams on various accounts. Agencies charge fees or retainers, receive commissions from the media, or mark up outside purchases made for their clients.

Some advertisers develop in-house agencies to save money by keeping agency commissions for themselves. However, they risk losing objectivity and creativity.

Most agencies get clients through referrals, publicity on successful campaigns, advertising, personal solicitation, or networking. The client/agency relationship goes through four stages: prerelationship, development, maintenance, and termination. Numerous factors affect the relationship, including chemistry, communication, conduct, and changes.

The suppliers in advertising are all the people and organizations that assist in the business. Examples are art studios and Web designers, printers, photoengravers, film and video houses, talent agencies, research firms, and consultants.

The media of advertising include the traditional mass media of print, electronic, and out-of-home as well as more specialized channels such as direct mail, digital interactive media, and specialty advertising.

Print media refer to magazines and newspapers as well as directories, Yellow Pages, school yearbooks, and special-event programs. Electronic media include radio, TV, and cable TV. Out-of-home refers to billboard and transit advertising. Direct-mail advertising is the most expensive medium on a cost-per-exposure basis but also typically the most effective at generating inquiries or responses. Interactive media let customers participate, turning advertising from a monolog to a dialog.

In foreign markets, advertisers are faced with different media mixes, different legal constraints, and different economies of advertising.

Important **Terms**

account executives (AEs), *98*

account planning, *98*

advertising agency, *92*

art director, *100*

art studio, *111*

Association of National Advertisers (ANA), *86*

brand manager, *91*

business-to-business agency, *96*

centralized advertising department, *88*

classified advertising, *84*

clearance advertising, *84*

cooperative (co-op) advertising, *85*

copy, *100*

copywriter, *100*

creative boutique, *97*

creative director, *100*

decentralized system, *90*

departmental system, *102*

development stage, *107*

digital interactive media, *112*

direct-mail advertising, *113*

electronic media, *112*

fee-commission combination, *104*

foreign media, *114*

full-service advertising agency, *95*

general consumer agency, *95*

global marketers, *92*

group system, *102*

horizontal cooperative advertising, *86*

in-house agency, *104*

incentive system, *104*

independent production house, *111*

independent research company, *111*

institutional advertising, *84*

integrated marketing communications (IMC), *85*

interactive agency, *97*

international agency, *94*

international media, *114*

international structure, *90*

local advertising, *83*

local agency, *94*

maintenance stage, *107*

management (account) supervisors, *98*

markup, *103*

media, *111*

media-buying service, *97*

media commission, *103*

multinational corporation, *92*

national advertiser, *86*

national agency, *94*

outdoor advertising, *113*

point, *87*

prerelationship stage, *107*

print media, *112*

printer, *111*

product advertising, *84*

regional advertiser, *86*

regional agency, *94*

regular price-line advertising, *84*

sale advertising, *84*

sales promotion department, *101*

speculative presentation, *105*

straight-fee (retainer) method, *104*

supplier, *110*

termination stage, *108*

transit advertising, *113*

vertical cooperative advertising, *86*

Web design house, *111*

Review **Questions**

1. What roles do the major organizations involved in the advertising business perform?

2. What's the difference between a local advertiser and a national advertiser?

3. What services might a modern full-service advertising agency offer a large business-to-business advertiser?

4. What are the most important things an advertiser should consider when selecting an agency?

5. How does an agency make money? What is the best way to compensate an agency? Explain your answer.

6. If you owned an ad agency, what would you do to attract new business? Be specific.

7. What are the advantages and disadvantages of an in-house agency?

8. What are the major influences on the client/agency relationship? What can clients and agencies do to maintain a good relationship?

9. What is meant by the term *interactive media?* Give some examples.

10. If you were planning to advertise your brand of computers in Europe, would you likely use foreign or international media? Why?

Exploring the **Internet**

The Internet Exercises for Chapter 3 cover two of the four areas of the advertising world that were discussed: advertising agencies (Exercise 1) and advertisers (Exercise 2).

A good place to start surfing the Web for information on advertising is "The Internet Resource Guide to Advertising" (www.adweb.com) or the "Advertising Worldwide Information" (www.awinet.com) site.

1. Advertising Agencies

   Ad agencies often specialize in a particular type of business or focus on a special market and/or consumer.

   Visit the Web sites for the following agencies.

   - Bates USA **www.batesusa.com**
   - BBDO **www.techsetter.com**
   - CKS Partners **www.cks.com**
   - Dailey & Associates **www.daileyads.com**
   - DDB Needham **www.ddbniac.com**
   - Fallon McElligott **www.fallon.com**
   - Foote, Cone & Belding (FCB) **www.fcb-tg.com**
   - GroundZero **www.groundzero.com**
   - Kirshenbaum Bond & Partners **www.kb.com**
   - Leo Burnett **www.leoburnett.com**
   - McCann-Erickson **www.mccann.com**
   - Muse Cordero Chen **www.musecordero.com**
   - Ogilvy & Mather Worldwide **www.ogilvy.com**
   - Poppe Tyson **www.poppe.com**
   - Rubin/Postaer Associates **www.rpa.com**
   - Saatchi & Saatchi Business Communications **www.saatchibuscomm.com**
   - TBWA Chiat/Day **www.tbwachiat.com**
   - TeamOne Advertising **www.teamoneadv.com**
   - The Phelps Group **www.phelpsgroup.com**
   - J. Walter Thompson **www.jwtworks.com**
   - Young & Rubicam **www.YandR.com**

   Answer the following questions for each.

   a. What is the focus of the agency's work (e.g., consumer, business-to-business, ethnic, general market)?
   b. What is the scope and size of the agency's business? Who makes up its clientele?
   c. What is the agency's mission statement and/or philosophy? How does that affect its client base?
   d. What is the agency's positioning (e.g., creative-driven, strategy (account)-driven, media-driven)?
   e. What is your overall impression of the agency and its work?

2. Agencies and Clients (Advertisers)

   The advertising industry is truly vast, and advertisers and their agencies focus on a wide range of businesses in a broad scope of markets. Visit the following Web sites and familiarize yourself further with the nature and scope of the advertising world.

   ### Advertisers
   - Global: International Advertising Association (IAA) **www.iaaglobal.org**
   - National: Association of National Advertisers (ANA) **www.ana.net**

   ### Advertising Agencies
   - Global: International Federation of Advertising Agencies (IFAA) **www.ifaa.com**
   - National: American Association of Advertising Agencies (AAAA) **www.aaaa.org**
   - National: Institute of Canadian Advertising (ICA) **www.ica-ad.com**
   - Regional: Western States Advertising Agency Association (WSAAA) **www.wsaaa.org/left/wsaaa/**

   ### Advertising Practitioners
   - National: American Advertising Federation (AAF) **www.aaf.org**
   - Regional: Denver Advertising Federation (DAF) **www.daf.org**
   - Local: AdClub of Greater Boston **www.adclub.org**

   ### Advertising Publications
   - National: *Advertising Age* **www.adage.com**
   - Regional/Local: *AdWeek* **www.adweek.com**

   Answer the following questions for each site.

   a. What advertising group (advertiser, ad agency, practitioner, trade press) sponsors the site? Who is the intended audience?
   b. What is the size/scope of the organization?
   c. What is the organization's purpose? The site's purpose?
   d. What benefit does the organization provide individual members? The advertising community at large?
   e. How is this organization important to the advertising industry? Why?

Part Two

Crafting Marketing and Advertising Strategies

The success of any business depends on its ability to attract customers willing and able to buy its products and services. To do this, a business must locate, understand, and communicate with potential customers. Part Two examines the marketing process, the nature of consumers, the relationship between products and market groups, and the research and planning processes that make for marketing and advertising success.●

chapter **4**   *Marketing and Consumer Behavior: The Foundations of Advertising* describes products and markets and how advertisers use the marketing process to create effective advertising. The chapter presents the consumer as an acceptor or rejector of products and discusses how the consumer's complex decision-making process affects the design of advertising.

chapter **5**   *Marketing Segmentation and the Marketing Mix: Determinants of Advertising Strategy* discusses market segments, the aggregation of segments, and the influence of target marketing on a product company. It presents the elements of the marketing mix and discusses how advertisers use them to understand and improve a product concept.

chapter **6**   *Information Gathering: Inputs to Advertising Planning* points out the value of research in improving marketing and advertising effectiveness. It describes how to organize and gather data and discusses the objectives and techniques of concept testing, pretesting, and posttesting.

chapter **7**   *Marketing and Advertising Planning: Top-Down, Bottom-Up, and IMC* details the creation of marketing and advertising plans, particularly setting realistic objectives and developing creative strategies to achieve them. The chapter also presents methods for allocating resources.

chapter **8**   *Planning Media Strategy: Finding Links to the Market* introduces the media plan and the changing role of media planners. It discusses how to determine target audiences and establish objectives for reaching them. The chapter explains the elements of media strategy, how to select specific media vehicles, and how to schedule their use.

Chapter **Four**

Marketing and Consumer Behavior: The Foundations of Advertising

Objective   To highlight the significance of the marketing function in business and to define the importance of advertising and other marketing communications tools that present the company and its products to the market. The successful advertising practitioner must understand the relationship between marketing and the way consumers behave. Ideally, it is this relationship that shapes advertising.

After studying this chapter, you will be able to:

- Define marketing and explain advertising's role in the larger marketing context.

- Discuss the concept of product utility and the relationship of utility to consumer needs.

- Identify the key participants in the marketing process.

- Outline the consumer perception process and explain why "perception is everything."

- Describe the fundamental motives behind consumer purchases.

- Discuss the various influences on consumer behavior.

- Explain how advertisers deal with cognitive dissonance.

Nineteen eighty-four set new benchmarks for American culture, bringing us *Ghostbusters*, the Soviet boycott of the Los Angeles Summer Olympics, and the marketing genius of the brand-new Macintosh computer. And along with more episodes of "Dallas" and "The A-Team" came one of the world's biggest promises, and flops, of mass digital communication. • Prodigy Services Co. was born from the visions of executives at IBM; Sears, Roebuck & Co. (the pre-eminent retailer for Big Blue); and CBS. This all-star team foresaw a bright future in digital commerce and wanted to grab an early lead while the only real competition came from a company named CompuServe. Prodigy would spearhead this new wave of consumerism, where America married electronica and did its things online with a personal computer: buy airline tickets, check stock prices, and maybe even pay the bills. This was quite a dream at a time when people still talked to human tellers to do nearly all their banking. • From the start, the venture was much more reality than pipe dream. IBM dominated the personal computer market after years of technological advances. Sears was the champion, his-

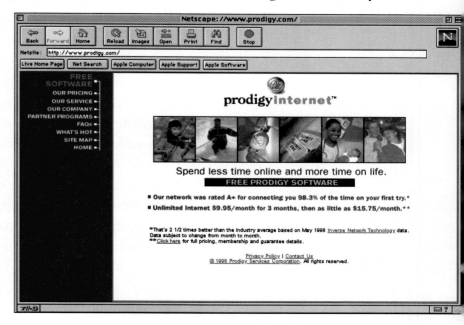

tory-making retailer. And CBS was, of course, one of the big three television networks that the country tuned to for all its news and entertainment. With such a powerful lineup, success seemed guaranteed. • Although CBS pulled out only two years later, Prodigy proudly opened its doors in 1988. The company was the envy of the fledgling online industry with its network services of business, education, and entertainment applications. It was fast and national in coverage and boasted a computer backbone built to handle 10 million users. When it hit the national circuit in 1990, Prodigy had 500,000 accounts after just one month.[1] • Despite its fantastic start, Prodigy's demise was already in the making. The original business plan assumed that the price of personal computers would drop to just a few hundred dollars and they would be found in over half of all American homes. Based on this premise, Prodigy prematurely marketed its product to a mass audience that didn't yet exist. In fact, by 1992 only about 23 percent of American homes owned personal computers, and that didn't necessarily mean they even wanted to go online.[2] • Prodigy also suffered from a lack of direction in its service and a conservatism passed down from its parent companies. It never planned to become a communications medium, where members chatted with each other via e-mail and electronic bulletin boards. "They (IBM and Sears) didn't understand that customers felt they were part of the service. They didn't understand how 'two-way' the medium was," says consultant Esther Dyson.[3] • So when gay-rights activists and Christian fundamentalists began "flame" wars with each other over the bulletin boards, Prodigy heavy-handedly prohibited all such dialog. The company also cut off service to a few subscribers who complained online about its ubiquitous advertising and promptly removed criticism of a price increase from the bulletin board. Then in June of 1991, Prodigy began charging its customers for use of its increasingly popular e-mail feature. Customers were billed if they sent over 30 pieces of e-mail each month, which outraged members who had grown accustomed to getting the service for free. ● Nevertheless, Prodigy continued to lead the online business. It advertised frequently in magazines and newspapers and launched direct marketing campaigns that included its start-up software for free with other software packages and new computer systems. And on September 6, 1991, just one year after its national inception, Prodigy hit 1 million users. ● However, Prodigy's business practice suffered terribly. While it managed an early lead in online services, it had yet to make any money. IBM and Sears had invested nearly $1 billion into Prodigy and were now demanding immediate profits. Meanwhile, as the online industry blossomed in the mass market, America Online became a publicly traded stock in 1992. At the time, AOL had only 155,000 users compared to Prodigy's 1.2 million, but in four short years the company racked up a whopping 5 million subscribers against Prodigy's modest 1.5 million.[4] ● So where did such a promising company, a prodigy, blunder so badly? Prodigy was structured and staffed to conform to the ideals of long-standing corporations that did not want to take big risks. As a result, the company reacted slowly to consumer desires, unlike its competitors. This spelled doom in the rough-and-tumble online industry. America Online and CompuServe both leaped at the opportunity to upgrade to new, Windows-compatible software, while Prodigy held onto its clumsy and dated graphics long past their usefulness. Prodigy waited a full nine years after AOL to incorporate a real-time chat feature, which was a key value of the competing providers.[5] In the end, Prodigy remained out of touch with its members and refused to accomodate their desires. And in this cutthroat business, the competition was more than willing to take up the slack of the lumbering giant. ● Prodigy has since been sold by Sears and IBM for a scant $250 million. It now acts as a moderately sized Internet service provider, not the gigantic online content provider it once was.[6] ● The Prodigy story offers good lessons. To succeed in business, a company's top managers cannot assume anything about their market. Rather, they have to respect the importance of marketing and know how to interpret the data uncovered by their research people. They must know who their customers are, and they must listen and respond to them. Companies that suffer from the *assumption syndrome* court failure and end up as their own "prodigies." ● The story demonstrates another important principle: even superior advertising can't save a product that isn't marketed correctly. Unfortunately, advertising often becomes the scapegoat for management's marketing misfires. ●

The Larger **Marketing Context** of Advertising

All advertisers face a perennial challenge: how to present their products, services, and ideas effectively through the media to buyers. To do this, they must comprehend the important relationship between the product and the marketplace. This relationship is the province of marketing.

Unfortunately, marketing's role is often misunderstood and occasionally overlooked. For example, everybody knows that a business can't survive without proper financing, and without production, there are no products to sell. But how does a company know what products or services to produce? Or to whom to distribute them, or through what channels? That's where marketing comes in.

The ability to attract and keep customers who are willing and able to pay for the firm's goods and services is the key to a company's prosperity. This means a company must be able to locate prospective customers—where they live, work, and play—and then understand their needs, wants, and desires; create products and services to satisfy those desires; and finally communicate that information to them.

This chapter (in fact, this whole unit) defines and outlines marketing issues to clarify advertising's proper role in the marketing function and to introduce the human factors that ultimately shape advertising. As we shall see, the relationship between advertising and marketing is critical.

The Relationship of Marketing to Advertising

As we discussed in Chapter 1, **marketing** is the business process management uses to plan and execute the conception, pricing, *promotion,* and distribution of its products, whether they be goods, services, brands, or even ideas. The ultimate purpose of marketing is to create exchanges that satisfy the perceived needs, wants, and objectives of individuals and organizations.

Advertising is just one of the numerous tools used in the promotion, or communication, aspect of marketing. But how the advertising is done, and where it is run, depends largely on the other aspects of the marketing mix and for whom the advertising is intended to reach.

Customer Needs and Product Utility

This definition of marketing shows that one of the important elements is the special relationship between a customer's *needs* and a product's *need-satisfying potential.* This is known as the product's utility. **Utility** is the product's ability to satisfy both functional needs and symbolic (or psychological) wants.[7] One of the roles of advertising is to communicate this utility. Thus, some ads promote how well a product works; others tout glamour, sex appeal, or status. Ad Lab 4–A discusses the important relationship between needs and utility.

Through the use of marketing research, companies try to discover what needs and wants exist in the marketplace and to define a product's general characteristics in the light of economic, social, and political trends. The goal is to use this information for *product shaping*—designing products, through manufacturing, repackaging, or advertising, to satisfy more fully the customers' needs and wants. In England, for example, automakers noted that more women were buying cars. In fact, by the mid-90s, they bought 55 percent of all small cars. Research revealed that women see their cars as a means of independence and status. So Ford launched a soft-focus campaign in women's magazines highlighting features such as superior seat belts and chip-resistant paint. Realizing the same opportunity in

Superior quality will not close a sale by itself. Marketing people must make the product available and promote its advantages, whether it's a graphite tennis racket, a high-performance sports car, or even the prompt, friendly service of a bank.

A key fact in any product's success is that it must satisfy consumers' needs. The capability to satisfy those needs is called utility. Five types of *functional utility* are important to consumers: *form, task, possession, time,* and *place.* A product may provide *psychic utility* as well as functional utility.

Companies create *form utility* whenever they produce a tangible good, like a bicycle. They provide *task utility* by performing a task for others. However, merely producing a bicycle—or repairing it—doesn't guarantee consumer satisfaction. Consumers must want the bicycle or require the repair, or no need is satisfied and no utility occurs. Thus, marketing decisions should guide the production side of business too.

Even when a company provides form or task utility, marketers must consider how consumers can take possession of the product. This includes distribution, pricing strategies, shelf availability, purchase agreements, and delivery. Money is typically exchanged for *possession utility.* An antique bicycle on display, but not for sale, lacks possession utility because the customer cannot purchase it.

Providing the consumer with the product when he or she wants it is known as *time utility.* Having an ample supply of jam, cars, or bank tellers on hand when the consumer has the need is thus another marketing requirement.

Place utility—having the product available where the customer can get it—is also vital to business success. Customers won't travel very far out of their way to get bicycles or cars. They're even less likely to travel long distances for everyday needs. That's why banks have branches. And that's why 24-hour convenience markets, which sell gasoline and basic food items, are so popular.

Finally, consumers gain *psychic utility* when a product offers symbolic or psychological need satisfaction, such as status or sex appeal. Psychic utility is usually achieved through product promotion (advertising) and may fulfill esteem and self-actualization needs.

Whether it be psychic utility or the functional utilities of form, task, possession, time, and place, product utility is an essential component of marketing success.

Laboratory Application

Select an ad from a weekly newsmagazine and describe in detail what it offers in terms of psychic utility and the functional utilities of form, task, possession, time, and place.

---

the United States, Ford exclusively sponsored a 1997 episode of "Murphy Brown" that dramatized the title character's fight against breast cancer. In addition to its woman-oriented commercials during the program, the company underwrote the airing of two public service announcements and a 30-second message from Candice Bergen about raising money for cancer research.[8]

Businesspeople all too often give the marketing process short shrift. Some companies introduce a product without a clear idea of its utility to the customer, hoping advertising will move the product off the shelf. As Prodigy found out, the consequences of such a shortsighted policy can be severe.

Exchanges, Perception, and Satisfaction

The purpose of marketing is "to create exchanges that satisfy the perceived needs, wants, and objectives of individuals and organizations." There are three important concepts here: *exchanges, perception,* and *satisfaction.*

Exchanges: The Purpose of Marketing and Advertising

Any transaction in which one person or organization trades something of value with someone else is an **exchange.** Exchange is the traditional, theoretical core of marketing. We all engage in exchanges to better our situation. It's a natural part of our human self-interest.

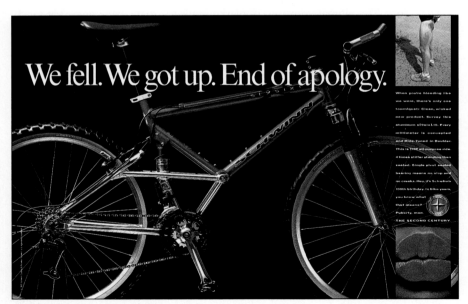

To satisfy its target market, Schwinn *(www.schwinn.com)* shapes its product and then its advertising to suit specific needs. The technical specifications and durability showcased in this Schwinn ad are clearly geared toward biking enthusiasts who demand premiere equipment for their sporting needs.

Advertisers know that satisfying a consumer's self-interest is central to affecting purchase behavior. This ad for the Yamaha WaveRunner (www.yamaha.com) provides a solution to the midlife crisis of the office culture, while appealing to the buyer's responsibility toward the family and day-to-day life.

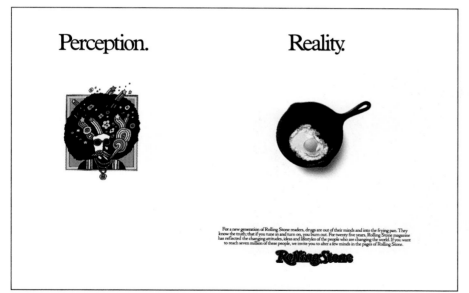

From the viewpoint of the customer, perception is reality. Companies must therefore carefully monitor the messages they send, since those messages may either enhance their image or damage it. Some advertisers, for example, perceive the readers of Rolling Stone *to be hedonistic dopeheads—leftovers from the hippie era. So the magazine (www.rollingstone.com) attempts to change this perception by specifically addressing it and offering a counter argument of what the reality actually is. This highly successful campaign has garnered inumerable awards for creativity from the advertising industry.*

Marketing facilitates these exchanges, thus increasing our potential for satisfaction. How does it do this? In a variety of ways: by developing goods and services we might want; by pricing them affordably; by distributing them to convenient locations; and by informing us about them through advertising and other communication tools. By providing information, advertising makes people aware of the availability of products and of the selection alternatives among different brands. Advertising communicates product features and benefits, various price options, and locations where the product can be found. In the case of *direct marketing,* advertising may even close the sale.

Perception Is Everything

People who are about to engage in a business exchange sometimes feel apprehensive. They may worry that the exchange is not equal, even when it is truly fair. This is where *perception* comes in. The perception of inequity is more likely if the customer has little knowledge of the product. In this case, the more knowledgeable party (the seller) must reassure the buyer—perhaps through advertising—that an equal exchange is possible. If the seller can provide the information and inspiration the buyer seeks, the two may recognize that a *perceived equal-value exchange* exists. Without this perception, though, an exchange is unlikely. If people don't believe the benefits Prodigy has to offer are worth $20 a month, they won't subscribe to the service—no matter how much Prodigy spends on advertising.

Thus, marketing is actually concerned with two levels of customer perception: the perception of the product or service, and the perception of needs, wants, and objectives.

So advertisers must first develop customers' perception of the *product* itself (awareness, attitude, interest) and then a belief in the product's ability (*value*) to satisfy the customers' perceived want or need (*utility*). The greater a customer's need, the greater the potential value or utility of the need-satisfying product.

Advertising may use a variety of techniques to accomplish this. By using just the right mood lighting or music, for example, a TV commercial can simultaneously capture customers' attention and stimulate their emotions toward the goal of need or want fulfillment. If customers are aware of the product and its value, and if they decide to satisfy the particular want or need the product addresses, they are more likely to act.[9] Since perception is so important to advertisers, we discuss it more fully later in this chapter.

Satisfaction: The Goal of the Customer

Even after an exchange occurs, *satisfaction* remains an issue. Satisfaction must occur every time customers use the product, or people won't think they got an equal-value exchange. Satisfaction leads to more exchanges; satisfied customers create more sales. Satisfaction must be the basic goal of any sophisticated marketer.

Advertising *reinforces* satisfaction by reminding customers why they bought the product, helping them defend the purchase against skeptical friends and associates, and enabling them to persuade other prospects to buy it. If a product performs poorly, the negative effect will be even more far-reaching. And good advertising for a poor product can actually run a manufacturer out of business. The better the advertising, the more people will try the product once. And the more who try an unsatisfactory product, the more who will reject it—and tell their friends.

Thus we can think of marketing as the process companies use to make a profit by satisfying their customers' needs and desires.

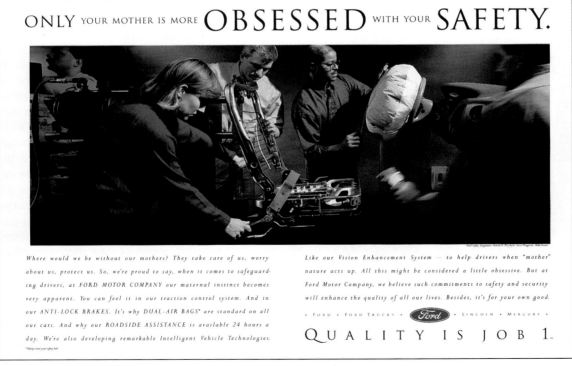

Corporate ads that promote the company's social responsibility as well as specific product benefits are useful because they reinforce the purchaser's decision to buy. By restating these benefits through advertising, Ford (www.ford.com) reassures customers that their decision to buy was the right one, and that increases the likelihood that these customers will return for subsequent purchases.

The **Key Participants** in the Marketing Process

People's needs and wants change daily, and marketers constantly advertise a plethora of products for customer attention and interest. This makes the marketing process very dynamic. At times, it seems like everybody is searching for an exchange. At other times, it seems nobody is. Marketing exchanges depend on three types of participants: *customers, markets* (groups of customers), and *marketers.*

Customers

Customers are the people or organizations who consume products and services. They fall into three general categories: *current customers, prospective customers,* and *centers of influence.*

Current customers have already bought something from a business; in fact, they may buy it regularly. One way to measure a business's success is by calculating the number of its current customers and their repeat purchases. **Prospective customers** are people about to make an exchange or considering it. **Centers of influence** are those customers, prospective customers, or opinion leaders whose ideas and actions others respect. A center of influence is often the link to many prospective customers.

Markets

The second participant in the marketing process is the **market,** which is simply a group of current customers, prospective customers, and noncustomers who share a common interest, need, or desire; who have the money to spend to satisfy needs or solve problems; and who have the authority to make expenditure decisions.[10] As we discuss more fully in Chapter 5, a market never includes everybody. Companies advertise to four broad classifications of markets:

$185

Same material. Same designer. Same sweater. We don't get it either.

$90

We sell the same cashmere sweater they sell. We just sell it for less. Up to 60% off every single thing, every single day. **You Could Pay More, But You'll Have To Go Somewhere Else.** Stein Mart.

Consumer ads, like this one for Stein Mart (www.steinmart.com) are targeted at people who buy goods and services for their own use. Food, clothing, and automobiles are just a few of the kinds of consumer goods that make up this $5 trillion industry.

1. **Consumer markets** include people who buy products and services for their own use. Both Nissan and Ford, for example, aim at the consumer market. But they cater to different groups within that market. They advertise some vehicles to single women; others to upscale young families; and still others to retired people. The consumer market is huge, spending close to $5 trillion every year on products and services in the United States alone.[11] Chapter 5 discusses ways to categorize consumer segments.

2. **Business markets** are composed of organizations that buy services, natural resources, and component products that they resell, use to conduct their business, or use to manufacture another product. As consumers we have a natural bias toward consumer marketing and advertising. And certainly consumer marketers rely on advertising more than business marketers do. However, virtually half of all marketing is business-to-business. In the United States, business buyers purchase over $1 trillion worth of manufactured goods every year, billions more of raw materials, and billions more for the services of law firms, accountants, airlines, and advertising agencies.[12] So business marketing is a very important field that requires special skills and is worthy of our consideration in every chapter. As we pointed out in Chapter 1, there are several subtypes of business markets. The two most important are *reseller markets* and *industrial markets.*

   Reseller markets buy products to resell them. Ford, for example, aims a portion of its marketing activities at its dealers. Similarly, Sunkist first needs to convince food wholesalers and

The Digital Video Disk

Digital technology has been growing by leaps and bounds over the past couple of years. From phones to personal digital assistants (PDAs), we have seen the emergence of tomorrow's technology today. One of the newest developments, the digital video (or versatile) disk (DVD), can be played on both TVs and computers. The new DVD looks just like an audio CD, but it contains both audio and video. It is similar to the laserdisk system of the 1980s, but in compact form. One DVD can contain nearly 16 gigabytes of information (compared to 650 megabytes for an hour-long CD).

The DVD is the latest format in the home entertainment market. It offers much better picture quality than the current standard VHS tape. Its technology allows for many features that simply blow away today's TV and VCR standards. For example, the resolution rate of VHS is 325 scan lines; the DVD has 720 scan lines, making for a much brighter, sharper picture.

The DVD has been called the downfall of the VCR. When the format is introduced into industry, it will be useful to advertising account executives whose duties include presentations to clients. Instead of taking a bulky VCR and VHS tapes to a presentation, the AE will be able to take a laptop with an audiovisual connection, or, for a small meeting, play the video directly from the notebook. The presentation will let the client see DVD's advantages over other media options.

In the future, DVDs may get small enough to fit inside a handheld PDA. Account executives will then be able to present their firm's portfolio to a client from the palm of their hand. This portability will enable them to give client presentations in a small office or even a restaurant without the need for a large dog-and-pony show.

Sources: The Audio Video Pros, http://avpros.net/dvd.htm; Jim Shatz-Atkin, "DVD Comes to Mac," *Mac User,* July 1997, pp. 74–7.

	DVD	CD	VHS Tape
Number of soundtracks	Multiple; allows for multilingual formats	Single format (audio)	Analog tape format
Amount of Information per disk	Four capacity levels (4.38–15.9 GB)	About 650 MB (1 hour audio)	About 2–8 hours
Multiple video tracks	Allows for multiple camera angles	Not available	Not available
Digital format	Allows clear freeze-frame and slow motion	Digital audio tracks from analog	Not available
Parental control	Lock out specific areas so that children cannot access them	Not available	Not available
Different movie tracks	The viewer can set the version of a movie such as the director's cut	Not availble	Have to purchase different versions (uncensored, director's cut)

retail grocers to carry its brand of fruits, or they will never be sold to consumers. Reseller markets, therefore, are extremely important to most companies, even though most consumers are unaware of the marketing or advertising activities aimed at them.

Industrial markets include more than 13 million firms that buy products used to produce other goods and services.[13] Manufacturers of plant equipment and machinery advertise to industrial markets, as do office suppliers, computer companies, and telephone companies. Chapter 5 categorizes industrial markets by factors of industry segment, geographic location, and size.

3. **Government markets** buy products for municipal, state, federal, and other government activities. Some firms are immensely successful selling only to government markets. They advertise post office vehicles, police and military weapons, and tax collector office equipment in trade magazines read by government buyers.

4. **Transnational** (or **global**) **markets** include any of the other three markets located in foreign countries. Every country has consumers, resellers, industries, and governments. So what's the difference between the transnational market and the domestic U.S. or Canadian market for the same product? Environment. The environment in France differs from that in Japan. The environment in Brazil differs from that in Saudi Arabia. Sometimes, as in the case of Switzerland, environments even vary widely within a single country. Targeting markets across national boundaries presents interesting challenges—and important

Een Italia, we lika ze louda opera, but we lika our carsa quieta.

Transnational ads are those that appear in foreign countries. If they are to succeed, advertisers must be aware of the often-subtle differences in environment and culture. In this example, Korean car manufacturer Daewoo (www.daewoo.com) touts the Italian design of its Leganza model in an ad created for the Australian market.

opportunities—for contemporary advertisers, so we deal with this subject wherever applicable throughout this book.

Marketers

The third participant in the marketing process, **marketers,** includes every person or organization that has products, services, or ideas to sell. Manufacturers market consumer and business products. Farmers market wheat; doctors market medical services; banks market financial products; and political organizations market philosophies and candidates. To be successful, marketers must know their markets intimately—*before* they start advertising.

Consumer Behavior: The Key to Advertising Strategy

Take a look at your friends in class, or the people you work with. How well do you know them? Could you describe their lifestyles and the kinds of products they prefer? Do they typically eat out or cook for themselves? Do they ski? Play tennis? If so, what brands of equipment do they buy? Do you know which radio stations they listen to? What TV programs they watch? Do they read a daily newspaper? If you wanted to advertise a new soft drink to these people, what type of appeal would you use? What media?

The Importance of Knowing the Consumer

Advertisers spend a lot of money to keep individuals and groups of individuals (markets) interested in their products. To succeed, they need to understand what makes potential customers behave the way they do. The advertiser's goal is to get enough relevant market data to develop accurate profiles of buyers—to find the common ground (and symbols) for communication. This involves the study of **consumer behavior:** the mental and emotional processes and the physical activities of people who purchase and use goods and services to satisfy particular needs and wants.[14] The behavior of **organizational buyers** (the people who purchase products and services for use in business and government) is also very important. We examine this aspect of buying behavior in Chapter 5.

The Consumer Decision-Making Process: An Overview

Social scientists develop many theories of consumer behavior to explain the process of making a purchase decision. Let's look at this information from the viewpoint of the advertiser.

Advertising's primary mission is to reach prospective customers and influence their awareness, attitudes, and buying behavior. We discussed in Chapter 1 that to succeed, an advertiser must make the marketing communications process work very efficiently.

The moment a medium delivers an advertising message to us, our mental computer runs a rapid evaluation called the **consumer decision-making process.** The conceptual model in Exhibit 4–1 on page 130 presents the fundamental building blocks in the consumer decision-making process. As you can see, the process involves a series of personal subprocesses that are affected by many influences.

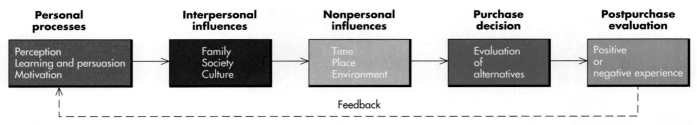

Exhibit 4–1

The basic consumer decision process comprises a set of fundamental steps that the consumer experiences during and after the purchase process. Advertising can affect the consumer's attitude at any point in this process. For the complete model of the process, see RL 4–1 in the Reference Library.

Note in the first box that three **personal processes** govern the way we discern raw data (*stimuli*) and translate them into feelings, thoughts, beliefs, and actions. These are the *perception,* the *learning and persuasion,* and the *motivation processes.*

Second, our mental processes and behavior are affected by two sets of influences. **Interpersonal influences** include our *family, society,* and *culture.* **Nonpersonal influences**—factors often outside the consumer's control—include *time, place,* and *environment.* These influences further affect the personal processes of perception, learning, and motivation.

After dealing with these processes and influences, we face the pivotal decision: to buy or not to buy. But taking that final step typically requires yet another process, the **evaluation of alternatives,** in which we choose brands, sizes, styles, and colors. If we do decide to buy, our **postpurchase evaluation** will dramatically affect all our subsequent purchases.

Like the marketing communications process, the decision-making process is circular in nature. The advertiser who understands this process can develop messages more likely to reach and make sense to consumers.

Personal **Processes** in Consumer Behavior

Assume you are the advertising manager on the launch of a new high-tech, vitamin-laden beverage brand for athletes and sports participants. We'll call it MonsterMalt. What's your first objective?

The first task in promoting any new product is to create awareness (*perception*) that the product exists. The second is to provide enough compelling information (*learning and persuasion*) about the product for prospective customers to find interest and make an informed decision. Finally, you want your advertising to stimulate customers' desire (*motivation*) to satisfy their needs and wants by trying the product. If they find MonsterMalt satisfying, they likely will continue to purchase it. These three personal processes of consumer behavior—perception, learning and persuasion, and motivation—are extremely important to advertisers. By studying these, advertisers can better evaluate how their messages are perceived.

The Consumer Perception Process

As we mentioned earlier, perception is everything. It guides everything we do, from the activities we enjoy to the people we associate with and the products we buy. How a consumer perceives each of the different brands in a category determines which ones he or she uses.[15] The perception challenge, therefore, is the first and greatest hurdle advertisers must cross. Some marketers spend millions of dollars on national advertising, sales promotion, point-of-purchase displays, and other marketing communications only to discover that many consumers don't remember the product or the promotion. The average adult is exposed to over 1,500 ads each day but notices only a handful and remembers even fewer.[16] How does this happen? The answer lies in the principle of perception.

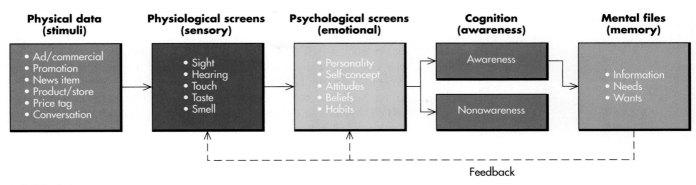

Physical data (stimuli)	Physiological screens (sensory)	Psychological screens (emotional)	Cognition (awareness)	Mental files (memory)
• Ad/commercial • Promotion • News item • Product/store • Price tag • Conversation	• Sight • Hearing • Touch • Taste • Smell	• Personality • Self-concept • Attitudes • Beliefs • Habits	Awareness Nonawareness	• Information • Needs • Wants

Feedback

Exhibit 4–2

The model of the consumer perception process portrays how consumers perceive, accept, and remember an ad or other stimulus to buy.

We use the term **perception** to refer to the personalized way we sense, interpret, and comprehend various *stimuli*. This definition suggests there are several key elements to the consumer perception process, as shown in Exhibit 4–2.

Stimulus

A **stimulus** is physical information we receive through our senses. When we look at a new car, we receive a number of stimuli. We might note the color of the paint, the smell of the leather, the purr of the engine. When we look at a theater ad in the newspaper, we see a collection of type, art, and photography arranged in a way that we interpret as an ad. That's the stimulus. So, for our purposes, assume that a stimulus is any ad, commercial, or promotion that we see.

Advertising stimuli can appear in a variety of forms: a window display at a local department store, the brightly colored labels on cans of Campbell's tomato soup, or even the red price tag on a pair of skis at the Sport Chalet. These objects are all physical in nature; they stimulate our senses (with varying degrees of intensity) in ways that can be measured.

Perceptual Screens

The second key element in perception is the personalized way of sensing and interpreting the data. Before any data can be perceived, they must first penetrate a set of **perceptual screens,** the subconscious filters that shield us from unwanted messages. There are two types of screens, *physiological* and *psychological*.

The **physiological screens** comprise the five senses: sight, hearing, touch, taste, and smell. They detect the incoming data and measure the dimension and intensity of the physical stimuli. A sight-impaired person can't read an ad in *Sports Illustrated*. And if the type in a movie ad is too small for the average reader, it won't be read, and perception will suffer. Similarly, if the music in a TV commercial for a furniture store is not congruent with the message, the viewer may tune out, change channels, or even turn off the TV. The advertiser's message is effectively screened out when the viewer can't interpret it; perception does not occur, and the furniture goes unsold.[17]

We are limited not only by the physical capacity of our senses but also by our feelings and interests. Each consumer uses **psychological screens** to evaluate, filter, and personalize information according

10% OF YOUR CLIENTS WOULD LOVE BERMUDA THIS WINTER. IF FOR NO OTHER REASON THAN TO AVOID THE OTHER 90%.

Bermuda from November through March isn't for everyone. And thank goodness. Our overworked visitors have always enjoyed our uncrowded paradise, its winding walks and pastel landscapes. Not to mention the absence of the thong-wearing, "I live to be bronze" population found at the sun resorts. • In fact, 80% of our winter *Mopeds instead of traffic* visitors are couples, sophisticated and weary clients that come through your door every day. To them club hopping means going from a 5 wood to a 3 iron. Drinking conjures up visions of high tea at 4:00. And tanning? Well, that's perfectly acceptable for leather. • But please, don't think our guests are unsocial. It's just that they don't travel to find themselves surrounded by the same people they left in the first place. For more information contact your Bermuda Department of Tourism representative.   *Not just teatime, tee-time*

BERMUDA
NOVEMBER THROUGH MARCH

Screens are physical and psychological barriers that advertisers must penetrate in order to convey their message. This trade advertisement from the Bermuda Department of Tourism (www.bermudatourism.com) must first grab the attention of all travel agents and then narrow its focus to those who serve a clientele of potential winter vacationers for an uncrowded paradise.

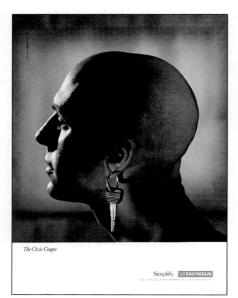

The Civic Coupe

Simplify. **HONDA**

Advertisers frequently capitalize on the consumers' concept of themselves to generate attention and interest in a particular product. The more the audience can identify with a particular lifestyle in an ad, the more likely the audience will find interest in the product. In this ad, Honda tries to appeal to consumers whose self-concept is one of youth, uniqueness, and independence.

to subjective emotional standards. These screens evaluate data based on *innate factors,* such as the consumer's personality and instinctive human needs, and *learned factors,* such as self-concept, interests, attitudes, beliefs, past experiences, and lifestyle. They help consumers summarize unwieldy or complex data. For example, perceptual screens help us accept or reject symbolic ideas, such as the commercial for Nestlé's Aero brand candy bar in which a woman basks in a bathtub of liquid chocolate. The commercial is targeted to women who seek a balance between work and self-indulgence.[18]

After extensive consumer research, Bally's Health & Tennis determined that the perfectly chiseled body, glorified by health club advertising of the 80s and exemplified by such icons as Cher, Victoria Principal, and Don Johnson, wasn't penetrating the psychological screens of its 4.5 million members. In the 90s, that premise no longer fit their **self-concept** (the image we have of who we are and who we want to be). In a major strategy shift, Bally's now relies on customers like Beth from Costa Mesa, California, who is seen rock climbing in a TV commercial while telling viewers, "I think I climb because I'm afraid of heights. . . . There is nothing better than being able to conquer that fear. That's why I work out at Bally's, so I can do more on the rocks." The tagline: "If you can get here [Bally's], you can get there [a mountaintop]."

As this example shows, advertisers face a major problem dealing with consumers' perceptual screens. As overcommunicated consumers, we unconsciously screen out or modify many of the sensations that bombard us, rejecting those that conflict with our experiences, needs, desires, attitudes, and beliefs.[19] We simply focus on some things and ignore others. This is called **selective perception.** Hence, Panasonic may run excellent ads in the daily newspaper, but they won't penetrate the psychological screens of consumers who don't need new camcorders. Later these people won't even remember seeing the ads.

Cognition

The third key element in perception is comprehending the stimulus, or **cognition.** Once we detect the stimulus and allow it through our perceptual screens, we can comprehend and accept it. Now perception has occurred, and the stimulus reaches the consumer's reality zone.

But each of us has his or her own reality. For example, you may consider the tacos advertised by Taco Bell to be "Mexican" food. That perception is your reality. But someone from Mexico might tell you that a fast-food taco bears little resemblance to an authentic Mexican taco. That person's reality, based on another perception, is considerably different. Advertisers thus seek commonly shared perceptions of reality as a basis for their advertising messages.

Mental Files

The mind is like a memory bank, and the stored memories in our minds are called the **mental** (or *perceptual*) **files.**

Just as stimuli bombard our senses, information crowds our mental files in today's highly communicative society. To cope with the complexity of stimuli like advertising, we rank products and other data in our files by importance, price, quality, features, or a host of other descriptors. Consumers can rarely hold more than seven brand names in any one file—more often only one or two. The remainder either get discarded to some other file category or rejected altogether.[20] How many brands of running shoes can you name, for example?

Because of our limited memory, we resist opening new mental files, and we avoid accepting new information inconsistent with what is already filed. The experience consumers receive from using a brand solidifies their perceptions of it. These fixed perceptions can rarely be changed through advertising alone.[21] But once a new perception does enter our mental files, the information alters the database on which our psychological screens feed.

Since perceptual screens are such a major challenge to advertisers, it's important to understand what's in the consumer's mental files and, if possible, modify them in favor of the advertiser's product. That brings us to the second process in consumer behavior: *learning and persuasion.*

Learning and Persuasion: How Consumers Process Information

Each time we file a new perception in our minds, it's a learning process. **Learning** is a relatively permanent change in thought process or behavior that occurs as a result of reinforced experience. Like perception, learning works off the mental files and at the same time contributes to them. Learning produces our habits and skills. It also contributes to the development of interests, attitudes, beliefs, preferences, prejudices, emotions, and standards of conduct—all of which affect our perceptual screens and our eventual purchase decisions.

Learning and persuasion are closely linked. **Persuasion** occurs when the change in belief, attitude, or behavioral intention is caused by promotion communication (such as advertising or personal selling).[22] Naturally, advertisers are very interested in persuasion and how it takes place.

The Elaboration Likelihood Model

Researchers have identified two ways promotion communication can persuade consumers: the *central* and *peripheral routes to persuasion.* Which route is used depends on the consumer's level of involvement with the product and the message. When the consumer's level of involvement is higher, the central route to persuasion is more likely. On the other hand, the peripheral route to persuasion is more likely when consumer involvement is low.[23]

We can see how this works by looking at the **Elaboration Likelihood Model** in Exhibit 4–3. In the **central route to persuasion,** consumers have a higher level of involvement with the product or the message, so they are motivated to pay attention to the central, product-related information, such as product attributes and benefits or demonstrations of positive functional or psychological consequences. Because of their high involvement, they tend to comprehend this information at deeper, more elaborate levels. This can lead to product beliefs, positive brand attitudes, and purchase intention.[24]

Exhibit 4–3
The Elaboration Likelihood Model.

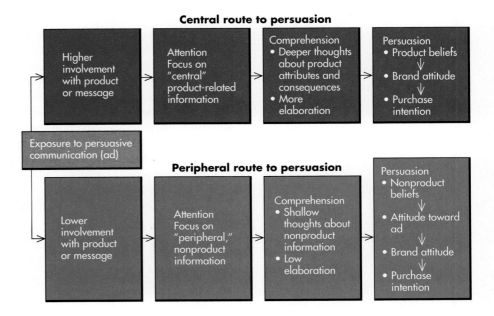

Must've been something he ate.

Next time uninvited guests show up for dinner, serve Thiodan Insecticide from FMC. Nothing controls early to mid-season insects more effectively. Not Guthion, Bolstar or any other organophosphate. Ask your dealer for information. Or give us a call at 1-800-468-0441. Seconds anyone? Hello? Anyone?

Opposite to central persuasion is the peripheral route. Peripherally processed ads, like this humorous one from FMC (www.FMC.com), tend to be "attention-getters" because they aim to create a lasting memory of a brand even though the consumer may have only low involvement with the product at the time the ad runs. These ads hope to create a positive attitude so that consumers will remember the brand once they are in the market to purchase.

Suppose you are in the market for a significant purchase, say a new camera or a computer. Since the purchase is relatively expensive, your level of involvement is higher. Perhaps you ask for advice from some friends or family members. You may shop different stores to compare models and prices. And you probably read ads for these products thoroughly to understand the variety of product features and benefits. That's central processing. And in that situation, a well-written, informative ad can be very persuasive.

The **peripheral route to persuasion** is very different. People who are not in the market for a product typically have low involvement with the product message. They have little or no reason to pay attention to it or to comprehend the central information of the ad. As a result, direct persuasion is also low, and consumers form few if any brand beliefs, attitudes, or purchase intentions. However, these consumers might attend to some peripheral aspects—say, the pictures in an ad or the actors in a commercial—for their entertainment value. And whatever they feel or think about these peripheral, nonproduct aspects might integrate into a positive attitude toward the ad. At some later date, if a purchase occasion does arise and the consumer needs to make some brand evaluation, these ad-related meanings could be activated to form some brand attitude or purchase intention.

Since very few people are actually in the market at any given time, most mass media advertising probably receives peripheral processing. We all know that most of the ads we see have little relevance to our immediate goals or needs, so we are not motivated to pay attention to them. Our involvement is very low. That's why we also have very little recall of ads we saw yesterday. In cases where there is little product differentiation, advertisers may actually *want* us to engage in peripheral processing. Their ads focus more on image or entertainment than product features. This is typical of advertising for many everyday low-involvement purchases, such as soap, cereal, toothpaste, and chewing gum.

But when a product has a distinct advantage, the advertiser's goal should be to encourage central route processing by increasing consumers' involvement with the message. This is where we see a lot of comparative advertising.[25]

One key to learning and persuasion is repetition. Just as a student prepares for an exam by repeating key information to memorize it, an advertiser must repeat key information to prospective and current customers so they remember the product's name and its benefits. Repeat messages penetrate customers' perceptual screens by rekindling memories of information from prior ads. Quebec-based Cossette Communications-Marketing used pairs of billboards for the Provigo grocery store chain. They featured similar strong visual elements and were positioned to be seen in succession. The repetition proved highly successful, producing $100 million in sales in just six months.

Learning Produces Attitudes and Interest

An **attitude** is our acquired mental position regarding some idea or object. It is the positive or negative evaluations, feelings, or action tendencies that we learn and cling to. To advertisers, gaining positive consumer attitudes is critical to success. Attitudes must be either capitalized on or changed. New ads for Grey Poupon mustard, for example, suggest readers "Poupon the potato salad" and "class up the

Brand interest is one of the most important components of marketing for familiar, frequently purchased products. Creatives strive to gain additional awareness and enhance interest in the brand, often through enjoyable and entertaining advertisements like this one for Edy's (www.edys.com).

(Open on close-up of a baby, pacifier in mouth, crawling across the floor.)
SFX: Baby babbling. Padding of hands and feet as baby crawls on floor.
MOM VO: That's my big boy.

(Mom is looking down with outstretched arms, urging baby on.)
MOM: Good! There you go! C'mon.
(Mom turns and disappears into kitchen.)
MOM: Mommy's gonna put you in your high chair . . .

(Cut to POV of baby. Mom is beckoning. Mom picks up scoop in front of a package of Edy's Cookie Dough Ice Cream.)
MOM VO: . . . and fix you some Edy's Cookie Dough ice cream.

(Baby stops and spits out pacifier with a grin.)
SFX: Pacifier being spit out.
(The baby suddenly stands up on two feet and dances to the music across the room and into the kitchen.

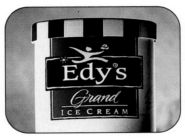

SFX: Music and baby giggles.
(Edy's package shot.)
(Double churn shot.)
(Cookie Dough ice cream shot.)

ANNCR VO: Edy's Cookie Dough. Double churned with real cookie dough. What could be better?
(Logo shot.)

Dreyer's Grand Ice Cream, Inc. is marketed and distributed as Edy's Grand Ice Cream in states east of the Rocky Mountains.

cold cuts." The campaign is aimed at changing the attitude of consumers who view Poupon as strictly a premium brand and reserve it for special occasions.[26]

For mature brands in categories with familiar, frequently purchased products, *brand interest* is even more critical for motivating action. **Brand interest** is an individual's openness or curiosity about a brand.[27] Enjoyable, entertaining advertising can enhance interest in the brand and reduce the variety-seeking tendencies of consumers who become bored with using the same old product.[28]

Learning Leads to Habits and Brand Loyalty

Attitude is the mental side and *habit* the behavioral side of the same coin. **Habit**— the acquired behavior pattern that becomes nearly or completely involuntary—is the natural extension of learning. We really are creatures of habit.

Most consumer behavior is habitual for three reasons: it's safe, simple, and essential. First, regardless of how we learned to make our purchase decision (through either central or peripheral route processing), if we discover a quality product, brand, or service, we feel *safe* repurchasing it through habit.

Second, habit is *simple*. To consider alternatives we must evaluate, compare, and then decide. This is difficult, time-consuming, and risky.

Finally, because habit is both safe and easy, we rely on it for daily living. Imagine rethinking every purchase decision you make. It would be virtually impossible, not to mention impractical. So it's really *essential* to use habit in our lives.

The major objective of all brand marketers is to produce *brand loyalty,* a direct result of the habit of repurchasing and the reinforcement of continuous advertising. **Brand loyalty** is the consumer's conscious or unconscious decision, expressed through intention or behavior, to repurchase a brand continually.[29] It occurs because the consumer *perceives* that the brand offers the right product features, image, quality, or relationship at the right price.

In the quest for brand loyalty, advertisers have three aims related to habits:

1. *Breaking habits.* Get consumers to unlearn an existing purchase habit and try something new. Advertisers frequently offer incentives to lure customers away from old brands or stores. Or they may use comparative advertising to demonstrate their product's superiority.

2. *Acquiring habits.* Teach consumers to repurchase their brand or repatronize their establishment. To get you started, Columbia House advertises free CDs when you sign up, tied to a contract to purchase more later on.

3. *Reinforcing habits.* Remind current customers of the value of their original purchase and encourage them to continue purchasing. Many magazines, for example, offer special renewal rates to their regular subscribers.

Developing brand loyalty is much more difficult today due to consumers' increased sophistication and to the legions of habit-breaking, *demarketing* activities of competitive advertisers.[30] Only recently have advertisers come to realize that their years of habit-breaking activities have undermined their own *habit-building* objectives. In the quest for instant results, they shifted much of their advertising budgets to sales promotions (deals, coupons, price cuts). But advertising, unlike sales promotion, is an integral part of what makes a brand salable. It's advertising that reinforces brand loyalty and maintains market share.[31] We revisit this topic in our discussion of sales promotion in Chapter 9.

Learning Defines Needs and Wants

The learning process is both immediate and long term. The moment we file a perception, some learning takes place. When we see a succulent food ad, we may suddenly feel hungry; we *need* food. As we collate the information in our mental files, comparing new perceptions with old ones, further learning takes place. The need may become a *want.* This leads to the next personal process, motivation.

The Consumer Motivation Process

Motivation refers to the underlying forces (or motives) that contribute to our purchasing actions. These motives stem from the conscious or unconscious goal of satisfying our needs and wants. **Needs** are the basic, often instinctive, human forces that motivate us to do something. **Wants** are "needs" that we learn during our lifetime.[32]

Motivation cannot be observed directly. When we see people eat, we assume they are hungry, but we may be wrong. People eat for a variety of reasons besides hunger: they want to be sociable, it's time to eat, or maybe they're bored.

People are usually motivated by the benefit of satisfying some combination of needs, which may be conscious or unconscious, functional or psychological. *Motivation research* offers some insights into the underlying reasons for unexpected consumer behavior. The reasons (*motives*) some people stop shopping at Lucky Supermarket and switch to Vons may be that the Vons market is closer to home, it has a wider selection of fresh produce, and (most likely) they see other people like themselves shopping at Vons. Any or all of these factors might make a shopper switch even if prices are lower at Lucky.

Exhibit 4-4

The hierarchy of needs suggests that people meet their needs according to priorities. Physiological and safety needs carry the greatest priority.

In advertising, the message must match the need of the market or the ad will fail.

Advertisers use marketing research to understand the need levels of their markets and use this information in determining the marketing mix.

Need	Product	Promotional appeal
Self-actualization	Golf clubs	"Time is to enjoy"
Esteem	Luxury car	"Be in control of the road"
Social	Pendant	"Show her you care"
Safety	Tires	"Bounces off hazards"
Physiological	Breakfast cereal	"The natural energy source"

To better understand what motivates people, Abraham Maslow developed the classic model shown in Exhibit 4-4 called the **hierarchy of needs.** Maslow maintained that the lower, physiological and safety needs dominate human behavior and must be satisfied before the higher, socially acquired needs (or wants) become meaningful. The highest need, self-actualization, is the culmination of fulfilling all the lower needs and reaching to discover the true self.

The promise of satisfying a certain level of need is the basic promotional appeal for many ads. In such affluent societies as the United States, Canada, Western Europe, and Japan, most individuals take for granted the satisfaction of their physiological needs. So advertising campaigns often portray the fulfillment of social, esteem, and self-actualization needs, and many offer the reward of satisfaction through personal achievement (Apple: "The power to be your best.").

We all have needs and wants, but we are frequently unaware of them. Before the advent of the desktop computer, people were completely unaware of any need for it. But the moment a consumer consciously recognizes a product-related want or need, a dynamic process begins. The consumer first evaluates the need and either accepts it as worthy of action or rejects it. Acceptance converts satisfaction of the need into a goal, which creates the dedication (the *motivation*) to

Maslow's hierarchy of needs explains the levels of physical and psychological needs that humans must fulfill. Mercedes-Benz (www.mercedes.com) hints at several levels of needs in its ad touting the car's "ultimate" comfort.

Sends chills down your orthopedically supported spine.

The E320. 10-way adjustable leather seats with lumbar support. 217 horses. Double-wishbone front suspension. Stabilizer bars. Traction control. 10-hole alloy wheels. Xenon headlamps. The hair on your neck will stand straight up. Mercedes-Benz

Exhibit 4–5

The eight fundamental purchase and usage motives.

Negatively originated (informational) motives	Positively originated (transformational) motives
1. Problem removal	6. Sensory gratification
2. Problem avoidance	7. Intellectual stimulation or mastery
3. Incomplete satisfaction	8. Social approval
4. Mixed approach–avoidance	
5. Normal depletion	

reach a particular result. In contrast, rejection removes the necessity for action and thereby eliminates the goal and the motivation to buy.

Modern researchers translated Maslow's theory about needs and motives into more strategic concepts for use by marketers and advertisers. Rossiter and Percy, for example, identify eight fundamental purchase and usage motives (see Exhibit 4–5). They refer to the first five as *negatively originated (informational) motives* and the last three as *positively originated (transformational) motives.*[33]

Negatively Originated (Informational) Motives

The most common energizers of consumer behavior are the **negatively originated motives,** such as problem removal or problem avoidance. Whenever we run out of something, for instance, we experience a negative mental state. To relieve those feelings, we actively seek a new or replacement product. Thus, we are temporarily motivated until the time we make the purchase. Then, if the purchase is satisfactory, the drive or motivation is reduced.

These are also called **informational motives** because the consumer actively seeks information to reduce the mental state. In fact, Rossiter and Percy point out, these could also be called "relief" motives because they work by relieving the negative state.

Positively Originated (Transformational) Motives

From time to time, we all want to indulge ourselves by buying some brand or product that promises some benefit or reward. With the **positively originated motives,** a positive bonus is promised rather than the removal or reduction of some negative situation. The goal is to use positive reinforcement to increase the consumer's motivation and to energize the consumer's investigation or search for the new product.

The three positively originated motives—sensory gratification, intellectual stimulation, and social approval—are also called **transformational motives** because the consumer expects to be transformed in a sensory, intellectual, or social sense.

Some critics believe China is especially vulnerable to exploitation. A couple living in a cramped Beijing apartment may have a $270 refrigerator, $700 foreign-made color TV, a telephone that came with a $600 installation charge, $600 Panasonic VCR, a $1,200 Toshiba air conditioner, and a $1,200 piano—all purchased on a salary of $300 a month. In Mexico, companies pitch credit cards to people earning as little as $650 a month. The National Association of Credit Card Holders estimates 5 million Mexicans carry credit cards, but a million of them can't pay their bills.

Critics say that companies act irresponsibly when they target these groups for marketing and advertising activities, because the average consumer can't afford the products being advertised.

However, researchers have investigated how advertising messages influence people to act. One finding, known as the third-person effect, holds that people generally believe others are more influenced by the media than they are. Perhaps the critics should consider this. They can resist advertising appeals, but they seem to believe the average consumer lacks their sophistication. So where do you draw the line between what is ethical (marketing) and what is not (exploitation)?

Questions

1. Do you think playing on people's desire for material possessions has a place in advertising? When does this become exploitation?

2. Is it the advertiser's responsibility to determine whether prospective customers can afford a product or service? Why or why not?

3. Do you think the third-person effect applies to consumers in the developing countries? If so, how can marketers avoid exploiting them?

Sources: Rachel Rosenthal, "Program Takes Sponsors to School," *Advertising Age,* September 5, 1994, p. 30; Ira Teinowitz and Steven W. Colford, "RJR, B&W Hit Anti-Smoking Blaze with Ads," *Advertising Age,* May 30, 1994, p. 8; Leah Rickard, "No Brood of New Ads for Baby Formula," *Advertising Age,* April 18, 1994, p. 35; Kathleen Barnes, "Changing Demographics: Middle Class," *Advertising Age International,* October 17, 1994, pp. I-14–16; and Esther Thorson and James Coyle, "The Third-Person Effect in Three Genres of Commercials: Product and Greening Ads and Public Service Announcements," paper presented to the annual conference of the American Academy of Advertising, April 8–11, 1994.

They could also be called "reward" motives because the transformation is a rewarding state.[34]

For some consumers, the purchase of a particular product (say, a new suit) might represent a negatively originated motive (they don't really want to spend the money on it, but they have to have it for work). But for other consumers, it might be positively originated (they love to shop for new clothes). This suggests two distinct target markets that advertisers must understand and that may call for completely different advertising strategies.

Before creating messages, advertisers must carefully consider the goals that lead to consumer motivations. Denny's Restaurants would make a costly mistake if its ads portrayed the reward of a romantic interlude if the real motive of most Denny's customers is simply to satisfy their need to reduce hunger with a filling, low-priced meal.

Negative motivation is a powerful tool to affect human behavior. This ad by St. Patrick's Church in England evokes a sense of religious or civil responsibility to help renovate the religious sanctuary and historical landmark. The implication in the ad is that one can eliminate negative feelings of responsibility or guilt by donating to the church's repair.

VISUAL: Inside St. Patrick's Church, we see a statue of the Virgin Mary. A tear seems to fall from the statue's eye. We follow this tear, and other droplets that seem to come from the statue's eye, down the length of its body until they drip from the statue's foot and into a bucket underneath.

As we cut to the head of the statue, we see drips of water falling onto the head and over the face. We follow the drips up and see that the water is coming from a hole in the ceiling above the statue.

Cut to exterior shot of the St. Patrick's Church sign. It's raining heavily.
SUPER: Donations needed for urgent repairs.

FOR THE RICH
THERE'S THERAPY.
FOR THE REST OF US,
THERE'S BASS.

Positive motivation promises a bonus to the consumer, rather than addressing problem avoidance issues found in negative motivation ads. This ad for Shimano (www.shimano.com) offers sensory gratification by recalling idyllic days of fishing in the great outdoors.

The issues of high-involvement and low-involvement products and informational and transformational motives are so important that we will revisit them in Chapter 7 when we discuss the planning of marketing and advertising strategies.

Interpersonal Influences
on Consumer Behavior

For advertisers, it's not enough just to know the personal processes of perception, learning and persuasion, and motivation. Important **interpersonal influences** affect—sometimes even dominate—these processes. They also serve as guidelines for consumer behavior. These influences can best be categorized as the *family,* the *society,* and the *cultural environment* of the consumer.

Family Influence

From an early age, family communication affects our socialization as consumers—our attitudes toward many products and our purchasing habits. This influence is usually strong and long-lasting. A child who learns that the "right" headache relief is Bayer aspirin and the "right" name for appliances is General Electric has a well-developed adult purchasing behavior.

Research, however, indicates that family influence is diminishing in the United States as working parents take a less active role in raising their children, and youngsters look outside the family for social values.[35] As this happens, the influence of the social and cultural environments intensifies.

Society's Influence

The community we live in exerts a strong influence on all of us. When we affiliate with a particular societal division or identify with some reference group or value the ideas of certain opinion leaders, it affects our views on life, our perceptual screens, and eventually the products we buy.

Societal Divisions: The Group We Belong to

Sociologists traditionally divided societies into **social classes:** upper, upper-middle, lower-middle, and so on. They believed that people in the same social class tended toward similar attitudes, status symbols, and spending patterns.

But today this doesn't apply to most developed countries. U.S. society, especially, is extremely fluid and mobile—physically, socially, and economically. Americans believe strongly in getting ahead, being better than your peers, and winning greater admiration and self-esteem. As the famous Army campaign illustrates, advertisers capitalize on this desire to "be all you can be."

Because of this mobility, dramatic increases in immigration, and the high divorce rate, social-class boundaries have become quite muddled. Single parents, stockbrokers, immigrant shopkeepers, retired blue-collar workers, and bankers all see themselves as part of the great middle class. So "middle class" doesn't mean anything anymore. From the advertiser's point of view, social class seldom represents a functional or operational set of values.

To deal with these often bewildering changes, marketers seek new ways to classify societal divisions and new strategies for advertising to them. We discuss some of these in Chapter 5. Exhibit 4–6 outlines some of the classifications marketers use to describe society today: for example, Midlife Success, Movers and Shakers, Stars

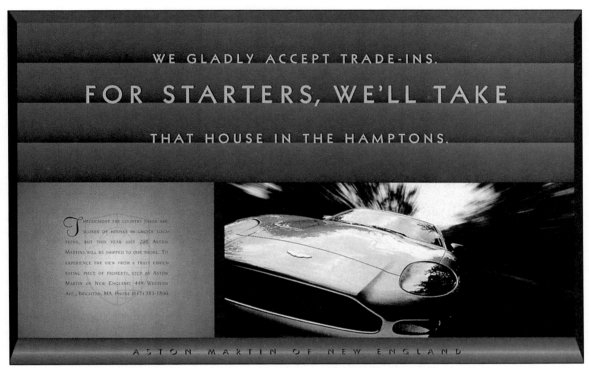

WE GLADLY ACCEPT TRADE-INS.

FOR STARTERS, WE'LL TAKE

THAT HOUSE IN THE HAMPTONS.

Throughout the country there are scores of houses in choice locations, but this year just 200 Aston Martins will be shipped to our shore. To experience the view from a truly exhilarating piece of property, stop by Aston Martin of New England, 449 Western Ave., Brighton, MA. Phone (617) 783-1800.

ASTON MARTIN OF NEW ENGLAND

Sometimes social class can affect how we see ourselves and how we fit into the larger social fabric. Although class differences are not as pronounced in the United States as in many parts of the world, marketers of high-end purchases often capitalize on class distinction for product positioning purposes. Aston Martin (www.astonmartin.com) makes no bones about its aristocratic airs and targets its advertising directly at such high-end purchasers for whom social class does play an important role.

Exhibit 4–6

Contemporary social classes. The groups outlined in this exhibit are just 10 of 50 Microvision lifestyle segments defined by National Decision Systems. This division of Equifax wants to know what financial services various consumers are likely to need.

Upper Crust
Metropolitan families, very high income and education, manager/professionals; very high installment activity

Midlife Success
Families, very high education, managers/professionals, technical/sales, high income; super-high installment activity

Movers and Shakers
Singles, couples, students, and recent graduates, high education and income, managers/professionals, technical/sales; average credit activity, medium-high installment activity

Successful Singles
Young, single renters, older housing, ethnic mix, high education, medium income, managers/professionals; very high bankcard accounts, very high installment activity, very low retail activity

Stars and Stripes
Young, large school-age families, medium income and education, military, precision/craft; average credit activity

Social Security
Mature/seniors, metro fringe, singles and couples, medium income and education, mixed jobs; very low credit activity

Middle of the Road
School-age families, mixed education, medium income, mixed jobs; very high revolving activity, very high bankcard accounts

Trying Metro Times
Young, seniors, ethnic mix, low income, older housing, low education, renters, mixed jobs; low credit activity, medium-high retail activity

Low-Income Blues
Minorities, singles and families, older housing, low income and education, services, laborers; low credit activity, medium-high retail activity

University USA
Students, singles, dorms/group quarters, very low income, medium-high education, technical/sales; low credit activity, high percent new accounts

and Stripes, and University USA. People in the same group tend to have similar patterns of behavior and product usage.

Reference Groups: The People We Relate to

Most of us care how we appear to people whose opinions we value. We may even pattern our behavior after members of some groups we affiliate with. This is the significance of **reference groups**—people we try to emulate or whose approval concerns us. Reference groups can be personal (family, friends, co-workers) or impersonal (political parties, religious denominations, professional associations). A special reference group, our peers, exerts tremendous influence on what we believe and how we behave. They determine which brands are cool and which are not.[36] To win acceptance by our peers (fellow students, co-workers, colleagues), we may purchase a certain style or brand of clothing, choose a particular place to live, and acquire behavioral habits that will earn their approval.

Often an individual is influenced in opposite directions by two reference groups and must choose between them. For example, a college student might feel pressure from some friends to join a Greek house and from others to live independently off campus. In ads targeted to students, a local apartment complex might tap the appeal of reference groups by showing students splashing in the complex's pool.

Opinion Leaders: The People We Trust

An **opinion leader** is some person or organization whose beliefs or attitudes are respected by people who share an interest in some specific activity. All fields (sports, religion, fashion, politics) have opinion leaders. An opinion leader may be a knowledgeable friend or some expert we find credible. We reason, "If Picabo Street thinks Marker makes the best ski bindings, then it must be so. She knows more about the sport than I do." Thus the purchasing habits and testimonials of opinion leaders are important to advertisers.

When choosing an opinion leader as a spokesperson for a company or product, advertisers must understand the company's target market thoroughly. Even if executives in the company do not relate to the spokesperson, they must follow market tastes and interests. A spokesperson out of sync with the market undermines his or her credibility—and the company's. On the other hand, an internal person like Dave Thomas, the founder of Wendy's, might turn out to be a highly credible spokesperson without the risks associated with outside celebrities and athletes.[37]

The Influence of Culture and Subculture

Culture has a tenacious influence on consumers. **Culture** refers to the whole set of meanings, beliefs, attitudes, and ways of doing things that are shared by some homogeneous social group and typically handed down from generation to generation.[38] Americans love hot dogs, peanut butter, corn on the cob, and apple pie.

As the old saying goes, you must feed a cold and starve a fever, or at least that's what we say in the West. Every culture is characterized by unique idiosyncrasies that advertisers must be very aware of when addressing a particular audience. This ad from the Ai Sin Foot Reflexology Centre capitalizes on the frequent notion of Asian expertise in holistic therapies.

Canada, Russia, Germany—every country has its own favorite specialties. And advertisers find it much easier to work with these tastes than try to change them.

Global marketers are especially concerned with the purchase environment. Of all business functions, marketing activities are the most susceptible to cultural error.[39]

For example, while both demographic and psychographic traits figure importantly in U.S. consumer marketing, age and sex are better indicators of behavior and lifestyles in Japan, where income is largely proportional to seniority and sex roles tend to be standardized.[40] When creating ads for foreign consumption, marketers must consider many environmental factors: cultural trends, social norms, changing fads, market dynamics, product needs, and media channels.[41]

In countries where people earn little income, demand for expensive products is low. So the creative strategy of an automobile advertiser might be to target the small group of wealthy, upper-class consumers. In a country with a large middle class, the same advertiser might be better off mass-marketing the car and positioning it as a middle-class product.

The United States and Canada embrace many subcultures, some of them quite large. They may be based on race, national origin, religion, language, or geographic proximity. The advertiser must understand these subcultures, for differences among them may affect responses to both products and advertising messages.

The United States, in particular, is a great melting pot of minority subcultures. A **subculture** is a segment within a culture that shares a set of meanings, values, or activities that differ in certain respects from those of the overall culture.[42] According to the U.S. Census, 31 million African-Americans, 22 million Hispanics, and 7 million Asians live in the United States (plus an unknown number of undocumented foreign nationals). These three minority groups alone account for close to 25 percent of the American population.[43] Canada has two major subcultures, anglophones and francophones, based on language (English and French), plus a mosaic of many other cultures based on ethnic and national origin.

ESTARÁN ORGULLOSOS DE ESTAR AQUÍ.

El Army ofrece a los jóvenes la oportunidad de aprender a tener disciplina y confianza en sí mismos. Éstas son cualidades útiles para toda la vida.

Y NOSOTROS, DE MANDARLOS ALLÁ.

ARMY
SÉ TODO LO QUE PUEDES SER

Además, pueden obtener hasta $40,000 para la universidad si califican para el Montgomery GI Bill y el Army College Fund.

LLAME AL 1-800-USA-ARMY   www.goarmy.com

Increasingly, advertisers realize that English-speakers are not the only market in the United States. Other ethnic and linguistic cultures exist, and pose enormous markets for the culturally saavy. Here, the U.S. Army encourages the Spanish-speaking audience to "Sé Todo Lo Que Puedes Ser," or "Be All You Can Be."

Subcultures tend to transfer their beliefs and values from generation to generation. Racial, religious, and ethnic backgrounds affect consumers' preferences for styles of dress, food, beverages, transportation, personal care products, and household furnishings, to name a few. As we saw in Chapter 3, many ad agencies now specialize in minority markets as more advertisers realize that tailoring their appeals to minorities makes good business sense. Recognizing the rapid growth of the Hispanic population, for example, Procter & Gamble spends over $30 million per year to understand and tap this market. Other major Hispanic marketers include Philip Morris, Anheuser-Busch, and Coca-Cola.[44]

The social environments in countries from Italy to Indonesia, from Sweden to Surinam are also based on language, culture, literacy rate, religion, and lifestyle. Advertisers who market products globally can't ignore these distinctions.

In North America, advertising encourages us to keep our mouths clean, our breath fresh, and our teeth scrubbed. But people in some southern European countries consider it vain and improper to overindulge in toiletries. Consumers in the Netherlands and the United Kingdom use three times as much toothpaste as those in Spain and Greece. To communicate effectively with Spanish consumers, who view toothpaste as a cosmetic product, advertisers use chic creative executions rather than dry, therapeutic pitches.[45]

Clearly, many interpersonal factors influence consumers. They have an important effect on our mental files, screens, and subsequent purchase decisions. Awareness of these interpersonal influences helps marketers, both domestic and international, create the strategies on which much advertising is based.

Nonpersonal Influences on Consumer Behavior

Numerous nonpersonal influences may affect a consumer's final purchase decision. The most important **nonpersonal influences**—*time, place,* and *environment*—are typically beyond the consumer's control, but not necessarily beyond the advertiser's.

Time

The old saw "timing is everything" certainly applies to marketing and advertising. A special weekend sale may provide just the added incentive to penetrate customers' perceptual screens and bring them into a store. But running an ad for that sale on Sunday evening would be a waste of advertising dollars.

Likewise, the consumer's particular need may be a function of time. Forecasts of an unusually wet winter from the El Niño phenomenon in 1998 motivated special ads from a variety of national advertisers as well as many small retailers of linens, boots, snow shovels, and rock salt. Consumers don't need snow tires and rock salt in the summer (although some off-season promotions do work). But if we unexpectedly get a flat on the highway, tire ads suddenly become timely. As we will see in our chapters on media, companies must plan all their marketing activities (including advertising) with the consumer's clock in mind.

Place

Once consumers decide to purchase a certain product, they will still hesitate if they don't know where to buy it or if it isn't available in a convenient or preferred location. Similarly, if consumers believe a particular brand is a specialty good but it suddenly appears everywhere, their perception of the product's "specialness" may diminish. Thus, marketers carefully weigh consumer demand when planning distribution strategy, and they devote much advertising to communicating the convenience of location. Distribution is an important element of the marketing mix and will be discussed further in Chapter 5.

Environment

Many **environments**—ecological, social, political, technical, economic, household, and point-of-sale location, to mention a few—can affect the purchase decision. For example, during a recession, advertisers can't expect to penetrate the perceptual screens of consumers who don't have enough money to buy. And no matter how good the advertising or how low the price, memberships in the National Rifle Association aren't likely to be a hot item with members of the Audubon Society. On the other hand, an enticing display next to the cash register can improve sales of low-cost impulse items. Advertisers must consider the influence of the purchase environment on the consumer's decision processes.

Likewise, the state of technological development affects economic and social conditions—and the prospects for advertisers of certain products and services. For example, countries that don't manufacture computers might be poor markets for components such as disk drives and microprocessors. On the other hand, advertisers of low-priced, imported computers might do very well.

Finally, some governments exert far greater control over their citizens and businesses than the U.S. government does. For example, until recently, virtually no American-made products could be sold in many Eastern bloc countries or China. They simply weren't allowed. Political control often extends to which products companies may advertise and sell, which media they use, and what their ads say.

The Purchase Decision and Postpurchase Evaluation

Now that we understand the elements in the consumer purchase decision process, let's examine how it might work in a typical situation. A hypothetical consumer named Chris is thinking about buying a CD player. To help follow this process and see the interrelationship of the many behavioral factors we've discussed, see the complete model of the consumer decision-making process shown in RL 4–1 in the Reference Library.

Ad Lab 4-B

Applying Consumer Behavior Principles to Ad Making

When Polaroid needed to capture the attention of photography enthusiasts it turned to the creatives at Leonard/Monahan to design a series of ads that would exhibit the advantages of the instantaneous film over other photo products. (See the ad in the margin below.)

The first challenge for the creative design team was to break through the consumers' resistance, the subtle barrier that begins with the perceptual screens. Second, the team had to present the picture as being worth a thousand words while avoiding clichés.

The advertisement's headline—"The victim refuses to speak. The pictures refuse to keep quiet."—commands your attention and expresses the big idea with urgency. The ad's black-and-white visual of a battery victim suggests the subject's grave nature while allowing the color Polaroids to jump out, emoting a raw portrayal of reality. The ad becomes credible by demonstrating the benefits of Polaroids and how they can be successfully used (to investigate, prosecute, and win). The tag line, "Instant evidence," sums up the product's features and helps the prospective consumer recall the product's benefits. These factors show clearly the product's benefits to those who may be critical of their purchase decision.

Laboratory Application

Choose an ad from a popular magazine and explain how the visuals, the words, and the overall design of the ad accomplish the following tasks. Provide specific details to support your answers.

1. Penetrate consumer perceptual screens.
2. Stimulate consumer learning.
3. Use the consumer's existing perceptual files.
4. Stimulate consumer wants and needs to achieve motivation.

Chris is enrolled at a state university and financed in part by a small scholarship. He also has a part-time job but must act conservatively when it comes to spending money because tuition, books, and expenses are costly.

One day, thumbing through a consumer electronics magazine, Chris sees an exciting ad for a new top-of-the line CD player. A beautiful photograph shows the product's modern yet understated design. The ad copy highlights the CD player's special features. They exude high-tech class—it's just the right style. The ad's signature: "Exclusively at Tech 2000." (See Ad Lab 4-B: "Applying Consumer Behavior Principles to Ad Making.")

In a split second Chris leaps from perception to motivation. Got to have it! He is highly involved and he wants this personal reward for all his hard work.

The next day Chris visits Tech 2000. While looking for the advertised CD player, he encounters a variety of alternative styles and models by well-known manufacturers.

The ad has already done its work; the purchase decision process is well under way. At the point of making a purchase decision, though, consumers typically search, consider, and compare alternative brands.

Consumers evaluate selection alternatives (called the **evoked set**). To do this, they establish **evaluative criteria,** the standards they use to judge the features and benefits of alternative products. Not all brands make it to the evoked set. In fact, based on their mental files, most consumers usually consider only four or five brands—which presents a real challenge to advertisers. If none of the alternatives meets the evaluative criteria, the consumer may reject the purchase entirely or postpone the decision.

Chris finally finds the advertised CD player. But it looks smaller on the shelf than it did in the ad. Two other good players are also displayed; both are attractive, both expensive. While trying out the sound systems, Chris considers other unique qualities of style and design. "This one may be a little too bulky." "This one would fit on my desk." "This one would be okay for me, but I'm not sure about using it for parties."

Using central route processing, Chris compares the CD players, considering their style, technology, possible advantages, and price (the models are all within $35 of each other). The advertised player really is the best buy and would be the most satisfying. None of Chris's friends has one like it. The purchase decision is complete when Chris writes out a check for the CD player.

On the way home, the **postpurchase evaluation** *begins. Chris suddenly envisions some friends' possible negative reactions to the purchase. Maybe it wasn't wise to spend so much money on a luxury CD player. Chris starts to worry—and to plan.*

"It's really a great player. It's excellent quality and worth the money. I'll get a lot of use out of it."

A key feature of the postpurchase evaluation is *cognitive dissonance*. The **theory of cognitive dissonance** (also called **postpurchase dissonance**) holds that people strive to justify their behavior by reducing the dissonance, or inconsistency, between their cognitions (their perceptions or beliefs) and reality.[46] In fact, research shows that, to combat dissonance, consumers are more likely to read ads for brands they've already purchased than for new products or competing brands.[47]

Back at the dorm, Chris puts the magazine on the desk with a Post-it note marking the ad (for his roommate to discover). Then he phones a friend and describes the purchase, emphasizing its technology, its great design, the enjoyment it will bring, and how expensive it was.

During the postpurchase period, the consumer may enjoy the satisfaction of the purchase and thereby receive reinforcement for the decision. Or the purchase may turn out to be unsatisfactory for some reason. In either case, feedback from the postpurchase evaluation updates the consumer's mental files, affecting perceptions of the brand and similar purchase decisions in the future.

This story is common for a high-involvement purchase decision. Of course, if Chris's decision had merely involved the purchase of a pack of gum, the process would have been significantly simpler.

Chris may typify a particular group of consumers, and that is important to marketers. Marketers are interested in defining target markets and developing effective marketing strategies for groups of consumers who share similar characteristics, needs, motives, and buying habits. These are the subjects of market segmentation and the marketing mix, the focus of Chapter 5.

Chapter **Summary**

Marketing is the process companies use to make a profit by satisfying their customers' needs for products. Marketing focuses on the special relationship between a customer's needs and a product's functional or psychic utility. The essence of marketing is the perceived equal-value exchange. Need satisfaction is the customer's goal and should be the marketer's goal as well.

Advertising is concerned with the promotion aspect of the marketing process. It is one of several tools marketers use to inform, persuade, and remind groups of customers (markets) about the need-satisfying value of their products and services. Advertising's effectiveness depends on the communication skill of the advertising person. It also depends on the extent to which firms correctly implement other marketing activities, such as market research, pricing, and distribution.

There are three categories of participants in the marketing process: customers, markets, and marketers. To reach customers and markets, advertisers must effectively blend data from the behavioral sciences with the communicating arts. Advertisers study the behavioral characteristics of large groups of people to create advertising aimed at those groups.

Successful advertising people understand the complexity of consumer behavior, which is governed by three personal processes: perception, learning and persuasion, and motivation. These processes determine how consumers see the world around them, how they learn information and habits, and how they actualize their personal needs and motives. Two sets of influences also affect consumer behavior: interpersonal influences (the consumer's family, society, and culture) and nonpersonal influences (time, place, and environment). These factors combine to determine how the consumer behaves, and their influence differs considerably from one country to another. Advertisers evaluate the effect of these factors on groups of consumers to determine how best to create their messages.

Once customers or prospects are motivated to satisfy their needs and wants, the purchase process begins. Based on certain standards they have established in their own minds, they evaluate various alternative products (the evoked set). If none of the alternatives meets their evaluative criteria, they may reject or postpone the purchase. If they do buy, they may experience cognitive dissonance in the form of postpurchase doubt and concern. An important role of advertising is to help people cope with dissonance by reinforcing the wisdom of their purchase decision. The result of the postpurchase evaluation will greatly affect the customer's attitude toward future purchases.

Important **Terms**

attitude, *134*

brand interest, *135*

brand loyalty, *136*

business markets, *127*

centers of influence, *127*

central route to persuasion, *133*

cogntion, *132*

consumer behavior, *129*

consumer decision-making process, *129*

consumer markets, *127*

culture, *142*

current customers, *127*

Review **Questions**

1. What is marketing, and what is advertising's role in the marketing process?

2. How does product utility relate to advertising?

3. Why is the perceived equal-value exchange an important advertising issue?

4. What's the difference between a customer and a market? What are the different types of markets?

5. What does the term *consumer behavior* refer to, and why is it important to advertisers?

6. Which consumer behavior process presents the greatest challenge to advertisers?

7. What is the difference between the central route and the peripheral route to persuasion?

8. What is the significance of negatively originated motives and positively originated motives to advertisers?

9. What are some of the environmental influences on consumer behavior in international markets?

10. How does the theory of cognitive dissonance relate to advertising?

Exploring the **Internet**

The Internet exercises for Chapter 4 address the two main areas covered in the chapter: marketing (Exercise 1) and consumer behavior (Exercise 2).

1. Marketing

   Visit the following Web sites and apply what you learned from this chapter by identifying the marketer, product utility, customer(s), and type of market(s) for each:

   - www.att.com
   - www.caterpillar.com
   - www.delta-air.com
   - www.dhl.com
   - www.fox.com
   - www.gm.com
   - www.johnsonandjohnson.com
   - www.kodak.com
   - www.marriott.com
   - www.nba.com
   - www.pg.com
   - www.siemens.com
   - www.sony.com
   - www.transamerica.com
   - www.unisys.com
   - www.visa.com
   - www.wal-mart.com

2. Consumer Behavior

   Understanding consumer behavior is essential to the contemporary advertiser. Browse the Web sites listed below, keeping in mind what you learned about culture/subculture, social class, reference groups, family/household, and opinion leaders. Identify and describe the major social influences that enable each organization to be successful in reaching its consumers.

   - alt.Culture **www.altculture.com**
   - America Online **www.aol.com**
   - Beechnut **www.beechnut.com**
   - Ben & Jerry's **www.benjerry.com**
   - Cars & Culture **www.carsandculture.com**
   - Motorola **www.motorola.com**
   - Music Television (MTV) **www.mtv.com**
   - Rollerblade **www.rollerblade.com**
   - Sega **www.sega.com**
   - Tower Records **www.towerrecords.com**

   It may help to browse through "Social Influence: The Science of Persuasion & Compliance" (found at www.public.asu.edu/~kelton/) and read about persuasion and propaganda before surfing the above sites.

Chapter Five

Market Segmentation and the Marketing Mix: Determinants of Advertising Strategy

Objective To describe how marketers use behavioral characteristics to cluster prospective customers into market segments. Since no product or service pleases everybody, marketers need to select specific target markets that offer the greatest sales potential. Thus, they can fine tune their mix of product-related elements (the four Ps), including advertising, to match the needs or wants of the target market.

After studying this chapter, you will be able to:

- Identify the methods used to segment consumer and business markets.
- Explain the process and the importance of aggregation to marketing.
- Discuss the target marketing process.
- Describe the elements of the marketing mix and their roles.
- Explain the role and importance of branding.

The trip was the most daring of adventures: 17,000 miles and five months on a clipper ship from New York, around South America, then to a rowdy frontier town aflame with gold fever. Imagine the awe and the excitement of Mr. Strauss, a young German immigrant, when he stepped off the ship in San Francisco in 1853. • Strauss came to San Francisco at the invitation of his brother-in-law, David Stern. Seeing the city's gold rush economy, Stern sensed an opportunity for a thriving dry-goods business.

Strauss brought a variety of supplies for the business with him, including canvas for tents and Conestoga wagon covers. • By the time he reached San Francisco, though, Strauss had sold virtually all his merchandise to the other passengers—everything except the canvas. Before long, the inventive young entrepreneur came up with an idea for selling that as well. • "Should'a brought pants," the prospectors and gold miners told him. "Pants don't wear worth a hoot in the diggins!" • Strauss immediately took the heavy brown canvas to a tailor and created pants that he called "waist-high overalls." These were the world's first jeans, a term derived from the cotton trousers (called *genes* by the French) worn in ancient days by sailors from Genoa, Italy. • Word of the quality of "those pants of Levi's" spread quickly, and young Levi Strauss began turning out dozens of pairs. Exhausting his original supply of canvas, Levi switched to a sturdy serge fabric made in Nimes, France, called serge de Nimes (pronounced *sayrzjh da neem*). Later the name of the fabric was conveniently shortened to "denim." With the development of an indigo dye, the natural brown color turned to the now familiar

deep blue. • While Levi's new product achieved rapid acceptance, prospectors found that the weight of gold nuggets caused the pockets to rip. Ever alert for ways to improve quality, Strauss was quick to adopt—and patent—the idea of riveting the pocket corners for added strength. To this day, rivets remain one of the hallmarks of the stiff, shrink-to-fit, button-fly pants now known as Levi's 501 jeans. • Young Levi achieved success beyond his wildest dreams. His pants, now sold in over 70 countries worldwide, became the flagship product of a diversified global company. Today, almost 150 years later, Levi's worldwide sales exceed $5.5 billion. The family-owned business Levi left to his nephews is the largest apparel company in the world and a trailblazer in corporate social responsibility. Thanks to years of brilliant marketing and advertising on a global scale, virtually everybody in the world knows Mr. Strauss's first name.[1] •

The **Market Segmentation** Process

Today's competitive economy demands that companies research potential consumer groups and focus their strategies. Market segmentation enables companies to save money by creating campaigns that concentrate on the markets with the greatest potential. The Australian "Loose Fit" campaign for Levi's (www.levi.com) does just that, focusing on those customers who need or prefer a looser fitting denim trouser.

Recall from our discussion in Chapter 1 that marketing and advertising strategies evolved over time as more and more products entered the marketplace and competed for consumer dollars and approval. During the 1950s and 60s, the unique selling proposition held sway as marketers built new and different properties into their products to tout in their advertising. Then in the 60s and 70s, as me-too products glutted mass markets, the strategy of market segmentation came to the fore. This meant developing products and marketing mixes to meet the needs and wants of particular market segments. Over time, as major market segments became saturated and product life cycles grew shorter, marketers developed new approaches, such as positioning, marketing warfare, niche marketing, micro marketing, and now even one-to-one marketing. All of these are variations on basic market segmentation strategy, except that today segments are getting smaller. Thanks to modern technology, companies can satisfy the needs of smaller segments and still make a profit. It's important for advertising people to have a solid understanding of the principles of market segmentation. In the 21st century, the task of finding profitable market segments will become even more challenging.

Marketing and advertising people constantly scan the marketplace to see what various consumer groups need and want and how they might be better satisfied. The process of **market segmentation** is actually a two-step strategy of *identifying* groups of people (or organizations) with certain shared needs and characteristics within the broad markets for consumer or business products and *aggregating* (combining) these groups into larger market segments according to their mutual interest in the product's utility. This process gives a company a selection of market segments large enough to target and lays the foundation for developing the proper mix of marketing activities—including advertising.

Markets often consist of many segments. A company may differentiate products and marketing strategy for every segment, or concentrate its marketing activities on only one or a few segments. Either task is far from simple. Levi Strauss identified and targeted a single market segment and catered to it with specific products and services. The diverse markets Levi's serves today are really combinations of numerous smaller groups that share certain interests or product needs. Catering to all these needs on a global level requires a sophisticated marketing and communications system. In this chapter, we look first at how marketers identify and categorize *consumer markets* and second at the techniques they use to segment *business markets*. Then we discuss various strategic options companies use to match their products with markets and create profitable exchanges.

Segmenting the Consumer Market: Finding the Right Niche

The concept of *shared characteristics* is critical to market segmentation. Marketing and advertising people know that, based on their needs, wants, and mental files, consumers leave "footprints in the sand"—the telltale signs of where they live and work, what they buy, and how they spend their leisure time. By following these footprints, marketers can locate and define groups of consumers with similar needs and wants, create messages for them, and know how and where to send their messages. The goal is to find that particular niche, or space in the market, where the advertiser's product or service will fit.

Marketers group these characteristics into categories (*behavioristic, geographic, demographic,* and *psychographic*) to identify and segment consumer markets. (RL 5–1 in the Reference Library shows typical breakdowns of the variables.) The marketers' purpose is twofold: first, to identify people who are likely to be responsive; and second, to create rich descriptions of them in order to better understand them, create marketing mixes for them, and reach them with meaningful communications.

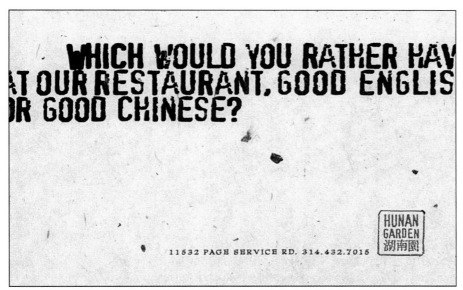

Behavioristic segmentation is one of the best ways to organize consumer markets. Purchase behavior variables, such as the benefits sought by the consumer, determine how the segmentations are made. In this ad, Hunan Garden targets Chinese food afficionados with a tongue-in-cheek promise that the Chinese food eaten is better than the English spoken.

While Guess (www.guess.com) is better known for its line of clothing, it uses its strong brand name to promote its home collection. For sole users this ad reinforces the brand and for repertoire users—those most likely to alternate between brands they believe to be equally superior—it enhances brand perception.

Behavioristic Segmentation

One of the best ways to segment markets is to group consumers by purchase behavior. This is called **behavioristic segmentation.** Behavioral segments are determined by many variables, but the most important are *user status, usage rate, purchase occasion,* and *benefits sought.* These categories tell us who our customers are now, when and why they buy, and how much they consume.

User-status variables   Many markets can be segmented by the **user status** of prospective customers. Stephan and Tannenholz identified six categories of consumers based on user status.

Sole users are the most brand loyal and require the least amount of advertising and promotion. *Semisole users* typically use brand A but have an alternate selection if it is not available or if the alternate is promoted with a discount. *Discount users* are the semisole users of competing brand B. They don't buy brand A at full price but perceive it well enough to buy it at a discount. *Aware nontriers* are category users but haven't bought into brand A's message. A different advertising message could help, but these people rarely offer much potential. *Trial/rejectors* bought brand A's advertising message, but didn't like the product. More advertising won't help; only a reformulation of brand A will bring them back. *Repertoire users* perceive two or more brands to have superior attributes and will buy at full price. They are the primary brand switchers and respond to persuasive advertising based on their fluctuating wants and desires. They should be the primary target for brand advertising.[2]

Usage-rate variables   It's usually easier to get a heavy user to increase usage than a light user. In **volume segmentation,** marketers measure **usage rates** to define consumers as light, medium, or heavy users of products (see Exhibit 5–1 on page 152). Often, 20 percent of the population consumes 80 percent of the product. Marketers want to define that 20 percent and aim their advertising at them. For example, one-third of all households purchase 83 percent of Levi's products—worldwide!

By finding common characteristics among heavy users of their products, marketers can define product differences and focus ad campaigns more effectively. For example, heavy users of bowling alleys tend to be working-class men between 25 and 50 who watch more than three and a half hours of television a day and prefer sports programs. So a bowling equipment company would probably want to advertise on TV sports programs.

Marketers of one product sometimes find that their customers are also heavy users of other products and can define target markets in terms of the usage rates of the other products. Research indicates that heavy users of home computers are also heavy users of foreign luxury cars, sports cars, backpacking equipment, binoculars, expensive bicycles, and literary magazines.[3] Similarly, of the 94 percent of teenage boys who use shampoo, 36 percent also use hair spray, 32 percent use conditioner, 31 percent use hair-styling products, and 19 percent use blow dryers.[4]

Exhibit 5–1
Usage rates vary for different products. For example, of all households, 64 percent never buy 35-millimeter film (nonusers), 12 percent account for nearly a third (31 percent) of sales (light users), and about a quarter of the households (24 percent) make two-thirds (69 percent) of the purchases (heavy users). Note the extreme difference between nonusers and heavy users of golf equipment.

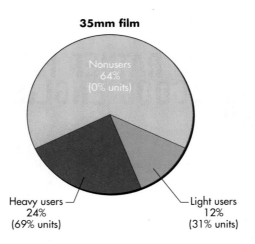

35mm film

Nonusers
64%
(0% units)

Heavy users
24%
(69% units)

Light users
12%
(31% units)

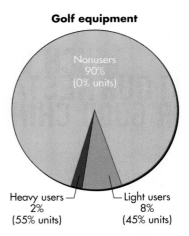

Golf equipment

Nonusers
90%
(0% units)

Heavy users
2%
(55% units)

Light users
8%
(45% units)

Purchase-occasion variables   Buyers can also be distinguished by when they buy or use a product or service—the **purchase occasion.** Air travelers, for example, may fly for business or vacation so one airline might promote business travel while another promotes tourism. The purchase occasion might be affected by frequency of need (regular or occasional), a fad (candy, computer games), or seasons (water skis, raincoats). The Japan Weather Association tracked buying patterns on 20,000 items and correlated them to the outside temperature. Not surprisingly, when the temperature goes up, people buy more sunshades, air conditioners, watermelons, and swimwear. When there's a chill in the air, sales of suits, sweaters, and heaters take off.[5] A marketer who discovers common purchase occasions for a group has a potential target segment and can better determine when to run specials and how to promote certain product categories.

Benefits-sought variables   Consumers seek **benefits** in the products they buy: high quality, low price, status, sex appeal, good taste. For example, people buy Levi's jeans for work, for play, or to make a fashion statement. Often, consumers are motivated by symbolism—what the product means to them, to associates, or to some social reference group.[6] Marketers may segment consumers based on the benefits being sought. **Benefit segmentation** is the prime objective of many consumer attitude studies and the basis for many successful ad campaigns.

Some product categories are characterized by substantial brand switching from one purchase occasion to the next. Researchers have determined that switching occurs in response to different "need states" consumers experience from one occasion to another. Thus a soft drink company competes not just for *drinkers* (users) but for *drinks* (occasions) based on the benefits the consumer is seeking at that moment. By measuring the importance of occasion-based motives, an advertiser can determine if a campaign needs to reposition the product.[7]

Seasonal usage is a common way to distinguish users. In fact, the purchase occasion provides insight into the most opportune sales periods. For this reason, Columbia Sportswear Company (http://columbia.com) runs its ski parka ads in fall and winter—just before and during the peak of the snow sport season.

Changing demographics in many international markets open up new opportunities for advertisers. This Audi ad, printed in both English and Chinese by Volkswagen Asia-Pacific, targets customers in the Pacific Rim area (www.audi.com). The translation reads: If you could, you would. Where permitted, the Audi Quattro's permanent four-wheel drive system gives you unparalleled road-holding.

Behavioristic segmentation accomplishes the first step of identifying likely prospects for marketing and advertising efforts. The next step of developing rich profiles of these customers involves using geographic, demographic, and psychographic characteristics.

Geographic Segmentation

One simple way to segment markets is by **geography.** People in one region of the country (or the world) have needs, wants, and purchasing habits that differ from those in other regions. People in Sunbelt states, for example, buy more suntan lotion. Canadians buy special equipment for dealing with snow and ice—products many Floridians have never seen in stores.

When marketers analyze geographic data, they study sales by region, country size, city size, specific locations, and types of stores. Many products sell well in urban areas but poorly in suburban or rural ones, and vice versa. As we'll see in Chapter 8, this information is critical in developing advertising media schedules because, with limited budgets, marketers want to advertise in areas where their sales potential is best.

Even in local markets, geographic segmentation is important. For example, a local progressive politician might send a mailer only to precincts where voters typically support liberal causes, and a local retail store rarely draws customers from outside a fairly limited *trading area.*

Demographic Segmentation

Demographics refer to a population's statistical characteristics: sex, age, ethnicity, education, occupation, income, and other quantifiable factors. Demographics are often combined with geographic segmentation to select target markets for advertising. This is called **geodemographic segmentation.** For example, research shows that people who identify themselves as "strongly Hispanic" tend to be very loyal to certain brands. And, as Exhibit 5–2 reveals, Hispanic media have recently experienced a boom. Many blue-chip advertisers, such as Procter & Gamble, McDonald's, Coca-Cola, and Levi's, now aim a significant portion of their advertising specifically at this $350 billion market.[8] To do so efficiently, they measure the size of the "strongly Hispanic" community in each marketing area they plan to target, as well as its income, age distribution, and attitudes. JCPenney, for example, discovered that its Sandra Salcedo line of clothing for Hispanic women sold well in Texas and Northern California stores but not in heavily Mexican-American Los Angeles, where urban influences hold greater sway. In other words, people's lives are influenced by their environment as well as by their ethnicity.[9]

Exhibit 5–2
Estimated annual ad spending in U.S. Hispanic market ($ millions).

	1994	1995	1996	1997
Total ad spending	$952.8	$1,060	$1,200	$1,400
Percentage growth from previous year	15%	11%	13%	17%

Exhibit 5–3

Heavy usage patterns of various age groups.

Age	Name of age group	Merchandise purchased
0–5	Young children	Baby food, toys, nursery furniture, children's wear
6–19	Schoolchildren and teenagers	Clothing, sporting goods, records and tapes, school supplies, fast food, soft drinks, candy, cosmetics, movies
20–34	Young adults	Cars, furniture, housing, food and beer, clothing, diamonds, home entertainment equipment, recreational equipment, purchases for younger age segments
35–49	Younger middle-aged	Larger homes, better cars, second cars, new furniture, computers, recreational equipment, jewelry, clothing, food and wine
50–64	Older middle-aged	Recreational items, purchases for young marrieds and infants, travel
65 and over	Senior adults	Medical services, travel, pharmaceuticals, purchases for younger age groups

As people grow older, their responsibilities and incomes change, and so do their interests in various product categories (see Exhibit 5–3). Buick, for instance, found a huge untapped market of mature single women who were financially secure and good prospects for its brand. The company now sponsors a newsletter specifically targeted to this group.[10]

In the 1960s and 70s, blue jeans were the basic uniform of young males, and Levi's was the "in" brand. In the 80s, the baby-boomer population grew older and the number of young adults dwindled. The big market of men approaching middle age needed professional clothes for work and wanted looser-fitting clothes for relaxation, so they bought fewer jeans. Levi's needed to evolve the basic blue jean or risk losing this market forever. It responded by targeting its basic, five-pocket, button-fly jeans to 15- to 24-year-olds. Then it developed more comfortable, looser-fitting jeans for men 25 to 34. Finally, Levi's introduced Dockers, cotton casual slacks targeted at men 25 to 54. Dockers soon became the fastest-growing brand in apparel industry history and now includes a whole family of casual clothing for men, women, and boys.

In international markets, population demographics of many populations are changing rapidly. From Kuala Lumpur to Brazil to Poland, middle-class life is becoming available to more people in former Third World countries. This emerging middle class has an apparently insatiable appetite for consumer goods—everything from color TVs and CD players to video cameras, cars, and refrigerators.[11] In China, for example, only 1 percent of the population has hot running water, but 84 percent have television sets![12] In Poland, Coca-Cola spent $350 million to build a bottling plant to serve Eastern Europe, and Procter & Gamble invested over $10 million advertising its Pampers diapers, Wash & Go shampoo, and Ariel detergents. According to *Advertising Age,* that's about 11 percent of Poland's entire ad spending.[13]

Geographic and demographic data provide information about markets but little about the psychology of individuals. Marketers want to reach people who are current or prospective customers, but people in the same demographic or geographic segment have widely differing product preferences and TV viewing habits. Rarely can demographic criteria alone predict purchase behavior.[14] That's why marketers developed the study of *psychographics.*

Psychographic Segmentation

For certain products, customers are more likely to be swayed by appeals to their emotions and cultural values. So some advertisers use **psychographic segmentation** to define consumer markets. **Psychographics** groups people by psychological

Ads for Dr. Martens
(www.drmartens.com) capture the atti-
tude and lifestyle of its target market—
young people who know who they are
and like to make their own fashion state-
ment. Segmentation along psychographic
lines is difficult because it is not easily
quantifiable. Nevertheless, lifestyle
advertisements play a critical role in
marketing products that involve feelings,
personalities, values, and attitudes.

makeup—their values, attitudes, personality, and lifestyle. It views people as individuals with feelings and tendencies, and it classifies people according to what they feel, what they believe, the way they live, and the products, services, and media they use.[15]

For years, marketers have tried to categorize consumers by personality and lifestyle types to determine advertising appeals. One classification system, VALS™, originated by Stanford Research Institute (now SRI International), was quickly adopted by marketers across the country. In 1989, SRI released VALS2, a new psychographic profile for segmenting U.S. consumers and predicting their purchase behavior (see Exhibit 5–4).

The Values and Lifestyles (VALS) typology breaks consumers into eight groups based on the concept of self-orientation and resources. *Self-orientation* is the pattern of attitudes and activities that helps people reinforce, sustain, or modify their social and self-image. Three particular patterns relate to consumer behavior: principles, status, and action. The VALS2 system organizes people into these three categories: those who are principle-oriented, status-oriented, and action-oriented. *Resources* in the VALS2 system relate to the range of psychological, physical, demographic, and material capacities that consumers can draw upon. These include education, income, self-confidence, health, eagerness to buy, intelligence, and energy level. People with the most resources are placed at the top of the typology; those with the least at the bottom. Each of the eight VALS2 groups exhibits distinctive behavior, decision-making patterns, and product/media usage traits.[16]

Abundant resources

Principle oriented   Status oriented   Action oriented

Actualizers

Fulfilleds   Achievers   Experiencers

Believers   Strivers   Makers

Strugglers

Minimal resources

Exhibit 5–4

The VALS2™ (Values and Lifestyles) classification system places consumers with abundant resources—psychological, physical, and material means and capacities—near the top of the chart and those with minimal resources near the bottom. The chart segments consumers by their basis for decision making: principles, status, or action. The boxes intersect to indicate that some categories may be considered together. For instance, a marketer may categorize Fulfilleds and Believers together.

Revlon tried to strike a note of nostalgia in a perfume commercial by using footage of African-American singer Nat King Cole crooning his classic "Unforgettable" to praise a parade of "unforgettable" women—all of whom were white. When Revlon belatedly tried to remedy the gaffe by tacking on a shot of black model Beverly Johnson, the effort seemed clumsy and contrived.

Madison Avenue's awkward efforts to embrace black consumers leave almost 60 percent of the nation's 31 million African-American consumers feeling most commercials and print ads are designed for white people. Such insensitivity can be hazardous to business, as Anheuser-Busch found out.

The "Bud Light Spotlight" commercials showing actual Bud Light drinkers at bars in a dozen cities having a good time while holding bottles of the brew were successful, so the campaign expanded to include many more cities, including Atlanta. Anheuser-Busch wanted to picture whites in Dugan's, a local tavern, even though the bar's clientele is overwhelmingly black. Dugan's owner asked the film crew to leave due to the crowd's negative reaction.

The crew obliged, without incident; but Dugan's no longer serves Bud Light or any other Anheuser-Busch product; and the owner considered yanking those brands out of 22 other establishments in which he has an interest.

Today, advertisers recognize that alienating or stereotyping minorities and women in their ads doesn't pay. They protray Hispanics, African-Americans, Chinese, gays, and other minority group members more favorably, not only because of pressure from watchdog groups, but also because it's good business; these consumers represent sizable target markets.

In efforts to capture similarities and simplify messages, mass marketers may resort to undesirable stereotypes. However, show a traditional "housewife" agonizing over her family's dirty laundry and you may irritate the two-thirds of American women who work outside the home, other householders who do the laundry, and the more than one-quarter of all households consisting of only one person.

Significant gaps often exist among market segment, program target, and program audience. Take daytime TV and its greatly changed audience. At 11 AM, a spot for Clorox bleach won't necessarily reach people who do laundry. Thus daytime ads have shifted their target from housewives to the unemployed and underem-

Radio is a good medium to reach some of the VALS2 groups. Conservative, blue-collar people with traditional values (the VALS2 Believer and Maker segments, comprising 29 percent of the U.S. population) often choose country music stations. Higher-income consumers over 45 (the VALS2 Actualizer, Fulfilled, and Achiever categories) typically listen to news and talk radio. Since radio has only a few formats, SRI's eight typologies fit radio audiences reasonably well.[17]

Numerous advertising agencies jumped on the VALS bandwagon. Young & Rubicam used VALS for clients Mercury, Dr Pepper, Kodak Instant Cameras, and Merrill Lynch, but then developed its own system, Cross Cultural Consumer Characterization (4Cs). Meanwhile, SRI developed Japan VALS to determine the consumer effect of changing values and social behavior in Japan. Since it believes that no one segmentation system can be applied cross-culturally, SRI has developed VALS systems for Germany, Norway, France, Italy, and the United Kingdom.[18]

In Europe and Asia, numerous lifestyle studies have produced a variety of other classification systems intended to help marketers understand the product use of different target groups across national boundaries. The research company RISC investigated how people react to social changes in 12 European countries. The basis of the research was the belief that when individuals share similar values, perceptions, and sensitivities, their purchasing behavior will also show consistent similarities. The resulting study, called Anticipating Change in Europe (ACE), identified six overall groups, or Eurotypes, of consumers. Each comprised a significant percentage of the European population: Traditional, 18 percent; Homebody, 14 percent; Rationalist, 23 percent; Pleasurist, 17 percent; Striver, 15 percent; and Trendsetter, 13 percent. The goal for global marketers is to identify and understand the similarities (and differences) between target groups in order to develop advertising and communication strategies with a common appeal.[19]

Limitations of Consumer Segmentation Methods

Advocates of all these psychographic systems claim they help address the emotional factors that motivate consumers. However, because the markets for many products comprise such a broad cross-section of consumers, psychographics may in fact offer little real value—especially since it oversimplifies consumer personalities and purchase behavior. Some typologies, like VALS, are also criticized for being complicated and lacking proper theoretical underpinnings.[20]

ployed who have bad credit. Ads for personal-injury lawyers and car insurance replace ads that chided wives for not removing ring around the collar. Today ads often portray women as having an attitude about, rather than a preoccupation with, perfection in the home. For example, comic Elayne Boosler doesn't fret about kitchen odors for Lemon Fantastik; she wisecracks about them.

One dilemma for advertisers today is recognizing who they might inadvertently insult next. A group of women complained on a national computer network about Sony's commercial for a portable MiniDisc player. The spot depicts a stud, clad in a tight T-shirt, draped over his 1958 Chevrolet Impala convertible. Each time Stud punches buttons on the MiniDisc programmed to display female names, a new leggy lady shows up. In the final shot, all the women are sitting in or lying around the car. The slogan: "If you play it, they will come." This blatant objectification of women as automatons that can be ordered up with push-button ease offended the protesters.

While market selection may be a logical consequence of the marketing concept, it raises ethical issues about *which* consumers are included and *how* they are targeted, as well as which consumers are *excluded* and the benefits they are denied. Marketing and advertising managers must be sensitive and balance the rights of different stakeholders.

Questions

1. Is targeting an advertising campaign to a niche market inherently insensitive to other groups? Do you believe a lack of sensitivity by an ad maker is the same as a bias?

2. How can advertisers avoid using stereotypical images? What are some other ethical problems in targeting minorities as a specific target market?

Sources: Laura Bird, "Marketers Miss Out by Alienating Blacks," *The Wall Street Journal,* April 9, 1993, p. B3; Bob Garfield, "Daytime Audience Does a Makeover," in Special Report: Marketing to Women, *Advertising Age,* October 4, 1993, p. S-11; Kevin Goldman, "Atlanta Tavern Says Budweiser Was Racially Insensitive on Ad," *The Wall Street Journal,* June 4, 1993, p. B6; Kevin Goldman, "Sexy Sony Ad Riles a Network of Women," *The Wall Street Journal,* August 23, 1993, p. B5; N. Craig Smith and John A. Quelch, "Ethical Issues in Researching and Targeting Consumers," in *Ethics in Marketing* (Burr Ridge, IL: Richard D. Irwin, 1993), pp. 188–95.

Much like consumer markets, business and government markets can also be segmented according to several variables which assist marketers develop effective strategies. This ESAB Welding & Cutting Products (www.esab.com) ad is not targeted for individual consumer use, but rather for large-scale business-to-business transactions.

Still, marketers need to monitor and understand their customers. It helps them select target markets, create ads that match the attributes and image of their products with the types of consumers who use them, develop effective media plans, and budget their advertising dollars wisely. (For an interesting twist on market segmentation, see Ad Lab 5–A.)

Segmenting Business and Government Markets: Understanding Organizational Buying Behavior

Business (or *industrial*) **markets** include manufacturers, government agencies, wholesalers, retailers, banks, and institutions that buy goods and services to help them operate. These products may include raw materials, electronic components, mechanical parts, office equipment, vehicles, or services used in conducting the business. Products sold to business markets are often intended for resale to the public, as in the case of Levi's apparel when it is sold to retailers.

Identifying target markets of prospective business customers is just as complex as identifying consumer markets. Many of the variables used to identify consumer markets can also be used for business markets—for example, geography and behavior (purchase occasion, benefits sought, user status, and usage rate).

Business markets also have special characteristics. They employ professional buyers and use systematic purchasing procedures. They are categorized by Standard Industrial Classification (SIC) codes. They may be concentrated geographically. And in any single market there may be only a small number of buyers.[21]

Business Purchasing Procedures

When businesspeople evaluate new products, they use a process far more complex and rigid than the consumer purchase process described in Chapter 4. Business marketers must design their advertising programs with this in mind.

157

Large firms have purchasing departments that act as professional buyers. They evaluate the need for products, analyze proposed purchases, weigh competitive bids, seek approvals from users and managers, make requisitions, place orders, and supervise all product purchasing. This structured purchase decision process implies a rational approach. Recent research, however, showed that professional buyers often exhibit significant brand-equity behaviors, such as willingness to pay a substantial premium for their favorite brand. This was especially true for buyers concerned about the negative consequences of a product failure. In other words, the buyers perceived well-known brands as a way to reduce risk. Moreover, their feelings about brands tended to transfer from one product category to another, even when the products were very different (for example, from fax machines to floppy disks).[22] This suggests that advertising may play a larger role in business-to-business marketing than previously thought.

 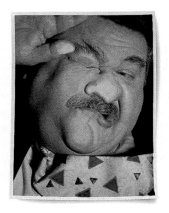 

Looks like color copying and printing just got a little too easy.

Although business purchases are often made according to a company's well-defined needs and policies, the actual purchasers are people who might be persuaded by traditional forms of product branding. For this reason, business-to business advertising for Hewlett Packard (www.hp.com) places great significance on establishing and reinforcing the HP brand name.

Making a sale in business markets may take weeks, months, or even years, especially to government agencies. Purchase decisions often depend on factors besides price or quality, among them product demonstrations, delivery time, terms of sale, and dependability of supply. Marketers often emphasize these issues in advertising and promotional appeals.

Business marketers should consider the purchase decision process of various segments before deciding on a target market. New companies, for instance, may target small firms where the purchase decision can be made quickly. Or they may use commission-only reps to call on the larger prospects that require more time. These decisions dictate where advertising should be placed.

Standard Industrial Classification

Industrial customers need different products, depending on their business. For example, apparel manufacturers like Levi's are the main customers for buttons and zippers. Marketing managers need to focus their sales and advertising efforts on those firms that are in the right business for their products.[23] The Department of Commerce classifies all U.S. businesses—and collects and publishes data on them—by **Standard Industrial Classification (SIC) codes.** These codes are based on broad industry categories (food, tobacco, apparel) subdivided into major divisions, subgroups, and then detailed classes of firms in similar lines of business. Exhibit 5–5 breaks down SIC codes in the apparel industry. The federal government reports the number of firms, sales volumes, and number of employees by geographic area for each code. SIC codes help companies segment markets and do research, and advertisers can obtain lists of companies in particular SIC groups for direct mailings.

Exhibit 5–5
A business marketer selling goods or services to firms in the apparel industry can use SIC codes in directories or on subscription databases to locate prospective companies.

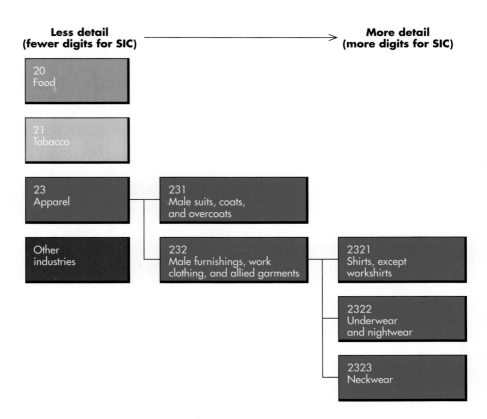

Market Concentration

Many countries' markets for industrial goods are concentrated in one region or several metropolitan areas. In the United States, for example, the industrial market is heavily concentrated in the Midwest, the South, and California (see Exhibit 5–6). Market concentration reduces the number of geographic targets for an advertiser.

Moreover, business marketers deal with fewer buyers than consumer marketers. Fewer than 22 percent of U.S. manufacturers employ nearly 70 percent of all production workers and account for over 80 percent of all manufacturing dollars.[24] Customer size is critical for market segmentation. A firm may concentrate its marketing and advertising efforts on a few large customers, many smaller ones, or both.

Levi Strauss markets through three channels: independent department stores; specialty stores (like Miller's Outpost); and chain stores (like Sears and JCPenney). Its top 100 accounts provide 80 percent of the company's annual sales and are made through 13,000 retail outlets. Its remaining accounts (20 percent of sales) represent another 13,000 stores. Major accounts are served by sales reps from Levi's various divisions, smaller accounts by telemarketers and pandivisional sales reps. TBWA/Chiat Day creates and coordinates advertising for most Levi Strauss divisions in the United States.

Business marketers can also segment by end users. For example, a firm may develop software for one industry, such as banking, or for general use in a variety of industries. That decision, of course, affects advertising media decisions.

Aggregating Market Segments

Once marketers identify and locate broad product-based markets with shared characteristics (behavioristic, geographic, demographic, or psychographic), they can proceed to the second step in the market segmentation process. This involves (1) selecting groups that have a mutual interest in the product's utility and (2) reorganizing and aggregating (combining) them into larger market segments based on their potential for sales and profit. Let's take a look at how this process might work for Levi Strauss & Co. in the U.S. market.

Exhibit 5–6
The states in this map are represented in proportion to the value of their manufactured products.

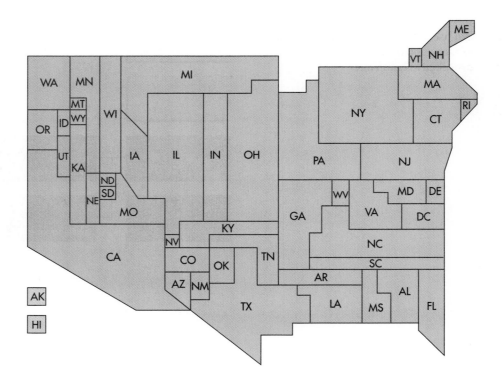

First, the company's management needs to know the market potential for jeans and casual pants in various market areas; that is, it needs to discover the **primary demand trend** of the total U.S. market for its pants. To do this it uses a variety of *marketing research* techniques (discussed in Chapter 6).

Then management must identify the needs, wants, and shared characteristics of the various groups within the casual apparel marketplace who live near the company's retail outlets. It may use the services of a large market segmentation company like National Decision Systems, which collects data on people's purchasing behavior and creates profiles of geographic markets across the country.

The company finds a huge market of prospective customers throughout the United States: students, blue-collar workers, young singles, professional people, homemakers, and so on. It then measures and analyzes household groups in each major retail area by demographic, lifestyle, and purchasing characteristics, sorts them into 50 geodemographic segments, and refers to them with terms like those in Exhibit 5–7: Established Wealth, Movers & Shakers, Family Ties, Intercity Singles, and the like. All these people have apparel needs, and many may be interested in the style, cachet, and durability of the Levi's brand.

Selecting Groups Interested in Product Utility

Levi Strauss next selects groups that would like and be able to afford the utilities or benefits of Levi's apparel—suitability for work or play, comfort, style, low cost, durability, and so on. Groups interested in all these features make up the total possible market for Levi's clothes.

Part of the challenge of market segmentation is estimating the profits the company might realize if it (1) aims at the whole market or (2) caters only to a specific market segment. Apparel is a highly competitive market, but 10 percent of 1,000 is always larger than 90 percent of 100. So for a company like Levi Strauss, the target market must be a large mass market or it won't be profitable.[25]

Exhibit 5–7
National Decision Systems' MicroVision system classifies prospective customers in the Chicago area by census tract and labels each area by the residents' shared characteristics.

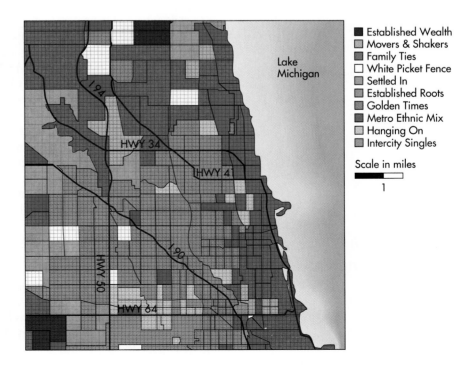

EVER HEARD A CHILD SAY "WHADAYA MEAN WE'RE ALREADY THERE?"

BMW engineers designed the 525iT Wagon to drive like a BMW, not a station wagon. And the reviews from the back seat are nothing but positive. **THE ULTIMATE DRIVING MACHINE!**

No product appeals universally to every customer, so advertisers must carefully choose their target markets. Although BMW (www.bmw.com) typically targets consumers in the market for more sporty luxury automobiles, this ad is aimed at parents who want the prestige of the BMW brand and the utility of a station wagon.

Combining Groups to Build Target Market Segments

The company needs to find groups that are relatively homogeneous (similar) and offer good potential for profit. Market data turn up a large number of demographic and lifestyle groups, including ethnically diverse families, young singles, and seniors with lower education and income who often live in rented homes or apartments: On Their Own (3.4 percent), Back Country (6.0 percent), and Settled In (5.1 percent). Because of their minimal retail or credit activity, these groups are not prime targets for premium-branded department store products.

Other segments offer even greater potential: young to middle-aged households with medium to high incomes and average to high retail activity: Movers & Shakers (2.5 percent), Prosperous Ethnic Mix (2.8 percent), and Home Sweet Home (5.7 percent). By combining these (and similar) groups with the young professionals in the Good Step Forward (2.1 percent) and Great Beginnings (3.6 percent) segments, Levi Strauss can target young to middle-aged people on their way up. Nationally, that amounts to 20 million U.S. households. That's not everybody, but it's a large and potentially very profitable mass-market segment. These people might like the style and comfort of Levi's 550s as well as the tradition of a brand they know and trust, and the company could develop a campaign to appeal to their particular needs, wants, and self-image.

The **Target** Marketing Process

Once the market segmentation process is complete, a company can proceed to the **target marketing process.** This will determine the content, look, and feel of its advertising.

Target Market Selection

The first step in target marketing is to assess which of the newly created segments offer the greatest profit potential and which can be most successfully penetrated. The company designates one or more segments as a **target market**—that group of segments the company wishes to appeal to, design products for, and tailor its marketing activities toward.[26] It may designate another set of segments as a secondary target market and aim some of its resources at it.

Let's look at the most likely target market for loose-fitting jeans: young to middle-aged customers with moderate to high income and education who like the style, comfort, and fashion of Levi's apparel. This group represents a large percentage of the apparel market, and, if won, will generate substantial profits. Levi's offers what these prospects need and want: the style and fashion of the jeans they grew up with, updated to be more comfortable for the adult body.

If the young, comfort-oriented segment wasn't large enough to be profitable, the company would select a different target market, and its other marketing and advertising activities would have to change as well. For an example, look at Ad Lab 5–B and consider how Starbucks selected its new target market.

The Marketing Mix: A Strategy for Matching Products to Markets

Once a company defines its target market, it knows exactly where to focus its attention and resources. It can shape the product concept and even design special features for its target market (such as certain colors or special sizes). It can establish proper pricing. It can determine the need for locating stores or dealers and prepare the most convincing advertising messages.

As we discussed in Chapter 4, a product offers a number of utilities, perceived by the consumer as a *bundle of values*. With this in mind, marketers and advertisers generally try to shape their basic product into a total **product concept:** the

Understanding the Product Element—Starbucks Coffee

America's java giant began as the idea of a man with a dream, whose tender care and commitment built the familiar coffee empire of today. While on a trip to Italy in 1983, Howard Schultz discovered and fell in love with the coffee bars of Milan and Verona. They were a combination of coffee and community. He was sure Americans would love this concept.

At the time, Starbucks was a little 11-store chain of roasted coffee stores in Seattle. Schultz was in charge of marketing. He pitched the coffee-bar concept to the company's management but received only a lukewarm response. They didn't want to be in the beverage business. Howard held on to his vision, though. Leaving Starbucks in 1987, he launched a handful of coffee bars on his own and named them Il Giornales. Two years later, with some investor backing, his demonstrated success enabled him to buy Starbucks out. Today, he is chairman and CEO of a publicly traded company that boasts over 1,500 outlets throughout the United States, Canada, and Japan. Serving 6 million Americans each week, Starbucks has definitely become a household name.

To Schultz, the most important component for success is consistent product quality. "Our long-range goal is to be nothing less than the most recognized and respected brand of coffee in the world," Schultz says.

Thanks to management's demand for consistency, a double-tall latte tastes the same in New York as it does in Seattle; and a perfectly pulled espresso won't sit for more than 10 seconds before being poured into the cup. This attention to detail has earned Starbucks its place in the premium coffee category.

Of course a good product is best prepared and served by skilled, happy employees. And that also adds to an organization's profitability. Starbucks' management believes that if it takes care of its workers, they in turn take care of the public. Employees who work at least 20 hours a week receive full benefits including dental, extended health benefits, and eyeglass and contact lens prescriptions—after only 90 days with the company. To further ensure consistent product quality, Starbucks implemented procedures for monitoring the working conditions of the overseas producers who supply materials to the company.

Today the coffee market is quite competitive, but Starbucks retains its leading position by continually introducing new products. It created a specially formulated coffee flavor, the "Nordstom Blend," for sale in all Nordstorm's Espresso bars. With Pepsi-Cola, Starbucks formed a partnership to produce its Frappuccino beverage and recently it entered into a joint venture with Dreyers Grand Ice Cream to market "Starbucks Coffee Ice Cream." So, if you're drinking a cup of coffee these days, it may well have been created by Starbucks—even if it doesn't say so on the label.

Laboratory Application

A basic rule of advertising is that the most ingenious campaign in the world cannot save a bad product. Think of a product in the marketplace that you consider successful and analyze the elements that make it profitable and unique. Are there any similarities to the product elements found in Starbucks? If so, what?

Sources: Elaine Sosa, "A Little Something about the Big 'S'," *Sally's Place* (www.bpe.com/drinks/coffee/starbucks/index.html), 1998; Lori Ioannou, "Howard Schultz, Interview: King Bean; Starbucks CEO Howard Schultz Runs a $1 Billion Company That Has a Successful Message for Small Business: Create Value and Always Focus on Customer Service," *Your Company,* April 1, 1998, p. 66; "About Starbucks" (www.occ.com/starbucks/about/history.htm), 1998; Carol Polsky, "Brewing Ambition: There's More to Starbucks' Mission than Being No. 1 as the Gourmet Coffee Chain Expands on L.I.," *Newsday,* November 27, 1995, p. C01.

---

consumer's perception of a product as a bundle of utilitarian and symbolic values that satisfy functional, social, psychological, and other wants and needs.

Companies engage in many activities to enhance the product concept and effect marketing exchanges (sales). These activities can be categorized under four generic functions that must be fulfilled for an exchange to come about: (1) *product,* (2) *price,* (3) *distribution,* and (4) *communication.*[27] For convenience, marketing educators developed a mnemonic device for these four functions: *product, price, place,* and *promotion*—or the **four Ps (4 Ps).**[28]

The 4 Ps are a simple way to remember the basic elements of the **marketing mix.** But within each element are numerous marketing activities a company can employ to fine-tune its product concept and improve sales. Advertising, for example, is one instrument of the communication (promotion) element. The remainder of this chapter focuses on the relationship between advertising and the other elements of the marketing mix.

Advertising and the Product Element

In developing a marketing mix, marketers generally start with the **product element.** Major activities typically include the way the product is designed and classified, positioned, branded, and packaged. Each of these affects the way the product is advertised.

Product Life Cycles

Marketers theorize that just as humans pass through stages in life from infancy to death, products (and especially product categories) also pass through a **product life cycle** (see Exhibit 5–8).[29] A product's position in

THE GREAT THING ABOUT THIS THERMOMETER IS THAT CHILDREN HAVE YET TO LEARN HOW TO CLENCH THEIR EARS SHUT.

If there's one thing kids are good at, it's figuring out how to make it difficult to take their temperature.

They squirm. They wiggle. They whine. They even cry. But don't give up hope. Just throw out your old thermometer. And replace it with a Thermoscan® Instant Thermometer.

In one short second, it takes a temperature at the ear. It's easy. It's accurate. It's safe. (No wonder over a half-billion temperatures are being taken this way every year in doctors' offices and hospitals.)

And now you can get it for a new lower price. Which means the perfect family thermometer just got better.

The first name in fast temperatures
THERMOSCAN®
INSTANT THERMOMETER

Most of us might stick a thermometer in our mouths when we come down with a fever, but the Braun Thermoscan (www.braun.com) isn't just any thermometer. The company's product concept, using the ear rather than the mouth, differentiates its thermometer as one that is gentle yet effective for the temperament of children.

the life cycle influences the kind of advertising used. There are four major stages in the product life cycle: *introduction, growth, maturity,* and *decline.*

When a company introduces a new product category, nobody knows about it. To educate consumers, the company has to stimulate **primary demand**—consumer demand for the whole product category, not just its own brand.

When cellular telephones were introduced in the late 1980s, advertisers had to first create enough consumer demand to pull the product through the channels of distribution (called **pull strategy**). Advertising communications educated consumers about the new product and its category, explained what cellular phones are, how they work, and the rewards of owning one. Sales promotion efforts aimed at the retail trade (called **push strategy**) encouraged distributors and dealers to stock, display, and advertise the new products (see Chapter 9).

During the **introductory** (pioneering) **phase** of any new product category, the company incurs considerable costs for educating customers, building widespread dealer distribution, and encouraging demand. It must spend significant advertising

Exhibit 5–8
A product's life cycle curve may vary, depending on the product category. Marketing objectives and strategies change as the product proceeds from one stage to the next.

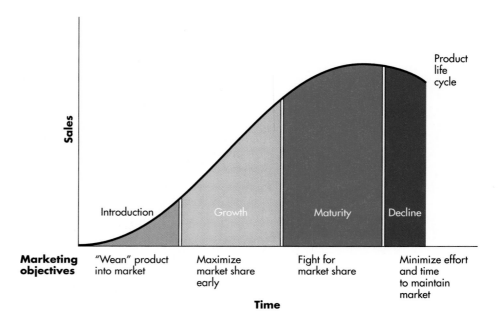

Advertisers use a variety of strategies to extend the life cycle of a product in its mature stage. Proctor & Gamble (www.pg.com), testing two new flavors of Crest toothpaste in mass-merchant chains, used Telestar Interactive's MicroTalk shelf units to play audio messages about the products to approaching consumers.

sums at this stage to establish a position as a market leader and to gain a large share of market before the growth stage begins.

When sales volume begins to rise rapidly, the product enters the **growth stage.** This period is characterized by rapid *market expansion* as more and more customers, stimulated by mass advertising and word-of-mouth, make their first, second, and third purchases. Competitors jump into the market, but the company that established the early leadership position reaps the biggest rewards. As a percentage of total sales, advertising expenditures should decrease, and individual firms will realize their first substantial profits.

During the early 1990s, the demand for cellular phones exploded, and category sales quadrupled every year. Many competitors suddenly appeared. With increased production and competition, prices started to fall, which brought even more people into the market. Now, some 40 percent of all U.S. families own cellular phones.

In the **maturity stage,** the marketplace becomes saturated with competing products and the number of new customers dwindles, so industry sales reach a plateau. Competition intensifies and profits diminish. Companies increase their promotional efforts but emphasize **selective demand** to impress customers with the subtle advantages of their brand. At this stage, companies increase sales only at the expense of competitors (*conquest sales*). The strategies of market segmentation, product positioning, and price promotion become more important during this shakeout period as weak companies fall by the wayside and those remaining fight for small increases in market share. By 1994, for example, cellular phones that had once sold for $1,500 were advertised regularly for $100 to $200. Ads emphasized features and low prices, and the product became a staple of discount merchandisers.

Late in the maturity stage, companies often scramble to extend the product's life cycle. They may try to find new users, develop new uses for the product, change the size of packages, design new labels, or improve quality. Without innovation, name brands eventually see their sales erode. If the advertised brand is really no better, people will buy whatever's cheapest and most convenient. Gillette realized that and spent 10 years and hundreds of millions of dollars to develop and market Sensor, a breakthrough shaving system that was successful beyond all expectations.[30] Keds shoes, on the other hand, didn't innovate. During a back-to-basics consumer fad, the brand made a comeback with baby boomers, and the company milked the brand for the windfall profits. But then the brand suddenly experienced declining sales and lost market share in 1993.[31]

Finally, products enter the **decline stage** due to obsolescence, new technology, or changing consumer tastes. Companies may cease all promotion and phase the products out quickly, as in the case of record turntables and LP albums, or let them fade slowly with minimal advertising, like most sheer hosiery brands.[32]

Product Classifications

The way a company classifies its product is important in defining both the product concept and the marketing mix. As Exhibit 5–9 shows, there are many ways to classify tangible goods: by markets, by the purchasing habits of buyers, by the consumption rate or degree of tangibility, or by physical attributes.

Unlike tangible products, a **service** is a bundle of *intangible* benefits that satisfy some need or want, are temporary in nature, and usually derive from completion of a task.[33] Thus we have *task utility,* as described in Chapter 4. Rail service is transitory, used and priced by time and distance. It offers the functional benefits of transporting people, livestock, and freight. But it can also offer psychological benefits. Just think of the romance and leisure of a train trip across Europe aboard the Orient Express. The railroad relies on the use of *specialized equipment*—vehicles able to pull huge loads over a unique track. This makes it an **equipment-based service.**

In contrast, an ad agency, like a law firm or a bank, is a **people-based service;** it relies on the creative talents and marketing skills of individuals. As one agency CEO said, "My inventory goes up and down the elevators twice a day."[34]

Product Positioning

Once an advertising person understands the product's stage in the life cycle and how it's classified, the first strategic decision can be made: how to **position** the product. The basic goal of positioning strategy is to own a word in the prospect's mind. Levi's owns "jeans." FedEx owns "overnight." And Volvo owns "safety." At a breakfast celebrating the 25th anniversary of positioning strategy, Al Ries quipped, "What Volvo is exploiting is the fact that the car looks like a tank. They can fire the designers."[35]

Products may be positioned in many different ways. Generally, they are ranked by the way they are differentiated, the benefits they offer, the particular market segment to which they appeal, or the way they are classified. Xerox has repositioned itself as "The Document Company," moving from the narrow, glutted,

Exhibit 5–9
Product classifications.

By market	By rate of consumption and tangibility	By purchasing habits	By physical description

Consumer goods
  Products and services we use in our daily lives (food, clothing, furniture, cars).
Industrial goods
  Products used by companies for the purpose of producing other products (raw materials, agricultural commodities, machinery, tools, equipment).
	Durable goods
	  Tangible products that are long-lasting and infrequently replaced (cars, trucks, refrigerators, furniture).
	Nondurable goods
	  Tangible products that may be consumed in one or a few uses and usually need to be replaced at regular intervals (food, soap, gasoline, oil).
	Services
	  Activities, benefits, or satisfaction offered for sale (travel, haircuts, legal and medical services, massages).
		Convenience goods
		  Purchases made frequently with a minimum of effort (cigarettes, food, newspapers).
		Shopping goods
		  Infrequently purchased items for which greater time is spent comparing price, quality, style, warranty (furniture, cars, clothing, tires).
		Specialty goods
		  Products with such unique characteristics that consumers will make special efforts to purchase them even if they're more expensive (fancy photographic equipment, special women's fashions, stereo components).
			Packaged goods
			  Cereals, hair tonics, and so forth.
			Hard goods
			  Furniture, appliances.
			Soft goods
			  Clothing, bedding.
			Services
			  Intangible products.

IT'S NOT A MATTER OF NO ONE ELSE BEING ABLE TO KEEP UP. IT'S A MATTER OF NO ONE ELSE BEING ABLE TO FOLLOW.

At a time when sport utility vehicles are popular among a suburban office crowd, Hummer (www.hummer.com)
positions itself as the hardcore and rugged vehicle that does the dirty jobs. Positioning is important in tight markets to as-
sist in differentiation between like products.

copier market to the broader, growing, document-handling market. With one stroke, Xerox redefined the business it is in, differentiated itself from the competition, and created a new number-one position for itself.[36]

Product Differentiation

Product differentiation creates a product difference that appeals to the preferences of a distinct market segment. In advertising, nothing is more important than being able to tell prospects truthfully that your product is new and different. Unfortunately, in response to increased competitive pressures, burgeoning innovation and technology, and various constraints on distribution, new-product development cycles have shortened dramatically. As a result, many brand managers find themselves launching new products that are "only 85 percent there."[37] So it's not surprising that most "new" products fail to impress consumers.[38] (See Exhibit 5–10.) Simply adding new colors might differentiate a product enough to attract a new set of customers, but not all product differences need be that obvious. Differences between products may be *perceptible, hidden,* or *induced.* Hank Seiden says every successful product must have a "unique advantage." Bob Pritikin humorously calls that differentiating quality the AMAZING NEW![39]

Differences between products that are readily apparent to the consumer are called **perceptible differences.** Snapple, for example, received its initial impetus because of its unique taste, and the company now spends $10 million annually to advertise this difference to consumers nationwide.[40] **Hidden differences** are not so readily apparent. Trident gum may look and taste the same as other brands, but it is differentiated by the use of artificial sweeteners. While hidden differences can enhance a product's desirability, advertising is usually needed to let consumers know about them.

For many product classes, such as aspirin, salt, gasoline, packaged foods, liquor, and financial services, advertising can create **induced differences.** Banks, brokerage houses, and insurance companies, for example, which offer virtually identical

Exhibit 5–10
What's new? Not much. Consumers didn't think these products were as new as they claimed to be.

Product	New and different	Purchase probability	Price/ Value	Overall Grade
Airwick Botanicals	F	A	A	B
Mr. Clean Glass & Surface Cleaner	F	A	A	B
Spic & Span with Bleach	F	A	B	B
Aspirin-Free Bayer Select	F	B	B	C
Sugar Twin Plus low-calorie sweetener	F	B	A	C
Lady Power Clear Roll-On antiperspirant	F	B	A	C

Source: Reprinted with permission from the March 13, 1997 issue of *Advertising Age.* Copyright, Crain Communications, Inc. 1994.

services and financial products, use advertising and promotion to differentiate themselves. However, few have yet discovered the image asset of branding as used by the national packaged-goods marketers. That is created through the accumulation of consistent advertising campaigns, favorable publicity, and special-event sponsorship.[41]

As Sunkist so successfully demonstrated (see Chapter 1), the ability to create the perception of differences in functionally similar products and services depends on the effective use of branding, packaging, and advertising.

Product Branding   The fundamental differentiating device for all products is the **brand**— that combination of name, words, symbols, or design that identifies the product and its source and distinguishes it from competing products. Without brands, consumers couldn't tell one product from another, and advertising them would be nearly impossible.

Branding decisions are difficult. A manufacturer may establish an **individual brand** for each product it produces. Unilever, for example, markets its toothpastes under the individual brand names Aim, Pepsodent, and Close-Up. Such companies designate a distinct target market for each product and develop a separate personality and image for each brand. However, this strategy is very costly.

On the other hand, a company might use a **family brand** and market different products under the same umbrella name. When Heinz promotes its ketchup, it hopes to help its relishes too. This decision may be cost effective, but one bad product in a line can hurt the whole family.

Creating a brand name is key to differentiation for a product. Without this, the consumer is left with a generic commodity. Large companies can actually oversee many different products and brand names, as in the case of the many popular and well-known items marketed by Procter & Gamble.

Because it is so expensive for manufacturers to market **national brands** (also called *manufacturer's brands*), some companies use a *private-labeling strategy.* They manufacture the product and sell it to resellers (distributors or dealers), who put their own brand on the product. **Private labels,** typically sold at lower prices in large retail chain stores, include such familiar names as Kenmore, Craftsman, Cragmont, Kroger, and Party Pride. They now account for 18.7 percent of all grocery-product purchases.[42] The responsibility for creating brand image and familiarity rests with the distributor or retailer, who is also the principal benefactor if the brand is successful. Recent trends have moved toward premium private labels, like President's Choice, which has enjoyed immense success. These products feature better packaging, superior quality, and a higher price, comparable to national brands.

Branding decisions are critical because the brands a company owns may be its most important capital asset. Imagine the value of owning a brand name like Coca-Cola, Nike, Porsche, or Levi's. *Financial World's* annual brand-value report ranks Coca-Cola as the most valuable brand in the world, followed by Marlboro, Nescafé, Kodak, and Microsoft (see Exhibit 5–11).[43] Some companies pay a substantial fee for the right to use another company's brand name. Thus, we have **licensed brands** like Sunkist vitamins, Coca-Cola clothing, Porsche sunglasses, and Mickey Mouse watches.

Exhibit 5–11
Top worldwide brands for 1993.

		Brand value ($ millions)
1.	Coca-Cola	$35,950
2.	Marlboro	33,045
3.	Nescafé	11,549
4.	Kodak	10,020
5.	Microsoft	9,842
6.	Budweiser	9,724
7.	Kellogg's	9,372
8.	Motorola	9,293
9.	Gillette	8,218
10.	Bacardi	7,163

The Role of Branding

For consumers, brands offer instant recognition and identification. They also promise consistent, reliable standards of quality, taste, size, or even psychological satisfaction, which adds value to the product for both the consumer and the manufacturer. In a study by McKinsey & Co., a computer's brand name ranked second (behind performance) in what consumers considered important when choosing a personal computer. Price, by the way, ranked fifth.[44]

Brands must be built on differences in images, meanings, and associations. It's up to manufacturers to differentiate their products clearly and deliver value competitively. The product has to taste better, or get clothes cleaner, or be packaged in a more environmentally friendly container.[45] Advertising for an established brand, particularly a well-differentiated one, is much more effective if it exploits the brand's positioning.[46] Ideally, when consumers see a brand on the shelf, they instantly comprehend the brand's promise and have confidence in its quality. Of course, they must be familiar with and believe in the brand's promise (a function of advertising effectiveness). And the advertiser wants to achieve brand preference or, as we pointed out in Chapter 4, *brand loyalty.*

The ultimate goal of all brand advertising and promotion is to build greater **brand equity,** the totality of what consumers, distributors, dealers—even competitors—feel and think about the brand over an extended period of time. In short, it's the value of the brand's capital. Young & Rubicam, the New York ad agency that handles Sears, uses an approach called the BrandAsset Valuator™ to determine brand equity. This model measures a matrix defined by *brand stature* (a blend of familiarity and esteem) and *vitality* (relevance and differentiation).

High brand equity offers a host of blessings to the product marketer: customer loyalty, price inelasticity, long-term profits. A loyal customer can be nine times as profitable as a disloyal one.[47] But building brand equity requires time and money. Brand value and preference drive market share, but share points and brand loyalty are usually won by the advertisers who spend the most. And increasing brand loyalty requires a spending increase of 200 to 300 percent to affect loyalty dramatically.[48]

Charlotte Beers, the head of Ogilvy & Mather, points out the importance of "brand stewardship." She believes companies must maintain consistency in their message by integrating all their marketing communications—from packaging and advertising to sales promotion and publicity—to maintain and reinforce the brand's personality in a real-life context and avoid doing something stupid like changing the distinctive color of a Ryder rental truck.[49]

Product Packaging

The product's package is a component of the product element and is also an *exhibitive medium* that can determine the outcome of retail shelf competition. Package designers (who sometimes work in agencies) must make the package exciting, appealing, and at the same time functional. The four considerations in package design

With integrated marketing communications strategies, all contact with the consumer is expected to make an impact, right down to the design of the product packaging. For this reason, companies like Iomega (www.iomega.com) invest time and resources into making their packaging as appealing and exciting to the consumer as possible.

are *identification; containment, protection, and convenience; consumer appeal;* and *economy.* These functions may even become **copy points**—copywriting themes—in the product's advertising.

Identification

Packaging is such an important identification device that some companies use the same package and label design for years. Why? Because the unique combination of trade name, trademark, or trade character, reinforced by the package design, quickly identifies the product's brand and differentiates it from competitors. For example, the traditional contoured Coke bottle was so unusual and popular that in 1992 Coca-Cola reintroduced it to U.S. markets. The company never stopped using it in many international markets, since it differentiated Coke so well from other cola products.

Packages must offer high visibility and legibility just to penetrate shoppers' *physiological screens.* Product features must be easy to read and color combinations must provide high contrast to differentiate the product. To penetrate consumers' *psychological screens,* the package design must reflect the tone, image, and personality of the product concept. In many product categories (wine, cosmetics), the package quality largely determines the consumer's perception of the product's quality.

Containment, Protection, and Convenience

The basic purpose of any package is to hold and protect the product and make it easy to use. While marketers must design an interesting package, they must also make sure it will keep the product fresh and protect its contents from shipping damage, water vapor (for frozen goods), grease, infestation, and odors. And packages must adhere to legal protection requirements.

Retailers want packages that are easy to stack and display; they also want a full range of sizes to fit their customers' needs. Consumers want packages that are easy to carry, open, and store, so these are important design considerations. But convenience can't interfere with protection. Spouts make pouring easier, but they may also limit a package's physical strength.

Packaging must have consumer appeal to be effective, since even minor changes in color can significantly affect sales. Companies can find even more success if the packaging appeal is great evough for consumers to want to keep and use the package long after the initial purchase.

Consumer Appeal

Consumer appeal in packaging is the result of many factors: size, color, material, and shape. Certain colors have special meanings to consumers. It's not uncommon for even a subtle change in color to result in as much as a 20 percent change in sales.[50]

In this age of environmental awareness, *green marketing* is an important issue for many companies and consumers alike. New technology has made ecologically safe packaging available and affordable for many product categories. Many companies now advertise their packages as environmentally responsible.

A package's shape also offers an opportunity for consumer appeal based on whimsy, humor, or romance. Heart-shaped packages of Valentine's Day candy instantly tell what the product is. Some companies design packages with a secondary use in mind. Kraft's cheese jar, once emptied, can be used for serving fruit juice. Some tins and bottles even become collectibles (Chivas Regal). These packages are really premiums that give buyers extra value for the dollars they spend.

Consumers frequently associate higher prices with higher quality. Volvo (www.volvo.com) capitalizes on that concept by reinforcing that the safety value of its automobiles is worth a slightly higher cost.

Economy

The costs of identification, protection, convenience, and consumer appeal add to basic production costs, but this increase may be more than offset by increased customer appeal. These benefits may make a considerable difference to the consumer and affect both the product concept and the way it is advertised.

Advertising and the **Price** Element

Many companies, especially small ones, request input from their advertising people about pricing strategies. That's because, as we all know, the **price element** of the marketing mix influences consumer perceptions of the brand dramatically.

Key Factors Influencing Price

Companies typically set their prices based on market demand for the product, costs of production and distribution, competition, and corporate objectives. Interestingly, though, a company often has relatively few options for determining its price strategy, depending on the desired product concept.

Market Demand

If the supply of a product is static but the desire (demand) for it increases, the price tends to rise. If demand drops below available supply, the price tends to fall. This may affect advertising messages in a major way (see Exhibit 5–12).

Exhibit 5–12
This graph plots demand versus price and supply versus price. The demand curve shows the amounts purchased at various prices. The supply curve shows the amounts offered for sale at various prices. The point where the two curves cross is called the market clearing price, where demand and supply balance. It is the price that theoretically sells out the product.

In the last recession, many auto manufacturers faced a glut of unsold new cars and declining demand. Several companies offered substantial factory rebates—price cuts—to motivate prospective buyers. Dealers immediately sold more cars. No amount of image or awareness advertising would have had the same effect. But, of course, advertising was essential to communicate the price cut.

Some marketing researchers theorize that for new durable goods, advertising works with word-of-mouth communication to generate awareness of and belief in the product's attributes. Once consumers perceive that the product's value warrants the purchase price, sales occur. As product experience and information spread, the risks typically associated with new products diminish, which effectively increases consumers' willingness to purchase at a higher price.[51]

Production and Distribution Costs

The price of goods depends to some extent on the costs of production and distribution. As these costs increase, they must be passed on to the consumer, or the company will be unable to meet its overhead and be forced out of business. One common advertising strategy is to tout the materials used in manufacturing a product. This can also help justify the prices manufacturers must charge to cover their production costs.

Competition

Marketers believe that, in many product categories, consumers are less concerned with a product's actual price than with its perceived price relative to competitors. For the advertiser, maintaining the value perception during periods of intense price competition and fluctuation is challenging and critically important.[52]

Corporate Objectives and Strategies

A company's objectives also influence price. When introducing new products, companies often set a high price initially to recover development and start-up costs. On the other hand, the objective may be to position the brand as an inexpensive convenience item aimed at a broad target market. In this case, ads stress the product's economy.

Price also depends on the company's marketing strategy, and image advertising may be used to justify a higher price. Many premium-priced brands, like L'Oréal, are touted for the very fact that they do cost more. The important thing is that the price be consistent with the brand image; you can't charge a Rolex price for a Timex watch.

As products enter the maturity stage of their life cycle, corporate objectives tend to aim at increasing, or at least maintaining, market share. To accomplish this, competitive advertising and promotion heat up, and prices tend to drop.

Variable Influences

Economic conditions, consumer income and tastes, government regulations, marketing costs, and other factors also influence prices and thus advertising. Marketing management must consider all these to determine an appropriate pricing strategy and then create advertising that justifies the product's price. Consider the alternatives listed in RL 5–2, Checklist of Strategies for Setting Prices, in the Reference Library. Each strategy will have a different effect on a company's choice of advertising.

The "place" (or distribution) element of marketing strategy is always integral to successful business. You may have the most wonderful product in the world—but nobody will buy it if they can't find it.

Starbucks is a phenomenon that changed the way people view coffee. This can be explained, in a large part, by the creative use of the place element. You'll notice that Starbucks cafés are found in high-traffic, easily noticeable locations in each market area. In some markets, Starbucks is even found on virtually every street corner. While the average consumer may find this excessive, Starbucks actually picks and plans each retail location with great care.

With a company like Starbucks, street space is the same as shelf space. In this sense, buying out existing coffee houses is the same as Coca-Cola buying shelf space in a supermarket. Starbucks management believes that chain expansion is as much a part of the company's success as is its coffee bar and customer service concepts. Stores have sprouted up in San Diego, Denver, Minneapolis, Boston, Atlanta, and nearly everywhere in between. The company has also opened its first stores in Japan. The goal is to have opened 2000 stores by the year 2000.

Aside from it's store locations, Starbucks' unique coffee blends are now found in selected airlines, restaurants, hotels, and supermarkets. Additional venues include a mail-order business with catalog distribution, Nordstrom department stores where the "Nordstrom Blend" coffee is sold, a coast-to-coast alliance with Barnes & Noble bookstores, a partnership with Star Markets in Boston, distribution to the Washington State Ferry system, Holland America Line–Westours cruises, the Seattle Kingdome, and Chicago's Wrigley Field.

Obviously, Starbucks intends to fully saturate every coffee market. When consumers go shopping for groceries, they aren't likely to make a separate trip to Starbucks for coffee. So Starbucks now competes directly with other specialty coffees sold in supermarkets. The company even hopes to soon surpass even Folgers, the leading coffee brand of Procter & Gamble.

Laboratory Application

Take the product you used in Ad Lab 5–B and compare the distribution principles used by Starbucks with your product. In addition, think about the factors that should be considered when placing your product or service in other venues. How does it compare with Starbucks?

Sources: Elaine Sosa, "A Little Something About the Big 'S'," *Sally's Place* (www.bpe.com/drinks/coffee/starbucks/index.html), 1998; Lori Ioannou, "Howard Schultz, Interview: King Bean; Starbucks CEO Howard Schultz Runs a $1 Billion Company That Has a Successful Message for Small Business: Create Value and Always Focus on Customer Service," *Your Company,* April 1,1998, p. 66; "About Starbucks" (www.occ.com/starbucks/about/history.htm), 1998; Carol Polsky, "Brewing Ambition: There's More to Starbucks' Mission than Being No. 1 as the Gourmet Coffee Chain Expands on L.I.," *Newsday,* November 27, 1995, p. C01 (sbaeweb2.fullerton.edu).

Advertising and the **Distribution** (Place) Element

Before the first ad can be created, the **distribution element,** or *place,* must be decided. It is important for marketers to understand that the method of distribution, like the price, must be consistent with the brand's image. People will not pay Nordstrom prices at Kmart. To understand Starbucks' distribution strategy, see Ad Lab 5–C, "Starbucks and the Place Element." Companies use two basic methods of distribution: *direct* or *indirect.*

Direct Distribution

When companies sell directly to end users or consumers, they use **direct distribution.** Avon, for example, employs sales reps who work for the factory rather than for a retailer and sell directly to consumers. Encyclopedia publishers and insurance companies often sell and distribute their products and services directly to customers without the use of wholesalers or retailers. In these cases, the advertising burden is carried entirely by the manufacturer.

One of the fastest-growing methods of direct distribution today is **network marketing** (also called *multilevel marketing*), in which individuals act as independent distributors for a manufacturer or private-label marketer. These people sign up friends and relatives to consume the company's products and recruit others to join. Through a gradual, word-of-mouth process, they form a "buying club" of independent distributors who buy the products wholesale direct from the company, use them, and tout them to more and more friends and acquaintances.

If successful, the rewards for the network marketing company (and many of the distributors) can be staggering. Amway International, the granddaddy of network marketing, now boasts international sales in excess of $5 billion, and many of its longtime distributors became multimillionaires in the process. Other companies have broken the billion-dollar sales mark, too, among them Nikken (Japan), Herbalife, and Shaklee. These companies brag about the fact that they do *no media advertising*. Since they usually sell consumer products (that would typically carry a heavy advertising and sales promotion burden), they save a tremendous

Some advertising addresses the distribution element of the marketing mix by targeting wholesalers and/or retailers of the product. Haggar's trade ad, for example, uses tongue-in-cheek humor to get the attention of the retailers who sell the company's brand of clothing directly to the consumer. The implication, of course, is that Haggar retailers are so successful that they live in beautiful estates like the one pictured.

amount of money. Most marketing communications are simply word-of-mouth. The companies do provide attractive product packaging, catalogs, brochures, and other sales material—which the distributors typically pay for at cost. Today, companies using this distribution method include subsidiaries or spinoffs of well-known public corporations such as Gillette, U.S. Sprint, and Rexall Sundown.

Indirect Distribution

Manufacturers usually don't sell directly to end users or consumers. Most companies market their products through a *distribution channel* that includes a network of *resellers*. A **reseller** (also called a *middleman*) is a business firm that operates between the producer and the consumer or industrial purchaser. It deals in trade rather than production.[53] Resellers include both wholesalers and retailers, as well as manufacturers' representatives, brokers, jobbers, and distributors. A **distribution channel** comprises all the firms and individuals that take title, or assist in taking title, to the product as it moves from the producer to the consumer.

Indirect distribution channels make the flow of products available to customers conveniently and economically. Appliance companies, for example, contract with exclusive regional distributors that buy the products from the factory and resell them to local dealers, who then resell them to consumers. Many industrial companies market their products through reps or distributors to *original-equipment manufacturers (OEMs)*. These OEMs may use the product as a component in their own product, which is then sold to their customers.

The advertising a company uses depends on the product's method of distribution. Much of the advertising we see is not prepared or paid for by the manufacturer, but by the distributor or retailer. Members of a distribution channel give enormous promotional support to the manufacturers they represent.

A part of marketing strategy is determining the amount of coverage necessary for a product. Procter & Gamble, for example, distributes Crest toothpaste to virtually every supermarket and discount, drug, and variety store. Other products might need only one dealer for every 50,000 people. Consumer goods manufacturers traditionally use one of three distribution strategies: *intensive, selective,* or *exclusive.*

Intensive Distribution

Soft drinks, candy, Timex watches, and other convenience goods are available at every possible location because of **intensive distribution.** In fact, consumers can buy them with a minimum of effort. The profit on each unit is usually very low, but the volume of sales is high. The sales burden is usually carried by the manufacturer's national advertising. Ads in trade magazines **push** the product into the retail "pipeline," and in mass media they stimulate consumers to **pull** the products through the pipeline. As a manufacturer modifies its strategy to more push or more pull, special promotions may be directed at the trade or at consumers to build brand volume (see Chapter 9).

Selective Distribution

By limiting the number of outlets through **selective distribution,** manufacturers can cut their distribution and promotion costs. Many hardware tools are sold selectively through discount chains, home-improvement centers, and hardware stores. Levi

Strauss sells through better department and chain stores. Manufacturers may use national advertising, but the sales burden is normally carried by the retailer. The manufacturer may share part of the retailer's advertising costs through a **cooperative advertising** program, as we discussed in Chapter 3. For example, a Levi's retailer may receive substantial allowances from the manufacturer for advertising Levi's clothing in its local area. In return, the retailer agrees to display the clothing prominently.

Exclusive Distribution

Some manufacturers grant **exclusive distribution** rights to a wholesaler or retailer in one geographic region. For example, a town of 50,000 to 100,000 people will have only one Chrysler dealer and no Mercedes dealer. This is also common in high fashion, major appliances, and furniture lines. What is lost in market coverage is often gained in the ability to maintain a prestige image and premium prices. Exclusive distribution agreements also force manufacturers and retailers to cooperate closely in advertising and promotion programs.

Vertical Marketing Systems: The Growth of Franchising

To be efficient, members of a distribution channel need to cooperate closely with one another. This need gave rise to the **vertical marketing system (VMS),** a centrally programmed and managed distribution system that supplies or otherwise serves a group of stores or other businesses.

There are many types of vertical marketing systems. Today, the greatest growth is in **franchising**—like McDonald's or Mailboxes, Etc.—in which dealers (*franchisees*) pay a fee to operate under the guidelines and direction of the parent company or manufacturer (the *franchisor*). An estimated 33 percent of all retail sales in the United States are made through franchise outlets,[54] though there are only 4,500 franchisors throughout the United States and Canada (compared to some 20 million businesses in the United States alone).[55]

Franchising and other vertical marketing systems offer both manufacturers and retailers numerous advantages, not the least of which are centralized coordination of marketing efforts and substantial savings and continuity in advertising. Perhaps most important is consumer recognition: the moment a new McDonald's opens, the franchisee has instant customers. Moreover, a single newspaper ad can promote all of a chain's retailers in a particular trading area.

Many marketers find that franchising is the best way to introduce their services into global markets. Subway sandwich shops, for example, is the fastest-growing

The vertical marketing system gave rise to successful business plans like franchising in which dealers pay a fee to operate under the guidelines of a parent company. Advertising and marketing activities are developed by a central organization and used by all the franchise companies under this umbrella, providing continuity in the advertising as well as substantial savings.

franchise operation in North America with a total of 7,000 stores (400 in Canada). With a solid base at home, the company entered the 90s by aggressively approaching new markets in Australia, Japan, Israel, Ireland, Mexico, Portugal, and South Korea.[56]

The European Union, a market of 340 million people, is now opening to innovative marketers. As a result, franchising is starting to grow rapidly in the United Kingdom, France, Germany, Spain, Belgium, and the Netherlands. Though franchising is less regulated in Europe, advertising is more regulated. This again points out the need for local experts to manage the advertising function in foreign markets.[57]

Advertising and the **Communication** (Promotion) Element

Once it determines product, price, and distribution, a company is ready to plan its marketing communications, of which advertising is just one component. (See Ad Lab 5–D, "Price and Promotion.")

The **communication element** includes all marketing-related communications between the seller and the buyer. A variety of marketing communications tools comprise the **communications mix.** These tools can be grouped into *personal* and *nonpersonal communication* activities.

Personal communication includes all person-to-person contact with customers. **Nonpersonal communication** activities—which use some medium as an intermediary for communicating—include *advertising, direct marketing,* certain *public relations* activities, *collateral materials,* and *sales promotion.* Today, successful marketing managers blend all these elements into an *integrated marketing communications program.*

Personal Selling

Some consumer products are sold by clerks in retail stores, others by salespeople who call on customers directly. Personal selling is very important in business-to-business marketing. It establishes a face-to-face situation in which the marketer can learn firsthand about customer wants and needs, and customers find it harder to say no. We discuss personal selling further in Chapter 9.

Advertising

Advertising is sometimes called mass or nonpersonal selling. Its usual purpose is to inform, persuade, and remind customers about particular products and services. In some cases, like mail order, advertising even closes the sale.

Certain products lend themselves to advertising so much that it plays the dominant communications role. The following factors are particularly important for advertising success:

- High primary demand trend.
- Chance for significant product differentiation.
- Hidden qualities highly important to consumers.
- Opportunity to use strong emotional appeals.
- Substantial sums available to support advertising.

Where these conditions exist, as in the cosmetics industry, companies spend large amounts on advertising, and the ratio of advertising to sales dollars is often quite high. For completely undifferentiated products, such as sugar, salt, and other raw materials or commodities, price is usually the primary influence, and advertising is minimally important. Sunkist is an interesting exception. As we saw in Chapter 1, this farmers' cooperative successfully brands an undifferentiated commodity (citrus fruit) and markets it internationally.

Direct Marketing

Direct marketing is like taking the store to the customer. A mail-order house that communicates directly with consumers through ads and catalogs is one type of company engaged in direct marketing. It builds its own database of customers and uses a variety of media to communicate with them.

Ad Lab 5–D

Price and Promotion

Starbucks classifies its product as a "gourmet" coffee—in other words, it's positioned as a premium product. That suggests it probably costs more than the typical coffee in the supermarket. However, since Starbucks targets a younger demographic of 20- to 49-year-olds, it must still be careful about how much it charges. Currently, regular brewed coffee at Starbucks costs only 80¢, but the most expensive beverage runs approximately $3.65. Whole-bean coffee ranges from $7.95 to $17.95 per pound. So overall Starbucks coffee may be a bit more pricey, but it offers a higher-quality product and tries to add value through superior employee service.

To promote awareness, many new companies dedicate enormous budgets toward advertising. However, this is not always necessary. Starbucks certainly never dreamed it could establish the degree of brand loyalty that it did in such a short time. But it managed to do so—and with only a minimal amount of advertising. It wasn't that they didn't believe in advertising, they just didn't think they could afford it. So they focused on creating product value and giving better service.

Initially, the only promotional elements the company used were public relations and some small sales promotions. These were designed to create some initial awareness and interest in their gourmet coffees. To demonstrate its social concern, Starbucks also ventured into philanthropic activities. In fact, it is now the largest corporate sponsor of C.A.R.E., an international relief and development organization that aids the very communities from which the company buys its coffee.

With the 90s coffee culture phenomenon approaching boom proportions, increased competition has surfaced, forcing Starbucks to spend more on advertising to maintain its market share. While Starbucks continues its public relations involvement with communities, it recognizes the growing need to invest in mass media advertising. Initially, Starbucks spent $17.8 million on a direct-response campaign. It also sold merchandise bearing the Starbucks logo on mugs, coffee grinders, espresso machines, and gourmet food via catalog and America Online. Starbucks also increased its ad expenditures from $14 million in 1995 to approximately $50 million in 1996.

Then in 1997, under the creative design of Goodby, Silverstein & Partners, Starbucks launched the largest advertising blitz in its history to promote its new Frapuccino beverage. Three television and three radio spots were created for the campaign, focusing on the jingle, "Starbucks, purveyors of coffee, tea, and sanity." In the fall of 1997, though, Starbucks changed agencies and hired BBDO West, claiming that with Goodby they hadn't yet found the right "creative voice" for Starbucks. They hoped BBDO could help them achieve that.

Laboratory Application

When constructing the marketing mix for your chosen product or service (refer to Ad Labs 5–B and 5–C), consider these last two elements: price and promotion. What should your product's price be and why? Should you offer some kind of credit terms? Also, what media should you use to advertise your product or service and why? Do you think Starbucks should advertise in more traditional mass media or stick to public relations? What creative voice would you suggest for Starbucks?

Sources: Elaine Sosa, Lori Ioannou, "Howard Schultz, Interview: King Bean; Starbucks CEO Howard Schultz Runs a $1 Billion Company That Has a Successful Message for Small Business: Create Value and Always Focus on Customer Service," *Your Company,* April 1,1998, p. 66; Adrienne W. Fawcett, "The Marketing 100: Starbucks: Scott Bedbury," *Advertising Age,* June 30, 1997, p. S18; Ronald Henkoff and Amy R. Kover, "Cover Stories: Growing Your Company: Five Ways to Do It Right; This Implies, Of Course, That You Can Do It Wrong Too. Here's How Some Shrewd Companies Avoided the Pitfalls," *Fortune,* November 25, 1996, p. 78; "Advertising and Marketing; THE PERSUADERS: A Look at Creative People Making a Difference; Starbucks' Schultz: Making His Macchiato," *Home Edition, Los Angeles Times,* September 25, 1997, p. D–5.

Direct marketing promotions are not always aimed at the consumer. In this instance, BMW (www.bmw.com) sent promotional material to their dealers and tied it into the James Bond film, Tomorrow Never Dies.

The field of direct marketing is growing rapidly as companies discover the benefits of control, cost efficiency, and accountability. For example, many companies like Levi Strauss use **telemarketing** (a direct-marketing technique) to increase productivity through person-to-person phone contact. By using the phone to follow up direct-mail advertising, a company can increase the response rate substantially. Moreover, through telemarketing, it can develop a valuable database of customers and prospects to use in future mailings and promotions.[58] We discuss this topic more thoroughly in Chapter 9.

Public Relations

Many firms supplement (or replace) their advertising with various public relations activities such as **publicity** (news releases, feature stories) and **special events** (open houses, factory tours, VIP parties, grand openings) to inform various audiences about the company and its products and to build corporate credibility and image. Public relations activities, as we discuss in Chapter 10, are extremely powerful tools that should always be integrated into a company's communications mix.

Collateral Materials

As mentioned in Chapter 3, **collateral materials** are the many accessory items companies produce to integrate and supplement their advertising or PR activities. These include booklets, catalogs, brochures, films, sales kits, and annual reports. Collateral materials should always be designed to reinforce the company's image or the brand's position in the minds of customers.

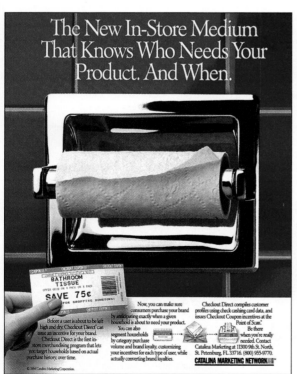

Checkout Coupon is an electronic in-store sales promotion that delivers incentives to shoppers at the checkout counter, based on what they buy. Catalina Marketing Network helps the retailer coordinate the campaigns with tie-in of the coupons to in-store posters, shelf-talkers, savings on related store products, and newspaper ads.

Sales Promotion

As we discuss in Chapter 9, **sales promotion** is a category of demand-influencing instruments and activities that supplement the basic instruments of the marketing mix for short periods of time by stimulating channel members or prospective customers to some immediate, overt behavior.[59] This broad category includes trade deals, free samples, displays, trading stamps, sweepstakes, cents-off coupons, and premiums, among others. *Reader's Digest,* for example, is famous for its annual sweepstakes designed to increase circulation. And grocery manufacturers print and distribute over 322 billion coupons per year, saving consumers $2.5 billion to $3 billion annually.[60]

Some promotions are linked mainly to the communications function of the marketing mix (displays, events, trade shows), while others are linked more to the product element (free samples, premiums) or the price element (coupons, volume discounts, end-of-month sales). And some complement the distribution element (trade deals, sales contests). Sales promotion (often referred to simply as *promotion*) is used primarily as a tactical adaptation to some external situation such as competitive pressure, changing seasons, declining sales, or new-product introductions.[61] Since advertising people are frequently called on to solve a variety of marketing problems, it is critical that they understand and know how to integrate the whole mix of communications techniques.

The **Marketing Mix** in Perspective

With the target market designated and the elements of the marketing mix determined, the company has a complete product concept and a strategic basis for marketing to that target. Now it can formalize its strategies and tactics in a written marketing and advertising plan. As part of the planning process, companies use marketing and advertising research. We discuss this in Chapter 6 before dealing with the formal planning process in Chapter 7.

Tech Talk

Segmentation Software

Knowing just who your customers are and where you can find them is perhaps the most important part of advertising. Almost intuitively we understand that the better you understand your target audience, the better you can create and place advertising that influences their purchasing behavior. Today, companies like The Marketing Task Group, ABC Technologies, SPSS Inc., Arbitron New Media, and Knowledge Seeker provide a variety of sophisticated market segmentation software just for this purpose: to help advertisers locate exactly where their consumers are.

These software analyze market regions via psychographic and demographic research, and act as a "consultant" by providing advice and graphs for a specific area. For example, the program TEAMS™, developed by The Marketing Task Group, acts as a "Virtual Consultant on a Disk" to eliminate guesswork from the creation of marketing plans. Users begin by answering detailed questions about their markets, the competition, promotional strategies, pricing, profitability, and sales force management. After the questions are completed, the computer analyzes the data and produces a detailed report.

Other programs like Retail Direct, developed by Arbitron New Media, outline the consumers' direct behavior. Retail Direct provides account executives with the ability to describe customers and media audiences in terms of their socioeconomic status, lifestyle, shopping behavior, purchase intentions, and media usage. The service delivers local consumer categories (e.g., automotive, audio-visual, soft drinks) as well as local media usage categories (radio, television, newspapers, advertising circulars) and key retail categories of who spends the most advertising dollars in a given market.

Research is consistently an underperformed task because of the time and resources it requires, but with the development of software like TEAMS™ and Retail Direct we can expect to see increased efforts in this direction.

Sources: The Marketing Task Group, Quick Facts about TEAMS™ (**T**otal **E**valuation and **A**nalysis of **M**arketing and **S**ales), retrieved from (www.mtg-teams.com/facts.htm), May 1998, and "Retail Direct: Your Local Market Qualitative Source," Arbitron New Media, retrieved from (http://www.arbitron.com/nmretaildirect.html), May 1998.

Chapter **Summary**

Market segmentation is the process of identifying groups of people with certain shared characteristics within a broad product market and aggregating these groups into larger market segments according to their mutual interest in the product's utility. From these segments, companies can then select a target market. Marketers use a number of methods to identify behavioral groups and segment markets. The most common are behavioristic, geographic, demographic, and psychographic.

Business markets are often segmented in the same way as consumer markets. They may also be grouped by business purchasing procedures, SIC code, or market concentration.

In the target marketing process, companies designate specific segments to target and develop their mix of marketing activities. The product concept is the consumer's perception of the product as a bundle of utilitarian and symbolic need-satisfying values.

Every company can add, subtract, or modify four major elements in its marketing program to achieve a desired marketing mix. These elements are product, price, distribution (place), and communications (promotion)—the 4 Ps.

The *product* element includes the way the product is designed and classified, positioned, branded, and packaged. Just as humans pass through a life cycle, so do products—and product categories. The stage of a product's life cycle may determine how it is advertised.

To satisfy the variety of consumer tastes and achieve competitive advantages, marketers build differences into their products. Even the product's package is part of the product concept. The concept may also be developed through unique positioning against competing products.

Price refers to what and how a customer pays for a product. Companies use many common pricing strategies. Some products compete on the basis of price, but many do not.

Distribution refers to how the product is placed at the disposal of the customer: where the product is distributed, how it is bought, and how it is sold. Companies may use direct or indirect methods of distribution. Consumer goods manufacturers use several types of distribution strategies.

Communications refers to all marketing-related communications between the seller and the buyer. Tools of the communications element include personal selling, advertising, direct marketing, public relations activities, collateral materials, and sales promotion. Marketers try to integrate all their marketing communications programs for greater effectiveness and consistency.

Important **Terms**

behavioristic segmentation, *151*

benefit segmentation, *152*

benefits, *152*

brand, *168*

brand equity, *169*

business markets, *157*

collateral materials, *178*

communication element, *176*

communications mix, *176*

cooperative advertising, *175*

copy points, *170*

decline stage, *166*

demographic segmentation, *153*

demographics, *153*

direct distribution, *173*

direct marketing, *176*

distribution channel, *174*

distribution element, *173*

equipment-based service, *166*

exclusive distribution, *175*

family brand, *168*

four Ps, *163*

franchising, *175*

geodemographic segmentation, *153*

geographic segmentation, *153*

growth stage, *165*

hidden differences, *167*

Review **Questions**

1. How does the concept of shared characteristics relate to the market segmentation process?
2. How could you use VALS to develop the marketing strategy for a product of your choice?
3. How does the segmentation of business markets differ from that of consumer markets?
4. What is the most important factor to consider when determining the elements of the marketing mix?
5. What is the difference between a product and a product concept?

6. What are some examples of product positioning not discussed in this chapter?
7. What effect does the product life cycle have on the advertising a company uses?
8. What factors influence the price of a product?
9. How do the basic methods of distribution affect advertising?
10. What product characteristics encourage heavy advertising? Little advertising? Why?

Exploring the **Internet**

The Internet exercises for Chapter 5 address the following areas covered throughout the chapter: marketing and the marketing mix (Exercise 1), and market segmentation and target marketing (Exercise 2).

1. World of Marketing

   Part I: Marketing.   You already learned the importance of marketing to the study and application of advertising. Visit the sites below to get a better feel about the scope of the marketing world and the importance of a good marketing strategy. Be sure to answer the questions below for each site.

   • American Marketing Association (AMA) **www.ama.org**
   • Business Marketing Association (BMA) **www.marketing.org**
   • American Business Press (ABP) **www.americanbusinesspress.com**
   • Business-to-Business Online **www.btb.com**
   • *BrandWeek* **www.brandweek.com**
   • *Business Marketing* **www.crain.co.uk/crain/busmar.html**
   • *Business-to-Business Marketing* **www.business2business.on.ca**
   • *Marketing* **www.marketing.haynet.com**

   • *Marketing Magazine* **www.marketingmag.ca**
   • *Marketing Tools* **www.marketingtools.com**
   • *Sales & Marketing Management* **www.salesandmarketing.com**

   a. What group sponsors the site? Who is the intended audience?
   b. What is the site's purpose? Does it succeed? Why?
   c. What is the size/scope of the organization? What is the organization's purpose?
   d. Who makes up the organization's membership? Its constituency?

   Part II: Marketing Mix. Visit Levi Strauss's site (www.levi.com) and then answer the following questions about one of its products.

   a. Identify the product, price, place, and promotion. (If there are multiple products, choose one.)
   b. Identify the stage in the product life cycle.
   c. What is the product's positioning?
   d. What are the key elements of the product's differentiation?

2. Market Segmentation and Target Marketing

   Segmenting markets and generating sound demographic, geographic, psychographic, and behavioristic profiles are critical to formulating advertising strategy. There is an abundance of market segmentation data available on the Internet from both the government and private sector. Peruse the following sample of online resources for target market information.

   - U.S. Census Bureau **www.census.gov**
   - USA Data **www.usadata.com**
   - Forrester Research **www.forrester.com**
   - *American Demographics* **www.demographics.com**
   - Target Marketing **www.napco.com/tm/tmcover.html**

   - Market Segment Resource Locator **www.awool.com**
   - Target Marketing & Creative Services **www.targetweb.com**

   Now choose a company with a Web site and use one of these online resources to answer the following questions. Be sure to cite any online resources you used besides the above.

   a. What type of segmentation approach did they take (single-market, multiple-market, aggregate market)?

   b. Develop a demographic profile, including age, income, education, and gender, for the target market.

   c. Describe the general geographic skew for the company's market.

   d. What consumption patterns are evident in the company's consumers?

Chapter Six

Information Gathering: Inputs to Advertising Planning

Objective To examine how advertisers gain information about the marketplace and how they apply their findings to marketing and advertising decision making.

After studying this chapter, you will be able to:

- Discuss how research helps advertisers locate market segments and identify target markets.

- Explain the basic steps in the research process.

- Discuss the differences between formal and informal research and primary and secondary data.

- Explain the methods used in qualitative and quantitative research.

- Define and explain the concepts of validity and reliability.

- Recognize the issues in creating survey questionnaires.

- Explain the challenges international advertisers face in collecting research data abroad.

- Debate the pros and cons of advertising testing.

In the mid-80s, Healthtex was a $350 million concern. But by the early 90s, the 75-year-old company was barely hanging on. Fortunately, VF Corp., the parent of Wrangler jeans, realized the value of the brand and bought the company. Healthtex had been a leading manufacturer of children's clothing for many decades, but with the emergence of sophisticated competition, the company had not kept up. VF moved it to offices close to Wrangler in Greensboro, North Carolina; installed new management; and proceeded to turn Healthtex around. John Martin was appointed director of marketing services and he brought in a new ad agency, The Martin Agency (no relation), in Richmond, Virginia.[1] • "Frankly, we needed help," says Martin. "And we weren't shy about requesting it. We didn't just need brilliant creative work; we needed extraordinarily savvy marketing counsel, too." • They got it. The people at The Martin Agency knew they had to know the product quickly. Beth Rilee-Kelley, now the agency's director of creative services, remembers the first days working on the account. "We went right out into the field and talked to retailers that carried the line and consumers that bought it," she says: "And we learned a lot—fast." • They got good news and bad news. • The bad news was that the trade was

disappointed in the company and lost confidence in the brand. Healthtex had missed shipping dates; customer service had declined; retailers saw the brand as underfunded in advertising and marketing; and even the product quality had slipped. In short, the long relationships Healthtex had enjoyed with retailers were rapidly deteriorating. • The good news was that consumers were unaware of these problems and still had great confidence in the Healthtex name. Moms saw the brand as high-quality, everyday playwear that lasts. They loved it.[2] • The agency also discovered that moms, the busiest customers on the planet, didn't find anything compelling or inspiring in advertising for any brand of kidswear. Magazines were full of ads showing beautiful, cuddly children in spotless clothes. But that just didn't resonate with these moms. There was no recognition of the hectic, untidy lives that moms of small children actually lead. • This was the nugget of insight the agency—and Healthtex—needed. This provided the opportunity for a unique position in the marketplace, for Healthtex to establish itself as the brand that understands moms and their lives. • In a series of award-winning ads, The Martin Agency made this position clear, sometimes explicitly, always implicitly. In one of the first ads, the headline reads: "Your baby's naked. Your phone's ringing. And your mother-in-law's walking up the driveway. Let's talk snaps." This was followed by four columns of factual, informative copy to explain precisely the practical, functional differences built into Healthtex infant wear. In another ad, the headline warns: "You've got 23 seconds to get your 2-year-old from the sandbox to the potty. Go." ● To say the least, these ads resonated with parents. They showed that Healthtex really understood just how chaotic it can be to raise (and dress) small children. In short order, Healthtex became the only brand with a position that had more substance than cuteness. Thanks to good research, the campaign enabled Healthtex to reverse its decline immediately, increase its market share, and regain its lost luster with the trade. It also made The Martin Agency a household name in the advertising business.[3] ●

The **Need** for **Research** in Marketing and Advertising

Marketing research is the important process of gathering, recording, and analyzing information about customers and prospects. Companies such as A. C. Nielsen (http://acnielsen.com) collect data for their clients and provide critical insight into current and potential markets.

Every year companies spend millions of dollars creating ads and promotions that they hope their customers and prospects will notice and relate to. Then they spend millions more placing their communications in print and electronic media, hoping their customers will see and hear them and eventually respond.

Advertising is expensive. In the United States the cost of a single 30-second commercial on prime-time network TV averages around $100,000. Likewise, a single, full-page color ad in a national business magazine averages $150 to reach every thousand prospects.[4] That's too much money to risk unless advertisers have very good information about who their customers are, what they want and like, and where they spend their media time. And that's why advertisers need research. Research provides the information that drives marketing and advertising decision making. Without that information, advertisers are forced to use intuition or guesswork. In today's fast-changing, highly competitive, global economy, that invites failure.

What Is Marketing Research?

To help managers make marketing decisions, companies develop systematic procedures for gathering, recording, and analyzing new information. This is called **marketing research** (it should not be confused with *market research,* which is information gathered about a *particular* market or market segment).[5] Marketing research does a number of things: it helps identify consumer needs and market segments; it provides the information necessary for developing new products and devising marketing strategies; and it enables managers to assess the effectiveness of marketing programs and promotional activities. Marketing research is also useful in financial planning, economic forecasting, and quality control.

Research is a big business today. Worldwide, the top 25 research companies earn over $6 billion per year in revenues for marketing, advertising, and public opinion research. In fact, these top 25 U.S. research organizations, led by the global A. C. Nielsen Co., account for about 60 percent of the worldwide total—much of it coming from foreign clients.[6] Exhibit 6–1 lists the top 10 research companies by revenues.

Exhibit 6–1

Top research companies by U.S. research revenues in 1996 ($ millions).

Rank	Organization	Total research revenues
1.	ACNielsen Corp.	$1,358.6
2.	Cognizant Corp.	1,223.8
3.	Information Resources Inc.	405.6
4.	The Arbitron Co.	153.1
5.	PMSI/Source Informatics	152.2
6.	Westat Inc.	146.5
7.	Maritz Marketing Research Inc.	133.6
8.	NFO Research Inc.	109.2
9.	The Kantar Group	103.3
10.	The NPD Group	99.6

In the marketing research process, companies gather a lot of different types of information. It may be easiest to think of all these in terms of what one researcher terms the *three Rs* of marketing: *recruiting* new customers, *retaining* current customers, and *regaining* lost customers.[7]

For example, to *recruit* new customers, researchers may study different market segments and create product attribute models to match buyers with the right products and services. Marketers need answers to many questions: What new products do consumers want? Which ideas should we work on? What are the most important product benefits to our customers? What changes in the product's appearance and performance will increase sales? What price will maintain the brand's image, create profits, and still be attractive and affordable to consumers? Answers may lead to product design and marketing decisions that directly affect the product's nature, content, packaging, pricing—and advertising.[8]

On the other hand, to *retain* existing customers, a marketer may use *customer satisfaction studies. Databases* of customer transactions may identify reasons for customer satisfaction or dissatisfaction.[9] Today, companies realize that the best sales go to those who develop good relationships with individual customers.[10] As a result, customer satisfaction is now the fastest-growing field in marketing research.

Information gained for the first two Rs helps the third, *regaining* lost customers. For example, if an office equipment manufacturer discovers through research that an increase in service calls typically precedes cancellation of a service contract, it can watch for that pattern with current customers and then take preventive action. Moreover, it can review service records of former customers and (if the pattern holds true) devise some marketing action or advertising appeal to win them back.[11]

In short, good marketing research enables the company to devise a sophisticated, integrated mix of product, price, distribution, and communication elements. It gives the advertiser and its agency the information they need to decide which strategies will enhance the brand's image and lead to greater profits. Finally, it enables them to judge the effectiveness of past programs and campaigns.

When companies falter in their efforts to satisfy market expectations, regaining lost customers can be a formidable problem. What is needed is innovative marketing and outstanding communications. Ads like this one from Healthtex (www.healthtex.com), which demonstrate an understanding of modern mothers' concerns, can help restore faith in the company's brand.

What Is Advertising Research?

Before developing any ad campaign, a company needs to know how consumers perceive its products, how they view the competition, and what brand or company image would be most credible. To get this information, companies use *advertising research*. A subset of marketing research, **advertising research** is the systematic gathering and analysis of information to help develop or evaluate advertising strategies, individual ads, and whole campaigns.

In this chapter, we consider the importance of information gathering to the development of advertising plans and strategies, look at how research can be used to test the effectiveness of ads before and after they run, and explore a number of specific research techniques.

Applying Research to Advertising **Decision Making**

Advertising research serves various purposes, most of which can be grouped into four categories: *strategy research, creative concept research, pretesting,* and *posttesting*.

1. *Advertising strategy research*. Used to help define the product concept or to assist in the selection of target markets, advertising messages, or media vehicles.
2. *Creative concept research*. Measures the target audience's acceptance of different creative ideas at the concept stage.
3. *Pretesting of ads*. Used to diagnose possible communication problems before a campaign begins.
4. *Posttesting of ads*. Enables marketers to evaluate a campaign after it runs.

As Exhibit 6–2 shows, marketers use the different categories of advertising research at different stages of ad or campaign development. The techniques they use at each stage also vary considerably. We'll examine each of these categories briefly before moving on to discuss the research process.

Category 1: *Advertising Strategy Research*

Companies develop advertising strategies by blending elements of the *creative mix*: the *product concept*, the *target audience*, the *communication media*, and the *creative message*. Advertising strategy research seeks information about these various elements.

	Category 1: Advertising Strategy Research	Category 2: Creative Concept Research	Category 3: Pretesting	Category 4: Posttesting
Timing	Before creative work begins	Before agency production begins	Before finished artwork and photography	After campaign has run
Research problem	Product concept definition Target audience selection Media selection Message-element selection	Concept testing Name testing Slogan testing	Print testing TV storyboard pretesting Radio commercial pretesting	Advertising effectiveness Consumer attitude change Sales increases
Techniques	Consumer attitude and usage studies	Free-association tests Qualitative interviews Statement-comparison tests	Consumer juries Matched samples Portfolio tests Storyboard test Mechanical devices Psychological rating scales	Aided recall Unaided recall Attitude tests Inquiry tests Sales tests

Exhibit 6–2
Categories of research in advertising development.

Through the applied use of marketing research, Healthtex discovered that customers wanted more than just cute clothing. They needed clothing that was designed to be practical and would allow them to spend more quality time with their children. This ad, created by The Martin Agency, highlighted those qualities in the Healthtex brand.

Product Concept Definition

As we saw at the beginning of this chapter, advertisers need to know how consumers perceive their brands. They also want to know what qualities lead to initial purchases and, eventually, to brand loyalty.

The Martin Agency asked consumers what would entice them to put their kids in Healthtex. They discovered that, overall, moms look for cuteness, durability, ease of dressing, and washability. Cuteness is the price of entry into the category—but to succeed a brand must have more than that.

Healthtex did. But they also discovered that mothers with full-time jobs want to spend any spare time they have with their kids. They don't want to waste time shopping. They want to be able to go in, pick out a trusted brand, and get home to spend time with the family.[12]

It's this kind of information that can lead to an effective positioning strategy for the brand. Advertising can shape and magnify a brand's position and image over time. In fact, this is one of the most important strategic benefits of advertising. But to use media advertising effectively, strategy research is essential to develop a blueprint for creatives to follow.[13]

Advertising works differently for different product categories and, often, even for different brands within a category. This means that each brand must develop a template for the creative based on an understanding of its particular consumers' wants, needs, and motivations. Only if this is done correctly over time (say, one to two years), can brand equity be built.[14]

To determine how brands are built and how they derive their strength Young & Rubicam developed the BrandAsset Valuator™. This model measures brands in terms of familiarity, relevance, differentiation, and esteem. In the mid-90s, a Y&R study in 19 countries found that Disney was one of the highest-valued brands around the world, even in France, home of the troubled Disneyland Paris theme park.[15]

Target Audience Selection

In Chapters 4 and 5 we pointed out that no market includes everybody. Therefore, a major purpose of research is to develop a rich profile of the brand's target markets and audiences. The marketer needs to know which customers are the primary users of the product category and then will study them carefully to understand their demographics, geographics, psychographics, and purchase behavior.

In the case of Healthtex, the agency discovered two distinct markets for its client's clothes: new mothers and experienced mothers. New mothers were categorized as first-time moms with infants from birth to 20 months old. The children of experienced mothers were between 2 and 4 years old. These were the primary markets and audiences for Healthtex's advertising. When the agency discovered later that grandparents were also a viable target market, it designed a program to appeal to them also.

With any new product, the biggest problem is invariably the budget. There is never enough money to attack all geographic or demographic markets effectively at the same time. So the advertiser often decides to employ the *dominance concept*—researching which markets (geographic or otherwise) are most important to product sales and targeting those where it can achieve advertising dominance.

Media Selection

To develop media strategies, select media vehicles, and evaluate their results, advertisers use a subset of advertising research called **media research.** Agencies subscribe to syndicated research services (such as A. C. Nielsen, Arbitron, Simmons, or Standard Rate & Data Service) that monitor and publish information on the reach and effectiveness of media vehicles—radio, TV, newspapers, and so on—in every major geographic market in the United States and Canada. (We'll discuss these in Part Five: "Using Media.")

The Martin Agency researched what media were regularly used by mothers. It discovered that new moms read publications like *American Baby* and *Baby Talk*, while more experienced mothers read *Parents* magazine and *Parenting*.

Message-Element Selection

Companies hope to find promising advertising messages by studying consumers' likes and dislikes in relation to brands and products. That was certainly what happened to Healthtex.

Similarly, AT&T wanted to create a corporate campaign to tell consumers how the company was developing high-tech products and services to improve their lives. The company's agency, N. W. Ayer, conducted a series of qualitative consumer attitude studies and discovered numerous potential themes. Next, the agency used concept testing to pinpoint which message-element options might prove most successful. This was now category 2 research aimed at developing creative advertising concepts.

Category 2: Creative Concept Research

Ayer prepared several tentative ad concepts in the form of *animatics,* rough commercials using stills instead of action. Each scene stressed a different service AT&T would offer consumers in the future, such as sending faxes from the beach with a personal communicator, paying road tolls without slowing down, or buying concert tickets with a "smart" card. The agency then conducted focus groups in its unique developmental lab, which combines intensive qualitative interviews with quantitative techniques. While a discussion leader moderated the conversation, each group viewed the animatics. The groups' reactions were measured, taped, and observed by Ayer staff behind a one-way mirror.

Once the most appealing products and services were determined, Ayer developed a campaign to verbally and nonverbally express AT&T's benefits to consumers. The theme was simply: "You will." The commercials posed questions such as "Have you ever tucked your baby in from a phone booth?" Answer: "You will. And the company that will bring it to you . . . AT&T." This embodied the company's mission of being the world's leader in bringing people together, giving them

The "You will" campaign from AT&T (www.att.com) received high marks from advertising critics—a result of good creativity and adequate testing.

AVO: Have you ever paid a toll . . . without slowing down?

AVO: Bought concert tickets . . .
FIRST GIRL: "There we go."

SECOND GIRL: "Yeah, perfect."

AVO: Or tucked your baby in . . . from a phone booth?

MOTHER: "Hi, pretty girl."
AVO: You will.

AVO: And the company that will bring it to you . . . AT&T.

easy access to each other and to the information and services they want and need—anytime, anywhere.

The campaign was so successful that the Advertising Research Foundation named Ayer a finalist for its prestigious David Ogilvy Award, given to the most effective ad campaign supported by research.[16]

Categories 3 and 4: Testing and Evaluating of Advertising

Advertising is often the largest single cost in a company's marketing budget. No wonder its effectiveness is a major concern! Companies want to know what they are getting for their money—and whether their advertising is working.

The Purpose of Testing

Testing is the primary tool advertisers use to ensure their advertising dollars are spent wisely. Testing can prevent costly errors, especially in judging which advertising strategy or medium is most effective. And it can give the advertiser some measure (besides sales results) of a campaign's value.

To increase the likelihood of preparing the most effective advertising messages, companies use **pretesting.** Some agencies, like DDB Needham, pretest all ad copy for communication gaps or flaws in message content before recommending it to clients.[17] When companies don't pretest their ads, they may encounter a surprising reaction from the marketplace. Schering Canada received a torrent of complaint letters from customers who said they didn't like its commercial introducing the antihistamine Claritin to the over-the-counter market in Canada. Most negative responses, though, are more insidious: consumers simply turn the page or change the channel, and sales mysteriously suffer. This is why it's also important to evaluate the effectiveness of an ad or campaign *after* it runs. **Posttesting** (also called *ad tracking*) provides the advertiser with useful guidelines for future advertising.

Claritin's (www.claritin.com) first commercial of a heavy metal rock musician was very memorable but received mixed reactions from the public, so the agency created new testimonial spots spoofing its own commercials.

"There's this TV ad that's driving me nuts."
SFX: Heavy metal guitar.
"It's this new antihistamine . . .
Uh . . . Claritin."
"He does something with his face . . ."

SFX: Heavy metal guitar.
"Claritin's great . . . it's the ad."
SFX: Heavy metal guitar.
"I think I'm allergic to the commercial . . .
Quick, gimme a Claritin."

AVO: New Claritin. Fast, 24-hour relief of seasonal allergies that lets you stay alert. From the makers of ChlorTrippolon.

Testing Helps Make Important Decisions

Advertisers use pretesting to help make decisions about a number of variables. It's easiest to think of these as the five Ms: *merchandise, markets, motives, messages,* and *media*. Many of these can be posttested too. However, in posttesting, the objective is to evaluate, not diagnose. We'll discuss each of the five Ms briefly.

Merchandise   For purposes of alliteration, we refer to the product concept here as **merchandise.** Companies may pretest a number of factors: the package design, how advertising positions the brand, or how well the advertising communicates the product's features.

In a process called *benefit testing,* The Martin Agency presented 10 to 12 product benefits to consumers in a focus group. The idea was to test which benefits the group considered most persuasive or compelling.[18]

A company called MarketWare Simulation Services introduced a virtual-reality testing program called Visionary Shopper, which allows people in the test to "shop" on a realistic on-screen shelf, using a touch-sensitive monitor and a trackball. They can "pull" products off the shelf, study them in 3-D, and rotate them to read side and back panels. They select items by touching an on-screen shopping cart, and the computer tracks the products examined and/or chosen, instantly gauging the impact of whatever the client is testing.[19]

Markets   Advertisers may pretest an advertising strategy or particular commercials with various audience groups representing different **markets.** The information they gain may cause them to alter their strategy and target the campaign to a different market. In posttesting, advertisers want to know if the campaign succeeded in reaching its target markets. Changes in awareness and increases in market share are two indicators of success.

Motives   Consumers' **motives** are outside advertisers' control, but the messages they create to appeal to those motives are not. Pretesting helps advertisers identify and appeal to the most compelling needs and motives. Posttesting can indicate how effective they were.

Messages   Pretesting helps identify outstanding, as well as underperforming, ads and commercials. It helps determine what (from the customer's point of view) a **message** says and how well it says it. Advertisers might test the headline, the text, the illustration, the typography—or the message concept. Most importantly, pretesting guides the improvement of commercials.[20]

However, pretesting is not foolproof. The only way to know for sure if the advertising works is through continuous tracking or posttesting. Here the advertiser determines to what extent the message was seen, remembered, and believed. Changes in consumer attitude, perception, or brand interest indicate success, as does consumers' ability to remember a campaign slogan or identify the sponsor.

Media   The cost of media advertising is soaring, and advertisers today demand greater accountability. Information gained from pretesting can influence several types of media decisions: classes of media, media subclasses, specific media vehicles, media units of space and time, media budgets, and scheduling criteria.

The broad media categories of electronic, print, outdoor, and direct mail are referred to as **media classes.** Within these categories, **media subclasses** are radio or TV, newsmagazines or business publications, and so on. The specific **media vehicle** is the particular program or publication. **Media units** are the size or length of an ad: half-page or full-page ads, 15- or 30-second spots, 60-second commercials, and so forth.

After a campaign runs, posttesting can determine how effectively the media mix reached the target audience and communicated the desired message. We discuss audience measurement further in Chapters 14 through 17.

A constant question facing all advertisers is how large the company's advertising budget should be. How much should be allocated to various markets and media? To specific products? Advertisers can use a number of pretesting techniques to determine optimum spending levels before introducing national campaigns. (Chapter 7, "Marketing and Advertising Planning," provides further information on budgeting.)

Media scheduling is another nagging question for many advertisers. Through pretesting, advertisers can test consumer response during different seasons of the year or days of the week. They can test whether frequent advertising is more effective than occasional or one-time insertions, or whether year-round advertising is more effective than advertising concentrated during a gift-buying season. (Chapter 8, "Planning Media Strategy," discusses the most common types of media schedules.)

Overall results   Finally, advertisers want to measure overall results to evaluate how well they accomplished their objectives. Posttesting is most helpful here to determine whether and how to continue, what to change, and how much to spend in the future. We'll discuss the methods advertisers use for pre- and posttesting toward the end of the chapter, in the section on conducting formal research.

Steps in the Research Process

Now that we understand the various types of decision-related information that marketers seek, let's explore how they gather this information by looking at the overall research process and some of the specific techniques they use.

There are five basic steps in the research process (see Exhibit 6–3 on page 192):

1. Situation analysis and problem definition.
2. Informal (exploratory) research.
3. Construction of research objectives.
4. Formal research.
5. Interpretation and reporting of findings.

Step 1: Analyzing the Situation and Defining the Problem

The first step in the marketing research process is to *analyze the situation* and *define the problem*. Many large firms have in-house research departments. Often the marketing department also maintains a **marketing**

Exhibit 6–3
The marketing research process begins with evaluation of the company's situation and definition of the problem.

information system (MIS)—a sophisticated set of procedures designed to generate a continuous, orderly flow of information for use in making marketing decisions. These systems ensure that managers get the information they need when they need it.[21]

Most smaller firms don't have dedicated research departments, and their methods for obtaining marketing information are frequently inadequate. These firms often find the problem-definition step difficult and time-consuming. Yet good research on the wrong problem is a waste of effort.

Step 2: Conducting Informal (Exploratory) Research

The second step in the process is to use **informal** (or *exploratory*) **research** to learn more about the market, the competition, and the business environment, and to better define the problem. As we saw with Healthtex, researchers may discuss the problem with wholesalers, distributors, or retailers outside the firm; with informed sources inside the firm; with customers; or even with competitors. They look for whoever has the most information to offer.

There are two types of research data: *primary* and *secondary*. Information collected from the marketplace about a specific problem is called **primary data;** acquiring it is typically expensive and time-consuming. So during the exploratory stage, researchers frequently use **secondary data**—information previously collected or published, usually for some other purpose, by the firm or by some other organization. This information is readily available, either internally or externally, and can be gathered more quickly and inexpensively than primary data.

Assembling Internal Secondary Data

Company records are often a valuable source of secondary information. Useful internal data include product shipment figures, billings, warranty-card records, advertising expenditures, sales expenses, customer correspondence, and records of meetings with sales staffs.

A well-developed marketing information system can help researchers analyze sales data, review past tracking studies, and examine previous marketing research data. This information might point the way toward an interesting headline or positioning statement such as Jiffy Lube's: "America's favorite oil change."

Gathering External Secondary Data

Much information is available, sometimes for little or no cost, from the government, market research companies, trade associations, various trade publications, or computerized databases. Most large companies subscribe to any of a number of syndicated research reports about their particular industry. For example, as the advertising manager for a large nutritional company introducing a new line of vitamins, you might need to know the current demand for vitamins and food supplements, the number of competitors in the marketplace, the amount of advertising each is doing, and the challenges and opportunities the industry faces. RL 6–1 in the Reference Library lists sources of information on the vitamin market. Many of these sources apply to other markets as well.

In the United States, frequently used sources of secondary data include:

- Library reference materials (*Business Periodicals Index* for business magazines, *Reader's Guide to Periodical Literature* for consumer magazines, *Public Information Service Bulletin,* the *New York Times Index,* and the *World Almanac and Book of Facts*).

- Government publications (*Statistical Abstract of the United States*).

- Trade association publications (annual fact books containing government data gathered by various industry groups listed in the *Directory of National Trade Associations*).

- Research organizations and their publications or syndicated information (literature from university bureaus of business research, Nielsen retail store audits, MRCA consumer purchase diaries, Simmons' Study of Media and Markets, IRI's InfoScan market tracking service, and Standard Rate & Data Service).

- Consumer/business publications (*Business Week, Forbes, Fortune, American Demographics, Advertising Age, Computer Marketing,* and thousands more).

- Computer database services (DIALOG Information Service, ABI/Inform, Electric Library, IQuest and Knowledge Index from CompuServe, and Dow Jones News Retrieval Service).

The Internet has evolved into a wellspring of secondary data that can be put to use for marketing purposes. Several well-known market research firms publish abbreviated market data on the World Wide Web, while other Internet services like Electric Library (www.elibrary.com) act as databases of news articles published in a wide range of trade and business journals. However, marketers must beware of the danger of potentially unreliable data sources on the Internet, as many sites may publish information that has not been verified by any independent organizations.

It's important to understand that secondary data carry some potential problems. Information may be out of date and therefore obsolete. Much of it is not relevant to the problem at hand. Some information from purported research is just wrong, so the findings are invalid. In other cases, the source may be unreliable. Finally, there is now so much information available (thanks to the Internet) that it's just overwhelming; it's virtually impossible to wade through it all.

Using Secondary Data for International Markets

In developing countries, the research profession is not as sophisticated or organized as in North America and Europe.[22] The available secondary research statistics may be outdated or invalid. When evaluating secondary data, advertising managers should ask: Who collected the data and why? What research techniques did they use? Would the source have any reason to bias the data? When were the data collected? International advertising managers should exercise caution when dealing with "facts" about foreign markets.

Step 3: Establishing Research Objectives

Once the exploratory research phase is completed, the company may discover it needs additional information that it can get only from doing primary research. For example, it may want to identify exactly who its customers are and clarify their perceptions of the company and the competition. To do so, the company must first establish *specific research objectives*.

A concise written statement of the research problem and objectives should be formulated at the beginning of any research project. A company must be clear about what decisions it has to make that the research results will guide. Once it knows the application, it can set down clear, specific research objectives.[23] For example, a department store, noticing that it is losing market share, might write its problem statement and research objectives as follows:

Market Share
Our company's sales, while still increasing, seem to have lost momentum and are not producing the profit our shareholders expect. In the last year, our market share slipped 10 percent in the men's footwear department and 7 percent in the women's fine apparel department. Our studies indicate we are losing sales to other department stores in the same malls and that customers are confused about our position in the market. We need to make decisions about how we position ourselves for the future marketplace.

Research Objectives
We must answer the following questions: (1) Who are our customers? (2) Who are the customers of other department stores? (3) What do these customers like and dislike about us and about our competitors? (4) How are we currently perceived? and (5) What do we have to do to clarify and improve that perception?

This statement of the problem is specific and measurable, the decision point is clear, and the questions are related and relevant. The research results should provide the information management needs to decide on a new positioning strategy for the company. The positioning strategy facilitates the development of marketing and advertising plans that will set the company's course for years to come.

Step 4: Conducting Formal Research

When a company wants to collect primary data directly from the marketplace about a specific problem or issue, it uses **formal research.** There are two types of formal research: qualitative and quantitative.

To get a general impression of the market, the consumer, or the product, advertisers typically start with *qualitative research*. This enables researchers to gain insight into both the population whose opinion will be sampled and the subject matter itself. Then, to get hard numbers about specific marketing situations, they may perform a survey or use some other form of *quantitative research*. Sophisticated

Exhibit 6–4

Differences between qualitative and quantitative research.

	Qualitative	Quantitative
Main techniques for gathering data	Focus groups and in-depth interviews.	Surveys and scientific samples.
Kinds of questions asked	Why? Through what thought process? In what way? In connection with what other behavior or thoughts?	How many? How much?
Role of interviewer	Critical: interviewer must think on feet and frame questions and probes in response to whatever respondents say. A highly trained professional is advisable.	Important, but interviewers need only be able to read scripts. They should not improvise. Minimally trained, responsible employees are suitable.
Questions asked	Questions vary in order and phrasing from group to group and interview to interview. New questions are added, old ones dropped.	Should be exactly the same for each interview. Order and phrasing of questions carefully controlled.
Number of interviews	Fewer interviews tending to last a longer time.	Many interviews in order to give a projectable scientific sample.
Kinds of findings	Develop hypotheses, gain insights, explore language options, refine concepts, flesh out numerical data, provide diagnostics on advertising copy.	Test hypotheses, prioritize factors, provide data for mathematical modeling and projections.

agencies use a balance of both qualitative and quantitative methods, understanding the limits of each and how they work together.[24] (See Exhibit 6–4.)

Basic Methods of Qualitative Research

To get people to share their thoughts and feelings, researchers use **qualitative research** that elicits in-depth, open-ended responses rather than yes or no answers. Some marketers refer to this as *motivation research*. Unfortunately, no matter how skillfully posed, some questions are uncomfortable for consumers to answer. When asked why they bought a particular status car, for instance, consumers might reply that it handles well or is economical or dependable, but they rarely admit that it makes them feel important. The methods used in qualitative research are usually either *projective* or *intensive techniques*.

Projective techniques   Advertisers use **projective techniques** to understand people's underlying or subconscious feelings, attitudes, interests, opinions, needs, and motives. By asking indirect questions (such as "What kind of people do you think shop here?"), the researcher tries to involve consumers in a situation where they can express feelings about the problem or product.

Projective techniques were adapted for marketing research after their use by psychologists in clinical diagnosis. But such techniques require highly experienced researchers.

Intensive techniques   **Intensive techniques,** such as in-depth interviews, also require great care to administer properly. In the **in-depth interview,** carefully planned but loosely structured questions help the interviewer probe respondents' deeper feelings. The big pharmaceutical company Schering, for example, uses in-depth interviews with physicians to find out what attributes doctors consider most important in the drugs they prescribe and to identify which brands the doctors associate with different attributes.[25]

While in-depth interviews help reveal individual motivations, they are also expensive and time-consuming, and skilled interviewers are in short supply.

One of the most common intensive research techniques is the **focus group,** in which the company invites six or more people typical of the target market to a group session to discuss the product, the service, or the marketing situation. The session may last an hour or more. A trained moderator guides the often freewheeling discussion, and the group interaction reveals the participants' true feelings or behavior toward the product. Focus-group meetings are usually recorded and often viewed or videotaped from behind a one-way mirror.

Focus groups don't represent a valid sample of the population, but the participants' responses are useful for several purposes. They can provide input about the viability of prospective spokespeople, determine the effectiveness of visuals and strategies, and identify elements in ads that are unclear or claims that don't seem plausible. Focus groups are best used in conjunction with surveys. In fact, focus-group responses often help marketers design questions for a formal survey.[26] Following a survey, focus groups can put flesh on the skeleton of raw data.[27]

As in the case of Healthtex, focus groups are particularly useful to gain a deeper understanding of particular market segments. A *show-and-tell* focus group conducted by Grieco Research Group in Colorado offers a glimpse beyond the statistics to some core values of baby boomers. Participants were asked to bring to the session three or four items that they felt represented their ideal environment. Items ranged from photographs to magazine pictures to mementos and souvenirs. One mother of two brought tickets to a retro rock concert; a conservative corporate executive brought in a pack of cigarettes to show he was still rebellious; a middle-aged father brought a lucky fishing lure given to his kids by his father.

The process uncovered five key themes regarding what matters most to urban boomers. Family love and support and a good home life are viewed as important achievements. Long-term friendships are also very important and provide continuity to boomers. City-dwelling boomers are driven to "get away from it all" and escape to the big outdoors. Spiritual fitness is as important as physical fitness, so they love to develop their intellectual potential. They also feel that they're never too old to improve themselves. Clearly, all these values can translate into interesting platforms for commercials.[28]

Basic Methods of Quantitative Research

Advertisers use **quantitative research** to gain reliable, hard statistics about specific market conditions or situations. There are three basic research methods used to collect quantitative data: *observation, experiment,* and *survey.*

A focus group is an intensive research technique used to evaluate the effectiveness of the various elements of a sponsor's ad or advertising campaign. Focus groups are especially effective used in conjunction with market surveys.

The Universal Product Code on packaging is scanned at checkout counters. It improves checkout time and inventory control, and provides a wealth of accessible data for use in measuring advertising response.

Observation   In the **observation method,** researchers monitor people's actions. They may count the traffic that passes by a billboard, count a TV audience through instruments hooked to TV sets, or study consumer reactions to products displayed in the supermarket. Most observation method research is performed by large, independent marketing research companies, such as the A. C. Nielsen Co., Information Resources, Inc., and Audits and Surveys Worldwide, whose clients subscribe to their various services. Healthtex, for example, subscribes to the services of NPD (National Panel Diary), which tracks the clothing purchases of 16,000 homes as a nationwide sample. From this, Healthtex can find out its market share and better understand statistical trends in the marketplace.

Technology has greatly facilitated the observation method. One example is the **Universal Product Code (UPC)** label, an identifying series of vertical bars with a 12-digit number that adorns every consumer packaged good. By reading the codes with optical scanners, researchers can tell which products are selling and how well. The UPC label not only increases speed and accuracy at the checkout counter; it also enables timely inventory control and gives stores and manufacturers accurate point-of-purchase data sensitive to the impact of price, in-store promotion, couponing, and advertising.

For example, A. C. Nielsen's ScanTrack service provides weekly data on packaged-goods sales, market shares, and retail prices from 3,000 UPC scanner-equipped supermarkets. A companion service, ScanTrack Electronic Household Panel, provides packaged goods purchase data via in-home UPC scanning based on 40,000 U.S. households. As a result, marketers suddenly have reliable data on the effectiveness of the tools they use to influence consumers. With that information, they can develop empirical models to evaluate alternative marketing plans, media vehicles, and promotional campaigns.[29]

In one case, data indicated that a 40-cent coupon for toothpaste could create $147,000 in profits, but a 50-cent coupon on the same item would create a $348,000 loss.[30]

Advertisers used to assume that changes in market share and brand position happen slowly. But observation shows that the packaged-goods market is complex and volatile. At the local level, weekly sales figures may fluctuate considerably, making it difficult to measure advertising's short-term effectiveness.

Video cameras have also affected observation techniques. Envirosell, a New York-based research company, uses security-type cameras to capture consumer in-store shopping habits. To determine the effectiveness of packaging and displays, the company analyzes how much time people spend with an item and how they read the label.[31]

Experiment   To measure actual cause-and-effect relationships, researchers use the **experimental method.** An experiment is a scientific investigation in which a researcher alters the stimulus received by a *test group* and compares the results with that of a *control group* that did not receive the altered stimulus. This type of research is used primarily for new-product introductions. Marketers go to an isolated geographic area, called a **test market,** and introduce the product in that area alone or test a new ad campaign or promotion before a *national rollout.* For example, a new campaign might run in one geographic area but not another. Sales in the two areas are then compared to determine the campaign's effectiveness. However, researchers must use strict controls so the variable that causes the effect can be accurately

This video frame from Envirosell shows how the company uses security-type cameras to capture in-store consumer shopping habits.

Research Statistics Can Be Friends or Foes

Research—the systematic gathering of facts and statistics—is the basis for most advertising claims. Marketing research gives the advertiser and its agency the data they need to identify consumer needs, develop new products and communication strategies, and assess the effectiveness of marketing programs.

The way advertisers use research causes many ethical dilemmas. People can hide, shape, and manipulate statistics in many ways. Companies have deliberately withheld information, falsified figures, altered results, misused or ignored pertinent data, compromised the research design, and misinterpreted the results to support their point of view.

TRIUMPH BEATS MERIT. Triumph, at less than half the tar, preferred over Merit. In fact, an amazing 60% said 3 mg. Triumph tastes as good or better than 8 mg. Merit.

Lorillard, the manufacturer of Triumph cigarettes, obtained the data for this claim from a survey. But in a classic illustration of selective facts and omissions, the ads did not say how Lorillard arrived at the 60 percent figure.

Industry regulators contradicted Triumph's claim. Thirty-six percent of respondents preferred Triumph; 24 percent said the two were equal; the remaining 40 percent preferred Merit. So an even more "amazing" 64 percent (40 plus 24) said Merit tasted as good as or better than Triumph. Philip Morris's Merit was the real winner of Lorillard's survey. Philip Morris sued Lorillard and won a prohibition of false claims.

Consider the Joe Camel controversy. The Coalition on Smoking OR Health petitioned the FTC to prohibit RJR Nabisco from using the cartoon trade character Joe Camel in Camel cigarette advertising. Its petition was based on three articles in the *Journal of the American Medical Association (JAMA)*. The articles claimed Camel ads targeted minors.

After many months, the FTC "acquitted" Joe Camel for lack of evidence. The FTC case files included several briefs from marketing and advertising professors that challenged the validity of the studies cited in the *JAMA* articles.

One brief pointed out that, on the charge of inducing minors to smoke, the *JAMA* articles used the wrong measure. The charge required data addressing *primary demand,* the use of the whole product category. But the articles examined only brand share data, a measure of *selective demand* for brands within a category. And the University of Michigan's "Monitoring the Future" study, an annual survey of high school seniors, showed no change in the level of smoking after the Joe Camel campaign debuted.

A brief filed by University of Michigan professor Claude Martin found a gross misquotation in one *JAMA* reference. In an attempt to prove RJR's intent to target minors, coauthor Dr. Joseph DiFranza quoted from an RJR document—except that he omitted key words, as well as parentheses around the words "new users." The RJR statement follows, with the words that DiFranza deleted underlined. (First read the quote without the underlined portions; then go back and read the whole quote.)

Exhibit 6–5

Comparison of data collection methods.

	Personal	Telephone	Mail
Data collection costs	High	Medium	Low
Data collection time required	Medium	Low	High
Sample size for a given budget	Small	Medium	Large
Data quantity per respondent	High	Medium	Low
Reaches widely dispersed sample	No	Maybe	Yes
Reaches special locations	Yes	Maybe	No
Interaction with respondents	Yes	Yes	No
Degree of interviewer bias	High	Medium	None
Severity of nonresponse bias	Low	Low	High
Presentation of visual stimuli	Yes	No	Maybe
Fieldworker training required	Yes	Yes	No

determined. Because it's hard to control every marketing variable, this method is difficult and expensive to use.

Survey The most common method of gathering primary research data is the **survey,** in which the researcher gains information on attitudes, opinions, or motivations by questioning current or prospective customers (political polls are a common type of survey). Surveys can be conducted by *personal interview, telephone,* or *mail.* Each has distinct advantages and disadvantages (see Exhibit 6–5).

Considerations in Conducting Formal Quantitative Research

Quantitative research requires formal design and rigorous standards for collecting and tabulating data to ensure its accuracy and usability. When conducting formal research, advertisers must consider certain issues carefully, especially whether the research is *valid* and *reliable.* For more on the pros and cons of research statistics, see the Ethical Issue.

Validity and reliability Assume you want to determine a market's attitude toward a proposed new toy. The market consists of 10 million individuals. You show a prototype of the toy to five people and four say they like it (an 80 percent favorable attitude). Is that test valid? Hardly. For a test to have **validity,** results must be free of bias and reflect the true status of the market.[32] Five people aren't enough for a minimum sample, and the fact that *you* showed a prototype of *your* toy to these people would probably bias their response.

Whose behavior are we trying to affect?: <u>Demographics:</u> <u>adults—male (predominantly), females (must not be excluded), 18–34; emphasis 18–24</u> (new users). The goal is optimizing product and user imagery of Export A [Camels] against young starter smokers.

The *Washington Times* alleged that DiFranza had not conducted an objective study. Based on memos he wrote in pursuit of funding, the *Times* charged that DiFranza set out to develop evidence that would prove his predetermined conclusion.

In another critique, St. Joseph's University professor Joel Dubow asked, "Was Joe Camel Framed?" Dubow obtained DiFranza's original data and discovered that DiFranza had actually deleted from his article data that contradicted the charge that Joe Camel's maximum appeal was to "children." Dubow (himself an advocate of tobacco control) reported that with the critical data included and the advertising data broken down by age, the maximum appeal of Joe Camel was among 18- to 24-year-olds—just the market RJR said it was targeting. He concluded that Joe Camel had indeed been framed. In a simultaneously published response to Dubow's article, DiFranza did not deny the charge.

Consumer goodwill is vital for most marketing research. In an activity that rarely yields any direct benefit to the individual respondent, unethical practices lessen the likelihood of consumer cooperation.

Honest surveys provide excellent consumer information and can give advertisers legitimate selling points. As the FTC noted, "The existence of a survey as support for a claim of superiority may well imply to many consumers a measure of precision and accuracy that they would be less willing to attribute to the same claim made without reference to any statistical support. We assume this is why advertisers wish to use surveys."

Questions

1. Do you feel that DiFranza, in pursuing his "noble" purpose, was justified in his actions? How do you feel about the misquote of the RJR document? What about the manner in which he reported his data?

2. Are there any circumstances that might justify a portrayal of research findings in a biased or distorted fashion?

3. Why is it so important when discussing marketing research results with a client to report all results, not just those that put the client in a good light?

Sources: Ivan L. Preston, *The Tangled Web They Weave: Truth, Falsity and Advertisers* (Madison, WI: The University of Wisconsin Press, 1994), pp. 142, 143, 145; Ira Teinowitz, "Nielsen in Turmoil," *Advertising Age,* November 15, 1993, pp. 21, 24; N. Craig Smith and John A. Quelch, "Ethical Issues in Researching and Targeting Consumers," in *Ethics in Marketing* (Burr Ridge, IL: Richard D. Irwin, 1993), pp. 145, 177; University of Michigan, "Monitoring the Future Study," *News and Information Services,* January 27, 1994; "Now All We Need Is Some Data," *The Washington Times,* August 4, 1992; Claude R. Martin, "Research Validity and Resulting Public Policy: The Case of the DiFranza 'Old Joe' Cigarette Study," Annual Conference of the American Association of Public Opinion Research, May 1993; Joel S. Dubow, "Was Joe Camel Framed?" *Food & Beverage Marketing,* July 1993, pp. 28–30.

Moreover, if you repeated the test with five more people, you might get an entirely different response. So your test also lacks **reliability.** For a test to be reliable, it must be repeatable—it must produce approximately the same result each time it is administered (see Exhibit 6–6 on page 200).

Validity and reliability depend on several key elements: the sampling methods, the survey questionnaire design, and the data tabulation and analysis methods.

Sampling methods   When a company wants to know what consumers think, it can't ask everybody. But its research must reflect the **universe** (the entire target population) of prospective customers. Researchers select from that population a **sample** that they expect will represent the population's characteristics.[33] To accomplish this, they must decide who to survey, how many to survey, and how to choose the respondents. Defining **sample units**—the individuals, families, or companies being surveyed—is very important.

A sample must be large enough to achieve precision and stability. The larger the sample, the more reliable the results. However, reliability can be obtained with even very small samples, a fraction of 1 percent of the population. There are two types of samples: random probability samples and nonprobability samples. Both are derived from mathematical *theories of probability.*

The greatest accuracy is gained from **random probability samples** because everyone in the universe has an equal chance of being selected.[34] For example, a researcher who wants to know a community's opinion on an issue selects members of the community at random. But this method has difficulties. Every unit (person) must be known, listed, and numbered so each has an equal chance of being selected, an often prohibitively expensive and sometimes impossible task, especially with customers of nationally distributed products.

Validity

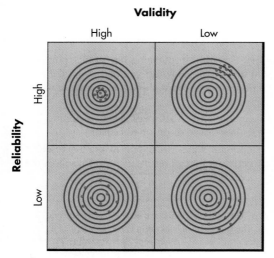

Exhibit 6–6

The reliability/validity diagram. Using the analogy of a dart board, the bull's-eye is the actual average of a value among a population (say, the average age in the community). The *top row* shows high reliability (repeatability) because the darts are closely clustered. When reliability drops, the darts land more randomly and spread across a wider area, as in both examples in the *bottom row*. The *left column* demonstrates high validity because in both examples the darts center around the bull's-eye. The *right column* represents low validity because bias in the testing process drew all the darts to one side. In the *upper-right quadrant,* members of a fraternity are in the same age group (high reliability or repeatability), but their ages do not reflect the average of the community (low validity). The *lower-left quadrant* suggests the testing of our average age sample is highly valid, but it is not reliable because it includes people with a wide range of ages. The *upper-left quadrant* reflects the truest picture of the data.

Instead, researchers use **nonprobability samples** extensively because they're easier than probability samples, as well as less expensive and time-consuming. Nonprobability samples don't give every unit in the universe an equal chance of being included, so there's no guarantee the sample is representative. As a result, researchers can't be as confident in the validity of the responses.[35] Most marketing and advertising research needs general measures of the data. For example, the nonprobability method of interviewing shoppers in malls may be sufficient to determine the shopping preferences, image perceptions, and attitudes of customers.

How questionnaires are designed Constructing a good questionnaire requires considerable expertise. Much bias in research is blamed on poorly designed questionnaires. Typical problems include asking the wrong types of questions, asking too many questions, using the wrong form for a question (which makes it too difficult to answer or tabulate), and using the wrong choice of words. Exhibit 6–7 shows some typical questions that might be used in a survey for a retail store.

Consider the simple question: "What kind of soap do you use?" The respondent doesn't know what *soap* means. Hand soap, shampoo, laundry detergent, or dishwashing soap? Does *kind* mean brand, size, or type? Finally, what constitutes *use?* What a person buys (perhaps for someone else) or uses personally—and for what purpose? In fact, one person probably uses several different kinds of soap, depending on the occasion. It's impossible to answer this question accurately. Worse, if the consumer does answer it, the researcher doesn't know what the answer means and will likely draw an incorrect conclusion. For these reasons, questionnaires *must* be pretested. (See the Checklist for Developing an Effective Questionnaire on page 203.)

Effective survey questions have three important attributes: *focus, brevity,* and *clarity.* They focus on the topic of the survey. They are as brief as possible. And they are expressed simply and clearly.[36]

The four most common types of questions are *open-ended, dichotomous, multiple choice,* and *semantic differential* (*scale*) (see Exhibit 6–8). But there are many ways to ask questions within these four types. More choices, for example, can be added to the multiple-choice format. Neutral responses can be removed from the semantic differential question so the respondent must answer either positively or negatively. And there is obvious bias in the dichotomous question.

Questions should elicit a response that is both accurate and useful. By testing questionnaires on a small subsample, researchers can detect any confusion, bias, or ambiguities.

Data tabulation and analysis Collected data must be validated, edited, coded, and tabulated. Answers must be checked to eliminate errors or inconsistencies. For example, one person might answer two years, while another says 24 months; such responses must be changed to the same units for correct tabulation. Some questionnaires may be rejected because respondents' answers indicate they misunderstood the questions. Finally, the data must be counted and summarized, usually by computer.

Many researchers want *cross-tabulations* (for example, product use by age group or education). Software programs such as MINITAB® Statistical Software make it possible for small advertisers as well as large corporations to tabulate data on a personal computer and apply advanced statistical techniques.[37] Many cross-tabulations are possible, but researchers must use skill and imagination to select only those that show significant relationships. On small samples, using additional cross-tabs dramatically reduces the level of confidence. (For information on PC software for research analysis, see RL 6–2 in the Reference Library.)

Exhibit 6–7

A personal questionnaire like this helps determine shoppers' feelings toward a chain of stores, its merchandise, and its advertising.

1. Do you intend to shop at _(Store name)_ between now and Sunday?
Yes   1   No   2   (If no, skip to question 5)

2. Do you intend to buy something in particular or just to browse?
Buy   1   Browse   2

3. Have you seen any of the items you intend to buy advertised by _(Store name)_ ?
Yes   1   (continue)   No   2   (skip to question 5)

4. Where did you see these items advertised? Was it in a _(Store name)_ advertising flyer included with your newspaper, a _(Store name)_ flyer you received in the mail, the pages of the newspaper itself, on TV, or somewhere else?
☐ Flyer in newspaper   ☐ On TV
☐ Flyer in mail   ☐ Somewhere else (specify) _____
☐ Pages of newspaper   ☐ Don't recall

5. Please rate the _(Store name)_ advertising insert on the attributes listed below. Place an X in the box at the position that best reflects your opinion of how the insert rates on each attribute. Placing an X in the middle box usually means you are neutral. The closer you place the X to the left or right phrase or word, the more you believe it describes the _(Store name)_ insert.

Looks cheap							Looks expensive
Unskillful							Cleverly done
Unappealing							Appealing
Does not show clothing in an attractive manner							Shows clothing in an attractive manner

1   2   3   4   5   6   7

6. Please indicate all of the different types of people listed below you feel this _(Store name)_ advertising insert is appealing to.

☐ Young people   ☐ Quality-conscious people
☐ Bargain hunters   ☐ Low-income people
☐ Conservative dressers   ☐ Budget watchers
☐ Fashion-conscious people   ☐ Older people
☐ Rich people   ☐ Middle-income people
☐ Professionals   ☐ Blue-collar people
☐ High-income people   ☐ Women
☐ Men   ☐ Office workers
☐ Someone like me   ☐ Smart dressers
☐ Career-oriented women   ☐ Other (specify) _____

Collecting Primary Data in International Markets

International marketers face a number of challenges when they collect primary data. For one thing, research overseas is often more expensive than domestic research. Many marketers are surprised to learn that research in five countries costs five times as much as research in one country; there are no economies of scale.[38]

But advertisers must determine whether their messages will work in foreign markets. (Maxwell House, for example, had to change its "great American coffee" campaign when it discovered that Germans have little respect for U.S. coffee.)

Control and direction of the research is another problem. Some companies want to direct research from their headquarters but charge it to the subsidiary's budget. This creates an instant turf battle. It also means that people less familiar with the country—and therefore less sensitive to local cultural issues—might be in charge of the project, which could flaw the data. Advertisers need more than just facts about a country's culture. They need to understand and appreciate the nuances of its cultural traits and habits, a difficult task for people who don't live there or speak the language. Knowledgeable international advertisers like Colgate-Palmolive work in

Exhibit 6–8

Different ways to phrase research questions.

Type	Questions
Open-ended	How would you describe (_Store name_) advertising?
Dichotomous	Do you think (_Store name_) advertising is too attractive? _____ Yes _____ No
Multiple choice	What description best fits your opinion of (_Store name_) advertising? _____ Modern _____ Unconvincing _____ Well done _____ Old-fashioned _____ Believable
Semantic differential (scale)	Please indicate on the scale how you rate the quality of (_Store name_) advertising. _____ _____ _____ _____ _____ 1 2 3 4 5 Poor Excellent

partnership with their local offices and use local bilingual marketing people when conducting primary research abroad.[39]

For years, Mattel tried unsuccessfully to market the Barbie doll in Japan. It finally sold the manufacturing license to a Japanese company, Takara, which did its own research. Takara found that most Japanese girls and their parents thought Barbie's breasts were too big and her legs too long. It modified the doll accordingly, changed the blue eyes to brown, and sold 2 million dolls in two years.

Conducting original research abroad can be fraught with problems. First, the researcher must use the local language, and translating questionnaires can be tricky. Second, many cultures view strangers suspiciously and don't wish to talk about their personal lives. U.S. companies found that mail surveys and phone interviews don't work in Japan; they have to use expensive, time-consuming personal interviews.[40]

Despite these problems—or perhaps because of them—it's important for global advertisers to perform research. Competent researchers are available in all developed countries, and major international research firms have local offices in most developing countries. The largest of these companies, which serve the largest multinational clients, organize their services globally based on the type of specialized research they conduct regularly. Research International Group, for instance, has global research directors for advertising research and for customer satisfaction research and global account directors for clients' projects worldwide.[41]

Marketers are often surprised by some of the differences they encounter when trying to conduct international research. Lead times to begin projects are typically longer, with the Far East being particularly troublesome. Groups can take twice as long to set up overseas. The structures differ too. Focus groups, for instance, rarely use more than four to six people rather than the eight to 10 typical of the United States. Screening requirements for participants abroad are typically less rigid, and foreign moderators tend to be much less structured than their U.S. counterparts. Finally, the facilities don't usually have all the amenities of U.S. offices, but the costs are frequently twice as high in Europe and three times as high in Asia.[42]

Two goals for international research are flexibility and standardization, and both are necessary for the best results. Flexibility means using the best approach in each market. If you're studying the use of laundry products, it's just as irrelevant to ask Mexicans about soy-sauce stains as it is to ask Thais how they get _mole_ out of their clothes.[43]

On the other hand, standardization is important so that information from different countries can be compared.[44] Otherwise the study will be meaningless. Balance is required to get the best of flexibility and standardization.

_____ **List specific research objectives.** Don't spend money collecting irrelevant data.

_____ **Write short questionnaires.** Don't tax the respondent's patience; you may get careless or flip answers.

_____ **State questions clearly** so there is no chance for misunderstanding. Avoid generalities and ambiguities.

_____ **Write a rough draft first,** then polish it.

_____ **Use a short opening statement.** Include the interviewer's name, the name of the organization, and the purpose of the questionnaire.

_____ **Put the respondent at ease** by opening with one or two inoffensive, easily answered questions.

_____ **Structure questions so they flow logically.** Ask general questions before more detailed ones.

_____ **Avoid questions that suggest an answer or could be considered leading.** They bias the results.

_____ **Include a few questions that cross-check earlier answers.** This helps ensure validity.

_____ **Put the demographic questions (age, income, education) and any other personal questions at the end of the questionnaire.**

_____ **Pretest the questionnaire** with 20 to 30 people to be sure they interpret the questions correctly and that it covers all the information sought.

Thanks to a combination of computer-based interviewing, the Internet, e-mail, telephones, faxes, and courier services, the time required to conduct worldwide business-to-business research has been drastically reduced. Experts point to several key factors such as international disk-by-mail (DBM) surveys: mail questionnaires on computer disks formatted for DOS; mail only one disk; incorporate

These examples from Nestlé's Malaysian campaign (www.nestle.com) illustrate some of the difficulties inherent in international advertising. In a country characterized by three widely spoken languages, several religions, and 19.5 million people, careful research had to be conducted so that Nestlé could reach all its target markets without offending current or prospective customers.

Database Management Software

With clients demanding increasingly specialized information about their audiences, software companies like Microsoft, Borland, and Oracle have provided database management programs to assist with this challenge.

Database programs act as a librarian to the mountain of knowledge that the advertising industry inevitably collects during the course of its research. These software programs organize data so that users may retrieve demographic and psychographic information about their audiences quickly and efficiently.

Microsoft's programs use relational database power to make data easy to access. The company's Access package allows users to generate, analyze, and create reports without hours of work; import data from numerous databases and spreadsheets; and share the information over vast computer networks. The applications can be scaled from the simple needs of the home business to the rigorous demands of large corporations.

The packages available from Borland and Oracle perform many of the same functions but are written specifically with large networking purposes in mind.

Statistical software from MINITAB® also serves as a database tool with pull-down menus and dialog boxes that provide easy prompts each step of the way. Without a lengthy learning process or unwieldy manuals, MINITAB® allows users to spend more time exploring their data, and less time telling the computer what it is they want to do.

Whether one is just a novice or a seasoned veteran, the responsibility of keeping apace with the market cannot be left solely in the hands of the research department. By becoming more knowledgeable with statistical software people can become more valuable to their clients.

Source: Microsoft Products Information (www.microsoft.com) and MINITAB Database Program (www.minitab.com).

---

graphics if possible to present the product concept; and use global field services with the language capabilities needed to recruit respondents and retrieve the disks. With the global adoption of the World Wide Web, these experts anticipate further cuts in costs and time for getting valuable customer input for marketing decision making.[45]

Basic Methods for Testing Ads

Although there is no infallible way to predict advertising success or failure, pretesting and posttesting can give an advertiser useful insights if properly applied.

Pretesting methods   Advertisers often pretest for likability and perception analysis by using a variety of qualitative and quantitative techniques.

For example, when pretesting print ads, advertisers often ask direct questions: What does the advertising say to you? Does the advertising tell you anything new or different about the company? If so, what? Does the advertising reflect activities you would like to participate in? Is the advertising believable? What effect does it have on your perception of the merchandise offered? Do you like the ads?

Through **direct questioning,** researchers can elicit a full range of responses from people and thereby infer how well advertising messages convey key copy points. Direct questioning is especially effective for testing alternative ads in the early stages of development, when respondents' reactions and input can best be acted on. Other techniques for pretesting print ads include *focus groups, order-of-merit tests, paired comparisons, portfolio tests, mock magazines, perceptual meaning studies,* and *direct-mail tests.* (See the Checklist of Methods for Pretesting Ads.)

Several methods are used specifically to pretest radio and TV commercials. In **central location tests,** respondents are shown videotapes of test commercials, usually in shopping centers, and questions are asked before and after exposure. In **clutter tests,** test commercials are shown with noncompeting control commercials to determine their effectiveness, measure comprehension and attitude shifts, and detect weaknesses.

Many companies' own employees are an important constituency. FedEx, for example, pretests new commercials by prescreening them on its in-house cable TV system for its 90,000 employees and soliciting feedback.[46]

The challenge of pretesting   There is no best way to pretest advertising variables. Different methods test different aspects, and each has its own advantages and disadvantages—a formidable challenge for the advertiser.

Print Advertising

_____ **Direct questioning.** Asks specific questions about ads. Often used to test alternative ads in early stages of development.

_____ **Focus group.** A moderated but freewheeling discussion and interview conducted with six or more people.

_____ **Order-of-merit test.** Respondents see two or more ads and arrange them in rank order.

_____ **Paired-comparison method.** Respondents compare each ad in a group.

_____ **Portfolio test.** One group sees a portfolio of test ads interspersed among other ads and editorial matter. Another group sees the portfolio without the test ads.

_____ **Mock magazine.** Test ads are "stripped into" a magazine, which is left with respondents for a specified time. (Also used as a posttesting technique.)

_____ **Perceptual meaning study.** Respondents see ads in timed exposures.

_____ **Direct-mail test.** Two or more alternative ads are mailed to different prospects on a mailing list to test which ad generates the largest volume of orders.

Broadcast Advertising

_____ **Central location projection test.** Respondents see test commercial films in a central location like a shopping center.

_____ **Trailer test.** Respondents see TV commercials in trailers at shopping centers and receive coupons for the advertised products; a matched sample of consumers just get the coupons. Researchers measure the difference in coupon redemption.

_____ **Theater test.** Electronic equipment enables respondents to indicate what they like and dislike as they view TV commercials in a theater setting.

_____ **Live telecast test.** Test commercials are shown on closed-circuit or cable TV. Respondents are interviewed by phone and/or sales audits are conducted at stores in the viewing areas.

_____ **Sales experiment.** Alternative commercials run in two or more market areas.

Physiological Testing

_____ **Pupilometric device.** Dilation of the subject's pupils is measured, presumably to indicate the subject's level of interest.

_____ **Eye-movement camera.** The route the subject's eyes traveled is superimposed over an ad to show the areas that attracted and held attention.

_____ **Galvanometer.** Measures subject's sweat gland activity with a mild electrical current; presumably the more tension an ad creates, the more effective it is likely to be.

_____ **Voice-pitch analysis.** A consumer's response is taped and a computer used to measure changes in voice pitch caused by emotional responses.

_____ **Brain-pattern analysis.** A scanner monitors the reaction of the subject's brain.

Pretesting helps distinguish strong ads from weak ones. But since the test occurs in an artificial setting, respondents may assume the role of expert or critic and give answers that don't reflect their real buying behavior. They may invent opinions to satisfy the interviewer, or be reluctant to admit they are influenced, or vote for the ads they think they *should* like.

Researchers encounter problems when asking people to rank ads. Respondents often rate the ones that make the best first impression as the highest in all categories (the **halo effect**). Also, questions about the respondent's buying behavior may be invalid; behavior *intent* may not become behavior *fact*. And some creative people mistrust ad testing because they believe it stifles creativity.

Despite these challenges, the issue comes down to dollars. Small advertisers rarely pretest, but their risk isn't as great, either. When advertisers risk millions of dollars on a new campaign, they *must* pretest to be sure the ad or commercial is interesting, believable, likable, and memorable—and reinforces the brand image.

Posttesting methods   Posttesting is generally more costly and time-consuming than pretesting, but it can test ads under actual market conditions. As mentioned earlier, some advertisers benefit from pretesting *and* posttesting by running ads in select test markets before launching a campaign nationwide.

As in pretesting, advertisers use both quantitative and qualitative methods in posttesting. Most posttesting techniques fall into five broad categories: *aided recall, unaided recall, attitude tests, inquiry tests,* and *sales tests.* (See the Checklist of Methods for Posttesting Ads.)

Advertisers can avert potential disaster by pretesting ads for their affectiveness prior to a campaign. While pretesting incurs yet another cost, advertisements that confuse or even offend consumers can cost a company millions of dollars in damages or lost sales. Tabasco (www.tabasco.com) pretested its "Exploding Mosquito" in spot advertisements around the country before airing it in front of millions of viewers around the world during the 1998 Super Bowl.

Open on a man sitting outside on his porch enjoying a pizza with McIlhenny Tabasco Pepper Sauce.

There are two empty bottles at his feet.

SFX: Mosquito hum.

Cut to mosquito biting the man on the leg.

The man has a bemused expression.

The mosquito flys off and explodes in mid-flight. The man smiles.

Some advertisers use **attitude tests** to measure a campaign's effectiveness in creating a favorable image for a company, its brand, or its products. Presumably, favorable changes in attitude predispose consumers to buy the company's product.

Impact Research in Montreal developed a proprietary posttest called TES (Tracking Efficiency Study) that it administers regularly for clients.[47] Using a random sample of 200 people in each market, Impact researchers phone or visit respondents and ask 8 to 10 questions to determine what ads or commercials they remember seeing, if they can identify the sponsor, which message elements they remember, and how well they liked the ads. Then Impact develops statistics on the real reach and frequency of the campaign—that is, how many people *actually* saw the ads or commercials and how often.

Similarly, Nissan interviews 1,000 consumers every month to track brand awareness, familiarity with vehicle models, recall of commercials, and shifts in attitude or image perception. If a commercial fails, it can be pulled quickly.[48]

Following its initial campaign, Healthtex conducted some posttesting and discovered that, while the new moms appreciated the information in the long copy format of their ads, more experienced mothers didn't. For them, the headline and one line of copy were sufficient to get the point across. They already understood the rest. As a result, The Martin Agency redesigned the ads aimed at experienced moms to the shorter format.

The challenge of posttesting Each posttesting method has limitations. **Recall tests** reveal the effectiveness of ad components, such as size, color, or themes. But they measure what respondents noticed, *not* whether they actually buy the product.

Starch Readership Reports (www.roper.com) posttest magazine ad effectiveness by interviewing readers. The summary tab at the top of this ad indicates that 51 percent of women readers noted the ad; 49 percent associated the ad with the advertiser (Hanes); and 27 percent read most of the copy.

For measuring sales effectiveness, attitude tests are often better than recall tests. An attitude change relates more closely to product purchase, and a measured change in attitude gives management the confidence to make informed decisions about advertising plans. Unfortunately, many people find it difficult to determine and express their attitudes. For mature brands, *brand interest* may be a better sales indicator, and advertisers now measure that phenomenon.[49]

By using **inquiry tests**—in which consumers respond to an ad for information or free samples—researchers can test an ad's attention-getting value, readability, and understandability. These tests also permit fairly good control of the variables that motivate reader action, particularly if a *split-run test* is used (split runs are covered in Chapter 14). The inquiry test is also effective for testing small-space ads.

Unfortunately, inquiries may not reflect a sincere interest in the product, and responses may take months to receive. When advertising is the dominant element or the only variable in the company's marketing plan, **sales tests** are a useful measure of advertising effectiveness. However, many other variables usually affect sales (competitors' activities, the season of the year, and even the weather). Sales response may not be immediate, and sales tests, particularly field studies, are often costly and time-consuming. Finally, sales tests are more suited for gauging the effectiveness of campaigns than of individual ads or components of ads.

Step 5: Interpreting and Reporting the Findings

The final step in the research process involves interpreting and reporting the data. Research is very costly (see Exhibit 6–9), and its main purpose is to help solve problems. The final report must be comprehensible to the company's managers and relevant to their needs.

Exhibit 6–9
The cost of professional research.

Type of research	Features	Cost
Telephone	500 20-minute interviews, with report	$15,000–$18,000
Mail	500 returns, with report (33 percent response rate)	$8,000–$10,000
Intercept	500 interviews, four or five questions, with report	$15,000
Executive interviews (talking to business administrators)	20 interviews, with report	$2,500–$7,500
Focus group	One group, 8 to 10 people, with report and videotape	$2,500–$3,800

Tables and graphs are helpful, but they must be explained in words management can understand. Technical jargon (such as "multivariate analysis of variance model") should be avoided, and descriptions of the methodology, statistical analysis, and raw data should be confined to an appendix. The report should state the problem and research objective, summarize the findings, and draw conclusions. The researcher should make recommendations for management action, and the report should be discussed in a formal presentation to allow management feedback and to highlight important points.

Chapter **Summary**

Marketing research is the systematic procedure used to gather, record, and analyze new information to help managers make decisions about the marketing of goods and services. Marketing research helps management identify consumer needs, develop new products and communication strategies, and assess the effectiveness of marketing programs and promotional activities. The many types of information gathered can help marketers recruit, retain, and regain customers.

Advertising research, a subset of marketing research, is used to gather and analyze information for developing or evaluating advertising. It helps advertisers develop strategies and test concepts. The results of research help define the product concept, select the target market, and develop the primary advertising message elements.

Advertisers use testing to make sure their advertising dollars are spent wisely. Pretesting helps detect and eliminate weaknesses before a campaign runs. Posttesting helps evaluate the effectiveness of an ad or campaign after it runs. Testing is used to evaluate several variables including merchandise, markets, motives, messages, media, and overall results.

The research process involves several steps: analyzing the situation and defining the problem, conducting informal (exploratory) research by analyzing internal data and collecting external secondary data, setting research objectives, conducting formal research using qualitative or quantitative methods, and, finally, interpreting and reporting the findings.

Marketers use qualitative research to get a general impression of the market. The methods used may be projective or intensive. Quantitative techniques include observation, experiment, and survey.

The validity and reliability of quantitative surveys depend on the sampling methods used and the design of the survey questionnaire. The two sampling procedures are random probability and nonprobability. Survey questions require focus, brevity, and simplicity.

In international markets, research is often more expensive and less reliable than in the United States. But advertisers must use research to understand cultural traits and habits in overseas markets.

Techniques used in pretesting include central location tests, clutter tests, and direct questioning. Pretesting has numerous problems, including artificiality, consumer inaccuracy, and the halo effect of consumer responses. The most commonly used posttesting techniques are aided recall, unaided recall, attitude tests, inquiry tests, and sales tests.

Important **Terms**

advertising research, *186*

attitude test, *206*

central location test, *204*

clutter test, *204*

direct questioning, *204*

experimental method, *197*

focus group, *196*

formal research, *194*

halo effect, *205*

in-depth interview, *195*

informal research, *192*

inquiry test, *207*

intensive techniques, *195*

marketing information system (MIS), *191*

marketing research, *184*

markets, *190*

media classes, *191*

media research, *188*

media subclasses, *191*

media units, *191*

media vehicles, *191*

Review **Questions**

1. How does research help advertisers meet the challenge of the three Rs of marketing?
2. Give an example that demonstrates the difference between marketing research and market research.
3. Which kind of research data is more expensive to collect, primary or secondary? Why?
4. How have you personally used observational research?
5. Do people use quantitative or qualitative research to evaluate movies? Explain.
6. Which of the major surveying methods is most costly? Why?
7. When might research offer validity but not reliability?
8. When could research help in the development of an advertising strategy for an international advertiser? Give an example.
9. How could the halo effect bias a pretest for a soft-drink ad?
10. How would you design a controlled experiment to test the advertising for a chain of men's clothing stores?

Exploring the **Internet**

The Internet exercises for Chapter 6 address the following areas related to marketing and advertising research: marketing research organizations and publications (Exercise 1) and market research companies (Exercise 2).

1. Marketing Research Organizations and Publications

   Many advertisers choose not to hire a company to conduct their research. When collecting research data by themselves, there are a number of advertising- and marketing-specific research sources available on the Web. Visit the research organizations' and publications' Web sites and answer the questions that follow.

   - Advertising Research Foundation (ARF) **www.arfsite.org**
   - *Journal of Advertising Research* **www.arfsite.org/webpages/jar_pages/jarhome.htm**
   - *Journal of Marketing* **www.ama.org/pubs/jm/index.html**
   - *Journal of Marketing Research* **www.ama.org/pubs/jmr/index.html**
   - *Marketing Research* **www.ama.org/pubs/mr/index.html**
   - Marketing Research Association (MRA) **www.mra-net.org**

   a. What research group sponsors the site? Who is/are the intended audience(s)?
   b. What is the site's purpose? Does it succeed? Why?
   c. What is the size/scope of the organization?
   d. What is the organization's purpose?

2. Market Research Companies

   Marketers and advertisers depend heavily on timely and accurate research in preparation for advertising planning. Market research companies are numerous and available to serve nearly every marketing and advertising research need. Visit the following syndicated and independent research companies' Web sites and answer the questions that follow.

   - A.C. Nielsen **www.acnielsen.com**
   - ASI Market Research Center **www.asiresearch.com**
   - Audits & Surveys Worldwide **www.surveys.com**
   - Burke **www.burke.com**
   - Diagnostic Research International (DRI) **www.diagnostic.com**
   - Dun & Bradstreet **www.dbisna.com/dbis/dnbhome.htm**
   - FIND/SVP **www.findsvp.com**
   - Gallup & Robinson **www.gallup.com**
   - IntelliQuest **www.intelliquest.com**
   - International Data Corporation (IDC) **www.idc.com**
   - J. D. Power and Associates **www.jdpower.com**
   - Research International **www.research-int.com**
   - Roper Starch **www.roper.com**
   - SRI Consulting **www.sriconsulting.com**

   a. What type(s) of research does the company specialize in?
   b. What industries/companies would be best suited to utilize the company's resources?
   c. What specific services, products, or publications does the company offer?
   d. Are the information services offered by the company primary or secondary data?
   e. How useful is the company for conducting advertising and marketing research? Why?

Chapter **Seven**

Marketing and Advertising Planning: Top-Down, Bottom-Up, and IMC

Objective   To describe the process of marketing and advertising planning. Marketers and advertisers need to understand the various ways plans are created. They must also know how to analyze situations; set realistic, attainable objectives; develop strategies to achieve them; and establish budgets for marketing communications.

After studying this chapter, you will be able to:

- Explain the role and importance of a marketing plan.

- Describe how marketing and advertising plans are related.

- Explain the difference between objectives and strategies in marketing and advertising plans.

- Give examples of need-satisfying and sales-target objectives.

- Discuss the suitability of top-down, bottom-up, and integrated marketing communications planning.

- Explain how advertising budgets are determined.

- Describe how share-of-market/share-of-voice budgeting can be used for new product introductions.

A decade ago, Japanese cars were the stars of the automotive world. But in the 90s, a player as down-home American as fried chicken entered the scene. • It all started in the mid-80s, when then-chair of GM, Roger Smith, vowed to find a better way to manufacture and market cars by building partnerships between management and labor, company and supplier. GM's mission was to produce a car that would be a powerful import fighter and to build the best-liked automotive company in America.[1] • The company eschewed its Detroit roots for the rural foothills of Spring Hill, Tennessee, where it built the most modern auto plant in America. Working with its target

market of typical import buyers, the company designed the vehicle they wanted: small, economical, safe, attractive, comfortable, and affordable—the Saturn. • In partnership with its employees, the company discarded assembly-line methods and developed teams to build its cars. Quality was paramount. • By 1987, Saturn officials started looking for an ad agency to introduce the first all-new American car since the Edsel. After an exhaustive search, they selected a San Francisco shop—Hal Riney & Partners—29 months before the first car would go on sale. Riney executives

immediately traveled to Saturn's headquarters to immerse themselves in the product plans and to undergo the orientation to Saturn culture given to all new employees. • Many key brand-building decisions were made well before the launch with contributions from Riney and a panel of 16 dealer advisers. "Most people start and stop with the car," says Donald Hudler, Saturn VP of sales, service, and marketing. But to Saturn, the product concept included not just the car's but the company's image, the customers' perceptions, and the whole shopping, buying, and owning experience. With Riney's help, the company meticulously crafted Saturn's brand image. • Saturn emphasized straight talk. Red cars would be called red, not "raspberry red." Customers would not have to haggle over price, and dealers would be called retailers ("we're not in the deal business"). Even the models would be designated by letters or numbers rather than names that might detract from the Saturn image. "The truth," Hal Riney says, "is far better than anything we can make up. Saturn has to represent honesty and directness." Moreover, all communications had to be integrated and consistent. • Before producing any consumer advertising, the agency created several internal communications pieces about the company. A short film documented the plant start-up and the workers' incredible commitment. The company used the film to train new employees and help introduce itself to suppliers and the press. Retailers used it in presentations for bank loans and zoning variances. After the launch, Riney even ran it as a "documercial" on cable TV. The film showed Saturn team members explaining in their own words, often emotionally, what the project meant to them. ● When the agency began creating consumer ads, it took the same tack: "A different kind of company. A different kind of car." ● The cars were such an immediate success that production couldn't keep up with demand. Riney had to create ads apologizing for delivery delays. In 1992, despite production restraints, Saturn sold 196,126 cars, or more than twice as many as the year before—outselling Hyundai, Subaru, Mitsubishi, and Volkswagen. Touted by the critics for its high quality-to-price ratio, the company also finished third in the J. D. Power & Associates survey of new-car buyer satisfaction, right behind Lexus and Infiniti, which cost several times more than Saturn's frugal $10,000. With its fanatic devotion to integrated marketing communications, Riney helped Saturn build a brand.[2] And in 1993, thanks largely to its work on the Saturn account, Hal Riney & Partners was named agency of the year by *Advertising Age.* ● Since that time, Saturn has continued to grow and today it is considered by both academics and practitioners to be the quintessential example of the successful application of integrated marketing communications. As a result, virtually every marketing and advertising textbook on the market cites the Saturn case. ●

The **Marketing** Plan

The Saturn story demonstrates that business success often depends more on careful marketing and advertising planning than on advertising creativity. Yet, every year, companies waste millions and millions of dollars on ineffective advertising due to a woeful lack of prior planning.

The Importance of Marketing Planning

Since marketing is typically a company's *only* source of income, the marketing plan may well be its most important document.

The **marketing plan** assembles all the pertinent facts about the organization, the markets it serves, and its products, services, customers, competition, and so on. It forces all departments—product development, production, selling, advertising, credit, transportation—to focus on the customer. Finally, it sets goals and objectives for specified periods of time and lays out the precise strategies and tactics to achieve them.

The written marketing plan must reflect the goals of top management and be consistent with the company's mission and capabilities. Depending on its scope, the plan may be long and complex or, in the case of a small firm or a single product line, very brief. Formal marketing plans are typically reviewed and revised yearly, but planning is not a one-time event; it's a continuous process that includes research, formulation, implementation, evaluation, review, and reformulation.

The Effect of the Marketing Plan on Advertising

The marketing plan has a profound effect on an organization's advertising program. It helps managers analyze and improve all company operations, including marketing and advertising programs. It dictates the role of advertising in the marketing mix. It enables better implementation, control, and continuity of advertising programs, and it ensures the most efficient allocation of advertising dollars.

Seven years ago, when we first started building Saturns, we discovered something really interesting. The federal crashworthiness standards all call for the use of 5'8", 179-lb. dummies. Which would be fine with us, except for one thing.

Everybody deserves a safe car. Not just average-sized males. So, in addition to simulating crashes with the standard dummies, we simulate them with ones ranging from 45-lb. six-year-olds to 4'11", 112-lb. females to burly 6', 234-lb. males.

All these extra tests make life rough for our biofidelic (that's engineering lingo for really lifelike) Hybrid III dummies. But we know of no better way to make sure a Saturn's steel spaceframe bends where it's supposed to and doesn't bend where it's not. Or to figure out how to shape our seats to help prevent smaller folks from sliding under the seatbelts in an impact.

It comes down to this. We like all the people who drive Saturns. We don't want to lose a single one.

A DIFFERENT KIND *of* COMPANY. A DIFFERENT KIND *of* CAR.
This 1998 Saturn SL2 comes with an M.S.R.P. of $13,195, including AC, retailer prep and transportation. Of course, options, tax and license are extra. We'd be happy to provide more information at 1-800-522-5000, or visit us on the Internet at www.saturn.com. ©1997 Saturn Corporation.

Part of Saturn's marketing plan is to satisfy the need of small-car buyers for a safe, reliable, economical vehicle. Many of these buyers, though, are women who, on average, are smaller than the 5'8", 179-lb. men for whom federal crash worthiness standards are designed. This led to Saturn's use of crash dummies of various sizes and to the creation of this information-packed ad that explains Saturn's commitment to safety and further illustrates the company's desire to build good customer relationships.

Exhibit 7–1
Traditional top-down marketing plan.

Successful organizations do not separate advertising plans from marketing. They view each as a vital building block for success. Companies typically employ one of three types of marketing planning models today: the traditional top-down or bottom-up marketing plans and, increasingly, integrated marketing communications (IMC) planning. We'll look at the first two briefly before delving into the new discipline of IMC.

Top-Down Marketing

The traditional **top-down marketing** plan is still the most common format. It has been used for over 30 years and fits the hierarchical organization of most companies. It is often appropriate for companies planning to launch completely new products. As Exhibit 7–1 shows, the top-down plan has four main elements: *situation analysis, marketing objectives, marketing strategy,* and *tactics* (or *action programs*). Large companies with extensive marketing plans sometimes include additional sections. At the end of the book, Appendix A outlines a complete top-down marketing plan.

Situation Analysis

The **situation analysis** section is a *factual* statement of the organization's current situation and how it got there. It presents all relevant facts about the company's history, growth, products and services, sales volume, share of market, competitive status, markets served, distribution system, past advertising programs, results of marketing research studies, company capabilities, strengths and weaknesses, and any other pertinent information. To plan successfully for the future, company executives must agree on the accuracy of the data and its interpretation. See the Reference Library, RL 7–1, Checklist for Situation Analysis, for the most important elements to consider.

Once the historical information is gathered, the focus changes to potential threats and opportunities based on key factors outside the company's control—for example, the economic, political, social, technological, or commercial environments in which the company operates.[3]

Look at the situation GM faced at the beginning of the 90s. American cars were perceived as lacking the quality or value of Japanese and German competitors. Detroit's management and manufacturing systems were considered outmoded bureaucracies, and people questioned the productivity of American workers.[4] Roger Smith believed that Americans wanted to buy domestic cars but had to be given a good reason. In a nutshell, that was the situation.

Marketing Objectives

The organization's next step is to determine specific marketing objectives. These must consider the amount of money the company has to invest in marketing and production, its knowledge of the marketplace, and the competitive environment. General Motors, for example, invested $5 billion in the Saturn project before the first car ever rolled out.[5]

Marketing objectives follow logically from a review of the company's current situation, management's prediction of future trends, and the hierarchy of company objectives. For example, **corporate objectives** are stated in terms of profit or return on investment, or net worth, earnings ratios, growth, or corporate reputation. **Marketing objectives,** which derive from corporate objectives, relate to the needs of target markets and to specific sales goals. These are called general *need-satisfying objectives* and specific *sales-target objectives*.

To shift management's view of the organization from a producer of products or services to a satisfier of target market needs, companies set **need-satisfying**

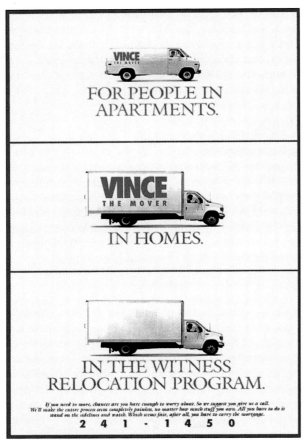

Companies often find it useful to frame their marketing strategies in terms of need-satisfying objectives. This often helps broaden the scope of their business. By understanding what consumers want, or how consumers use the company's product or service, marketers can more easily plan how to deliver on those expectations. With tongue-in-cheek humor, Vince the Mover showed that he had expanded his perspective from being a simple moving service to one that could satisfy a variety of customer needs under often-difficult circumstances.

objectives. These enable the firm to view its business broadly. Since customer needs change, a narrow view may lead the company into markets where its products are obsolete.[6] Revlon founder Charles Revson once said a cosmetic company's product is hope, not lipstick. An insurance company sells financial security, not policies.

The second kind of marketing objectives are **sales-target objectives.** These are specific, quantitative, realistic marketing goals to be achieved within a specified time period. Saturn defined its goal as selling 75,000 cars nationwide in 1991 and 196,000 in 1992. These objectives were specific by product and market, quantified by time and amount, and judging by the results, fairly realistic. In 1991, Saturn sold 74,493 cars; in 1992, it sold 196,126. Only by setting specific objectives can management measure its marketing success. Saturn's objectives for 1993 and 1994 were 235,000 and 300,000 respectively. Sales for those two years were 229,356 and 286,003.[7]

Sales-target objectives may be expressed in several ways: total sales volume; sales volume by product, market segment, or customer type; and market share, growth rate of sales volume, or gross profit in total or by product line.

Marketing Strategy

The **marketing strategy** describes how the company plans to meet its marketing objectives (see Ad Lab 7–A, "The Strategies of Marketing Warfare"). Marketing strategy typically involves three steps: (1) defining the particular target markets; (2) determining the strategic position; and (3) developing an appropriate marketing mix for each target market. A company's marketing strategy has a dramatic impact on its advertising. It determines the role and amount of advertising in the marketing mix, its creative thrust, and the media employed.

Selecting the target market In top-down marketing, the first step in strategy development is to define and select the target market, using the processes of market segmentation and research discussed in Chapters 5 and 6.

Saturn, for instance, defined its target market as "college-educated import owners and intenders"—highly educated young adults (18 to 34) considering their first or second car purchase. They were further defined as 60 percent female, living in one- or two-person households, and seeking a vehicle with sporty styling, fun performance, fuel economy, a good warranty, and sound quality/reliability/dependability.[8] They typically drive a Honda Civic, Toyota Corolla, or Nissan 240SX.

Positioning the product David Ogilvy said one of the first decisions in marketing and advertising is also the most important: how to position the product. To Ogilvy, positioning means "what the product does and who it is for."[9] His agency (Ogilvy & Mather), for example, differentiated Dove soap in 1957 by positioning it as a *complexion bar for women with dry skin.* Now, some 40 years later, every commercial still uses the same cleansing cream demonstration, and Dove is consistently the number-one brand, spending some $33 million in advertising annually to maintain its 14 percent share of the $1.5 billion bar soap market.[10]

Companies usually have a number of positioning options. They might pick a position similar to a competitor's and fight for the same customers. Or they might find a position not held by a competitor—a hole in the market—and fill it quickly, perhaps through product differentiation or market segmentation.

Saturn positioned its car as an American alternative to the Japanese imports, offering comparable styling, performance, and quality at a lower price, and its company as the "caring" car company.[11] In recent years, the National Pork Producers Council slowed declining pork consumption with a national TV campaign that *repositioned* pork as "the other white meat."[12]

Determining the marketing mix The next step in developing the marketing strategy is to determine a cost-effective marketing mix for *each* target market the company pursues. As we discussed in Chapter 5, the mix blends the various marketing elements the company controls: *product, price, distribution,* and *communications.*

Saturn manufactured a solidly engineered, driver-oriented *product* and supported it with a 24-hour roadside assistance program and a money-back guarantee for dissatisfied customers who returned their cars within 30 days or 1,500 miles. Then, to reinforce its commitment to doing business differently, it established a

Positioning is important for both the advertiser and the consumer because it differentiates a product or service from those of competitors. With over $450 billion in assets, Hong Kong Bank (part of the huge HSBC Group) is one of the largest players in the world of banking. Here, HSBC Australia (www.hongkongbank.com/home.html) positions itself as a bank with a storehouse of options, compared to the simple offerings of most other banks.

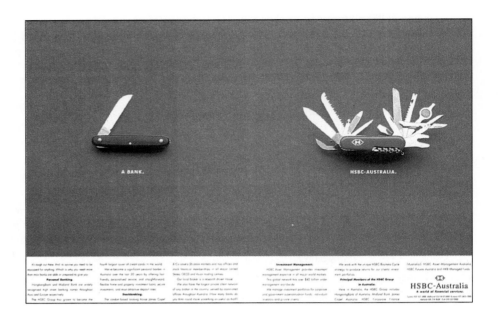

manufacturer's suggested retail *price* (MSRP) well below Honda Civic and Toyota Corolla, and decided not to use factory rebates or dealer incentives.[13]

GM created a completely new, wholly owned subsidiary and nationwide retail *distribution* system for Saturn, separate from the GM network. Finally, Saturn initiated an integrated *communications* program that included extensive training for retailer sales and service staffs (personal selling), innovative Media Days at the Spring Hill factory (public relations), and a full TV, magazine, and radio ad campaign to develop a distinct Saturn personality—not just for the car, but for the company as well.

Companies have a wide variety of marketing strategy options. They might increase distribution, initiate new uses for a product, change a product line, develop entirely new markets, or start discount pricing. Each option emphasizes one or more marketing mix elements. The choice depends on the product's position in the market and its stage in the product life cycle.

Marketing Tactics (Action Programs)

A company's objectives indicate where it wants to go; the strategy indicates the intended route; and the **tactics** (or **action programs**) determine the specific short-term actions to be taken, internally and externally, by whom, and when. Advertising campaigns live in the world of marketing tactics. These tactics are the key to *bottom-up marketing*.

Bottom-Up Marketing: How Small Companies Plan

In a small company, everybody is both player and coach, and the day-to-day details seem to come first, leaving little or no time for formal planning. However, there is a solution to this dilemma: **bottom-up marketing** (see Exhibit 7–2).

Jack Trout and Al Ries think the best way for a company to develop a competitive advantage is to focus on an ingenious tactic first and then develop that tactic into a strategy. By reversing the normal process, advertisers sometimes make important discoveries.[14] Researchers at Vicks developed an effective liquid cold remedy but discovered that it put people to sleep. Rather than throw out the research, Vicks positioned the formula as a nighttime cold remedy. NyQuil went on

Exhibit 7–2
Bottom-up marketing plan.

to become the number-one cold remedy and the most successful new product in Vicks's history.

The *tactic* is a singular, competitive mental angle. By planning from the bottom up, entrepreneurs can find unique tactics to exploit. Advertisers should find just one tactic, not two or three. The advertiser can then focus all elements of the marketing mix on the tactic. The tactic becomes the nail, and the strategy is the hammer that drives it home.

The combination of tactic and strategy creates a position in the consumer's mind. When Tom Monaghan thought of the tactic of delivering pizza to customers' homes, he focused his whole strategy on this singular idea and ended up making a fortune with Domino's Pizza.

A company's advertising plan is an excellent place to discover a competitive tactic. But opportunities are hard to spot because they often don't look like opportunities—they look like angles or gimmicks.

Managers of small companies have an advantage here. Surrounded by the details of the business, they are more likely to discover a good tactic that can be developed into a powerful strategy. However, that's not to say that a large company cannot profit from bottom-up marketing. Many have, like 3M with its Post-it notes.

The New Marketing Mantra: **Relationship** Marketing

Today, many advertisers are discovering what Saturn figured out going in: the key to building brand equity in the 21st century will be to develop interdependent, mutually satisfying relationships with customers.

A market-driven firm's overriding purpose is to create happy, loyal customers. Customers, not products, are the lifeblood of the business.[15] This realization has created a new trend away from simple *transactional marketing* to **relationship marketing**—creating, maintaining, and enhancing long-term relationships with customers and other stakeholders that result in exchanges of information and other things of mutual value.[16]

Today's affluent, sophisticated consumers can choose from a wide variety of products and services offered by producers located around the world. As a result, customer relationships—in which the sale is only the beginning—are the key strategic resource of the successful 21st-century business.[17] As Dartmouth professor Frederick Webster points out: "The new *market-driven* conception of marketing will focus on *managing strategic partnerships* and positioning the firm between vendors and customers in the value chain with the aim of delivering *superior value* to the customer."[18]

We define value as the ratio of *perceived benefits* to the price of the product.[19]

The Importance of Relationships

To succeed, companies must focus on managing loyalty among carefully chosen customers and **stakeholders** (employees, centers of influence, stockholders, the financial community, and the press).[20] This is important for a number of reasons:

You are a raindrop.

Not just any raindrop, but a raindrop with an attitude.

Pancake-big and ready to splat.

You're a frog-strangling, car-stalling, game-cancelling kind of raindrop and you don't care whose parade you screw up.

Just then you realize.

No, it can't be. It is.

You're headed straight for a Siplast roof.

Some days, it's just not worth getting out of the cloud.

Considering what you're up against, you need more than a roof, you need a partnership. And what better partner than the company that pioneered the SBS process? That's Siplast. The company with over 30 years of success in the roofing business. Not somebody who just fell into it. 1.800.922.8800.

NOTHING STANDS UP TO THE ELEMENTS LIKE A SIPLAST ROOF

⚡ **siplast**

The traditional transactional marketing approach, which focused on short-term profits, is now being replaced by a new model called relationship marketing. The purpose of relationship marketing is to create, maintain, and enhance long-term relationships with good customers and other stakeholders so that business can continue beyond periodic fluctuations in the economy. In this ad, Siplast (www.siplast.com), the largest commercial roofing manufacturer in the world, addresses the need for long-standing partnerships with its contractor clients. This is particularly important for high-cost, high-think products and services.

1. *The cost of lost customers.* No amount of advertising is likely to win back a customer lost from shoddy products or poor service. The real profit lost is the customer's *lifetime value* to a firm. For example, the average customer of one major transportation firm represented a lifetime value of $40,000. The company had 64,000 accounts and lost 5 percent of them due to poor service—an unnecessary loss of $128 million in revenue and $12 million in profits![21]

2. *The cost of acquiring new customers.* Defensive marketing typically costs less than offensive marketing because it requires a great deal of effort to lure satisfied customers away from competitors.[22] The fragmentation of media audiences and the resistance of sophisticated consumers to advertising messages make it increasingly difficult for a brand to break out of the ghetto of advertising clutter by stepping up the advertising volume.[23] In fact, it costs five to eight times as much in marketing, advertising, and promotion to acquire a new customer as it does to keep an existing one.[24]

3. *The value of loyal customers.* Lester Wunderman, the founder of Cato Wunderman Johnson (the second largest direct-response agency in the world), says that 90 percent of a manufacturer's profit comes from repeat purchasers; only 10 percent comes from trial or sporadic purchasers.[25] Reducing customer defections by even 5 percent can improve profit potential by 25 to 85 percent.[26] And the longer customers stay with a company, the more willing they are to pay premium prices, make referrals, increase their annual buying, and the less hand-holding they need.[27]

An overwhelming proportion of most business is conducted with repeat customers. This places a premium on the importance of customer retention. Retention can be achieved by offering special benefits to loyal customers, effectively rewarding and thanking them for past business and providing an incentive for future business. The airline industry offers frequent flyer miles as an incentive for customer loyalty. Hilton hotels (www.hilton.com) provides a similar service to their Hhonors members, offering free overnight stays to customers that provide repeat business.

If taken too far, comparative advertising can also be illegal. If the comparison is false, misleading, or deceptive, even ads that are literally correct can be found liable. According to one court, "innuendo, indirect intimations, and ambiguous suggestions" can unjustly injure a competitor. McNeil Consumer Products' Extra-Strength Tylenol, for example, successfully sued American Home Products' Maximum Strength Anacin even though Anacin's ad was literally true. Anacin had implied superiority over Tylenol when in fact both products contain the same amount of pain reliever.

The ethical problem is even stickier, because moral beliefs are typically personal. Many consumers don't like advertising that names competitors, and many in the industry feel similarly. To keep comparison battles from getting out of hand, numerous groups—including the American Association of Advertising Agencies, the National Association of Broadcasters, the FTC, and the TV networks—have issued guidelines for comparative ads, often stricter than current laws. NBC, for example, insists that "advertisers shall refrain from discrediting, disparaging, or unfairly attacking competitors, competing products, or other industries."

This is a good step, but the legal language governing comparisons is vague, obscuring the line between healthy one-upmanship and illegal behavior. As competition continues to increase, and ethical and legal guidelines remain fuzzy, the public will no doubt continue to be blitzed by comparative ads. The responsibility falls on consumers to sift the facts and figures and to separate truth from fiction.

Questions

1. How do you feel about ads that compare the features and benefits of competitive products and services? Do you believe they are unethical even if the comparisons are honest? Why or why not?

2. Select a comparative ad and study the copy. What points of comparison does the ad make? Are the points made honestly and directly, or are they masked by innuendo and implication? Is the ad literally true but still potentially misleading? Do you think the ad is ethical or not?

Sources: Gary Levin, "Marketers Get Really Nasty with In-Your-Face Advertising," *Advertising Age,* October 17, 1994, p. 2; Jim Henry, "Comparative Ads Speed Ahead for Luxury Imports," *Advertising Age,* September 12, 1994, p. 10; Thomas E. Barry, "Comparative Advertising: What Have We Learned in Two Decades?" *Journal of Advertising Research,* March/April 1993, pp. 19–29; A. Andrew Gallo, "False and Comparative Advertising under Section 43(a) of the Lanham Trademark Act," in Theodore R. Kupferman, ed., *Advertising and Commercial Speech* (CN: Meckler Corp., 1990), pp. 49–76; Steven A. Meyerowitz, *Marketing, Sales, and Advertising Law* (Detroit: Visible Ink Press, 1994).

Thus, a company's first market should always be its current customers. In the past, most marketing and advertising effort focused on *presale* activities aimed at acquiring new customers. But today sophisticated marketers are shifting more of their resources to *postsale* activities, making customer retention their first line of defense. They have discovered the primary benefit of focusing on relationships: increasing retention and optimizing **lifetime customer value (LTCV).**[28]

Levels of Relationships

Kotler and Armstrong distinguish five levels of relationships that can be formed between a company and its various stakeholders, depending on their mutual needs:

- *Basic transactional relationship.* The company sells the product but does not follow up in any way (Kmart).

- *Reactive relationship.* The company (or salesperson) sells the product and encourages customers to call if they encounter any problems (Men's Wearhouse).

- *Accountable relationship.* The salesperson phones customers shortly after the sale to check whether the product meets expectations and asks for product improvement suggestions and any specific disappointments. This information helps the company to continuously improve its offering (Acura dealers).

- *Proactive relationship.* The salesperson or company contacts customers from time to time with suggestions about improved product use or helpful new products (CompuServe).

- *Partnership.* The company works continuously with customers (and other stakeholders) to discover ways to deliver better value (Apple Computer).[29]

Different stakeholders require different types of relationships. The relationship a company seeks with a customer will rarely be the same as it seeks with the press. However, there is often significant overlap in stakeholder roles. An employee may also be a customer and own stock in the company. Knowing intimately the customers and stakeholders is critical to the success of relationship marketing.

Saturn (www.saturn.com) pretends to give away a trade secret in this ad: treating people the same way you'd want to be treated. In fact, the deeper secret is that Saturn knows how to develop relationships with its customers. That's why it has succeeded in becoming what it claims to be: "a different kind of company."

The number of stakeholders is also important. The more there are, the more difficult it is to develop an extensive personal relationship with each. Moreover, some customers may not want anything more than a transactional relationship.[30] Most people wouldn't want a phone call from Oscar Mayer asking if the hot dogs tasted good or from Pepsi-Cola to ascertain the quality of fizz. However, when Coca-Cola changed its formula in the early 80s, legions of Coke loyalists besieged the company with angry letters and phone calls. They believed their relationship with the brand had been violated. The company quickly brought back Classic Coke. Clearly, brand relationships can be psychological or symbolic as well as personal, and they can be created by brand advertising as well as by people.

The final consideration is the profit margin. High-profit product or service categories make deeper, personal relationships more desirable (see Exhibit 7–3). Low profit margins per customer suggest that the marketer should pursue basic transactional relationships augmented by brand image advertising.[31]

Using **IMC** to Make Relationships Work

This interest in relationship marketing coincided with the interest in *integrated marketing communications* (IMC). In fact, according to Northwestern professor Don Schultz, IMC is what makes relationship marketing possible.[32]

The link is *interdependence*, the fundamental characteristic of all relationships. As Drake University professor Lou Wolter points out, "IMC is the management of interdependence in the marketplace."[33]

IMC: The Concept and the Process

Technology has enabled marketers to adopt flexible manufacturing, customizing products for customized markets. "Market driven" today means bundling more services together with products to create a "unique product experience." As with Saturn, it means companies and customers working together to find solutions.[34]

The counterpart to flexible manufacturing is flexible marketing—and integrated marketing communications—to reach customers at different levels in new and better ways.

IMC is both a concept and a process. The *concept* of integration is *wholeness*. Achieving this wholeness in communications creates *synergy*—the principal benefit of IMC—because each element of the communications mix reinforces the others for greater effect.[35]

Tom Duncan, director of the IMC graduate program at the University of Colorado at Boulder, points out that IMC is also a *process* in which communication becomes the driving, integrating force in the marketing mix and throughout the organization.

The Evolution of the IMC Concept

As we discussed in Chapter 1, with the phenomenal technological changes of the last decade came a host of specialized media and the fragmentation of the mass market. At the same time we witnessed a flood of mergers and acquisitions, the ascension of the global marketplace, the escalation of competition between various internal departments and external suppliers, and the arrival of more sophisticated,

Profit margins

	High	Medium	Low
Many	Accountable	Reactive	Basic
Medium	Proactive	Accountable	Basic
Few	Partnership	Accountable	Reactive

Number of customers

Exhibit 7–3
Relationship levels as a function of profit margin and number of customers.

critical, and demanding customers. Suddenly, companies faced costly redundancies and inefficiencies as company departments with different missions and agendas all sought to achieve their particular goals, often at odds with either corporate or customer needs. For efficiency, companies needed to coordinate the multiplicity of inconsistent company and product messages being issued.[36]

Many companies initially took a narrow, *inside-out* view of IMC. They saw it as a way to coordinate and manage their marketing communications (advertising, sales promotion, public relations, personal selling, and direct marketing) to give the audience a consistent message about the company.[37]

A broader, more sophisticated, *outside-in* perspective of IMC sees customers as partners in an ongoing relationship, recognizes the references they use, acknowledges the importance of the whole communications system, and accepts the many ways they come into contact with the company or the brand. Companies committed to IMC realize their biggest asset is not their products or their plants or even their employees, but their customers.[38] Defined broadly:

> **Integrated marketing communications** is the process of building and reinforcing mutually profitable relationships with employees, customers, other stakeholders, and the general public by developing and coordinating a strategic communications program that enables them to have a constructive encounter with the company/brand through a variety of media or other contacts.

Whether a company employs the narrow view or the broad view depends to a great extent on its corporate culture. Some companies enjoyed rapid growth and strong customer relationships because they intuitively integrated and focused all corporate and marketing activities. Saturn, Apple, Honda, Nike, and Banana Republic are just a few.

Tom Duncan identified four distinct levels of integration that companies use: unified image, consistent voice, good listener, and at the most integrated, world-class citizen (see Exhibit 7–4). These levels demonstrate how IMC programs range from narrowly focused corporate monologs to broad, interactive dialogs, resulting in a corporate culture that permeates an organization and drives everything it does, internally and externally.[39]

Exhibit 7–4
Levels of integration.

Level	Name	Description/focus	Examples
1	Unified image	One look, one voice; strong brand image focus	3M
2	Consistent voice	Consistent tone and look; coordinated messages to various audiences (customers, trade, suppliers, etc.)	Hallmark, Coca-Cola
3	Good listener	Solicits two-way communication, enabling feedback through toll-free numbers, surveys, trade shows, etc.; focus on long-term relationships	Andersen windows, Saturn
4	World-class citizen	Social, environmental consciousness, strong company culture; focus on wider community	Ben & Jerry's, Apple, Honda

How the Customer Sees Marketing Communications

To truly understand IMC, we have to look through the customer's eyes. In one study, consumers identified 102 different media as "advertising"—everything from TV to shopping bags to sponsored community events.[40] Customers also develop perceptions of the company or brand through a variety of other sources: news reports, word-of-mouth, gossip, experts' opinions, financial reports, and even the CEO's personality.

All these communications or brand contacts, sponsored or not, create an *integrated product* in the consumer's mind.[41] In other words, customers automatically integrate all the brand-related messages that emanate from the company or some other source. The way they integrate those messages determines their perception of the company. IMC gives companies a better opportunity to manage or influence those perceptions and create a superior relationship with those stakeholders.

The Four Sources of Brand Messages

To influence customers' perceptions, marketers must understand one of the basic premises of IMC: that *everything we do (and don't do) sends a message.* That is to say, every corporate activity has a message component. Duncan categorized four types of company/brand-related messages stakeholders receive: *planned, product, service,* and *unplanned.* They each influence a stakeholder's relationship decision, so marketers must know where these messages originate, what impact they have, and the costs to influence or control them.

1. *Planned messages.* These are the traditional marketing communication messages—advertising, sales promotion, personal selling, merchandising materials, publicity releases, event sponsorships. These often have the *least* impact because they are seen as self-serving. They may also include help-wanted or financial offering ads, engineering articles in professional journals, and new contract announcements. Planned messages should work toward a determined set of communications objectives. This is the most fundamental aspect of IMC.

2. *Product messages.* In IMC theory, every element of the marketing mix sends a message. Messages from the product, price, or distribution elements are typically referred to as product (or inferred) messages. For example, customers and other stakeholders receive one product message from a $2,500 Rolex watch and a totally different one from a $30 Timex.

    Product messages have great impact. When a product performs well, the customer infers a positive message that reinforces the purchase decision. However, a gap between the product's performance and advertised promises is likely to infer a negative message. Managers must realize that marketing mix decisions are also communication decisions.

3. *Service messages.* Many messages result from employee interactions with customers. In many service organizations, customer service people are supervised by operations, not marketing. Yet the service messages they send have greater impact than the planned messages. With IMC, marketing people work with operations to minimize negative messages and maximize positive ones.

4. *Unplanned messages.* Companies have little or no control over the unplanned messages that emanate from employee gossip, unsought

Product messages, which are often implied by the various aspects of the product, price, and distribution elements of the marketing mix, can assist in providing an overall image for a product or service. Advertising, as a planned message, helps convey the product message. Therefore, it is important for companies to create ads that are consistent with the desired product message and that appropriate media be selected for carrying the ad. Over the years, DeBeers has consistently provided a planned message of elegance and romance through its famous "A diamond is forever" campaign. To learn more about this interesting advertiser, check out DeBeers (www.adiamondisforever.com) on the World Wide Web.

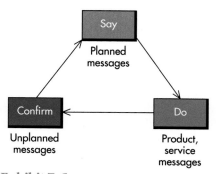

Exhibit 7–5
The integration triangle.

news stories, comments by the trade or competitors, word-of-mouth rumors, or major disasters. Unplanned messages may affect customers' attitudes dramatically, but they can sometimes be anticipated and influenced, especially by managers experienced in public relations.[42]

The Integration Triangle

The integration triangle developed by Duncan and Moriarty is a simple illustration of how perceptions are created from the various brand message sources (see Exhibit 7–5). Planned messages are *say* messages, what companies say about themselves. Product and service messages are *do* messages because they represent what a company does. Unplanned messages are *confirm* messages because that's what others say and confirm (or not) what the company says and does. Constructive integration occurs when a brand does what its maker says it will do and then others confirm that it delivers on its promises.[43]

The Dimensions of IMC

To maximize the synergy benefits of IMC, Duncan suggests three dimensions to an organization's integration process. It should first ensure consistent positioning, then facilitate purposeful interactivity between the company and its customers or other stakeholders, and finally actively incorporate a socially responsible mission into the organization's relationships with its stakeholders. As Duncan's IMC macro model in Exhibit 7–6 shows, the goal of all IMC efforts is an enhanced relationship with customers and other stakeholders, which leads to stakeholder loyalty and ultimately to brand equity.[44] See RL 7–2 in the Reference Library for more details on this model.

The interest in IMC is already global, moving from North America to Europe, Asia, and Latin America.[45] The $38 billion Swiss company Nestlé, for example, used a variety of IMC strategies, such as building highway rest stops for feeding and changing babies, designed to establish deep, caring relationships between families and the Nestlé Baby Foods division in France.[46]

In short, IMC offers accountability by maximizing resources and linking communications activities directly to organizational goals and the resulting bottom line.[47]

The IMC Approach to Marketing and Advertising Planning

Integrated marketing communications suggest a new approach to planning marketing and communications activities. It differs substantially from the traditional process by mixing marketing and communications planning together rather than separating them. Using the outside-in process, the IMC approach starts

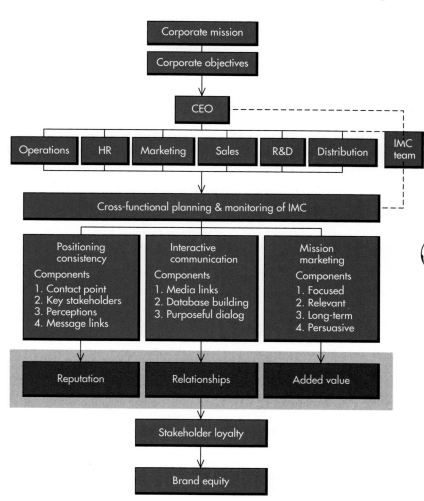

Exhibit 7–6
IMC macro model.

Source: ©Tom Duncan, Ph.D., University of Colorado, 1995.

Companies have control over their advertising, but they must be careful about any unplanned messages they may inadvertently engender. Over the years, the fashion designer Benetton (www.Benetton.com) has developed a number of highly controversial ads addressing social issues and, much like Calvin Klein, Benetton has suffered criticism for its advertising. However, some critics maintain that these messages are by no means unplanned but, rather, are very deliberate attempts to generate inexpensive press.

with the customer. Marketers study what media customers use, the relevance of their message to the customers, and when customers and prospects are most *receptive* to the message. They begin with the customer and work back to the brand.[48]

Thanks to computer technology, marketers of mass merchandise have a wealth of information at their fingertips. With supermarket scanner data, for instance, packaged-goods marketers can (1) identify specific users of products and services; (2) measure their actual purchase behavior and relate it to specific brand and product categories; (3) measure the impact of various advertising and marketing communications activities and determine their value in influencing the actual purchase; and (4) capture and evaluate this information over time.[49]

This ever-expanding database of customer behavior can be the basis for planning all future marketing and communications activities, especially if the database contains information on customer demographics, psychographics, purchase data, and brand or product category attitudes (see Exhibit 7–7).

Starting the whole planning process with the database forces the company to focus on the consumer, or prospect, not on the company's sales or profit goals. These marketing objectives are moved farther down in the planning process.[50]

Wang and Schultz developed a seven-step IMC planning model. The first step segments the customers and prospects in the database—either by brand loyalty, as illustrated, or by some other measurable purchase behavior (heavy usage, for instance).

The second step analyzes the information on customers to understand their attitudes, their history, and how they enter into contact with the brand or product—in other words, determining the best time, place, and situation to communicate with them.

Next, the planner sets marketing objectives based on this analysis. In the illustrated example, these objectives relate to building and maintaining usage or nurturing brand loyalty.

The marketer then identifies what brand contacts and what changes in attitude are required to support the consumer's continuance or change of purchase behavior.

The fifth step sets communications objectives and strategies for making contact with the consumer and influencing his or her attitudes, beliefs, and purchase behavior. The marketer can then decide what other elements of the marketing mix (product, price, distribution) can be used to further encourage the desired behavior.

Finally, the planner determines what communications tactics to use—media advertising, direct marketing, publicity, sales promotion, special events—to make contact and influence the consumer's behavior.[51]

By following this model, the marketer sets objectives based on an understanding of the customer or prospect and of what must be communicated. All forms of marketing are turned into communication, and all forms of communication into marketing.[52]

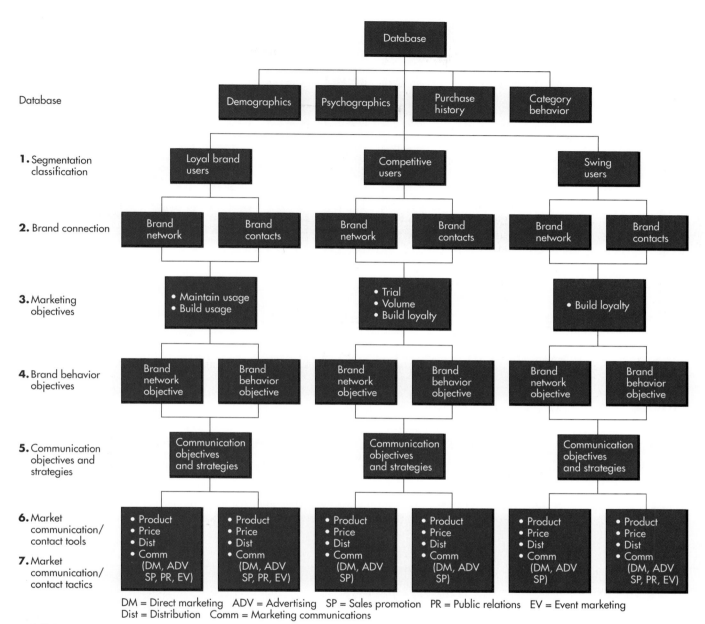

Exhibit 7–7

Wang-Schultz IMC planning model.

The Importance of IMC to the Study of Advertising

Since customers see all sponsored communications as advertising, advertising people (account managers, creatives, media planners) must grow beyond their traditional specialty to become enlightened generalists, familiar with and able to integrate all types of marketing communications.

In a survey of 100 company marketing executives, most respondents thought integration of advertising, promotion, public relations, and other communications activities would influence companies' marketing strategies more in the next three to five years than economic trends, globalization, and even pricing (see Exhibit 7–8).[53] However, studies also suggest that most practitioners today lack the broad knowledge required to develop, supervise, and execute full IMC programs.[54]

Exhibit 7–8
Factors expected to influence marketing strategies.

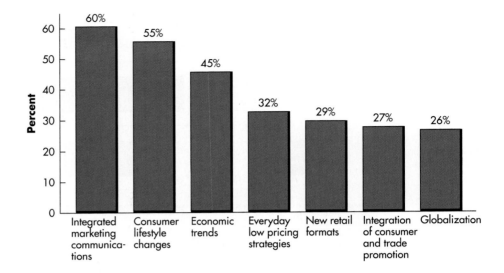

The **Advertising** Plan The **advertising plan** is a natural outgrowth of the marketing or IMC plan and is prepared in much the same way. In IMC planning, the advertising plan is an integral part of the overall procedure. Appendix B at the end of the book outlines a top-down advertising plan, and Appendix C shows an IMC plan outline.

Reviewing the Marketing Plan The advertising manager first reviews the marketing plan to understand where the company is going, how it intends to get there, and what role advertising plays in the marketing mix. The first section of the advertising plan should organize information from the marketing plan's situation analysis into four categories: internal *strengths* and *weaknesses* and external *opportunities* and *threats* (SWOT). This **SWOT analysis** briefly restates the company's current situation, reviews the target market segments, itemizes the long- and short-term marketing objectives, and cites decisions regarding market positioning and the marketing mix.

To prevent consumer confusion, companies must ensure that their positioning strategies remain consistent over the course of several ad campaigns. In each of its ads, BMW (www.BMW.com) positions its automobiles consistently to ensure that consumers always recognize the brand as "The Ultimate Driving Machine."

Setting Advertising Objectives

The advertising manager then determines what tasks advertising must take on. What strengths and opportunities can be leveraged? What weaknesses and threats need to be addressed? Unfortunately, some corporate executives (and advertising managers) state vague goals for advertising, like "increasing sales and maximizing profits by creating a favorable impression of the product in the marketplace." When this happens, no one understands what the advertising is intended to do, how much it will cost, or how to measure the results. Advertising objectives should be specific, realistic, and measurable.

Understanding What Advertising Can Do

Most advertising programs encourage prospects to take some action. However, it is usually unrealistic to assign advertising the whole responsibility for achieving sales. Sales goals are marketing objectives, not advertising objectives. Before an advertiser can persuade customers to buy, it must inform, persuade, or remind its intended audience about the company, product, service, or issue. A simple adage to remember when setting objectives is: "Marketing sells, advertising tells." In other words, advertising objectives should be related to communication effects.

The Advertising Pyramid: A Guide to Setting Objectives

Suppose you're advertising a new brand in a new product category, but you're not sure what kind of results to expect. The pyramid in Exhibit 7–9 shows some of the tasks advertising can perform. Obviously, before your product is introduced, prospective customers are completely unaware of it. Your first advertising objective therefore is to create *awareness*—to acquaint people with the company, product, service, and/or brand.

The next task might be to develop *comprehension*—to communicate enough information about the product such that some percentage of the aware group recognizes the product's purpose, image, or position, and perhaps some of its features.

Next, you need to communicate enough information to develop *conviction*—to persuade a certain number of people to actually believe in the product's value. Of those who become convinced, some may be moved to *desire* the product. Finally, some percentage of those who desire the product will take *action*. They may request additional information, send in a coupon, visit a store, or actually buy the product.

The pyramid works in three dimensions: time, dollars, and people. Advertising results may take time, especially if the product is expensive or not purchased regularly. Over time, as a company continues advertising, the number of people who become aware of the product increases. As more people comprehend the product, believe in it, and desire it, more take the final action of buying it.

Let's apply these principles to Saturn's advertising pyramid. In 1992, Saturn introduced an entry-level 2 + 2 coupe, the SC1. Specific advertising objectives for this car might have read as follows:

Exhibit 7–9

The advertising pyramid depicts the progression of advertising effects on mass audiences—especially for new products. Compared to the large number of people aware of the product (the base of the pyramid), the number motivated to act is usually quite small.

1. Within two years, communicate the existence of the Saturn SC1 to half of the more than 500,000 people who annually buy foreign economy cars.
2. Inform two-thirds of this "aware" group that the Saturn is a technologically superior economy car with many design, safety, and performance features; that it is a brand-new nameplate backed with unmatched service, quality, and value; and that it is sold only through dedicated Saturn dealers.
3. Convince two-thirds of the "informed" group that the Saturn is a high-quality car, reliable, economical, and fun to drive.
4. Stimulate desire within two-thirds of the "convinced" group for a test drive.
5. Motivate two-thirds of the "desire" group to visit a retailer for a test drive.

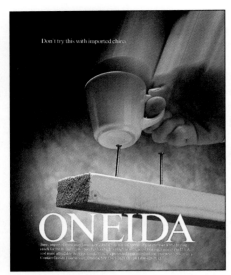

The advertising pyramid represents the learn-feel-do model of advertising effects. Oneida (*www.Oneida.com*), for instance, is renowned for its quality glassware and china. It uses the learn-feel-do approach in this ad, where consumers learn *about the resiliency of the* porcelain, feel *positively about the* durability, and fulfill the do element by visiting the store and/or purchasing the product.

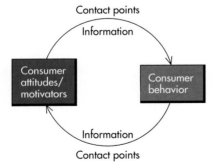

Exhibit 7–10
Messages go to the customer through advertising and other communication channels. Messages come back via direct response, surveys, and a purchase behavior database. The marketer's message can evolve based on this feedback.

These advertising objectives are specific as to time and degree and are quantified like marketing objectives. Theoretically, at the end of the first year, a consumer attitude study could determine how many people are aware of the Saturn SC1, how many understand the car's primary features, and so on, thus measuring the program's effectiveness.

Saturn's advertising may accomplish the objectives of creating awareness, comprehension, conviction, desire, and action. But once the customer is in the store, it's the retailer's responsibility to close the sale with effective selling and service.

With the advent of integrated marketing communications, we can look at the pyramid in another way. By using a variety of marketing communications (marcom) tools and a wide menu of traditional and nontraditional media, we can accomplish more efficiently the communications objectives suggested by the pyramid. For creating sheer *awareness* of the new coupe as well as brand image for the car and the company, mass media advertising is the marcom tool of choice. *Comprehension* and *conviction* can be augmented by media advertising, press publicity, direct mail brochures, and special events like a sports car show. *Desire* can be enhanced by a combination of the buzz created by media advertising plus good reviews in car enthusiast magazines, beautiful brochure photography, and the excitement generated by a sales promotion (such as a sweepstakes). Finally, *action* can be stimulated by direct-mail solicitation, sales promotion, and the attentive service of a retail salesperson in an attractive new-car showroom. After the sale, media advertising should continue to reinforce the purchase decision. At the same time, telemarketing calls from the retailer can be used to thank the customer, solicit feedback on that customer's experience, and offer any needed assistance. This acknowledges that the sale was just the beginning of a valuable relationship.

The Old Model versus the New

The advertising pyramid represents the *learn-feel-do* model of advertising effects. That is, it assumes that people rationally consider a prospective purchase, and once they feel good about it, they act. The theory is that advertising affects attitude, and attitude leads to behavior. That may be true for certain expensive, high-involvement products that require a lot of consideration. But other purchases may follow a different pattern. For example, impulse purchases at the checkout counter may involve a *do-feel-learn* model, in which behavior leads to attitude. Other purchases may follow some other pattern. Thus, there are many marketing considerations when advertising objectives are being set, and they must be thought out carefully (see RL 7–3, Checklist for Developing Advertising Objectives, in the Reference Library).

The advertising pyramid also reflects the traditional mass-marketing monolog. The advertiser talks and the customer listens.[55] That was appropriate before the advent of computers and databases, and it may still be appropriate in those categories where the marketer has no choice.

But today, as the IMC model shows, many marketers have databases of information on their customers, about where they live, what they buy, and what they like and dislike. When marketers can have a dialog and establish a relationship, the model is no longer a pyramid but a circle (see Exhibit 7–10). Consumers and business customers can send messages back to the marketer in the form of coupons, phone calls, surveys, and database information on purchases. With interactive media, the responses are in real time. This feedback can help the marketer's product, service, and messages evolve.[56] And reinforcement advertising, designed to build brand loyalty, will remind people of their successful experience with the product and suggest reuse.

By starting with the customer and then integrating all aspects of their marketing communications—package and store design, personal selling, advertising, public relations activities, special events, and sales promotions—companies hope to accelerate the communications process, make it more efficient, and achieve lasting loyalty from *good* prospects, not just prospects.[57]

Advertising Strategy and the Creative Mix

The advertising (or communications) *objective* declares where the advertiser wants to be with respect to consumer awareness, attitude, and preference; the advertising (or creative) *strategy* describes how to get there.

Advertising strategy blends the elements of the **creative mix:** *target audience, product concept, communications media,* and *advertising message.*

The Target Audience: Everyone Who Should Know

The **target audience,** the specific people the advertising will address, is typically larger than the target market. Advertisers need to know who the end user is, who makes the purchase, and who influences the purchasing decision. Children, for example, often exert a strong influence on where the family eats. So while McDonald's target market is adults, its target audience also includes children, and it spends much of its advertising budget on campaigns directed at kids.

Similarly, while companies may target heavy users of a product, many light and nonusers are exposed to the advertising as well. That's good, because research shows that brand popularity (which advertising is uniquely good at creating) cuts across all levels of purchasing frequency.[58] The dominant brands are purchased the most by both heavy and light users (see Exhibit 7–11). It's the accumulation of all these sales that makes a product the dominant brand.

The Product Concept: Presenting the Product

The "bundle of values" the advertiser presents to the consumer is the **product concept.** Quaker Oats Life cereal and Plus Fiber are similarly priced brands aimed at the U.S. ready-to-eat breakfast cereal market. However, Life is presented as a cereal kids will like, Plus Fiber as a healthful cereal for adult needs.

When writing the advertising plan, the advertising manager must develop a simple statement to describe the product concept—that is, how the advertising will present the product. To create this statement, the advertiser first considers how

Exhibit 7–11
Greater popularity occurs at each level of frequency.

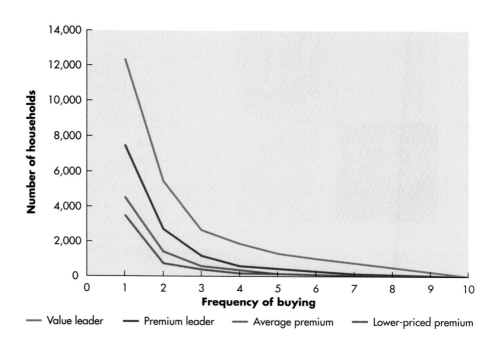

Product concept embodies the sum total of values that customers receive from a product or service and can also be used in product differentiation. While UPS, Federal Express, and the U.S. Postal Service all provide reliable parcel delivery services, the U.S. Postal Service (www.usps.com) differentiates its product concept in terms of price.

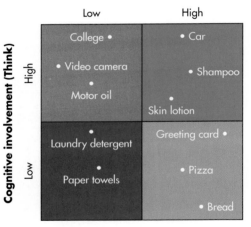

Exhibit 7–12
The Kim-Lord grid.

consumers perceive the product and then weighs this against the company's marketing strategy.

Recall from chapter 4 our discussion of the Elaboration Likelihood Model and the role of involvement with the product message. Some years ago, Richard Vaughn at Foote, Cone & Belding noted that different kinds of products typically evoke different levels of consumer involvement (either high or low) and different types of involvement, either *cognitive* (think) or *affective* (feel). This meant different products called for different kinds of advertising. He created a two-dimensional model known as the FCB grid, which categorized consumer products into four quadrants based on "high involvement" or "low involvement," and "think" or "feel." By positioning brands in the grid based on the degree and type of involvement consumers brought to the purchase decision, the agency could determine which type of advertising would be most appropriate. Rossiter and Percy extended this research with the six-cell grid you saw in Exhibit 4–3, which also suggested different creative executions.

More recently, Kim and Lord recognized that people can be both cognitively and affectively involved at the same time. So they developed the enhanced Kim-Lord grid, shown in Exhibit 7–12. It too depicts the degree and the kind of involvement a consumer brings to the purchase decision for different products. Some purchases, like cars, require a high degree of personal involvement on both the cognitive and affective levels.[59] For others, like detergent, involvement is low on both axes. Sometimes a marketer uses an advertising strategy aimed at shifting the product to higher involvement on either axis. A product's location on the grid also indicates how the product is purchased (learn-feel-do or feel-learn-do) and how advertising copy should be written (more emotional or more rational).[60]

The Communications Media: The Message Delivery System

As an element of creative strategy, the **communications media** are all the vehicles that might transmit the advertiser's message. They include traditional media such as radio, TV, newspapers, magazines, and billboards and, in an integrated communications program, direct marketing, public relations, special events, sales promotion, and personal selling.

Introducing a new product is a daunting task, particularly if the advertiser's budget is lower than competitors'—as was the case with Saturn. Hal Riney & Partners invited the media to build a relationship with Saturn and then limited advertising media purchases to those that responded. As a result, Saturn got choice back-cover positions with magazines, received economical placements on the Fox TV network, and (in a single deal with Patrick Media Group) became the largest brand advertiser on outdoor boards in California.[61]

The Advertising Message: What the Advertising Communicates

What the company plans to say in its ads and how it plans to say it, both verbally and nonverbally, make up the **advertising message.** As we discuss in Chapter 11, the combination of copy, art, and production elements forms the message, and there are infinite ways to combine these elements (see Portfolio Review: Strategic Use of the Creative Mix).

Riney broke new creative ground for Saturn. Rather than focusing on product features, standard fare in automotive advertising, Riney used Saturn employees and customers to symbolize the company and its philosophy.[62]

The Secret to Successful Planning Whether the advertiser is a large corporation or a small company, the key to successful planning is information. But the genius of business is in interpreting what the information means. This leads to direction, which makes planning easier and more rewarding.

Project Planning Software

Deadlines are the most important goals in the advertising business. From developing a campaign to executing the media placement, you need more than a pencil and paper to keep organized. To help along the way, Microsoft, Claris, and other companies have developed a whole gamut of project planning software.

These programs are geared to generate PERT (program evaluation and review technique) and Gantt charts that help managers see the entire project from beginning to end, including deadlines and project delegations. This helps keep the sales or creative team up-to-date on projects in order to meet deadlines and goals. Being informed is half the battle in the communications arena.

Microsoft Project, Mac Project Pro, and other programs are available at local software retailers, or you can visit the companies' Web sites on the Internet. The chart gives Web site addresses for companies that offer project planning software.

Product	Description	Platform	Publisher
Microsoft Project	Powerful analysis, management tools	Windows 95/NT	Microsoft Corp. www.microsoft.com
Power Planner	Critical path analysis, resource scheduling	Windows 3.1	Sphygemzic Software Ltd. www.agoron.com
Project Scheduler	Basic talk scheduling using SQL database	Windows 95/NT	Scitor Corp. www.scitor.com
SureTrak Project Manager	Scheduling small to medium projects from start to finish. Timetables and management resources like budgeting and cash flow	Windows 3.1	Primavera Systems Inc. www.primavera.com
TASKey Personal	Project and task manager that integrates a planner, time bar scheduler, to-do list, calendar, resource manager	Windows 95/NT	Task Solutions www.taskey.com
Group Works	Workgroup collaboration package, tasks, meetings, people. Network file sharing using network object linking and embedding (OLE)	Windows 3.1	Group Works www.ftp.com
Mac Project Pro	Complete planning, professional charting, management flexibility, report generation, resource management, seamless data sharing	Mac OS	Claris Corp. www.claris.com

Allocating **Funds** for Advertising

In 1990, after eight years of unprecedented growth, the United States and Canada experienced the first throes of a recession. Interest rates were high, real estate sales dropped, construction of new homes slowed, defense spending was cut, and unemployment began to rise. To make matters worse, threats of war in the Persian Gulf caused fear of higher fuel prices. Consumer confidence sank, and with it sank retail sales.

As sales dropped, many executives cut back their advertising budgets, some to zero. Two years later, when the government announced the recession was over, these executives wondered why sales were still down and how their companies had lost so much market share.

Money is the motor that drives every marketing and advertising plan. If you suddenly shut the motor off, the car may coast for a while, but before long it will stop running. The marketing department has to convince management that advertising spending makes good business sense, even in an adverse economic climate.

continued on page 236

The advertising message represents what a company plans to say about its product and how it plans to say it. The advertising message for Seattle Chocolates (www.seattlechocolate.com) is that its candies provide sweet tooth decadence and gratification to consumers willing to indulge themselves for a moment. The "how" is through tongue-in-cheek humor by parodying the nutritional facts on other food products.

231

During the marketing and advertising planning process,

companies need to carefully consider who their target markets are and then who should be the targets of their advertising. They also need to consider the elements of advertising strategy. This brings up a lot of questions: what product concept are they trying to communicate; what various media will be used to communicate the message; and what should the nature of our advertising message be? Once these things are decided, the creative team can begin its work.

The ads in this portfolio demonstrate some good creative thinking, but more important, some outstanding strategic thinking. See if you can determine which element(s) of the creative mix is emphasized in each ad.

Developing a product concept for a product is necessary for the advertiser, the consumer, and other stakeholders so that all parties understand completely the nature of the product or service being sold. It's often effective, too, to think outside of the "box," which helps find metaphors for presenting the product concept. Digital Equipment Corp. (www.digital.com) is a manufacturer of networking software that is able to integrate several different computer operating systems. How does this ad present their product concept?

When Macintosh released its new G3 computer processor, the agency creatives conceived this clever ad as a direct comparison—a daring one— against the industry's behemoth leader, Intel. The G3 processor allowed Macintosh to break the computer speed benchmarks that had, up to that time, been set by Intel. With this ad, the underdog Macintosh (www.apple.com) was able to create a product concept around the speed idea. Visit Apple's Web site and see how the company uses that medium to follow up on this concept.

When companies plan to advertise, they should use marketing research to understand the buying habits of their target audience. The degree and kind of involvement (think/feel) also needs to be taken into consideration. In this very surreal ad for Sega Saturn video game system, who do you think the target audience is and why was the ad developed in such a manner? A look at Sega's Web page (www.sega.com/welcome.html) might help answer these questions.

"Theater of the Eye" :60

(Open on close-up of an eye. Push in on the pupil)

ANNCR. (VO): Welcome to the Theater of the Eye.

SFX: Movie projector sound.

(Cut to bored looking Rods and Cones.)

ROD: (in monotone) How nice . . .

(Cut to reveal the Rods and Cones watching disgusting toenails being trimmed. Cut to the theater screen. A disc is inserted into a Sega Saturn component. Cut to reveal the game screens.)

SFX: Fast paced, high energy game sound effects and music in the background throughout. Telephone ring.

(Cut to a shot of the Optic Nerve against the screen.)

OPTIC NERVE: Optic Nerve.

(Cut to a shot of an older, graying man.)

MAN: This is the Brain . . . what's going on down there?

OPTIC NERVE: (unsure) Uhh . . . pfff . . .

(Cut to a guy with protective head phones on, gripping a door through which we see the Ear Drum maniacally playing the drums.)

GUY: The Ear Drum's going off . . . go get hellllp!!!

(Cut to the Nervous System room. Two uptight guys are staring up at a monitor.)

NERVOUS SYSTEM GUY 1: (extremely fast) We're having a breakdown, we're having a breakdown.

NERVOUS SYSTEM GUY 2: Aaaaaaaaahhhhhhhhhhh!!!

(The Rods and Cones tilt their bodies as they follow a moving race car on the screen.)

BRAIN: What else can go wrong?

(Cut to the Cerebral Cortex.)

SECRETARY: Urgent, synapse on line two . . . it's the Sphincter.

(Cut to the chubby Sphincter, freaking out. He's trapped between two walls closing in on him.)

SFX: Slurping noises.

SPHINCTER: (yelling) What . . . is . . . going . . . on . . . up . . . there?

TAG ANNCR. (VO): (harmonically altered) Sega . . .

(The eye blinks. The Saturn logo replaces the eye ball. Sega Saturn is tattooed onto the skin.)

TAG ANNCR. (VO): . . . Saturn.

Just as with consumer advertising, business-to-business ads also target a specific audience. Self-promotionals, such as this example from professional photographer John Huet, are just one form of business-to-business advertising that provides a target audience (other businesses) with valuable information about certain products or services. Who might be the potential target audience for this ad?

According to the IMC model of advertising, every piece of communication with the public or other stakeholders will affect their relationship with a company. This includes the selection of media. When Altoids *(www.altoids.com)* began its "The Curiously Strong Mint" compaign, the company chose to advertise on billboards and in transit shelters. Why do you think this medium was chosen and what impact might it have had on consumers?

'NICE ALTOIDS'
THE CURIOUSLY STRONG MINTS

©1995 Callard & Bowser-Suchard Inc.

Southwestern Bell 1998 Radio

VO Southwestern Bell Wireless presents a modern-day tale — "Jack and Jill." And, yeah, a hill. Jack and Jill went up a hill together. Call it the buddy system.

JACK It's best to go with someone you know.

VO That was their climber's wisdom.

JILL You should also be prepared for anything, like, say, a nasty spill.

VO Lo and behold, Jack took a tumble — he spilled; he fell. Lucky for him, Jill had a wireless phone from Southwestern Bell.

JACK Uhm, I think I broke my crown.

JILL Wow, that was a long way down.

VO She called for help with that reliable phone because with Southwestern Bell it worked wherever she roamed, and soon enough Jack was medevacked home. And the moral is: Go with someone you know and you'll live happily ever after.

ANNCR Sign up now and pay only nine ninety-eight a month for one year. Plus get a free Motorola phone with nationwide coverage from Southwestern Bell.

SFX PIXIE DUST

ANNCR Your friendly neighborhood global communications company.

Limited time offer good on select rate plans. Requires two-year commitment. Other conditions and restrictions apply. Product and promotion may vary by location. See store for details. Service provided by Southwestern Bell Wireless, who reminds you to use your phone safely while driving.

Your friendly neighborhood global communications company.

○ **Southwestern Bell**

Radio is often selected as an advertising medium because every station's demographics can be determined with great accuracy. This knowledge provides marketers, like Southwestern Bell Mobile Systems *(www.swbell.com)*, with a precise way to selectively target those audiences best suited for the product. What, if any, are some possible unplanned messages that might occur because of the use of this medium?

What a company plans to say in its ads and how it plans to say it constitute the advertising message. Both verbal and nonverbal communication are components of the advertising message, manifested in copy that can be happy-go-lucky or photos and illustrations that can exude excitement or perhaps even melancholy. What is the advertising message of this ad for Isuzu (www.Isuzu.com) and what does it communicate to the consumer?

Although the relationship between advertising and sales can at times be difficult to ascertain, certain profit trends can be linked directly to the intensity and frequency of advertising. A locally based business like the Kelsey Seybold Clinic (www.kelsey-seybold.com) can expect to have some sales even if it does not advertise, mostly through word-of-mouth. But advertising in a high-exposure medium like outdoor is likely to provide significant sales improvement. Local businesses are hit particularly hard during times of recession, but, if at all possible, they should maintain advertising levels to prevent losing ground over the long run.

continued from page 231

Advertising: An Investment in Future Sales

Accountants and the Internal Revenue Service consider advertising a current business expense. Consequently, many executives treat advertising as a budget item to be trimmed or eliminated like other expense items when sales are either extremely high or extremely low. This is understandable but shortsighted.

The cost of a new plant or distribution warehouse is an investment in the company's future ability to produce and distribute products. Similarly, advertising—as one element of the communications mix—is an investment in future sales. While advertising is often used to stimulate immediate sales, its greatest power is in its cumulative, long-range, reinforcement effect. Advertising builds consumer preference and promotes goodwill. This enhances the reputation and value of the company name and brand. It also encourages customers to make repeat purchases.

So while advertising is a current expense for accounting purposes, it is also a long-term capital investment. For management to see advertising as an investment, however, it must understand how advertising relates to sales and profits.

The Relationship of Advertising to Sales and Profits

Many variables, both internal and external, influence the effectiveness of a company's marketing and advertising efforts. Methods to measure the relationships between advertising and sales and between sales and profits are far from perfect. However, research does verify the following.

In consumer goods marketing, increases in market share are more closely related to increases in the marketing budget than to price reductions. And market share is a prime indicator of profitability.[63]

● Sales normally increase with additional advertising. At some point, however, the rate of return declines (see Ad Lab 7–B, "How Economists View the Effect of Advertising on Sales").

● Sales response to advertising may build over time, but the durability of advertising is brief, so a consistent investment is important.[64]

● There are minimum levels below which advertising expenditures have no effect on sales.

● There will be some sales even if there is no advertising.

● Culture and competition impose saturation limits above which no amount of advertising can increase sales.

To management, these facts might mean: Spend more until it stops working. In reality, the issue isn't that simple. Advertising isn't the only marketing activity that affects sales. A change in market share may occur because of quality perceptions,

Ad Lab 7–B

How Economists View the Effect of Advertising on Sales

Normally, the sales of a product depend on the number of dollars the company spends advertising. Within reasonable limits (if its advertising program is not too repugnant), the more dollars spent on advertising, the more a company will sell—up to a point. Even the most enthusiastic ad agencies admit, reluctantly, that it is possible to spend too much.

Management must know how much more it can sell per additional dollar of advertising and when additional advertising dollars cease being effective. It doesn't need a fixed number representing potential demand, but a graph or a statistical equation describing the relationship between sales and advertising.

In our illustration, most of the curve goes uphill as we move to the right (it has a positive slope). This means that additional advertising will continue to bring in business until (at a budget of x million dollars) people become so saturated by the message that it begins to repel them and turn them away from the product.

Even if saturation cannot be reached within the range of affordable outlays, the curve is likely to level off, becoming flatter and flatter as the amount spent on advertising gets larger and

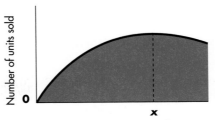

larger and saturation is approached. Advertising results begin to diminish at the point where the curve begins to flatten out. When the total advertising budget is small, even a $1 addition to the campaign may bring in as much as $10 in new sales. But when the market approaches saturation, each additional dollar may contribute only 30 cents in new sales.

Laboratory Applications

1. When would an advertising expenditure curve have a negative slope?

2. Economists suggest that sales depend on the level of advertising expenditures. Is that a safe assumption? Discuss.

---

word-of-mouth, the introduction of new products, the opening of more attractive outlets, better personal selling, or seasonal changes in the business cycle.

Furthermore, most companies don't have a clear-cut way to determine the relationship between sales and profit. What if the company sells a variety of products? Which advertising contributes to which sales?

One thing remains clear. Since the response to advertising is spread out over an extended time, advertising should be viewed as a long-term investment in future profits. Like all expenditures, advertising should be evaluated for wastefulness. But historically, companies that make advertising the scapegoat during tough times end up losing substantial market share before the economy starts growing again.[65]

The corollary is also true. Sustained ad spending during difficult times protects, and in some cases even increases, market share and builds brands. During the last global recession, the leading European marketers recognized this fact, and fewer than 40 percent of the top spenders in Italy, Austria, Germany, France, and Spain cut their budgets.[66]

The Variable Environments of Business

Before attempting to determine advertising allocations, the advertising manager must consider the company's economic, political, social, and legal situation. These factors affect total industry sales and corporate profits on sales. The manager must consider the institutional and competitive environments. What is the level of sales within the industry? How much are competitors spending and what are they doing that might either help or hinder the company's marketing efforts?

Finally, the manager must consider the internal environment. Do the company's current policies and procedures allow it to fulfill the promises its advertising intends to make?

Methods of Allocating Funds

Most business executives will spend more money on advertising as long as they are assured it will mean more profit. However, the point of equilibrium is hard to predict when advertising budgets are being developed.

Companies use a number of methods to determine how much to spend on advertising, including the *percentage-of-sales, percentage-of-profit, unit-of-sale, competitive-parity, share-of-market,* and *objective/task methods* (see the Checklist of Ways to Set Advertising Budgets).

Ways to Set Advertising Budgets

_____ **Percentage of sales.** Advertising budget is determined by allocating a percentage of last year's sales, anticipated sales for next year, or a combination of the two. The percentage is usually based on an industry average, company experience, or an arbitrary figure.

_____ **Percentage of profit.** Percentage is applied to profit, either past years' or anticipated.

_____ **Unit of sale.** Also called the _case-rate method._ A specific dollar amount is set for each box, case, barrel, or carton produced. Used primarily in assessing members of horizontal co-ops or trade associations.

_____ **Competitive parity.** Also called the _self-defense method._ Allocates dollars according to the amounts spent by major competitors.

_____ **Share of market/share of voice.** Allocates dollars by maintaining a percentage share of total industry advertising comparable to or somewhat ahead of desired share of market. Often used for new-product introductions.

_____ **Objective/task.** Also referred to as the _budget buildup method,_ this method has three steps: defining objectives, determining strategy, and estimating the cost to execute that strategy.

_____ **Empirical research.** By running experimental tests in different markets with different budgets, companies determine which is the most efficient level.

_____ **Quantitative mathematical models.** Computer-based programs developed by major advertisers and agencies rely on input of sophisticated data, history, and assumptions.

_____ **All available funds.** Go-for-broke technique generally used by small firms with limited capital, trying to introduce new products or services.

No technique is adequate for all situations. The three methods discussed here are used primarily for national advertising budgets. However, local retailers can use them too.

Percentage-of-Sales Method

The **percentage-of-sales method** is one of the most popular techniques for setting advertising budgets. It may be based on a percentage of last year's sales, anticipated sales for next year, or a combination of the two. Businesspeople like this method because it is the simplest, it doesn't cost them anything, it is related to revenue, and it is considered safe. The problem is knowing what percentage to use. As Exhibit 7–13 shows, even leaders in the same industry use different percentages. Across industries, they range from just 1.3 percent to almost 15 percent.

Usually the percentage is based on an industry average or on company experience. Unfortunately, it is too often determined arbitrarily. An industry average assumes that every company in the industry has similar objectives and faces the same marketing problems. Company experience assumes that the market is highly static, which is rarely the case.

However, when applied against future sales, this method often works well. It assumes that a certain number of dollars will be needed to sell a certain number of units. If the advertiser knows what the percentage is, the correlation between advertising and sales should remain constant, assuming the market is stable and competitors' advertising remains unchanged. And since this method is common in the industry, it diminishes the likelihood of competitive warfare.

The greatest shortcoming of the percentage-of-sales method is that it violates a basic marketing principle. Marketing activities are supposed to _stimulate_ demand and thus sales, not occur as a _result_ of sales. If advertising automatically increases when sales increase and declines when sales decline, it ignores all other factors that might encourage an opposite move.

Share-of-Market/Share-of-Voice Method

In markets with similar products, a high correlation usually exists between a company's share of the market and its share of industry advertising.

The **share-of-market/share-of-voice method** is a bold attempt to link advertising dollars with sales objectives.[67] It holds that a company's best chance of maintaining its share of market is to keep a share of advertising (voice) somewhat ahead of its market share. For example, a company with a 30 percent share of the market should spend 35 percent of the industry's advertising dollars.

The share-of-market/share-of-voice method is commonly used for new products.[68] According to this formula, when a new brand is introduced, the advertising budget for the first two years should be about one and a half times the brand's targeted share of the market in two years. This means that if the company's two-year sales goal is 10 percent of the market, it should spend about 15 percent of total industry advertising during the first two years.

One hazard of this method is the tendency to become complacent. Simply maintaining a higher percentage of media exposure usually isn't enough to accomplish the desired results. The top national packaged-goods marketers still spend 25 percent of their marketing budgets on consumer and trade promotion rather than con-

Exhibit 7–13
Advertising expenditures by the top 15 leading advertisers in 1993 ($ millions, rounded).

Rank	Company	U.S. advertising expenditures	U.S. sales	Advertising as percentage of U.S. sales
1	Procter & Gamble	$2,398	$ 15,579	7.3
2	Philip Morris	1,844	38,387	5.1
3	General Motors	1,539	109,668	1.8
4	Sears Roebuck	1,311	50,838	4.7
5	PepsiCo	1,039	18,309	6.3
6	Ford Motor	958	75,661	2.3
7	AT&T	812	61,580	*
8	Nestlé	794	*	5.0
9	Johnson & Johnson	763	7,203	12.6
10	Chrysler	762	37,847	*
11	Warner-Lambert	751	2,747	5.7
12	Unilever	738	8,550	3.4
13	McDonald's	737	3,931	14.6
14	Time Warner	695	4,414	*
15	Toyota Motor	690	*	1.3

*Figures not provided.

sumer advertising.[69] Companies must be aware of all their competitors' marketing activities, not just advertising.

Objective/Task Method

The **objective/task method,** also known as the *budget buildup method,* is used by the majority of major national advertisers in the United States. It considers advertising to be a marketing tool to help generate sales.

The task method has three steps: defining objectives, determining strategy, and estimating cost. After setting specific, quantitative marketing objectives, the advertiser develops programs to attain them. If the objective is to increase the sales of cases of coffee by 10 percent, the advertiser determines which advertising approach will work best, how often ads must run, and which media to use. The estimated cost of the program becomes the basis for the advertising budget. Of course, the company's financial position is always a consideration. If the cost is too high, objectives may have to be scaled back. If results are better or worse than anticipated after the campaign runs, the next budget may need revision.

The task method forces companies to think in terms of accomplishing goals. Its effectiveness is most apparent when the results of particular ads or campaigns can be readily measured. The task method is adaptable to changing market conditions and can be easily revised.

However, it is often difficult to determine in advance the amount of money needed to reach a specific goal. Techniques for measuring advertising effectiveness still have many weaknesses.

Additional Methods

Advertisers also use several other methods to allocate funds. In the **empirical research method,** a company runs a series of tests in different markets with different budgets to determine the best level of advertising expenditure.

Computers can generate quantitative mathematical models for budgeting and allocating advertising dollars. Foote, Cone & Belding developed a response-curve database from tracking studies on more than 40 clients' products and services. The program analyzes media programs and estimates customer response.[70] Many other sophisticated techniques facilitate marketing and advertising planning, budget allocation, new-product introductions, and media analysis.[71] However, most are not easily understood by line executives, and all rely on data that may be unavailable or estimated.[72] While widely employed by major national advertisers, these methods require very sophisticated users and, for the most part, are still too expensive for the average business.

The Bottom Line Unfortunately, all these methods rely on one of two fallacies. The first is that advertising is a *result* of sales. Advertisers know this is not true, yet they continue to use the percentage-of-sales method.

The second fallacy is that advertising *creates* sales. In certain circumstances (where direct-action advertising is used), advertising closes the sale. But advertising's real role is to locate prospects, build brand equity, and stimulate demand. It may even stimulate inquiries and product trial.

But the principal job of advertising is to influence perception by informing, persuading, and reminding. Advertising *affects* sales, but it is just one of many influences on consumer perception. Advertising managers must keep this in mind when preparing their plans and budgets.

Chapter **Summary**

The marketing plan may be the most important document a company possesses. It assembles all the pertinent and current facts about a company, the markets it serves, its products, and its competition. It sets specific goals and objectives and describes the precise strategies to use to achieve them. It musters the company's forces for the marketing battlefield and, in so doing, dictates the role of advertising in the marketing mix and provides focus for advertising creativity.

There are three types of marketing planning models: top-down, bottom-up, and integrated marketing communications planning.

The top-down marketing plan contains four principal sections: situation analysis, marketing objectives, marketing strategy, and tactics (action programs). A company's marketing objectives should be logical deductions from an analysis of its current situation, its prediction of future trends, and its understanding of corporate objectives. They should relate to the needs of specific target markets and specify sales objectives. Sales-target objectives should be specific, quantitative, and realistic.

The first step in developing a marketing strategy is to select the target market. The second step is to determine the product's positioning. The third step is to construct a cost-effective marketing mix for each target market the company pursues. The marketing mix is determined by how the company blends the elements it controls: product, price, distribution, and communications. Advertising is a communications tool.

One way for small companies to fulfill the marketing and advertising plan is to work from the bottom up, taking an ingenious tactic and building a strategy around it.

Integrated marketing communications can help build long-term relationships with customers. IMC planning is driven by technology. Thanks to computers and databases, marketers can learn more about their customers' wants and needs, likes and dislikes. IMC is both a concept and a process that offers the synergy of various communications media, strategically managed to enhance the relationship between the customer and the brand or company. Starting with the customer, the IMC planning model uses seven steps to segment the customer database by product-purchase-related attributes; determine the best place, situation, and time to reach the prospect; develop behavior-related marketing and communications objectives and strategies; and develop specific communications tactics to implement the plan. In the IMC model, all marketing becomes communications and all communications become marketing.

Advertising is a natural outgrowth of the marketing plan, and the advertising plan is prepared in much the same way as the top-down marketing plan. It includes a SWOT (strengths, weaknesses, opportunities, and threats) analysis, advertising objectives, and strategy.

Advertising objectives may be expressed in terms of moving prospective customers up through the advertising pyramid (awareness, comprehension, conviction, desire, action). Or they may be expressed in terms of generating inquiries, coupon response, or attitude change.

The advertising (or creative) strategy is determined by the advertiser's use of the creative mix. The creative mix is composed of the target audience, product concept, communications media, and advertising message. The target audience includes the specific groups of people the advertising will address. The product concept refers to the bundle of product-related values the advertiser presents to the customer. The communications media are the vehicles used to transmit the advertiser's message. The advertising message is what the company plans to say and how it plans to say it.

Several methods are used to allocate advertising funds. The most popular are the percentage-of-sales approach and the objective/task method. The share-of-market/share-of-voice method is often used in markets with similar products.

Important **Terms**

advertising message, *230*
advertising plan, *226*
advertising strategy, *229*

bottom-up marketing, *216*
communications media, *230*
corporate objectives, *213*

creative mix, *229*
empirical research method, *239*
integrated marketing communications (IMC), *221*

Review **Questions**

1. What is a marketing plan and why is it a company's most important document?

2. What examples illustrate the difference between need-satisfying objectives and sales-target objectives?

3. What are the three types of marketing plans? How do they differ?

4. What basic elements should be included in a top-down marketing plan?

5. How can small companies use bottom-up marketing to become big companies?

6. What are the elements of an advertising plan and an advertising strategy?

7. What types of involvement do consumers bring to the purchase decision?

8. What is the best method of allocating advertising funds for a real estate development? Why?

9. What types of companies tend to use the percentage-of-sales method? Why?

10. How could a packaged-foods manufacturer use the share-of-market/share-of-voice method to determine its advertising budget?

Exploring the **Internet**

The Internet exercises for Chapter 7 address the following areas covered throughout the chapter: strategic advertising planning (Exercise 1) and integrated marketing communications (Exercise 2).

1. Strategic Advertising Planning

   You studied in this chapter the various means of planning advertising strategy—top-down, bottom-up, and IMC. Browse through the Web sites of the following marketers, and answer the questions regarding the various means of planning advertising strategy.

   • American Automobile Association (AAA) **www.aaa.com**
   • Bristol Myers Squibb **www.bms.com**
   • Connett Insurance **www.automobile-insurance.com**
   • Conroy's Flowers **www.conroysflowers100.com**
   • Hudson Moving & Storage **www.moving-storage.com**
   • Metro Goldwyn Mayer/UA **www.mgm.com**
   • General Electric **www.ge.com**
   • Hewlett-Packard **www.hp.com**
   • Intel **www.intel.com**
   • Kellogg's **www.kelloggs.com**
   • Walt Disney **www.disney.com**

   a. What is the size/scope of the company and its business? What is the company's purpose?

   b. Identify the target audience, product concept, communications media, and advertising message for each.

   c. What is the company's position within the industry? Type of communication used? Target market?

   d. Where does the company's product(s) fall within the Kim-Lord grid?

2. Integrated Marketing Communications (IMC)

   Integrated marketing communications (IMC) is an important part of modern advertising strategy. However, the exact role of IMC is still up-in-the-air and has many applications industry-wide. Browse the following five Web sites, and provide a summary of the organization's IMC role and its implications to the advertising industry. Also answer the questions listed below.

   • IMC Strategic Development **www.imcstrategic.com**
   • Integrated Marketing Communications, Inc. **www.intmark.com**
   • The Phelps Group **www.phelpsgroup.com**
   • Medill's IMC Graduate Program at Northwestern University **www.medill.nwu.edu/imc/**
   • CU Boulder's IMC Graduate Program **http://128.138.144.96/ej/projects/imc_home.html**

   a. Who is the intended audience of the site?

   b. What type of organization sponsors the site?

   c. What specific IMC vehicles or services (if any) are mentioned/offered?

   d. What benefit does the organization provide individual clients/students? The advertising community, at large?

Chapter Eight

Planning Media Strategy: Finding Links to the Market

Objective To show how communications media help advertisers achieve marketing and advertising objectives. To get their messages to the right people in the right place at the right time, media planners follow the same procedures as marketing and advertising planners: setting objectives, formulating strategies, and devising tactics. To make sound decisions, media planners must possess marketing savvy, analytical skill, and creativity.

After studying this chapter, you will be able to:

- **Describe** how a media plan helps accomplish marketing and advertising objectives.

- **Explain** the importance of creativity in media planning.

- **Define** reach and frequency and debate the controversy surrounding effective frequency.

- **Discuss** how reach, frequency, and continuity are related.

- **Calculate** gross rating points and cost per thousand.

- **Name** some of the secondary research sources available to planners and describe how they are used.

- **Describe** different types of advertising schedules and the purpose for each.

On August 24, 1995, there were 700 babies born in Australia. When they opened their eyes for the first time, there was light, there was mother's face, and there was a brand-new copy of Windows 95, compliments of Microsoft Corp. Awarding a free copy of its long-awaited software to all the bouncing Australian babies born that day was just the beginning of Microsoft's incredible marketing communications event that ended one day, $700 million, and 20-some countries later.[1] • The Windows 95 launch was a global phenomenon that strategically integrated every medium and marketing scheme imaginable, ranging from TV to print and co-op ads to massive in-store promotions, public relations, and publicity stunts. • Londoners, for example, awoke to free copies of the *Times*—sponsored by Microsoft, which had bought out the whole edition. The Empire State Building in New York was festooned with the colors of the new Windows 95 logo. In Hong Kong, champagne flowed; in software stores around America, midnight pizza was on the house. Computer stores like CompUSA gave away discount certificates for American Airlines flights and MCI long-distance services with purchases of the software. In Poland, reporters were even taken down in a submarine to see what the world would be like "without windows." • Key to the event was a massive $200 million mass-media advertising campaign, the biggest in Microsoft's history. Teaser ads in consumer newspapers and trade magazines created the initial buzz and alerted people to the importance of August 24. The global TV campaign then started on launch day with a spot featuring the Rolling Stones'

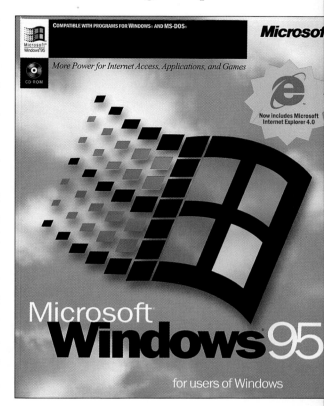

song "Start Me Up." In the United States, an eight-page ad ran in *USA Today* and *The Wall Street Journal*. More ads appeared in consumer and business publications as well as computer-enthusiast magazines. The omnimedia campaign reached 22 countries in more than a dozen languages, including Spanish, French, German, and Italian. • Microsoft's whole objective was to get tens of millions of people excited enough to trade up. Windows was already the standard operating system on most PCs, but Microsoft worried that people wouldn't buy the new software immediately. So creating interest and excitement about the launch became the paramount strategy for overcoming the natural inertia in the marketplace. Microsoft's advertising agency, Wieden & Kennedy, chose television as the medium of excitement. With the Rolling Stones music, the agency incorporated fast cuts of people using Windows 95 and employed the software's Start button as an icon to symbolize how people could now do PC tasks in new and different ways. The product's name wasn't even mentioned until the end. But the spots, along with all the promotion and hype, did create sensory appeal. One man who walked out of a store with a new Windows 95 box didn't even own a computer. "I just thought I ought to have it," he said. • With

TV providing the air coverage, Wieden & Kennedy sent in the ground forces in the form of print ads. Not limited by 30 or 60 seconds, these could focus on the real and specific features and benefits of the software. Here, too, the Start-button icon was widely used as an invitation to people to participate in something new and exciting by joining the movement to Windows 95. Not content with just its own forces, Microsoft enlisted the aid of its allies—its channel members (distributors and retailers), as well as the computer manufacturers, peripheral suppliers, and software developers who would also rise or fall on the success of Windows 95. These companies ended up contributing another $500 million worth of advertising, making August 24 not just the launch of a new product but an unprecedented, world-class event in marketing communications. ● In addition to all the advertising Microsoft and its stakeholders bought, the public relations effort also garnered an incredible amount of free publicity for the event: over 3,000 headlines, 6,528 news stories, and 3 million words of coverage.[2] Talk about integrated marketing communications! It was, in fact, one of the biggest news stories of the year. ● The total synergistic effect of the campaign can be seen in the sales results. In the first three weeks after the launch, consumers worldwide bought an estimated 5 million copies of Windows 95. By the end of 1997, they had bought over 100 million copies—exceeding many observers' original expectations.[3] ●

Media Planning: Integrating Science with Creativity in Advertising

In today's overcommunicated society, advertising media planners need the analytical competence of top financial officers and the creativity of senior art directors and copywriters. Since most money in advertising is spent on media, solid media decisions are critical to the success of the overall marketing communications plan.

The purpose of **media planning** is to conceive, analyze, and creatively select channels of communication that will direct advertising messages to the right people in the right place at the right time. It involves many decisions. For example:

- Where should we advertise? (In what countries, states, or parts of town?)
- Which media vehicles should we use?
- When during the year should we concentrate our advertising?
- How often should we run the advertising?
- What opportunities are there to integrate our media advertising with other communication tools?

Some of these decisions require hard scientific research and detailed, mathematical analysis, aided by sophisticated computer software programs. But understanding and interpreting what all the numbers really mean, and then conceiving and implementing a truly masterly media plan like the launch of Windows 95, demand human intelligence and creativity.[4]

The Challenge

Historically, the people who plan and buy media have enjoyed relative anonymity compared to the "stars" in the creative and account service departments. As evidence of this, witness the fact that entry-level media positions are still among the lowest-paid jobs in the business. This may be due to two facts.

Flagrant spending without a well-conceived media plan can produce an advertising disaster. However, as Microsoft (www.microsoft.com) demonstrated with the release of its Windows 95 software, well-planned media campaigns generate enormous positive publicity. Microsoft can attribute much of its current success to the mastery of the Windows 95 launch campaign.

First, lower-ranking media jobs are still fairly routine and uncreative, so they don't require employees with high levels of training and competence. They are a good entry point for young people in the business, however, and those with superior skill or ability can move up quickly. Second, in many agencies and companies, conventional media planning is still relatively archaic, based on a bygone era when just a few spots on prime-time network television would easily reach the majority of an advertiser's target audience. These dinosaur media-planning organizations have been able to grind along with their obsolete systems for some time, but this situation is now changing rapidly due to the pressures of competition.

The fact is that today the media planner's assignment is just as critical as the creative director's: One media planner can be responsible for millions of client dollars. The planner's work attests to an agency's strategic ability to negotiate the best prices and use effectively the incredible array of media choices available today. Jack Klues, the senior VP/director of U.S. media services for Leo Burnett USA, says, "Our mission is to buy and plan media so effectively that our clients obtain an unfair advantage versus their competitors."[5]

In the 90s, the media department suddenly gained new prominence. Clients are taking an "a la carte" approach to agency services and agencies are competing for media-planning and buying assignments as well as the creative business.[6] It's big news when an agency like McCann-Erickson and a number of other roster agencies lose the planning portion of the $450 million Coca-Cola account to D'Arcy Masius Benton & Bowles, or when Campbell Soup Co. consolidates its $130 million media services account at TN Media, an offshoot of True North Communications (the holding company for Foote, Cone & Belding).[7]

As the complexity of the field increases, media decisions become more critical and clients more demanding. Advertisers want agencies to be more than efficient. They want accountability and information, particularly about media options. And they want creative buys.[8]

What makes media planning today so much more complicated than it was just a few years ago?

Increasing Media Options

With the advent of modern electronic technology and the natural maturation of the marketplace, there are many more media to choose from today, and each offers more choices. As we mentioned earlier, it wasn't long ago that major advertisers could ensure a big audience by simply advertising on TV. Not anymore. Today it's

Technology provides marketers with unparalleled media options when considering the best strategy to reach potential markets. The most prominent and promising new media is, of course, the Internet, now utilized for events as popular as the Superbowl (www.superbowl.com). However, lesser-known media options are also available, such as clever product placements in movies, various niche publications, ATM machines and kiosks, and even parking meters.

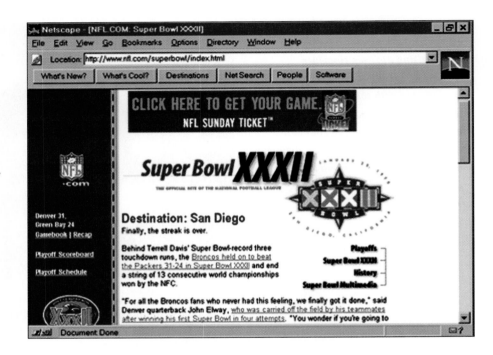

much more difficult to reach a big audience. As Stacey Lippman, director of corporate media at TBWA Chiat/Day, says, "There's too much to keep track of and too many things to explore."[9]

TV is now fragmented into network, syndicated, spot, and local television, as well as network and local cable. Specialized magazines now aim at every possible population and business segment. Even national magazines publish editions for particular regions or demographic groups. Exhibit 8–1 shows the breakdown of total (local and national) advertising expenditures by traditional media in the United States.

Nontraditional media—from videotape and movie advertising to computer online services, the Internet, electronic kiosks, and even shopping carts—also expand the menu of choices. (Ad Lab 8–A describes some nontraditional media available today.) In addition, many companies spend a considerable portion of their marketing budgets on specialized communications like direct marketing, sales promotion, public relations activities, and personal selling, topics we'll discuss in the next two chapters. In fact, these "below-the-line" activities are the fastest-growing segments at some of the large agency holding companies, like WPP and Interpublic.[10]

Exhibit 8–1
U.S. ad spending by medium.

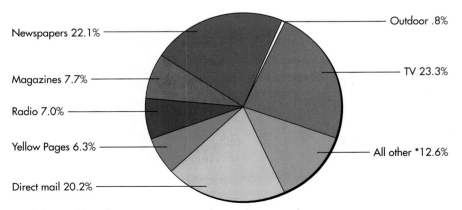

* Includes weeklies, shoppers, pennysavers, bus, and cinema advertising.

Ad Lab 8–A

Off-the-Wall Media That Pull Customers Off the Fence

Advertising can be found everywhere these days—even places where we least expect it.

Videotapes
Advertisers either sponsor their own videos, such as Mr. Boston's *Official Bartender's Guide* and Red Lobster Inns' *Eat to Win,* or place ads on videos of popular films.

Aerial Banners and Lights
Banners carrying ad messages can be pulled by low-flying planes. After dark, traveling aerial lights can display messages of up to 90 characters. Slow-flying helicopters can carry 40- by 80-foot signs lit by thousands of bulbs.

Blimps
In addition to Goodyear, blimps now carry ads for many companies, including Citibank, Coca-Cola, and Fuji Film, among others. Computer-operated lighting systems allow the blimps to advertise at night.

In-Flight Ads
Many airlines' in-flight audio and video entertainment runs ads. The travel industry and advertisers that want to reach business fliers are the primary users.

Newspaper Bags
The protective bags of newspapers are used for full-color advertising and can be enhanced by adding product samples. This method is desirable because it does not have to compete with other advertisers.

Parking Meters
In Calgary and Baltimore, parking meters carry signs of national products and local businesses. Newer, solar-powered versions have liquid crystal displays that exhibit ad messages.

Electronic Billboards
Most modern sports stadiums and arenas sell ad space on giant electronic displays.

Inflatables
Giant inflatable beer cans, mascots, and even cereal boxes are used for advertising purposes.

Taxicab Advertising
In addition to the familiar ads on the roofs and backs of taxis, some companies sell ad space inside, facing the riders. In one sophisticated system, an electronic message scrolls across a screen in the riders' view.

Painted Vehicles
Buses, trucks, and cars are completely decorated with patterns, larger-than-life illustrations, and messages to attract attention. Some vehicles are "wrapped" with a material that covers the entire vehicle to present the greatest visual impact. Advertising on wrapped vehicles can be quickly changed and does not require repainting.

Trash Receptacles
Uniquely designed and decorated trash bins, boxes, and baskets bear advertising logos and messages. Some major cities offer ad space on concrete litter receptacles at major commercial intersections.

Kiosks
Stand-alone kiosks can be painted with eye-catching designs and messages. Unique constructions can be attached to the top and sides to draw attention. Electronic displays running presentation software can show colorful fast-action video clips, slide images, and interactive text. These systems can also play synchronized sounds and music.

Lavatory Advertising
Numerous venues use advertising in lavatories. Print ads can be found on the inner side of stalls and above urinals in the men's restrooms.

Gobo/Cookie Advertising
The gobo (or cookie) is a piece of metal stenciled with a logo, through which light is projected against a wall or other suitable background. This is ideal for huge outdoor or indoor events.

CD-ROMs
Consumers now find advertising for products in video games and other software. Advertisements are also seen during the installation of programs or as a prelude to programs.

Train Cars
Train cars are wrapped with advertisements instead of graffiti these days. In Chicago, an eight-car commuter train was wrapped with Illinois lottery ads.

Rollerblades
Park security officers in New York have skated their best foot forward by wearing Rollerblade in-line skates on their beat.

Fruit
Many major motion picture companies are placing their feature film's titles on stickers that are put on Granny Smith and Fuji apples. The stickers, featured in New York's and Los Angeles' grocery stores, promote movie video releases.

Cab Receipts
In 55 cities from Boston to Denver, the face of CBS news anchor Dan Rather is printed on the back of the taxi cab receipts. According to a CBS spokesperson, "Cab receipts have an interesting life. After the rider sees it, the company accountant sees it. And then, maybe the IRS."

Grocery Receipts
Today, most major supermarket chains print coupons on the back of grocery receipts. The coupons feature discounts at local retailers.

Laboratory Applications

1. How effective are off-the-wall media?

2. What other off-the-wall media can you think of?

Source: "Ads Losing Creative Touch?" *USA TODAY,* September 8, 1997, p. 8B.

The **San Diego Union Tribune** *uses painted trucks to deliver newspapers and its advertising message.*

Duncan and Moriarty point out that for companies practicing integrated marketing communications, their "media menu" needs to include everything that carries a message to and/or from customers and other stakeholders. The proliferation of toll-free phone numbers, faxes, the Internet, and company Web sites makes it easy and cost-effective to facilitate customer feedback. The result is that advertisers can be very creative in designing systems for both sending and receiving messages. That means that companies and agencies need to think in terms of *message handling,* being as responsible for *receiving* messages as for sending them. Mark Goldstein, the president of integrated marketing at Fallon McElligott in Minneapolis, says, "Media is no longer planned and bought; instead it's created, aggregated, and partnered." Perhaps, as Duncan and Moriarty say, the media department of the future will be called the *connect department.*[11]

Increasing Fragmentation of the Audience

Further evidence of the maturing marketplace is the fragmentation of the media audience. This also complicates the media planner's job. Readers and viewers have scattered to all the new media options, selectively reading only parts of magazines or newspapers, watching only segments of programs, and listening to many different radio stations. This makes it very difficult to find the prospect in the marketplace, even though consumers are spending more time with media than ever before—an average of over 3,400 hours per year.[12] (See Exhibit 8–2.)

Increasing Costs

At the same time that there are more media choices, the number of messages that need to be communicated has also proliferated—so much so, in fact, that they have outstripped the ability of consumers to process them. People can cope with

Exhibit 8–2

Hours per person per year using consumer media.

	1990	1991	1992	1993	1994	1995	1996	1997	1998	1999	2000	2001
Network-affiliated stations	780	838	914	920	919	836	803	759	730	690	666	642
Independent stations*	340	227	159	162	172	183	177	183	177	183	188	188
Total broadcast television	1,120	1,065	1,073	1,082	1,091	1,019	980	942	907	873	854	830
Basic networks[†]	260	340	359	375	388	468	498	528	547	571	592	612
Premium channels	90	90	78	78	81	88	89	94	98	104	109	109
Total subscription video services	350	430	437	453	469	556	587	622	645	675	701	721
Total TV	1,470	1,495	1,510	1,535	1,560	1,575	1,567	1,564	1,552	1,548	1,555	1,551
Radio	1,135	1,115	1,150	1,082	1,102	1,091	1,091	1,089	1,085	1,076	1,074	1,072
Recorded music	235	219	233	248	294	289	289	296	303	313	325	336
Daily newspapers	175	169	172	170	169	165	161	158	157	155	154	153
Consumer books	95	98	100	99	102	99	99	97	96	97	98	99
Consumer magazines	90	88	85	85	84	84	83	81	80	80	79	79
Home video[‡]	38	40	42	43	45	45	49	52	54	56	58	60
Movies in theaters	12	11	11	12	12	12	12	12	12	12	12	12
Video games	12	18	19	19	22	24	26	29	31	33	35	37
Consumer on-line	1	1	2	2	3	7	16	22	30	33	37	39
General-interest and educational software	§	1	1	1	2	2	2	2	2	2	2	2
Total	3,263	3,255	3,325	3,296	3,395	3,393	3,395	3,402	3,402	3,405	3,429	3,440

*Affiliates of the Fox network are counted as network affiliates for part of 1991 and all of 1992, but as independent stations in earlier years. Includes UPN and WB affiliates, 1995–2001.   †Includes TBS beginning in 1992.   ‡Playback of prerecorded tapes only.   §Less than one hour.

Note: Estimates of time spent were derived using rating data for television and radio, survey research and consumer purchase data for recorded music, newspapers, magazines, books, home video, admissions for movies, consumer on-line services, and general-interest and educational software. Adults 18 and older were the basis for estimates except for recorded music, movies in theaters, and video games, where estimates included persons 12 and older.

Exhibit 8–3
The most attractive value-added options.

According to advertisers	According to agencies
1. Targeted promotional mailings	1. Research surveys
2. Research surveys	2. Free list rental
3. Advertorials	3. Targeted promotional mailings
4. Free list rental	4. Special editorial sections
5. Focus groups	5. Postcard mailings
6. Special editorial sections	6. Advertorials
7. Postcard mailings	7. Exclusive event sponsorship
8. Telemarketing services	8. Convention, seminar, or trade show tie-ins

only so many messages, so the media have to restrict the number of ads they sell. As a result, the cost of reaching target audiences is increasing for almost all media. In the last decade, the cost of exposing 1,000 people to each of the major media (called *cost per thousand*) rose faster than inflation. Shows that can deliver a big audience are sold at a premium. To run a 30-second spot on "Friends" or "ER," for instance, now costs around $500,000.[13] Rising costs make media planning more challenging than ever, especially for advertisers with small budgets. Clients want proof that planners are squeezing the most they can out of every media dollar.[14]

Increasing Complexity in Media Buying and Selling

As the process of buying media has become more complex, so has the process of selling media. In the battle for additional sales, many print and broadcast media companies developed "value-added" programs to provide extra benefits.[15] Besides selling space or time at rate-card prices or below, these companies now offer reprints, merchandising services, special sections, event sponsorships, and mailing lists (see Exhibit 8–3). To get a bigger share of the advertiser's budget, larger media companies are bundling the various stations, publications, or properties they own and offering them in integrated combos as further incentives. International Data Group (IDG), for example, which publishes *PC World* and *Computer World* magazines, offers a marketing access program (MAP) that gives major business-to-business advertisers access to IDG's research subsidiary, its world exposition unit (for trade shows), and its book company.[16]

Television networks work with major sports associations and professional teams to develop integrated marketing "partnerships" for sports and event sponsors. General Motors and NBC, for example, raised the bar on Olympic sponsorships in 1997 with a 12-year, $600 million deal to make GM the official domestic car and truck of the U.S. Olympic Team. The NBC portion of the deal gives GM domestic category exclusivity and media placement for the network's coverage of the 2000, 2002, 2004, 2006, and 2008 Olympics. GM is expected to spend an additional $300 million to leverage its Olympics involvement. As Phil Guarasco, GM's VP/general manager of marketing and advertising says, "This isn't about dollars, it's about value. What we have here is a strong, cost-effective marketing initiative for the company."[17]

Value-added packages often employ communications vehicles outside traditional media planning, such as public relations activities, sales promotion, and direct marketing. With BMW, for instance, *Yachting* magazine sponsors sailing weeks in various markets and displays the advertiser's cars on site. So people who can afford expensive sailboats are also exposed to the cars, to BMW signage at the event, and to any premium giveaways the sponsors might offer.[18] Integrated events like these help advertisers build relationships with their customers and prospects, and that's a major goal today. But placing a value on these deals is difficult because the nonmedia elements are hard to quantify.

The trend toward integrated marketing communications and relationship marketing is creating a new breed of media planner: younger, computer literate, and schooled in marketing disciplines

Increasing media options also means increasing complexity within the buying and selling environments. Today, media is often sold in negotiable packages, with value-added incentives to encourage larger purchases. General Motors (www.gm.com), for instance, has signed a 12-year deal with NBC to be the official domestic car and truck sponsor for the U.S. Olympic Team until the year 2008.

Political Advertising: Positively Negative?

While we criticize some commercial advertising for its reliance on puffery (which at times may even border on deception) nobody even thinks about puffery in political advertising. In that arena, critics are far more concerned with negatively slanted comparative ads and outright mudslinging. Nasty political ads are nothing new; mudslinging between candidates is as old as politics itself. However, many insiders believe negative political ads reached a new low in 1994.

In Massachusetts, for instance, incumbent U.S. Senator Ted Kennedy ran negative ads for the first time in his 32-year career, calling opponent Mitt Romney a "vulture capitalist" and accusing him of running a "misleading" and "deceptive" campaign. Romney retorted by accusing Kennedy of supporting a "big government takeover" of health care, being out of touch on welfare, and being soft on crime. Romney was so busy differentiating himself from Kennedy that he spent no time establishing his own image.

The California Senate race between incumbent Dianne Feinstein and Michael Huffington was no better. Huffington accused Feinstein of being a career politician, a supporter of strong government, a dealmaker, and an insider. Feinstein called Huffington "a Texas oil millionaire Californians can't trust."

In the consumer products arena, companies sometimes demean their competition (see Ethical Issue on comparative advertising in Chapter 7). But commercial advertising is highly regulated. Not so in politics. The First Amendment protects political advertising from legal restrictions and regulation. The most basic American freedom is freedom of political speech. So politicians can get as nasty as they want, regardless of whether their messages are misleading or unfair.

Moreover, politicos believe negative ads work. Campaign handlers say the increasingly cynical and angry electorate responds to negative messages and that politicians under attack have little choice but to fight back.

Critics charge that negative political ads carry serious consequences. *TV Guide* and "Entertainment Tonight" polled voters and found that negative ads offended 75 percent of the respondents. Of the people who didn't vote, 58 percent said negative ads contributed to their decision to stay home.

Some people believe negative political ads may harm society. Unlike product advertising, where the dissatisfied consumer can choose not to buy again, political advertising can leave voters stuck with a choice that may affect their lives for years.

Political ads even offend advertising professionals. Dianne Snedaker, former head of Ketchum Advertising's San Francisco office, got so angry that she took out an ad in *The New York Times* and *The Wall Street Journal* insisting "Don't call it advertising" (see

beyond traditional media. George Hayes, McCann-Erickson's senior VP/media director, points out that the good media specialist today is actually "a real advertising generalist."[19] And with many of the biggest client billing changes happening in *media-only* agency reviews, it's apparent that the media professionals are finally coming into their own.[20]

Increasing Competition

Independent media-buying services have grown dramatically in the last decade, attracting some of the best and brightest talent in the business to compete with agencies for what was once a private domain (see Exhibit 8–4). The independents buy advertising space and time at lower bulk rates and then sell it at a higher rate or for a handling commission to advertisers or ad agencies that don't have a fully staffed media department. By 1994, the independents already handled over a quarter of all national advertising media accounts. And, today, as Exhibit 8–5 shows, the top 20 independents account for over $9.3 billion in media purchasing power.[21]

Exhibit 8–4

Top accounts that independent media-buying services won from ad agencies in 1997–1998.

Advertiser	Buying service	Previous ad agency	Estimated billings ($ millions)
Citgo Petroleum Corp	Media First International	Bozell	$10–12
Bank of America	GSD&M	Ketchum	32.9
Encore Media Group	SFM Media	Jordan McGrath Case & Taylor	45
Stroh's Old Milwaukee	SFM Media	Hal Riney & Partners	15
Carter Wallace	Zenith Media	Bates USA and Avrett, Free & Ginsberg	20–30
Alberto Culver	Carat Europe	Lois Chicago	50
Glaxo Wellcome	Media Edge	Grey Healthcare	60

Chapter 2). She said, "If a reputable corporation produced advertising with the same exaggerated claims and promises for their products and then failed to deliver on those claims, the company's executives would be fined or led off to jail in handcuffs."

Advertising observers want politicians to take responsibility. Some think political parties should create standards of ethical campaign conduct; others recommend creating a bipartisan committee to screen ads and suggest establishing legal limits on the content of political speech.

However, politicos scoff at the critics' self-righteousness and naiveté. Alan Secrest, a Washington-based Democrat strategist, answered Snedaker's ad by letter. "Dear Advertising Cretin," he wrote, "You plainly have no clue what the political process is all about, and it will be a cold day in hell when any of us submits to your vision of 'standards' in the political marketplace."

According to Secrest, voters "have nothing short of a craving for information that helps them distinguish . . . between two candidates. And as messy as the process sometimes is, that requires setting forth the differences between the two candidates."

Certainly voters want to know the differences. But are catchy soundbites and vicious attacks really the differentiation that voters seek, especially when there's no guarantee that they are ethical or true? Until some agreement is reached on the style and content of political advertising and some self-regulatory mechanism put in place, the old adage applies: *Caveat emptor*—let the buyer (voter) beware.

Questions

1. Voters want information that helps them distinguish between two political candidates. Is there a way to communicate this information without being negative? Explain.

2. If millions were invested in TV ads by one brand of toothpaste arguing that a competing brand rotted your teeth, would you buy the advertiser's brand? By the same token, would you vote for a candidate who trashed his or her opponent?

3. Should political advertising be held to the same regulations as commercial advertising? Why or why not?

Sources: Mark Z. Barabak, "Political Ads Have Gotten So Bad They Offend Even Ad Executives," *San Diego Union-Tribune,* January 7, 1995, p. A3; Reginald K. Brack, Jr., "How to Clean Up Gutter Politics," *New York Times,* December 27, 1994, p. A21; John Carroll, "Campaign Ads '94: Massachusetts," *Adweek,* November 7, 1994, pp. 28–29; Bob Gardner, "Campaign Ads '94: California," *Adweek,* November 7, 1994, pp. 36–37; Kenneth Roman and Jane Maas, *The New How to Advertise* (New York: St. Martin's Press, 1992), p. 145; Spencer F. Tinkham and Ruth Ann Weaver-Lariscy, "Ethical Judgments of Political Television Commercials as Predictors of Attitude toward the Ad," *Journal of Advertising,* September 1994, pp. 44–57.

Exhibit 8–5
Media powerhouses (Top U.S. independent media services ranked by billings).

Rank	Service	Headquarters	Billings	Representative clients
1	Western International Media	Los Angeles	$3.2 billion	Walt Disney Corp., American Honda Motor Co.'s Acura, Home Depot
2	SFM Media	New York	$1 billion	American Isuzu Motors, Canon, Intel Corp.
3	Carat North America	New York	$650 million	Hardee's Food Systems, PrimeStar, Borders Books & Music
4	Botway Group	New York	$600 million	Lever Bros., Ross Laboratories, Bayer Corp.
5	Advanswers	St. Louis	$504 million	Walgreen Co., Reckitt & Coleman, Energizer
6	Creative Media	New York	$400 million	Polaroid Corp., Avon Products, Porsche Cars North America
7	Media That Works	Cincinnati	$400 million	Andrew Jergens Co., Nine West Corp., Transitions Optical
8	TBS Media Management	New York	$360 million	Radio Shack, PacificTelesis, No Fear
9	Focus Media	Santa Monica, CA	$350 million	Dayton Hudson Corp.'s Mervyn's and Target Stores, Universal Home Video
10	DeWitt Media	New York	$225 million	BMW of North America, National Hockey League, Rite Aid
11	KSL Media	New York	$225 million	Revlon, Lea & Perrins, The Limited/Victoria's Secret, Ringling Brothers
12	Cash Plus	Minneapolis	$215 million	U S West, Anderson Corp., International Dairy Queen
13	JL Media	Union, NJ	$210 million	Beiersdorf, General Motors Corp.'s Buick dealers
14	VSM	New York	$200 million	Volvo Cars of North America, Dunkin Donuts
15	Horizon Media	New York	$185 million	Midas International Corp., A&E Television Networks
16	Freeman & Associates	Wellesley, MA	$150 million	America Online, Bay Networks
17	Media First International	New York	$150 million	Northwest Airlines, Marriott Corp.
18	Corinthian Media	New York	$135 million	Barney's, Six Flags
19	CPM	Chicago	$130 million	Kinko's, Columbia Healthcare Corp.
20	Media Inc.	New York	$100 million	Meineke Muffler Discount Shops, Conair

The Role of Media in the Marketing Framework

As we've discussed in previous chapters, the key to successful advertising is proper planning. Thus, before media planning begins—indeed, before advertising is even considered—companies must first establish their overall marketing and advertising plans for their products.

Marketing Objectives and Strategy

As we saw in Chapter 7, the top-down marketing plan defines the market need and the company's sales objectives and details strategies for attaining those objectives. Exhibit 8–6 shows how objectives and strategies result from the marketing situation (or SWOT) analysis, which defines the company's strengths and weaknesses and uncovers any marketplace opportunities and threats. Marketing objectives may focus on solving a problem ("regaining sales volume lost to major competitive introductions over the past year") or seizing an opportunity ("increasing share in the female buyer segment of the athletic-shoe market").

Marketing strategies lay out the steps for meeting these objectives by blending the four elements of the marketing mix. A company whose marketing objective is to increase sales of a particular brand in a certain part of the country has many options. For example, it can adapt the product to suit regional tastes (*product*); it can lower the price to compete with local brands (*price*); it can devise deals to gain additional shelf space in retail outlets (*distribution*); and it can reposition the product through intensive trade and consumer advertising (*communication*). Thus, advertising is just one of the many strategic tools a company may use to achieve its marketing objectives.

Advertising Objectives and Strategy

The objectives and strategies of an advertising plan unfold from the marketing plan. But advertising objectives focus on communication goals, such as:

To be able to quantitatively measure the success of the campaign, companies should always set well-defined goals prior to the start of any media campaign. Microsoft has consistently set such goals with all the media it uses, including print, television, the Internet, and exhibitive media.

- Convincing 25 percent of the target market during the next year of the brand's need-satisfying abilities.
- Positioning the brand as a cost-effective alternative to the market leader in the minds of 30 percent of men ages 18–34 during the next two years.
- Increasing brand preference by 8 percent in the South during the next year.
- Improving the target stakeholder group's attitude toward the company's environmental efforts by at least 15 percent by campaign end.

To achieve these objectives, companies devise advertising strategies that employ the elements of the **creative mix:** the product concept, target audience, advertising message, and communications media.

The media department makes sure the advertising message (developed by the creative department) gets to the correct target audience (established by the marketing managers and account executives) in an effective manner (as measured by the research department).

The Media-Planning Framework

In the age of integrated marketing communications, many agencies have moved the task of media planning earlier in the advertising management process, because people typically make contact with the brand through some medium. Before determining what creative approach to employ, it's important to know when, where, and under what conditions contact can best be made with the customer or other stakeholder and to plan for that. This sets the strategic direction for the creative department.

Development of a media plan involves the same process as marketing and advertising planning. First, review the marketing and advertising objectives and strategies and set relevant, measurable objectives that are both realistic and

The situation analysis
Purpose: To understand the marketing problem. The company and its competitors are analyzed on:
1. Internal strengths and weaknesses.
2. External opportunities and threats.

The marketing plan
Purpose: To plan activities that will solve one or more of the marketing problems.
Includes the determination of:
1. Marketing objectives.
2. Product and spending strategy.
3. Distribution strategy.
4. Which marketing mix to use.
5. Identification of "best" market segments.

The advertising plan
Purpose: To determine what to communicate through ads.
Includes the determination of:
1. How product can meet consumer needs.
2. How product will be positioned in ads.
3. Copy themes.
4. Specific objectives of each ad.
5. Number and sizes of ads.

Setting media objectives
Purpose: To translate marketing and advertising objectives and strategies into goals that media can accomplish.

Determining media strategy
Purpose: To translate media goals into general guidelines that will control the planner's selection and use of media. The best strategy alternatives should be selected.

Selecting broad media classes
Purpose: To determine which broad class of media best fulfills the criteria. Involves comparision and selection of broad media classes: newspapers, magazines, radio, television, and others. Audience size is a major factor used in comparing the various media classes.

Selecting media within classes
Purpose: To compare and select the best media within broad classes, again using predetermined criteria. Involves making decisions about the following:
1. If magazines were recommended, then which magazines?
2. If television was recommended, then
   a. Broadcast or cable TV?
   b. Network or spot TV?
   c. If network, which program(s)?
   d. If spot, which markets?
3. If radio or newspapers were recommended, then
   a. Which markets shall be used?
   b. What criteria shall buyers use in making purchases in local media?

Media use decisions–broadcast
1. What kind of sponsorship (sole, shared participating, or other)?
2. What levels of reach and frequency will be required?
3. Scheduling: On which days and months are commercials to appear?
4. Placement of spots: In programs or between programs?

Media use decisions–print
1. Numbers of ads to appear and on which days and months.
2. Placement of ads: Any preferred position within media?
3. Special treatment: Gatefolds, bleeds, color, etc.
4. Desired reach or frequency levels.

Media use decisions–other media
1. Billboards:
   a. Location of markets and plan of distribution.
   b. Kinds of outdoor boards to be used.
2. Direct mail or other media: Decisions peculiar to those media.
3. Interactive media:
   a. Which kind of interactive media.
   b. How will responses be handled.

Exhibit 8–6
This diagram outlines the scope of media-planning activities.

Exhibit 8–7
How media objectives are expressed.

ACME Advertising
Client: Econo Foods
Product/Brand: Chirpee's Cheap Chips
Project: Media plan, first year introduction

Media Objectives

1. To target large families with emphasis on the family's food purchaser.
2. To concentrate the greatest weight of advertising in urban areas where prepared foods traditionally have greater sales and where new ideas normally gain quicker acceptance.
3. To provide extra weight during the announcement period and then continuity throughout the year with a fairly consistent level of advertising impressions.
4. To deliver advertising impressions to every region in relation to regional food store sales.
5. To use media that will reinforce the copy strategy's emphasis on convenience, ease of preparation, taste, and economy.
6. To attain the highest advertising frequency possible once the need for broad coverage and the demands of the copy platform have been met.

Marketing research helps advertisers determine specific characteristics of media audiences. This ad for Men's Health *magazine (www.menshealth.com) addresses the athletic, active men they hope to reach by showing role reversal between the sled driver and the sled dogs. Demographics help media planners ascertain which media will reach the largest portion of their target market.*

achievable by the media. Next, try to determine an ingenious strategy for achieving these objectives. Finally, develop the specific tactical details of media scheduling and selection.

Defining Media **Objectives**

Media objectives translate the advertising strategy into goals that media can accomplish. Exhibit 8–7 shows general media objectives for a new food product. They explain who the target audience is and why, where messages will be delivered and when, and how much advertising weight needs to be delivered over what period of time.

Media objectives have two major components: *audience objectives* and *message-distribution objectives.*

Audience Objectives

Audience objectives define the specific types of people the advertiser wants to reach. Top-down planners typically use geodemographic classifications to define their target audiences. In Exhibit 8–7, for example, the target audience is food purchasers for large families who live in urban areas across the country.

The target audience may consist of people in a specific income, educational, occupational, or social group—any of the segments we discussed in Chapter 5. And the target audience is not necessarily the product's actual consumers. Often it is considerably larger. In the case of Windows 95, we saw that the target audience included channel members, computer and peripheral manufacturers, and even the media themselves.

Many advertisers have to defend their media decisions with the retailers who stock and resell their products. Why? If these people construed a change in media strategy as a loss of advertising support, they might reduce the shelf space for the advertiser's products. Therefore, most consumer campaigns are supported by a concurrent campaign directed to the trade.

The consumer target audience may be determined from the marketer's research. However, planners rely largely on secondary research sources, such as Arbitron and Nielsen Media Research, which provide basic demographic characteristics of media audiences. Others, such as Simmons Market Research Bureau (SMRB) and Mediamark Research, Inc. (MRI), describe media audiences based on purchase tendencies (see Exhibit 8–8). These syndicated reports give demographic profiles of heavy and light users of various products and help planners define the target audience. The reports also specify which TV programs or magazines heavy and light users watch and read, which helps planners select media with large audiences of heavy users. Planners can then select **media vehicles**—particular magazines or shows—according to how well they "deliver" or expose the message to the media audience that most closely resembles the desired target consumer.

Advertisers using the IMC planning model start by segmenting their target audiences according to brand-purchasing behavior (for example, loyal users, brand switchers, new prospects) and then ranking them by profit to the brand.[22] Communications objectives are then stated in terms of reinforcing or modifying customer purchasing behavior or creating a perceptual change about the brand over time.[23]

Unfortunately, due to cost restraints, most media research does not provide the specificity that marketers would really like. Most radio, TV, newspaper, and outdoor audience reports, for example, are limited to age and gender. So media planners often have to rely on their judgment and experience to select the right media vehicles.[24]

Exhibit 8–8
A media planner's toolbox.

Secondary sources of information help media planners do their jobs.

- **Simmons Market Research Bureau (SMRB) and Mediamark Research, Inc. (MRI)** (www.mediamark.com): report data on product, brand, and media usage by both demographic and lifestyle characteristics.
- **Broadcast Advertisers Reports (BAR), Leading National Advertisers (LNA), and Media Records:** report advertisers' expenditures by brand, media type, market, and time period.
- **Standard Rate & Data Service (SRDS)** (www.srds.com): provides information on media rates, format, production requirements, and audience.
- **Audit Bureau of Circulations (ABC)** (www.accessabc.com): verifies circulation figures of publishers.
- **The Arbitron Company** (www.arbitron.com): measures local radio audiences in 265 markets and offers access to data through printed reports, computer tape, and software applications. Arbitron also provides syndicated measurement of local market media and consumer and retail behavior in 60 top markets. RetailDirect is Arbitron's local market, integrated audience measurement service for television stations, radio stations, and cable systems in 44 small- to medium-size markets. In 132 medium and small markets, Arbitron offers the Qualitative Diary Service to collect consumer behavior in a number of key local market, retail categories. Arbitron New Media offers survey research, consulting, and methodological services to the cable, telecommunications, direct broadcast satellite, online, and new media industries.
- **Competitive Media Reporting (CMR)** (www.usadata.com/cmr/cmr.htm): delivers strategic advertising intelligence to advertising agencies, advertisers, broadcasters, and publishers. The tracking technologies collect occurrence and expenditure data, as well as the creative executions of over 750,000 brands across 15 media.
- **Nielsen Media Research** (www.nielsenmedia.com): Nielsen is the leading provider of television information services in the United States and Canada. Nielsen Media Research is a subsidiary of Cognizant Corporation. It is no longer associated with ACNielsen.
- **ACNielsen Company** (http://acnielsen.com): a global provider of market research information and analysis to the consumer products and service industry. It provides TV ratings service to countries outside the United States and Canada. As a result of the split-up of The Dun & Bradstreet Corporation in 1996, both ACNielsen and Cognizant Corporation were spun off as independent, publicly traded companies.
- **Roper Starch Worldwide** (www.roper.com): Starch Ad Readership Reports measure ad readership within specific publications and each year measure over 25,000 ads in over 500 magazine issues.

Message-Distribution Objectives

Distribution objectives define where, when, and how often advertising should appear. To answer these questions, a media planner must understand a number of terms, including *message weight, reach, frequency,* and *continuity.*

Audience Size and Message Weight

Marketers are naturally interested in having their messages exposed to as many customers and prospects as they can afford. So they are also logically most interested in those media opportunities that offer the largest audiences.[25] The basic way to express audience size is simply to count the number of people in a medium's audience. This is what media research firms like Nielsen and Arbitron do for the broadcast media, typically using a statistical sample to project the total audience size. For print media, firms like the Audit Bureau of Circulations actually count and verify the number of subscribers (the **circulation**) and then multiply by the number of **readers per copy (RPC)** to determine the total audience.

Media planners often define media objectives by the schedule's **message weight,** the total size of the audience for a set of ads or an entire campaign, because it gives some indication of the scope of the campaign in a given market. There are two ways to express message weight: *gross impressions* and *gross rating points.*

Once planners know the audience size, they can easily calculate the number of advertising impressions in a media schedule. An **advertising impression** is a possible exposure of the advertising message to one audience member. It is sometimes referred to as an **opportunity to see (OTS).** By multiplying a medium's total

Exhibit 8–9
Gross impressions analysis for Brand X
in the second quarter, 1997.

Media vehicle	Target audience*	Messages used	Gross impressions
"TV Ch. 6 News"	140,000	15	2,100,000
Daily newspaper	250,000	7	1,750,000
Spot radio	10,000	55	550,000
Total gross impressions			4,400,000

*Average.

audience size by the number of times an advertising message is used during the period, planners arrive at the **gross impressions,** or potential exposures, possible in that medium. Then, by summing the gross impressions for each medium used, they know the total gross impressions for the schedule.[26] (See Exhibit 8–9.)

With large media schedules, though, gross impressions can run into the millions and become very awkward to handle, so media planners have developed an alternative way to express message weight—as a percentage. Percentages are not only simpler numbers to deal with, they are also more useful in making comparisons.[27] In media terminology, percentages are expressed as *ratings*. The **rating** is simply the percentage of homes (or individuals) exposed to an advertising medium. Thus, one rating point is equal to one percent of a given population group. If a particular TV show garnered a 20 rating, it means 20 percent of the households with TV sets (**television households,** or **TVHH**) were tuned in to that show. The higher a program's rating, the more people are watching.[28] This definition applies to many media forms, but it is most commonly used for radio and TV.

By adding the ratings of several media vehicles (as we did for gross impressions) we can determine the message weight of a given advertising schedule, only now it's expressed as **gross rating points (GRPs)** (see Exhibit 8–10). When we say a schedule delivered 180 GRPs, that means the gross impressions generated by our schedule equaled 180 percent of the target market population. For broadcast media, GRPs are often calculated for a week or a month. In print media, they're calculated for the number of ads in a campaign. For outdoor advertising, they're calculated on the basis of daily exposure.

Media planners may use GRPs to determine the optimal level of spending for a campaign. The more GRPs they buy, the more it costs. However, because of discounting, the unit cost per GRP decreases as more GRPs are bought. Beyond a certain point, the effectiveness of additional GRPs diminishes. Through the use of computer models and certain assumptions based on experience, planners can determine the optimal objective based on *return on investment (ROI)* and frequently save their clients substantial sums.[29]

In the calculation of message weight, advertisers disregard any overlap or duplication. As a result, certain individuals within the audience may see the message several times while others don't see it at all. While message weight gives an indication of size, it does not reveal much about who is in the audience or how often they are reached. This fact necessitated the development of other media objectives, namely *reach, frequency,* and *continuity.*

Exhibit 8–10
Gross rating points analysis for Alpha
brand in the second quarter, 1997.

Media vehicle	Adult Rating*	Messages used	Gross rating points
"TV Ch. 6 News"	14	15	210
Daily newspaper	25	7	175
Spot radio	1	55	55
Total gross rating points			440

*Assumes market size of 1 million people.

Audience Accumulation and Reach

The term **reach** refers to the total number of *different* people or households exposed, at least once, to a medium during a given period of time, usually four weeks.[30] For example, if 40 percent of 100,000 people in a target market tune in to radio station WKKO at least once during a four-week period, the reach is 40,000 people. Reach may be expressed as a percentage of the total market (40 percent) or as a raw number (40,000). Reach should not be confused with the number of people who will actually be exposed to and consume the advertising, though. It is just the number of people who are exposed to the medium and therefore have an *opportunity to see* the ad or commercial.

An advertiser may accumulate reach in two ways: by using the same media vehicle over time or by combining two or more media vehicles. Naturally, as more media are used, some duplication occurs. Exhibit 8–11 is a statistical table that shows how unduplicated reach builds as additional media are added.[31]

Exposure Frequency

To express the number of times the same person or household is exposed to a message—a radio spot, for example—in a specified time span, media people use the term *frequency*. **Frequency** measures the *intensity* of a media schedule, based on repeated exposures to the medium or the program. Frequency is important because repetition is the key to memory.

Frequency is calculated as the *average* number of times individuals or homes are exposed to the medium. For instance, suppose in the radio example that 20,000 people tune in to WKKO and have three OTSs during a four-week period, and another 20,000 have five OTSs. To calculate the average frequency, divide the total number of exposures by the total reach:

$$\text{Average frequency} = \text{Total exposures} \div \text{Audience reach}$$

$$= ((20{,}000 \times 3) + (20{,}000 \times 5)) \div 40{,}000$$

$$= 160{,}000 \div 40{,}000$$

$$= 4.0$$

Exhibit 8–11
Random combination table.

		Reach of first medium													
		25	30	35	40	45	50	55	60	65	70	75	80	85	90	95
Reach of second medium	25	46	47	51	55	59	62	66	70	74	77	81	85	89	92	95
	30	—	51	54	58	61	65	68	72	75	79	82	86	90	93	95
	35	—	—	58	61	64	67	71	74	77	80	84	87	90	93	95
	40	—	—	—	64	67	70	73	76	79	82	85	88	91	94	95
	45	—	—	—	—	70	72	75	78	81	83	86	89	92	94	95
	50	—	—	—	—	—	75	77	80	82	85	87	90	92	95	95
	55	—	—	—	—	—	—	80	82	84	86	89	91	93	95	95
	60	—	—	—	—	—	—	—	84	86	88	90	92	94	95	95
	65	—	—	—	—	—	—	—	—	88	89	91	93	95	95	95
	70	—	—	—	—	—	—	—	—	—	91	92	94	95	95	95
	75	—	—	—	—	—	—	—	—	—	—	94	95	95	95	95
	80	—	—	—	—	—	—	—	—	—	—	—	95	95	95	95
	85	—	—	—	—	—	—	—	—	—	—	—	—	95	95	95
	90	—	—	—	—	—	—	—	—	—	—	—	—	—	95	95
	95	—	—	—	—	—	—	—	—	—	—	—	—	—	—	95

For the 40,000 listeners reached, the average frequency, or number of exposures, was four.

Once we understand reach and frequency, we have another, simple way to determine the message weight. To calculate GRPs, just multiply a show's reach (expressed as a rating percentage), by the average frequency. In our radio example, 40 percent of the radio households (a 40 rating) had the opportunity to hear the commercial an average of four times during the four-week period:

$$\text{Reach} \times \text{Frequency} = \text{GRPs}$$

$$40 \times 4 = 160 \text{ GRPs}$$

Continuity

Media planners refer to the duration of an advertising message or campaign over a given period of time as **continuity.** Few companies spread their marketing efforts evenly throughout the year. They typically *heavy up* before prime selling seasons and slow down during the off-season. Likewise, to save money, a media planner for a new product might decide that after a heavy introduction period of, say, four weeks, a radio campaign needs to maintain *continuity* for an additional 16 weeks but on fewer stations. We'll discuss some common scheduling patterns in the section on media tactics.

While frequency is important to create memory, continuity is important to *sustain* it. Moreover, as people come into and out of the market for goods and services every day, continuity provides a means of having the message there when it's most needed. Ads that hit targets during purchase cycles are more effective and require less frequency.[32]

Optimizing Reach, Frequency, and Continuity: The Art of Media Planning

Good media planning is both an art and a science. The media planner must get the most effective exposure on a limited budget. As Exhibit 8–12 shows, the objectives of reach, frequency, and continuity have inverse relationships to each other. To achieve greater reach, some frequency and/or continuity has to be sacrificed, and so on. Research shows that all three are critical. But since all budgets are limited, which is most critical? This is currently the subject of hot debate in advertising circles.

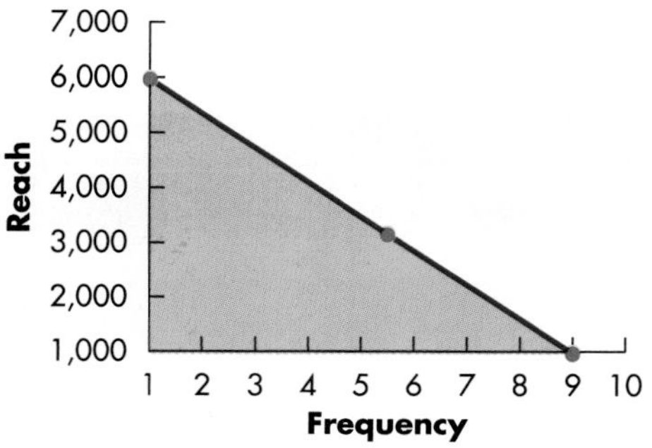

Effective Reach

One of the problems with reach is that, by themselves, the numbers don't take into account the *quality* of the exposure. Some people exposed to the medium still won't be aware of the message. So, on the surface, reach doesn't seem to be the best measure of media success. Media people use the term **effective reach** to describe the quality of exposure. It measures the number or percentage of the audience who receive enough exposures to truly receive the message. Some researchers maintain that three OTSs over a four-week period are usually enough to reach an audience.[33]

Exhibit 8–12
Reach, frequency, and continuity have an inverse relationship to one another. For instance, in the example above, an advertiser can reach 6,000 people once, 3,000 people 5.5 times, or 1,000 people 9 times for the same budget. However, to gain continuity over time, the advertiser would have to sacrifice some reach and some frequency.

Effective Frequency

Similar to the concept of effective reach is **effective frequency,** defined as the average number of times a person must see or hear a message before it becomes effective. In theory, effective frequency falls somewhere between a minimum level that achieves message awareness and a maximum level that becomes overexposure, which leads to "wearout" (starts to irritate consumers).

Following the publication of Michael Naples's classic book *Effective Frequency* in 1979, most of the industry fell in love with his claim that, in most cases, effective frequency could be achieved by an average frequency of three over a four-week period. Here was a nice, simple conclusion that all the low-level media planners could use. Naples's conclusion seemed to be intuitively correct, and it was supported by some researchers who viewed advertising effects as a learning situation. While this might be true for some new products, most of the time advertising is for established products and therefore is not about "learning" but rather about "reminding." Syracuse University professor John Philip Jones writes that "a massive, multitiered edifice" of belief was built on the evidence in Naples's book—evidence he believes led the industry down the wrong path.[34]

While the concepts of effective reach and frequency are now hotly debated, virtually all agencies still use them. Cannon and Riordan point out that conventional media planning is based on *media vehicle exposure* (the number of people in a medium's audience), but effectiveness should relate to *advertising message exposure.* For example, only 20 percent of viewers may pay attention when a commercial runs. It may take 10 opportunities-to-see to reach an average frequency of one!

Cannon and Riordan would replace effective frequency with *optimal frequency.* Most studies of the **advertising response curve** indicate that incremental response to advertising actually diminishes—rather than builds—with repeated exposures (see Exhibit 8–13). The optimal frequency concept moves the focus of media planning from exposure effectiveness to *effective exposures per dollar.*

> With a response curve that is characterized by continually diminishing returns, the first ad will be the most profitable. But subsequent exposures—advertising frequency—are still important. How important depends on the slope of the response curve and the cost of advertising. Obviously, the less money it costs per exposure to advertise, the more the firm can afford to advertise. The profit-maximizing firm will continue to spend until the revenue resulting from an additional advertisement placed is offset by its cost.[35]

The implications of Cannon and Riordan's theory are immense. Historically, media planning has emphasized frequency as the most important media objective. This assumes an S-shaped advertising response curve in which the first two or three exposures don't count. But Cannon and Riordan's analysis indicates that response curves are convex. The first exposure is the most effective, followed by diminishing returns. If that's the case, then the basic emphasis in advertising should switch from maximizing frequency to maximizing target market reach, adding less profitable second exposures only as the budget permits.[36]

This approach is now supported by numerous researchers who believe effective frequency planning is seriously flawed and who make a strong case for the primacy of reach and continuity as the most important media objectives.[37] In fact, for fast-moving consumer products, researcher Erwin Ephron suggests the concept of **recency planning,** based on "the sensible idea that most advertising works by influencing the brand choice of consumers who are ready to buy." Therefore, the important thing for advertising is to be there when the consumer is ready to buy, and that suggests continuity.[38] His theories have gained the attention of many of the nation's largest advertisers, among them Procter & Gamble, Kraft Foods, and Coca-Cola.[39]

For most media planners, the only solution to this debate is to establish first which type of response curve is most likely to apply to the particular situation and then to develop their media objectives accordingly.

Once the media objectives have been determined—that is, the optimum levels of message weight, reach, frequency, and continuity—the media planner can develop the strategy for achieving them.

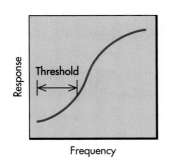

a. S-shaped response curve   b. Convex response curve

Exhibit 8–13

Two advertising response curves. The S-shaped curve would be applicable for products that require a frequency of more than one to reach a threshold of greatest response. After that threshold is reached, the response diminishes for each subsequent exposure. The convex curve applies to products for which the first exposure produces the best return and all subsequent exposures produce slightly lower response.

Developing a Media **Strategy**: The Media Mix

The media strategy describes how the advertiser will achieve the stated media objectives: which media will be used, where, how often, and when. Just as marketers determine marketing strategy by blending elements of the marketing mix, media planners can develop media strategies by blending the elements of the *media mix*.

Elements of the Media Mix: The Five Ms

Many factors go into developing an effective media strategy. For simplicity and ease of memory, we have sorted them into five categories and given them the alliterative moniker of the **five Ms** (5Ms): *markets, money, media, mechanics,* and *methodology.*

Markets refers to the various targets of a media plan: trade and consumer audiences; global, national, or regional audiences; ethnic and socioeconomic groups; or other stakeholders. In an integrated marketing communications plan, the IMC planner wants to find the reasons and motivations for the prospect's purchase and usage patterns and then create a media plan based on those findings.[40]

Using intuition, marketing savvy, and analytical skill, the media planner determines the second element, **money**—how much to budget and where to allocate it. How much for print media, how much in TV, how much to nontraditional or supplemental media, how much to each geographic area? We discuss this issue in depth in the chapters on using and buying media (Chapters 14–17).

Today, the **media** element includes all communications vehicles available to a marketer, such as radio, TV, newspapers, magazines, outdoor, and direct mail, plus sales promotion, direct marketing, public relations activities and publicity, special events, and collateral materials.[41] Good media planners champion the integration of all marketing communications to help achieve their companies' marketing and advertising objectives. They look at the media element both analytically and creatively.

The media planner also has to deal with the complex **mechanics** of advertising media and messages. Electronic commercials come in a variety of time units, and print ads are created in a variety of sizes and styles. IMC planners may also deal with the mechanics of nontraditional media, everything from shopping bags to multimedia kiosks to the Internet. The myriad media options now available offer exciting, creative ways to enhance consumer acceptance of the advertiser's message and offer the consumer a relevant purchase incentive.[42]

This ad for Kinko's (www.kinkos.com) exemplifies three of the five Ms of the media mix. Addressing business owners and executives (market), this ad ran in trade publications such as Fast Company *magazine (media). The two-page spread and effective wording (mechanics) are intended to make a big impression on the reader. Methodology is the sum of processes used to create the ad, and money is affected by the four other elements.*

The **methodology** element refers to the overall strategy of selecting and scheduling media vehicles to achieve the desired message weight, reach, frequency, and continuity objectives. It offers the opportunity for creativity in planning, negotiating, and buying.[43]

Factors That Influence Media Strategy Decisions

Media decisions are greatly influenced by factors over which the media planner has little or no control. These include the scope of the media plan, sales potential of different markets, competitive strategies and budget considerations, availability of different media vehicles, nature of the medium, mood of the message, message size and length, and buyer purchase patterns.

Scope of the Media Plan

The location and makeup of the target audience strongly influence the breadth of the media plan, thereby affecting decisions regarding the *market,* the *money,* and the *media* elements.

Domestic markets   A media planner normally limits advertising to areas where the product is available. If a store serves only one town, or if a city has been chosen to test market a new product, then the advertiser will use a *local* plan.

A *regional* plan may cover several adjoining metropolitan areas, an entire state or province, or several neighboring states. Regional plans typically employ a combination of local media, regional editions of national magazines, and/or spot TV and radio.

Advertisers who want to reach several regions or an entire country use a *national* plan. This may call for network TV and radio, full-circulation national magazines and newspapers, and nationally syndicated Sunday newspaper supplements.

International markets   Foreign media can be a challenge for U.S. advertisers. While many broadcast stations are being privatized in countries as diverse as Israel and Russia, governments around the world still control many broadcast media, and some still do not permit commercials. Others limit advertising to a certain number of minutes per hour or per day.[44]

In countries that do allow TV advertising, advertisers face other problems: how many people own TV sets, who they are, and what channels they receive. While this is not an issue in Europe and is becoming less so in Latin America, it is still a problem in many of the less-developed nations of Africa and Asia.[45] There, TV ownership may be limited to upper-income consumers, or the availability of commercial channels may be severely limited. In those markets, advertisers must use a different media mix.

Even in Europe, over 60 percent of total advertising expenditures are still spent in print media versus 25 percent on television. However, like the United States, Europe and Asia are experiencing a virtual explosion of new media and technology. Advertisers and agencies alike are realizing the importance of developing integrated marketing communications plans to build their brands and establish long-term relationships with their customers.[46]

Most marketers develop an international media plan by formulating individual national plans first. But it's not as simple as it sounds. Depending on the country, precise media information may not be available, circulation figures may not be audited, audience demographics may be sketchy, and even ad rates may be unreliable. Finally, the methodology used in media research may be considerably different from one market to another, making comparisons virtually impossible.[47] At the same time, in some European

The Arab world is watching, tell them something!

Reaching international markets presents unique challenges to advertisers. There are many unknown variables in regulations, viewers, potential audience, and language and cultural barriers. This ad claims to solve these problems as MBC TV will take the guesswork out of media planning and ad preparation when targeting audiences in the Arab world.

and Asian countries, media research and planning are probably more sophisticated than in the United States, which creates another problem for U.S. advertisers who are unfamiliar with European terms, concepts, and methodologies.[48]

Because of the media variations from country to country, most international and global advertisers entrust national media plans to in-country foreign media specialists rather than risk faulty, centralized media planning.[49]

Sales Potential of Different Markets

The *market* and *money* elements of the media mix also depend on the sales potential of each area. National advertisers use this factor to determine where to allocate their advertising dollars. Planners can determine an area's sales potential in several ways.

The brand development index   The **brand development index (BDI)** indicates the sales potential of a particular brand in a specific market area. It compares the percentage of the brand's total U.S. sales in an area to the percentage of the total U.S. population in that area. The larger the brand's sales relative to the area's percentage of U.S. population, the higher the BDI and the greater the brand's sales potential. BDI is calculated as:

$$\text{BDI} = \frac{\text{Percent of the brand's total U.S. sales in the area}}{\text{Percent of total U.S. population in the area}} \times 100$$

Suppose sales of a brand in Los Angeles are 1.58 percent of the brand's total U.S. sales and the population of Los Angeles is 2 percent of the U.S. total. The BDI for Los Angeles is:

$$\text{BDI} = \frac{1.58}{2} \times 100 = 79$$

An index number of 100 means the brand's performance balances with the size of the area's population. A BDI index number below 100 indicates poor potential for the brand.

The category development index   To determine the potential of the whole product category, media planners use the **category development index (CDI),** which works on the same concept as the BDI and is calculated in much the same way.

$$\text{CDI} = \frac{\text{Percent of the product category's total U.S. sales in the area}}{\text{Percent of total U.S. population in the area}} \times 100$$

If category sales in Los Angeles are 4.92 percent of total U.S. category sales, the CDI in Los Angeles is:

$$\text{CDI} = \frac{4.92}{2} \times 100 = 246$$

The combination of BDI and CDI can help the planner determine a media strategy for the market (see Exhibit 8–14.) In our example, low BDI (under 100) and high CDI (over 100) in Los Angeles indicate that the product category has high potential but the brand is not selling well. This may represent a problem or an opportunity. If the brand has been on the market for some time, the low BDI raises a red flag; some problem is standing in the way of brand sales. But if the brand is new, the low BDI may not be alarming. In fact, the high CDI may indicate the brand can grow substantially, given more time and greater media and marketing support. At

Exhibit 8–14
Media buyers compare the brand development index with the category development index for their products to better understand which markets will respond best to advertising. Advertising can be expected to work well when BDI and CDI are both high, but probably not when both are low.

	Low BDI	High BDI
High CDI	Low market share *but* Good market potential	High market share *and* Good market potential
Low CDI	Low market share *and* Poor market potential	High market share *but* Monitor for sales decline

this point, the media planner should assess the company's share of voice (discussed in Chapter 7) and budget accordingly.

Competitive Strategies and Budget Considerations

Advertisers always consider what competitors are doing, particularly those that have larger advertising budgets. This affects the *media, mechanics,* and *methodology* elements of the media mix. Several services, like Competitive Media Reports, report competitive advertising expenditures in the different media. By knowing the size of competitors' budgets, what media they're using, the regionality or seasonality of their sales, and any new-product tests and introductions, advertisers can better plan a counterstrategy.[50]

Again, the media planner should analyze the company's share of voice in the marketplace. If an advertiser's budget is much smaller than the competition's, the brand could get lost in the shuffle. Advertisers should bypass media that competitors dominate and choose other media that offer a strong position.

When Karen Ritchie, senior vice president/director of media services at McCann-Erickson, Detroit, had to develop a media plan for the introduction of Buick's Roadmaster Wagon, she didn't have the budget of Honda Accord or Ford Mustang to work with. So she didn't want to place her ads where theirs were. Ritchie and her team creatively fashioned a targeted media plan that included preprinted inserts in seven national magazines, ads in other magazines featuring special ink-jet printing of the subscriber's name, national TV spots on the A&E and Discovery cable channels, and outdoor advertising and network radio targeted to affluent car buyers in the suburbs. The response was excellent.[51]

It sometimes makes sense to use media similar to the competition's if the target audiences are the same or if the competitors are not using their media effectively.

Media Availability and Economics: The Global Marketer's Headache

North American advertisers are blessed—or cursed—with an incredible array of media choices, locally and nationally. Such is not always the case in other areas of the world, which is one reason their per capita advertising expenditures are so much lower than in the United States (Exhibit 8–15 shows the total local ad agency billings for the top 10 advertising cities outside the U.S.)

Every country has communications media, but they are not always available for commercial use (especially radio and television) and coverage may be limited. Lower literacy rates and education levels in some countries restrict the coverage of print media. Where income

ONCE YOU OUTGROW zip, AVOID THE rip.

FUJITSU

Sometimes a competitor's strategies can provide enormous marketing leverage. Here, Fujitsu (www.fcpa.com) advertises its portable data drive as a superior alternative to the industry standard Zip and Jaz drives, manufactured by Iomega. And it's cheaper, too.

Exhibit 8–15

Top 10 non-U.S. advertising cities by volume ($ millions), 1996.

Rank	Market	Total local shop billings
1	Tokyo	$32,406.5
2	London	12,611.1
3	Paris	10,406.6
4	Frankfurt	4,184.6
5	Sao Paulo	4,169.0
6	Duesseldorf	3,760.9
7	Madrid	3,535.3
8	Milan	3,492.1
9	Seoul	3,455.8
10	Sydney	3,344.6

Source: Reprinted with permission from the April 12, 1997 issue of *Advertising Age.* Copyright, Crain Communications, Inc. 1997.

ONE FOR ME, AND ONE FOR ME.

What could make your taste buds happier than one of our wondrous medleys of fresh pecans, hazelnuts or cashews wrapped in caramel and chocolate? Partake of these caramel nut bouchées, and your sweet tooth will positively swoon.

1-800-9-GODIVA   www.godiva.com   AOL (keyword: GODIVA)

New York   Paris   GODIVA   Tokyo   Brussels
                           Chocolatier

The language and imagery of this Godiva chocolate (www.godiva.com) ad exudes a sense of elegance that suits the audience of the medium selected. Godiva placed the ad in magazines such as Architectural Digest *to reach a target audience of affluent, well-educated individuals. The photo, type, and layout elements reflect the nature of the magazine, the advertiser, and even the audience.*

levels are low, TV ownership is also low. These factors tend to segment markets by media coverage.

To reach lower-income markets, radio is the medium of choice, as both Coke and Pepsi have demonstrated successfully for years. Auto manufacturers make good use of TV and magazine advertising to reach the upper class. And movie advertising can reach whole urban populations where TV ownership is low because motion picture attendance in such countries is very high. The Checklist for International Media Planning outlines some basic considerations for media buyers entering international markets.

Some companies are attempting to become true global marketers of their brands with centralized control of media and standardized creative. As a group, global media are growing, which is good news for global marketers.[52] However, there are still few true global media. So these major advertisers must continue to use local foreign media in the countries where they do business and localize their campaigns for language and cultural differences.

Finally, there's the problem of **spillover media,** local media that many consumers in a neighboring country inadvertently receive. For example, media from Luxembourg regularly spill over into France, Belgium, and Holland. Media often spill over into countries lacking indigenous-language publications, particularly specialty publications. English and German business media enjoy a large circulation in Scandinavian countries, for example, where there are relatively few specialized trade publications written in Swedish, Danish, or Norwegian.

Spillover media pose a threat for the multinational advertiser because they expose readers to multiple ad campaigns. If the advertiser runs both international and local campaigns for the same products, discrepancies in product positioning, pricing, or advertising messages could confuse potential buyers. Advertisers' local subsidiaries or distributors need to coordinate local and international ad campaigns to avoid such confusion. On the positive side, spillover media offer potential cost savings through regional campaigns.

Nature of the Medium and Mood of the Message

An important influence on the *media* element of the mix is how well a medium works with the style or mood of the particular message.

Advertising messages differ in many ways. Some are simple messages: "Just do it" (Nike). Others make emotional or sensual appeals to people's needs and wants: "The great taste of fruit squared" (Jolly Rancher candies). Many advertisers use a reason-why approach to explain their product's advantages: "Twice the room. Twice the comfort. Twice the value. Embassy Suites. Twice the hotel."

Complex messages, such as ads announcing a new product or concept, require more space or time for explanation. Each circumstance affects the media selection as well as the *methodology* of the media mix.

A new or highly complex message may require greater frequency and exposure to be understood and remembered. A dogmatic message like Nike's may require a surge at the beginning, then low frequency and greater reach.

Once consumers understand reason-why messages, pulsing advertising exposures at irregular intervals is often sufficient. Emotionally oriented messages are usually more effective when spaced at regular

Checklist

International Media Planning

Basic Considerations (Who Does What?)

_____ **What is the client's policy regarding supervision and placement of advertising?** When, where, and to what degree is the client and/or client branch office abroad involved?

_____ **Which client office is in charge of the campaign?** North American headquarters or foreign office or both? Who else has to be consulted? In what areas (creative or media selection and so forth)?

_____ **Is there a predetermined media mix?** Can international as well as foreign media be used?

_____ **Who arranges for translation of copy if foreign media are to be used?**
  - Client headquarters in North America.
  - Client office in foreign country.
  - Agency headquarters in North America.
  - Foreign media rep in North America.

_____ **Who approves translated copy?**

_____ **Who checks on acceptability of ad copy in foreign country?** Certain ads need approval by foreign governments.

_____ **What is the advertising placement procedure?**
  - From agency branch office in foreign country directly to foreign media.
  - From North American agency to American-based foreign media rep to foreign media.
  - From North American agency to American-based international media.
  - From North American agency to affiliated agency abroad to foreign media.

_____ **What are the pros and cons of each approach?** Is the media commission to be split with foreign agency branch or affiliate office? Can the campaign be run from North America? Does the client save ad taxes by placing from North America? In what currency does the client want to pay?

_____ **Who receives checking copies?**

_____ **Will advance payment be made to avoid currency fluctuation?**

_____ **Who bills?** What currency? Who approves payment?

Budget Considerations

_____ **Is budget predetermined by client?**

_____ **Is budget based on local branch or distributor recommendation?**

_____ **Is budget based on agency recommendation?**

_____ **Is budget related to sales in the foreign market?**

_____ **What is the budget period?**

_____ **What is the budget breakdown for media,** including ad taxes, translation, production, and research costs?

_____ **What are the tie-ins with local distributors, if any?**

Market Considerations

_____ **What is the geographic target area?**
  - Africa and Middle East.
  - Asia, including Australasia.
  - Europe, including Eastern Europe.
  - Latin America.

_____ **What are the major market factors in these areas?**
  - Local competition.
  - GDP growth over past four years and expected future growth.
  - Membership of country in a common market or free trade association.
  - Literacy rate.
  - Attitude toward North American products or services.
  - Social and religious customs.

_____ **What is the basic target audience?**
  - Management executives in business and industry.
  - Managers and buyers in certain businesses.
  - Military and government officials.
  - Consumers; potential buyers of foreign market goods.

Media Considerations

_____ **Availability of media to cover market:** Are the desired media available in the particular area?

_____ **Foreign media and/or international media:** Should the campaign be in the press and language of a particular country, or should it be a combination of foreign and international?

_____ **What media does the competition use?**

_____ **Does the medium fit?**
  - Optimum audience quality and quantity.
  - Desired image, editorial content, and design.
  - Suitable paper and color availability.
  - Justifiable rates and CPM (don't forget taxes on advertising, which can vary by medium).
  - Discount availability.
  - Type of circulation audit.
  - Availability of special issues or editorial tie-ins.

_____ **What are the closing dates at North American rep and at the publication headquarters abroad?**

_____ **What is the agency commission?** (When placed locally abroad at the agency, commission is sometimes less than when placed in North America.)

_____ **For how long are contracted rates protected?**

_____ **Does the publication have a North American rep** to help with media evaluation and ad placement?

intervals to create enduring feelings about the product. We discuss these scheduling methods further in the next section, on media tactics.

Message Size, Length, and Position Considerations

The particular characteristics of different media, over which the media planner has no control, affect the *mechanics* element of the media mix. For example, in print, a full-page ad attracts more attention than a quarter-page ad and a full-color ad more than a black-and-white one. Color and larger units of space or time cost dearly in terms of reach and frequency (see Exhibit 8–16).

Should a small advertiser run a full-page ad once a month or a quarter-page ad once a week? Is it better to use a few 60-second commercials or many 15- and 30-second ones? The planner has to consider the nature of the advertising message; some simply require more time and space to explain. Competitive activity often dictates more message units. The product itself may demand the prestige of a full page or full color. However, it's often better to run small ads consistently rather than one large ad occasionally. Unfortunately, space and time units may be determined by someone other than the media planner—creative or account service, for example—in which case the planner's options are limited.

The position of an ad is another consideration. Preferred positions for magazine ads are front and back covers; for TV, sponsorship of prime-time shows. Special positions and sponsorships cost more, so the media planner must decide whether the increased reach and frequency are worth the higher costs.

As we can see, the nature of the creative work has the potential to greatly affect the media strategy. This means that media planners have to be flexible, since the initial media plan may well have been determined prior to beginning the creative work.

Buyer Purchase Patterns

Finally, the customer's product purchasing behavior affects every element of the media mix. The media planner must consider how, when, and where the product is typically purchased and repurchased. Products with short purchase cycles (convenience foods and paper towels) require more constant levels of advertising than products purchased infrequently (refrigerators and furniture). For a practical checklist of these points, see RL 8–1 in the Reference Library.

Stating the Media Strategy

A written rationale for the media strategy is an integral part of any media plan. Without one, it's difficult for client and agency management to analyze the logic and consistency of the recommended media schedule.

Exhibit 8–16

a. Readership scores for ads of various sizes. b. Readership scores for ads with various degrees of color. Readership is the greatest for four-color, two-page ads, but increased readership may not offset the additional cost in some publications.

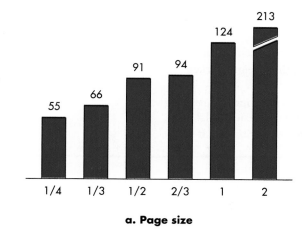

a. Page size

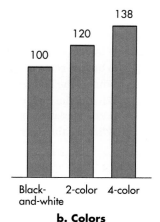

b. Colors

Generally, the strategy statement begins with a brief definition of target audiences (the *market* element) and the priorities for weighting them. It explains the nature of the message and indicates which media types will be used and why (the *media* element). It outlines specific reach, frequency, and continuity goals and how they are to be achieved (the *methodology* element). It provides a budget for each medium (the *money* element) including the cost of production and any collateral materials. Finally, it states the intended size of message units, any position or timing considerations (the *mechanics* element), and the effect of budget restrictions.

Once the strategy is delineated, the plan details the tactics to be employed, the subject of the next section.

Media **Tactics:** Selecting and Scheduling Media Vehicles

Once the general media strategy is determined, the media planner can select and schedule particular media vehicles. The planner usually considers each medium's value on a set of specific criteria (see Ad Lab 8–B on page 268).

Criteria for Selecting Individual Media Vehicles

In evaluating specific media vehicles, the planner considers several factors: overall campaign objectives and strategy; size and characteristics of each medium's audience; attention, exposure, and motivational value of each medium; and cost efficiency. (For a comparative evaluation of various media types, see RL 8–2 in the Reference Library.)

Overall Campaign Objectives and Strategy

The media planner's first job is to review the nature of the product or service, the intended objectives and strategies, and the primary and secondary target markets and audiences. The characteristics of the product often suggest a suitable choice. A product with a distinct personality or image, such as a fine perfume, might be advertised in media that reinforce this image. The media planner considers how consumers regard various magazines and TV programs—feminine or masculine, highbrow or lowbrow, serious or frivolous—and determines whether they're appropriate for the brand.

After a general media strategy is selected, the media planner can move forward to begin selecting and scheduling ads to run in the appropriate media. Software developers like Telmar (www.telmar.com) provide media planners with sophisticated tools for determining the most effective media plans, employing statistical analysis for the most mathematically accurate course of action.

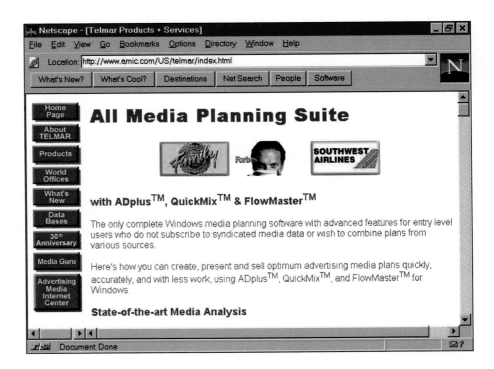

Ad Lab 8–B

Media Selection: Quicklist of Advantages

Medium	Advantages
Newspapers	Many ad sizes available. Quick placement, local targeting.
Magazines	High-quality graphics/reproduction. Prestige factor. Color.
TV	Combines sight, sound, movement. A single message. Demonstration.
Radio	Intimacy. Loyal following. Ability to change message quickly.
Direct mail	Measurable. Graphics, color. 3-D. Highly personal.
Outdoor/Transit	Local targeting. Graphics, color. Simple message. Larger than life.

An extensive list of media appears as RL 8–2 in the Reference Library.

Laboratory Applications

1. If you wanted a set of complementary media to cover all the creative advantages, which mix would you select?
2. What creative advantages can you add to the list?

The content and editorial policy of the media vehicle and its compatibility with the product are important considerations. *Tennis* magazine is a poor vehicle for cigarette or alcohol ads even though its demographic profile and image might match the desired target audience.

Consumers choose a particular media vehicle because they gain some "reward": self-improvement, financial advice, career guidance, or simply news and entertainment. Advertising is most effective when it positions a product as part of the solution that consumers seek. Otherwise, they may see it as an intrusion.[53]

If the marketing objective is to gain greater product distribution, the planner should select media that influence potential dealers. If the goal is to stimulate sales of a nationally distributed product in isolated markets, ads should be placed in local and regional media that penetrate those markets. Pricing strategy influences media choices too. A premium-priced product should use prestigious or classy media to support its market image.

Characteristics of Media Audiences

An **audience** is the total number of people or households exposed to a medium. The planner needs to know how closely the medium's audience matches the profile of the target market and how interested prospective customers are in the publication or program. A product intended for a Latino audience, for example, would likely appear in specific media directed toward Hispanics. Simmons Market Research Bureau provides research data on age, income, occupational status, and other characteristics of magazine readers. Simmons also publishes demographic and psychographic data on product usage of consumers. Likewise, Nielsen provides audience statistics for TV programs and Arbitron for radio stations.

The *content* of the medium usually determines the type of people in the audience. Some radio stations emphasize in-depth news or sports; others feature jazz, rock, or classical music. Each type of programming attracts a different audience.

Exposure, Attention, and Motivation Value of Media Vehicles

The media planner has to select media that will not only achieve the desired *exposure* to the target audience, but also attract *attention* and *motivate* people to act.

Exposure To understand the concept of **exposure value,** think of how many people an ad "sees" rather than the other way around. How many of a magazine's 3 million readers will an ad actually see? How many of a TV program's 10 million viewers will a commercial actually see?

As we discussed earlier, just because someone reads a particular magazine or watches a certain program doesn't mean he or she sees the ads. Some people read only one article, set the magazine aside, and never pick it up again. Many people change channels during commercial breaks or leave to get a snack. Comparing the exposure value of different media vehicles is very difficult. Without statistics, media planners have to use their best judgment based on experience.

Five factors that affect the probability of ad exposure are:[54]

1. The senses used to perceive messages from the medium.
2. How much and what kind of attention the medium requires.
3. Whether the medium is an information source or a diversion.

Even the most superb ad will be wasted without the sufficient exposure required to reach a substantial number of consumers. E*Trade (www.etrade.com) was one of the first excursions into online brokerage services, but the company took its advertising to television to generate the desired exposure for their product.

4. Whether the medium or program aims at a general or a specialized audience.
5. The placement of the ad in the vehicle (within or between broadcast programs; adjacent to editorial material or other print ads).[55]

Attention   Degree of attention is another consideration. Consumers with no interest in motorcycles or cosmetics won't remember ads for those products. But someone in the market for a new car tends to notice every car ad.

Exposure value relates only to the medium; **attention value** concerns the advertising message and copy, as well as the medium. Special-interest media, such as boating magazines, offer good attention value to a marine product. But what kind of attention value does the daily newspaper offer such a product? Do sailors think about boats while reading the newspaper? Much research still needs to be done, but six factors are known to increase attention value:[56]

1. Audience involvement with editorial content or program material.
2. Specialization of audience interest or identification.
3. Number of competitive advertisers (the fewer, the better).
4. Audience familiarity with the advertiser's campaign.
5. Quality of advertising reproduction.
6. Timeliness of advertising exposure.

Motivation   These same factors affect a medium's **motivation value,** but in different ways. Familiarity with the advertiser's campaign may affect attention significantly but motivation very little. The attention factors of quality reproduction and timeliness can motivate someone, however.

Media planners analyze these values by assigning numerical ratings to their judgments of a medium's strengths and weaknesses. Then, using a weighting formula, they add them up. Planners use similar weighting methods to evaluate other factors, such as the relative importance of age versus income.

Cost Efficiency of Media Vehicles

Finally, media planners analyze the cost efficiency of each medium. A common term used in media planning and buying is **cost per thousand,** or **CPM** (M is the Roman numeral for 1,000). If a daily newspaper has 300,000 subscribers and charges $5,000 for a full-page ad, the cost per thousand is the cost divided by the number of thousands of people in the audience. Since there are 300 *thousands* of subscribers, you divide $5,000 by 300:

$$CPM = \frac{\$5,000}{300,000 \div 1,000} = \frac{\$5,000}{300} = \$16.67 \text{ per thousand}$$

The quality and presentation of advertising messages affect the consumer's degree of attention and motivation to respond. This Italian in-your-face anti-smoking ad certainly captures the consumer's attention. And the fact that the sponsor is an undertaker who includes his telephone number adds credibility and urgency to the message. Translation: How much of you goes up in smoke every day?—Eugenio Fabozzi, Undertaker. Telephone: 23 23 23 23.

Media Planning Software

Imagine: You've just developed a fabulous ad campaign, replete with print and electronic media. Now all that's left is to spend your client's money effectively, exacting the most bang for the buck, but without overspending the budget. Fortunately, several software developers provide packages that make this daunting road to success a little easier.

As discussed in the chapter, media placement can make or break a campaign. Knowing this, the developers of Telmar software designed programs to help plan media strategy and placement both properly and effectively. Telmar calculates all aspects of media placement, from reach and frequency planning to cost analysis to creating graphical flowcharts for media schedules, all designed for use by novices and experts. Telmar software supports analysis for television, radio, and print media and can accommodate planning for a complete media mix.

In addition to projected media placement, Telmar displays media variables of GRP, reach and frequency for national and local markets, television dayparts, and cable TV networks. The program provides a complete analysis of all Audit Bureau of Circulation (ABC) audited newspapers in the country and supports county, metro, state, DMA, census, and marketing regions. Radio planning is also simple with displays of reach and frequency, frequency distribution, and cost analysis before or after purchases are made.

Another developer, Stone House Systems Inc., designed MacOS-based software to plan media strategy and placement. The company's premiere package, "Go Chart," allows users to create media flowcharts, prepare budget analyses, formulate summaries, and develop presentation packages. The program will also specify advertising flights in GRPs, allow costs to be analyzed in CPP (cost per point), and can balance budgets instantly by adjusting the GRP.

Media planning is an essential part of the advertising business, and placement is a key factor to success. These software packages greatly simplify this complex procedure and are integral to many agencies today.

Source: Telmar Media Buying Software, retrieved from
http://www.telmar.com/software/N3P/

However, media planners are more interested in **cost efficiency**—the cost of exposing the message to the target audience rather than to the total circulation. Let's say the target audience is males ages 18 to 49, and 40 percent of a weekly newspaper's subscriber base of 250,000 fits this category. If the paper charges $3,000 for a full-page ad, the CPM is computed as follows:

$$\text{Target audience} = 0.40 \times 250,000 = 100,000$$

$$\text{CPM} = \frac{\$3,000}{100,000 \div 1,000} = \$30 \text{ per thousand}$$

The daily paper, on the other hand, might turn out to be more cost efficient if 60 percent of its readers (180,000) belong to the target audience:

$$\text{CPM} = \frac{\$5,000}{180,000 \div 1,000} = \$27.78 \text{ per thousand}$$

Comparing different media by CPMs is important but does not take into account each medium's other advantages and disadvantages. The media planner must evaluate all the criteria to determine:

1. How much of each medium's audience matches the target audience.
2. How each medium satisfies the campaign's objectives and strategy.
3. How well each medium offers attention, exposure, and motivation.

To evaluate some of these issues, the media planner may want to calculate the **cost per point (CPP)** of different broadcast programs. This is done the same way as cost per thousand, except you divide the cost by the rating points instead of the gross impressions.

Economics of Foreign Media

The main purpose of media advertising is to communicate with customers more efficiently than through personal selling. In some developing countries, though, it's cheaper to send people out with baskets of samples. For mass marketers in the United States, this kind of personal contact is virtually impossible.

In many foreign markets, outdoor advertising enjoys far greater coverage than in the United States because it costs less to have people paint the signs and there is also less government restriction.

Cost inhibits the growth of broadcast media in some foreign markets, but most countries now sell advertising time to help foot the bills. China and Vietnam, for example, have recently become booming markets for advertising.[57] As more countries allow commercial broadcasts and international satellite channels gain a greater foothold, TV advertising will continue to grow.

The Synergy of Mixed Media

A combination of media is called a **mixed-media approach.** There are numerous reasons for using mixed media:

- To reach people who are unavailable through only one medium.
- To provide repeat exposure in a less expensive secondary medium after attaining optimum reach in the first.
- To use the intrinsic value of an additional medium to extend the creative effectiveness of the ad campaign (such as music on radio along with long copy in print).
- To deliver coupons in print media when the primary vehicle is broadcast.
- To produce **synergy,** where the total effect is greater than the sum of its parts.

Newspapers, for example, can be used to introduce a new product and give immediacy to the message. Magazine ads can then follow up for greater detail, image enhancement, longevity, and memory improvement.

A mixed-media campaign was effective for General Electric's lighting products. The promotion used a combination of network TV spots, print advertising, Sunday supplement inserts, in-store displays in over 150,000 stores, and a highly creative publicity program. By using an integrated, mixed-media approach, the campaign produced "unprecedented" consumer awareness and dealer support. It achieved synergy.[58]

Methods for Scheduling Media

After selecting the appropriate media vehicles, the media planner decides how many space or time units to buy of each vehicle and schedules them for release over a period of time when consumers are most apt to buy the product.

Continuous, Flighting, and Pulsing Schedules

To build continuity in a campaign, planners use three principal scheduling tactics: *continuous, flighting,* and *pulsing.* (see Exhibit 8–17).

In a **continuous schedule,** advertising runs steadily and varies little over the campaign period. It's the best way to build continuity. Advertisers use this scheduling pattern for products consumers purchase regularly. For example, a commercial is scheduled on radio stations WTKO and WRBI for an initial four-week period. Then, to maintain continuity in the campaign, additional spots run continuously every week throughout the year on station WRBI.

Flighting alternates periods of advertising with periods of no advertising. This intermittent schedule makes sense for products and services that experience large fluctuations in demand throughout the year (tax services, lawn-care products, cold remedies). The advertiser might introduce the product with a four-week flight and then schedule three additional four-week flights to run during seasonal periods later in the year.

The third alternative, **pulsing,** mixes continuous and flighting strategies. As the consumer's purchasing cycle gets longer, pulsing becomes more appropriate. The

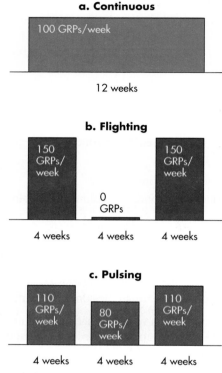

Exhibit 8–17

Three ways to schedule the same number of total gross rating points: continuous, flighting, and pulsing.

The advent of computer software has taken some of the more grueling, laborious chores out of media planning. Planners can now crunch numbers, track results, and compute GRPs and CPMs right at their desktops. This saves an enormous amount of time and money. The screen capture of the SRDS Media Planning System shown here is an example of one of the many programs available.

advertiser maintains a low level of advertising all year but uses periodic pulses to heavy up during peak selling periods. This strategy is appropriate for products like soft drinks, which are consumed all year but more heavily in the summer.

Additional Scheduling Patterns

For high-ticket items that require careful consideration, **bursting**—running the same commercial every half hour on the same network during prime time—can be effective. A variation is **roadblocking,** buying air time on all three networks simultaneously. Chrysler used this technique to give viewers the impression that the advertiser was everywhere, even if the ad showed for only a few nights. Digital Equipment used a scheduling tactic called **blinking** to stretch its slim ad budget. To reach business executives, it flooded the airwaves on Sundays (on both cable and network TV channels) to make it virtually impossible to miss the ads.[59] (For guidelines on determining the best reach, frequency, continuity, and pulsing combinations, study RL 8–1 in the Reference Library.)

Once the scheduling criteria are determined, the media planner creates a flowchart of the plan. The flowchart is a graphic presentation of the total campaign to let the creative department, media department, account services, and the client see the pattern of media events that will occur throughout the period, usually one year (see Exhibit 8–18).

Computers in Media Selection and Scheduling

The last decade has seen a profusion of new desktop computer software to assist media planners. Computers perform the tedious number crunching needed to compute GRPs, CPMs, reach, frequency, and the like. They also save time and money. One agency found it could plan the entire TV, radio, and print co-op budgets for one of its largest clients in two days with only three people and one software

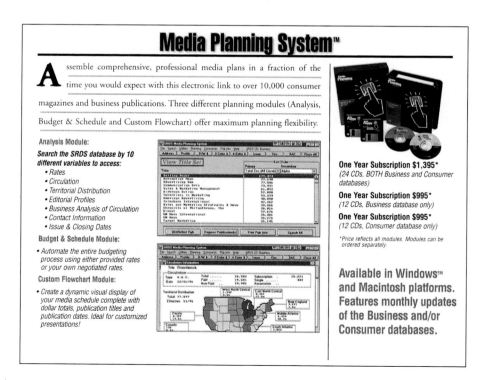

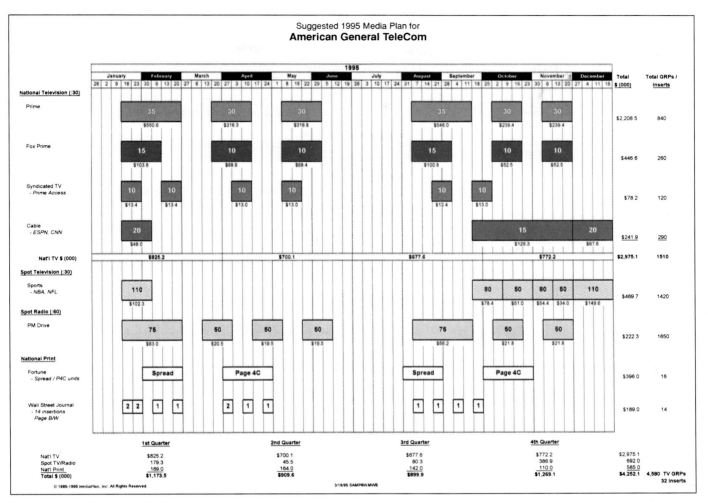

Exhibit 8–18

A media plan flowchart like this computerized printout by MediaPlan, Inc., gives a bird's-eye view of the major media purchases and where and when they will appear over a specified period of time.

system. Previously, that task required 70 staffers working manually for a week and a half.

Advertising executives may now gather information from their media directories electronically and then create timely budgets for their clients. An SRDS CD-ROM program, called Media Planning System, includes monthly updates. Planners can reconfigure budgets on-screen according to circulation, CPM, or other variables using any of the 10,000 publications in the SRDS database.[60]

Similarly, Interactive Market Systems (IMS) has introduced PC software and on-line data for the business-to-business computer marketplace. The software analyzes readership of various business publications for the customized target audience and ranks the publications on any of 10 variables. The program also creates an optimized schedule within the parameters specified by the user.[61]

Many other programs calculate reach, frequency, and GRPs of broadcast and print schedules using sophisticated mathematical models. These are typically known by acronyms such as CANEX, MEDIAC, ADMOD, or VIDEAC, and each touts features or areas of accuracy that the others don't have.[62]

In Europe, two of the most widely known simulation models are the CAM model of the London Press Exchange and the Simulmatics model out of New York. Both have been in use for almost 20 years. More recent models are TOM, developed by CMC in Paris, and Ecotel's model, developed by Ecotel S.A. in Spain (the same company that operates the Spanish People Meter for measuring TV audiences). With any of these models, the computer instantly recalculates results whenever one of the basic factors in the program changes, so the planner can perform what-ifs on the schedule.[63]

But even with technological timesavers and shortcuts, it's still up to the media planner to know the product, the market, and the media, and to make the call. Computers can't decide which medium or environment is best for the message. They can't evaluate the content of a magazine or the image of a TV program. They can't judge whether the numbers they're fed are valid or reliable, and they can't interpret the meaning of the numbers. What they can do is help the process along.

Chapter **Summary**

Media planning directs the advertising message to the right people at the right time. It involves many decisions: where to advertise and when, which media to use, and how often to use them. Media planners need both financial skills and creativity. Like good art and copy ideas, media decisions should be based on sound marketing principles and research.

The task of media planners has become more complicated and competitive in recent years due to the dramatic increase in media options, the continuing fragmentation of audiences, the rising cost of space and time, and the increasing complexity in the way media buys are made. But this has also given the professionals who work in media departments new prominence.

The media function involves two basic processes: planning media strategy and selecting media vehicles. Media planning begins with defining audience objectives—the specific types of people the advertising message will be directed to—and then setting the goals for communicating with those audiences. The target audience is often determined from the marketer's past experience, through special research studies, or through secondary research sources such as Simmons Market Research Bureau and Mediamark Research. Planners who follow an IMC model start by segmenting their audiences according to brand purchasing behavior and then ranking these segments by profit to the brand. Once the target audience is determined, the planner sets the message-distribution objectives. These specify where, when, and how often the advertising should appear. They may be expressed in terms of message weight, reach, frequency, and continuity. In this process, the planner considers the amount of advertising needed to achieve effectiveness.

To create the appropriate media strategy, the planner develops the best blend of the five Ms: markets, money, media, mechanics, and methodology. The planner must also consider many uncontrollable variables: the scope of the media plan, which is determined by the location and makeup of the target audience; the sales potential of different markets for both the brand and the product category; competitive strategies and budget considerations; media availability and economics; the nature of the medium and the mood of the message; the size, length, and position of the message in the selected media; and buyer purchase patterns. IMC planners try to discover the reasons and motivations for people's purchase and usage patterns and then create media plans based on those findings.

For international markets, media planners have to consider the availability and cost structure of foreign media and the differing cultural markets they serve. Some advertisers attempt to standardize their messages through the use of global media, but these media are still quite limited.

After the media strategy is developed, the planner selects specific media vehicles. Both the quantitative and qualitative criteria used to make this decision are important in the evaluation process. Factors that influence the selection process include campaign objectives and strategy; the size and characteristics of each medium's audience; geographic coverage; the exposure, attention, and motivation value of each medium; cost efficiency; and the advisability of a mixed-media approach.

Once media vehicles are selected, the media planner decides on scheduling—how many of each medium's space or time units to buy over what period of time. A media campaign can run continuously or in erratic pulses. These decisions are affected by consumer purchase patterns, the product's seasonality, and the balance of reach, frequency, and continuity that meets the planner's media objectives and budget.

The media planner must spend money wisely to maximize the campaign's effectiveness. To that end, many computer models have been developed, both in the United States and overseas, to help planners determine optimum levels of expenditure or compare alternative media schedules.

Important **Terms**

advertising impression, *255*
advertising response curve, *259*
attention value, *269*
audience, *268*
audience objectives, *254*
blinking, *272*
brand development index (BDI), *262*
bursting, *272*
category development index, *262*
circulation, *255*
continuity, *258*
continuous schedule, *271*
cost efficiency, *270*
cost per point (CPP), *271*
cost per thousand (CPM), *269*

creative mix, *252*
distribution objectives, *255*
effective frequency, *258*
effective reach, *258*
exposure value, *268*
five Ms, *260*
flighting, *271*
frequency, *257*
gross impressions, *256*
gross rating points (GRPs), *256*
markets, *260*
mechanics, *260*
media, *260*
media planning, *244*
media vehicles, *254*

message weight, *255*
methodology, *261*
mixed-media approach, *271*
money, *260*
motivation value, *269*
opportunity to see (OTS), *255*
pulsing, *271*
rating, *256*
reach, *257*
readers per copy (RPC), *255*
recency planning, *259*
roadblocking, *272*
spillover media, *264*
synergy, *271*
television households (TVHH), *256*

Review **Questions**

1. What major factors contribute to the increased complexity of media planning?
2. What must media planners consider before they begin?
3. What secondary research sources are available to planners?
4. How does the IMC approach differ from the top-down media planning approach?
5. What are the "right" reach and frequency for a given message?
6. How are GRPs and CPMs calculated?
7. What are the 5Ms of the media mix, and how are they determined?
8. What major factors influence the choice of individual media vehicles?
9. Why might an advertiser use a mixed-media approach?
10. What are the principal methods used to schedule media?

Exploring the **Internet**

The Internet exercises for Chapter 8 address the following areas covered in the chapter: media buying services (Exercise 1) and media organizations (Exercise 2).

1. Media Buying Services

   There are three sides to the media business: those who plan; those who buy; and those who sell. Media planning and media buying are often in-house functions at an advertising agency, while sellers are those who represent the various media to clients, agencies, and media buying services.

   Visit the Web sites for the media companies listed below, consider the impact and importance of each to advertisers and their agencies, and answer the questions that follow.

   - International Communications Group (ICG) **www.icg-media.com**
   - Media Solutions **www.mediasol.com**
   - The Davis Group **www.thedavisgrouptx.com**
   - Time Buying Services **www.tbsmm.com**
   - WebConnect **www.webconnect.net**
   - Western International Media **www.wimc.com**
   - Zenith Media Services **www.zenithmedia.com**

   a. Who is the intended audience(s) of the site?
   b. What is the site's purpose? Does it succeed? How?

   c. What is the company's purpose?
   d. Does the company specialize in any particular segment (consumer, business-to-business, agriculture, automotive)?

2. Media Organizations

   The world of media is vast and constantly changing. Many media giants own properties in several media categories and are major forces in the world of advertising. Visit the Web sites for the following media companies and answer the questions below.

   - Advo Inc. **www.advo.com**
   - Cox Enterprises **www.cox.com**
   - Gannett **www.gannett.com**
   - McGraw-Hill **www.mcgraw-hill.com**
   - NyNex **www.nynex.com**
   - Time-Warner **www.pathfinder.com**
   - Tribune Communications **www.tribune.com**
   - Turner Entertainment Group **www.turner.com**
   - Viacom **www.viacom.com**

   a. Who is the intended audience of the site?
   b. What is the size/scope of the organization?
   c. What is the organization's purpose? The site's purpose?
   d. How important is this organization to the advertising industry? Why?

Part Three

Integrating Advertising with Other Elements of the Communications Mix

Today, corporate managers worldwide are becoming more and more aware of the important benefits of relationship marketing and integrated marketing communications. By maximizing resources and linking communications activities directly to organizational goals and the resulting bottom line, these activities offer unparalleled accountability. Integral to these topics, though, are a number of specialized communications tools and processes besides mass-media product advertising. The most important of these are direct marketing, personal selling, sales promotion, certain public relations activities, various types of sponsorships, and corporate advertising.

Chapter **9**   **Relationship Building: Direct Marketing, Personal Selling, and Sales Promotion** focuses on some of the methods marketers can use today to communicate one-on-one with their customers and add tangible value to their relationships.

Chapter **10**   **Relationship Building: Public Relations, Sponsorship, and Corporate Advertising** explores how companies integrate a variety of public relations and corporate advertising activities into their communication mixes to enhance their relationships and build their reputation with a wide variety of stakeholders.

Chapter Nine

Relationship Building: Direct Marketing, Personal Selling, and Sales Promotion

Objective   To emphasize the importance of relationship marketing in today's high-tech, overcommunicated world and to demonstrate how various forms of marketing communications can be integrated with advertising to manage an organization's relations with its various stakeholders. Relationship marketing and IMC are two of the most important trends in marketing and advertising today. Direct marketing, personal selling, and sales promotion play different but often overlapping roles that are vitally important to IMC programs. Each offers many opportunities but also has limitations that advertisers should be aware of.

After studying this chapter, you will be able to:

- Discuss the importance of relationship marketing and IMC.
- Define direct marketing and discuss its role in IMC.
- Explain the importance of databases to direct marketers.
- Discuss the role of personal selling in an IMC program.
- Describe the advantages and drawbacks of personal selling.
- Define sales promotion and discuss its importance as a communications tool.
- Identify the benefits and drawbacks of sales promotion.
- Explain the difference between push and pull strategies and give some tactical examples of each in sales promotion.

Andersen Corporation, maker of Andersen Windows and Patio Doors, believes in relationships. The company is still located in Bayport, Minnesota, where it was founded by Danish immigrant Hans Jacob Andersen and his sons in 1903. Its nearly 4,000 employees own a significant portion of the company. And Andersen has worked with the same hardware supplier and advertising agency since 1932 and 1933, respectively. In fact, Andersen was the first client of Campbell Mithun Esty (CME). • Andersen also knows that when it comes to buying new windows for their homes, people don't buy on impulse. The details involved make the purchase very complex. To establish its brand identity, Andersen uses a highly informative approach, teaching consumers about its products and helping them through the planning and buying process. It also uses a sophisticated blend of media advertising, direct marketing, public relations, sales promotion, retailing, computer-aided design, and after-sale follow-up—all aimed at learning about the customer and creating a mutually beneficial relationship. • Working with CME, Andersen uses innovative ads (both print and broadcast) to highlight the features, advantages, and benefits of buying quality products from the market leader. The ads are based on substantiated facts and testimonials from builders, remodelers, and homeowners. The copy is as inviting as the photography. Once engaged, the reader can check the Yellow Pages for a local Andersen dealer, call a toll-free number, or contact the company's Web site at www.andersenwindows.com. • All 800-number responses are fielded by a professional fulfillment house. Phone respondents provide their names, addresses, and basic information about their plans to build, remodel, or replace windows. This information is collected in Andersen's extensive computer database. • Respondents are then sent literature featuring the company's handsome windows and doors along with a multitude of innovative ideas and tools to use in evaluating and selecting windows. Each packet contains a card that asks customers for more information about their project and offers additional literature from Andersen's extensive library. • The literature opens a dialog with the customer. It also draws customers to the retail store, the ultimate objective of the direct marketing effort. Each issue's address label contains a custom message inviting the customer to visit Andersen and gives the local dealer's address and phone number. All ancillary materials—publications, brochures, videos—use the same glamorous photos, reinforcing Andersen's high-quality image to further enhance the company's relationship with consumers. • Andersen has developed a proprietary computer program that allows dealers to specify, quote, and prepare a purchase order for shipment from the company that is five times faster than doing the work by hand. The order is captured in Andersen's database, which assigns a

tracking number to the job and follows it from the assembly line through the warehouse. This helps ensure that what the customer ordered is what gets shipped. In one year, the company ships over four million products, with 98.5 percent of orders shipping without backorders. ● From advertising to selling to delivery, the whole process is consistent and seamless. This has contributed to Andersen's reputation as a management mecca, a place where people from other companies come to learn how the best do it. ● For anyone who questions the effectiveness of relationship marketing or the power of integrated marketing communications, one thing is obvious: Andersen's program works. Andersen is the leader in the window market, recognized by consumers more than two to one over its nearest competitor and larger than its next two competitors combined.[1] ●

In the past, a large company could often muscle its marketing strategies against the consumer. But with tighter markets, corporations realize that the most seemingly mundane contact with the consumer is a prime opportunity to build and maintain relationships that result in future sales. Companies that adopt such IMC strategies are much more likely to succeed over the long run.

The Importance of **Relationship Marketing** and IMC

In Chapter 7, we pointed out that due to a variety of environmental factors, the key to building brand equity in the 21st century will be to develop interdependent, mutually satisfying relationships with customers and other stakeholders. Further, to manage these relationships, companies will need to consciously (and *conscientiously*) integrate their marketing communications activities with all their other company functions so that all the messages the marketplace receives about the company are consistent.

However, this is a lot easier said than done, since everything a company does (and doesn't do) sends a message. Seamless, consistent communication—from every corner of the company—is how a firm earns a good reputation. And that is the principal objective of IMC.

Andersen Corp. is a good example of how IMC works. To attract prospects and initiate the relationship-building process, Andersen integrates its advertising efforts with a host of other marketing communications tools: direct marketing, sales promotion, personal selling, and even certain public relations activities. These are then integrated with other company functions—design, manufacturing, assembly, inventory control, and shipping—to reduce errors and assure a consistently high level of quality. The result of all this is happier, more satisfied customers whose expectations have been not just met but exceeded. That contributes to Andersen's glowing reputation.

A simple adage: Advertising can create an image, but a reputation must be earned.

While the integration of marketing with other company functions is beyond the scope of this book, it is important for advertising people to understand how to integrate the various tools of marketing communications. As they plan a campaign, advertising practitioners need a basic understanding of what other communications tools are available to them and how they can best be used in the overall marketing communications mix. In this chapter, we will discuss the interactive, one-to-one communication tools of direct marketing and personal selling. We'll also look at sales promotion, which might be called the "value-added" tool. In the next chapter, we'll address the "credibility" tools companies use to enhance their reputations. These include various public relations activities, sponsorships, and corporate advertising.

Understanding **Direct** Marketing

There is a lot of confusion surrounding the term *direct marketing,* even among the experts. In fact, Lester Wunderman, the man who coined the term some 30 years ago, now thinks it may be due for a change.

The Direct Marketing Association (DMA) has traditionally defined **direct marketing** as "an interactive system of marketing which uses one or more advertising media to effect a measurable response and/or transaction at any location." However, in a major 1997 study on the economic impact of direct marketing the DMA broadened its definition to include "*any direct communication* to a consumer or business recipient that is designed to generate a response in the form of an order (direct order), a request for further information (lead generation), and/or a visit to a store or other place of business for purchase of a specific product(s) or service(s) (traffic generation)."[2]

Direct Marketing magazine goes even further: "Direct marketing is a measurable system of marketing that uses one or more advertising media to effect a measurable response and/or transaction at any location, with this activity stored in a database." From this definition a virtually synonymous term has emerged: **database marketing.** Database marketers build and maintain a pool of data on current and prospective customers (and other stakeholders) and communicate with them using a variety of media (from personal contact to direct mail to mass media). Database marketing is one of the fastest-growing marketing methods because it has proven to be a cost-efficient method for increasing sales.[3] A good **database** enables marketers to target, segment, and grade customers. It helps them to know who their customers and prospects are, what and when they purchase, and how to contact them. That, of course, leads to the possibility of a relationship. So today, database marketing is a major component of most integrated marketing communications programs.

What we see from these various definitions is that, first and foremost, direct marketing is a *system of marketing* and it is *interactive,* meaning buyers and sellers can exchange information with each other directly. In fact, Joan Throckmorton, a prominent direct marketing consultant and writer, has urged that direct marketing be dropped completely and replaced with *interactive marketing.*[4] Wunderman, on the other hand, is leaning toward *dialog marketing* or *membership marketing*—anything, he says, to get rid of the confusion that surrounds this business.[5]

A second important part of the definition is the concept of *one or more advertising media.* Part of the confusion with the name is its similarity to *direct mail.* While direct mail is often used in direct marketing, it is just one of the many media that direct marketers use. We saw how Andersen, for instance, uses a variety of mass media, including TV and magazines (as well as direct mail), to elicit responses from people who are considering new windows. In fact, experienced direct marketers know that using more than one medium tends to be far more productive than using a single medium.[6]

The third key point of the direct marketing definition is a *measurable response.* In fact, the kind of advertising direct marketers use is called **direct-response** (or **action**) **advertising.** This is because direct

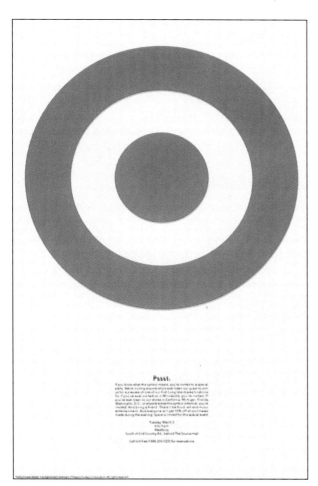

Direct marketing is an interactive system of marketing in which buyers and sellers participate in a dialog. Direct marketing is intended to stimulate a response in the form of a request for information, a store visit, or an actual purchase, as demonstrated by this ad for Target (www.target.com). The invitation singles out existing and past customers, and welcomes them to the opening of Target's first location in New York. By requiring reservations, Target makes customer response easy to measure, and gives the opening an air of distinction.

marketing efforts are typically aimed at stimulating some action or response on the part of the customer or prospect. It may be in the form of a request for information, a store visit, or an actual purchase. Since these responses can be tallied and analyzed, direct marketing becomes accountable. And that, more than any other reason, accounts for the tremendous growth of direct marketing in recent years. Managers like it because they can see what they got for their money.

The final point most of the definitions make is that the response can be at *any location*. In other words, direct marketing is *not* restricted to mail order or catalog sales. Customers may respond by telephone, via mail-in coupons, over the Internet, at a retail store or other place of business, or even at a kiosk.

The **Role** of Direct Marketing in IMC

As we saw in the Andersen case, sophisticated companies today can use the skills developed by direct marketers to establish, nourish, and maintain relationships, not just with customers, but with all stakeholders.

Andersen, for instance, first uses magazine and TV advertising as **linkage media**—media that help prospects and customers link up with a company—to inform prospects how to inquire about its products. Next, it uses these responses to build its database of names and addresses. Then it uses the database to communicate with prospects, open a dialog, and establish a relationship. Usually it sends a catalog with ordering information that enables prospects to further connect with Andersen directly or to visit a retail store. At the store, the Andersen computer program is another linkage medium between the retailer and the manufacturer.

The Evolution of Direct Marketing

Direct marketing is the oldest marketing method, and today it is growing incredibly fast, propelled by the major social and technological changes of recent decades. About 59.3 percent of American women now work outside the home.[7] So while families have more income, they have less time to spend shopping, thus making the convenience of telephones and credit cards important factors in direct marketing.

Likewise, the expanding use of credit cards has revolutionized the way consumers buy goods and services. Electronic, cashless transactions make products (especially large, costly items) easier and faster to purchase. And now, with advances in credit-card security technology, people are even shopping right from their computers.

In 1997, sales attributed to direct marketing totaled $1.2 *trillion* in the United States alone. Of this, $684.6 billion were sales to consumers—an increase of 7 percent over 1996. And business-to-business direct marketing sales grew 9.1 percent, to $541.6 billion, over the same period. The annual growth rate is expected to increase to over 10 percent by 2002.[8] The business is strong, and the BTB sector is growing at a disproportionately fast pace.

Working with direct-response specialists, marketers are fueling this growth by pouring money into direct marketing campaigns. Exhibit 9–1 shows the largest direct-response agencies in the United States. Overall media spending for direct marketing initiatives reached $153 billion in 1997, up 7.7 percent over 1996. This amount was split almost evenly between consumer and BTB efforts. However, the BTB *growth* in media expenditures was considerably higher than the consumer growth—8.6 percent to 7.4 percent.

The boom in telecommunications and computer technology is spurring the growth of direct marketing worldwide. In 1994, for instance, European spending on direct marketing jumped by more than 23 percent to $46 billion. Germany is by far the largest national market, accounting for 30 percent of spending in Europe. Britain is in second place, followed closely by France.[9]

Telephone companies worldwide now provide toll-free numbers for customers to place orders or request information. Toll-free numbers give companies

This Wired *ad for Webmonkey (www.webmonkey.com) exemplifies the use of linkage media (helping people to link up with companies). Placing the ad in a magazine dedicated to computer technology reaches the audience most likely to be interested in developing a Web page, and directs prospective customers to Webmonkey's URL. A database of these customers can then be generated from* Wired's *subscription list as well as those who contact Webmonkey through their Web site.*

Exhibit 9–1
Largest direct response agencies in the United States.

Rank	Agency	Headquarters	U.S. direct response revenue ($000)
1	Rapp Collins Worldwide	New York	$105,831
2	DIMAC Direct	Bridgeton, MO	88,778
3	Bronner Slosberg Humphrey	Boston	83,200
4	Wunderman Cato Johnson	New York	81,003
5	Barry Blau & Partners	Wilton, CT	63,723
6	OgilvyOne Worldwide	New York	57,800
7	DraftDirect Worldwide	Chicago	57,097
8	Carlson Marketing Group	Minneapolis	46,440
9	Customer Development Corp.	Peoria, IL	37,887
10	Gage Marketing Group	Minneapolis	36,738

Source: Reprinted with permission from the July 21, 1997 issue of *Advertising Age.* Copyright, Crain Communications, Inc. 1997.

immediate, direct responses and help them collect information to create and refine their databases.

However, certain challenges in foreign markets have limited the growth of direct marketing efforts. There are, of course, a wide variety of legal and regulatory environments to contend with. Likewise, payment systems in different countries are at different stages of maturity. And finally, cultural nuances and language can get in the way. For example, the same name can indicate different genders in different countries. In England Abigail is a woman's name, but in Portugal it's a man's name. Most men are put off when they are referred to as "senora." Again, though, technology comes to the rescue. A French company, OBIMD, has developed a solution to these problems with its universal mailing software. It makes sure the correct salutation and gender code are used for some 118,000 given names in various countries and also enables marketers to satisfy the differing postal regulations of more than 180 countries.[10]

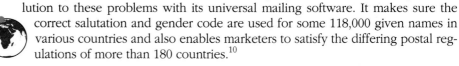

The Impact of Databases on Direct Marketing

Modern computer technology enables marketers to compile and analyze important customer information in unprecedented ways. Pitney Bowes, for instance, is the dominant company in the postal meter business. However, its growth rate and profitability were flattening. So the company used its database to identify its best customers, their value to the organization, and their needs and buying behavior. From this, Pitney Bowes created a **customer lifetime value (LTV)** model based on historical and potential share of wallet. Computing and ranking the *lifetime value* of all of its 1.2 million customers showed that more than two-thirds of the customer base value resided in fewer than 10 percent of the customers. The company also found it had a major retention problem within its low-volume, low-cost accounts. Cancellation rates were running as high as 40 percent per year in some segments. This analysis enabled Pitney Bowes to develop a distinct direct marketing strategy for both its best and its worst customers. It began a sophisticated *loyalty program* for its best customers and a *retention program* for its problem accounts. By the end of the first year, the program had reduced attrition by 20 percent, and the reduction in cost of sales alone paid back the entire direct marketing investment.[11]

The database is the key to direct marketing success, especially in an IMC program. It enables marketers to target, segment, and grade customers. It is the corporate memory of all important customer information: name and address, telephone number, SIC code (if a business firm), source of inquiry, cost of inquiry, history of purchases, and so on. It should record every transaction across all points of contact with both channel members and customers. The company that understands its customers' needs and wants better than any of its competitors, and retains more of its

American Airlines (www.Americanair.com) Interactive Travel Network "AAccess" serves the needs of customers, as well as the company's marketing needs. For customers, it facilitates travel planning, ticket purchasing, and access to special deals. For the company, it enables the marketing department to track all customer activity and develop Customer Lifetime Value (LTV) estimates. The comparison between Ned and Marie in this ad for AAccess shows how LTV measures past buying behavior and can be used to anticipate future buying patterns.

best customers, will create a sustainable competitive advantage. Strategically, therefore, companies have to determine if they will focus on share of market or on retention and loyalty (share of customer).[12] More often than not, this is a short-term versus long-term trade-off.

The database also lets the company measure the efficiency of its direct-response advertising efforts to see, for instance, which radio or TV commercials, or which mailing lists, perform the best.

Working with a marketing database requires two processes: data management and data access. **Data management** is the process of gathering, consolidating, updating, and enhancing the information about customers and prospects that resides in the database. For most companies of any significant size, this requires a mainframe computer due to the complexity and volumes of the processes involved.

Most importantly, the database gives marketers **data access,** enabling them to manipulate, analyze, and rank all the information to make better marketing decisions. Thanks to new software, this can now usually be accomplished on Windows-based desktop PCs hooked up to client-server computers.

Direct magazine's "database doctor," Rob Jackson, suggests that database marketing should start with *customer profiling.* Profiling allows marketers to get a snapshot of what their customers look like at any given time by identifying common characteristics and ranking their relative importance in different segments.[13]

In the same vein, direct marketing expert Bob Stone recommends using an **RFM formula** (recency, frequency, monetary) to identify the best customers—the ones most likely to buy again (see Exhibit 9–2). The best customers have bought recently, they buy frequently, and they spend the most. Customers may be further ranked by the type of merchandise or services they buy, information that becomes very useful in the effort to cross-sell other merchandise.[14]

Some companies may simply purchase a mailing list as its initial database. There are typically three types of data available for purchase: demographics, lifestyle (leisure interests), and behavioristics (purchase habits).[15]

The Importance of Direct Marketing to IMC

Perhaps the greatest reason for direct marketing's current growth is that marketers and agencies realize they can't do the job with just one medium anymore. As the mass audience fragmented and companies began to integrate their marketing communications, customer databases became key to retaining and growing customers.

Direct marketing is the best way to develop a good database. The database enables the marketer to build a relationship by learning about customers in-depth: their nuances, what and where they buy, what they're interested in, and what they need. With a database, companies can choose the prospects they can serve most effectively and *profitably*—the purpose of all marketing. "You don't want a relationship with every customer," says Philip Kotler. "In fact, there are some bad customers out there."[16]

People like to see themselves as unique, not part of some 100-million-member mass market. Through direct marketing, especially addressable electronic media, companies can send discrete messages to individual customers and prospects.[17] With different types of sales promotion (discussed in the last part of this chapter), a company can encourage individuals, not masses, to respond and can develop a

Database Marketing Tools

Keeping in touch with a target audience for direct marketing purposes is difficult at best. Today's consumers are highly mobile and from day to day they continually change their views—or their addresses. Fortunately, software developers like American Business Lists (ABL) understand this trend and have designed programs to assist with direct mail campaigns. ABL provides software that helps keep in touch with over 10 million businesses and 94 million households, offering valuable information such as names and complete addresses, age and gender, estimated income, approximate home value, length of residence, and geographic region.

The information is concise and easy to read. When time is short, it's critical to have quick access to the data and to be able to manipulate it with minimal hassle.

Other companies sell database-oriented programs that assist direct mail campaigns in different ways. Mailer's 4+ program for Windows provides tools that verify and standardize addresses nationwide (certified by the U.S. Postal Service) and eliminate costly duplicate entries. In addition, 4+ can print POSTNET bar codes, required for automation discounts. This package not only organizes pre-mail logistics, but can also determine gender by referencing a database of over 12,000 common first names.

relationship with each person. By responding, the prospect self-selects, in effect giving the marketer permission to begin a relationship.[18] The direct marketing database, then, becomes the company's primary tool to initiate, build, cultivate, and measure the effectiveness of its loyalty efforts.[19]

By providing a tangible response, direct marketing offers accountability. Marketers can count the responses and determine the cost per response. They can also judge the effectiveness of the medium they're using and test different creative executions. They like that a lot.

Direct marketing offers convenience to time-sensitive consumers, and it offers precision and flexibility to cost-sensitive marketers. For example, to reach small

Exhibit 9–2

RFM (recency, frequency, monetary) analysis of accounts, December 1998.

Account number	Month of purchase	Recency points	No. of purchases	Frequency points	Dollar purchases	Monetary points	Total points	Carryover points	Cumulative points
701	7	12	1	4	37.45	3.75	19.75	16	35.75
701	10	24	2	8	17.86	1.79	33.79	16	49.79
702	6	6	2	8	25.43	2.54	16.54	4	20.54
703	4	6	1	4	33.22	3.32	13.32	7	20.32
703	8	12	2	8	42.34	4.23	24.23	7	44.56
703	11	24	1	4	18.95	1.90	29.90	7	74.45
704	9	12	1	4	109.45	9.00	25.00	23	48.00
705	5	6	2	8	37.65	3.77	17.77	0	17.77
705	7	12	3	12	49.63	4.96	28.96	0	46.73
706							0.00	43	43.00

Notes:

• Points assigned by recency of puchase: current quarter—24 points; last six months—12 points; last nine months—6 points; and last twelve months—3 points.

• Frequency points: number of purchases × 4.

• Monetary points: 10 percent of dollar purchase, with a ceiling of 9 points.

• Carryover points: Points carried over from previous calendar year.

• Cumulative total points: Total account points plus carryover from previous calendar year.

The RFM formula is a mathematical model that provides marketers with a method for determining the most valuable customers in a company's database, according to recency, frequency, and monetary variables. Recency points are assigned according to the date of the customer's last purchase (24 points if the purchase was made within the current quarter, 12 points if within the last 6 months, 6 points if within the last 9 months, and 3 points if the purchase was made within the last 12 months). Frequency points are equal to the number of purchases made multiplied by a factor of 4. Monetary points are equal to 10 percent of the dollar purchase, with a maximum of 9 points to prevent artificial distortion by an unusually large purchase. The R, F, and M variables are summed to provide total points. The cumulative total is a measure of relative customer importance to the company—the larger the value, the more likely a customer is to make additional purchases of significant value. The higher-value customers, such as account numbers 701 and 703, who make multiple purchases, are likely prospects for targeted mailings and special offers.

Database marketing was much more difficult before the development of computers because of the intense organizational requirements. Today with the cost of personal computers under $1,000, even the smallest companies can engage in complex database building and marketing strategies.

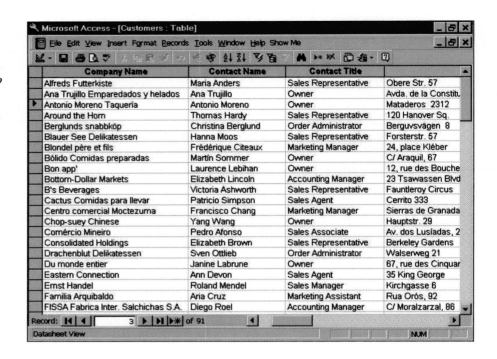

BTB markets, there is no more cost-effective method than the database-driven direct-response media.

Also, the economics of direct marketing are becoming more competitive. It used to be easy for big companies to spend a few million dollars for prime-time network TV spots when everybody was home watching and the average cost was only a penny to 10 cents per person. But those days are over. Everybody's not home today. And if they are, they're watching 150 different channels or a video. They have a remote control to mute ads. Further, network TV advertising is far more expensive than it used to be. So targeted direct-response media (magazines, niche TV, direct mail, e-mail, kiosks) are more cost-effective than ever before.

Finally, unlike the public mass media, direct-response media can be more private. A company can conduct a sales letter campaign without the competition ever knowing about it.

Drawbacks to Direct Marketing

At the same time, direct marketing still faces some challenges. In the past, direct marketers were sales oriented, not relationship oriented. This gave direct marketing a bad reputation in the minds of many consumers. Some people enjoy the experience of visiting retail stores and shopping. They like to see and feel the goods personally, and they're hesitant to buy goods sight unseen. This is why many direct marketing campaigns are now used to help drive traffic to retail locations.

Direct marketing efforts often have to stand on their own without the content support of the media that advertising enjoys. They don't always get the prestigious affiliation offered by some media. This makes it more difficult (and costly) to build image for the product, something mass-media advertising is particularly good at.

Direct marketing also suffers from clutter. People are deluged with mail, cable channels are filled with infomercials, and telemarketing pitches intrude on consumers at home and at work.

While direct mail has proven to be an incredibly effective marketing strategy, it also presents severe drawbacks. Anybody with a mailbox can attest to the large volume of unwanted "junk" mail received each week. Direct mail marketers must constantly fight against competitive advertising clutter.

Many consumers are also concerned with privacy. They don't like having their names sold by list vendors. At one national forum of direct marketers, attendees were told they must self-regulate, give consumers more control, and treat privacy like a customer service issue—or risk legislation restricting access to the information they desperately need.[20] Wise marketers heeded these warnings and have developed methods for responsible direct marketing. Using IMC theory, they integrate all their marketing communications and focus on building the *relationship value* of their brands.

Types of Direct Marketing **Activities**

All direct marketers face two basic strategy decisions: the extent to which they will use *direct sales* and the extent to which they will use *direct-response advertising*. They can use one or the other or both.

Direct Sales

In a **direct-sales strategy,** marketers' representatives sell to customers directly, either at home or at work, rather than through a retail establishment or some other intermediary. Direct sales feature *personal* (face-to-face) *selling* or *telemarketing*.

Personal Direct Selling

Professors Robert Peterson and Thomas Wotruba define **direct selling** as face-to-face selling away from a fixed retail location. In this sense, direct selling usually refers to a method of marketing consumer goods—everything from encyclopedias and insurance to cosmetics and nutritional products. Companies like Avon, Amway, Herbalife, Mary Kay Cosmetics, World Book, and Tupperware have achieved very high levels of success in direct sales.[21] In personal direct selling, the representative introduces the product to the customer, convinces the customer of the product's value, and, if successful, completes the sale. There are two main forms of personal selling: person-to-person and group sales. In some *network marketing* organizations, such as Amway, Rexall Showcase International, and Shaklee, the direct salespeople are both distributors (sellers) and end users. They often do very little actual retailing of the products. Their effort is usually to recruit new distributors who will buy the products at wholesale and consume them personally.

The Peterson-Wotruba definition of direct selling could also apply to business-to-business marketing, since it typically occurs "away from a fixed retail location." However, the common term for this is simply *personal selling*. And since it is so important to BTB marketers, we will deal with that subject more completely in the next section of this chapter.

Telemarketing

As a method of direct sales, telemarketing has been used for decades, but the term is relatively new. **Telemarketing** includes selling and prospecting by telephone, answering phone inquiries, and providing sales-related services to callers. The resulting information updates the company's customer database. Telemarketing is the major source of income for some companies and organizations, such as nonprofit and charitable causes, political candidates, and home-study courses. It is also cited as the direct marketing medium of choice. In 1997, marketers spent 38 percent of all their direct marketing media expenditures, or an estimated $58.1 billion,

Advertising agencies have long accepted commissions as remuneration and advised clients to distribute gifts and specialty items to reinforce marketing messages. But more and more people are calling these exchanges unethical.

Ad agencies traditionally make money from three sources: commissions, markups, and fees or retainers. Of the three, agency commissions generate the most income but also receive the most criticism. Just one national ad can yield huge profits for an agency (especially compared to the amount of time directly spent earning that money). Since ad agencies realize greater profits when clients buy additional advertising space or air time, some observers regard an agency's so-called expert and impartial advice to the advertiser about commissionable media spending as tainted, and some agency critics see commissions as kickbacks.

It might help to understand how this system began. In 1843, when the advertising industry was young and formless, the first advertising agent, Volney Palmer, solicited orders as a media agent, not an advertising agent, and received a commission on what he sold. Later, when advertising agents began working for the clients, the commission system remained. The tradition is now over 150 years old, but the legions of its detractors are growing.

Some clients balk at the system. Most large national accounts now negotiate the commission with their agencies, which may receive substantially less than the standard 15 percent. Others negotiate a fee against which commissions are credited. Some now use an incentive system—a base fee supplemented by bonuses for meeting specific goals. Both of these latter approaches help answer the ethical question.

However, the whole area of promotions, gifts, and premiums raises some people's hackles. From advertising's earliest days, agency and media people have presented gifts, offered special incentives, and wined and dined prospects. They also recommended that their clients do the same.

on outbound telemarketing calls to both consumers and businesses. This generated an estimated $424.5 billion in total sales.[22]

The reasons for all this are economics and consumers' acceptance of teleculture. First, telemarketing costs a lot less money than personal selling. In the insurance business, for example, the expense ratio for car and home insurance is currently running at 27 percent for all insurers. The most efficient insurers, though, employ high-tech database marketing techniques from phone centers and operate at around a 20 percent expense ratio.[23] That difference goes straight to the bottom line.

Second, people have come to accept the idea of shopping by phone. It's convenient, hassle-free, and inexpensive. In fact, in the United States, the toll-free telephone business is booming. In any given week, 30,000 to 50,000 toll-free numbers are added across North America. In fact, due to the large demand, the phone companies ran out of 800 numbers in 1996 and had to add 888 as a second prefix for toll-free calls.[24]

Each year telemarketing generates an estimated $424.5 billion in sales in the United States. It is cited as the direct marketing medium of choice, providing elements of direct personal sales yet at a substantially lower cost. Telemarketing also integrates easily into database management campaigns for gathering new data and for utilizing the collected data.

As an IMC medium, telemarketing is the next best thing to a face-to-face, personal sales call. In the BTB arena, for example, good telemarketers can develop strong, lasting relationships with customers they have never met but with whom they speak every week. Stand Out Designs in San Diego employs highly skilled telemarketers who call on zoos, museums, and boutique retailers all across the country to get them to order and stock the company's unique line of silk-screened T-shirts. The telemarketers don't just take orders; they counsel the dealers with display and promotion suggestions, offer advertising tips, and arrange for special imprints on the shirts when appropriate.

When combined with other direct-response media, telemarketing becomes even more effective. For example, experience shows that when telemarketing is combined with direct mail, there is usually at least a 10 percent increase in responses—often a lot more.

For example, in the past, brewery executives commonly accepted gifts from outside suppliers. When Anheuser-Busch investigated whether senior executives had accepted gifts from companies handling A-B's sales promotion, the numerous gifts lined both sides of the corridors in the company headquarters.

Some of the sales promotion and advertising agencies involved contended that they needed the gifts to obtain business and that the brewers didn't dissuade them in their gift-giving practices.

However, in today's highly competitive atmosphere, business ethics in general have come under increased scrutiny, especially since the insider trading and savings and loan scandals.

Now, agencies are very cautious when advising clients about incentive programs. They could lose an account by suggesting practices that conflict with their client's ethical code. NCR's code of ethics on "gifts and favors," for example, offers guidelines useful to advertising people as well as clients: "Giving and receiving gifts in our business dealings can create conflicts of interest; such situations require careful thought. The purpose of gifts and favors is generally to create goodwill. If they do more than that, and unduly influence judgment or create a feeling of obligation, we should not give or accept them."

Fortunately, ad agencies today are becoming more sensitive to the issue of questionable exchanges—particularly regarding the commission system and gift giving—that could lead people to question the industry's integrity.

Questions

1. Compare the advantages and disadvantages of the commission system versus those of the fee or incentive system.

2. When, if ever, is it appropriate for companies to give gifts to customers? Should some limit be placed on the value of gifts given or received? Who should make that judgment call?

Sources: Jonathan D. Hibbard, "Anheuser-Busch," in N. Craig Smith and John A. Quelch, eds., *Ethics in Marketing* (Homewood, IL: Richard D. Irwin, 1993), pp. 651–54; Robert J. Kopp, "Ethical Issues in Personal Selling and Sales Force Management," in N. Craig Smith and John A. Quelch, eds., *Ethics in Marketing,* pp. 539–54; Steven Fox, *The Mirror Makers* (New York: Vintage Books, 1985), pp. 14–17.

Direct-Response Advertising

Advertising that asks the reader, viewer, or listener to provide feedback straight to the sender is called **direct-response advertising.** Any medium can be used for direct response, but the most common are direct mail, catalogs, magazines, and TV.

Direct Mail

Next to personal selling and telemarketing, direct mail is the most effective method for closing a sale or generating inquiries. It's very useful to direct marketers seeking an immediate response. In 1997, marketers spent approximately $37.4 billion on direct mail advertising, or 24.4 percent of all direct marketing expenditures. Sales directly attributed to direct-mail advertising reached $145.7 billion in the BTB category and $244.3 billion in the consumer segment.[25]

Direct mail is an important medium to many advertisers, which we'll explore in greater detail in Chapter 16.

Catalog Sales

The largest direct marketers are the catalog companies. **Catalogs** are reference books (and now also CD-ROMs) that list, describe, and usually picture the products sold by a manufacturer, wholesaler, jobber, or retailer. With more high-income families shopping at home, specialized catalogs are becoming very popular. Some catalog retailers prosper with specialized approaches like outdoor clothing and equipment (L.L. Bean, Lands' End), electronic gadgets (Sharper Image), and gourmet foods (Balducci's).

Catalogs are big business. In 1997, the catalog industry spent some $10 billion in advertising and generated more than $78 billion in both BTB and consumer sales.[26] The top 10 catalog companies did over $25 billion in business in 1996 (see Exhibit 9–3). And Dell Computer, the leading catalog marketer, alone sold over $7.5 *billion* worth of merchandise.[27]

To increase readership and stand out from the glut of other catalogs, some marketers have added editorial and slick photography, all designed to sell a certain image. Abercrombie & Fitch, for instance, publishes its *A&F Quarterly,* a thick, glossy "magalog" that offers advice on how to attain a "cool" lifestyle beyond what you wear: by acquiring the right mode of transportation (a Vespa scooter), drinking the right beer (Belgian Chimay), and using the right accessories (a Nokia personal communicator). By selling the Abercrombie lifestyle, A&F hopes to bring more people into the stores.[28]

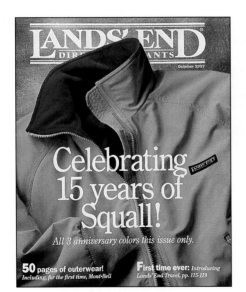

Catalog sales make up the largest portion of direct marketing. Catalogs display a company's products and enable customers to order at their convenience via mail, phone, or Internet. J. Crew, Victoria's Secret, the Sharper Image, and this example from Lands' End (www.landsend.com), are just a few of the multitude of consumer catalogs available today.

Exhibit 9–3

The top 10 catalog companies.

Rank	Company	1996 sales	1995 sales
1	Dell Computer Corp.	$7,554	$5,144
2	Gateway 2000	5,035	3,676
3	JCPenney	3,772	3,378
4	Digital Equipment	3,300*	3,000*
5	Micro Warehouse	1,916	1,308
6	Spiegel	1,681	1,760
7	Fingerhut	1,638	1,782
8	Viking Office Products	1,182.3	920.7
9	Land's End	1,112	1,030
10	CDW	927.9	634.5

Notes: All sales in millions; * = estimate.

Source: Reprinted with permission of CATALOG AGE magazine, an Intertec publication.

Direct-Response Print Advertising

As Andersen Windows so aptly demonstrated, magazine ads and inserts featuring coupons or listing toll-free phone numbers can be very effective at stimulating customer responses. Today the same is true with newspapers. Moreover, in magazines, advertisers can devote most of the space to image-building, thus maximizing the medium's power. We discuss the use of print media further in Chapter 14.

Direct-Response Broadcast Advertising

Direct marketers' use of TV and radio has increased dramatically in recent years. Avon, whose products are normally sold door to door, advertised its catalog and a toll-free number in a 15-second network TV commercial and print ad. The campaign garnered 35,000 phone calls in four days. The response was so great that Avon developed a 30-minute infomercial featuring TV star Linda Gray.[29] Cher reportedly earned over $1 million for appearing in an infomercial for Lori Davis Hair Products.[30] As Exhibit 9–4 shows, more people are watching infomercials and buying the advertised products.

Until recently, radio was uncharted territory for direct-response advertising. But that has made the medium all the more intriguing to some marketers and ad agencies.[31] Radio industry executives expect to see a dramatic increase in the number of direct-response ads on radio in the next few years.[32] We discuss radio, TV, and infomercials further in Chapter 15.

Exhibit 9–4

Who watches (and buys from) infomercials.

	Seen an infomercial in the past year?	Ever purchased anything using a toll-free number at the end of an infomercial?	Ever purchased anything in a store based on information provided in an infomercial?
Sex			
Male	57%	8.0%	20.0%
Female	54	9.0	19.0
Age			
18–24	70	4.0	19.0
25–34	63	9.0	19.0
35–49	58	12.0	20.0
50–64	55	10.0	26.0
65+	33	3.0	13.0
Income			
Under $15,000	53	4.5	22.5
$15,000–$20,000	52	11.0	24.0
$20,000–$30,000	62	8.0	21.0
$30,000–$40,000	63	9.0	25.0
$40,000+	60	11.0	16.0
Region			
Northeast	56	7.0	24.0
North Central	52	9.0	14.0
South	57	8.0	21.0
West	55	10.0	17.0
Total	55%	8.5%	19.0%

Note: Data from a survey of 1,005 men and women ages 18 and older.

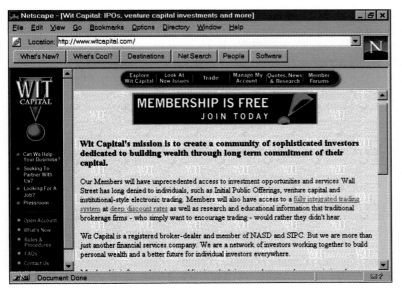

Technology has provided marketers with increasingly interactive media such as the Internet. Today's more sophisticated Web sites, like this example from Wit Capital (www.witcapital.com), provide consumers with genuine interactive options. Wit Capital allows its customers to engage in stock market trading from their own personal computers. Within a short period of time, we can expect this technology to develop into complete multimedia presentations.

Interactive Media

Interactive media systems allow customers and prospects to control both the content and the pace of presentations and to order merchandise directly from the system. The most popular interactive media currently are online personal computers (see Exhibit 9–5). Although still in the development stage, interactive TV may allow viewers to respond to questions during a commercial, giving advertisers a wealth of demographic information for future promotions. The use of the new digital interactive media is explored in depth in Chapter 16. For now, let's take a brief look at the ultimate interactive communication tool, personal selling.

Personal Selling: The Human Medium

"If it is to be, it is up to me."

Ten little words, two letters each. That's Sid Friedman's philosophy for success. Typical sales rep, right?

Well, not exactly. Sid Friedman sells insurance. He's been doing it for some time. He's the president and chair of the Philadelphia-based insurance, financial planning, and consulting firm Corporate Financial Services. Friedman manages his 200-plus employees, runs three other companies, and directs the Philadelphia chapter of the children's Make-a-Wish Foundation. *Forbes* magazine's article "People at the Top, What Do They Earn?" included Sid, along with the likes of Arnold Schwarzenegger, Tom Clancy, and Ralph Lauren.

Exhibit 9–5

How consumers are using interactive media to shop (1,200 online consumers using new media between April 1996 and April 1997).

	Percent
Respondents who made interactive purchase within the year	58%
Of these, number that shopped via online service	86
Of these, number that used credit card	83
Number that shopped via Internet	43
Of these, number that used credit card	70
Number that switched to 800 number	16
Number that shopped via e-mail	8
Number that shopped via CD-ROM	5
Number making 2–4 purchases in last six months	47
Number making 5–10 purchases in last six months	12
Number who spent $26–$50 on each interactive purchase	46
Number who spent over $100 on each purchase	11
Types of products purchased:	
Books, music CDs, and videos	57
Computer-related equipment	55
Flowers	20
Clothing	18
Travel	14
Respondents that also made purchases from catalogs or TV shopping channels	50

Sid made the *Forbes* article because his selling techniques, augmented by the use of direct marketing, resulted in personal commissions of $2.6 million—in one year. Sid likes telephone marketing. It works for him. Every week he calls 100 people, gets 15 appointments, sells three, and earns lots of money.

"Sometimes," he says, "you earn even more money, but only when you do three things: See the people, see the people, and see the people."[33]

That's what personal selling is all about. Seeing the people. And that's also why personal selling is the best marketing communication tool for relationship building—because the sales rep and the customer are face to face. It's the ultimate one-to-one medium.

Personal selling can be defined in a number of ways, depending on the orientation of the company using it. In an integrated marketing communications program, though, the sales effort of the reps must be consistent with the mission, vision, and strategies of the firm and with all the firm's other communications.

Therefore, for our purposes we define **personal selling** as the interpersonal communication process by which a seller ascertains and then satisfies the needs of a buyer, to the mutual, long-term benefit of both parties.[34]

Thus, the task of personal selling is a lot more than just making a sale. In an IMC program, the objective of personal selling is to build a relationship, a partnership, that will provide long-term benefits to both buyer and seller (a win-win situation). The salesperson discovers the buyer's needs by helping the customer identify problems, offers information about potential solutions, assists the buyer in making decisions, and provides after-sale service to ensure long-term satisfaction. Influence and persuasion are only one part of selling. The major part is problem solving.

Types of Personal Selling

Everyone sells, at one time or another. Children sell lemonade, magazine subscriptions, and Girl Scout cookies. Students sell prom tickets, yearbook ads, and term papers. Doctors sell diets to unwilling patients. Lawyers sell briefs to skeptical judges. And cops sell traffic safety to nervous motorists.

As a business process and a profession, though, personal selling is something else. It's just one of a company's mix of communications tools, and its relative importance depends on the type of business or industry, the nature of the product or service, and the strategy of the business.

The fact is that everything has to be sold, by someone to somebody. A retail clerk may sell you a pocket calculator. Behind that clerk is a virtual army of other salespeople who sold processed materials to the manufacturer, capital equipment for use in the manufacturing process, business services such as human resources and accounting, plant and office furniture, vehicles, advertising services, media space and time, and insurance. Then the manufacturer's salespeople sold the calculator (and a few others) to a wholesaler who, of course, had to buy transportation services and warehousing from other salespeople. And then the wholesaler's sales reps sold the calculator to the retail outlet where you bought it.

As this scenario shows, people in sales work for a wide variety of organizations and

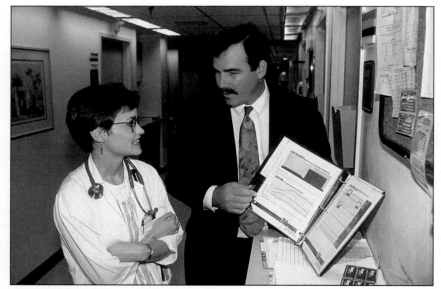

This pharmaceutical salesperson is engaging in missionary selling when he presents the benefits of his products to a doctor. The salesperson understands that the doctor will not place an order, but he is attempting to get the doctor to prescribe the pharmaceutical for her patients so his company will get an order from the patient's drugstore.

call on an equally wide variety of customers. They may call on other businesses to sell products or services used in the manufacture of other products. They may call on resellers—people who buy the product, add value, and resell it. Or they may sell to consumers, either in a retail store or, as we discussed earlier, in a direct selling situation away from a fixed retail location.

Since advertising is basically a support service for a company's sales efforts, advertising people (whether in the company or at an agency) have to understand the selling environment their companies or clients deal in. Many companies have their advertising people make calls with the sales force for this very reason. The advertising person can experience firsthand what questions prospects ask, how customers view the company (and its competitors), how people use the company's product, and what information (in either an ad or a piece of sales material) might help the salesperson communicate better with the prospect.

Advantages of Personal Selling

The greatest strength of personal selling is its personal nature. Nothing is as persuasive as personal communication. A skilled salesperson can observe a prospect's body language and read between the lines to detect what's troubling the customer. The rep can ask questions and answer queries as they arise. The face-to-face situation facilitates instant feedback. And the rep has the flexibility to adjust the presentation, tailoring it specifically to the needs and interests of the particular prospect. Not only that, the salesperson can demonstrate the product live. And the rep can negotiate, finding those terms that best suit the buyer's needs.

Time is on the rep's side, too. The sale doesn't have to be made today. The relationship has to be established, though, and a human being is better at doing that than any nonpersonal medium.

Drawbacks of Personal Selling

Personal selling is very labor intensive, so it's the most costly method of communicating with prospects. This is its single biggest weakness. A business-to-business sales call today costs well in excess of $300. Not only that, it's time-consuming. Since it is basically a one-on-one medium, there are few economies of scale. In fact, two or three salespeople will sometimes go to an important customer's office to make a presentation. In personal selling we don't talk about cost per thousand.

This is why one important role of advertising is to reduce the cost of sales by communicating as much relevant information as possible about the company and its products to prospects and customers before the salesperson even calls. That information may be functional (specifically about the product) or symbolic (building image and credibility for the company).

Another drawback is the poor reputation of personal selling with many people. Decades of "suede shoe" salesmen employing high-pressure tactics, usually in retail venues, have sullied the profession. Thus the common jibe: "Would you buy a used car from that man?" In health care services, for example, selling activities have limited philosophical acceptance. Salespeople are frequently given fancier titles like marketing associate, marketing representative, admissions coordinator, clinical liaison, professional services representative, or program manager in an attempt to reduce guilt or the rejection associated with personal selling.[35]

Moreover, one bad apple can ruin a previously unblemished association. Imagine spending millions of dollars on a nationwide advertising campaign to communicate your good customer service and then sending out an unprofessional salesperson who is improperly groomed or, worse, arrogant and rude. Unfortunately, it happens all the time. The salesperson has incredible power to either make or break a delicate relationship. As a result, sophisticated firms go to great lengths to screen sales applicants to find the right personality attributes and then invest heavily in training.

Personal selling is one of the most important facets of an IMC strategy, because individually the salespeople take on the persona of the company in its relationship with customers. Saturn's (www.saturn.com) philosophy of great attention to customer care revolves largely around superb personal selling, that human element that most often dictates the direction of any sale. In the end, a bad advertisement is less likely to spread negative word-of-mouth about a company as a bad personal sales experience.

The **Role** of Personal Selling in IMC

Salespeople are the company's communicators. They are the human medium. In fact, to the customer who doesn't know anybody else at the company, the salesperson doesn't just represent the firm. He or she *is* the firm. The customer's impression of the salesperson, therefore, will frequently govern his or her perception of the company. Again, this makes the sales rep a very important person.

In an integrated marketing communications program, personal selling can play a very important role. Salespeople provide four distinct communications functions: information gathering, information providing, order fulfillment, and relationship building.

Gathering Information

Sales reps often serve as the eyes and ears of the company. Because they are out in the field talking to customers or attending trade shows, they have access to information and they can see trends. For example, salespeople provide information on who's new in the business, how customers are reacting to new products or styles, what the competition is doing, and where new sales might be made. Generally, information gathering by the sales force relates to prospecting; determining customer wants, needs, and abilities; and monitoring the competition.

Providing Information

Salespeople not only gather information, they impart it. In fact, the stereotype (both negative and positive) of a good salesperson is someone who is a good talker, articulate and persuasive. In truth, a superior salesperson is a good listener first and a good talker second. Salespeople impart information both upstream and downstream within their organization. They deliver information to customers about the company and its products, they recommend solutions to problems, and they use information to communicate value and to build relationships and trust.

Personal selling incorporates all three legs of the IMC triangle, the "say → do → confirm," because what the rep says and does will either confirm or contradict the company's other messages. The rep's skill, therefore, will definitely color the relationship between the company and the customer. It's critically important that the salesperson's performance be consistent with the firm's positioning and reinforce its other marketing communications.

Fulfilling Orders

There comes a time in every relationship when someone has to make a commitment. Asking for that commitment can be very difficult if the preceding steps have not been handled well. The inevitable tasks of personal selling are to motivate the customer to action, close the sale, and then make sure the goods and services are delivered correctly.

An important part of personal selling is following up after the sale, making sure the goods or services are delivered in a timely fashion, and seeing to it that the customer is completely satisfied. This is a combination of the "do" and "confirm" steps, and it's critical to continued relationship building.

This is also where cross-functional management and open communication come back into play. If there is any kind of manufacturing glitch or delay in shipping, the salesperson needs to notify the customer immediately. But to do that, the

This advertisement for AOL is an interesting study in hyperbole. When the company first announced its new unlimited access time, it touted the service in ads such as this one. The ads were successful. However, AOL's telephone infrastructure was incapable of handling the deluge of eager callers, causing a traffic jam with hours of delays and busy signals for irate customers. AOL eventually upgraded its equipment to handle the massive volume of incoming calls. But in the meantime, it angered customers by continuing to advertise the new service.

salesperson must be informed. Similarly, goods need to be protected and shipped with care. Salespeople hate to receive calls from new customers saying their first shipment arrived with damaged goods. Every employee, including those in the warehouse, needs to understand the impact of unplanned product messages.

Likewise, if the company is advertising a certain model of a product and the salesperson closes the sale on the product, that model had better be in stock. Again, good internal communication is a key to good external relationships.

Building Relationships

A company's sales reps should be the ultimate relationship marketers. The fact is that often people will buy a product more because they like the salesperson than for any other reason. Salespeople build relationships by paying attention to three simple things: keeping commitments, servicing their accounts, and solving problems. Interestingly, those are also probably the three basic requirements for any company's success.

Here again, advertising people can help. When a company advertises, it is making a commitment to its customers and prospects. It is very difficult for a salesperson to keep those commitments if the advertising has overpromised. So puffery should be avoided wherever possible, since by its very nature, it tends to overpromise.

Likewise, it's difficult for customer service reps to adequately service their accounts if every time people call they get a busy signal. This happened to U.S. West when it downsized and reengineered the company. Meanwhile, it kept on running ads touting its great services. Not smart. The advertising people have to know what's going on in the company, and sometimes they should recommend that advertising be stopped.

Finally, advertising as well as salespeople should be concerned with solving problems. If the sales staff uncovers a problem that customers frequently encounter, and the company's product can help solve that problem, then that should become the focus of some planned communications—either advertising or publicity.

The Role of **Sales Promotion** in IMC

Imagine walking into the fresh-fruit section of your local grocery store, picking up a big, juicy mango, and discovering a sticker on it stating: "Now available in Snapple. Mango Madness." You turn around and suddenly notice that there, right next to the fresh-fruit bin, stands a big Snapple display of, you guessed it, Mango Madness.

It actually happened. New York agency Kirshenbaum, Bond & Partners launched Snapple's new Mango Madness drink nationally on the back of 30 million pieces of fruit.[36] Talk about out-of-the-box thinking and creative media planning! Moreover, it was an outstanding example of how sales promotion can be perfectly integrated with a company's positioning, in this case Snapple's overall "100% natural" message strategy.

The term *sales promotion* is often misunderstood or confused with advertising or publicity. This may be because sales promotion activities often occur simultaneously and use both advertising and publicity as part of the process. In truth, though, it is a very specific marketing communications activity.

Sales promotion is a direct inducement that offers extra incentives anywhere along the marketing route to enhance or accelerate the product's movement from producer to consumer. There are three important elements to this definition. Sales promotion:

Snapple's clever promotion of its new flavor, Mango Madness, demonstrates an ingenious integration of sales promotion and product positioning. By placing a sticker ad on actual mangoes in the fresh fruit section, Snapple reinforced its slogan of "100% natural" and grabbed the attention of customers not necessarily looking to buy the beverage. The marketing strategy was supported by placing bottles of Mango Madness within close proximity of the fruit.

- May be used anywhere along the marketing route: from manufacturer to dealer, dealer to customer, or manufacturer to customer.
- Normally involves a direct inducement (such as money, prizes, extra products, gifts, or specialized information) that provides extra incentives to buy, visit a store, request literature, display a product, or take some other action.
- Is designed to speed up the selling process.

Let's see how this definition applies to Snapple. In an interesting combination of both consumer advertising and *trade promotion* (sales promotion aimed at members of the distribution channel), Snapple used the fresh mangoes as an unusual new advertising medium to introduce its Mango Madness to consumers and to stimulate initial demand for the drink. The magnitude of that media effort (30 million pieces of fruit) served as a huge incentive to retailers to grant Snapple extra floor space (very expensive real estate, by the way) to display Mango Madness right next to the fresh-fruit stand. The result: Snapple (and the retailers) sold a lot more Mango Madness a lot faster, and for a lot less money, than they would have if they had just placed some expensive ads in consumer magazines or on TV. Moreover, by creatively integrating different forms of marketing communications, Snapple simultaneously bolstered its positioning strategy and enhanced its relationship with the retail trade—its primary customer.

Some marketers consider sales promotion supplemental to advertising and personal selling because it binds the two together, making both more effective. In reality, however, sales promotion is far more than supplemental. Sales promotion expenditures in some companies consume 75 percent of the advertising/promotion budget, compared to 25 percent for advertising.[37] We'll see why shortly.

Sales promotion is expensive. But it's also effective. Unfortunately, it has serious drawbacks, which lead to furious battles in marketing circles between proponents of sales promotion and proponents of advertising. Each approach has an important role to play, but advertisers must consider the positives and negatives and get the balance right.

The Positive Effect of Sales Promotion on Brand Volume

Effective sales promotion accomplishes a number of things. First of all, it adds tangible, immediate, extra value to the brand. Snapple's creative media buy suddenly made Mango Madness more valuable to the retail trade. This induced retailers to stock up on the new product and display it prominently. Similarly, when Publishers Clearinghouse runs a million-dollar sweepstakes, it's adding instant value to the service it sells in an effort to induce consumers to order their magazine subscriptions through it. This is why we refer to sales promotion as the value-added tool.

Second, by adding immediate value, sales promotion maximizes sales volume. While advertising helps develop and reinforce a quality, differentiate brand reputation, and build long-term *market value,* sales promotion helps build *market volume.* To become a market leader, therefore, a brand needs both advertising and sales promotion.

Finally, when all brands appear to be equal, sales promotion can be more effective than advertising in motivating customers to select a specific brand. It can also motivate some customers who might be unmoved by advertising efforts. And certain sales promotions generate a more immediate, measurable payoff than traditional advertising campaigns. In fact, we might also refer to sales promotion as the "sales accelerator."

To succeed, sales promotions should be creative and hard to imitate. Kirshenbaum, Bond & Partners certainly demonstrated that. The Checklist for Creating Effective Sales Promotions outlines some basic ideas to consider in designing promotions.

Creating Effective Sales Promotions

____ **Set specific objectives.** Undisciplined, undirected creative work is a waste of time and resources.

____ **Set a theme that is relevant.** Start with a strategy, preferably from a unified marketing or advertising plan. Stay on track: A Nynex promotion reinforced its "If it's out there, it's in here" campaign with a sweepstakes asking consumers to look up the "heading of the day" in the phone book and note the page.

____ **Involve the trade.** Build relationships. Carrier air conditioning sponsored the Junior Olympics in key markets, sharing sponsorship with its dealer in each city.

____ **Coordinate promotional efforts with other marketing plans.** Be sure to coordinate schedules and plans. A consumer promotion should occur simultaneously with a trade promotion; a free sample promotion should be timed to the introduction of a new line.

____ **Know how basic promotion techniques work.** A sweepstakes shouldn't be used to encourage multiple purchases or a refund to get new customers. A price-off deal can't reverse a brand's downward sales trend.

____ **Use simple, attention-getting copy.** Most promotions are built around a simple idea: "Save 75 cents." Emphasize the idea and don't try to be cute.

____ **Use contemporary, easy-to-track graphics.** Don't expect to fit 500 words and 20 illustrations into a quarter-page freestanding insert.

____ **Clearly communicate the concept.** Words and graphics must work together to get the message across.

____ **Add advertising when you need measurable responses.** When part of a promotion, advertising directed at a broad audience is usually wasted. Trial-building promotions designed to build loyalty among current users, however, can be helped by advertising.

____ **Reinforce the brand's advertising message.** Tie promotions to the brand's ad campaign.

____ **Support the brand's positioning and image.** This is especially important for image-sensitive brands and categories, like family-oriented Kraft.

____ **Know the media you work through.** Determine which media will work best. Should samples be distributed in stores, door to door, or through direct mail? Does the promotion need newspaper or magazine support?

____ **Pretest promotions.** Pretesting doesn't have to be expensive. For packaged goods, small samplings in a few stores can reveal how to maximize coupon redemption rates by testing various values, creative approaches, and delivery methods.

The Negative Effect of Sales Promotion on Brand Value

Advertisers need to understand the negative effects of sales promotion, too. For instance, excessive sales promotion at the expense of advertising hurts profits. Some marketers believe a proper expenditure balance for consumer packaged-good products is approximately 60 percent for trade and consumer promotion, 40 percent for advertising.

A high level of trade sales promotion relative to advertising and consumer sales promotion has a positive effect on short-term market share but may have a negative effect on brand attitudes and long-term market share. Without an effective advertising effort to emphasize brand image and quality, customers become deal-prone rather than brand loyal. And overemphasis on price (whether in advertising or sales promotion) eventually destroys brand equity.[38]

Another drawback of sales promotion is its high cost. One analysis showed that only 16 percent of sales promotions were profitable. In other words, the manufacturer spent more than $1 to generate an extra $1 of profits.[39]

Finally, overly aggressive sales promotion or advertising can draw competitors into a price war, which leads to reduced sales and profits for everyone.

Thus, if too much of the marketing mix is allocated to advertising, the brand may gain a high-quality, differentiated image but not enough volume to be a market leader. On the other hand, as Larry Light, chair of the AAAA's Coalition for Brand Equity, says, "Too much [sales] promotion, and the brand will have high volume but low profitability. Market leadership can be bought through bribes, but enduring profitable market leadership must be earned through building both brand value as well as volume."[40]

Sales Promotion **Strategies** and Tactics

To move their products through the distribution channel from the point of manufacture to the point of consumption, marketers employ two types of strategies: push and pull. **Push strategies** are primarily *defensive* tactics designed to secure the cooperation of retailers, gain shelf space, and protect the product against competitors. **Trade promotions**—sales promotions

As published in 1994.

Trade promotions are business-to-business communications that are strategically aimed at pushing products into the distribution channel and securing shelf-space. This Kleenex (www.kimberlyclark.com) ad promotes the benefits that retailers gain by stocking Kleenex: increased sales, strong support from Kleenex (TV promotion, coupons, etc.), brand recognition, and a history of quality.

aimed at members of the distribution channel—are one of the principal tactics marketers use to *push* products through the distribution pipeline and gain shelf space. We'll discuss some of these tactics in the next section. Marketers may also use **trade advertising** (advertising in publications read by members of the trade) as a push tactic.

Pull strategies, on the other hand, are *offensive* tactics designed to attract customers and increase demand for the product. Consumer advertising and **consumer sales promotions** are examples of pull strategies because they are designed to induce consumers to seek out or ask for the product, in effect *pulling* the product through the pipeline. Today, national advertisers typically spend significantly more dollars on trade sales promotions than on consumer sales promotions or media advertising.

Giving Brands a Push with Trade Promotions

In supermarkets today, shelf space and floor space are hard to come by. To maintain their own images, department stores set standards for manufacturers' displays. This means that retailers often can't use the special racks, sales aids, and promotional literature supplied by manufacturers.

These are minor problems; major ones have to do with control of the marketplace. **Trade concentration**—more products going through fewer retailers—gives greater control to the retailers and less to the manufacturers. Increased competition for shelf space gives retailers even more power, enabling them to exact hefty deals and allowances. As a result, manufacturers of national brands often don't have enough money left to integrate consumer advertising or sales promotion.[41]

Despite these problems, many manufacturers still implement effective push strategies. And the smart ones safeguard enough money for consumer advertising. Trade tactics include slotting allowances, trade deals, display allowances, buyback allowances, advertising allowances, cooperative advertising and advertising materials, dealer premiums and contests, push money, and company conventions and dealer meetings.

Slotting Allowances

In response to the glut of new products, some retailers charge manufacturers **slotting allowances**—fees ranging from $15,000 to $40,000 for the privilege of obtaining shelf or floor space for a new product. The practice is highly controversial because manufacturers think they're being forced to subsidize the retailer's cost of doing business. The Federal Trade Commission and the Bureau of Alcohol, Tobacco, and Firearms looked into the legality of such allowances, and determined they were acceptable as long as the same promotional allowances were offered to all retailers on "proportionally equal terms."[42]

In an effort to avoid slotting allowances, some marketers have made major shifts in strategy. H. J. Heinz, for example, reduced spending on both slotting allowances and coupons by shifting its focus to consumer outreach programs, primarily direct mail and PR, in the product areas that offered the greatest growth potential.[43]

Trade Deals

Manufacturers make **trade deals** with retailers by offering short-term discounts or other dollar inducements. To comply with the Robinson-Patman Act, trade deals must be offered equally to all dealers. Dealers usually pass the savings on to customers through short-term sale prices, or "specials."

Excessive trade deals threaten brand loyalty because they encourage customers to buy whatever brand is on sale. Furthermore, marketers who use trade discounts extensively find themselves in a vicious circle: if they cut back on the promotions, they may lose shelf space and then market share.

In addition, some retailers abuse trade discounts by engaging in forward buying and diverting. With **forward buying,** a retailer stocks up on a product when it is on discount and buys smaller amounts when it sells at list price. **Diverting** means using the promotional discount to purchase large quantities of an item in one region, then shipping portions of the buy to areas where the discount isn't offered.

Display allowances

More and more stores charge manufacturers **display allowances**—fees to make room for and set up displays. In-store displays include counter stands, floor stands, shelf signs, and special racks that give the retailer ready-made, professionally designed vehicles for selling more of the featured products.

Buyback Allowances

When introducing a new product, manufacturers sometimes offer retailers a **buyback allowance** for the old product that hasn't sold. To persuade retailers to take on their product line, some manufacturers even offer a buyback allowance for a competitor's leftover stock.

Advertising Allowances

Manufacturers often offer **advertising allowances** as either a percentage of gross purchases or a flat fee paid to the retailer. Advertising allowances are more common for consumer than industrial products. They are offered primarily by large companies, but some smaller firms give them to high-volume customers.

Display allowances for in-store retail displays and shelf signs provide retailers like De Walt with promotional materials they would not produce on their own. Both the manufacturer and the retailer benefit from such trade promotions.

Co-op Advertising and Advertising Materials

With **cooperative (co-op) advertising,** national manufacturers reimburse their dealers for advertising the manufacturer's products or logo in their trading area. The manufacturer usually pays 50 to 100 percent of the dealer's advertising costs based on a percentage of the dealer's sales. Special co-op deals are used to introduce new products, advertise certain lines, or combat competitors.

Unlike advertising allowances, co-op programs typically require the dealer to submit invoices and proof of the advertising (tearsheets from the newspaper or affidavits of performance from radio or TV stations). Many manufacturers also give their dealers prepared advertising materials: ads, glossy photos, sample radio commercials, and so on. To control the image of their products, some advertisers insist that dealers use these materials to qualify for the co-op advertising money.

Dealer Premiums and Contests

To encourage retail dealers and salespeople to reach specific sales goals or stock a certain product, manufacturers may offer special prizes and gifts. Ethics can be a thorny issue when companies award prizes and gifts to dealers and salespeople.

Push Money

Retail salespeople are often encouraged to push the sale of particular products. One inducement is called **push money (PM),** or **spiffs.** For example, a shoe salesperson may suggest shoe polish or some other high-profit extra; for each item sold, the salesperson receives a 25- to 50-cent spiff.

Company Conventions and Dealer Meetings

Most major manufacturers hold **company conventions** and **dealer meetings** to introduce new products, announce sales promotion programs, or show new advertising campaigns. They may also conduct sales and service training sessions. Meetings can be a dynamic sales promotion tool for the manufacturer.

Push strategies are virtually invisible to consumers. Yet successful inducements mean the product gets more shelf space, a special display, or extra interest and enthusiasm from salespeople. And extra interest can spell the difference between failure and success.

Using Consumer Promotions to Pull Brands Through

One reason for today's increased focus on consumer sales promotions is the change in TV viewing habits. With cable TV and VCRs, fewer people watch any one program. Advertising audiences are more fragmented, and major manufacturers must turn to new methods to reach these moving targets.

Common consumer sales promotions include point-of-purchase materials, coupons, electronic coupons and convenience cards, cents-off promotions, refunds, rebates, premiums, sampling, combination offers, contests, and sweepstakes. Exhibit 9–6 shows the percentages of firms that use various consumer sales promotions. A successful IMC campaign may integrate several of these techniques along with media advertising, product publicity, and direct marketing.

Exhibit 9–6

Consumer sales promotion scorecard.

Types of sales promotion	Percent of respondents
Couponing consumer direct	100%
Cents-off promotions	90
Couponing in retailer's ad	88
Money-back offers/cash refunds	80
Premium offers	78
Sampling established products	78
Sweepstakes	63
Contests	51
Prepriced products	51

Point-of-Purchase (P-O-P) Materials

Walk into any store and notice the number of display materials and advertising-like devices that are designed to build traffic, exhibit and advertise the product, and promote impulse buying. Collectively, these are all referred to as **point-of-purchase (P-O-P) materials.**

P-O-P works best when used with other forms of advertising. For example, by advertising its gum and candy, one marketer increased sales by about 150 percent. But when P-O-P was added to the same program, the purchase rate jumped 550 percent.[44] Ad Lab 9–A offers the opportunity to apply what you've learned about push and pull strategies to the marketing of textbooks.

In a 1994 Gallup poll, 56 percent of mass-merchandise shoppers and 62 percent of grocery shoppers said they noticed point-of-purchase materials. More than half reported noticing signs and displays, 18 percent remembered coupon dispensers, and 14 percent could recall samplings and demonstrations.[45]

Today's consumers make their decisions in the store 66 percent of the time and make unplanned (impulse) purchases 53 percent of the time, so P-O-P can often be the major factor in stimulating purchases.[46]

P-O-P materials may also include window displays, counter displays, floor and wall racks to hold the merchandise, streamers, and posters. Often, the product's shipping cartons are designed to double as display units. A complete information center may even provide literature, samples, product photos, or an interactive computer in a kiosk.

The trend toward self-service retailing has increased the importance of P-O-P materials. With fewer and less knowledgeable salespeople available to help them, customers are forced to make purchasing decisions on their own. Eye-catching, informative displays can give them the nudge they need. Even in well-staffed stores, display materials can offer extra selling information and make the product stand out from the competition.

The proliferation of P-O-P displays has led retailers to be more discriminating in what they actually use. Most are beginning to insist on well-designed, attractive materials that will blend harmoniously with their store atmosphere.

The emphasis on P-O-P has led to a variety of new approaches, including ads on shopping carts, "talking" antacid boxes, beverage jingles activated when in-store refrigerator doors are opened, and interactive computers for selecting everything from shoe styles to floor coverings. Digital technology has led to Hallmark Cards' Touch-Screen Greetings interactive kiosks, which print a customer's personal message onto any card.[47]

Consumer sales promotions expose potential customers to a product and induce them to seek it out. While trade promotions push products through distribution channels, consumer sales promotions are intended to pull the product through due to customer demand. This Nokia (www.nokia.com) point-of-purchase display can serve as both a trade and consumer promotional tool.

Most coupons reach consumers through newspaper free-standing inserts (FSIs), which have a higher redemption rate than regular newspaper or magazine coupons.

Coupons

A **coupon** is a certificate with a stated value presented to the retail store for a price reduction on a specified item. Over 300 billion coupons were distributed in the United States in 1996, but only about 1.8 percent were ever redeemed.[48]

Coupons may be distributed in newspapers or magazines, door to door, on packages, in stores, and by direct mail. Most reach consumers through colorful preprinted newspaper ads called **freestanding inserts (FSIs).** FSIs have a higher redemption rate than regular newspaper and magazine coupons; coupons in or on packages have the highest redemption levels of all.[49]

Manufacturers lose hundreds of millions of dollars annually on fraudulent coupon submissions. Some coupons are counterfeited; others are submitted for products that were never purchased. To fight this problem, some companies have developed computerized systems to detect fraudulent submissions and charge them back to the retailers who made them.

Electronic Coupons and Convenience Cards

High-tech **electronic coupons** work like paper coupons in that they entitle the shopper to a discount, but their method of distribution is entirely different. Interactive touch-screen videos at the point of purchase generate instant-print discounts, rebates, and offers to try new brands. Electronic coupons are spreading quickly in the nation's supermarkets, though they still represent only a small percentage of the total coupons distributed annually.

Nonetheless, all the nation's top brand marketers are currently involved in tests being conducted by the two leaders in the field, Catalina Marketing and Advanced Promotion Technologies. Catalina's system is installed in more than 8,000 supermarkets, and recent growth in this category has exceeded 50 percent per year.[50]

Electronic couponing gives the retailer access to information about consumers that would not be available with paper coupons.[51] Many supermarket chains now issue customers convenience cards entitling them to instant discounts at the checkout counter. When customers use the card, a record of their purchases is sent to a database and sorted into various lifestyle groups. The card saves customers the hassle of clipping paper coupons, and it allows retailers to better understand its customers' purchasing behaviors.[52]

Similar systems are used in Europe. Multipoints is an interactive system that lets customers collect points for visiting stores or watching commercials on TV. The points can be redeemed for prizes and discounts on various products at participating stores. Quick Burger, France's second-largest restaurant chain, noticed a significant increase in traffic after joining Multipoints, even when the system was less than a year old.[53]

Cents-off Promotions, Refunds, and Rebates

Cents-off promotions are short-term reductions in the price of a product in the form of cents-off packages, one-cent sales, free offers, and boxtop refunds. Some packages bear a special cents-off sticker, which the clerk removes at the checkout counter.

Some companies offer *refunds* in the form of cash or coupons that can be applied to future purchases of the product. To obtain the refund, the consumer must supply proof of purchase, such as three boxtops.

Rebates are larger cash refunds on items from cars to household appliances. Large rebates (like those given on cars) are handled by the

Pick 'n Save's VIP Stations use a consumer's membership card to issue a list of manufacturer discounts and to calculate customer purchase patterns.

seller. For small rebates (like those given for coffeemakers), the consumer sends in a certificate.

Research indicates that many people purchase a product because of an advertised rebate but never collect the rebate because of the perceived inconvenience.[54]

Premiums

A **premium** is an item offered free or at a bargain price to encourage the consumer to buy an advertised product. Premiums affect purchase behavior the same way as rebates but tend to be more effective at getting consumers to buy a product they didn't really need (see Exhibit 9–7). Premiums are intended to improve the product's image, gain goodwill, broaden the customer base, and produce quick sales.

A premium should have strong appeal and value and should be useful or unusual. It may be included in the product's package (*in-pack premium*), on the package (*on-pack premium*), mailed free or for a nominal sum on receipt of proof of purchase (boxtop or label), or given with the product at the time of purchase. Cosmetics companies often hold department store promotions in which scarves, purses, and cosmetic samplers are given free or for a low price with a purchase.

The purchased cosmetics sampler is an example of a *self-liquidating premium:* the consumer pays enough that the seller breaks even but doesn't make a profit. A variation is the *continuity premium,* given weekly to customers who frequent the same store. With a minimum dollar purchase of other items, the customer receives a dish or book each week to complete a set.

Sampling

Sampling is the most costly of all sales promotions. It is also one of the most effective for new products, because it offers consumers a free trial in hopes of converting them to habitual use. Sampling should be supported by advertising and must involve a product available in small sizes and purchased frequently. Successful sampling depends heavily on the product's merits. It offers the greatest credibility and can turn a nonuser into a loyal customer instantly—if the product lives up to its promise.

Samples may be distributed by mail, door to door, via coupon advertising, or by a person in the store. They may be given free or for a small charge. Sometimes samples are distributed with related items, but this limits their distribution to those

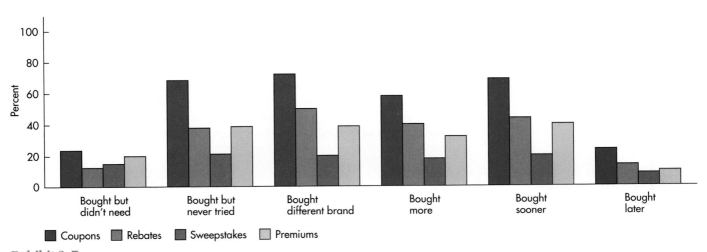

Exhibit 9–7
Next to coupons, premiums are one of the most effective sales promotion techniques for changing consumer behavior.

The EPSON STYLUS PHOTO PRINTER brings brilliant colors to your world. And now Epson brings you the opportunity to see a world of brilliant color. Send us your photographic version of the brilliant tropics. in digital or traditional film formats (please identify as such).   What do we mean by tropics... How about a backyard pool,a garden scene or vacation shot from any exotic tropical odyssey?

The grand prize will be a 5 day trip for 2 to colorful Puerto Rico. Runner-ups will receive an EPSON STYLUS PHOTO PRINTER or an EPSON PHOTOPC 600 Digital Camera. The winning images will also be published in SPRING 1998 issues of POPULAR PHOTOGRAPHY and American PHOTO. (See below for details).

Entries are due by January 31, 1998. So, start shooting now for a chance to see the world in Epson color.

Epson's (www.epson.com) photo sweepstakes reaches and generates interest in people who enjoy photography, but may not have been considering a purchase of computer hardware. While the sweepstakes entry does not require purchase—which would be illegal—it provides exposure to and promotion for Epson printers and assists in the creation of a customer database from the pool of sweepstakes entrants.

who buy the other product. In **polybagging,** samples are delivered in plastic bags with the daily newspaper or a monthly magazine. This enables distribution to targeted readers and lets publications give their subscribers added value at no cost.[55]

In-store sampling is very popular. Most in-store sampling programs are tied to a coupon campaign. Depending on the nature of the product, samples can be used as either a push strategy or a pull strategy.

Combination Offers

Food and drug marketers use **combination offers,** such as a razor and a package of blades or a toothbrush with a tube of toothpaste, at a reduced price for the two. For best results, the items should be related. Sometimes a combination offer introduces a new product by tying its purchase to an established product at a special price.

Contests and Sweepstakes

A **contest** offers prizes based on entrants' skill. A **sweepstakes** offers prizes based on a chance drawing of entrants' names. A **game** has the chance element of a sweepstakes but is conducted over a longer time (like local bingo-type games designed to build store traffic). A game's big marketing advantage is that customers must make repeat visits to the dealer to continue playing.

Both contests and sweepstakes encourage consumption of the product by creating consumer involvement. These devices pull millions of entries. Usually contest entrants must send in some proof of purchase, such as a boxtop or label. For more expensive products, consumers may only have to visit the dealer to pick up an entry blank.

To encourage entries, sponsors try to keep their contests as simple as possible. The prize structure must be clearly stated and rules defined. National contests and sweepstakes are handled and judged by independent professional contest firms.

Sweepstakes and games are now more popular than contests because they are much easier to enter and take less time. Sweepstakes require careful planning by the advertiser. Companies cannot require a purchase as a condition for entry or the sweepstakes becomes a lottery and therefore illegal. Marketers must obey all postal laws. If they run the sweepstakes in Canada, they may have to pay a percentage of the prizes to the Quebec government.

Contests and sweepstakes must be promoted and advertised to be successful, and this can be expensive. And sales promotions need dealer support. To ensure dealer cooperation, many contests and sweepstakes require the entrant to name the product's local dealer. They may also award prizes to the dealer who made the sale.

Chapter **Summary**

The key to building brand equity in the 21st century is to develop interdependent, mutually satisfying relationships with customers and other stakeholders. To manage these relationships, companies will need to consciously integrate their marketing communications activities with all their other company functions so that all the messages the marketplace receives about the company are consistent. The idea is to not just meet customer expectations but exceed them.

As part of this process, it is important for advertising people to understand how to integrate the various tools of marketing communications. Advertising practitioners need to have a basic understanding of what other tools are available to them and how they can best be used in the overall communications mix.

In direct marketing, the marketer builds and maintains a database of customers and prospects and uses anything from personal contact to mass media to communicate with them directly in the effort to generate a response, a transaction, or a visit to a retail store.

The database is the key to direct marketing success, especially in an IMC program. Databases let marketers target, segment, and grade customers. This allows them to identify their best customers, their value to the organization, and their needs and buying behavior. They can then calculate the customer's lifetime value. The database is the corporate memory of all important customer information. It should record every transaction across all points of contact with both channel members and customers. The database also enables the company to measure the efficiency of its direct-response advertising efforts. Working with a marketing database requires two processes: data management and data access.

Advertisers and agencies now realize they can't do the job with one medium. Databases let companies choose the prospects they can serve most effectively and profitably. By providing a tangible response, direct marketing offers accountability. Direct marketing offers convenience to time-sensitive consumers and precision and flexibility to cost-sensitive marketers.

Direct marketing is a rapidly growing industry, but it still suffers from problems of cost, clutter, and image.

Direct marketers use a variety of activities, from direct sales (personal selling and telemarketing) to direct-response advertising. Telemarketing, followed by direct mail, is the medium of choice for most direct marketers, but more are beginning to use other media, especially TV infomercials. Interactive TV may be the direct marketing medium of the future.

Personal selling is actually the ultimate interactive medium. It is the interpersonal communication process by which a seller ascertains and then satisfies the needs of a buyer, to the mutual, long-term benefit of both parties.

There are many types of personal selling: retail, business-to-business, and direct selling. Since advertising is a support service for a company's sales efforts, advertising people have to understand the selling environment their companies deal in.

The greatest strength of personal selling is its personal nature. Nothing is as persuasive as personal communication. The one-to-one situation facilitates instant feedback. And the rep has the flexibility to adjust the presentation, tailoring it specifically to the needs and interests of the particular prospect.

Like all communications tools, personal selling also has some drawbacks. It is very labor intensive and therefore very expensive. One important role of advertising is to reduce the cost of sales by communicating as much relevant information as possible about the company and its products before the salesperson even calls. The salesperson has incredible power to either make or break a delicate relationship. So one of the risks is that one bad apple can ruin a previously unblemished association.

Salespeople provide four communications functions: information gathering, information providing, order fulfillment, and relationship building.

Sales promotion complements advertising and personal selling by stimulating sales. It includes direct inducements (such as money, prizes, or gifts) aimed at salespeople, distributors, retailers, consumers, and industrial buyers.

Marketers must balance sales promotion with advertising. Advertising creates market value for a brand; promotion creates market volume. Advertising has a positive effect on profits; promotion can have a negative effect. Sales promotion techniques are used in the trade to push products through the distribution channels and with consumers to pull them through.

Manufacturers use many sales promotion techniques with dealers: slotting allowances, trade deals, display allowances, buyback allowances, advertising allowances, co-op advertising and advertising materials, dealer premiums and contests, push money, and company conventions and dealer meetings. Sales promotions aimed at the ultimate purchaser include point-of-purchase materials, coupons, electronic coupons and convenience cards, cents-off promotions, refunds, rebates, premiums, sampling, combination offers, contests, and sweepstakes.

Important **Terms**

advertising allowance, *299*

buyback allowance, *299*

catalog, *289*

cents-off promotion, *302*

combination offer, *304*

company conventions and dealer meetings, *300*

consumer sales promotion, *298*

contest, *304*

cooperative (co-op) advertising, *300*

coupon, *302*

customer lifetime value (LTV), *283*

data access, *284*

data management, *284*

database, *281*

database marketing, *281*

direct marketing, *281*

direct-response (action) advertising, *281*

direct-sales strategy, *287*

direct selling, *287*

display allowance, *299*

diverting, *299*

electronic coupon, *302*

forward buying, *299*

freestanding insert (FSI), *302*

game, *304*

in-store sampling, *304*

linkage media, *282*

personal selling, *292*

point-of-purchase (P-O-P) materials, *300*

polybagging, *304*

premium, *303*

pull strategies, *298*

push money (PM) (spiff), *300*

push strategies, *297*

rebate, *302*

RFM formula, *284*

sales promotion, *295*

sampling, *303*

slotting allowance, *298*

sweepstakes, *304*

telemarketing, *287*

trade advertising, *298*

trade concentration, *298*

trade deal, *299*

trade promotion, *297*

Review **Questions**

1. Who are a company's best prospects for additional sales and profits? Why?

2. How should a large insurance company view integrated marketing communications?

3. What are the basic strategic and tactical decisions direct marketers face?

4. How can an advertiser use a newspaper for direct-response advertising?

5. What distinct communications functions do salespeople provide?

6. What are the three things salespeople must do to build relationships?

7. What are the main purposes of sales promotion?

8. Why is trade promotion controversial?

9. What are the most common pull strategies? Which would you use to launch a new soft drink?

10. Why is there a trend away from push strategies and toward pull strategies?

Exploring the **Internet**

The Internet Exercises for Chapter 9 address the following main areas covered in the chapter: direct marketing and direct response (Exercise 1) and sales promotion (Exercise 2).

1. Direct Marketing and Direct Response

   Direct marketing is not only vast, it's ever-changing in all its facets—direct sales, direct mail, direct response. Likewise, direct-marketing agencies tend to differ in strategy, organization, and clientele from traditional advertising agencies. Take a look at some of the Web sites below and answer the questions that follow for each site.

   Direct Marketing Organizations

   • Canadian Direct Marketing Association (CDMA) **www.cdma.org**

   • *DIRECT* **www.mediacentral.com/direct**

   • Direct Marketing Association (DMA) **www.the-dma.org**

   • Direct Marketing Club of Southern California (DMCSC) **www.dmcsc.com**

   • *Direct Marketing News* **www.dmnews.com**

   • Direct Marketing Resources **www.direct-marketing.com**

   • Direct Marketing World **www.dmworld.com**

   • Direct Response.com **www.directresponse.com**

   • National Informercial Marketing Association (NIMA) **www.nima.org**

   • The 900 Advertising Club **www.infoguru.com**

   a. What group sponsors the site? Who is the intended audience(s)?

   b. What are the size, scope, and purpose of the organization?

   c. What benefits does the organization provide to individual members or subscribers? To the overall advertising and direct marketing communities?

   d. How important do you feel this organization is to the direct marketing industry? Why?

   Direct Firms

   Select five of the following direct-marketing firms, visit their Web sites, and answer the questions that follow.

   • AGA Catalog Marketing & Design **www.aganet.com**

   • Cohn and Wells **www.cohn-wells.com**

   • CPS Direct **www.cpsDIRECT.com**

   • Direct Resources International (DRI) **www.go-direct.com**

   • Direct Results Group **www.directresults.com**

   • DRTV World **www.drtvworld.com**

   • Gage Marketing Group **www.gage.com**

   • Harte-Hanks **www.harte-hanks.com**

   • Hunt Marketing Group **www.huntgroup.com**

   • Response Marketing Group (RMG) **www.rmgusa.com**

   • Wunderman Cato Johnson **www.wcj.com**

   Answer the following questions for each site:

   1. Who is the intended audience of the site?

   2. What are the scope and size of the agency's business?

   3. How does the agency position itself (i.e., creative-driven, strategy (account)-driven, media-driven, etc.)?

   4. What is your overall impression of the agency and its work? Why?

2. Sales Promotion

   Sales promotion vehicles are often key elements in integrated marketing communication campaigns. Browse the Web sites of the following support organizations for the sales promotion field and answer the questions for each site.

   Sales Promotion Organizations

   • *PROMO* **www.promomagazine.com**

   • Promotion Marketing Association of America (PMAA) **www.pmaalink.org**

   • Promotional Product Association International (PPAI) **www.ppa.org**

   • *Creative Magazine* **www.creativemag.com**

   • *P.O.P. Magazine* **www.popmag.com**

   a. What group sponsors the site? Who is the intended audience(s)?

   b. What is the organization's purpose?

   c. Who makes up the organization's membership? Its constituency?

   d. What benefit does the organization provide individual members/subscribers? The overall advertising and sales promotion communities?

Sales Promotion Agencies

Promotional companies, like their direct-marketing counterparts, differ somewhat from traditional advertising firms. Visit five of the Web sites for the following sales promotion companies, and answer the questions below for each.

- AdSolution **www.adsolution.com**
- Advanced Promotion Technologies **www.apt.com**
- BIC Special Markets Division **www.bicpromo.com**
- Boulder Blimp Company **www.salespromotion.com**
- InterPromo, Inc. **www.interpromo.com**

- Jornik Promotional Products **www.promotions.com**
- StorePoint Communications **www.storepoint.com**
- Val-Pak Coupons **www.valpak.com**

a. What is the focus of the company's work (i.e., consumer or trade)?

b. What are the scope and size of the company's business?

c. What promotional services does the company offer?

d. What is your overall impression of the company and its work? Why?

Chapter Ten

Relationship Building: Public Relations, Sponsorship, and Corporate Advertising

Objective To explain the role of public relations, sponsorships, and corporate advertising in relationship marketing and integrated marketing communications. By using public relations, event sponsorships, and institutional advertising, a company can improve the effectiveness of all its marketing efforts.

After studying this chapter, you will be able to:

- Distinguish between advertising and public relations.
- Discuss the key elements of crisis communications.
- Describe the difference between press agentry and publicity.
- Identify the tools used by public relations practitioners.
- Explain how event sponsorships can fit into an IMC plan.
- Define advocacy advertising and debate its role in a free society.
- Explain the role of corporate identity advertising.

Intel, an American success story, is one of the world's largest corporations, controlling nearly 80 percent of the personal computer-chip market. It was the first semiconductor company to produce annual sales over $10 billion, and its $2.3 billion research and development budget alone is greater than most of its competitors' annual revenues. Intel's work with Novell, Microsoft, and Hewlett-Packard has made it one of the few corporations capable of defending America's economic future in the new world order.[1] ● On November 7, 1994, a mathematics professor with the unassuming name of Nicely announced that Intel's Pentium processing chips produced miscalculations of certain extremely large numbers. His discovery would eventually cost Intel $6 million in legal fees and as much as $475 million in replacement costs.[2] The ripple effect would hit the owners

of 5.5 million Pentium-based computers, thousands of individual retailers, and many other Intel stakeholders such as Hewlett-Packard, the largest seller of Pentium-chip computers.[3] ● Overnight the Internet was buzzing with the bad news. Then came reports of concerned Pentium owners being stalled by Intel reps, an early sign that a huge public relations debacle was in the making. Some users were promised replacement chips in a matter of days. But after waiting weeks, they shared their frustration across the Internet, fueling the impression that the problem was much bigger than Intel was willing to admit. ● Although Intel was monitoring the Internet, it didn't respond well—the second sign of problems. Alex Stanton, head of a New York marketing consulting and communications company, said,

"Despite its technological savvy, the company seemed not to appreciate the 'real time' dynamics of the Net and online chat groups, and the communications problems that are created when there is a disconnect."[4] ● Finally, Intel CEO Andrew Grove promised Intel would replace the chips for customers it deemed to have been affected.[5] This was the third blunder. Suddenly the Internet was aflame with threats of lawsuits and, worse, jokes. Question: How many Pentium designers does it take to screw in a lightbulb? Answer:1.9904274014, but that's close enough for nontechnical people.[6] ● At the peak of the Christmas shopping season, on December 12, the fourth hit came. IBM halted shipments of Pentium computers. It believed the frequency of math errors was far greater than Intel had admitted.[7] According to Alex Stanton, "Intel squandered the opportunity to take decisive action during the critical two-week period between receiving bona-fide user complaints of processing flaws and IBM's preemptive announcement of its decision to withhold shipments."[8] ● The press went wild. Article titles included "Pentium Means Having to Say You're Sorry," "When Good Chips Go Bad," "Unsafe at Any Speed," and "Intel's Tainted Tylenol?" The editor-in-chief of *Computerworld*, Bill Laberis, wondered why Intel did not heed its own CEO's words, "There are only two kinds of companies: the quick and the dead."[9] ●

Intel's size seemed to affect its public relations effort, insulating it from day-to-day shifts in market conditions. "It's a classic example of a product-driven company that feels its technical expertise is more important than buyers' feelings," said management consultant Barton Goldenberg, head of Information Systems Marketing in Washington, DC.[10] Intel management didn't have a crisis communication plan. As Alex Stanton points out, companies should establish a party line, deliver it with one voice, and correct misimpressions quickly and convincingly.[11] ● After six weeks and thousands of phone calls from consumers and the trade, Intel relented by promising to replace all flawed chips. "The company could have turned this into a positive experience by immediately falling on its sword," stated Laberis, "and offering to replace what would likely have been very few chips for users who wanted to bother. But noooooooo."[12] ● Intel's credibility was tarnished, particularly among computer owners, and many of these people remain hostile today. According to Bill Slater, publisher of *Microprocessor Report,* "Intel had an aggressive, arrogant style of doing business that alienated a lot of people. This was their chance for revenge."[13] ●

The Role of **Public Relations**

The primary role of public relations is to manage a company's reputation and help build public consent for its enterprises. Today's business environment has become so competitive that public consent can no longer be assumed; it must be earned continuously.[14]

The term *public relations* is widely misunderstood and misused. Part of the confusion is due to the fact that public relations covers a very broad area. Depending on the context and one's point of view, it can be a concept, a profession, a management function, or a practice. For our purposes, we define **public relations (PR)** as the management function that focuses on the relationships and communications that individuals and organizations have with other groups (called *publics*) for the purpose of creating mutual goodwill.

As we've already discussed, every company, organization, or government body has relationships with groups of people who are affected by what it does or says. They may be employees, customers, stockholders, competitors, suppliers, legislators, or the community in which the organization resides. Marketing professionals refer to these people as *stakeholders* because they all have some vested interest in the company's actions. In PR terminology, each of these groups is considered one of the organization's **publics,** and the goal of PR is to develop and maintain goodwill with most, if not all, of its publics. Failure to do so may mean loss of customers and revenues, time lost dealing with complaints or lawsuits, and loss of esteem (which weakens the organization's brand equity as well as its ability to secure financing, make sales, and expand).

A company's publics change constantly. As soon as word of Intel's defective chip got out, Intel's publics multiplied rapidly. There were the Internet surfers, frustrated computer owners that Intel never had to deal with before, lawyers for upset computer manufacturers, members of the trade and consumer press, and retailers that sold Pentium-based computers.

37% of our subscribers are millionaires. What do you think they drive? Yugos?

Every advertiser forms relationships with groups of people, including its current and potential customers, who are affected by what it does or says. The Crain's Chicago Business *ad shown here compliments a portion of its subscribers and piques the interest of potential customers.*

Because of the powerful effect of public opinion, companies and organizations must consider the breadth of impact of their actions. This is especially true in times of crisis, emergency, or disaster. But it also holds true for major policy decisions: changes in management or pricing, labor negotiations, introduction of new products, or changes in distribution methods. Each decision affects different groups in different ways. Effective public relations can channel groups' opinions toward mutual understanding and positive outcomes.

In short, the goals of public relations are to improve public opinion, build goodwill, and establish and maintain a satisfactory reputation for the organization. PR efforts may rally public support, obtain public understanding or neutrality, or simply respond to inquiries. Well-executed public relations is an ongoing process that molds good long-term relationships and plays an important role in relationship marketing and integrated communications.[15]

The Difference between Advertising and PR

Since they both use the media to create awareness or to influence markets or publics, advertising and public relations are similar—but they're not the same. Advertising reaches its audience through media the advertiser pays for. It appears just as the advertiser designed it, with the advertiser's bias built in. Knowing this, the public views ads with some skepticism or ignores them outright. So in an integrated marketing communications program, advertising may not be the best vehicle for building credibility.

Certain public relations communications, like publicity, are not openly sponsored or paid for. People receive these communications in the form of news articles, editorial interviews, or feature stories after the messages have been reviewed and edited—filtered—by the media. Since the public thinks such messages are coming from the medium rather than a company, it trusts them more readily. For building credibility, therefore, public relations is usually a better approach.[16]

However, since advertising is carefully placed to gain particular reach and frequency objectives, PR is less precise. Public relations communications are not easily quantifiable. In fact, the results gained from public relations activities depend greatly on the experience and skill of the people executing it. Moreover, PR can go only so far. Editors won't run the same story over and over, but an ad's memorability comes from repetition. While PR activities may offer greater credibility, advertising offers greater awareness and control.[17] This is why some companies relay their public relations messages through *corporate advertising,* which we discuss later in this chapter.

Advertising and PR in the Eyes of Practitioners

Another major difference between public relations and advertising is the orientation of professional practitioners. Advertising professionals see *marketing* as the umbrella process companies use to determine what products and services the market needs and how to distribute and sell them. To advertising professionals, advertising and public relations are "good news" marketing tools used to promote sales.

Public relations professionals take a totally different view. With their background typically in journalism rather than marketing, they believe *public relations* should be the umbrella process. They think companies should use PR to maintain relationships with all publics, including consumers. As *Inside PR* magazine says, "Public relations is a management discipline that encompasses a wide range of activities, from *marketing and advertising* to investor relations and government affairs."[18] To PR professionals, public relations should be integrated "corporate" communications, which is certainly broader than what most people consider integrated "marketing" communications.

Texaco (www.texaco.com) produced this corporate image program-length documercial *to inform customers about its new CleanSystem³ gasoline. It featured interviews with Texaco scientists who developed the product, and day-in-the-life stories of people discussing the importance of their cars in their personal and professional lives. The only commercial was a 30-second spot at the end.*

To date, few companies are structured with a public relations orientation; most are marketing oriented, perhaps due to marketing's bottom-line orientation. But in today's world of downsizing, reengineering, and total quality management (TQM), marketing people would be well advised to adopt the multiple-stakeholder approach and relationship consciousness that PR people bring to the table.

Moreover, in times of crisis, the candid, open-information orientation of PR is invariably the better perspective to adopt. Fortunately, with the growing interest in relationship marketing, two-way interactivity, and IMC, companies are finally beginning to embrace a public relations philosophy.

When PR activities are used for marketing purposes, the term **marketing public relations (MPR)** is often used. In support of marketing, public relations activities can raise awareness, inform and educate, improve understanding, build trust, make friends, give people reasons or permission to buy, and create a climate of consumer acceptance—usually better than advertising.[19]

In an integrated marketing communications program, advertising and MPR need to be closely coordinated. Many ad agencies now have PR departments for this very purpose. And many companies now have communications departments that manage both advertising and PR.

The Public Relations **Job**

The public relations job comprises a variety of activities, from crisis communications to fundraising. And practitioners use many tools besides press conferences and news releases.

PR Planning and Research

The first function of a PR practitioner is to plan and execute the public relations program. Part of this task may be integrated with the company's marketing efforts (for instance, product publicity), but the PR person typically takes a broader view. He or she must prepare an overall public relations program for the whole organization.

Since public opinion is so important, the PR person must constantly monitor, measure, and analyze changes in attitudes among a variety of publics. Several years ago, Perrier used research to monitor its standing with the general consuming public after traces of benzene, a carcinogen, were found in bottles of Perrier water. Perrier found that 82 percent of its customers knew about the contamination, but 80 percent planned to buy the product when it became available again.[20]

A common form of public relations research is **opinion sampling** using techniques discussed in Chapter 6: shopping center or phone interviews, focus groups, analysis of incoming mail, and field reports. Some advertisers set up toll-free phone lines and invite consumer feedback.

The practitioner analyzes the organization's relationships with its publics; evaluates people's attitudes and opinions toward the organization; assesses how company policies and actions relate to different publics; determines PR objectives and strategies; develops and implements a mix of PR activities, integrating them whenever possible with the firm's other communications; and solicits feedback to evaluate effectiveness.

Aside from advertising, publicity can help companies distribute information or shape an image. A company's public relations department will notify the press when new products are introduced, a business is bought or sold, or a crisis is afoot. The idea is to disseminate important information while maintaining the company's public reputation.

To maintain credibility with the press, news releases should be distributed only for newsworthy events—those that affect some significant segment of the company's various publics.

Kodak, Intel put heads together

By Kevin Maney
USA TODAY

Eastman Kodak is teaming with Intel to try to make it easier for consumers to get their photos into computers without having to buy expensive digital cameras or scanners.

The partnership, announced Thursday, involves technology development, sharing of patents and up to $150 million in joint consumer marketing over three years. One of the first tangible moves will be to upgrade technology in Kodak photofinishing labs. The labs could then inex-

pensively digitize film photos and put them on CD-ROM disks, called Kodak Picture CDs.

Consumers would be able to take pictures using a 35mm camera and get the film developed as usual. On the developer's envelope would be a box for the CDs. Check the box, and you get back both the regular prints and the CD when you pick up your photos. The CD could be loaded into a PC and the photos could be dumped into documents or e-mail.

Kodak already has a CD-ROM offering called PhotoCD. But the Kodak-Intel version is supposed to be

cheaper — less than $10 extra per roll of film — and have turnaround times equal to those of film processing. Eventually, consumers should be able to get a CD at a one-hour photo shop. The idea is to let mass-market consumers get into digital images no matter what kind of camera people own.

"We want the lines between analog and digital photography to be completely blurred," says Don Whiteside, general manager of Intel digital imaging. Adds Kodak executive Willy Shih, "It lowers the entry point for getting into the digital format."

Reputation Management

One of the principal tasks of public relations is to manage the standing of the firm with various publics. **Reputation management** is the name of this long-term strategic process.[21] PR practitioners employ a number of strategies and tactics to help them manage their firm's or client's reputation, including publicity and press agentry, crisis communications management, and community involvement.

Publicity and Press Agentry

For many public relations professionals, their primary task is to generate news and get it placed in the media for their companies or clients. A major activity of public relations, **publicity** is the generation of news about a person, product, or service that appears in print or electronic media. Companies employ this activity either for marketing purposes or to enhance the firm's reputation.

Some people think of publicity as "free" because the media don't charge firms to run it (they also don't guarantee they'll use it). This is a misnomer, though. Someone still gets paid to write the release and coordinate with the press. However, as a marketing communications vehicle, publicity often offers a considerably greater return on money invested than other communications activities. A large ad campaign might require an investment of 5 to 20 percent of sales; a major publicity program, only 1 to 2 percent.

To be picked up by the media, publicity must be *newsworthy.* Typical publicity opportunities include new-product introductions, awards, company sales and earnings, major new contracts, mergers, retirements, parades, and speeches by company executives. Sometimes publicity accrues unintentionally, as in the case of Intel. And since publicity can originate from any source, it may be difficult—or impossible—to control. In IMC terms, unintentional publicity is an *unplanned message.*

The planning and staging of events to generate publicity is called **press agentry.** Most PR people engage in press agentry to bring attention to new products or services or to portray their organizations favorably. For print media, the publicity person deals with editors and feature writers. For broadcast media, he or she deals with program directors, assignment editors, or news editors. Successful PR practitioners develop and maintain close, cordial relations with their editorial contacts. An MPR professional practicing IMC sees the press as an important *public,* and writers and editors as important *stakeholders.* PR people pay atention to the phenomenon of stakeholder overlap: A company's customer might also work for the press. An employee might also be a stockholder and a customer. Awareness of these potentially multifaceted relationships helps create consistent communications, the hallmark of IMC.

Crisis Communications Management

As the Intel episode illustrates, one of the most important public relations tasks for any corporation is **crisis management.** Even companies that earn the public's trust and goodwill over decades can lose their status fast if they mismanage their response to a crisis.

The classic case of exemplary crisis communication management was Johnson & Johnson's handling of a product-tampering episode in 1982. Several people died when a criminal laced bottles of J&J's Extra-Strength Tylenol with cyanide on retail shelves. The moment they received the news, management strategists at J&J and McNeil Products (the J&J subsidiary that markets Tylenol) formulated three stages of action:

1. Identify the problem and take immediate corrective action. J&J strategists got information from the police, FBI, FDA, and press; identified the geographic area affected; corrected rumors; and immediately withdrew the product from the marketplace.

2. Actively cooperate with authorities in the investigation. Johnson & Johnson was proactive. It helped the FBI and other law enforcement agencies generate leads and investigate security at the plants, and it offered a $100,000 reward.

3. Quickly rebuild the Tylenol name and capsule line, including Regular Strength capsules, which were recalled, too. Although J&J believed the poisoning had taken place at the retail end of the chain, it first made sure that the tampering hadn't occurred at McNeil. The company's two capsule production lines were shut down, and dog teams were brought in to search for cyanide.

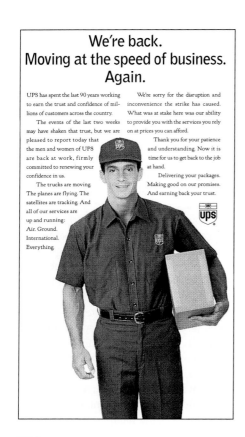

Years of hard work and millions of dollars of investment can quickly disappear if a company does not have an effective system for crisis management. In the fall of 1997, UPS's (www.ups.com) union workers unilaterally voted to strike, plunging the company into a crisis that impacted the country's mail delivery service. Shortly after the company's resolution with labor union officials, UPS ran this ad to counteract the ill effects of the strike and buffer the damage caused by the event.

sources by including fact-oriented text, graphs, and documentary-like imagery. The result is an innocence by association, where the advertorial reflects the higher ideals and honest objectivity that are usually associated with journalism and academia.

However, disguising a point of view as objective, unbiased editorial material poses ethical dilemmas with real consequences. A major criticism of advocacy advertising is simply that it persuades without appearing to do so. Advertisers may also be tempted to use the advertorial as a veiled technique for deflecting serious criticism about the advertiser's policies, products, or practices—an approach often considered unethical. There's also potential for advertorials to intentionally mislead the public into supporting policies of questionable social value.

Corporations have the same right as anyone else to express their views, and advocacy ads provide an effective medium for doing so. But in addition to adhering to the law, advocacy advertisers must judge the ethical issues of fairness (recognizing what is good for everyone involved), loyalty (the individual good versus that of the group and the "public's right to know"), truth (the lack of fabrication, falsification, and distortion), and duty (sacrificing the individual's interests to support principles like rightness over

utility). Advertising practitioners must therefore carefully examine the integrity of their client's message and its impact on society as a whole—not merely focus on the client's immediate interests.

Questions

1. Should corporations use persuasive advertising techniques to influence key decision makers? Explain.
2. How can you determine if an advocacy ad is deceptive? If deception is established, what should the penalty be?

Sources: Denise M. Bostdorff and Steven L. Vibbert, "Values Advocacy: Enhancing Organizational Images, Deflecting Public Criticism, and Grounding Future Arguments," *Public Relations Review*, Summer 1994, p. 153; Eugene H. Fram, S. Prakash Sethi, and Nabauki Namiki, "Newspaper Advocacy Advertising: Molder of Public Opinion?" *USA Today*, July 1993, p. 92; Richard Alan Nelson, "Issues Communication and Advocacy: Contemporary Ethical Challenges," *Public Relations Review*, Fall 1994, p. 226; Marc Rosenberg, "The Power of Advocacy Advertising in Newspapers," *Editor & Publisher*, February 11, 1995, pp. 36, 48; Dennis Sandler and Eugene Seconda, "Point of View: Blurred Boundaries—Where Does Editorial End and Advertising Begin?" *Journal of Advertising Research*, May/June 1993, pp. 73–74.

The insatiable appetite of the news media plus a flood of inquiries from anxious consumers put J&J's PR people under enormous pressure. All communications between the media and the company were channeled through the corporate communications department. All customer, trade, and government communications were coordinated within the company. This way, J&J maintained open, clear, consistent, legal, and credible communications and avoided rumors, political backbiting, and corporate defensiveness.

In the first 48 hours after the news broke, phone calls to Johnson & Johnson and McNeil were incessant. In the basement at McNeil, a bank of phones usually used for sales was staffed by employees who were briefed on what to say, what not to say, and where to refer tough questions.

At the same time, management and employees had to be informed, authorities contacted, and many others notified. J&J and McNeil public relations managers and staff had to plan, coordinate, and supervise this enormous task.

As infrequent as disasters are, there is no more important activity for PR professionals and public information officers than crisis communications management—especially those in highly sensitive fields such as airlines, government agencies, the military, law enforcement, chemical and oil companies, and public utilities.

Since the Tylenol incident, many companies in normally nonsensitive industries have prepared crisis management plans. The manner in which a company handles communications during emergencies or catastrophes will determine to a great extent how the public responds to the news. When corporations have no plans for coping with crisis, the resulting press coverage can be disastrous. Experts on crisis management encourage all companies to follow J&J's example by being open and candid. Withholding information or evading questions inevitably backfires, as many politicians have learned.

Community Involvement

The goal of **community involvement** is to develop a dialog between the company and the community.[22] This is best done by having company officers, management, and employees contribute to the community's social and economic development. Every community offers opportunities for corporate involvement: civic and youth groups, charitable fundraising drives, cultural or recreational activities, and so on. As

"Green" Advertising Takes Root

Over the past decade, the environmental movement has exploded onto the minds of mainstream consumers, a fact not lost on marketers and advertisers. In fact, according to Robert Rehak, a senior VP/creative director of Ogilvy & Mather South in Houston, environmental advertising has already entered a third wave of its development.

Green advertising started in the mid-1980s when issues of the environment muscled their way to the forefront of marketing. Advertisers saw the consumer desire for environmentally safe products and tried to meet the demand as quickly as possible. Not surprisingly, this first wave suffered from rough and poorly conceived marketing efforts. Many advertisers embraced a genuine concern for the environment. But consumers realized that some companies made false claims and exploited the movement, using such nebulous terms as "environmentally friendly" and "green."

Consumers grew wary of environmental appeals, and advertisers reacted by reducing its emphasis. To avoid future trouble, many companies waited for state and federal governments to define terms and provide legal guidelines, which paved the road to a second wave.

In 1992 the Federal Trade Commission established guidelines for green marketing, followed shortly by the state governments. California passed particularly stringent laws, setting definitions for terms like "ozone friendly," "biodegradable," and "recycled." According to the state's court, "California seeks to guard against . . . potentially specious claims or ecological puffery about products with minimal environmental attributes." Texas, Massachusetts, Minnesota, Tennessee, Connecticut, and Washington soon followed the Golden State's lead.

Green marketing has since grown into a specialty industry, supported by two organizations that certify product compliance with environmental standards. Scientific Certification Systems, founded in 1990, verifies claims of recycled content in products. They recently created the environmental report card, which measures a product's total environmental impact. Green Seal, founded in 1994, focuses "on the measure of environmental damage that scientists have found to be most important in certain product categories," says Norman Dean, president. Certification by either organization is not cheap. Scientific Certification Systems charges $3,000 to $5,000 to verify each claim; the environmental report card costs approximately $20,000 to $50,000. Green Seal bills its clients at about $3,000 per claim.

The rigid regulations have left a number of advertisers confused and frustrated, although some feel that environmental claims have already peaked and are on their way out. This is where Robert Rehak believes that we've now entered green advertising's third wave, where environmental concern is now part of the mainstream.

Today's new marketing sensitivity toward the environment and social consciousness focuses on consumer purchasing behavior. Seventy-nine percent of Americans consider themselves environmentalists; 83 percent say they have changed their shopping habits to help protect the environment; and 67 percent say they would be willing to pay 5 to 10 percent more for environmentally friendly products. The data, however, is contradicted by more recent studies that reveal that people in America do not actually buy the products they claim to prefer. Even though studies show a high concern for the environment, the public lacks a behavior consistent with such concerns.

Researchers believe that this attitude-behavior gap exists when the competitive advantage of green products is overcome by factors of price, quality, and convenience. Businesses also find it difficult to inform potential customers about product benefits because of the strict definitions of many environmentally related terms.

But in an increasingly competitive marketplace, firms must ultimately benefit from their green actions. A survey, conducted by Lester D. Lave and H. Scott Mathews, with 54 "environmentally aware" companies revealed that these businesses would take measures to reduce pollution only if it did not involve too much effort or cost.

Even though we see examples of big, environmentally friendly companies such as Cadillac and The Body Shop, consumer behavior must follow consumer attitudes before substantial changes can be made. Once this occurs, we may begin to correct the problems facing the environment and create more markets for green products and services.

Laboratory Applications

1. Imagine you are marketing a new product that sells for $1.25 and is environmentally safe. Would you spend thousands of dollars for a green seal on your impulse product if consumers are ambivalent toward such environmentally safe goods as observed in the first wave? Explain.

2. Imagine that you just made manufacturing changes to your product so that it is now easily recyclable. Would you advertise these changes, knowing the restrictions on the term "recycle"?

we discussed in Chapter 7, a company should ideally adopt one program relevant to its expertise and focus its *mission marketing* activities. The PR department may help set up such programs and publicize them to the community (see Ad Lab 10–A).

Other Public Relations Activities

In addition to planning and reputation management, public relations professionals are often involved in activities like public affairs and lobbying, speechwriting, fundraising and membership drives, creation of publications, and special-events management.

Public Affairs and Lobbying

Organizations often need to deal with elected officials, regulatory and legislative bodies, and various community groups—the realm of **public affairs.** Public affairs usually requires a specialist. Many experts think PR and public affairs should be-

If you believe in tact, diplomacy, the entente cordiale and going through the proper channels, find another charity.

Life is a human right.

To meet demanding operating budgets, nonprofit organizations often devote a significant proportion of their advertising to raising funds. Medecins Sans Frontieres (Doctors Without Borders), an international emergency relief agency in the United Kingdom, ran this emotionally jarring ad to drum up financial support for its worldwide humanitarian aid.

come more integrated to combine the skills and policy expertise of the specialist with the PR person's media and community relations savvy.[23]

Lobbying refers to informing government officials and persuading them to support or thwart administrative action or legislation in the interests of some client. Every organization is affected by the government, so lobbying is big business.

Speechwriting

Since company officials often have to speak at stockholder meetings, conferences, or conventions, PR practitioners often engage in **speechwriting.** They are also frequently responsible for making all the arrangements for speaking opportunities and developing answers for questions company representatives are likely to be asked. Since the PR people may sometimes represent their employers at special events, press conferences, and interviews, they too should be articulate public speakers.

Fundraising and Membership Drives

A public relations person may be responsible for soliciting money for a nonprofit organization or for a cause the company deems worthwhile, such as the United Way or a political action committee (PAC).

Charitable organizations, labor unions, professional societies, trade associations, and other groups rely on membership fees or contributions. The PR specialist must communicate to potential contributors or members the goals of the organization and may integrate promotional tie-ins to publicize the drive or encourage participation. In the process, the company PR people may work closely with the advertising department or agency to create ads promoting the particular cause or to publicize the company's involvement with the cause in product ads.

Publications

Public relations people prepare many of a company's communications materials: news releases and media kits; booklets, leaflets, pamphlets, brochures, manuals, and books; letters, inserts, and enclosures; annual reports; posters, bulletin boards, and exhibits; audiovisual materials; and speeches and position papers. Here again, they may work with the advertising department or agency to produce these materials. The advertising people need to keep the company's overall strategy in mind while trying to help accomplish the particular PR objectives.

Special-Events Management

The sponsorship and management of special events is a rapidly growing field. In fact, it has become such an important topic that we devote the next major section of this chapter to it, following our discussion of PR tools.

Public Relations Tools The communications tools at the PR person's disposal vary widely, from news releases and photos to audiovisual materials and even advertising. We'll discuss some of the more common ones briefly.

How to Write a News Release

The Role of the News Release

The news release is an effective tool for publicizing information for several reasons. It helps to protect the publicist and the client from being misquoted. It permanently records the preferred word usage, specific terms, key phrasing, and unique details.

Its standardized format also speeds up the process. It eliminates debate over how to format the information, highlights the data most needed by the recipient (contact person's name and telephone, date, etc.), and spells out the source and topic of the story.

The news release also simplifies dissemination by providing a form that is easily reproduced and transferred (e-mail, fax, postal mail, etc.) and by assuring that all recipients receive the same message.

Preparing the News Release

The news release follows a format generally accepted throughout the news industry.

____ **Triple-space the text and use wide margins.**

____ **At the top of the page (left or right side) place the name and phone number of your contact person.** If your page is not preprinted with your company's name and address, add it below the contact person. Finally, write FOR IMMEDIATE RELEASE or TO BE RELEASED AFTER [date].

____ **Write a headline that signals the key fact or issue of the story.** For example, TECHCO PRESIDENT SPEAKS TO BAY CITY LIONS CLUB THURSDAY.

____ **Place the most important information first.** The editors may shorten your news release by cutting from the bottom.

    ____ **Lead sentence:** The lead sentence is the most important. Keep it focused strictly on who, what, where, when, why, and how. For example, "Techco President Ralph J. Talk will address the Bay City Lions Club at 8 PM Thursday, September 16, 1999."

    ____ **Body text:** Add directly related support information. "Mr. Talk's speech will be 'Technology in Albania.' Mr. Talk served five years as assistant to the president of the Albania Travel Association."

    ____ **Final text:** Fill in background details. "Mr. Talk was born on April 30, 1956, and is married to Alice Johnson of Bay City. They have two children. Mr. Talk is a board member of the Bay City Little League."

____ **Keep the text as factual, direct, and short as possible.**

____ **Carefully proof your copy.**

Etiquette

____ **Don't call to see whether the editor received your release.** Editors don't like to be pressured. Don't ask for tearsheets. An editor has little time to send you a copy. Don't promise you'll advertise if the item is published; the editor will be offended at the suggestion that news can be bought. If the article is run, send a thank-you letter to the editor.

Mailing List

____ **Prepare a list of local publications.** You may want to group them so that you don't mail out news releases to publications that don't use your type of information. Update your list regularly, because editors change and offices move.

News Releases and Press Kits

A **news release** (or **press release**), the most widely used PR tool, consists of one or more typed sheets of information (usually 8½ by 11 inches) issued to generate publicity or shed light on a subject of interest. News releases cover time-sensitive hard news. Topics may include the announcement of a new product, promotion of an executive, an unusual contest, landing of a major contract, or establishment of a scholarship fund. For pointers in preparing releases, see the Checklist on How to Write a News Release.

A **press kit** (or **media kit**) supports the publicity gained at staged events such as press conferences or open houses. It includes a basic fact sheet of information about the event, a program or schedule of activities, and a list of the participants and their biographical data. The kit also contains a news story about the event for the broadcast media, news and feature stories for the print media, and photos and brochures.

Photos

Photos of events, products in use, new equipment, or newly promoted executives can lend credence or interest to a dull news story. In fact, a photo tells the story faster. Photos should be high quality and need little or no explanation. Typed captions should describe the photo and accurately identify the people shown.

kinko's

Contact: Laura McCormick
805/652-4129
Lauram@kinkos.com

Kinko's, Inc. • World Headquarters
255 West Stanley Avenue
Ventura, California 93002-8060
TEL (805)652-4000

FOR IMMEDIATE RELEASE

KINKO'S, INC., ACQUIRES ELECTRONIC DEMAND PUBLISHING,INC.

Kinko's launches Corporate Document Solutions division
providing total business solutions to large corporate customers

May 7, 1997 -- Kinko's, Inc., today announced the acquisition of Electronic Demand Publishing, Inc. (EDP), a global document management and manufacturing company. The acquisition, the first in Kinko's 27-year history, signals a major commitment by the company toward the integration of digital production and information technologies.

"This acquisition positions Kinko's extremely well in the $200 billion knowledge management market. EDP's unique capabilities, specialized technology and extensive information management experience will enable Kinko's to fully meet the increasing demand from our commercial customers for complex document management and manufacturing needs," said Kinko's Chairperson Paul J. Orfalea. "We are firmly committed to providing total business solutions for our customers' intellectual property needs. This move clearly demonstrates Kinko's aggressive pursuit of high-end document management clients, an important strategic market for the company domestically and globally in the coming decade."

EDP's technologies, products, services and employees will be fully integrated into Kinko's, forming the core of a newly-created, separate Kinko's division named **Corporate Document Solutions**. The new division will be directed out of EDP's headquarters facility in Rochester, NY, and continue operations in the company's current locations in Chicago, Ill., Marlborough, Mass., and Hoofddorp, The Netherlands. John M. Lacagnina, co-founder and chief executive officer of EDP, will lead the operations of the new division.

-- more --

More than 850 Kinko's locations worldwide. For the location nearest you, call 1-800-2-KINKOS or visit our web site at http://www.kinkos.com.

A news release is used to announce the important events of a company, including grand openings, responses to a crisis, or changes of leadership. In this example from Kinko's (www.kinkos.com), the company gives information about a new acquisition. News releases are sent to the press in the hope that the information will be used to generate a story about the event in local or national papers or even on television. Through the PR Newswire, companies can even place their news releases on the Internet.

Feature Articles

Many publications, especially trade journals, run **feature articles** (soft news) about companies, products, or services. They may be written by a PR person, the publication's staff, or a third party (such as a freelance business writer). As an MPR tool, feature articles can give the company or product great credibility. Editors like them because they have no immediate deadline and can be published at the editor's convenience.

Features may be case histories, how-to's (such as how to use the company's product), problem-solving scenarios (how one customer uses the company's product to increase production), or state-of-the-art technology updates. Other formats include roundups of what's happening in a specific industry and editorials (such as a speech or essay by a company executive on a current issue).

Printed Materials

Printed materials are the most popular tools used by public relations professionals.[24] They may be brochures or pamphlets about the company or its products, letters to customers, inserts or enclosures that accompany monthly statements, the *annual report* to stockholders, other reports, or house organs.

A **house organ** is a publication about happenings and policies at the company. An internal house organ is for employees only. External house publications go to company-connected people (customers, stockholders, suppliers, and dealers) or to the public. They may take the form of a newsletter, tabloid-size newspaper, or magazine. Their purpose is to promote goodwill, increase sales, or mold public opinion. A well-produced house organ can do a great deal to motivate employees and appeal to customers. However, writing, printing, and distributing can be expensive—and very time-consuming.

Posters, Exhibits, and Bulletin Boards

Posters can be used internally to stress safety, security, reduction of waste, and courtesy. Externally, they can impart product information, corporate philosophy, or other news of interest to consumers.

Companies use **exhibits** to describe the organization's history, present new products, show how products are made, or explain future plans. Exhibits are often prepared for local fairs, colleges and universities, and trade shows.

Internally, the public relations staff often uses **bulletin boards** to announce new equipment, new products, meetings, promotions, construction plans, and recreation news to employees.

Audiovisual Materials

Slides, films, filmstrips, and videocassettes are all forms of **audiovisual materials** and may be used for training, sales, or public relations. Considered a form of *corporate advertising,* nontheatrical or sponsored films (developed for public relations reasons) are often furnished without charge to movie theaters, organizations, and special groups, particularly schools and colleges. Classic examples include *Why Man Creates,* produced for Kaiser Aluminum, and Mobil Oil's *A Fable,* starring the famous French mime Marcel Marceau.

Many PR departments provide **video news releases (VNRs)**—news or feature stories prepared by a company and offered free to TV stations, which may use the

Presentation Technology

These days sophisticated computing has all but replaced the simple overhead projector and dry erase sketch presentation. The value of a well-planned and visually powerful advertising presentation cannot be overstated. To this end, numerous software packages now offer the tools used to create a fully integrated multimedia display. These programs provide the means to create transparencies, 35mm slides, and even full-motion videos with sound and music.

The most simple package available is Microsoft's PowerPoint® which uses on-screen "cue cards" for step-by-step instructions through the most common presentation scenarios. PowerPoint is programmed to perform over 100 common tasks, including file and object manipulation and editing, and its compatibility with other Microsoft applications (Excel, Word) minimizes the hassle of file conversions from other programs. Its abilities, however, stop short of the full-motion video.

The industry standard for multimedia presentations is Director, by Macromedia®. This package provides the most sophisticated multimedia tools used to show presentations for companies, prospective clients, and seminars. The program allows users to create high-quality digital movies that combine video, animation, still images, and graphics to set the most creative presentation into motion. Presentations can thus be designed to showcase an entire advertising campaign from print and collateral to Web and television.

---

whole video or just segments. Video news releases are somewhat controversial. Critics see them as subtle commercials or even propaganda and object when stations run the stories without disclosing that they came from a public relations firm, not the station's news staff.

Sponsorships and Events

One day not long ago in Minneapolis, Bennett Gibbs sent a couple of his mechanics to lend a hand at an American Lung Association-sponsored bicycle race. Gibbs owned Bennett's Cycle, a small retail shop doing about $200,000 a year in business. He figured that, in addition to helping a good cause, his mechanics could pick up on what bike enthusiasts were saying about his shop and his competitors.

After the race he was surprised when many of the riders started showing up in his store. So Gibbs started to get involved in other events. Today he participates in about 100 races every year and actually sends his staff members to 30 of them. He even has one full-time employee dedicated to hunting down projects that will increase traffic at Bennett's Cycle.

Like most small bike shops, Bennett's initially couldn't afford to participate in many annual projects; it started out small, donating a couple of hundred dollars' worth of mechanics' services or water bottles at each event. Now, with bigger, more costly events, Gibbs makes sure that riders notice Bennett's Cycle's involvement.

For example, at a recent Iron Man ride, a 100-mile event for 5,700 hard-core bike riders, Bennett's opened its doors for registration prior to the event and offered seminars to the participants on fitness and bicycle maintenance. At the ride, the company gave away bags filled with bike accessories and discount coupons on bike tune-ups and helmets. Printed on the bags was an offer for a 20 percent discount on all the merchandise shoppers could fit into their bags when they visited Bennett's Cycle. Within a week 30 participants had come into the store.

After one Iron Man ride, Gibbs discovered that 2,500 of the 5,300 participants had bought goods at Bennett's Cycle. "I support them, and they support us," says Gibbs. That relationship has been good for business. Today, his 16,000-square-foot retail and repair shop produces annual revenues of $3 million.[25]

That's the power of sponsorship when integrated with a good relationship marketing program.

The Growth of Sponsorship

Advertising and public relations people get involved in sponsoring many kinds of special events. In fact, sponsorship may be the fastest-growing form of marketing today. It actually embraces two disciplines: sales promotion and public relations. Some sponsorships are designed to create publicity, others to improve public relations through personal contact and affiliation with a worthy cause, and others to immediately improve the bottom line.

Corporations engage in various types of sponsorships (e.g., events, festivals, and causes) for a multitude of reasons ranging from publicity to genuine good-will. The Internet has become one of the hottest locations for corporate sponsor-ships for both events and content areas on Web pages. One such example is Quicken (quicken.excite.com), a developer of financial management soft-ware, which sponsors the finance section of the Internet search engine Excite.

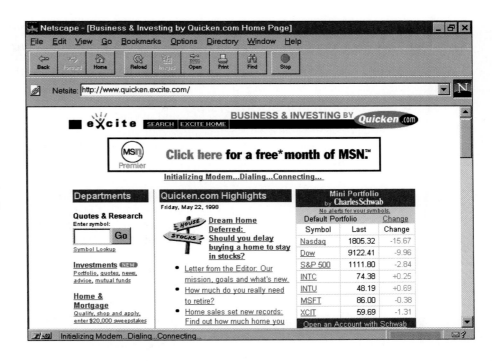

A **sponsorship** is a cash or in-kind fee paid to a property (which may be a sports, entertainment, or nonprofit event or organization) in return for access to the exploitable commercial potential associated with that property.[26] In other words, just as advertisers pay a fee to sponsor a program on radio or TV, they may also sign on to sponsor a bike race, an art show or chamber music festival, a fair or ex-hibition, or the Olympics. The sponsorship fee may be paid in cash or **in kind** (that is, through a donation of goods and services). For instance, if a local TV sta-tion signs on as a sponsor of a 10K run, it will typically pay for some part of its sponsorship with advertising time for the event.

While the sponsored event or organization may be nonprofit, sponsorship is not the same as philanthropy. **Philanthropy** is support of a cause without any com-mercial incentive. Sponsorship (and a related strategy, *cause marketing*) is used to achieve commercial objectives.[27]

Today, companies spend millions of dollars on sponsorships, and the industry is growing very fast. In the United States before 1990, sponsors spent less than a bil-lion dollars per year. In 1996, they spent over $5 billion, an 11 percent growth over the previous year, and experts predicted a 20 percent increase between 1996 and 1997. Worldwide, companies will spend over $17 billion on sponsorships in 1998.[28]

The reasons for this phenomenal growth relate to the economics of marketing we discussed earlier: the escalating costs of traditional advertising media, the frag-mentation of media audiences, the growing diversity in leisure activities, and the ability to reach targeted groups of people economically. Initial growth probably came from the tobacco and alcohol companies, which many governments banned from broadcast advertising. Recent legislation in the United Kingdom, Canada, and the United States threatens to end tobacco sponsorships alto-gether, but their success at sponsoring sports and events has shown the way for mainstream advertisers, who are rapidly picking up the slack.

Today, there is greater media coverage of sponsored events—everything from beach volleyball to grand prix horse shows to Xtreme games to cultural events. This provides a highly desirable venue for advertisers seeking young, upwardly mobile, educated consumers. Likewise, for transnational marketers, there is growing interest in global events like World Cup soccer, the Olympics, and the Super Bowl. Even traditional business-to-business marketers, like Sweden's Ericsson Corp., are making a play for greater brand awareness in the United States by sponsoring the World Championships of Beach Volleyball, which is staged and marketed by Nike.[29]

Benefits of Sponsorship

In the past, for marketers with limited media alternatives (like tobacco and alcohol companies), sponsorship simply offered a means of communication with customers and prospects. Today, the many benefits of sponsorship are well documented and more far-reaching.

Certainly one benefit of sponsorship is that the public approves of it. One study by Roper Starch Worldwide reported that 80 percent of Americans believe corporate sponsorship is an important source of money for professional sports and 74 percent believe sponsorships provide benefits to the cities where events occur.[30] Supporting this view, an economic analysis by the American Coalition for Entertainment and Sports Sponsorship showed that the 100 events it studied pumped over $1.8 billion into local economies.[31] In the Roper Starch study, 74 percent of the people also said government should have little or no influence on which types of companies sponsor professional sports events. This is a far higher approval rating than most companies would get for their advertising programs.

More than almost any other marketing communications tool, sponsorships and events have the ability to involve customers, prospects, and other stakeholders. Naturally, events vary in degree of participation. A person attending a seminar or workshop will have greater involvement with the sponsor than someone attending a sponsored stock-car race.[32] However, events are also highly self-selective of their target audience. Someone who actually attends a stock-car race will most likely have a higher degree of interest than the average person. So marketers that define their audiences tightly can select just those sponsorships that offer the closest fit. Of course marketers that sponsor an event simply because it has a large audience are misusing this tool.[33]

Unlike advertising, sponsorships and events can provide face-to-face access to current and potential customers. Depending on the venue, this access can be relatively clean and uncluttered by competition. Sponsoring a seminar, for instance, creates an opportunity for both customer education and brand involvement. In some cases, it even enables product demonstrations and the opportunity to give a personal sales pitch to multiple prospects at a time when they are open to new information.[34] This is especially good for business-to-business marketers.

A significant benefit is the opportunity to enhance the company's public image or merchandise its positioning through affiliation with an appropriate event.

Also important, but often overlooked, is the impact sponsorship can have on employees. Affiliating with a dynamic event can really boost the morale and pride of the troops in the trenches. And many companies offer attendance at the event (Super Bowl, Olympics, etc.) as an incentive to their sales staff.[35]

Some marketers have discovered that sponsorships can rapidly convert fan loyalty into sales. For example, 70 percent of stock-car racing fans report that they often buy products they see promoted at the racetrack. This is also true for other sports: 58 percent for baseball, 52 percent for tennis, 47 percent for golf. One fan told Greg Penske, president/CEO of Penske Motorsports, how upset he was that NASCAR driver Rusty Wallace had switched from Pontiac to Ford: "I'm only one year into my Pontiac lease and it's costing me $3,000 to get out of it and into a Ford."[36]

Finally, sponsorships can be very cost-efficient. Volvo International believes the media exposure it gets from its $3 million sponsorship of local tennis tournaments is equivalent to $25 million worth of advertising time and space.[37]

Exhibit 10–1
Corporate sponsor bucks

Sports*	$4.6 billion
Entertainment†	$675 million
Festivals/fairs/annual events	$587 million
Causes	$454 million
Arts	$413 million

Sponsorship spending by North American companies is expected to rise 15 percent this year, to $6.8 billion.

* Olympics, motor racing, pro leagues, etc.
† Tours and attractions.
Source: Copyright 1998, *USA Today,* Reprinted with permission.

Drawbacks of Sponsorship

Like all marketing communications tools, sponsorship has some drawbacks. First, it can be very costly, especially when the event is solely sponsored. For this reason, most companies participate in co-sponsored events, which spreads the cost among several participants.

The problem with co-sponsored events is clutter. Some events have so many sponsors that getting one marketer's message through is extremely difficult. Look again at stock-car racing. How many logos do those cars sport?

Finally, evaluating the effectiveness of a particular sponsorship can be tricky at best—especially since it rarely happens in a vacuum. The problem is in separating the effects of a sponsorship from the effects of other concurrent marketing activities. We'll deal with these issues shortly.

Types of Sponsorship

While there are many, many avenues and events available for sponsorship, *USA Today* groups most of them into five categories: sports; entertainment; festivals, fairs, and annual events; causes; and the arts (see Exhibit 10–1).[38]

Sports Marketing

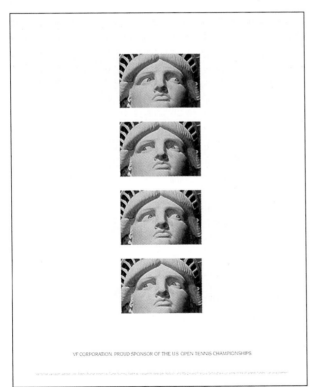

VF CORPORATION. PROUD SPONSOR OF THE U.S. OPEN TENNIS CHAMPIONSHIPS

Sporting events have a long history of corporate sponsorship. Virtually every major sporting event in the United States is subsidized in part by corporate sponsors who wish to have their names associated with the event. This often provides high visibility and publicity for the company. VF Corporation (www.vfcorporation.com), which sponsors the U.S. Open Tennis Championships, is just one such example.

Corporations spend billions of dollars a year on sports marketing. The most popular of these are golf and tennis tournaments, auto racing, and running events.[39] In fact, the vast majority of sponsorship money, over 65 percent, is spent on sports events. This includes everything from the Olympics to motor-car racing to professional athletic leagues. And as we saw from the Bennett Gibbs story, companies don't have to be big multinationals to reap rich rewards from sponsorships—if they do it properly.

By buying the rights to serve Gatorade on the sidelines of professional basketball and football games, that brand has received more credibility than any television ad could provide, at a fraction of the cost. During every game, TV cameras show pros drinking the product in big Gatorade cups. And it's clear they're doing it because they want to, not because their agent told them to.[40]

In hotly contested markets, the giants in their fields fight over sponsorship rights. Nike battles Reebok and Adidas, Coke spars with Pepsi, Kodak runs up against Fuji, Visa struggles against American Express, and AT&T battles it out with both MCI and Sprint. This has certainly contributed to the rising cost of sponsorships. General Motors, for instance, signed an unprecedented $1 billion, eight-year sponsorship deal to assure its exclusivity as the automotive sponsor for the U.S. Olympic Committee through 2008. Its investment in the 1998 Winter Games in Nagano, though, was estimated at only $500,000.[41]

Similarly, in an effort to unseat Adidas as the king of soccer mountain, Nike agreed to pay $120 million over eight years to sponsor the U.S Soccer Federation. That was a tenfold increase over Nike's previous contract and a hundredfold increase over what Adidas had paid when it was the sponsor. But soccer shoes and apparel account for $5 billion in annual sales worldwide, so Nike wants to improve its third-place position in that segment.[42]

In the meantime, Adidas is trying to outflank Nike in the basketball segment by sponsoring high school basketball summer camps. It signed a $10 million promotional deal with teenage prodigy Kobe

Exhibit 10–2

U.S. companies spending more than $10 million on event sponsorship.

$90–$95 million	$20–$25 million
Philip Morris Cos. (includes Philip Morris USA, Kraft General Foods, Miller Brewing)	Quaker Oats
	Chrysler
	Mars
	AT&T
	McDonald's
$85–$90 million	**$15–$20 million**
Anheuser-Busch	Sara Lee
$35–$40 million	Procter & Gamble
RJR Nabisco	American Airlines
Coca-Cola	Visa USA
General Motors	Bausch & Lomb
Eastman Kodak	**$10–$15 million**
$30–$35 million	3M
IBM	Adolph Coors
	Du Pont
$25–$30 million	MasterCard International
PepsiCo	Delta Air Lines

Note: Figures reflect fees paid for sponsorship rights.

Bryant, who was making his NBA debut, and took a major $12 million gamble with another teenager, Tracy McGrady, drafted by Toronto.[43]

Many sports events are strictly local and therefore cost much less while giving the sponsor closer access to attendees and participants. Firms with modest event-marketing budgets, for example, use options ranging from local golf tournaments and tennis matches to surfing contests (see Exhibit 10–2).

An increasingly popular promotion is the company-sponsored sports event. The event can serve as an effective focal point for an IMC campaign if it ties the company to the local community hosting the event as well as to the event's regional or national audience. But without a concerted effort to tie an event to other marketing communications activities, the money spent on sponsorships is generally wasted.[44]

Some companies associate their names with existing events. AT&T, Nike, Mountain Dew, Pringles, Taco Bell, and Volkswagen, for instance, are the "gold" sponsors of ESPN's Winter X Games and regularly renew their sponsorships.[45]

But controversy often swirls around big sports sponsorships. The most controversial practice is **ambush marketing,** a promotional strategy nonsponsors use to capitalize on the popularity or prestige of an event or property by giving the false impression that they are sponsors. Ambush marketing techniques, like buying up all the billboard space around an athletic stadium, are often employed by the competitors of the property's official sponsor. Fuji did this to Kodak in Nagano. One of the reasons this works is because people are often confused about who the official sponsors actually are—again, the problem is clutter. Just because a company advertises on the Olympic broadcast, for instance, does not mean it is an official sponsor. Ambush marketers take advantage of this.[46]

Sports marketing is now a worldwide phenomenon. In Latin America, sponsorship of soccer teams has grown dramatically. In Argentina alone, it rose from $820,000 in 1983 to $12 million in 1996. Out of 20 Argentine soccer teams, 17 now have official sponsors. The largest local sponsor is Quilmes beer, which paid $3 million to have its logo on the shirts of the country's most popular team, the Boca Juniors.[47]

In India, a new intercity cricket league sells sponsorships, in-stadium advertising, merchandising licenses, and TV rights. Teams sport U.S.-style names, like the Bangalore Braves and the Calcutta Tigers.[48]

Entertainment

After sports marketing, the largest area of sponsorship is **entertainment,** which includes things like concert tours, attractions, and theme parks. For instance, numerous attractions at Disneyland and Disney World are sponsored by major corporations such as GE, AT&T, ARCO, Kodak, and Carnation.

Likewise, Nokia, Chevrolet, and Wrangler jeans cosponsor the George Strait Country Music Festival tour. This entertainment tour, in fact, has borrowed an idea from pro sports and introduced its version of *fan fests,* a festival area outside a stadium that offers amusement rides, sponsor displays, and opportunities to tie the brand to a fun and involving "experience." At "Straitland," for instance, fans can also enjoy live music at the Jack Daniels saloon and the Skoal Music dance tent.[49]

In 1997, U.S. companies spent $675 million on this category.

Festivals, Fairs, and Annual Events

In 1997, IEG Network surveyed 1,000 members of the International Association of Fairs and Expositions. The findings revealed a very healthy, growing environment. The average yearly sponsorship increased a whopping 20 percent over the previous four years, with the biggest growth (30 percent) occurring between 1996 and 1997. Moreover, renewal rates averaged 88 percent!

One of the largest annual events in the state of Michigan is the National Cherry Festival in Traverse City. Held every year around the Fourth of July, it boasts an impressive lineup of events and promotional activities that drives both attendance and sponsor visibility. Events include band parades, races, concerts, tournaments, an antiques show, an air show, Native American exhibits, and much more. Among the official sponsors are Ameritech, American Eagle/American Airlines, Pepsi, NorthMed, and Pontiac-GMC.

Similarly, annual events like business-to-business trade shows attract large numbers of sponsors as well as exhibitors because of the economics of being able to talk to prospects and customers in the same place at the same time (see Exhibit 10–2).

Sometimes the competition to sponsor an event even comes from within the same company. The Florida Renaissance Festival, for instance, received calls from three AT&T entities inquiring about sponsorship availabilities. Two calls were from different departments and the third was from one of AT&T's agencies. The festival ultimately signed with the phone company's Hispanic marketing department.[50]

Causes

Sponsorship of charity events and educational institutions is a tried-and-true PR activity that often fits with the IMC strategy of mission marketing. A number of large corporations (including Chevrolet, AT&T, American Airlines, Pepsi, and Kodak) cosponsored the Live Aid concerts, for instance.

The vice president for corporate relations at Philip Morris, the nation's largest event sponsor, refers to mission marketing activities as "enlightened self-interest." People appreciate the fact that the business does not really get anything tangible out of them to put in the bank.[51]

Health care marketers such as hospitals, HMOs, and managed-care companies are increasing their sponsorship activities. Oxford Health Plans, for example, signed up with the Franklin Institute Science Museum to host Cyber Seniors, a free seminar at the Philadelphia museum that teaches older people how to use the Internet.[52]

Arts and Culture

Symphony orchestras, chamber music groups, art museums, and theater companies are always in desperate need of funding. In 1997, sponsors spent $413 million to support the arts—the least funded activity in *USA Today*'s report. This relatively untapped area provides outstanding sponsorship and underwriting opportunities for both national and local firms interested in audiences on the high end of the income scale.

 Unfortunately, this group is likely to be hardest hit by any legislation aimed at ending tobacco sponsorships. For instance, The Gallaher Group, Northern Ireland's largest cigarette manufacturer, regularly donates about a million pounds (U.S. $1.5M) to the Ulster Orchestra, the flagship of the arts in Northern Ireland. In the face of government plans to curtail tobacco advertising and sponsorships, the Association for Business Sponsorship for the Arts gave Gallaher its highest award for outstanding corporate citizenship, citing it for investing in the cultural life of the community in which it operates.[53]

Venue Marketing

Finally, an area not covered by *USA Today*'s report is **venue marketing,** a form of sponsorship that links a sponsor to a physical site such as a stadium, arena, auditorium, or racetrack. In 1997, for instance,

While the most common form of sponsorship involves sporting events, there are many arts and cultural activities that attract widespread corporate support. The audiences of such events tend to be smaller, but they also tend to be more affluent and they provide the sponsor with an association to more upscale, cultural refinement.

A hot form of sponsorship today is venue marketing, in which corporations pay money to associate their name with a sports arena, theater, or civic center. Often, these companies will invest money into desperately needed repairs or improvements to existing facilities, as Qualcomm (www.qualcomm.com) did with San Diego's former Jack Murphy Stadium. The company saved the city $18 million in stadium renovations and received the right to name the venue Qualcomm Stadium for the next 20 years.

the cellular technology company Qualcomm made a good name for itself by offering the city of San Diego $18 million to help it meet its shortfall on construction funds for its football stadium. All Qualcomm wanted was the name changed for 20 years. The city agreed (and said thank you)—and the San Diego Chargers now play at Qualcomm Stadium.

Likewise, Denver has Coors Field, and Charlotte, North Carolina, has Ericsson Stadium. Candlestick Park in San Francisco is now 3Com Park. And Pacific Bell is putting its name on San Francisco's new baseball park. Venue marketing is changing the economics of professional sports. Sponsorships help pay for stadium renovations and upgrades and may assist the home team in defraying the high cost of leasing. Many teams keep the money from their stadium luxury suites, stadium advertising, naming rights, and food and beverage concessions. Under the new economic rules, big stadium revenues are essential to signing big-name players and staying competitive.[54]

Methods of Sponsorship

Companies interested in sponsorship have two choices: buy into an existing event or create their own. Event marketing specialist Paul Stanley predicts that corporate event sponsorships will likely become "sponsownerships," where the sponsor owns and controls the entire event. This would allow more control and would likely be more cost-effective. It would also help the company achieve its marketing objectives.[55]

For most companies, though, it's easier to buy into an existing event, either as the sole sponsor (the Buick Tournament of Champions) or as one of many cosponsors. What's most important is to get a good fit between the sponsor and the event. KFC, for instance, snagged the LeAnn Rimes/Bryan White 85-market concert tour. The artists were approached by several other sponsors, but they signed with KFC because they felt it had the right blend of demographics and family values. KFC has a history of sponsoring bluegrass and gospel, and more recently it sponsored Colorado's Country Jam USA.[56]

In his book *Aftermarketing,* Terry Vavra suggests several guidelines for selecting the right sponsorship opportunity or event. See the Checklist on How to Select Events for Sponsorship.

Measuring Sponsorship Results One of the problems with event sponsorship (as with public relations activities in general) has historically been how to evaluate results. Experts suggest there are really only three ways to do this:

1. Measure changes in awareness or image through pre- and post-sponsorship surveys.

2. Measure spending equivalencies between free media exposure and comparable advertising.

3. Measure changes in sales revenue with a tracking device such as coupons.

Unfortunately, none of these methods covers all the reasons for sponsoring. For example, how do you measure the effect on employee morale? What if the sponsorship is aimed at rewarding current customers or enhancing relationships within the trade? These are important possible objectives, but they are very difficult to measure.

Still, most companies are very concerned about the bottom line and look for a substantial return on investment for their sponsorship dollars. Delta Airlines, for example, is said to require $12 in new revenue for every dollar it spends on sponsorship—a ratio the airline claims to have achieved during its Olympic sponsorship.[57]

The International Events Group (IEG) suggests the following pointers for measuring the value of event sponsorships[58]:

- Have clear goals and narrowly defined objectives.
- Set a measurable goal.
- Measure against a benchmark.
- Do not change other marketing variables during the sponsorship.
- Incorporate an evaluation program into the overall sponsorship and marketing program.
- At the outset establish a budget for measuring results.

Corporate Advertising When a company wants to communicate a PR message and control its content, it may use a form of *corporate advertising*. In an integrated marketing communications program, corporate advertising can set the tone for all of a company's public communications. **Corporate advertising** covers the broad area

327

Corporate advertising is used to communicate a name, presence, or even the philosophy of a company within business circles. These ads do not provide information about a particular product or service, but rather communicate information about the company as a whole. Andersen Consulting (www.ac.com) uses corporate advertising to promote its name and service philosophy to large corporate clients.

of nonproduct advertising, including public relations advertising, institutional advertising, corporate identity advertising, and recruitment advertising.

Public Relations Advertising

To direct a controlled public relations message to one of its important publics, a company uses **public relations advertising.** PR ads may be used to improve the company's relations with labor, government, customers, suppliers, and even voters.

When companies sponsor art events, programs on public television, or charitable activities, they frequently place public relations ads in other media to promote the programs and their sponsorship, enhance their community citizenship, and create public goodwill. If the public relations people don't have advertising experience, they will typically turn to the firm's advertising department or agency for help.

Corporate/Institutional Advertising

In recent years, the term *corporate advertising* has come to denote a particular type of nonproduct advertising aimed at increasing awareness of the company and enhancing its image. The traditional term for this is **institutional advertising.** These ad campaigns may serve a variety of purposes: to report company accomplishments, position the company competitively in the market, reflect a change in corporate personality, shore up stock prices, improve employee morale, or avoid communications problems with agents, dealers, suppliers, or customers (for some excellent examples, see the Portfolio of Corporate Advertising on pages 330–33).

Historically, companies and even professional ad people have questioned, or misunderstood, the effectiveness of corporate advertising. Retailers in particular cling to the idea that institutional advertising, although attractive and nice, "doesn't make the cash register ring." A series of marketing research studies, however, offered dramatic evidence to the contrary. Companies using corporate advertising registered significantly better awareness, familiarity, and overall impression than those using only product advertising. Five corporate advertisers in the study drew higher ratings in every one of 16 characteristics measured, including being known for quality products, having competent management, and paying higher dividends.[59] Ironically, the companies in the study that did no corporate advertising spent far more in total advertising for their products than the corporate advertisers did. Yet, despite the higher expenditures, they scored significantly lower across the board.

David Ogilvy, founder and former creative head of Ogilvy & Mather, is an outspoken advocate of corporate advertising, but he is appalled by some corporate ads. For more on Ogilvy's views, see Ad Lab 10–B.

Responding to such criticisms and to marketplace forces, corporations now design their corporate advertising to achieve specific objectives: develop awareness of the company and its activities, attract investors, improve a tarnished image, attract quality employees, tie together a diverse product line, and take a stand on important public issues. The primary media companies use for corporate advertising are consumer business magazines and network TV.

A variation on corporate advertising is **advocacy advertising.** Companies use it to communicate their views on issues that affect their business (to protect their position in the marketplace), to promote their philosophy, or to make a political or

David Ogilvy Talks about Corporate Advertising

David Ogilvy, founder and former creative director of Ogilvy & Mather, has worked with Shell, Sears, IBM, International Paper, Merrill Lynch, General Dynamics, Standard Oil of New Jersey, and other successful corporations.

According to Ogilvy, big corporations are increasingly under attack from consumer groups, environmentalists, governments, and antitrust prosecutors who try their cases in the newspapers. If a corporation does not take the time to cultivate its reputation, it loses by default.

"If it were possible, it would be better for corporations to rely on public relations (i.e., favorable news stories and editorials) rather than paid advertising. But the media are too niggardly about disseminating favorable information about corporations. That is why an increasing number of public relations directors have come to use paid advertising as their main channel of communication. It is the only one they can control with respect to content, with respect to timing, and with respect to noise level. And it is the only one which enables them to select their own battleground," he says.

"So I guess that corporate advertising is here to stay. Why is most of it a flop?"

First, because corporations don't define the purpose of their corporate campaigns.

Second, because they don't measure the results. In a survey conducted by *The Gallagher Report,* only one in four U.S. corporate advertisers said it measured changes in attitude brought about by its corporate campaigns. "The majority fly blind," says Ogilvy.

Third, because so little is known about what works and what doesn't work. The marketing departments and their agencies know what works in brand advertising, but when it comes to corporate advertising they are amateurs.

Fourth, very few advertising agencies know much about corporate advertising. It is only a small part of their business. "Their creative people know how to write chewing-gum jingles for kids and how to sell beer to blue-collar workers. But corporate advertising requires copywriters who are at home in the world of big business. There aren't many of them," believes Ogilvy.

"I am appalled by the humbug in corporate advertising. The pomposity. The vague generalities and the fatuous platitudes. Corporate advertising should not insult the intelligence of the public."

Unlike product advertising, Ogilvy says, a corporate campaign is the voice of the chief executive and his or her board of directors. It should not be delegated.

What can good corporate advertising hope to achieve? Ogilvy thinks at least one of four objectives:

1. It can build awareness of the company. Opinion Research Corp. states, "The invisibility and remoteness of most companies is the main handicap. People who feel they know a company well are five times more likely to have a highly favorable opinion of the company than those who have little familiarity."

2. Corporate advertising can make a good impression on the financial community, enabling you to raise capital at lower cost—and make more acquisitions.

3. It can motivate your present employees and attract better recruits. "Good public relations begins at home," Ogilvy says. "If your employees understand your policies and feel proud of your company, they will be your best ambassadors."

4. Corporate advertising can influence public opinion on specific issues. Abraham Lincoln said, "With public opinion against it, nothing can succeed. With public opinion on its side, nothing can fail."

"Stop and go is the typical pattern of corporate advertising. What a waste of money. It takes years for corporate advertising to do a job. It doesn't work overnight. Only a few companies have kept it going long enough to achieve measurable results," Ogilvy concludes.

Laboratory Application

Find and discuss a corporate ad that demonstrates what Ogilvy refers to as the humbug in corporate advertising, the pomposity, vague generalities, and fatuous platitudes.

---

social statement. Such ads are frequently referred to as **advertorials** since they are basically editorials paid for by an advertiser.

Corporate advertising can also build a foundation for future sales, traditionally the realm of product advertising. Many advertisers use umbrella campaigns, called **market prep corporate advertising,** to simultaneously communicate messages about the products and the company.

While corporate advertising is an excellent vehicle for promoting the company's desired image, it cannot succeed if the image doesn't fit. If a big high-tech corporation like GE, for example, tried to project a homey, small-town image, it would likely lose credibility.

Corporate Identity Advertising

Companies take pride in their logos and corporate signatures. The graphic designs that identify corporate names and products are valuable assets, and companies take great pains to protect their individuality and ownership. What does a company do when it changes its name, logos, trademarks, or corporate signatures, as when it merges with another company? This is the job of **corporate identity advertising.**

continued on page 335

Corporate Advertising

Companies use public relations activities and various forms of public relations advertising to communicate with a wide constituency. PR people refer to these groups of people as *publics.* Marketing people call them *stakeholders.*

• *As you study the ads in this portfolio, see if you can determine what stakeholders the company was targeting. Then analyze the ad to determine what objective the company was trying to achieve and if they succeeded.*

Corporate advertising is employed by all manner of companies, and it is by no means limited to rigid and conservative business-to-business advertisements. In this example, Augustine Land & Development, Inc. used an upside-down photograph of a marvelously pristine lakefront to reflect its desired image. Even though this is a corporate advertisement, the intention is to stir emotions of awe within the audience.

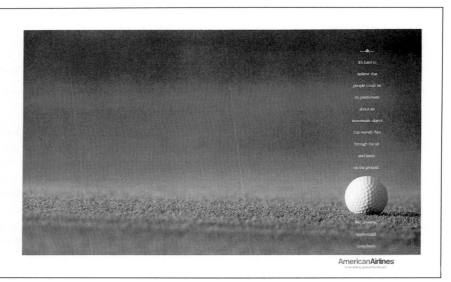

American Airlines (www.amrcorp.com) uses the graceful imagery and metaphors of golf to present itself in this ad. Aside from the company's obvious message of attention to safety, the choice of golf as the vehicle for the concept reflects important characteristics of the target audience: conservative, business-minded travelers.

Corporate ads can reinforce the company name and image through repeat exposures, similar to reinforcing brand image in consumer product ads. Corporate ads are also not limited to business audiences; they may target consumer audiences, too. Mercedes Benz (*www.mercedes-benz.com*) succinctly used its famous logo in just such a manner with this artful Valentine's season ad that ran on the back cover of Wired magazine.

Love

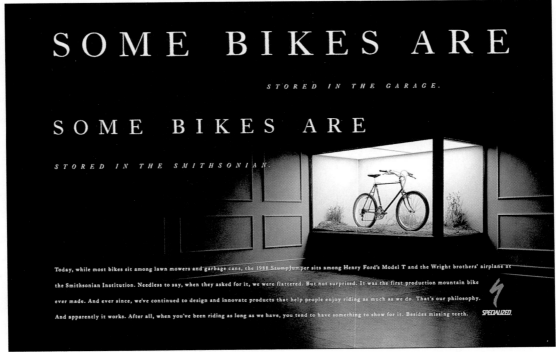

A corporate ad from Specialized Bicycles (*www.specialized.com*) demonstrates the company's positioning strategy. By showcasing its StumpJumper bicycle as a piece of history in the Smithsonian Institution, it establishes credence as a leading bicycle manufacturer.

In this ad, Motorola (*www.mot.com*) employs a strategy similar to Specialized Bicycles by framing the company from a venerable perspective. By featuring a modern cellular phone and the original wireless radio manufactured for the U.S. military, Motorola establishes its credibility within both the business and consumer markets.

As we have seen, using longevity to establish credibility is a common technique in corporate advertising. The strategy cements notions of strength, durability, and reliability into the minds of the audience. Kelly-Springfield (*www.kelly-springfield.com*) provides yet another such example, telling the story of its roots that date back to when the American flag had only 44 stars.

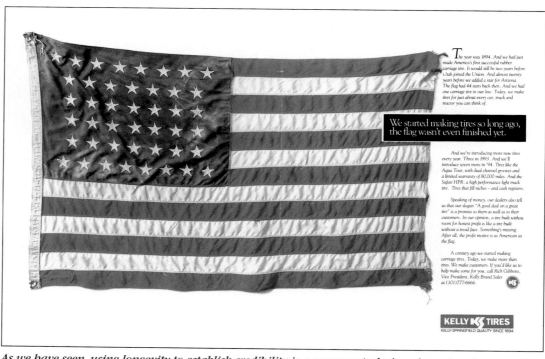

Their grandparents used letters to share a funny story.

Their parents used a wire to confess an intimate thought.

They use a cell phone to reveal a piece of gossip.

What will their kids use to make each other smile?

Translator Radio   Home VCR   Handycam®   Digital Cell Phone   What's next?   **SONY**

This ad for Sony (www.sony.com) focuses on the ever-quickening pace of technological advancement, but it sets a tone of tenderness and hope with the use of these three young girls. Although the correlation is not direct, Sony attaches its brand to such technological innovations through simple name association with the message.

Climate change: a degree of uncertainty

 The debate on climate change has been long, complex and intense. Governments, corporations, scientists, economists and private citizens have all helped to frame this debate. Today, we respectfully submit our message to the officials who are gathered in Kyoto to consider actions to reduce emissions of carbon dioxide and other greenhouse gases.

Mobil shares the widespread concern about the potential impact of these emissions on the global climate. At the same time, we are concerned that mandated emission cutbacks <u>now</u> will produce grave economic consequences for <u>all</u> nations.

Fossil fuels dominate the world's energy picture today. For at least several decades, they will continue to be the major source of the world's energy needs. Government and the private sector should begin <u>now</u> to expand the array of technology options that can help reduce our emission of greenhouse gases in the future.

The mission of the delegates at the Kyoto conference should not be driven by the politics of an artificial deadline, nor should it be constrained by only the several proposals under consideration.

Two factors argue for nations to move prudently. First, there is a high degree of uncertainty over the timing and magnitude of the potential impacts that man-made emissions of greenhouse gases have on climate. Second, the emission-reduction policies being considered carry with them very large economic risks. Objectives and actions to deal with climate change can only be determined as additional knowledge is gained and uncertainties minimized. Nations should commit themselves to meaningful actions, including:

■ Governments should encourage and accelerate cooperative research on climate change while harnessing free markets and voluntary measures to deliver optimum emission reductions while preserving sustained economic growth.
■ To address the scientific uncertainty, governments, universities and industry should form global research partnerships to fill in the knowledge gap, with the goal of achieving a consensus view on critical issues within a defined time frame.
■ During the fact-finding period, governments should encourage and promote voluntary actions by industry and citizens that reduce emissions and use energy wisely. Governments can do much to raise public awareness of the importance of energy conservation.

Mobil is already participating in such efforts. Through cooperative endeavors, we are funding research on technologies that promise greater energy savings or lower greenhouse gas emissions. We are continuing to create energy-saving products, reducing our own emissions and undertaking forestation projects to remove carbon dioxide from the atmosphere.

In proposing these recommendations, we ask the Kyoto delegates to avoid mandates based on uncertain science and to resist agreements that could inflict great economic pain. Take steps to curtail emissions, develop more energy-efficient technologies and improve scientific understanding: These are the challenges nations should lay before their citizens. Collectively, we can accomplish a lot.

The Kyoto delegates should know that there is time to make it right. Advances in climate science can remove a degree of uncertainty from decisions on how best to protect our planet and its inhabitants.

 The energy to make a difference.

http://www.mobil.com/climatechange   ©1997 Mobil Corporation

When companies want to communicate their views on business, philosophical, social, or political issues, they use advocacy advertising. Some advocacy advertising is intended to affect the business climate, while others are aimed at generating goodwill toward a company for its social responsibility. Mobil Oil (www.mobil.com) has a long history of advocacy advertising. It often promotes social and political issues like conservation of energy and the environment through lengthy and informative advertorials.

When companies change their name, logo, or trademark, they use corporate identity ads to communicate the change. These ads are intended to inform other businesses of the new identity, while still retaining the prior reputation. This Imation (www.imation.com) ad ties the company's identity to the technology and reputation of the renowned 3M corporation from which it was spun off.

concluded from page 329

When software publisher Productivity Products International changed its name to Stepstone, Inc., it faced an interesting dilemma. It needed to advertise the change. But in Europe, one of its key markets, a corporate name change implies that a bankrupt business is starting over with a new identity. So rather than announcing its new name in the print media, Stepstone used direct mail targeted at customers, prospects, investors, and the press. The campaign was a success.

More familiar corporate name changes include the switch from American Harvester to Navistar International, the change from Consolidated Foods to Sara Lee Corp., and the creation of Unisys to replace the premerger identities of Burroughs and Sperry.

Recruitment Advertising

Companies use **recruitment advertising** to attract new employees. Most recruitment advertising appears in the classified help-wanted sections of daily newspapers and is placed by the human resources department rather than the advertising department. But many ad agencies now employ recruitment specialists, and some agencies specialize in recruitment advertising.

Chapter **Summary**

Public relations is a process used to manage an organization's relationships with its various publics, including employees, customers, stockholders, competitors, and the general populace. The term *public relations* can describe a concept, a profession, a management function, and a practice. Many PR activities involve media communications. However, unlike product advertising, these communications are not normally sponsored or paid for.

Public relations activities include planning and research, reputation management (publicity and press agentry, crisis management, and community involvement), public affairs and lobbying, speech-writing, fundraising and membership drives, publication preparation, and special-events management.

The tools used in public relations include news releases and press kits, photos, feature articles, all sorts of printed materials, posters and exhibits, and audiovisual materials.

Sponsorship is one of the fastest-growing forms of marketing today. It actually embraces two disciplines: sales promotion and public relations. A sponsorship is a cash or in-kind fee paid to a property (which may be a sports, entertainment, or nonprofit event or organization) in return for access to the exploitable commercial potential of that property. It should not be confused with philanthropy.

Sponsorship offers many benefits. It meets with public approval. It has the ability to involve customers, prospects, and other stakeholders. Most events are highly self-selective of their target audience. Sponsorships and events can provide face-to-face access to current and potential customers. They can enhance the company's public image or reinforce its positioning through affiliation with an appropriate event. And they can boost employee morale.

However, sponsorships can be very costly, and they are also subject to clutter, which reduces their effectiveness.

Types of sponsorships include: sports marketing; entertainment; festivals, fairs, and annual events; causes; the arts; and venue marketing. Sports marketing is by far the largest category, consuming over two-thirds of all sponsorship dollars.

Companies may either buy into an existing event or start their own. One problem with sponsorship is evaluating the results. Three methods include measuring changes in awareness, measuring spending equivalencies with advertising, and measuring changes in sales revenue.

To help create a favorable reputation in the marketplace, companies use various types of corporate advertising, including public relations advertising, institutional advertising, corporate identity advertising, and recruitment advertising.

Important **Terms**

advertorials, *329*	house organ, *319*	public affairs, *316*
advocacy advertising, *328*	in kind, *321*	public relations (PR), *310*
ambush marketing, *324*	institutional advertising, *328*	public relations advertising, *328*
audiovisual materials, *319*	lobbying, *317*	publicity, *313*
bulletin board, *319*	market prep corporate advertising, *329*	publics, *310*
community involvement, *315*	marketing public relations (MPR), *312*	recruitment advertising, *335*
corporate advertising, *327*	news (press) release, *318*	reputation management, *313*
corporate identity advertising, *329*	opinion sampling, *312*	speechwriting, *317*
crisis management, *314*	philanthropy, *321*	sponsorship, *331*
entertainment, *324*	poster, *319*	venue marketing, *325*
exhibit, *319*	press agentry, *313*	video news release, *319*
feature article, *319*	press (media) kit, *318*	

Review **Questions**

1. How does public relations differ from advertising?
2. How is the perspective of advertising practitioners different from that of PR professionals? How is marketing public relations used?
3. What is the role of public relations in relationship marketing and integrated marketing communications?
4. What are some activities used in reputation management?
5. Why is it important to establish a crisis management plan? What types of companies are most likely to need one?
6. What types of sponsorship activities are available to marketers today?
7. Which sponsorships are likely to offer the best return on investment, and how can that be measured?
8. What are the various types of corporate advertising? Describe them.
9. What is the purpose of corporate identity advertising?
10. What is the purpose of recruitment advertising? Why is it under the domain of corporate advertising and public relations?

Exploring the **Internet**

The Internet Exercises for Chapter 10 address the following areas covered in the chapter: public relations firms and corporate advertising (Exercise 1) and PR organizations (Exercise 2).

1. **Public Relations Firms and Corporate Advertising**

    Chapter 9 discussed the difference between traditional advertising agencies and direct marketing or sales promotion firms. Public relations firms, too, differ substantially from ad agencies. And, in some cases, they are stealing corporate advertising duties away from traditional advertising shops. It is important to explore the function of public relations firms. Visit the Web sites for five of the following PR companies and answer the questions that follow.

    - Ballard Communications
      www.ballardcommunications.com
    - Burson-Marsteller **www.bm.com**
    - Creamer Dickson Basford **www.cdbpr.com**
    - Hill & Knowlton **www.hillandknowlton.com**
    - Ketchum Public Relations **www.ketchum.com**
    - Minkus & Dunne Communications
      www.minkus-dunne.com
    - Rowan & Blewitt **www.rowanblewitt.com**
    - S&S Public Relations, Inc. **www.sspr.com**
    - Stanton Communication **www.stantoncomm.com**
    - Stoorza, Ziegaus & Metzger **www.stoorza.com**
    - The Rowland Company **www.rowland.com**

    a. Who is the intended audience of the site?
    b. What are the scope and size of the firm's business?
    c. What is the focus of the firm's work (i.e., consumer, business-to-business, not-for-profit)?
    d. What is your overall impression of the firm and its work? Why?

2. PR Organizations

As you learned in Chapter 10 of *Contemporary Advertising,* perhaps no other marketing communications function plays a more integrated role with advertising than public relations. Now take a moment to explore the world of PR a bit further by visiting the Web sites for the following public relations-related organizations and answer the following questions for each site.

- American Association for Public Opinion Research (AAPOR) **www.aapor.org**
- PR Newswire **www.prnewswire.com**
- Public Relations Society of America (PRSA) **www.prsa.org**

- Public Relations Student Society of America (PRSSA) **www.prssa.org**
  a. What is the organization's purpose?
  b. Who makes up the organization's membership? Its constituency?
  c. What benefit does the organization provide individual members/subscribers? The overall advertising and PR communities?
  d. How important is this organization to the public relations community? Why?

Part Four

Creating Advertisements and Commercials

Once the marketing, advertising, and media strategies are set, the advertiser prepares a creative brief for the people in the creative department. They, in turn, develop a message strategy to guide the conception and production of ads and commercials. Part Four looks at this process in detail, examining how the creative process works, how we apply creativity to ad making, and how advertisers adapt their message strategies to a variety of print and electronic media. ●

Chapter **11** *Creative Strategy and the Creative Process* examines the development of advertising strategies, creative briefs, message strategies, and advertising concepts, including the "big idea." It explains how our preferred style of thinking modifies the creativity within all of us. The chapter presents a simple, flexible, four-step model of the creative process that can be used in all walks of life.

Chapter **12** *Creative Execution: Art and Copy* depicts the complexity of preparing copy and art for a variety of media forms. The discussion includes common copy and art terminology, as well as the typical formats art directors and copywriters use in creating print ads, radio and TV spots, and Web sites.

Chapter **13** *Producing Ads for Print, Electronic, and Digital Media* presents an overview of how advertisers create ads and commercials for the print, broadcast, and digital media. The chapter discusses the techniques and equipment used in the process and the dynamic impact of computerization. It explores the printing process and the advantages and limitations of various print media. It concludes by examining in detail how a print ad and a TV commercial for the Toyota 4Runner were created from initial concept through final production.

A perfect shade, no matter what your bathroom walls are presently wearing.

ROYAL VELVET.
100% Cotton. 1,000% Color.
by *Fieldcrest*

Chapter Eleven

Creative Strategy and the Creative Process

Objective   To show how advertising strategies are translated into creative briefs and message strategies that guide the creative process. The chapter examines the characteristics of great advertising, styles of thinking, the nature of creativity, its importance in advertising, and the role of the agency creative team. We discuss how research serves as the foundation for creative development and planning, and we review common problems and pitfalls faced by members of the creative team.

After studying this chapter, you will be able to:

- Discuss the meaning and the importance of creativity.
- Identify the members of the creative team and their primary responsibilities.
- Tell how to differentiate great advertising from the ordinary.
- Explain the role of the creative brief and its effect on the artistic expression in an ad or commercial.
- Enumerate the principal elements that should be included in a creative brief.
- Explain the purpose of the message strategy and how it differs from the creative strategy.
- Discuss the relevance of thinking styles to creativity.
- Define the four roles in the creative process.
- List several techniques creatives can use to enhance their productivity.

Bob Taylor has designed and assembled guitars for more than two decades. He's an artisan, and his instruments show it. The average Taylor guitar sells for around $2,000, some for as much as $7,000. The company makes some of the best guitars in the world. But its sales volume didn't reflect that fact. • So Taylor and Kurt Lustig, the company's CEO, put in a call to John and John—Vitro and Robertson, that is. John Vitro had been an outstanding art director for some time, and John Robertson was a great copywriter. But when they got together, they were even better. Call it *creative synergy*.

The two Johns had been the principal creative team at Taylor Guitar's previous ad agency but had gone out on their own. Now, not only Taylor Guitar but also AirTouch Cellular (formerly PacTel) and Thermoscan wanted them back. And Chiat/Day, the L.A. agency they had worked for prior to moving to San Diego, wanted them to do some freelance work. • What did these guys have that everybody wanted? • For starters, they were winning more awards than any other creative team around. And not just local medals, but

SOME PEOPLE CAN'T SEE THE FOREST FOR THE TREES. SOME PEOPLE CAN'T SEE THE TREES FOR THE FOREST. WE JUST HEAR GUITAR MUSIC.

SShhh. Listen real closely and you can hear the sound of handcrafted guitars being shaped from special woods. Oddly enough, the sound's coming from El Cajon, California. Write us: 1940 Gillespie Way, El Cajon, CA 92020.

major national honors from the New York Art Director's Club, the One Show, and the leading trade press. Vitro and Robertson never had great notions about owning an agency of their own, but with clients knocking their doors down, there seemed little choice. They formed VitroRobertson, and the clients started coming. • The first meetings with Taylor Guitar were successful. The agency and the client saw eye to eye and seemed to share similar values. Lustig and Taylor both understood marketing and advertising. They wanted advertising that would make a statement about the company and its ideals—not just words and pictures, but something genuine and visceral, yet subtle. • Their marketing problem was clear. In limited circles, people recognized the Taylor guitar as a quality instrument. But to the vast majority of amateur guitar enthusiasts, Taylor was completely unknown. Dealers told Rick Fagan, Taylor's national sales rep, "We know Taylor makes a great guitar, but our customers have never heard of it. Nobody knows the name." Vitro and Robertson had to develop a creative strategy that would put the Taylor name on the tongue of every serious guitarist. If the campaign was successful, these people would *ask* to strum a Taylor when considering their next instrument. • "We had plenty of research data to give them," said Fagan. The Johns looked at the research, listened to the founders, and reviewed guitar publications. Competitors used two general approaches: feature comparisons or celebrity artist endorsements. ● Vitro and Robertson understood the parameters. To increase name recognition, Taylor's ads had to be completely different. They had to stand out, and they had to reflect the quality that goes into every Taylor guitar. Moreover, they had to appeal to the sensibilities of today's musicians. The ads should talk *to* them, not *at* them. ● The creative process began. Vitro-Robertson started playing with ideas, putting them down on paper. "A lot of times, it's based on their gut instinct," says AirTouch/San Diego's marketing manager Mary Bianchetti, "and their gut instinct is usually very good." ● The challenge was to integrate all the concepts into a single *big idea*. If they could accomplish that, they could develop individual messages for a series of ads. Unfortunately, finding the big idea is rarely a simple task. It's usually a frustrating, laborious process of developing an initial stream of concepts—5, 10, 20, whatever it takes. Sifting, sorting, evaluating, throwing them out, and starting over again. It's 90 percent perspiration and 10 percent inspiration. ● Vitro and Robertson plugged away, discarding one concept after another. And then suddenly it came. The big idea was *trees*. Because *wood* comes from trees. ● They would use magnificent photos of trees: trees alone, trees in a forest, trees in the fog. Big photos. Not just a full-page ad but a *spread,* two full pages. And they would use very short, slightly humorous copy lines to speak about wood's subtle relationship with people's lives. In contrast to Taylor's competitors, they would appeal to the sensitive, emotional side of the marketplace *and* make their prospects think. ● They prepared two-page, horizontal layouts of their ideas for Taylor and Lustig to evaluate. One ad featured a lone tree in a barren landscape. The headline read: "In its simplest form, a guitar is just a hollow box made of wood. It's up to you to decide how to fill it." Taylor and Lustig loved it. The proposed campaign passed the review, and the rest is history. ● "The recognition has been fantastic," reports Rick Fagan. "No one mentions the name problem since these ads have appeared. And sales are up." ● The recognition has also been good for VitroRobertson. The Taylor Guitar campaign has won national awards and been applauded in *Advertising Age* and *Adweek.* And when the Magazine Publishers of America invited Ken Mandelbaum, CEO of the New York agency Mandelbaum Mooney Ashley, to choose a favorite for its "I wish I'd done that ad" series, he chose a VitroRobertson ad for Taylor Guitars.[1] ●

The **Creative** Team: The Authors and Encoders of Advertising

In Chapter 1 we discussed the marketing communications process, in which a source encodes a message that is sent through a channel to be decoded by a receiver. The source is multidimensional, comprising a sponsor, an author, and a persona. In advertising, the *encoding* of messages—the conversion of mental concepts into symbols—is the responsibility of the creative team. While the client is the sponsor of the advertising, the creative team is the *author*.

Each member of the creative team plays an essential role. The team's **copywriter** develops the *verbal* message, the copy (words) within the ad spoken by the imaginary persona. The copywriter typically works with an **art director** who is responsible for the *nonverbal* aspect of the message, the design, which determines the visual look and intuitive feel of the ad. Together, they work under the supervision of a **creative director** (typically a former copywriter or art director), who is ultimately responsible for the creative product—the form the final ad takes. As a group, the people who work in the creative department are generally referred to as **creatives,** regardless of their specialty.

In the Taylor Guitar ads, we see how the creative team's taste, talent, and conceptual skill determine an ad's overall character and its ability to communicate.

This chapter focuses on the creative process: where it comes from, how it's developed, and how it relates to a company's marketing and advertising strategy. But to get a proper perspective on creativity, we need to understand the characteristics of great advertising. What is it? Where does it come from?

What Makes **Great** Advertising?

We've all seen ads we love, and we've all seen ads we hate (probably a lot more of the latter). The ads we love we refer to as "great." We don't need to say what we call the other ones, because it's only greatness that we're concerned with here. But what do we really mean when we say an ad is great?

If we look at some of the classic ads in history, we may get a clue: Volkswagen's famous "Think small" ad; DeBeers' "A diamond is forever" line; Clairol's "Does she or doesn't she?" Arpege's "Promise her anything, but give her Arpege;" the Army's "Be all you can be;" and Coca-Cola's "The real thing." What do all these ads and campaigns have in common that have made them univerally considered great?

This is a very important question, since most recent research indicates that "ad liking" has a tremendous impact on "ad success." No wonder, then, that agencies want to author, and advertisers want to sponsor, ads that people like. But is liking all that is required for an ad to be great?

Whether the "ad" is a billboard, a page in a magazine, a TV or radio spot, or a hot new Web site, great ads do have certain commonalities. We can probably lump most of these characteristics into two dimensions of greatness: *audience resonance* and *strategic relevance.*[2]

The Resonance Dimension

To resonate means to echo, reverberate, or vibrate. It also means to boom, ring, or chime. And that's what a great ad does with the audience. It rings their chimes. It echoes in their ears. It reverberates and gives them good vibes. It *resonates.*

Why? Because of the boom factor.

In the Hindu Kush, it's fashionable simply to arrive.

A great ad is one so remarkable, so stunning, or so convincing that it leaves a long-lasting impression of the product or service on the audience. Advertisers typically begin with a headline or visual that quickly grabs attention and resonates with the audience. This ad for Land Rover (www.landrover.com) draws attention with a treacherous hillside and asks the reader to wonder how the truck navigated the perilous terrain, a question answered within the informative copy.

IN ITS SIMPLEST FORM, A GUITAR IS JUST A HOLLOW BOX MADE OF WOOD.

IT'S UP TO YOU TO DECIDE HOW TO FILL IT.

When you think about it, it's amazing that those sweet sounds can come from a wooden box. But quit thinking about it. And play. Write us at 1940 Gillespie Way, El Cajon, CA 92020 for the dealer near you.

Every advertisement should seek to achieve the elusive "boom factor," that essential quality that makes an immediate and lasting impression on the mind of the reader or viewers. Through their Taylor Guitar series, VitroRobinson has become famous for their knack of putting the boom factor into all the ads they create.

When a cannon goes "boom," it gets your attention—right now! The same is true with an ad. It's the surprise element—the "aha," the "gee," or the "wow." But in advertising, it not only gets your attention, it catches your imagination. In this sense it's like great art. It invites you to stop and think about the message. In fact, often it doesn't tell you as much as it invites you to tell yourself.

Look at the Taylor Guitar ad, juxtaposing the image of a box with a musical instrument. They're both made of wood. So they are the same, but oh so different! We recognize this reality at an instinctive level, and we are left to think about it. More important, we associate the profundity of the question with the company that thinks to pose it. We like it, and we respect Taylor for it. The ad resonates.

Other ads may resonate for different reasons. In some of the classic cases we just mentioned, it's simply the headline that resonates—so much so that it becomes a part of our daily lexicon. Other memorable classics include Alka-Seltzer's "Try it, you'll like it" and Wendy's "Where's the beef?"

Recall from Chapter 4 our discussion of consumer motives. *Negatively originated motives,* such as problem avoidance or problem removal, provide the foundation for many great ads. These resonate with the audience by being highly **informational,** by offering relief from some real or perceived problem (FedEx's "When it absolutely, positively has to be there overnight."). Other motives are *positively originated* as consumers seek sensory gratification, intellectual stimulation, or social approval. Here, ads may achieve greatness by being **transformational,** using positive reinforcement to offer a reward ("Be all you can be.").

Ads that appeal to the avoidance or removal of a problem are based on negatively originated motives. This ad for the Minnesota Motorcycle Safety Center encourages motorcyclists to wear safety gear to avoid injury by depicting the highway as a cheese grater. The copy reinforces the ad's visual by referring to the "feel" of the road.

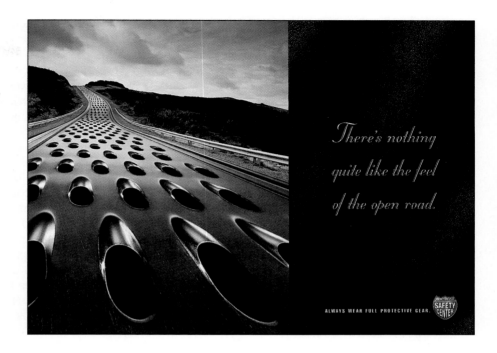

There's nothing quite like the feel of the open road.

ALWAYS WEAR FULL PROTECTIVE GEAR.

Unfortunately, most ads, whether they're informational or transformational, fail to resonate with the audience. Why? Because they fall down in the *execution*. The copy may be uninspiring, the visual may be less than attractive, or the production techniques used may be low quality. From the consumer's point of view, these ads are just a waste of time.

From the advertiser's point of view, ads that don't resonate are a terrible waste of money. In fact, for them the greatness of the advertising is in the "bang per buck." Great ads give their sponsors much more advertising effectiveness per dollar spent. Given this reality, isn't it amazing how much money is invested in ads that are simply not great?

The Relevance Dimension

The second dimension of great advertising is strategic relevance. An ad may get you to think, but what does it get you to think about? A classic example is the old Alka-Seltzer ad "I can't believe I ate the whole thing." It captured everyone's imagination, but it reinforced the wrong feeling—the feeling of the problem (overeating) rather than the solution (Alka-Seltzer). The agency lost the account.

While the text and the visual carry the ad message, behind the creative team's choice of tone, words, and ideas lies an advertising strategy. When the ad is completed, it must be relevant to the sponsor's strategy, or it will fail—even if it resonates with the audience. In other words, it may be great entertainment, but not great advertising. Great advertising always has a strategic mission to fulfill. In fact, strategy is the key to great creative work.

Formulating Advertising **Strategy**: The **Key** to Great Creative

Let's look at the advertising (or creative) strategy Vitro and Robertson developed for Taylor Guitar. Then we'll see how they translated that into a message strategy and a big idea and, finally, into effective ads.

Recall from Chapter 7 that advertising strategy consists of four elements: the *target audience,* the *product concept,* the *communications media,* and the *advertising message.*

What is Taylor Guitar's **target audience?** Taylor's target audience comprises resellers, consumers, and centers of influence. Resellers (or retailers) are Taylor's *primary market*—that's who the company sells to. So Taylor definitely wants them to see its advertising. Since Taylor guitars are handcrafted from the highest-quality materials, they command premium prices. Therefore, the primary target audience also includes a segment of the retailer's customers—serious musical enthusiasts who play acoustic guitars and are willing to spend $2,000 to $5,000 for a superior instrument. Professional guitarists typically circumvent the normal distribution channels, so there was no reason to include them in the target market. However, they might act as *centers of influence* (or *key influentials*), in which case they would be a *secondary target audience* for the advertising.

What is Taylor Guitar's **product concept?** Taylor's acoustic guitars are top-quality, handcrafted musical instruments made from the finest woods available. They are designed and constructed differently from other guitars, which gives them a unique, distinguishable sound quality—a certain ring in the tone—that customers like. In other words, there is something special about a Taylor guitar that makes it worth more.

What **communications media** does Taylor use? The company has a small budget and uses limited media. It advertises in special-interest consumer magazines targeted to well-defined segments of the guitar enthusiast market. The magazines offer high-quality reproduction and color and are read by members of the trade as well as professional musicians. The company also produces high-quality brochures and price lists that detail the instruments' features and construction.

What is Taylor Guitar's **advertising message?** In its simplest terms, message strategy is determined by *what* a company wants to say and *how* it wants to say it. Although Taylor was well-known in the trade for its quality guitars, the word was not filtering down to the larger guitar-buying public. The goal (or *message objective*) was to get prospective customers to ask for the Taylor name when they shopped for a guitar. To accomplish this, the ads had to exude an aura of quality. So the agency creative team chose a message strategy that was simple yet thoughtful, entertaining, credible, and most of all, distinctive.

The agency and client team must understand and agree to these four elements of the advertising strategy—target, product, media, and message—before any creative work begins. In most agencies, the account management group is responsible for developing the advertising strategy. In some agencies, account planners spend a great deal of time researching the market. Then they prepare the advertising strategy with input from, and the approval of, account management. When the strategy-development task is completed, the account people prepare a *creative brief* to communicate the strategy to the creative department.

Writing the Creative Brief (Copy Platform)

With the overall advertising objectives and strategy determined, the account managers (or, often, account planners) write a brief statement of the intended advertising strategy. The **creative brief** serves as the creative team's guide for writing and producing the ad. In some agencies it may be referred to as a *copy platform,* a *work plan,* or a *copy* (or *creative*) *strategy document.* Regardless of the name, it is a simple written statement of the most important issues to consider in the development of the ad or campaign: the who, why, what, where, and when.

- *Who?* Who is the prospect in terms of behavioristic, geographic, demographic, and/or psychographic qualities? What is the typical prospect's personality?
- *Why?* Does the consumer have specific wants or needs the ad should appeal to? Advertisers use two broad categories of appeals. **Rational appeals** are directed at the consumer's practical, functional need for the product or service; **emo-**

Exhibit 11–1
Selected advertising appeals.

Approach / Needs	Selected advertising appeals		
	Rational	**Emotional**	
Self-actualization	Opportunity for more leisure Efficiency in operation or use	Ambition Avoidance of laborious task Curiosity Entertainment	Pleasure of reaction Simplicity Sport/play/ physical activity
Esteem	Dependability in quality Dependability in use Enhancement of earnings Variety of selection	Pride of personal appearance Pride of possession	Style/beauty Taste
Social	Cleanliness Economy in purchase	Cooperation Devotion to others Guilt Humor Home comfort	Romance Sexual attraction Social achievement Social approval Sympathy for others
Safety	Durability Protection of others Safety	Fear Health	Security
Physiological	Rest or sleep	Appetite	Personal comfort

tional appeals target the consumer's psychological, social, or symbolic needs. For a sampling of specific appeals within these categories, see Exhibit 11–1.

- *What?* Does the product have special features to satisfy the consumer's needs? What factors support the product claim? How is the product positioned? What personality or image (of the product or the company) can be or has been created? What perceived strengths or weaknesses need to be dealt with?

- *Where* and *when* will these messages be communicated? Through what medium? What time of year? What area of the country?

- Finally, *what style, approach,* or *tone* will the campaign use? And, generally, what will the copy say?

The creative brief identifies the benefits to be presented to consumers, but it doesn't cover execution. *How* the benefits will be presented is the creative team's job.

Procter & Gamble and Leo Burnett use a simple creative brief with three parts:[3]

1. *An objective statement.* A specific, concise description of what the advertising is supposed to accomplish or what problem it is supposed to solve. The objective statement also includes the name of the brand and a brief, specific description of the target consumer. For example:

   Advertising will convince serious guitar players that the Taylor guitar is a distinctive, high-value instrument and persuade them to consider it the next time they are in the market for an acoustic guitar.

2. *A support statement.* A brief description of the evidence that backs up the product promise; the reason for the benefit. For example:

   Support is that Taylor guitars are handcrafted from the finest woods available, which gives the instrument a distinctive sweet sound.

3. *A tone or brand character statement.* A brief statement of either the advertising's tone or the long-term character of the brand. Tone statements are short-term emotional descriptions of the advertising strategy. Brand character statements are long-term descriptions of the enduring values of the brand—things that give the product brand equity. A tone statement might be phrased:

> The tone of Taylor Guitar advertising should convey beauty, quality, sophistication, and value, with just a touch of good-natured humor.

On the other hand, a brand character statement might be phrased:

> Taylor Guitars—handcrafted from the finest materials to give the sweetest sound.

The delivery of the creative brief to the creative department concludes the process of developing an advertising strategy. It also marks the beginning of the next step: the *advertising creative process,* in which the creative team develops a *message strategy* and begins the search for the *big idea.* After writing the first ad, the copywriter should review the copy platform to see if the ad measures up on the resonance and relevance dimensions. If it doesn't, the team must start again.

Elements of Message Strategy

The creative team is responsible for developing creative ideas for ads, commercials, and campaigns and for executing them. From the information given by the account team (in the creative brief) and any additional research it may perform, the creative team develops the message strategy. This may occur before, during, or after the creative process of searching for the big idea.

The **message strategy** (or **rationale**) is a simple description and explanation of an ad campaign's overall creative approach—what the advertising says, how it says it, and why. The message strategy has three components:

- **Verbal.** Guidelines for what the advertising should say; considerations that affect the choice of words; and the relationship of the copy approach to the medium (or media) that will carry the message.
- **Nonverbal.** Overall nature of the ad's graphics; any visuals that must be used; and the relationship of the graphics to the media in which the ad will appear.
- **Technical.** Preferred execution approach and mechanical outcome, including budget and scheduling limitations (often governed by the media involved); also any **mandatories**—specific requirements for every ad, such as addresses, logos, and slogans.

This print ad for the Mercedes SLK (www.mercedes.com) exemplifies the art of nonverbal communication in advertising. Well-known brands benefit from name or logo identification, which can eliminate entirely the need for copy in an ad such as this. In this example, all of the photo's elements—whether the car is parked or in motion, if the top is up or down, how the car is lit, and of course the skid marks—are decided well in advance, as part of the message strategy.

Because all these elements of the message strategy intertwine, they typically evolve simultaneously. Language affects imagery, and vice versa. However, the verbal elements are the starting point for most advertising campaigns.

The message strategy helps the creative team sell the ad or the campaign concept to the account managers and helps the managers explain and defend the creative work to the client. Of course, the message strategy must conform to the advertising strategy outlined in the creative brief or it will probably be rejected.

In the development of message strategy, certain basic questions need to be answered: How is the market segmented? How will the product be positioned? Who are the best prospects for the product? Is the target audience different from the target market? What is the key consumer benefit? What is the product's (or company's) current image? What is the product's unique advantage?[4] At this point, research data are important. Research helps the creative team answer these questions.

How Creativity **Enhances** Advertising

The powerful use of imagery, copy, and even humor in the Taylor Guitar campaign demonstrates how creativity enhances advertising. But what exactly is creativity or the creative process? What is the role of creativity in advertising? And where does creativity come from?

What Is Creativity?

To create means to originate, to conceive a thing or idea that did not exist before. Typically, though, **creativity** involves combining two or more previously unconnected objects or ideas into something new. As Voltaire said, "Originality is nothing but judicious imitation."

Many people think creativity springs directly from human intuition. But as we'll see in this chapter, the creative process is actually a step-by-step procedure that can be learned and used to generate original ideas.

The Role of Creativity in Advertising

Advertisers often select an agency specifically for its creative style and its reputation for coming up with original concepts. While creativity is important to advertising's basic mission of informing, persuading, and reminding, it is vital to achieving the boom factor.

Creativity Helps Advertising Inform

Advertising's responsibility to inform is greatly enhanced by creativity. Good creative work makes advertising more vivid, and many researchers believe vividness attracts attention, maintains interest, and stimulates consumers' thinking.[5] A common technique is to use plays on words and verbal or visual metaphors, such as "Put a tiger in your tank," "Fly the friendly skies," or "Own a piece of the rock." The metaphor describes one concept in terms of another, helping the reader or viewer learn about the product.[6]

Other creative techniques can also improve an ad's ability to inform. Advertising writers and artists must arrange visual and verbal message components according to a genre of social meaning so that readers or viewers can easily interpret the ad using commonly accepted symbols. For example, aesthetic cues such as lighting, pose of the model, setting, and clothing style can instantly signal viewers nonverbally whether a fashion ad reflects a romantic adventure or a sporting event.[7]

Creativity Helps Advertising Persuade

The ancients created legends and myths about gods and heroes—symbols for humankind's instinctive, primordial longings and fears—to affect human behavior and thought. To motivate people to some action or attitude, advertising copywriters have created new myths and heroes, like the Jolly Green Giant and the Energizer

International ads must appeal to the target audience within a given country; what works in the United States may not work elsewhere. Nike (www.nike.com) tailored this ad specifically for an Australian market, but maintains consistency with its omnipresent Nike "swoosh" and typeface throughout all its markets. However, the word choice of rugby language, the tone, and the spokesperson are all relevant almost exclusively to Australian audiences.

Ad Lab 11–A

The Psychological Impact of Color

National origin or culture can play a role in color preferences. For example, warm colors—red, yellow, and orange—tend to stimulate, excite, and create an active response. People from warmer climes, apparently, are most responsive to these colors. Certain color combinations stimulate ethnic connotations. Metallic golds with reds, for example, are associated with China. Turquoise and beige are associated with the Indian tribes of the American Southwest.

Colors can impart lifestyle preferences. Vivid primary colors (red, blue, yellow) juxtaposed with white stripes exude decisiveness and are often used in sporting events as team colors. Thus, they are associated with a sporting lifestyle.

The colors we experience during the four seasons often serve as guides for combining colors and for guessing the temperaments of individuals who dress themselves or decorate their house in specific seasonal colors. Spring colors such as yellows, greens, and light blues, for example, suggest a fresh, exuberant character. Winter colors such as dark blues, deep violets, and black are associated with cool, chilly attitudes.

Because we usually feel refreshed from sleeping, we associate the colors of the morning—emerald green, raspberry, and pale yellow—with energy. And because the mellow colors of sunset predominate when we're usually home relaxing after work, we may associate sunset colors—peach, turquoise, and red-orange—with relaxation and reflective moods.

Some colors are ambiguous. Violet and leaf-green fall on the line between warm and cool. They can be either, depending on the shade.

Here are some more observations:

■ Red

Symbol of blood and fire. Second to blue as people's favorite color but more versatile, the hottest color with highest "action quotient." Appropriate for soups, frozen foods, and meats. Conveys strong masculine appeal, so is often used for shaving cream containers.

■ Brown

Another masculine color, associated with earth, woods, mellowness, age, warmth, comfort. Used to sell anything, even cosmetics (Revlon's Braggi).

■ Yellow

High impact to catch consumer's eye, particularly when used with black. Good for corn, lemon, or suntan products.

■ Green

Symbol of health and freshness; popular for mint products and soft drinks (7UP).

■ Blue

Coldest color with most appeal; effective for frozen foods (ice impression); if used with lighter tints becomes "sweet" (Yoplait yogurt, Lowenbrau beer, Wondra flour).

■ Black

Conveys sophistication and high-end merchandise, and is used to stimulate purchase of expensive products. Good as background and foil for other colors.

■ Orange

Most "edible" color, especially in brown-tinged shades; evokes autumn and good things to eat.

Laboratory Application

Explain the moods or feelings that are stimulated by two color ads or packages illustrated in this text.

Bunny. A creative story or persona can establish a unique identity for the product in the collective mindset, a key factor in helping a product beat the competition.[8]

Creativity also helps position a product on the top rung of consumers' mental ladders. The Taylor Guitar ads, for example, suggest metaphorically that the personal touch of Taylor's artisans can caress trees into making beautiful music. The higher form of expression creates a grander impression. And when such an impression spreads through the market, the product's perceived value also rises.

To be persuasive, an ad's verbal message must be reinforced by the creative use of nonverbal message elements. Artists govern the use of these elements (color, layout, and illustration, for example) to increase vividness. Research suggests that, in print media, *information graphics* (colorful explanatory charts, tables, and the like) can raise the perception of quality for some readers.[9] Artwork can also stimulate emotions. Color, for example, can often motivate consumers, depending on their cultural background and personal experiences (see Ad Lab 11–A, The Psychological Impact of Color).

Creativity Helps Advertising Remind

Imagine using the same invitation, without any innovation, to ask people to try your product again and again, year after year. Your invitation would become stale very quickly—worse, it would become tiresome. Only creativity can transform your boring reminders into interesting, entertaining advertisements. Nike is proof.

Several commercials in a Nike campaign never mentioned the company name or even spelled it on the screen. The ads told stories. And the only on-screen cue identifying the sponsor was the single, elongated "swoosh" logo inscribed on the final scene. A Nike spokesperson said the ads weren't risky "given the context that the Nike logo is so well known."[10] We are entertained daily by creative ads—for soft drinks, snacks, and cereals—whose primary mission is simply to remind us to indulge again.

Creativity Puts the "Boom" in Advertising

Successful comedy also has a boom factor, the punchline. It's that precise moment when the joke culminates in a clever play on words or turn of meaning, when the audience suddenly gets it and guffaws its approval.

Good punchlines are the result of taking an everyday situation, looking at it creatively, adding some slight or great exaggeration, and then delivering it as a surprise. Great advertising often does the same thing.

When the cute little chihuahua walks up to the man eating a taco, cocks its head, and then suddenly speaks in Spanish (*Yo quiero Taco Bell*), the audience is caught completely off guard and roars with laughter. Boom!

In advertising, though, the boom doesn't always have to be funny. It may come from the sudden understanding of a subtle profundity, as in the case of Taylor Guitars. Or from the gentle emotional tug of a Hallmark Cards commercial. Or the breathtaking beauty of a magnificent nature photograph for Timberland shoes. In a business-to-business situation, it may come from the sudden recognition of how a new high-tech product can improve workplace productivity. In short, the boom factor may come from many sources. But it always requires the application of creativity.

Understanding Creative Thinking

Some people may exhibit more of it than others, but creativity lives within all of us. Human creativity, developed over millions of years, enabled our ancestors to survive. Without creativity we wouldn't have discovered how to harness fire, domesticate animals, irrigate fields, or manufacture tools. As individuals, we use our natural creativity every time we select an outfit to wear, style our hair, contrive an excuse, decorate our home, or cook a meal.

Creativity attracts attention and stimulates interest but also enhances the ability of an ad to inform consumers about a product. In this ad, the creatives working for Jeep (www.jeepunpaved.com) used an allegory of mountain peaks, formed out of the teeth of a Jeep key, to reinforce the company's long-standing image as a premiere manufacturer of 4×4 vehicles. The play on words in the copy drives the point home—use your key to start your Jeep and drive (start) up a mountain.

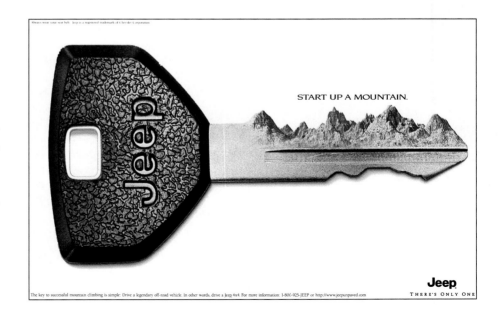

Styles of Thinking

At the turn of the century, the German sociologist Max Weber determined that people think in two ways: an objective, rational, fact-based manner and a qualitative, intuitive, value-based manner. For example, while studying for a test, we use our rational, fact-based style of thinking. But when we buy a car, we call on taste, intuition, and knowledge to make a qualitative value judgment of the car's features, styling, and performance weighed against its price.

In the late 1950s, the theories of convergent and divergent thinking described how one can process concepts by narrowing or expanding one's assortment of ideas.[11] In the late 1970s, researchers discovered that the left side of the brain controls logical functions and the right controls intuitive functions. In the 1980s, social scientists Allen Harrison and Robert Bramson defined five categories of thinking: the synthesist, the idealist, the pragmatist, the analyst, and the realist. They concluded that the analyst and realist fit Max Weber's fact category and the synthesist and idealist fit his value category.[12]

Roger von Oech defined this dichotomy as hard and soft thinking. *Hard thinking* refers to concepts like logic, reason, precision, consistency, work, reality, analysis, and specificity. *Soft thinking* refers to less tangible concepts: metaphor, dream, humor, ambiguity, play, fantasy, hunch. On the hard side, things are right or wrong, black or white. On the soft side, there may be many right answers and many shades of gray.[13]

Also in the 80s, Alessandra, Cathcart, and Wexler developed a model featuring four types of personalities and relationship behaviors based on assertiveness and responsiveness factors (the relater, the socializer, the director, and the thinker).[14] The relater and the socializer exhibit value-based characteristics; the director and the thinker display fact-based traits.

Fact-Based versus Value-Based Thinking

Most theories of thinking fit into two general categories: value-based or fact-based. Let's examine these styles of thinking more closely.

People whose preferred style of thinking is **fact-based** tend to fragment concepts into components and to analyze situations to discover the one best solution. Although fact-based people can be creative, they tend to be linear thinkers and prefer to have facts and figures—hard data—they can analyze and control. They are not comfortable with ambiguous situations. They like logic, structure, and efficiency.[15]

In contrast, **value-based** thinkers make decisions based on intuition, values, and ethical judgments. They are better able to embrace change, conflict, and paradox. This style fundamentally relies on melding concepts together. Value-based thinkers, for example, attempt to integrate the divergent ideas of a group into an arrangement that lets everyone win. They are good at using their imagination to produce a flow of new ideas and synthesizing existing concepts to create something new.[16]

How Styles of Thinking Affect Creativity

If the creative team prefers a value-based thinking style, it tends to produce ads like those in the Taylor Guitar and Nike campaigns—soft, subtle, intuitive, metaphorical. That's fine if the client also prefers that style of thinking.

Nike (www.nike.com) is always finding new and creative ways to remind consumers about the company and the brand. This ad draws attention with a spectacular rock formation in the splendor of a desert color palette that dwarfs the determined pole vaulter. With Nike's "swoosh" logo, the consumer is subtly reminded of the brand as well as the company's message to "just do it."

On the other hand, clients who prefer a fact-based style often seek agencies that produce practical, hard-edged work characterized by simple, straightforward layouts, rational appeals, and lots of data. A fact-based client may even find a value-based campaign to be unsettling.

The Saatchi & Saatchi ad campaign for Hewlett-Packard's laser printers, for example, created a stir internally. The ads simulated interviews. The actors portrayed harried customers, talking about how they didn't have time to think about their printers. "Some people within Hewlett-Packard are somewhat uncomfortable with the direction of the campaign," reported Arlene King, a marketing communications manager for H-P, "because we are a high-tech company and the ads don't focus on any aspect of the technology."[17]

The creative team needs to understand the campaign's target audience. In some market segments (high-tech, for example) customers may tend toward one style of thinking over another. And that could dictate which approach to use.

As we shall see in the next section, the best art directors and copywriters use both styles to accomplish their task. In the creative process, they need to use their imagination (value-based thinking) to develop a variety of concepts. But to select the best alternative and get the job done, they probably have to use the fact-based style.

The Creative **Process**

The **creative process** is the step-by-step procedure used to discover original ideas and reorganize existing concepts in new ways. By following it, people can improve their ability to unearth possibilities, cross-associate concepts, and select winning ideas.

The new generation of advertising creatives will face a world of ever-growing complexity. They must handle the many challenges of integrated marketing communications (IMC) as they help their clients build relationships with highly fragmented target markets. They will need to understand the wide range of new technologies affecting advertising (computer hardware and software, electronic networking, high-definition television, and more). And they will have to learn how to advertise to emerging international markets. To do this, they need a model that handles many situations simply.

Over the years, many notions of the creative process have been proposed. Although most are similar, each format has unique merits. In 1986, Roger von Oech published a four-step creative model used today by many Fortune 100 companies. It offers flexibility for fact-based and value-based thinkers alike. Von Oech describes four distinct, albeit imaginary, roles (Explorer, Artist, Judge, and Warrior) that every art director and copywriter has to take on at some point in the creative process:[18]

1. *The Explorer* searches for new information, paying attention to unusual patterns.
2. *The Artist* experiments and plays with a variety of approaches, looking for an original idea.
3. *The Judge* evaluates the results of experimentation and decides which approach is most practical.
4. *The Warrior* overcomes excuses, idea killers, setbacks, and obstacles to bring a creative concept to realization.

The **Explorer** Role: Gathering Information

Copywriters and art directors thrive on the challenge of creating advertising messages—the encoding process. But first they need the raw materials for ideas: facts, experiences, history, knowledge, feelings.

Taking on the role of the **Explorer,** the creatives examine the information they have. They review the creative brief and the marketing and advertising

Ads may appeal to decision makers either through a fact-based or value-based approach, as demonstrated by this pair of ads from The Red Chip Review *(www.redchip.com) and Royal Life insurance.* The Red Chip Review *takes a fact-based tack, using charts, simple illustrations, straightforward copy with statistics, and a conservative double-column layout. On the other hand, the Royal Life ad appeals to value-based thinkers, relying solely on the subtle and sardonic humor within the visual ad to communicate the message.*

LIKE INSIDER TRADING WITHOUT ALL THAT UNPLEASANT JAIL TIME.

INSIDER TRADING. So tempting, yet so illegal. Still, as an investor, there are probably lots of times you've wished someone had given you the inside scoop on a new stock before you plunked down your money. That's where *The Red Chip Review* comes in. We're an investment publication committed to finding promising small-cap companies long before they show up on Wall Street's radar. We provide the sort of information which, until we came along, was almost impossible to come by. Legally, anyway.

THINK OF us as your small-cap research department. We focus in on roughly 300 companies chosen from 28 industries. And we focus hard. Each report gives you a wealth of information—from a 52-week trading history to calculations of projected value. We also analyze the current status and future prospects of each company, and issue recommendations and ratings. Better yet, this exceptional information is completely unbiased. We

accept no research fees. Our income is from subscription fees alone.

OUR MODEL portfolio would indicate that our approach works. Since inception in August 1993, annual returns have averaged 41%.

YOU CAN subscribe three ways. The full subscription brings you 24 *Red Chip* books a year. You receive a new book about every two weeks, plus biweekly updates of our model portfolio, industry reviews, and news affecting our stocks. There's also *Highlights*, a convenient monthly digest. And a six-week trial subscription, at a special price. No matter which you choose, you'll feel like you suddenly know someone who knows someone on the inside. Because, in fact, you will. For more information and to get a free copy, call the toll-free number below today.

The companies we profile give us access to top management. Sometimes the executive washroom.

SUBSCRIPTION LEVELS

Full Subscription $315
Monthly Digest $129
Trial Subscription $ 60

THE RED CHIP REVIEW
The unbiased word on small-cap stocks.

For a free copy, call 1-800-460-2785 *(7am-5pm PST). Or* http://www.redchip.com

It should not be assumed future results will match past performance. A list of recommendations for the past 12 months is available upon request.

plan; they study the market, the product, and the competition (see RL 11–1, Checklist of Product Marketing Facts for Creatives, in the Reference Library). They may seek additional input from the agency's account managers and from the client side (sales, marketing, product, or research managers).

When John Vitro and John Robertson began work for Taylor Guitar, they first assumed the Explorer role. They spoke with people about the nature of the company, its products, its marketing history, its competitors, and the competitors' styles of advertising. They reviewed all appropriate sources of advertising for acoustic guitars and studied the company's marketing environment.

Develop an Insight Outlook

In advertising, it's important that when creatives play the Explorer role, they get off the beaten path to look in new and uncommon places for information—to discover new ideas and to identify unusual patterns. Vitro and Robertson might have hiked in the wilderness to spark a new idea for Taylor Guitar. Or they could have opened a book on national parks and experienced the same flash.

Von Oech suggests adopting an "insight outlook" (a positive belief that good information is available and that you have the skills to find and use it). This means opening up to the outside world to receive new knowledge. Ideas are everywhere: visit a museum, an art gallery, a hardware store, an airport. The more diverse the sources, the greater your chance of uncovering an original concept.

Know the Objective

If people know what they're looking for, they have a better chance of finding it. Think about the color blue. Now look around you. Note how blue suddenly jumps out at you. If you hadn't been looking for it, you probably wouldn't have noticed it.

Philosopher John Dewey said, "A problem well-stated is a problem half-solved." This is why the creative brief is so important. It helps define what the creatives are looking for. The creatives typically start working on the message strategy during the Explorer stage because it, too, helps them define what they're looking for.

To get their creative juices flowing, most copywriters and art directors maintain an extensive library of advertising award books and trade magazines. Many also keep a *tickler* (or *swipe*) *file* of ads they like that might give them direction.

Brainstorm

As Explorers, the art director and copywriter look first for lots of ideas. One technique is **brainstorming,** a process (conceived by Alex Osborn, the former head of BBDO) in which two or more people get together to generate new ideas. A brainstorming session is often a source of sudden inspirations. To succeed, it must follow a couple of rules: all ideas are above criticism (no idea is "wrong"), and all ideas are written down for later review. The goal is to record any inspiration that comes to mind, a process that psychologists call *free association,* allowing each new idea an opportunity to stimulate another.

Von Oech suggests other techniques for Explorers: leave your own turf (look in outside fields and industries for ideas that could be transferred); shift your focus (pay attention to a variety of information); look at the big picture (stand back and see what it all means); don't overlook the obvious (the best ideas are right in front of your nose); don't be afraid to stray (you might find something you weren't looking for); and stake your claim to new territory (write down any new ideas or they will be lost).

The Explorers' job is to find new information that they can use when they take on the next role: the Artist. To be effective Explorers, they must exercise flexibility, courage, and openness.[19]

The **Artist** Role: Developing and Implementing the Big Idea

The next step in the creative process, playing the Artist's role, is both the toughest and the longest. But it's also the most rewarding. The **Artist** must actually accomplish two major tasks: searching for the big idea and then implementing it.

Task 1: Develop the Big Idea

The first task for Artists is the long, tedious process of reviewing all the pertinent information they gathered when they played the Explorer role, analyzing the problem, and searching for a key verbal or visual concept to communicate what needs to be said. It means creating a mental picture of the ad or commercial before any copy is written or artwork begun.

This step (also called **visualization** or **conceptualization**) is the most important in creating the advertisement. It's where the search for the **big idea**—that flash of insight—takes place. The big idea is a bold, creative initiative that builds on the strategy, joins the product benefit with consumer desire in a fresh involving way, brings the subject to life, and makes the audience stop, look, and listen.[20]

What's the difference between a strategy and a big idea? A strategy describes the direction the message should take. A big idea gives it life. For example, the creative brief discussed earlier for the Taylor Guitar campaign contains a strategic brand character statement:

Taylor Guitars—handcrafted from the finest materials to give the sweetest sound.

Vitro and Robertson could have used that strategy statement as a headline. But it would have been dreadfully dull for an ad aimed at musicians. It lacks what a big idea headline delivers: a set of multiple meanings that create interest, memorability, and, in some cases, drama. Note the long, provocative, slightly poetic, and very witty headline that Vitro and Robertson chose to convey the same strategic concept:

In one pair of hands, a piece of wood can become a living room coffee table.

In another pair of hands, that piece of wood can become the sweetest-sounding guitar.

This is for everyone who has no desire to play the coffee table.

John O'Toole said, "While strategy requires deduction, a big idea requires inspiration."[21] The big idea in advertising is almost invariably expressed through a combination of art and copy. Most ads use a specific word or phrase to connect the text to the visual, like "wood" in the Taylor Guitar ad. Think what this ad would look like without the beautiful photograph of the trees in the background, with just the headline and body copy on an otherwise bare page. It would have saved a lot of money. But it would have greatly reduced the boom factor and lost a lot more money due to low readership.

Transforming a Concept: Do Something to It

Creative ideas come from manipulating and transforming resources. Von Oech points out that when we take on the Artist role, we have to do something to the materials we collected as Explorers to give them value. That means asking lots of questions: What if I added this? Or took that away? Or looked at it backward? Or compared it to something else? The Artist has to change patterns and experiment with various approaches.

Vitro and Robertson had two concepts to begin with: "guitar" and "music." Looking at the guitar, they noted it was made of wood—special wood. So "wood" became a third concept. Thinking about wood led them to "trees." Interesting notion. But now they had to figure out how to turn these four concepts into a "big idea."

At this point in the creative process, a good Artist may employ a variety of strategies for transforming things. Von Oech suggests several techniques for manipulating ideas:[22]

1. *Adapt.* Change contexts. Think what else the product might be besides the obvious. A Campbell's Soup ad showed a steaming bowl of tomato soup with a bold headline underneath: "HEALTH INSURANCE."

2. *Imagine.* Ask what if. Let your imagination fly. Be zany. What if people could do their chores in their sleep? What if animals drank in saloons? Clyde's Bar in Georgetown actually used that idea. The ad showed a beautifully illustrated elephant and donkey dressed in business suits and seated at a table toasting one another. The headline: "Clyde's. The People's Choice."

3. *Reverse.* Look at it backward. Sometimes the opposite of what is expected has great impact and memorability. A cosmetics company ran an ad for its moisturizing cream under the line: "Introduce your husband to a younger woman." A vintage Volkswagen ad used "Ugly is only skin deep."

4. *Connect.* Join two unrelated ideas together. Ask yourself: What ideas can I connect to my concept? A Sunkist billboard showed a saltshaker cap on a lemon. The headline: "S'alternative." To get people to send for its catalog, Royal Caribbean Cruises ran an ad that showed the catalog cover under the simple headline: "Sail by mail."

5. *Compare.* Take one idea and use it to describe another. Ever notice how bankers talk like plumbers? "Flood the market, laundered money, liquid assets, cash flow, take a bath, float a loan." The English language is awash in metaphors because they help people understand. Jack in the Box advertised its onion rings by picturing them on a billboard and inviting motorists to "Drive thru for a ring job." An elegant magazine ad for the Parker Premier fountain pen used this sterling metaphor: "It's wrought from pure silver and writes like pure silk."

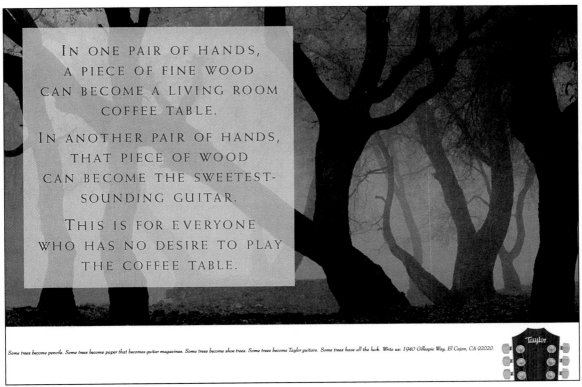

IN ONE PAIR OF HANDS,
A PIECE OF FINE WOOD
CAN BECOME A LIVING ROOM
COFFEE TABLE.

IN ANOTHER PAIR OF HANDS,
THAT PIECE OF WOOD
CAN BECOME THE SWEETEST-
SOUNDING GUITAR.

THIS IS FOR EVERYONE
WHO HAS NO DESIRE TO PLAY
THE COFFEE TABLE.

Some trees become pencils. Some trees become paper that becomes guitar magazines. Some trees become shoe trees. Some trees become Taylor guitars. Some trees have all the luck. Write us: 1940 Gillespie Way, El Cajon, CA 92020.

Taylor Guitar ads run as large, high-quality two-page spreads in guitar magazines. The small print in this reduced reproduction continues the witty approach of the headline: Some trees become pencils. Some trees become paper that becomes guitar magazines. Some trees become shoe trees. Some trees become Taylor guitars. Some trees have all the luck.

6. *Eliminate.* Subtract something. Or break the rules. In advertising, there's little virtue in doing things the way they've always been done. For example, 7UP became famous by advertising what it wasn't ("the Uncola") and succeeded in positioning itself as a refreshing alternative. And FedEx exceeded all the guidelines for length of copy in a TV commercial with its famous fast-talking Mr. Spleen. It also won all the advertising awards that year, and business skyrocketed.

7. *Parody.* Fool around. Have some fun. Tell some jokes—especially when you're under pressure. There is a close relationship between the *ha-ha* experience of humor and the *aha!* experience of creative discovery. Humor stretches our thinking and, used in good taste, makes for some great advertising. A classical radio station ran a newspaper ad: "Handel with care." Fila USA got a rave review from *Advertising Age* for its "bizarre, absolutely hilarious, and totally cool" spot of a praying mantis racing up a leaf stem in Fila sneakers to escape his murderous mate.[23]

Blocks to Creativity

Everybody experiences times when the creative juices just won't flow. There are many causes: information overload, mental or physical fatigue, stress, fear, insecurity. Often, though, the problem is simply the style of thinking being used.

In the Explorer stage, when creatives study reams of marketing data, the facts and figures on sales and market share may put them in a fact-based frame of mind. But to create effectively, they need to shift gears to a value-based style of thinking.

Creatives employ various strategies for transforming ideas into the unique form of advertising. This Tabasco (www.tabasco.com) ad connects two seemingly unrelated ideas together, hot sauce and a tongue piercing, to clearly convey the product concept.

As von Oech says, "Creative thinking requires an attitude that allows you to search for ideas and manipulate your knowledge and experience."[24] Unfortunately, it is sometimes difficult for creatives to make that mental switch instantly. Von Oech recommends some techniques to stimulate integrative thinking. For example: look for the second right answer (there is usually more than one answer to any problem, and the second may be more creative); seek cross-fertilization (TV people could learn a lot from teachers, and vice versa); slay a sacred cow (sacred cows make great steaks); imagine how others would do it (stretch the imagination by role playing); laugh at it (make up jokes about what you're doing); and reverse your viewpoint (open up your thinking and discover things you typically overlook).[25]

George Gier, the creative partner and cofounder of the Leap Partnership, says, "The only thing agencies have left to sell to clients that they can't get anywhere else is creative ideas."[26] Creative blocks can indeed be bad for an agency.

Creative blocking may occur when people in the agency start "thinking like the client," especially if the client is a fact-based thinker. This can also be hazardous to the agency's creative reputation and is one reason agencies sometimes resign accounts over "creative differences." An agency can eliminate a lot of frustration and wasted time and money by evaluating the client's corporate culture, its collective style of thinking, and its creative comfort level in advance.

Creative fatigue sometimes happens when an agency has served an account for a long time and all the fresh ideas have been worked and reworked. It can also happen when a client has rejected a series of concepts; the inspiration is lost and the creatives start trying to force ideas. They suddenly find it hard to shift their style of thinking or to crank up the creative process again. If this becomes chronic, the only solutions may be to appoint an entirely new creative team or resign the account.

Incubating a Concept: Do Nothing to It

When the brain is overloaded with information about a problem, creatives sometimes find it's best to just walk away from it for a while, do something else, and let the unconscious mind mull it over. This approach yields several benefits. First, it puts the problem back into perspective. It also rests the brain, lets the problem incubate in the subconscious, and enables better ideas to percolate to the top. When they return to the task, the creatives frequently discover a whole new set of assumptions.

Parody is often used to modify concepts and to create a humorous appeal to audiences. Here, Honda (www.honda.com) parodied its owner's manual, changing it from an instruction book for operating the car to one for a successful and safe day at the beach. The images are cute and lighthearted, and appeal to the beach-goers in the market.

Task 2: Implement the Big Idea

Once the creatives latch onto the big idea, they have to focus on how to implement it. When Vitro and Robertson suddenly thought "trees" and connected that idea to "guitars" and "music," they then had to translate that concept into a tangible ad. This is where the real art of advertising comes in—writing the exact words, designing the precise layout. To have a sense of how advertising creatives do that, we need to understand what *art* is in advertising, how artistic elements and tools are selected and used, and the difference between good art and bad art.

In advertising, art shapes the message into a complete communication that appeals to the senses as well as the mind. So while **art direction** refers to the act or process of managing the visual presentation of the commercial or ad, the term **art** actually refers to the whole presentation—visual, verbal, and aural. For example, the artful selection of words not only communicates information but also stimulates positive feelings for the product. An artfully designed typeface not only makes reading easier, it also evokes a mood. By creatively arranging format elements—surrounding the text with lines, boxes, and colors, and relating them to one another in proportion—the art director can further enhance the ad's message. Art also shapes the style of photography and illustration. An intimate style uses soft focus and close views, a documentary style portrays the scene without pictorial enhancements, and a dramatic style features unusual angles or blurred action images.

In short, if *copy* is the verbal language of an ad, *art* is the body language. TV uses both sight and sound to involve viewers. Radio commercials use sound to create *word pictures* in the minds of listeners. The particular blend of writing, visuals, and sounds makes up an ad's expressive character. So while the quality may vary, every ad uses art.

In advertising, balance, proportion, and movement are guides for uniting words, images, type, sounds, and colors into a single communication so they relate to and enhance each other. We'll discuss more of these concepts in Chapter 12: Creative Execution: Art and Copy.

The Creative Pyramid: A Guide to Formulating Copy and Art

Depending on the product category and the situation, the **creative pyramid** is a model that can help the creative team convert the advertising strategy and the big idea into the actual physical ad or commercial.

Ethical Issue

Does Sex Appeal?

It's one of the more provocative billboard ads in recent memory—a photograph of a woman who seems to be naked, lips slightly parted, and a simple slogan: "Body shots." Another ad features a very muscular man and carries the same implication—that this tequila is more than just a drink. It's an aphrodisiac. Nothing about the ad says this explicitly, but suggestion is more important than directness when it comes to advertising.

While advertisers frequently use the power of suggestion to imply sex and allow the viewer to fill in as much as their brain can imagine, some consumer activist groups object to such implied tension (something as simple as two people embracing with their lips close together can hint at sex) or anything else which they consider obscene or indecent.

Advertisers who run such risqué ads must contend with these critics and the legal distinction between obscenity and indecency. Obscenity is illegal and carries criminal charges, while indecency doesn't. Obscenity involves three conditions—it appeals to prurient interests, it is patently offensive, and it lacks any redeeming value. In general, most ads with sexual appeals don't meet the criteria for obscenity.

However, some ads might seem indecent, since indecency is in the eye of the beholder. If enough people believe sexually oriented material is indecent, the community standards reflect this belief. In such a case, citizen pressure groups and media organizations enforce community standards by disallowing advertising that offends those standards.

As an example, take Calvin Klein's infamous campaign that featured seemingly underage youths in provocative positions (see Chapter 2). The suggestion of pederasty sparked enough controversy to force Klein to pull the ads. However, the resulting "scandal" generated millions of dollars' worth of free publicity for his flagging product. Was this exploitation or just a savvy marketing tactic? Was it obscene or indecent? Some people actually appreciated the ads for touching on the same realities that the film *Kids* did. Others found them patently offensive, even though Klein was never officially charged with any legal wrongdoing. While it's hard to believe that Klein would not be able to predict the ensuing outrage over the campaign, the ads did generate enormous publicity. Other advertisers, too, find it increasingly difficult to toe the line between exploitation and simple sex appeal.

There is no easy solution to this dilemma, especially since research shows that sexual appeals can be effective when sexuality relates to the product. However, when it doesn't, it can distract audiences from the main message and severely demean the advertiser in the consumer's eyes. Another consideration is how sex in advertising creates *externalities*—social costs to consumers outside the target market, such as children who might be indirectly affected.

Advertisers must examine, on a case-by-case basis, at what point sexual appeals become unethical and therefore counterproductive. Diet Coke, for example, raised a few eyebrows when its commercial showed women gathering at an office window to ogle a shirtless male construction worker taking a Diet Coke break. Since women comprise 65 percent of all soft-drink buyers, it's no surprise that Nancy Gibson, worldwide brand manager for Diet

Based on the cognitive theory of how people learn new information, it uses a simple five-step structure (see Exhibit 11–2).

The purpose of much advertising copy and design is to either persuade prospective customers to take some action to satisfy a need or want or to remind them to take the action again. In a new-product situation, people may first need to be made aware of the problem or, if the problem is obvious, that a solution exists. For a frequently purchased product, the advertiser simply has to remind people of the solution close to the purchase occasion. In either case, the advertiser's first job is to get the prospect's *attention*. The second step is to stimulate the prospect's *interest*—in either the message or the product itself. Next, it's important, especially for new products, to build *credibility* for the product claims. Then the ad can focus on gen-

Exhibit 11–2

The creative pyramid offers an excellent simple guide for establishing copy-writing objectives.

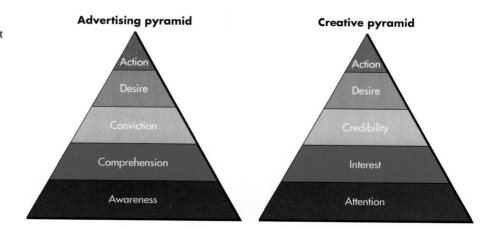

Advertising pyramid

Action
Desire
Conviction
Comprehension
Awareness

Creative pyramid

Action
Desire
Credibility
Interest
Attention

Coke, says, "Usually, we have made absolutely sure the female appeal is there."

Advertising Age columnist Bob Garfield suggests the Diet Coke ad offers women "psychic benefits" by taking a particular point of view, but it does so at the expense of men. However, not all men agree with him. Women in the Diet Coke focus groups loved the ad, and the younger men in the study also saw it favorably. In another case, an executive on the Valvoline advertising account justified using "girlie calendars" for mechanics by noting, "It may offend some groups—but they aren't your customers."

Cultural norms strongly influence our ethics, and consumer activist groups have successfully changed some of these norms. Before World War II, advertisers portrayed women as managers of the household, but afterward they treated women more as objects of desire. Ads also told women that housework was the way to please a man or get one. Feminist leader Betty Friedan notes that the advertising industry's move away from selling "this endless sacrificial housework" is "real progress" for women.

To address changing cultural views, ad agencies have sought the advice of women's advocates. Most feminists, for example, don't object to sexual appeals in advertising if the woman is in control of her sexuality rather than being shown passively or as a victim. Some agencies now retain feminist consultants to review ads to ensure they are not offensive; not using such consultants can sting an agency. After getting burned by adverse publicity over a 1991 Swedish Bikini Team campaign for its Old Milwaukee beer, Stroh Brewery now stays away from anything that could be remotely sexist. The campaign supposedly parodied both old beer ads and the brand's own old ads, but consumers didn't find the parody funny.

Nonetheless, it remains difficult for industry or government policymakers to know how to treat ad sex in a way satisfactory to everyone—or perhaps anyone.

Questions

1. How would you explain the "redeeming value" of sexual appeals in advertising?

2. If ad sex is considered okay by audiences that are directly targeted, what responsibility does the advertiser have for any effect on indirect targets, such as children? How can advertisers protect themselves from this problem?

Sources: Adrienne Ward Fawcett, "Friedan Sees Real Progress in Woman's Ads," *Advertising Age Special Report: Marketing to Women,* October 4, 1993, pp. S-1, S-2; John S. Ford and Michael S. LaTour, "Different Reactions to Female Role Portrayals in Advertising," *Journal of Advertising Research,* September/October 1993, p. 43; Stephen J. Gould, "Sexuality and Ethics in Advertising: A Research Agenda and Policy Guideline Perspective," *Journal of Advertising,* September 1994, pp. 73–79; Michael S. LaTour and Tony L. Henthorne, "Ethical Judgments of Sexual Appeals in Print Adver-tising," *Journal of Advertising,* September 1994, pp. 80–90; N. Craig Smith and John A. Quelch, "Ethical Issues in Researching and Targeting Consumers," *Ethics in Marketing* (Homewood, IL: Richard D. Irwin, 1993), pp. 190–92; Daniel Riffe, Patricia C. Place, and Charles M. Mayo, "Game Time, Soap Time and Prime Time TV Ads: Treatment of Women in Sunday Football and Rest-of-Week Advertising," *Journalism Quarterly,* Summer 1993, pp. 437–46; Delia M. Rios, Newhouse News Service, "Provocative Coke Ads Engender Delight, Disgust," *San Diego Union-Tribune,* January 31, 1994, p. E-4; Ira Teinowitz, "Days of 'Beer and Babes' Running Out," *Advertising Age Special Report: Marketing to Women,* October 4, 1993, p. S-8.

erating *desire* and finally on stimulating *action*. These five elements should be addressed in just about every ad or commercial. We'll deal with each step briefly.

Attention

An ad or commercial is a *stimulus*. It must break through consumers' physiological screens to create the kind of attention that leads to perception. *Attention,* therefore, is the first objective of any ad and the fundamental building block in the creative pyramid. The Artist may spend as much time and energy figuring out how to express the big idea in an interesting, attention-getting way as searching for the big idea itself.

The attention step is critically important to triggering the ad's boom factor. Print ads often use the headline as the major attention-getting device. The copywriter's goal is to write a headline that expresses the big idea with verve. Usually designed to appear in the largest and boldest type in the ad, the headline is often the strongest focal point conceptually as well as visually. Many other devices also help gain attention. In print media, they may include dynamic visuals, unusual layout, vibrant color, or dominant ad size. In electronic media, they may include special sound effects, music, animation, or unusual visual techniques.

Some factors are beyond the creatives' control. The budget may determine the size of the ad or length of the commercial. And that may influence how well or quickly it penetrates consumers' screens. Similarly, a TV spot's position in a cluster of commercials between shows or an ad's position in a publication may determine who sees it.

The attention-getting device should create drama, power, impact, and intensity. It must also be appropriate, relating to the product, the tone of the ad, and the needs or interests of the intended audience. This is especially true in business-to-business advertising, where rational appeals and fact-based thinking dominate.

This ad for Lexus (www.lexus.com) exemplifies the five steps of the creative pyramid. The ad gains attention with its stark imagery and gothic typeface, then retains interest with the larger poetic text drawn from Ray Bradbury. Credibility is established with the secondary, smaller copy, which enumerates technical details. The tagline, "Faster. Sleeker. Meaner.", combines with the image on the facing page to enable the reader to visualize driving and creates a sense of desire. The price and contact information at the bottom of the page serves as a subtle call to action.

Headlines that promise something but fail to deliver in a credible manner won't make a sale; in fact, they may alienate a potential customer. Ads that use racy headlines or nude figures unrelated to the product often lose sales because prospects can't purchase the item that first attracted their attention.

Interest

The second step in the creative pyramid, *interest,* is also extremely important. It carries the prospective customer—now paying attention—to the body of the ad. The ad must keep the prospect excited or involved as the information becomes more detailed. To do this, the copywriter may answer a question asked in the attention step or add facts that relate to the headline. To maintain audience interest, the tone and language should be compatible with the target market's attitude. As we discussed earlier, the successful ad *resonates.*

The writer and designer must lead prospects from one step to the next. Research shows that people read what interests them and ignore what doesn't, so the writer must maintain prospects' interest at all times.[27] One way to do so is to sneak through prospects' psychological screens by talking about their problems, their needs, and how the product or service will answer them. Copywriters use the word *you* a lot.

There are many effective ways to stimulate interest: a dramatic situation, a story, cartoons, charts. In radio, copywriters use sound effects or catchy dialog. Television frequently uses quick cuts to maintain interest. We discuss some of these techniques in the chapter on advertising production.

Credibility

The third step in the creative pyramid is to establish *credibility* for the product or service. Customers today are sophisticated and skeptical. They want claims to be backed up by facts. Comparison ads can build credibility, but they must be relevant to customers' needs—and fair.

Well-known presenters may lend credibility to commercials. For example, Candice Bergen effectively represents Sprint with her personable, believable, down-to-earth style.

Advertisers often show independent test results to substantiate product claims. To work, such "proofs" must be valid, not just statistical manipulation. Advertisers and agencies must remember that many consumers have extensive product knowledge, even in specialized areas.

Desire

In the *desire* step, the writer encourages prospects to picture themselves enjoying the benefits of the product or service. Essentially, they are invited to visualize.

In print ads, copywriters initiate visualization by using phrases like "Picture yourself" or "Imagine." In TV, the main character pulls a sparkling clean T-shirt from the washer, smiles, and says "Yeah!" In radio, the announcer says, "You'll look your best."

The desire step hints at the possibilities and lets the consumer's mind take over. If prospects feel they're being led by the nose, they may feel insulted, resent the ad, and lose interest in the product. In some cases, writers maintain this delicate balance by having a secondary character agree with the main character and prattle off a few more product benefits. The secondary character allows the main character, the one audiences relate to best, to retain integrity.

In print advertising, the desire step is one of the most difficult to write (which may be why some copywriters omit it). In TV, the desire step can simply show the implied consumer experiencing the benefit of the product. Ever notice how cosmetics advertisers almost invariably show the happy life that awaits their product users?

Action

The final step up the creative pyramid is *action*. The purpose is to motivate people to do something—send in a coupon, call the number on the screen, visit the store—or at least to agree with the advertiser.

This block of the pyramid reaches the smallest audience but those with the most to gain from the product's utility. So the last step is often the easiest. If the copy is clear about what readers need to do and asks or even nudges them to act, chances are they will (see Ad Lab 11–B: Applying the Creative Pyramid to Advertising).

The call to action may be explicit—"Call for more information"—or implicit— "Fly the friendly skies." Designers cue customers to take action by placing dotted lines around coupons to suggest cutting and by highlighting the company's telephone number with large type or a bright color.

With today's technology, it's important to not only ask people to act but facilitate their action, through either a toll-free phone number or an attractive Web site. In relationship marketing, the ad basically enables people to select themselves as

Applying the Creative Pyramid to Advertising

Notice how the five objectives of advertising copy apply to the ad shown here.

Attention This headline snares our attention with its large, calligraphy-like type. It tugs at our mental files with humor—dieters diving for a Twinkie before it hits the floor. We suddenly spot the fishing lure and—boom—we take the hook, swallowing the metaphoric cue to a second mental image: hungry fish with open mouths and thrashing tails rushing to hit the lure.

Interest The first line of the body copy suggests that fishing enthusiasts picture a subject of particular interest to them, a starving largemouth hitting the lure with exceptional vigor.

Credibility The credibility step casts specifics, the product name and two features ("one of a kind wiggle" and "irresistible to lunker bass").

Desire The last line begins with the assertion that the reader is on a diet. This lifestyle technique symbolically applies to the target market, identifying them as fishing enthusiasts who suffer from lunker bass deprivation and are in need of the Shore's River Shiner lure to blow their fishless diet!

Action If the reader has taken the bait, then all he or she needs to know is the identity of the product (represented here by the logo) because we assume that it's sold at the closest sporting-goods store or tackle shop.

Laboratory Applications

1. Find an ad that exhibits the five elements of the creative pyramid. *(A print ad will be the easiest to find and talk about, but radio and TV commercials also feature the five elements. Beware: The desire step may be hard to find.)*

2. Why do so many good ads lack one or more of the five elements listed here? How do they overcome the omission?

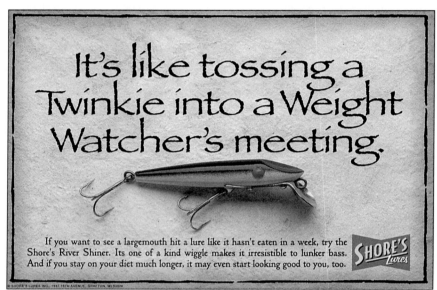

being interested in a relationship. Then the marketer can use more efficient one-on-one media to develop the relationship.

The **Judge** Role: Decision Time

The next role in the creative process is the **Judge.** This is when the creatives evaluate the practicality of their big ideas and decide whether to implement, modify, or discard them.[28]

The Judge's role is delicate. On the one hand, the creatives must be self-critical enough to ensure that when it's time to play the Warrior they will have an idea worth fighting for. On the other hand, they need to avoid stifling the imagination of their internal Artist. It's easier to be critical than to explore, conceptualize, or defend. But the Judge's purpose is to help produce good ideas, not to revel in criticism. Von Oech suggests focusing first on the positive, interesting aspects of a new idea. The negatives will come soon enough.

When playing the Judge, the creatives need to ask certain questions: Is this idea an aha! or an uh-oh? (What was my initial reaction?) What's wrong with this idea? (And what's right with it?) What if it fails? (Is it worth the risk?) What is my cultural bias? (Does the audience have the same bias?) What's clouding my thinking? (Am I wearing blinders?)

Risk is an important consideration. When the advertising scores a hit, everybody's happy, sales go up, people get raises, and occasionally there's even positive publicity. But when a campaign flops, all hell breaks loose, especially on high-profile accounts. Sales may flatten or even decline, competitors gain a couple of points in market share, distributors and dealers complain, and the phone rings incessantly

Ad Lab 11–C
The Creative Gymnasium

The Explorer

Here's a visual calisthenics exercise for your Explorer. Find a perfect star in the pattern:

The Judge and the Warrior

As a creative person, what verdict would your Judge give ads that feature creative gymnastics like the ones below? How would your Warrior present these two ads to a client for approval?

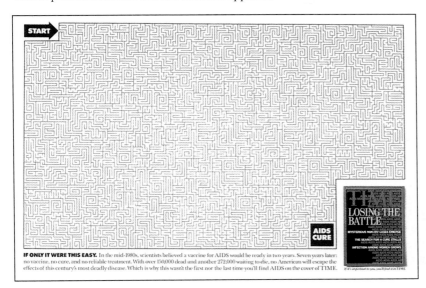

The Artist

The artist uses humor and absurd what-if questions to mentally loosen up. Try these warm-up techniques:

1. Think up a new set of conversion factors:
   10^{12} microphones = 1 megaphone
   10^{12} pins = 1 terrapin
   $3\frac{1}{3}$ tridents = 1 decadent
   4 seminaries = 1 binary
   10^{21} piccolos = 1 gigolo
   1 milli-Helen = the amount of beauty required
   to launch 1 ship

2. Another mental muscle stretcher is to change the context of an idea. You can turn the roman numeral for 9 into a 6 by adding only a single line:

   IX

   Some people put a horizontal line through the center, turn it upside down, and then cover the bottom. This gives you a roman numeral VI. A more artistic solution might be to put "S" in front of the IX to create "SIX." What we've done here is take the IX out of the context of Roman numerals and put it into the context of "Arabic numerals spelled out in English."
   Another right answer might be to add the line "6" after the IX. Then you get IX6, or one times six.

Laboratory Applications

1. Attempt to solve the exercises above. Explain your choices.
2. Create a metaphor for each of these paired concepts:
   a. Boxing + Water.
   b. Magnet + Library.
   c. Rainbow + Clock.

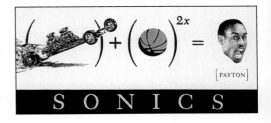

with calls from disgruntled client executives. Perhaps worst of all is the ridicule in the trade. Advertising pundits say nasty things about the ads in TV interviews; reviewers write articles in *Ad Age* and *Adweek;* and even the big daily papers get in their licks. In one article, for instance, *The Wall Street Journal* panned the campaigns of four high-profile advertisers: Diet Coke, Subaru, AT&T, and American Express.[29] This is not good for either the agency's stock or the client's. And it's how agencies get replaced. So the Judge's role is vital.

If the Artist-as-Judge does a good job, the next role in the creative process, the Warrior, is easier to perform.

The **Warrior** Role: Overcoming Setbacks and Obstacles

In the final step of the creative process, the **Warrior** wins territory for big new ideas in a world resistant to change. The Warrior carries the concept into action. This means getting the big idea approved, produced, and placed in the media. Von Oech says Warriors must be bold, sharpen their sword (skills), strengthen their shield (examine criticism in advance), follow through (overcome obstacles), use their energy wisely, be persistent, savor their victories, and learn from defeat.[30]

To get the big idea approved, the Warrior has to battle people within the agency and often the client, too. So part of the Warrior's role is turning the agency account team into co-warriors for the presentation to the client. At this point, it's imperative that the creatives finish their message strategy document to give their rationale for the copy, art, and production elements in the concept they're trying to sell. And the message strategy had better mesh with the creative brief, or the valiant Warrior will likely face a wide moat with no drawbridge (see Ad Lab 11–C: The Creative Gymnasium).

Part of the Warrior's task may be to help the account managers present the campaign to the client. Bruce Bendinger says, "How well you *sell* ideas is as important as how *good* those ideas are." To give a presentation maximum selling power, he suggests five key components:[31]

1. *Strategic precision.* The selling idea must be on strategy. The presenting team must be able to prove it, and the strategy should be discussed first, before the big selling idea is presented.

2. *Savvy psychology.* The presentation, like the advertising, should be receiver-driven. The idea has to meet the client's needs.

3. *Slick presentation.* The presentation must be prepared and rehearsed; it should use great visuals and emotional appeals. A good presentation makes people want to do the campaign.

4. *Structural persuasion.* The presentation should be well-structured, since most clients relate well to organized thinking. The opening is all-important because it sets the tone for the entire presentation.

5. *Solve the problem.* Clients have needs, and they frequently report to big shots who ask tough questions about the advertising. Solve the client's problem and you'll sell the big idea—and do it with style.

For clients, recognizing a big idea and evaluating it are almost as difficult as coming up with one. When the agency (or the in-house advertising department) presents the concepts, the client is suddenly in the role of the Judge, without having gone through the other roles first. David Ogilvy recommends that clients ask themselves five questions: Did it make me gasp when I first saw it? Do I wish I had thought of it myself? Is it unique? Does it fit the strategy to perfection? Could it be used for 30 years?[32]

As Ogilvy points out, campaigns that run five years or more are the superstars: Dove soap (33 percent cleansing cream), Ivory soap (99 and 44/100 percent pure), Perdue chickens ("It takes a tough man to make a tender chicken"), the U.S. Army

("Be all you can be"). These campaigns are still running today, and some have run for as long as 30 years. Those are big ideas!

When the client approves the campaign, the creative's role as a Warrior is only half over. Now the campaign has to be executed. That means the Warriors shepherd it through the intricate details of design and production to see that it is completed on time, under budget, and with the highest quality possible. At the same time, the creatives revert to their Artist roles to design, write, and produce the ads.

The next step in the process, therefore, is to implement the big idea, to produce the ads for print and electronic media—the subject of our next two chapters.

Chapter **Summary**

In the marketing communications process, the creative team is responsible for encoding advertising messages. It is the author of the communications. The creative team typically comprises an art director and a copywriter who report to a creative director.

Their job is to create great advertising for their clients. Great advertising is characterized by two dimensions: audience resonance and strategic relevance. To truly resonate, ads need the boom factor—that element of surprise that instantly attracts the audience's attention, gets them involved, and stirs their imagination. Some ads are informational and resonate with the audience by offering relief from some real or perceived problem. Other ads are transformational and achieve resonance through positive reinforcement by offering some reward.

The second dimension of great advertising, strategic relevance, is behind the visuals and the text of every ad. In fact, advertising strategy is the key to great creative work.

Typically written by the account management team, the advertising (or creative) strategy includes four elements: the target audience, the product concept, the communications media, and the advertising message. Once the general parameters of the plan are developed, the account managers prepare a creative brief that outlines the key strategic decisions. The creative brief should contain at least three elements: an objective statement, a support statement, and either a tone statement or a brand character statement. The brief gives strategic guidance to the art director and copywriter, but it is their responsibility to develop a message strategy that lays out the specifics of how the advertising will be executed. The three elements of message strategy are copy, art, and production.

Copy is the verbal and art the nonverbal (visual) presentation of the message strategy. Production refers to the mechanical details of how the ads and commercials will be produced.

To create means to originate, and creativity involves combining two or more previously unconnected elements, objects, or ideas to make something new. Creativity helps advertising inform, persuade, and remind customers and prospects by making the advertising more vivid. All people have creativity; they just differ in degree.

Scholars believe certain styles of thinking are more conducive to creativity than others. The two basic thinking styles are fact-based and value-based. People who prefer the fact-based style tend to be linear thinkers, analytical, and rational. Value-based thinkers tend to be less structured, more intuitive, and more willing to use their imagination. They are good at synthesizing diverse viewpoints to arrive at a new one. And, with their ability to think metaphorically, they tend to be more creative.

In one model of the creative process, the creative person must play four roles along the way to acceptance of a new idea: the Explorer, Artist, Judge, and Warrior. The Explorer searches for new information, paying attention to unusual patterns. The Artist experiments with a variety of approaches looking for the big idea. The Artist also determines how to implement it. For this, the creative pyramid may help. The pyramid models the formation of an ad after the way people learn new information, using five steps: attention, interest, credibility, desire, and action.

The Judge evaluates the results of experimentation and decides which approach is most practical. The Warrior overcomes excuses, idea killers, setbacks, and obstacles to bring a creative concept to realization. Each role has unique characteristics, and there are many techniques for improving performance in each role. During the creative process, it's better to use a value-based style of thinking; during the Judge and Warrior phases, a fact-based style is more effective.

One of the worst blocks to creativity is getting stuck in the wrong mindset, the wrong style of thinking, for the task at hand. However, there are numerous techniques for escaping these mental blocks.

Important **Terms**

advertising message, *346*

art, *359*

art direction, *359*

art director, *353*

Artist role, *355*

big idea, *355*

brainstorming, *355*

communications media, *346*

conceptualization, *355*

copywriter, *343*

creative brief, *346*

creative director, *343*

creative process, *353*

creative pyramid, *359*

creatives, *343*

creativity, *349*

emotional appeal, *346*

Explorer role, *353*

fact-based thinking, *352*

informational, *344*

Judge role, *364*

mandatories, *348*

message strategy (rationale), *348*

nonverbal, *348*

product concept, *346*

rational appeal, *346*

target audience, *346*

technical, *348*

transformational, *344*

value-based thinking, *352*

verbal, *348*

visualization, *355*

Warrior role, *366*

Review **Questions**

1. Select an ad from an earlier chapter in the book. What do you believe is the sponsor's advertising and message strategy? What is the ad's boom factor?

2. What are the most important elements of a creative brief?

3. What are the elements of message strategy and how does it differ from advertising (or creative) strategy?

4. In what ways have you exercised your personal creativity in the last week?

5. What qualities characterize the two main styles of thinking? Which style do you usually prefer? Why?

6. What are the four roles of the creative process? Have you played those roles in preparing a term paper? How?

7. What is the difference between a strategy statement and a big idea?

8. Select five creative ads from a magazine. What techniques of the Artist can you recognize in those ads?

9. In those same ads, can you identify each step of the creative pyramid?

10. What are the important things to remember about making a presentation?

Exploring the **Internet**

The Internet exercises for Chapter 11 address the following areas related to the chapter: creative strategy and execution (Exercise 1) and account planning (Exercise 2).

1. Effective Creative Strategy and Execution

   Apply the creative process and the various means of deriving and judging "good" advertising to the following Web sites, noting the quality of the creative and the strategic intent behind the work. Be sure to answer the questions below.

   - Adidas **www.adidas.com**
   - Energizer **www.energizer.com**
   - Nintendo **www.nintendo.com**
   - Nissan **www.nissan-usa.com**
   - Pacific Bell **www.pacbell.com**
   - Sea World **www.seaworld.com**
   - Taco Bell **www.tacobell.com**
   - Toys "R" Us **www.toysrus.com**

   a. Who is the intended audience of the site?

   b. What is it that makes the site's creative good or bad? Why?

   c. Identify the "who, why, what, when, where, style, approach, and tone" of the communication.

   d. Write an objective statement, support statement, and brand character statement for each.

2. Account Planning

   Account planners help ensure the research process has reaped the proper information for the creatives. The function of account planning—namely the gathering of research and the formulation of strategy for the creative team, cannot be understated. Browse through the documents held on the Account Planning Group's (APG) Web sites listed below and answer the questions that follow.

   - Account Planning Group, U.K. (APG) **www.apg.org.uk**
   - Account Planning Group, U.S. (APG) **www.apgus.org**
   - Account Planning Group, San Francisco (APG) **www.apgsf.org**

   a. Who is the intended audience of the site?

   b. What is account planning? Why is it important?

   c. What is the primary document that the account planning function generates? What are the main elements in the document?

   d. Choose an essay or article on any of the APG sites and discuss at length, explaining the relevance of the topic to account planning and the advertising business.

Chapter Twelve

Creative Execution: Art and Copy

Objective   To present the role of art and copy—the nonverbal and verbal elements of message strategy—in print, radio, and television advertising. Artists and copywriters include a variety of specialists who follow specific procedures for conceptualizing, designing, writing, and producing advertising materials. To be successful, advertising people must be conversant with the copywriting and commercial art terms and formats used in the business. They must also develop an aesthetic sensitivity so they can recognize, create, evaluate, or recommend quality work.

After studying this chapter, you will be able to:

- Describe the roles of the various types of artists in the advertising business.
- Explain the use of advertising layouts and the steps in creating them.
- Explain the creative approval process.
- Explain the role of the copywriter in relation to other members of the creative team.
- Describe the format elements of an ad and discuss how they relate to the objectives of advertising copywriting.
- Explain the art director's role in radio commercials.
- Discuss the advantages of the major types of TV commercials.

For 17 years, Timberland Co.'s award-winning ads featured witty copy and beautifully lit studio shots of its all-weather gear. One ad pictured a column of water rolling out of a spigot onto the golden-rough, natural leather toe of a Timberland boot. The headline: "For long wear and rugged good looks, just add water." But Timberland wanted a new direction for the 90s. • John Doyle, an art director for Boston-based Mullen Advertising, was assigned to the job. Doyle chose to break with the studio look and take the client's products outdoors into nature's expansive settings and full spectrum of light.

"We wanted people to be visually transported to a different place," says Doyle, "where they could feel the environment and the elements." • The big idea was Timber Land, an imaginary place that played off the company's name. Timber Land would be a utopian setting of extraordinary landscapes and crystalline waters where the mountains dramatically disappeared into the clouds. Great creativity, as well as photographic skill, was needed to express such a wondrous place. • Noted New York photographer Eric Meola is a master at capturing the look and feel of monumental subject matter. He is also known for his work in portraits and architecture. Doyle hired him, noting that Meola's "shots are so intriguing, a viewer is compelled to spend time with them—which is just what we needed for this campaign." • They spent 44 days shooting in Alaska, Arizona, and Scotland. They auditioned over 200 models, struggled through blinding snow gusts, and rented six planes to stage shots 7,000 feet up Mount McKinley. After all this effort, Meola and Doyle captured only nine shots of Timber Land that they deemed usable, just enough to start the campaign. • With the photos in hand, Doyle had to finalize the ads. Brainstorming with copywriter Paul Silverman produced a lot of ideas but only a few real winners. • Finally it all came together. Meola's stunning wide-angle shots across lakes, plains, and mountainous landscapes with a lone person in the foreground were capped by Silverman's headlines: "Timberland. Because the earth is two-thirds water," and "Timberland. Where the elements of design are the elements themselves." Doyle's design included a special typeface whose character added elegance. • This was the look and concept that expressed the mystique of Timber Land, the place. And the image that would carry Timberland, the company, successfully into the new decade.[1] •

Delivering on the **Big Idea:** Integrating the Visual and the Verbal

The Timberland campaign was applauded worldwide in a variety of advertising competitions, and it set the tone for the company's unprecedented growth in the 90s. What characterized this campaign more than anything else was the nonverbal message strategy, the *art,* created by Doyle's thoughtful design and execution and Meola's magnificent photography.

In advertising, what is shown is just as important as what is said—sometimes more. The nonverbal aspect of an ad or commercial carries fully half the burden of communicating the message. It creates the mood of the ad, determining the way it *feels* to the audience. That mood flavors the verbal message, embodied in the *copy.*

In this chapter, we discuss how advertising concepts are executed from the standpoint of both art and copy. We examine the visual and the verbal details, first of print advertising and then of electronic media.

The Art of Creating **Print** Advertising

Timberland's ad campaign stands out because of its vivid presentation of the big idea. To conceive of the big idea demanded rare artistic vision. But to resonate with the audience and be relevant to the company's objectives and strategy, Doyle had to *execute* the design with brilliance and precision.

Designing the Print Ad

The term **design** refers to how the art director and graphic artist (or graphic designer) choose and structure the artistic elements of an ad. A designer sets a *style*—the manner in which a thought or image is expressed—by choosing particular artistic elements and blending them in a unique way.

The Timberland designs enhance the message through a feeling of spaciousness. First, the sheer size of the photograph captures attention. Sparse text gives the ad breathability. The copy is set in a neat, easy-to-read format with lots of *white space.* This space gives the ad unity and balance in spite of the diversity of elements.

A number of designers, working under the art director, may produce initial layouts of the ad concept. In collaboration with copywriters, these artists draw on their expertise in graphic design (including photography, typography, and illustration) to create the most effective ad or brochure.

The Use of Layouts

A **layout** is an overall orderly arrangement of all the format elements of an ad: visual(s), headline, subheads, body copy, slogan, seal, logo, and signature.

The layout serves several purposes. First, it helps both the agency and the client develop and evaluate, in advance, how the ad will look and feel. It gives the client (usually not an artist) a tangible item to correct, change, comment on, and approve.

Second, the layout helps the creative team develop the ad's psychological elements: the nonverbal and symbolic components. Sophisticated advertisers want their advertising to do more than just bring in store traffic. They want their ads to create personality for the product—image, if you will—and to build the brand's (and the company's) equity with the consumer. To do this, the "look" of the ad needs to elicit an image or mood that reflects and enhances both the advertiser and the product.

Therefore, when designing the initial ad layout, the creative team must be very sensitive to the desired image of the product or business. In the Timberland ads, image was the primary reason for combining a dominant, spacious photograph with sparse, elegant copy. The ad makes a credible instant impression on its target audience, and that *adds value to the brand.*

Third, once the best design is chosen, the layout serves as a blueprint. It shows the size and placement of each element in the ad. Once the production manager knows the dimensions of the ad, the number of photos, the amount of typesetting,

When designing an ad, the layout is the preliminary version of the ad that shows where all the key formatting elements are placed. It is used by both the agency and the client to evaluate and develop the ad's look and feel. In this ad for San Francisco's new Pacific Bell Baseball Park, we can see that the layout was designed to grab attention and build a psychological association with baseball by using the name of Giants' great Willie Mays as the dominant headline. The ad copy follows the format of the newspaper story, and goes on to detail the Giant's past and Pacific Bell's role in their future.

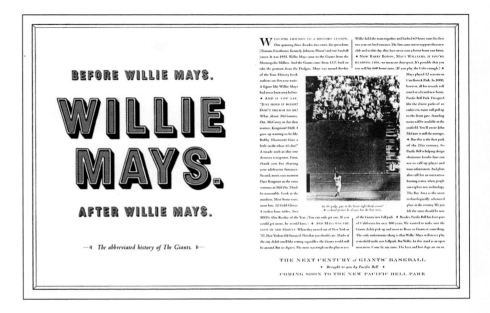

and the use of art elements such as color and illustrations, he or she can determine the cost of producing the ad (see Ad Lab 12–A: The Role of the Advertising Artist).

Advertising Design and Production: The Creative and Approval Process

The design process is both a creative and an approval process. In the creative phase, the designer uses thumbnails, roughs, dummies, and comprehensives—in other words, *nonfinal art*—to establish the ad's look and feel. Then in the *prepress* (or *production art*) phase, the artist prepares a mechanical: the final artwork with the actual type in place along with all the visuals the printer or the media will need to reproduce the ad.

The approval process takes place at each step along the way. At any point in the design and production process, the ad—or the ad concept—may be altered or even canceled.

Thumbnail Sketches

The thumbnail sketch, or **thumbnail,** is a very small (about three- by four-inch), rough, rapidly produced drawing that the artist uses to visualize layout approaches without wasting time on details. Thumbnails are very basic. Blocks of straight or squiggly lines indicate text placement, and boxes show placement of visuals. The best sketches are then developed further.

Rough Layout

In a rough, the artist draws to the actual size of the ad. Headlines and subheads suggest the final type style, illustrations and photos are sketched in, and body copy is simulated with lines. The agency may present roughs to clients, particularly cost-conscious ones, for approval.

Comprehensive

The **comprehensive layout,** or **comp,** is a highly refined facsimile of the finished ad. A comp is generally quite elaborate, with colored photos, the final type styles and sizes, subvisuals, and a glossy spray coat. Today, copy for the comp is typeset on computer and positioned with the visuals, and the ad is printed as a full-color proof. At this stage, all visuals should be final.

The Role of the Advertising Artist

All the people employed in commercial art are called artists, but they may perform entirely different tasks. Some can't even draw well; instead, they're trained for different artistic specialties.

Art Directors

Art directors are responsible for the visual presentation of the ad. Along with a copywriter, they develop the initial concept. They may do initial sketches or layouts, but after that they may not touch the ad again. Their primary responsibility is to supervise the ad's progress to completion.

The best art directors are good at presenting ideas in both words and pictures. They are usually experienced graphic designers with a good understanding of consumers. They may have a large or small staff, depending on the organization. Or they may be freelancers (independent contractors) and do more of the work themselves.

Graphic Designers

Graphic designers are precision specialists preoccupied with shape and form. In advertising they arrange the various graphic elements (type, illustrations, photos, white space) in the most attractive and effective way possible. While they may work on ads, they usually design and produce collateral materials, such as posters, brochures, and annual reports.

In an agency, the art director often acts as the designer. Sometimes, however, a separate designer is used to offer a unique touch to a particular ad.

Illustrators

Illustrators paint or draw the visuals in an ad. They frequently specialize in one type of illustrating, such as automotive, fashion, or furniture. Very few agencies or advertisers retain full-time illustrators; most advertising illustrators freelance. Typically, agencies hire different illustrators for different jobs, depending on an ad's particular needs, look, and feel.

Photographers

Like the illustrator, the advertising photographer creates a nonverbal expression that reinforces the verbal message. Photographers use the tools of photography—cameras, lenses, and lights—to create images. They select interesting angles, arrange subjects in new ways, carefully control the lighting, and use many other techniques to enhance the subject's image quality. A studio photographer uses high-powered lights to photograph products in front of a background or as part of an arranged setting. A location photographer generally shoots in real-life settings like those in the Timberland ads. Many photographers specialize—in cars, celebrities, fashion, food, equipment, or architecture. Agencies and advertisers rarely employ staff photographers. They generally hire freelancers by the hour or pay a fee for the assignment. Photographers also sell stock photography, photos on file from prior shootings.

Production Artists

Production (or pasteup) artists assemble the various elements of an ad and mechanically put them together the way the art director or designer indicates. Good production artists are fast, precise, and knowledgeable about the whole production process. Production artists today must be computer literate; they use a variety of software programs for pagemaking, drawing, painting, and photo scanning. Most designers and art directors start their careers as production artists and work their way up. It's very difficult work, but it is also very important, for this is where an ad actually comes together in its finished form.

Laboratory Applications

1. Select an ad in the Portfolio Review (pp. 386–89). Explain which advertising artists were probably involved in its creation and what the responsibility of each artist was.

2. Which ad in the Portfolio Review do you think needed the fewest artists? How many?

Dummy

A dummy presents the handheld look and feel of brochures, multipage materials, or point-of-purchase displays. The artist assembles the dummy by hand, using color markers and computer proofs, mounting them on sturdy paper, and then cutting and folding them to size. A dummy for a brochure, for example, is put together, page by page, to look exactly like the finished product.

Mechanical (Pasteup)

The type and visuals must be placed in their exact position for reproduction by a printer. Today, most designers do this work on the computer, completely bypassing the need for a mechanical. Some advertisers, however, still make traditional mechanicals, where black type and line art are pasted in place on a piece of white artboard (called a **pasteup**) with overlay sheets indicating the hue and positioning of color. Printers refer to the mechanical or pasteup as **camera-ready art** because they photograph it using a large production camera before starting the reproduction process—creating color keys, prints, and films of the finished ad.

At any time during the design process—until the printing press lays ink on paper—changes can be made on the art. However, the expense may grow tenfold with each step from roughs to mechanicals to printing.

Thumbnails and a rough layout of an ad by the Muse Cordero Chen agency celebrate the firm's philosophy and "out-of-the-box" approach to advertising. The final sketch humorously shows the firm's cultural diversity. The body copy emanating from the pipe proclaims: advertising. bold. culturally hip. t.v. radio. print. out-of-the-box. award winning. on target. fresh. impactful. relevant. generation x. latino. black. asian. diverse. the new america. dare to be different. challenge the status quo.

Approval

The work of the copywriter and art director is always subject to approval. The larger the agency and the larger the client, the more formidable this process becomes (see Exhibit 12–1). A new ad concept is first approved by the agency's creative director. Then the account management team reviews it. Next, the client's product managers and marketing staff review it, often changing a word or two or sometimes rejecting the whole approach. Both the agency's and client's legal departments scrutinize the copy and art for potential problems. Finally, the company's top executives review the final concept and text.

The biggest challenge in approval is keeping approvers from corrupting the style of the ad. The creative team works hard to achieve a cohesive style. Then a group of nonwriters and nonartists have the opportunity to change it all. Maintaining artistic purity is extremely difficult and requires patience, flexibility, maturity, and the ability to articulate an important point of view and explain why artistic choices were made.

Impact of Computers on Graphic Design

By using graphics or imaging programs on computers, today's graphic artist or designer can do much of the work previously performed by staff artists. On the screen, the artist can see an entire page layout, complete with illustrations and photos, and easily alter any of them in a few minutes. Before

Exhibit 12–1

The copy approval process begins within the agency and ends with approval by key executives of the client company. Each review usually requires some rewrite and a presentation to the next level of approvers. When the agency and the advertiser are large companies, the process can require long lead times.

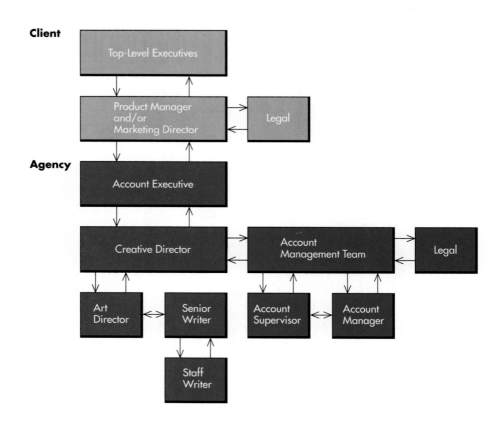

computers, designing a variety of layouts could take days, and final art was not so detailed or complete as designs created today on the computer.

Small PC- and Macintosh-based systems are ideal for computer design, and sophisticated PC graphics software is now available for pagemaking (QuarkXPress and PageMaker), painting and drawing (CorelDraw!, FreeHand, Adobe Illustrator), and image manipulation (ColorStudio, PhotoStyler, Adobe Photoshop). For word processing the most popular programs include Microsoft Word, WordPerfect, and Claris MacWrite.[2] Their moderate cost makes such software accessible to freelancers, small businesses, and agency creative departments. Today's graphic artist, illustrator, and retoucher must be computer literate in addition to having a thorough knowledge of aesthetics, rendering, and design.

Principles of Design: Which Design Formats Work Best

Ads must be designed to attract the customer, and they have to do it fast. Typically, the advertiser has only a second or two to grab the reader's attention. Indeed, studies of ad readership show that 85 percent of ads don't even get looked at.[3] They also show virtually no relationship between how much the advertiser spends and how well the ad is recalled. But the *quality* of the advertising is important.[4] Good design not only commands attention but holds it. Good design also communicates as much information as possible in the shortest amount of time and makes the message easier to understand.[5]

Advertisers use many different types of layouts (see Exhibit 12–2). Traditionally, the ads that score the highest recall employ a standard, **poster-style format** (also called a **picture-window layout** and **Ayer No. 1** in the trade) with a single, dominant visual that occupies 60 to 70 percent of the ad's total area.[6] In fact, some research shows that ads scoring in the top third for stopping power devote an average of 82 percent of their space to the visual.[7] Next in ranking are ads that have one large picture and two smaller ones. The visuals are intended to stop the reader and arouse interest, so their content must be interesting.

Exhibit 12–2

Art directors use many types of layouts. To create an ad for the Underwater Kinetics (UK) industrial strength utility flashlight, the company's agency Market Design prepared thumbnails of a number of layouts first to see which would work best.

Mondrian *The Mondrian layout uses series of vertical and horizontal lines, rectangles, and squares to give geometric proportion to an ad.*

Frame *The copy is surrounded by the visual. Or, as in this case, the visual may be surrounded by the copy.*

Silhouette *Irregular shaped white space surrounds the main elements in the ad creating a silhouette effect.*

Picture window *A single, large visual occupies about two-thirds of the ad. The headline and copy may appear above or below the "window."*

Copy heavy *When you have a lot to say and visuals won't say it, use text. But let the headlines and subheads make it interesting.*

Circus *Filled with multiple illustrations, oversize type, reverse blocks, tilts, and other gimmicks to bring the ad alive and make it interesting.*

Band *A series of elements lined up in one column with, usually, only one major element outside this band.*

As we discuss in the next section, headlines also stop the reader and may actually contribute more to long-term memory than the visual.[8] As a design element, the total headline area should normally fill only 10 to 15 percent of the ad, so the type need not be particularly large. Headlines may appear above or below the visual, depending on the situation. However, when the headline appears below the illustration, the ad typically gains about 10 percent more readership.[9]

Research also shows that readership drops considerably if ads have more than 50 words. So to attract a large number of readers, copy blocks should be kept to less than 20 percent of the ad. However, with many high-involvement products, the more you tell, the more you sell. If selling is the objective, then informative body copy becomes important. And long copy works when it's appropriate—when the advertiser is more interested in *quality* of readership than *quantity*.[10]

Finally, most people who read ads want to know who placed the ad. Company signatures or logos need not be large or occupy more than 5 to 10 percent of the area. For best results, they should be placed in the lower right-hand corner or across the bottom of the ad.

Advertising author Roy Paul Nelson points out that the principles of design are to the layout artist what the rules of grammar are to the writer. The basic rules include the following:

- The design must be in *balance*.
- The space within the ad should be broken up into pleasing *proportions*.
- A directional pattern should be evident so the reader knows in what *sequence* to read.
- Some force should hold the ad together and give it *unity*.
- One element, or one part of the ad, should have enough *emphasis* to dominate all others.[11]

For more on the basic principles of advertising design (balance, proportion, sequence, unity, and emphasis), see RL 12–1, Checklist of Design Principles, in the Reference Library.

The Use of Visuals in Print Advertising

Th e artists who paint, sketch, and draw in advertising are called **illustrators.** The artists who produce pictures with a camera are **photographers.** Together they are responsible for all the **visuals,** or pictures, we see in advertising.

Purpose of the Visual

When confronted with a print ad, most prospects spot the picture first, then read the headline, and then peruse the body copy, in that order. Since the visual carries so much responsibility for an ad's success, it should be designed with several goals in mind. Some of the most obvious follow:

- Capture the reader's attention.
- Clarify claims made by the copy.
- Identify the subject of the ad.
- Show the product actually being used.
- Qualify readers by stopping those who are legitimate prospects.
- Help convince the reader of the truth of copy claims.

- Arouse the reader's interest in the headline.
- Emphasize the product's unique features.
- Create a favorable impression of the product or advertiser.
- Provide continuity for the campaign by using a unified visual technique in each ad.[12]

Determining the Chief Focus for Visuals

The Timberland ads are dominated by a large, single visual that demonstrates the environment in which the product is used rather than the product itself. The visuals capture a mood and create a feeling, a context for the consumer's perception of the product.

Selecting the focus for advertising visuals is a major step in the creative process. It often determines how well the big idea is executed. Print advertising uses many standard subjects for ad visuals, including:

1. *The package containing the product.* Especially important for packaged goods, it helps the consumer identify the product on the grocery shelf.

Ads that employ a standard poster-style format tend to gain higher readership and recall scores than other types of layouts. As this ad for Wallis clothing shows, the visual is the dominant element in a poster-style ad. The comic element of unseen danger stops the reader and arouses interest. The center of attention, a glamorously dressed woman, exudes a sexy lifestyle for Wallis clothing and provides a lasting image. The company name and additional information are secondary, but still identifiable to the reader.

Showing the product in use is one method of visually creating a context for consumer perception. In this ad for Stren Powerbraid fishing line (www.stren.com), the strength and dependability of the line is shown by the fact that Stren can support an anvil without breaking. Most fishermen would be happy to catch a fish much lighter than an anvil, so they know they can rely on Stren to withstand the weight and resistance of the average fish.

2. *The product alone.* This doesn't work well for nonpackaged goods.

3. *The product in use.* Automobile ads typically show a car in use while talking about its ride, luxury, handling, or economy. Cosmetic ads usually show the product in use with a close-up photo of a beautiful woman or a virile man.

4. *How to use the product.* Recipe ads featuring a new way to use food products historically pull very high readership scores.

5. *Product features.* Computer software ads frequently show the monitor screen so the prospect can see how the software features are displayed.

6. *Comparison of products.* The advertiser shows its product next to a competitor's and compares the important features of the two.

7. *User benefit.* It's often difficult to illustrate intangible user benefits. However, marketers know that the best way to get customers' attention is to show how the product will benefit them, so it's worth the extra creative effort.

8. *Humor.* If used well, a humorous visual can make an entertaining and lasting impression. It can also destroy credibility if used incorrectly.

9. *Testimonial.* Before-and-after endorsements are very effective for weight-loss products, skin-care lotions, and bodybuilding courses.

10. *Negative appeal.* Sometimes visuals point out what happens if you don't use the product. If done well, that can spark interest.

Selecting the Visual

The kind of picture used is often determined during the conceptualization process (see RL 12–2: Techniques for Creating Advertising Visuals). But frequently the visual is not determined until the art director or designer actually lays out the ad.

Selecting an appropriate photo or visual is a difficult creative task. Art directors deal with several basic issues. For example, not every ad needs a visual to communicate effectively. Some all-type ads are quite compelling. If the art director determines that a visual is required, how many should there be: one, two, or more? Should the visual be black-and-white or color? These may be budgetary decisions.

The art director must then decide the subject of the picture. Should it be one of the standard subjects listed earlier? Or something else altogether? And how relevant is that subject to the advertiser's creative strategy? The art director also has to decide how the visual should be created. Should it be a hand-rendered illustration? A photograph? What about a computer-generated illustration?

Finally, the art director has to know what technical and/or budgetary issues must be considered. With so many options, selecting visuals is obviously no simple task. In Chapter 13, we'll see how all these decisions come together in the process of producing the final ad.

Copywriting and **Formats** for Print Advertising

Now that we understand the objectives and format elements of good design, let's examine some basic copywriting formats to see how art and copy are linked.

Imitation, Plagiarism, or Flattery?

When two companies run strikingly similar ads, is it imitation, plagiarism, or coincidence? In the early 1990s, Leo Burnett Advertising created a commercial featuring astronaut Scott Carpenter and his son comparing an Oldsmobile to a spaceship. At the end, the Olds rotated on end and blasted off like a rocket. Larry Postaer, creative director at Rubin Postaer & Associates for American Honda, claimed, "That was a direct steal from us," referring to an ad published five years earlier. But Burnett executives denied pilfering the visual. Burnett president Rick Fizdale said he wasn't even familiar with the Honda ad.

Advertisers and media commonly point to "coincidence." Several newspapers across the country, for example, use some form of, "If you don't get it, you don't get it," a federally registered trademark of the *Washington Post.* When the same slogan appeared in an ad campaign for the *Orange County Register,* it claimed no knowledge of the *Post*'s trademark. Also proclaiming innocence were the *San Francisco Chronicle* ("You don't get the Bay Area if you don't get the *Chronicle*"), the *Austin American Statesman* ("The *Statesman.* Either you get it or you don't"), and the *Oregonian* ("When you get it, you'll get it").

Stephen Bergerson, an attorney specializing in advertising and promotion law at Fredrikson & Byron, Minneapolis, is skeptical. "When you get four or five words that are so specific, simultane-

ously used by people in the same category, the nose starts to quiver." But Ron Redfern, senior vice president of sales and marketing for the *Orange County Register,* calls it "coincidental invention. It's like the automobile being invented in France and in the U.S. within weeks of each other."

Some advertisers try to ignore the problem by convincing themselves that being copied is actually good. Hugh Thrasher, executive VP of marketing for Motel 6, says of his often-imitated Tom Bodett commercials: "We think these copycat ads just remind people of the originality of our concept." Nancy Shalek, president of L.A.'s Shalek Agency, maintains, "If you haven't been ripped off, you're really in trouble."

But Ellen Kozak, a Milwaukee copyright and publishing lawyer, warns against this form of flattery. "There's a fine line between the kind of borrowing that constitutes an admiring bow to a classic work and the kind that's really the theft of another writer's efforts."

Unfortunately, plagiarism is almost impossible to prove, as long as you make a few changes. It's also hard to define, making it tough for advertisers to know just when they cross the line. There is no set number of words that make up a plagiarized effort. And plagiarism covers not only words but ideas, plots, and characters. According to Boston University, plagiarism can occur simply through the borrowing of a "particularly apt term." "The only gray area is when the words that are identical are very common,

In print advertising, the key format elements are the *visual(s), headlines, subheads, body copy, slogans, seals, logos,* and *signatures.* As Exhibit 12–3 shows, copywriters can correlate the visual, headline, and subhead to the *attention* step of the creative pyramid (discussed in Chapter 11). The *interest* step typically corresponds to the subhead and the first paragraph of body copy. Body copy handles *credibility* and *desire,* and the *action* step takes place with the logo, slogan, and signature block. We'll discuss these elements first and then look at the formats for radio and television commercials.

Headlines

The **headline** contains the words in the leading position in the advertisement—the words that will be read first and are situated to draw the most attention. That's why headlines usually appear in larger type than other parts of the ad.

Role of Headlines

Effective headlines attract attention, engage the audience, explain the visual, lead the audience into the body of the ad, and present the selling message.

One popular way to attract attention is to occupy the entire top half of the ad with a headline written in large letters. This technique can be just as eye-catching as a dramatic photo or illustration.

Another goal of a headline is to engage the reader—fast—and give a reason to read the rest of the ad. If the headline lacks immediacy, prospects turn their attention to another subject and pass the ad's message by.[13]

An ad for Esser's wine store is a good example of a headline leading the reader into the body copy.

Headline: "Esser's Knows."

Body copy: "Manfred Esser's nose knows a good wine . . ."

The headline is the most important thing an advertiser says to the prospect. It explains or gives greater meaning to the visual and then immediately dictates the

ordinary words and expressions," says Walter Stewart of the National Institutes of Health and a freelance scholar of academic improprieties.

The crux of the problem is that imitation is an accepted part of the business, at least unofficially. Clients tend to avoid the debate, perhaps because they're more comfortable with well-worn ideas than with bold, original concepts. Many art directors and writers collect competitive ads for inspiration. And advertising is such a highly collaborative process that it's often difficult to determine each individual's creative contribution. With personal responsibility so unclear, it becomes easier to ignore professional ethics.

But every so often, someone creates an ad that moves beyond the gray zone of imitation into outright plagiarism. Cyrix, a small microprocessor manufacturer, lifted the swirled trademark of its huge competitor Intel. Cyrix's ads play off the graphics and type of the successful and expensive "Intel inside" campaign. The ads, which feature the familiar swirl around the word "ditto" in Intel's typeface, use the tagline "Cyrix instead." Intel sued Cyrix, calling its ads a "spurious imitation." Frank Priscaro, co-creative director of Cyrix's ad agency, Priscaro & Hukari, makes no bones about the issue. With Cyrix's ad budget at about $2.5 million to Intel's $100 million, Priscaro says, "The lawsuit's going to give Cyrix a million dollars in free publicity."

Even flagrant infringement cases are very hard to win because ideas aren't protected by copyright laws, and creative advertising is an idea business. That's why some industry leaders are passionate about the need for personal ethics. Jim Golden, executive producer of DMH MacGuffin, says, "All we have in this business are creativity and ideas. The moment someone infringes on that, they're reaching into the very core of the business and ripping it out." Ultimately, advertisers must stop "borrowing" ideas from each other and demand greater creativity from themselves.

Questions

1. Some art directors claim that "independent invention" explains why many ads look the same. Is that possible? If so, does it excuse running imitative advertising—or should the originator of an idea be the only one allowed to use it?

2. Should clients be more concerned about the ethics of copycat advertising? What would you do if a client asked you to copy an ad that was already running?

Sources: Tim Clark, "Intel Drags Rival Cyrix and Its Shop into Court over 'Ditto' Ad Campaign," *Advertising Age,* December 6, 1993, p. 8; Morris Freedman, "The Persistence of Plagiarism, the Riddle of Originality," *Virginia Quarterly Review,* Summer 1994, pp. 504–17; Philip J. Hilts, "When Does Duplication of Words Become Theft?" *New York Times,* March 29, 1993, p. A10; Ellen M. Kozak, "The ABCs of Avoiding Plagiarism," *Writer's Digest,* July 1993, pp. 40–41; Kathy Tyrer, "Some Get It; Some Don't," *Adweek,* May 30, 1994, p. 6.

advertiser's position in that person's mind, whether or not the prospect chooses to read on.[14]

Ideally, headlines present the complete selling idea. Research shows that, on average, three to five times as many people read the headline as read the body copy. So if the ad doesn't sell in the headline, the advertiser is wasting money.[15] Nike uses beautiful magazine and outdoor ads featuring just an athlete, the logo, and the memorable headline: "Just do it." Working off the visual, the headline creates the mood and tells the reader to take action (through implication, buy Nikes). Headlines help trigger a recognition response, which reinforces brand recognition and brand preference.

The traditional notion is that short headlines with one line are best but a second line is acceptable. Many experts believe that headlines with 10 words or more gain greater readership.[16] In one study of over 2,000 ads, most headlines averaged eight words in length.[17] David Ogilvy says the best headline he ever wrote contained 18 words—and became a classic: "At 60 miles an hour, the loudest noise in the new Rolls-Royce comes from the electric clock."[18]

A good headline draws attention to the ad and induces the reader to read the copy. In this ad for Yale New Haven Health System (www.image-matrix.com/ yalenew.htm), the headline explains the photo of Alice, and leads the reader into the body text by lamenting that the modern health care system is more convoluted than Alice's trip through Wonderland. The statement implies that Yale New Haven thinks it has a simpler solution, and this is the inducement to read on. The headline would be most effective, of course, with those readers familiar with Lewis Carrol's fairy tale and in need of a friendlier health care system.

381

Exhibit 12–3

An ad's success depends on the viewer's ability to absorb and learn its message. The creative pyramid helps the copywriter present the conceptual elements of the message. The format elements (headlines, subheads, body copy, slogan) segment the copy to help audiences decode the message.

Creative pyramid

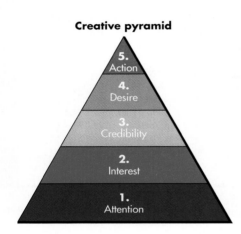

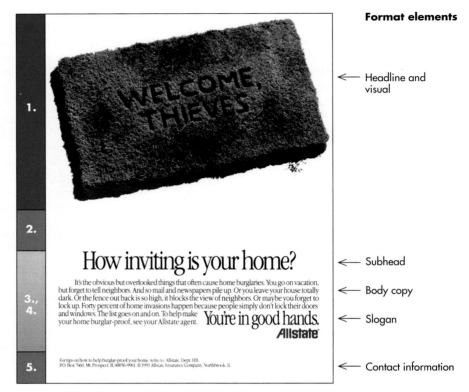

Format elements

← Headline and visual

← Subhead

← Body copy

← Slogan

← Contact information

Headlines should offer a benefit that is apparent to the reader and easy to grasp. For example: "When it absolutely, positively has to be there overnight" (FedEx) or "Folds flat for easy storage" (Honda Civic Wagon).[19]

Finally, headlines should present *product news*. Consumers look for new products, new uses for old products, or improvements on old products. If they haven't been overused in a category, "power" words that suggest newness can increase readership and improve the boom factor of an ad. They should be employed whenever *honestly* applicable.[20] Examples include *free, now, amazing, suddenly, announcing, introducing, it's here, improved, at last, revolutionary, just arrived,* and *important development.*

Types of Headlines

Copywriters use many variations of headlines depending on the advertising strategy. Typically, they use the headline that presents the big idea most successfully. Headlines may be classified by the type of information they carry: *benefit, news/information, provocative, question,* and *command.*

Advertisers use **benefit headlines** to promise the audience that experiencing the utility of the product or service will be rewarding. Benefit headlines shouldn't be too cute or clever, just simple statements of the product's most important benefit.[21] Two good examples are

Gore-Tex® Fabrics
Keep you warm and dry.   and   Speak a foreign language in
Regardless of what falls   30 days or your money back.
Out of the sky.

Note that both of these headlines focus on the benefit of using the product, not the features of the product itself.[22]

Provocative headlines are aimed at piquing the reader's curiosity. A successful provocative headline stops readers, makes them think, and, with the aid of visuals, entices them to read the copy to satisfy their curiosity. This headline from an ad for Galaxy Army & Navy Store grabs attention by comparing actual combat zones to New York City. It makes the reader wonder what kind of things one would need for a weekend in Lebanon or Nicaragua that can also be useful in New York. To find out, one would have to go to the store.

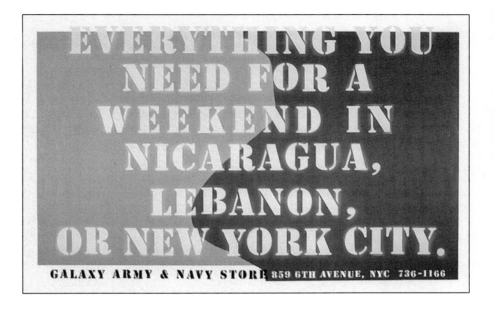

The **news/information headline** announces news or promises information. Sea World began its TV announcement of a new baby whale with the headline "It's a girl." The information must be believable, though. A claim that a razor "shaves 200% smoother" isn't.[23]

Copywriters use **provocative headlines** to provoke the reader's curiosity—to stimulate questions and thoughts. For example: "My chickens eat better than you do" (Perdue Chickens). To learn more, the reader must read the body copy. The danger, of course, is that the reader won't read on. To avoid this, the creative team designs visuals to clarify the message or provide some story appeal.

A **question headline** asks a question, encouraging readers to search for the answer in the body of the ad. An ad for 4day Tire Stores asks: "What makes our tire customers smarter & richer than others?" A good question headline piques the reader's curiosity and imagination. But if a headline asks a question the reader can answer quickly (or even worse, negatively) the rest of the ad may not get read. Imagine a headline that reads: "Do you want to buy insurance?" The reader answers, "No," and turns the page.[24]

A **command headline** orders the reader to do something, so it might seem negative. But readers pay attention to such headlines. Ocean Spray targets youth with the hip headline: "Crave the wave."[25] Some command headlines make a request: "Please don't squeeze the Charmin" (bathroom tissue).

Many headline types are easily combined. But the type of headline used is less important than the way it's used. Copywriters must always write with style—for the audience's pleasure, not their own.[26]

Subheads

The **subhead** is an additional smaller headline that may appear above the headline or below it. A subhead above the headline, called a **kicker** (or *overline*), is often underlined. Subheads may also appear in body copy.

Subheads are usually set smaller than the headline but larger than the body copy or text. Subheads generally appear in **boldface** (heavier) or *italic* (slanted) type or a different color. Like a headline, the subhead transmits key sales points fast. But it usually carries less important information than the headline. Subheads are important for two reasons: most people read only the headline and subheads, and subheads usually support the interest step best.

_____ **Get to the main point—fast.**

_____ **Emphasize one major idea simply and clearly.**

_____ **Be single-minded.** Don't try to do too much. If you chase more than one rabbit at a time, you'll catch none.

_____ **Position the product clearly.**

_____ **Keep the brand name up front and reinforce it.**

_____ **Write with the consumer's ultimate benefit in mind.**

_____ **Write short sentences.** Use easy, familiar words and themes people understand.

_____ **Don't waste words.** Say what you have to say—nothing more, nothing less. Don't pad, but don't skimp.

_____ **Avoid bragging and boasting.** Write from the reader's point of view, not your own. Avoid "we," "us," "our."

_____ **Avoid clichés.** They're crutches; learn to get along without them. Bright, surprising words and phrases perk up readers and keep them reading.

_____ **Write with flair.** Drum up excitement. Make sure your own enthusiasm comes through in the copy.

_____ **Use vivid language.** Use lots of verbs and adverbs.

_____ **Stick to the present tense, active voice.** It's crisper. Avoid the past tense and passive voice. Exceptions should be deliberate, for special effect.

_____ **Use personal pronouns.** Remember, you're talking to just one person, so talk as you would to a friend. Use "you" and "your."

_____ **Use contractions.** They're fast, personal, natural. People talk in contractions (listen to yourself).

_____ **Don't overpunctuate.** It kills copy flow. Excessive commas are the chief culprits. Don't give readers any excuse to jump ship.

_____ **Read the copy aloud.** Hear how it sounds; catch errors. The written word is considerably different from the spoken word.

_____ **Rewrite and write tight.** Edit mercilessly. Tell the whole story and no more. When you're finished, stop.

Subheads are longer and more like sentences than headlines. They serve as stepping stones from the headline to the body copy, telegraphing what's to come.[27]

Body Copy

The advertiser tells the complete sales story in the **body copy,** or **text.** The body copy comprises the interest, credibility, desire, and often even the action steps. It is a logical continuation of the headline and subheads, set in smaller type. Body copy covers the features, benefits, and utility of the product or service.

The body copy is typically read by only one out of 10 readers, so the writer must speak to the reader's self-interest, explaining how the product or service satisfies the customer's need.[28] The best ads focus on one big idea or one clear benefit. Copywriters often read their copy aloud to hear how it sounds, even if it's intended for print media. The ear is a powerful copywriting tool.[29]

Some of the best copywriting techniques of leading experts are highlighted in the Checklist for Writing Effective Copy.

Body Copy Styles

Experienced copywriters look for the technique and style with the greatest sales appeal for the idea being presented. Common copy styles include *straight sell, institutional, narrative, dialog/monolog, picture caption,* and *device.*

In **straight-sell copy,** writers immediately explain or develop the headline and visual in a straightforward, factual presentation. The straight-sell approach appeals to the prospect's reason. Since it ticks off the product's sales points in order of importance, straight-sell copy is particularly good for high think-involvement products or products that are difficult to use. It's very effective in direct-mail advertising and industrial or high-tech situations. Advertisers use the straight-sell approach more than all other techniques combined.[30]

Advertisers use **institutional copy** to promote a philosophy or extol the merits of an organization rather than product features. The Timberland ad at the beginning of this chapter uses an institutional copy style to explain the company's design philosophy. Institutional copy is intended to lend warmth and credibility to the organization's image. Banks, insurance companies, public corporations, and large manufacturing firms use institutional copy in both print and electronic media. However, David Ogilvy warns against the "self-serving, flatulent pomposity" that characterizes the copy in many corporate ads.[31]

Copywriters use **narrative copy** to tell a story. Ideal for the creative writer, narrative copy sets up a situation and then resolves it at the last minute by having the product or service come to the rescue. Narrative copy offers good opportunities for emotional appeals. An insurance company, for example, might tell the poignant story of the man who died unexpectedly but, fortunately, had just renewed his policy.[32]

By using **dialog/monolog copy,** the advertiser can add the believability that narrative copy sometimes lacks. The characters portrayed in a print ad do the sell-

This ad for Bell Helmet (www.echo.it/ echo/echo/bell/index.html) exemplifies the narrative copy style. Narrative copy tells a story about the product or the type of people who use the product and resolves the narrative with the product as the hero. To give credibility to their safety claims, Bell uses testimonials from accident survivors who avoided head injury because they were wearing a helmet.

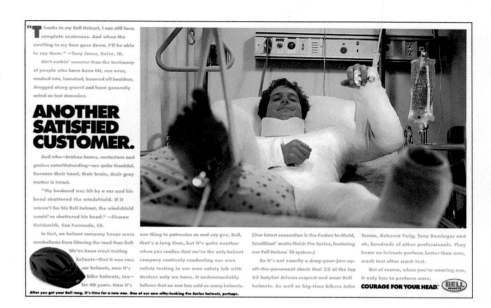

ing in their own words. A caution: poorly written dialog copy can come off as dull or, even worse, hokey and unreal.

Sometimes it's easier to tell a story with illustrations and captions. A photo with **picture-caption copy** is especially useful for products that have a number of different uses or come in a variety of styles or designs.

With any copy style, the copywriter may use some device copy to enhance attention, interest, and memorability. **Device copy** uses figures of speech (like puns, alliteration, assonance, and rhymes) as well as humor and exaggeration. Verbal devices help people remember the brand and tend to affect attitude favorably.[33] The Timberland headline ("Where the elements of design are the elements themselves") plays off the double meaning of the word *element*.

Humor can be effective when the advertiser needs high memorability in a short time, wants to dispel preconceived negative images, or needs to create a distinct personality for an undifferentiated product. However, humor should always be used carefully and never be in questionable taste. Some researchers believe humor distracts from the selling message and can even be detrimental when used poorly or for serious services like finance, insurance, and crematoriums.[34]

Formatting Body Copy

The keys to good body copy are simplicity, order, credibility, and clarity. Or, as John O'Toole says, prose should be "written clearly, informatively, interestingly, powerfully, persuasively, dramatically, memorably, and with effortless grace. That's all."[35] (See the Portfolio Review: The Creative Director's Greatest Ads, on pages 386–89 for some good examples.)

Four basic format elements are used to construct long copy ads: *the lead-in paragraph, interior paragraphs, trial close,* and *close.*

Lead-in paragraph   The **lead-in paragraph** is a bridge between the headline and the sales ideas presented in the text. Like a subhead, the lead-in paragraph is part of the *interest* step. It must be engaging and able to convert a prospect's reading interest to product interest.

continued on page 390

The Creative Director always wants to produce the most

effective advertising possible in order to give the client the greatest bang for the buck. That means conceiving a brilliant idea that will both resonate with the particular target audience and relate to the client's marketing and advertising strategy, and then executing that idea in a masterful way.

● *Study all the award-winning ads in this portfolio and consider how well they measure up to this definition of greatness. To do this, start by analyzing whether the ad is informational or transformational. Then evaluate and describe the "boom" factor each one uses. Next, see if you can determine from the ad what the company's advertising strategy was and discuss how relevant the ad is to that strategy. And finally, examine how well the creative director executed the concept.*

Metaphors are an effective method of writing copy for an advertisement. Here Norfolk Southern asserts its care for the customer by explaining it will act as the safe deposit box to the client's precious metal goods. In the background a wild horse races across the prairie, symbolizing the company slogan: The Thoroughbred of Transportation.

The "boom" factor of this ad comes from the irony in the copy. For fishing enthusiasts, the copy reaffirms the personal importance of fishing in pristine waters, rod and Shimano reel in hand. Additionally, the body copy provides technical information of concern to those who are comparing potential brands or models.

Sometimes a value-based approach is the only realistic means to showcase a product. Oneida produces the desire for its stemware with a goldfish trio who gaze enviously at their friend who basks happily in the company's goblet. The imagery also contrasts the harsh angles of the aquarium against the warm elegance of the goblet, creating a subtle impression of imprisonment for the group in the tank.

ONEIDA

Shown: Heiress Gold Goblet.

BECAUSE WE'LL RECYCLE OVER 200 MILLION PLASTIC BOTTLES THIS YEAR, LANDFILLS CAN BE FILLED WITH OTHER THINGS. LIKE LAND, FOR INSTANCE.

We can't make more land. But we can do more to protect what we have. In fact, this year Phillips Petroleum's plastics recycling plant will process over 200 million containers. This effort will help reduce landfill waste and conserve natural resources. And that will leave another little corner of the world all alone. At Phillips, that's what it means to be The Performance Company.

PHILLIPS PETROLEUM COMPANY

For an annual report on Phillips' health, environmental and safety performance, write to: HES Report, 16 A1 PB, Bartlesville, OK 74004, or visit us at www.phillips66.com.

This advertisement is an example of the importance of well-written copy. With an image of a serene autumn forest, this message changes people's perception of a petroleum corporation from being environmentally unfriendly to one of ecological responsibility.

KILLER COLOR

WORLD'S FINEST GRAIN COLOR. WORLD'S FASTEST DIGITAL COLOR COPIERS.

Look like a bigger fish with a Ricoh digital color copier. The world's smallest toner particles deliver the finest color presentations ever. Faster than ever. The world's fastest first copy. The most copies per minute. And computer connectable. All in the same full line of digital color copiers. This means unmatched performance and unprecedented productivity. It also means Ricoh now leads the world in digital color copier technology. Make a bigger splash. Call us at 1-800-63-RICOH.

THE NAME TO KNOW
RICOH

By using the creative pyramid as a guideline, advertisers can ensure that their ads will address the needs of both the reader and their company or client. In this spectacular example by Ricoh, the ad first grabs the readers' attention with its rich and attractive colors, which also turns out to be part of the credibility component: a quality copier company must, after all, reproduce quality colors. Interest is generated by the selection of a grotesque fish for the image, and both desire and action steps can be found in the body copy.

Advertisements must, of course, be tailored to address a specific market audience. Allen Edmonds, maker of high-end dress shoes, has a client base composed mainly of businessmen with tastes on the more conservative side. The question headline, thus, intends to pique the interest of those routinely involved in finance issues and is tied to the product with the soft photograph of a brown leather shoe.

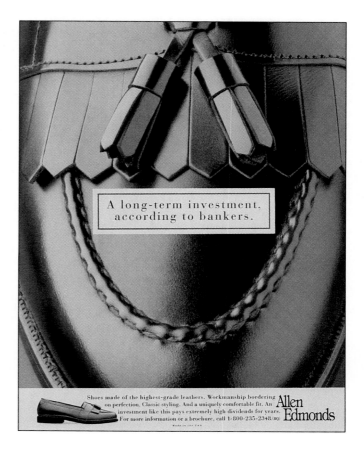

A long-term investment,
according to bankers.

Shoes made of the highest-grade leathers. Workmanship bordering on perfection. Classic styling. And a uniquely comfortable fit. An investment like this pays extremely high dividends for years. For more information or a brochure, call 1-800-235-2348.

Allen
Edmonds

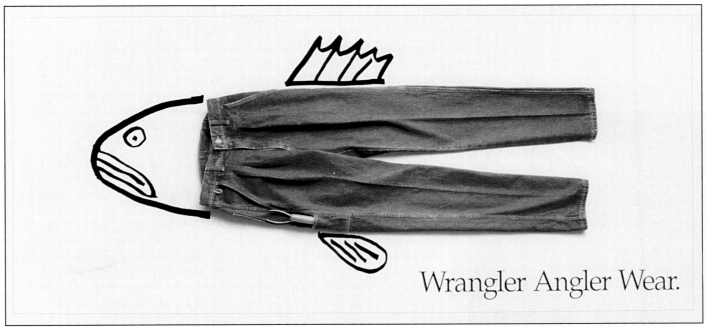

Wrangler Angler Wear.

Body copy is not always necessary, particularly with lifestyle ads that don't need to explain a product. With lifestyle ads, both image and headline copy are extremely important to grab audience attention long enough for readers to process the information from an ad. Wrangler Jeans uses a sing-songy play on words to get its point across in this ad.

continued from page 385

Interior paragraphs The **interior paragraphs** of the body copy should develop *credibility* by providing proof for claims and promises and they should build *desire* by using language that stirs the imagination. Advertisers should support their product promises with research data, testimonials, and warranties. Such proofs help avoid costly lawsuits, convince customers of the validity of the product, improve goodwill toward the advertiser, and stimulate sales.

Trial close Interspersed in the interior paragraphs should be suggestions to *act* now. Good copy asks for the order more than once; mail-order ads ask several times. Consumers often make the buying decision without reading all the body copy. The **trial close** gives them the opportunity to make the buying decision early.

Close The **close** is the real *action* step. A good close asks consumers to do something and tells them how. The close can be indirect or direct (a subtle suggestion or a direct command). A *direct close* seeks immediate response in the form of a purchase, a store or Web site visit, or a request for further information.

The close should simplify the audience's response, making it easy for them to order the merchandise, send for information, or visit a showroom or a Web site. A business reply card or a toll-free phone number may be included.

Of course, not all ads sell products or services. Advertisers may want to change attitudes, explain their viewpoints, or ask for someone's vote. By giving a Web site address, the advertiser can offer additional information to those readers who are interested in learning more at their leisure.

Slogans

Many **slogans** (also called **themelines** or **taglines**) begin as successful headlines, like AT&T's "Reach out and touch someone." Through continuous use, they become standard statements, not just in advertising but for salespeople and company employees.

Slogans have two basic purposes: to provide continuity to a series of ads in a campaign and to reduce an advertising message strategy to a brief, repeatable, and memorable positioning statement. The Southern California ski resort Snow Valley, for example, positions itself as "The mountain of youth." And ads for DeBeers still use the famous "Diamonds are forever" slogan. But Miller Lite's corny "It's it and that's that" was "major league pathetic," according to one *Wall Street Journal* article. Lacking the creativity, freshness, and power to become a full-fledged slogan, it was short-lived.[36]

Seals, Logos, and Signatures

A **seal** is awarded only when a product meets standards established by a particular organization such as the Good Housekeeping Institute, Underwriters Laboratories, or Parents Institute. Since these organizations are recognized authorities, their seals provide an independent, valued endorsement for the advertiser's product.

Logotypes (*logos*) and **signature cuts** (*sig cuts*) are special designs of the advertiser's company or product name. They appear in all company ads and, like trademarks, give the product individuality and provide quick recognition at the point of purchase.

Copywriting for **Electronic** Media

For electronic media, the fundamental elements—the five steps of the creative pyramid—remain the primary guides, but the copywriting formats differ. Radio and television writers prepare *scripts* and *storyboards*.

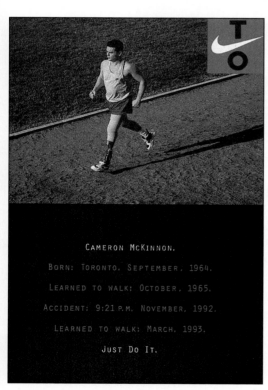

Nike (www.nike.com) uses its "Just Do It" slogan in just about all of its ads. In this example, the slogan also serves as the close. It is not a direct call to action since it does not ask the reader to purchase Nike products. However, as a finale to the tale of Cameron McKinnon, it does say to readers that they can do the things in life that they want to, and it implies that Nike products can help them succeed.

Writing Radio Copy A **script** resembles a two-column list. On the left side, speakers' names are arranged vertically, along with descriptions of any sound effects and music. The right column contains the dialog, called the **audio.**

Copywriters first need to understand radio as a medium. Radio provides entertainment or news to listeners who are busy doing something else—driving, washing dishes, reading the paper, or even studying. To be heard, an advertising message must be catchy, interesting, and unforgettable. Radio listeners usually decide within five to eight seconds if they're going to pay attention. To attract and hold the attention of listeners, particularly those not attracted to a product category, radio copy must be intrusive.

Intrusive, yes; offensive, no. An insensitive choice of words, overzealous effort to attract listeners with irritating everyday sounds (car horn, alarm clock, screeching tires), or characters that sound too exotic, odd, or dumb can cause listener resentment and ultimately lose sales. Tom Bodett's famous ads for Motel 6 demonstrate the effectiveness of a personal, relaxed, and cheerful style. Other guidelines are given in the Checklist for Creating Effective Radio Commercials.

One of the most challenging aspects is making the script fit the time slot. The delivery changes for different types of commercials, so writers must read the script

A radio script format resembles a two-column list, with speakers' names and sound effects on the left and the dialog in a wider column on the right. The quality of radio commercials depends on the actor/announcer's delivery of the message and the background music and sound effects.

McCANN-ERICKSON

RADIO SCRIPT

Client:	United Nations	**Date:**	4/95
Product:	50th Anniversary	**Length:**	:30
Title:	Health/Disease		

As Produced....

SFX - V/O	Audio
SFX: Small girl coughing	
AVO	Darjhi has whooping cough. And without medical care she might die. But today, in a United Nations' mobile health clinic, she's on the road to recovery.
SFX: Background sounds of doctor's office	
Doctor's voice	Take a deep breath.
AVO	For 50 years, the UN has developed initiatives like mobile medical units. So while 80% of the world's children *are* vaccinated against whooping cough, the UN also ensures that patients like Darjhi can receive treatment.
SFX: Background sounds of doctor's office.	
Doctor's voice	All better.
AVO	The United Nations proudly celebrates 50 years of work for better medical care. And proudly continues nursing the world back to health.

_____ **Make the big idea crystal clear.** Concentrate on one main selling point. Radio is a good medium for building brand awareness, but not for making long lists of copy points or complex arguments.

_____ **Mention the advertiser's name early and often.** If the product or company name is tricky, consider spelling it out.

_____ **Take time to set the scene and establish the premise.** A 30-second commercial that nobody remembers is a waste of money. Fight for 60-second spots.

_____ **Use familiar sound effects.** Ice tinkling in a glass, birds chirping, or a door shutting can create a visual image. Music also works if its meaning is clear.

_____ **Paint pictures with your words.** Use descriptive language to make the ad more memorable.

_____ **Make every word count.** Use active voice and more verbs than adjectives. Be conversational. Use pronounceable words and short sentences.

_____ **Be outrageous.** The best comic commercials begin with a totally absurd premise from which all developments follow logically. But remember, if you can't write humor really well, go for drama.

_____ **Ask for the order.** Try to get listeners to take action.

_____ **Remember that radio is a local medium.** Adjust your commercials to the language of your listeners and the time of day they'll run.

_____ **Presentation counts a lot.** Even the best scripts look boring on paper. Acting, timing, vocal quirks, and sound effects bring them to life.

---

out loud for timing. With electronic compression, recorded radio ads can now include 10 to 30 percent more copy than text read live. Still, the following is a good rule of thumb:

10 seconds: 20–25 words.	30 seconds: 60–70 words.
20 seconds: 40–45 words.	60 seconds: 130–150 words.[37]

Radio writing has to be clearer than any other kind of copywriting. For example, the listener can't refer back, as in print, to find an antecedent for a pronoun. Likewise, the English language is so full of homonyms (words that sound like other words) that one can easily confuse the meaning of a sentence ("who's who is whose").[38]

Writing Television Copy

Radio's basic two-column script format also works for television. But in a TV script, the left side is titled "Video" and the right side "Audio." The video column describes the visuals and production: camera angles, action, scenery, and stage directions. The audio column lists the spoken copy, sound effects, and music.

Broadcast commercials must be believable and relevant. And even zany commercials must exude quality in their creation and production to imply the product's quality. While the art director's work is very important, the copywriter typically sets the tone of the commercial, establishes the language that determines which visuals to use, and pinpoints when the visuals should appear. Research shows the techniques given in the Checklist for Creating Effective TV Commercials work best.

To illustrate these principles, let's look at a particular commercial. Many people want smooth, soft skin and consider a patch of rough, flaky skin anywhere on their body a disappointment. If you were the copywriter for Lubriderm skin lotion, how would you approach this somewhat touchy, negative subject?

The creative staff of J. Walter Thompson crafted an artistic solution for Lubriderm. An alligator was the big idea. The gator's scaly sheath was a metaphor for rough, flaky skin. Its appearance ignited people's survival instincts; they paid attention, fast. A beautiful, sophisticated woman with smooth, feminine skin was seated in a lounge chair, completely unruffled by the passing gator. The swing of the animal's back and tail echoed the graceful curves of the two simple pieces of furniture on the set, and its slow stride kept the beat of a light jazz tune.

_____ **Begin at the finish.** Concentrate on the final impression the commercial will make.

_____ **Create an attention-getting opening.** An opening that is visually surprising or full of action, drama, humor, or human interest sets the context and allows a smooth transition to the rest of the commercial.

_____ **Use a situation that grows naturally out of the sales story.** Avoid distracting gimmicks. Make it easy for viewers to identify with the characters.

_____ **Characters are the living symbol of the product.** They should be appealing, believable, nondistracting, and most of all, relevant.

_____ **Keep it simple.** The sequence of ideas should be easy to follow. Keep the number of elements in the commercial to a minimum.

_____ **Write concise audio copy.** The video should carry most of the weight. Fewer than two words per second is effective for demonstrations. For a 60-second commercial, 101 to 110 words is most effective; more than 170 words is too talky.

_____ **Make demonstrations dramatic but believable.** They should always be true to life and avoid the appearance of camera tricks.

_____ **Let the words interpret the picture and prepare viewers for the next scene.** Use conversational language; avoid "ad talk."

_____ **Run scenes five or six seconds on average.** Rarely should a scene run less than three seconds. Offer a variety of movement-filled scenes without "jumping."

_____ **Keep the look of the video fresh and new.**

This commercial opened with an attention-getting big idea that was visually surprising, compelling, dramatic, and interesting. It was also a quasi-demonstration: we saw the alligator's scaly, prickly skin, and the woman's confidence and willingness to touch the alligator as it passed by symbolized the confidence Lubriderm can bring.

This ad follows the creative pyramid. The alligator captures attention visually while the announcer's first words serve as an attention-getting headline: "A quick reminder." The ad commands us to listen and sets up the interest step that offers this claim: "Lubriderm restores lost moisture to heal your dry skin and protect it." Now for the credibility step: "Remember, the one created for dermatologists is the one that heals and protects." Then a quick trial close (action): "Lubriderm." And then the desire step recaps the primary product benefit and adds a touch of humor: "See you later, alligator."

The Role of **Art** in **Radio** and **TV** Advertising

According to *Advertising Age* columnist Bob Garfield, the best commercial in the world in 1997 was from Delvico Bates, Barcelona, for Esencial hand cream. The spot opens with a woman riding her bicycle to the persistent squeak of its unlubricated chain. She dismounts, opens a jar of Esencial, and rubs some of the cream onto the chain. Then she rides away—but the squeak is still there. Why? Because, as the voiceover points out, "Esencial moisturizes, but it has no grease."

No big production. No digital effects. No jingle. No celebrity. No big comedy payoff. Just a pure advertising idea: a problem/resolution spot where the brand pointedly cannot solve the problem. It's a vivid demonstration of brand nonattributes. Inspired. Cunning. Brilliant.

Unfortunately, it did not win the Cannes film festival because the agency missed the deadline.[39]

Developing the Artistic Concept for Commercials

Creating the concept for a radio or TV commercial is similar to creating the concept for print ads. The first step is to determine the big idea. Then the art director and copywriter must decide what commercial format to use. Should a celebrity present the message? Or should the ad dramatize the product's benefits with a semifictional story? The next step is to write a script containing the necessary copy or dialog plus a basic description of any music, sound effects, and/or camera views.

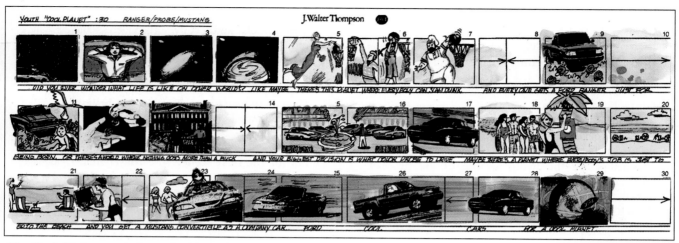

After the initial concepts for a television ad are finalized, creatives develop a storyboard rough composed of small sketches that depict the various scenes of the ad. The storyboard rough is used to provide a visual guideline for the various scenes for the final production phase, including camera angles and script.

In both radio and TV, the art director assists the copywriter in script development. But in television, artistic development is much more extensive. Using the TV script, the art director creates a series of **storyboard roughs** to present the artistic approach, the action sequences, and the style of the commercial. When the storyboard is approved, it serves as a guide for the final production phase.

Good casting is critical. The most important consideration is relevance to the product; agencies don't use a comic to sell financial products—or cremation services. And in spite of Michael Jordan's success for Nike, Gatorade, and McDonald's, some experts don't believe in using celebrities. David Ogilvy, for example, thinks viewers remember the celebrity more than the product.[40] As the concept evolves, the creative team defines the characters' personalities in a detailed, written **casting brief.** These descriptions serve as guides in casting sessions when actors audition for the roles. Sometimes agencies discover a Tony and Sharon (of Taster's Choice fame): solid, memorable characters who go beyond a simple role and actually create a personality or image for the product.

Formats for Radio and TV Commercials

Similar to print advertising, the format for a broadcast ad serves as a template for arranging message elements into a pattern. Once the art director and copywriter establish the big idea, they must determine the commercial's format.

Many radio and TV commercial styles have been successful. Some of these are listed in Ad Lab 12–B, Creative Ways to Sell on Radio. Hank Seiden, the former chair of Ketchum Advertising, developed the Execution Spectrum: 24 basic formats that range from frivolous to serious (see Exhibit 12–4). Here we consider eight common commercial formats that can be used in either radio or television: *straight announcement, presenter, testimonial, demonstration, musical, slice of life, lifestyle,* and *animation.*

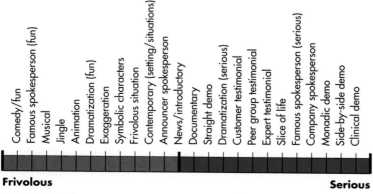

Frivolous — Comedy/fun · Famous spokesperson (fun) · Musical · Jingle · Animation · Dramatization (fun) · Exaggeration · Symbolic characters · Frivolous situation · Contemporary (setting/situations) · Announcer spokesperson · News/introductory · Documentary · Straight demo · Dramatization (serious) · Customer testimonial · Peer group testimonial · Expert testimonial · Slice of life · Famous spokesperson (serious) · Company spokesperson · Monadic demo · Side-by-side demo · Clinical demo — **Serious**

Exhibit 12–4
The Execution Spectrum, developed by Hank Seiden, shows 24 execution formats ranging in style from frivolous to serious, for both print and electronic advertising.

Creative Ways to Sell on Radio

Product demo   The commercial tells how a product is used or the purposes it serves.

Voice power   A unique voice gives the ad power.

Electronic sound   Synthetic sound-making machines create a memorable product-sound association.

Customer interview   A spokesperson and customer discuss the product advantages spontaneously.

Humorous fake interview   The customer interview is done in a lighter vein.

Hyperbole (exaggeration) statement   Overstatement arouses interest in legitimate product claims that might otherwise pass unnoticed; often a spoof.

Fourth dimension   Time and events are compressed into a brief spot involving the listener in future projections.

Hot property   Commercial adapts a current sensation: a hit show, performer, or song.

Comedian power   Established comedians do commercials in their own unique style, implying celebrity endorsement.

Historical fantasy   Situation with revived historical characters is used to convey product message.

Sound picture   Recognizable sounds involve the listener by stimulating imagination.

Demographics   Music or references appeal to a particular segment of the population, such as an age or interest group.

Imagery transfer   Musical logo or other sound reinforces the memory of a TV campaign.

Celebrity interview   Famous person endorses the product in an informal manner.

Product song   Music and words combine to create a musical logo, selling the product in the style of popular music.

Editing genius   Many different situations, voices, types of music, and sounds are combined in a series of quick cuts.

Improvisation   Performers work out the dialog extemporaneously for an assigned situation; may be postedited.

Laboratory Applications

1.   Select three familiar radio commercials and discuss which creative techniques they use.

2.   Select a familiar radio commercial and discuss how a different creative technique would increase its effectiveness.

Straight Announcement

The oldest and simplest type of radio or TV commercial and probably the easiest to write is the **straight announcement.** One person, usually a radio or TV announcer, delivers the sales message. Music may play in the background. Straight announcements are popular because they are adaptable to almost any product or situation. In radio, a straight announcement can also be designed as an **integrated commercial**—that is, it can be woven into a show or tailored to a given program.

For TV, an announcer may deliver the sales message **on camera** or off screen, as a **voiceover,** while a demonstration, slide, or film shows on screen. If the script is well written and the announcer convincing, straight announcements can be very effective. Since they don't require elaborate production facilities, they save money, too.

Straight announcements are commonly used on late-night TV programs, by local advertisers, and by nonprofit or political organizations.

Presenter

The **presenter commercial** uses one person or character to present the product and carry the sales message. Some presenters are celebrities, like Lindsay Wagner for Ford. Others are corporate officers of the sponsor, like Dave Thomas, the president of Wendy's, or actors playing a role (the lonely Maytag repairman). However, a presenter doesn't have to be a real person. Remember Tony the Tiger?

A **radio personality**, like Rush Limbaugh or Larry King, may *ad lib* an ad message live in his or her own style. Done well, such commercials can be very successful, as evidenced by the initial success of Snapple. However, the advertiser surrenders control to the personality. The main risk, outside of occasional blunders, is that the personality may criticize the product. Even so, this sometimes lends an appealing realism. The personality gets a highlight sheet listing the product's features, the main points to stress, and the phrases or company slogans to repeat. But he or she can choose the specific wording and mode of delivery.

Advertisers commonly use presenter testimonials to lend credibility to their ads. In this example by Adidas (www.adidas.com), U.S. soccer goalie Tony Meola attests to the high performance of the company's athletic shoes. Other famous presenters include Candice Bergen for Sprint, Michael Jordan for Nike, Jerry Seinfeld for American Express, and even Tony the Tiger for Kellogg's Frosted Flakes.

SUPER: Tony Meola, U.S. goalkeeper. CUT to Tony in goal in practice situation. We hear Tony's voiceover.

TONY VO: In my twenty years in the nets, I've never seen a ball do this. We see a dramatic swerve shot.

Quick cuts of balls hitting all four sweet spots of the net. TONY VO: Or this.

CUT to a speed gun recording a fast ball. TONY VO: Or this.

CUT back to a less-than-happy Tony. TONY VO: In a word, this shoe sucks.

CUT to shoe spinning in stylized environment.

Testimonial

The true **testimonial**—where a satisfied user tells how effective the product is—can be highly credible in both TV and radio advertising. Celebrities may gain attention, but they must be believable and not distract from the product. Actually, people from all walks of life endorse products, from known personalities to unknowns and nonprofessionals. Which type of person to use depends on the product and the strategy. Satisfied customers are the best sources for testimonials because their sincerity is usually persuasive. Ogilvy suggests shooting candid testimonials when the subjects don't know they're being filmed.[41] Of course, advertisers must be sure to get their permission before using the piece.

Demonstration

Television is uniquely suited to visual demonstration. And a **demonstration** convinces an audience better and faster than a spoken message. So don't say it, show it.[42] Naturally, it's easier to demonstrate the product on TV than on radio, but some advertisers have used radio to create humorous, tongue-in-cheek demonstrations.

Products may be demonstrated in use, in competition, or before and after. These techniques help viewers visualize how the product will perform for them.

Musical

The **musical commercials,** or **jingles,** we hear on radio and TV are among the best—and worst—ad messages produced. Done well, they can bring enormous success, well beyond the average nonmusical commercial. Done poorly, they can waste the advertising budget and annoy audiences beyond belief.

Ads that appeal to lifestyle present the type of user associated with the product, rather than the product itself. In this ad, Sprite (www.sprite.com) presents itself as the drink for Everyman. By contrasting two different lifestyles—the carefree beautiful people and the average working stiff—Sprite crosses social barriers, pointing out that we all get thirsty and that Sprite can quench one's thirst regardless of lifestyle or image.

(MUSIC: OPERA)
ANNCR (WITH FRENCH ACCENT): What do the really, really beautiful people drink when they get thirsty? The same thing as the rest of us.

SUPER: IMAGE IS NOTHING.
SUPER: THIRST IS EVERYTHING.

SUPER: OBEY YOUR THIRST.
ANNCR: Sprite.

Musical commercials have several variations. The entire message may be sung; jingles may be written with a **donut** in the middle (a hole for spoken copy); or orchestras may play symphonic or popular arrangements. Many producers use consistent musical themes for background color or to close the commercial. An example is the Rolling Stones' "Start Me Up," used in commercials for Windows 95 software. This is called a **musical logo.** After many repetitions of the advertiser's theme, the listener begins to associate the musical logo with the product. To achieve this, the jingle should have a **hook**—that part of the song that sticks in your memory.[43]

Advertisers have three sources of music. They can buy the right to use a tune from the copyright owner, which is usually expensive. They can use a melody in the public domain, which is free. Or they can hire a composer to write an original song. Some original tunes, including Coke's famous "I'd like to teach the world to sing," have become hits.

Slice of Life (Problem Solution)

Commercials that dramatize real-life situations are called **slice of life.** It usually starts with just plain folks, played by professional actors, discussing some problem or issue. Often the situation deals with a problem of a personal nature: bad breath, loose dentures, dandruff, body odor, or yellow laundry. A relative or a co-worker drops the hint, the product is tried, and the next scene shows the result—a happier, cleaner, more fragrant person off with a new date. The drama always concludes with a successful trial. Such commercials can get attention and create interest, even though they are often irritating to viewers and hated by copywriters.

The key to effective slice-of-life commercials is simplicity. The ad should concentrate on one product benefit and make it memorable. Often a **mnemonic device** can dramatize the product benefit and trigger instant recall. Users of Imperial margarine, for example, suddenly discover crowns on their heads.

Believability in slice commercials is difficult to achieve. People don't really talk about "the sophisticated taste of Taster's Choice," so the actors must be highly credible to put the fantasy across. That's why most *local* advertisers don't use the slice-of-life technique. Creating that believability takes very professional talent and money. In all cases, the story should be relevant to the product and simply told.

Lifestyle

To present the user rather than the product, advertisers may use the **lifestyle technique.** For example, Levi's targets its 501 Jeans messages to young, contemporary men by showing characters working in various occupations and participating in many pastimes. Likewise, beer and soft-drink advertisers frequently target their messages to active, outdoorsy young people, focusing on who drinks the brand rather than on specific product advantages.

Animation

Cartoons, puppet characters, and demonstrations with computer-generated graphics are very effective **animation techniques** for communicating difficult messages and reaching specialized markets, such as children. The way aspirin or other medications affect the human system is difficult to explain. Animated pictures of headaches and stomachs can simplify the subject and make a demonstration understandable.

Computer animation requires a great deal of faith on the part of advertisers. Since most of this very expensive work is done on the computer, there's nothing to see until the animation is well developed and a good bit of money has been spent (this is more fully discussed in Chapter 13).

Exhibit 12–5

Cut, zoom, and wipe, please! (Common abbreviations used in TV scripts.)

CU: Close-up. Very close shot of person or object.

ECU: Extreme close-up. A more extreme version of the above. Sometimes designated BCU (big close-up) or TCU (tight close-up).

MCU: Medium close-up. Emphasizes the subject but includes other objects nearby.

MS: Medium shot. Wide-angle shot of subject but not whole set.

FS: Full shot. Entire set or object.

LS: Long shot. Full view of scene to give effect of distance.

DOLLY: Move camera toward or away from subject. Dolly in (DI), dolly out (DO), or dolly back (DB).

PAN: Scan from one side to the other.

ZOOM: Move in or out from the subject without blurring.

SUPER: Superimpose one image on another (as showing lettering over a scene).

DISS: Dissolve (also DSS). Fade out one scene while fading in another.

CUT: Instantly change one picture to another.

WIPE: Gradually erase picture from screen. (Many varied effects are possible.)

VO: Voiceover. An off-screen voice, usually the announcer's.

SFX: Sound effects.

DAU: Down and under. Sound effects fade as voice comes on.

UAO: Up and over. Voice fades as sound effects come on.

Basic Mechanics of Storyboard Development

After the creative team selects the big idea and the format for a TV commercial, the art director and the writer develop the script. Television is so visually powerful and expressive that the art director's role is particularly important. Art directors must be able to work with a variety of professionals—producers, directors, lighting technicians, and set designers—to develop and produce a commercial successfully.

Storyboard Design

Once the basic script is completed, the art director must turn the video portion of the script into real images. This is done with a **storyboard,** a sheet preprinted with a series of 8 to 20 blank windows (frames) in the shape of TV screens. Below each frame is room to place the text of the commercial, including the sound effects and camera views as abbreviated in Exhibit 12–5. The storyboard works much like a cartoon strip.

Through a process similar to laying out a print ad (thumbnail, rough, comp) the artist carefully designs how each scene should appear, arranging actors, scenery, props, lighting, and camera angles to maximize impact, beauty, and mood. The storyboard helps the creatives visualize the commercial's tone and sequence of action, discover any conceptual weaknesses, and make presentations for management approval. It also serves as a guide for filming.

Even when designed to the level of a comp, though, the storyboard is only an approximation. Actual production often results in many changes in lighting, camera angle, focal point, and emphasis. The camera sees many things that the artist couldn't visualize, and vice versa (see Chapter 13 for more details on working with storyboards).

Animatic: The Video Comp

To supplement the storyboard or pretest a concept, a commercial may be taped in rough form using the writers and artists as actors. Or an **animatic** may be shot—a film strip of the sketches in the storyboard accompanied by the audio portion of the commercial synchronized on tape. Even a standard animatic now costs more than $10,000 to produce. But computers are cutting costs. Avid Technologies, for example, developed a Macintosh-based editing system that lets the agency create moving pictures on the screen, lay sound behind them, and transfer the entire package onto videotape to send to the client. This system cuts the cost to produce testable material from about $11,000 to $1,100. This kind of technology is being adopted by many agencies as they look for ways to serve clients' creative needs better for less money.

Upon approval of the storyboard and/or the animatic, the commercial is ready for production, a subject we cover in detail in Chapter 13.

Creating Ads for International Markets

In international markets, the most important consideration for copywriters and creative directors is language. In Western Europe, people speak at least 15 different languages and more than twice as many dialects. A similar problem exists in Asia, Africa, and, to a lesser extent, South America. International advertisers have debated the transferability of campaigns for years. One side believes it's too expensive to create a unique campaign for each national group. They simply translate one overall campaign into each language. Timberland, for example, thinks globally but acts locally. It creates ads for various language groups in those languages, but the overall themes are consistent around the world. Other advertisers believe the only way to ensure success is to create a special campaign for each market. Still others find both solutions expensive and unnecessary. They run their ads in English worldwide.

Advertisers must look at each situation individually. Moreover, they have to weigh the economics of various promotional strategies.

Translating Copy

Regardless of strategy, translation remains a basic issue. Classic examples of mistranslations and faulty word choices abound in international advertising. A faulty Spanish translation for Perdue chickens reads, "It takes a sexually excited man to make a chick affectionate," instead of, "It takes a tough man to make a tender chicken."[45]

A poorly chosen or badly translated product name can undercut advertising credibility in foreign markets. A classic case was when Coke's product name was

Global advertisers often use a single basic ad, translating it into the languages of the various countries where it will run.

widely translated into Chinese characters that sounded like "Coca-Cola" but meant "bite the wax tadpole."[46]

People in the United States, Canada, England, Australia, and South Africa all speak English, but with wide variations in vocabulary, word usage, and syntax. Similarly, the French spoken in France, Canada, Vietnam, and Belgium may differ as much as the English spoken by a British aristocrat and a Tennessee mountaineer. Language variations exist even within countries. The Japanese use five lingual "gears," ranging from haughty to servile, depending on the speaker's and the listener's respective stations in life. Japanese translators must know when to change gears.

Advertisers should follow some basic rules in using translators:

- *The translator must be an effective copywriter.* In the United States and Canada, most people speak English, yet relatively few are good writers and even fewer are good copywriters. Too often advertisers simply let a translation service rewrite their ads in a foreign language. That's not good enough.

- *The translator must understand the product.* The translator must also know the product's features and its market. It is always better to use a translator who is a product or market specialist rather than a generalist.

    - *Translators should translate into their native tongue.* Ideally, they should live in the country where the ad will appear. This way the advertiser can be sure the translator has a current understanding of the country's social attitudes, culture, and idioms.

    - *The advertiser should give the translator easily translatable English copy.* The double meanings and idiomatic expressions that make English such a rich language for advertising rarely translate well. They only make the translator's job more difficult.

There is no greater insult to a national market than to misuse its language. The translation must be accurate and punctuated properly, and it must also be good copy.

English is rapidly becoming the universal language for corporate ad campaigns directed to international businesspeople. Some firms still print their instructional literature and brochures in English as well. But this approach can incite nationalistic feelings against the company. Worse yet, it automatically limits a product's use to people who understand technical English.[47]

Art Direction for International Markets

Philosophers often refer to the arts as a kind of international language whose nonverbal elements translate freely regardless of culture. A nice idea but, in advertising, a very costly one. People ascribe different meanings to color depending on their culture. When designing ads for use in other countries, the art director must be familiar with each country's artistic preferences and peculiarities.

Some consider color to indicate emotion: someone "has the blues" or is "green with envy" (refer back to Ad Lab 11–A, The Psychological Impact of Color). National flags—the Canadian maple leaf, the red, white, and blue of the United States, the tricolor of France—are nonverbal signals that stir patriotic emotions, thoughts, and actions. However, these same symbols could hurt sales. For example, a promotion using the colors in the U.S. and French flags could easily fail in Southeast Asia, where some people still have painful memories of wars fought against the two countries.

When preparing an ad for an international market, the art director must be sure that the language and imagery will not offend or alienate the target audience. Cultural differences and preferences make it essential that ad copy and visuals (icons or models) are in sync with the tastes of the potential readers. This German ad for Schiesser (www.waesche-shop.de/TopSalesman) underwear uses the humor of a rhyming headline to say, in effect, that being "always nude is pretty crude."

An **icon,** a visual image representing some idea or thing, can have a meaning that cuts across national boundaries and reflects the tastes and attitudes of a group of cultures. An ad with a snake (an icon for the devil and eroticism in many Western cultures) could easily lose sales in North American markets. But in the Far East, where the snake represents renewal (by shedding its skin), the same visual might work as a dynamic expression of a product's staying power.

On a more personal level, a culture's icons can express social roles. When an agency calls a casting company or talent agent in search of a model, the agency, in essence, seeks an icon. It hopes the model will effectively symbolize the product's benefits or help the target market relate better to the ad. A model considered attractive in one culture is not necessarily seen that way in another, however.

Catchy phrases popular in a local culture are often used for advertising. But even if the idea translates verbally into another language, which is rarely the case, the art director may still have difficulty using the same imagery. Advertisers working in global markets must pretest art and design concepts with natives of each country.

Legal Restraints on International Advertisers

Finally, all advertising creativity, including what the ads say, show, or do, is at the mercy of foreign governments and cultures. As we discussed in Chapter 2, many countries strongly regulate advertising claims and the use of particular media.

Chapter **Summary**

The nonverbal aspect of an ad or commercial carries half the burden of communicating the big idea. In fact, the nonverbal message is inseparable from the verbal. Either can enhance the other or destroy it.

Design refers to how the art director and graphic artist conceptually choose and structure the artistic elements that make up an ad's appearance or set its tone. For print advertising, the first work from the art department is a simple, undeveloped design of the ad's layout. The layout has several purposes: it shows where the parts of the ad are to be placed; it is an inexpensive way to explore creative ideas; it helps the creative team check the ad's psychological or symbolic function; and it serves as a blueprint for the production process.

As advertising copy goes through the editing process, copywriters must be prepared for an inevitable (and sometimes lengthy) succession of edits and reedits from agency and client managers and legal departments. Copywriters must be more than creative; they must be patient, flexible, mature, and able to exercise great self-control.

Several steps are used to develop an ad's design: thumbnail sketch, rough layout, and comprehensive layout. The mechanical is the final art ready for reproduction. Brochures and other multipage materials use a three-dimensional rough called a dummy.

The computer has dramatically affected graphic design. Inexpensive PC software programs allow artists to paint and draw, make up pages, and manipulate images in ways that would not be possible manually. Every graphic designer must now be computer literate.

In print advertising, the visual has a great deal of responsibility for an ad's success. The picture may be used to capture the reader's attention, identify the subject of the ad, create a favorable impression, or serve a host of other functions.

The two basic devices for illustrating an ad are photos and drawings. Photography can contribute realism; a feeling of immediacy; a feeling of live action; the special enhancement of mood, beauty, and sensitivity; and speed, flexibility, and economy. Drawn illustrations do many of these things, too, and may be used if the artist feels they can achieve greater impact than photos. The chief focus for visuals may be the product in a variety of settings, a user benefit, a humorous situation, a testimonial, or even some negative appeal.

The key format elements for writing print ads are headlines, subheads, body copy, slogans, seals, logos, and signatures. Many headline types and copy styles are used in print advertising. There are five basic types of advertising headlines: benefit, provocative, news/information, question, and command. Copy styles also fall into several categories: straight sell, institutional, narrative, dialog/monolog, picture caption, and device.

The creative pyramid and the format elements come together in creating effective print ads. The headline carries the attention step, the subhead and lead-in paragraph hold the interest step, and the interior paragraphs, trial close, and close of body copy contain the credibility and desire steps. The action step takes place with the last line of copy or with the logo, slogan, and signature block.

In electronic media, copy is normally spoken dialog that is prepared using a script; it is referred to as the audio portion of the commercial. The copy may be delivered as a voiceover by an unseen announcer or on camera by an announcer, spokesperson, or actor.

Radio commercials must be intrusive to catch and hold the attention of people who are usually doing something else. Radio copy must be more conversational than print copy and should paint word pictures for listeners to see in their mind's eye.

Television copywriters use scripts and storyboards to communicate the verbal and nonverbal ideas of a commercial. When writing TV ads, the creative team must strive for credibility, relevance, and consistency in tone. While TV commercials should be entertaining, the entertainment should not interfere with the selling message.

In radio and TV advertising, art plays an important role. Art includes concept development, character definition, set and scene design, costuming, lighting, scripting, camera angles—everything having to do with the visual value of the commercial.

Common formats for radio and TV commercials include straight announcement, presenter, testimonial, demonstration, musical, slice of life, lifestyle, and animation. The art director works with a writer to develop the artistic qualities of the big idea, the format, and the storyboard. The storyboard, the basic rough design of a TV commercial, contains sketches of the scenes along with the script. To supplement the storyboard and pretest a commercial, an animatic may be used.

When creating ads for international markets, advertisers must consider the variations in language and the legal restrictions imposed by foreign governments or cultures. Art direction for international markets requires an in-depth knowledge of the foreign culture. Even if the verbal message translates well, the icons and images may not.

Important **Terms**

Review **Questions**

1. What is a layout? What is its purpose?
2. What are the steps in the design process for a print ad?
3. What color is white space?
4. From any chapter in the book, select an ad that contains a visual. What is the visual's purpose? How would you improve the visual if you were the art director?
5. What kind of headline does the ad from question 4 have? How well has the creative team followed the steps up the creative pyramid? Explain.
6. Choose an ad you don't like. Rewrite the headline using three different styles.
7. What is a storyboard, and what is its role?
8. Give examples of television spots that typify the eight major types of TV commercials.
9. Find an international ad or commercial you like. What is its message strategy? Can you discern the copy style? Do you think the copy and headline reflect the strategy? What do you like about the ad? Why?
10. What guidelines can you cite for preparing an ad in a foreign language?

Exploring the **Internet**

The Internet exercises for Chapter 12 address the following areas related to the chapter: creative boutiques (Exercise 1) and copywriting and art direction (Exercise 2).

1. Creative Boutiques

   One of the growing trends in advertising is the increased use of creative boutiques. Many of these smaller shops have stolen business from larger, full-service advertising agencies. Peruse the small sampling of creative boutiques below and answer the questions that follow.

   - AdWorks **www.adworks.com**
   - Bertha Communications **www.bertha.com**
   - B Creative **www.bcreative.com**
   - JDG Designs **www.jdgdesign.com**
   - Jan Collier Represents Online **www.collierreps.com**
   - Lightstream, Inc. **www.lightpage.com**
   - Rough Guys **www.roughguys.com**
   - Virtual Access **www.virtualaccesscorp.com**

   a. What is the focus of the company's work (consumer, business-to-business, ethnic, general market)?

   b. What are the scope and size of the company's business?

   c. What services does the company offer?

   d. What is your overall impression of the company and its work? Why?

2. Creative Resources

   As you saw in this chapter with Timberland (**www.timberland. com**), a lot goes into writing good copy and developing effec-

tive visuals. With the Internet, many new resources are available to the creative team when developing their concept.

Copywriters often rely on different sources to aid them in developing their copy. Visit the following Web sites and explain how each relates to copywriters and their task of developing effective copy.

- Copy Chef **www.copychef.com**
- Copywriting.com **www.copywriting.com**
- The Slot **www.theslot.com**
- Writers Guild of America **www.wga.org**

Like copywriters, art directors require many resources while developing their art. Familiarize yourself further with art direction by browsing the following Web sites. Be sure to discuss the importance of each to art directors.

- American Institute of Graphic Arts **www.aiga.org**
- Art Directors Club **www.adcny.org**
- Creative Cafe **www.creativity.net**
- Design & Publishing Center **www.graphic-design.com**
- designOnline **www.dol.com**
- DesktopPublishing.com **www.desktoppublishing.com**
- Digital Directory **www.digitaldirectory.com**
- Iconomics **www.iconomics.com**
- PhotoDisc **www.photodisc.com**
- Photographer Listing **www.photoscape.com/photoscape**
- Portfolios Online **www.portfolios.com**
- Right Brain Works **www.gocreate.com**

Chapter Thirteen

Producing Ads for Print, Electronic, and Digital Media

Objective To present an overview of how ads and commercials are produced for print, electronic, and digital media. With their dynamic effect on the production process, computers now give advertisers many more options for saving money and time and enhancing production quality. But to control cost and quality, advertisers still need a basic knowledge of the processes and methods used in printing and broadcasting as well as in the new digital media.

After studying this chapter, you will be able to:

- Discuss the role of computers in the print production process.
- Explain the development process for ads and brochures from initial concept through final production.
- Discuss how materials for printing are prepared for the press.
- Explain the development process for radio and TV commercials from initial concept through final production.
- Describe the major types of TV commercials.
- Understand how to save money in television production.
- Discuss the opportunities for special effects in television.
- Explain how the major types of digital media are useful to advertisers.

They decided to give the job to Kim and Kim (they like to do things in pairs at Saatchi & Saatchi). It was to be a four-color print ad for the new 1998 Toyota 4Runner. And it had to mesh perfectly with the umbrella branding campaign they had just launched for Toyota (see The Epilogue: The Complete Campaign, immediately following Chapter 17).

• Kim Edward was the copywriter and Kim Wright the art director. They were not only a creative team, they were office mates. So they spent eight hours a day together, every day, and had become quite good at playing ideas off one another. Working closely with them to see the job through to completion would be Alicia Perez, the agency's print producer assigned to that ad. Supervising the project was Joe McDonagh, Saatchi's executive creative director. Joe was demanding. The client was demanding. Toyota is the biggest client of Saatchi & Saatchi Los Angeles. In fact, it's the largest advertiser west of the Mississippi River. And the four-wheel-drive 4Runner is an important product in Toyota's lineup. This ad had to be good. • Research showed the primary target market for the 4Runner to be upper-income, middle-aged men—hardworking, upwardly mobile executives and professionals who bring home more than $60,000 a year. They're married and educated, and half of them have kids under the age of 18. On the surface, they're baby boomers. • But what

counted was who these men are under the surface. Working with McDonagh and David Purdue, the 4Runner account executive, Sally Reinman (Saatchi's director of account planning) had developed a creative brief that shed some interesting light on the target market. Her studies pointed out that, while many of these men work in the corporate rat race, struggling to climb the ladder and get ahead, what they yearn for is freedom, independence, and a little adventure in the great outdoors. In their hustle-bustle world, they ache for the peace and serenity of nature. • To Wright and Edward, this meant the 4Runner should epitomize the rugged outdoors. It could symbolize that opportunity to be off in another world. After all, the 4Runner is one of the few sport utility vehicles (SUVs) built on a truck platform. It offers the rugged, tough performance of a truck as well as the highest ground clearance in its class. That, combined with Toyota's 40-year history of building off-road vehicles, means it can go where other vehicles can't. At the same time, it offers beautiful styling and a comfortable, luxurious interior, features important to this class of customer. • So there was the germ of an idea: the spiritual concept of nature beckoning, of this wonderful world just waiting for you. Now the question was how to say that—and how to link it to the 4Runner as the enabling device for the customer to do what he wants, to actually experience the feeling of the great outdoors right now. The ad needed to capture the poetry of nature and, at the same time, appeal viscerally to the child in the man, giving him permission to experience the peace he sought. ● As the agency team looked at the variety of directions they could take, someone suggested the famous Jack London title: *The Call of the Wild*. Now there was a phrase everyone could relate to. Kim Edward started to play with that. She really liked it. Suddenly that became their theme. What is the call of the wild? It's crystalline glacial lakes, snow-capped mountains, gurgling streams, a vast blue sky, and whispering pines—it's nature. And it's calling to you, no, *whispering* . . . your name. The call of the wild is nature, beckoning to you to come out and play for a while. ● That was it! ● Kim Wright quickly worked up some sketches of the layout while Kim Edward refined the headline and worked out the body copy. Then they took it to Joe McDonagh. The layout showed an idyllic mountain lake that reflected the surrounding mountains, in the full bloom of spring but with traces of snow still left on their crests. Above the visual, Wright had placed the four-line headline with the body copy running in smaller type between each of the lines. Separating the copy from the visual would be a small inset photo of the 4Runner. ● Joe read the headline: ●

> "the call of the wild whispers your name and asks if you can come out and play."

In smaller type between the headlines ran the body copy: ●

> The wild is waiting. And so is the 4Runner, ready to take you places you've only dreamt of before—and to some you never knew existed. All in a sophisticated, roomy comfort that will embrace not only your body, but your sense of adventure. The 1998 Toyota 4Runner. Answer the call.

"Beautiful. I love it," said Joe. "Let me show it to Dave. He'll want to get Mike's approval" (Michael Bevan, Toyota's national advertising manager). "In the meantime, let's plan to really do it right. Call Alicia." ● With their approval, the ad would go into production. Print producer Alicia Perez's job would now begin, and her work would either make or break the ad.[1] ●

Managing the Advertising Production Process

The average reader has little idea of the intricate, technical stages that ads go through from start to finish. But experienced advertising people do, especially art directors, designers, print production managers, and producers. They know that details give an ad added impact and com-

While the copy may require only 15 seconds for a reader to embrace the "Call of the Wild," most people don't realize that, from initial concept to completion, an ad of this caliber may require from three weeks to a month, or even longer, to create. As ideas are born and discarded and then meticulously crafted into a finished work, an advertisement passes through many hands before it is finally ready to make its first public appearance.

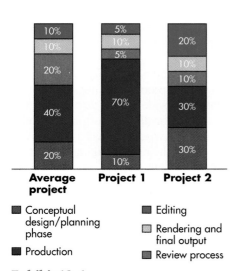

Average project   **Project 1**   **Project 2**

■ Conceptual design/planning phase
■ Production

■ Editing
■ Rendering and final output
■ Review process

Exhibit 13–1
Time allocation comparison.

pleteness. Since careful management is the key to success in producing advertising, we'll discuss some of the management issues before examining the details of the production processes.

The Role of the Production Manager or Producer

Every ad or commercial represents the completion of a highly complex process that includes many steps, such as the reproduction of visuals in full color, the shooting and editing of scenes, the precise specification and placement of type, and the checking, approving, duplicating, and shipping of final art, negatives, tape, or film to various communications media (newspapers, magazines, radio and TV stations, and sometimes even computer stores).

These tasks are usually the responsibility of a **print production manager** or, for electronic media, a **producer** (at Saatchi & Saatchi, they're all called producers). The overall responsibility of this manager is to keep the project moving smoothly and under budget, while maintaining the required level of quality through every step of the production process.

Essentially, production managers and producers perform the four classic functions of management: *planning, organizing, directing,* and *controlling.* At Saatchi, for example, Alicia Perez had to review the conceptual art and then *plan* which production process would resolve each requirement. Next she *organized* the tasks and established priorities in order to meet the client's media schedule. She then *directed* the production staff in completing each section of the art. Finally, to perform the *control* function—essential for optimizing quality, economy, and speed—she carefully reviewed the work of each staffer and subcontractor and solicited feedback from her supervisor and the art director, just to be sure they were all on the same track. Supervising Alicia was Charlene Washburn, Saatchi's director of print services.

Planning and Organizing

An important facet of management is the *allocation of time.* Each phase of a project comprises many tasks, so the production manager must anticipate where irregularities may occur within each phase. For example, five phases are needed to complete one animated commercial, but the amount of time required for each may vary greatly from spot to spot, as shown in Exhibit 13–1.[2]

Directing and Controlling

Supervising the production staff and suppliers is another challenge. If artists fail to follow the art director's design correctly, they can kill an ad's power, beauty, and effectiveness. Improper printing processes, papers, or inks can also weaken the impact of the image, increase costs, and even lead to time-consuming reprinting. Print production managers can lose tens of thousands of their client's or agency's dollars (and sometimes their jobs) by forgetting to double-check the details of print production and the work of the production staff.

Charlene Washburn points out that the producer also has to keep up with all the technological changes occurring in print and electronic production, including the emerging forms of *digital media* (multimedia, interactive media, and online networks). And since virtually all ad agency employees now use computers, the manager must also understand how computers serve the production process and which software programs offer the best results.[3]

Managing Production Costs When Saatchi began working on the 4Runner ad, it submitted an estimate for anticipated production costs, including computer artwork and subcontracted work like photography, reproduction services, and delivery. When Perez received the approved ad concepts a couple of weeks later, it was understood that she would keep the actual costs below the estimate.

A good production manager continually monitors the time spent on a job and the charges submitted by outside suppliers so as to not exceed the budget. The big effort is to control *unplanned costs*.

Common Budget Busters

There are five problems that commonly break budgets. The most frequent cause of cost overruns is *inadequate planning* and lack of preparation. Another culprit is *production luxuries*. When the creative director wants to reward the staff by taking everyone to lunch at the company's expense, the first question should be: "Was money budgeted for this?" The third budget buster is *overtime:* night and weekend work. Whenever possible, managers should develop alternative plans to avoid overtime hours. *Special equipment* for unusual production effects can also wreak havoc on budgets. It's often far more expensive to use an exotic computer gizmo than standard equipment. Finally, a complex *hierarchy* of decision makers, approvers, and lawyers can stall decision making, cause negative debate, and stop progress.

International advertisers should also be aware that foreign taxation on production costs varies widely from country to country. Argentina, for instance, charges a blanket 21 percent VAT (value-added tax) on all production costs as well as on media-buying commissions. In 1996 it imposed a further 10.5 percent tax on media placement.[4]

Some other budget issues are peculiar to each medium.

Managing the Cost of Print Production

The term *print production* refers to the systematic process an approved design goes through from concept to final publication in a printed medium such as magazines, newspapers, or collateral materials like brochures and direct-mail packages.

For print media, production managers can choose from more than 60 techniques to execute the creative team's design and get it printed on any of a variety of materials (usually paper).[5] They must translate the rough or comprehensive design into a final assembly of black-and-white artwork called a *mechanical* or *paste-up*. Then they make sure the mechanical is converted into a correct set of negatives for the printer to use to make printing plates. We'll discuss this process in detail shortly.

A big cost factor in the production of the 4Runner ad was the *reprographic service bureau* that provided all the color separations, proofs, and negatives. Many production managers prefer using their printer to provide all the *prepress graphic services* (such as processing negatives from artwork or disk). Most printers today offer digital graphic services in-house, and they know exactly which processing specifications yield the most suitable negatives for their platemaking equipment and printing presses. They also tend to charge less than outside service bureaus. Other production managers feel safer ordering the negatives from a reprographics service bureau because it's a specialized service and they get to proof the negatives before the printer mounts them for platemaking (a process called *stripping*).

Paper costs affect budgets, too. When agencies place ads in print media, the cost of paper is included in the charge for the ad. They don't notice this pass-along cost. But when an agency prints collateral materials such as data sheets, brochures, or packaging for a client, the cost of paper is noticeable. For example, on a full-color job, a short run of 2,000 units would require only a few thousand sheets of paper (a variable cost), while the prepress and press set-up charges (fixed costs) would comprise the bulk of the final selling price. But if the same job had a long run of 100,000 or more units, the prepress and press setup charges would remain the same, while the cost for paper would rise according to the volume used—a cost increase of 700 to 1,000 percent. Thus, paper costs could greatly outweigh press costs.

For *sheetfed* printing jobs (where individual sheets are fed into the press), the cost of paper averages about 22 percent of the selling price of the job. Huge *web presses,* frequently used by catalog publishers and magazines, require rapid printing, so they use rolls of paper and inks that dry instantly when heated (*heat set*). The paper cost for this process averages about 35 percent of the printer's selling price.[6]

Managing the Cost of Electronic Production

The term **electronic production** refers to the process of converting a script or storyboard to a finished commercial for use on radio, TV, or digital media. While the overall process is similar to print production, the technical details and the costs of electronic production are quite different. And the end result, rather than print film or negatives, may be audio or videotape, motion picture film, or some digital format like CD-ROM or floppy disk.

Radio   Radio is the least expensive electronic medium to produce because it deals only with the dimension of sound. Equipment and labor costs are less than for, say, TV production. There's no need for hairstylists, makeup artists, or cue-card holders. And commercials are duplicated on inexpensive audiotape.

The primary control factors in producing radio spots, therefore, are the costs of talent and music. Celebrity talent, especially, can be very expensive. But even the cost of standard union talent, paid at **scale** (the regular charge agreed to in the union contract), can mount rapidly if there are multiple voices or if the commercial is aired in many markets or for an extended period of time. The advertiser, for example, may initially contract for a four-week or a thirteen-week run. If the commercial is extended beyond that time, the advertiser will have to pay a **residual fee** to the talent again.

Likewise, the cost of original music (composing, scoring, and orchestration) can range from very inexpensive to frightful, depending on the talent and scope of use. For this reason, many clients—especially small local and regional advertisers—prefer to use prerecorded music available for commercial use from the studio or radio station.

Television   Many companies require the broad coverage and impact offered by TV. However, the television industry is susceptible to prohibitive costs of equipment and labor. In 1996, the average cost of producing a 30-second national television spot was $278,000.[7] With costs like that, clients become very picky very quickly (see Exhibit 13–2).

There is a belief in the industry that high-priced celebrity talent and extravagant effects get attention and increase memorability. It turns out that's not true. A recent study showed that advertising that features a brand differentiation message along with a demonstration of the product is actually more effective and costs on average 28 percent less. The study further indicated that advertisers sometimes use lavish production values to compensate for having nothing to say.[8]

Numerous factors can torture TV production budgets. They include the use of children and animals, superstar talent and directors, large casts, animation, involved opticals, special effects, stop-motion photography, use of both location and studio shooting for one commercial, expensive set decoration or construction, additional shooting days, and major script changes during a shoot.[9] Commercial producers have to be aware of all these factors and plan for them very carefully.

Exhibit 13–2

Average cost to produce a TV commercial ($ thousands).

Commercial type	1996 National advertisers
Special effects	$453
Interview/testimonial	143
Multistory line/vignettes	313
Single situation—voiceover	274
Single situation—dialog	257
Animation	284
Large-scale product performance	336
Song and dance	372
Monolog	161
Tabletop/ECU products, food	172

The Power of Color on the Internet

Before the introduction of computers into graphic design, advertisers used only swatches from color palettes, like PANTONE®, to match colors and reproduce eye-catching ads. In fact, until the advent of computers, the CMYK and PANTONE MATCHING SYSTEM® processes worked well for print production. But computer monitors reproduce colors on-screen through a completely different color system known as RGB. This created problems at first. Today, though, most graphic design software can easily convert the RGB color values of computers into the PANTONE® numbering system used by printers.

While the Internet has become an incredible new medium for advertisers, the color configurations of HTML (the language used by World Wide Web graphic designers) pose a similar problem to the RGB dilemma. Because of the nature of HTML and the differences in complex computer hardware, Web page colors viewed on one monitor can change dramatically when viewed on another monitor. To solve the problem, PANTONE® developed PANTONE® Color-Web™ Pro software, that facilitates color conversions from HTML to RGB and the PANTONE MATCHING SYSTEM® provides consistent Web page color reproduction from any computer monitor.

Now, PANTONE® engineers are developing other techniques, as well as calibration devices, to assist software and hardware developers to create products and color systems that support universal, device-independent color standards. Software companies such as Adobe, Corel, and Macromedia use these most recent innovations in color to help designers create visuals with the most stunning and technically accurate color palettes possible.

Digital media   The computer has engendered a whole new class of digital media. This has dramatically increased the importance of the tasks performed by the agency producer and creative staff and made it critical for them to stay current with new recording and duplicating processes as well as special-effects technology.

In the past, to display their portfolios dramatically, agencies created **multimedia presentations** with fast-paced slide shows using multiple projectors and synchronized, recorded sound. Today's multimedia presenter aims a laser beam at the screen, and a sensor signals a portable computer to fade the slide machine and brighten the RGB projector. Then it runs a short animated video, complete with computer graphics and special effects. The creative team may write these multimedia sales presentations, but the production managers and producers are typically responsible for actually creating them.[10] Doing this in a cost-effective manner can be a challenge.

One of the new media created by the computer is the stand-alone electronic **kiosk.** While there were some 70,000 kiosks in the United States in 1995, that number was expected to explode to over 600,000 by 1998. Kiosks feature a computerized interactive touch screen, a printer, and in some cases, a credit-card reader. Agencies are busy preparing storyboards, electronic images, and presentations for them. Advertising production managers now must know about presentation and image software and know reliable suppliers for cabinet fabrication and computer hardware installation.[11]

Finally, some ads are totally created by computer for use on computers—electronic images and text designed for transmission around the world via the Internet or some online service such as CompuServe, Prodigy, or America Online. The production manager can construct ads using off-the-shelf image and text development software. But to go onto the Internet, the completed files

Advertisements created by a computer for use on another computer are commonplace to anybody who surfs the World Wide Web. As they peruse the Internet from their home, office, or school, consumers in search of information now see multitudes of computer-produced online advertisements. As an example, check out the auto channel on the Excite search engine (www.excite.com).

have to be combined with computer programming. For this service, most production managers subcontract the work—but they have to know the suppliers, and charges can range from $30 to $100 per hour.[12] Saatchi & Saatchi, for instance, has a special design and interactive media group that creates Internet advertising for Toyota, but for the computer programming, it subcontracts to Nova Media in San Francisco.[13]

The overall production process for creating images, graphic design, texts, and interactive digital programs for various electronic media is similar to working in print. Final output, though, is to a medium suitable for storage and transmission: CD-ROM, diskette, data cartridge, or a transmittable computer file.

With digital media, costs rise dramatically when multiple copies are made. CD-ROMs can cost as little as $3 each if you purchase 1,000 copies or more. This is because of the up-front, fixed cost of making a master. Computer diskettes can cost less than $1 each to duplicate, but they hold only a few hundred pages of information. Cartridges hold up to 1,200 pages, but at $40 or more each, they are not yet suitable for mass marketing.

The **Print** Production Process

Once Joe McDonagh and Michael Bevan, Toyota's national advertising manager, gave the go-ahead on the 4Runner ad concept, Alicia Perez could turn her full attention to it. The process she used was the same as for any other print job, whether a brochure, a poster, or a direct-mail piece. Her goal is always the same—to produce the job as closely as possible to the concept intended by the creative team.

The **print production process** consists of four major phases: *preproduction, production, prepress,* and *printing and distribution.* For a simple model of this process, see Exhibit 13–3 (a more detailed version appears in RL 13–1 in the Reference Library).

The Preproduction Phase: Planning the Project

The first step, **preproduction,** begins when the creative department submits the approved creative concepts—rough or comprehensive layout and copy—to the production department. The production manager's first task is to log the project into the department's *traffic system* and open a **job jacket** for storing the various pieces of artwork and ideas that will be generated throughout the process. The next task is to examine the general nature of the job and consider several questions pertinent to managing it efficiently. For example:

- What equipment will be needed?
- How will we get it? (Will we have to lease another machine?)
- What materials are necessary? (If this is a packaging job, what material will we be printing on: tin, paper, cardboard?)
- What human resources are needed? (Do we need to hire any freelancers?)
- How many production artists will be needed? (Is the deadline so near that we'll have to call up the reserves?)

Working backward from publication **closing dates** (deadlines), the production manager decides when each step of the work must be completed. Deadlines can vary from months to hours. The manager tries to build extra time into each step because every word, art element, and aesthetic choice may need some last-minute change.

Once these general questions are answered, the production manager can look more closely at the specific needs of the project.

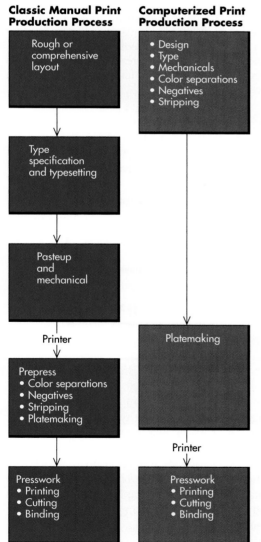

Classic Manual Print Production Process

Rough or comprehensive layout

Type specification and typesetting

Pasteup and mechanical

Printer

Prepress
• Color separations
• Negatives
• Stripping
• Platemaking

Presswork
• Printing
• Cutting
• Binding

Computerized Print Production Process

• Design
• Type
• Mechanicals
• Color separations
• Negatives
• Stripping

Platemaking

Printer

Presswork
• Printing
• Cutting
• Binding

Exhibit 13–3
The print production process.

The Characteristics of Type

Readability

The most important consideration in selecting a typeface is readability. As David Ogilvy says, good typography helps people read; bad typography prevents them from doing so. General factors that contribute to readability include the type's style, boldness, and size; the length of the line; and the spacing between words, lines, and paragraphs. An ad is meant to be read, and reduced readability kills interest. Difficult-to-read typefaces should be used infrequently and only to create special effects.

Large, bold, simply designed typefaces are the easiest to read. However, the amount of space in the ad and the amount of copy that must be written limit the use of these type forms. The length of the line of copy can also affect the readability. Newspaper columns are usually less than 2 inches wide; magazine columns slightly wider. For ads, columns of copy should be less than 3 inches (18 picas) wide.

Spacing between lines also influences an ad's readability. Space between lines of type allows for descenders (the part of the letter that extends downward, as in the letters j, g, p) and ascenders (the part of the letter that extends upward, as in the letters b, d, k). When this is the only space between lines, type is said to be "set solid." Sometimes an art director adds extra space between lines (called **leading,** pronounced "ledding") to give a more "airy" feeling to the copy. The name comes from the thin lead strips that used to be inserted between lines of metal type.

Kerning (spreading or narrowing the spaces between letters) also improves an ad's appearance and readability. The narrower the kerning, the more type can fit into the available space. Narrow kerning is effective in headlines because people read large type faster when the letters are close together. But narrow kerning is hard to read if overdone or in smaller type sizes.

Appropriateness

A typeface must be appropriate to the product being advertised. Each typeface and size conveys a mood and feeling quite apart from the meanings of the words themselves. One typeface whispers "luxury," another screams "bargain!" A typeface that looks old-fashioned is probably inappropriate for an electronic watch.

Harmony/Appearance

Advertising novices often mix too many typefaces, creating disharmony and clutter. Type should harmonize with the other elements of an ad, including the illustration and layout. Skilled artists choose typefaces in the same family or faces that are closely related in appearance.

Emphasis

Contrast creates emphasis. Artists often use more than one type style or mix italic and roman, small and large type, lowercase and uppercase. But they must be careful not to emphasize all elements or they won't emphasize any.

Classes of Type

There are two classes of type used in advertising.

Display type is larger and heavier than text type; useful in headlines, subheads, logos, and addresses, and for emphasis.

Text type is smaller and finer, used in body copy.

Type Groups

Serif (roman) type is the most popular type group due to its readability and warm personality. It is distinguished by small lines or tails called serifs that finish the ends of the main strokes and by variations in the thickness of the strokes. It comes in a wide variety of designs and sizes.

Sans serif (gothic) type is the second most popular type group; also referred to as block or contemporary. Characterized by lack of serifs (hence the name sans serif) and relatively uniform thickness of the strokes, it is not as readable as roman but is widely used because the simple, clean lines give a slick, modern appearance (see **a**).

Roman type	Square serif type
Typography	**Typography**
Typography	
Typography	**Script type**
Typography	*Typography*
	Typography
Sans serif type	
Typography	**Ornamental type**
Typography	Typography
TYPOGRAPHY	Typography

a.

Typography and Copy Casting Art directors select type styles to enhance the desired personality of the product and complement the tone of the ad. Typefaces affect an ad's appearance, design, and readability. Good type selection can't compensate for a weak headline, poor body copy, or an inappropriate illustration, but it can create interest and attract readers.

It's imperative that production managers as well as graphic artists understand **typography,** the art of selecting and setting type. Advertising artists have to know the five major type groups, the artistic variations within a type family, and the structure of type. They should consider four important concepts when selecting type: *readability, appropriateness, harmony or appearance,* and *emphasis.* Ad Lab 13–A, The Characteristics of Type, describes these and other type-related topics.

Square serif type combines sans serif and serif typefaces. It has serifs, but letter strokes have uniform thickness.

Cursive or script type resembles handwriting; letters often connect and may convey a feeling of femininity, formality, classicism, or beauty. It is difficult to read and is used primarily in headlines, formal announcements, and cosmetic and fashion ads.

Ornamental type uses novel designs with a high level of embellishment and decorativeness. It adds a "special effects" quality but is often difficult to read.

Type Families

A **type family** is made up of related typefaces. The serif typeface you are reading now is called Garamond Light. Within a family, the basic design remains the same but varies in the proportion, weight, and slant of the characters. The type may be light, medium, bold, extra bold, condensed, extended, or italic. Variations enable the typographer to provide contrast and emphasis without changing the family (see **b**).

A **font** is a complete assortment of capitals, small capitals, lowercase letters, numerals, and punctuation marks for a particular typeface and size.

Measuring Type

Type characters have height, width, weight, and, for some ornamental typefaces, depth. They also come in shapes called a case. And with the advent of computers, type comes in a variety of resolutions.

Size is the height of a character (or letter) measured in **points** (72 points to the inch) from the bottom of the descenders to the top of the ascenders (see **c**).

The set width of a letter, known as an em space, is usually based on the maximum width and proportions of the capital letter "M" for that particular typeface. Set width of the letter "N" is called an en space.

Capital letters are uppercase, small letters lowercase (in the hot-type era, compositors stacked the case containing the capital letters above the one with the small letters). It's easiest to read a combination of uppercase and lowercase. Type may be set in all caps (for emphasis) or in commoncase (caps and small caps).

Resolution refers to the fineness of the type. The goals of fine typesetting are readability, clarity, and smoothness of appearance. Type on a computer screen is usually 72 to 78 dots per inch (dpi). A dot-matrix printer outputs type at 360 dpi, a laser printer at over 600 dpi. The preferred level of quality for magazines and brochures begins at 1,000 dpi; advertisers often use resolutions of 2,400 to 3,750 dpi.

Laboratory Applications

Use the various figures and terms in this Ad Lab to answer the following:

1. Describe the class, group, family, and size of the type used in the title "Producing Ads for Print, Electronic, and Digital Media," which appears on the first page of this chapter.

2. Do the same for the captions that appear with the exhibits in this book.

Garamond Book	Garamond Condensed Book
Garamond Book Italic	*Garamond Condensed Book Italic*
Garamond Bold	**Garamond Condensed Bold**
Garamond Bold Italic	***Garamond Condensed Bold Italic***
Garamond Light	Garamond Condensed Light
Garamond Light Italic	*Garamond Condensed Light Italic*
Garamond Ultra	**Garamond Condensed Ultra**
Garamond Ultra Italic	***Garamond Condensed Ultra Italic***

b.

Text type	Display type
6 pt. Type size	16 pt. Type size
8 pt. Type size	18 pt. Type size
9 pt. Type size	20 pt. Type size
10 pt. Type size	24 pt. Type size
12 pt. Type size	30 pt. Type size
14 pt. Type size	36 pt. Type size

c.

Artists who plan to buy type outside must **copy cast** (or *copyfit*) to calculate the total block of space the type will occupy in relation to the typeface's letter size and proportions. This is an important task because type is expensive to buy and costly to change. There are two ways to fit copy: the word-count method and the character-count method.

With the **word-count method,** the words in the copy are counted and divided by the number of words per square inch that can be set in a particular type style and size, as given in a standard table. The **character-count method** is more accurate. Someone counts the actual number of characters (letters, word spaces, and punctuation marks) in the copy, finds the average number of characters per *pica*

continued on page 419

Creative Department: From Concept through Production of a Magazine Ad and TV Commercial

Marketing Considerations

In the 1990s, the U.S. automobile business experienced a major shift as people became more focused on family and relationships and more concerned with quality-of-life issues rather than material possessions. As a result, sales of high-status luxury cars and sports cars declined, and the most popular vehicle segments became sedans and sports utility vehicles (SUV).

The Situation

By 1997, most auto manufacturers understood the trends and were jumping on the SUV bandwagon. While Toyota had a big head start with its 40-year heritage of building off-road vehicles, it still faced increased competition. Moreover, the company offered 13 different auto and truck models—far more than most other manufacturers—which had the effect of fragmenting its advertising dollars. Toyota's 4Runner SUV was a very popular vehicle, but it still represented less than one-fifth of the company's total sales. Its share of advertising voice, therefore, would not be large, making it even more difficult to break through the clutter of automotive ads. When media dollars are limited, that means the creative work must be outstanding.

Marketing and Advertising Objectives

National automotive advertising traditionally aims at generating awareness and building brand imagery so that the company's vehicles will enter the consumer's evoked set, or consideration list. Toyota and its agency, Saatchi & Saatchi, set specific communication objectives for the 4Runner campaign: to build the 4Runner's image as the most rugged SUV in its class.

Target Markets

Demographically, the primary target market was men 35 to 40 years old, mostly married, and with a household income over $60,000. The psychographic character of the market, described next, was the real key to the campaign.

Creative Strategy

The creative strategy included a mix of product concept, target audience, communications media, and advertising message.

1. *Product concept.* The 4Runner enables its owner to answer the call of the wild and enhances his sense of self-reliance. One of the few SUVs built on a truck platform, it offers the rugged, tough performance of a truck. High ground clearance lets it go where others can't. And luxurious appointments add comfort and style to the experience.

2. *Target audience.* The campaign would focus on upwardly mobile men aged 35 to 40. The 4Runner man is not just interested in transportation. He likes to think of himself as adventurous, independent, capable, and in control of his own destiny. While he may be an urban dweller, his soul belongs to the outdoors. He longs for the peace and serenity—and adventure—that nature offers.

3. *Communications media.* Saatchi & Saatchi proposed a mixed-media campaign of print ads in upscale consumer and auto/outdoor enthusiast magazines, as well as radio and TV. In addition, the 4Runner campaign theme would be carried over to Toyota's Internet Web site.

4. *Advertising message.* The message strategy was to portray the 4Runner as the means to answer the "call of the wild." This theme would be sophisticated and understated, acknowledging the inherent intelligence and self-assurance of the target market. In print, this meant beautiful visuals and elegant typography, with minimal copy written in a quiet, almost-poetic voice. The TV approach would be slice of life—thoughtful, introspective, and revealing.

Production Planning

Once the creative roughs were approved, the production supervisors prepared the schedule for both TV and print production. Considerations included Toyota's marketing and media deadlines; logistical concerns such as location filming permits and security; seasonal conditions; and production factors such as equipment needs, production support people, and facilities. The production department also prepared cost estimates for approval by agency and client managers.

4Runner print ad production schedule

To ensure precise and timely execution in ad production, agencies develop production schedules that outline all the major project deadlines. For the 4Runner, the production schedule provided concrete deadlines for headlines and layouts, body copy, art, mechanicals, proofs, and final shipping. Also included in the schedule were the necessary approvals by client personnel and various legal departments.

SAATCHI & SAATCHI / LOS ANGELES
PRINT PRODUCTION SCHEDULE   **Rev #:**

FROM:	David Purdue	DATE:	6/10/97
TO:	Alicia Perez	CLIENT:	TMS
JOB:	'98 4Runner Print Ad	JOB#	PT8-062

DUE DATES	ACTION	MISCELLANEOUS INFORMATION
	HEADLINE/LAYOUT:	* first close is August 4th
6/23	▪ Approval by AE/Creative	
6/25	▪ Approval by Client	** Job calls for PG 4/C Bleed
6/27	▪ Approval by TMS Legal	
6/27	▪ Approval by S&S Legal	
6/30	PRE-PRODUCTION MEETING	
7/2	ESTIMATE TO AE/AAE	
7/3	ESTIMATE APPROVAL	
	COPY:	
7/4	▪ Approval by AE/Creative	
7/8	▪ Approval by Client	
7/14	▪ Approval by TMS Legal	
7/14	▪ Approval by S&S Legal	
7/15	JOB TICKET TO STUDIO	
	ART:	
N/A	PROCEED WITH ART/PHOTO SHOOT	
7/7	▪ Internal Review of Art/Photos	
7/14	▪ Approval by Client/Legal	
7/15	▪ Art to Production	
7/16-7/21	RETOUCHING	
	MECHANICAL(S):	
7/17	▪ Internal Approvals	
7/18	▪ Client Approval of mechanical(s)	
7/21	▪ Mechanical(s) to Production	
	PROOF(S):	
7/24	1ST PROOF DUE (patch proof)	
7/28	2ND PROOF DUE (stripped)	
7/29	CLIENT APPROVAL OF PROOF	
7/30	**FINAL PROOF DUE**	
8/1	**SHIP MATERIALS**	
8/4	**FIRST MATERIAL CLOSING**	

Please note the following:
▪ If for any reason the above deadlines cannot be met, AAE Internal Operations must be informed immediately.
▪ Unless otherwise notified, AAE Internal Operations assumes management approval has been obtained when necessary.

CC: J. McDonagh, M. Turpin, T. Balagia, K. Edward, K. Wright, I. Beavis, E. Franco, P. Oyague, E. Graffeo, K. Lopez, D. Bergin, J. Caprini, T. DiOrio, A. M. Jeffrey, J. Kelly, S. Martin, T. Meridith, D. Millette, S. Migliaccio, S. Mistry, J. Phillips, C. Washburn, E. Weiss, Cost Control

Print Production Process

The print ad would show the 4Runner to identify it, but not large enough to detract from the beauty of the nature photograph or the elegance of the typography. The verbal and nonverbal messages had to work in perfect concert, so balance was a key decision issue.

Kim Wright prepared the initial layouts using a 4Runner photo supplied by Toyota. The nature photo came from a photographer's stock library. It was well shot, but required computer retouching to add more light to some areas and adjust the colors. The photo actually required two transparencies; one of them had better mountains than the other, so Alicia Perez stripped in the sky from one over the mountains of the other.

4Runner print—mountains retouching
Although advertising photographs are often commissioned and shot with a specific ad in mind, they may also be obtained from a stock photography company. In this case, Saatchi & Saatchi actually used two stock photos. After digitally enhancing them, the agency then spliced together the best elements of each to create the final image of the mountains. Stock agencies license generic photographs for use in advertisements. The license agreement typically covers only the original advertising use and is good for a limited run of the ad. Photographers who sell their photos to stock agencies are paid according to where and how often their work is used.

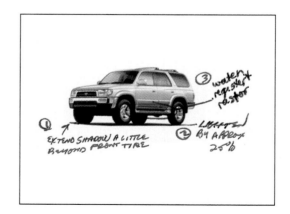

Print Production and Distribution

The production team assembled the approved copy and photography and opened a computer graphics file featuring guide-marked pages based on the specs provided by the magazines in which the ads would appear. The photo was rescanned larger and with higher resolution. The final mechanicals were sent to the reprographic service bureau for color separations, proofs, and negs. Once these were all approved, the service bureau forwarded the negs to the appropriate media.

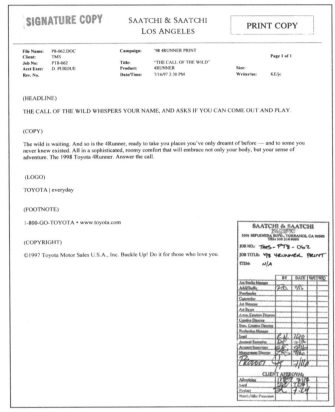

4Runner print copy approval

This is the copy approval form used by Saatchi & Saatchi for the "Call of the Wild" print ad. Before the ad was produced, approvals were obtained from the various management, creative, and legal departments of both parties.

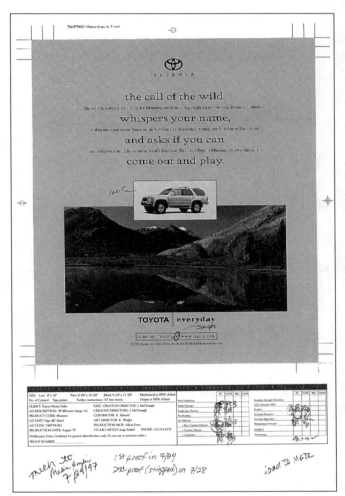

4Runner print black and white mechanical with changes and approvals

In the early phases of production, when the focus is on copy and overall design, mechanical layouts are produced in black and white, which speeds up the process and reduces cost.

Yellow

4 R U N N E R

the call of the wild

The wild is waiting. And so is the 4Runner, ready to take you places you've only dreamt of

whispers your name,

before — and to some you never knew existed. All in a sophisticated, roomy comfort that will embrace

and asks if you can

not only your body, but your sense of adventure. The 1998 Toyota 4Runner. Answer the call.

come out and play.

TOYOTA | *everyday*

4 process colors combined

4Runner print final proof with final approvals

Near the end of the production schedule, print ads enter the final proofing stage. Here the ad is viewed in full color to check for any final corrections before going to press.

Television Production Process

Sally Reinman and Joe McDonagh drafted a creative brief based on the advertising strategy determined by Saatchi & Saatchi and Toyota and presented it to copywriter Mike Whitlow and art director Doug Van Andel for scripting. They developed the Epiphany approach, wrote the script, and gave a final draft to the agency account people for critique and approval.

A set of storyboards was prepared from the approved script. Van Andel selected thumbnails for several sets of frames and sent them to broadcast producer Jeff Beverly and Joe McDonagh for review. The approved thumbnails were then rendered into final frames, and copy was typeset and printed on desktop computers. The frames and text were mounted for presentation to Toyota's marketing people, to the director, and to other company approvers. With creative approval granted, the production budget and schedule were finalized and work began.

Preproduction

Reactor Films was chosen to produce the TV spots. Working with T. K. Knowles, Reactor's executive producer, Jeff Beverly organized the project. Director John Mastromonaco, the creative team, and Beverly reviewed the script, breaking it down into elements and scenes. They reviewed each scene for the imagery and sound effects required. Casting began two weeks before the shoot. The talent was selected and the streets and subways of New York City were chosen for location shooting.

The cinematographer reviewed the storyboard, chose camera angles and individual shots, determined equipment needs, gathered and scheduled camera crews, and prepared a shooting schedule with daily filming goals. Executing the project also required negotiating contracts and hiring a variety of services and personnel, among them insurance, catering, special equipment (lighting, cranes, dollies, cellular phones), film processing labs, motor homes, permits, and transportation.

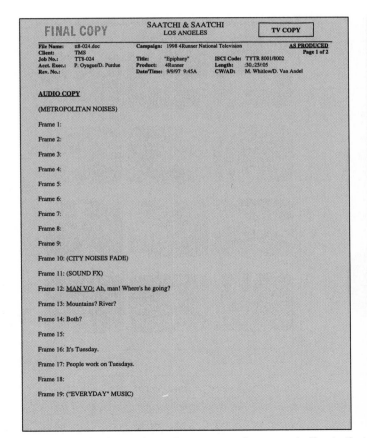
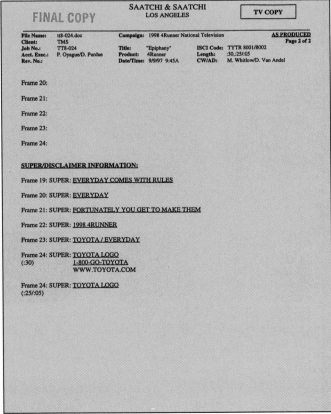

Television ads also go through an approval process similar to that of print. One of the initial steps is to write out the script for the ad and to obtain all necessary permissions.

Production

A two-day shooting schedule ran during the weekend from early morning until late each night. In fact, the subway scene required an all-night shoot since that was the only time it could be closed down. The shoot called for one camera crew, talent and wardrobe time, and filming sequences for a variety of purposes and camera angles. Planned shots had the executive walking in the subway station and on the city streets surrounded by extras. Other shots included sequences where he visually caressed every angle of the vehicle. And then there were shots of the 4Runner taken from a multitude of angles, showing it driving up, stopping at the light, and driving off. Each day's rolls of film—the *dailies*—were shipped to the processing lab.

Postproduction: Dailies to Distribution Prints

The day after the shoot, the postproduction phase began. The film was digitally converted and viewed on an Avid computer to select key sequences. In a 10-day editing process, each scene was polished and then assembled into a final, intriguing spot with no music but lush sound effects. Over the next three days, the spot was presented within Saatchi & Saatchi and revised. It was then taken to Toyota, and final revisions were completed on the last day. Dubs of the commercial were distributed to the appropriate media.

Campaign Results

The 4Runner SUV is not the largest segment of Toyota's business, but it's an important one. It is also one of the fastest-growing segments. Based on informal surveys of the target audience following the campaign launch, the agency and client believe it is achieving its goal of positioning the 4Runner as the best SUV to get you to the great outdoors.

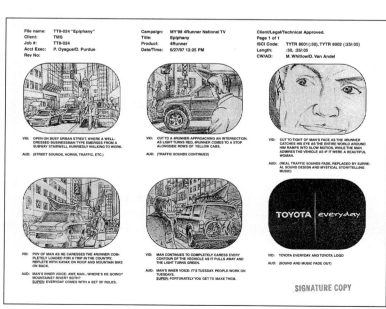

Storyboard of "Epiphany" TV commercial

The storyboard for television ads is developed simultaneously with the copy. The storyboard is a visual representation of the ad, made up of sketches that indicate the art director's concept of the various scenes, camera angles, sound effects, and special effects to be used in the final production.

Final "Epiphany" commercial

Following the shoot, the footage goes to the editing studios where music, voice overs, special effects, and supers are all incorporated into the finished ad. This is the final "Epiphany" commercial, as aired.

continued from page 413
for each typeface and size, and determines how much space the copy will fill (there are six picas to an inch).

Just a decade ago, copyfitting ability was essential for all artists; but now type can be manipulated in minutes on computers. However, copyfitting is still useful in the preproduction phase for avoiding typesetting problems later. When local advertisers, for instance, provide the agency with text for printed materials, they expect the artist to make the type "look good," even though there may be far too much or too little text to fit properly in the space available. By measuring the copy early in the process, the artist has enough time to suggest that the text be rewritten to fit. Once production begins, deadlines may be missed while the agency waits for text rewrites.

To make their ads unique and exclusive, some advertisers even commission a new type design. Other companies tailor their typography to blend with the magazines or newspapers their advertising appears in. This gives the ad an editorial look and, the advertiser hopes, enhanced credibility (or at least interest). For Toyota, Saatchi & Saatchi uses a particular type family called *Artcraft* in all its ads. But each vehicle model has its own typeface, selected to match the car's personality, which is used in the "everyday" slogan in the logo. The 4Runner ads, for instance, use a typeface called *Jazz,* which imparts a hand-etched, woodcut feeling that is at once both rustic and classic (see The Epilogue: The Complete Campaign).

Planning the Job

The overall purpose of preproduction is to plan the job thoroughly, which usually entails making a number of strategic choices before launching into full production. For example, since the art director's conceptual rough layouts are often made with marker colors that do not match printing inks, the production manager should consult with the art director to formally select a color palette in advance, using a color guide like the PANTONE® system.

For brochures, there is also the question of which printing process and which type of printing press to use for the job (see RL 13–3: Choosing the Best Method of Printing, in the Reference Library). This will affect the budget and dictate how art is prepared in the production and prepress phases.

Similarly, the art director and production manager usually consult on the paper to be used. Three categories of paper are used for advertising purposes: *writing, text,* and *cover stock.* Letters and fliers, for example, commonly use **writing paper.** Bond writing paper is the most durable and most frequently used. For brochures, there are many types of **text papers,** such as news stock, antique finish, machine finish, English finish, and coated. These range from the inexpensive, coarse, porous papers (*newsprint*) used by newspapers to the smooth, expensive, coated stocks used in upscale magazines, industrial brochures, and fine-quality annual reports. **Cover papers,** available in many finishes and textures, are used on soft book covers, direct-mail pieces, and brochure covers, so they're thicker, tougher, and more durable.

Finally, the production manager must decide early which is most important for a particular project: *speed, quality,* or *economy.* Typically, the manager must sacrifice one in favor of the other two. The answer determines the production methods used and the personnel employed. Once all these decisions are made, the manager can begin the production phase.

The Production Phase: Creating the Artwork

Following the preproduction phase of the 4Runner ad, Alicia Perez passed the job to the production staff in Charlene's art studio to produce the actual ad for the intended print media. Essentially, the **production phase** involves setting up the artwork and typesetting, completing ancillary functions such as illustration or photography, and then melding all these components into a final tangible form for the printer or publisher.

In a multicolor piece of art, the printer needs layers that can be reproduced individually. This is done by computer or assembled by hand with plastic overlays. The total image is then reconstructed as each layer is printed over the other.

Preparing Mechanicals

To create the art for an ad, brochure, or package, the production artist normally begins by marking out a grid on which to lay the type and art. Artists used to do this by hand on a piece of artboard in light-blue pencil. Today, pagemaking computer software does this with commands for setting up columns and guides. The grid provides an underlying consistency to the spacing and design of the piece.

The production artist then specifies the style and size of the typefaces for the text and inputs this information, along with the copy, into the computer. If the company doesn't have its own typesetting machines or computer systems, the artist must still specify the type so the typesetting company can understand the data. The type may be positioned electronically or output onto paper and glued onto the artboard within the image area.

The 4Runner ad design was quite simple. Kim Wright had indicated a large dominant photograph occupying most of the lower half of the ad, the headline and body copy centered in the top half, and these two elements separated by the inset photo of the vehicle, positioned right in the center of the page. Below the large photo would be the Toyota signature, slogan, and **mandatories** (phone, Web address, etc.).

Perez, with the studio artists, studied the comps to visualize how the various art and copy elements could be isolated in individual layers in the mechanical art and the pagemaking software.

When an additional color is to be printed, a second artboard marked to the same dimensions is used for the second image. The second image may be glued onto a clear plastic **overlay** that lies on top of the first image (called the **base art**). The production artist places crossmarks in the corners of the base art and then superimposes crossmarks on the transparent overlay precisely over those on the base art. This registers the exact position of the two layers of art in relation to one another.

The art elements must be properly positioned in the artwork (whether mechanical or computer generated) because the printer needs to have layers of art that can be reproduced individually. The total image is then constructed as each layer is printed over the previous one. Since the printer must photograph each layer to make separate plates, this kind of artwork is called **camera-ready art.**

This procedure is easily performed in the computer. The various elements of art are assigned to a layer the operator names and can be run out as separate film negatives or paper positive images as needed.

The biggest problem Perez faced was what color background to use. Saatchi's art directors had made an early decision to use a range of background colors for all the Toyota ads. Charlene Washburn had had these printed up on a sheet for each art director to use (see Exhibit 13–4). But choosing which one to use for a particular ad could be a daunting dilemma, solved only by trial and error and continous consultation with the art director. The background had to do double duty: complement the main visual and the photo of the vehicle, as well as attracting the target audience. After many tries they settled on a creamy yellow color that was sedate yet displayed some energy. Alicia could now move on to preparing the camera-ready materials.

Camera-Ready Art and Halftones

Production art for the printing process is like an on/off switch: where the art is black, ink will stick; where the art is white, ink won't stick. The production artist adheres to this printing principle by using black-and-white artwork that is called *line art* and by converting gray images to a form of line art called *halftones.*

Exhibit 13–4
Background colors for Toyota ads.

420

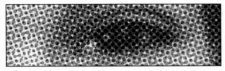

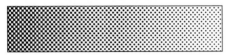

A halftone screen breaks up continuous tone artwork into tiny dots. The combination of printed dots produces an optical illusion of shading, as in a photograph. The color dots show the separation for the color photo above. The other set of dots show the range that would appear in a black and white photo.

Line art   Normal photographic paper (like snapshots made with a camera) produces images in **continuous tones**—black and white with shades of gray in between. But printing presses cannot print gray. So printers use special **orthographic film,** a high-contrast film yielding only black-and-white images with no gray tones. The artwork is simply photographed as is, and the result is called a **line film.** From that a **line plate** is produced for printing.

A *continuous-tone photograph* or other illustration requiring gradations in tone cannot be reproduced on orthographic film or a plate without an additional process, the *halftone screen.*

Halftone screens   While line plates print lines and solid areas (like type), **halftone plates** print dots. The key element is the **halftone screen,** which breaks up continuous-tone artwork into tiny dots. The combination of dots, when printed, produces an optical illusion of shading, as in a photo. In the dark areas of the image, the dots bump into each other and make the paper appear nearly black. In the gray areas, the size of the black dots equals the amount of white paper showing through; in the white areas, the black dots are surrounded by a lot of white or are almost completely missing. The human eye perceives the dots as gradations of tone.

The fineness of the halftone screen determines the quality of the illusion. Glossy magazine ads are printed with halftone screens as fine as 200 lines per inch (lpi), while newspaper photos appear very coarse at 80 to 100 lpi. Coarser screens are used to print on coarse, ink-absorbent paper (like newsprint) because the ink spreads when it hits the paper and fills in the white areas. Fine-quality, glossy magazine paper can take fine-screen halftones because the compressed chalk surface doesn't let the ink spread into the white areas. The dots in a coarse screen can be seen quite easily with the naked eye. To create special effects, the artist may employ different types of screens with interesting irregularities.

The artist's final step is to mark any halftones and line art for size and indicate where they should be placed. The artist simply sticks a photocopy of the visual to the artboard in its exact location with the letters "FPO" (for position only) written across the image. That way the printer doesn't think the copy is the actual final art.

The Prepress Phase: Stripping, Negs, and Plates   When Saatchi & Saatchi had completed all the production for the 4Runner ad on its computers, the next step was to get the finished artwork ready for the press. In addition to running the ads in the media, it also needed prints of the ad for use by the agency, the client, and Toyota's dealers.

In the **prepress phase,** the printer makes a plate from the base art and one from each overlay. Each pasteup (mechanical) has to be photographed separately.

65-line screen

100-line screen

150-line screen

Halftone screens help the printer control ink flow when trying to emulate the continuous-tone quality of photos. On newsprint, where the ink soaks in and spreads, a coarse 65-line screen gives the ink some room between dots. The finer, 150-line screen gives a better appearance, but it works best with magazine-quality paper that has a compressed chalk coating to keep ink from spreading.

Special screens lend an artistic look to photos. Whether the screens use lines, scratches, or some other technique, they work on the same principle as the halftone dot screen.

Two-color texture

Random line

Mezzo tint

Wavy line (dry brush)

The various layers of line art and halftones are converted to film negatives, which are carefully mounted together in perfect registration—through a process known as **stripping**—onto opaque plastic sheets called **flats.** A completed flat is a mask that allows light to pass through only where lines and dots are to appear on the plate. The flat is pressed against the printing plate, and ultraviolet light exposes the plate's photosensitive emulsion. Once exposed, the emulsion is developed, etching the plate in the process. This leaves some areas of the plate capable of holding ink and others unable to do so. Once dry, the plates are "hung" on the press, ready for printing.

Printing in Color

A printing plate can print only one color at a time. An advertiser who wants to print an ad or a brochure in blue, green, and black needs three different plates (one for each color), and the job is referred to as a three-color job. To print in full color, though, the **four-color process** is used. This process can simulate nearly all colors by combining the four primary colors: *process blue* (cyan), *process yellow, process magenta,* and *black* (which provides greater detail and density as well as shades of gray). In the parlance of the trade, this is also called **CYMK printing,** the K standing for black. To print in full color, therefore, the printer prepares four different printing plates—one for each process color plus black.

Designs that don't need full color are printed in blended inks rather than process colors. For example, it would take two process colors (magenta and yellow) to make red or three process colors (magenta, yellow, and cyan) to make burgundy. To print a brochure in black and burgundy, it's cheaper to use only two ink colors rather than black plus three process colors.

A PANTONE® color, one of a spectrum of colors that makes up the PANTONE MATCHING SYSTEM®(PMS), is a single ink premixed according to a formula and given a specific color number. The PANTONE® swatch book features over 100 colors in solid and screened blocks printed on different paper finishes.[14]

Four-Color Separations

Four separate halftone negatives are needed to make a set of four-color plates: one each for cyan, yellow, magenta, and black. Each of the resulting negatives appears in black and white, and the set is called the **color separation.** In printing, the process color inks are translucent, so two or three colors can overlap to create another color. For example, green is reproduced by overlapping yellow and cyan dots (see the transvision overlays in the Portfolio Review: Creative Department: Production of a Magazine Ad and TV Commercial).

Until recently, most color separations were done using a photographic process. Today, sophisticated electronic scanning systems—such as the workstations from Silicon Graphics, Hell ScriptMaster, Scitex, and Crosfield—can produce four-color separations and screens in one process, along with enlargements or reductions. And all this can be accomplished in minutes instead of the hours or days previously needed for camera work and hand etching.

Regardless of the separation method used, when properly printed, tiny clusters of halftone dots in various colors, sizes, and shapes give the eye the illusion of seeing the colors of the original photograph or painting.

The Duplication and Distribution Phase: Printing, Binding, and Shipping

The last phase of the print production process involves the actual printing, proofing, and finishing steps of drying, cutting, binding, and shipping.

The Press Run

Once the paper, plates, and ink are readied, the press is started and stopped a few times to adjust the image's alignment on the paper. In multicolored printing, proper alignment of all the colors is critical. When the initial proofs show good alignment, the presses are started again and gradually sped up to maximum output.

Finishing

Once all the pieces are printed, the ink must dry (unless heat-set or cold-set inks were used). Then the excess paper (or other material) is cut away using huge cutting machines. Depending on the nature of the job, the pieces may be delivered to special subcontractors who emboss or die-cut or perform other special techniques to enhance the final printed piece. The final stop may be the bindery for two- and three-hole drilling, wire stapling, and folding.

Quality Control in Print Production

At various stages of the print production process, the production manager needs to verify the quality. Artwork for a newspaper or magazine ad, for example, must be camera-ready. Many agencies now just send a disk, and the publisher converts the computer image to negatives. Magazines provide specific instructions and measurements for each ad size they offer. If there is any question, the production manager should call the publication and ask how current the data are.

Finally, the production manager must check all proofs for errors and obtain approvals from agency and client executives before releasing ads to publications or artwork to printers. Proofing is a time-consuming task made more so by the fact that not everyone is available when the work is ready for approval.

For the production process to run smoothly, everyone concerned must understand the procedure. The later in the process errors are discovered, the more expensive they are to fix. Changing a single comma may cost as much as $50 after copy is typeset, or $500 once negatives are made, or $5,000 if the job is already printed.[15]

Production Phase Quality Issues

The task of quality control really begins in the production phase. Proofs of the production art, with all its type and images, must be carefully inspected for misspellings, mismeasured lines, improperly sized images, misplaced cropmarks, or a myriad of other minutiae that could lead to a problem later.

Prepress Quality Issues   The slightest flaw in the final printed piece can have serious repercussions. The production manager must check and double-check, even triple-check, the film negatives before they're sent off to a magazine. An analog or digital proof (described below) of the negatives should be carefully checked and sent with the negatives.

Ways to Proof Print Production

When printing collateral materials or projects like brochures, the production manager will typically see a *blueline, color key, analog* or *digital proof,* and *press proof* from the printer.

Blueline proof   A **blueline** is a proof that is created by shining light through the negatives and exposing a light-sensitive paper that turns from white to blue. The blueline helps reveal scratches and flaws in the negatives as well as any assembly errors, such as a reversed illustration. The blueline is usually trimmed, folded, and stapled like the final product to check if the crop and fold marks have been properly registered.

Color keys and analog or digital proofs   The **analog proof** (also called a **Chromalin**) uses a series of four very thin sheets of plastic pressed together. Each layer's light-sensitive emulsion turns one of the process colors when exposed to certain wavelengths of light. Together they form a full, four-color image proof. The **color key** is a less expensive form of the Chromalin with relatively thick plastic sheets that can be lifted up. The plastic makes the overall image grayer than the final printed piece. The most recent innovation is the **digital proof** (also called an **Iris**). It uses ink-jet technology and offers accuracy as well as lower cost and faster turnaround time.[16]

Press proof   When the presses begin printing, the press operator "pulls" a few proofs to align the press and check ink densities. At this time the production manager should sign one of these actual press proofs as a guide for the operator to follow and for the agency's protection if something goes wrong later in the printing process.

What to Look for in a Proof

When checking proofs, production managers and art directors look for any scratches, minute holes or dots, blemishes, or unevenness of ink coverage. Using a *loupe* (magnifying glass), they inspect the dot pattern in halftones to make sure the registration of color is perfectly tight. Then they check *traps* and *bleeds*.

Traps   A **trap** occurs where the edge of one color or shade overlaps its neighbor by a fraction of an inch to make sure the white paper underneath doesn't show through. If the production artist fails to trap the artwork properly, the printer has to slightly overexpose one negative (sometimes called a *fatty*) or slightly underexpose another (a *skinny*) (see Exhibit 13–5).

To save money and avoid trapping problems, designers often plan for the typesetting to *overprint* (print on top of) the background color with black ink. But when colored type is printed over a differ-

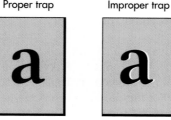

Letter overprints background   Reverse knockout   Proper trap   Improper trap

Exhibit 13–5
Black ink can overprint a background color (*far left*). However, art or text printed in a color other than black should have no background color underneath. For example, if a blue letter "a" appears on a red field, a white reverse knockout will keep the blue from being affected by the red (*second from left*). If the blue letter and the reverse knockout aren't properly aligned or the blue letter is smaller than the white knockout, the letters will not trap, and white paper will show between the two colors (*far right*).

ent background color, the background color must let white show to avoid distorting the true color of the colored type. This **reverse knockout** requires careful trapping.

For full-color ads, it's often wise to overprint text in black ink. When ads or brochures reprint, advertisers often make type changes. If all the text is black, as in the case of the 4Runner ad, the advertiser needs only to change the black negative and plate. If the text is any other color, all the negatives, stripping, and plating will have to be changed.

Bleeds   Finally, designers also need to consider **bleeds**—colors, type, or visuals that run all the way to the edge of the page. Production artists must set up their artwork for at least a quarter inch of extra color *outside* the image area to accommodate variations in the printing and cutting processes.

The **Radio Commercial** Production Process

Radio commercials, called **spots,** are among the quickest, simplest, and least expensive ads to produce. In fact, many stations provide production services free to local advertisers.

Some commercials are delivered live by the announcer, in which case the station gets a script or highlight sheet and any recorded music to be used. The material must be accurately timed. A live commercial script should run about 130 to 150 words per minute so the announcer can speak at a normal, conversational pace. The best way to do this is to use a popular DJ and let him or her improvise. It's a lot more entertaining and links the DJ's credibility to the product.[17]

The disadvantages of live commercials are that announcers may be inconsistent in their delivery, and sound effects are quite limited. Uniform delivery requires a recorded commercial. The process of producing a recorded commercial includes *preproduction, production,* and *postproduction* (or finishing) phases (see Exhibit 13–6).

Preproduction

In the **preproduction phase,** the advertiser and agency perform a variety of tasks that allow production to run smoothly, on time, and within budget. The agency assigns a radio producer from its staff or hires a freelance producer. Based on the script, the producer selects a studio and a director, determines

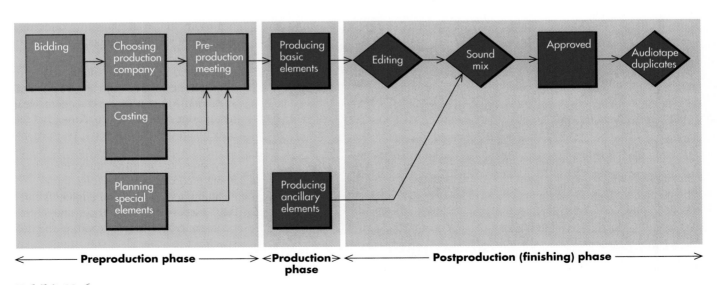

Exhibit 13–6

Radio commercials have three production phases. The preproduction and finishing phases are usually the most complex. Preproduction and postproduction editing and mixing typically require far more time than the actual recording session.

what talent will be needed, estimates costs, and prepares a budget for the advertiser's approval.

To control the production process and get the finest sound reproduction, most ad agencies use independent recording studios. The best audio studios have experienced sound directors and technicians, close ties to well-known talent, and the latest recording equipment.

During the preproduction phase, the producer (or a casting director) searches for the right talent. This is an important decision, because talent is a form of icon or symbol for the product. The advertiser and the agency consider several factors before arriving at a decision: the person's tone of voice, vocal acting skills and creativity, intelligence, style of thinking, and reputation. The unusual effect of Tom Bodett's vocal style for Motel 6, for instance, shows how valuable good talent can be. In just three years, Motel 6 went from near-bankruptcy to incredible profitability and became the largest chain of budget motels in the United States—using only radio and Bodett's folksy commercials ("We'll only charge you 20 bucks and we'll leave the light on for ya").

If the script calls for music, the producer decides whether to use prerecorded music or hire a composer and/or arranger. Any needed sound effects can be created or, most often, collected from prerecorded sources. All these decisions, of course, affect the budget, but they also have a dramatic impact on the effectiveness of the spots.

Once the talent is hired and music prepared, the **director** supervises rehearsals until everything is ready for recording.

Production: Cutting the Spot

All the elements to be used in the commercial—voices, music, sound effects—come together and are recorded at a **session.** Depending on the nature of the spot, a session can last from a half-hour to more than a day. Since studios charge by the hour, rehearsals are important in the preproduction phase.

A sophisticated audio console manipulates sound electronically, making sounds sharper or fuzzier, with more echo, or more treble or bass. Its multitrack mixing and sound enhancement capabilities are most useful during postproduction.

The Sound Studio

At the session, the voice and music talent perform in a studio, which has sound-dampening wall surfaces, a carpeted floor, microphones, a window to a control room, and wall plugs for connecting equipment and instruments to the control room.

Standard items in the sound studio are microphones, headphone sets, and speakers. Announcers and singers wear headphones to hear instructions from the director in the control room or to monitor prerecorded instrumental tracks as they sing (keeping the music track from being recorded onto the voice track).

Studio technicians and engineers carefully select, disperse, and aim the appropriate microphones to capture the full spectrum of sounds. The studio may have a separate sound booth (a small windowed room or partitioned area) to isolate drums or louder backup talent so the sound technicians can better balance the overall group of sounds.

The Control Room

The agency producer, director, and sound engineer (and often the client and account executive) sit in the **control room,** where they can monitor all the sounds generated in the sound studio. The control room is separated from the studio by a thick glass window and soundproofed walls, so the people monitoring the session can hear the sounds on quality speakers and discuss the various takes.

The director and sound engineer work at an **audio console** (also called a **board**), the central "switchboard" for controlling the sounds and channeling them to the appropriate recording devices. As they monitor the sounds coming from the studio, they keep the pitch and loudness within acceptable levels for broadcast.

The board also serves as a sound mixer, blending both live and prerecorded sounds for immediate or delayed broadcast. The board connects to a range of recording and playback units, including multitracking, reel-to-reel or cartridge ("cart") tape recorders, and CD recorders.

Postproduction: Finishing the Spot

After the commercial is recorded a number of times, a selection is made from the best takes. The sound engineer usually records music, sound effects, and vocals separately and then mixes and sweetens them during the **postproduction** (or *finishing*) **phase.** The final recording is referred to as the **master tape.**

From the master tape, the engineer makes duplicates called **dubs,** records them onto quarter-inch magnetic tape, and sends them to radio stations for broadcast.

The **Television Commercial** Production Process

While the Kims were creating the 4Runner print ad, another creative team across the office was working on the television commercial. Mike Whitlow was the copywriter and Doug Van Andel the art director. While they were given the same brief as the print creatives, they came up with a very different solution—a little drama that would work beautifully on television. They called it "Epiphany."

They wanted to show a moment in the life of that harried executive in the print ad. So they thought about who he is and where he works. They saw him as 35 to 40 years old. White collar. Maybe he works in an ad agency, or maybe he's a lawyer. Making good money, riding the treadmill everyday, putting in his nine-to-nine days in the city. He's getting ahead, doing well. But then there's that other part of him, wondering, is it all really worth it?

Then one day, as he walks from the subway to his building, he sees a man similar to himself. Not a wealthy guy who doesn't need to work, but a guy just like him. Except for one distinction: he made a different choice about his life. Stopped at a traffic light, there he is in his 4Runner, and it's loaded up with bikes and kayaks. This guy is taking off for some time in the wilderness. As the executive watches, visually caressing the vehicle, words appear on the screen: "Every day comes with a set of rules." The next screen says, "Fortunately you get to make them." As the 4Runner pulls away, the man suddenly experiences a moment of epiphany: It isn't Friday, or Saturday, or even Monday morning. It's Tuesday. The middle of the week. Here's somebody making his own rules, answering the call of the wild.

Boom! A poignant yet highly tangible spot. Right on the button strategically. Translating this concept to television, though, would be no simple task. It would have to be produced exceedingly well to communicate the idea credibly and resonate with the audience. That meant bringing in one of the agency's top TV producers. After discussing the spot with Damon Webster, Saatchi's head of TV production, the team decided to give the job to Jeff Beverly.

The Role of the Commercial Producer

Today, advertising agency producers must be generalists, able to work with a variety of technicians to bring a spot's creative essence to life. And they must have the savvy to budget large amounts of money and spend them wisely.[18]

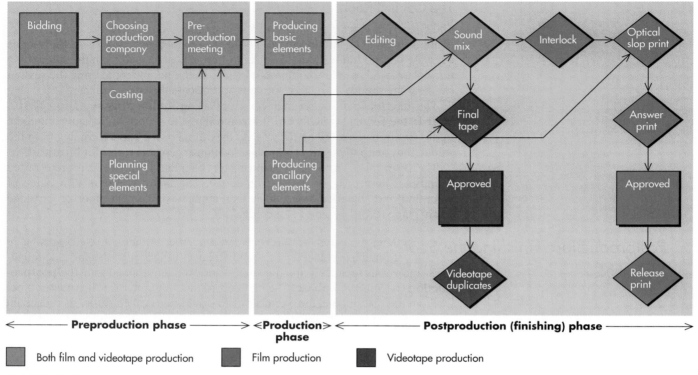

Exhibit 13–7
The production processes for film and videotape are very similar to that for radio until the sound-mixing stage. Computerized editing speeds up the finishing phase for videotape.

Students of advertising need to know basic TV production concepts to understand how commercials are made, why production is so expensive, and what methods they can use to cut costs without sacrificing quality or effectiveness.

As with radio, the process of producing a TV commercial always involves three stages, as shown in Exhibit 13–7:

1. Preproduction: all the work prior to the actual day of filming.
2. Production: the actual day (or days) the commercial is filmed or videotaped.
3. Postproduction (or finishing): all the work done after shooting to edit and finish the commercial.

In the preproduction stage, art directors, copywriters, and producers carefully hash out the details required for filming one 30-second ad. During this stage, the production team will develop and sketch a storyboard that depicts, in rough form, how an ad will appear. Any major changes should be made at this time, because alterations in script or direction after filming begins can drive production costs up exponentially.

Each step has a dramatic impact on cost and quality. For a look at how all three affect the end product, see the Portfolio Review: Creative Department: Production of a Magazine Ad and TV Commercial (pp. 414–18).

The Preproduction Phase

Good planning before production can save advertisers a lot of money. That's the purpose of the **preproduction phase.** The first thing the producer must do, therefore, is study the script and storyboard and analyze the production techniques that will be called for in the commercial. Three major categories of production techniques are used today: *live action, animation,* and *special effects.*

Live Action

To portray people and things in lifelike, everyday situations, like typical slice-of-life TV commercials, advertisers use the **live action** technique.

Van Andel and Whitlow planned to use live-action shots to illustrate the bustling urban scene. They wanted to put the vehicle someplace where it didn't really fit—because that's what would predicate the man's epiphany. They concluded that the man worked in a tall building, maybe a skyscraper: New York, for instance, where amid all the cabs, small sedans, and commuter cars, the gleaming 4Runner would be completely out of place, standing there in all its majestic glory. To get the greatest impact, they wanted to shoot this spot in the valley of glass and steel.

If a commercial calls for live action, the producer must consider whether the action will be staged indoors in a studio, outside on a studio lot, or on location away from the studio. Will it be taped or filmed? All these factors will have a bearing on what equipment and personnel are required, where costumes are obtained, what permissions may be required, what talent can be used, and, of course, what the commercial costs. When children are used, rehearsals are a must. Children and animals are unpredictable and often cause production delays.

Jeff Beverly concurred that the best place to shoot the spot would be on location in New York. This would require coordinating with the city to get the necessary permits, police security, and street clearances. As it turned out, they would even take over a whole subway station on Broadway.

Animation

Animation—cartoons, dancing puppets, and demonstrations in which inanimate objects come to life—can effectively communicate difficult messages or reach special markets such as children.

Traditional animation techniques include *cartoons, photo animation, stop-motion photography,* and *video animation.* Cartoons often score the highest viewer interest and the longest life, so over time they cost the least per showing. However, initial production is very expensive. A fully animated commercial can cost over $200,000.[19]

Special Effects

Today, much video animation and most **special effects,** such as moving titles and whirling logos, are done with a joystick. All major video production companies use dedicated **digital video effects (DVE) units** that can manipulate graphics on the screen in many ways: fades, wipes, zooms, rotations, and so on.

Special effects entertain viewers and win advertising awards. But if the sales message is complex or based on logic, another technique might be better. No technique should so enthrall viewers that they pay more attention to it than to the product—or the strategic message. Further, more than one fantasy or **mnemonic device** (Energizer bunny or Jolly Green Giant) might confuse audiences. David

Manipulating Morphing's Magic

Digital photographer Laurence Gartel was thumbing through a copy of *Byte* magazine when a computer-rendered illustration of a man with a clock face caught his eye. It looked amazingly similar to an illustration he had once created. Certain details convinced him his illustration had been digitally copied from a book of published photographs and then edited and distorted. He immediately called the magazine. The editor apologized and printed a clarification.

To morph or not to morph is a big ethical question in computer-generated art and design these days. Only recently has it become possible to *metamorphose*—change something in form or character—with a few computer keystrokes. The effect is usually dramatic. Take a television spot for Chanel No. 5, in which a mousy moviegoer transforms magically into Marilyn Monroe.

The dowdily dressed young woman is eating popcorn and watching Marilyn on a large movie screen when suddenly a button pops open on the viewer's dress, and, to her shock, out bursts . . . cleavage! Next, her moussed-back hair begins to grow and the black-and-white scene turns to Technicolor. Her dark hair becomes blonde and, thanks to digital metamorphosis, she becomes the ravishing Monroe. The popcorn container turns into a 2-quart bottle of Chanel No. 5 and Marilyn coos, "You know what I mean? No. 5!" Then, in the blink of a heavy-lidded eye, Marilyn reverts to the moviegoer, hugging her $15,000 bottle of perfume as she settles in her seat for more movie magic.

Blame computers and photo manipulation technology for defying the adage, "Seeing is believing." Image manipulation can be obvious, as in *TV Guide*'s cover photo of Oprah Winfrey's head on the body of Ann Margret. Or it can be subtle, as when *National Geographic* moved one of the great pyramids closer to the others for a more esthetic cover shot.

According to Fred Ritchin, professor of photography and interactive telecommunications at New York University, the news media jeopardize their integrity with each doctored photo. While readers have always accepted that text is rewritten and sometimes edited with a point of view, they have relied on photos to represent the unvarnished truth.

So vital is the question of news integrity that the American Society of Media Photographers has adopted a policy that a photo used in a news context may not be altered in any fashion. Major news organizations have adopted the same hands-off policy. For other kinds of photography, such as advertising and creative work, the rule is "no alteration without permission."

Animation or special effects are often used to create the boom factor in a television ad. Tony the Tiger, the longtime spokescritter for Kellogg's Frosted Flakes, is just one famous example of how animation can be used in advertising. With sophisticated computer technology, companies now produce seemingly impossible special effects, like the little boy who sucked himself through a straw and into a bottle in this classic summertime ad from Pepsi (www.pepsi.com).

"Inner Tube" :30
SFX: Sound of waves, seagulls squawking.
(Camera pans in on a young kid drinking a bottle of Pepsi from a straw. His sister sits in the sand. The camera pans in on the Pepsi bottle as the young boy sips the soda. The bottle is down to the last drops of soda as he continues to

drink. When he finishes, the top of his hat starts to move.)
SFX: Sucking noise.
(The camera pans in with a close-up of an old woman as she looks around. As the young boy sips through the straw his ears start to wiggle. Suddenly the boy's head is sucked into the bottle along with

the rest of his body. The bottle bounces off the inner tube and we see a close-up of the young boy inside the bottle. His sister runs over and stares at the bottle. She picks it up and turns it upside down to try to get her brother out.)
LITTLE GIRL: Mom, he's done it again!
SUPER: Nothing else is a Pepsi.

Skilled photographers with razor blades and airbrushes have moved objects and people in and out of photographs for decades, but the issue today is the sheer number of people who can do this. Making composites and doctoring photos is easy, thanks to the myriad digital scanners and software available.

Morphing also poses the question: Who owns the final product? If one photographer takes the shot of a head, another provides the body, and a third party actually makes the composite, are they all entitled to ownership? FCL/Colorspace, the New York City–based studio that designs *Spy*'s covers, addresses the question case by case. "If we shoot all the photography and do all the photo manipulation, then the image is ours," explains Phil Heffernan, creative director.

But what about manipulating an image of a cloud to create steam coming out of an engine? Is it ethical to take a picture of a tree and use the bark as background texture in another image? "The line between photography and illustration is blurring," says Heffernan.

To help educate digital artists about the integrity of published images, the Center for Creative Imaging published *Ethics, Copyright and the Bottom Line*. Director Ray DeMoulin notes that changing images is becoming more acceptable. "This is the most talked-about issue in graphics today," he says.

Until copyright laws address this gray area, the advertising industry will have to rely on its own code of ethics and the integrity of its people.

Questions

1. What ethical issues should an advertiser be aware of when considering alteration of an existing photograph or illustration? Enumerate and explain them.

2. Should photos and illustrations in ads carry some small-type disclaimer when the visual has been changed or computer enhanced? Why or why not?

Sources: Bob Garfield, "Wondrous Chanel No. 5 Spot Deftly Nurtures the Product," *Advertising Age,* December 12, 1994, p. 3; Jean Marie Angelo, "Photo Manipulation, Retouching Stirs Legal, Ethical Questions," *Computer Pictures,* March/April 1993, pp. 20–25; "FPG Wins Digital Plagiarism Suit," *New Media,* January 1995, p. 28; Christopher R. Harris and Don E. Tomlinson, "The Lanham Act and Copyright: Application vis-à-vis Computer Manipulation of Photographic Imagery," paper presented to the annual conference of the Association for Education in Journalism and Mass Communication, Montreal, Quebec, August 8, 1992.

Ogilvy suggests that, to make the strongest impression on the viewer, fantasies should relate to the product's claims and be repeated heavily.[20]

Planning Production

The commercial is a group effort; the team includes a writer, art director, producer, director, and sometimes a musical composer and choreographer. The agency producer, who is responsible for completing the job on schedule and within budget, usually sends copies of the storyboard to three studios for competitive bids.

When the studio is chosen, the producer and casting director select the cast and hire the announcer. Next the set is built, and the crew and cast rehearse under the director's supervision.

During this period, preproduction meetings are necessary among the agency producer, the account representative, the writer, the art director, the commercial director, possibly the advertiser, and anyone else important to the production. This is where they iron out any last-minute problems and make final decisions about the scenes, the actors, and the announcer. They should review everything—music, sets, action, lighting, camera angles. A finished 60-second film commercial takes only 90 feet of film, but the shooting often requires several days and 3,000 to 5,000 feet of film. And unlike videotape, film can't be used again (see Ad Lab 13–B: The Film versus Tape Decision).

The soundtrack may be recorded before, during, or after actual production. Recording sound in advance ensures that the commercial will be neither too long nor too short; it also helps when the subject has to move or dance to a specific rhythm.

Production: The Shoot

The actual shooting day (or days) can be very long and tedious. It may take several hours just to light the set to the director's liking. The 4Runner spot, for instance, took three full days to shoot. Today producers can use technology to control sound, lighting, and staging.

Quiet on the Set: Sound

Procedures for recording and controlling music and sound effects are similar to those used in radio. Microphones capture sound; recorders transfer the sound and store it on a medium like magnetic tape. Then, with the use of a multichannel

The Film versus Tape Decision

Today, live TV commercials are rare. Even those that look live are usually videotaped, and most national commercials are shot on color film. Film projects a soft texture that live broadcasts and videotape do not have. Because film is the oldest method, producers have a large pool of skilled talent to choose from. Also, film is extremely versatile. It works for numerous optical effects, slow motion, distance shots, mood shots, fast action, and various animation techniques. While film stock is expensive (and most of it ends up on the cutting-room floor) duplicate film prints are cheaper than videotape dupes.

However, magnetic videotape offers a more brilliant picture and better fidelity. It looks more realistic and more "live." Tape is also more consistent in quality than film stock. The chief advantage of tape is that it provides immediate playback, so scenes can be checked and redone while the props and actors are still to-

gether on the set. Moreover, computerization has cut editing time up to 90 percent. Videotape can be replayed almost forever, but a film commercial can be run only about 25 times.

Today, many directors shoot their commercials on film for texture and sensitive mood lighting, but then they dub the processed film onto videotape for editing. This process is more costly, but it gives them faster finishing and lets them see optical effects instantly. Some directors, however, still prefer to edit on film because they get the wider range of effects and thus achieve a higher level of creative storytelling.

Laboratory Application

Some products and some types of commercials are more effective shot on film, while others are better on videotape. Make a list of three product categories (or three brands) and three types of commercials. Describe which medium (film or tape) you think would be more effective in each case and why.

---

control board, a sound engineer manipulates sounds for effect and records them onto film, video, or a playback system synchronized with film.

But the original recording is the key to success for two reasons. First, the original sound recording is synchronized with the original visual recording and with the action and the emotion expressed by the actors. A re-creation never quite matches the timing or feel of the original.

Second, before it reaches its final form, the original recording undergoes rerecording many times, with some loss of fidelity each time. So high-quality sound-recording equipment is mandatory.

Lights

The director and the cinematographer must deal with a variety of light sources. For example, a scene with a person standing close to a window may have three light sources: daylight through the window, high-intensity studio lighting for brightening the subject and the room's interior, and a regular table lamp serving as a prop. All these shed different types of light that could adversely affect the scene. To control this effect, technicians need to measure the light and style it to suit the scene.

Experienced **cinematographers** (motion picture photographers) can guess the range and intensity of light by briefly studying its source. However, they use light meters to determine how to set the camera's lens **aperture,** the opening that controls the amount of light that reaches the film or videotape. To record the correct color and brightness, all light sources must be in balance.

The arrangement of lights—whether in the studio, on the studio lot, or on location—establishes a visual mood. Intense light from a single source gives a harsh appearance and may be used to

Different types of lighting can enhance a scene and create special moods. Here, strong keylights light up the actors. The fainter light of the window screen casts a window-shaped pattern onto the background. The effect light above enhances the reflected glow of the candle on the table top. To bystanders the scene appears very bright, but when the camera's aperture is set properly, the film sees a darker, more shadowy play of lights and darks.

create anxiety in the viewer. By using filters, warmer lights, diffusion screens, and reflectors, the cinematographer can create a reddish, more consistent, softer illumination—and a more romantic mood. The director works with the art director, the cinematographer, and the lighting engineer to choose the most appropriate placement, types, and intensities.

Camera

Professional film cameras used for making TV commercials shoot 16 millimeter, 35 mm, and 75 mm film, the diagonal measurement of a single film frame.

Producers of local TV commercials used to shoot with the grainier but less expensive 16 mm film; national spots were shot on 35 mm for extra quality and precision; and 75 mm film provides the highest quality image. While film is still widely used for national spots because of the atmosphere it brings to an image, most local spots are now shot on video.

Heavy-duty studio video cameras mounted on a stand with wheels can carry a number of accessories. One of the most important is the lens-mounted **Teleprompter,** which allows the camera to see a spokesperson through the back of a two-way mirror while he or she reads moving text reflected off the front.

Unlike film cameras, studio video cameras are tied to a control room by large electronic cables. In the control room, multiple video screens and sound channels are wired to a control panel. Working at the control panel, the director can switch from one camera to another and simultaneously set the input and output levels of sound and visuals. Control panels also have DVE units for creating text or visual effects on screen.

Action: Staging and Talent

Staging for a commercial may be done in the isolation of a studio, outside on a studio lot, or on location. The studio offers the most control.

Most film and video studios have heavy soundproofing to eliminate outside noises such as sirens and low-flying aircraft. The studios are lightproof, which allows for complete lighting control. Special equipment is easier to use in the controlled environment of a studio. But studio lighting can make a scene appear artificial.

For scenes requiring large amounts of space, historic or unique architecture, scenery, and the full effect of outdoor lighting, the studio lot offers the best control. The **lot** is outside acreage shielded from stray, off-site sounds. The lot is convenient to the studio's carpentry shop, and sets can be left standing until all shootings and retakes are completed.

Although it adds realism, **location** shooting is often a technical and logistical nightmare. Every location has natural and manufactured features that create obstacles. Natural lighting creates bright highlights that contrast with harsh shadows. Large reflective screens and high-intensity lights are required to brighten up shadows for a more even-toned exposure. Energy sources for lighting and equipment may be insufficient, requiring long cables and mobile generators. But since sets don't have to be built, location shooting can be good for some low-budget commercials. However, natural events like rain and fog can cause costly interruptions. On the last day of

This studio camera has a video viewfinder that is plugged into a TV screen for simultaneous viewing, as shown in the TV monitor to the left of the camera operator.

After filming or videotaping the scenes for an ad, the video material goes to the production studio for assembly of the final product. At this stage, the director and editor will select and splice scenes into their respective order, removing all the unneeded footage. Next they add off-camera special effects like supers and incorporate any necessary music or voiceovers.

the 4Runner shoot, the filmmakers were suddenly notified of a huge storm moving into the area. They had 20 minutes to devise and take the final shot of the 4Runner driving off or they would have to bring the whole crew and cast back to New York a week later. They got the third take just as the rain began to fall. Whew!

Shooting on location sets up special challenges for directors using video. A truck, van, motor home, or trailer is wired for video and sound control recording. Inside, a row of TV monitors and a multichannel control panel direct the recording from one or more cameras running simultaneously.

Whether at the studio or on location, most scenes require several takes for the **talent** (actors) to get them right. Lighting may need readjusting as unexpected shadows pop up. Each scene is shot from two or three different angles: one to establish the characters, one to show only the speaker, and one to show the listener's reaction.

Scenes aren't necessarily shot in order. Those with no synchronized sound are usually shot last since they don't require the full crew.

It may take a long time between scenes to move the camera, reset the lights, reposition the talent, and pick up the action, sound, and look to match the other scenes. Each action must match what comes before and after. Commercials with disconcerting jumps destroy credibility.

Once all the scenes are "in the can," the commercial enters the postproduction, or finishing, phase.

Postproduction

In the **postproduction phase,** the film editor, sound mixer, and director actually put the commercial together.

With computer and videotape technology, editors can convert the film to tape and add effects like wipes and dissolves electronically. While the director spent many hours editing the 4Runner commercial, it was still considerably less than he would have needed for film editing and lab work.

Many professionals, however, still prefer film. The visual portion of the commercial appears on one piece of celluloid without the effects of dissolves, titles, or **supers** (words superimposed on the picture). The sound portion is assembled on another piece of celluloid. This is the **work print** stage (also called the *rough cut* or *interlock*).

External sound is recorded next. The sound engineer records the musicians and singers, as well as the announcer's voiceover narrative. Prerecorded stock music may be bought and integrated into the commercial. The mixing also includes any sound effects, such as doorbells ringing or doors slamming.

Once sound editing is complete, the finished sound is put on one piece of celluloid. That, combined with the almost-completed visual celluloid, yields the **mixed interlock.** The addition of optical effects and titles results in the **answer print.** This is the final commercial. If it is approved, **dupes** (duplicate copies) are made for delivery to the networks or TV stations.

In the postproduction phase, the director editor can save a lot of time and money by using computerized video and sound editing equipment.

Producing Advertising for **Digital Media**

Did you see the Academy Awards show this year? It was a multimedia extravaganza. On one side of the stage was a podium with multiple microphones for the emcee, the speakers, the award presenters, and the many recipients. Center stage was left open for performers—the dancers and singers—but was lavishly decorated by a top Hollywood set designer. Above and to the sides of the stage were large screens to show the lists of the nominated individuals and films, as well as short clips from those movies.

Thanks to the miracle of television, millions of people around the world saw it simultaneously. We were all participants in a huge digital media event, one form of the hottest and most dynamic emerging medium since the advent of TV.

The Emergence of Digital Media

The roots of this new phenomenon really go back to the 35 mm camera and the lowly slide show. Remember when the neighbors got back from Paris and came over to show their slides?

Boring as it was, the home slide show was rapidly adopted by the business world and became a staple of sales presentations, corporate shareholder meetings, and luncheon speeches.

Some enterprising person thought the slide show could be perked up with a little music, or a professional announcer. The professional slide presentation was born—and so was a new medium for advertising. The slide presentation was quickly adopted by sales forces, and companies sprang up all over the country to write, photograph, and produce high-quality, professional slide shows for business.

Sound + Music + Motion = Multimedia

Then came the idea of using multiple screens and multiple projectors. Quick cuts from one slide to another, in sync with the music and sound effects, created the feeling of motion. This was the birth of the **multimedia presentation,** which simply refers to presenting information or entertainment using several communications media simultaneously.

It wasn't long before video and animation were added to the mix. In one multimedia presentation, a prospect might be treated to both slides and video playing on two to twelve screens simultaneously, plus professional narration, music, and sound effects. It was very compelling.

Multimedia + Computer Technology = Digital Media

Then along came the personal computer, the breakup of AT&T, the deregulation of the broadcast and cable TV industry, the development of CD-ROM technology and fiberoptics, and the stage was set for the media revolution now taking place—the emergence of digital media. Basically, **digital media** are channels of communication that join the logic of multimedia formats with the electronic system capabilities and controls of modern telecommunications,

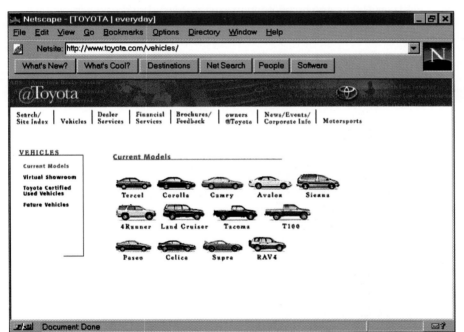

The emergence of digital media required the development of an entirely new set of skills to produce ads. Art directors and designers must understand how to integrate print and video into a single medium, and they must also comprehend the features and limitations of the computer languages used to produce such work.

Since 1994 Hot Wired *(www.hotwired.com) has been* the *hot online magazine for informed computer wonks. Visit the Web site and see how* Hot Wired *incorporates animation, video, and other multimedia forms into this interactive, personal audience venue.*

television, and computer technologies. Digital media are a subset of electronic media. We already see them in many venues (settings).

Venues for Digital Media

The three categories of places where we experience digital media today are based on audience size: *mass audience, private audience,* and *personal audience venues.*

The Academy Awards show is a good example of a **mass audience venue.** With hundreds of people in the live audience and millions more watching at home, the multimedia presentation had a huge reach. Multimedia is also used in major sporting events, the Olympics opening ceremonies, political conventions, and other mass audience events.

Many digital media events are in **private audience venues,** though some of these may be quite large. A major marketer's national sales meeting, large corporate conferences, sales meetings with 10 people in attendance, educational conferences, training seminars, and local information centers all use computer-driven multimedia presentations, utilizing software programs such as Powerpoint to inform, persuade, remind, and entertain people.

The **personal audience venue** is experiencing the most growth today. One person sitting in front of a personal computer can receive multimedia information off the Internet from an online database service like Prodigy or America Online, or from software bought in a computer store. People can even create their own mini-multimedia programs with slides and limited animation by buying a turnkey *authoring program* (Hypercard®, Supercard®, Macromedia Director®) at any software store.

The landscape is rapidly becoming dotted with *kiosks,* interactive computers in a stand-alone cabinet (discussed earlier in this chapter). Kiosks offer a station from which one person at a time can interact with the computer. They are used to sell products, inform, and entertain.

Finally, **interactive TV** is becoming available as another personal audience venue. While watching TV, people can use a remote control system to gain immediate access to the Internet or, in some limited cases, even tailor the programming to their personal tastes. Ironically, the most massive form of media—television—is now becoming one of the most personal.

The Role of Digital Media in Advertising

With the trend toward integrated marketing communications, the various digital media give marketers new ways to reach prospects and begin a relationship—or improve their relationship with current customers.

In some cases, the medium itself is the ad, as in the case of a multimedia sales presentation or a dedicated kiosk offering information about one company's wares. In other cases, though, the digital media are a form of narrowcasting in which advertisers can buy space or time for their commercial announcements. Often the spot is just an electronic billboard with the company or brand name. In Internet advertising, the advertiser sets up a virtual storefront, called a **Web page,** or places a billboard ad on some other company's Web page. When viewers click certain "buttons" on the home page, a new page comes up with more detailed information about the company and its products, policies, or prices. We've gone back to the basics; it's a fancy slide show. But, in fact, it's multimedia. And the technology is getting better, faster, cheaper, and more impressive every day.

For the agency producer, this presents exciting challenges and opportunities. Not all the opportunities are available yet, but everybody knows what's around the corner: touch a button on the screen and a full video commercial or technical film will run; click on another button and a personal representative will come online with you. The possibilities are endless. The challenge will be to keep current.

The People Who Produce Digital Media Advertising

Some experts predict a virtual revolution in creative style and effectiveness as creative people learn to deal with the new media, offering more information and less glitz.[21] The ranks of production managers and producers are already swelling as media vehicles multiply beyond anybody's recent imagination. New titles are suddenly appearing on agency rosters: multimedia producers, directors, and technicians; interactive planners and writers; computer programmers and system designers; kiosk media buyers; and so on. At Saatchi & Saatchi, Dean Van Eimeren holds the title of creative director, Design & Interactive Media Group. Working with him is a staff of art directors, copywriters, and producers who specialize in creating interactive ads for Saatchi's clients. Outside the agencies are a host of new suppliers: kiosk manufacturers, interactive software developers, CD-ROM manufacturers, digital media-buying services, and so on.

The Production Process

For digital media, the production process is a hybrid of all the other processes we've discussed. That's because some of the digital media are akin to print and outdoor media (computer billboards and Web pages), while others are closely associated with TV and radio.

As we've seen in this chapter, regardless of medium, the production manager or producer goes through a planned sequence of activities: preproduction, production, and postproduction. Preproduction includes the planning, costing, and hiring activities. The production stage is when the artwork is created, the video and audio recorded, or the computer program developed. Postproduction includes the editing, duplicating, and distribution activities. The difference for digital media is in the details of activities in the production and postproduction stages (see RL 13–2, Production Process for Digital Media, in the Reference Library).

The new media have introduced new costs.[22] One of these is **platform licensing,** a fee paid to original software developers for the special key codes that access multimedia programs on certain computer networks. There is the cost of buying and leasing new equipment and the cost of manufacturing or duplicating CD-ROMs, diskettes, or whatever new medium comes along to transport the advertiser's message.

An exciting new world awaits us out there. And it's not just around the corner. It's already here.

Chapter **Summary**

Careful management is the key to success in producing advertising. If the production process is not handled correctly, an otherwise beautiful ad or commercial can be destroyed. The task of managing this process is the responsibility of a print production manager or an electronic media producer. The manager's job is to keep the project moving smoothly and under budget, while maintaining the required level of quality through every step of the production process.

Production managers perform the classic functions of management: planning, organizing, directing, and controlling. They also have to keep up with changing technology, monitor costs, and meet budgets.

Many factors can destroy budgets. The five most common are inadequate planning and preparation, production luxuries, overtime, special equipment, and too many decision makers. Factors specific to each medium can also affect budgets drastically.

The print production process consists of four phases: preproduction, production, prepress, and printing and distribution. In the preproduction phase, the manager plans the overall job carefully and then starts to deal with the specific needs of the job, such as typography.

Typography affects an ad's appearance, design, and legibility. There are four important concepts when selecting type: readability, appropriateness, harmony or appearance, and emphasis. A key skill is copy casting, knowing how to fit type into a particular space in a layout. The production manager also considers what kind of paper will be used, since it affects the way the art is prepared.

In the production phase, artists prepare mechanicals (or paste-ups) of the art to be printed. Most agencies today use sophisticated desktop publishing. The artists prepare the mechanicals as line art and use a photographic process to turn continuous-tone artwork into halftones. Halftone images (illustrations and photos) simulate gradations of tone with different sizes of black dots.

In the prepress stage, the printer makes a plate from the base art and one from each overlay. Each mechanical must be photographed separately. For full color, four halftone plates are used (one for each color process color plus black). The set of negatives used to make the four plates is called a color separation. This work is now mostly done on large computerized scanner systems.

The final phase of the production process includes the actual printing of the job, as well as cutting, embossing, binding, and shipping. Quality control is critical throughout the process. The production manager has to make sure computer disks are compatible with the reprographics service bureau and contain all the elements needed to produce the negatives. Along the way, the manager must check several printer's proofs for scratches or blemishes and to make sure traps and bleeds are handled correctly.

Radio spots are among the quickest, simplest, and least expensive ads to produce. A producer manages the production process through the preproduction, production, and postproduction stages. The producer contracts with a recording studio, selects talent, and collects music and sound effects for the recording session. At the session, the talent works in a studio, while the director and sound engineer work in the control room at an audio console, monitoring and modulating the sound as it's recorded.

In the postproduction phase, the director and sound engineer select the best takes, splice them together, mix in sound effects and music, and then edit the sound until the master tape is completed. Dubs are made from this and sent to radio stations for airing.

Television production involves the same three stages. In preproduction, the producer determines which production technique is most suitable for the script: live action, animation, special effects, or a combination. The studio is chosen, the cast selected, and rehearsals held. As much work as possible is done during preproduction to reduce the shooting time required.

The production phase is when the commercial is actually shot, in a studio, on a lot, or on location. Specialized technicians are responsible for the sound, lights, and cameras, all of which can diminish the commercial if not handled correctly. Scenes are shot and reshot until the director and producer feel they have a good take. For cost reasons, scenes are frequently not shot in order. The sound track may be recorded before or after the shoot.

In the postproduction stage, the commercial is actually put together on either film or videotape. External sound and music are added to the video and the soundtrack until the master (or answer print for film) is completed. Then dupes are made and shipped to TV stations.

A multimedia presentation provides information or entertainment using several communications media simultaneously, typically slides, video, and audio. The electronic capabilities of computer technology were added to the multimedia presentation to create digital media.

Digital media are used in mass audience venues, private audience venues, and personal audience venues. The personal audience venue includes PC applications such as advertising on the Internet, with online database services, or via interactive TV and kiosks.

Digital media are a whole new industry. The overall production process is similar to those of print and electronic media, but the details involve new technologies, terminologies, and costs that advertisers and agencies are not yet familiar with. This means opportunities for new people coming into the field.

Important **Terms**

analog proof (Chromalin), *424*

animation, *429*

answer print, *434*

aperture, *432*

audio console (board), *427*

base art, *420*

bleeds, *425*

blueline, *424*

camera-ready art, *420*

character-count method, *413*

cinematographer, *432*

closing date, *411*

color key, *424*

color separation, *423*

continuous tones, *421*

control room, *427*

copy cast, *413*

cover paper, *419*

CYMK printing, *422*

digital media, *435*

digital proof (Iris), *424*

digital video effects (DVE) units, *429*

director, *426*

display type, *412*

dubs, *427*

dupes, *434*

electronic production, *409*

flats, *422*

font, *413*

four-color process, *422*

halftone plate, *421*

halftone screen, *421*

interactive TV, *436*

job jacket, *411*

kerning, *412*

kiosk, *411*

leading, *412*

line film, *421*

line plate, *421*

live action, *429*

location, *433*

lot, *433*

mandatories, *420*

mass audience venue, *436*

master tape, *427*

Review **Questions**

1. What are the five common budget busters every production manager should be aware of?
2. What is the primary role of the print production manager?
3. What does copy casting mean? Explain how it is done.
4. What is a halftone? Why is it important, and how is it produced?
5. How are color photographs printed? What are the potential problems with printing in color?
6. What are the advantages and disadvantages of animation?
7. What leads to the greatest waste of money in TV commercial production? Explain.
8. When is it better to use film and when is it better to use videotape? Why?
9. What are the most common forms of digital media? How do they differ from media in the past?
10. What are some ways an advertiser like McDonald's could use digital media to enhance its IMC program? Explain.

Exploring the **Internet**

The Internet exercises for Chapter 13 address the following areas covered in the chapter: print production and broadcast production.

1. Print Production

   Take a moment to go online and learn more about print production. Numerous organizations and companies that specialize in some aspect of print production are on the Web. Visit the sites listed below and answer the questions that follow.

   • Acme Printing www.acmeprinting.com
   • AlphaGraphics www.alphagraphics.com
   • Chromapress International www.chromapress.com
   • Color Masters www.colormasters.com
   • ColorArts www.colorarts.com
   • Digital XPress www.digitalxpress.com
   • Graphic Communications Association (GCA) www.gca.org
   • Hart Graphics www.hartgr.com
   • National Association of Printers & Lithographers (NAPL) www.napl.org
   • PANTONE® www.pantone.com
   • Printing Industries of America (PIA) www.printing.org
   • Screen Printing & Graphic Imaging Association (SGIA) www.sgia.org

   a. Who is the intended audience of the site?
   b. What type of company or organization is it? What are the scope and size of its operations?
   c. What print-related activities does the company or organization specialize in?

   d. What is your overall impression of the company and its work? Why?

2. Broadcast Production

   Producing broadcast commercials is even more complex than the print production process. Peruse the Web sites below of these broadcast production-related organizations. Then answer the questions that follow.

   • Aardman Animation www.aardman.com
   • @radical.media www.radicalmedia.com
   • Directors Guild of America www.dga.org
   • Duck Soup Produckions www.ducksoupla.com
   • EDS Digital Studios www.edsdigital.com
   • Film Planet www.filmplanet.com
   • Hollywood Digital www.hollydig.com
   • Johnson Burnett www.johnsonburnett.com
   • Jones Film & Video www.jonesinc.com
   • Screen Actors Guild (SAG) www.sag.com

   a. What type of production-related company or organization is it? What seem to be the scope and size of its operations?
   b. What kind of broadcast production activities does the company specialize in? Are these typically preproduction, production, or postproduction activities?
   c. What benefit does the company or organization provide the advertising community?
   d. What impresses you most about this organization and its work? Least? Why?

Part Five

Using Advertising Media

Advertising media are the channels of communication through which advertising messages are conveyed. Choosing the best media for an advertising campaign is a critical task, requiring a sound knowledge of the benefits each channel provides for the audiences being targeted and the products being advertised. ●

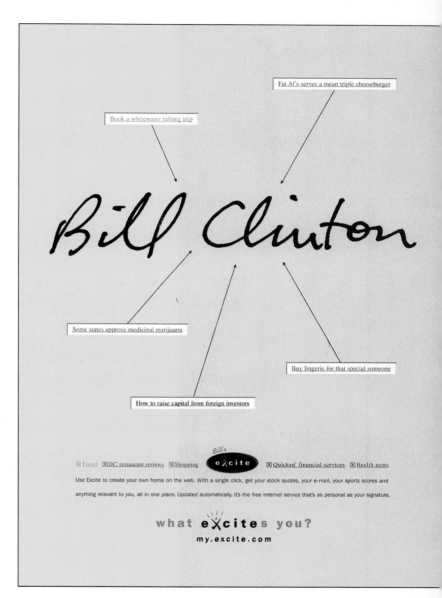

Chapter Fourteen

Using Print Media

Objective To examine how print advertising enhances the advertiser's media mix. Newspapers and magazines, with their unique qualities, can complement broadcast, direct mail, and other media. By using print wisely, advertisers can greatly expand the reach and impact of their campaigns and still stay within their budget.

After studying this chapter, you will be able to:

- Explain the advantages and disadvantages of magazine advertising.
- Discuss the various ways to analyze a magazine's circulation.
- Describe how newspapers are categorized.
- Define the major types of newspaper advertising.
- Explain the advantages and disadvantages of newspaper advertising.
- Discuss how rates are determined for print media.
- List several sources of print media data.

Americans celebrate their down-to-earth origins. These are often reflected in a wide range of popular culture artifacts and even the fine arts, from the colorful portraits of Normal Rockwell to the icons of the friendly neighborhood milkman of the "Leave it to Beaver" generation. But for today's increasingly health- and image-conscious public, the steak and egg meals of yesteryear have lost their appeal. Today, people count their calories meticulously, right down to a simple can of soda. • Given this changing atti-

tude, the National Fluid Milk Processor Promotion Board faced a considerable dilemma. How could it reestablish its product as sufficiently savvy for the country's modern beverage consumption? Milk from the dairies of the heartland didn't have the panache sought by the majority of consumers. Fortunately, unlike many food marketers, the milkboard held a trump card of superior nutritional value that it knew would complete a winning hand. What it needed was to educate the public about its special secret and overcome fears of what had become that most taboo "F word": fat. • Science (and nature) worked in the organization's favor. Nutritionists began publishing study after study that confirmed that most Americans did not receive enough calcium from their diet. And calcium is easily obtained through the consumption of milk. The National Institutes of Health (NIH) warned that without enough calcium, middle-aged people (especially women) suffer from the bone-degenerating disease osteoporosis. It reported that after the age of 11, no age group of females achieves even 75 percent of the recommended levels of calcium and that only one out of three

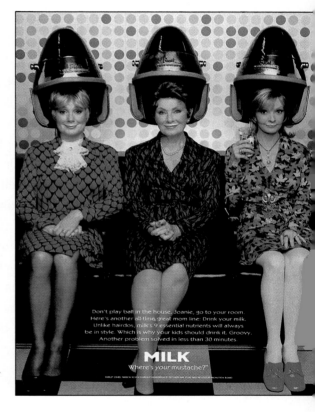

males receives the levels recommended for adults.[1] Armed with this information, the milk board set out to create a campaign that would spark public interest in its solution to this health problem. • The board hired Bozell Worldwide, an advertising agency well-known for its print ads. The puzzle was to create a campaign that would resonate with the times, one that would create appeal for a new era of milk, and one that could be supported by the data from the NIH. • From a marketing perspective, the beauty of print media is the ability to target audiences selectively and achieve maximum exposure for a product. Magazines open avenues to very specific niches of the public and facilitate high-quality presentations in the brilliance of full-color spreads. Thus, the efforts culminated in the "Milk, where's *your* mustache?" campaign, featuring celebrities from all walks with not-so-debonair milk mustaches smeared across their upper lip. Accompanying the quirky photos, Bozell incorporated testimonials from the models praising the positive effects of the vitamins, minerals, and protein from milk that helped them to achieve their success. • The campaign's initial phase focused on women to eliminate the stigma of milk's supposed high fat content. Ads featuring the likes of supermodel Kate Moss and actress Daisy

Fuentes played up their glamour and health consciousness. (Moss' ad even joked that the waif look was out.) The accompanying testimonials touted milk's bone-fortifying effects while assuring the audience of its minimal fat content. Another ad featured America's most famous home-maker, Martha Stewart, with a caption that advised the audience to sub-stitute milk for water in their cooking recipes. ● The ads ran in such consumer magazines as *Vogue, Cosmopolitan, People,* and *Good House-keeping,* carefully targeting each publication's audience of consumption-oriented women. Follow-up research after the campaign revealed a 17 percent increase in the belief by women that milk's health benefits out-weigh its fat and calories. This success emboldened the National Fluid Milk Processor Promotion Board to double the campaign's advertising budget and led to more ambitious plans to target teenage boys and girls, college students, and men.[2] ● By carefully selecting the vehicles, the milk board changed the public's attitude toward an entire industry. Use of consumer magazines emphasized the rich colors of the photos and displayed the desired tone of athleticism, sensuality, and humor to the fullest degree in each of the easily identified celebrities. And the long shelf life of magazines let readers explore the inherent message of milk's health benefits in a manner that would not have been as effective in an-other medium. ● In the end, the milk processors' $110 million "Where's *your* mustache?" integrated campaign endowed milk with its current and much-needed image of fun, glamour, and health. Note that the campaign was good for the entire industry, not just one dairy. That's why it was sponsored by a trade association to which many dairies across the coun-try belong. Most industries have trade associations that promote primary demand for the product category rather than for a specific brand. ●

The Role of the Print Media **Buyer**

Once all the strategic marketing, advertising, and media planning is ac-complished and the creative direction is set, the advertiser can turn to the tactical details of actually scheduling and buying media time on radio and tele-vision and media space in magazines and newspapers. This is where the big money is spent in advertising—on the actual placement of ads in the media. So the competent performance of the media-buying task is critical to getting the most bang for the advertiser's buck.

The person in charge of negotiating and contracting with the media is called a **media buyer.** Media buyers often specialize in one medium or another, so there are print media buyers, spot TV media buyers, network media buyers, and so on. The degree of specialization depends on the size of the advertiser or the agency or the independent media-buying firm the buyer works for. In small agencies, for ex-ample, buyers frequently don't specialize. They do it all.

Success as a *print media buyer* requires a range of knowledge and abilities. First, media buyers must have a broad and basic understanding of all the various forms of print media available and the terminology used in the field. They need to know, for example, how magazines and newspapers are categorized, the advertising possibilities each form offers, and the pros and cons of using various types of print media vehicles. Today, they should also have an understanding of the impact of new technologies on the print media.

Second, buyers need to know how to buy magazine and newspaper space. They must understand how to analyze circulation, how to read rate cards, where to go to get reliable information, and how to calculate and negotiate the most efficient media buys.

Finally, media buyers can exercise their creativity by developing ingenious, sophisticated ways to integrate the advertiser's print media efforts into the whole creative mix.

Obviously, this is no small task. But for the student of advertising who may begin his or her career in a media department, a basic understanding of all these issues is quite important. Explaining them is the purpose of this chapter and, in fact, this whole part.

Using **Magazines** in the Creative Mix

Advertisers use magazines in their creative mix for many reasons. First and foremost, magazines allow an advertiser to reach a particular target audience with a high-quality presentation. The National Fluid Milk Processor Promotion Board is just one of many leading advertisers that use magazines as an important element of their creative mix (Exhibit 14–1 lists the top U.S. magazine advertisers).

The Pros and Cons of Magazine Advertising

Magazines offer a wide variety of benefits to advertisers. The milk mustache campaign depended on the outstanding color reproduction available only from magazines. Further, by running in consumer magazines read by women of particular ages and lifestyles, the Milk Board could target its audience more precisely. Magazines offer a host of other features too: flexible design options, prestige, authority, believability, and long shelf life. Magazines may sit on a coffee table or shelf for months and be reread many times. People can read a magazine ad at their leisure; they can pore over the details of a photograph; and they can study carefully the information presented in the copy. This makes it an ideal medium for high-involvement think and feel products.

However, like every medium, magazines also have a number of drawbacks (see the Checklist on the Pros and Cons of Magazine Advertising). They are expensive (on a cost-per-thousand basis), especially for color ads. And since they typically come out only monthly, or weekly at best, it's difficult to build up reach and frequency quickly. For these reasons, many advertisers use magazines in combination with other media—such as newspapers, which we'll discuss later in this chapter (see Ad Lab 14–A: Magazines and the Creative Mix).

Special Possibilities with Magazines

Media buyers need to be aware of the many creative possibilities magazines offer advertisers through various technical or mechanical features. These include bleed pages, cover positions, inserts and gatefolds, and special sizes, such as junior pages and island halves. We discuss these elements briefly here.

When the dark or colored background of the ad extends to the edge of the page, it is said to **bleed** off the page (see the Nikon ad in the Portfolio Review of Outstanding Magazine Ads in this chapter). Most magazines offer bleed pages, but they charge 10 to 15 percent more for them. The advantages of bleeds include greater flexibility in expressing the advertising idea, a slightly larger printing area, and more dramatic impact.

Exhibit 14–1

Top 10 magazine advertisers in the United States in 1996.

Rank	Advertiser	Magazine ad spending 1996 ($ millions)
1	General Motors Corp.	$456.4
2	Philip Morris Cos.	343.1
3	Procter & Gamble Co.	280.2
4	Ford Motor Co.	280.2
5	Chrysler Corp.	269.5
6	Time Warner	156.4
7	Johnson & Johnson	154.6
8	Toyota Motor Corp.	126.1
9	Unilever	125.2
10	Nestlé	118.9

Source: Reprinted with permission from the September 1997 issue of *Ad Age International.* Copyright, Crain Communications, Inc., 1997.

The Pros

_____ **Flexibility** in readership and advertising. Magazines cover the full range of prospects; they have a wide choice of regional and national coverage and a variety of lengths, approaches, and editorial tones.

_____ **Color** gives readers visual pleasure, and color reproduction is best in slick magazines. Color enhances image and identifies the package. In short, it sells.

_____ **Authority and believability** enhance the commercial message. TV, radio, and newspapers offer lots of information but lack the depth needed for readers to gain knowledge or meaning; magazines often offer all three.

_____ **Permanence,** or long shelf life. Magazines let the reader appraise ads in detail, allowing a more complete education/sales message and the opportunity to communicate the total corporate personality.

_____ **Prestige** for products advertised in upscale or specialty magazines like _Architectural Digest, Connoisseur,_ and _Town and Country._

_____ **Audience selectivity** is more efficient in magazines than any other medium except direct mail. The predictable, specialized editorial environment selects the audience and enables advertisers to pinpoint their sales campaigns. Examples: golfers _(Golf Digest),_ businesspeople _(Business Week),_ 20-something males _(Details),_ or teenage girls _(Seventeen)._

_____ **Cost efficiency** because wasted circulation is minimized. Print networks give advertisers reduced prices for advertising in two or more network publications.

_____ **Selling power** of magazines is proven, and results are measurable.

_____ **Reader loyalty** that sometimes borders on fanaticism.

_____ **Extensive pass-along readership.** Nonsubscribers read the magazine after subscribers finish it.

_____ **Merchandising assistance.** Advertisers can generate reprints and merchandising materials that help them get more mileage out of their ad campaigns.

The Cons

_____ **Lack of immediacy** that advertisers can get with newspapers or radio.

_____ **Shallow geographic coverage.** They don't offer the national reach of broadcast media.

_____ **Inability to deliver mass audiences at a low price.** Magazines are very costly for reaching broad masses of people.

_____ **Inability to deliver high frequency.** Since most magazines come out only monthly or weekly, the advertiser can build frequency faster than reach by adding numerous small-audience magazines to the schedule.

_____ **Long lead time** for ad insertion, sometimes two to three months.

_____ **Heavy advertising competition.** The largest-circulation magazines have 52 percent advertising to 48 percent editorial content.

_____ **High cost per thousand.** Average black-and-white CPM in national consumer magazines ranges from $5 to $12 or more; some trade publications with highly selective audiences have a CPM of more than $40 for a black-and-white page.

_____ **Declining circulations,** especially in single-copy sales, is an industrywide trend that limits the reach of an advertiser's message.

If a company plans to advertise in a particular magazine consistently, it may seek a highly desirable **cover position.** Few publishers sell ads on the front cover, commonly called the _first cover._ They do sell the inside front, inside back, and outside back covers (the _second, third,_ and _fourth covers,_ respectively), usually through multiple-insertion contracts at a substantial premium.

A less expensive way to use magazine space is to place the ad in unusual places on the page or dramatically across spreads. A **junior unit** is a large ad (60 percent of the page) placed in the middle of a page and surrounded with editorial matter. Similar to junior units are **island halves,** surrounded by even more editorial matter. The island sometimes costs more than a regular half-page, but because it dominates the page, many advertisers consider it worth the extra charge. Exhibit 14–2 shows other space combinations that create impact.

Sometimes, rather than buying a standard page, an advertiser uses an **insert.** The advertiser prints the ad on high-quality paper stock to add weight and drama to the message, and then ships the finished ads to the publisher for insertion into the magazine at a special price. Another option is multiple-page inserts. Calvin Klein once promoted its jeans in a 116-page insert in _Vanity Fair._ The insert reportedly cost more than $1 million, but the news reports about it in major daily newspapers gave the campaign enormous publicity value. Advertising inserts may be devoted exclusively to one company's product, or they may be sponsored by the magazine and have a combination of ads and special editorial content consistent with the magazine's focus.

A **gatefold** is an insert whose paper is so wide that the extreme left and right sides have to be folded into the center to match the size of the other pages. When the reader opens the magazine, the folded page swings out like a gate to present the ad. Not all magazines provide gatefolds, and they are always sold at a substantial premium.

Some advertisers create their own **custom magazines.** These look like regular magazines and are often produced by the same companies that publish traditional magazines. However, they are essentially magazine-length ads, which readers are expected to purchase at newsstands. Custom magazines have been published for Sony, General Motors, General Electric, Jenny Craig, and Ray-Ban sunglasses.[3] In 1995, Apple Computer solely sponsored a special issue of *Scientific American* entitled "The Computer in the 21st Century." It was touted as a sign of things to come since it was the "first complete computer-to-plate magazine production without using film."[4]

Ad Lab 14–B discusses other innovations in magazine advertising.

How Magazines Are Categorized

In the jargon of the trade, magazines are called *books,* and media buyers commonly categorize them by *content, geography,* and *size.*

Content

One of the most dramatic developments in publishing is the emergence of magazines with special content, which has given many books good prospects for long-term growth. The broadest classifications of content are *consumer magazines,*

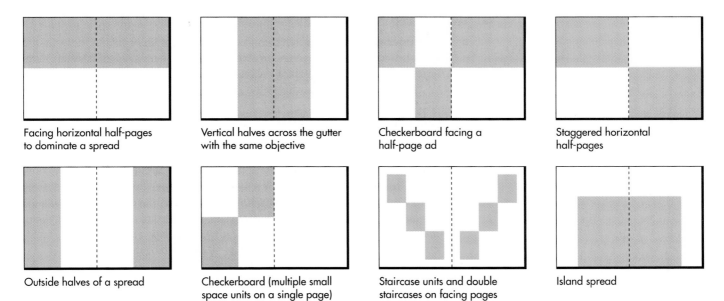

Facing horizontal half-pages to dominate a spread	Vertical halves across the gutter with the same objective	Checkerboard facing a half-page ad	Staggered horizontal half-pages
Outside halves of a spread	Checkerboard (multiple small space units on a single page)	Staircase units and double staircases on facing pages	Island spread

Exhibit 14–2

An ad's position on the page influences its effectiveness. The size and shape of the ad often determine where it will fall on the page. These eight two-page spreads show most of the positions an ad can take.

Innovations in Magazine Advertising

Magazines work closely with advertisers to develop new technologies for presenting ideas and products. From these efforts have come such innovations as fragrance strips, color strips, and pop-ups.

In the early 1980s, **fragrance strips** became a great favorite with perfume advertisers. With the Scentstrip, readers sample a scent by opening a sealed insert tucked into a magazine. Despite some consumer complaints, Scentstrips proved incredibly popular. Odors are useful for other products as well; a Rolls-Royce ad in *Architectural Digest* carried a Scentstrip bearing the essence of leather.

Cosmetics manufacturers insert **color strip** samples of eye shadow, blush, lipstick, and other makeup that readers can try immediately. Color strips are expensive to produce, but many advertisers think they're worth it.

Another costly innovation is the **pop-up ad,** shown here. Corporate advertisers such as Honeywell and TransAmerica were among the first to try this eye-catching approach. Product ads, such as a pop-up Dodge Dakota, followed.

Other intriguing approaches include **3-D ads** (complete with 3-D glasses), product samples (facial tissues and paper towels), and unusual shapes and sizes for preprinted inserts. An ad for Sara Lee cheesecake used a single heavy-stock page with what appeared to be a bite taken out of a large-as-life cheesecake slice. A half-page insert for Gleem toothpaste featured a metallic graphic of a mirror with the slogan "Check your mirror."

Researchers are probing the possibilities of holograms and ads that talk when readers pass a device across the page. Already ads can sing—liquor companies included microchips that played Christmas carols in their December magazine ads, and Camel cigarette ads played "Happy Birthday" on the brand's 75th anniversary.

Such innovative approaches not only attract readers' attention but also involve them in the experience by appealing to more than just the visual sense.

Laboratory Application

What products besides perfumes and cars could Scentstrips be used to advertise?

HFC, Direct Mail/DDB Needham Worldwide

farm magazines, and *business magazines.* Each may be broken down into hundreds of categories.

- **Consumer magazines,** purchased for entertainment, information, or both, are edited for consumers who buy products for their own personal consumption: *Time, Sports Illustrated, Glamour, Good Housekeeping.* The Portfolio Review of Outstanding Magazine Ads shows the range of creativity in consumer magazine advertising.

- **Farm publications** are directed to farmers and their families or to companies that manufacture or sell agricultural equipment, supplies, and services: *Farm Journal, Progressive Farmer, Prairie Farmer, Successful Farming.*

- **Business magazines,** by far the largest category, target business readers. They include *trade publications* for retailers, wholesalers, and other distributors (e.g., *Progressive Grocer, Bakery News*); *business* and *industrial magazines* for businesspeople involved in manufacturing and services (*Electronic Design, American Banker*); and *professional journals* for lawyers, physicians, architects, and other professionals (*Archives of Ophthalmology*).

Geography

A magazine may also be classified as *local, regional,* or *national.* Today most major U.S. cities have a **local city magazine:** *San Diego Magazine, New York, Los Angeles, Chicago, Palm Springs Life.* Their readership is usually upscale, professional people interested in local arts, fashion, and business.

5. North Central   10. Chicago   3. Great Lakes†   9. Mid-Atlantic‡   1. New England

2. New York

- Major market
* Pacific Ed. excludes counties covered by Metro L.A. Edition
† Great Lakes Ed. excludes counties covered by Metro Chicago
‡ Mid-Atlantic Ed. excludes counties covered by Metro N.Y.

Exhibit 14–3
Advertisers benefit from selecting regional editions similar to the 10 geographic editions of *Reader's Digest* shown on the map. With regional binding and mailing, advertisers can buy ad space for only the amount of distribution they need.

Regional publications are targeted to a specific area of the country, such as the West or the South: *Sunset, Southern Living.* National magazines sometimes provide special market runs for specific geographic regions. *Time, Newsweek, Woman's Day,* and *Sports Illustrated* allow advertisers to buy a single major market. Exhibit 14–3 shows the 10 major geographic editions of *Reader's Digest.*

National magazines range from those with enormous circulations, such as *TV Guide,* to small, lesser-known national magazines, such as *Nature* and *Volleyball Monthly.* The largest circulation magazine in the United States today is *Modern Maturity,* distributed to the 20 million members of the American Association of Retired Persons.[5]

continued on page 454

Magazines that cater to specific geographic areas are regional publications. Most metropolitan areas publish magazines specific to their particular city, such as this example from Chicago *magazine (www.chicagomag.com), providing news and information on issues and events of interest to the local population.*

Magazines provide creative people with an unlimited palette for their imagination.

Offering permanence, color, unmatched reproduction quality, and excellent credibility, magazines are a powerful weapon in the advertiser's arsenal. In this portfolio, we've selected some outstanding examples of magazine advertising.

See if you can look past the beauty of these ads, though, and determine the underlying strategy that guided the artists' thinking. Who is the target audience? Is that different from the target market? What are they trying to say about the advertiser? How is the advertiser positioned? Once you determine what the strategy is, try to think which magazines you would have placed these ads in?

Outstanding Magazine Ads

This ad for Nikon (www.nikon.com) takes advantage of the different sizes and styles of advertising found in magazines. Employing a double-page bleed, the image dominates the ad and provides the reader with a sense of the product in use. The headline is simple and the body text informative. The striking shadows and light in the photo reinforce Nikon's claim to "the art of mastering light."

Some of the most elegant and captivating advertisements are created by nonprofit organizations such as art exhibitions, dance performances, or museums. In this case, the Delta Blues Museum (www.clarksdale.com/bluesed/) uses vintage photos to impart the rapture of the people for the music of their time. The headline copy is critical here as it provides a distinctly soulful African-American voice when tied into the photograph, reflecting the historic importance of blues music to this culture.

Effective use of language is a key element to the success of any advertisement.
Mongoose Bicycles (www.mongoose.com) plays on the dual meaning of scream in
this example. The copy refers to the real act of screaming, while the visual refers to the
colloquial use of "scream," meaning to move very fast. The image of the cyclist is
blurred to show the visceral rush of the rider's high speed, but in the body copy the
audience can rationally read technical drawings and information about the bike.

Pioneer Electronics (www.pioneerelectronics.com) advertises its car stereo without
actually featuring the product for most of the ad. The company captures the readers'
attention with the strange lead copy of "The Road Kill Diaries," followed up by a
humorously irreverent story, meant to capture a youthful audience. Sound quality
is emphasized in the subhead as rock music was the last sound the "Road Kill" heard
before the narrator was run over. The product itself is only mentioned in the small
copy at the bottom of the ad, demonstrating the reliance on brand name and lifestyle
focus of the marketing approach.

Nissan (www.nissan-usa.com) finds an exemplary way to use print with this ad that showcases some of the more inventive uses of the medium. The audience first sees the image of the off-road, dirtied truck (above), which is actually a translucent overlay for the image of a clean version of the same truck on a desert highway (below). The medium itself conveys much of the message, because it has been manipulated to provide a physical interaction with the reader. The final version of the ad uses copy to contrast the two forms and purposes of the truck, and reinforce the aesthetic qualities of the vehicle.

Striking visuals and clever headline copy draw immediate attention to this ad for Peak 1 Outdoor Equipment (www.coleman-eur.com). The body copy then appeals to reason in the audience, explaining that the only truly important features of outdoor equipment are those that are useful—the kind found on Peak 1 gear. This ad artfully combines elements of parody, informative copy, and user benefit styles.

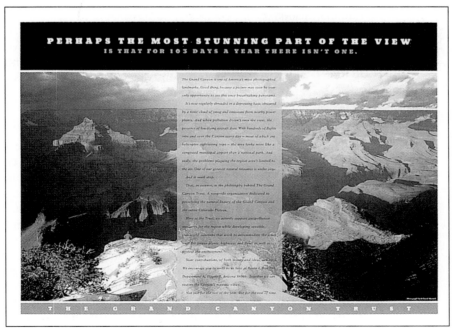

It is critical for advertisers to use images and copy that an audience can relate to, particularly when addressing an issue that affects a diverse group of people. The Grand Canyon Trust (www.grandcanyontrust.org), an organization dedicated to the preservation of the national park, must first appeal to an audience that instinctively empathizes with environmental issues. But it must also attempt to extend the ad's effects to mainstream consumers as well. To achieve this goal, the trust uses a familiar desert panorama of the Southwest, contrasting the grandeur of the vista with ironic copy that hints at the crisis at hand.

continued from page 449

Size

It doesn't take a genius to figure out that magazines come in different shapes and sizes, but it might take one to figure out how to get one ad to run in different-size magazines and still look the same. Magazine sizes run the gamut, which can make production standardization a nightmare. The most common magazine sizes follow:

Size classification	Magazine	Approximate size of full-page ad
Large	*Life*	4 col. × 170 lines (9³/₈ × 12¹/₈ inches)
Flat	*Time, Newsweek*	3 col. × 140 lines (7 × 10 inches)
Standard	*National Geographic*	2 col. × 119 lines (6 × 8¹/₂ inches)
Small or pocket	*Reader's Digest, TV Guide*	2 col. × 91 lines (4¹/₂ × 6¹/₂ inches)

Buying **Magazine** Space

When analyzing a media vehicle, media buyers consider readership, cost, mechanical requirements, and ad closing dates (deadlines). To buy effectively, they must thoroughly understand the magazine's circulation and rate-card information.

Understanding Magazine Circulation

The first step in analyzing a publication's potential effectiveness is to assess its audience. The buyer studies circulation statistics, primary and secondary readership, subscription and vendor sales, and any special merchandising services the magazine offers.

Guaranteed versus Delivered Circulation

A magazine's rates are based on its circulation. The **rate base** is the circulation figure on which the publisher bases its rates; the **guaranteed circulation** is the number of copies the publisher expects to circulate. The latter assures advertisers they will reach a certain number of people. If the publisher does not reach its *delivered figure,* it must provide a refund. For that reason, guaranteed circulation figures are often stated safely below the average actual circulation. However, this is not always true. Circulation actually gets overstated more often than people think. As many as 30 percent of consumer magazines audited by the Audit Bureau of Circulations (ABC) each year don't meet the circulation levels they guarantee to advertisers.[6]

So media buyers expect publications to verify their circulation figures. Publishers pay thousands of dollars each year for a **circulation audit**—a thorough analysis of the circulation procedures, outlets of distribution, readers, and other factors—by companies like ABC. Directories such as those published by Standard Rate & Data Service (SRDS) feature the logo of the auditing company in each listing for an audited magazine.

Primary and Secondary Readership

Data from the ABC or other verified reports tell the media buyer the magazine's total circulation. This **primary circulation** represents the number of people who buy the publication, either by subscription or at the newsstand. **Secondary** (or

Advertising Age **is a good example of a vertical publication. The magazine is geared toward a variety of issues specific to the advertising industry and read by people throughout the industry. Unlike horizontal publications,** Advertising Age **does not focus on a single job function across various industries.**

pass-along) readership is very important to magazines; some have more than six readers per copy. Multiplying the average pass-along readership by, say, a million subscribers can give a magazine a substantial audience beyond its primary readers.

Vertical and Horizontal Publications

There are two readership classifications of business publications: *vertical* and *horizontal.* A **vertical publication** covers a specific industry in all its aspects. For example, Cahners Publishing produces *Restaurants & Institutions* strictly for restaurateurs and food-service operators. The magazine's editorial content includes everything from news of the restaurant industry to institutional-size recipes.

Horizontal publications, in contrast, deal with a particular job function across a variety of industries. Readers of *Purchasing* work in purchasing management in many different industries. Horizontal trade publications are very effective advertising vehicles because they usually offer excellent reach and they tend to be well read.[7]

Subscription and Vendor Sales

Media buyers also want to know a magazine's ratio of subscriptions to newsstand sales. Today, subscriptions account for the majority of magazine sales. Newsstands (which include bookstore chains) are still a major outlet for single-copy sales, but no outlet can handle more than a fraction of the many magazines available.

From the advertiser's point of view, newsstand sales are impressive because they indicate that the purchaser really wants the magazine and is not merely subscribing out of habit. According to the Magazine Publishers Association, single-copy sales account for 34 percent of total revenues for a representative sampling of leading magazines.

Paid and Controlled Circulation

Business publications may be distributed on either a *paid circulation* or *controlled circulation* basis. A paid basis means the recipient must pay the subscription price to receive the magazine. *Business Week* is a **paid circulation** business magazine.

In **controlled circulation,** the publisher mails the magazine free to individuals who the publisher thinks can influence the purchase of advertised products. Managers of corporate video departments receive *Corporate Video Decisions.* To qualify for the subscription list, people must indicate in writing a desire to receive it and must give their professional designation or occupation. Dues-paying members of organizations often get free subscriptions; members of the National Association for Female Executives receive free copies of *Executive Female.*

Publishers of paid-circulation magazines say subscribers who pay are more likely to read a publication than those who receive it free. But controlled-circulation magazines can reach good prospects for the goods and services they advertise.

Merchandising Services: Added Value

Magazines, and newspapers too, often provide liberal *added-value services* to their regular advertisers, such as:

- Special free promotions to stores.
- Marketing services to help readers find local outlets.
- Response cards that allow readers to request an advertiser's brochures and catalogs.

- Help handling sales force, broker, wholesaler, and retailer meetings.
- Advance editions for the trade.
- Research into brand preferences, consumer attitudes, and market conditions.

If a publication's basic factors—editorial, circulation, and readership—are strong, these additional services can increase the effectiveness of its ads.[8] Magazines offer great potential for relationship marketing since they already have a relationship with their subscribers. New added-value options might include using magazines' custom publishing, editorial, and production knowledge, along with their databases, to help clients develop videos, books, and guides that create added value for the brand.[9]

Reading Rate Cards

Magazine rate cards follow a standard format (see RL 14–1 in the Reference Library). This helps advertisers determine costs, discounts, mechanical requirements, closing dates, special editions, and additional costs for features like color, inserts, bleed pages, split runs, or preferred positions.

Three dates affect magazine purchases. The **cover date** is the date printed on the cover. The **on-sale date** is the date the magazine is actually issued. And the **closing date** is the date all ad material must be in the publisher's hands for a specific issue. Lead time may be as much as three months.

Rates

As we discussed in Chapter 8, one way to compare magazines is to look at how much it costs to reach a thousand people based on the magazine's rates for a one-time, full-page ad. You compute the **cost per thousand (CPM)** by dividing the full-page rate by the number of *thousands* of subscribers:

$$\frac{\text{Page rate}}{(\text{Circulation} \div 1{,}000)} = \text{CPM}$$

If the magazine's black-and-white page rate is $10,000, and the publication has a circulation of 500,000, then:

$$\frac{\$10{,}000}{(500{,}000 \div 1{,}000)} = \frac{10{,}000}{500} = \$20 \text{ CPM}$$

Consider this comparison. In 1997, the page rate for a full-color, one-page ad in *Car & Driver* was $65,710 on total paid circulation of 1,110,869; *Road & Track* offered the same ad for $58,395 on total paid circulation of 733,444. Which was the better buy?[10]

Exhibit 14–4 lists the circulations and color page rates for 18 leading consumer magazines. Using this data, you can calculate which national buys offer the best CPMs.

Discounts

Magazines and newspapers often give discounts. **Frequency discounts** are based on the number of ad insertions, usually within a year; **volume discounts** are based on the total amount of space bought during a specific period. Most magazines also offer *cash discounts* (usually 2 percent) to advertisers who pay right away, and some offer discounts on the purchase of four or more consecutive pages in a single issue. In fact, more than half of all magazine publishers now negotiate their rates. According to Harold Shain, executive VP/publisher of *Newsweek,* "Every piece of business is negotiated. I don't believe we will ever return to the industry we were 10 years ago."[11]

Premium Rates

Magazines charge extra for special features. Color normally costs 25 to 60 percent more than black and white. Some publications, such as *Money,* even offer metallic inks and special colors. Bleed pages can add as much as 20 percent to regular rates, although the typical increase is about 15 percent.

Second and third cover rates (the inside covers) typically cost less than the fourth (back) cover. *Newsweek* charges $154,750 for a normal color page and the same for second and third covers, but $198,365 for the fourth cover.

Magazines charge different rates for ads in geographic or demographic issues. **Geographic editions** target geographic markets; **demographic editions** reach readers who share a demographic trait, such as age, income level, or professional status. *Time* offers one-page, four-color ads (one-time insertion) in Boston for $13,126 (135,000 circulation), in its top management edition for $68,000 (798,460 circulation), and in the nation's highest income zip codes for $98,000 (1.3 million circulation).

Using **Newspapers** in the Creative Mix

Exhibit 14-4

Selected consumer magazine circulation and cost.

Magazine	Total paid circulation	Page cost for four-color ad
Modern Maturity	20,390,755	$248,800
Reader's Digest	15,038,708	208,000
TV Guide	13,103,187	155,200
National Geographic	9,013,113	167,310
Better Homes & Gardens	7,605,187	213,900
Family Circle	5,107,477	161,510
Good Housekeeping	4,739,592	174,385
Ladies' Home Journal	4,590,155	137,000
Woman's Day	4,163,248	140,055
Time	4,155,806	169,000
Sports Illustrated	3,280,233	170,000
Newsweek	3,276,457	154,750
Playboy	3,169,697	96,210
Redbook	2,889,466	99,300
Cosmopolitan	2,701,916	99,550
National Enquirer	2,324,678	49,800
People Weekly	3,608,111	131,500
Star	1,948,247	40,300

When a small, alternative newspaper in Manhattan asked one of the newest and hottest creative shops in the city for help in promoting subscriptions, it had no idea what the little agency with the funny name, Mad Dogs & Englishmen, would do for it.

The *Village Voice* newspaper had always knocked the Establishment with its radical coverage of social issues, politics, media, and culture. So perhaps it shouldn't have come as a surprise when the Mad Dogs took the newspaper's own prose style and turned it around in a series of impertinent, self-mocking ads.

"Hell, I wouldn't have my home contaminated with a subscription to your elitist rag if you were giving away five-speed blenders," rants one ad in the series. "You people think New York is the friggin' center of the world." But then a second paragraph offers a dramatic alternative: "YES, I want to buy a year's subscription to the *Village Voice,*" along with a coupon.

The paper's readers aren't spared either. One ad skewers New Age tree-huggers: "Murderers! Trees are being systematically swallowed up by the jaws of industry and still you insist I take part in this horror by subscribing?"

Newspaper is an important medium in the creative mix, second only to television in advertising volume, but costing much less. This ad for the Village Voice *(www.villagevoice.com) shows how a niche business can use newspaper advertising to expand sales. Mimicking the freewheeling tone of the newspaper, the advertiser targeted those who already read the* Village Voice *but were not subscribers.*

Mad Dogs principal Nick Cohen said he thought the *Voice* would like the campaign because the newspaper is honest. "It really stands behind the freedom of the writers, even when they criticize the management itself," he said.

Selecting the medium was easy. Since most people who would be interested in a subscription are *Village Voice* readers, the campaign ran in the paper itself. It proved to be a wise choice. In the first year of the campaign, the *Voice* saw a 30 percent increase in its subscriber base, surpassing all expectations.[12]

Who Uses Newspapers?

Newspapers are now the second largest medium (after television) in terms of advertising volume, receiving 21.9 percent of the dollars spent by advertisers in the United States.[13]

Consider these important facts:

- More than 114.7 million U.S. adults read daily papers each weekday; nearly two out of three Americans read a paper every day.
- Almost 60 percent of American adult newspaper readers read every page of the newspaper, while almost all (95 percent) read the general news sections.
- Approximately 60 million daily papers are circulated in the United States each day, with an average of 2.1 readers per copy.
- In 1997, there were 1,520 daily newspapers in the United States, with a total circulation of 59.8 million. The same year, the nation's 10,000-plus weekly newspapers and shoppers had a combined circulation of more than 105 million.[14]
- Advertising volume in daily newspapers increased by 5.7 percent in 1996, with total sales of more than $38 billion.[15]

Although the newspaper is the major community-serving medium for both news and advertising, more and more national advertisers are shifting to radio and television. As a result, radio and TV carry most of the national advertising in the United States, while 88 percent of newspaper advertising revenue comes from local advertising. As Exhibit 14–5 shows, retailers are the primary local advertisers in newspapers.

The Pros and Cons of Newspaper Advertising

The *Village Voice* promotion shows how small businesses with even smaller budgets can benefit from creative newspaper advertising. Print ads in general and newspapers in particular provide a unique, flexible medium for advertisers to express their creativity—especially with businesses that rely on local customers.

Newspapers offer advertisers many advantages. One of the most important is *timeliness;* an ad can appear very quickly, sometimes in just one day. Newspapers also offer geographic targeting, a broad range of markets, reasonable cost, and more. But newspapers suffer from lack of selectivity, poor production quality, and clutter. And readers criticize them for lack of depth and follow-up on important issues.[16]

Use the Checklist of Pros and Cons of Newspaper Advertising to answer the questions in Ad Lab 14–C: Newspapers and the Creative Mix.

How Newspapers Are Categorized

Newspapers can be classified by *frequency of delivery, physical size,* or *type of audience.*

Exhibit 14–5

Top 10 newspaper advertisers in the United States (1996).

Rank	Advertiser	Newspaper ad spending 1996 ($ millions)
1	Federated Department Stores	$339.5
2	May Department Stores Co.	326.1
3	Circuit City Stores	250.3
4	Sears, Roebuck & Co.	193.1
5	Dayton Hudson Corp.	158.8
6	Dillard Department Stores	126.9
7	Time Warner	124.0
8	Walt Disney Co.	118.7
9	JCPenney Co.	105.2
10	Kmart Corp.	97.9

Source: Reprinted with permission from the September 1997 issue of *Ad Age International.* Copyright, Crain Communications, Inc., 1997.

Frequency of Delivery

A **daily newspaper** is published as either a morning or evening edition at least five times a week, Monday through Friday. Of the 1,520 dailies in the United States, 846 are evening papers and 686 are morning papers. (The total exceeds 1,520 because 12 consider themselves morning and evening papers, or "all-day" newspapers.)[17] Morning editions tend to have broader geographic circulation and a larger male readership; evening editions are read more by women.

With their emphasis on local news and advertising, **weekly newspapers** characteristically serve small urban or suburban residential areas and farm communities. They are now the fastest-growing class of newspapers. A weekly newspaper's cost per thousand is usually higher than a daily paper's, but a weekly has a longer life and often has more readers per copy.

Physical Size

There are two basic newspaper formats, standard size and tabloid. The **standard-size newspaper** is about 22 inches deep and 13 inches wide and is divided into six columns. The **tabloid newspaper** is generally about 14 inches deep and 11 inches wide. National tabloid newspapers like the *National Enquirer* and the *Star* use sensational stories to fight for single-copy sales. Other tabloids, such as the *New York Daily News,* emphasize straight news and features.

Newspapers used to offer about 400 different ad sizes. But in 1984, the industry introduced the **standard advertising unit (SAU)** system, which standardized the newspaper column width, page sizes, and ad sizes. An SAU column inch is $2^{1}/_{16}$ inches wide by 1 inch deep. There are now 56 standard ad sizes for standard papers and 32 for tabloids. Virtually all dailies converted to the SAU system (some at great expense) and so did most weeklies.

Type of Audience

Some dailies and weeklies serve special-interest audiences, a fact not lost on advertisers. They generally contain advertising oriented to their special audiences and they may have unique advertising regulations.

Some serve specific ethnic markets. Today more than 200 dailies and weeklies are oriented to the African-American community. Others serve foreign-language groups. In the United States there are newspapers printed in 43 languages other than English.

Specialized newspapers also serve business and financial audiences. *The Wall Street Journal,* the leading national business and financial daily, enjoys a circulation of nearly 2 million. Other papers cater to fraternal, labor union, or professional organizations, religious groups, or hobbyists.

Other Types of Newspapers

The United States has 890 Sunday newspapers, mostly Sunday editions of daily papers, with a combined circulation of more than 63 million.[18] Sunday newspapers generally combine standard news coverage with special functions like these:

● Increased volume of classified ads.

● Greater advertising and news volume.

● In-depth coverage of business, sports, real estate, literature and the arts, entertainment, and travel.

● Review and analysis of the past week's events.

● Expanded editorial and opinion sections.

We are all familiar with the daily newspaper, from the local city paper to The Wall Street Journal *to* The Washington Daily Post *and* USA Today *(www.usatoday.com). Daily newspapers cover a wide range of demographics and provide advertisers with one of the most timely media for presenting current news and information.*

The Pros and Cons of Newspaper Advertising

The Pros

_____ **Mass medium** penetrating every segment of society. Almost all consumers read the newspaper.

_____ **Local medium** with broad reach. Covers a specific geographic area that comprises both a market and a community of people sharing common concerns and interest.

_____ **Comprehensive in scope,** covering an extraordinary variety of topics and interests.

_____ **Geographic selectivity** is possible with zoned editions for specific neighborhoods or communities.

_____ **Timeliness.** Papers primarily cover today's news and are read in one day.

_____ **Credibility.** Studies show that newspaper ads rank highest in believability. TV commercials are a distant second.

_____ **Selective attention** from the relatively small number of active prospects who, on any given day, are interested in what the advertiser is trying to tell them or sell them.

_____ **Creative flexibility.** An ad's physical size and shape can be varied to give the degree of dominance or repetition that suits the advertiser's purpose. The advertiser can use black and white, color, Sunday magazines, or custom inserts.

_____ **An active medium** rather than a passive one. Readers turn the pages, clip and save, write in the margins, and sort through the contents.

_____ **A permanent record,** in contrast to the ephemeral nature of radio and TV.

_____ **Reasonable cost.**

The Cons

_____ **Lack of selectivity** of specific socioeconomic groups. Most newspapers reach broad, diverse groups of readers, which may not match the advertiser's objectives.

_____ **Short life span.** Unless readers clip and save the ad or coupon, it may be lost forever.

_____ **Low production quality.** Coarse newsprint generally produces a less impressive image than the slick, smooth paper stock of magazines, and many newspapers can't print color.

_____ **Clutter.** Each ad competes with editorial content and with all the other ads on the same page or spread.

_____ **Lack of control** over where ad will appear unless the advertiser pays extra for a preferred position.

_____ **Overlapping circulation.** Some people read more than one newspaper. Advertisers may be paying for readers who were already reached in a different paper.

Most Sunday newspapers also feature a **Sunday supplement** magazine. Some publish their own supplement, such as _Los Angeles Magazine_ of the _Los Angeles Times._ Other papers subscribe to syndicated supplements; _Parade_ magazine is now received by over 37 million people every week.[19]

Printed by rotogravure on heavier, coated paper stock, Sunday supplements are more conducive to color printing than newsprint, making them attractive to national advertisers who want better reproduction quality.

Another type of newspaper, the **independent shopping guide** or free community newspaper, offers advertisers local saturation. Sometimes called _pennysavers,_ these shoppers offer free distribution and extensive advertising pages targeted at essentially the same audience as weekly newspapers—urban and suburban community readers. Readership is often high, and the publishers use hand delivery or direct mail to achieve maximum saturation.

North Americans also read national newspapers, including the _Globe and Mail_ in Canada, _USA Today,_ and the _Christian Science Monitor._ With a circulation of 1.5 million, _USA Today_ is second only to _The Wall Street Journal_ in national distribution and first among U.S. general-interest dailies, surpassing the _New York Daily News._ _USA Today_ is now the print vehicle of choice for automotive ads due to its high-quality color reproduction.[20]

Types of Newspaper Advertising

The major classifications of newspaper advertising are _display, classified, public notices,_ and _preprinted inserts._

Display Advertising

Display advertising includes copy, illustrations or photos, headlines, coupons, and other visual components—like the ads for the _Village Voice_ discussed earlier. Display ads vary in size and appear in all sections of the newspaper except the first page of major sections, the editorial page, the obituary page, and the classified section.

Ad Lab 14–C

Newspapers and the Creative Mix

Study the Checklist: The Pros and Cons of Newspaper Advertising and see if you can apply that information to the following situation:

You're the product manager for a major brand of bar soap and you wish to go nationwide with an ad featuring a coupon.

Laboratory Applications

1. Which newspaper would be best?
   a. A weekly.   b. A daily.
2. If you use a daily, in what section of the paper do you want your ad to appear?
3. If you decided on the Sunday supplement, which of the following would you choose and why:
   a. *Parade* magazine?   b. Color coupon supplement?

One common variation of the display ad, the **reading notice,** looks like editorial matter and sometimes costs more than normal display advertising. To prevent readers from mistaking it for editorial matter, the word *advertisement* appears at the top.

As we discussed in Chapters 3 and 5, retailers often run newspaper ads through **cooperative** (or **co-op**) **programs** sponsored by the manufacturers whose products they sell. The manufacturer pays fully or partially to create and run the ad, which features the manufacturer's product and logo along with the local retailer's name and address.

Classified Advertising

Classified ads provide a community marketplace for goods, services, and opportunities of every type, from real estate and new-car sales to employment and business opportunities. A newspaper's profitability often depends on a healthy classified section.

Classified ads usually appear under subheads that describe the class of goods or the need the ads seek to satisfy. Most employment, housing, and car advertising is classified. To promote the use of classified ads in the *Village Voice,* MD&E created a series of display ads that used humorous "Situation Wanted" ads as the main visuals.

Classified rates are typically based on how many lines the ad occupies and how many times the ad runs. Some newspapers accept **classified display ads,** which run in the classified section of the newspaper but feature larger type and/or photos, art borders, abundant white space, and sometimes even color.

Public Notices

For a nominal fee, newspapers carry legal **public notices** of changes in business and personal relationships, public governmental reports, notices by private citizens and organizations, and financial reports. These ads follow a preset format.

Preprinted Inserts

Like magazines, newspapers carry **preprinted inserts.** The advertiser prints the inserts and delivers them to the newspaper plant for insertion into a specific edition. Insert sizes range from a typical newspaper page to a double postcard; formats include catalogs, brochures, mail-back devices, and perforated coupons.

Some large metropolitan dailies allow advertisers to limit their inserts to specific circulation zones. A retail advertiser that wants to reach only those shoppers in its immediate trading area can place an insert in the local-zone editions. Retail stores, car dealers, and large national advertisers are among those who find it less costly to distribute their circulars this way than to mail them or deliver door to door.

How Advertisers **Buy** Newspaper **Space**

To get the most from the advertising budget, the media buyer must know the characteristics of a newspaper's readership: the median age, sex, occupation, income, educational level, and buying habits of the typical reader.

Understanding Readership and Circulation

Readership information is available from various sources, such as Simmons Market Research Bureau and Scarborough Research Corp. Most large papers also provide extensive data on their readers.

In single-newspaper cities, reader demographics typically reflect a cross-section of the general population. In cities with two or more newspapers, however, these characteristics may vary widely. The *Los Angeles Times* is directed to a broad cross-section of the community and *La Opinion* to the area's large Hispanic population.

Advertisers must understand the full extent of the newspaper's circulation. The paper's total circulation includes subscribers and single-copy newsstand buyers, as well as secondary readers.

Rate Cards

Like the magazine rate card, the newspaper **rate card** lists advertising rates, mechanical and copy requirements, deadlines, and other information. Because rates vary greatly, advertisers should calculate which papers deliver the most readers and the best demographics for their money.

Local versus National Rates

Most newspapers charge local and national advertisers at different rates. The **national rate** averages 75 percent higher, but some papers charge as much as 254 percent more.[21] Newspapers attribute higher rates to the added costs of serving national advertisers. For instance, an ad agency usually places national advertising and receives a 15 percent commission from the paper. If the advertising comes from another city or state, then additional costs, such as long-distance telephone calls, are also involved.

But many national advertisers reject the high rates and take their business elsewhere. Less than 5 percent of national ad money now goes to newspapers, and that proportion may shrink even further.[22] In response to declining national advertising revenue, newspapers are experimenting with simplified billing systems and discount rates for their national clients.

Flat Rates and Discount Rates

Many national papers charge **flat rates,** which means they allow no discounts; a few newspapers offer a single flat rate to both national and local advertisers.

Newspapers that offer volume discounts have an **open rate** (their highest rate for a one-time insertion) and **contract rates,** whereby local advertisers can obtain discounts of up to 70 percent by signing a contract for frequent or bulk space purchases. **Bulk discounts** offer advertisers decreasing rates (calculated by multiplying the number of inches by the cost per inch) as they use more inches. Advertisers earn **frequency discounts** by running a given ad repeatedly in a specific time period. Similarly, advertisers can sometimes get **earned rates**, a discount applied retroactively as the volume of advertising increases through the year. More than 1,000 newspapers also participate in Newsplan, a Newspaper Advertising Bureau (NAB) program that gives national and regional advertisers discounts for purchasing six or more pages per year.

Short Rate

An advertiser who contracts to buy a specific amount of space during a one-year period at a discount and then fails to fulfill the promise is charged a **short rate,** which is the difference between the contracted rate and the earned rate for the actual inches run. Conversely, an advertiser who buys more inches than contracted may be entitled to a rebate or credit because of the discounted earned rate for the additional advertising space.

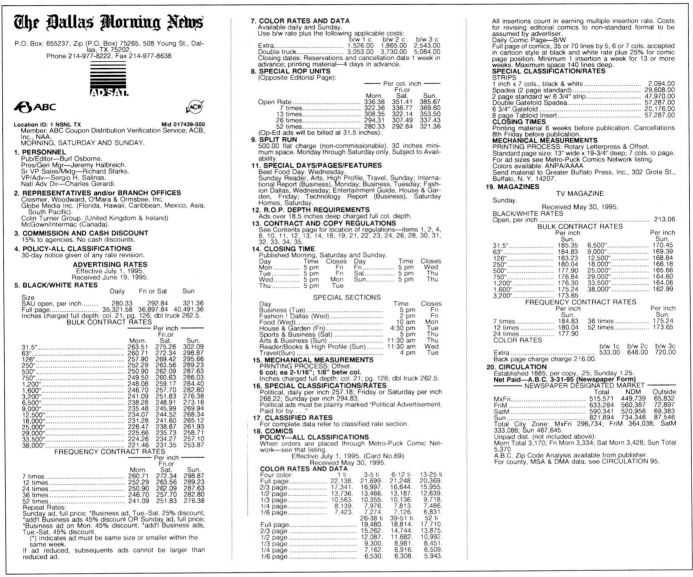

The newspaper rate card for The Dallas Morning News *(www.dallasnews.com) is similar to that for magazines. It shows the variety of ad sizes and their costs.*

Combination Rates

Combination rates are often available for placing a given ad in (1) morning and evening editions of the same newspaper; (2) two or more newspapers owned by the same publisher; and (3) in some cases, two or more newspapers affiliated in a syndicate or newspaper group.

Run of Paper versus Preferred Position

Run-of-paper (ROP) advertising rates entitle a newspaper to place a given ad on any newspaper page or in any position it desires. Although the advertiser has no control over where the ad appears in the paper, most newspapers try to place an ad in the position the advertiser requests.

An advertiser can ensure a choice position for an ad by paying a higher **preferred-position rate.** A tire manufacturer, for example, may pay the preferred rate to ensure a position in the sports section.

Ethics, Ergonomics, and Economics

Who is likely to be injured at work? Repetitive stress injuries (RSIs) cause half of all workplace injuries, the kind that affect advertising agency staffs: computer operators (administrative and creative), graphics artists, audiovisual specialists, and anyone who performs the same set of motions many times daily. These disorders cost business $20 billion annually just in workers' compensation expenses, according to Dr. Barbara Silverstein, special assistant for ergonomics at the Occupational Safety & Health Administration (OSHA).

Until very recently, relatively few ad agency managers were even aware of RSIs. Occasionally artists and typists reported back and neck problems, but managers infrequently took action because no one could prove that the office environment caused these problems. The problems seemed minor and no one even thought they were related to ethics. But, in fact, they were. And since business managers weren't meeting their obligation to protect workers and workplaces, the government moved in to fill the ethical void.

Federal and state OSHA regulations now protect workplace safety and are making regulations stricter—requiring, among other things, an ergonomics risk factor checklist. Key risk factors are

force, the repetitive nature or frequency of a task, awkward postures, the time spent on a task, and the pace of work. "The human body is simply not designed to sit," says Rajendra Paul, corporate ergonomist at Haworth, Inc. in Michigan. "Yet between 70 and 75 percent of today's workforce is sitting and working on computers.

Other regulations affect equipment. While buying a monitor based on something like ergonomics may sound like a big headache, consider that using the wrong monitor can cause migraines and even worse. According to one estimate, as many as 10 million people may suffer from an ailment known as CVS (computer vision syndrome), which has an array of symptoms including eyestrain, fatigue, blurred vision, double vision, and headaches. California's Cal OSHA, for example, wants those who work at video display terminals (VDT) or computers to be positioned so that the screen's entire primary viewing area is less than 60 degrees below the horizontal plane passing through the eyes of the operator. After two hours of repetitive work, each operator must get a 15-minute break or be assigned to 15 minutes of alternate work.

Even the quality of an agency's equipment has ethical implications. For example, some poorly designed computer monitors generate high levels of low-frequency electromagnetic fields, which some studies associated with miscarriages and cancer. Al-

There also are preferred positions on a given page. The preferred position near the top of a page or at the top of a column next to reading matter is called **full position.** It's usually surrounded by reading matter and may cost the advertiser 25 to 50 percent more than ROP rates. Slightly less desirable is placement *next to reading matter (NR),* which generally costs 10 to 20 percent more than ROP rates.

Color Advertising

Color advertising is available in many newspapers on an ROP basis. Because of their high-speed presses and porous paper stock, newspapers are not noted for high-quality color printing. So advertisers frequently preprint ads using processes known as HiFi color and Spectracolor. The cost of a color ad is usually based on the black-and-white rate plus an extra charge for each additional color.

Split Runs

Many newspapers (and magazines) offer **split runs.** The advertiser runs two ads of identical size but different content for the same product in the same or different press runs on the same day. This lets the advertiser test the *pulling power* of each ad. Newspapers set a minimum space requirement and charge extra for this service.

Co-ops and Networks

As an aid to national advertisers, the NAB created the Newspaper Co-op Network (NCN). Salespeople from participating newspapers helped national advertisers line up retailers for dealer-listing ads. The advertiser would produce the ad and include a blank space for each paper to insert local retailers' names. The system also helped manufacturers manage local advertising tie-ins to national campaigns and themes. Before the development of NCN, national advertisers had to place ads and recruit local dealers individually.

In 1992 the Newspaper Advertising Bureau merged with the American Newspaper Publishers Association and five other marketing associations to form the **Newspaper Association of America (NAA),** which continued to simplify national newspaper ad buys. In 1994 the NAA launched a *one-order, one-bill system* for

though there is no conclusive proof that emissions from computers or monitors cause adverse health effects, OSHA has developed standards for measuring emissions. When dealing with a gray area such as this, ethics are often our only guide.

Materials can also require ethical review. For years, advertising artists used marker pens and spray glues (that use vaporous chemicals as solvents) to create and mount artwork. Once trade publications began reporting a link between spray glue and tingling and numbing in the fingers, agencies set up spray booths to capture floating solvent and glue particles. They also adopted the OSHA standards for good ventilation to disperse toxic fumes.

Agency managers now realize that offices (in contrast to manufacturing work sites) have unique and potentially harmful elements to take into consideration when designing work areas, distinct types of lighting, furniture, and tools such as computers, keyboards, and telephones. The think tank Orincon hired an ergonomic consultant when setting up its in-house agency and graphics department at its San Diego headquarters. The consultant helped select the chairs, proposed the layout for the computer stations, and talked to employees about their individual needs.

Agencies can learn from other types of companies. At Minneapolis-based IDS Financial Services (which hires 6,000 employees), each individual gets a choice of chairs, footrests, and options for computer location. Anyone at IDS with an ergonomics complaint gets a personal evaluation of his or her workstation.

While all this may seem like coddling, nonbelievers should remember that one bout of monitor migraine, carpal tunnel syndrome, or incapacitating backache—not to mention the stress of a resultant lawsuit stemming from such an injury—could debilitate the smooth operation of any agency. Ethical behavior can pay big dividends when workplace safety is the issue.

Questions

1. Would the possibility of being called a troublemaker by your company's managers stop you from telling your employer that the company was not meeting its ethical ergonomic responsibilities? Describe your reasoning.

2. If you owned a company with 15 employees, do you think an ergonomic evaluation of each person's workstation would be important? Explain your answer by informally estimating the cost of the survey and the potential savings (from work loss, hiring replacement workers, and legal damages).

Sources: Michael A. Verespej, "Ergonomics: An Unfounded Fear?" *Industry Week,* December 5, 1995, pp. 36–42; Winn L. Rosch, "In Search of the Safest Monitor," *Mac User,* February 1994, pp. 92–105.

national advertising, called the Newspaper National Network. Advertisers can make multimarket newspaper buys by placing one order and paying one bill, instead of having to contact—and pay—each paper individually.[23]

Chrysler was the first marketer to use the new network, placing ads for its national minivan sale in 75 newspapers in March 1994.[24] The Newspaper National Network offers advertisers competitive CPM pricing and guaranteed positioning, in addition to its one-order, one-bill appeal.[25] It also allows smaller papers to participate in national advertising.[26]

Insertion Orders and Tearsheets

When advertisers place an ad, they submit an **insertion order** to the newspaper stating the date(s) on which the ad is to run, its size, the desired position, the rate, and the type of artwork accompanying the order.

An insertion order serves as a contract between the advertiser (or its agency) and the publication. If an advertiser fails to pay the agency, the agency still must pay the publication. To avoid this liability, many agencies now place a disclaimer on their insertion orders stating that they are acting solely as an *agent for a disclosed principal* (legal terminology meaning the agency is just a representative for the advertiser

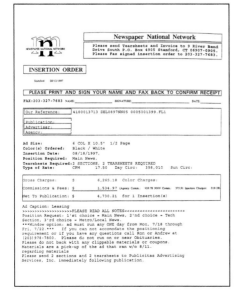

Co-ops and networks help simplify the ad buying process for advertisers by consolidating the purchasing paperwork and requirements for all local papers in a single location. In 1997, the Newspaper National Network (www.naa.org/national/) placed advertising in 864 newspapers for companies like Coors, Procter & Gamble, and Chrysler, posting sales of nearly $84 million. This is an example of a typical insertion order—providing run date, size, desired position—used to purchase newspaper space.

and is therefore not liable for the payment). Some publications refuse to accept insertion orders with disclaimers unless payment accompanies the order. In 1991 the American Association of Advertising Agencies recommended to its agency members that they no longer accept sole liability for their client's bills.[27] However, many agencies do still accept liability, perhaps out of some insecurity about possibly losing their agency commission—or their client.

When a newspaper creates ad copy and art, it gives the advertiser a **proof copy** to check. In contrast, most national advertising arrives at the newspaper *camera ready,* either in the form of a photo print or electronically via modem. To verify that the ad ran, the newspaper tears out the page on which the ad appeared and sends it to the agency or advertiser. Today most **tearsheets** for national advertisers are handled through a private central office, the Advertising Checking Bureau.

When a tearsheet arrives, the advertiser examines it to make sure the ad ran according to instructions: in the right section and page position, and with the correct reproduction. If the ad did *not* run per instructions, the agency or advertiser is usually due an adjustment—a discount or even a free rerun.

Print: A Worldwide Medium

Every country has newspapers and magazines to serve its population (see Exhibit 14–6). U.S. advertisers in foreign markets generally use either international or local media, depending on their campaign objectives and intended audience. Whether at home or abroad, advertisers must study the audience and remember the basics of print advertising, some of which are enumerated in the Checklist of What Works Best in Print.

Several large U.S. publishers, including Time-Warner and Scientific American, circulate international editions of their magazines abroad. The *International Herald Tribune, The Wall Street Journal,* and London's *Financial Times* are widely read in Asia, Europe, and the Middle East. In China, numerous publications such as *Elle* and *Avenue China* are now distributed to the country's wealthiest and most influential residents.[28]

Well-educated, upper-income consumers read these publications, typically printed in English, so they are the closest to global media for reaching this audience. *Reader's Digest,* the oldest international mass-audience medium, reaches 170 foreign countries. However, the publisher prints the magazine in local languages and tailors it to each country, so advertisers often view it as a local medium.

The number of international business, trade, or specialty publications is growing. Switzerland's *European Business* and Belgium's *Electronic Product News,* both English-language magazines, are distributed throughout Europe.

Political changes in the former Soviet Union and Eastern bloc countries are spurring many new trade publications. Most are published locally in association with foreign publishers. In 1990, McGraw-Hill launched Russian-language editions of *Aviation Week & Space Technology* and *Business Week.* And International Data

International magazines are yet another print advertising venue, of particular interest to large transnational corporations. These magazines may be international editions of American publications like Reader's Digest *or* National Geographic, *or they may be native to a particular country, like Germany's* Der Spiegel *(www.spiegel.de). Advertisements from global companies like Unilever, Coca-Cola, and Mercedes Benz are common in both types of magazines.*

Exhibit 14–6

International consumer magazine paid circulation.

Argentina		Australia		Canada	
Title	**Circulation**	**Title**	**Circulation**	**Title**	**Circulation**
Gente	220,150	*Australian Women's Weekly*	1,152,000	*Reader's Digest*	1,220,049
Mia	141,698	*Woman's Day*	1,122,631	*Chatelaine*	899,909
Conozca Mas	118,197	*New Idea*	954,374	*TV Guide*	810,436
Billiken	117,339	*TV Week (National)*	563,845	*National Geographic*	684,467
Week End	116,547	*Reader's Digest*	480,438	*Leisure Ways*	594,716

France		Japan		Mexico	
Title	**Circulation**	**Title**	**Circulation**	**Title**	**Circulation**
Télé 7 Jours	2,969,674	*The Television*	1,021,447	*TV y Novelas*	699,028
Téléstar	1,990,756	*Ie-No-Hikari*	1,017,731	*Teleguia*	498,905
Télé Z	1,781,095	*Shukan Bunshun*	766,897	*Selecciones*	314,505
Femme Actuelle	1,768,822	*Josei Seven*	765,662	*Vanidades*	220,946
Télé Poche	1,507,457	*Josei Jishin*	758,480	*Muy Interesante*	186,239

Spain		United Kingdom		United States	
Title	**Circulation**	**Title**	**Circulation**	**Title**	**Circulation**
Pronto	750,436	*Reader's Digest*	1,660,170	*Modern Maturity*	22,166,294
Teleprograma	693,484	*What's on TV*	1,571,892	*Reader's Digest*	15,240,615
Supertele	681,100	*Radio Times*	1,485,759	*TV Guide*	14,093,144
Hola	651,967	*TV Times*	1,021,966	*Better Homes & Gardens*	7,497,838
Tele Indiscreta	642,256	*Woman's Weekly*	795,230	*National Geographic*	7,329,499

Group launched several trade publications, including *Mir PK Russia* (formerly *PC World USSR*) and *ComputerWorld Poland.*[29]

In the past, international advertising media consisted mainly of newspapers and magazines. Today, satellite-to-cable broadcast options, such as Superchannel and Sky Channel in Europe and Star TV in Asia, supplement print media.

Print Media and New Technologies

With computers have come revolutionary media options, such as the Internet and CD-ROM, challenging both traditional print media and advertisers to adapt. Newspapers and magazines are rushing to make alliances with cable, regional telephone, and online companies to get a toehold in the interactive information market.

Over the last five years, for example, virtually all metropolitan news organizations and national magazines have incorporated electronic services. News organizations are information-rich, and much of the specialized information they don't run in the paper or the magazine fits perfectly with the online world's narrower interests.[30] They are still, however, trying to figure out how to incorporate advertising into their new ventures. Most ads are still simply banners, but customers who are interested can click on the banners and drill down to more in-depth information. This becomes a value-added service for the print medium's advertising customers. George Gilder, media expert and author, believes that the newspaper industry is in a particularly advantageous position, because "the convergence of text and video will cause a revolution in advertising, with targeted messages leading consumers step-by-step to a transaction."[31]

We'll deal with these issues in greater depth in Chapter 16.

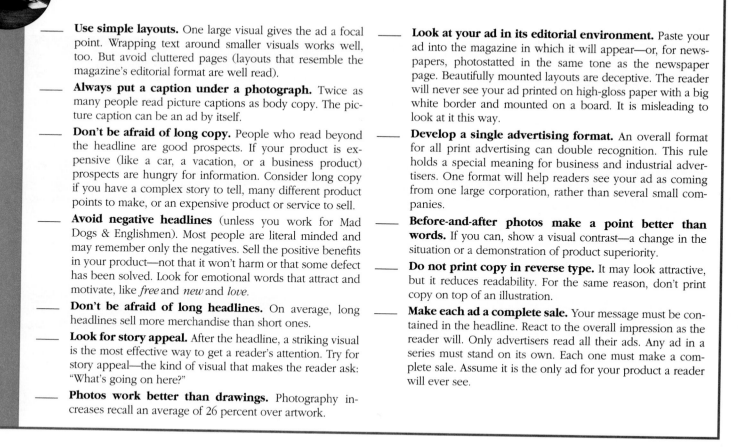

_____ **Use simple layouts.** One large visual gives the ad a focal point. Wrapping text around smaller visuals works well, too. But avoid cluttered pages (layouts that resemble the magazine's editorial format are well read).

_____ **Always put a caption under a photograph.** Twice as many people read picture captions as body copy. The picture caption can be an ad by itself.

_____ **Don't be afraid of long copy.** People who read beyond the headline are good prospects. If your product is expensive (like a car, a vacation, or a business product) prospects are hungry for information. Consider long copy if you have a complex story to tell, many different product points to make, or an expensive product or service to sell.

_____ **Avoid negative headlines** (unless you work for Mad Dogs & Englishmen). Most people are literal minded and may remember only the negatives. Sell the positive benefits in your product—not that it won't harm or that some defect has been solved. Look for emotional words that attract and motivate, like *free* and *new* and *love*.

_____ **Don't be afraid of long headlines.** On average, long headlines sell more merchandise than short ones.

_____ **Look for story appeal.** After the headline, a striking visual is the most effective way to get a reader's attention. Try for story appeal—the kind of visual that makes the reader ask: "What's going on here?"

_____ **Photos work better than drawings.** Photography increases recall an average of 26 percent over artwork.

_____ **Look at your ad in its editorial environment.** Paste your ad into the magazine in which it will appear—or, for newspapers, photostatted in the same tone as the newspaper page. Beautifully mounted layouts are deceptive. The reader will never see your ad printed on high-gloss paper with a big white border and mounted on a board. It is misleading to look at it this way.

_____ **Develop a single advertising format.** An overall format for all print advertising can double recognition. This rule holds a special meaning for business and industrial advertisers. One format will help readers see your ad as coming from one large corporation, rather than several small companies.

_____ **Before-and-after photos make a point better than words.** If you can, show a visual contrast—a change in the situation or a demonstration of product superiority.

_____ **Do not print copy in reverse type.** It may look attractive, but it reduces readability. For the same reason, don't print copy on top of an illustration.

_____ **Make each ad a complete sale.** Your message must be contained in the headline. React to the overall impression as the reader will. Only advertisers read all their ads. Any ad in a series must stand on its own. Each one must make a complete sale. Assume it is the only ad for your product a reader will ever see.

Sources of Print Media Information

Publications provide information about their readership, circulation, rates, advertising policies, and editorial focus. Media planners can also consult the following sources:

- **Audit Bureau of Circulations (ABC)** was formed in 1914 to verify circulation and other marketing data on magazines and newspapers. Each publication submits a semiannual statement, which is checked by specially trained ABC field auditors. The publisher supplies data on paid circulation (for a specified period) for its regional, metropolitan, and demographic editions, broken down by subscription, single-copy sales, and average paid circulation. The ABC also analyzes new and renewal subscriptions by price, duration, sales channel, and type of promotion.

- **Classified Advertising Network of New York (CANNY)** is a statewide affiliation of daily newspapers that reaches over 3.5 million New Yorkers. It enables advertisers to place classified ads in daily papers throughout the state easily and inexpensively.

- **Magazine Publishers Association (MPA)** has a total membership of more than 230 publishers, representing 1,200 magazines. This trade group provides the circulation figures of all ABC member magazines (general and farm) from 1914 to date, with annual figures related to population. It estimates the number of consumer magazine copies sold by year from 1943, and it lists the 100 highest-circulation ABC magazines.

- **Mediamark Research Inc. (MRI)** conducts personal interviews to determine readership patterns. In addition to reporting the audiences and readership demographics for leading consumer magazines and national newspapers, MRI

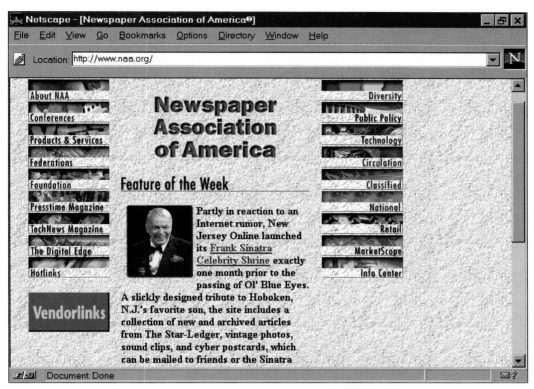

Many resources for advertisers and media buyers are now available, on demand, through the Internet. Today, most large organizations, like the Newspaper Association of America (www.naa.org), provide such information online, giving media personnel instant access to critical information. Some organizations even offer direct online transactions to purchase information or media space.

publishes annual studies on the affluent market, business-purchase decision makers, and the top 10 local markets.

- **Newspaper Association of America (NAA)** is the promotional arm of the American Newspaper Publishers Association and the nation's newspaper industry. The association provides its newspaper members with market information by conducting field research and collecting case histories. It also administers the National Newspaper Network one-order, one-bill system.

- **Newspaper Space Bank (NSB)** is an online database service through which advertisers can buy canceled, unsold, or remnant space in major market newspapers across the country at deeply discounted rates after normal closings.

- **Simmons Market Research Bureau (SMRB)** is a respected syndicated research organization that publishes magazine readership studies. Its annual study of media and markets provides data on readers' purchase behavior and demographics based on personal interviews. In addition, SMRB publishes the National College Study and the Simmons Teen-Age Research Study twice a year.

- **Standard Rate & Data Service (SRDS)** publishes *Newspaper Rates and Data, Consumer Magazine and Agri-Media Rates and Data,* and *Business Publication Rates and Data,* as well as other monthly directories, so advertisers and their agencies don't have to obtain rate cards for every publication.

- *Audience studies provided by publications.* Newspapers and magazines also offer media planners many other types of statistical reports, including reader income, demographic profiles, and percentages of different kinds of advertising carried.

Chapter **Summary**

The printed page—in magazines and newspapers—provides a unique, flexible medium for advertising creativity.

In selecting magazines for advertising, the media buyer must consider a publication's circulation, its readership, its cost, and mechanical requirements. A magazine's rates may be determined by several factors: its primary and secondary readership, the number of subscription and vendor sales, and the number of copies guaranteed versus those actually delivered.

Magazine rate cards follow a standard format so advertisers can readily compare advertising costs. They list black-and-white and color rates, discounts, issue and closing dates, and mechanical requirements.

Magazines offer distinct advantages. They are the most selective of all mass media and are flexible in both readership and advertising. They offer unsurpassed color, excellent reproduction quality, authority and believability, long shelf life, and prestige at an efficient cost. However, they often require long lead times, have problems offering reach and frequency, and are subject to heavy advertising competition. The cost of advertising in some magazines is also very high.

The newspaper is a mass medium read by almost everybody. It offers great flexibility, which assists creativity, and its printed message lasts longer than ads in electronic media. However, newspapers also have disadvantages: lack of audience selectivity, short life span, poor production quality, heavy advertising competition, po-

tentially poor ad placement, and overlapping circulation. Still, the newspaper is the major community-serving medium today for both news and advertising.

The newspaper's rate card lists prices, deadlines, mechanical requirements, and other pertinent information. Rates vary for local and national advertisers. Also listed are the newspaper's short-rate policy, combination rates, frequency discounts, run-of-paper rates, and other data.

Print is a worldwide medium; every country has newspapers and magazines. The international advertiser may have to choose between local and international media. The most educated consumers in many countries often read English-language publications. Political changes in Eastern Europe spurred the introduction of many trade and business publications in the local language. Advertisers must study the audience they wish to reach before buying any media, whether at home or abroad.

Newspapers and magazines are making alliances with cable, regional telephone, and online computer companies to enter the interactive information market. They are still experimenting with ways to sell advertising on their electronic publications. Some experts believe that the convergence of text, video, and graphics will cause a creative revolution in advertising, with targeted, information-rich messages able to lead consumers step by step to a transaction without ever leaving home.

Important **Terms**

Audit Bureau of Circulations (ABC), *468*

bleed, *445*

bulk discount, *462*

business magazines, *448*

circulation audit, *454*

classified ad, *461*

Classified Advertising Network of New York (CANNY), *468*

classified display ad, *461*

closing date, *456*

color strip, *448*

combination rate, *463*

consumer magazines, *448*

contract rate, *462*

controlled circulation, *455*

cooperative (co-op) program, *461*

cost per thousand (CPM), *456*

cover date, *456*

cover position, *446*

custom magazines, *447*

daily newspaper, *459*

demographic editions, *457*

display advertising, *460*

earned rate, *462*

farm publications, *448*

flat rate, *462*

fragrance strip, *448*

frequency discount, *456, 462*

full position, *464*

gatefold, *446*

geographic editions, *457*

guaranteed circulation, *454*

horizontal publication, *455*

independent shopping guide, *460*

insert, *446*

insertion order, *465*

island half, *446*

junior unit, *446*

local city magazine, *448*

Magazine Publishers Association (MPA), *468*

media buyer, *444*

Mediamark Research Inc. (MRI), *468*

national magazines, *449*

national rate, *462*

Newspaper Association of America (NAA), *464, 469*

Newspaper Space Bank (NSB), *469*

on-sale date, *456*

open rate, *462*

paid circulation, *435*

pop-up ad, *448*

preferred-position rate, *463*

preprinted insert, *461*

primary circulation, *454*

proof copy, *466*

public notice, *461*

rate base, *454*

rate card, *462*

reading notice, *461*

regional publications, *449*

run-of-paper (ROP) advertising rate, *463*

secondary (pass-along) readership, *454*

short rate, *462*

Simmons Market Research Bureau (SMRB), *469*

split run, *464*

standard advertising unit (SAU), *459*

Standard Rate & Data Service (SRDS), *469*

standard-size newspaper, *459*

Sunday supplement, *460*

tabloid newspaper, *459*

tearsheet, *466*

3-D ad, *448*

vertical publication, *455*

volume discount, *456*

weekly newspaper, *459*

Review **Questions**

1. If you worked in the advertising department of a premium-priced furniture manufacturer, would you recommend magazine advertising? Why or why not?

2. If you were the advertising manager for a magazine aimed at senior citizens, what advantages would you cite to potential advertisers?

3. What is the advantage of magazine advertising to businesses that sell to other businesses?

4. What is the importance of the Audit Bureau of Circulations?

5. Why do retailers advertise so heavily in local newspapers?

6. How can advertisers improve the selectivity of their newspaper ads?

7. What factors should advertisers consider in deciding among several local papers (including dailies and weeklies)?

8. Should national advertisers be charged a higher rate than local advertisers? Support your position.

9. Should agencies be liable for their clients' advertising bills? Why or why not?

10. How could a local newspaper use an online database service or the Internet to help itself or its advertisers?

Exploring the **Internet**

The Internet exercises for Chapter 14 address the following areas related to the chapter: print media organizations (Exercise 1) and print media tools (Exercise 2).

1. Print Media Organizations

   Visit the following print industry Web sites and familiarize yourself further with the size and scope of the print media world. Be sure to answer the questions for each site.

   - American Newspaper Network **www.amnewsnet.com**
   - American Society of Newspaper Editors (ASNE) **www.asne.org**
   - Association of Alternative Newsweeklies (AAN) **www.aan.org**
   - International Newspaper Marketing Association (INMA) **www.inma.org**
   - National Newspaper Association (NNA) **www.oweb.com/nna**
   - National Newspaper Publishers Association (NNPA) **www.nnpa.org**
   - Newspaper Association of America (NAA) **www.naa.org**
   - Canadian Newspaper Association **www.cna-acj.ca/english**

   a. What is the purpose of the organization that sponsors this site?

   b. Who is the intended audience(s) of this site?

   c. Who makes up the organization's membership? Its constituency?

   d. How important do you feel this organization is to the advertising industry? Why?

2. Print Media Tools

   Were it not for the products and services offered by the following companies, planning and buying print vehicles could be an overwhelming task for media professionals. From audit reports to media kits, agencies and media houses are aided every day by companies who specialize in easing the lives of media planners and buyers. Visit the following syndicated and independent media companies' Web sites and answer the questions that follow:

   - Advertising Checking Bureau **www.acbcoop.com**
   - Advertising Media Internet Center (AMIC) **www.amic.com**
   - Audit Bureau of Circulations **www.accessabc.com**
   - Business Publications Audit of Circulation (BPA) **www.bpai.com**
   - Certified Audit of Circulations **www.certifiedaudit.com**
   - Competitive Media Reporting (CMR) **www.usadata.com/**
   - MediaCentral **www.mediacentral.com**
   - MediaFinder **www.mediafinder.com**
   - Mediamark Research, Inc. **www.mediamark.com**
   - Print Measurement Bureau (PMB) **www.pmb.ca**
   - Scarborough **www.scarborough.com**
   - Standard Rate & Data Service (SRDS) **www.srds.com**

   a. Who is the intended audience of the site?

   b. What is the size/scope of the company?

   c. What type(s) of print media information does the company specialize in?

   d. How useful do you feel the company or organization is for obtaining print media information? Why?

Chapter Fifteen

Using Electronic Media: Television and Radio

Objective   To present the important factors advertisers weigh when considering the use of radio and television in the creative mix. Each medium has its own characteristics, advantages, and drawbacks. Advertisers must be able to compare their merits and understand the most cost-effective ways to buy advertising time.

After studying this chapter, you will be able to:

- Describe the advantages and drawbacks of broadcast television as an advertising medium.

- Outline the advantages and drawbacks of cable TV as an advertising medium.

- Compare the process of buying cable versus broadcast TV time.

- Describe different types of TV advertising and the process of audience measurement.

- Discuss the main factors to consider when buying television time.

- Analyze the pros and cons of using radio in the creative mix.

- Explain the major factors to consider when buying radio time.

SFX: Music under, throughout.
FLIGHT ATTENDANT: Captain, here's your cookie!

PILOT: (Mumbles)
SUPER: California Fluid Milk Processor Advisory Board.

PILOT: Come to papa!
ANNC: (VO): Got milk?

Milk may "do a body good," but for the dairy industry, the bottom line remains the same: how can we sell more of it? Unlike the "Milk, where's *your* mustache?" magazine campaign, the California milk producers weren't as concerned with changing consumer attitudes toward milk as increasing its consumption. The late 80s and early 90s were characterized by slumping sales that needed to be bolstered, not with an image enhancer but with an action campaign—one that would move more moo juice out of the supermarkets and into the homes of consumers. • The problem of declining milk consumption was not unique to California, of course. It plagued the industry nationwide. People simply weren't drinking the beverage on the scale they once did; milk was losing out to sexy colas and snappy fruit drinks. And while the campaigns of "Milk does a body good" and "America's favorite health kick" had managed to create a fun and healthy image for milk, they had done little to improve sales. • Enter Jeff Manning, executive director for the California Milk Processor Board. Founded by the state's milk producers in 1993, the board set out to solve the problem of poor sales. Manning started with a hunch—that people don't drink milk by itself. Previous ads featured milk alone, but he believed that *food* was a key component, and it was missing from the picture. "If you ask people when milk is crucial, they'll tell you it's when they have cereal in the bowl or cookies in their mouth," Manning explained. "The driver is not the milk. It's the food."[1] • With this idea, Manning hired San Francisco-based Goodby, Silverstein & Partners to develop an advertising campaign that would target people who already consume milk and encourage them to drink more. Research revealed that 88 percent of milk is consumed at home and, as Manning suspected, it is usually accompanied by other food. People most often drink milk with cereal, but cookies, pastries, peanut butter and jelly sandwiches, and brownies are also popular milk partners. • The agency asked a group of research participants to go without milk for one week and then to share their experiences. The group quickly discovered the anguish of not having milk when they really needed it. One person woke up early in the morning and poured himself a bowl of cereal but then discovered there was no milk in the fridge. "It's so bad, you'd even steal milk from your kid," said one man, to which another replied, "Never mind your kid. You're so desperate you'd even steal it from your cat!"[2] ● These stories found their way into the creative TV commercials that we all know: the businessman who dies and finds himself in what appears to be heaven with a plateful of cookies, only to discover that there is no milk; the angry Santa who takes back his gifts when he finds that no milk was left with the cookies. And cross-promotionals with co-marketers have taken off too, such as the Oreo cookie parody of *Citizen Kane*. The question "Got milk?" became a punchline to jokes, not just a tagline for commercials. ● Television proved to be the perfect vehicle for the "Got milk?" campaign because of its ability to tell the story in a unique manner and to dramatize the dilemma faced by milk-starved consumers. Using offbeat camera perspectives and lighting techniques that are possible only through television, the campaign offered immense visual appeal. And the ultimate medium for reaching the masses brought an action component to the campaign. People began buying milk again. So successful was the regional advertising campaign, in fact, that the national dairy industry board quickly licensed it to run on the national circuit. ●

The Medium of **Television**

Back in 1950, U.S advertisers spent $171 million, or about 3 percent of total U.S. advertising volume, on the new medium of television. It didn't take long, though, for the nation's advertisers to discover the power of this new vehicle to reach mass audiences quickly and frequently. TV also offered unique creative opportunities to imbue their brands with personality and image like never before. By 1996, TV advertising had grown to more than $42.5 *billion* and accounted for over 24 percent of all U.S. ad spending, finally surpassing newspapers as the leading U.S. advertising medium.[3] Exhibit 15–1 lists the top network television advertisers in the United States and their annual expenditures.

Today, the medium of television is available to advertisers in two principal forms: broadcast and cable TV. **Broadcast TV** reaches its audience by transmitting electromagnetic waves through the air across some geographic territory. **Cable TV** reaches its audience through wires, either strung from telephone poles or laid underground.

Broadcast TV

Until the advent of the Internet, broadcast television grew faster than any other advertising medium in history. As both a news and entertainment medium, it caught people's fancy very quickly. From its beginnings after World War II, broadcast TV rapidly emerged as the only medium that offered sight, sound, and motion. People could stay home and still go to the movies. As TV's legions of viewers grew, the big national-brand advertisers quickly discovered they could use the medium very efficiently to expand distribution across the country and sell products like never before. Not only that, the medium was ideal for building an image for their brands—

Exhibit 15–1

Top 10 network TV advertisers.

Rank	Advertiser	Network TV spending ($ millions, 1996)
1	General Motors Corp.	$613.9
2	Procter & Gamble Co.	589.5
3	Johnson & Johnson	504.8
4	PepsiCo	423.4
5	Philip Morris Cos.	403.1
6	McDonald's Corp.	372.0
7	Ford Motor Co.	319.7
8	Grand Metropolitan	294.4
9	Chrysler Corp.	280.5
10	Walt Disney Co.	267.2

Source: Reprinted with permission from the May 21, 1998 issue of *Advertising Age.* Copyright, Crain Communications, Inc. 1998.

better even than magazines, which had previously been the image-building medium of choice. It didn't take long for marketers to switch their budgets from radio, newspapers, and magazines. Today, broadcast TV still attracts the largest volume of *national* advertising, more than $36 billion in 1996.[4]

The United States now has over 1,500 commercial TV stations; Canada has another 127.[5] About half the U.S. stations are **VHF** (very high frequency, channels 2 through 13); the rest are **UHF** (ultrahigh frequency, channels 14 through 83). Stations in the United States operate as independents unless they are affiliated with one of the national networks (ABC, NBC, CBS, Fox). Both network affiliates and independent stations may subscribe to nationally syndicated programs as well as originate their own programming. However, increasing competition from cable TV is taking viewers from the national network programs. To compensate, some networks are investing in cable TV systems or starting their own. NBC, for example, started CNBC and MSNBC, and ABC (which is now owned by Disney) has an 80 percent interest in ESPN.

Cable TV For more than 30 years, broadcast TV, especially network TV, was the dominant entertainment medium for most Americans. Today, other electronic media are changing that dominance. Chief among the challengers is cable television.

Cable TV has been around since the late 1940s. Initially, it carried TV signals by wire to areas with poor reception like mountainous regions. But in the 1970s, the advent of satellite TV signals, the proliferation of channels, and the introduction of uncut first-run movies via pay-cable channels such as Home Box Office and Showtime made cable more attractive to all viewers, even those in urban areas.

At first, many subscribers valued cable simply for the full array of regional channels and access to premium services like HBO. But once this novelty wore off, subscribers wanted more. A variety of advertiser-supported cable networks soon appeared with specialized programming in arts, history, sports, news, and comedy, along with diversified pay services and many more local shows. All of this attracted more and more subscribers—and simultaneously drew viewers away from the big broadcast networks.

In the last two decades, cable's growth has been extraordinary. In 1975, only 13 percent of TV households in the United States had cable. By 1997, cable reached over 65 percent of all homes.[6]

Subscribers to cable TV pay a monthly fee to receive over 80 cable channels, most of which are privately owned and commercially operated. These include local network affiliates and independents, cable networks, superstations, local cable system channels, and community access channels.[7] The cable fees represent about one-third of cable TV revenues; advertising makes up the remainder. Networks such as CNN, USA, the Discovery Channel, Arts & Entertainment, Lifetime, Comedy Central, and The Nashville Network now compete for advertisers' dollars, each selling its own niche audience.[8] For an additional price, subscribers can receive premium services like HBO, Showtime, and Cinemax, and see special events such as first-run films, boxing matches, and baseball games (pay-per-view service).

There are now some 55 national cable networks in the United States and a growing number of regional networks. Exhibit 15–2 lists the most widely carried ones.[9] There are also a handful of *superstations,* local over-the-air TV stations whose signals are delivered via satellite to cable systems across the country and that carry some national advertising.

TV Audience Trends As a way to reach a mass audience, no other medium today has the unique creative abilities of television: the combination of sight, sound, and motion; the opportunity to demonstrate the product; the potential to use special effects; the empathy of the viewer; and the believability of seeing it happen

Exhibit 15–2
Major cable TV networks.

Network	Estimated home coverage (millions)	Cost range*	Program type
Arts & Entertainment	55.4	$4,500–7,000	Family/variety
Black Entertainment TV	34.0	350–1,000	Sports/family/entertainment/news/gossip/ethnic/music video/information
CNBC	47.1	500–2,000	Educational information/business/news/information/general
Cable News Network	64.2	5,000–11,000†	News/information
The Discovery Channel	58.0	550–4,000	Educational information/family/health/original/news/information/technology/science
ESPN	60.4	N/A	Sports
The Family Channel	55.8	500–4,000	Family/general/original
Headline News	52.8	5,000–11,000†	News/information
Lifetime Television	56.0	450–12,650	Women's interest/family/general/health/news/information
MTV	57.0	2,500–7,500	Music video
Nickelodeon	58.9	2,000–15,000	Youth interest
Nick at Nite	58.9	1,700–3,000	Family/variety
TBS	63.0	1,000–12,000	Family/general/music video/sports/women's interest/youth interest
The Nashville Network	56.7	500–15,000	Family/sports/music video/news/information/variety/general/women's interest
Turner Network Television	61.2	1,000–6,500	Family/general/sports/women's interest/youth interest
The Weather Channel	52.6	250–1,050	News/information
USA	59.2	550–2,500	Entertainment/movies/sports

*Refers to average prime-time costs only.
†CNN and Headline News sold in combination.

right before your eyes (see the Checklist of Pros and Cons of Broadcast TV Advertising). As Exhibit 15–3 shows, 57 percent of viewers believe TV is the most authoritative advertising source, compared to only 20 percent for newspapers, 11 percent for magazines, and 9 percent for radio.[10]

The heaviest viewers of broadcast TV are middle-income, high school-educated individuals and their families, so most programming is directed at this group. People with considerably higher incomes and more education typically have a more diverse range of interests and entertainment options.

The number of TV viewing hours continues to increase. In the average U.S. home, viewers watch TV/cable/VCR for 8.5 hours *every day*. Children and teenagers view an average of 17.5 to 17.8 hours per week, four hours less than their parents and one hour less than they watched just five years ago (thanks to the

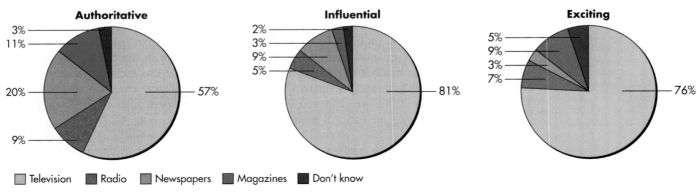

Exhibit 15–3
Viewers rate television as the most influential medium.

Checklist

The Pros and Cons of Broadcast TV Advertising

The Pros

Contemporary broadcast television offers advertisers many advantages over competing media.

_____ **Mass coverage.** A full 98 percent of all U.S. homes have a TV (most have more than one), and viewing time for the average household increased from about five hours a day in 1960 to eight and a half hours a day in 1996.

_____ **Low cost.** Despite the often huge initial outlays for commercial production and advertising time, TV's equally huge audiences bring the cost per exposure down to $2 to $10 per thousand viewers.

_____ **Some selectivity.** Television audiences vary a great deal depending on the time of day, day of the week, and nature of the programming. Advertising messages can be presented when potential customers are watching, and advertisers can reach select geographic audiences by buying local and regional markets.

_____ **Impact.** Television offers an immediacy that other forms of advertising cannot achieve, displaying and demonstrating the product with sound and full color right before the customer's eyes.

_____ **Creativity.** The various facets of the TV commercial—sight, sound, motion, and color—permit infinite original and imaginative appeals.

_____ **Prestige.** Since the public considers TV the most authoritative and influential medium, it offers advertisers a prestigious image. Hallmark, Xerox, Mobil, Exxon, and IBM increase their prestige by regularly sponsoring cultural TV programs.

_____ **Social dominance.** In North America, most people under age 35 grew up with TV as a window to their social environment. They continue to be stirred by TV screenings of the Olympics, space travel, assassinations, wars, and political scandals.

The Cons

Sometimes broadcast TV just doesn't "fit" the creative mix because of cost, lack of audience selectivity, inherent brevity, or the clutter of competitive messages.

_____ **High production cost.** One of broadcast TV's greatest handicaps is the high cost of producing quality commercials. Depending on the creative approach, the cost of filming a national commercial today may run from $200,000 to more than $1 million.

_____ **High air-time cost.** The average cost of a prime-time network commercial is close to $400,000. A single 30-second commercial for a top-rated show in prime time may cost over $500,000. Special attractions like the Super Bowl cost almost $2 million. The cost of large coverage, even at low rates, prices small and medium-size advertisers out of the market.

_____ **Limited selectivity.** Broadcast TV is not cost-effective for advertisers seeking a very specific, small audience. And it is losing some of its selectivity because of changing audience trends. More women are working outside the home or watching cable TV, hurting advertisers on network soap operas.

_____ **Brevity.** Studies show that most TV viewers can't remember the product or company in the most recent TV ad they watched—even if it was within the last five minutes. Recall improves with the length of the commercial; people remember 60-second spots better than 30-second spots.

_____ **Clutter.** TV advertising is usually surrounded by station breaks, credits, and public service announcements, as well as six or seven other spots. All these messages compete for attention, so viewers become annoyed and confused and often misidentify the product.

_____ **Zipping and zapping.** VCR users who skip through commercials when replaying taped programs are zipping; remote-control users who change channels at the beginning of a commercial break are zapping.

---

impact of video games and the Internet).[11] By age 18, the average child has still spent more than two and a half years watching TV.

Around the world, older women watch TV the most (36 hours per week in both the United States and Canada). This makes the medium very popular with advertisers like Weight Watchers, whose primary target is middle-aged and older women.

Cable in North American homes has significantly altered TV viewing patterns and the use of other media. Households with cable spend less time watching broadcast TV. They also spend less time listening to the radio, reading, or going to the movies. Cable seems to reach an audience that is difficult to get to in any other way. As a result of this *audience fragmentation,* advertising on broadcast networks has become less cost effective. Video rentals have also increased dramatically, drawing more viewers away from advertiser-supported TV, both broadcast and cable (which is why ads have now started appearing on videos).

Cable households watch more television than noncable households: 56.2 hours per week versus 41.6 hours. Cable households watch about 22.8 hours of cable programming a week.[12]

National advertisers have been using cable since the late 1970s and cable advertising revenues have grown steadily, reaching $4.7 billion in 1996.[13] One reason is that cable's upscale audience buys proportionately more goods and services than

Ethical Issue

Children's Advertising: Child's Play?

Kids make up a considerable consumer group whose number and purchasing power are growing. By the year 2030, it is estimated that children aged 13 and under will comprise over 62 percent of the population, up almost 10 percent from 1994. Already, kids make up an enviable market: 52 million children spend an estimated $100 billion annually. And with the rise in single-parent and dual-income homes, kids are taking on more household chores and having a greater say in the purchasing process.

These facts aren't lost on advertisers and marketers, who are targeting children in more and more creative ways. Saturday morning cartoons are the traditional vehicles for ads promoting cereals, candy, and toys. But marketers are now reaching children in the classroom, through video games and computer programs, and by direct mail, which overrides parental rejection.

The benefits of reaching children are great. "If treated right today, they can contribute substantially to the future success of a business when they reach their peak buying period as adults," says James McNeal, marketing professor at Texas A&M University. "In fact, if won over now, they are likely to be more loyal than customers obtained through brand-switching or store-switching strategies."

Besides selling *to* children, advertisers also sell *through* children. From the frequency of ads for toys and sugary foods targeted at children, it is clear that some companies believe they can sell more by appealing to children than to adults. This must mean that many kids ask their parents to buy the items advertised on TV, and a significant number of parents do just that. Parents become simply "purchasing agents" for their children. Though advertising through children creates the problem of connecting kids' desires with parents' purchase decisions, the process does work. The effectiveness of children's advertising can be partly attributed to parental desires to satisfy their children.

But kids aren't sophisticated consumers. Their conceptions of self, time, and money are immature. As a result, they know very

Television is absolutely unique in its ability to creatively communicate an advertiser's message. No other medium can deliver a product in action and with as much dynamic energy, directly to the consumer, as television. Imagine the impossibility of trying to communicate this message for Nissan (www.nissan-usa.com) outside of the scope of television.

"Doggy Mind Control" :60
(Open on a suburban neighborhood at night.)
SFX: Dog bark.
(Inside on the kitchen floor, a dog hears a bark outside and raises his head. The

dog gets up and leaves the frame. Cut to the dog heading up the stairs. Cut to the bedroom where the dog is staring at his master in bed, exercising doggy mind control. The guy's eyes pop open and he sits up in bed.)

GUY: I think I'll take Ralphie for a ride.
(Cut to a shot from the hood of the Pathfinder that reveals that the dog is driving. They put on some music and head out into the night.)
SFX: Music.

(The car stops at various homes and other dogs run out to join them.)
SFX: Music.
(The dogs all pile into the car where the master has been relegated to the back seat. The car stops for a dog waiting by

the side of the road and there is no room for it in the car. Cut to the man standing on the street as the car, filled with dogs, pulls away. Cut to Mr. K smiling knowingly.)

MR. K: Dogs love trucks.
(Cut to Nissan badge and titles.)
SUPER: Enjoy the ride.™

little about their own desires, needs, and preferences—or how to use economic resources rationally to satisfy them. And the nature of children's conceptual ability makes it likely that child-oriented advertising can lead to false beliefs or highly improbable product expectations.

The new truth is that while most children and parents are still joint consumers, more and more children are becoming sole decision makers. To protect them, both critics and defenders agree that advertisers should not intentionally deceive children. The central issue is how far advertisers should go to ensure that children are not misled by their ads.

Questions

1. If you were an advertiser introducing a brand of healthy granola cereal, would you plan your campaign *to* or *through* children? How would you sell differently to the children and to the parents?

2. According to Robert Reiher of Youth Market Systems, up to the age of 7, the brain structure of kids is set up for fantasy and play. He says that cognitively they're not ready to plan for the future until the age of 12. They can't think in gray, only in black and white. Knowing this, how would you target a food ad to a 7-year-old who has to start preparing dinner when she gets home from school?

Sources: Ad in "Special Report: Marketing to Kids," *Advertising Age,* February 14, 1994, p. S-3; Adrienne Ward Fawcett, "'Sunday Best' Becoming More of a Daily Ritual," in "Special Report: Marketing to Kids," *Advertising Age,* February 14, 1994, p. S-10; Glenn Heitsmith, "Promoting to Kids: Is It Exploitation or Socialization?" *Promo: The International Magazine for Promotion Marketing,* December 1993, pp. 42–44, 88–92; Junu Bryan Kim, "For Kids, It's a Fast Spinning, Real World," in "Special Report: Marketing to Kids," *Advertising Age,* February 14, 1994, pp. S-1, S-10; Lynne Sharp Paine, "Children as Consumers: The Ethics of Children's Television Advertising," N. Craig Smith and John A. Quelch, eds., *Ethics in Marketing* (Burr Ridge, IL: Richard D. Irwin, 1993), pp. 672–86; Betsy Sharky, "Kid Stuff," in *ADWEEK,* October 18, 1993, p. 32.

noncable subscribers (see Exhibit 15–4). Procter & Gamble traditionally spends the most on network cable, as shown in Exhibit 15–5. However, local retailers also find local cable a good place to advertise. Fisher Big Wheel, a discount department store in Midvale, Ohio, became a cable devotee after its first cable promotion brought an extra 15,000 customers into the store.

Recent studies suggest that the number of TV channels will more than double by 2005, when the average U.S. household will have 165 channels—130 of them advertising-supported. But that number won't translate into more TV viewing. For most families, the number of regularly viewed channels (those that are watched for 30 minutes or more each week) is 10. That number is expected to rise only slightly, to 12, by 2005.[14]

But there lies the crux of one of the major issues of modern media. While there is no doubt that the media play an ever-expanding role in our daily lives, there is a finite limit to the number of advertising exposures people can absorb. When that limit is reached (and we're certainly getting close to it now), any new media will simply be fighting for market share. This is the reason for the increasing fragmentation of the audience and the precipitous decline in the huge share of audience once held by the broadcast networks. This is also why media buyers and planners are growing in importance as advertisers search for the elusive audience and fight for their share of that audience in an overcrowded media environment.

The Use of Television in IMC

Television today is very versatile. For many years it was strictly a mass medium, used to great advantage by the manufacturers of mass consumption goods: toiletries and cosmetics, food, appliances, and cars. But today, thanks to the narrowcasting ability of cable TV, television can also be a highly selective niche medium. It's not unusual, for instance, to see ads for special feed for thoroughbreds and show horses on ESPN's Grand Prix of Jumping. And thanks to local cable, TV is now affordable for even small local advertisers. This makes it a very viable option for use in an integrated marketing communications program.

While single programs don't deliver the mass audience they once did, television is still the most cost-effective way to deliver certain kinds of messages to large, well-defined audiences. For awareness and image advertising, for instance, television has no rival. The same is true for brand reinforcement messages.[15]

Since marketing integrators are looking to establish, nourish, and reinforce relationships with many groups of stakeholders, television serves another role quite

Within the IMC paradigm, television plays an important role in its ability to impart brand meaning—or the personality of the brand—for a company or product. Television communicates with many stakeholders simultaneously and can deliver a "big idea" in a uniquely creative manner. Campbell Soup (www.campbellsoup.com), with its emotional "Good For The Body. Good For The Soul." television campaign did just that, creating an image of down-home comfort and caring for the company's brand.

Exhibit 15–4

Cable households more likely to purchase goods and services than non-cable households.

Products or Services	Cable Households versus US Average (Index)	Noncable Households versus US Average (Index)	Products or Services	Cable Households versus US Average (Index)	Noncable Households versus US Average (Index)
Travel			**Consumer electronics**		
Business travel	111	81	Cellular phone	118	68
Vacation travel	107	87	Telephone pagers—beepers	115	74
Car rental (heavy)	118	69	Home computer	111	80
3+ plane trips	117	71	Compact disc player (in last year)	111	81
Member frequent flyer program	114	76	Video camcorder	114	75
Spent $2,500+ on travelers checks	118	69	Bought large screen TV (27"+)	112	79
Leisure activities			Own video game system	110	82
Play golf	120	66	**Financial/investment**		
Attend live theatre	111	81	Second mortgage (equity loan)	114	75
Go boating	107	87	Belong to credit union	110	82
Health clubs	109	84	Education loan	111	81
Snow skiing	111	80	Retirement loan	112	79
Movie attendance (2–3 times per month)	108	86	Use ATM	109	84
Member of online service	129	49	U.S. savings bonds	111	81
Food and beverage			Money market accounts	110	82
Family restaurants/steak houses*	107	87	Mutual funds	112	79
Instant iced tea mix*	105	91	Use credit card (personal)	109	84
Bottled water and seltzer*	104	92	Use credit card (business)	112	79
Diet cola drinks*	110	83	**Home appliances†**		
Champagne, cold duck, and sparkling wines	105	91	Burglar alarm	116	72
Imported beer*	109	84	Water softener	104	93
Imported wine*	112	80	Microwave oven	104	94
Automotive			Gas grill	117	70
Bought a new car last year	115	73	Continuous cleaning oven	118	68
Own new luxury automobile	109	85	Hot tub/whirlpool spa	112	78
Own an imported automobile	109	85	Fireplace	117	70
Bought new domestic car	109	84	Air conditioner	112	79
Own new sport/utility truck	111	80	**Home furnishings†**		
Own new mini-van	114	75	Sofa/sectional	109	84
Shopping and retail			Wall unit	111	81
Spend $159+ per week in food stores	108	86	Wall-to-wall carpeting	110	83
Dry cleaning ($100+ in last 6 months)	117	71	Spent $700+ on dining room furniture	115	73
Flowers by wire (in last 6 months)	115	73	Spent $700+ on family room furniture	117	71
Spent $750+ on jewelry (in last year)	117	70	Spent $2,500+ on big ticket furniture	125	56
Have a telephone calling card	108	86			

*Denotes heavy use.
†Purchased in the past year.

efficiently. It can speak to many different kinds of stakeholders—not just customers—at the same time. Moreover, through its unique ability to deliver a creative big idea, television can impart *brand meaning* (the symbolism or personality of the brand) to either attract people to the brand or reinforce their current relationship with it.

Exhibit 15–5
Top 10 cable network advertisers.

Rank	Advertiser	Cable TV spending ($ millions, 1996)
1	Procter & Gamble Co.	$201.2
2	General Motors Corp.	116.6
3	AT&T Corp.	98.5
4	Time Warner	94.0
5	Sprint Corp.	76.2
6	Philip Morris Cos.	74.9
7	Grand Metropolitan	72.0
8	Unilever	62.6
9	Kellogg Co.	61.3
10	Hasbro	60.6

Television is also a good leverage tool. That is, an advertiser might take advantage of the relatively low CPM of television to reach out to many prospects. Prospects can identify themselves by responding to the commercial, and then the advertiser can follow up with less expensive, one-to-one or addressable media.[16]

What's important to remember in all this is that the high visibility of TV forces the sponsor to create ads that people find interesting and that consistently reinforce the brand's strategic position (remember our definition of great advertising). The brands that succeed are the ones that are the most popular. And "ad liking" has a lot to do with brand popularity.

Types of TV Advertising

Advertisers use different strategies to buy time on broadcast and cable TV. The major broadcast networks offer a variety of programs that appeal to different audiences. So the advertiser buys ads based on the viewing audience of each program. A national advertiser that wants to reach a broad cross-section of women ages 18 to 35, for example, might find "Dharma and Greg" an efficient buy, especially at the cost of only $210,000 for a 30-second commercial (which is about half the average cost of a prime-time network show).

When buying cable TV, an advertiser can buy ads over the full schedule of a channel because cable networks typically aim their overall programming to relatively specific audiences. The Lifetime and Family channels heavily weigh programs toward women; MTV targets viewers 16 to 25. Cable companies sell their network channels in bundles at a discount and offer discounts for *run-of-schedule* positioning—multiple ad purchases they can place throughout a channel's daily schedule (see the Checklist of Pros and Cons of Cable TV Advertising).

There are various ways advertisers can buy time on TV. They include sponsoring an entire program, participating in a program, purchasing spot announcements between programs, and purchasing spots from syndicators. Exhibit 15–6 shows how much money is spent nationally on the various types of television advertising.

Network Advertising

Historically, major U.S. advertisers purchased air time from one of the national broadcast **networks:** ABC, CBS, NBC, or Fox. In 1995, relaxed FCC rules enabled two of the biggest producers of prime-time shows, Warner Bros. and Paramount, to launch their own broadcast networks—WB and UPN—giving them captive distribution outlets for programs they produce and buy.[17] With 31 affiliated stations, UPN immediately covered 80 percent of the country, even though it initially programmed only a couple of nights a week.[18]

Cable has slowly eroded the audience of the broadcast networks. At one time the big three (ABC, CBS, and NBC) had over 90 percent of the prime-time audience; today their total share is about 62 percent, while the cable networks hold about 32 percent.[19]

Exhibit 15–6
Where does all the money go?
(Measured TV spending in $ millions).

	1996	1995	Percent change
Network TV	$14,739.60	$12,402.20	18.8
Spot TV	14,017.70	13,017.20	7.7
Syndicated TV	2,326.10	2,316.80	0.4
Cable TV networks	4,728.40	3,418.80	38.3
Total	$35,811.80	$31,155.00	14.9

Source: Reprinted with permission from the September 15, 1997 issue of *Advertising Age.* Copyright, Crain Communications, Inc. 1997.

Networks offer large advertisers convenience and efficiency because they broadcast messages simultaneously across many affiliate stations throughout the country. Broadcast networks tend to reach masses of American consumers—a cross-section of the population—while cable networks tend to reach more selective niches.

An advertiser who underwrites the total cost of a program is engaging in **sponsorship.** In a sole sponsorship, the advertiser is responsible for both the program content and the cost of production. Sponsorship is so costly that single sponsorships are usually limited to specials. Companies that sponsor programs (AT&T, Xerox, and Hallmark, for example) gain two important advantages. First, the public more readily identifies with the product(s) due to the prestige of sponsoring first-rate entertainment. Second, the sponsor controls the placement and content of its commercials. The commercials can be fit to the program and run any length the sponsor desires so long as they remain within network or station regulations. Further, because networks are centralized, the advertiser gets only one bill.

Sponsorship offers so many opportunities that Procter & Gamble signed a sweeping deal with Paramount in 1995, making it a full partner with the studio in at least 10 new series to be produced for network TV. P&G not only has a guaranteed venue for its advertising, but also shares in the development costs as well as any profit or loss on the shows.[20] To save money and reduce risks, many advertisers cosponsor programs, sponsoring on alternate weeks or dividing the program into segments. NFL games, for instance, are always sold as multiple sponsorships.

Most network TV advertising is sold on a **participation basis,** with several advertisers buying 30- or 60-second segments within a program. This enables them to spread their budgets and avoid long-term commitments to any one program. It also lets smaller advertisers buy a limited amount of time and still get nationwide coverage.

Network advertising also has several disadvantages: lack of flexibility, long lead times, inconvenient restrictions, and forced adherence to network standards and practices, not to mention high prices. Costs average about $388,000 for a 30-second prime-time spot and range from a low of $55,000 to a high of $560,000 for a spot on "ER" (see Exhibit 15–7). For this reason, most advertisers opt to buy *spot announcements.*

Spot Announcements

National **spot announcements** run in clusters between programs. They are less expensive than participations and more flexible than network advertising because they can be concentrated in specific regions of the country. An advertiser with a small budget or limited distribution may use spots to introduce a new product into one area at a time. Or an advertiser can vary its message by market to suit promotional needs.[21]

Spots may run 10, 15, 30, or 60 seconds and be sold nationally or locally. Spot advertising is more difficult to buy than network advertising because it involves

Exhibit 15–7

Top 10 shows by ad rates.

Rank		Price per :30
1	Seinfeld (NBC)	$575,000
2	ER (NBC)	560,000
3	Friends (NBC)	410,000
4	Veronica's Closet (NBC)	400,000
5	Monday Night Football (ABC)	360,000
6	Home Improvement (ABC)	350,000
7	Union Square (NBC)	310,000
8	The X-Files (FOX)	275,000
9	The Drew Carey Show (ABC)	275,000
10	Frasier (NBC)	275,000

Source: Reprinted with permission from the May 21, 1998 issue of *Advertising Age.* Copyright, Crain Communications, Inc. 1998.

contacting each station directly. This is a headache with cable channels, since one city may be served by 10 or more cable companies. For the broadcast stations, the *national rep system,* in which individuals act as sales and service representatives for a number of stations, alleviates this problem through the use of *electronic data interchange (EDI).*[22] This technology enables agency buyers to electronically process orders, makegoods, and revisions, and maintain an electronic audit trail through the life of a schedule. Likewise, reps can transmit orders directly to their stations via satellite while keeping in day-to-day contact with agency buyers.[23] In 1994, Media Technologies created the AdValue Network, a computerized media-buying system that automates spot TV buys. The service quickly attracted agency interest, signing up McCann-Erickson, Backer Spielvogel Bates, N. W. Ayer, Grey Advertising, and Ogilvy & Mather Worldwide.[24]

Meanwhile, a trio of large cable rep firms is now working to make the purchase of spot cable more convenient for national advertisers through satellite technology and digital systems that **interconnect** various cable companies in a region.[25]

The last decade saw a significant shift toward greater regional advertising by national advertisers. Campbell Soup, for example, increased its local spot TV ad budget to address regional differences in eating habits. But spot advertising is available only at network station breaks and when network advertisers purchase less than a full lineup, so spot ads may get lost in the clutter—which is why they tend to have lower viewership and lower ad spending.

Spot announcements are generally regionally based advertisements, used when an advertiser wants to reach only certain geographic areas or as an alternative to high-cost network advertising. Advertisers have no commitments to specific programming, and the spots are purchased on a station-by-station basis. This works well for regional companies, such as Lotto, for instance.

"Born to be Wild" :30
(Open on a relatively regular looking guy riding a Harley-Davidson motorcy-

cle in eastern Washington. The song "Born to be Wild" plays throughout. Cut to the rider rounding curves. He reaches

a stop sign and a small station wagon overloaded with PA equipment and blar-

ing the Steppenwolf song, pulls alongside him. The biker leans over and yells.)

BIKER: You're gonna have to keep up because sometimes I can't hear the music.

WOMAN (VO): OK.
ANNCR (VO): Six little numbers. Just think. (The biker continues on.)

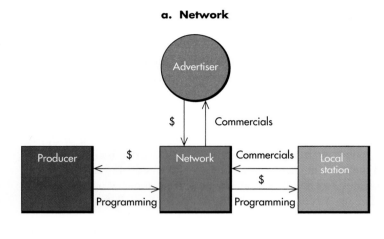

a. Network

b. Syndication

Exhibit 15–8
TV network and syndication distribution.
a. The networks are essentially middlemen.
b. Syndication is often a more efficient way of financing and distributing programs.

Syndication

As audiences fragment, syndicated programs become an increasingly popular adjunct or alternative to network advertising. In a little over 10 years, the syndication industry has grown from almost nothing into a $2 billion advertising medium.[26]

Syndication is the sale of programs on a station-by-station, market-by-market basis.[27] In other words, the producer (for example, Warner Bros. or Disney) deals directly with the stations, often through a distribution company, rather than going through the networks. This efficient "direct-from-the-factory" approach gives local TV stations more programming control and greater profits. It also gives advertisers access to **inventory** (commercial time) for their spots that they might not get on network programs—often at better prices.[28] Syndication has become the largest source of programming in the United States (see Exhibit 15–8).

Television syndication comes in three forms: off-network, first-run, and barter. In **off-network syndication,** former popular network programs (reruns) are sold to individual stations for rebroadcast. Examples include "Home Improvement" and "Seinfeld." **First-run syndication** involves original shows, like "Rosie O'Donnell," "Xena: Warrior Princess," and "Entertainment Tonight," which are produced specifically for the syndication market. One of the fastest-growing trends in television is **barter syndication** (also called *advertiser-supported syndication*). These are first-run programs offered free or for a reduced rate, but with some of the ad space (usually 50 percent) presold to national advertisers. "Wheel of Fortune," "Jeopardy," and "The Oprah Winfrey Show," all distributed by King World Productions, are some of the most popular examples.[29]

Although infomercials were once chided as nonsense programming for late-night television viewers, the industry has turned into a multibillion-dollar business. Today, well-respected advertisers ranging from Philips Magnavox (www.philipsmagnavox.com) to presidential candidate Ross Perot have made excellent use of infomercials. Infomercials provide an extended period of time to convey in-depth information that cannot be covered in a 30-second spot.

Exhibit 15–9
Syndication viewing shares for total and daytime dayparts. Although syndication holds a respectable 13 percent share relative to total overall viewing, it commands a full one-third of viewing share of all national broadcast. During prime time dayparts, when competing with network sitcoms and dramas, syndication's share of audience drops way off. But, during early prime time it is responsible for over 75 percent share of national broadcast viewing, and during late fringe it commands close to 50 percent share. Syndication ranks high in early prime time and late fringe segments because the only broadcast competition comes from early evening news programs and late-night talk shows.

Viewing Shares for All Dayparts

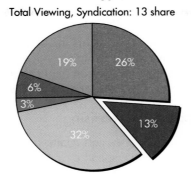
Total Viewing, Syndication: 13 share

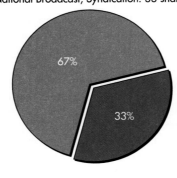
National Broadcast, Syndication: 33 share

Viewing Shares for Daytime Dayparts

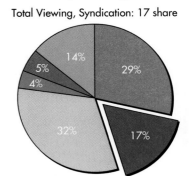
Total Viewing, Syndication: 17 share

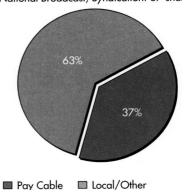
National Broadcast, Syndication: 37 share

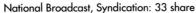
■ Network   ■ Syndication   □ Cable   ■ PBS   ■ Pay Cable   □ Local/Other

Syndication is a powerful tool for building reach. Advertisers like it because they can affiliate with popular programs and maximize their use of broadcast TV, gaining back much of the audience they used to reach through the networks (see Exhibit 15–9).

Program-Length Ads (PLAs)

In the fall of 1992, independent presidential candidate Ross Perot sat in front of a TV camera for 30 minutes with homemade flip charts and a down-home pitch for the White House and drew 20 million viewers. A month later, he pulled a respectable 19 percent of the vote.

Perot made advertising history by catapulting the **program-length advertisement (PLA),** or **infomercial,** into the limelight. He also proved what companies that produce and sell infomercials have been saying for years: long-form advertising can communicate a message in a way other forms can't.[30] As a result, *Advertising Age* named Perot its adman of the year.

Infomercials aren't new, but their respectability is. Before Perot, most PLA users were off-Madison Avenue marketers of hand mixers, juicers, and car waxes. Today, major marketers like Toshiba, Lexus, and Magnavox are venturing into the infomercial arena.[31] In Colorado, long-form ads were used as a negotiating tool in a labor dispute.[32] And now even networks air some of these ads, which were once relegated to independents and cable channels.[33] The reasons for this sudden growth are simple:

1. Consumers pay attention and can respond immediately.
2. Brand managers want the competitive edge of going where the competition isn't.
3. PLAs can fulfill some message objectives, like product demonstration and brand differentiation, far better than 30-second commercials.

4. Results are both measurable and accountable.
5. The ad campaign can pay for itself while supporting the retail trade.
6. PLAs combine the power of advertising, direct response, and sales promotion.[34]

Add to these factors the benefits of lower (though rising) production costs and attractive, upscale audience demographics, and it's easy to see why national marketers have jumped on the PLA bandwagon. They spent some $500 million on infomercials in 1996, 60 percent of which went to cable.[35]

Local TV Advertising

Local businesses and retailers, often in cooperation with nationally known manufacturers, now spend over $10 billion annually on local broadcast and cable TV.[36] Most local stations sell spot announcements, but some local advertisers develop and sponsor local programs or buy the rights to a syndicated series.

TV **Audience** Measurement

Efficient advertisers study the audiences of various programs and analyze their impact and cost effectiveness against other media vehicles. To do this, they must understand the techniques and terminology of audience measurement.

Rating Services: The Book

The companies that measure the program audiences of TV and radio stations for advertisers and broadcasters are called **rating services.** These firms attempt to pick a representative sample of the market and furnish data on the number and characteristics of the viewers or listeners. Several research organizations gather the data at their own expense and publish it. Companies subscribe to a service and use it as a basis for planning, buying, or selling media advertising.

In the United States, Nielsen Media Research, a division of Cognizant Corp., is the major rating service for television. Its flagship service, the Nielsen Television Index (NTI), uses a national sample of 5,000 households equipped with *people meters* to develop audience estimates for all national TV programming sources: six broadcast networks, 41 cable networks, and 100 syndicators. At the local level, Nielsen uses people meters in 35 markets and diary surveys in 211 markets to measure viewing for more than 1,500 local TV stations, 140 cable operators, 48 syndicators, and 2,000 local advertising agencies.[37] It publishes the information at least twice a year in a publication commonly called *the Book* (see Ad Lab 15–A).

Since 1993, when the Arbitron Co. discontinued its local-market TV audience rating service, Nielsen has enjoyed a virtual monopoly. This may be short-lived, though; many advertisers and broadcasters maintain that Nielsen overreports cable TV viewing in its sample and underreports network TV viewing by people under age 50.[38] Don Ohlemeyer, president of NBC West Coast, says, "Nielsen is an antiquated, inaccurate monopoly that hasn't kept up with the way people watch television today. Norway has better TV measurement than we do in this country."[39] In fact, Nielsen's biggest problem may be the low cooperation rate among viewers who are supposed to fill out diaries. When they aren't consistent, the results can be very quirky ratings.[40]

The issues are critical to the networks and advertisers alike, since Nielsen's numbers determine the fate of billions of dollars' worth of advertising every year. In fact, the big three major networks are so dissatisfied with Nielsen's methodology that they have funded a $30 million project to test a new rating system in the Philadelphia area by Statistical Research, Inc.[41] Called SMART-TV (Systems for Measuring and Reporting Television), SRI's system is currently being tested in 500 homes. It is intended to be more user friendly and less intrusive than Nielsen's system, while providing more accurate numbers on who is actually watching what programs and when.

For demographic studies of TV audiences, advertisers also use the Simmons Market Research Bureau and Mediamark Research. These companies perform ex-

Where Do Those Infamous TV Ratings Come From?

For four decades, the life and death of network TV programs have been in the hands of the Nielsen families, households chosen with the aid of national census and other data to reflect the country's demographics. Originally there were two measuring types: those who kept diaries and those who had a black box attached to their TV sets. Someone in each of 2,400 diary homes kept a written record of which shows each person watched during the week. In the 1,700 black-box households, an audimeter attached to the TV kept track of when the set was on and what channel it was tuned to. Nielsen Media Research paid these families for gathering data from their viewing patterns and computed its Nielsen Television Index (NTI), the sole source of national TV ratings.

But that method of determining national ratings has been replaced by the more accurate people meter (see illustration), an electronic device that automatically records a household's TV viewing. The people meter records the channels watched, the number of minutes of viewing, and who in the household is watching. Each person must punch in and punch out on a keypad. The microwave-based people meter keeps track of second-by-second viewing choices of up to eight household members and relays the data to a central computer, which tabulates the data overnight.

The original people meter was developed by AGB Research, a British company. AGB found clients in ad agencies, cable networks, and syndicators—all of whom believed NTI overreported

broadcast network shows and underreported other types. However, Nielsen developed its own people meter, and AGB abandoned the U.S. market.

Unfortunately, Nielsen's people meter had its share of problems. At one point, Nielsen's numbers showed millions of people suddenly stopped watching TV. The networks hit the roof, but Nielsen officials defended their system. The networks gave advertisers $150 million worth of free time, since they hadn't met rating guarantees, and decided to use eight-year trends for rating guarantees instead of just the current year's ratings. And critics are still convinced that people meter numbers are flawed.

Nielsen has since developed a passive people meter that actually records how many people watched the commercial, something advertisers have always wanted to know. It uses digital scanning technology to record and remember participants' faces. Every two seconds, it scans the room to see who's there and who is actually watching the TV. Nielsen's competitor Arbitron is developing a passive people meter whose portable technology can register TV viewing and radio listening anywhere respondents are using them, even out of home. The new pocket people meter would be carried or worn by each panelist. Currently, Arbitron is using meters and diaries to collect TV and radio ratings.

Nielsen conducts its survey sweeps twice a year in major market areas and publishes sweeps books that are the basis for network and local station ad rates. With the advent of the passive people meter, advertisers may once again believe in the ratings they're paying for.

An interesting development in audience measurement is the single-source data made available by supermarket scanners. Once information on a family's viewing habits has been gathered, its packaged-goods purchases are measured. The implications are monumental for marketing and media planners. The leaders in single-source measurement are Information Resources, Inc. (IRI), with its BehaviorScan service, and Nielsen, with its Home Scan service. The U.S. Justice Department is evaluating the competitive nature of certain market behavior. If the department finds pricing is not competitive, it may mean the end of discounted scanner data services.

Laboratory Applications

1. What are the advantages and disadvantages of the various measurement methods?
2. Which method do you consider best? Why?

tensive surveys of the U.S. marketplace and publish their findings on consumer lifestyles, product usage, and media habits. Advertisers use the results for strategic planning purposes.

Cable Ratings Reliable information on cable programs is even harder to gather. Traditional techniques often rely on too small a sample to be statistically significant, so major cable programming services provide their own reports of daypart division and audience viewership by show. Interpreting cable ratings is a confusing process, since the media planner has to integrate so much information from so many different sources. Some companies are trying to remedy the situation. ADcom Information Services, for example, is a ratings service that installs in-home recording devices to provide more reliable information. Its recent test with Continental Cablevision in Jacksonville, Florida, confirmed that Nielsen had been underreporting cable TV audiences—in some cases dramatically.[42] Nielsen, meanwhile, has introduced its own cable TV ratings service but has been criticized for using older broadcast reporting technology.[43] This controversy is destined to rage for some time.

Defining Television Markets Television rating services define geographic television markets to minimize the confusion of overlapping TV signals. The Nielsen station index uses the term **designated market areas (DMAs)** for geographic areas (cities, counties) in which the *local* TV stations attract the most viewing. For example, the DMA for Casper-Riverton, Wyoming (see Exhibit 15–10), is all counties in which the Casper or Riverton County TV stations are the most watched.

Dayparts Advertisers must decide *when* to air commercials and on *which programs.* Unlike radio listeners, TV viewers are loyal to programs, not stations. Programs continue to run or are canceled depending on their *ratings* (percentage of the population watching). Ratings also depend on the time of day a program runs.

Television time is divided into dayparts as follows:

	Daytime:	9 AM–4 PM (EST)
	Early fringe:	4–5:30 PM (EST)
Combine as	Early news:	5 or 5:30–7:30 PM (EST)
early fringe	Prime access:	7:30–8 PM (EST)
	Prime:	8–11 PM (EST)
Combine as	Late news:	11–11:30 PM (EST)
late fringe	Late fringe:	11:30 PM–1 AM (EST)

Viewing is highest during **prime time** (8 to 11 PM Eastern Standard Time; 7 to 10 PM Central Standard Time). Late fringe ranks fairly high in most markets among adults, and daytime and early fringe tend to be viewed most heavily by women. To reach the greatest percentage of the advertiser's target audience with optimal frequency, the media planner determines a **daypart mix** based on TV usage levels reported by the rating services.

Audience Measures Rating services and media planners use many terms to define a station's audience, penetration, and efficiency. **TV households (TVHH)** refers to the number of households that own television sets. The number of TVHH in a particular market gives an advertiser a sense of the market's size. Likewise, the number of TVHH tuned in to a particular program helps the advertiser estimate the program's popularity and how many people a commercial is likely to reach.

The percentage of homes in a given area that have one or more TV sets turned on at any particular time is expressed as **households using TV (HUT).** If there are 1,000 TV sets in the survey area and 500 are turned on, HUT is 50 percent.

The **program rating** refers to the percentage of TV households in an area that are tuned in to a specific program. The rating is computed as follows:

$$\text{Rating} = \frac{\text{TVHH tuned to specific program}}{\text{Total TVHH in area}}$$

Networks want high ratings because they measure a show's popularity. More popular shows can command higher advertising rates. Local stations often change their programming (buy different syndicated shows, for example) to increase their popularity and thereby their ratings (and their revenues).

The percentage of homes with sets in use (HUT) tuned to a specific program is called the **audience share.** A program with only 500 viewers can have a 50 *share*

MARKET DATA

CASPER-RIVERTON, WY
DMA RANK # 194

APRIL 27 - MAY 24, 1995

TABLE 1 - UNIVERSE ESTIMATES - JAN. 1995

AREA	TOTAL HOUSEHOLDS	TV HOUSEHOLDS	TV HOUSEHOLDS BY COUNTY SIZE † A	B	C	D
METRO	37.300	36.410				
DMA	48.800	47.580			24.340	23.240
%		100			51	49
NSI	180.100	175.860			53.990	121.870
%		100			31	69

TOTAL HOUSEHOLDS are estimated by Market Statistics (MSI) used by special permission of that organization. They are the base against which television ownership percentages have been applied.
TELEVISION OWNERSHIP PERCENTS are Nielsen estimates based on combining historical projections from the 1960 and 1970 Censuses with estimates from the NSI telephone interviews from a number of all market measurement periods.
HOUSEHOLDS ARE OCCUPIED HOUSING UNITS. The household universe estimates shown in Table 1 are estimates of year-round households. i.e., housing units occupied year round. Seasonal housing units which are occupied only during certain seasons of the year are not included in the Household Universe Estimates. Thus, the number of households during the survey period may differ from the estimate in Table 1.

† See NSI Reference Supplement for definition of county size.　　　　LT Less than 1%.

TABLE 2 - PENETRATION ESTIMATES

	PERCENT OF TV HOUSEHOLDS				
AREA	BLACK %	HISPANIC %	MULTI-SET %	CABLE TV %	VCR %
METRO	1	3	60	65	
DMA	LT	3	58	67	81
CASPER	1	3	NA	NA	NA
RIVERTON	LT	5	NA	NA	NA

Black and Hispanic estimates are as of January 1, 1995. Multi-set. Cable TV and VCR estimates are based on the latest available data.

See NSI Reference Supplement for detail regarding the derivation of these estimates and for information regarding response and sampling error.

TABLE 3 - SAMPLE SIZES: HOUSEHOLDS

	INITIALLY DESIGNATED HOUSEHOLDS			IN-TAB DIARY HOUSEHOLDS		
AREA	LISTED	UNLISTED	TOTAL	LISTED	UNLISTED	TOTAL
METRO	236	91	327	107	27	134
DMA(INCL METRO)	316	113	429	149	36	185
NSI(INCL. DMA)	826	287	1113	436	112	548

For sample selection procedures used in Total Telephone Frame sampling, see NSI Reference Supplement. This DMA, being a Type D market, has an advance household sample estimate of 180 or more during this measurement period. A minimum in-tab household sample size of 50 is required to report multi-week DMA or Station Total Audience data. Weekly ratings not reported in Type D markets.

TABLE 4 - TELEVISION STATIONS

CITY OF ORIGIN	STATION	CHANNEL	AFFILIATION
LANDER	KCWC	4	P
CASPER	*KFNB+	20	A
RIVERTON	*KFNE	10	SATELLITE OF KFNB
RAWLINS	*KFNR	11	SATELLITE OF KFNB
CASPER	*KGWC+	14	C
LANDER	*KGWL	5	SATELLITE OF KGWC
ROCK SPRINGS	*KGWR	13	SATELLITE OF KGWC
CASPER	*KTWO+	2	N
CHEYENNE	*KKTU	33	SATELLITE OF KTWO
DENVER	*KCNC (D)	4	N
DENVER	*KRMA (D)	6	P
DENVER	*KWGN (D)	2	I
ATLANTA	*WTBS (D)	17	T
CABLE	CNN (D)		
CABLE	TNT (D)		
CABLE	USA (D)		

(D) THIS OUTSIDE STATION IS REPORTABLE IN THE DAYPART SECTION ONLY

TABLE 5 - TV HOUSEHOLDS AND IN-TAB DIARY HOUSEHOLDS BY SAMPLING AREA

ADJ DMA CNTY	COUNTY & STATE	MRS TERRI-TORY†	EST. TV HHLDS JAN. 1995	CABLE TV HHLDS % MAY 1995	CNTY SIZE†	IN-TAB DIARY HHLDS
#3	SEVIER	UT P	5,110	59	D	4
#1	ALBANY	WY WC	12,860	69	D	14
#2	BIG HORN	WY WC	3,910	57	D	24
#1	CAMPBELL	WY WC	10,550	77	D	9
#1	CARBON	WY WC	5,370	96	D	5
D	CONVERSE	WY WC	3,910	71	D	22
MD	FREMONT	WY WC	12,070	53	D	41
	GOSHEN	WY WC	4,930	47	D	26
D	HOT SPRINGS	WY WC	1,870	82	D	6
D	JOHNSON	WY WC	2,210	63	D	11
	LARAMIE	WY WC	29,650	76	C	150
	LINCOLN	WY WC	4,290	50	D	13
MD	NATRONA	WY WC	24,340	71	C	93
#2	PARK	WY WC	9,110	56	D	43
#1	PLATTE	WY WC	3,240	62	D	4
	SHERIDAN	WY WC	9,510	82	D	32
#3	SUBLETTE	WY WC	1,870	64	D	1
#3	SWEETWATER	WY WC	14,200	88	D	17
#3	TETON	WY WC	5,340	96	D	3
#3	UINTA	WY WC	6,040	66	D	13
D	WASHAKIE	WY WC	3,180	75	D	12
	WESTON	WY WC	2,300	76	D	5
METRO TOTAL			36,410	65		134
DMA TOTAL			47,580	67		185
NSI AREA TOTAL			175,860	71		548

#1 = DENVER　　　　#2 = BILLINGS
#3 = SALT LAKE CITY
NOTE: VIEWING IN ADJACENT DMA'S IS NOT LIMITED TO NSI AREA COUNTIES IN TABLE 5. THE ABOVE LIST OF COUNTIES DOES NOT NECESSARILY REPRESENT ENTIRE AREA FOR WHICH VIEWING OCCURS TO STATIONS IN THIS MARKET. SEE INSIDE BACK COVER FOR FURTHER STATION TOTAL AREA DESCRIPTION.

CASPER-RIVERTON, WY

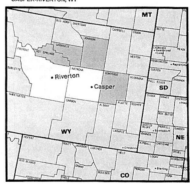

Nielsen Station Index

Measurement Schedule 1995–96

Report Month		Dates	# Markets
October	1995	Sept. 28 – Oct. 25	25
November	1995	Nov. 2 – Nov. 29	(All Markets)*
January	1996	Jan. 4 – Jan. 31	17
February	1996	Feb. 1 – Feb. 28	(All Markets)
March	1996	Feb. 29 – Mar. 27	4
May	1996	April 25 – May 22	(All Markets)**
July	1996	July 11 – Aug. 7	(All DMAs)

*Thanksgiving is Nov. 23, 1995　　　**Memorial Day is May 27, 1996

Audience estimates are computed separately for each week. Reported multi-week averages are the average of the appropriate individual week audience estimates. Some of the above counties may have been combined for projecting individual week audience estimates. Viewing among the households in the in-tab sample for all counties that are combined are projected to the Total TV Households for the combined counties. These county groupings are available upon request.

M = Metro County. D = Designated Market Area County (for definition, see Section II).
† See NSI Reference Supplement for explanation of MRS Territory and County Size.

* = NSI Client　　　　　I = Independent Station　　　　I-F = Independent-Fox Network Affiliate
I-S = Independent-Subscription TV Station　　　　T = Turner Broadcasting System
P = Educational and Public Broadcasting Service Stations　　P-C = Public Broadcasting-Commercial
Network affiliation as shown herein is based on information supplied by the networks for use in Nielsen Television Index (NTI). For additional details, see the NSI Reference Supplement.

1

Exhibit 15–10

Market data from Nielsen Media Research for Casper–Riverton, Wyoming.

if only 1,000 sets are turned on. *Ratings,* in contrast, measure the audience as a percentage of *all* TVHH in the area, whether the TV sets are on or off.

The total number of homes reached by some portion of a program is called **total audience.** This figure is normally broken down to determine **audience composition** (the distribution of the audience into demographic categories).

Gross Rating Points

In television, **gross rating points (GRPs)** are the total rating points achieved by a particular media schedule over a specific period. As we discussed in Chapter 8, a weekly schedule of five commercials on programs with an average household rating of 20 would yield 100 GRPs. Recall that GRPs are computed as follows:

Reach (average rating) × Frequency = Gross rating points

GRPs allow advertisers to draw conclusions about the different markets available for a client's ads by providing a comparable measure of advertising weight. However, GRPs do not reflect a market's size. For example, while campaigns in Knoxville and Charlotte might have the same GRPs, they would differ significantly in their reach:

	TV homes (000s)	Average cost per spot	Average rating	No. of spots	GRPs
Knoxville	1,002	$1,500	15	5	75
Charlotte	638	$1,250	15	5	75

To better determine the relative value of television advertising markets, other measures are used, such as *cost per rating point* (CPP) and *cost per thousand* (CPM), which were described in Chapter 8.

Buying Television Time

The process of buying TV time can be lengthy and, depending on the number of stations in the buy, quite involved. Advertisers or media buyers must:

- Determine which programs are available at what cost.
- Analyze the various programs for efficiency.
- Negotiate price with station reps.
- Determine what reach and frequency they are achieving.
- Sign broadcast contracts.
- Review affidavits of performance to be sure the commercials ran as agreed.

These procedures are so complex that most large advertisers use ad agencies or media-buying services. Buying services are gaining in popularity because they charge less and can save advertisers money by negotiating for desirable time slots at reduced rates. Local advertisers typically rely on station reps to determine the best buys for the money.

Requesting Avails

To find out which programs are available, media buyers contact stations' sales reps—local station salespeople, national media rep organizations that sell for one station in each market, or network reps. The media buyer gives the rep information about the advertiser's media objectives and target audiences and asks the rep to supply a list of **avails** (available time slots) along with prices and estimated ratings. Many media buyers ask for the information based on the last two or three Nielsen books to see whether a show's ratings are consistent, rising, or falling.

Selecting Programs for Buys

The media buyer selects the most efficient programs in relation to the target audience using the **cost per rating point (CPP)** and the **cost per thousand (CPM)** for each program:

$$CPP = \frac{Cost}{Rating} \qquad\qquad CPM = \frac{Cost}{Thousands\ of\ people}$$

For example, assume "Ally McBeal" has a rating of 25, reaches 200,000 people in the primary target audience, and costs $2,000 for a 30-second spot with a fixed guarantee on station WALB-TV in Albany, Georgia. Then,

$$CPP = \frac{\$2,000}{25} = \$80 \qquad\qquad CPM = \frac{\$2,000}{(200,000 \div 1,000)} = \$10$$

The lower the cost per thousand, the more efficient the show. The media buyer substitutes stronger programs for less efficient ones to get the best buys within the available budget (see Ad Lab 15–B: Getting "You're Out" on TV).

Negotiating Prices and Contracts

TV stations and cable companies publish rate cards to sell their air time. However, since TV audiences are estimated at best, television reps will always negotiate prices.

The media buyer contacts the rep and explains what efficiency the advertiser needs in terms of delivery and CPM to make the buy. The buyer has numerous ways to negotiate lower rates: work out a package deal, accept *run-of-schedule positioning* (the station chooses when to run the commercials), or take advantage of preemption rates. A **preemption rate** is lower because the advertiser agrees to be "bumped" (preempted) if another advertiser pays the higher, nonpreemption rate.

The media buyer must read the advertising contract carefully before signing it. The contract indicates the dates, times, and programs on which the advertiser's commercials will run, the length of each spot, the rate per spot, and the total amount. The reverse side of the contract defines payment terms and responsibilities of the advertiser, agency, and station. After the spots run, the station returns a signed and notarized **affidavit of performance** to the advertiser or agency, specifying when the spots aired and what makegoods are available. **Makegoods** refer to free advertising time an advertiser receives to compensate for spots the station missed or ran incorrectly or because the program's ratings were substantially lower than guaranteed.[44]

Other **Forms** of Television

Cable isn't the only electronic challenger to traditional broadcast TV. Cable has its own (minor) competitors: DBS, MDS, STV, and SMATV.

- DBS (direct broadcast satellite) beams programs from space via satellites to satellite dishes mounted in the home or yard. For a monthly fee, consumers can subscribe to one of the DBS program distributors, such as DirectTV or United States Satellite Broadcasting (USSB), to receive from 20 to 150 channels.[45]

Getting "You're Out" on TV

"You're Out" baseball mitts have expanded to television. As the marketing director, you choose to examine the gross rating points (GRPs) for placing your advertising. You have an idea of the days and times you want the ads to be placed. Chart 1 indicates the best programs for Memphis, Tennessee, and relevant planning data your assistant has gathered according to your preferences. Due to time constraints the chart is incomplete, but there are enough data available for you to finish the chart.

Chart 1 shows the marketing figures for a single city, but now you decide to determine which of the three major cities in Tennessee will serve "You're Out" baseball mitts the best. Your assistant didn't quite finish Chart 2, but with the help of Chart 1 you can complete the needed calculations.

Laboratory Applications

1. Using the formulas in the text as a guide, complete Chart 1.

2. Assuming your budget is $68,000, use Chart 1 to decide which programs would be most effective for reaching children. Explain your selection.

3. Using Chart 1, complete the "per spot" and "rating" figures in Chart 2. Next, calculate how many GRPs each city will deliver if you buy five spots of advertising.

4. Using the completed Chart 2, calculate for each city the number of household impressions.

5. Knowing that you are running five spots, find the CPP and CPM for all three cities.

6. Based on the completed Chart 2, what city is ideal for "You're Out" baseball mitts?

Chart 1: Best Programs for Memphis, TN

Program	Rating	Cost	Spots	GRP
"Family Matters" (early evening daily, rerun, 30/70 adults to kids)	15	$34,000	32	—
Saturday morning cartoons (kids ages 2–12)	—	$34,000	30	300.0
Major league baseball game (weekends, mostly adults)	7.8	$34,000	29	—
After-school special (kids ages 7–13, afternoon, daily)	—	$34,000	27	205.0

Chart 2

TV homes (000s)	Average cost per spot	Average % of rating	GRP
1,002	$1,500	15	—
638	$1,250	15	—
847	$___	—	—

Frequency: 5 spots

- MDS (multipoint distribution system), a microwave delivery system that can carry a dozen channels, is usually offered in rural areas where cable isn't available.

- STV (subscription television) is over-the-air pay TV. Subscribers buy a descrambler that allows them to watch programs carried over a regular TV channel.

- SMATV (satellite master antenna television) uses a satellite dish to capture signals for TV sets in apartment buildings and other complexes, acting as a sort of minicable system.

Most of these systems are more expensive or carry fewer channels, so none has yet captured the public's imagination the way cable has.

Advertising on **Video** Rentals

Ever since Pepsi sponsored the successful home-video release *Top Gun* a decade ago, industry analysts have been expecting advertising on video rentals to become a major new medium.

Research shows that home-video renters are younger and more upscale than the general population. And the majority of video renters do watch the commercials that precede the movie—sometimes more than once. A Schweppes ad starring comedian John Cleese was viewed by an astounding 95 percent of households renting Cleese's movie *A Fish Called Wanda*.[46] However, more recent research has shown that video renters find ads on tape intrusive and somewhat offensive. Many just zip through them to get to the movie.[47]

When metered viewer data becomes widely available, more advertisers may place commercials on videos. In the meantime, the primary users of the medium are the movie studios themselves, advertising coming attractions.

Daily Reach: Adults 18+

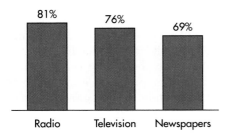

Weekly Reach: Adults 18+

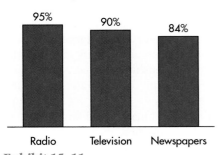

Exhibit 15–11
Daily and weekly reach of radio for people 18 and older exceeds other media.

Depending on a company's advertising needs, radio has many uses within the IMC model. For the National Fluid Milk Processor Promotion Board, the "Got Milk?" radio campaign (www.got-milk.com) proved to be an excellent way to achieve imagery transfer from its television ads. Local retailers, on the other hand, benefit from radio's low cost and targeted neighborhood markets.

The Medium of **Radio**

Radio is a personal, one-on-one medium; people listen alone. And radio is mobile. It can entertain people who are driving, walking, at home, or away from home. It's a particularly strong way to reach people who commute by car.

Radio is also adaptable to moods. In the morning, people may want to hear the news, upbeat music, or interesting chatter; in the afternoon, they may want to unwind with classical or easy-listening music.

Who Uses Radio?

In an average week, 96 percent of the U.S. population listens to radio; in an average day, almost 80 percent. The average American listens to the radio more than three hours every weekday and almost six hours on the weekend. In fact, during the prime shopping hours of 6 AM to 6 PM, the average U.S. adult spends more time with radio than any other medium.[48] As Exhibit 15–11 shows, radio is also cost-effective. In the last decade, the CPM for radio advertising has risen less than for any other major medium and substantially less than the consumer price index.[49] As a result, radio's advertising revenues have grown steadily.

More national advertisers are discovering radio's reach and frequency potential. Look at Snapple, for instance. Back when it was still a little company in Queens, New York, and strapped for money, Snapple Natural Beverages decided to use radio. It put its entire ad budget into a year-long schedule with a young, relatively unknown radio show host named Howard Stern. Snapple liked the way he delivered its spots as a live reader. Snapple has been with Stern ever since.

> MAN: I . . . I . . . I love you.
> WOMAN: Awwww.
> MAN: No, I mean . . . I . . . I mean. I don't . . . just . . .
> WOMAN: What (GIGGLES), go ahead . . .
> MAN: I just . . . don't think I'd be anything without you . . .
> WOMAN: Aw . . . that's so nice . . .
> MAN: I, uh, made these for you . . .
> (SFX: Baking pan and foil sounds.)
> WOMAN: Aw . . . you didn't have to do this . . .
> MAN: They're just brownies.
> WOMAN: Ooh, and they're still warm too.
> MAN: I was gonna get you something good.
> WOMAN: Aww, don't be silly, could I have one?
> MAN: (Laughs.) Well, yeah sure . . . go ahead . . .
> WOMAN (Mouth full.): You know . . . ?
> MAN: What . . . you don't like brownies?
> WOMAN: No . . . no . . . (Slight gag.) miggkkk . . .
> MAN: I'm sorry. I can't understand you.
> WOMAN: Neet . . . dmiggkk.
> MAN: You need Mick?
> WOMAN: Miccliggkk!
> MAN: A guy named Mick! I can't believe this . . .
> WOMAN: Pleeeease miiigggggglllkk . . .
> MAN: Yeah, yeah, okay you don't have to scream his name in ecstasy. I get the message. All right I got it, I'm gone.
> WOMAN: No, umbhum, no, miiiiiigggglllkk!
> MAN: Look, I gotta go, I'm sorry I'm gonna need my CDs back . . . and
> WOMAN: No, no, miiiggllk.
> MAN: . . . and I'm sorry for this whole thing . . .
> WOMAN: . . . No, miiigggllkk . . .
> MAN: No, it's Scott remember?
> WOMAN: No . . . miigggkkkfffff . . .
> ANNCR: True love means never having to say, "Got Milk?"

A few years later, Snapple began receiving letters and phone calls from people in the Midwest and West, where it didn't even have distribution. It seems that nationally syndicated talk show host Rush Limbaugh, on a restricted-calorie diet, had been giving enthusiastic on-air endorsements for Snapple Diet Iced Tea. The firm moved quickly to sign him as a paid endorser. What it learned was the power of radio, especially when combined with a popular radio personality. This combination doubled Snapple's sales every year for five years, propelled it into national distribution, and turned it into a major national advertiser, spending over $30 million every year advertising in more than 100 U.S. radio markets.[50]

The Use of Radio in IMC

While television is a passive medium that people simply watch, they get actively involved with radio. They listen intently to their favorite personalities; they call in to make requests, participate in a contest, or comment on a discussion; they use their ears and imaginations to fill in what they cannot see. Most people listen faithfully to two or three different radio stations with different types of programming. This means that smart advertisers can use the medium to establish an immediate, intimate relationship with consumers and other stakeholders. That makes radio an ideal medium for integrated marketing communications.

With radio, national companies can tie in to a local market and target the specific demographic group they want to reach. Most important, radio enables advertisers to maintain strategic consistency and stretch their media dollars through **imagery transfer** (see Exhibit 15–12). Research shows that when advertisers run a schedule on TV and then convert the audio portion to radio commercials, fully 75 percent of consumers replay the video in their minds when they hear the radio spot.[51] That extends the life and builds the impact of a TV campaign at greatly reduced cost.[52] In an IMC campaign, where message consistency is a primary objective, this is a very important feature of radio.

Local retailers like the medium for the same reasons. Also, they can tailor it to their needs. It offers defined audiences; its recall characteristics are similar to TV's; and retailers can create an identity by doing their own ads. Finally, since radio is so mobile, retailers can reach prospects just before they purchase. Hence, recent years have seen major spending increases by local grocery stores, car dealers, banks, and home-improvement, furniture, and apparel stores.[53]

Radio Programming and Audiences

Radio stations plan their programming carefully to reach specific markets and to capture as many listeners as possible. The larger the audience, the more a station can charge for commercial time. Therefore, extensive planning and research go into radio programming and program changes.

Stations can use tried-and-true formats, subscribe to network or syndicated programming, or devise unique approaches. Programming choices are greatly influenced by whether a station is on the AM or FM band. FM has much better sound fidelity, fewer commercial interruptions, and more varied programming.

Here's how imagery transfer works

1. Consumer sees TV commercial

3. Consumer recalls TV images

2. Consumer hears radio spot with similar soundtrack

This is what it does
- Extends campaigns
- Builds brand awareness
- Increases awareness during a TV flight hiatus
- Generates greater impact
- Keeps costs down
- Helps maintain brand equity
- Increases media productivity

Exhibit 15–12
How imagery transfer from TV to radio works, and what it does.

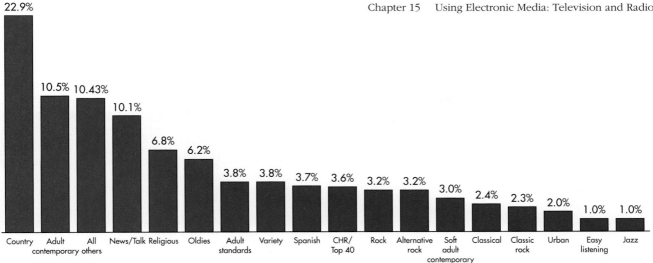

CHR: Contemporary hit radio

Exhibit 15–13
Each radio station's programming produces a unique and loyal audience.

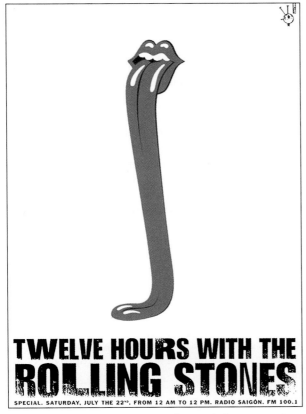

A radio station's programming format is important to advertisers because it is the best indicator of the demographics of the audience. While broadcast television audiences are driven largely by specific programs, radio audiences are determined almost entirely by the station's overall format. However, when advertising overseas on a station like Radio Saigon in Spain, marketers must realize that radio audiences there may not be as predictable as in the United States.

To counteract FM's inroads, many AM stations switched to programs that don't rely on sound quality, such as news, talk, and sports. Some stations are experimenting with all comedy, midday game shows with audience participation, or formats geared to specific regions, such as KHJ's "car radio" in Los Angeles. AM stations are also trying to win back music listeners by improving their sound quality and offering stereo broadcasting.

When buying radio time, advertisers usually buy the station's *format,* not its programs. Most stations adopt one of the dozen or so standard **programming formats:** contemporary hit radio (CHR-TOP 40), adult contemporary, country, rock, easy listening, news/talk, adult standards, classical, religious, and so on, as shown in Exhibit 15–13. Each format tends to appeal to specific demographic groups. The most popular format is country music, which is programmed by 22.9 percent of the stations in the United States (both AM and FM) and appeals to a broad cross-section of Americans from 25 to 54 years old.

Contemporary hit radio (CHR), always found on FM stations, appeals to teenagers and women under 30. It provides a constant flow of top 40 hits, usually with minimal intrusion by disk jockeys. Another popular format, adult contemporary (or "easy oldies"), is often advertised as "light rock, less talk." This format aims at the desirable target group of working women between 25 and 54. The news/talk, easy-listening, and nostalgia formats tend to have high listenership among men and women over 35.[54]

A major trend in radio today is the resurgence of radio networks, which offer services and programs that complement a station's local programming. A station might subscribe to ABC Radio's daily Paul Harvey news and commentary, CBS's weekly "House of Blues Radio Hour," and Westwood One's "Larry King Show."

There are now over 20 national radio networks, including the multiple "mini-networks" of ABC, CBS, Westwood One, and Unistar (see Exhibit 15–14), and numerous syndicators offer programs from live rock concerts to public-affairs discussions. To stand out, 80 percent of licensed radio stations are opting for syndicated and network offerings.[55] As more stations carry these programs and more listeners tune in, national advertisers find them increasingly attractive.

Exhibit 15–14

The radio mininetworks provide various types of programming including news, talk, and sports. Each network targets a specific demographic group such as Adults 25–54 (CBS) or Men 18 years and older (ESPN).

ABC Radio Networks			Westwood One Radio Networks		
Network	**Target demo**	**Affiliates**	**Network**	**Target demo**	**Affiliates**
Prime	A 25–54	2,566	Westwood One Mutual	A 25–54	1,385
Platinum	A 25–54	2,566	Westwood One NBC	A 25–54	1,338
Galaxy	A 12+	1,030	Westwood One Source	A 12–34	115
Genesis	A 12–34	317	Westwood One Programming	A 12–54	3,600
Excel	A 18–49	111	Westwood One Play by Play Sports	A 18+	1,192
ESPN	M 18+	231	Westwood One Talk	A 25–54	1,236
ABC Special Programming	A 12+	3,829			

CBS Radio Networks			Unistar Radio Networks		
Network	**Target demo**	**Affiliates**	**Network**	**Target demo**	**Affiliates**
CBS Radio Network	A 25–54	470	Super	A 25–54	1,256
CBS Spectrum	A 25–54	570	Power	A 18–49	218
CBS Radio Sports	A 25–54	300	CNN+	A 25–54	1,248
CBS Radio Programs	A 18–54	126	CNBC Business Radio	A 25–54	72
CBS Hispanic Radio Network	A 25–54	39	Unistar Weekly Music/ Personality Programs	A 12–49	1,700

The largest national radio advertisers are major retailers, car companies, beer and wine producers, telecommunications companies, and packaged-goods marketers (see Exhibit 15–15.) But of the almost $12.4 billion spent on radio ads in 1996, over $9.8 billion came from local advertisers—an 8 percent jump over the prior year.[56] Advertisers like radio's reach and frequency, selectivity, and cost efficiency (see the Checklist of Pros and Cons of Radio Advertising).

Buying **Radio Time**

Advertisers need a basic knowledge of the medium to buy radio time effectively: the types of radio advertising available for commercial use, a basic understanding of radio terminology, and the steps involved in preparing a radio schedule.

Exhibit 15–15

Radio's top 10 national advertisers, 1994.

Rank	Advertiser	Radio expenditures ($ 000s)
1	Sears, Roebuck & Co.	$100,026
2	AT&T	36,604
3	GM Dealers Assn.	31,569
4	News Corp., Ltd.	28,668
5	Chrysler Dealers Assn.	26,551
6	Tandy	25,242
7	Kmart	24,860
8	General Motors	24,499
9	U.S. government	24,198
10	Warner-Lambert	18,697

Types of Radio Advertising

An advertiser may purchase network, spot, or local radio time. Local purchases account for 79 percent of all radio time sold; national spot radio, another 17 percent; and networks, 4 percent.[57]

Networks

Advertisers may use one of the national radio networks to carry their messages to the entire national market simultaneously via stations that subscribe to the network's programs. In addition, more than 100 regional radio networks in the United States operate with information oriented toward specific geographic markets.

Networks provide national and regional advertisers with simple administration and low effective net cost per station. Disadvantages include lack of flexibility in choosing affiliated stations, the limited number of stations on a network's roster, and the long lead times required to book time.

The Pros and Cons of Radio Advertising

The Pros

The principal advantages of radio are high reach and frequency, selectivity, and cost efficiency.

_____ **Reach and frequency.** Radio offers an excellent combination of reach and frequency. The average adult listens more than three hours a day, radio builds a large audience quickly, and a normal advertising schedule easily allows repeated impact on the listener.

_____ **Selectivity.** Specialized radio formats, with prescribed audiences and coverage areas, enable advertisers to select the market they want to reach: a specific sex, age group, ethnic or religious background, income group, employment category, educational level, or special interest.

_____ **Cost efficiency.** Radio offers its reach, frequency, and selectivity at one of the lowest costs per thousand, and radio production is inexpensive. National spots can be produced for about one-tenth the cost of a TV commercial. And local stations often produce local spots for free.

_____ **Other advantages.** Radio also offers timeliness, immediacy, local relevance, and creative flexibility.

The Cons

In spite of these advantages, radio has limitations: it's an aural medium only, its audience is highly segmented, the advertiser's commercials are short-lived and often only half-heard, and each ad must compete with the clutter of other advertising.

_____ **Limitations of sound.** Radio is heard but not seen, a drawback if the product must be seen to be understood. Some agencies think radio restricts their creative options.

_____ **Segmented audiences.** If a large number of radio stations compete for the same audience, advertisers who want to blanket the market have to buy multiple stations, which may not be cost-effective.

_____ **Short-lived and half-heard commercials.** Radio commercials are fleeting. They can't be kept like a newspaper or a magazine ad. Radio must compete with other activities for attention, and it doesn't always succeed.

_____ **Clutter.** Stations with the greatest appeal for advertisers have more commercials. Advertisers must produce a commercial that stands out from the rest.

Spot Radio

Spot radio affords national advertisers great flexibility in their choice of markets, stations, air time, and copy. They can put commercials on the air quickly—some stations require as little as 20 minutes' lead time, and advertisers can build local acceptance by using local personalities. Radio rep firms, like Katz Radio, represent a list of stations and sell spot time to national advertisers and agencies.

Local Radio

Local time denotes radio spots purchased by a local advertiser or agency. It involves the same procedure as national spots.

Radio advertising is either live or taped. Most radio stations use recorded shows with live news in between. Likewise, nearly all radio commercials are prerecorded to reduce costs and maintain broadcast quality.

Radio Terminology

Much radio terminology is the same as for other media, but some terms are peculiar to radio. The most common of these are the concepts of *dayparts, average quarter-hour audiences,* and *cumes* (cumulative audiences).

Dayparts

The radio day is divided into five dayparts:

6 AM–10 AM	Morning drive
10 AM–3 PM	Daytime
3 PM–7 PM	Afternoon (or evening) drive
7 PM–midnight	Nighttime
Midnight–6 AM	All night

Rating services measure audiences for only the first four dayparts because all-night listening is very limited and not highly competitive. Ad Lab 15–C describes the major radio audience rating services. Heaviest radio use occurs during **drive times**

The Reports That Make or Break Radio Stations

Media buyers use the data from three major audience rating services to determine which programs and stations will deliver the greatest number of target listeners.

Arbitron

The Arbitron rating service chooses a group of representative listeners in each of 257 cities and gives them a diary for tracking the time they spend listening to radio. Listeners return the diaries to Arbitron at the end of each week for tabulation, and Arbitron compiles the results into a quarterly report.

The Arbitron *Book,* available by subscription, reports the number of listeners to particular stations and shows their ages, sexes, and preferred listening times. Major clients are radio stations, but some ad agencies and radio sales reps also subscribe.

Birch Research

Birch Research uses phone surveys rather than diaries to obtain listener data. Interviewers talk to representative listeners in 130 major radio markets. Results are published monthly and summarized quarterly. Birch also offers Birchscan, a monthly computerized report.

RADAR

RADAR (Radio's All-Dimension Audience Research) rates network radio programs based on phone interviews with listeners. Each listener is called daily for a week and asked about listening habits from the day before until that moment. RADAR conducts research year-round and publishes results annually in *Radio Usage and Network Radio Audiences.* A number of specialized reports are also available.

Laboratory Applications

1. What are the advantages and the disadvantages of these radio audience measurement methods?

2. Which audience measurement method, diary or phone interview, is best? Why?

(6–10 AM and 3–7 PM) during the week (Monday through Friday), when many listeners are commuting to or from work or school.

Radio stations base their rates on the time of day the advertiser wants commercials aired, but the rates are negotiable according to supply and demand at any given time. RL 15–1 in the Reference Library shows standard rates for air time on KWOD-FM in Sacramento, California. For the lowest rate, an advertiser orders spots on a **run-of-station (ROS)** basis, similar to ROP in newspaper advertising. However, this leaves total control of spot placement up to the station. So most stations offer a **total audience plan (TAP)** package rate, which guarantees a certain percentage of spots in the better dayparts if the advertiser buys a total package of time.

Average Quarter-Hour Audience

Average quarter-hour audience (AQH persons) identifies the average number of people listening to a specific station for at least five minutes during a 15-minute period of any given daypart. For example, station KKDA in Dallas/Fort Worth, Texas, has an average quarter-hour listenership of 33,800, meaning that any day, during any 15-minute period between 3 and 7 PM, about 33,800 people ages 12 and older are tuned in (see RL 15–2 in the Reference Library).

The **average quarter-hour rating** expresses the AQH persons as a percentage of the population. Since KKDA is located in an area of 3,072,727 people, its average quarter-hour persons could be expressed as an average quarter-hour *rating* of 1.1:

$$\frac{\text{AQH persons}}{\text{Population}} \times 100 = \text{AQH rating}$$

$$\frac{33,800}{3,072,727} \times 100 = 1.1\%$$

The same idea can be expressed in terms of **average quarter-hour share:** the station's audience (AQH persons) expressed as a percentage of the total radio listening audience in the area. For example, if the total average quarter-hour persons for all stations is 676,000, then radio station KKDA's average quarter-hour *share* is 5:

$$\frac{\text{AQH persons of a station}}{\text{AQH persons of all stations}} \times 100 = \text{AQH share}$$

Because advertisers typically buy radio spots according to station format, rather than by specific program, the AQH is typically a strong indicator of the most opportune time to run ads. However, public service announcements, such as this humorous spot from the Utah Transit Authority, are frequently aired during dayparts with low listenership because the advertising time could otherwise be sold commercially for a profit. For this reason, some organizations who sponsor PSA's, like the Partnership for a Drug Free America, now often purchase radio time instead of relying on time donated by the station.

> "Lip Rings" :60
> SFX: Piano-driven public-service type music up and under.
> TEEN: (Unintelligible.) I'be-looind-ry-rife.
> FEMALE INTERPRETER: I've ruined my life.
> TEEN: (Frustrated.) I-ast-ry-budder-fo-a-wide-to-duh-mawl-atty-ted-no-bay-deeb.
> INTERPRETER: I asked my brother for a ride to the mall and he said, "No way, dweeb."
> TEEN: (Emotional.) I-fel-twapt.
> INTERPRETER: I felt trapped.
> TEEN: (More emotion.) So-o-poob-by-ireperense-I-perst-ry-riss-n-pur-dis-irenwing-tro-dem.
> INTERPRETER: So to prove my independence, I pierced my lips and put this iron ring through them.
> TEEN: (Losing it.) Naw-et-hurs-do-tauk.
> INTERPRETER: Now it hurts to talk.
> TEEN: Ad-by-rom-is-rakeen-be-wer-id-duh-ho-sumuh.
> INTERPRETER: And my mom is making me wear it the whole summer.
> TEEN: Fogus!
> INTERPRETER: Bogus.
> PSA-ISH ANNCR: Please, teenagers. Piercing body parts is no way to prove your independence. Buy a UTA Summer Youth Pass. It's a rippin' dog tag to wear around your neck. And a Summer Youth Pass gets you around without help from mom or your gomer brother.
> TEEN: (Under control again.) Sukin-denah-troo-a-sraw-boes.
> INTERPRETER: Sucking dinner through a straw blows.
> ANNCR: Kids seventeen and under get one for twenty-five dollars or two or more for twenty each. Call BUS-INFO for details.
> TEEN: (Emotional again.) Den dere's my navel wing.

$$\frac{33,800}{676,000} \times 100 = 5\%$$

The **gross rating points** of a radio schedule are the sum of all ratings points delivered by that schedule, or the *gross impressions* (see Chapter 8) expressed as a percentage of the population being measured:

$$\text{AQH rating} \times \text{Number of spots} = \text{GRPs}$$

$$1.1 \times 24 = 26.4$$

or

$$\frac{\text{Gross impressions}}{\text{Population}} \times 100 = \text{GRPs}$$

$$\frac{33,800 \times 24}{3,072,727} \times 100 = 26.4$$

Cume Estimates

The **cume persons** is the total number of *different* people who listen to a radio station for at least five minutes in a quarter-hour within a reported daypart (also called *unduplicated audience*).

In the example, our schedule on station KKDA generated 811,200 gross impressions, but that does not mean that 811,200 different people heard our commercials. Many people heard the commercials three, four, or five times. By measuring the cumulative number of different people who listened to KKDA, rating services provide the *reach potential* of our radio schedule, which in this case is 167,800.

The **cume rating** is the cume persons expressed as a percentage of the population being measured. For example,

$$\frac{167,800 \times 100}{3,072,727} = 5.5\%$$

The Seven Steps in Preparing a Radio Schedule

The procedure advertisers use to prepare radio schedules is similar to that used for TV schedules.

1. Identify stations with the greatest concentration (cume) of the advertiser's target audience by demographics (say, men and women ages 35 to 49).
2. Identify stations whose format typically offers the highest concentration of potential buyers.
3. Determine which time periods (dayparts) on those stations offer the most (average quarter-hour) potential buyers.
4. Using the stations' rate cards for guidance, construct a schedule with a strong mix of the best time periods. At this point, it is often wise to give the advertiser's media objectives to the station reps, suggest a possible budget for their station, and ask what they can provide for that budget. This gives the media buyer a starting point for analyzing costs and negotiating the buy.
5. Assess the proposed buy in terms of reach and frequency.
6. Determine the cost for each 1,000 target people each station delivers. The key word is *target*; the media buyer isn't interested in the station's total audience.
7. Negotiate and place the buy (see RL 15–3 in the Reference Library).

Chapter **Summary**

As a means of reaching the masses, no other medium today has the unique creative ability of television. Broadcast TV grew faster than any previous advertising medium because of the unique advantages it offered advertisers: mass coverage at efficient cost, impact, prestige, and social dominance.

Television is a powerful creative tool, but the medium still has many drawbacks, including high actual cost, limited selectivity, brevity, clutter, and susceptibility to zipping and zapping.

Broadcast TV dominance is being challenged by new electronic media, particularly cable. Cable offers the visual and aural appeal of TV at much lower cost and with greater flexibility. Cable audiences are highly fragmented, which helps advertisers target specific markets but is a drawback for those wanting to reach a mass audience.

TV advertising can be done at the national, regional, or local level and can take the form of program sponsorships, segment sponsorships, and spots of varying lengths, including program-length infomercials.

To determine which shows to buy, media buyers select the most efficient ones for their target audience. They compare the packages of each station, substitute stronger programs for less efficient ones, and negotiate prices to get the best buy. Media buyers must have a firm grasp of certain important terms: designated market areas (DMAs), TV households (TVHH), households using TV (HUT), program rating, share of audience, gross rating points, and cost per thousand.

Like TV, radio is a highly creative medium. Its greatest attribute is its ability to offer excellent reach and frequency to selective audiences at a very efficient price. Its drawbacks are the limitations of sound, segmented audiences, and its short-lived and half-heard commercials.

Radio stations are normally classified by the programming they offer and the audiences they serve. Radio stations may be AM or FM. They may use network or syndicated programs and follow any of a dozen or more popular formats. Advertisers purchase radio time in one of three forms: local, spot, or network. Buying radio time requires a basic understanding of radio terminology. The most common terms are dayparts, average quarter-hour, and cumulative audiences.

Important **Terms**

affidavit of performance, *491*

audience composition, *490*

audience share, *488*

avails, *490*

average quarter-hour audience (AQH persons), *498*

average quarter-hour rating, *498*

average quarter-hour share, *498*

barter syndication, *484*

broadcast TV, *474*

cable TV, *474*

cost per rating point (CPP), *491*

cost per thousand (CPM), *491*

cume persons, *499*

cume rating, *499*

daypart mix, *488*

designated market areas (DMAs), *488*

drive time, *497*

first-run syndication, *484*

gross rating points (GRPs), *490, 499*

households using TV (HUT), *488*

imagery transfer, *494*

infomercial, *485*

interconnect, *483*

inventory, *484*

local time, *497*

makegoods, *491*

networks, *481*

off-network syndication, *484*

participation basis, *482*

preemption rate, *491*

prime time, *488*

program-length advertisement (PLA), *485*

Review **Questions**

1. What are the advantages of broadcast TV advertising for a product like milk?
2. What steps can advertisers take to overcome zipping and zapping?
3. Why has advertising on network TV become less desirable in recent years?
4. In what ways is cable TV's selectivity a strength? A drawback?
5. What are the various ways to buy broadcast television time?
6. How can TV be best used in an integrated marketing communications program?

7. How can radio be best used in an IMC program?
8. What is the format of the radio station you listen to most? How would you describe the demographics of its target audience?
9. What is the difference between average quarter-hour and cume audiences? Which is better?
10. What is the significance of dayparts in radio and TV advertising? What are the best dayparts for each?

Exploring the **Internet**

The Internet exercises for Chapter 15 address the following areas related to the chapter: TV organizations (Exercise 1) and broadcast media tools (Exercise 2).

1. TV Organizations

   The size of the television industry and the advertising dollars that are spent within it are extraordinary. Many TV-related organizations were formed to help service the industry. Discover a little more about the nature and scope of the television industry as you peruse the following Web sites. Be sure to answer the questions below.

   - Broadcast Education Association (BEA) **www.beaweb.org**
   - Cable Television Administration & Marketing Society (CTAM) **www.ctam.com**
   - Cable World **www.mediacentral.com/cableworld**
   - CableTVad.com **www.cabletvad.com**
   - National Association of Broadcasters (NAB) **www.nab.org**
   a. Who is the intended audience(s) of the site?
   b. What is the site's purpose? Does it succeed? Why?
   c. What is the organization's purpose?
   d. What benefit does the organization provide individual members/subscribers? The overall advertising and television and cable communities?

2. Broadcast Media Tools

   Broadcast advertising reports and audience studies are critical to the development and implementation of effective media strategy. As with print media, advertisers have a set of "staple" companies and reports they regularly use to help plan and implement their broadcast media buys. Visit the following syndicated and independent broadcast media companies' Web sites and answer the questions that follow:

   - Arbitron **www.arbitron.com**
   - Bureau of Broadcast Measurement (BBM) **www.bbm.ca**
   - Cabletelevision Advertising Bureau (CAB) **www.cabletvadbureau.com**
   - Nielsen Media Research **www.nielsenmedia.com**
   - Radio Advertising Bureau **www.rab.com/rabinfo/rabinfo.html**
   - Radio Marketing Bureau (RMB) **www.rmb.ca**
   - Television Bureau of Advertising **www.tvb.org**
   - Television Bureau of Canada (TVB) **www.tvb.ca**
   - TV RunDown **www.tvrundown.com**
   a. What type(s) of broadcast media information does the company specialize in and what specific services, products, or publications does the company offer?
   b. What industries/companies would be best suited to utilize the company's media resources?
   c. Does the company represent syndicated or independent research?
   d. How useful do you feel the company is for gathering broadcast media information? Why?

Chapter Sixteen

Using Digital Interactive Media and Direct Mail

Objective To present the important factors advertisers weigh when considering the new digital interactive media and direct mail. Each medium has its own characteristics, advantages, and drawbacks. Advertisers must be able to compare their merits and understand the most cost-effective ways to buy advertising time.

After studying this chapter, you will be able to:

- Discuss the opportunities and challenges presented by the new digital interactive media.

- Explain the evolution of interactive media.

- Debate the pros and cons of the Internet as an advertising medium.

- Discuss the Net's audience and the challenges involved in measuring it.

- Explain the best ways to get access to the Net.

- Define the various kinds of Internet advertising.

- Explain how Internet advertising is sold and how much it costs.

- Enumerate the various types of direct-mail advertising.

- Assess which kinds of mailing lists are best.

Like many children, Chad Steelberg had a mind full of curiosity that could never be sated. At the tender age of eight, Chad began taking apart light switches to try to figure out a better way to design them. When he was ten, he started a diary to record his assorted schematics, business plans, and ideas of new ways to do old things. And by the seventh grade, young Steelberg had written a computer program for posting e-mail to bulletin boards. "I sold it for $3,000, which I promptly went out and spent on a 20-megabyte hard drive," Chad recalls. • Much has changed since those days. Today, for less than $3,000 he could get a 20-*gigabyte* hard drive. Chad is now 26. Along with his younger brother Ryan, he heads the multimillion-dollar company IMGIS, the technological leader in the management and targeting of Internet advertising. • Iron Mountain Global Information Systems (IMGIS) has made its mark on the electronic superhighway by innovating the infrastructure for managing the placement of ads on the World Wide Web. Using AdForce, IMGIS's proprietary software program, advertisers can target their Web-page ads to spe-

cific types of users. When a consumer clicks onto a Web site that uses AdForce, the computer reaches into IMGIS data banks and pulls out an appropriate ad based on what the server reads about the computer making the ad request. The facilitating software combines various sources of demographic and psychographic information about the user, then displays an ad according to selected criteria. Thus, Web publishers can charge a premium for their ad space and marketers benefit by more precise targeting. • IMGIS also acts as a complete online advertising manager. With point-and-click ease, clients can build and customize their media plans and schedules according to AdForce's targeting parameters. Once that's done, clients can receive real-time reports on the entire campaign at any time of the day or night. • The technological and creative savvy of the brothers Steelberg shone in their early business dealings. The duo pioneered the first advertising contracts for the WWW search engine Excite. But their first real payoff came when they smartly bought up the advertising rights to selected keywords on various search engines. In just a few short months, marketers from around the globe began demanding the licensing rights to these same words so they could add them to their own advertising arsenals, and the few thousand dollars the Steelbergs had invested in the keywords suddenly turned into many thousands. • Now, with clients like GeoCities, WebChat, and 24/7 Media, IMGIS finds itself at the management helm of over 750 million WWW ads that are served to consumers each month. And the brothers have yet to take a course in computer programming.[1] •

The New Digital Interactive Media

Today, we are all participating in the beginning of a new media revolution, brought on by incredible achievements in communications technology. We're talking, of course, about **digital interactive media** and the *information superhighway.* Chad and Ryan Steelberg are just two of the many pioneers that have turned the information highway—the Internet—into the fastest-growing medium in history.

To understand the dramatic effect this is having on marketing and advertising, imagine for a moment what life was like before radio and TV. Back then, if you had a product to sell, you made your appeal to the consumer directly, often on her front door step. If she didn't like what you were peddling, she slammed the door in your face. She was in complete control of the selling environment.[2] Then along came radio and, 30 years later, TV. Now mass marketers had a captive audience, people who would willingly pay for an evening's entertainment at home by simply sitting through the commercials. Advertisers prospered—and so did consumers, as they participated in a rapidly growing standard of living.

But now the sands are shifting across the advertising landscape. The remote control was the first step toward convenient interactivity, and it had a major impact on commercial viewership. Instead of watching commercials, people could now use the station breaks to channel surf, effectively slamming the door in the sales rep's face.

Right on its heels came the widespread distribution of cable TV. In less than a decade, the network TV audience plunged from 90 percent to 60 percent. SLAM!

Then, of course, came the VCR. People could now record shows and watch them later at their convenience, zipping through the commercials. Or they could just rent a movie and skip the commercials altogether. SLAM!

Keith Reinhard, the chair and CEO of DDB Needham Worldwide, acknowledged the sound of all the slamming doors in a 1994 speech: "Our consumer society is undergoing a fundamental power shift from the marketer to the consumer." Reinhard pointed out that consumers are becoming "active controllers" of the messages they see and hear.[3] His message to the assembled agency people was to "adapt [to the new media environment] or die," because there are plenty of other people waiting in the wings to help marketers reach and satisfy these new, in-control consumers.

Meanwhile, technology keeps on going and going and going. It's already given us the personal computer, the cellular phone, the Internet and the World Wide Web, fiberoptics, satellite communications, CD-ROM, and the software to make it all simple enough for virtually everybody to use. And on the launching pad, about to blast off, is interactive TV. With growing consumer acceptance of all this wizardry, prices have plummeted, making most of it affordable to the masses.

These are not just advertising media. In many cases, they represent completely new ways of living and doing business. The fastest-growing advertising medium in history is also opening the door to

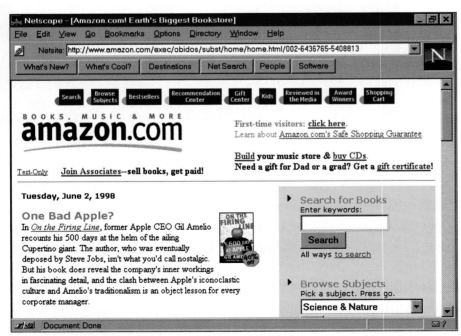

Digital interactive media brings us full-circle back to when the consumer controlled the selling environment before the advent of mass media. Sites like online bookseller Amazon.com offer interactivity with the consumer, to a degree unmatched by any other advertising medium. Amazon.com not only serves as an Internet-based mail order retailer, but also provides customers with extensive search capabilities, book reviews, and book suggestions tailored to each specific user.

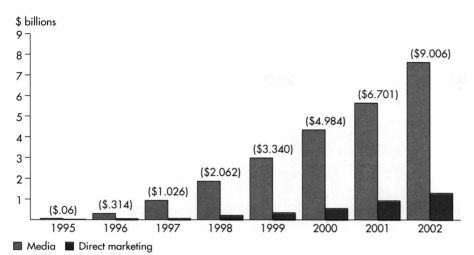

$ billions

■ Media   ■ Direct marketing

Exhibit 16–1
Total online advertising and direct marketing revenues (1995–2002).

electronic commerce. From the convenience of your own personal computer you can bank online, buy a car or a beautiful piece of art, trade on the stock exchange, book your airline reservations, order concert tickets, or buy a complete new wardrobe from your favorite retailer. The Internet has also changed the way we send mail, eliminating the need for an overseas airmail stamp if you want to communicate with your brother in Bonn. You can do library research in the comfort of your den, or you can start your own home-based business and market your products worldwide.

The new media are truly revolutionary in their effect on our daily lives, and it's a revolution for marketers too. While the new media accounted for only about 2 percent of total revenue for direct marketers in 1996, the potential is incredibly huge.[4] In fact, Forrester Research predicts that Internet commerce will grow from $8 billion in 1997 to $327 billion in 2002.[5] Moreover, by offering true interactivity, the new media enable businesses and other organizations to develop and nurture relationships with their customers and other stakeholders, in a way never before available, on a global scale at very efficient costs (see Exhibit 16–1).

The new interactive media include the Internet and commercial online services, CD-ROM catalogs and magazines, stand-alone kiosks, and interactive TV. Most prominent of all is the Internet, so that is what we will focus on in this chapter. We need to understand what the medium is, how it's organized, how people get to it, and how advertisers buy it and use it in their marketing plans. Following that discussion, we'll examine some of the other new media briefly and then look at the most prominent form of *addressable media:* direct mail.

The **Internet** as a Medium

The Internet has come a long way from its simple roots. While some people assume it was just recently created by today's commercial online providers, like America Online (AOL) and CompuServe, in fact the technological infrastructure of the Internet has been around for some 30 years.

The Evolution of the Internet

The **Internet** actually began in the early 1960s as a twinkle in the eye of the U.S. Department of Defense, which saw it as a means of supercomputer communication for researchers and military facilities across the country. Until its commercial explosion in the 90s, the Internet remained a relatively obscure network of linked computers used mostly by academics, military researchers, and scientists around the world to send and receive electronic mail, transfer files, and find or retrieve information from databases.

Commercial Online Services

During the 80s, a number of commercial online services began their operations by capitalizing on the phenomenon of local *electronic bulletin board services (BBSs)* that computer wonks used in increasing numbers. These new online providers managed to create, in effect, nationwide BBSs that delivered e-mail between subscribers, supplied catalogs for online shopping, provided chat rooms for discussion, organized interactive game playing, and offered software downloading capabilities,

continued on page 510

As the fastest growing medium in history, the Internet offers incredible opportunities for a wide range of people in both business and advertising. For advertisers, there is a whole new world of potential customers out there, waiting to be engaged.

Without question, what we are witnessing is a new creative revolution that will continue well into the new millenium.

- *In this portfolio, study the ads and see if you can express how the creative approach has changed from advertising in previous media arenas. Evaluate how each site capitalizes on the truly interactive nature of the medium or how it could better incorporate interactivity with the audience. Try to determine how the Web site fits into the company's overall strategy and how the site either complements or can perhaps replace a more traditional media approach. Could the company benefit by incorporating additional features into the Web site, such as the ability to purchase products or services online, providing games or entertainment, offering additional tips or advice, or providing content in other languages?*

Hot Web Sites

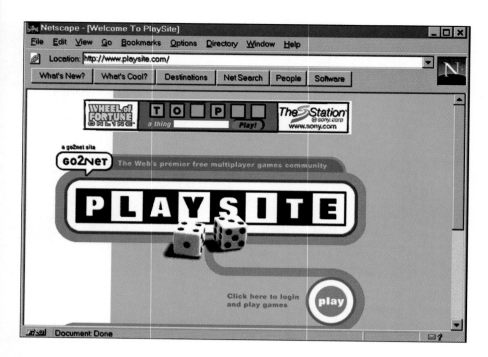

Although most online companies originally charged a subscription fee to the public, most have now abandoned this approach due to the competition from advertising-supported sites. Playsite (www.playsite.com) is just one such example, providing WWW users with free recreational diversion through familiar and original games like chess and tangleword. Playsite is just one of several advertising-supported services offered by Go2Net, one of the Internet's premiere interactive technology providers.

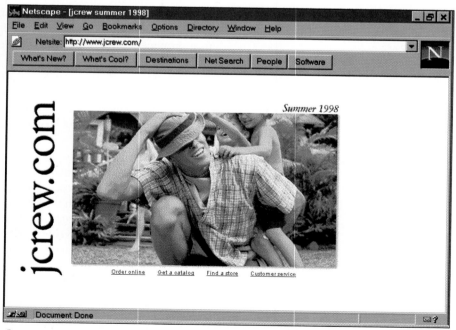

Consumer commerce is a rapidly growing segment of the online industry, particularly as consumers gain confidence in the security of Internet credit transactions. Increasingly, retailers are establishing Web storefronts, where consumers may purchase goods that are typically available through department stores or mail-order catalogs. The mail-order giant J. Crew (www.jcrew.com) is just one such example.

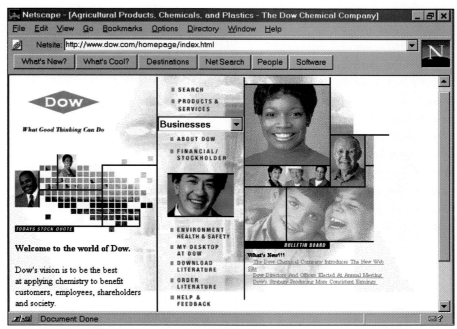

Corporate Web pages can also be considered a form of corporate advertising. These sites provide the public, businesses, and other stakeholders with information about a company while simultaneously reflecting a certain image or philosophy of the company, as shown in this Web site for Dow Chemical (www.dow.com). Corporate Web pages are often used for recruitment purposes, too.

Both print and broadcast news media have taken advantage of digital technologies as a means for coverage expansion. Virtually every major newspaper, magazine, and television network publishes online editions of its organization's news, much of which is increasingly exclusive to the Internet. Many daily newspapers, like the New York Times (www.nytimes.com), update their pages each day to remain abreast with the latest news and sometimes even update hourly as news breaks over the wire services.

Some Web sites are content publishers of information based entirely online, with no print or broadcast counterpart. "Beatrice's Guide" (*www.bguide.com*) is just one such example, providing lifestyle articles dedicated to women's issues. Online periodicals are perhaps even more diverse in content than print publications because of the relatively low cost of publishing and distribution.

Interactivity takes many different forms on the World Wide Web. United Parcel Service (*www.ups.com*) capitalized on the latest technology by allowing its customers to check up on their own shipment orders directly from the business office or at home. The Web site also serves as a form of corporate and consumer advertising for UPS.

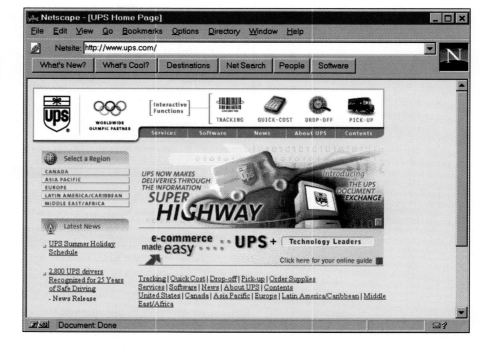

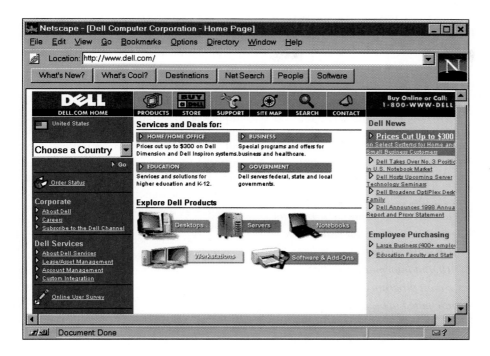

Dell Computers (www.dell.com) may well be a barometer and testament to the future of online commerce. Each month the personal computermaker sells over $1 million of computer goods and services from its online store in transactions with large corporate accounts and consumers. The company provides online troubleshooting help for its customers, as well as software upgrades available for download. On the corporate side, businesses like Dell are now developing private infrastructures with clients that allow for rapid and large-scale transactions over secure communications lines.

MSNBC (www.msnbc.com) began as an online news partnership between Microsoft and NBC. The Web site provides original news coverage and works in association with the cable news channel of the same name.

```
┌─────────────────────────────────────────────────────────────────────┐
│   keri_johnson@mcgrawhill.com,5/19/98  7:47  PM,GeoCities  Home      1 │
│             To:  keri_johnson@mcgrawhill.com                          │
│           From:  mhruby@cyberconnect.com                              │
│        Subject:  GeoCities Home                                       │
│                                                                       │
│   This is a screen shot of the GeoCities Home page.  I was oringally to send │
│   it to  Keri Johnson, but the email address I was given, kept bouncing. │
│                                                                       │
│   Thanks,                                                             │
│   ac                                                                  │
│                                                                       │
│   Attachment converted: Hard Disk:GeoHome3.gif (GIFf/8BIM) (0000D9C4) │
│              *                                                        │
│   A  l  l  e  n      C  o  m  p  t  o  n                              │
│         Design Director                                               │
│                                                                       │
│     acompton@geocities.com                                            │
└─────────────────────────────────────────────────────────────────────┘
```

Computers and the Internet are rapidly evolving to meet the demands of a growing number of technology-oriented consumers. While the Internet has not reached the consumer penetration levels of television or radio, it is the single fastest-growing medium in the history of mass communications. Digital information, online commerce, and global communications through e-mail programs like Eudora all compose the medium of the Internet. These are anticipated to become the mainstays of our technology-driven economy.

continued from page 505

along with a host of other features. People could even advertise in the CompuServe or AOL classifieds just like in the newspaper.

Now, anyone with a modem-equipped PC could join the several million members of CompuServe, Prodigy, and America Online for a basic fee of around $10 a month plus a charge for any time spent online beyond the basic monthly allowance. One drawback, though, was that subscribers were limited to sharing e-mail and information with users of the same service provider.

Still, it didn't take long for the country's largest advertisers to understand the potential of being able to communicate with this lucrative market of computer users via a new medium. General Motors, Chrysler, MCI, 1-800-FLOWERS, *Business Week* magazine, and Lands' End jumped on the bandwagon. Soon thousands of product marketers and business services were using the online services as a medium of both advertising and commerce.[6]

Commercial applications of the Internet itself were not as well received as online services until the development of graphical browsers. The Internet offered a tremendous wealth of information; if AOL and CompuServe were nuggets of gold, the Internet was the mother lode. But the Internet wasn't as easy to use as the online services. First of all, to even get access to the Internet, people had to find an **Internet service provider** and sign on directly by getting a *SLIP/PPP account* or a *shell account.* Once they were online, there was no simple way to navigate around the Internet unless they possessed a lot of technical know-how. The first form of the World Wide Web, for instance, was entirely text-based; it had no graphics, and the initial ads resembled simple print classifieds.

When the first commercially available **Web browser** software that accommodated graphics, Netscape Navigator, was released in 1994, the Internet drew even more public attention. People could now simply point and click on icons and pictures to find their way around in cyberspace. This made the Internet almost as user-friendly as the online services.

The World Wide Web

The **World Wide Web (WWW)** is composed of an enormous amount of information found mostly in the form of **home pages.** These can best be likened to book covers or gateways, since they act as starting points to additional information. These pages are created by millions of online users and businesses, with content varying from culinary tips to sports commentary to corporate and business information. Early Internet sites on the Web typically consisted of a home page that resembled a poorly designed brochure cover, with perhaps some limited information on subsequent *Web pages* about the company and its products. These were, in effect, storefronts.

Once business (and the media) sensed the lucrative potential of the Internet, they bombarded the public with messages about how the technology would revolutionize global communication. This became a self-fulfilling prophecy, and the gold rush of the Information Age began. CompuServe, AOL, and Prodigy, with

The World Wide Web, where people come to "browse" or "surf the Internet" is the best-known feature of cyberspace. Although the name is often used interchangeably with the Internet, the World Wide Web is actually just one facet of the medium: the graphical and multimedia interface used to view Web sites like that of the Discovery Channel (www.discovery.com).

The development of the search engine greatly facilitated the explosion of the Internet because it provided a centralized source of information that made the medium accessible to the mainstream user. Without search engines like Yahoo! (www.yahoo.com), the World Wide Web would not have captured such a significant consumer audience, and the Internet may have developed for use only by technology-based businesses.

their multimillion-customer databases, rushed to marry their services to the Internet to provide communication to users worldwide. The Web exploded from about 50 sites in 1993 to over 70,000 sites in 1995, with 3 to 5 million Web pages.[7]

Internet Search Engines

Imagine trying to find a book in the Library of Congress without the aid of a card catalog. It would be next to impossible. That's the problem people faced in their initial efforts to find information on the World Wide Web. And that's what created the demand for another software program: the search engine. In rapid succession, a number of programs with catchy names like Yahoo!, Excite, and InfoSeek emerged to act as **search engines** for the cyberspace traveler. The user could simply type in a name, a word, or a phrase, and the search engine would scour the Net for relevant information and Web site addresses.

Because of their usefulness, many millions of people pass through the major search engines each month, and marketers quickly realized the advertising potential of these and other high-traffic Internet sites. Actual Internet advertising began in earnest in October 1994, when the first *banner ads*—little billboards of various sizes that pop up when a visitor lands on a particular Web page—were sold by *Hotwired* (the online edition of *Wired* magazine). Soon, other companies followed suit, buying banner advertising on other popular Web sites.

Today, Web surfers can browse everything from university libraries to the Louvre museum in Paris. Along the way, they can click on an ad banner and visit the commercial sites set up by IBM, AT&T, the city of Berlin, Ford, Merrill Lynch, JCPenney, and Mitsubishi, to mention just a few. By 1995, there were already over 71,000 officially registered commercial "domains," the Internet equivalent of storefront addresses. By 1997, that number had jumped to 1.3 million.[8]

Since the online services and the search engines are the gateways to all these sites, they also attract the greatest number of "hits" (visits), as well as the

Exhibit 16–2
The Web's greatest hits (June 1998).

Publisher	Number of unique visitors (in 000s)*
Yahoo/Four11	30,431
AOL.com	23,184
Excite Network	18,934
Netscape	18,470
Microsoft	18,018

*Age 12 and older in the United States.
Source: Relevant Knowledge, 1998
(www.relevantknowledge.com). Copyright Relevant
Knowledge, 1998.

Exhibit 16–3
Online products mix in 2000.

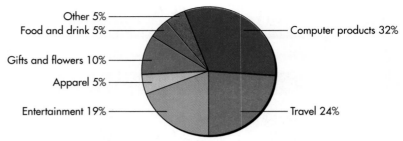

Note: The mix of products sold over the Internet, shown here as percentages of total sales, won't change much through 2000. Computer products, which total $2.1 billion, travel ($1.58 billion), and entertainment ($1.3 billion) will account for the lion's share.

greatest amount of advertising. In October 1997, the top Web site by number of hits was Yahoo! (see Exhibit 16–2).[9]

The Internet's growth has been exponential. Over 50 million U.S. adults accessed the Internet in 1997, a 46 percent increase over the previous year.[10] Some 10 million children are also on the Internet, making them the fastest-growing segment of new Internet users. By 2002, the Internet is expected to reach some 400 million people (including 45 million children) through 42,000 different computer networks.[11]

Businesses ranging from your local florist to global manufacturers are using the Internet to develop multimedia menus that include bulletin boards, interesting or entertaining information, product data, and even games. Many of them, like E*Trade and Amazon.com, conduct all their commerce right on the Web (see Exhibit 16–3). Users move from page to page and site to site depending on what they are looking for. In other words, the user is in control. The consumer chooses what screens to watch, what banners to click, and what to ignore.[12]

That means marketers have to provide information that is useful and relevant. They have to keep updating it to get repeat visits. And a little entertainment with a

Push technology is the Internet's closest resemblance to television, with the major exception that users must actively request the information. Users set up push technology software, like PointCast (www.pointcast.com) to automatically search for and retrieve the most current information on news, sports, entertainment, or hundreds of other subjects of interest. The service and software are free to the consumer with just one caveat—they must also download advertisements onto their computer along with the requested information.

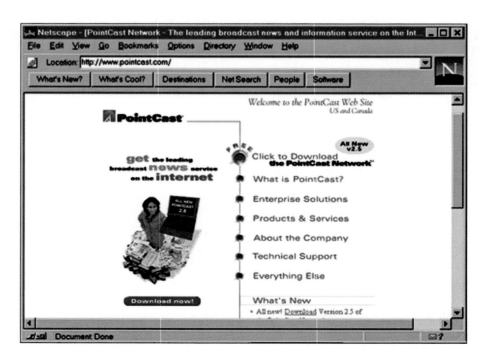

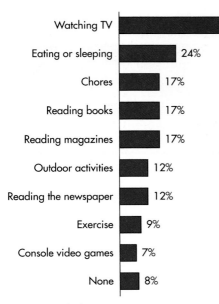

Exhibit 16–4

Which activities do people take time from to spend on the computer?

Note: Multiple responses accepted.

few freebies tossed in doesn't hurt. Even Ragú (www.ragu.com) spaghetti sauce has a site that offers Italian phrases, recipes, and a sweepstakes.[13] Learning how to use this new medium challenges the creativity of the whole advertising community. And with the amount of daily updating that is required to keep Web sites current, the opportunity for growth and specialization is great.

The latest development in online advertising, **push technology,** now brings advertising directly to the user. Instead of having to visit a Web site, the user can program the PC to automatically retrieve information from the Internet. The user pays nothing for the service because advertising often accompanies this information, allowing for more intrusive ads similar to those on TV.

The Internet Audience

The last several years have seen a steady migration of people who used to spend time in front of the TV moving over to the computer. In a 1997 Forrester Research study, researchers asked PC users which activities they were giving up most to spend more time on their computers. Over three-quarters said they were watching less TV; eating or sleeping was second at 24 percent (see Exhibit 16–4). Interestingly, this coincides with other studies that showed the online audience had doubled in just 12 months and that a million fewer U.S. households were watching prime-time TV during Nielsen's February 1997 ratings sweeps than in the same period a year earlier (see Exhibit 16–5).[14]

Who Uses the Net

Media budgets tend to be very pragmatic. As audiences migrate, so do the media dollars. As a result, media spending on Internet advertising is growing exponentially. And one of the great draws of the Internet from the marketer's point of view is its demographics. Many of the people who cruise the Internet are still well-educated, upscale males who use the Net for business purposes. However, a 1997 CommerceNet/Nielsen survey of Internet demographics found that women now represent some 42 percent of the online population. Also, the average age of Web users has been increasing steadily, to 34.9 in 1997.[15]

In 1996, a survey by the Media Futures Program of SRI Consulting revealed that more than 65 percent of Internet users have household incomes of $50,000 or more, compared with 35 percent of the U.S. population as a whole. Moreover, the *average* household income of Internet users is $60,800. The same study also showed that more than 75 percent of Internet users have attended college (as opposed to 46 percent of the total U.S. population). To marketers this is a very attractive audience, especially for business-to-business advertisers (see Exhibit 16–6).

However, this group is quickly broadening and will expand the medium's advertising opportunities to an even wider range of marketers. The growing number of women on the Net is pushing many advertisers (such as makers of packaged goods) to consider the medium seriously. Numerous Web sites now catering exclusively to women's personal interests

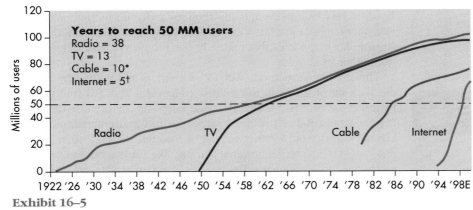

Exhibit 16–5

Adoption curves for various media—the Internet is the fastest-growing communications medium in history.

E = Morgan Stanley Technology Research Estimate.
*The launch of HBO in 1976 was used to estimate the beginning of cable as an entertainment/advertising medium.
†Morgan Stanley Technology Research Estimate.

Exhibit 16–6
Advertising expenditures by market ($ millions).

	1994	1996	1997	1998	2002	Compound Annual Growth 1994–97	1997–2002
Total	$11.0	$144.0	$275.0	$546.0	$3,480.0	189.3%	66.1%
Consumer	3.5	50.7	99.6	201.9	1,330.6	202.5	67.9
Business-to-business	7.5	93.3	175.4	344.1	2,149.4	182.7	65.1

include iVillage (www.ivillage.com), Ladies' Home Journal Online (www.lhj.com), and Hearst New Media's HomeArts Network (see Exhibit 16–7).

How People Access the Net

Currently, there are four effective means people use to get online. By far, the most used method is via dial-up modem through an Internet service provider. All you need is a modem-equipped desktop computer (PC or Mac). You simply contact one of the hundreds of ISP companies that advertise regularly in local newspapers and computer publications to get an e-mail account and access to the Internet for a small monthly fee, usually under $20. Similarly, you can join AOL, CompuServe, or Prodigy, which also act as ISPs for a similar monthly fee. With this method, you use the computer's modem to dial up the local ISP number and type in a password, and the connection to the Internet is made.

The second method, called **cable-modem,** is quickly growing in popularity. This system offers enormously high-speed data transfer direct to the computer. It's available only from cable TV companies that offer one of the new cable-modem

Exhibit 16–7
Online activities.

What do you do when you go online?*		
Activity	1997	1996
Gather news or information	87.8%	82.0%
Send e-mail	83.2	80.5
Conduct research	80.5	69.1
Surf various sites	75.3	66.9
Play games	33.7	23.8
Participate in chats	30.8	25.3
Post to bulletin boards	30.0	39.3
Shop	17.8	14.9

What do you do on a company's homepage?**	
Activity	1997
Look for product information	90.5%
Look for company information	87.8
Shop for products	34.5
Receive pricing, discounts, coupons, etc.	31.7
Enter contests	18.9

Notes: Respondents could choose more than one answer.
*Based on 584 U.S. residents who have been online in the past six months.
**Based on 419 U.S. online users who have visited a company's home page.

services, such as Roadrunner or @Home. No phone lines are involved, and you don't have to dial up anyone. Once the coaxial cable is plugged into an ethernet card inside your computer, you're online. However, start-up costs for a cable-modem connection are substantially more expensive than for dial-up modem, and its availability is still limited.

Another method, called DirecPC, is satellite based. Developed by Hughes Electronics, the same company that pioneered the DirecTV satellite system, **DirecPC** offers even faster downloading than cable. But it is very expensive and still requires a dial-up modem and separate phone line to *send* data out of your computer. This method is most suitable for companies that regularly need to download extensive files from other locations.

The last viable method, **WebTV®** system, is still quite new but has the backing of giants in the industry: Microsoft and TCI (the nation's largest cable company). This system is based on the premise that some people would rather use the Internet for fun and entertainment, not business, and would rather receive it through their TV than a computer.[16] WebTV Internet terminal is much like cable-modem except the receiving and viewing device used is the family TV and an analog phone line instead of a computer. It includes a set-top box and remote, which sell for around $99–$199, and offers constant connection to the Internet, even while the TV is playing. This is the newest turn in the search for interactive TV technology and is really aimed at those people who don't want the cost and complexity of having a computer at home but would still like to have Internet access. Once the equipment is purchased, the cost of this service is simply a small monthly fee.

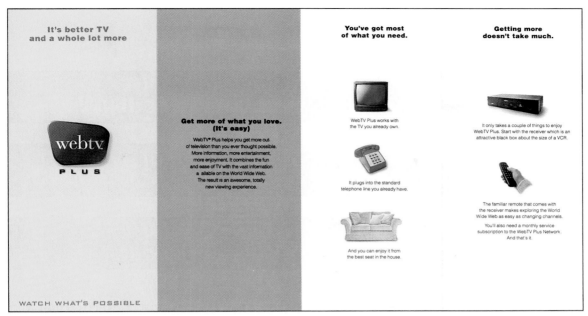

Critics contend that the Internet will never be as pervasive as television because many people either don't need to purchase an expensive computer or have no desire to use one. However, developers of WebTV (www.webtv.com) are attempting to incorporate the easy-to-use and interactive aspects of the World Wide Web directly into a typical television. The goal is, of course, to bring the Internet into mainstream use.

Types of Internet Advertising

Ads on the Internet can take a variety of forms, and as the Net matures, the number of forms continues to expand. Most advertising opportunities today can be classified as Web sites, banners, buttons, sponsorships, interstitials, or classifieds. We'll discuss each briefly.

Web Sites

Some companies view their whole Web site as an ad. And in some ways it is. But in truth the Web site is more than an ad—it's an alternative "storefront," a location where customers, prospects, and other stakeholders can come to find out more about the company, its products and services, and what it stands for. Some companies use their Web site like an extended brochure to promote their goods and services; others act as information and entertainment publishers and try to create a cool environment that people will visit often; still others treat their Web site as an online catalog store, conducting business right on the Net. Thus, except when being used like a brochure, the Web site is not really an ad; it's an "ad-dress" (see Exhibit 16–8).

Web sites typically consist of a *home page* and an indefinite number of subsequent pages that users can visit for further information. A **Web page** does not refer to an $8\frac{1}{2}$ by 11-inch page. It refers to a single HTML (*hypertext markup language*) file, which, when viewed with a browser, may actually be several screens long. A large Web site may have hundreds of these pages of information. This means the site contains hundreds of different documents of various lengths (from one to 10 or more screens), each probably covering a different subject.[17]

Banners

The most basic form of Web advertising is the ad banner. A **banner** is a little billboard that spreads across the top or bottom of the Web page. When users click their mouse pointer on the banner, it sends them to the advertiser's site or a buffer page. The standard

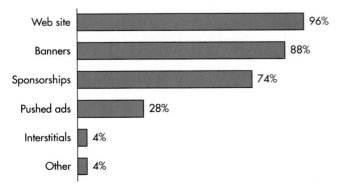

Exhibit 16–8
What form of Internet advertising do the top 50 advertisers plan to use in the next two years?

Banners are by far the advertising medium of choice on the Internet, second perhaps only to the business home page. Although the effectiveness of the banner is still untested and underresearched, most advertisers accept the branding opportunities it can provide. This sequence of banners from usa.net is typical of this form of advertising.

size for an ad banner is 468 pixels (picture elements) wide by 60 pixels high. That means that on a standard $8\frac{1}{2}$ by 11-inch page, the banner would measure just over $4\frac{1}{2}$ inches wide by one-half inch high.

The cost of banners fluctuates wildly, from free to over $15,000 per month. It depends entirely on the number and type of visitors the site regularly receives.

Buttons

Similar to banners are **buttons,** small versions of the banner that often look like an icon and usually provide a link to an advertiser's home page. Since buttons take up less space than banners, they also cost less.

Today, a host of new software technologies, like Shockwave, Java, Acrobat, and Enliven, have greatly enhanced the once-static banner and button ads. Full motion and animation, for example, are now commonplace. The Excite and Webcrawler search engines also offer audio features, available to advertisers at additional cost, that accompany a click on the banner. Warner Bros., in fact, sells three-second slots for some of its Web audio programming. In other words, the banner and button are becoming more interactive. A banner ad from John Hancock Mutual Life Insurance, for instance, lets users input their children's ages to find out how much money they need to invest each month for a college education.[18] We can anticipate seeing more audio and animation integrated into these ads as improving technology accommodates them.[19]

Sponsorships

A form of advertising on the Internet that is growing in popularity is the **sponsorship** of Web pages. Corporations sponsor entire sections of a publisher's Web page or sponsor single events for a limited period of time, usually calculated in months. In exchange for sponsorship support, companies are given extensive recognition on the site. Sometimes this is done by integrating the sponsor's brand with the publisher's content, as a sort of advertorial, or with banners and buttons on the page.

IBM has exclusively sponsored the Super Bowl Web page since 1996, at an estimated cost of $1 million for each event. Other forms of sponsorships have included Web serials, sites devoted to women's issues, contests, and giveaways. Levi's Dockers brand sponsored *HotWired*'s Dream Jobs Web site, with a gauge that measures a job's dress requirements. The dress code usually centers on khakis as a reminder that Dockers can be worn at almost any dream job.[20] Because of their high cost, sponsorships are most common on sites with high traffic, where the opportunity for exposure is greatest.

Shockwave Brings Internet Ads Alive

While banners and icons provide at least branding opportunities for Internet advertisers, the real power of the medium lies in full-motion animation and its ability to truly interact with the user. Technology developments now allow advertisers to move beyond static banners or banners that scroll a sequence of copy and images for the user. Macromedia, the leader in WWW animation with its popular Shockwave software, gives creatives ammunition to fulfill the computer's much-touted role as a genuine, interactive multimedia provider.

Today's most sophisticated banner and interstitial ads include Shockwave in the computer code to provide animation beyond simple static images. These animations can either be video or illustrations, and often tie in music, sounds, and voice-overs, pro-viding ads that could possibly become the Internet's equivalent of the 30-second TV commercial. Shockwave also facilitates user-interactivity with the ads. Hewlett-Packard, for example, created the first truly interactive ad by incorporating a playable version of the famous video game Pong directly into the banner. Advertisers anticipate that such interactivity, for which the creative possibilities are endless, will become a driving force in the effectiveness of online ads.

Unfortunately, as with most online advertising, technological limitations still prevent Shockwave and similar programs from realizing their full potential. Slow download times are still a major barrier to online advertising, particularly for users who are too impatient to wait for the larger, Shockwave-driven banners and interstitials to download. But with the passing of only a little more time, we can anticipate that this problem will be overcome.

Interstitials

A new form of Net advertising is the **interstitial** (or *intermercial*). This is an animated ad that pops up on the screen while the computer downloads a Web site that the user has clicked on. In 1997, interstitials were so new that they accounted for only 1 or 2 percent of Internet ads. However, a study by entertainment software company Berkeley Systems found that interstitial ads are twice as effective at generating higher brand awareness as online banners.[21] So we may see them grow in popularity if actual practice shows them to be as effective as the research indicates. Jupiter Communications predicts that by 2001, advertisers looking for more intrusive and powerful online ad models will spend 25 percent of their online ad budgets on interstitials, 25 percent on sponsorships, and 50 percent on banner ads.[22]

Classified Ads

Another growing area for Internet advertisers, and an excellent opportunity for local advertisers, is the plethora of **classified ad Web sites.** Many of these offer *free* classified advertising opportunities because they are typically supported by ad banners of other advertisers. In style, the classifieds are very similar to what we are all familiar with from newspapers. You can search for homes, cars, jobs, computer equipment, business opportunities, and so on. Moreover, the search can be narrowed to your city or expanded nationwide. Many of these sites are sponsored by the search engines themselves or by local newspapers around the country. To date, most sites promise more volume than they deliver; most still have relatively few listings in each category. However, this is still a new area and can be expected to grow substantially in the near future. For now, the lack of volume actually gives the local antique dealer or auto showroom a better shot at being seen.

Problems with the Internet as an Advertising Medium

The Internet, like any medium, has its drawbacks. It is not a mass medium in the traditional sense, and it may never offer mass-media efficiency (see the Checklist: Pros and Cons of Internet Advertising). Some marketers may decide it's too complex, too cumbersome, too cluttered, or not worth the time and effort. It is not controlled by any single entity, so security (for credit-card purchases over the Net) is still a concern. It has all the problems of any new, untried medium. The technology for running television-quality video is still not in place, and the long-term cost of full participation in the Internet is anybody's guess. The final drawback is also one of the Net's greatest appeals: it is the most democratic of media—anybody can get on it and do or say anything.[23]

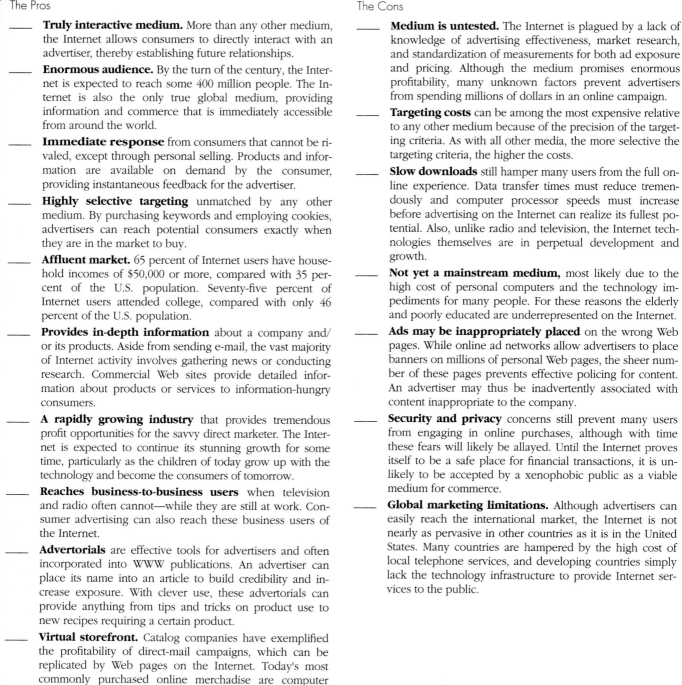

Checklist

The Pros and Cons of Internet Advertising

The Pros

_____ **Truly interactive medium.** More than any other medium, the Internet allows consumers to directly interact with an advertiser, thereby establishing future relationships.

_____ **Enormous audience.** By the turn of the century, the Internet is expected to reach some 400 million people. The Internet is also the only true global medium, providing information and commerce that is immediately accessible from around the world.

_____ **Immediate response** from consumers that cannot be rivaled, except through personal selling. Products and information are available on demand by the consumer, providing instantaneous feedback for the advertiser.

_____ **Highly selective targeting** unmatched by any other medium. By purchasing keywords and employing cookies, advertisers can reach potential consumers exactly when they are in the market to buy.

_____ **Affluent market.** 65 percent of Internet users have household incomes of $50,000 or more, compared with 35 percent of the U.S. population. Seventy-five percent of Internet users attended college, compared with only 46 percent of the U.S. population.

_____ **Provides in-depth information** about a company and/ or its products. Aside from sending e-mail, the vast majority of Internet activity involves gathering news or conducting research. Commercial Web sites provide detailed information about products or services to information-hungry consumers.

_____ **A rapidly growing industry** that provides tremendous profit opportunities for the savvy direct marketer. The Internet is expected to continue its stunning growth for some time, particularly as the children of today grow up with the technology and become the consumers of tomorrow.

_____ **Reaches business-to-business users** when television and radio often cannot—while they are still at work. Consumer advertising can also reach these business users of the Internet.

_____ **Advertorials** are effective tools for advertisers and often incorporated into WWW publications. An advertiser can place its name into an article to build credibility and increase exposure. With clever use, these advertorials can provide anything from tips and tricks on product use to new recipes requiring a certain product.

_____ **Virtual storefront.** Catalog companies have exemplified the profitability of direct-mail campaigns, which can be replicated by Web pages on the Internet. Today's most commonly purchased online merchadise are computer products, travel arrangements, and entertainment-related products.

The Cons

_____ **Medium is untested.** The Internet is plagued by a lack of knowledge of advertising effectiveness, market research, and standardization of measurements for both ad exposure and pricing. Although the medium promises enormous profitability, many unknown factors prevent advertisers from spending millions of dollars in an online campaign.

_____ **Targeting costs** can be among the most expensive relative to any other medium because of the precision of the targeting criteria. As with all other media, the more selective the targeting criteria, the higher the costs.

_____ **Slow downloads** still hamper many users from the full online experience. Data transfer times must reduce tremendously and computer processor speeds must increase before advertising on the Internet can realize its fullest potential. Also, unlike radio and television, the Internet technologies themselves are in perpetual development and growth.

_____ **Not yet a mainstream medium,** most likely due to the high cost of personal computers and the technology impediments for many people. For these reasons the elderly and poorly educated are underrepresented on the Internet.

_____ **Ads may be inappropriately placed** on the wrong Web pages. While online ad networks allow advertisers to place banners on millions of personal Web pages, the sheer number of these pages prevents effective policing for content. An advertiser may thus be inadvertently associated with content inappropriate to the company.

_____ **Security and privacy** concerns still prevent many users from engaging in online purchases, although with time these fears will likely be allayed. Until the Internet proves itself to be a safe place for financial transactions, it is unlikely to be accepted by a xenophobic public as a viable medium for commerce.

_____ **Global marketing limitations.** Although advertisers can easily reach the international market, the Internet is not nearly as pervasive in other countries as it is in the United States. Many countries are hampered by the high cost of local telephone services, and developing countries simply lack the technology infrastructure to provide Internet services to the public.

Using the Internet in IMC As we discussed in Chapter 7, one of the keys to successfully developing an integrated marketing communications program is to promote purposeful dialog between the company and its stakeholders. That is what interactivity really means. And that is where the Internet offers its greatest potential.

For the first time, customers and other stakeholders can truly respond to a company's media communications in real time, using the same channel for feedback that the company used for promotion. This means that even if a customer finds herself accidentally at the company's Web site and, if something there strikes her fancy, she can commence a dialog (relationship) with the company immediately. Of course, this also means that, if the Web site triggers her memory of a less-than-satisfactory experience with the company, she can use the same mechanism for complaining. But that's actually good, because a customer that complains usually cares. And a complaint gives the company the opportunity to correct the situation and set things right. It also gives the company information on how to improve. Sophisticated marketers cherish complaints.

While all of this is well and good, it also brings up a new problem for marketers today. In the good old days of simple mass-media advertising, manufacturers placed their ads on network TV and went on about their business. The retailers took care of customers, so the manufacturers didn't really have to be concerned about them. In the new age of integrated marketing communications, that is no longer the case. Yes, the retailer is still there. But Mrs. Consumer doesn't want to talk to the retailer. She's a pretty sophisticated person. She knows who makes the product and if she's got a complaint that's who she wants to talk to. So it's not good enough for companies to put a pretty Web site up on the Internet and then walk away from it. It has to be staffed—daily—and it must be kept up to date—daily. If you log on the Internet Sunday morning and check your local newspaper's Web site for yesterday's baseball scores, you don't want to read about how your team got whipped Friday night. You already read about that yesterday. While this may seem obvious, the fact is that these problems still occur regularly and they defeat the whole purpose of having an interactive location for your customers to visit. Realizing this, companies are now finally beginning to staff up. But this is very expensive—often requiring companies to double or triple their Internet budget with no increase in advertising exposure. So the decision to use the Internet for integration is a big one and cannot be taken lightly.

Measuring the Internet
Audience

When marketers and the media first began trumpeting the marvels of the Internet, they quickly noted the potentially vast size of its population. Today it's already up to 51 million people in the United States alone. Around the world, hundreds of millions of people use the Internet, and only citizens of the developing countries are left without access.

While most large companies have been caught by the allure of the Internet, advertisers are still nervous about spending millions of dollars in this largely unregulated and uncharted medium. Research firms like Media Metrix (www.mediametrix.com) specialize in gathering and testing Internet market data, from user demographics to advertisement effectiveness.

Exhibit 16–10

An example of a rate card for WWW banner ads from the search engine Metacrawler.

The "exclusive keywords" category provides advertisers with the opportunity to have their ad appear whenever someone conducts a search using a particular word. "Front page promotions" is for banners on the home page of the Metacrawler site. "Search results pages" provides rates for banners that appear after a search has been conducted. And "targeting filters" provides advertisers with selectivity criteria for their ads. These rates for Metacrawler are based on a minimum of 200,000 impressions per month, and calculated according to CPM. In this example, gross CPM reflects the cost to the advertiser, which includes the agency commission, and net CPM is the price the agency pays Metacrawler.

MetaCrawler Keyword Packages:
Advertisers may select an industry-specific package of keywords such as travel, sports, business, or software.

Exclusive keywords

Gross CPM	Net CPM	Impressions	
$47.06	$40	200,000	$ 8,000

MetaCrawler front page promotions*

Gross CPM	Net CPM	Impressions	
$23.53	$20	200,000	$ 4,000
$17.65	$15	1 million	$15,000

*Exclusivity pricing is available on a case-by-case basis.

MetaCrawler search results pages (run-of-site)

Gross CPM	Net CPM	Impressions	
$17.65	$15	500,000	$ 7,500
$16.41	$13.95	1 million	$13,950

MetaCrawler targeting filters*

	Gross CPM	Net CPM
One filter	$35.29	$30 CPM
Two filters	$43.52	$37 CPM

1. Operating system (Mac, Unix, Win95).
2. Browser type (Netscape, IE).

*Available on run-of-site purchases only.

Continuity discount

	2–3 months	4–6 months	7–11 months	12+ months
Program duration				
Discount from base rate	5%	7%	10%	15%

increase as the buyer targets a more selective audience. Costs are tiered according to thousands, hundreds of thousands, or even millions of page requests per month (see Exhibit 16–10).

Another augmentation to the general banner purchase is the **keyword** purchase, available on major search engines. Advertisers may buy specific keywords that bring up their ads when a user's search request contains these words. Keywords may be purchased individually or in packages that factor in the information categories and subcategories of a search engine site. As we mentioned at the beginning of this chapter, some keyword entrepreneurs, like the Steelbergs, purchased certain keywords from the search engines early in the game. They were later able to license these words to third parties at a substantial profit.

Some publishers charge their clients according to **click-throughs**—that is, when a user actually clicks on an ad banner to visit the advertiser's home page. Although the CPM cost is considerably higher, this method is still unpopular with most publishers because it may expose the user to an advertiser's banner message without the publisher being able to charge for the service. Some publishers, like Interactive Imaginations, have developed hybrid pricing that combines low-cost page request rates with click-through rates.

A relatively new ad form on the Internet comes from push technology. *Push* is generally defined as information that's delivered to Web users via their PCs over personal broadcast services or e-mail. It's basically a targeted Web medium that delivers news, information, and marketers' messages directly to consumers who have signed up for it.[29] In 1997, approximately 25 percent of Web users said they also used some push service like Pointcast Network or BackWeb. Push ads are fully animated and may even appear as screen savers when the user isn't active on the computer. Typically, the ads cost from $12,000 to $15,000 per month, or they may be set by CPM. PointCast, one of the pioneers of push technology, guarantees click-throughs on banners purchased in monthly packages of 5,000, at $2 per click-through.

For advertisers involved in e-commerce, some publishers charge a commission percentage of the transaction cost. For example, a site devoted to music reviews may have a banner link to an online music retailer. When consumers buy music from the retailer, the site publisher receives a percentage of the sale for showing the banner.

The Cost of Targeting

The very selective nature of the Internet can, for additional cost, be combined with the tracking technology described earlier. This makes for a very focused campaign. Companies like IMGIS work behind the scenes to meet the advertiser's CPM guarantees by using software that directs specific ads to a highly selective audience. Because IMGIS technology "tags" users, it can build a consumer profile and show those ads that are likely to be of the greatest interest to that specific Web user.

But contrary to popular belief, consumer targeting on the Internet is very cost intensive. While it is true that millions of people do indeed scour the Net each day, it is still difficult to find and reach the specific consumers that you want. Thus, prices for precision WWW targeting can eclipse even those of direct mail.

Stretching Out the Dollars

One of the problems facing most Net marketers is how to get enough reach from their Internet advertising. The enormous proportion of users who utilize the major search engines make these sites attractive for advertisers. However, Web browsers surf millions of other Web pages each day, many of which are potential sites for effective ads. However, contacting all these sites and negotiating advertising contracts on each is a nearly impossible task.

For this reason, most advertisers work through **ad networks** that act as brokers for advertisers and Web sites. Ad networks pool hundreds or even thousands of Web pages together and facilitate advertising across these pages. The advantage is that this allows advertisers to gain maximum exposure by covering even the smaller sites. The drawback is that such advertising is more difficult to monitor. The advertiser must watch each site for traffic and content, which creates problems when trying to calculate costs. A few Web masters have been known to try to cheat the system by artificially increasing the number of page requests. So, as with any new medium, caution is always the watchword.

The **Global** Impact of the Internet

The United States overwhelmingly outspends the rest of the world in Internet advertising. U.S. Web ad expenditures in 1996 topped $139 million, while Japan came in second at a meager $1.8 million and the United Kingdom third at $985,000 (see Exhibit 16–11).[30]

Currently, the United States enjoys fairly heavy international Web traffic, caused mostly by a lack of telephone and Internet infrastructure and Web sites overseas. In Europe, online penetration was less than 4 percent in 1996. International Web sites also tend to remain primitive in design and function compared to U.S. competitors, which are strongly consumer-oriented. Furthermore, the international appeal of U.S. brands, especially companies like Coca-Cola and Disney, is strong.[31]

But as the Internet increasingly becomes a household word, the content of Web sites for local businesses overseas will also grow. Already the search engine Yahoo! has staked an early claim by servicing Japan, Germany, France, Norway, Sweden, Denmark, and Korea in their native languages. And while today most

Exhibit 16–11

Leading non-U.S. online ad markets in 1996 ($ thousands).

Japan	$1,799
United Kingdom	985
Germany	982
Netherlands	964
Australia/New Zealand	765
Scandinavia	148

The Internet's largest potential is perhaps its ability to instantaneously create global commerce. Although currency exchanges can still be problematic, global consumer commerce is becoming a common occurrence. Because of the enormous economic potential, many of the large search engines now provide their services in a variety of languages, including French, German, Swedish, Korean, and Japanese, as shown in this example from Excite (jp.excite.com).

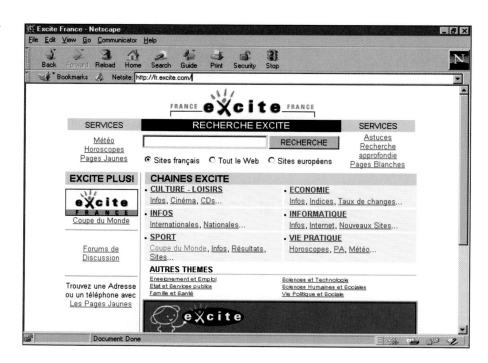

international Web surfers are proficient in English, this can be expected to change. As local online markets grow, so will the number of non-English-speaking users.

With the growth of an overseas online market, we can anticipate that American companies will try harder to cater to the native population. Although Europe is not expected to reach 1996 U.S. spending levels until the year 2000, it will spend approximately $1.2 billion in online advertising by 2002. These are not numbers that marketers can ignore (see Exhibit 16–12).[32]

Expanding their horizons to encompass the whole world will be the key to businesses' success in the 21st century.

Other New **Media**   In addition to the Internet, advertisers now also use other new media vehicles, such as CD-ROMS, kiosks, and interactive TV. While they are not major media forms, they do warrant some brief discussion (see Exhibit 16–13).

CD-ROM Catalogs and Magazines   Virtually every new personal computer today comes equipped with **CD-ROM** (compact disk-read only memory) capabilities, and the CD is the fastest growing segment of the software industry. The benefit of this technology is storage space; a high concentration of data, combined with full-motion video and high-quality audio, can be stored on one disk.

Exhibit 16–12

Total estimated world online ad revenue, 1997–2000 ($ thousands).

Year	United States	Non-United States	Total
1997	1,101,146	24,919	1,126,065
1998	2,206,578	138,179	2,344,757
1999	3,610,318	350,272	3,960,590
2000	5,041,647	703,614	5,745,261

Exhibit 16–13

What interactive media have you used for marketing purposes?

World Wide Web	87.4%
Online service	40.2%
CD-ROM	35.9%
Kiosk	17.3%
Interactive phone	16.3%

Source: Reprinted with permission from the March 10, 1997 issue of Advertising Age. Copyright, Crain Communications, Inc. 1997.

The stand-alone digital kiosk provides businesses and municipal organizations with a new technology for communication and advertising. Kiosks today are used for a variety of purposes, ranging from the sale of train tickets to distribution of coupons to information about tourist attractions.

Marketers like the CD-ROM format because of its high quality and versatility. In fact, CompuServe, which already publishes a monthly magazine for its customers, is enhancing its online electronic mall with sound and video and mailing it as a bimonthly CD magazine. A number of its advertisers are participating. One of them, *Chef's Catalog,* included video clips about the creation of cookware and the proper way to carve a turkey.[33] The CD-ROM is also being used as a sound and video catalog that can be connected via modem to its source and used to make transactions online.[34]

Kiosks

The immense storage capacity of the CD makes it an ideal medium for saving the detailed information housed in stand-alone sales and information **kiosks.** In fact, kiosks were used for voter education during the 1994 national elections in South Africa. The project used video messages from 19 political parties, plus text, graphics, and sound—recorded in 11 languages—to detail information for the largely illiterate electorate on why, where, and how to vote. The kiosks made the information available 24 hours a day even in remote areas. Over a three-month period, the information in the 30 kiosks was regularly updated, and more than a million people used them. The experiment was so successful that the South African government put two of the kiosks in museums to be part of the country's history.[35]

Kiosks are used around the globe for many purposes. The Singapore Postal Service has an award-winning, computerized vending kiosk that allows customers to pay utility bills; buy postcards, stamps, and envelopes; and get government information. The architectural firm Szabo International in Irvine, California, uses an elegant custom-built kiosk in its offices for impressive presentations of the firm's capabilities. BVR Group, the firm that developed Szabo's kiosk, won a gold medal for its creativity.[36]

Interactive TV Imagine you're watching "Friends," and a spot for State Farm Insurance appears. You remember you're not happy with your current insurance carrier. You pick up your remote control and click it on a box in the corner of the screen: "For more information." A menu appears. You click on "Auto insurance," and a multimedia presentation begins. At various prompts, you click your remote to get more information. At the end you request the location of a State Farm agent. The directions appear from a PC printer attached to your TV. Then it's back to "Friends."[37]

That's **interactive TV (ITV).** It already exists in test form in New Jersey, Florida, Montreal, and London. Other interactive TV tests are being conducted on a smaller scale in cooperative efforts by Sears and Viacom Cable with the help of AT&T. Most experts believe it will be several years before one system emerges as preeminent and grows to any significant reach. Interactive Network, in San Jose, California, successfully test-marketed an interactive service that lets viewers play along with their TV for prizes. The multichannel service allows TV viewers to interact with live sports, game shows, and other programming. Advertisers such as Chrysler, American Airlines, and Sprint are experimenting with it. The company expects the service to be incorporated into the national rollout of ITV services by the cable and telco operators.[38] But for the general category of interactive TV, the issues are still costs, equipment, and technology. So, for the immediate future, most interactive systems will continue to center on the PC.

Direct-Mail Advertising: The Addressable Medium

Applied Communications, Inc. (ACI) was known for its sophisticated banking and retail computer systems, but few people knew about ASTech, its new Applied Communications Support and Technical Ser-

Is Privacy Going Public?

With just a scrap of information, such as a name or phone number, a marketer can access hundreds of databanks for demographic data on individuals: their credit history, income, marital status, number of children, and more. The decrease in cost and complexity of equipment combine with the widespread availability of data to make information-based marketing feasible for companies that never considered it before.

Even consumers benefit from this movement. Companies can offer more personalized service. And marketers are better able to target the right customers, reducing irrelevant junk mail.

However, some marketers are using personal information without restraint or sensitivity to the consumer—and consumers feel violated. A 1993 survey by the Louis Harris Co. found that 83 percent of Americans were concerned about threats to their personal privacy, 55 percent worried that consumer information would be less protected by the year 2000, and 68 percent believed the present uses of computers threaten their privacy.

Consumers accept marketing in general—it's the loss of control over personal information that concerns them. There are two fundamental issues: insensitivity and security.

Consumers don't like to receive mail and phone calls from strangers armed with highly personal information such as their income, where they traveled last year, the names and ages of their children, or the phone numbers they call most frequently. Advertisers that use this data insensitively risk damaging their relationship with customers. An insurance agent, for example, irritated many prospective customers when he mailed postcards with the amount of their mortgage openly listed on the card. As Patricia Faley, vice president of public responsibility and chair of the Task Force on Privacy at American Express, states, "Clearly, the information we have on our customers is one of our greatest assets. If our customers don't trust us, we lose the ability to use that tremendous asset."

Security is another worry for consumers. "If I go in the hospital, I don't want that going into some database that gives intelligence to a credit-card company," says Laurie Petersen, editor-in-chief of the *Cowles Report on Database Marketing.*

The list rental business is so profitable that many list owners are willing to overlook how the names are used. But they should be concerned, for consumer discomfort can easily turn into legislation. In Germany, it is against the law for marketers to phone or fax a person without prior permission. Britain has also passed a code of advertising practice that covers the accumulation and use of information. Many in the industry say it is time to self-regulate, before the government steps in.

But who should be responsible for protecting privacy in direct marketing? And what ethical guidelines are effective?

One possible answer is the Direct Marketing Association (DMA), which offers mail and phone preference services to consumers who want their names removed from solicitation lists. Unfortunately, their usefulness is limited. The DMA's membership includes about 3,500 companies of the 10 million that operate in the United States, and only 60 or 70 percent of those members actually use the preference services.

The DMA believes it is the marketer's duty to act responsibly. "We came to the conclusion that the ultimate categorical pro-

vices division. ASTech needed an awareness campaign for its on-site computer technical support service. So ACI turned to Webster Design, a marketing communications design firm in Omaha, Nebraska, that had specialists in **creative dimensional direct mailing (CDDM).**

"We witnessed Webster Design's great success using dimensional mailings," states Ken Simpson, ASTech's vice president, "and believed their expertise could do the same for us."

Dave Webster, president of Webster Design and the creative director/designer for the company, says, "We started doing creative dimensional direct mailing a dozen years ago, with the idea that the most difficult task of any mailing is to stay out of the trash can long enough to deliver a message." An additional plus, he feels, is that CDDM is generally very cost-effective for mailings in quantities under 500. Webster reports that he won his first dimensional project for ACI by being lowest bidder against agencies recommending traditional brochure mailings. And he delivered a 100-to-1 return on ACI's investment.

ASTech's corporate communications department and Webster decided to send ACI's customer base a series of mailings with the sales goal of securing contracts from at least 5 percent of the list. They estimated this would bring a 2-to-1 return on investment (ROI). Following several creative meetings, Webster's designers and copywriters decided on a four-phase program using a baseball theme: "Cover all the bases." This would be a foil for promoting ASTech's ability to provide the "pinch-hitting" services its clients needed.

ASTech's primary obstacle was that potential customers already employed trained personnel to handle the day-to-day responsibilities of keeping large computer systems up and running. The Webster Design team had to convey that smart managers know when to call for extra help, the pinch-hitters. A number of factors combined to make baseball the home-run analogy: the potential customers' demo-gram is an in-house suppression system whereby Jane Doe tells the individual company, 'Send me your mailings, but don't rent my name to others,'" says James Crowe, assistant to the DMA's vice president for consumer affairs. *Plow & Hearth,* which sells products for country living, has maintained an in-house mail preference service since 1992. An explanation of the list rental process and how to remove one's name from catalog mailing and rental lists is on the mail-order envelope; *Plow & Hearth* estimates that about 3 percent of customers have requested that their names be removed.

The British Code of Advertising Practice successfully protected all the parties involved in the privacy issue. In 1990, nearly half (44 percent) of letters received by the British Registrar of Data Protection were complaints about direct mail. After the code, letters dropped to only 4 percent—and most of these were just asking for information. The code's provisions include telling customers how survey data will be used, allowing consumers to opt out of mailings, safeguarding against improper handling, releasing to consumers the source of lists from direct-mail companies, and requiring consent from individuals before sensitive personal information is used.

Dr. Alan Westin, a leading authority on privacy issues, says, "The right focus for the privacy effort is to move direct marketing into a choice or consumer-controlled environment. If I'm right, the marketplace will show that more consensual, pinpointed marketing is better than psychographics-based marketing without consent."

Most businesses continue to depend on traditional methods of direct marketing, arguing that it's impossible to provide as much

protection as privacy advocates demand. But when eight out of every ten Americans are concerned about threats to their personal privacy, marketers have to stop and listen—before the choice is taken out of their hands.

Questions

1. The example of the insurance agent who placed mortgage amounts on postcards broke no laws: mortgages are listed in government records and available to the public. And post office personnel are, theoretically, the only people to see the mortgages written on the postcards. Should the individuals in the target market really be so concerned? Explain your answer.

2. The British government established a code that controlled complaints about direct mail. Can industry self-regulation work in the United States, or should the government follow Britain's lead? Discuss your reasoning.

Sources: Karl Dentino, "Taking Privacy into Our Own Hands," *Direct Marketing,* September 1994, pp. 38–42; William Dunn, "Membership Has Its Privileges," *Marketing Tools,* November/December 1994, pp. 42–43; Peter F. Eder, "Privacy on Parade," *Futurist,* July/August 1994, pp. 38–42; Denison Hatch, "Privacy: How Much Data Do We Really Need?" *Target Marketing,* February 1994, pp. 35–40; Ed McLean, "Privacy Big Issue for Mailers," *Advertising Age,* July 4, 1994, p. 14; Claudia Montague, "Privacy," *Marketing Tools,* November/December 1994, pp. 41–52; Claudia Montague, "Common Hazards, Commonsense Advice," *Marketing Tools,* November/December 1994, pp. 48–49; Claudia Montague, "It's Not a Big Deal at All,'" *Marketing Tools,* November/December 1994, pp. 44–45; Keith Wardell, "Meeting Privacy Concerns Head On," *Catalog Age,* August 1994, p. 107.

Webster Design created this dimensional direct-mail campaign for Applied Communications, Inc., to help introduce the firm's new ASTech division. The awareness campaign theme of "Cover all the bases" conveyed the message that smart managers need to know when to call for pinch-hitters to help out. The campaign hit a grand slam home run, with a 20-to-1 return on ASTech's investment.

graphics, the time of year, ASTech's team structure, and the overall mainstream understanding of baseball jargon.

The program was divided into four mailings over a three-month period in the spring and summer:

Phase One: A custom-designed package containing an official league baseball, imprinted with the ACI logo. The package also served as a file folder for a brochure portraying ASTech's services, a business reply card, and an incentive offer for those who responded in a given time frame.

Phase Two: A set of baseball cards that popped up when the mailer was opened. The detachable cards featured the actual ASTech team members in baseball uniforms with the ASTech logo, as well as their "stats."

Phase Three: An ACI baseball cap in a custom-designed, wedge-shaped box bearing the message "Cover your head with ASTech," and the implication that ASTech could be useful when other areas needed covering.

Phase Four: The incentive of a genuine, official Louisville Slugger bat for those who signed contracts.

The promotion was an immediate winner. It generated a total response of 59 percent via the business reply card and phone requests and, according to a telephone survey, an 87 percent awareness rate. Sales attributed to the campaign totaled $1.2 million for a 20-to-1 return on ASTech's investment. Webster Design's sluggers had hit a grand slam.

All forms of advertising sent directly to prospects through a government or private mail delivery service are called **direct-mail advertising.** In dollars spent, direct mail is the third-ranked advertising medium today, surpassed only by newspapers and TV.

Both large and small companies use direct mail. New firms usually use direct mail as their first advertising medium. The reason is clear: of all media, direct-mail advertising offers the straightest line to the desired customer.

Growth of Direct Mail

Direct methods of advertising and selling have grown astronomically in the last decade. Robert Coen of McCann-Erickson estimates that national advertisers spent $36 billion on direct mail in 1997, a 6 percent increase over the previous year; that represents a full third of total advertising expenditures. Further, Ad Audit Services predicts that advertiser spending on direct mail will more than double to $80 billion over the next five years.[39]

Direct mail is successful for two reasons. First, it meets the needs of today's fast lifestyles. Families have less time, so shopping by mail is convenient. Second, it's the most effective medium for generating immediate results.

Marketers are expanding their profits by stuffing monthly credit-card statements with tempting mail-order offers. Today's leading mail-order products include insurance and financial services, department-store merchandise, and the other products and services listed in Exhibit 16–14.

Types of Direct-Mail Advertising

Direct-mail advertising comes in a variety of formats, from handwritten postcards to dimensional mailings like ASTech's. The message can be one sentence or dozens of pages. And within each format—from tiny coupon to thick catalog or box—the creative options are infinite. In addition to the dimensional direct mail category are the following:

Sales letters, the most common direct-mail format, are often mailed with brochures, price lists, or reply cards and envelopes. **Postcards** are used to announce sales, offer discounts, or generate customer traffic. National postal services regulate formats and dimensions. Some advertisers use a double postcard, enabling them to send both an advertising message and a perforated reply card. A recipient who wants the product or service tears off the reply card and mails it back to the advertiser. To encourage response, some advertisers use **business reply mail** so the recipient can respond without paying postage. The advertiser needs a special first-class postal permit and must print the number on the face of the return card or envelope. On receiving a response, the advertiser pays postage plus a handling fee of a few cents. "Postage-free" incentives usually increase response rates.

Folders and **brochures** are usually printed in multiple colors with photos or other illustrations on good paper stock that reproduces printed images well. **Broad-**

Exhibit 16–14

Top 10 mail-order product categories.

Rank	Category	Sales ($ billions)
1	Insurance/financial	$13.3
2	Department stores	11.7
3	General merchandise	9.5
4	Apparel	8.6
5	Major catalog retailers	6.2
6	Magazines	5.8
7	Unclassified merchandise	4.2
8	Sporting goods	3.6
9	Electronic goods	2.7
10	Collectibles	2.1

sides are larger than folders and are sometimes used as window displays or wall posters in stores. They fold to a compact size to fit in a mailbag.

Self-mailers are any form of direct mail that can travel without an envelope. Usually folded and secured by a staple or seal, they have special blank spaces for the prospect's name and address to be written, stenciled, or labeled.

Statement stuffers are ads enclosed in monthly customer statements from department stores, banks, oil companies, and the like. To order, customers write in their credit-card number and sign the reply card.

House organs are publications produced by associations or business organizations—for example, stockholder reports, newsletters, consumer magazines, and dealer publications.

Catalogs are reference books that list, describe, and often picture the products sold by a manufacturer, wholesaler, jobber, or retailer. With more high-income families shopping at home, specialized catalogs are becoming very popular. Some mail-order companies prosper with specialized approaches, like outdoor clothing and equipment (L.L. Bean, Lands' End), electronic gadgets (Sharper Image), or gourmet foods (Balducci's).

Catalogs are big business. In 1995, the catalog industry generated more than $60 billion in revenues. And the industry's success was not limited to the United States. In Japan, for instance, major American catalogs like L.L. Bean, Land's End, Patagonia, and Eddie Bauer have made substantial inroads into that country's $20 billion catalog market. L.L. Bean, in fact, reported that its $200 million of sales in Japan accounted for 80 percent of its international sales.[40] And JCPenney, the leading catalog marketer, alone sold over $3.5 billion worth of merchandise.[41]

Using Direct Mail in the Media Mix

Direct mail is an efficient, effective, and economical medium for sales and business promotion (see the Checklist of The Pros and Cons of Direct-Mail Advertising). That's why it's used by a wide variety of companies, charity and service organizations, and individuals. Direct mail can increase the effectiveness of ads in other media. Publishers Clearinghouse uses TV spots to alert viewers to the impending arrival of its direct-mail sweepstakes promotions.

Direct mail has two main drawbacks: cost and the "junk mail" image, both of which are almost inescapable. No other medium (except personal selling and consumer targeting on the Internet) has such a high cost per thousand. For this reason, many small advertisers participate in cooperative mailings with companies like ADVO, which serves most major U.S. cities. ADVO mails an envelope containing a coupon for each participating company to targeted zip codes.

Some large advertisers don't send unsolicited mail. To locate prospects, they use other direct-response media. Then they use direct mail to respond to inquiries. They save money by mailing only to qualified prospects, and by sending higher-quality materials, they build their image and improve their chances of establishing a worthwhile relationship.

Buying Direct-Mail Advertising

Direct-mail advertising has three basic costs: list acquisition, creative production, and distribution.

Acquiring Direct-Mail Lists

The heart of any direct-mail program is the mailing list. Each list actually defines a market segment. Direct-mail advertisers use three types of lists: *house, mail-response,* and *compiled.*

House lists   The company's relational database of current, recent, and long-past customers as well as future prospects comprises the **house list** for direct-mail programs. Since customers are its most important asset, every company should focus sufficient resources on developing a rich database of customer and

Doubleday Book Club

Doubleday List Marketing

Location ID: 10 DCLS 564   Mid 019884-000
Member: D.M.A.
Participant D.M.A. Mail Preference Service.
Doubleday Mailing Lists.
501 Franklin Ave., Garden City, NY 11530. Phone 516-
873-4477. Fax: 516-873-4774.
**Specific list selections are located in each
appropriate classification in their normal alphabetical
sequence.**
1. **PERSONNEL**
   Manager, List Marketing—Diane Silverman.
   Assistant Manager, List Mktg.—Liz Maletta.
   List Mktg. Coordinator—Linda Jackson.
   Broker and/or Authorized Agent
   All recognized brokers.
2. **DESCRIPTION**
   Doubleday Book Club members.
   ZIP Coded in numerical sequence 100%.
3. **LIST SOURCE**
   Direct mail and space ads.
4. **QUANTITY AND RENTAL RATES**
   Rec'd Mar. 8, 1990.

	Total Number	Price per/M
Members	900,000	75.00
Hotline	479,000	80.00
Completers (1989-90)	433,000	40.00
Age-coded names	2,130,000	80.00

   Selections: enrollment date, 5.00/M extra; dollar select,
   6.00/M extra; Mr./Mrs./Miss/Ms., sex, 3.00/M extra;
   state, SCF, ZIP tape, 4.00/M extra.
5. **COMMISSION, CREDIT POLICY**
   20% commission to all recognized brokers. Payments
   due 30 days after billing.
6. **METHOD OF ADDRESSING**
   4/5-up Cheshire labels. 4-up pressure sensitive labels,
   5.00/M extra. Magnetic tape (9T 1600/6250 BPI).
7. **DELIVERY SCHEDULE**
   Ten working days.
8. **RESTRICTIONS**
   Sample mailing piece required for approval.
9. **TEST ARRANGEMENT**
   Minimum 10,000.
11. **MAINTENANCE**
    Cleaned and updated quarterly.

Exhibit 16–15

Typical listing from *Direct Mail List Rates and Data (Consumer Lists),* published by Standard Rate & Data Service.

prospect information and profiles. There are several ways a company can build its own house list, from offering credit plans to sending useful information to exchanging names with other businesses with similar customer profiles.

Consumer product companies like General Electric gather customer data by enclosing an owner registration form with their products. On the mail-in form, purchasers give their name, address, phone number, birth date, occupation, income range, credit-card preferences, home ownership status, and number of children. They also indicate their hobbies and interests (such as golf, foreign travel, photography, or bowling). Companies use this information for their own mailings and sell it to other direct-mail advertisers.

Mail-response lists   The advertiser's second most important prospects are people who respond to direct-mail pieces from other companies—especially those with complementary products or services. **Mail-response lists** are the house lists of other direct-mail advertisers, and they can be rented with a wide variety of demographic breakdowns.

Compiled lists   The most readily available lists are those that some entity compiles for a different reason and then rents or sells—for example, lists of car owners, new-home purchasers, business owners, and so on. **Compiled lists** typically offer the lowest response rate, so experts suggest using numerous sources, computer merging them with mail-response and house lists, and then purging them of duplicate names.[42]

Direct-mail lists can be bought or rented. Purchased lists can be used without limit; rented lists may be used for a single mailing only. List owners plant decoy names in the list to be sure renters don't use it more than once.

Some list owners pay a **list broker** a commission (usually 20 percent) to handle the rental details. The advertiser, in turn, benefits from the broker's knowledge of list quality without having to pay more than the rental cost.

Lists can be brokered or exchanged with list houses or other noncompetitive companies. And they can be tailored to reflect customer location (zip code); demographics such as age, income, and credit-card ownership; or psychographic characteristics such as personality and lifestyle. The SRDS *Direct Mail List Rates and Data* comes in two volumes, *Consumer Lists* and *Business Lists,* and contains more than 50,000 list selections in hundreds of classifications (see Exhibit 16–15).

The quality of mailing lists varies enormously. The wrong list can have out-of-date addresses and names of people who live too far away, don't use the product advertised, and can't afford it anyway. Mailing list prices vary according to quality. Rental rates average about $55 per thousand names but can be as little as $35 per thousand or as much as $400 per thousand. The more stringent the advertiser's selection criteria, the more expensive the list. An extra $10 per thousand is often well worth the savings in mailers and postage that would otherwise be wasted.

The average mailing list changes more than 40 percent a year as people relocate, change jobs, get married, or die. So mailing lists must be continually updated *(cleaned)* to be sure they're current and correct. Advertisers can also test the validity and accuracy of a given list. They rent or buy every *n*th name and send a mailer to that person. If the results are favorable, they purchase additional names, usually in lots of 1,000.

Production and Handling

To create a direct-mail package, the advertiser may use in-house staff, an ad agency, or a freelance designer and writer. Some agencies specialize in direct mail.

The direct-mail piece normally goes through the same production process as any other print piece. The size and shape of the mailing package, as well as the

Developing Effective Direct-Mail Packages

Good direct-mail campaigns help build relationships between advertisers and customers. As with an ad, the effectiveness of a direct-mail campaign relies strongly on both its message and its appearance.

Shaping the Message

When Air France wanted to reach valued customers, its agency, Wunderman Cato Johnson, New York, created the direct-mail pieces shown here. The strategy was to emphasize an upscale design style with the *Paris Bistro Cooking* book and *Savoir Faire* newsletter to make the recipient feel truly valued as an Air France customer.

To develop the message element in direct mail, experts suggest several techniques: stress the benefits; repeat your offer more than once; offer an incentive; offer a guarantee; don't be afraid of long

copy; don't write copy that is over the reader's head; and give the customer more than one option for responding.

Integrating the Message with the Direct-Mail Pieces

Creating direct mail involves fitting the message with the key physical components of the direct-mail package. As discussed in Chapter 12, the five steps of the creative pyramid (attention, interest, credibility, desire, and action) may be guidelines for forming the message. Next, this information must be incorporated into all the components of the direct-mail package: the mailing envelope, the sales letter, the color piece or brochure, and the response device.

Paris Bistro Cooking and *Savoir Faire* attract *attention* with their large type and color. The sales letter's color logo and signature catch the recipient's eye and keep his or her *interest* on the letter and its contents.

The specifics within the letter and the matching travel survey card build *credibility* by providing data useful in the purchase decision. Details include the features and benefits of the product, the deadline and value of the offer, and instructions the recipient should follow.

The cookbook features images suggesting how the airline puts the recipient in touch with the elegance of life, whetting the recipient's *desire* to purchase the product.

In the last step, the postage-free business reply card as well as telephone and fax numbers make it easy for the recipient to take *action* to buy the product.

Some Secrets of Direct Mail

Research has revealed countless direct-mail techniques that improve response rates: indent type and set it flush left with a ragged right edge; avoid printing in reverse type; list dollars saved in your offer rather than percentages; use the word "you" in text; provide a reason for sale pricing (almost any will do); and do not paste labels over old addresses—print new materials.

This elegant, three-dimensional mailing is part of a series providing positive recognition to valued Air France customers while maintaining the airline's upscale image. The target market received a personalized cover letter, a monthly newsletter, a travel survey, and a book, **Paris Bistro Cooking.** *Air France received a substantial response, including dozens of thank-you notes.*

Laboratory Applications

1. Locate a direct-mail package that has the four components common to most mailings and list how the elements of the creative pyramid are integrated throughout the components.

2. Review the copywriting in your direct-mail package and identify how many of the techniques mentioned in this Ad Lab are used or could be improved.

---

type, illustrations, and colors, all affect printing costs. Special features such as simulated blue-ink signatures, cardboard pop-ups, and die-cutting (the cutting of paper stock into an unusual shape) add to the cost. But the larger the printing volume, or *run,* the lower the printing cost per unit (see Ad Lab 16A: Developing Effective Direct-Mail Packages).

Remaining production and handling tasks can be done by a local **letter shop** (or *mailing house*), or the advertiser can do them internally. On a cost-per-thousand basis, letter shops stuff and seal envelopes, affix labels, calculate postage, and sort, tie, and stack the mailers. Some shops also offer creative services. If the advertiser is using third-class bulk mail, the letter shop separates mailers by zip code and ties them into bundles to qualify for low bulk rates. Then the letter shop delivers the mailers to the post office.

Distribution

Distribution costs are based chiefly on the weight of the mailer and the delivery method. U.S. advertisers can use the U.S. Postal Service, air freight, or private delivery services like UPS and FedEx. The most common, the U.S. Postal Service, offers several types of delivery (for more postal information, see RL 16–1 in the Reference Library). Direct-mail advertising is most effective when it arrives on Tuesdays, Wednesdays, and Thursdays.

Chapter **Summary**

The new digital interactive media, which include online database services, the Internet and the World Wide Web, CD-ROM catalogs, magazines, kiosks, and interactive television, represent a revolution in the making. From an advertising standpoint, the new media offer an opportunity to develop customer relationships rather than volume. The new media are still in flux, but they're growing at an exponential rate and offer an array of challenges and opportunities for advertising creativity.

The commercialization of the Internet really began with the commercial online services that offered a large subscriber base to potential advertisers. However, the Internet itself dwarfed the online services in potential since it reached so many people around the globe. Once Web browser software became available, it made the Internet user-friendly to noncomputer specialists.

Similarly, search engines made sites on the World Wide Web available to PC users with just the click of a mouse. When people began migrating to the Web, so did advertisers. The first banner ad was sold by *Hotwired* magazine.

Web users tend to be upscale, college-educated men and women. This is an ideal target, especially for business-to-business advertisers. This group is rapidly broadening, which will make the Web even more attractive to many mainline advertisers. People currently access

the Net through Internet service providers, cable-modems, and satellites. The most common, though, is dial-up modem through an ISP.

The most common types of Net advertising are banners, buttons, sponsorships, interstitials, and classifieds. Like all media, the Internet has many advantages and disadvantages.

Most Internet advertising is sold by CPM. Some, though, is sold by click-through and/or results. In some cases marketers conducting commerce on the Net take a commission on what is sold.

Direct mail attracts nearly 20 percent of all ad dollars. While it has historically been the most expensive major medium on a cost-per-exposure basis, it has also always been the most effective in terms of tangible results. Marketers like direct mail for its accountability. There are many types of direct-mail advertising, from catalogs and brochures to statement stuffers.

One of the great features of direct mail is that it can increase the effectiveness of ads in other media. However, direct mail has many drawbacks too—primarily its cost and the junk-mail image.

The two most important things that affect direct-mail success are the mailing list and the creativity used. The direct-mail piece normally goes through the same production process as any other print piece. The size and shape of the mailing package, as well as the type, illustrations, and colors, all affect printing costs.

Important **Terms**

ad networks, *523*

ad request, *520*

banner, *515*

broadside, *528*

brochure, *528*

business reply mail, *528*

button, *516*

cable-modem, *514*

catalog, *529*

CD-ROM, *524*

classified ad Web site, *517*

click rate, *520*

click-throughs, *522*

compiled lists, *530*

cookies, *520*

creative dimensional direct mailing, *526*

digital interactive media, *504*

DirecPC, *514*

direct-mail advertising, *528*

folder, *528*

home page, *510*

house lists, *529*

house organ, *529*

interactive TV (ITV), *525*

Internet, *505*

Internet service provider, *510*

interstitial, *517*

keyword, *522*

kiosk, *525*

letter shop, *531*

list broker, *530*

mail-response lists, *530*

postcard, *528*

push technology, *513*

sales letter, *528*

search engine, *511*

self-mailer, *529*

sponsorship, *516*

statement stuffer, *529*

Web browser, *510*

Web page, *515*

WebTV, *514*

World Wide Web (WWW), *510*

Review **Questions**

1. How did the Internet evolve to its present status as an advertising medium?
2. Which companies on the Internet receive the greatest amount of advertising revenue? Why?
3. What are the different ways of advertising on the Net?
4. What are cookies, and what are they used for?
5. What are the different ways Web publishers charge for advertising on the Net?
6. How would you describe the advantages the Internet offers advertisers over traditional media?
7. How does audience measurement on the Web differ from that for traditional media?
8. What is the importance of the new interactive media to small advertisers?
9. How could you use direct mail in an integrated marketing communications program for a particular product? Give an example.
10. What factors have the greatest influence on the success of a direct-mail campaign?

Exploring the **Internet**

The Internet exercises for Chapter 16 address the following areas related to the chapter: internet advertising (Exercise 1) and direct mail (Exercise 2).

1. Internet Advertising

    Advertising banners on the Internet are akin to outdoor billboards and fill the information superhighway with advertising messages, corporate signage, and hyperlinks. But, as is the case with all new media, the future of ad banners is uncertain. The only thing that is certain is that they will exist—in one form or another. Many advertisers are unsure about putting their advertising dollars towards cyberspace, and companies like Iron Mountain Global Information Systems (www.imgis.com) are flourishing as they introduce new and better ways of managing Web advertising—helping advertisers to feel more confident about the banner programs they place.

    Visit the following ad banner-related sites on the Internet and discover more about this fast-changing segment of the advertising industry. Then answer the questions that follow.
    - ChannelSeven.com www.channelseven.com
    - Classifieds 2000 www.classifieds2000.com
    - DoubleClick www.doubleclick.com
    - I/PRO www.ipro.com
    - IMGIS www.imgis.com
    - Internet Marketing and Advertising Association (IMAA) www.imaa.org
    - Internet Advertising Bureau (IAB) www.iab.net
    - Internet Advertising Resource Guide www.admedia.org
    - "Regulating Internet Advertising" www.brownraysman.com/doclib/complaw596.html
    - Jupiter Communications www.jup.com

    a. What group sponsors the site and what is the organization's purpose?
    b. What is the size/scope of the organization?
    c. Who is the intended audience(s) of the Web site?
    d. What services does the organization offer Web advertisers?

2. Direct Mail

    Direct-mail advertising is one of the advertiser's best tools to execute highly targeted relationship-building communications. Take a few moments to familiarize yourself further with this side of the advertising business. Browse the direct-mail-related Web sites below and then answer the questions that follow.
    - Advertising Mail Marketing Association (AMMA) www.amma.org
    - Advo, Inc. www.advo.com
    - Alamo Direct www.alamodirect.com
    - American List Counsel www.amlist.com
    - Catalyst Direct Marketing www.catalystdm.com
    - Community Mailers www.communitymailers.com
    - Direct Mail Express www.dmenet.com
    - Direct Mailing Systems www.dirmailsys.com
    - L.I.S.T. Incorporated www.l-i-s-t.com
    - Mail Advertising Service Association (MASA) www.masa.org
    - PostMaster Direct Response www.postmasterdirect.com
    - Response Mail Express www.responsemail.com
    - United States Postal Service www.usps.com

    a. What company or group sponsors the site?
    b. What is the organization's purpose?
    c. Who makes up the organization's membership? Its constituency?
    d. What benefit does the organization provide individual members and the advertising community?

Chapter Seventeen

Using Out-of-Home, Exhibitive, and Supplementary Media

Objective To present the factors advertisers consider when evaluating various out-of-home, exhibitive, and supplementary media. Many advertisers use these media to either complement or replace print and electronic media, so it's important to understand how advertisers buy these media and the advantages and disadvantages of each.

After studying this chapter, you will be able to:

- Discuss the pros and cons of outdoor advertising.
- Explain how to measure exposure to outdoor media.
- Describe the types of standard outdoor advertising structures.
- Detail the various options available in transit advertising.
- Discuss the variables that influence the cost of transit and other out-of-home media.
- Discuss the importance of exhibitive media in a company's marketing mix.
- Explain the issues advertisers face when considering a change in packaging.
- Identify several types of supplementary media.

It was spring in Buffalo, and love was in the air. One Monday morning, as people were driving to work, they suddenly noticed a big new billboard. In large white letters against a siren-red background, it displayed a very personal message: ● Angel in Red: ● Saw You at Garcia's Irish Pub. ● Love to meet you.—William. ● For the next nine weeks, commuters discovered a new message every Monday morning, each more romantic—and more desperate—than the last.

"Angel in Red: Still waiting. Garcia's Pub. Friday? —William." "Angel in Red: I'm going broke with these billboards. Garcia's . . . Please! —William." ● People started going to Garcia's to see if they could spot Angel, or meet William. Soon a board appeared authored by Frankie warning William that his angel was out of bounds. William responded with a board saying: "Angel in Red: Frankie be damned! I'd risk it all to meet you at Garcia's." Women started calling the local billboard company to see how they could get to meet romantic William. ● The story became the talk of the town. And for nine weeks, nobody caught on, not even the employees at Garcia's. ● Finally, the board everyone was waiting for appeared: "Dear William: I must be crazy. Garcia's, Friday, 8:30.—Angel." ● That night the place was jammed. Garcia's had to hire two models to play William and Angel. Yes, William finally found his angel, and they danced to (what else?) "Lady in Red." ● The final board appeared the next week. "Angel: Thanks for Friday at Garcia's. I'm in heaven.—Love, William." ● The campaign was the brainchild of Crowley Webb & Associates, the ad agency next door to Garcia's. The owner of Garcia's was nervous about a new restaurant chain's plans to open a pub on the lakefront. So he hired Crowley Webb to come up with something really "way out"—for under $20,000. ● The agency demonstrated to Garcia's (and the world) that with a little imagination, outdoor advertising is an ideal medium for achieving local reach, frequency, and continuity on a very limited budget.[1] ●

Exhibit 17–1
Breakdown of out-of-home media.

Mall advertising 1%
Supplemental forms 5%
Bus shelters 5%
Sports stadiums 8%
30-sheet posters 22%

2% Airport advertising
4% 8-sheet posters
6% Transit
12% In-store
35% Bulletins

Out-of-Home Media

Media that reach prospects outside their homes—like outdoor advertising, bus and taxicab advertising, subway posters, and terminal advertising—are part of the broad category of **out-of-home media** (see Exhibit 17–1). Today, there are over 30 different types of out-of-home media, generating revenues of some $3.7 billion annually. Many of these did not even exist five or 10 years ago.[2] The most common are *on-premise signs,* which promote goods and services, or identify a place of business, on the property where the sign is located.[3] The golden arches at McDonald's franchises are a good example. On-premise signs are important for helping us find a place of business, but they don't provide any kind of market coverage and they aren't an organized medium like, for instance, the standardized outdoor advertising business.

In the past three chapters, we've looked at the traditional mass media forms as well as some of the interesting new media vehicles that have burst upon the advertising scene in recent years. Now, to round out our discussion of advertising media, we'll present in this last chapter some of the other vehicles that advertisers use today.

We'll start with the last major media category: the organized out-of-home media. These include standardized outdoor advertising and transit advertising. We'll also briefly discuss some other out-of-home vehicles that are gaining in popularity: mobile billboards, electronic signs and displays, and even the ads that are now cropping up on phone booths and parking meters.

Next we'll discuss a category we call *exhibitive media,* which includes product packaging and trade shows and exhibits. Finally, we'll examine some of the media that advertisers typically consider supplementary to their other advertising activities—things like promotional products (specialty advertising), directories, and Yellow Pages—as well as some of the emerging media that are beginning to gain advertiser interest.

Billboards are one of the most commonly used forms of out-of-home media. This medium appeals to the YMCA (www.ymca.com) as a nonprofit organization, because it has the lowest cost per thousand of any major medium. Billboards such as the one depicted here would be placed in areas trafficked by commuters, who would be most likely to join a gym. The visual is a very effective choice for a billboard—a larger-than-life gut would grab just about anyone's attention and make them look at their own gut for reassurance.

Outdoor Advertising

As a national and global medium, outdoor advertising has achieved great success. It was probably the first advertising medium ever used, dating back over 5,000 years to when hieroglyphics on obelisks directed travelers. In the Middle Ages, bill posting was an accepted form of advertising in Europe. And in the 19th century, it evolved into a serious art form, thanks to the poster paintings of both Manet and Toulouse-Lautrec.[4]

Today, from Africa to Asia to Europe to South America, both local and global marketers use outdoor media for the same

Exhibit 17–2

Outdoor advertising expenditures, 1994.

Category	1994 ($ millions)
1. Entertainment and amusements	127.2
2. Cigarettes, tobacco, and accessories	121.9
3. Retail	103.2
4. Business and consumer services	99.4
5. Automotive, auto accessories, and equipment	86.2
6. Travel, hotels, and resorts	81.8
7. Publishing and media	57.2
8. Beer and wine	52.5
9. Insurance and real estate	38.4
10. Liquor	28.8

reasons as Garcia's Irish Pub: to communicate a succinct message or image in the local language to a mass audience quickly and frequently at the lowest cost per thousand of any major medium.

In 1996, U.S. advertisers spent a total of $1.96 billion in standardized outdoor advertising, a whopping 15 percent increase over 1994 figures.[5] This growth is expected to continue as advertisers seek alternatives to the declining audiences and ad clutter of other mass media forms. Now that TV viewers can choose from more than 50 channels, it has become increasingly difficult for national advertisers to tell their story to mass audiences. But there's still one medium that can carry their message 24 hours a day, seven days a week, day and night, without interruption. It's never turned off, zipped, zapped, put aside, or left unopened. And it's big. That's outdoor. For that reason, some experts now refer to billboards as the *last* mass medium.[6]

Standardization of the Outdoor Advertising Business

Standardized outdoor advertising uses scientifically located structures to deliver an advertiser's message to markets around the world.

In the United States, there are approximately 390,000 outdoor ad structures owned and maintained by some 3,000 outdoor advertising companies, known as *plants.*[7] Plant operators find suitable locations (usually concentrated in commercial and business areas), lease or buy the property, acquire the necessary legal permits, erect the structures in conformance with local building codes, contract with advertisers for poster rentals, and post the panels or paint the bulletins. Plant operators also maintain the outdoor structures and keep surrounding areas clean and attractive.

The plant operator may have its own art staff to supply creative services for local advertisers; ad agencies usually do the creative work for national advertisers. The biggest outdoor advertisers are traditionally in the entertainment and amusement category (see Exhibit 17–2). In fact, this group increased its spending by 85 percent in one year. Tobacco companies are the next largest spenders. However, with the new antismoking legislation, it's anticipated that the revenue from tobacco will decline dramatically in coming years. The next largest category is local retail. Typically, the smaller the market, the larger the percentage of local advertisers.

Types of Outdoor Advertising

To buy outdoor advertising effectively, the media planner must understand its advantages and disadvantages and the types of structures available (see the Checklist of Pros and Cons of Outdoor Advertising). Standardized structures come in three basic forms: *bulletins, 30-sheet poster panels,* and *eight-sheet posters.* For extra impact, some companies use the nonstandard *spectacular.*

Bulletins

Where traffic is heavy and visibility good, advertisers find that large **bulletin structures** work best, especially for long-term use. Bulletins measure 14 by 48 feet, plus any extensions, and may carry either

This ad for the Louisville Zoo (www.louisvillezoo.org) is an example of a bulletin structure, used in outdoor advertising. The boa constrictor that wraps around and slithers across the top of the structure is called an extension. It is very eye-catching, and perhaps even daunting. Advertisers use this type of billboard in locations with heavy traffic and good visibility. They are intended for long-term use and hold up well.

Continued on page 542

As the oldest medium on earth,

outdoor advertising benefits from its inherent nature as a "sign" as well as the modern features of graphic design and technology. In fact, thanks to technology, advertisers can do things in outdoor today they couldn't have dreamed of just a few years ago. Plus, no other medium is this big—commanding attention from motorists and pedestrians 24 hours a day, seven days a week at a fraction of the cost of other media. However, outdoor is limited in what it can say. For normal outdoor structures on the highway, seven words is the rule-of-thumb. That places an additional burden on the nonverbal (artistic) aspects of the ad, and this definitely challenges the creative muscle of every advertiser's ad agency.

Study the ads in this portfolio to see how big, strategic ideas get translated into outstanding outdoor advertising. Then consider why the advertiser chose outdoor as the medium. Was outdoor the right choice for this advertiser? Why? Or why not? Could the same concept be used in other media? How?

Out-of-Home Advertising

Creativity is essential to the success of an ad no matter what medium one chooses. This creative ad for the Tigra from Vauxhall (www.vauxhall.co.uk) makes exceptional use of the medium chosen. The ad literally sticks to, and wraps around, the corner of the building just as it claims the car can stick to the road. A visually stunning ad, it may make a reader think that if the car could hug corners even half as well as the ad does it would be worth driving.

Out-of-home advertising offers many ways to reach consumers at almost any time in any place. United Airlines makes exceptional use of the space available on the backs of seats on buses, as shown in this ad. As a passenger on the bus, one has little choice where to look, and United (www.ual.com/home/default.asp) has provided a more interesting view than the back of someone's head. The passenger is a captive audience. The invitation to put one's feet in the space provided involves the reader, and most people would likely attempt to do so. Plus, the passenger can relate to the message by the reality of the leg room available on the bus.

This series of billboards for the Pacific Science Center (www.pacsi.org) and its new film on sharks would typically be placed one after the other, a short distance apart alongside of the freeway. The absence of one person in the second billboard draws attention and signifies that this is not the same billboard the reader just passed. The absence of all four people on the last board provides humor, plays on people's fear of sharks (and perhaps even brings to mind the movie Jaws), and again lets the reader know they are looking at a new billboard. Interesting billboards like these can achieve the repetition necessary to get the point across and, by entertaining readers, they avoid alienating them.

Mutual Community targets its audience in a most unusual way. Perhaps the person on the stretcher can read it as he's being carried off the field, but the creative use of upside-down text also draws the attention of the uninjured spectators. The creative team came up with an entertaining way to utilize space that will most certainly draw attention to this ad and away from the many other competing ads lining the stadium.

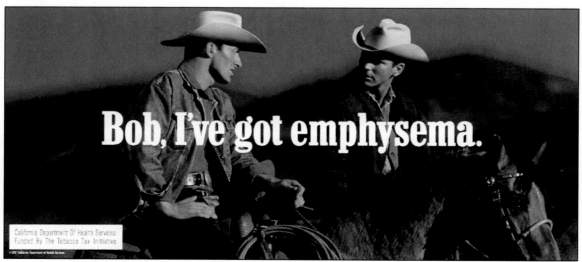

The California Department of Health Services (www.dhs.cahwnet.gov) uses the familiar faces and scenery of Marlboro country in its antismoking campaign. Since the advertiser uses the same medium and visual style as the cigarette ads, people will immediately think of Marlboro before they even read the headline. Once the headline is read, the implication is clear—smoking cigarettes causes emphysema. The Department of Health doesn't have to come right out and say it because the reader has already made the association with cigarettes as a result of the visual clues.

Out-of-home advertising can be very suitable for particular industries, such as restaurants that court hungry travelers to stop for food. McDonald's (*www.mcdonalds.com*) is no exception, frequently advertising on billboards to attract local consumers and reinforce the company name. Over the years, McDonald's has developed such a ubiquitous identity that the mere sight of the golden arches creates an immediate mental association with the brand.

The body outline in this ad is eye-catching and creates curiosity. It is a symbol everyone is familiar with and the mental association with a dead body is immediate. The advertisers for Brian Bohr Karate use this association to their advantage. The message is made clear in the reader's mind just by the visual. All they have to do is provide a solution. The solution here is to learn karate and avoid becoming a chalk outline. The headline also serves as a call to action—something along the lines of kill or be killed—of course, the message is really to learn to defend yourself.

A unique use of transit advertising can be seen on the roof of this bus. The "Don't Jump" headline addresses everyone looking down from the windows above. Whether or not they are considering jumping, the headline grabs their attention—leading them to the ad for The Guardian (*www.guardian.co.uk*). The creative team hit on a very interesting use of transit advertising to reach people who are above the street, rather than the usual audience of motorists and pedestrians on the street.

The Pros and Cons of Outdoor Advertising

The Pros

_____ **Accessibility.** Outdoor carries the message 24 hours per day and cannot be fast-forwarded, put aside, zapped, or turned off.

_____ **Reach.** For the same dollars, outdoor delivers a reach of 86.4 percent compared to spot TV (76.5 percent), radio (72.3 percent), and newspaper (72.2 percent) for the same target audience in the same city. The audience is mostly young, educated, affluent, and mobile—an attractive target to many national advertisers.

_____ **Frequency.** Nine out of 10 people reached with a 100 GRP showing receive an average of 29 impressions each over a 30-day period.

_____ **Geographic flexibility.** Outdoor advertisers can place their advertising where they want it nationally, regionally, or locally in more than 9,000 markets across North America.

_____ **Demographic flexibility.** Messages can be concentrated in areas frequented or traversed by young people, upper-income people, or people of specific ethnic backgrounds. With computerization, it's possible to characterize outdoor audiences by age, sex, income, and lifestyle down to the block level.

_____ **Cost.** Outdoor offers the lowest cost per exposure of any major advertising medium. Rates vary depending on market size and intensity, but the GRP system makes cost comparisons possible from market to market.

_____ **Impact.** Since advertisers can build up GRPs very fast, outdoor is ideal for those with a short, simple, dogmatic message.

_____ **Creative flexibility.** Outdoor offers a large display and the spectacular features of lights, animation, and brilliant color. New fiberoptics, giant video screens, and backlit display technologies offer more creative options.

_____ **Location.** Outdoor can target consumers by activity, reaching shoppers on their way to the store, businesspeople on their way to work, or travelers on their way to the airport, thereby influencing shoppers just before they make a purchase decision.

The Cons

_____ **Fleeting message.** Customers pass quickly, so outdoor advertising must intrude to be effective. The design and copy must tell a story briefly and crisply, and the words must sell.

_____ **Environmental influence.** Outdoor messages are influenced by their environment. Placement in a run-down area can detract from a product's image.

_____ **Audience measurement.** Audience demographics are difficult to measure. Not every passerby sees or reads the ad, so some buyers distrust the space seller's reach estimates.

_____ **Control.** Unlike print and broadcast ads, it's hard to physically inspect each outdoor poster panel.

_____ **Planning and costs.** Outdoor messages usually require six to eight weeks of lead time for printing and posting. High initial preparation cost may discourage local use. And for national advertisers, buying outdoor is complex. As many as 30 companies may sell ad space in a single market.

_____ **Availability of locations.** Outdoor is so popular that demand now exceeds supply.

_____ **Visual pollution.** Some people object to outdoor advertising as visual pollution. They have a negative reaction to advertisers who use it.

Continued from page 537

painted or printed messages. They are created in sections in the plant's shop and then brought to the site, where they are assembled and hung on the billboard structure.

Painted displays are normally lighted and are repainted several times each year (color is very important to readability; see Ad Lab 17–A). Some bulletins are three-dimensional or embellished by extensions (or cutouts) that stretch beyond the frames of the structure. Variations include cutout letters, backlighting, moving messages, and electronic time and temperature units called jump clocks.

Painted bulletins are very costly, but some advertisers overcome this expense by rotating them to different choice locations in the market every 60 or 90 days. Over time, this gives the impression of wider coverage than the advertiser is actually paying for.

Poster Panels

The **30-sheet poster panel** (_standard billboard_) is less costly per unit and is the basic outdoor advertising structure. A poster consists of blank panels with a standardized size and border. Its message is first printed at a lithography or screen plant on large sheets of paper, then mounted by hand on the panel.

Poster sizes are referred to in terms of _sheets_. The poster sheets are mounted on a board with a total surface of 12 by 25 feet and usually change every 30 days.

Some local advertisers get high-quality outdoor advertising at reduced cost by using **stock posters.** These ready-made, 30-sheet posters are available in any

How to Use Type and Color in Outdoor Advertising

Outdoor advertising is generally viewed from 100 to 500 feet away by people in motion. So it must be simple, brief, and easy to discern. Large illustrations, bold colors, simple backgrounds, clear product identification, and easy-to-read lettering are essential for comprehension.

Type Weight and Spacing

The recommended maximum for outdoor copy is seven words. Bold typefaces appear blurred and thin ones seem faded. Ornate typefaces are too complicated. Simple sans serifs are the most effective. Spacing between letters and words (kerning) should be separated to reduce confusion.

Color Contrast and Value

In outdoor advertising, a full range of colors can be vividly and faithfully reproduced. A huge poster or bulletin alive with brilliant reds, greens, yellows, and blues produces an effect unmatched by any other medium.

In choosing colors for outdoor, the designer should seek high contrast in both hue (the identity of the color, such as red, green, yellow) and value (the color's lightness or darkness) to make it more readable. Contrasting colors work well at outdoor-viewing distances; colors lacking contrast in value blend together and obscure the message.

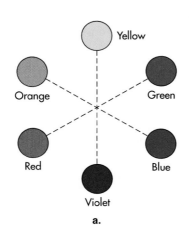

a.

The color wheel illustrates the need for contrast in both hue and value. For example, green and red are opposite each other on the wheel (dashed line) and are therefore complementary colors. They contrast well in hues—but when their values are similar, they can create an annoying visual vibration. The same is true of blue and orange.

Blue and green, and orange and red, are especially poor combinations because they are generally similar in both hue and value.

Yellow and violet (dissimilar in both hue and value) provide a strong, effective contrast for outdoor. White goes well with any dark-value color, while black is good with colors of light value.

Most readable	Least readable
Upper & Lower Case	ALL UPPER CASE
Regular Kerning	Tight Kerning
Bold Face	Light Face
Uniform Thicknesses	**Too Thick & Thin**

b.

c.

Color Impact

Among the color combinations shown below, legibility ranges from best in combination 1 (upper left) to poorest in combination 18 (lower right).

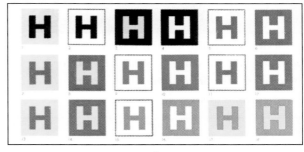

d.

Laboratory Applications

1. Which outdoor ads in this chapter use color the most effectively? Explain.

2. What outdoor ads have you seen that don't use color effectively? How can they be improved?

---

quantity and often feature the work of first-class artists and lithographers. Local florists, dairies, banks, or bakeries simply place their name in the appropriate spot.

Eight-Sheet Posters

Manufacturers of grocery products, as well as many local advertisers, use smaller poster sizes. Called **eight-sheet posters** (or *junior panels*), these offer a 5- by 11-foot printing area on a panel surface 6 feet wide by 12 feet deep. They are typically concentrated in urban areas, where they can reach pedestrian as well as

Spectaculars are expensive, elaborate animated signs found primarily in the heart of large cities. They incorporate movement, color, and flashy graphics to grab attention in high-traffic areas.

Exhibit 17–3
Billboard locations throughout the San Diego metropolitan area that achieve at least 100 GRPs each day for four weeks.

vehicular traffic. In an integrated marketing communications campaign, they are also an excellent medium for coverage close to the point of purchase.

Spectaculars

Times Square in New York is well known for its **spectaculars**—giant electronic signs that incorporate movement, color, and flashy graphics to grab attention in high-traffic areas. Spectaculars are very expensive to produce and are found primarily in the world's largest cities, such as Tokyo, London, Atlanta, Los Angeles, and, of course, Las Vegas (see the Portfolio Review of Out-of-Home Advertising).

Buying Outdoor Advertising

Advertisers use outdoor advertising for a variety of purposes. For example, to introduce a new product or announce a change in package design, advertisers want to saturate the market. Outdoor advertising makes broad coverage possible—overnight. For a small portion of its total media budget, for example, Saturn was able to buy 400 billboards and dominate the outdoor medium in the important California market, contributing significantly to the car's introduction. California is the state with the most import car owners, Saturn's key competitive target.[8]

The basic unit of sale for billboards, or posters, is *100 gross rating points daily,* or a **100 showing.** One rating point equals 1 percent of a particular market's population. Buying 100 gross rating points does *not* mean the message will appear on 100 posters; it means the message will appear on as many panels as needed to provide a daily exposure theoretically equal to the market's total population. Actually, a showing of 100 gross rating points achieves a *daily* reach of about 88.1 percent of the adults in a market over a 30-day period.[9]

For less saturation, units of sale can be expressed as fractions of the basic unit, such as 75, 50, or 25 gross rating points. If a showing provides 750,000 total impression opportunities daily in a market with a population of 1 million, it delivers 75 GRPs daily. Over a period of 30 days, the showing would earn 2,250 GRPs (30 × 75).

Location, Location, Location

As in real estate, location is everything in outdoor advertising. Advertisers that want more saturation can increase the number of posters or purchase better locations to achieve 200 or 300 GRPs per day. The map in Exhibit 17–3 shows the billboard locations in San Diego County, California, that would total 100 or more GRPs per day. Rates vary considerably from market to market due to variations in property rentals, labor costs, and market size. As Exhibit 17–4 shows, locations

New Innovative Technologies in Advertising

The advent of computer graphic interactive (CGI) provides the world of advertising with a new avenue to produce commercials and display logos. During the 1998 World Cup Tournament in France, Anheuser-Busch signed up as a major sponsor. However, the company was prohibited from displaying any banners or logos in the venue where the finals were to be held because of French laws governing the advertising of alcoholic beverages.

Unfortunately for Anheuser-Busch, it was predicted that the 64 matches would draw a cumulative audience of 30 billion people in 100 countries. Furthermore, the company had spent more than $20 million just for the right to name Budweiser the official beer of the World Cup and to use the cup logo in its advertising.

The firm "non" from the French led Anheuser-Busch to seek other options to avoid the potential disaster. What they came up with was an ingenious idea—to leave the billboards inside the stadium blank. And then, in television transmissions outside of France, they would project a computer-generated Budweiser image on the blank billboards.

This technology is customarily called blue screen (or chroma key). By filming against a blue or green image, a CGI technician can digitally enhance and replace the blue or green screen with the desired image of choice; in this case, the Anheuser-Busch logo. Many motion picture and television production companies use this technique to place people or things in areas that do not exist or would be otherwise too dangerous for the actors or crew.

While CGI has been around for awhile, its use in the advertising industry is new. In fact, the success of the 1998 movie *Titanic* now has advertising folk asking director James Cameron for advice on whether to use "real life" actors in some spots or digitally enhanced images and people like he used in the movie.

---

in larger markets with high traffic volume have higher rates. However, as a rule of thumb, a standard billboard costs around $500 per month. At that rate, billboards still offer the lowest cost per thousand (an average of $1.55) of any major mass medium.[10]

Technology in Outdoor Advertising

In the past it was always a problem for a media buyer in New York to adequately supervise the posting of outdoor boards in Peoria, Illinois. A buyer can't just jump on a plane and travel to all the cities where the client's boards are posted to verify the value of the locations. Fortunately, though, new technology has helped solve this dilemma and has thus made outdoor an even more attractive medium to national advertisers. Today, outdoor companies can use sophisticated **global positioning systems (GPS)** to give the exact latitude and longitude of particular boards using satellite technology. Media buyers, equipped with sophisticated new software on their desktop computers, can then integrate this information with demographic market characteristics and traffic counts to determine the best locations for their boards.[11]

Some outdoor companies even provide digitized video of their locations so the buyer can see the actual board and the environment in which it is located. Other

Exhibit 17–4

Monthly rates for standard posters (12 by 25 feet) in selected metropolitan markets.

Market	25 daily GRPs		50 daily GRPs		100 daily GRPs		Average cost of a poster for 100 daily GRPs
	Number	Cost	Number	Cost	Number	Cost	
Atlanta	30	$ 15,000	60	$ 30,000	120	$ 60,000	$500
Denver	21	11,700	39	21,000	78	41,000	526
Detroit Metro	45	33,525	90	67,050	180	134,100	745
Las Vegas	9	5,175	17	9,518	33	17,599	533
Los Angeles Metro	120	85,200	240	169,000	480	333,600	695
Minneapolis/St. Paul	56	30,800	112	61,600	224	123,200	550
Baton Rouge	10	5,215	20	9,710	40	14,205	355
Tucson	10	5,700	20	10,900	40	20,500	513
Seattle/Tacoma	40	25,800	80	51,660	160	103,200	645
St. Louis Metro	32	16,000	64	32,000	128	64,000	500

Note: Costs are for space only; they do not include production. Based on four-week posting period.

The marketers of cigarettes and hard liquor, banned by law from advertising on television and radio, have become heavy users of outdoor and transit advertising. Even though existing codes prevent such advertising from appearing too close to schools, it is virtually impossible to keep minors from becoming exposed to it due to the *spillover* nature of out-of-home media.

Regulation of outdoor advertising has focused on the *location* of billboards, not the *content*. The Outdoor Advertising Association's Code of Industry Principles says billboard companies can "reject advertising that is misleading, in poor taste, or otherwise incompatible with community standards." But it's unknown how often this clause is invoked. The trend is toward sexually explicit ads in the outdoor arena, especially in highly urban areas. Some consumers have gotten so steamed they've defaced billboards with graffiti or even created campaigns of their own to fight sexist and sexually explicit ads.

The real problem, as the critics see it, is that outdoor is the most public mass medium. You can't turn it off. It's there 24 hours a day, for all to see—even children. It's understandable that when nudity appears in Calvin Klein billboards, or sexually suggestive poses are used for Horizon cologne, some parents rebel. That's happening not just in the United States, but around the world. In fact, there was a miniscandal in 1995 over bus signs in Italy featuring U.S. supermodel Naomi Campbell stretched out in the altogether.

The ethical issues involved with spillover media are complex, often relating to the nature of the advertised product or to the kind of advertising appeal used.

Cigarette smoking, for example, kills thousands of people a year, and many smokers become addicted as teenagers. A ban on cigarette advertising seems the primary solution, if without advertising no child too young to make an informed decision would crave a cigarette.

"But are the ads really to blame?" asks Herbert Rotfeld, associate professor of marketing at Auburn University. National and local surveys, he says, repeatedly show that the laws against selling cigarettes to minors are among the least enforced in the nation. Everyone is quick to criticize cigarette advertising; rarely is a call heard for stricter law enforcement. That, of course, has changed recently with new calls for stricter enforcement and greater advertising restrictions.

---

new developments include bar coding of materials so they can be tracked, posted, and authenticated, all by computer. Computerized painting on flexible vinyl is another recent breakthrough that guarantees a high-quality, high-resolution, faithful reproduction of the advertiser's message regardless of the market.[12]

Regulation of Outdoor Advertising

The Highway Beautification Act of 1965 controls outdoor advertising on U.S. interstate highways and other federally subsidized highways. It was enacted partly in response to consumer complaints that outdoor advertising was spoiling the environment. Over 700,000 billboards were removed by 1991, the year Congress banned the construction of new billboards on all scenic portions of interstate highways.[13] Since that time, the image of outdoor has improved dramatically. Today, most people polled say they like billboards, believe they promote business, and find them useful travel information for drivers.[14]

Each state also regulates, administers, and enforces outdoor advertising permit programs through its department of transportation. Some states (Maine, Vermont, Hawaii, and Alaska) prohibit outdoor advertising altogether. Ironically, though, some of these states use outdoor advertising themselves in other states to promote tourism (see the Ethical Issue: Does Spillover Need Mopping Up?).

Transit Advertising

Campbell Soup started advertising around 1910. The company spent its first $5,000 placing ads on one-third of the buses in New York City for one year. The ads were so successful that after only six months, Campbell enlarged the contract to include all surface vehicles in the city. People started trying more Campbell's and in short order sales were up 100 percent. For the next 12 years, transit advertising was the only medium Campbell employed. Today, Campbell is still a major user of transit advertising.

Transit advertising is a category of out-of-home media that includes bus and taxicab advertising as well as posters on transit shelters, terminals, and subways. Though transit is not considered a major medium by most advertising practitioners, standardization, better research, more statistical data, and measured circulation have made transit advertising more attractive to national advertisers. National marketers of designer apparel and movies, for example, are two of the many cate-

Alcohol also spills over, in more ways than one. A federal trial court upheld a Baltimore city ban on billboard advertising of alcoholic beverages. The American Advertising Federation's legal counsel found the decision disturbing, because the trial judge simply presumed that advertising stimulated demand and that prohibiting ads would cut consumption.

Anheuser-Busch challenged the ban on constitutional grounds, arguing that it would not "directly advance" the city's interest in protecting its youth. It said its advertising was not designed to increase overall consumption, but rather to increase the company's market share among adults who already drink. A-B claimed Baltimore officials could not deprive adults of their right to receive information about lawful products in order to protect children. The court rejected all arguments and held that the goal of protecting children justified special treatment.

Regardless of the courts' positions in these cases, the ethical issues remain. Advertisers, agencies, and media companies must be sensitive to public opinion and seek creative solutions to the issues of protecting minors from legal adult products. Further, they must realize that when they create or allow in-your-face, shock-tactic advertising to run where consumers have no control of the medium, those outraged consumers will find ways to take control.

And then the industry will risk severe restriction and regulation for having failed to responsibly and conscientiously assert firm ethical standards itself.

Questions

1. Do you believe the goal of protecting children justifies banning advertising for legal products? Which products specifically?

2. Should ads in spillover media be censored for sexually explicit content? If so, who should the censors be, and what specifically should they prohibit?

3. What alternatives might be available to fight teenage smoking, drinking, and sexual promiscuity besides banning advertising for legal adult products?

Sources: Joel Dubow, "Say It Isn't So, Joe!" *Academy of Food Marketing,* St. Joseph's University, Philadelphia, PA, September 28, 1994; *Billboard Basics* (New York: Outdoor Advertising Association of America, 1994), p. 4; "Advertisers Asked to Abstain," *San Diego Union-Tribune,* January 20, 1994, p. B2; Michael Antebi, "Reaction to Distasteful Ads Endangers All of Advertising," *Advertising Age,* February 13, 1995, p. 14; Herbert Rotfeld, "Don't Blame Cigarette Ads, Enforce Law on Minors," *Advertising Age,* December 5, 1994, p. 29; Anne Burke, "Billboard Ban Case Clouds Future," *Admonth,* September 1994, p. 13.

The Jeff Wyler Dealer Group (www.wyler.com) uses transit advertising creatively to reach potential customers. By painting the image of a car on the side of a bus, they achieve the visual equivalent of an oversized car driving down the street. It is difficult to tell that one is looking at a bus at first; this is what draws attention to the Jeff Wyler Dealer Group name, and gets the message across.

gories of advertisers spending dramatically more in this medium, replacing the traditional transit advertising leaders such as tobacco companies, petroleum products, financial services, and proprietary medicines.[15]

Transit advertising is especially suitable for reaching middle- to lower-income urban consumers and providing supplemental coverage of these groups. Patrick Media and Gannett Outdoor Group are using innovative marketing strategies to highlight both outdoor boards and transit ads in Hispanic communities, catering to marketers' increasing desire to tap into the $240 billion Hispanic market. Today, marketers like Coke, Pepsi, and Modelo Beer spend over $20 million a year on out-of-home ads aimed at Hispanic consumers.[16]

Transit advertising is equally popular with local advertisers. Retailers can expand their reach inexpensively and often receive co-op support from national marketers, which thrive on the local exposure[17] (see the Checklist of Pros and Cons of Transit Advertising).

Types of Transit Advertising

Transit advertising targets the millions of people who use commercial transportation (buses, subways, elevated trains, commuter trains, trolleys, and airlines), plus pedestrians and car passengers, with a variety of formats: transit shelters; station, platform, and terminal posters; inside cards and outside posters on buses; and taxi exteriors.

The Pros

_____ **Long exposure.** The average transit ride is 25 minutes.

_____ **Repetitive value.** Many people take the same routes day after day.

_____ **Eagerly read messages.** Riders get bored, so readership is high and ad recall averages 55 percent.

_____ **Low cost.** Transit ads cost less than any other medium.

_____ **Creative flexibility.** Special constructions and color effects are available at relatively low cost.

_____ **Need satisfying.** Transit can target the needs of riders—with ads for cool drinks in summer, for example. Food ads do well as evening riders contemplate dinner.

_____ **Environmentally sensitive.** As social pressure to use public transportation increases, transit is well positioned as a medium of the future.

The Cons

_____ **Status.** Transit lacks the status of a major advertising medium.

_____ **Crowded environment.** Rush-hour crowding limits the opportunity and ease of reading. The vehicle itself, if dirty, may tarnish the product's image.

_____ **Selectivity.** Transit reaches a nonselective audience, which may not meet the needs of some advertisers.

_____ **Clutter.** Cards are so numerous and look so similar they may be confusing or hard to remember.

_____ **Location.** With outlying shopping malls, fewer shoppers make trips downtown.

_____ **Creative restrictions.** Although transit cards may carry longer messages than billboards, copy is still limited.

Transit Shelters

In cities with mass-transit systems, advertisers can buy space on bus shelters and on the backs of bus-stop seats. **Transit shelter advertising** is a relatively new out-of-home form enjoying great success. It reaches virtually everyone who is outdoors: auto passengers, pedestrians, bus riders, motorcyclists, bicyclists, and more. It is extremely inexpensive and available in many communities that restrict billboard advertising in business or residential areas. In fact, shelter advertising is sometimes the only form of outdoor advertising permitted. It's also an excellent complement to outdoor posters and bulletins, enabling total market coverage in a comprehensive outdoor program.

Terminal Posters

In many bus, subway, and commuter train stations, space is sold for one-, two-, and three-sheet **terminal posters.** Major train and airline terminals offer such special advertising forms as floor displays, island showcases, illuminated cards, dioramas (3-D scenes), and clocks with special lighting and moving messages.

In Paris, Nike made a splash at the French Open tennis tournament even though a competitor had locked up advertising rights within the stadium. Nike covered the city by buying space on some 2,500 buses during the tournament. As the coup de grace, it bought up every bit of signage space at the Porte d'Auteuil metro (subway) station close to the stadium and turned it into a Nike gallery of terminal posters featuring famous tennis players from around the world.[18]

This ad for Volvo (www.volvo.com) typifies the kind of one-sheet-poster advertising that is common in bus, train, and airline terminals. The ad copy complements the location of the ad with its reference to the baggage carousel in the background.

Inside and Outside Cards and Posters

The **inside card** is placed in a wall rack above the vehicle windows. Cost-conscious advertisers print both sides of the card so it can be reversed to change the message, saving on paper and shipping charges. Inside **car-end posters** (in bulkhead positions) are usually larger, but sizes vary. The end and side positions carry premium rates.

Outside posters are printed on high-grade cardboard and often varnished for weather resistance. The most widely used outside posters are side, rear, and front of bus. (See RL 17–1 in the Reference Library for common sizes and placement of inside cards and outside posters.)

Advertisers may also buy space on **taxicab exteriors,** generally for periods of 30 days, to display internally illuminated, two-sided posters positioned on the roofs. Some advertising also appears on the doors or rear of taxicabs. In some major areas, sponsors can buy cards mounted on the trunks. In Southern California, advertisers can rent cards mounted on the tops of cabs that travel throughout Los Angeles, Orange, and San Diego counties, serving major airports and traveling the busiest freeways in the country. Costing from $110 to $130 per month per cab, this is a very cost-effective way to reach the mobile public. Major tobacco advertisers are now experimenting with this medium (before traditional outdoor becomes off-limits to them).

Buying Transit Advertising

The unit of purchase is a **showing,** also known as a *run* or *service.* A **full showing** (or *No. 100 showing*) means that one card will appear in each vehicle in the system. Space may also be purchased as a *half* (No. 50) or *quarter* (No. 25) *showing.*

Rates are usually quoted for 30-day showings, with discounts for 3-, 6-, 9-, and 12-month contracts. Advertisers supply the cards at their own expense, but the transit company can help with design and production.

Cost depends on the length and saturation of the showing and the size of the space. Rates vary extensively, depending primarily on the size of the transit system. Advertisers get rates for specific markets from local transit companies and the Transit Advertising Association's *TAA Rate Directory of Transit Advertising.*

The Transit Advertising Association is the national trade organization and promotion arm of the industry. It performs research and supplies industry data on the number of vehicles, trends, and rider demographics. TAA members represent 80 percent of the transit advertising volume in the United States and Canada.

Special Inside Buys

In some cities, advertisers gain complete domination by buying the **basic bus**—all the inside space on a group of buses. For an extra charge, pads of business reply cards or coupons (called **take-ones**) can be affixed to interior ads for passengers to request more detailed information, send in application blanks, or receive some other benefit.

Special Outside Buys

Some transit companies offer **bus-o-rama signs,** jumbo full-color transparencies backlighted by fluorescent tubes and running the length of the bus. A bus has two bus-o-rama positions, one on each side. A single advertiser may also buy a **total bus**—all the exterior space, including the front, rear, sides, and top.

Gannett Outdoor has extended the idea of the total bus to the subway system in New York. Now advertisers can buy a complete *brand train*—all the subway cars that run in a particular corridor. Clothing designer Donna Karan's DKNY line, for example, bought a 10-car brand train that runs under Lexington Avenue on Manhattan's East Side. It stops right under Bloomingdale's, where DKNY's "supershop" is. The brand train costs advertisers from $65,000 to $85,000, depending on the number of cars in a train and the length of the run. National advertisers like the exclusivity it gives them.[19]

Clever outdoor buys can give public exposure and cut through advertising clutter in a spectacular way. In New York, fashion designer Donna Karan bought a 10-car train that provides advertising exclusivity to the DKNY (www.donnakaran.com) line of clothes and does so in a high-traffic location.

Other Out-of-Home Media

As mentioned earlier, there are many forms of out-of-home media. Some are so new that they are still unproven. However, several seem to be gaining in popularity, and they demonstrate how far advertisers will go to get their messages seen by the consuming public.

Mobile Billboards

The **mobile billboard,** a cross between traditional billboards and transit advertising, was first conceived as advertising on the sides of tractor-trailer trucks. Today in some large cities, specially designed flatbed trucks carry long billboards up and down busy thoroughfares. Local routes for mobile ads are also available on delivery trucks in San Francisco, Los Angeles, and Seattle.

Electronic Signs and Display Panels

Electronic signs display text and graphic messages much like the big screens in sports stadiums. The signs transmit commercial messages to retail stores, where shoppers see them. The stores pay nothing for the signs and receive 25 percent of the advertising revenue. In Montreal, Telecite used its new visual communication network (VCN) technology to install electronic display panels on subway cars. Advertisers got a powerful, inexpensive, and flexible medium with a large, captive audience; the transit authority got a modern, self-financed emergency and public information system; and passengers got something to watch while they ride.[20] Telecite is negotiating with numerous U.S. and European cities to install the systems in their subway and metro cars.

Parking Meters and Public Phones

Thanks to a couple of enterprising companies, American Parking Meter Advertising and American Telephone Advertising (ATA), marketers can now advertise on parking meters and public phones. ATA offers 20 market segments, such as hotels and restaurants, airports, college campuses, and convenience stores.

Exhibitive Media

Some media are designed specifically to help bring customers eyeball to eyeball with the product—often at the point of sale or close to it. These **exhibitive media** include *product packaging* and *trade-show booths and exhibits*. When successful, the synergy of combining exhibitive media with other media can improve product or brand awareness by as much as 500 percent.[21]

Product Packaging

In 1996, U.S. companies spent some $95 billion on packaging (as much as they spent on media advertising).[22] Since upward of 70 percent of all buying decisions are made at the point of purchase, packages play a major role in both advertising and selling. And in the world of integrated marketing comunications, the package is not only the last "ad" a consumer sees before purchasing the product, it is the only "ad" the consumer sees when using the product. So it is more than just another planned message; it is part of the product message as well.

Packaging encompasses the physical appearance of the container and includes design, color, shape, labeling, and materials. Packaging serves marketers in four major ways: protection, preservation, information, and promotion.[23] Although the protection and preservation aspects reduce the costly effects of damage, pilferage, and spoilage, the importance of packaging as an informational and promotional tool cannot be underestimated. An attractive package can create an immediate relationship with the customer, influence in-store shopping decisions, help set the product apart from competitors, and inform customers of the product's features and benefits.

Designers consider three factors: the package's stand-out appeal, how it communicates verbally and nonverbally, and the prestige or image desired.

Consumers respond to packaging intuitively, so packaging design can be as important as advertising in building a product's brand image. Packaging establishes or reinforces the brand's personality at the point of sale. So if status is the goal, the

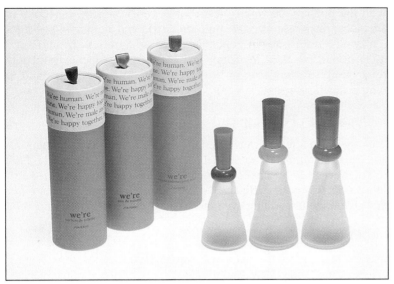

Packaging is an essential part of advertising, as it serves as the only advertising consumers take home with them. While the packaging shown here looks plain, the message it delivers presents the image that Shiseido (www.shiseido.co.jp/e/index5/htm) wants associated with its products. The text uses the product name "we're" as the first word in several simple, positive statements of men and women living happily together. The implication of the text is that such happiness can be achieved by wearing the perfume contained inside and the repetition of the product name keeps it fresh in the consumer's mind.

package designer must consider what consumers regard as prestigious. This is especially important for so-called nonrational products—cosmetics and perfumes, sports accessories, confection gifts, and certain luxury products—in which fantasy, impulsiveness, or mystique supersedes rational choice.

To sell products off the shelf, packages may use shape, color, size, interesting visuals, or even texture to deliver a marketing message, give product information, and indicate application. Packages continue promoting the product in the home, reinforcing the brand's image, so they should open and close with minimal effort and be easy to handle.

Buying packaging includes two major phases: *concept* and *production*. The *conceptual process* involves input from five major groups: consumers, manufacturers, marketing intermediaries, consumer advocacy groups, and government agencies.[24] The conflicting concerns of these groups strongly influence the nature of packaging (see Exhibit 17–5).

Environmental Issues in Packaging

As manufacturers continue to produce environmentally safe packaging, the marketer's cost of materials rises. And what some consumers expect from *green packaging* is not necessarily what manufacturers traditionally offer nor what marketing intermediaries prefer to use.[25]

Exhibit 17–5
Expectations and concerns in packaging development.

Consumers	Manufacturers	Marketing intermediaries (retailers/wholesalers)	Consumer advocacy groups	Government agencies

• Ease (to handle and store)
• Convenience
• List of ingredients
• Instructions
• Life of product
• Disposal method
• Toll-free phone number for emergencies
• Performance guarantees
• Safety guarantees
• Environmental safety (biodegradability)
• Reusable
• Recyclable
	• Sturdiness
	• Suppleness
	• Attractiveness
	• Safety (to users and for the product)
	• Cost of:
	  – materials
	  – fabrication
	  – labor
	  – inventory
	  – shipping
	  – storage
	• Need to change
	• Lighter weight (with safety)
	• Tamper proof
	• Package size (promotion space versus materials cost and environmental safety)
	• Availability of materials
		• Sturdiness (of case and packages)
		• Convenience (of removal)
		• Tamper proof
		• Identifiable
		• Safety (to users and for the product)
		• Ease of:
		  – storage
		  – shelving stacking
		  – package stacking
		  – inventory (by computer)
		• Room for price stickers
			• Package safe to:
			  – handle
			  – use
			• Environmentally safe (biodegradability, etc.)
			• Package free of health hazards
			• Self-informative
			  – List of ingredients
			  – Instructions
			  – Disposal method
			  – Toll-free phone number for emergencies
			  – Warranties
			  – Expiration date
			• Recyclable
			• Adherence to federal and local regulations
				• Free of deception
				• Free of harmful effects to ecology
				• Biodegradable
				• Free of health hazards
				• All-around safety
				  – Safe to handle
				  – Safe to use
				• Labeled properly
				  – List of ingredients
				  – Nutritional facts with guidelines
				• Expiration date for certain products
				• Recyclable
				• Adherence to federal and local regulations

There are many different types of packaging available. Cardboard boxes, such as the one shown, are ideal for computer hardware. The styles range from a large box for a PC or monitor to the small flat disk jacket. However, they are all consistent in design and therefore create a unified image for Digital Equipment Corp. (www.digital.com). Each box bears the company name and logo, as well as various images and text. Such elements would be consistent with the overall ad campaign. Packaging such as this plays a significant role in IMC.

 With the public's growing concern for the environment, especially in international markets, recyclable tin-coated steel and aluminum packages are enjoying a resurgence in popularity. Because European countries are so densely populated, their regulations requiring environmentally friendly packaging are far more stringent than in North America. Such regulations add to the cost of doing business overseas.

Government Impact on Packaging

Government agencies also affect package design. The Food and Drug Administration (FDA), for example, and the Nutrition Labeling and Education Act of 1990 (which went into effect in 1994) imposed stricter labeling requirements for nutrition and health products. And sometimes a state's packaging requirements differ from the federal government's, adding even more complexity for manufacturers.

Package Manufacturing

Packages may come in many forms: wrappers, cartons, boxes, crates, cans, bottles, jars, tubes, barrels, drums, and pallets. And they may be constructed of many materials, from paper and steel ("tin" cans) to wood, glass, and burlap. Newer packaging materials include plastic-coated papers, ceramics, metal foils, and even straw. Improvements in packaging include amber-green glass bottles that protect the contents from light damage and heavy-duty, gray computer-disk jackets that reflect heat and protect the disk. The plastic film pouch for food products has become a substitute for tin cans and is more flexible, light, and compact. For pharmaceutical products, consumers prefer plastic containers.[26]

The second phase of packaging, the *production process,* may require the use of many packaging specialists: experts in package engineering (box designers, packaging materials consultants, and specialists in equipment configuration); graphic artists (designers, production/computer artists, illustrators, and photographers); label producers (printers and label manufacturers); die-cutters for custom packages; and package warehousing companies (wholesalers of prefabricated packages and package manufacturers). (See RL 17–2: The Packaging Production Process, in the Reference Library.)

Ad agencies are not usually involved in packaging decisions. This is typically the realm of specialists. However, it's not uncommon for an agency to be consulted on the design of labels and packages, and some may even prepare the copy that goes on them. In an IMC program, the agency can be very helpful in coordinating this work with the overall theme of the ad campaign.

Generally, the package's design should be kept simple for three reasons: typical packaging materials (such as corrugated cardboard) cannot support high-resolution printing, intricate folding and die-cutting can be very expensive, and packaging that requires exact folding and fitting often creates excessive assembly costs and leads to structural challenges that most cost-effective packaging materials cannot support.[27]

When Should a Package Be Changed?

There are many reasons to change a package: product alteration or improvement, substitution in packaging materials, competitive pressure, environmental concerns, changes in legislation, or the need to increase brand recognition.[28]

Advertisers spend millions researching and promoting new images. And packages have to reflect a contemporary brand image consistent with constantly changing consumer perceptions and desires. However, marketers should always exercise caution. Designers often change packaging very gradually to avoid confusing consumers.

Trade-Show Booths and Exhibits

Every major industry sponsors annual **trade shows**—exhibitions where manufacturers, dealers, and buyers get together for demonstrations and discussion. More than 9,000 industrial, scientific, and medical shows are held in the United States each year, and many companies exhibit at more than one show.

Trade shows are also very important for global marketers, since they may be the only place where an advertiser can meet the company's major international prospects at one time. Moreover, some of the world's largest trade shows (the Paris Air Show, for example) are held overseas.

The construction of trade-show **booths** and **exhibits** has become a major factor in sales promotion plans. To stop traffic, a booth must be simple and attractive and have good lighting and a large visual. It should also provide a comfortable atmosphere to promote conversation between salespeople and prospects. Many regular trade-show exhibitors use state-of-the-art technology, such as holograms, fiberoptics, and interactive computer systems, to communicate product features quickly and dramatically.

When establishing an exhibit booth program, managers should consider planning, budgeting, promotion, people, and productivity.[29]

Planning

Planning pivots on four major areas: the budget, the image of the company or brand, the frequency of the shows, and the flexibility of booth configuration.[30] In planning the actual exhibits or trade-show booths, advertisers need to consider numerous factors: size and location of space; desired image or impression of the exhibit; complexities of shipping, installation, and dismantling; number of products to be displayed; need for storage and distribution of literature; use of preshow advertising and promotion; and the cost of all these factors.

This booth for Reebok exemplifies how a company can promote itself and generate traffic at trade shows. The oversized ads and the sign reading "Planet Reebok" welcome attendees into another realm—differentiating Reebok (www.reebok.com) from the many other companies present at such exhibitions. Once within the halls of Planet Reebok, attendees are exposed to the many different sports that one would wear athletic shoes for through ads lining the walls. Hanging from the ceiling are signs displaying the names of the many specialized sneakers the company has to offer.

Budgeting

Trade shows are expensive, and costs have increased substantially in the last decade. A large company may spend $1 million or more on a booth for one trade show. With staffers' travel, living, and salary expenses added to booth costs and preshow promotion, the cost per visitor reached rises to more than $185.[31] Despite the expense, trade shows can still be a cost-effective way to reach sales prospects.

Budgeting for trade shows and a booth may require an extensive review of over 60 factors (see RL 17–3: Trade-Show Budgeting Checklist, in the Reference Library).

Promotion

To build traffic for a trade-show booth or exhibit, marketers send out personal invitations, conduct direct-mail campaigns,

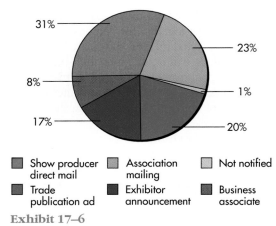

Show producer direct mail

Association mailing

Not notified

Trade publication ad

Exhibitor announcement

Business associate

Exhibit 17–6
How do customers learn about trade shows?

place ads in trade publications, issue news releases, and perform telemarketing. The pie chart in Exhibit 17–6 portrays how customers typically learn about a trade show.[32]

At the show itself, activities at the booth and promotional materials (handouts, brochures, giveaway specialty items, raffles) can stimulate customer interest and improve product exposure. 3M's Telcomm Products Division mailed 6,000 potential show attendees a Pony Express theme folder that invited them to pick up a trail map at the booth. The map guided the visitors (Pony Express riders) through a series of stations shared by seven product groups within the huge booth. Once the visitors' maps had been stamped at each station, they were given a "pay envelope" containing replicas of 1850 coins and vouchers redeemable for merchandise awards.[33]

People

The company representatives staffing the booth personify the kind of service the customer can expect to receive. They should be articulate, people-oriented, enthusiastic, knowledgeable about the product, and empathetic listeners.[34]

The primary goal of a trade-show booth is to meet with qualified prospects face to face. However, research shows that 58 percent of the people visiting a booth will not wait more than one minute to meet a representative (see Exhibit 17–7). Ideally, 80 percent of the salesperson's time should be spent listening and 20 percent talking.[35]

Productivity

A company's trade-show effort may be wasted if prospects' names are not collected properly. Each lead should be evaluated as to the prospect's readiness to receive another contact (A = now; B = 2 weeks; C = 6 months; D = never).[36] The resulting lead list is the link to future sales and augments the company's prospect database.

Supplementary Media

Many promotional media are difficult to classify because they're tailored to individual needs. Such supplementary media include specialty advertising, directories and Yellow Pages, and a variety of emerging alternative media vehicles.

Specialty Advertising

41%

28%

14%

11%

6%

Will not wait | 30 sec. | 1 min. | 3 min. | 5 min.

Exhibit 17–7
How long a visitor will wait for a sales rep at a trade show booth.

The Promotional Products Association International (PPAI) defines an **advertising specialty** as a promotional product, usually imprinted with an advertiser's name, message, or logo, that is distributed free as part of a marketing communications program.[37] Today, nearly every business uses advertising specialties. As many as 15,000 different specialty items, ranging from coffee mugs to ballpoint pens, key chains, and T-shirts, represent an annual volume of more than $6 billion.[38]

An advertising specialty is different from a premium. **Premiums** are also promotional products; they are typically more valuable and usually bear no advertising message. However, to get a premium, recipients must buy a product, send in a coupon, witness a demonstration, or perform some other action advantageous to the advertiser. An advertising specialty, on the other hand, is always given *free* as a goodwill item. Some specialty items may be kept for years and serve as continuous, friendly reminders of the advertiser's business. Companies often spend substantial sums for goodwill items to promote customer referrals. In fact, studies show that recipients of advertising specialties are typically better referrers than nonrecipients.[39]

Fossil Watches (www.fossil.com) used this specialty packaging as a gift to consumers. The container is modeled after automotive oil cans (a good gift for men) and is reusable. This novelty gift is more useful and appealing than the typical key chain or pencil. The text proclaims the quality and style of the watch that can be found inside and serves as both a reminder to the customer and an ad for others who see it.

Consumer Specialties

Consumers tend to associate the quality of a specialty item with the quality of the company providing it, so companies lean toward more expensive gifts for consumers. Items costing $3 to $5 have become the norm, as opposed to cheap key rings and pencils. Specialties work best when they are integrated into a broader marketing program or service strategy. Some businesses, like banks and savings and loans, are subject to government regulation of the value of gifts they can give.

Business-to-Business Specialties

In the business-to-business arena, companies use more structured specialty promotions to improve their goodwill standing over competitors. In one case, including an ad specialty with a thank-you letter improved customer attitude by 34 percent over sending a thank-you letter alone. At the same time, customers' general feelings about the company and its sales reps improved 52 percent.[40]

In one test, a group of Realtors received a $1.49 ballpoint pen imprinted with a mortgage company's name, a second group received a $10 sports bag (also imprinted), and a third group got nothing. In a follow-up questionnaire, Realtors who received nothing were least inclined to recommend the product, but both the sports bag and ballpoint groups responded equally positively. Evidently, gift recipients felt obliged to reciprocate, but the value of the gift was not crucial. So the $1.49 pen was the better return on investment.[41]

Inappropriate specialty items can backfire no matter what the cost. A recipient may perceive an overly expensive gift as a form of bribery, yet a cheap trinket could make a quality-conscious business look chintzy. As we discussed in Chapter 8, the value and nature of gifts can also become an ethical issue.

Directories and Yellow Pages

Thousands of **directories** are published each year by phone companies, trade associations, industrial groups, and others. They mainly serve as locators, buying guides, and mailing lists, but they also carry advertising aimed at specialized fields. When Yellow Pages advertising is combined with other media, reach increases significantly, as illustrated in Exhibit 17–8. In Yellow Pages ads, content is most important. The ad should tell people *how* to make the purchase, not why. As with most advertising media, the larger the ad, the more attention it attracts.[42]

The United States has about 6,000 local telephone directories with a combined circulation of 350 million. Since deregulation of the phone industry and the 1984 breakup of AT&T, the Yellow Pages business has boomed, with ad revenues reaching more than $10 billion in 1994.[43] In fact, the Yellow Pages is now the fourth largest medium, ahead of radio, magazines, and outdoor. The 10 largest publishers, shown in Exhibit 17–9, receive more than 90 percent of the industry's advertising revenues.[44] Some 200 other publishers also produce Yellow Pages directories (the

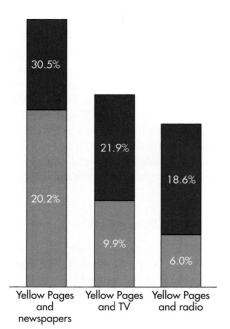

Exhibit 17–8
Overall advertising reach from media combinations. When Yellow Pages advertising is used in conjunction with other media, reach increases significantly.

Exhibit 17–9
Top Yellow Pages companies, 1996.

Company	Revenues ($ millions)
SBC Communications	$1,985.0
BellSouth Corp.	1,742.0
GTE Corp.	1,527.0
Bell Atlantic	1,222.5
US West	1,120.0
Nynex Corp.	969.5
Ameritech Corp.	860.1
DonTech	408.9
Dun & Bradstreet Corp.	377.5
Sprint	309.0

Source: Reprinted with permission from the August 18, 1997 issue of *Advertising Age.* Copyright, Crain Communications, Inc. 1997.

Yellow Pages name and the walking-fingers logo are not trademarked, so anyone can use them).

Stiff competition has forced phone and directory companies to differentiate their Yellow Pages with more user-friendly directories containing supplemental, general interest information. Techniques being used include:

● An alphabetical index that groups related headings beneath a consumer description of the product.

● A brand-name index listing the Yellow Pages heading where a specific brand can be found.

● A subject index that groups headings by broad areas, such as Automotive; Entertainment and Leisure; Health and Well-Being; Just for Kids; and Pets.

● Pages with local maps and information on parks, events, community services, transportation, and shopping.

● Free interactive voice services ("audiotext") that link the telephone with a host computer to allow the easy retrieval of information.

In addition, highly specialized directories aim at particular audiences, such as the Chinese-language Yellow Pages in San Francisco and the Paginas Amarillas in the border states.

Yellow Pages are often the sole advertising medium for local businesses, and nearly 87 percent of Yellow Pages revenue is derived from local advertisers.[45] But Yellow Pages directories can be an important medium for national advertisers, too. For example, U-Haul spends more than $20 million a year on Yellow Pages ads. The Yellow Pages Publishers Association created the BrandSell program for national packaged-goods advertisers whose products have no specific Yellow Pages heading. BrandSell enables a toothpaste manufacturer, say, to advertise under the "Dentists" heading and a telephone calling-card company to advertise in the "Airlines" section.

A growing number of publishers now offer a "ride-along" program that lets regional and national marketers deliver coupons and product samples along with the white and Yellow Pages directories. The ride-along program now reaches about 75 percent of the top 300 markets, resulting in a potential audience of 60 million households.[46]

Emerging Media

As traditional advertising media become more expensive and audiences become more fragmented, many advertisers seek new ways to reach their customers. Several types of alternative media are potentially viable options.

Videotapes

People rent millions of videos every week. However, as we discussed in Chapter 15, commercials on movie videos are controversial. In a less intrusive approach, ads are placed on the videocassette boxes. A third type of video advertising is the **video brochure,** which advertisers produce and mail to customers and prospects.

Cinema Advertising

Advertising in movie theaters (**cinema advertising**), is a growing but controversial practice. Some audiences boo and hiss during commercials, but studies show that 77 percent of viewers recall theater ads the following day, compared to 20 percent for TV ads.[47] Some movie theater chains prohibit filmed advertising for fear of offending their audience. Walt Disney Studios no longer allows U.S. theaters to run commercials before any of its movies.

Product placement is an increasingly popular way to discretely advertise consumer products. BMW (www.bmw.com) paid money to wrest away James Bond's traditional Aston Martin in the 1997 movie hit, Tomorrow Never Dies. *The movie featured scenes of the international superspy racing around in BMW's newest line of sassy automobiles.*

Product Placement

Another way to reach movie audiences is to pay a fee to have the product written into the movie. Such **product placement** is becoming more common—and more controversial. Notice the number of identifiable products in the next movie you see.

Increasingly, product placement in the multibillion dollar movie industry has become an important advertising medium. By getting their brands appearances, and sometimes roles, in movies, companies benefit from the association with top films and big-name actors.

Nokia Mobile Phones paid Paramount Pictures close to $1 million for placement in the 1996 blockbuster *Mission Impossible*. In the film, actor Tom Cruise is seen holding a Nokia phone and asking a costar to explain all of its functions. Mercedes-Benz of North America used a similar approach when it launched its M-Class all-activity vehicle in the film *The Lost World: Jurassic Park*. Products can also be placed on TV shows, on the Internet, and in computer games.

However, controversy surrounds some product placement categories. In response to severe new laws prohibiting most forms of tobacco advertising, the Canadian Tobacco Manufacturers' Council withdrew all product placements in films, videotapes, TV programs, and computer games.

ATMs

These days it seems you can't travel one city block without running into the omnipresent **automated teller machine (ATM),** a fact that is hardly lost on contemporary marketers. With so many thousands of money devices in service, it's only natural that the captive audience of this medium be targeted for creative promotional tactics.

Fleet Financial Group has capitalized on ATM technology by printing retailer coupons on the back of ATM receipts, the other piece of paper that customers receive from the machines. The coupons, which were initially redeemable at Bruegger's Bagels, Firestone, Great Cuts, Oil Doctor, and Pizza Hut, originated in Massachusetts and provided advertising that customers were likely to carry around in their wallets or cars.

The newest ATM innovation, developed by Electronic Data Systems Corp., puts full-motion video ads on the machine's screen as customers wait for their transaction to be processed. The 15-second ads, which debuted in 7-Eleven stores in San Diego, replace the "Transaction being processed" or "Please wait" messages that appeared on the screen. The original ads promoted Fox Searchlight Pictures' films *The Ice Storm* and *The Full Monty*.

Other promotions run through ATM machines include a MasterCard International and Coca-Cola USA collaboration on the "Coca-Cola incredible summer," in which customers could win cash instantly by using a special disposable ATM card.

Marketers are quickly filling every space where advertisements might be seen by an unsuspecting customer. From blimps to video game placements to parking meters, advertisers go where consumers congregate. Today we can even find short video clip ads played on selected ATM machines across the country.

Chapter **Summary**

Media that reach prospects outside their homes are called out-of-home media. They include outdoor advertising, transit advertising, and exotica like electronic signs and parking meters. Of the major advertising media, outdoor advertising is the least expensive per message delivered. It also offers other attractive features: instant broad coverage (reach), very high frequency, great flexibility, and high impact. Drawbacks include the limits of brief messages, long lead times, high initial preparation costs, and the difficulty of physically inspecting each billboard.

The standardized outdoor advertising industry consists of about 3,000 local and regional plant operators. National advertising makes up the bulk of outdoor business. The three most common forms of outdoor advertising structures are the 30-sheet poster, the eight-sheet poster, and the bulletin. A form of outdoor available in some cities is the spectacular, an expensive electronic display. The basic unit of sale for outdoor advertising is the 100 showing, or 100 GRPs, which means the message will appear on enough panels to provide a daily exposure equal to the market's total population.

Transit advertising includes transit shelters; station, platform, and terminal posters; inside cards and outside posters on buses; and taxi exteriors. This medium offers high reach, frequency, exposure, and attention values at very low cost. It gives long exposure to the advertiser's message and offers repetitive value and geographic flexibility. In addition, advertisers have a wide choice in the size of space used.

But transit advertising does not cover some segments of society. Also, it reaches a nonselective audience, it lacks prestige, and copy is still somewhat limited.

Other out-of-home media include mobile billboards, electronic signs and display panels, parking meters, and public phones.

Exhibitive media include product packaging and trade-show booths and exhibits. These media are designed to help bring consumers or business customers eyeball to eyeball with the product, often at the point of sale or close to it.

Supplementary media include specialty advertising, Yellow Pages directories, and emerging media like videotapes, movie theaters, product placements and ATMs. Product placement includes films, videos, computer games, and the Internet. The advantage of film is that it creates brand association with top movies and actors.

ATMs provide several means of exposure, from printed ads on receipts to full-motion video to promotionals like ATM-card cash giveaways. Because most Americans today use ATMs, they offer a high frequency of exposure.

Important **Terms**

advertising specialty, *554*	exhibitive media, *550*	spectaculars, *544*
automated teller machine (ATM), *557*	full showing, *544*	standardized outdoor advertising, *537*
basic bus, *549*	global positioning system (GPS), *545*	stock poster, *542*
booth, *553*	inside card, *548*	take-ones, *549*
bulletin structure, *537*	mobile billboard, *550*	taxicab exterior, *548*
bus-o-rama sign, *549*	100 showing, *544*	terminal poster, *548*
car-end poster, *548*	out-of-home media, *536*	30-sheet poster panel, *542*
cinema advertising, *556*	outside poster, *548*	total bus, *549*
directories, *555*	packaging, *550*	trade show, *553*
eight-sheet poster, *543*	premium, *554*	transit advertising, *546*
electronic sign, *550*	product placement, *557*	transit shelter advertising, *548*
exhibit, *553*	showing, *549*	video brochure, *556*

Review **Questions**

1. What is the difference between out-of-home media and outdoor advertising?
2. Why is outdoor advertising sometimes referred to as the last mass medium?
3. Which advertising objectives are the outdoor media most suitable for?
4. Is outdoor an effective advertising medium for a local political candidate? Why?
5. How do gross rating points for outdoor media differ from GRPs for electronic media?
6. What are the principal categories of transit advertising?
7. What is a brand train and what advantages does it offer over less expensive forms of transit advertising?
8. Which are the exhibitive media and why are they called that?
9. What is the principal benefit of trade shows and exhibitions?
10. How does specialty advertising differ from premiums? How could a local computer store use these media, and which would be better for the store to use?

Exporing the **Internet**

The Internet exercises for Chapter 17 address the following areas covered throughout the chapter: outdoor advertising (Exercise 1) and specialty advertising (Exercise 2).

1. Outdoor Advertising

    As you have learned in this chapter, out-of-home advertising and communication have been a mainstay in consumers' lives for quite some time. The outdoor advertising industry certainly makes up the largest portion of such advertising.

    Though often overlooked in advertising and media decision making, outdoor can have a powerful impact as a supplemental medium to broader print and/or broadcast campaigns. Now, find out more about this side of the advertising business by visiting five of the Web sites for the outdoor advertising organizations below and answer the questions that follow.

    - American Billboard Network **www.abn1.com**
    - Burkhart Advertising **www.burkhartadv.com**
    - Edwards Outdoor **www.edwards1.com**
    - Eight-Sheet Outdoor Association **www.eightsheet.com**
    - Eller Media **www.ellermedia.com**
    - Gallop & Gallop Advertising **www.gallop.ca**
    - Gannett Outdoor **www.macneil.com/gannett**
    - Outdoor Advertising Association of America, Inc. (OAAA) **www.oaaa.org**
    - Poster Publicity **www.posterpublicity.com**
    - *Sign Business* magazine **www.nbm.com/signbusiness**
    - *SignCraft* magazine **www.signcraft.com**
    - Steen Outdoor Systems **www.steen.com**
    - Whiteco Outdoor **www.whiteco.com**
    - Wilkins Outdoor Network (WON) **www.outdoor-ad.com**

    a. What organization sponsors the site? Who is the intended audience(s)?

    b. What is the purpose of the site? Does it succeed? Why?

    c. What services (if any) does the organization provide advertisers?

    d. How important do you feel this organization is to outdoor advertising today and in the future? Why?

2. Specialty Advertising

    Promotional specialty items are, perhaps, one of the oldest forms of media. Though consumers do not always think of these items as "advertising," they most certainly are—being clearly composed, nonpersonal communications by an identified sponsor. Many organizations and firms are involved in specialty advertising and the industry is still growing today. Peruse some of the Web sites below and learn more about the products, processes, and promotional power of specialty ad items. Then answer the questions that follow.

    - ADCOLOR, Inc. **www.logomall.com/adcolorinc**
    - Adsmart **www.tiac.net/users/adsmart**
    - BCG Creations **www.bcgcreations.com**
    - Bells Advertising **www.bells.com**
    - Corporate Graphics, Inc. **www.wearables.com**
    - Cowan Graphics Inc. **www.cowan.ca**
    - Image Pointe **www.imagepointe.com**
    - Keegan Tees **www.upbeat.com/keegants**
    - LogoZ **www.logoz.com**
    - PromoMart **www.promomart.com**
    - PROMO'S **www.coolgifts.com**
    - Promotional Product Association International (PPAI) **www.ppa.org**
    - Promotions Online **www.promosonline.com**
    - S-N-T Graphics **www.sntgraphics.com**
    - Top Line Apparel **www.net22.com/topline**

    a. What is the focus of the organization sponsoring this site?

    b. Who is the intended audience of the site?

    c. What services (if any) does the organization offer?

    d. What is your overall impression of the organization and its work? Explain?

The **Epilogue**

The Complete Campaign: Toyota/Everyday

It was the first commercial in the new campaign. But to the viewer, it was hard to tell what it was all about. It started with a group of girls jumping rope. Superimposed over the scene was scrawled a handwritten question: "All you have is today . . . How will you make it count?" And in the background played a familiar tune: Sly and the Family Stone singing the 70s hit "Everyday People."

Toyota used vignettes of a wide group of people making "Everyday" affirmations to demonstrate the company's understanding and caring for everyday life. Saatchi & Saatchi's creatives also employed the famous song "Everyday People" as a musical logo to link the Toyota brand concept to the minds of consumers. The overall campaign aim was to associate the positive messages in the copy and visuals with the company's own dedication and commitment to its customers.

Then the video quickly evolved into a fast-paced montage—a series of quick, one- and two-second cuts—of different types of people, from all walks of life, answering the initial question by declaring their aspirations. A middle-aged mother says, "I will remember what's really important." A young, African-American musician vows, "I will always speak my mind—everyday." One guy in a pick-up basketball game says, "I will never take my wife for granted." A female executive declares, "I'll spend more time with my kids—everyday." A little boy in the barber's chair says, "I will try to find something good in someone I don't like." And a crusty old rancher promises, "I'll be more romantic—everyday."

In some of the myriad scenes, a vehicle—either a car, or a van, or a pickup—is parked unobtrusively in the background. But you don't know what it is—until the very end. Finally an older gentleman says, "Isn't life wonderful." And the screen dissolves to the Toyota logo and the company's new slogan: "Everyday."

Sure doesn't look like a car commercial.

Created by Toyota's longtime agency, Saatchi & Saatchi Los Angeles, the novel Everyday campaign is part of a new genre of advertising that seeks to break the stereotypical hard-sell mold of auto advertising and connect with people's hearts and lives in an emotional, visceral way.[1]

This is a far cry from Toyota's previous "I love what you do for me" campaign that hammered the quality, reliability, and dependability of the company's cars. While these ads may not have been particularly memorable, they evidently did the job. Toyota has prospered in the United States. It's now the number four automaker in America—right behind GM, Ford, and Chrysler. And in 1997, the Toyota Camry was the top-selling car in the nation, outpacing even the Honda Accord and the Ford Taurus. So, for a company that was already considered by many to be one of the best-run corporations in the world, this was a completely new approach.

Why would they make this change? And how did they come up with this particular campaign? That's an interesting story that demonstrates one company's growing sophistication, its commitment to customer satisfaction, and its understanding of integrated marketing communications.

The Importance of a Brand Campaign

A *campaign* is a combination of unique advertisements, promotional events, and other marketing communications activities that all express the same selling proposition. The ads and promotions collectively present a singular strategic message to the customer or prospect. When implemented effectively, this cumulative process integrates the message into the consumer's everyday life, ties all the company's products together under a singular symbolic umbrella, distinguishes the company's offerings from the competition, and creates a rationale for the consumer to pay a little extra for the added value of the brand. Thus, the campaign is not only a very persuasive marketing tool, it's a good way to maintain customer loyalty while maximizing every ad dollar spent.

To achieve their full effect, ad campaigns require extensive development. A theme—or Big Idea—must be established early and communicated well to give the campaign consistency, and it must be adaptable to a wide variety of media.

When Toyota launched its Everyday campaign, some observers questioned: If Toyota is at the top of its class, why develop a new campaign? Are they trying to fix something that isn't broken? In fact, why advertise at all? Why not save the money and bank the profits?

if life came

Career Art. Family. An All-around your life is pretty good. After all, you pride yourself on always making educated choices. For you, there's the

with a report card

#1 selling car in America, the Toyota Camry. An available 194-hp V6 engine. Anti-lock Brake System. And a quiet, comfortable, rein-

you'd be bringing home

forced passenger cabin. So by owning an affordable 1998 Toyota Camry you can add another class to your report card of life. Can An

straight A's.

CAMRY
#1 SELLING CAR IN AMERICA

TOYOTA | everyday

1 800-GO-TOYOTA ◆ www.toyota.com

After the overall campaign theme was established by Toyota, the company's agency (Saatchi & Saatchi) created both television and print ads to showcase each vehicle model. In each of the ads, the agency maintained the Everyday theme and music, even though they were individually tailored to markets ranging from young parents to corporate executives to retired grandparents.

There's no question that Toyota was doing well. Its sales at the time were way up. *Consumer Reports* regularly rated Toyota products as the best buy. *Fortune* named Toyota one of its most-admired companies and designated it as the top company in the automotive industry. And, of course, the Camry was selling like gangbusters.[2]

But beneath this "bulletproof" exterior, there were potential problems. Fortunately, Toyota was savvy enough to not only discover them in advance, but to prepare a long-term, comprehensive plan to deal with them. By identifying and attacking critical problems early, a company can work from a position of strength rather than weakness. Toyota saw it simply as preventive maintenance.[3]

Situation Analysis—Understanding Your Strengths and Weaknesses

David Pelliccioni, the corporate marketing manager of Toyota Motor Sales USA, noted that while the company was selling more cars and trucks than ever before, research showed it was losing the emotional connection it had once had with the customer.

To understand what was happening, one had to look at the recent history of Japanese cars in America. Back in the 80s, consumers had gobbled up the Japanese imports enthusiastically because of their reliability and affordability. In fact, due to American import quotas, there was greater demand than Toyota could fill. Those people who were able to get them, loved them—and they actually scoffed at their neighbors who were still driving Detroit iron. However, with the cars selling themselves, dealers didn't need a degree in social skills to move a lot of product.

Then, in the 90s, things changed. Detroit finally responded—by improving the quality of their products and by offering lower prices. Toyota's advertising became more pragmatic and product-focused, or, as Pelliccioni called it, "more sterile." With the increased competition, the company placed more and more emphasis on monthly sales quotas—at any expense. This created continuing pressure on the dealerships, and that affected customer relationships.

So, while loyalty to the brand was exceptionally high, the company was slipping badly in J. D. Power's sales and service satisfaction rankings. Toyota's own internal research reflected the same information—customers were saying they loved the cars but, despite the advertising ("I love what you do for me"), they didn't like the way they were being treated in the dealerships. This set off the alarm bells at Toyota, and they attacked the problem aggressively.[4]

Restoring Brand Value through Integrated Marketing Communication

In 1997, under the new leadership of Toyota president Hiroshi Okuda, a marketing-savvy, global-view player, the company announced a corporatewide, global overhaul. They dubbed it their "New Era Business Strategy." New Era is an all-encompassing program that is designed to impact the way Toyota does everything—and most important, the way it communicates the Toyota brand both inside and outside the company.[5]

Recall our discussion of integrated marketing communications in Chapter 7. What New Era demonstrated was Toyota's understanding of the most basic principle of IMC—that *everything* a company does sends a message. Besides the *planned messages* of advertising and sales promotion, companies also send *product messages* and *service messages* through their product offerings and various actions. On top of that, they have to deal with the *unplanned messages* that may emanate from employees, customers, or even the press. Unfortunately, most of these messages have far greater long-term impact than all the planned messages a company pays for. Moreover, to avoid a communications misfire, the planned messages must be consistent with the other messages customers receive or they will inevitably confuse the customer, thereby impairing the relationship and damaging the brand's equity.

Understanding this, Pelliccioni says Toyota's New Era guidelines purposefully gave dealers greater latitude in employee training and local marketing and advertising. But they also put greater pressure on the dealers to provide customers with a positive experience in all departments: sales, service, and financing.[6]

Developing an IMC Campaign

The idea of IMC is to get *all* company activities in sync—not just the advertising—so that the messages emanating from every department are consistent with the desired overall brand image. But once the company's operations are working smoothly, the advertising itself must reflect the company's new reality. Thus, everybody agreed—the company, the agency, and the dealers—that Toyota needed a new branding campaign. They needed to go back out and re-establish friendship with the customer. And they needed to talk *to* them rather than *at* them.

Joe McDonagh, Saatchi & Saatchi's executive creative director, said, "No matter what focus groups you sit in on, whether they are talking about their beer or their sneakers or their cars, consumers are looking for brands they can believe in and brands that are relevant."[7]

Sophisticated brand campaigns are not developed overnight, though. And, to be truly effective internally as well as externally, a company as large as Toyota has to have participation and buy-in from all its disparate arms—corporate, dealer groups, and Toyota's 1,200 individual dealerships that are scattered all over the country.

As a result, the process of developing the campaign was collaborative between the agency and the client, and good research was critical. Michael Bevan, Toyota's national advertising manager, spent more than a year traveling the country to attend countless focus groups of Toyota owners, nonowners, dealers, and the general public. During this time, he also worked with Saatchi & Saatchi to develop and

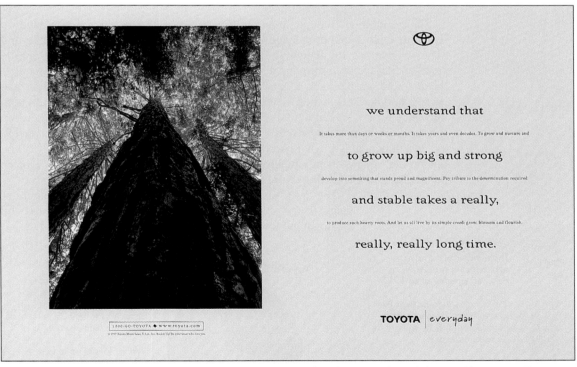

Majestic tall trees and deep roots form an interesting metaphor for strength, stability, and longevity. Here, Toyota talks in general terms about the length of time and the commitment needed for beautiful things (like people) to grow and mature. But, of course, after nearly 50 years in this country, perhaps Toyota is really talking about its own success in a very subtle and humble way. This type of corporate ad is often used to engender good morale among corporate employees.

test different concepts, and he held numerous consensus-building sessions between the agency, the company, and the dealers. "The exercise," said Bevan, "was exhausting. But it was also exciting. We learned so much about our own brand, the consumer, and the competition. And the process of everybody working together toward a common goal was incredibly rewarding."[8]

During this developmental period, one of the things they learned about the consumer was that today's auto purchasers are far more sophisticated people than even a decade ago. Customers today are well-informed, "professional" consumers. They are self-assured—optimistic, even—but they demand quality, integrity, and proper treatment. They believe they deserve the best, and they are interested in buying products they can relate to. They are also very focused on their families and personal relationships today. So they are interested in products that will help them function better as parents and spouses.

What they also learned was that, with the incredible fragmentation of the market and the heightened competition among automakers, Toyota's brand awareness was slipping. In fact, people today see cars more and more as parity commodities, with few differentiating features (see Exhibit E–1). Given the intensity of automotive advertising, this is actually not surprising. Despite the fact that it spends a substantial amount of money on advertising every year, Toyota's share of voice in the overall U.S. automotive market is only about 2 percent. Compare that to the Big Three American automakers who comprise over 50 percent share of voice. That's heavy competition—just to be heard. Moreover, Toyota's national advertising, which creates the image for the brand, comprises only about one-third of Toyota's total communications (the rest comes from dealer associations and individual dealers), and that has to be spread over 13 different models. This further fragments the company's ability to communicate any kind of brand message (see Exhibit E–2). Result: declining brand awareness.

The good news, though, was that Toyota enjoyed a very strong heritage on which to build a brand message. First, it offered a broad line of cars, trucks, and SUVs—something for everybody. This enabled the company to appeal to a wide cross-section of automotive buyers. Second, its products were current and state-of-the-art—and people liked them. Toyota had just introduced the RAV4 with great success and had relaunched the hot-selling Camry. Plus, the company was about to introduce a new, expanded family van, the Sienna. And a new full-sized pickup truck was in the planning stage. Third, people did trust in Toyota's quality, reliability, and dependability. That had been the company's hallmark, consistently borne out by high marks from virtually every independent rating organization. Finally, the company was enjoying unprecedented sales success.

The time was thus ripe for Toyota to initiate a strategic campaign that would reposition the brand in the marketplace by making a gut-level, emotional connection with the consumer.

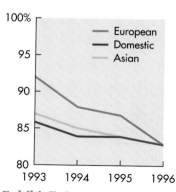

The number of car owners experiencing problems has declined steadily since 1993.

1996 marks the first year ever to see Asian, Domestic, and European makes merging into an identical score.

Exhibit E–1

Emerging product parity—percentage of car owners reporting problems in past year.

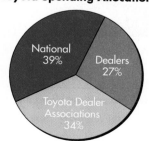

Over 60 percent of Toyota communications are dealer based. National advertising accounts for only 39 percent of Toyota's communications.

Within Toyota national advertising, the budget is fragmented further across 13 different models, making it more difficult to break through ad clutter.

Exhibit E–2

Toyota's voice has a fragmented message.

Self-image is often the deciding factor in people's auto-mobile purchases. With the RAV4, Toyota appeals to the individualism within all of us. And what a great tongue-in-cheek headline to get the point across!

Consumer Behavior and the Brand

As we discussed in Chapter 4, purchase behavior for certain high-involvement products (like cars) is centered around the concept of self-image. For a brand to be meaningful, it must provide a fit between the customer's self-image and the product's image. By understanding what issues are important to constructing the customer's self-image, and then attaching the brand to those concepts, marketers hope to forge the emotional bond that can lead to long-term, mutually profitable relationships.

Given the many "selves" that make up Toyota's base of customers and prospects, this was not an easy task. Adding to the complexity were certain "mandatories" that Toyota and Saatchi & Saatchi had agreed on. For instance, whatever they came up with had to be distinctive, memorable, and unique to Toyota. Moreover, while they needed to develop a simple, singular concept for Toyota, this same concept had to be flexible enough to also work across 13 different models, each of which has its own image and personality to defend. It also had to work across present and future scenarios. In other words, it had to be broad enough to evolve over time as the environment changed. Most important, the concept had to be inclusive of the audience, not talking at them. It had to present Toyota as caring, respectful, and genuinely interested in helping consumers fulfill their goals.

A very tall order.

From this consensus, though, the client and the agency developed a "core strategic thought" that stated clearly who Toyota was, how it intended to act, and how it wanted to be perceived. It was virtually a mission statement:

> Toyota is more than a car, a truck or an SUV. It is a company with integrity, dedicated to enabling consumers to meet their life needs, whatever they may be. It is a company that places the consumer first.[9]

From this core strategic thought a concept evolved. Joe McDonagh explained, "There are things we depend on in our lives. Things we count on to do what needs to be done each and every day . . . whether it's a person or a brand. Toyota is one of the select brands you can count on, every day of your life. We simply want to demonstrate Toyota's rightful place in people's everyday lives, nothing more, nothing less."[10]

And that's how the theme evolved. Toyota/Everyday.

Here suddenly was a campaign concept that could leverage Toyota's heritage—by focusing on how vehicles converge with people's everyday lives, and how Toyota delivers products designed to address a consumer's individual needs and wants . . . every day. McDonagh pointed out that one of the purposes of the campaign is to demonstrate an understanding of and caring for everyday life and to build off the hope and opportunity every day holds.

In fact, this was more than a concept. It was a position—subtle, but deep—and one that Toyota could uniquely occupy.

Now they had to execute the campaign.

Implementing the Campaign

On September 12, 1997, Toyota held a news conference at the Four Seasons Hotel in New York to announce the new branding campaign. That same day, the campaign broke with 30- and 60-second commercials on prime-time network television and full page ads in *USA Today* and *The Wall Street Journal*. The initial flight for the branding campaign lasted 12 days with heavy concentration on prime-time television. Immediately following that, they launched the premiere flight

As a print counterpart to its Portraits television spot, Toyota ran this full-page, four color newspaper ad in USA Today to launch the Toyota/Everyday campaign. The faces in the ad are many of the same people who appeared in the TV version.

of Everyday ads for the all-new '98 Toyota Corolla. Three weeks later they introduced the new Toyota Sienna minivan with a flight of Everyday ads that ran into early November (see Exhibit E–3).

Then, in February of 1998, they ran the "power unit"—an eight-page series of Everyday ads in seven Time, Inc., magazines, including *Time, Sports Illustrated,* and *People.* Emily Weiss, Saatchi & Saatchi's associate media director, explained that the power unit included a front cover gatefold, the center spread, the back cover, and the inside back cover. It actually did double duty since it was a brand advertising effort, but it included model-specific ads. Saatchi & Saatchi purposefully used the same print media for both the brand advertising and the model ads. It was more cost-efficient and the same customers could see both campaigns and mentally tie them together.[11]

Howard Gossage, one of the famed advertising gurus of the 60s, once said, "Nobody reads advertising. People read what interests them; and sometimes it's an ad."[12] Following this premise, Toyota and Saatchi & Saatchi have intentionally tried to create ads that are both varied and interesting. The Everyday campaign began with the "Portraits" spot we described at the beginning. This was designed to set the tone of the campaign and to get people thinking about what "Everyday" means. Dave Illingworth, senior vice president and general manager of Toyota Motor Sales, U.S.A., points out that each of the ads features a deliberate "communication gap"—so the audience will have to fill in the missing pieces. The idea is to provoke audience involvement.[13]

They've also had some fun with the ads. The Corolla spot, for instance, features an elderly couple arguing about whether to leave the windows up or down. The feud is finally settled by the foul odor emanating from the grandchild in the back seat. When they introduced the Sienna, they used the voiceover of a woman giving birth and then the sound of an infant crying as the minivan slowly emerged from its garage.[14] In all the spots, though, there is a unifying element—Sly and the Family Stone's seductive rendition of "Everyday People" which has already become a recognizable musical logo that instantly identifies a spot as a Toyota commercial.

		September				October				November				December				January				February				March				April				May				June				July				August				September
TOYOTA BRAND CAMPAIGN																																													
MY '98 MEDIA SCHEDULE																																													
MEDIA	**VEHICLE**																																												
PRINT	CONSUMER MAGAZINES																																												
	American Way																																												
	Bon Appetit																																												
	Forbes																																												
	Fortune																																												
	Life																																												
	Martha Stewart Living																																												
	People																																												
	Time																																												
	Regional Issues																																												
	NEWSPAPERS																																												
	USA Today																																												
BROADCAST	RADIO																																												
	TELEVISION																																												
	NETWORK TV																																												
	CABLE																																												
OTHER	OUT-OF-HOME																																												
	LOCAL BILLBOARDS																																												
	STADIUM SIGNAGE																																												
	INTERACTIVE																																												
	AD BANNERS																																												

cc: T. Balagia, J. Beverly, J. Caprini, G. DeCuir, N. Grimskog, A. Guillermo, J. Kelly, K. Lopez, S. Mistry, C. Mobeyen, K. Perea, J. Phillips, D. Purdue, A. Perez, M. Turpin, D. Van Andel, V. Voornas, C. Washburn, D. Webster, E. Weiss, R. Weig

Heavy / Sustaining

SAATCHI & SAATCHI / LOS ANGELES   **JUNE 17, 1997**

Exhibit E–3
Media flowchart spreadsheet.

Some of the Everyday commercials focused on a more humorous event, such as the spot involving the feuding grandparents. Regardless of approach, the Toyota message remained consistent throughout the campaign and continued to connect on a very human level across all advertising media.

The print campaign also utilizes a variety of ads, but continuity is gained through the use of a unified graphic design theme, copywriting style, and the use of similar background colors (see the Toyota 4Runner story in Chapter 13). While every ad incorporates the Toyota/Everyday slogan, Saatchi & Saatchi designed a different Everyday logotype to be used for each vehicle as well as a separate one for corporate use. These were designed to symbolically match the personality of each model. They were then distributed to dealers for use in their local advertising along with a graphic standards manual that explained their proper use.

Integrating the Campaign with Other Marketing Communication Tools

Toyota's Everyday campaign doesn't stop with just ads and commercials; it is truly an integrated marketing communications campaign. As mentioned earlier, the campaign actually began with a public relations activity—a press conference. That has been followed by innumerable stories in both the trade and consumer press about the campaign and Toyota's sales and introduction of new products.

TOYOTA	*everyday*	Brand & Sienna Marydale
TOYOTA	**everyday**	4Runner Jazz
TOYOTA	*everyday*	Avalon Snell bd BT
TOYOTA	everyday	Camry Bernhard Modern
TOYOTA	*everyday*	Celica AT French Script
TOYOTA	everyday	Corolla Regular Joe
TOYOTA	*everyday*	Land Crusier Embassy BT
TOYOTA	everyday	RAV4 Doghouse
TOYOTA	*EVERYDAY*	Supra Bank Gothic Lt BT italicized
TOYOTA	**EVERYDAY**	T100 Machine BT
TOYOTA	everyday	Tacoma Crudfont
TOYOTA	*everyday*	Tercel Bernhard Bold Italic

Toyota worked with Saatchi & Saatchi to develop a unique "Everyday" logo typeface that would be assigned to each automobile model. This decision was made, not just for the sake of aesthetic quality, but to subtly introduce each automobile's personality and lifestyle to the consumer.

With each of the media Toyota has engaged, it has also actively sought added-value opportunities. For instance, the introduction of the Sienna afforded a wonderful opportunity to make connections with its target demographic of busy, active, involved families who have outgrown their compact cars. Working with *Parenting* magazine and Borders bookstores, Toyota sponsored an education-based program that involved children as well as adults. This was a series of more than 200 fun, educational, storytelling events, called Reading '98, held at Borders' locations around the country. In addition, the magazine custom-produced and distributed 2 million glossy publications, also entitled *Reading '98,* that gave tips on how to enhance family reading. At each storytelling event, Toyota had a Sienna on-site so the families could sit in them and paw over them. While the events were primarily intended for image building, each of the attending parents was also given a coupon worth $250—not for buying a Sienna but for that amount of books at Borders if they did buy a Sienna. Amazingly, 55 coupons were redeemed within a month.[15]

Toyota hasn't been satisfied to just use traditional media, either. Posters for the Sienna were placed in 1,250 childcare centers nationwide. The company also distributed 3 million Sienna brochures to childcare facilities and to parents of newborns in hospitals around the country. In addition, Sienna signs appeared on shopping carts in 8,000 grocery stores and in key markets, Toyota wrapped Sienna images on buses that traveled past elementary schools, again aiming at parents.[16]

Taking advantage of the interactivity of the Internet early on, Toyota instituted an award-winning Web site back in 1995. Since then it has grown in size as well as popularity. Dean Van Eimeren, Saatchi & Saatchi's creative director for design and digital media, emphasizes that, as a new medium, the World Wide Web is being driven and developed by the demands of consumers.

In a sense, Toyota's Web site (www.toyota.com) is a direct extension of the everyday campaign's enabling strategy. It provides as much infor-

Toyota's Web site has become a very popular destination for Web surfers and Toyota customers alike. The splash page that greets visitors changes daily and offers some inspirational words for the day ahead.

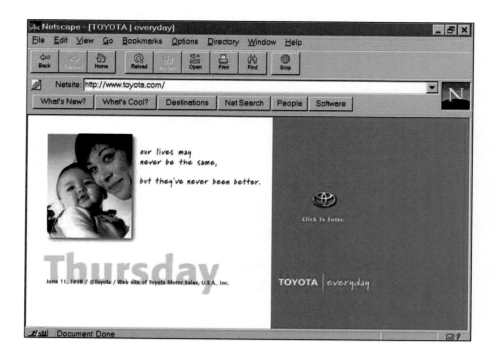

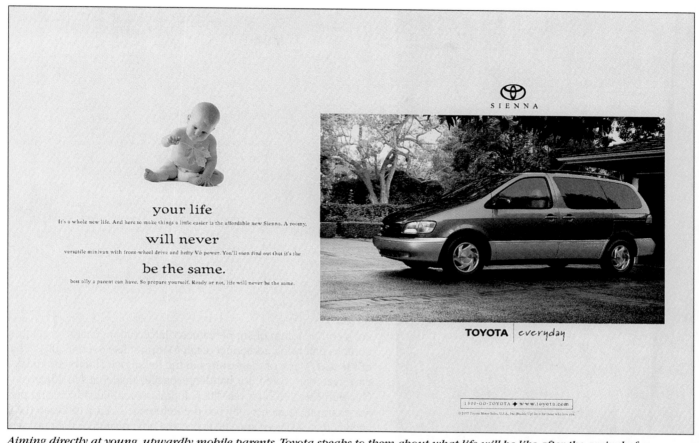

Aiming directly at young, upwardly mobile parents, Toyota speaks to them about what life will be like after the arrival of a newborn—it will never be the same. In the TV version, a mom searches for the baby's pacifier and in so doing demonstrates how easily the minivan's seats can be moved out of the way.

mation on Toyota and Toyota products as consumers need, on their terms, 24 hours a day, 7 days a week. This includes 3-dimensional exterior walkarounds, IPix photobubble views of each interior, and full specifications and charts for all the vehicles Toyota sells in the United States. In the near future, the Web site will make buying a Toyota even easier as credit applications, model and pricing configurators, and dealer inventory checks are perfected and rolled out nationwide.[17]

Finally, Toyota is involved in a plethora of sponsorships, from auto shows to mountain-bike racing. Some of its well-known participations include the Nabisco Dinah Shore Golf Tournament, the SCORE Baja 500 and 1,000 races, Jimmy Huega's Toyota Snow Express, and the Toyota Gator Bowl held every year in January.

While strategic consistency, interactivity, and mission marketing define IMC, they also define Toyota—every day.

Advertising Resources

The Reference Library and Appendixes
are a compendium of supplementary information, charts, checklists, and
outlines that bring additional detail to topics discussed in all 17 chapters
of the text. Many of the features in the Reference Library are quick reference materials, useful for handling specific challenges in advertising.
Our purpose is to offer real-life solutions to real-life advertising problems.
For example, students may use the Reference Library to locate the federal
agency that oversees specific aspects of advertising, or they may use the
practical checklist for planning and designing a trade show booth. We
hope you will find the Reference Library and Appendixes to be a useful
tool long after the completion of the course for which this book was
purchased.

Reference **Library**

RL 1–1

A synoptic history of advertising.

Stage	Characteristics of the stage				
	Dominant advertiser	**Advertising public**	**Object promoted**	**Role of advertising**	**Media**
Pre-industrial	Producers/sellers or merchants	Local consumers	Basic commodities and crafts	Promote immediate sales	Voice and signs
Industri-alizing	Wholesalers	Retailers	Unbranded products	Announce product availability and establish wholesaler reputation	Business newspapers ("price currents")
	Local businesspeople	Local consumers	Local products	Create awareness and desire	Newspapers
	Manufacturers	National consumers	New products	Create new product awareness, under-standing, and desire	Billboards, newspapers, magazines
	Mail-order retailers	National consumers	Specialty products	Announce availability and stimulate desire	Catalogs
Industrial	Manufacturers of differentiated brands	National consumers	Nationally differentiated brands	Create awareness and brand image	Magazines, network radio
	Manufacturers of segmented brands	National consumers	Nationally segmented brands	Create awareness and product positioning	Network TV, spot radio and TV, magazines
	Retail chains	National consumers	Assortments of related products	Create retail store image	National TV
Post-industrial	Retail chains	Lifestyle groups	Strategic assortments of products and services	Create store/family-brand image	Integrated systems of communication media
	Manufacturers	Retail chains	Family brands	Win retail support for product lines	Trade promotion and support
	Direct marketers	National customers	Strategic groups of products	Solicit and process immediate sales	All types of media
	Relationship marketers	Current customers	Current products and services	Service ongoing customer needs	Interactive media
	Business-to-business marketers	Organizational customers	Organizational products and services	Establish supplier credibility and generate sales leads	BTB and interactive media
	Global marketers	Global segments	Global products	Message requirements vary, depending on market needs	Global and local media
	Nonprofit organizations	Affluent and/self-actualizing consumers	Ideas, social and charitable causes	Stimulate social change, activity, and financial contributions	Integrated systems of communication media

Source: Copyright 1996 Hugh M. Cannon.

RL 1–2

Pioneers in advertising.

Advertising's evolution was influenced by two major factors: technological progress and the individual achievement of pioneers in the field. Technology was an external force that shaped the context surrounding advertising. It also provided additional tools to professionals. Individual achievement shaped advertising from within, each advertising professional's success serving as a model for others. Individual achievement is partially represented by the following people.

Formative Years

1729 Benjamin Franklin: Separated ads from text with white space; used large type for headlines; and used illustrations in ads.

1841 Volney Palmer: First "adman"; first to call himself an "agent" (media broker); paid by publishers; surveyed pricing; negotiated deals; hired writers or used client-provided text.

1880 John E. Powers: Hired by Wanamaker stores; "journalized" copy (newsy, informational, and accurate); updated text daily; said "My discovery was to print the news of the store."

1888 George E. Rowell: First agent to guarantee payment to publishers for space; started *Printers' Ink*, first magazine devoted to advertising.

Modern Period

1900s

Earnest Elmo Calkins: Initiated "original art" appearance for magazine ads (image advertising); in 1905, prepared first national advertising plan for Gillette safety razor.

1905 John E. Kennedy and Albert Lasker: Formed the Lord & Thomas agency with the primary focus of selling product. It was Kennedy who originally told Lasker, "Advertising is salesmanship in print," giving birth to the sales approach and "reason-why" advertising.

1911 Samuel Dobbs: Created truth in advertising codes for Advertising Clubs of America, now the American Advertising Federation.

1920s

1923 Raymond Rubicam and John Orr Young: Opened Young & Rubicam, featuring unique ads with intriguing headlines and emphasis on fresh ideas; hired George Gallup to make research essential to the creative process.

Stanley and Helen Resor: Worked at J. Walter Thompson; created the concepts of brand names, account services, and status appeal (nonwealthy imitating the habits of the wealthy). Helen was the first woman of real prominence in advertising, and Stanley also built a network of agencies (some outside the U.S.).

1930s

Claude Hopkins: Worked at Lord & Taylor; has been called the greatest copywriter of all time; wrote *Scientific Advertising* (1923), featuring results of tests conducted with his mail-order advertising.

Theodore McManus: Copywriter (at GM) who introduced image ads using a soft-sell appoach to develop long-term relationships with clients; soft sell worked through an accumulation of positive images.

1932 John Caples: VP for BBDO (Batton, Barton, Durstine & Osborn); published *Tested Advertising Methods*, featuring the pulling power of headlines; changed advertising by proving the effectiveness of one- or two-word headlines and short copy.

1940s

Clyde Bedell: Published *How to Write Advertising That Sells*, which featured "31 proved selling stratagems" that connect product features to selling points.

1950s

Rosser Reeves: Worked at the Ted Bates Agency; introduced the concept that an ad must offer a unique selling proposition (USP) containing a benefit to be effective ("M&M's melt in your mouth, not in your hands").

William Bernbach: An agency principal (Doyle, Dane & Bernbach) and copywriter with a keen sense for art. To him, advertising was the art of persuasion, a philosophy that made him look to the emotions for creative solutions.

1960s

Leo Burnett: Leader in the Chicago school of advertising, which finds the inherent drama in every product and then presents it as believably as possible. Created many personae: Jolly Green Giant, Tony the Tiger, Charlie the Tuna, Morris the Cat, and the Marlboro Man.

David Ogilvy: Established himself as a blend between the MacManus and Rubicam "image" school and the Lasker and Hopkins "claim" school. Story appeal and personae such as the Hathaway man and Commander Whitehead were hallmarks of Ogilvy's style. He wrote *Confessions of an Advertising Man* in 1963 and *Ogilvy on Advertising* in 1985.

Mary Wells Lawrence: Copywriter who became the first female founder of a major advertising agency in 1966. She attained notoriety with her Braniff Airlines campaign, which included painting the aircraft pastel colors. Her agency, Wells, Rich, Greene, was noted for its catchy Alka-Seltzer TV commercials, many of which became classics.

1970s

Barbara Gardner Proctor: Credited with bringing the Beatles to America before she entered the field of advertising, Proctor formed the first major agency owned and operated by a black woman and the first person granted a service loan by the Small Business Administration. She went on to build the agency into a $12.2-million business. Proctor became the recipient of over 40 awards by 1980, including *Business Week* magazine's "100 Top Corporate Women in America" and an Honorary Doctorate of Humane Letters by Southern Methodist University.

Jack Trout and Al Ries: Principals in Ries, Cappiello & Colwell; wrote *Positioning: The Battle for Your Mind* and later *Marketing Warfare* and *Bottom-Up Marketing*. Extended strategic thinking in advertising by demonstrating how consumers rank brands in their minds.

RL 2–1

Advertising regulations in selected countries of Western Europe.

| Country | General regulations | | Limitations on specific products |
	Comparative advertising	Advertising to children	Alcoholic beverages
European Union	OK if data accurate and verifiable	Ban on showing children in danger; exploiting their ignorance or credulity; or encouraging them to persuade adults to buy	TV advertising restricted
Austria	OK if based on objective, verifiable data	Direct appeal forbidden	Hard liquor banned on TV and radio
Belgium	Banned if denigrating	Follows EU guidelines	Strict labeling laws
Denmark	OK if accurate, relevant, and fair	Follows EU guidelines	Banned on radio and TV
France	OK if not disparaging	Generally follows EU guidelines, but stricter	Banned on TV and at sporting events; restrictions on ad content
Germany	Banned if denigrating	Voluntary restraints on direct appeals in radio and TV ads	Voluntary limits by industry
Italy	Direct comparisons restricted; indirect OK if substantiated	Ban on ads during cartoon programs	Follows EU guidelines
Netherlands	Indirect comparisons OK if complete, accurate, and not denigrating	Voluntary restraints on exploiting children's natural credulity	Strict industry regulations on ad content
Spain	Banned if denigrating or not objectively verifiable	Restricts exploitation	Some restrictions
Switzerland	OK if not denigrating; banned on TV	None	Banned on TV and radio; restricted in other media
United Kingdom	Banned if denigrating	Voluntary rules designed to protect children	Voluntary ban on TV advertising for hard liquor; content restrictions for other media

Limitations on specific products		Media regulations	
Tobacco	Pharmaceuticals	Restricted or banned media	Limitations on commercials
Banned on TV	Prescription drugs banned on TV	None	May not exceed 15 percent of daily broadcast time
Banned on TV and radio	Greatly restricted by pharmaceutical law	Billboards heavily regulated; telephone advertising prohibited	Follows EU guidelines
Heavily restricted in all media; banned on TV and radio	Banned on TV and radio; restricted in other media	Billboards heavily regulated	Follows EU guidelines
Banned on TV and radio	Prescription drugs banned on TV and radio; prior government approval for others	Telemarketing banned; outdoor heavily restricted	Follows EU guidelines
Banned in all media except press and posters	Prescription drugs banned in public media; others require prior approval	Outdoor restricted locally	Follows EU guidelines
Banned on radio and TV	Permitted with strict regulations on content	None	Follows EU guidelines
Banned in all media	Prescription drug ads banned; copy clearance needed for others	Outdoor restricted by local ordinances	Follows EU guidelines; prohibits interruptive ads
Strict but voluntary regulation by industry	Prior approval by industry board; consumer ads for prescription drugs banned	Outdoor restricted by local ordinances	Follows EU guidelines
Restricted on TV	Prior government approval for OTC drugs; consumer ads for prescription drugs banned	Outdoor restricted locally	Regulation of content and duration of commercials
Banned on TV and radio; restricted in other media	Banned on TV and radio	Only commercial radio is local	No noncommercial advertising; restrictions on commercial length
Banned on TV and radio	Ban on ads for prescription drugs; strict regulations for OTC drugs	Local restrictions on outdoor; many restrictions on other media	Code of Advertising Standards

RL 2–2

Federal regulators of advertising in the United States.

Federal Trade Commission

Regulates all commerce between the states. Formed in 1914, the FTC is the leading federal regulatory agency for advertising practices and the subject of much criticism by the advertising profession.

Food and Drug Administration

Has authority over the advertising, labeling, packaging, and branding of all packaged goods and therapeutic devices. The FDA requires full disclosure labels, regulates the use of descriptive words on packages, and has jurisdiction over the packaging of poisonous or otherwise hazardous products.

Federal Communications Commission

Formed by the Communications Act of 1934, the FCC has jurisdiction over the radio, TV, telephone, and telegraph industries. It maintains indirect control over advertising through its authority to license or revoke the license of all broadcast stations.

Patent and Trademark Office

Regulates registration of patents and trademarks. It enforces the Trade-Mark Act of 1947.

Library of Congress

Registers and protects all copyright material including ads, music, books, booklets, computer software, and other creative material.

Bureau of Alcohol, Tobacco, and Firearms

Has almost absolute authority over liquor advertising through its power to suspend, revoke, or deny renewal of manufacturing and sales permits for distillers, vintners, and brewers found to be in violation of regulations.

Office of Consumer Affairs

Is the chief consumer protection department in the federal government. Established in 1971, the OCA coordinates, maintains, and publicizes information on all federal activities in the field of consumer protection. Publications produced and circulated by the OCA include consumer education guidelines, monthly newsletters, and a consumer services column released to some 4,500 weekly newspapers.

U.S. Postal Service

Has authority to halt mail delivery to any firm or person guilty of misusing the mails. It maintains control over false and deceptive advertising, pornography, lottery offers, and deceptive guarantees.

U.S. Department of Agriculture

Closely monitors the distribution of misbranded or unregistered commercial poisons. The USDA works with the FTC to enforce regulations governing certain products. The USDA Grain Division has regulatory authority over false and deceptive advertising for seeds and grain products. The Grain Division can initiate action against violators.

Securities and Exchange Commission

Established in 1934, has jurisdiction over all advertising of stocks, bonds, and other securities sold via interstate commerce. The SEC requires that public offerings contain full disclosure of all pertinent information on the company and the securities offered so the prospective investor can make informed buying decisions. Disclosure must detail all risk factors that may affect the investment.

Department of Justice

Normally does not initiate legal action against people or firms charged with violating the federal laws governing advertising. Instead, it enforces these laws by representing the federal government in the prosecution of cases referred by other federal agencies.

Consumer Product Safety Commission

Established in 1972 to develop and enforce standards for potentially hazardous consumer products. It derives its power from four acts: the Flammable Fabrics Act of 1954, the Federal Hazardous Substances Act of 1960, the Children Protection Act of 1966, and the Standard for the Flammability of Children's Sleepwear of 1972. It has jurisdiction over placement of warning statements in ads and other promotional materials for covered products. Its authority extends to household products, toys, and hazardous substances that cause accidental poisoning. The Consumer Product Safety Commission investigates product advertising and labeling violations brought to its attention by consumers and consumer protection groups. Continued violations by product makers are grounds for prosecution and punitive action by the Attorney General.

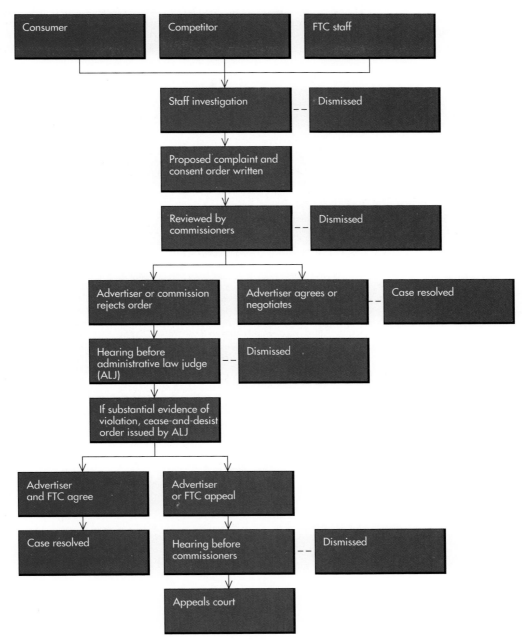

RL 2–3
Flowchart of the FTC complaint procedure.

RL 2–4
Trademark and copyright tips.

Ironically, advertising success can sometimes cause the loss of a trademark. That's what happened to *thermos, escalator,* and *cellophane.* The owners lost their trademark rights when the courts declared the trademarks "generic," meaning the names had come into common use and are now the dictionary names for the products.

Most trademark owners take precautions to prevent their trademarks from becoming generic. They capitalize the trademark and follow it with the generic name of the product (Band-Aid brand adhesive bandages, Scotch brand tape, Kleenex tissues, Jell-O brand gelatin). They never refer to the trademark in the plural or use it as a verb. Many companies even advertise the fact that their name is a registered trademark: "You can't Xerox a Xerox on a Xerox."

While a copyright prevents a whole ad from being legally used by another, it does not prevent others from using the general concept or idea of the ad or paraphrasing the copy.

Copyright protection exists from the time the work is created in fixed form; that is, it is incident to the process of authorship. So the copyright *immediately* becomes the property of the author who created it. Only the author or those deriving rights through the author can rightfully claim copyright. In the case of *works made for hire,* the employer and not the employee is considered to be the author. Work made for hire is defined as (1) work prepared by an employee within the scope of his or her employment or (2) work specially commissioned from a nonemployee if the parties expressly agree in writing that it is "work made for hire."

An advertiser that uses original written, musical, illustrative, or other material from an outside source without its creator's express written consent is infringing on the copyright and may be subject to legal action. Advertisers and agencies must obtain permission before they use creative material, like music or photography, from any outside source.

All works under copyright protection that are published in the United States are subject to the mandatory deposit provision of the copyright law. This law requires that the "owner of coyright or of the exclusive right of publication" deposits two copies of the best edition of every copyrightable work published in the United States with the Copyright Office within three months of publication.

While deposit for the collections of the Library of Congress is mandatory under section 407, *registration* of a copyright claim under section 408 is voluntary. Registration is not a condition of copyright protection, but under certain circumstances it may allow the owner a broader range of remedies in infringement suits. To satisfy requirements for both, the following must be sent in one package to the Register of Copyrights: (1) two mandatory deposit copies, (2) a completed application for registration, and (3) a $20 nonrefundable filing fee payable to the Register of Copyrights.

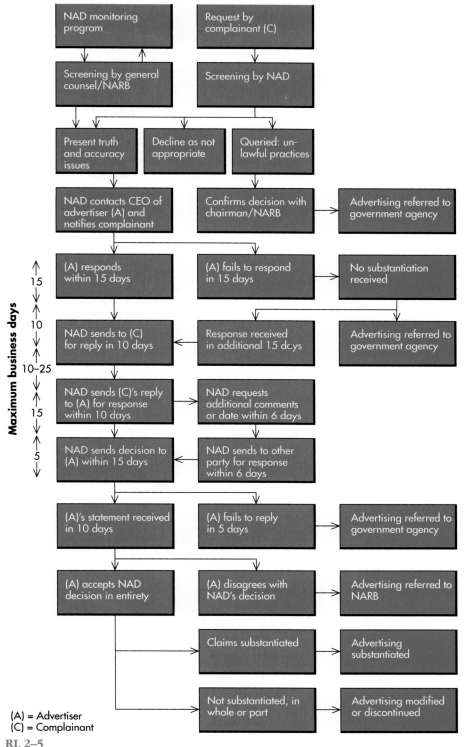

RL 2–5

Flowchart of the National Advertising Division/National Advertising Review Board (NAD/NARB) review process.

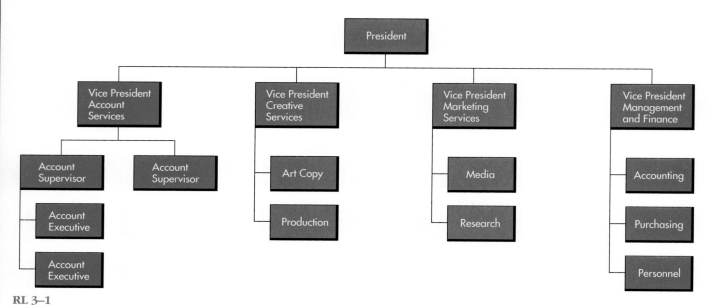

RL 3–1

In the department system, each function—account services, creative services, marketing services, and administration—is relatively independent and specialized. But departments can become too autonomous and inflexible.

RL 3–2

In the group system, each small "agency" or group has all the personnel needed to serve that group's clients. This system helps huge agencies remain flexible.

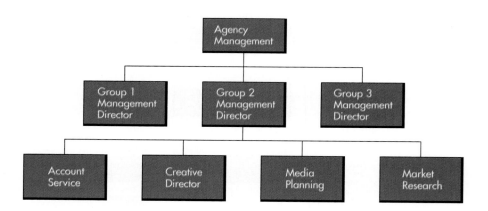

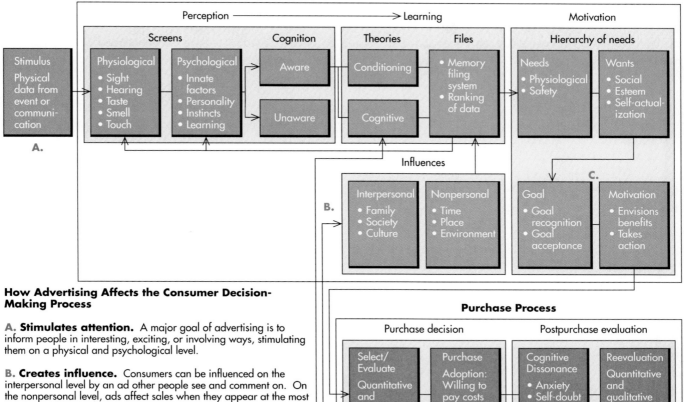

Personal Processes

Perception ⟶ Learning Motivation

Screens · Cognition · Theories · Files · Hierarchy of needs

Stimulus — Physical data from event or communication **A.**

Physiological
• Sight
• Hearing
• Taste
• Smell
• Touch

Psychological
• Innate factors
• Personality
• Instincts
• Learning

Aware / Unaware

Conditioning / Cognitive

• Memory filing system
• Ranking of data

Needs
• Physiological
• Safety

Wants
• Social
• Esteem
• Self-actual-ization

B.

Influences

Interpersonal
• Family
• Society
• Culture

Nonpersonal
• Time
• Place
• Environment

Goal
• Goal recognition
• Goal acceptance

Motivation
• Envisions benefits
• Takes action

C.

How Advertising Affects the Consumer Decision-Making Process

A. Stimulates attention. A major goal of advertising is to inform people in interesting, exciting, or involving ways, stimulating them on a physical and psychological level.

B. Creates influence. Consumers can be influenced on the interpersonal level by an ad other people see and comment on. On the nonpersonal level, ads affect sales when they appear at the most opportune time or place.

C. Presents goals. People act when they have a goal. An ad that uses imagery and picturesque wording helps customers visualize and recognize their goals. An ad can stimulate motivation by persuading customers that it is possible to attain their goal.

D. Promises product benefits. Ads give consumers quantitative and qualitative information. An ad is an implied contract, warranty, or promise of benefits that reassures doubting prospects.

E. Reinforces purchase decision. An ad can lower customers' postpurchase anxiety by reminding them of the product's positive features. The claims in an ad offer a rebuttal to negative comments by critical friends or family members.

Purchase Process

Purchase decision · Postpurchase evaluation

Select/Evaluate — Quantitative and qualitative analysis of evoked set

Purchase — Adoption: Willing to pay costs (makes purchase)

Cognitive Dissonance
• Anxiety
• Self-doubt

Reevaluation — Quantitative and qualitative analysis: Benefits versus costs

D.

Nonpurchase — Rejection of product: Unwilling to pay costs

Postpone — Needs new data: Adoption process on hold

E.

Not Satisfied — Rejection of product: Unwilling to pay costs

Satisfied — Readopts: Willing to pay costs

RL 4–1

The complete model of the consumer decision-making process.

RL 5–1

Methods for segmenting consumer markets.

Variables	Typical breakdowns	Variables	Typical breakdowns
Geographic		**Demographic**	
Region	Pacific; Mountain; West North Central; West South Central; East North Central; East South Central; South Atlantic; Middle Atlantic; New England	Age	Under 6, 6–11, 12–19, 20–34, 35–49, 50–64, 65+
County size	A, B, C, D	Sex	Male, female
Climate	Northern; southern	Family size	1–2, 3–4, 5+
City or SMSA size	Under 5,000; 5,000–19,999; 20,000–49,999; 50,000–99,999; 100,000–249,999; 250,000–499,999; 500,000–999,999; 1,000,000–3,999,999; 4,000,000 or over	Family life cycle	Young, single; young, married, no children; young, married, youngest child under six; young, married, youngest child six or over; young, unmarried, with children; older, married, with children; older, unmarried, with children; older, married, no children under 18; older, single; other
Density	Urban, suburban, rural		
Behavioristic		Income	Under $10,000; $10,000–20,000; $20,000–30,000; $30,000–40,000; $40,000–60,000; $60,000–100,000; $100,000 and over
Purchase occasion	Regular occasion, special occasion		
Benefits sought	Economy, convenience, prestige		
User status	Nonuser, ex-user, potential user, first-time user, regular user	Occupation	Professional and technical; managers, officials, and proprietors; clerical, sales; craftspeople, supervisors; operatives; farmers; retired; students; homemakers; unemployed
Usage rate	Light user, medium user, heavy user		
Loyalty status	None, medium, strong, absolute		
Readiness stage	Unaware, aware, informed, interested, desirous, intending to buy	Education	Grade school or less; some high school; graduated high school; some college; graduated college
Marketing-factor sensitivity	Quality, price, service, advertising, sales promotion-	Religion	Catholic, Protestant, Jewish, other
Psychographic		Race	White, Black, Asian
Societal divisions	Upper crust, movers and shakers, successful singles, social security, middle of the road, metro ethnic mix	Nationality	American, British, French, German, Scandinavian, Italian, Latin American, Middle Eastern, Japanese
Lifestyle	Straights, swingers, long-hairs		
Personality	Compulsive, gregarious, authoritarian, ambitious		

Checklist

Setting Prices

_____ **Competitive pricing strategy.** Prices set at or below competitors' prices. Ads show a variety of products with large, bold prices and boast, "We won't be undersold." Requires constant competitive monitoring; may invite retaliation.

_____ **Skimming strategy.** Initial prices set relatively high to recover the initial capital spent developing the product—or furnishing, decorating, stocking, and promoting a store. Ads feature quality, convenience, and service. As competition increases, prices may be lowered.

_____ **Penetration pricing.** Initial prices set low at first to penetrate the market quickly. As business develops, prices are gradually raised to a more profitable level. Initial ads feature low prices; later ads promote store services, quality products, wide selection, or convenience.

_____ **Promotional pricing.** Special low prices set to introduce new lines of equipment or to clear out old lines. Typical tactics include two-for-one specials or end-of-month sales. Designed to maintain traffic, stimulate demand, or make room for new merchandise.

_____ **Loss-leader pricing.** One piece of merchandise selected and advertised at well below cost to create store traffic and sell other regularly priced merchandise. Companies offering loss leaders must have the items in stock and be prepared to sell them without trying to "switch" customers to higher-priced items. Bait-and-switch advertising is illegal in many areas and unethical everywhere.

_____ **Prestige pricing.** Nonprice competition. The business offers the finest merchandise, the best service, free delivery, and friendly, knowledgeable clerks in plush, convenient surroundings. Ads may not even mention prices.

Marketing research sources for new vitamin product development.

General Reference Guidelines
Government. *U.S. Government Organizational Manual, Federal Statistical Directory,* government reports and announcements.
Trade and Other Organizations. *Encyclopedia of Associations.*
Consumer/Business Press. *Business Publications Rates & Data, Consumer Magazine & Agri-Media Rates & Data.*
Publications. *Business Periodicals Index, Funk & Scott Index of Corporations & Industries, Index Medicus, Thomas Register of American Corporations, Pharmaceuticals News Index, Reader's Guide to Periodical Literature.*

Issues Specific to the Vitamin Market
Nature of the product, vitamins and how they are used, new products, external issues influencing the market.
Government. National Technical Information Service (Dept. of Commerce), National Center for Health Statistics (HHS).
Trade and Other Organizations. Vitamin Information Bureau, American Dietetic Association, National Science Foundation.
Consumer/Business Press. *Consumer Reports, Today's Health, Drug Topics, Prevention, American Druggist, Product Marketing.*
Publications. *Journal of the AMA, New England Journal of Medicine, FDA Reports.*

Role of Government
Impact of existing and potential government rules and regulations.
Government. Food & Drug Administration (HHS), reports of congressional committees.
Trade and Other Organizations. The Proprietary Association, Pharmaceutical Manufacturers Association, consumer groups.
Consumer/Business Press. Articles in business and drug trade magazines and medical journals.
Publications. *Pharmaceutical News Index, FDA Reports.*

Consumer Behavior
Level of vitamin usage by consumers; consumers' perceptions and attitudes about vitamins.

Government. National Technical Information Service (Dept. of Commerce), National Center for Health Statistics (NCHS).
Consumer/Business Press. *Prevention,* readership studies of general consumer and trade magazines.
Publications. *Findex Directory of Market Research Reports, Studies & Surveys.*

Competition
Nature of the competition and extent of leverage in the market.
Government. Form 10-Ks (SEC).
Consumer/Business Press. Articles appearing in business and drug trade magazines.
Publications. *Moody's Industrial Manual,* Standard & Poor's corporation records, *Value Line Investment Survey, Dun & Bradstreet Reports,* National Investment Library annual report, Disclosure, Inc., annual report, *Thomas Register of American Corporations.*

Market Trends and Developments
Size of the market and growth rate, major vitamin categories and relative growth, traditional distribution channels and major retail outlets, seasonal patterns or regional skews.
Government. Census of Manufacturers (Dept. of Commerce), Survey of Manufacturers (Dept. of Commerce), current industrial reports (Dept. of Commerce).
Trade and Other Organizations. The Proprietary Association, Pharmaceutical Manufacturers Association.
Consumer/Business Press. *Product Marketing, Drug Topics, Supermarket Business,* articles in business and drug trade magazines.
Publications. *Standard & Poor's Industry Surveys, Pharmaceutical News Index.*

Advertising
Kinds and levels of advertising support, creative strategies employed by advertisers.
Consumer/Business Press. *Advertising Age, Marketing Communications.*
Publications. Leading national advertisers, Publishers Information Bureau.

RL 6–2

Software for PC research analysis.

As technological advances continue to lower the cost of research handling, more large corporations and even small local businesses are taking marketing and advertising research and statistical analysis in-house.

There are two major forms of software programs for marketing and advertising research using desktop computers: mathematical and database. Mathematical programs are useful for conducting statistical analysis and calculating mathematical formulas, X-Y graphing of research data, numeric sorting, cross-referencing statistics, and streamlining complex data such as regression modeling. Database programs calculate numeric statistics using fields of information such as names, addresses, dates, telephone numbers. Their advantage is that fields of data can be arranged in any number of report formats while the numeric calculations are performed automatically.

Common Database Management Programs			
Product	**Description**	**Platform**	**Publisher**
MINITAB	Statistical software: factor analysis, multivariate variance (MANOVA), regression, and more.	Windows	MINITAB, Inc. State College, PA 814-238-3280
SPSS (Statistics Package for the Social Sciences)	Statistical software: cross-tab, Npar, correlation, regression, t-test, and variance (ANOVA).	Windows, Mac OS	SPSS, Inc. Chicago, IL 800-543-2185
MS FoxPro	Relational database manager.	MS-DOS, Windows, Mac OS	Microsoft Redmond, WA 800-446-6955
dBase and Paradox	Relational database manager.	MS-DOS, Windows	Borland International Scotts Valley, CA 510-354-3828
Access	Flat-file database manager with relational tables.	Windows	Microsoft Redmond, WA 800-446-6955
Approach	Nonprogrammable, front-end manager of dBase, Paradox, and Oracle files.	Windows	Approach Software, Inc. Redwood City, CA 800-354-1122
4th Dimension/4D First	Relational database manager.	Mac OS, Windows	ACI Inc. Cupertino, CA 408-252-4444
FileMaker Pro	Flat-file database manager.	Mac OS, Windows	Claris Santa Clara, CA 800-3-CLARIS
Helix Express	Relational database manager.	Mac OS	Helix Technologies Cupertino, CA 800-364-4354
Oracle	Relational database manager—operates with Structured Query Language (SQL) used by mini- and mainframe computers.	Mac OS, Windows	Oracle Corp. Belmont, CA 800-ORACLE 1

Checklist
Situation Analysis

The Industry

____ **Companies in industry:** dollar sales, strengths.

____ **Growth patterns within industry:** primary demand curve, per capita consumption, growth potential.

____ **History of industry:** technological advances, trends.

____ **Characteristics of industry:** distribution patterns, industry control, promotional activity, geographic characteristics, profit patterns.

The Company

____ **The company story:** history, size, growth, profitability, scope of business, competence, reputation, strengths, weaknesses.

The Product or Service

____ **The product story:** development, quality, design, description, packaging, price structure, uses, reputation, strengths, weaknesses.

____ **Product sales features:** exclusive, nonexclusive differentiating qualities, competitive position.

____ **Product research:** technological breakthroughs, improvements planned.

Sales History

____ **Sales and sales costs:** by product, model, sales districts.

____ **Profit history.**

Share of Market

____ **Sales history industrywide:** share of market in dollars and units.

____ **Market potential:** industry trends, company trends, demand trends.

The Market

____ **Who and where is the market:** how was market segmented, how can it be segmented, what are consumer needs, attitudes, and characteristics? How, why, when, where do consumers buy?

____ **Past advertising appeals:** successful or unsuccessful.

____ **Who are our customers:** past and future? What characteristics do they have in common? What do they like about our product? What don't they like?

Distribution

____ **History and evaluation:** how and where product is distributed, current trend.

____ **Company's relationship:** with the distribution channel and its attitudes toward product/company.

____ **Past policies:** trade advertising, deals, co-op programs.

____ **Status:** trade literature, dealer promotions, point-of-purchase displays.

Pricing Policies

____ **Price history:** trends, relationship to needs of buyers, competitive price situation.

____ **Past price objectives:** management attitudes, buyer attitudes, channel attitudes.

Competition

____ **Who is the competition:** primary, secondary, share of market, products, services, goals, attitudes. What is competition's growth history and size?

____ **Strengths and competition:** sales features, product quality, size. Weaknesses of competition.

____ **Marketing activities of competition:** advertising, promotion, distribution, sales force. Estimated budget.

Promotion

____ **Successes and failures:** past promotion policy, sales force, advertising, publicity.

____ **Promotion expenditures:** history, budget emphasis, relation to competition, trend.

____ **Advertising programs:** review of strategies, themes, campaigns.

____ **Sales force:** size, scope, ability, cost/sale.

RL 7–2

How IMC builds relationships.

Tom Duncan, director of the IMC graduate program at the University of Colorado at Boulder, developed a model of the IMC process that portrays how a variety of functions work together sequentially. (The Schultz IMC model explained in Chapter 7 emphasizes the elements and processes involved in executing an IMC program.) The Duncan model uses a step-by-step approach to portray how IMC creates the synergy to build relationships.

Premises

Five premises affect the model's design:

1. **Integration is a continuum.** Companies may employ various levels of integration.
2. **IMC is a cross-functional process.** IMC is not just a departmental function—it must be companywide.
3. **All stakeholders are important.** Not just customers but also employees, stockholders, competitors, neighboring residents, the press.
4. **Customer-focused marketing drives IMC.** Company must proactively seek stakeholder input and listen to the customer's voice.
5. **All contact points deliver messages.** Every brand contact delivers a message—including seeing the package, noting a price, using the product, listening to an ad, talking to a receptionist, hearing a news story, reading an instruction manual, overhearing gossip. Stakeholders might receive four different types of messages: *planned, inferred, maintenance,* and *unplanned.* All have a bearing on a stakeholder's relationship decision, so marketers need to know where they originate, and what it costs to influence or control them.

The IMC Model

*The corporate mission (Section **a** on the chart).* A company's management must have a vision for the organization that can be translated into a mission statement and subsequently into corporate objectives.

*Cross-functional planning and monitoring of IMC (Section **b**).* The corporate objectives should guide all the departments to provide an overall consistent direction. To do this well, interaction must occur among all departments.

*Integration process (Section **c**).* An organization's integration process should (1) ensure consistent positioning; (2) facilitate interaction between the company and its customers or other stakeholders; and (3) actively incorporate a relevant, socially responsible mission into the firm's relationships with customers and other stakeholders.

1. *Positioning consistency.* Consistent positioning has four basic components the IMC team must study and understand to attain enhanced reputation:

    A **contact point** (or brand contact) is any type of direct or indirect cue a stakeholder uses in deciding to have a relationship with a

company. Every contact point delivers a message and thereby affects perceptions and ensuing relationships.

   Key stakeholders have a vested interest in the company and may include consumer and business-to-business customers and prospects, employees, vendors and suppliers, the press, competitors, local citizens, and the financial community. However, key stakeholders are more instrumental in the company's survival and growth. They must be identified, located, monitored, and ranked. Their needs are the primary focus of all the company's IMC activities.

   To reinforce a consistent **perception** of the company, all messages must have common elements that reflect the company's position (and mission). Coca-Cola's "Always" campaign features many different commercials. However, each commercial contains similar **message links** to reinforce the same message (for example: the "Always Coca-Cola" slogan, the red circle, the script graphics, the uniquely contoured bottle, and the jingle that serves as a musical logo).

   Graphic continuity is important, but the verbal message elements affect reputation and relationships the most, particularly those that position the brand, state product claims and benefits, and make promises. To monitor positioning consistency, Duncan recommends structured observation, evaluation of employee dialogs with customers and other stakeholders, and periodic perception studies of key stakeholders.

2. *Interactive communication.* The second dimension in the integration process is interactive communication, a dialog that builds relationships with stakeholders. This dimension has three components: linkage media, database building, and purposeful dialog. When exercised correctly, interactivity leads to relationships.

   IMC theory recognizes that stakeholders dictate when, where, and how they will use the vast array of media options available. Thanks to technology, they can control which commercial messages they will receive. To improve interaction, marketers use **linkage media**—the whole menu of interlinked media channels that serve as consumer-to-brand contact points.

   With digital interactive media, two-way communication with stakeholders is possible as never before. Prospective customers can self-identify, complain, and in some cases make purchases, using linkage media such as interactive television or kiosks. Once identified, prospects can be reached with more cost-efficient, addressable media such as direct mail.

   Interactive communication depends on building and maintaining a relational database of identified people who are or might be involved in the communication program. Thus, **database building** is necessary for companies to manage their relationships. This also makes the next component, purposeful dialog, possible.

Customers resent intrusive messages, but they welcome messages that, in their view, offer added value. Relationship marketing and IMC are not about stepping up the telemarketing effort or sending out more junk mail, but having a **purposeful dialog**—that is, one that is important and useful to the customer or stakeholder. The new communication technologies offer pathways that are more personal and immediate and less costly than ever—factors that reinforce message purposefulness and provide the perception of added value.

3. *Mission marketing.* In mission marketing, the firm's overall corporate mission and sense of social responsibility are fundamental to all its corporate communications. Mission marketing seeks to enrich a brand's reputation by integrating a noncommercial, socially redeeming value system into a company's business plan and operations. Mission marketing leads to added value because it gives stakeholders an extra reason to support the company.

Effective mission marketing should be **focused** on one long-term activity, value, or belief—not scattered across a number of "good causes." The mission should be **relevant** to the company's business and expertise. For example, publishers could sponsor literacy programs; paper companies could support environmental programs. **Longevity** gives mission marketing credibility. It means the company stands for something beyond its product and profits. The mission should be **pervasive** throughout the life of the firm.

By providing something extra, mission marketing enhances brand differentiation. Avon's support of breast cancer research, for example, allows the company to stand out from the crowd of competitors with similar product offerings.

*Enhanced relationships (Section **d**).* Once the company completes the three major phases of IMC development (the mission, interactivity, and positioning consistency), stakeholders will have formed feelings and opinions about the company's reputation, their relationship with the company, and the added value the company provides. If the IMC program has properly enhanced these areas, additional stakeholders will be loyal to the company and brand equity will be strengthened.

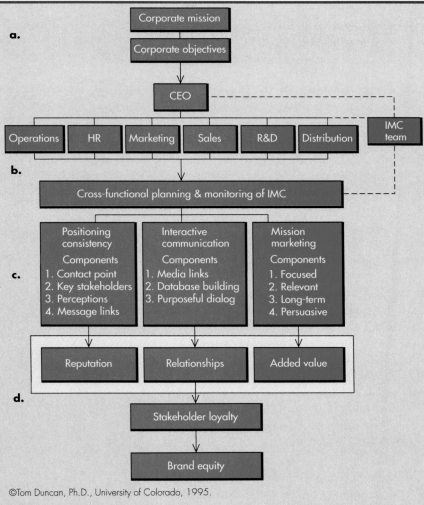

©Tom Duncan, Ph.D., University of Colorado, 1995.

Checklist
Developing Advertising Objectives

Does the advertising aim at immediate sales? If so, objectives might be:

—— Perform the complete selling function.

—— Close sales to prospects already partly sold.

—— Announce a special reason for buying now (price, premium, and so forth).

—— Remind people to buy.

—— Tie in with special buying event.

—— Stimulate impulse sales.

Does the advertising aim at near-term sales? If so, objectives might be:

—— Create awareness.

—— Enhance brand image.

—— Implant information or attitude.

—— Combat or offset competitive claims.

—— Correct false impressions, misinformation.

—— Build familiarity and easy recognition.

Does the advertising aim at building a "long-range consumer franchise"? If so, objectives might be:

—— Build confidence in company and brand.

—— Build customer demand.

—— Select preferred distributors and dealers.

—— Secure universal distribution.

—— Establish a "reputation platform" for launching new brands or product lines.

—— Establish brand recognition and acceptance.

Does the advertising aim at helping to increase sales? If so, objectives would be:

—— Hold present customers.

—— Convert other users to advertiser's brand.

—— Cause people to specify advertiser's brand.

—— Convert nonusers to users.

—— Make steady customers out of occasional ones.

—— Advertise new uses.

—— Persuade customers to buy larger sizes or multiple units.

—— Remind users to buy.

—— Encourage greater frequency or quantity of use.

Does the advertising aim at some specific step that leads to a sale? If so, objectives might be:

—— Persuade prospect to write for descriptive literature, return a coupon, enter a contest.

—— Persuade prospect to visit a showroom, ask for a demonstration.

—— Induce prospect to sample the product (trial offer).

How important are supplementary benefits of advertising? Objectives would be:

—— Help salespeople open new accounts.

—— Help salespeople get larger orders from wholesalers and retailers.

—— Help salespeople get preferred display space.

—— Give salespeople an entrée.

—— Build morale of sales force.

—— Impress the trade.

Should the advertising impart information needed to consummate sales and build customer satisfaction? If so, objectives may be to use:

—— "Where to buy it" advertising.

—— "How to use it" advertising.

—— New models, features, package.

—— New prices.

—— Special terms, trade-in offers, and so forth.

—— New policies (such as guarantees).

Should advertising build confidence and goodwill for the corporation? Targets may include:

—— Customers and potential customers.

—— The trade (distributors, dealers, retail people).

—— Employees and potential employees.

—— The financial community.

—— The public at large.

What kind of images does the company wish to build?

—— Product quality, dependability.

—— Service.

—— Family resemblance of diversified products.

—— Corporate citizenship.

—— Growth, progressiveness, technical leadership.

RL 8–1
Guidelines for determining reach, frequency, continuity, and pulsing combinations.

Considerations	Objectives			
	Reach	Frequency	Continuity	Pulsing
Needs				
New or highly complex message		✓		
Dogmatic message (surge at beginning)	✓			
Reason-why messages (high frequency at first)				✓
Emotionally oriented messages			✓	
Message is so creative or product so newsworthy that it forces attention	✓			
Message is dull or product indistinguishable		✓		
Consumer puchase patterns				
To influence brand choice of regularly purchased products		✓	✓	
As purchase cycle lengthens		✓		✓
To influence erratic purchase cycles				✓
To influence consumer attitudes toward impulse purchases		✓	✓	
For products requiring great deliberation, alternate	✓	✓		
To reinforce consumer loyalty	✓		✓	
To influence seasonal purchases	✓	✓		
Budget levels				
Low budget				✓
Higher budgets			✓	
Competitive activity				
Heavy competitive advertising		✓		
When competitive budgets are larger				✓
Marketing objectives				
For new, mass-market product introductions	✓			
To expand share of market with new uses for product	✓			
For direct response from advertising		✓		✓
To create awareness and recognition of corporate status	✓		✓	

RL 8–2
Comparative evaluation of advertising media.

	Spot TV	Network TV	Cable TV	Spot radio	Network radio	Consumer magazines	Business publications	Farm publications	Sunday supplements	Daily newspapers	Weekly newspapers	Direct mail	Outdoor	Transit
Audience considerations														
Attentiveness of audience	◐	◐	◐	◐	◐	◐	◐	◐	◐	◐	◐	●	○	○
Interest of audience	◐	●	●	◐	◐	●	●	●	●	●	●	○	○	○
Offers selectivity to advertiser	○	○	✓	◐	◐	●	●	●	○	○	○	●	○	○
Avoids waste	○	○	◐	○	○	●	●	●	◐	○	○	●	○	○
Offers involvement	◐	●	●	◐	◐	●	●	●	◐	◐	◐	●	○	○
Offers prestige	◐	●	◐	○	◐	●	●	◐	◐	◐	○	○	○	○
Good quality of audience data	◐	◐	◐	◐	◐	●	●	◐	◐	◐	○	◐	○	○
Timing factors														
Offers repetition	●	●	●	●	●	◐	◐	◐	○	◐	○	✓	●	●
Avoids irritation	○	○	○	○	◐	◐	◐	◐	◐	◐	◐	◐	◐	●
Offers frequency	●	●	●	●	●	◐	◐	◐	○	◐	○	◐	●	●
Offers frequency of issuance	●	●	●	●	●	✓	✓	○	○	◐	◐	✓	—	—
Offers flexibility in scheduling	●	●	●	●	●	✓	✓	○	○	◐	○	✓	—	—
Avoids perishability	○	○	○	○	○	●	●	◐	◐	○	◐	○	○	○
Allows long message	◐	◐	●	◐	◐	●	●	●	●	●	●	●	○	○
Geographic considerations														
Offers geographic selectivity	●	○	●	●	◐	◐	◐	◐	●	●	●	●	◐	◐
Offers proximity to point of sale	○	○	○	○	○	○	○	○	○	○	○	◐	◐	◐
Provides for local dealer "tags"	◐	○	●	◐	○	◐	◐	◐	●	●	●	◐	◐	◐
Creative considerations														
Permits demonstration	●	●	●	○	○	◐	◐	◐	◐	◐	◐	●	○	○
Provides impact	●	●	●	◐	◐	◐	◐	◐	◐	◐	◐	●	○	○
Permits relation to editorial matter	◐	◐	◐	○	◐	●	●	●	◐	◐	◐	●	—	—
Mechanical and production factors														
Ease of insertion	◐	●	◐	◐	●	●	●	●	◐	◐	○	●	◐	◐
High reproduction quality	◐	◐	◐	◐	◐	●	◐	●	●	✓	✓	●	✓	✓
Flexibility of format	◐	◐	◐	◐	◐	●	●	●	○	—	—	●	◐	○
Financial considerations														
Low total cost	◐	○	◐	◐	○	○	○	○	◐	●	●	○	◐	◐
High efficiency	◐	●	●	●	◐	◐	◐	◐	◐	◐	○	●	●	●

Note: ○ = Weak; ◐ = Medium; ● = Strong; — = Not a factor for this medium; ✓ = Varies from one vehicle to another within the medium.

Checklist

Product Marketing Facts for Creatives

____ **Proprietary information**

Product's trade name.

Trademark.

Product symbol.

Other copyrighted or patented information.

____ **History**

When was the product created or invented?

Who introduced it?

Has it had other names?

Have there been product changes?

Is there any "romance" to it?

____ **Research**

Are research results available?

What research about the product does the supplier have?

Which research will be most useful for each medium?

____ **Life cycle**

What is the product's life or use span?

What stage is it in now and what style of copy should be used for that stage?

What stages are competitors in?

____ **Market position**

What is the product's share of the total market?

Does its market share suggest a positioning strategy?

What position does the company wish to occupy?

____ **Competitive information**

Who are the product's competitors?

Does the product have any advantages over them?

Does it have any disadvantages?

Are they all about the same?

Do rival products present problems that this one solves?

____ **Product image**

How do people view the product?

What do they like about it?

What do they dislike about it?

Is it a luxury?

Is it a necessity?

Is it a habit?

Is it self-indulgent?

Do people have to have it but wish they didn't?

____ **Customer use**

How is the product used?

Are there other possible uses?

How frequently is it bought?

What type of person uses the product?

Why is the product bought?

   Personal use.

   Gift.

   Work.

What type of person uses the product most (heavy user)?

How much does the heavy user buy?

Where does the best customer live?

____ **Performance**

What does the product do?

What might it be expected to do that it does not?

How does it work?

How is it made or produced?

What's in it?

   Raw materials.

   Special ingredients.

   Preservatives.

   Chemicals.

   Nutrients.

____ **What are its physical characteristics?**

Smell.

Appearance.

Color.

Texture.

Taste.

Others.

____ **Effectiveness**

Is there proof the product has been tested and works well?

Do any government or other regulations need to be mentioned or observed?

How does it work compared to its competitors?

____ **Manufacturing**

How is the product made?

How long does it take?

How many steps are in the process?

How about the people involved in making it?

Are any special machines used?

Where is it made?

____ **Distribution**

How widely is the product distributed?

Are there exclusive sellers?

Is there a ready supply or a limited amount?

Is it available for a short season?

What channels of distributors must be reached?

____ **Packaging**

Unit size or sizes offered.

Package shape.

Package design.

   Styling.

   Color.

Special protection for product.

A carrier for product.

Package label.

Checklist
Design Principles

Balance

The **optical center** is the reference point that determines the layout's balance. The optical center is about one-eighth of a page above the physical center of the page. Balance is achieved through the arrangement of elements on the page—the left side of the optical center versus the right, above the optical center versus below. Example **a:** Arms in lap appear in the horizontal center, but are slightly above; face in upper left corner counterbalances type on the right.

_____ **Formal balance.** Perfect symmetry is the key to formal balance: matched elements on either side of a line dissecting the ad have equal optical weight. This technique strikes a dignified, stable, conservative image. Example **b.**

_____ **Informal balance.** A visually balanced ad has elements of different size, shape, color intensity, or darkness at different distances from the optical center. Like a teeter-totter, an object of greater optical weight near the center can be balanced by an object of less weight farther from the center. Many ads use informal balance to make the ad more interesting, imaginative, and exciting. Examples **a** and **c.**

Movement

Movement is the principle of design that causes the audience to read the material in the desired sequence. It can be achieved through a variety of techniques.

_____ People or animals can be positioned so that their eyes direct the reader's eyes to the next important element. Example **a.**

_____ Devices such as pointing fingers, boxes, lines, or arrows (or moving the actors or the camera or changing scenes) direct attention from element to element. Example **c.**

_____ Design can take advantage of readers' natural tendency to start at the top left corner of the page and proceed in a Z motion to the lower right. Examples **a** and **c.**

_____ Comic-strip sequence and pictures with captions force the reader to start at the beginning and follow the sequence in order to grasp the message. Example **c.**

_____ Use of white space and color emphasizes a body of type or an illustration. Eyes will go from a dark element to a light one, or from color to noncolor. Example **c.**

_____ Size itself attracts attention because readers are drawn to the biggest and most dominant element on the page, then to smaller elements. All examples, **b** and **c** stronger.

Proportion

_____ Elements should be accorded space based on their importance to the entire ad. Attention-getting elements are usually given more space. Avoid the monotony of giving equal amounts of space to each element. Examples **b** and **c.**

White Space (Isolation)

_____ White space is the part of the ad not occupied by other elements (note that white space may be some color other than white). White space helps focus attention on an isolated element—it makes the copy appear to be in a spotlight. White space is an important contributor to the ad's overall image. Examples **b** and **c.**

Contrast

_____ An effective way of drawing attention to a particular element is to use contrast in color, size, or style; for example, a reverse ad (white letters against a dark background) or a black-and-white ad with a red border. Example **c,** stop sign.

Clarity and Simplicity

_____ Any elements that can be eliminated without damaging the overall effect should be cut. Too many type styles; type that is too small; too many reverses, illustrations, or boxed items; and unnecessary copy make for an overly complex layout and an ad that is hard to read. Artful arrangement keeps this from happening in Example **a.** Note simplicity of Example **b.**

Unity

_____ Unity means that an ad's many different elements must relate to one another in such a way that the ad gives a singular, harmonious impression. Balance, movement, proportion, contrast, and color may all contribute to unity of design. Many other techniques can be used: type styles from the same family, borders around ads to hold elements together, overlapping one picture or element on another, judicious use of white space, graphic tools such as boxes, arrows, or tints. Examples **a** and **b** have stronger unity than **c.**

Continuity

_____ Continuity is the relationship of one ad to the rest of the campaign. This is achieved by using the same design format, style, and tone; the same spokesperson; or the same graphic element, logo, cartoon character, or catchy slogan. See the Taylor Guitar ads in Chapter 10.

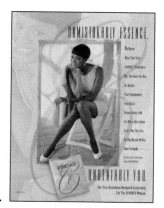

a.

b.

c.

RL 12–2

Techniques for creating advertising visuals.

Visuals in an ad help consumers envision a fact or concept with immediacy. The style and size of the visual depend on several factors: its role in the ad, cost, technical limitations, production time, effect desired, printing requirements, and the availability of the necessary professionals. Two types of visuals are used in advertising: photographs and illustrations (drawn, painted, or computerized).

PHOTOGRAPHY

A good photograph usually makes several important contributions to an ad.

Provides Realism Good color photography can give an exciting, realistic look to all kinds of products, from close-up views of high-tech products to wide landscape vistas. Photographs, especially news-type photos, put the reader at the scene. Knowing the photographer had to be there, the reader becomes personally involved in the action.

Adds Mood, Beauty, and Sensitivity Photography can deliver a mood or a tremendous emotional wallop—like a photograph of an abused child. And it also offers beauty.

Brings the "Cartoon Effect" to Life Photography lends realism to unusual or cartoonish subjects. A drawing of the famous eye-patched Hathaway man would have lacked the realism and story appeal of the actual man.

Offers Speed, Flexibility, and Economy An illustration usually takes considerably longer to complete than a photograph. Many photos can be taken and developed overnight.

Using photography is relatively simple. The photographer shoots a variety of poses at various angles and with various light settings. Then, in the case of print photography, the negatives are printed actual size on a contact sheet unretouched. With a magnifying glass, the art director finds and proofs the most suitable photo. Most color photos are shot as transparencies (slides), and the art director uses a light table or slide viewer to make selections.

Photography can be economical. Photos can be cropped to any size or shape and retouched by computer or with a paintbrush or airbrush to improve the image. Also, stock photo houses have tens of thousands of images, and they're usually cheaper than hiring a photographer.

Requires Precautions When photos are commissioned or bought by an advertiser or agency, any individuals who appear in the picture must sign a standard model release (available from many stationery stores), which gives the advertiser permission to use their picture.

Copyright laws state that the image belongs to the artist (photographer or illustrator); hence, it's customary to pay for each use. The price a photographer charges usually depends on the intended use, frequency of use, and size of the market—not to mention the renown of the photographer.

ILLUSTRATION

Hand-drawn or painted illustrations offer different benefits. Some things cannot be photographed: certain concepts and past and future events. Likewise, a line drawing may more clearly portray a product or instill the proper mood. Illustrations may also be used to exaggerate a subject.

Illustrators are limited only by their own skill. Unlike photographers, who must capture a scene (either in nature or with expensive staging), the illustrator can create the desired image and still add personal style.

Illustrators use a number of techniques (or media) to produce illustrations, including pencil, crayon, and charcoal; ink and ink wash; scratchboard; airbrush; oil, acrylic, tempera, and watercolor; and computers. Computer software such as Fractal Painter and Adobe Photoshop can now simulate the nature and effects of all of these media.

Drawing Ideal for sharp and clearly detailed subjects, line drawings are usually created in black and white, with no shades of gray. The media used include pencil, crayon, and charcoal, which are known for their dry, scratchy appearance; and ink and markers, which can appear wet. Sometimes referred to as pen-and-ink drawings, line drawings are less costly to reproduce than drawings with tonal values. Technical drawings and cartoons are frequently done as line drawings. Scratchboard is a line-drawing technique where a sharp tool is used to scratch away black ink that covers the soft, chalky surface of a special paper called scratchboard. The effect yields fine, white, etched lines on a black field. Overall, line drawings are usually inexpensive and often the least time-consuming type of illustration.

When tones and grays are desired, a wash drawing might be used. Ink is applied in various shades of one color using a brush filled with varying degrees of ink and water. A tight wash drawing is detailed, realistic, and done with both a pen and a brush. A loose wash drawing is more impressionistic and done with a brush only; this is used by fashion and furniture illustrators in newspaper advertising.

Painting Painted illustrations are best used for portraying concepts—recreations of events in history, fictional story characters and persona, emotional moments in daily life, or abstract inspirations. Because airbrush, oil, tempera, and watercolor tend to blur and soften as they are applied to various materials, especially paper, they are ideal for romantic and expressive images. An artist can make a message more expressive by splattering, smearing, and thickly applying paint. Painting is useful for executing smooth gradations from one color or tone to the next, a technique that can be very eye-catching. Because airbrush offers the best control of graduated tones, it is often used in technically oriented illustrations of products or futuristic scenes, and to retouch photographic prints for advertising.

Computer Computer technology has been used for several decades to create illustrations. Today's software can recreate the look of drawing and painting techniques. *Drawing* programs such as Adobe Illustrator are used to layer type and flat areas into which shades and colors can be inserted. *Painting* programs such as Fractal Painter allow illustrators to shape images as though they were applying watercolor or oil paint—very wet or very thick. *Image enhancement* programs such as Adobe Photoshop are used to digitally retouch or modify photographic images and to create montage images and composite illustrations.

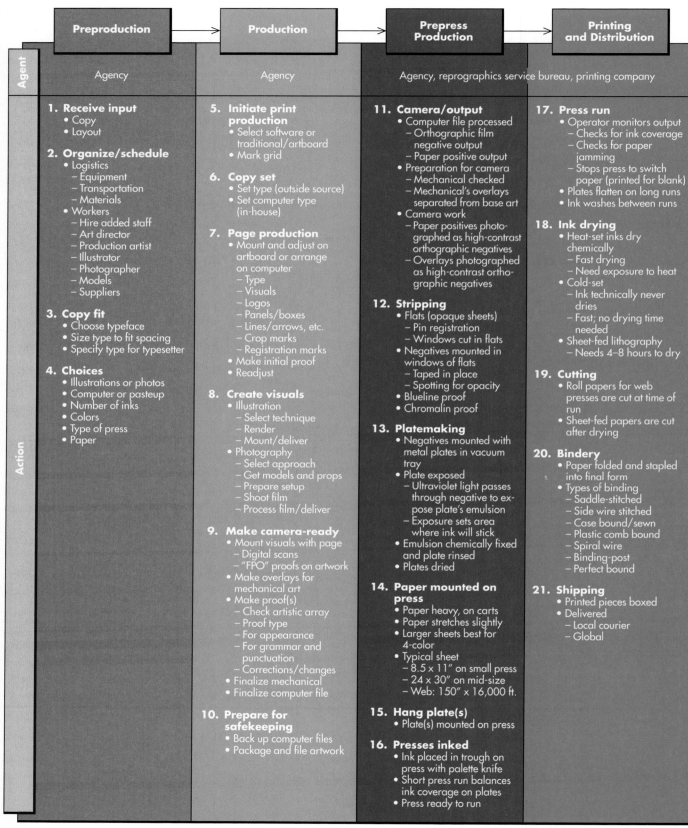

Preproduction	Production	Prepress Production	Printing and Distribution

Agent

| Agency | Agency | Agency, reprographics service bureau, printing company | |

Action

1. Receive input
- Copy
- Layout

2. Organize/schedule
- Logistics
  - Equipment
  - Transportation
  - Materials
- Workers
  - Hire added staff
  - Art director
  - Production artist
  - Illustrator
  - Photographer
  - Models
  - Suppliers

3. Copy fit
- Choose typeface
- Size type to fit spacing
- Specify type for typesetter

4. Choices
- Illustrations or photos
- Computer or pasteup
- Number of inks
- Colors
- Type of press
- Paper

5. Initiate print production
- Select software or traditional/artboard
- Mark grid

6. Copy set
- Set type (outside source)
- Set computer type (in-house)

7. Page production
- Mount and adjust on artboard or arrange on computer
  - Type
  - Visuals
  - Logos
  - Panels/boxes
  - Lines/arrows, etc.
  - Crop marks
  - Registration marks
- Make initial proof
- Readjust

8. Create visuals
- Illustration
  - Select technique
  - Render
  - Mount/deliver
- Photography
  - Select approach
  - Get models and props
  - Prepare setup
  - Shoot film
  - Process film/deliver

9. Make camera-ready
- Mount visuals with page
  - Digital scans
  - "FPO" proofs on artwork
- Make overlays for mechanical art
- Make proof(s)
  - Check artistic array
  - Proof type
  - For appearance
  - For grammar and punctuation
  - Corrections/changes
- Finalize mechanical
- Finalize computer file

10. Prepare for safekeeping
- Back up computer files
- Package and file artwork

11. Camera/output
- Computer file processed
  - Orthographic film negative output
  - Paper positive output
- Preparation for camera
  - Mechanical checked
  - Mechanical's overlays separated from base art
- Camera work
  - Paper positives photographed as high-contrast orthographic negatives
  - Overlays photographed as high-contrast orthographic negatives

12. Stripping
- Flats (opaque sheets)
  - Pin registration
  - Windows cut in flats
- Negatives mounted in windows of flats
  - Taped in place
  - Spotting for opacity
- Blueline proof
- Chromalin proof

13. Platemaking
- Negatives mounted with metal plates in vacuum tray
- Plate exposed
  - Ultraviolet light passes through negative to expose plate's emulsion
  - Exposure sets area where ink will stick
- Emulsion chemically fixed and plate rinsed
- Plates dried

14. Paper mounted on press
- Paper heavy, on carts
- Paper stretches slightly
- Larger sheets best for 4-color
- Typical sheet
  - 8.5 x 11" on small press
  - 24 x 30" on mid-size
  - Web: 150" x 16,000 ft.

15. Hang plate(s)
- Plate(s) mounted on press

16. Presses inked
- Ink placed in trough on press with palette knife
- Short press run balances ink coverage on plates
- Press ready to run

17. Press run
- Operator monitors output
  - Checks for ink coverage
  - Checks for paper jamming
  - Stops press to switch paper (printed for blank)
- Plates flatten on long runs
- Ink washes between runs

18. Ink drying
- Heat-set inks dry chemically
  - Fast drying
  - Need exposure to heat
- Cold-set
  - Ink technically never dries
  - Fast; no drying time needed
- Sheet-fed lithography
  - Needs 4–8 hours to dry

19. Cutting
- Roll papers for web presses are cut at time of run
- Sheet-fed papers are cut after drying

20. Bindery
- Paper folded and stapled into final form
- Types of binding
  - Saddle-stitched
  - Side wire stitched
  - Case bound/sewn
  - Plastic comb bound
  - Spiral wire
  - Binding-post
  - Perfect bound

21. Shipping
- Printed pieces boxed
- Delivered
  - Local courier
  - Global

RL 13–1

The print production process.

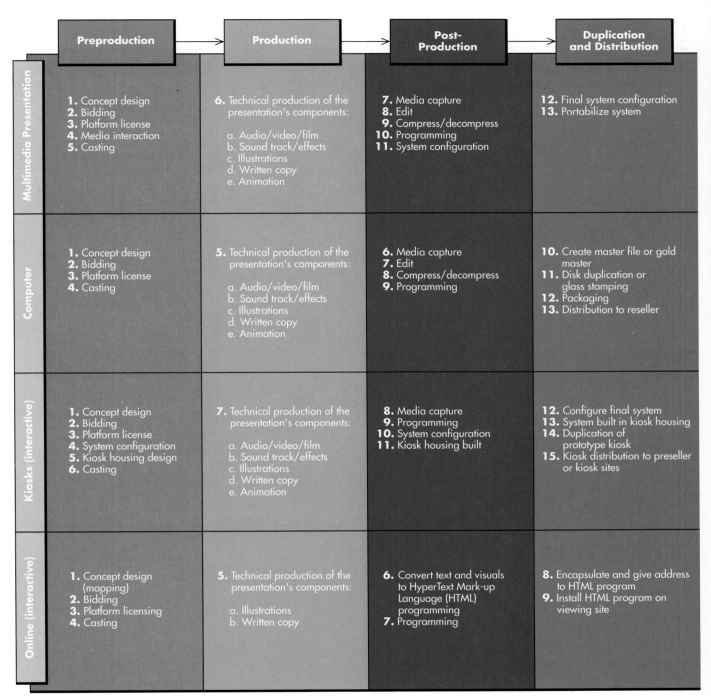

RL 13–2

The production process for digital interactive media.

RL 13–3
Choosing the best method of printing.

The objective of all printing methods is to transfer an image from one surface to another. Advertising materials are printed today by six major types of presses: offset lithography, letterpress, flexography, web-fed printing, rotogravure, and screen printing. There is a distinction between a method for transferring ink and a printing press. A web-fed press, for example, mechanically transfers ink using a lithographic process, meaning that oil-based inked areas are separated by areas moistened with water. Production managers should know which type of press will work best for a particular job and the strengths and weaknesses of each.

Offset Lithography

Pros Plates are relatively inexpensive, printing can be done on almost any quality paper, and preparation time is short. Ink goes on flat, without impressing the paper like letterpress. Ideal for books (including this one), direct-mail materials, and catalogs. Because it's suitable for printing on metal, most packaging materials, including cans, are printed by lithography (see Exhibits **a** and **c**).

Cons Plates wear down after 10,000 to 20,000 units. Can't compete with web-fed presses for jobs of 20,000 units or more.

Notes Offset lithography is currently the most popular printing process in the U.S. All you need is simple art pasted up for the printer's camera (camera-ready materials) or film for the platemaker. The underlying principle is that oil and water don't mix. To start, the material to be printed is photographed. The negative is then laid on top of a zinc or aluminum printing plate and exposed to light. Chemicals are applied to the plate after exposure, and the image takes the form of a greasy coating. The

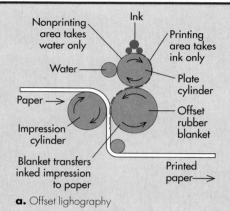

a. Offset lighography

plate is then attached to a cylinder on a rotary printing press, and water is applied with a roller. The greasy image repels the water, while the blank portions of the plate retain it. Next the plate is covered with an oily ink, which the moist, blank portions of the plate repel. The greasy-coated image transfers the ink to an intermediate rubber surface called a blanket, which contacts the paper and prints the image. Offset lithography is used for most inexpensive advertising materials prepared at instant printing shops.

Letterpress

Pros Small letterpresses are useful for hand-fed item work, such as printing names onto business cards or printing short-run announcement jobs. Larger letterpresses are used to print labels and books.

Cons Letterpress dents the printing material with an impression of the lettering. Uses etched metal plates and handset type, which can be labor intensive and time consuming. Cannot compete for jobs that offset lithography can do. Presses run slower than lithographic presses.

Notes For many years, letterpress was the universal method of printing. Johannes Gutenberg and Ben Franklin both used forms of letterpress. It was employed for newspapers and magazines that needed reasonable quality with sharp contrast. The letterpress prints from a metal or plastic printing plate onto a large drum or cylinder. Like a rubber stamp, the image to be transferred is backward ("wrong reading") on the plate. The ink is applied to the raised (relief) surfaces on the plate and then stamped onto the paper or other medium. With the advent of higher-quality methods, letterpress is rarely used to print publications in the U.S. anymore.

Flexography

Pros Ideal for printing on any flexible packaging, including frozen-food packages, multicolor corrugated point-of-sale displays, bread bags, diaper packages, multiwall pet-food bags, polyester, and nylon. Compares well with gravure, matching its long-run ability while taking less time and about half the cost.

Cons Not good for line screens exceeding 180 lines per inch. Flexible plate may cause minor distortions of type and images.

Notes Flexography is a form of letterpress—the raised surfaces transfer the ink to the paper. But instead of a metal plate, flexography uses a flexible rubber or plastic plate. This allows it to print on many different surfaces. In the trade, flexography is called "flexo."

Web-Fed Printing

Pros Appropriate for large-run color jobs from 10,000 units to 400,000 units. Gives accurate color registration even at high press speeds, making it ideal for magazines. Prints up to eight colors simultaneously and signatures up to 32 pages.

Cons Requires greater tolerances than other methods. Image area should be kept at least $\frac{1}{4}$ inch within trim lines and away from fold lines.

Notes Web-fed printing is a form of offset lithography that uses huge rolls of paper. The paper passes across a series of connected presses running each color, then through a heating unit that sets the inks.

Gravure and Rotogravure

Pros Good color reproduction on both newsprint and quality paper, able to stand up to long press runs. Inks dry fast. Can be used with fast web-fed presses as well as standard

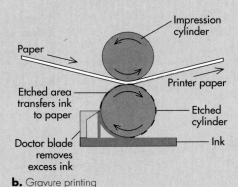

b. Gravure printing

Paper

Impression cylinder

Printer paper

Etched area transfers ink to paper

Etched cylinder

Doctor blade removes excess ink

Ink

c. The high-speed Heidelberg five-color offset press prints magazine-quality publications and advertising materials. The first four units are used for four-color process printing. The fifth can add a protective coat of clear varnish over the printing page or lay down a fifth color (some art directors may want a "company blue," a specific color of ink rather than a combination of process colors).

gravure and roto-gravure presses (see Exhibit **b**). Rotogravure prints foils well.

Cons The most expensive printing process. Preparing the plates or cylinders is time-consuming and costly, so rotogravure is most practical for long press runs.

Notes Gravure uses a sheetfed press and rotogravure a roll-fed press. Gravure uses two separate films, one for type and line illustrations and the other for halftones. The negatives are combined into a single film "positive." Every element of the image is screened, even type and line art. As with letterpress, the image is backward on the plate (wrong reading). The design is etched or electromechanically engraved into a metal plate or cylinder, leaving microscopic depressions. Ink left in the tiny depressions transfers to the paper by pressure and suction. Sunday newspaper supplements, mail-order catalogs, some major magazines, packaging, and other materials

requiring many photographs work well with this method.

Screen Printing (Serigraphy)

Pros Ideal for printing on materials that won't pass through a press, such as wood, metals, and plastics. Can achieve good registration.

Cons Slower than other methods. Not recommended for long runs.

Notes Used for signs, glass bottles, and billboards. Screen printing, an old process based on the stencil principle, requires no plates. A special screen is stretched tightly on a frame, which is placed on the printing surface. A stencil, either hand cut from film or photographically prepared, blocks out areas that won't be printed. A squeegee (rubber bar) is pushed across the surface, squeezing ink through the screen and transferring the image onto the paper or other surface. A separate stencil is made for each color.

RL 15–1

SRDS for radio station. The SRDS *Spot Rate & Data* listing for KWOD (FM) in Sacramento, California, provides data on the station and the rates for air time based on volume and dayparts.

KWOD (FM)

1957
SACRAMENTO
COUNTY: Sacramento

NAB

Location ID: 4 RLST CA   Mld 008767-000
Royce International Broadcasting Corp.
1425 River Park Dr., Sacramento, CA 95815. Phone 916-929-5000.

FORMAT DESCRIPTION
KWOD (FM): Programmed for adults 18-49; music, personalities & news format. MUSIC: Contemporary mass appeal, plus recurrent hits; 30-min uninterrupted sweeps hrly. FEATURES: interviews w/Contemporary & AOR recording artists 2x/day; wkly specials featuring music blocks & personal interviews w/popular artists Wed 11 pm; countdown of day's top hits M-F 8 pm; syndicated countdown programs w/artist interviews Sun 9 am-noon & 7-11 pm. 14 AIR PERSONALITIES; emphasis community involvement & promotion. NEWS: blocks M-Sat am & pm drives; local, reg'l & nat'l coverage; live & taped actualities employing earth satellite, mobile ENG vans & 2-way units; airborne traffic reports 2x/hr in drive; weather hrly; nat'l & local sports recap in AM drive. COMMERCIAL POLICY: 3 comm'l showcases w/12 comm'l units hrly. Rec'd 11/27/89.

1. PERSONNEL
President—Edward R. Stolz, II.
Local Sales Manager—Tom Miller.
Program Director—Gerry Cagle.

2. REPRESENTATIVES
CBS Radio Representatives.

2A. NETWORK/GROUP AFFILIATION
Affiliated with ABC FM Radio Network.
Affiliated with CBS RADIORADIO.

3. FACILITIES
ERP 50,000 w. (horiz.) 50,000 w. (vert.); 106.5 mhz. Stereo.
Antenna ht.: 1,100 ft. above sea level.
Operating schedule: 24 hours daily. PST.

4. AGENCY COMMISSION
15/2 time only; 10th of following month.

TIME RATES
No. 25 Eff 1/15/89—Rec'd 11/27/89.
AA—Mon thru Fri 6 am-8 pm; Sat & Sun 10 am-8 pm.
A—Mon thru Fri 8 pm-midnight; Sat & Sun 6-10 am & 8 pm-midnight.

6. SPOT ANNOUNCEMENTS

GRID—CLASS AA

PER WK:	— 1 min —				— 30 sec —			
	24 ti	18 ti	12 ti	6 ti	24 ti	18 ti	12 ti	6 ti
I	260	265	270	275	205	210	215	220
II	235	240	245	250	185	190	195	200
III	210	215	220	225	165	170	175	180
IV	185	190	195	200	145	150	155	160
V	160	165	170	175	125	130	135	140
VI	135	140	145	150	105	110	115	120

CLASS A

I	250	255	260	265	200	204	208	212
II	225	230	235	240	180	184	188	192
III	200	205	210	215	160	164	168	172
IV	175	180	185	190	140	144	148	152
V	150	155	160	165	120	124	128	132
VI	125	130	135	140	100	104	108	112

Fixed position, extra 25%.

10. SPECIAL FEATURES
News: adjacencies—1-min/30-sec, extra 25%.
Traffic report adjacencies—1 min/30-sec, extra 25%.

RL 15–2

The Arbitron *Radio Market Report* for station KKDA-FM, Dallas/Fort Worth.

		Specific Audience Monday–Friday, 3 P.M.–7 P.M.													
KKDA-FM		Persons 12+	Persons 18+	Men 18+	Men 18–24	Men 25–34	Men 35–44	Men 45–54	Men 55–64	Women 18+	Women 18–24	Women 25–34	Women 35–44	Women 45–54	Women 55–64	Teens 12–17
MET AQH	PER (00)	338	260	107	20	54	15	8	9	153	52	42	31	1	4	78
MET AQH	RATING	1.1	.9	.8	1.0	1.4	.4	.4	.7	1.0	2.5	1.1	.9		.3	2.5
MET AQH	SHARE	5.0	4.2	3.6	4.0	6.3	2.1	1.7	3.2	4.8	9.4	4.9	4.1	.2	1.5	14.9
MET CUME	PER (00)	1678	1282	626	93	314	117	45	35	656	224	202	141	8	17	396
MET CUME	RATING	5.2	4.4	4.5	4.6	8.2	3.5	2.2	2.7	4.4	11.0	5.3	4.3	.4	1.2	12.7
TSA AQH	PER (00)	368	283	123	29	58	15	8	12	160	53	45	31	3	4	85
TSA CUME	PER (00)	2021	1547	800	208	328	117	45	69	747	246	227	141	39	17	474

MET AQH PER (00) (Metropolitan Average Quarter Hour Persons) = Estimated number of persons who listened to a station for a minimum of five minutes within a quarter hour.

TSA (Total Survey Area may include counties surrounding the MET (metropolitan area).

MET AQH RATING (Rating Point) = Metropolitan Average Quarter Hour Persons estimate expressed as a percentage of the appropriate estimated population.

MET AQH SHARE = Metropolitan Average Quarter Hour Persons estimate for a given station expressed as a percentage of the total MET AQH estimate within a reported daypart.

MET CUME PER = Estimated number of *different* persons who listened to a station for a minimum of five minutes in a quarter-hour within a reported daypart. (Cume estimates may also be called *cumulative* or *unduplicated* estimates.)

MET CUME RATING = Estimated number of Cume Persons expressed as a percentage of the appropriate estimated metropolitan population.

FCB

Foote, Cone & Belding
11601 Wilshire Boulevard
Los Angeles, CA 90025
(310) 312-7000

Spot Commercial Instructions

Station:_____   Commercial Material:_____

Air Dates:_____   Live Copy No(s):_____

Client/Product:_____   Estimate No.:_____

Rotation:_____

Commercials to run per media time order.
Call with questions.

Issued by:_____FCB/LA Forwarding

Phone:_____

Date:_____

```
FCB/LOS ANGELES                    SPOT COMMERCIAL INSTRUCTIONS (RADIO)

11601 WILSHIRE BOULEVARD           Period JAN01/93 thru DEC31/93                  Page   1
LOS ANGELES, CA 90025                                                             Mon May 24, 1993
                                                                                  7:35 PM - 8JE
                                   Client                                         SP:TLETTER2
                                   Product EXP     EXPANSION

                                          Market   DOT AL  DOTHAN, AL.
                                          Station  WTVY-FM
                                          Phone             205-792-0047
                                          FAX               205-793-3947

          -------------------------------------------------------------------------------------
          Prod                    Start              ----------------------Commercial-----------------------
          Code Product name    Length Date  End Date    Code No.  Title                   (Rot'n)  Mat'ls
          -------------------------------------------------------------------------------------
          EXP  EXPANSION               MAR15/93 JUN13/93           Previously Trafficked

          EXP  EXPANSION          :60  JUN14/93 UFN      FA2102A   GRADUATION :60          25.0%  On Hand

                                                         FA2104A   BABY :60                25.0%  On Hand

          *****************************************       FA2106A   GUITAR :60              25.0%  On Hand
          * YOU HAVE THESE SPOTS.  CONTINUE RUNNING WITH TAGS AS  *
          * PREVIOUSLY INSTRUCTED.                    *       FA8013    RECRUITING - INSURE SUCCESS  12.5%  On Hand
          *                                           *
          * CALL JESSE BARNETT AT FCB (310) 312-7251 WITH QUESTIONS. *  FA8104    RECRUITING - LIKE WHAT YOU SEE  12.5%  On Hand
          *****************************************
                                                         *** Billboards ***
                                                         :05  FA2020
                                                         BROUGHT TO YOU BY THE LOCAL AGENTS OF THE
                                                              ASK THEM ABOUT LIFE INSURANCE.
                                                         :10  FA2020A
                                                         BROUGHT TO YOU BY                   YEAR AFTER YEAR,
                                                         MILLIONS OF FAMILIES ACROSS AMERICA DEPEND ON       FOR
                                                         HOME, AUTO, AND ESPECIALLY, LIFE INSURANCE.
                                                              ONE OF THE BIGGEST.  ONE OF THE BEST.

                                                         ** RADIO OPERATIONS DESK **
                                                         WTVY-FM
                                                         BOX 1089
                                                         DOTHAN, AL 36301
```

RL 15–3

Spot commercial instructions. Once the buy is completed, the agency's traffic department issues instructions to the station describing the rotation of commercials to be used. Shown here are the bare-bones instructions a station would require, as well as computerized instructions from FCB's internal buying/trafficking system.

RL 16–1
Advantages and disadvantages of the U.S. postal system.

Class*	Category	Advantages	Disadvantages
Express mail	Overnight	• Fastest delivery: overnight and 2 day for some addresses	• Highest cost: many dollars per unit, generally prohibitive for direct mail
Priority mail	Two-day	• Fast delivery: 2-day delivery	• Very high cost: a few dollars per unit, prohibitive for most direct-mail programs
First class	First class (single piece)	• Normal delivery: 2–7 days for U.S. • Items forwarded without additional charge or returned • Envelope provides best presentation	• Noticeable cost • Priced by the ounce of each item
	Post card (Can be first, third, or fourth class, depending on the rate paid, size of card, and permit used)	• Least expensive	• Slowest first-class mail (7–21 days in U.S.) • Poorest presentation • Over 4.24" × 6" requires higher rate
	Business reply: a. Mail	• Same advantages as first-class mail • Postage-paid envelope encourages responses	• Need permit
	b. Card	• Same advantages as post card • Postage-paid post card encourages responses	• Need permit • Slow
Second class	None (reserved for publishers)	• None	• Not directly available for advertising use
Third class (1–32 oz.)	Promotional materials	• Price is relatively low	• Slow delivery: 3–14 days for U.S. • Per-piece pricing
Fourth class (2–70 lbs.)	Parcel post	• Same low rate as third class • Large parcels up to 108" combined length and girth	• Slow delivery: 3–21 days for U.S. • Per-piece pricing
Bulk rate (1–15.9 oz.)	Bulk rate	• Least expensive • Ideal for catalogs	• Requires a permit • Slow delivery • Items must be provided to post office bundled by ZIP code

*Within the United States.

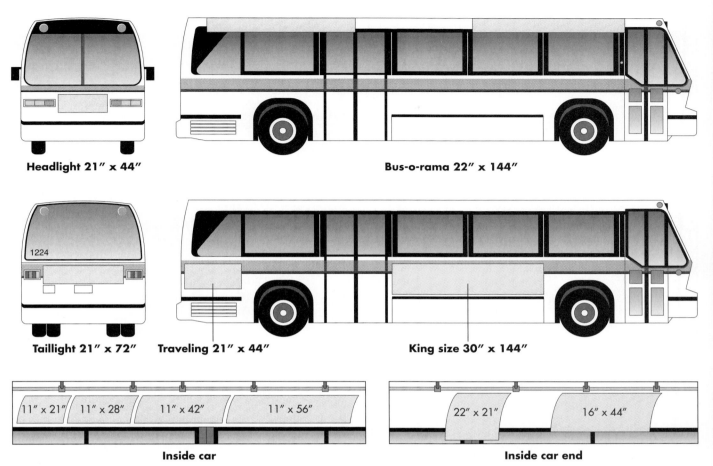

Headlight 21" x 44"

Bus-o-rama 22" x 144"

1224

Taillight 21" x 72"

Traveling 21" x 44"

King size 30" x 144"

| 11" x 21" | 11" x 28" | 11" x 42" | 11" x 56" |

Inside car

22" x 21"

16" x 44"

Inside car end

RL 17–1
Common sizes for outside posters and inside cards.

The package production process.

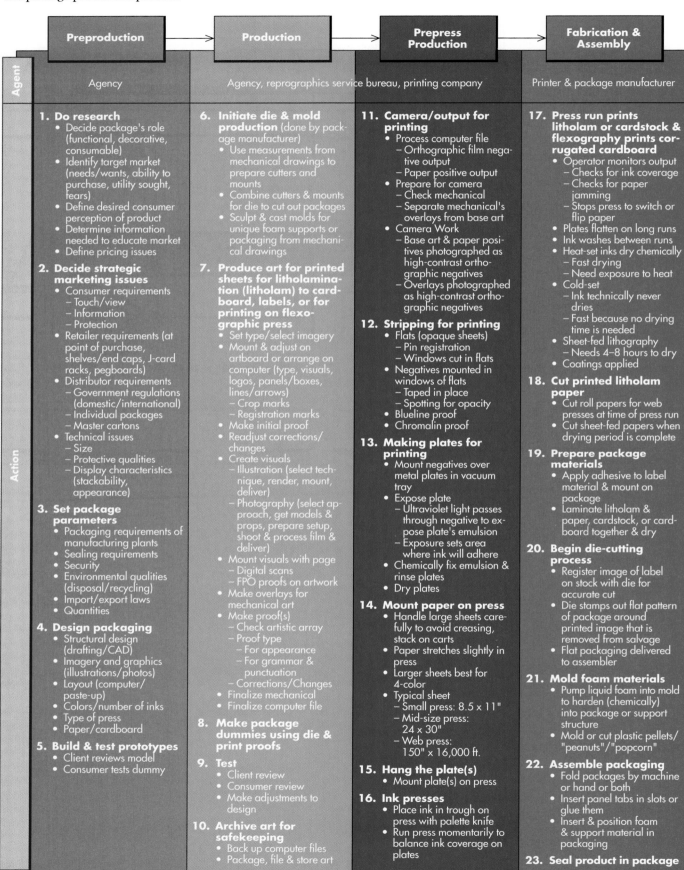

Preproduction	Production	Prepress Production	Fabrication & Assembly

Agent

| Agency | Agency, reprographics service bureau, printing company | | Printer & package manufacturer |

Action

Preproduction (Agency)

1. **Do research**
   - Decide package's role (functional, decorative, consumable)
   - Identify target market (needs/wants, ability to purchase, utility sought, fears)
   - Define desired consumer perception of product
   - Determine information needed to educate market
   - Define pricing issues

2. **Decide strategic marketing issues**
   - Consumer requirements
     – Touch/view
     – Information
     – Protection
   - Retailer requirements (at point of purchase, shelves/end caps, J-card racks, pegboards)
   - Distributor requirements
     – Government regulations (domestic/international)
     – Individual packages
     – Master cartons
   - Technical issues
     – Size
     – Protective qualities
     – Display characteristics (stackability, appearance)

3. **Set package parameters**
   - Packaging requirements of manufacturing plants
   - Sealing requirements
   - Security
   - Environmental qualities (disposal/recycling)
   - Import/export laws
   - Quantities

4. **Design packaging**
   - Structural design (drafting/CAD)
   - Imagery and graphics (illustrations/photos)
   - Layout (computer/paste-up)
   - Colors/number of inks
   - Type of press
   - Paper/cardboard

5. **Build & test prototypes**
   - Client reviews model
   - Consumer tests dummy

Production (Agency, reprographics service bureau, printing company)

6. **Initiate die & mold production** (done by package manufacturer)
   - Use measurements from mechanical drawings to prepare cutters and mounts
   - Combine cutters & mounts for die to cut out packages
   - Sculpt & cast molds for unique foam supports or packaging from mechanical drawings

7. **Produce art for printed sheets for litholamination (litholam) to cardboard, labels, or for printing on flexographic press**
   - Set type/select imagery
   - Mount & adjust on artboard or arrange on computer (type, visuals, logos, panels/boxes, lines/arrows)
     – Crop marks
     – Registration marks
   - Make initial proof
   - Readjust corrections/changes
   - Create visuals
     – Illustration (select technique, render, mount, deliver)
     – Photography (select approach, get models & props, prepare setup, shoot & process film & deliver)
   - Mount visuals with page
     – Digital scans
     – FPO proofs on artwork
   - Make overlays for mechanical art
   - Make proof(s)
     – Check artistic array
     – Proof type
       – For appearance
       – For grammar & punctuation
     – Corrections/Changes
   - Finalize mechanical
   - Finalize computer file

8. **Make package dummies using die & print proofs**

9. **Test**
   - Client review
   - Consumer review
   - Make adjustments to design

10. **Archive art for safekeeping**
    - Back up computer files
    - Package, file & store art

Prepress Production

11. **Camera/output for printing**
    - Process computer file
      – Orthographic film negative output
      – Paper positive output
    - Prepare for camera
      – Check mechanical
      – Separate mechanical's overlays from base art
    - Camera Work
      – Base art & paper positives photographed as high-contrast orthographic negatives
      – Overlays photographed as high-contrast orthographic negatives

12. **Stripping for printing**
    - Flats (opaque sheets)
      – Pin registration
      – Windows cut in flats
    - Negatives mounted in windows of flats
      – Taped in place
      – Spotting for opacity
    - Blueline proof
    - Chromalin proof

13. **Making plates for printing**
    - Mount negatives over metal plates in vacuum tray
    - Expose plate
      – Ultraviolet light passes through negative to expose plate's emulsion
      – Exposure sets area where ink will adhere
    - Chemically fix emulsion & rinse plates
    - Dry plates

14. **Mount paper on press**
    - Handle large sheets carefully to avoid creasing, stack on carts
    - Paper stretches slightly in press
    - Larger sheets best for 4-color
    - Typical sheet
      – Small press: 8.5 x 11"
      – Mid-size press: 24 x 30"
      – Web press: 150" x 16,000 ft.

15. **Hang the plate(s)**
    - Mount plate(s) on press

16. **Ink presses**
    - Place ink in trough on press with palette knife
    - Run press momentarily to balance ink coverage on plates

Fabrication & Assembly (Printer & package manufacturer)

17. **Press run prints litholam or cardstock & flexography prints corrugated cardboard**
    - Operator monitors output
      – Checks for ink coverage
      – Checks for paper jamming
      – Stops press to switch or flip paper
    - Plates flatten on long runs
    - Ink washes between runs
    - Heat-set inks dry chemically
      – Fast drying
      – Need exposure to heat
    - Cold-set
      – Ink technically never dries
      – Fast because no drying time is needed
    - Sheet-fed lithography
      – Needs 4–8 hours to dry
    - Coatings applied

18. **Cut printed litholam paper**
    - Cut roll papers for web presses at time of press run
    - Cut sheet-fed papers when drying period is complete

19. **Prepare package materials**
    - Apply adhesive to label material & mount on package
    - Laminate litholam & paper, cardstock, or cardboard together & dry

20. **Begin die-cutting process**
    - Register image of label on stock with die for accurate cut
    - Die stamps out flat pattern of package around printed image that is removed from salvage
    - Flat packaging delivered to assembler

21. **Mold foam materials**
    - Pump liquid foam into mold to harden (chemically) into package or support structure
    - Mold or cut plastic pellets/"peanuts"/"popcorn"

22. **Assemble packaging**
    - Fold packages by machine or hand or both
    - Insert panel tabs in slots or glue them
    - Insert & position foam & support material in packaging

23. **Seal product in package**

RL 17–3
Trade show budgeting checklist.

	Cost Estimated	Actual		Cost Estimated	Actual
1. Space			**5. Shipping & Storage**		
[ ] Booth	$_____	$_____	[ ] Freight	$_____	$_____
[ ] Hotel suite	$_____	$_____	[ ] Drayage	$_____	$_____
2. Display			[ ] Exhibit storage	$_____	$_____
[ ] Design & construction	$_____	$_____	[ ] Insurance	$_____	$_____
[ ] Graphics	$_____	$_____	**6. Advertising & promotion**		
[ ] Refurbishing	$_____	$_____	[ ] Preshow promotion	$_____	$_____
[ ] Products for display	$_____	$_____	[ ] On-site promotion	$_____	$_____
[ ] Booth rental	$_____	$_____	[ ] Postshow promotion	$_____	$_____
[ ] Used booth purchase	$_____	$_____	[ ] Direct mail	$_____	$_____
[ ] Literature holders	$_____	$_____	[ ] Special badges	$_____	$_____
[ ] Easels	$_____	$_____	[ ] Special uniforms	$_____	$_____
[ ] Tool kit	$_____	$_____	[ ] Handouts, giveaways	$_____	$_____
[ ] Lighting fixtures	$_____	$_____	[ ] Special show literature	$_____	$_____
3. Furnishing at booth			[ ] Telemarketing	$_____	$_____
[ ] Tables	$_____	$_____	**7. Personnel**		
[ ] Chairs	$_____	$_____	[ ] Travel reservations	$_____	$_____
[ ] Coat racks	$_____	$_____	[ ] Hotel reservations	$_____	$_____
[ ] Floor covering	$_____	$_____	[ ] Registrations at show	$_____	$_____
[ ] Floral arrangements	$_____	$_____	[ ] Meals	$_____	$_____
[ ] Computer rental	$_____	$_____	[ ] Out-of-pocket expenses	$_____	$_____
[ ] Imprinter rental	$_____	$_____	**8. Special activities**		
[ ] Audiovisual equipment	$_____	$_____	[ ] Client entertainment	$_____	$_____
4. Show services			[ ] Receptions	$_____	$_____
[ ] Set-up/tear-down labor	$_____	$_____	[ ] Sales meetings	$_____	$_____
[ ] Electricity	$_____	$_____	[ ] Speakers, training	$_____	$_____
[ ] Water, gas, air	$_____	$_____	**9. Other**		
[ ] Phone, fax	$_____	$_____	[ ] _____	$_____	$_____
[ ] Photos of display	$_____	$_____	[ ] _____	$_____	$_____
[ ] Security	$_____	$_____	[ ] _____	$_____	$_____
[ ] Fed Ex	$_____	$_____	[ ] _____	$_____	$_____
			Total show budget	$_____	$_____

Appendix **A**

Marketing Plan Outline

Date:
Company Name:
Brand or Service:

Encapsulation, for executive review, of entire marketing plan in no more than two or three pages.

I. Executive Summary
  A. Summary of situation analysis
  B. Summary of marketing objectives
  C. Summary of marketing strategies
  D. Budget summary

Complete statement of where the organization is today and how it got there. See Checklist for Situation Analysis (RL 7–1).

What business the organization is in and characteristics of the industry as a whole. Information available from industry trade publications, trade association newsletters, consumer business press, Department of Commerce publications.

II. Situation Analysis
  A. The industry
    1. Definition of industry and company business
    2. History of industry
      a. Technological advances
      b. Trends
    3. Growth patterns within industry
      a. Demand curve
      b. Per capita consumption
      c. Growth potential
    4. Characteristics of industry
      a. Distribution patterns and traditional channels
      b. Regulation and control within industry
      c. Typical promotional activity
      d. Geographical characteristics
      e. Profit patterns

All relevant information on the company and its capabilities, opportunities, and/or problems. Information may be found in annual reports, sales records, warranty card records, customer correspondence, sales staff reports.

  B. The company
    1. Brief history
    2. Scope of business
    3. Current size, growth, profitability
    4. Reputation
    5. Competence in various areas
      a. Strengths
      b. Weaknesses

Complete description and all relevant information on the product/service mix, sales, and the strengths and weaknesses therein. See sales literature, sales reports, dealer correspondence, and so on.

  C. The product/service
    1. The product story
      a. Development and history
      b. Stage of product life cycle
        (1) Introduction
        (2) Growth
        (3) Maturity
        (4) Decline
      c. Quality factors
      d. Design considerations

       e. Goods classification
- (1) Consumer or industrial good
- (2) Durable or nondurable good or service
- (3) Convenience, shopping, or specialty good
- (4) Package good, hard good, soft good, service

       f. Packaging
       g. Price structure
       h. Uses
- (1) Primary
- (2) Secondary
- (3) Potential

       i. Image and reputation
       j. Product/service strengths
       k. Product/service weaknesses
2. Product sales features
  a. Differentiating factors
- (1) Perceptible, imperceptible, or induced
- (2) Exclusive or nonexclusive

  b. Position in mind of customer
  c. Advantages and disadvantages (customer perception)
3. Product research and development
  a. Technological breakthroughs
  b. Improvements planned
  c. Technical or service problems
4. Sales history
  a. Sales and cost of sales
- (1) By product/service
- (2) By model
- (3) By territory
- (4) By market

  b. Profit history for same factors
5. Share of market
  a. Industry sales by market
  b. Market share in dollars and units
  c. Market potential and trends

D. The market

All relevant information about the people or organizations that comprise the current and prospective market for the firm's offerings. See market research reports, consumer/business press, trade publications, Census of Manufacturers, trade association reports.

1. Definition and location of market
  a. Identified market segments
- (1) Past
- (2) Potential

  b. Market needs, desires
  c. Characteristics of market
- (1) Geographic
- (2) Demographic
- (3) Psychographic
- (4) Behavioral

  d. Typical buying patterns
- (1) Purchase patterns
- (2) Heavy users/light users
- (3) Frequency of purchase

  e. Buying influences on market
2. Definition of our customers
  a. Present, past, and future

Complete information about the competition, the competitive environment, and the opportunities or challenges presented by current or prospective competitors. See SEC Form 10-Ks, consumer/business press articles, Moody's Industrial Manual, *Standard & Poor's reports, Dun & Bradstreet report,* Thomas Register of American Corporations.

Complete discussion of how the firm's products/services are distributed and sold, what channels are available, and characteristics of channel members. See dealer and distributor correspondence, sales staff reports, advertising reports, trade publication articles.

Background and rationale for firm's pricing policies and strategies, discussion of alternative options. Study sales reports, channel-member correspondence, customer correspondence, competitive information.

      b. Characteristics
        (1) Shared characteristics with rest of market
        (2) Characteristics unique to our customers
      c. What they like about us or our product
      d. What they don't like
   3. Consumer appeals
      a. Past advertising appeals
        (1) What has worked
        (2) What has not worked and why
      b. Possible future appeals
   4. Results of research studies about market and customers
E. The competition
   1. Identification of competitors
      a. Primary competitors
      b. Secondary competitors
      c. Product/service descriptions
      d. Growth and size of competitors
      e. Share of market held by competitors
   2. Strengths of competition
      a. Product quality
      b. Sales features
      c. Price, distribution, promotion
   3. Weaknesses of competition
      a. Product features
      b. Consumer attitude
      c. Price, distribution, promotion
   4. Marketing activities of competition
      a. Product positioning
      b. Pricing strategies
      c. Distribution
      d. Sales force
      e. Advertising, publicity
      f. Estimated budgets
F. Distribution strategies
   1. Type of distribution network used
      a. History of development
      b. Trends
   2. Evaluation of how distribution is accomplished
   3. Description and evaluation with channel members
   4. Promotional relationship with channel members
      a. Trade advertising and allowances
      b. Co-op advertising
      c. Use of promotion by dealer or middlemen
      d. Point-of-purchase displays, literature
      e. Dealer incentive programs.
   5. Strengths/weaknesses of distribution systems
   6. Opportunities/threats related to distribution
G. Pricing policies
   1. Price history
      a. Trends
      b. Affordability
      c. Competition

All relevant data concerning the firm's personal sales efforts and effectiveness as well as complete discussion of the firm's use of advertising, public relations, and sales promotion programs. Examine sales reports, advertising reports, articles in Advertising Age, Marketing Communications, *and so on, in-house data on advertising, sales, and training.*

Enumeration of environmental factors that may be beyond the firm's immediate control but affect the firm's business efforts. See government reports and announcements, consumer/business press, trade association articles.

Recitation of relevant attitudes and directives of management as they pertain to the firm's marketing and advertising efforts. Information available from corporate business plan, management interviews, internal memos and directives.

Enumeration or summary of problems considered most serious to the firm's marketing success.

Summary of those opportunities which offer the greatest potential for the firm's success. What general and specific needs the firm seeks to satisfy. Determine through study of situation analysis factors and management discussions and interviews.

2. Price objectives and strategies in past
   a. Management attitudes
   b. Buyer attitudes
   c. Channel attitudes
3. Opportunities/threats related to pricing
H. Communication strategies
   1. Past promotion policy
      a. Personal versus nonpersonal selling
         (1) Use of sales force
         (2) Use of advertising, public relations, sales promotion
      b. Successes and failures of past policy
   2. Sales force
      a. Size
      b. Scope
      c. Ability/training
      d. Cost per sale
   3. Advertising programs
      a. Successes and failures
      b. Strategies, themes, campaigns, media employed
      c. Appeals, positionings, and so on
      d. Expenditures
         (1) Past budgets
         (2) Method of allocation
         (3) Competitor budgets
         (4) Trend
   4. Opportunities/threats related to communications
I. Environmental factors
   1. Economy
      a. Current economic status
      b. Business outlook and economic forecasts
   2. Political situation
   3. Societal concerns
   4. Technological influences
J. Corporate objectives and strategies
   1. Profitability
      a. Sales revenue
      b. Cost reductions
   2. Return on investment
   3. Stock price
   4. Shareholder equity
   5. Community image
   6. New product development
   7. Technological leadership
   8. Mergers and/or acquisitions
   9. Overall corporate mission
K. Potential marketing problems
L. Potential marketing opportunities

III. Marketing Objectives
A. Market need objectives
   1. Market need-satisfying objectives
   2. Community need-satisfying objectives
   3. Corporate need-satisfying objectives

Organization sales goals defined for whole company or for individual products by target market, by geographic territory, by department, or by some other category. Must be specific and realistic based on study of company capabilities, funding, and objectives.

The method(s) by which the organization plans to achieve the objectives enumerated above.

A general description of the type of marketing strategy the organization intends to employ.

A detailed description of the marketing mix(es) the firm intends to use to achieve its objectives.

The detailed tactical plans for implementing each of the elements of the firm's marketing mix.

Description of the methods the firm will use to review, evaluate, and control its progress toward the achievement of its marketing objectives.

    B. Sales target objectives
      1. Sales volume
        a. Dollars
        b. Units
        c. Territories
        d. Markets
      2. Share of market
      3. Distribution expansion
      4. Other

IV. Marketing Strategy
    A. General marketing strategy
      1. Positioning strategy
      2. Product differentiation strategy
      3. Price/quality differentiation strategy
      4. Mission marketing strategy
    B. Specific market strategies
      1. Target market A
        a. Product
        b. Price
        c. Distribution
        d. Communication
          (1) Personal selling
          (2) Advertising
          (3) Direct marketing
          (4) Sales promotion
          (5) Public relations
      2. Target market B
        a. Product
        b. Price
        c. Distribution
        d. Communication
          (1) Personal selling
          (2) Advertising
          (3) Direct marketing
          (4) Sales promotion
          (5) Public relations

V. Action Programs (Tactics)
    A. Product plans
    B. Pricing plans
    C. Distribution plans
    D. Communication plans
      1. Sales plan
      2. Advertising plan
      3. Direct marketing plan
      4. Sales promotion plan
      5. Public relations plan
    E. Mission marketing plan
    F. Interactivity plan

VI. Measurement, Review, and Control
    A. Organizational structure
    B. Methodology for review and evaluation
    C. Interactivity monitoring

Determination of the amount of money needed to conduct the marketing effort, the rationale for that budget, and the allocation to various functions.

VII. Marketing Budget
   A. Method of allocation
   B. Enumeration of marketing costs by division
      1. New product research
      2. Marketing research
      3. Sales expenses
      4. Advertising, direct marketing, sales promotion, public relations

Details of information, secondary data, or research conducted to develop information discussed in the marketing plan.

VIII. Appendixes
   A. Sales reports
   B. Reports of market research studies
   C. Reprints of journal or magazine articles
   D. Other supporting documents

Appendix **B**

Advertising Plan Outline

Date:
Company (Brand/Service) Name:

Brief encapsulation, for executive review, of entire advertising plan in no more than two or three pages.

Condensed review of pertinent elements presented in the marketing plan.

I. Executive Summary
    A. Premises—summary of information presented in marketing plan
    B. Summary of advertising objectives
    C. Summary of advertising strategy
    D. Budget summary
II. Situation Analysis
    A. Company's (or product's) current marketing situation
        1. Business or industry information
        2. Description of company, product, or service
            a. Stage of product life cycle
            b. Goods classification
            c. Competitive or market positioning
        3. General description of market(s) served
        4. Sales history and share of market
        5. Description of consumer purchase process
        6. Methods of distribution
        7. Pricing strategies employed
        8. Implications of any marketing research
        9. Communications history
    B. Target market description
        1. Market segments identified
        2. Primary market
        3. Secondary markets
        4. Market characteristics
            a. Geographic
            b. Demographic
            c. Psychographic
            d. Behavioral
    C. Marketing objectives
        1. Need-satisfying objectives
        2. Long- and short-term sales target objectives
    D. Marketing mix for each target market—summarized from marketing plan
        1. Product
        2. Price
        3. Distribution
        4. Communication
    E. Intended role of advertising in the communications mix
    F. Miscellaneous information not included above

Analysis and statement of what the advertising is expected to accomplish—see Checklist for Developing Advertising Objectives (RL 7–3).

III. Advertising Objectives
    A. Primary or selective demand
    B. Direct action or indirect action
    C. Objectives stated in terms of:
        1. Advertising pyramid
        2. Purchase behavior
        3. Other
    D. Quantified expression of objectives
        1. Specific quantities or percentages
        2. Length of time for achievement of objectives
        3. Other possible measurements
            a. Inquiries
            b. Increased order size
            c. Morale building
            d. Other

Intended blend of the creative mix for the company as a whole, for each product, or for each target market.

IV. Advertising (Creative) Strategy
    A. Product concept—how the advertising will present the product in terms of:
        1. Product or market positioning
        2. Product differentiation
        3. Life cycle
        4. Classification, packaging, branding
        5. Kim-Lord grid purchase-decision position
            a. High/low think involvement
            b. High/low feel involvement
    B. Target audience—the specific people the advertising will address
        1. Detailed description of target audiences
            a. Relationship of target audience to target market
            b. Prospective buying influences
            c. Benefits sought/advertising appeals
            d. Demographics
            e. Psychographics
            f. Behavioristics
        2. Prioritization of target audiences
            a. Primary
            b. Secondary
            c. Supplementary

The strategy for selecting the various media vehicles that will communicate the advertising message to the target audience—see Chapters 8, 12–14.

    C. Communications media
        1. Definition of media objectives
            a. Reach
            b. Frequency
            c. Gross rating points
            d. Continuity/flighting/pulsing
        2. Determination of which media reach the target audience best
            a. Traditional mass media
               (1) Radio
               (2) Television
               (3) Newspapers
               (4) Magazines
               (5) Outdoor
            b. Other media
               (1) Direct mail
               (2) Interactive/digital media
               (3) Publicity

      c. Supplemental media
        (1) Trade shows
        (2) Sales promotion devices
        (3) Other media
        (4) Off-the-wall media
   3. Availability of media relative to purchase patterns
   4. Potential for communication effectiveness
   5. Cost considerations
      a. Size/mechanical considerations of message units
      b. Cost efficiency of media plan against target audiences
      c. Production costs
   6. Relevance to other elements of creative mix
   7. Scope of media plan
   8. Exposure/attention/motivation values of intended media vehicles

  D. Advertising message
   1. Copy elements
      a. Advertising appeals
      b. Copy platform
      c. Key consumer benefits
      d. Benefit supports or reinforcements
      e. Product personality or image
   2. Art elements
      a. Visual appeals
        (1) In ads and commercials
        (2) In packaging
        (3) In point-of-purchase and sales materials
      b. Art platform
        (1) Layout
        (2) Design
        (3) Illustration style
   3. Production elements
      a. Mechanical considerations in producing ads
        (1) Color
        (2) Size
        (3) Style
      b. Production values sought
        (1) Typography
        (2) Printing
        (3) Color reproduction
        (4) Photography/illustration
        (5) Paper
        (6) Electronic effects
        (7) Animation
        (8) Film or videotape
        (9) Sound effects
        (10) Music

What the company wants to say and how it wants to say it, verbally and nonverbally—see Chapters 9–11.

V. The Advertising Budget
  A. Impact of marketing situation on method of allocation
   1. New or old product
   2. Primary demand curve for product class
   3. Competitive situation
   4. Marketing objectives and strategy
   5. Profit or growth considerations
   6. Relationship of advertising to sales and profits
   7. Empirical experience

The amount of money to be allocated to advertising and the intended method of allocation—Chapters 7, 17.

The research techniques that will be used to create the advertising and evaluate its effectiveness—see Chapter 6.

  B. Method of allocation
    1. Percentage of sales or profit
    2. Share of market
    3. Objective/task method
    4. Unit of sale
    5. Competitive parity

VI. Testing and Evaluation
  A. Advertising research conducted
    1. Strategy determination
    2. Concept development
  B. Pretesting and posttesting
    1. Elements tested
      a. Markets
      b. Motives
      c. Messages
      d. Media
      e. Budgeting
      f. Scheduling
    2. Methodology
      a. Central location tests
      b. Sales experiments
      c. Physiological testing
      d. Aided recall tests
      e. Unaided recall tests
      f. Attitude tests
      g. Inquiry tests
      h. Sales tests
      i. Other
    3. Cost of testing

Appendix C

Integrated Marketing Communications Plan Outline

Author's note: To better understand the IMC Plan Outline, read Don E. Schultz, Stanley I. Tannenbaum, and Robert F. Lauterborn, Integrated Marketing Communications: Putting It Together & Making It Work *(Lincolnwood, IL: NTC Business Books, 1993), and Thomas R. Duncan and Sandra E. Moriarty,* Driving Brand Value: Using Integrated Marketing to Manage Stakeholder Relationships *(New York: McGraw-Hill, 1997).*

Executive Memo
Table of Contents
Executive Summary

I. Situation Analysis
  A. The marketplace
    1. The industry
    2. The category
    3. Trends
  B. The competition
    1. Primary competition
    2. Secondary competition
    3. Generic competition
    4. Sales and share-of-market (S-O-M)
    5. Promotion spending and share-of-voice (S-O-V)
  C. The company
    1. Background
    2. Sales/S-O-M
    3. Promotion spending/S-O-V
    4. Product portfolio analysis
    5. Brand and positioning status
  D. The customer/prospect
    1. Product category behavior/attitudes
    2. Purchase history
    3. Demographics/geographics
    4. Psychographics
II. Market Segmentation—Database Analysis
  A. Primary target market—loyal users
    1. Identify consumer's brand network—how consumers mentally store ideas about products, services, brands
      a. Perception of products in category
      b. How customers buy and use the brand
      c. Psychographics, attitude toward category and brand
      d. Perception of the company behind the brand
      e. Primary buying incentive to purchase brand (competitive benefit)

      2. Ascertain customer's brand contacts
        a. Where are customers when they need the product?
        b. Where are they most likely to receive and accept messages about the brand?
        c. When can the brand be of greatest benefit to them?
   B. Secondary target market—competitive users
      1. Identify brand network
      2. Ascertain brand contacts
   C. Tertiary target market—swing users
      1. Identify brand network
      2. Ascertain brand contacts

III. Marketing Objectives
   A. Primary target market
      1. Maintain usage
      2. Build usage (share of customer)
      3. Brand network and behavior objectives
   B. Secondary target market
      1. Generate trial
      2. Build volume
      3. Build loyalty to brand
      4. Brand network and behavior objectives
   C. Tertiary target market
      1. Build loyalty to brand
      2. Brand network and behavior objectives

IV. Communication Objectives and Strategies
   A. Determine principal target audiences for communications
   B. Determine overall product positioning and personality
   C. Determine best contact points for reaching and interacting with customer or prospect
   D. Determine the key customer benefit and principal selling message
   E. Determine value-added mission marketing objectives

V. Marketing Strategy
   A. Identify target markets and their needs
   B. Develop best marketing mix for each target market
      1. Product/service mix
      2. Distribution strategy/geographic coverage
      3. Pricing strategy
      4. Communication strategy based on contact point analysis
        a. Personal selling
        b. Advertising
        c. Sales promotion
        d. Direct marketing
        e. Public relations activities/corporate identity/sponsorships
        f. Merchandising, packaging, and collateral

VI. Advertising Program
   A. Advertising objectives
   B. Creative strategy
      1. Advertising assignment
      2. Creative objectives
      3. Message strategy
        a. Product concept
        b. Target audience
        c. Accepted consumer belief
        d. Key selling idea (USP)

   e. Support of promise
   f. Tone and manner
   g. Desired consumer response
   h. Justification for strategy
   i. Mandatory elements
 C. Media plan (based on contact point analysis)
  1. Media objectives
   a. Target audience
   b. Geographic coverage
   c. Seasonal coverage
   d. Reach, frequency, continuity objectives
   e. Scheduling/monetary objectives
  2. Media strategies
   a. Media mix and media types
    (1) Strategy
    (2) Rationale
   b. Media format and subclasses
    (1) Strategy
    (2) Rationale
   c. Media buying considerations
    (1) Geographic coverage
    (2) Seasonal coverage
    (3) Scheduling and continuity
    (4) Reach and frequency
    (5) Rationale
  3. Media tactics—media vehicles
   a. Broadcast
    (1) Television
     (*a*) Network
     (*b*) Spot
     (*c*) Cable
    (2) Radio
     (*a*) Network
     (*b*) Spot
   b. Print
    (1) Newspapers
     (*a*) Dailies
     (*b*) Weeklies
    (2) Magazines
     (*a*) Consumer
      i. General consumer
      ii. Specialty
     (*b*) Trade
   c. Direct Mail
    (1) Sales piece
    (2) Announcement
   d. Outdoor
    (1) Billboards
    (2) Transit (terminals, buses, taxis, trains, planes, blimps, etc.)
    (3) Stadium/sports arena boards
    (4) Posters/banners
   e. Interactive media
    (1) Web sites
    (2) Internet advertising banners

          (3) CD-ROMs

          (4) Kiosks

     f. Supplemental

          (1) Directories

              (*a*) Yellow Pages

              (*b*) Professional publications

          (2) Cinema/on-screen

          (3) Specialty advertising items (key chains, pens, etc.)

  4. Media tactics—media scheduling

     a. Media schedule

     b. Message effectiveness analyses

     c. Cost efficiency analyses

     d. Rationale

     e. Flowcharts

VI. Sales Promotion Program

  A. Trade promotions

    1. Push promotion objectives

    2. Push promotion strategies

    3. Push promotion tactics

       a. Trade shows/conferences

       b. Trade allowances

       c. Co-op advertising

       d. Dealer premiums

       e. Dealer contests/sweepstakes

    4. Rationale

    5. Payout (cost justification)

  B. Consumer promotions

    1. Pull promotion objectives

    2. Pull promotion strategies

    3. Pull promotion tactics

       a. Premiums

       b. Couponing

       c. Continuity programs

       d. Refunds/rebates

       e. Contests

       f. Sweepstakes

       g. Price-offs

    4. Rationale

    5. Payout

VII. Direct Marketing Program

  A. Objectives

  B. Strategies

  C. Tactics

    1. Database marketing

       a. Business reply cards (BRC)

       b. Toll-free number

       c. Web site

    2. Direct response

       a. Magazine advertisement

       b. Infomercial

       c. Web site

    3. Direct sales

       a. Internet marketing

       b. Catalog merchandising

       c. Television shopping

      D. Rationale

      E. Payout (cost justification)

VIII. Public Relations Program

      A. PR objectives

      B. PR strategies

      C. PR tactics

          1. Publicity

              a. Press releases

              b. Media kits

              c. Announcements

          2. Event marketing

              a. Special events

              b. Sponsorships

          3. Corporate communications

              a. Annual report

              b. Newsletter

              c. Web site

      D. Rationale

      E. Payout (cost justification)

IX. Merchandising Program

      A. Objectives

      B. Strategies

      C. Tactics

          1. Corporate identity and branding

              a. Logo

              b. Stationery

          2. Packaging

          3. Collateral

              a. Brochures

              b. Catalogs

          4. Point-of-purchase (POP)

              a. POP displays

              b. In-store promotions (posters, hang-tags, etc.)

      D. Rationale

      E. Payout (cost justification)

X. Action Plans

      A. Financial analysis

          1. Demand forecasting

          2. Contribution analysis

      B. Campaign budget

          1. Budgetary considerations

          2. Method of budget allocation

          3. Line-item budget

      C. Production

          1. Production considerations

          2. Schedule

          3. Rationale

      D. Implementation strategy

          1. Key issues

          2. Inventory levels

          3. Media timing

XI. Evaluation and Control

      A. Pretesting/posttesting

      B. Monitoring and control

      C. Customer feedback/database building

XII. Appendixes

Appendix **D**

Career Planning in Advertising

The cliché is old but true: Looking for a job is a full-time job in itself. Career research and planning (and lots of patience) are the way to a job in advertising—one that fits your abilities, interests, and career goals. The job-hunting process, in advertising or any other field, can be broken down into five main steps:

1. Self-assessment and goal setting.
2. Conducting the job search.
3. Preparing a résumé, cover letter, and portfolio.
4. Interviewing.
5. Following up.

Self-Assessment and Goal Setting

The first (and possibly the most important) step is to assess your interests, marketable skills, strengths and weaknesses, and other essentials needed to find and keep the kind of job you want. The goal: determine the kind of job you will do best.

Many books on career planning provide inventories and questionnaires for self-assessment. Some are listed at the end of this appendix. Self-evaluation helps you determine your career goals and objectives. What type of work would you like to do? What do you expect to get out of your work? Money? Power? Recognition? What work environment do you prefer? This is often called career planning. Make a list of *musts* and *preferences* about size of company, location, salary, benefits, training programs, and other employer characteristics. After completing your self-assessment, you may find you are simply unprepared to enter the career area of your choice or that your qualifications are not sufficient to get you the kind of job you really want.

At this point, you may undertake additional learning—either with more school or by getting experience. Schooling is certainly helpful, but job experience is mandatory. Consider taking a summer or part-time job in a related field or serving as an intern (unpaid worker) at an advertising agency, in a company advertising department, with the media, or with a supplier. Your objective should be to build your base of job experience so you can prove to an employer that you understand what needs doing and that you know how to do it.

Conducting the Job Search

Before looking into specific jobs, investigate what types of jobs best fit your career goals. The advertising field includes six main areas: creative (art direction, copywriting), account services (coordination, management, sales), media (planning, scheduling, buying), production (print, broadcast), research, and public relations. (See Exhibit D–1 for specific jobs and salaries.) Advertising jobs are found in agencies, in advertising departments of both large and small companies, in the media, and in allied services (such as media-buying firms or production

Exhibit D–1

Careers in advertising.

Job title	Job description	Requirements	Salary range	Entry level
Art director	Responsible for visual elements in print and broadcast ads; supervises or creates layouts; hires photographers, illustrators.	B.A. desirable but not required; art school degree helpful; portfolio a must.	$39,900–$66,300 (senior art director)	Assistant art director ($20,700)
Copywriter	Writes copy for print and broadcast advertisements; works with art director to develop ad concept; can work for ad agency or advertiser.	B.A. with courses in advertising, marketing, liberal arts, social sciences; portfolio a must.	$46,700–$60,000 (senior copywriter)	Junior copywriter ($20,700)
Account executive	Serves as a link between client and ad agency; acts as business manager for account; does market planning; coordinates advertising planning process; assists in new business acquisition.	B.A. in business; M.B.A. often preferred; marketing background desirable.	$25,000–$82,000	Junior account executive (B.A.: $20,700–$26,450; M.B.A.: $29,900–$39,100)
Media planner	Selects media to advertise in and plans media mix; chooses media vehicles; conducts media tests.	B.A. with emphasis in marketing, merchandising, or psychology.	$29,900–$172,500 (media director)	Trainee ($13,500–$16,100)
Media buyer	Buys space in print media and time in electronic media; negotiates price and position of ads; may work for ad agency or media-buying firm.	B.A. with emphasis in marketing, economics, mathematics, or statistics; M.B.A. preferred.	$29,900–$172,500 (media director)	Trainee ($13,000–$16,100)
Traffic manager	Schedules, supervises, and controls an ad agency's work flow.	B.A. not required but highly desirable; good general education helpful.	$23,000–$43,700	Traffic assistant ($15,525)
Print production manager	Prepares ads for printing; works with typesetters, color separators, printers, and other suppliers.	B.A. helpful but not essential; background in graphic arts, printing useful.	$25,300–$64,400	Production assistant ($14,950–$17,250)
Broadcast producer	Supervises all aspects of the production for radio and TV commercials, including hiring the director and production company and controlling the budget.	B.A. preferred; background in some area of broadcasting helpful.	$31,500–$102,350	Production assistant ($14,950–$17,250)
Market researcher	Conducts studies of consumers and their buying habits; conducts tests of consumer reactions to products and ads; may work in ad agency or with research firm.	Degree a must; M.B.A. or Ph.D. desirable; background in statistics useful; computer literacy an advantage.	$25,000–$73,000 (market research manager)	Trainee ($15,525)
Public relations manager	Obtains publicity for clients, serves as intermediary between client and public; handles contacts with press; may work for ad agency, client company, or public relations firm.	College degree with emphasis on liberal arts; journalism or marketing background helpful.	$29,900–$96,600	PR assistant or trainee ($17,250–$19,550)
Advertising director/manager	Responsible for the public image, fundraising, and overall day-to-day managerial responsibility of the organization.	B.A. or M.B.A. in marketing.	$38,000–$105,000	Advertising assistant ($19,550–$23,000)
Brand/product manager	Responsible for the marketing of a specific product or brand at a company, including sales and advertising.	B.A. in marketing or M.B.A.	$40,250–$52,900	Advertising assistant ($19,550–$23,000)
Copywriter for retail ad department	Writes copy for newspaper ads, catalogs, direct-mail pieces for retail business.	B.A. preferred, with courses in advertising, English, sociology, psychology; portfolio helpful.	$31,050–$36,800	($17,250–$25,300)
Artist for retail ad department	Designing and/or illustrating materials to sell a product or concept by print ads, catalogs, and direct-mail pieces for retail business.	B.A. desirable; commercial art courses useful; portfolio a must.	$24,000–$55,000	($22,500–$26,450)
Photographer	Photographs products, other setup shots for ad agency, or in-house ad department.	B.A. from professional art school; portfolio a must.	$13,000–$52,000	Usually freelance
Sales representative	Handles advertising sales for a particular newspaper, magazine, radio or TV station, or other medium.	B.A. preferred with emphasis on business.	Commission ($17,000–$60,000)	Sales trainee ($17,000)
Jingle creator	Writes the music and jingles used in radio and TV commercials, usually on a contract or freelance basis.	B.A. preferred (but not required), with emphasis on music and business.	$40,000–$690,000	($28,750)

companies). Read books about the field, write to organizations that have career information, and keep up with the most popular periodicals—especially *Advertising Age* and *Adweek* in the United States and *Marketing* or *Info-Press* in Canada.

Explore your local advertising industry by finding out the names of advertising people who are highly regarded in your community and ask for a brief, informative interview. Many will be flattered to be sought out as experts in their field. Be prepared to ask specific questions; don't take up too much of the person's time; and always follow up with a brief thank-you note.

When ready to conduct your actual job search, the most obvious source is the want ads in your local paper or in the city where you want to work. However, about 80 percent of jobs are filled before an ad ever appears. How do you hear about these job openings? Cracking this hidden job market requires time and effort—you need to create a network of people who are aware of and can help you find these unadvertised jobs. This entails letting everyone know that you are looking for a job—family, friends, distant relatives, teachers, and their associates. Join the local ad or PR club, attend their meetings, and participate in their activities. Follow up every lead and ask each new person for additional leads. Over time, networking should land you some interviews. While building your network, prepare a list of target employers—the companies you most want to work for. This requires research, such as checking the *Standard Directory of Advertisers*, the *Standard Directory of Advertising Agencies,* and the *Advertising Career Directory.* Make a file card for each company, including who is in charge of the specific department where you would like to work. Other leads include college placement offices, employment sections of industry trade papers, and employment agencies (some specialize in jobs in the advertising field).

Preparing a Résumé, a Cover Letter, and a Portfolio

Armed with your list of potential employers, your initial tools of contact will be a résumé and cover letter in most cases. Because they are such important tools for marketing your product—*you*—they must be carefully prepared to create a good first impression.

Your résumé should be attractive, well written, and professional in appearance and wording. Always proofread it carefully (better to have a more qualified person proof it) to be sure there are no grammatical, punctuation, or spelling errors. For an impressive-looking résumé stick with clean black type on white bond paper. Leave generous margins to enhance readability. And keep it short—two pages maximum. Employers are busy and usually go directly to the résumé's content, ignoring colored paper, professional typesetting, and slick design. The exception may be when you apply for a creative art position—but again, limit your creativity (do not use decorative typefaces and keep the design simple and clean).

The two most widely used résumé formats are *reverse-chronological* and *skill-based.* The reverse-chronological is based on your jobs held, presenting the most recent job first and ending with the oldest. In contrast, a skill-based format emphasizes your skills according to the interviewer's needs and those you wish to feature, allowing you to refer to job experience.

Job counselors and company recruiters usually advise job seekers to include the same elements in their résumés, but they often differ as to the order and emphasis of such elements. There is no question about the preferred format—78 percent of recruiters and 56 percent of counselors recommend the reverse-chronological résumé format. They also believe strongly in using bullet listings of items rather than paragraphs. They agree that references do not need to be shown. Though 78 percent of recruiters believe the grade point average (GPA) should be listed, 84 percent of counselors say GPA use depends on a number of factors (how high it is, what scale is used, if recruiters think you're hiding it) and most suggest that GPA not be listed.

Exhibit D–2
Résumé example.

James Sharpe
18 Central Park Street
Burr Ridge, IL 60521
(708) 546-1113

EDUCATION

B.S. Mass Communications, 1995
Syracuse University, Syracuse, New York.

Relevant Courses   **Advertising Account Management**
Scored first in a class project involving the creation and presentation of a proposed advertising campaign before the CEO, CFO, and marketing director of an actual company. Served as team leader and financial officer for the group, receiving a letter of praise from the CEO and a 4.0 grade for the project and class.

Advanced Marketing
Graduate-level course requiring a special application for undergraduates to enter. Received a 4.0 grade in the class and for my 58-page paper entitled "The Brünwell Effect Created by the Confluence of Comparative Advertising Messages With Various Media."

ACCOUNT MANAGEMENT EXPERIENCE

Account Planning Internship, Fastlane Advertising
Served as an intern working directly with the Assistant Account Planner for three Proctor and Gamble regional accounts. Attended 23 client meetings and interfaced with the clients' coordinator staff members.

Marketing and Sales Internship, Burden Marketing Communications
Worked directly for the Account Executive in the Midwest region for the Sara Lee account. Attended 15 client meetings and drafted correspondence, filed documentation, and monitored the production of presentation handouts and art.

COMPUTER SKILLS

Able to work on MS DOS, Windows, and Mac OS platforms. Proficient with MS Word (typing 50 wpm), WordPerfect, PageMaker, QuarkXpress, FrameMaker, Excel, dBase Pro, MacProject, Oracle, FileMaker Pro, and Quattro.

SALES EXPERIENCE

Sears, Roebuck and Co., Chicago
Sales Associate: Worked the counter in the automotive, sports and home furnishing departments for three years.

Floor Supervisor: Advanced to managing the home furnishings and appliances floor. Trained sales associates, scheduled work week, planned and subcontracted decorative promotions, approved checks, and supervised floor activities.

A sample résumé is shown in Exhibit D–2. Use the following tips for preparing your own résumé.

Heading

The heading should include a title (such as "Résumé") and basic information about you (name, address, phone number). It should also include your career objective stated as specifically as possible ("an entry-level position in the media department of a large ad agency with a long-term goal of media planning for major accounts"). Don't be vague ("a challenging position in the advertising industry" or "a job where I can put my enthusiasm and interpersonal skills to good use").

Education

Include any degrees you have earned and outstanding honors or scholarships. If you have little work experience, emphasize all applicable study programs, courses, and projects you have completed.

Work Experience

Emphasize past jobs relevant to your target field. Include part-time or volunteer work that reflects an interest in the type of job you are seeking. For all relevant work experience, be sure to include a brief description of your duties and any worthy accomplishments. Briefly list other jobs held to prove you can get and hold a job and have at least contributed to your own support.

Activities and Achievements

Include information that might interest an employer, such as language skills, relevant hobbies, and community activities.

References

If you wish to list past employers who can be contacted about your skills and experience, be sure to get their permission first. If you have good references it's best to list them. It's also acceptable to state "References available upon request."

The Cover Letter

Accompanying the résumé should be a cover letter that catches the reader's attention, provides evidence of your qualifications, and requests an interview (see Exhibit D–3). Like the résumé, the letter should be professionally presented (not

Exhibit D–3
Cover letter.

James Sharpe

18 Central Park Street, Burr Ridge, IL, 60521
(708) 546-1113

June 15, 1995

Phillip Lessler
Director, Human Resources
Ardmore & Associates
5602 Industry Plaza
Chicago, IL 60034

Dear Mr. Lessler:

Please accept this letter as application for the Assistant Account Executive position currently available with your company. My confidential résumé is enclosed for your review and consideration.

My experience as an intern with two Chicago advertising agencies has exposed me to numerous facets of the advertising process, including troubleshooting, problem solving, performance improvement projects, and quality assurance. I am confident that my experience in these areas will benefit Ardmore & Associates.

My current salary requirement would range mid- to high-20K's, with specifics flexible, negotiable, and dependent upon such factors as benefit structure, responsibility, and advancement opportunity.

I look forward to hearing from you in the near future to schedule an interview at your convenience, during which I hope to learn more about your corporation, its plans and goals, and how I might contribute to its continued success.

Sincerely,

James Sharpe
James Sharpe

JS

handwritten, for instance) and businesslike. It should contain no spelling, grammar, or punctuation errors. It should answer the employer's question, "What's in it for me?" A number of books that can provide help with writing good résumés and cover letters are listed at the end of this appendix.

Portfolio

For positions as an art director or a copywriter, you will need to prepare a portfolio, or "book," that shows potential employers your published works, pieces done for school courses, or self-projects. Remember: the fact that something you did was published does not automatically qualify it for your portfolio, especially if it is not among your best work. A portfolio should be carefully thought out and prepared, for it may be the sole basis on which some employers do their hiring. It should contain a small number of items that represent the kinds and quality of work you can do.

Artists and writers are often asked to mail or drop off their portfolios and then pick them up a week or two later. Therefore it's wise to prepare two or more portfolios.

One enterprising graduate of Glasboro State College skipped the standard résumé and portfolio process altogether. He used his education in advertising and direct marketing to prepare a direct-mail campaign that clearly demonstrated the skills he had to offer (see Exhibit D–4).

Interviewing

The purpose of the résumé and cover letter is to land a job interview. Employers hire on the basis of the interview (and your portfolio), so perfect your interviewing skills. Learn the most commonly asked interview questions and rehearse your answers. Read about preparing for an interview and follow suggestions for scheduling, attire, grooming, and appropriate interview behavior.

Before scheduling an interview, find out about the company. How large is it? How is it structured? What are its major accounts? Who are the major figures? Who will you be talking to, and what is the correct pronunciation of his or her name? This information will help you relate better with the interviewer and demonstrate your interest in the company.

At the close of the interview, be sure to thank the interviewer and to politely inquire about what will happen next. Should you expect additional interviews? Will someone from the company be in touch? Show that you are interested—but not desperate.

Follow Up

Record-keeping is a must. Keep files or cards for recording letters and résumés sent, dates of interviews, and so forth. If you do not receive responses to your letters to certain target employers within a reasonable time, write follow-up letters. After an interview, write a brief, typewritten, thank-you note. Reiterate your interest in the job.

Eventually these techniques and your persistent effort will lead to job offers. Accept the job that best fits your objectives, and you will be on your way to a career in advertising.

Good luck!

Attention Advertising Executives! When You're Ready To Make A Sound Investment . . .

Here Are Five Profitable Reasons Why You Should Hire This Adman

EXPERIENCE:
1. The main reason.

An adman is measured by his track record. Past performance is the best thing he can offer you. Hiring people without experience can be risky and costly. Karl Dentino comes to your firm with one year of part-time agency experience with Serpente, Wharton & Associates Advertising (May 1977 to May 1978). During that year he also worked with the Community Relations Department at Glassboro State College (September 1977 to May 1978).

Karl has previously worked for two retail establishments: Two Guys Department Store (1975-76), and Spencer Gifts (1974-75).

ADVERTISING SKILLS:
2. The tools.

Over the years, advertising has developed a body of research. Proven selling techniques have removed much costly guesswork. Facts, not opinions, make good ads. At Serpente, Wharton & Associates, Karl was taught the facts. He was trained in the direct response advertising philosophy. He learned the tested principles of direct response copywriting, and possesses the necessary ingredients for a career in direct response copywriter.

Karl also developed and administered market surveys for a major supermarket account, compiled mailing lists for a direct mail account, and developed media estimates for industrial accounts.

In addition, Karl worked for two years as a retail salesperson for Two Guys Department Store and Spencer Gifts. This experience served as the baptismal ground for a career where persuasiveness, reliability, and the ability to communicate effectively are so vital.

Karl also holds a 3rd Class FCC Broadcasting License.

EDUCATION:
3. Laying the groundwork.

A sound academic background is no longer a luxury for prospective advertising people. Today it's a necessity. Karl Dentino has solid training in the study of advertising. He brings to your firm a B.A. in Communications from Glassboro State College (May 1978), with a concentration in advertising, and a minor in marketing. He graduated with cum laude honors, a 3.50 grade point average.

Direct Marketing Honors!

Karl Dentino was one of thirty-three advertising students from across the country awarded a scholarship to the Direct Mail/Marketing Association (DMMA) Collegiate Institute. The week-long seminar, held in New York, covered all the principles of Direct Marketing and Direct Mail Advertising. This training gives Karl practical knowledge in an area not taught in most universities and colleges in the country.

LEADERSHIP QUALITIES:
4. How to recognize a leader.

A leader is a special breed of person. He accepts that extra responsibility which sets him apart from the others. You would know a leader – because you are one. And, you will recognize this potential in Karl Dentino.

For three years Karl served as Vice-President of the Advertising Club at Glassboro State College. He helped club membership grow from five to twenty-five. He coordinated field trips to advertising agencies and arranged for advertising professionals to speak at club meetings.

Karl also served as Advertising Director for Student Activities Board Concerts (SAB) for two years. He was responsible for the promotion, logo design, and naming of an annual outdoor music festival held at Glassboro. The "Sunshine Jam" attracts more than 2500 students each year. He also wrote and designed ads for other SAB events.

SELF MOTIVATION:
5. The deciding factor.

Self motivation is the personality trait that separates the superior adman from the mediocre. Mediocre advertising people come a dime a dozen. And they usually don't last too long. The self motivator comes with full realization that hard work gets results. He knows his potential, and he knows how to reach it.

Karl Dentino has the self motivation you are looking for. He is ready to roll up his sleeves and get things done. He seeks a career with your firm, not just a job.

Karl is never satisfied with his present knowledge of advertising and he's always eager to learn more. That's why he is currently enrolled at Charles Morris Price School of Advertising and Journalism in Philadelphia (evening classes). And that's why he served for two years on the Advertising Staff of his college newspaper handling copywriting, layout, and paste-up.

ADVERTISING PHILOSOPHY:

Karl believes that all advertising should be based on a marketing plan. The plan, in turn, should be based on research of the product, its market, and its distribution. The over-all plan objective should be to increase the sale of the product. So advertising is actually selling.

If your advertising meets these selling standards, then Karl Dentino will meet your standards. For a free demonstration of Karl's selling abilities, fill out and mail the enclosed reply card. Or better yet, call Karl today at (609) 662-0387. He'll show you how to make a sound investment.

Do it today! This offer expires as soon as Karl gets a job.

WHAT OTHERS SAY ABOUT KARL DENTINO

"Articulate, enthusiastic, lots of potential." - Joseph Serpente, President, Serpente, Wharton & Associates, Mt. Laurel, New Jersey.

"Fine student, bright future in advertising." - Steven Le Shay, President, Le Shay Advertising LTD., Malaga, New Jersey.

"Firm grasp on the direct response copy principles." - Frank Grazian, Associate Prof. of Communications, Glassboro State College, Glassboro, New Jersey.

KARL G. DENTINO
3350 Hollywood Circle
Pennsauken, New Jersey 08109
(609) 662-0387

6'1"
175 lbs.
September 19, 1956
Single

Exhibit D–4

Karl Dentino created this direct-mail ad to secure his first job out of college. After testing it in the Philadelphia area, he made some revisions and then mailed it to 24 chief executive officers of direct-response marketing agencies in New York. The approach secured nine interviews and landed him two job offers.

Career Planning, Job Search, and Résumé Preparation Publications

Anderson, Byron, editor. *Library Services for Career Planning, Job Search, and Employment Opportunities* (Haworth, 1992).

Battle, Carl W. *Smart Maneuvers: Taking Control of Your Career and Personal Success in the Information Age* (Allworth, 1994).

Gonyea, James C. *The Online Job Search Companion: A Complete Guide to Hundreds of Career Planning Job Resources Available via Your Computer* (McGraw-Hill, 1994).

Career Planning Publications

Lock, Robert D. *Taking Charge of Your Career Direction: Career Planning Guide* (Brooks-Cole, 1992), Books 1 and 2.

Martin, Mini. *Career Planning* (Kendall-Hunt, 1994).

McCorkle, Denny E. *The Self-Marketing Advantage for Business Careers: A Workbook and Resource Guide to Developing Self-Marketing Skills and Strategies for Student Career Planning and Job Search Success* (Self-Marketing Institute, 1993).

Mitchell, Joyce S. *College Board Guide to Jobs and Career Planning* (College Board, 1994).

Multiple authors. *Work, Sister, Work: How Black Women Can Get Ahead in the Workplace* (Carol Publishing Group, 1993).

Pick, Doris J.; Tondow, Murray; and Fox, Valerie S. *A Computerized Career Planning Guide Including Your Occupational Interests, Psychological Assessment and Personality Traits* (Behaviordyne, 1991).

Porterfield, Jim. *Business Career Planning Guide* (Southwestern, 1993).

Porterfield, Jim. *Career Planning Guide* (Wadsworth, 1993).

Powell, Randall. *Career Planning Today* (Kendall-Hunt, 1994).

Résumé Preparation Publications

Adams, Bob, and Morin, Laura. *The Complete Résumé and Job Search Book for College Students* (Adams, 1992).

Asher, Donald. *College to Career: Entry Level Résumés for Any Major* (Ten Speed, 1992).

Bloch, Deborah P. *How to Write a Winning Résumé* (NTC, 1993).

Brett, Pat. *Résumé Writing for Results: A Workbook* (Wadsworth, 1993).

Corbin, Bill, and Wright, Shelbi. *The Edge Résumé and Job Search Strategy* (Beckett-Highland, 1993).

Corwen, Leonard. *Your Résumé: Key to a Better Job* (Prentice Hall, 1993).

Downe, Robert P. *Better Book for Getting Hired: How to Write a Great Résumé, Sell Yourself in the Interview* (Self-Counsel, 1993).

Farr, J. Michael. *The Quick Résumé and Cover Letter Book: Write and Use a Superior Résumé within 24 Hours* (JIST Works, 1994).

Faux, Marian. *The Complete Résumé Guide* (Prentice Hall, 1993).

Good, C. Edward, and Fitzpatrick, William G. *Does Your Résumé Wear Blue Jeans? The Student's First Guide to Finding a Real Job* (Prima, 1993).

Gosmann, Carl E. *Résumé Reference Manual* (Career Connect, 1993).

Haft, Timothy D. *Trashproof Résumés: Your Guide to Cracking the Job Market* (Random House, 1995).

Jackson, Tom, and Buckingham, Bill. *Tom Jackson's Résumé Express: The Fastest Way to Write a Winning Résumé* (Random House, 1993).

Jackson, Tom. *Perfect Résumé Strategies: Seventy-Five Résumé Samples, Stories, and Techniques of Real People* (Doubleday, 1992).

Kennedy, Joyce L., and Morrow, Thomas J. *Electronic Job Search Revolution: Win with the New Technology That's Reshaping Today's Job Market* (Wiley, 1994).

Kennedy, Joyce L., and Morrow, Thomas J. *Electronic Résumé Revolution: Create a Winning Résumé for the New World of Job Seeking* (Wiley, 1993).

Krantman, Stan. *The Résumé Writer's Workbook* (Capital Writers, 1992).

Marino, Kim. *The College Student's Résumé Guide* (Ten Speed, 1992).

Morin, Laura. *Every Woman's Essential Job Hunting and Résumé Book* (Adams, 1994).

Provenzano, Steven A. *TOP SECRET Résumés for the '90s: Discover What Really Works and the Secrets "Professional" Résumé Writers Won't Tell You* (DeskTop, 1994).

Résumé Handbook (Kendall-Hunt, 1993).

Simons, Leslie. *Create a Résumé: A Step-by-Step Guide to Professional Quality Results* (Adrienne, 1993).

Smith, Michael H. *The Résumé Writer's Handbook: A Comprehensive, Step-by-Step Writing Guide and Reference Manual for Every Job Seeker* (HarperCollins, 1993).

Washington, Tom, and Allgood, Edith. *Résumé Power: Selling Yourself on Paper* (Mount Vernon, 1993).

Wendleton, Kate. *Through the Brick Wall: Résumé Builder for Hunters and Career Changers* (Five O'Clock, 1994).

Wilson, Robert F., and Rambusch, Erick H. *Conquer Résumé Objections* (Wiley, 1994).

Yate, Martin. *Cover Letters That Knock 'Em Dead* (Adams, 1995).

Appendix **E**

Industry Resources

Professional and Trade **Associations**

The Advertising Council, 261 Madison Avenue, New York, NY 10016-2303; (212) 922-1500.

Advertising Research Foundation, 641 Lexington Avenue, New York, NY 10022; (212) 751-5656.

American Advertising Foundation, 1101 Vermont Avenue N.W., Ste. 500, Washington, DC 20005; (203) 898-0089.

American Association of Advertising Agencies, 666 3rd Avenue, 13th Floor, New York, NY 10017; (212) 682-2500.

American Business Press, 675 3rd Avenue, Ste. 415, New York, NY 10017; (212) 661-6360.

American Marketing Association, 250 South Wacker Drive, Chicago, IL 60606; (312) 648-0536.

Association of National Advertisers, 155 East 44th Street, New York, NY 10017; (212) 697-5950.

Business Marketing Association, 150 North Wacker Drive, Ste. 1762, Chicago, IL 60606; (312) 409-4262.

Council of Better Business Bureaus, 4200 Wilson Boulevard, Arlington, VA 22203; (703) 276-0100.

Direct Marketing Association, Inc., 1120 Avenue of the Americas, New York, NY 10036-6700; (212) 768-7277.

International Advertising Association, 342 Madison Avenue, 20th Floor, Ste. 2000, New York, NY 10017; (212) 557-1133.

International Association of Business Communicators, 1 Hallidie Piazza, Ste. 600, San Francisco, CA 94102; (415) 433-3400.

Magazine Publishers Association, 575 Lexington Avenue, New York, NY 10022; (212) 752-0055.

Marketing Research Association, 2189 Silas Deane Highway, Ste. 5, Rocky Hill, CT 06067; (203) 257-4008.

National Advertising Review Board, 845 3rd Avenue, New York, NY 10022; (212) 832-1320.

National Association of Broadcasters, 1771 N Street, N.W., Washington, DC 20036; (202) 429-5300.

National Advertising Agencies Network, 245 5th Avenue, New York, NY 10016; (212) 481-3022/(212) 779-7504.

National Retail Federation (was National Retail Merchants Association), 701 Pennsylvania Avenue, N.W., Ste. 710, Washington, DC 20004-2608; (202) 783-7971.

Newspaper Advertising Bureau, 1180 Avenue of the Americas, New York, NY 10036; (212) 704-4547.

Outdoor Advertising Association of America, 1850 M Street, Ste. 1040, Washington, DC 20036; (202) 833-5566.

Point-of-Purchase Advertising Institute, 66 North Van Brunt Street, Englewood, NJ 07631; (201) 894-8899.

Promotional Product Association International (was Specialty Advertising Association), 3125 Skyway Circle North, Irving, TX 75038; (214) 580-0404.

Public Relations Society of America, 33 Irving Place, 3rd Floor, New York, NY 10003-2376; (212) 995-2230.

Radio Advertising Bureau, 304 Park Avenue South, New York, NY 10010; (212) 387-2100.

Sales and Marketing Executives International, Stratler Office Tower, No. 977, Cleveland, OH 44115; (216) 771-6650.

Television Bureau of Advertising, 850 3rd Avenue, 10th Floor, New York, NY 10022; (212) 486-1111.

Yellow Pages Publishers Association, 820 Kirts Boulevard, Ste. 100, 5th Floor, Troy, MI 48084; (810) 244-6200.

Selected **Periodicals**

Advertising Age, 740 North Rush Street, Chicago, IL 60611.

Advertising Techniques, 10 East 39th Street, New York, NY 10016.

Adweek, 49 East 21st Street, New York, NY 10010.

Adweek's Marketing Week, 49 East 21st Street, New York, NY 10010.

American Demographics, 127 West State Street, Ithaca, NY 14850.

Archive, P.O. Box 6338, Syracuse, NY 13217.

Art Direction, 10 East 39th Street, New York, NY 10016.

Broadcasting, 1735 DeSales Street N.W., Washington, DC 20036.

Business Marketing, 740 Rush Street, Chicago, IL 60611.

Canadian Journal of Communication, St. Thomas More College, 1437 College Drive, Saskatoon, Saskatchewan, Canada S7N 0W6.

Communication Arts, P.O. Box 10300, Palo Alto, CA 94304.

Direct Marketing, 224 Seventh Street, Garden City, NY 11530.

Editor & Publisher, 575 Lexington Avenue, New York, NY 10022.

Harvard Business Review, Soldiers Field, Boston, MA 02163.

Incentive Marketing, 633 Third Avenue, New York, NY 10017.

InfoPresse Communications, 4316 Boulevard Saint-Laurent, Bureau 400, Montreal, Quebec, Canada H2W 1Z3.

Interactive Age, 600 Community Drive, Manhasset, NY 11030-3875.

Journal of Advertising, American Academy of Advertising, c/o Ron Lane, School of Journalism, The University of Georgia, Athens, GA 30602.

Journal of Advertising Research, Advertising Research Foundation, 641 Lexington Avenue, New York, NY 10022.

Journal of Broadcasting, Broadcast Education Association, 1771 N Street N.W., Washington, DC 20036.

Journal of Marketing, American Marketing Association, 250 South Wacker Drive, Ste. 200, Chicago, IL 60606.

Marketing, Maclean-Hunter Ltd., 777 Bay Street, Toronto, Ontario, Canada, M5W 1A7.

Marketing News, American Marketing Association, 250 South Wacker Drive, Ste. 200, Chicago, IL 60606.

Marketing Tools, 127 West State Street, Ithaca, NY 14850.

Mediaweek, 1515 Broadway, New York, NY 10036.

MIN/Media Industry Newsletter, 145 East 49th Street, New York, NY 10017.

Modern Packaging, 205 East 42nd Street, New York, NY 10017.

Packaging Digest, Cahners Publishers, 275 Washington Street, Newton, MA 02158.

Print, 355 Lexington Avenue, New York, NY 10017.

Public Relations Journal, 845 Third Avenue, New York, NY 10020.

Sales and Marketing Management, 633 Third Avenue, New York, NY 10164.

Stores, National Retail Federation, 701 Pennsylvania Avenue, NW, Ste. 710, Washington, DC 20004.

Television/Radio Age, 1270 Avenue of the Americas, New York, NY 10020.

Winners, 49 East 21st Street, New York, NY 10010.

Zip, 401 North Broad Street, Philadelphia, PA 19108.

Reference **Books** and Directories

Standard Directory of Advertisers, National Register Publishing Company, Wilmette, IL 60091.

Standard Directory of Advertising Agencies, National Register Publishing Company, Wilmette, IL 60091.

Standard Rate and Data Service (Directory), 1700 Higgins Road, Des Plaines, IL 60018.

Research and **Information** Services

A. C. Nielsen Company, Nielsen Plaza, Northbrook, IL 60062.

Advertising Checking Bureau, 165 North Canal Street, Chicago, IL 60606.

The Arbitron Company, 1350 Avenue of the Americas, New York, NY 10019.

Audit Bureau of Circulations, 900 North Meacham Road, Schaumburg, IL 60195.

Broadcast Advertisers Report (BAR), 500 Fifth Avenue, New York, NY 10036.

Gallup & Robinson, Research Park, Princeton, NJ 08540.

Leading National Advertisers (LNA), 515 Madison Avenue, New York, NY 10022.

Mediamark Research, 341 Madison Avenue, New York, NY 10017.

Simmons Marketing Research Bureau, 219 East 42nd Street, New York, NY 10017.

Starch INRA Hooper, 566 East Boston Post Road, Mamaroneck, NY 10543.

Important Terms*

AAAA *(Ch. 2)* See *American Association of Advertising Agencies.*

AAF *(Ch. 2)* See *American Advertising Federation.*

ABC *(Ch. 12)* See *Audit Bureau of Circulations.*

abundance principle *(Ch. 1)* The idea that in an economy that produces more goods and services than can be consumed, advertising serves two purposes: keeping consumers informed of selection alternatives and allowing companies to compete more effectively for consumer dollars.

account executive (AE) *(Ch. 3)* The liaison between the agency and the client. The account executive is responsible both for managing all the agency's services for the benefit of the client and for representing the agency's point of view to the client.

account planning *(Ch. 3)* A hybrid discipline that bridges the gap between traditional research, account management, and creative direction whereby agency people represent the view of the consumer in order to better define and plan the client's advertising program.

action advertising *(Ch. 1)* Advertising intended to bring about immediate action on the part of the reader or viewer.

action programs *(Ch. 7)* See *tactics.*

actual consumers *(Ch. 1)* The people in the real world who comprise an ad's target audience. They are the people to whom the sponsor's message is ultimately directed.

ad networks *(Ch. 16)* Brokers for advertisers and Web sites. Ad networks pool hundreds or thousands of Web pages together and facilitate advertising across these pages, thereby allowing advertisers to gain maximum exposure by covering even the smaller sites.

ad request *(Ch. 16)* An opportunity to deliver an advertising element to a Web site visitor.

advertisers *(Ch. 3)* See *clients.*

advertising *(Ch. 1)* The structured and composed nonpersonal communication of information, usually paid for and usually persuasive in nature, about products (goods and services) or ideas by identified sponsors through various media.

advertising agency *(Ch. 3)* An independent organization of creative people and businesspeople who specialize in developing and preparing advertising plans, advertisements, and other promotional tools for advertisers. The agency also arranges for or contracts for purchase of space and time in various media.

advertising allowance *(Ch. 9)* Either a percentage of gross purchases or a flat fee paid to the retailer for advertising the manufacturer's product.

advertising impression *(Ch. 8)* A possible exposure of the advertising message to one audience member; see *opportunity-to-see (OTS).*

advertising manager *(Ch. 3)* The advertiser's person who is in charge of planning, coordinating, budgeting, and directing the company's advertising program.

advertising medium *(Ch. 1)* Any vehicle of communication that an advertiser may use; see *media.*

advertising message *(Ch. 7)* An element of the creative mix comprising what the company plans to say in its advertisements and how it plans to say it—verbally or nonverbally.

advertising plan *(Ch. 7)* The plan that directs the company's advertising effort. A natural outgrowth of the marketing plan, it analyzes the situation, sets advertising objectives, and lays out a specific strategy from which ads and campaigns are created.

advertising pyramid *(Ch. 7)* A simple five-step model for understanding some of the tasks advertising can perform and for setting advertising objectives. The five steps include awareness, comprehension, conviction, desire, and action.

advertising research *(Ch. 6)* The systematic gathering and analysis of information specifically to facilitate the development or evaluation of advertising strategies, ads and commercials, and media campaigns.

advertising response curve *(Ch. 8)* Studies of this indicate that incremental response to advertising actually diminishes—rather than builds—with repeated exposure.

advertising specialty *(Ch. 17)* A promotional product, usually imprinted with an advertiser's name, message, or logo, that is distributed free as part of a marketing communications program.

advertising strategy *(Ch. 7)* The methodology advertisers use to achieve their advertising objectives. The strategy is determined by the particular creative mix of advertising elements the advertiser selects, namely: target audience; product concept; communications media; and advertising message. (Also called the *creative mix.*)

advertorial *(Ch. 10)* An ad that is half advertising, half editorial, aimed at swaying public opinion rather than selling products.

advocacy advertising *(Ch. 10)* Advertising used to communicate an organization's views on issues that affect society or business.

affidavit of performance *(Ch. 15)* A signed and notarized form sent by a television station to an advertiser or agency indicating what spots ran and when. It is the station's legal proof that the advertiser got what was paid for.

affirmative disclosure *(Ch. 2)* Advertisers must make known their product's limitations or deficiencies.

agricultural advertising *(Ch. 1)* See *farm advertising.*

ambush marketing *(Ch. 10)* A promotional strategy utilized by nonsponsors to capitalize on the popularity or prestige of an event or property by giving the false impression that they are sponsors,

---

*Numbers in parentheses after term indicate chapter(s) where term is discussed.

such as by buying up all the billboard space around an athletic stadium. Often employed by the competitors of the property's official sponsor.

American Advertising Federation (AAF) *(Ch. 2)* A nationwide association of advertising people. The AAF helped to establish the Federal Trade Commission, and its early "vigilance" committees were the forerunners of the Better Business Bureaus.

American Association of Advertising Agencies (AAAA) *(Ch. 2)* The national organization of the advertising business. It has members throughout the United States and controls agency practices by denying membership to any agency judged unethical.

ANA *(Ch. 2)* See *Association of National Advertisers.*

analog proof *(Ch. 13)* See *Chromalin proof.*

animatic *(Ch. 12)* A rough television commercial produced by photographing storyboard sketches on a film strip or video with the audio portion synchronized on tape. It is used primarily for testing purposes.

animation *(Ch. 12, 13)* The use of cartoons, puppet characters, or demonstrations of inanimate characters come to life in television commercials; often used for communicating difficult messages or for reaching specialized markets, such as children.

annual report *(Ch. 10)* A formal document issued yearly by a corporation to its stockholders to reflect the corporation's condition at the close of the business year.

answer print *(Ch. 13)* The final print of a filmed commercial, along with all the required optical effects and titles, used for review and approval before duplicating.

aperture *(Ch. 13)* The opening in a camera that determines the amount of light that reaches the film or videotape.

art *(Ch. 11)* The whole visual presentation of a commercial or advertisement—the body language of an ad. Art also refers to the style of photography or illustration employed, the way color is used, and the arrangement of elements in an ad so that they relate to one another in size and proportion.

art direction *(Ch. 11)* The act or process of managing the visual presentation of an ad or commercial.

art director *(Ch. 3, 11)* Along with graphic designers and production artists, determines how the ad's verbal and visual symbols will fit together.

art studio *(Ch. 3)* Company that designs and produces artwork and illustrations for advertisements, brochures, and other communication devices.

artist role *(Ch. 11)* A role in the creative process that experiments and plays with a variety of approaches, looking for an original idea.

Association of National Advertisers (ANA) *(Ch. 2)* An organization composed of 400 major manufacturing and service companies that are clients of member agencies of the AAAA. These companies, which are pledged to uphold the ANA code of advertising ethics, work with the ANA through a joint Committee for Improvement of Advertising Content.

attention value *(Ch. 8)* A consideration in selecting media based on the degree of attention paid to ads in particular media by those exposed to them. Attention value relates to the advertising message and copy just as much as to the medium.

attitude *(Ch. 4)* The acquired mental position—positive or negative—regarding some idea or object.

attitude test *(Ch. 6)* A type of posttest that usually seeks to measure the effectiveness of an advertising campaign in creating a favorable image for a company, its brand, or its products.

audience *(Ch. 8)* The total number of people exposed to a particular medium.

audience composition *(Ch. 15)* The distribution of an audience into demographic or other categories.

audience objectives *(Ch. 8)* Definitions of the specific types of people the advertiser wants to reach.

audience share *(Ch. 15)* The percentage of homes with TV sets in use (HUT) tuned to a specific program.

audio *(Ch. 12)* The sound portion of a commercial. Also, the right side of a script for a television commercial, indicating spoken copy, sound effects, and music.

audio console board *(Ch. 13)* In a sound studio control room, the board that channels sound to the appropriate recording devices and that blends both live and prerecorded sounds for immediate or delayed broadcast.

audiovisual materials *(Ch. 10)* Slides, films, filmstrips, and videocassettes that may be used for training, sales, or public relations activities.

Audit Bureau of Circulations (ABC) *(Ch. 14)* An organization supported by advertising agencies, advertisers, and publishers that verifies circulation and other marketing data on newspapers and magazines for the benefit of its members.

author *(Ch. 1)* In Stern's communication model, a copywriter, an art director, or a creative group at the agency that is commissioned by the sponsor to create advertising messages.

autobiographical messages *(Ch. 1)* A style of advertising that utilizes the first person "I" to tell a story to the audience, "You."

automated teller machine (ATM) *(Ch. 17)* Automated machines that dispense cash to bank customers. ATMs are now used to display full-motion video ads while the transaction is processed.

avails *(Ch. 15)* An abbreviated term referring to the TV time slots that are *available* to an advertiser.

average quarter-hour audience (AQH persons) *(Ch. 15)* A radio term referring to the average number of people who are listening to a specific station for at least 5 minutes during a 15-minute period of any given daypart.

average quarter-hour rating *(Ch. 15)* The average quarter-hour persons estimate expressed as a percentage of the estimated population.

average quarter-hour share *(Ch. 15)* The radio station's audience (AQH persons) expressed as a percentage of the total radio listening audience in the area.

awareness advertising *(Ch. 1)* Advertising that attempts to build the image of a product or familiarity with the name and package.

Ayer No. 1 *(Ch. 12)* See *poster-style format.*

banner *(Ch. 16)* Little billboards of various sizes that pop up when a visitor lands on a particular Web page.

barter syndication *(Ch. 15)* Marketing of first-run television programs to local stations free or for a reduced rate because some of the ad space has been presold to national advertisers.

base art *(Ch. 13)* The first image on an artboard on which an overlay may be placed.

basic bus *(Ch. 17)* In transit advertising, all the inside space on a group of buses, which thereby gives the advertiser complete domination.

behavioristic segmentation *(Ch. 5)* Method of determining market segments by grouping consumers into product-related groups based on their purchase behavior.

benefit headline *(Ch. 12)* Type of headline that makes a direct promise to the reader.

benefits *(Ch. 5)* The particular product attributes offered to customers, such as high quality, low price, status, speed, sex appeal, good taste, and so on.

benefit segmentation *(Ch. 5)* Method of segmenting consumers based on the benefits being sought.

Better Business Bureau (BBB) *(Ch. 2)* A business-monitoring organization funded by dues from over 100,000 member companies. It operates primarily at the local level to protect consumers against fraudulent and deceptive advertising.

big idea *(Ch. 11)* The flash of creative insight—the bold advertising initiative—that captures the essence of the strategy in an imaginative, involving way and brings the subject to life to make the reader stop, look, and listen.

billboards *(Ch. 17)* See *30-sheet poster panel.*

bleeds *(Ch. 13, 14)* Colors, type, or visuals that run all the way to the edge of the page.

blinking *(Ch. 8)* A scheduling technique in which the advertiser floods the airwaves for one day on both cable and network channels to make it virtually impossible to miss the ads.

blueline *(Ch. 13)* A proof created by shining light through the negatives and exposing a light-sensitive paper that turns from white to blue; it helps reveal scratches and flaws in the negatives.

board *(Ch. 13)* See *audio console.*

body copy *(Ch. 12)* The text of an advertisement that tells the complete story and attempts to close the sale. It is a logical continuation of the headline and subheads and is usually set in a smaller type size than headlines or subheads.

boldface *(Ch. 12)* Heavier type.

booths *(Ch. 17)* At trade shows, a major factor in sales promotion plans. To stop traffic, it must be simple and attractive and have good lighting and a large visual.

bottom-up marketing *(Ch. 7)* The opposite of standard, top-down marketing planning, bottom-up marketing focuses on one specific tactic and develops it into an overall strategy.

brainstorming *(Ch. 11)* A process in which two or more people get together to generate new ideas; often a source of sudden inspiration.

brand *(Ch. 6)* That combination of name, words, symbols, or design that identifies the product and its source and distinguishes it from competing products—the fundamental differentiating device for all products.

brand development index (BDI) *(Ch. 8)* The percentage of a brand's total sales in an area divided by the total population in the area; it indicates the sales potential of a particular brand in a specific market area.

brand equity *(Ch. 5)* The totality of what consumers, distributors, dealers, and competitors feel and think about a brand over an extended period of time; in short, it is the value of the brand's capital.

branding *(Ch. 1)* A marketing function that identifies products and their source and differentiates them from all other products.

brand interest *(Ch. 4)* An individual's openness or curiosity about a brand.

brand loyalty *(Ch. 4)* The consumer's conscious or unconscious decision—expressed through intention or behavior—to repurchase a brand continually. This occurs because the consumer perceives that the brand has the right product features, image, quality, or relationship at the right price.

brand manager *(Ch. 3)* The individual within the advertiser's company who is assigned the authority and responsibility for the successful marketing of a particular brand.

broadcast TV *(Ch. 15)* Television sent over airwaves as opposed to over cables.

broadside *(Ch. 16)* A form of direct-mail advertisement, larger than a folder and sometimes used as a window display or wall poster in stores. It can be folded to a compact size and fitted into a mailer.

brochure *(Ch. 16)* Sales materials printed on heavier paper and featuring color photographs, illustrations, typography. See also *folders.*

budget buildup method *(Ch. 7)* See *objective/task method.*

bulk discounts *(Ch. 14)* Newspapers offer advertisers decreasing rates (calculated by multiplying the number of inches by the cost per inch) as they use more inches.

bulletin boards *(Ch. 10)* An internal public relations means for announcing new equipment, meetings, promotions, new products, construction plans, and recreation news.

bulletin structures *(Ch. 17)* A type of outdoor advertising meant for long-term use and works best where traffic is heavy and visibility is good. They carry printed or painted messages, are created in sections, and are brought to the site where they are assembled and hung on the billboard structure.

bursting *(Ch. 8)* A media scheduling method for promoting high-ticket items that require careful consideration, such as running the same commercial every half-hour on the same network in prime time.

business advertising *(Ch. 1)* Advertising directed at people who buy or specify goods and services for business use. Also called *business-to-business advertising.*

business magazines *(Ch. 14)* The largest category of magazines, they target business readers and include: *trade publications* for retailers, wholesalers, and other distributors; *industrial magazines* for businesspeople involved in manufacturing and services; and *professional journals* for lawyers, physicians, architects, and other professionals.

business markets *(Ch. 4, 5)* Organizations that buy natural resources, component products, and services that they resell, use to conduct their business, or use to manufacture another product.

business reply mail *(Ch. 16)* A type of mail that enables the recipient of direct-mail advertising to respond without paying postage.

business-to-business advertising *(Ch. 1)* See *business advertising.*

business-to-business agency *(Ch. 3)* Represents clients that market products to other businesses; also called high-tech agency.

bus-o-rama *(Ch. 17)* In transit advertising, a jumbo roof sign, which is actually a full-color transparency backlighted by fluorescent tubes, running the length of the bus.

button *(Ch. 16)* In Internet advertising, buttons are small versions of a banner and sometimes look like an icon, and they usually provide a link to an advertiser's home page. Since buttons take up less space than banners, they also cost less.

buyback allowance *(Ch. 9)* A manufacturer's offer to pay for an old product so that it will be taken off the shelf to make room for a new product.

cable-modem *(Ch. 16)* A system of connecting with the Internet which offers high-speed data transfer direct to the computer. Only available from those cable TV companies that offer one of the new cable-modem services such as Roadrunner or @Home.

cable TV *(Ch. 15)* Television signals carried to households by cable and paid by subscription.

camera-ready art *(Ch. 12, 13)* A finished ad that is ready for the printer's camera to shoot—to make negatives or plates—according to the publication's specifications.

car-end posters *(Ch. 17)* A transit advertisement of varying sizes, positioned in the bulkhead.

casting brief *(Ch. 12)* A detailed, written description of the characters' personalities to serve as guides in casting sessions when actors audition for the roles.

catalogs *(Ch. 16)* Reference books mailed to prospective customers that list, describe, and often picture the products sold by a manufacturer, wholesaler, jobber, or retailer.

category development index (CDI) *(Ch. 8)* The percent of a product category's total U.S. sales in an area divided by the percent of total U.S. population in the area.

CD-ROM *(Ch. 16)* Acronym for compact disc–read only memory; computer storage disk that offers a large amount of storage space and a high concentration of data, combined with full-motion video and high-quality audio.

cease-and-desist order *(Ch. 2)* May be issued by the FTC if an advertiser won't sign a consent decree; prohibits further use of an ad.

centers of influence *(Ch. 4)* Customers, prospective customers, or opinion leaders whose opinions and actions are respected by others.

centralized advertising department *(Ch. 3)* A staff of employees, usually located at corporate headquarters, responsible for all the organization's advertising. The department is often structured by product, advertising subfunction, end user, media, or geography.

central location test *(Ch. 6)* A type of pretest in which videotapes of test commercials are shown to respondents on a one-to-one basis, usually in shopping center locations.

central route to persuasion *(Ch. 4)* One of two ways researchers Petty, Cacioppo, and Schumann theorize that marketers can persuade consumers. When consumers have a high level of involvement with the product or the message, they are motivated to pay attention to the central, product-related information in an ad, such as product attributes and benefits, or demonstrations of positive functional or psychological consequences; see *elaboration likelihood model.*

cents-off promotion *(Ch. 9)* A short-term reduction in the price of a product designed to induce trial and usage. Cents-off promotions take various forms, including basic cents-off packages, one-cent sales, free offers, and box-top refunds.

channel *(Ch. 1)* Any medium through which an encoded message is sent to a receiver, including oral communication, print media, television, and the Internet.

channels of distribution *(Ch. 5)* See *distribution channels.*

character-count method *(Ch. 13)* A method of copy casting in which an actual count is made of the number of characters in the copy.

Chromalin proof *(Ch. 13)* This proof uses a series of four very thin plastic sheets pressed together; each layer's light-sensitive emulsion turns one of the process colors when exposed to certain wavelengths of light.

cinema advertising *(Ch. 17)* Advertising in movie theaters.

cinematographer *(Ch. 13)* A motion picture photographer.

circulation *(Ch. 14)* A statistical measure of a print medium's audience; includes subscription and vendor sales and primary and secondary readership.

circulation audit *(Ch. 14)* Thorough analysis of circulation procedures, distribution outlets, and other distribution factors by a company such as the Audit Bureau of Circulations (ABC).

classified ads *(Ch. 14, 16)* Newspaper, magazine, and now Internet advertisements usually arranged under subheads that describe the class of goods or the need the ads seek to satisfy. Rates are based on the number of lines the ad occupies. Most employment, housing, and automotive advertising is in the form of classified advertising.

Classified Advertising Network of New York (CANNY) *(Ch. 14)* A statewide affiliation of daily newspapers that enables advertisers to place classified ads in daily newspapers throughout the state easily and inexpensively.

classified ad Web site *(Ch. 16)* Web sites that specialize in providing classified advertisements, often provided for free. Many classified ad Web sites are supported by ad banners of other advertisers.

classified display ads *(Ch. 14)* Ads that run in the classified section of the newspaper but have larger-size type, photos, art borders, abundant white space, and sometimes color.

clearance advertising *(Ch. 3)* A type of local advertising designed to make room for new product lines or new models or to get rid of slow-moving product lines, floor samples, broken or distressed merchandise, or items that are no longer in season.

click rate *(Ch. 16)* In Internet advertising, the number of "clicks" on an advertisement divided by the number of ad requests. A method by which marketers can measure the frequency with which users try to obtain additional information about a product by clicking on an advertisement. Also called *click-through rate.*

click-through *(Ch. 13)* A term used in reference to when a World Wide Web user clicks on an ad banner to visit the advertiser's site. Some Web publishers charge advertisers according to the number of click-throughs on a given ad banner.

clients *(Ch. 3)* The various businesses that advertise themselves or their products and for whom advertising agencies work in an effort to find customers for their goods and services.

clip art *(Ch. 3)* Syndicated source for preprinted images that can be purchased and used by advertisers to illustrate ads.

close *(Ch. 12)*   That part of an advertisement or commercial that asks customers to do something and tells them how to do it—the action step in the ad's copy.

closing date *(Ch. 13, 14)*   A publication's final deadline for supplying printing material for an advertisement.

clutter tests *(Ch. 6)*   Method of pretesting in which commercials are grouped with noncompetitive control commercials and shown to prospective customers to measure their effectiveness in gaining attention, increasing brand awareness and comprehension, and causing attitude shifts.

cognition *(Ch. 4)*   The point of awareness and comprehension of a stimulus.

cognitive dissonance *(Ch. 4)*   See *theory of cognitive dissonance.*

cognitive theory *(Ch. 4)*   An approach that views learning as a mental process of memory, thinking, and the rational application of knowledge to practical problem solving.

collateral sales material *(Ch. 5)*   All the accessory nonmedia advertising materials prepared by manufacturers to help dealers sell a product—booklets, catalogs, brochures, films, trade-show exhibits, sales kits, and so on.

color key *(Ch. 13)*   A color proof that is a less-expensive form of the Chromalin, with thicker plastic sheets that can be lifted up.

color separations *(Ch. 13)*   Four separate continuous-tone negatives produced by photographing artwork through color filters that eliminate all the colors but one. The negatives are used to make four printing plates—one each for yellow, magenta, cyan, and black—for reproducing the color artwork.

color strip *(Ch. 14)*   Samples of eye shadow, blush, lipstick, and other makeup inserted into magazines.

combination offers *(Ch. 9)*   A sales promotion device in which two related products are packaged together at a special price, such as a razor and a package of blades. Sometimes a combination offer may be used to introduce a new product by tying its purchase to an established product at a special price.

combination rates *(Ch. 14)*   Special newspaper advertising rates offered for placing a given ad in (1) morning and evening editions of the same newspaper; (2) two or more newspapers owned by the same publisher; or (3) two or more newspapers affiliated in a syndicate or newspaper group.

command headline *(Ch. 12)*   A type of headline that orders the reader to do something.

communication element *(Ch. 5)*   Includes all marketing-related communications between the seller and the buyer.

communications media *(Ch. 7, 11)*   An element of the creative mix, comprising the various methods or vehicles that will be used to transmit the advertiser's message.

communications mix *(Ch. 5)*   A variety of marketing communications tools, grouped into personal and nonpersonal selling activities.

community involvement *(Ch. 10)*   A local public relations activity in which companies sponsor or participate in a local activity or supply a location for an event.

company conventions and dealer meetings *(Ch. 9)*   Events held by manufacturers to introduce new products, sales promotion programs, or advertising campaigns.

comparative advertising *(Ch. 2)*   Advertising that claims superiority to competitors in some aspect.

compiled list *(Ch. 16)*   A type of direct-mail list that has been compiled by another source, such as lists of automobile owners, new home purchasers, business owners, union members, and so forth. It is the most readily available type of list but offers the lowest response expectation.

comprehensive layout *(Ch. 12)*   A facsimile of a finished ad with copy set in type and pasted into position along with proposed illustrations. The "comp" is prepared so the advertiser can gauge the effect of the final ad.

conceptualization *(Ch. 11)*   See *visualization.*

conditioning theory *(Ch. 4)*   The theory that learning is a trial-and-error process. Also called *stimulus-response theory.*

consent decree *(Ch. 2)*   A document advertisers sign, without admitting any wrongdoing, in which they agree to stop objectionable advertising.

consumer advertising *(Ch. 1)*   Advertising directed at the ultimate consumer of the product, or at the person who will buy the product for someone else's personal use.

consumer advocates *(Ch. 2)*   Individuals and groups who actively work to protect consumer rights often by investigating advertising complaints received from the public and those that grow out of their own research.

consumer behavior *(Ch. 4)*   The activities, actions, and influences of people who purchase and use goods and services to satisfy their personal or household needs and wants.

consumer decision-making process *(Ch. 4)*   The series of steps a consumer goes through in deciding to make a purchase.

consumer information networks *(Ch. 2)*   Organizations that help develop state, regional, and local consumer organizations and work with national, regional, county, and municipal consumer groups. Examples include the Consumer Federation of America (CFA), the National Council of Senior Citizens, and the National Consumer League.

consumerism *(Ch. 2)*   Social action designed to dramatize the rights of the buying public.

consumer magazines *(Ch. 14)*   Information- or entertainment-oriented periodicals directed toward people who buy products for their own consumption.

consumer sales promotions *(Ch. 9)*   Marketing, advertising, and sales promotion activities aimed at inducing trial, purchase, and repurchase by the consumer. (Also called *pull strategy.*)

consumers, consumer market *(Ch. 1, 4)*   People who buy products and services for their own, or someone else's, personal use.

contest *(Ch. 9)*   A sales promotion device for creating consumer involvement in which prizes are offered based on the skill of the entrants.

continuity *(Ch. 8)*   The duration of an advertising message or campaign over a given period of time.

continuous schedule *(Ch. 8)*   A method of scheduling media in which advertising runs steadily with little variation.

continuous tone *(Ch. 13)*   Normal photographic paper produces images in black and white with shades of gray in between.

contract rate *(Ch. 14)* A special rate for newspaper advertising usually offered to local advertisers who sign an annual contract for frequent or bulk-space purchases.

controlled circulation *(Ch. 14)* A free publication mailed to a select list of individuals the publisher feels are in a unique position to influence the purchase of advertised products.

control room *(Ch. 13)* In a recording studio, the place where the producer, director, and sound engineer sit, monitoring and controlling all the sounds generated in the sound studio.

cookies *(Ch. 16)* Small pieces of information that get stored in a computer's Web browser when one loads certain Web sites. Cookies keep track of whether a certain user has ever visited a specific site and allows the site to give users different information according to whether or not they are repeat visitors.

cooperative (co-op) advertising *(Ch. 5, 9, 14)* The sharing of advertising costs by the manufacturer and the distributor or retailer. The manufacturer may repay 50 or 100 percent of the dealer's advertising costs or some other amount based on sales. See also *horizontal cooperative advertising, vertical cooperative advertising.*

copy *(Ch. 3)* The words that make up the headline and message of an advertisement or commercial.

copycast *(Ch. 13)* To forecast the total block of space the type in an ad will occupy in relation to the typeface's letter size and proportions.

copy points *(Ch. 5)* Copywriting themes in a product's advertising.

copyright *(Ch. 2)* An exclusive right granted by the Copyright Act to authors and artists to protect their original work from being plagiarized, sold, or used by another without their express consent.

copywriters *(Ch. 3, 11)* People who create the words and concepts for ads and commercials.

corporate advertising *(Ch. 1, 10)* The broad area of nonproduct advertising aimed specifically at enhancing a company's image and increasing lagging awareness.

corporate identity advertising *(Ch. 10)* Advertising a corporation creates to familiarize the public with its name, logos, trademarks, or corporate signatures, especially after any of these elements are changed.

corporate objectives *(Ch. 7)* Goals of the company stated in terms of profit or return on investment. Objectives may also be stated in terms of net worth, earnings ratios, growth, or corporate reputation.

corrective advertising *(Ch. 2)* May be required by the FTC for a period of time to explain and correct offending ads.

cost efficiency *(Ch. 8)* The cost of reaching the target audience through a particular medium as opposed to the cost of reaching the medium's total circulation.

cost per rating point (CPP) *(Ch. 15)* A simple computation used by media buyers to determine which broadcast programs are the most efficient in relation to the target audience. The CPP is determined by dividing the cost of the show by the show's expected rating against the target audience.

cost per thousand (CPM) *(Ch. 8, 14, 15)* A common term describing the cost of reaching 1,000 people in a medium's audience. It is used by media planners to compare the cost of various media vehicles.

coupon *(Ch. 9)* A certificate with a stated value that is presented to a retail store for a price reduction on a specified item.

cover date *(Ch. 14)* The date printed on the cover of a publication.

cover paper *(Ch. 13)* Paper used on soft book covers, direct-mail pieces, and brochure covers that are thicker, tougher, and more durable than text paper.

cover position *(Ch. 14)* Advertising space on the front inside, back inside, and back cover pages of a publication which is usually sold at a premium price.

CPM *(Ch. 8, 14)* See *cost per thousand.*

creative boutique *(Ch. 3)* An organization of creative specialists (such as art directors, designers, and copywriters) who work for advertisers and occasionally advertising agencies to develop creative concepts, advertising messages, and specialized art. A boutique performs only the creative work.

creative brief *(Ch. 11)* A written statement that serves as the creative team's guide for writing and producing an ad. It describes the most important issues that should be considered in the development of the ad (the who, why, what, where, and when), including a definition and description of the target audience; the rational and emotional appeals to be used; the product features that will satisfy the customer's needs; the style, approach, or tone that will be used in the copy; and, generally, what the copy will say.

creative department *(Ch. 3)* The department in an advertising agency that is responsible for conceiving, writing, laying out, and producing ads and commercials.

creative dimensional direct mailing (CDDM) *(Ch. 16)* Any form of nontraditional direct mail. Examples include baseball caps, creative packaging, and pop-up brochures.

creative director *(Ch. 3, 11)* Heads a creative team of agency copywriters and artists that is assigned to a client's business; is ultimately responsible for the creative product—the form the final ad takes.

creative mix *(Ch. 8)* Those advertising elements the company controls to achieve its advertising objectives, including the target audience, the product concept, the communications media, and the advertising message. (See also *advertising strategy.*)

creative process *(Ch. 11)* The step-by-step procedure used to discover original ideas and reorganize existing concepts in new ways.

creative pyramid *(Ch. 11)* A five-step model to help the creative team convert advertising strategy and the big idea into the actual physical ad or commercial. The five elements are: attention, interest, credibility, desire, and action.

creatives *(Ch. 11)* The people who work in the creative department, regardless of their specialty.

creativity *(Ch. 11)* Involves combining two or more previously unconnected objects or ideas into something new.

crisis management *(Ch. 10)* A company's plan for handling news and public relations during crises.

culture *(Ch. 4)* A homogeneous group's whole set of beliefs, attitudes, and ways of doing things, typically handed down from generation to generation.

cume persons *(Ch. 15)* The total number of different people listening to a radio station for at least one 15-minute segment over the course of a given week, day, or daypart.

cume rating *(Ch. 15)* The estimated number of cume persons expressed as a percentage of the total market population.

current customers *(Ch. 4)* People who have already bought something from a business and who may buy it regularly.

customer lifetime value (LTV) *(Ch. 9)* The total sales or profit value of a customer to a marketer over the course of that customer's lifetime.

customers *(Ch. 4)* The people or organizations who consume goods and services. See also *centers of influence, current customers,* and *prospective customers.*

custom magazine *(Ch. 14)* Magazine-length ads that look like regular magazines but are created by advertisers. They are sold at newsstands and produced by the same companies that publish traditional magazines.

CYMK printing *(Ch. 13)* See *four-color process.*

daily newspapers *(Ch. 14)* Often called *dailies,* these newspapers are published at least five times a week, in either morning or evening editions.

data access *(Ch. 9)* Characteristic of a database that enables marketers to manipulate, analyze, and rank all the information they possess in order to make better marketing decisions.

database *(Ch. 9)* The corporate memory of all important customer information: name and address, telephone number, SIC code (if a business firm), source of inquiry, cost of inquiry, history of purchases, and so on. It should record every transaction across all points of contact with both channel members and customers.

database marketing *(Ch. 9)* Tracking and analyzing the purchasing patterns of specific customers in a computer database and then targeting advertising to their needs.

data management *(Ch. 9)* The process of gathering, consolidating, updating, and enhancing the information about customers and prospects that resides in a company's database.

daypart mix *(Ch. 15)* A media scheduling strategy based on the TV usage levels reported by the rating services.

DBS *(Ch. 15)* See *direct broadcast satellite.*

decentralized system *(Ch. 3)* The establishment of advertising departments by products or brands or in various divisions, subsidiaries, countries, regions, or other categories that suit the firm's needs, which operate with a major degree of independence.

deceptive advertising *(Ch. 2)* According to the FTC, any ad in which there is a misrepresentation, omission, or other practice that can mislead a significant number of reasonable consumers to their detriment.

decline stage *(Ch. 5)* The stage in the product life cycle when sales begin to decline due to obsolescence, new technology, or changing consumer tastes.

decoding *(Ch. 1)* The interpretation of a message by the receiver.

demarketing *(Ch. 1)* The marketing and advertising techniques used by some companies and organizations to discourage the purchase or use of certain products.

demographic editions *(Ch. 14)* Magazines that reach readers who share a demographic trait, such as age, income level, or professional status.

demographics *(Ch. 5)* The statistical characteristics of the population.

demonstration *(Ch. 12)* A type of TV commercial in which the product is shown in use.

departmental system *(Ch. 3)* The organization of an ad agency into departments based on function: account services, creative services, marketing services, and administration.

design *(Ch. 12)* Visual pattern or composition of artistic elements chosen and structured by the graphic artist.

designated market areas (DMA) *(Ch. 15)* The geographical areas in which TV stations attract most of their viewers.

development stage *(Ch. 3)* In the agency-client relationship, the honeymoon period when both agency and client are at the peak of their optimism and are most eager to quickly develop a mutually profitable mechanism for working together.

device copy *(Ch. 12)* Advertising copy that relies on wordplay, humor, poetry, rhymes, great exaggeration, gags, and other tricks or gimmicks.

dialog/monolog copy *(Ch. 12)* A type of body copy in which the characters illustrated in the advertisement do the selling in their own words either through a quasi-testimonial technique or through a comic strip panel.

digital interactive media *(Ch. 3, 13, 16)* Electronic channels of communication—including online databases, the Internet, CD-ROMs, and stand-alone kiosks—with which the audience can participate actively and immediately.

digital media *(Ch. 13)* Channels of communication that join the logic of multimedia formats with the electronic system capabilities and controls of modern telephone, television, and computer technologies.

digital proof *(Ch. 13)* A prepress proof that uses inkjet technology and offers fairly accurate reliability as well as lower cost and faster turn-around time. Also called an *Iris.*

digital video effects (DVE) unit *(Ch. 13)* In video, special-effects equipment for manipulating graphics on the screen to produce fades, wipes, zooms, rotations, and so on.

DirecPC *(Ch. 16)* Satellite-based system to connect with the Internet that offers very fast downloading—faster even than cable—but is still very expensive and requires a dial-up modem and separate phone line for sending material.

direct broadcast satellite (DBS) *(Ch. 15)* A television delivery system that involves beaming programs from satellites to special satellite dishes mounted in the home or yard.

direct distribution *(Ch. 5)* The method of marketing in which the manufacturer sells directly to customers without the use of retailers.

direct-mail advertising *(Ch. 3, 16)* All forms of advertising sent directly to prospective customers without using one of the commercial media forms.

direct marketing *(Ch. 5)* A system of marketing in which companies build their own database of customers and use a variety of media to communicate with them directly such as through ads and catalogs.

director *(Ch. 9, 13)* The director supervises preproduction, production, and postproduction of radio and television commercials.

directories *(Ch. 16, 17)* Listings, often in booklet form, that serve as locators, buying guides, and mailing lists.

direct questioning *(Ch. 6)* A method of pretesting designed to elicit a full range of responses to the advertising. It is especially effective for testing alternative advertisements in the early stages of development.

direct-response advertising *(Ch. 9)* An advertising message that asks the reader, listener, or viewer to provide feedback straight to the sender. Direct-response advertising can take the form of direct mail, or it can use a wide range of other media, from matchbook covers or magazines to radio, TV, or billboards.

direct sales *(Ch. 9)* Strategy where representatives sell to customers directly at home or work rather than through a retail establishment or other intermediary.

direct selling *(Ch. 9)* Face-to-face selling away from a fixed retail location. Usually refers to a method of marketing consumer goods—everything from encyclopedias and insurance to cosmetics and nutritional products.

display advertising *(Ch. 14)* Type of newspaper advertising that includes copy, illustrations or photographs, headlines, coupons, and other visual components.

display allowances *(Ch. 9)* Fees paid to retailers to make room for and set up manufacturers' displays.

display type *(Ch. 13)* A style of typeface used in advertising that is larger and heavier than normal text type. Display type is often used in headlines, subheads, logos, and addresses, and for emphasis.

distribution channel *(Ch. 5)* The network of all the firms and individuals that take title, or assist in taking title, to the product as it moves from the producer to the consumer.

distribution element *(Ch. 5)* How and where customers will buy a company's product; either direct or indirect distribution.

distribution objectives *(Ch. 8)* Where, when, and how advertising should appear.

diverting *(Ch. 9)* Purchasing large quantities of an item at a regional promotional discount and shipping portions to areas of the country where the discount isn't being offered.

DMA *(Ch. 15)* See *designated market areas.*

donut *(Ch. 12)* When writing a jingle, a hole left for spoken copy.

drama *(Ch. 1)* One of the three literary forms of advertising messages in which the characters act out events directly in front of an imagined empathetic audience.

drive times *(Ch. 15)* Radio use Monday through Friday at 6–10 A.M. and 3–7 P.M.

dubs *(Ch. 13)* Duplicates of radio commercials made from the master tape and sent to stations for broadcast.

dummy *(Ch. 12)* A three-dimensional, hand-made layout of a brochure or other multipage advertising piece put together, page for page, just like the finished product will eventually appear.

dupes *(Ch. 13)* Copies of a finished television commercial that are delivered to the networks or TV stations for airing.

earned rate *(Ch. 14)* A discount applied retroactively as the volume of advertising increases through the year.

effective frequency *(Ch. 8)* The average number of times a person must see or hear a message before it becomes effective.

effective reach *(Ch. 8)* Term used to describe the quality of exposure. It measures the number or percentage of the audience who receive enough exposures for the message to truly be received.

8-sheet posters *(Ch. 17)* A type of outdoor advertising offering a 5' by 11' printing area on a panel surface 6' tall by 12' wide.

elaboration likelihood model *(Ch. 4)* A theory of how persuasion occurs due to promotion communication. Psychologists Petty, Cacioppo, and Schumann theorize that the method of persuasion depends on the consumer's level of involvement with the product and the message. When consumers have a higher level of involvement with the product or the message, they will tend to comprehend product-related information, such as product attributes and benefits or demonstrations, at deeper, more elaborate levels. This can lead to product beliefs, positive brand attitudes, and purchase intention. On the oter hand, people who have low involvement with the product or the message. have little or no reason to pay attention to it or to comprehend the central message of the ad. As a result, direct persuasion is also low, and consumers form few if any brand beliefs, attitudes, or purchase intentions. However, these consumers might attend to some peripheral aspects of the ad or commercial—say, the pictures in the ad or the actors in a commercial—for their entertainment value. And whatever they feel or think about these peripheral, nonproduct aspects might integrate into a positive attitude toward the ad. See also *central route to persuasion* and *peripheral route to persuasion.*

electronic couponing *(Ch. 9)* In supermarkets, the use of frequent-shopper cards that automatically credit cardholders with coupon discounts when they check out. Also using touch-screen videos at the point of purchase, instant-print discounts, rebates, and offers to try new brands.

electronic media *(Ch. 3)* Radio and television, which may be transmitted electronically through wires or broadcast through the air.

electronic production *(Ch. 13)* The process of converting a script or storyboard into a finished commercial for use on radio, TV, or digital media.

electronic sign *(Ch. 17)* Large displays that provide text and graphic messages, similar to those found in sports stadiums.

emotional appeals *(Ch. 11)* Marketing appeals that are directed at the consumer's psychological, social, or symbolic needs.

empirical research method *(Ch. 7)* A method of allocating funds for advertising that uses experimentation to determine the best level of advertising expenditure. By running a series of tests in different markets with different budgets, companies determine the most efficient level of expenditure.

encoding *(Ch. 1, 4)* Translating an idea or message into words, symbols, and illustrations.

endorsement *(Ch. 2)* See *testimonial.*

entertainment *(Ch. 10)* The second largest area of sponsorship, which includes things like concert tours, attractions, and theme parks.

environments *(Ch. 4)* Surroundings that can affect the purchase decision.

equipment-based service *(Ch. 5)* A service business that relies mainly on the use of specialized equipment.

ethical advertising *(Ch. 2)* Doing what the advertiser and the advertiser's peers believe is morally right in a given situation.

euphemism *(Ch. 8)* The substitution of an inoffensive, mild word for a word that is offensive, harsh, or blunt.

evaluation of alternatives *(Ch. 4)* Choosing among brands, sizes, styles, and colors.

evaluative criteria *(Ch. 4)* The standards a consumer uses for judging the features and benefits of alternative products.

evoked set *(Ch. 4)* The particular group of alternative goods or services a consumer considers when making a buying decision.

exchange *(Ch. 4)* The trading of one thing of value for another thing of value.

exclusive distribution *(Ch. 5)* The strategy of limiting the number of wholesalers or retailers who can sell a product in order to gain a prestige image, maintain premium prices, or protect other dealers in a geographic region.

exhibitive media *(Ch. 17)* Media designed specifically to help bring customers eyeball to eyeball with the product. These media include product packaging and trade show booths and exhibits.

exhibits *(Ch. 10, 17)* A marketing or public relations approach that involves preparing displays that tell about an organization or its products; exhibits may be used at fairs, colleges and universities, or trade shows.

experimental method *(Ch. 6)* A method of scientific investigation in which a researcher alters the stimulus received by a test group or groups and compares the results with those of a control group that did not receive the altered stimulus.

exploratory research *(Ch. 6)* See *informal research*.

explorer role *(Ch. 11)* A role in the creative process that searches for new information, paying attention to unusual patterns.

exposure value *(Ch. 8)* The value of a medium determined by how well it exposes an ad to the target audience. In other words, how many people an ad "sees" rather than the other way around.

externalities *(Ch. 1, 2)* The social costs (or benefits) of a transaction to people not involved in the transaction. The absence of externalities is one of the fundamental principles or assumptions of free-market economics.

fact-based thinking *(Ch. 11)* A style of thinking that tends to fragment concepts into components and to analyze situations to discover the one best solution.

family brand *(Ch. 5)* The marketing of various products under the same umbrella name.

farm advertising *(Ch. 1)* Advertising directed to farmers as businesspeople and to others in the agricultural business. Also called *agricultural advertising*.

farm publications *(Ch. 14)* Magazines directed to farmers and their families or to companies that manufacture or sell agricultural equipment, supplies, and services.

FCC *(Ch. 2)* See *Federal Communications Commission*.

FDA *(Ch. 2)* See *Food and Drug Administration*.

feature article *(Ch. 10)* Soft news about companies, products, or services that may be written by a PR person, the publication's staff, or a third party.

Federal Communications Commission (FCC) *(Ch. 2)* Federal regulatory body with jurisdiction over radio, television, telephone, and telegraph industries. Through its licensing authority, the FCC has indirect control over broadcast advertising.

Federal Trade Commission (FTC) *(Ch. 2)* The major federal regulator of advertising used to promote products sold in interstate commerce.

fee-commission combination *(Ch. 3)* A pricing system in which an advertising agency charges the client a basic monthly fee for its services and also retains any media commissions earned.

fee-commission method *(Ch. 3)* Compensation method whereby an ad agency establishes a fixed monthly fee for all its services to the client and retains any commissions earned for space or time purchased on behalf of the client.

feedback *(Ch. 1, 4)* A message that acknowledges or responds to an initial message.

first-run syndication *(Ch. 15)* Programs produced specifically for the syndication market.

five Ms *(Ch. 8)* The elements of the media mix that include markets, money, media, mechanics, and methodology.

flanking strategy *(Ch. 1, 7)* In marketing warfare, the strategy adopted by middle companies in the hierarchy, who must point out the qualities that make them different from the top-three companies.

flat rate *(Ch. 14)* A standard newspaper advertising rate with no discount allowance for large or repeated space buys.

flats *(Ch. 13)* Opaque plastic sheets that film negatives are mounted on in perfect registration; light passes through only where lines and dots are to appear on the printing plate.

flighting *(Ch. 8)* An intermittent media scheduling pattern in which periods of advertising are alternated with periods of no advertising at all.

focus group *(Ch. 6)* A qualitative method of research in which four or more people, "typical" of the target market, are invited to a group session to discuss the product, the service, or the marketing situation for an hour or more.

folders *(Ch. 16)* Large, heavy-stock fliers, often folded and sent out as self-mailers.

font *(Ch. 13)* A uniquely designed set of capital, small capital, and lowercase letters, usually including numerals and punctuation marks.

Food and Drug Administration (FDA) *(Ch. 2)* Federal agency that has authority over the labeling, packaging, and branding of packaged foods and therapeutic devices.

foreign media *(Ch. 3)* The local media of each country used by advertisers for campaigns targeted to consumers or businesses within a single country.

formal research *(Ch. 6)* Collecting primary data directly from the marketplace using qualitative or quantitative methods.

forward buying *(Ch. 9)* A retailer's stocking up on a product when it is discounted and buying smaller amounts when it is at list price.

four-color process *(Ch. 13)* The method for printing color advertisements with tonal values, such as photographs and paintings. This process is based on the principle that all colors can be printed by combining the three primary colors—yellow, magenta (red), and cyan (blue)—plus black (which provides greater detail and density as well as shades of gray).

four Ps *(Ch. 5)* See *marketing mix*.

fragrance strips *(Ch. 14)* Perfume samples included in sealed inserts in magazines.

franchising *(Ch. 5)* A type of vertical marketing system in which dealers pay a fee to operate under the guidelines and direction of the manufacturer.

free-standing inserts (FSIs) *(Ch. 9)* Coupons distributed through inserts in newspapers.

frequency *(Ch. 8)* The number of times the same person or household is exposed to a vehicle in a specified time span. Across a total audience, frequency is calculated as the average number of times individuals or homes are exposed to the vehicle.

frequency discounts *(Ch. 14)* In newspapers, advertisers earn this discount by running an ad repeatedly in a specific time period.

FTC *(Ch. 2)* See *Federal Trade Commission.*

full position *(Ch. 14)* In newspaper advertising, the preferred position near the top of a page or on the top of a column next to reading matter. It is usually surrounded by editorial text and may cost the advertiser 25 to 50 percent more than ROP rates.

full-service advertising agency *(Ch. 3)* An agency equipped to serve its clients in all areas of communication and promotion. Its advertising services include planning, creating, and producing advertisements as well as performing research and media selection services. Nonadvertising functions include producing sales promotion materials, publicity articles, annual reports, trade show exhibits, and sales training materials.

full-showing *(Ch. 17)* A unit of purchase in transit advertising where one card will appear in each vehicle in the system.

game *(Ch. 9)* A sales promotion activity in which prizes are offered based on chance. The big marketing advantage of games is that customers must make repeat visits to the dealer to continue playing.

gatefold *(Ch. 14)* A magazine cover or page extended and folded over to fit into the magazine. The gatefold may be a fraction of a page or two or more pages, and it is always sold at a premium.

general consumer agency *(Ch. 3)* An agency that represents the widest variety of accounts, but it concentrates on companies that make goods purchased chiefly by consumers.

geodemographic segmentation *(Ch. 5)* Combining demographics with geographic segmentation to select target markets in advertising.

geographic editions *(Ch. 14)* Magazines that target geographic markets and have different rates for ads.

geographic segmentation *(Ch. 5)* A method of segmenting markets by geographic regions based on the shared characteristics, needs, or wants of people within the region.

global advertising *(Ch. 1)* Advertising used by companies that market their products, goods, or services throughout various countries around the world with messages that remain consistent.

global corporations *(Ch. 3)* Multinational corporations that market global brands and use the same marketing and advertising in all countries.

global marketers *(Ch. 3)* Multinationals that use a standardized approach to marketing and advertising in all countries.

global positioning system (GPS) *(Ch. 17)* New satellite-based system whereby outdoor advertising companies give their customers the exact latitude and longitude of particular boards. Media buyers, equipped with sophisticated new software on their desktop computers, can then integrate this information with demographic market characteristics and traffic counts to determine the best locations for their boards without ever leaving the office.

goods *(Ch. 1)* Tangible products such as suits, soap, and soft drinks.

government markets *(Ch. 4)* Governmental bodies that buy products for the successful coordination of municipal, state, federal, or other government activities.

gross impressions *(Ch. 8)* The total of all the audiences delivered by a media plan.

gross rating points (GRPs) *(Ch. 8, 15)* The total audience delivery or weight of a specific media schedule. It is computed by dividing the total number of impressions by the size of the target population and multiplying by 100, or by multiplying the reach, expressed as a percentage of the population, by the average frequency. In television, gross rating points are the total rating points achieved by a particular media schedule over a specific period. For example, a weekly schedule of five commercials with an average household rating of 20 would yield 100 GRPs. In outdoor advertising, a 100 gross rating point showing (also called a number 100 showing) covers a market fully by reaching 9 out of 10 adults daily over a 30-day period.

group system *(Ch. 3)* System in which an ad agency is divided into a number of little agencies or groups, each composed of an account supervisor, account executives, copywriters, art directors, a media director, and any other specialists required to meet the needs of the particular clients being served by the group.

growth stage *(Ch. 5)* The period in a product life cycle that is marked by market expansion as more and more customers make their first purchases while others are already making their second and third purchases.

GRPs *(Ch. 8, 15)* See *gross rating points.*

guaranteed circulation *(Ch. 14)* The number of copies of a magazine that the publisher expects to sell. If this figure is not reached, the publisher must give a refund to advertisers.

habit *(Ch. 4)* An acquired or developed behavior pattern that has become nearly or completely involuntary.

halftone plate *(Ch. 13)* Plate that prints dots, the combination of which, when printed, produces an optical illusion of shading as in a photograph.

halftone screen *(Ch. 13)* A glass or plastic screen, crisscrossed with fine black lines at right angles like a window screen, which breaks continuous-tone artwork into dots so that it can be reproduced.

halo effect *(Ch. 6)* In ad pretesting, the fact that consumers are likely to rate the one or two ads that make the best first impression as the highest in all categories.

handbills *(Ch. 3)* Low-cost fliers or other simple brochures distributed by hand on the street, in parking lots, or door-to-door.

headline *(Ch. 12)* The words in the leading position of an advertisement—the words that will be read first or that are positioned to draw the most attention.

hidden differences *(Ch. 5)* Imperceptible but existing differences that may greatly affect the desirability of a product.

hierarchy of needs *(Ch. 4)* Maslow's theory that the lower biological or survival needs are dominant in human behavior and must be satisfied before higher, socially acquired needs become meaningful.

highly promotional strategy *(Ch. 3)* In retailing, doing a great deal of advertising in order to keep bringing customers in.

home page *(Ch. 13, 16)* In Internet advertising, an advertiser's virtual storefront or gateway to more specific information about the company and its products.

hook *(Ch. 12)* The part of a jingle that sticks in your memory.

horizontal cooperative advertising *(Ch. 14)* Joint advertising effort of related businesses (car dealers, realtors, etc.) to create traffic for their type of business.

horizontal publications *(Ch. 14)* Business publications targeted at people with particular job functions that cut across industry lines, such as *Purchasing* magazine.

households using TV (HUT) *(Ch. 15)* The percentage of homes in a given area that have one or more TV sets tuned on at any particular time. If 1,000 TV sets are in the survey area and 500 are turned on, the HUT figure is 50 percent.

house list *(Ch. 16)* A company's most important and valuable direct-mail list, which may contain current, recent, and long-past customers or future prospects.

house organs *(Ch. 10, 16)* Internal and external publications produced by business organizations, including stockholder reports, newsletters, consumer magazines, and dealer publications. Most are produced by a company's advertising or public relations department or by its agency.

icon *(Ch. 12)* A pictorial image that represents an idea or thing.

ideas *(Ch. 1)* Economic, political, religious, or social viewpoints that advertising may attempt to sell.

illustrators *(Ch. 12)* The artists who paint, sketch, or draw the pictures we see in advertising.

image advertising *(Ch. 15)* Type of advertising intended to create a particular perception of the company or personality for the brand.

imagery transfer *(Ch. 15)* When advertisers run a schedule on TV and then convert the audio portion to radio commercials, fully 75 percent of consumers replay the video in their minds when they hear the radio spot.

implied consumers *(Ch. 1)* The consumers who are addressed by the ad's persona. They are not real, but rather imagined by the ad's creators to be ideal consumers—acquiescing in whatever beliefs the text requires. They are, in effect, part of the drama of the ad.

incentive system *(Ch. 3)* A form of compensation in which the agency shares in the client's success when a campaign attains specific, agreed-upon goals.

independent production house *(Ch. 3)* Supplier company that specializes in film or video production or both.

independent research company *(Ch. 3)* Research firms that work outside of an agency. They may come in all sizes and specialties, and they employ staff statisticians, field interviewers, and computer programmers, as well as analysts with degrees in psychology, sociology, and marketing.

independent shopping guide *(Ch. 14)* Weekly local ad vehicles that may or may not contain editorial matter. They can be segmented into highly select market areas.

in-depth interview *(Ch. 6)* An intensive interview technique that uses carefully planned but loosely structured questions to probe respondents' deeper feelings.

individual brand *(Ch. 5)* Assigning a unique name to each product a manufacturer produces.

induced differences *(Ch. 5)* Distinguishing characteristics of products effected through unique branding, packaging, distribution, merchandising, and advertising.

industrial markets *(Ch. 4)* Individuals or companies that buy products needed for the production of other goods or services such as plant equipment and telephone systems.

infomercial *(Ch. 15)* A long TV commercial that gives consumers detailed information about a product or service; see also *program-length advertisement*.

informal research *(Ch. 6)* The second step in the research process, designed to explore a problem by reviewing secondary data and interviewing a few key people with the most information to share. Also called *exploratory research*.

informational motives *(Ch. 4, 11)* The negatively originated motives, such as problem removal or problem avoidance, that are the most common energizers of consumer behavior.

in-house agency *(Ch. 3)* Agency wholly owned by an advertiser and set up and staffed to do all the work of an independent full-service agency.

in kind *(Ch. 10)* The donation of goods and services as payment for some service such as a sponsorship.

inquiry test *(Ch. 6)* A form of test in which consumer responses to an ad for information or free samples are tabulated.

insert *(Ch. 14)* An ad or brochure which the advertiser prints and ships to the publisher for insertion into a magazine or newspaper.

insertion order *(Ch. 14)* A form submitted to a newspaper or magazine when an advertiser wants to run an advertisement. This form states the date(s) on which the ad is to run, its size, the requested position, and the rate.

inside card *(Ch. 17)* A transit advertisement, normally 11 by 28 inches, placed in a wall rack above the windows of a bus.

institutional advertising *(Ch. 1, 3, 11)* A type of advertising that attempts to obtain favorable attention for the business as a whole, not for a specific product or service the store or business sells. The effects of institutional advertising are intended to be long term rather than short range.

institutional copy *(Ch. 12)* A type of body copy in which the advertiser tries to sell an idea or the merits of the organization or service rather than the sales features of a particular product.

in-store sampling *(Ch. 9)* The handing out of free product samples to passing shoppers.

integrated commercial *(Ch. 12)* A straight radio announcement, usually delivered by one person, woven into a show or tailored to a given program to avoid any perceptible interruption.

integrated marketing communications *(Ch. 1, 3, 7)* The process of building and reinforcing mutually profitable relationships with employees, customers, other stakeholders, and the general public by developing and coordinating a strategic communications program that enables them to make constructive contact with the company/brand through a variety of media.

intellectual property *(Ch. 2)* Something produced by the mind, such as original works of authorship including literary, dramatic, musical, artistic, and certain other "intellectual" works, which may be legally protected by copyright, patent, or trademark.

intensive distribution *(Ch. 5)* A distribution strategy based on making the product available to consumers at every possible location so that consumers can buy with a minimum of effort.

intensive techniques *(Ch. 6)* Qualitative research aimed at probing the deepest feelings, attitudes, and beliefs of respondents through direct questioning. Typical methods include in-depth interviews and focus groups.

interactive agency *(Ch. 3)* An advertising agency that specializes in the creation of ads for a digital interactive medium such as Web pages, CD-ROMs, or electronic kiosks.

interactive media *(Ch. 1, 9, 13, 16)* These systems allow users to control both the content and the pace of presentations and to order merchandise directly from the system.

interactive TV *(Ch. 13, 16)* A personal audience venue where people can personally guide TV programming through a remote control box while watching TV.

interconnects *(Ch. 15)* Groups of cable systems joined together for advertising purposes.

interior paragraphs *(Ch. 12)* Text within the body copy of an ad where the credibility and desire steps of the message are presented.

international advertising *(Ch. 1)* Advertising aimed at foreign markets.

international agency *(Ch. 3)* An advertising agency that has offices or affiliates in major communication centers around the world and can help its clients market internationally or globally.

international markets *(Ch. 4)* Consumer, business, or government markets located in foreign countries. Also called *global markets*.

international media *(Ch. 3)* Media serving several countries, usually without change, available to an international audience.

international structure *(Ch. 3)* Organization of companies with foreign marketing divisions, typically decentralized and responsible for their own product lines, marketing operations, and profits.

Internet *(Ch. 16)* A worldwide network of computer systems that facilitates global electronic communications via e-mail, the World Wide Web, ftp, and other data protocol.

Internet service provider (ISP) *(Ch. 16)* Companies which offer consumer and business access to the Internet.

interpersonal influences *(Ch. 4)* Social influences on the consumer decision-making process, including family, society, and cultural environment.

interstitial *(Ch. 16)* Animated screens, often advertisements, which pop up momentarily as the computer searches for and downloads information for a requested Web page. Also known as "splash" pages.

interview *(Ch. 6)* See *in-depth interview*.

introductory phase *(Ch. 5)* The initial phase of the product life cycle (also called the *pioneering phase*) when a new product is introduced, costs are highest, and profits are lowest.

inventory *(Ch. 15)* Commercial time for advertisers.

island half *(Ch. 14)* A half-page of magazine space that is surrounded on two or more sides by editorial matter. This type of ad is designed to dominate a page and is therefore sold at a premium price.

italic *(Ch. 12)* A style of printing type with letters that generally slant to the right.

jingle *(Ch. 12)* A musical commercial, usually sung with the sales message in the verse.

job jacket *(Ch. 13)* In the preproduction phase, a place to store the various pieces of artwork and ideas that will be generated throughout the process.

judge role *(Ch. 11)* A role in the creative process that evaluates the results of experimentation and decides which approach is more practical.

junior unit *(Ch. 14)* A large magazine advertisement (60 percent of the page) placed in the middle of a page and surrounded by editorial matter.

kerning *(Ch. 13)* The measurement of the space between individual letters of text.

keyword *(Ch. 16)* A single word that a user inputs into an Internet search engine to request information that is similar in subject matter to that word. Advertisers may buy keywords from search engines so that their advertisements appear when a user inputs the purchased word.

kicker *(Ch. 12)* A subhead that appears above the headline.

kiosks *(Ch. 13, 16)* Interactive computers in a stand-alone cabinet that make information available 24 hours a day even in remote areas.

layout *(Ch. 12)* An orderly formation of all the parts of an advertisement. In print, it refers to the arrangement of the headline, subheads, visuals, copy, picture captions, trademarks, slogans, and signature. In television, it refers to the placement of characters, props, scenery, and product elements, the location and angle of the camera, and the use of lighting. See also *design*.

leading *(Ch. 13)* The measurement of the space between separate lines of text (pronounced *ledding*).

lead-in paragraph *(Ch. 12)* In print ads, a bridge between the headlines, the subheads, and the sales ideas presented in the text. It transfers reader interest to product interest.

learning *(Ch. 4)* A relatively permanent change in thought processes or behavior that occurs as a result of reinforced experience.

letter shop *(Ch. 16)* A firm that stuffs envelopes, affixes labels, calculates postage, sorts pieces into stacks or bundles, and otherwise prepares items for mailing.

Library of Congress *(Ch. 2)* The federal body that registers and protects all copyrighted material, including advertising.

licensed brands *(Ch. 5)* Brand names that other companies can buy the right to use.

lifestyle *(Ch. 12)* Type of commercial in which the user is presented rather than the product. Typically used by clothing and soft drink advertisers to affiliate their brands with the trendy lifestyles of their consumers.

lifetime customer value (LTCV) *(Ch. 7)* A measurement of a consumer's economic value to a company over the course of his or her entire lifetime which comes from developing lasting relationships.

line film *(Ch. 13)* The product of a photograph shot with orthographic film which yields a high-contrast black-and-white image with no gray tones.

line plate *(Ch. 13)* A printing plate used to produce black-and-white artwork from line film

linkage media *(Ch. 9)* In direct marketing, media that help prospects and customers link up with a company.

list broker *(Ch. 16)* An intermediary who handles rental of mailing lists for list owners on a commission basis.

live action *(Ch. 13)* The basic production technique in television that portrays real people and settings, as opposed to animation.

lobbying *(Ch. 10)* Informing government officials and persuading them to support or thwart administrative action or legislation in the interests of some client.

local advertising *(Ch. 1, 3)* Advertising by businesses within a city or county directed toward customers within the same geographical area.

local agency *(Ch. 3)* Advertising agencies that specialize in creating advertising for local businesses.

local time *(Ch. 15)* Radio spots purchased by a local advertiser.

local trading area *(Ch. 3)* Primary geographic area from which most of a company's customers come.

location *(Ch. 13)* Shooting away from the studio. Location shooting adds realism but can also be a technical and logistical nightmare, often adding cost and many other potential problems.

logotype *(Ch. 12)* Special design of the advertiser's name (or product name) that appears in all advertisements. Also called a signature cut, it is like a trademark because it gives the advertiser individuality and provides quick recognition at the point of purchase.

long-term macro arguments *(Ch. 2)* Criticisms of advertising that focus on the social or environmental impact of marketing.

lot *(Ch. 13)* Acreage outside a studio that is shielded from stray, off-site sounds.

Magazine Publishers Association (MPA) *(Ch. 14)* A trade group made up of more than 230 publishers who represent 1,200 magazines. It compiles circulation figures on ABC member magazines and promotes greater and more effective use of magazine advertising.

mail-response list *(Ch. 16)* A type of direct-mail list, composed of people who have responded to the direct-mail solicitations of other companies, especially those whose efforts are complementary to the advertiser's.

maintenance stage *(Ch. 3)* In the client-agency relationship, the day-to-day interaction that, when successful, may go on for years.

makegoods *(Ch. 15)* TV spots that are aired to compensate for spots that were missed or run incorrectly.

management (account) supervisors *(Ch. 3)* Managers who supervise account executives and who report to the agency's director of account services.

mandatories *(Ch. 13)* The address, phone number, Web address, etc., that the advertiser usually insists be included within an ad to give the consumer adequate information.

many buyers and sellers *(Ch. 1, 2)* One of the four fundamental assumptions of a free market system, the concept of many buyers and sellers means, among other things, that competition will keep prices down without interference from the government.

market *(Ch. 4, 8)* A group of potential customers who share a common interest, need, or desire; who can use the offered good or service to some advantage; and who can afford or are willing to pay the purchase price. Also, an element of the media mix referring to the various targets of a media plan.

marketer *(Ch. 4)* Any person or organization that has products, services, or ideas to sell.

marketing *(Ch. 1, 4)* The process of planning and executing the conception, pricing, promotion, and distribution of ideas, goods, and services to create exchanges that satisfy the perceived needs, wants, and objectives of individuals and organizations.

marketing communications *(Ch. 1)* The various efforts and tools companies use to initiate and maintain communication with customers and prospects, including solicitation letters, newspaper ads, event sponsorships, publicity, telemarketing, statement stuffers, and coupons, to mention just a few.

marketing information system (MIS) *(Ch. 6)* A set of procedures for generating an orderly flow of pertinent information for use in making market decisions.

marketing mix *(Ch. 5)* Four elements, called the 4Ps (product, price, place, and promotion), that every company has the option of adding, subtracting, or modifying in order to create a desired marketing strategy.

marketing objectives *(Ch. 7)* Goals of the marketing effort that may be expressed in terms of the needs of specific target markets and specific sales objectives.

marketing plan *(Ch. 7)* The plan that directs the company's marketing effort. First, it assembles all the pertinent facts about the organization, the markets it serves, and its products, services, customers, and competition. Second, it forces the functional managers within the company to work together—product development, production, selling, advertising, credit, transportation—to focus efficiently on the customer. Third, it sets goals and objectives to be attained within specified periods of time and lays out the precise strategies that will be used to achieve them.

marketing public relations (MPR) *(Ch. 1, 10)* The use of public relations activities as a marketing tool.

marketing research *(Ch. 6)* The systematic gathering, recording, and analysis of information to help managers make marketing decisions.

marketing strategy *(Ch. 7)* The statement of how the company is going to accomplish its marketing objectives. The strategy is the total directional thrust of the company, that is, the "how-to" of the marketing plan, and is determined by the particular blend of the marketing mix elements (the 4 Ps) which the company can control.

market prep corporate advertising *(Ch. 10)* Corporate advertising that is used to set the company up for future sales; it simultaneously communicates messages about the products and the company.

market segmentation *(Ch. 5)* Strategy of identifying groups of people or organizations with certain shared needs and characteristics within the broad markets for consumer or business products and aggregating these groups into larger market segments according to their mutual interest in the product's utility.

markup *(Ch. 3)* A source of agency income gained by adding some amount to a supplier's bill, usually 17.65 percent.

mass audience venue *(Ch. 13)* One category of digital media based on audience size, where hundreds of people are in the live audience and millions more are watching at home.

master tape *(Ch. 13)* The final recording of a radio commercial, with all the music, sound, and vocals mixed, from which dubs (duplicates) are recorded and sent to radio stations for broadcast.

maturity stage *(Ch. 5)* That point in the product life cycle when the market has become saturated with products, the number of new customers has dwindled, and competition is most intense.

MDS *(Ch. 15)* See *multipoint distribution system.*

mechanical *(Ch. 12, 13)* The set type and illustrations or photographs pasted into the exact position in which they will appear in the final ad. Also called a pasteup, this is then used as the basis for the next step in the reproduction process.

mechanics *(Ch. 8)* One of the five Ms of the media mix; dealing creatively with the available advertising media options.

media *(Ch. 1, 3, 8)* A plural form of *medium,* referring to communications vehicles paid to present an advertisement to its target audience. Most often used to refer to radio and television networks, stations that have news reporters, and publications that carry news and advertising.

media buyer *(Ch. 14)* Person responsible for negotiating and contracting the purchase of advertisement space and time in various media.

media-buying service *(Ch. 3)* An organization that specializes in purchasing and packaging radio and television time.

media classes *(Ch. 6)* Broad media categories of electronic, print, outdoor, and direct mail.

media commission *(Ch. 3)* Compensation paid by a medium to recognized advertising agencies, usually 15 percent (16 2/3 percent for outdoor), for advertising placed with it.

Mediamark Research, Inc. (MRI) *(Ch. 14)* MRI conducts personal interviews to determine readership patterns, reports the audience and demographics for leading magazines and newspapers, and publishes annual studies on markets and decision makers.

media planning *(Ch. 8)* The process that directs advertising messages to the right people in the right place at the right time.

media research *(Ch. 6)* The systematic gathering and analysis of information on the reach and effectiveness of media vehicles.

media subclasses *(Ch. 6)* Smaller divisions of media classes, such as radio, TV, magazines, newspapers, and so on.

media units *(Ch. 6)* Specific units of advertising in each type of medium, such as half-page magazine ads, 30-second spots, and so on.

media vehicles *(Ch. 8)* Particular media programs or publications.

medium *(Ch. 1)* An instrument or communications vehicle that carries or helps transfer a message from the sender to the receiver. Plural is media. See also *media.*

mental files *(Ch. 4)* Stored memories in the consumer's mind.

merchandise *(Ch. 6)* Synonymous with *product concept* when used in reference to the 5Ms of advertising testing.

message *(Ch. 1)* In oral communication, the idea formulated and encoded by the source and sent to the receiver.

message-distribution objectives *(Ch. 8)* Distribution objectives define where, when, and how often advertising should appear.

message strategy *(Ch. 11)* The specific determination of what a company wants to say and how it wants to say it. The elements of the message strategy include verbal, nonverbal, and technical components; also called *rationale.*

message weight *(Ch. 8)* The total size of the audience for a set of ads or an entire campaign.

methodology *(Ch. 8)* The overall strategy of selecting and scheduling media vehicles to achieve the desired reach, frequency, and continuity objectives.

mixed interlock *(Ch. 13)* The edited version of a filmed television commercial mixed with the finished sound track. Used for initial review and approval prior to being duplicated for airing.

mixed-media approach *(Ch. 8)* Using a combination of advertising media vehicles in a single advertising campaign.

mnemonic device *(Ch. 12, 13)* A gimmick used to dramatize the product benefit and make it memorable, such as the Imperial Margarine crown or the Avon doorbell.

mobile billboard *(Ch. 17)* A cross between traditional billboards and transit advertising; some specially designed flatbed trucks carry long billboards up and down busy thoroughfares.

money *(Ch. 8)* In media planning, one of the five elements in the media mix.

motivation *(Ch. 4)* The underlying drives that stem from the conscious or unconscious needs of the consumer and contribute to the individual consumer's purchasing actions.

motivation research *(Ch. 6)* Qualitative research used to give advertisers a general impression of the market, the consumer, or the product.

motivation value *(Ch. 8)* A consideration in selecting media based on the medium's ability to motivate people to act. Positive factors include prestige, good quality reproduction, timeliness, and editorial relevance.

motives *(Ch. 6)* Emotions, desires, physiological needs, or similar impulses that may incite consumers to action.

MPA *(Ch. 13)* See *Magazine Publishers Association.*

multimedia presentation *(Ch. 13)* Presenting information or entertainment using several communications media simultaneously.

multinational corporations *(Ch. 3)* Corporations operating and investing throughout many countries and making decisions based on availabilities worldwide.

multipoint distribution system (MDS) *(Ch. 15)* A microwave TV delivery system that can carry up to a dozen channels.

musical commercial *(Ch. 12)* See *jingle.*

musical logo *(Ch. 12)* A jingle that becomes associated with a product or company through consistent use.

NAD *(Ch. 2)* See *National Advertising Division.*

NARB *(Ch. 2)* See *National Advertising Review Board.*

NARC *(Ch. 2)* See *National Advertising Review Council.*

narrative copy *(Ch. 12)* A type of body copy that tells a story. It sets up a problem and then creates a solution using the particular sales features of the product or service as the key to the solution.

narrative message *(Ch. 1)* Advertising in which a third person tells a story about others to an imagined audience.

national advertisers *(Ch. 3)* Companies which advertise in several geographic regions or throughout the country.

national advertising *(Ch. 1)* Advertising used by companies that market their products, goods, or services in several geographic regions or throughout the country.

National Advertising Division (NAD) *(Ch. 2)* The National Advertising Division of the Council of Better Business Bureaus. It investigates and monitors advertising industry practices.

National Advertising Review Board (NARB) *(Ch. 2)* A five-member panel, composed of three advertisers, one agency representative, and one layperson, selected to review decisions of the NAD.

National Advertising Review Council (NARC) *(Ch. 2)* An organization founded by the Council of Better Business Bureaus and various advertising industry groups to promote and enforce standards of truth, accuracy, taste, morality, and social responsibility in advertising.

national agency *(Ch. 3)* Advertising agencies that produce and place the quality of advertising suitable for national campaigns.

national brands *(Ch. 5)* Product brands that are marketed in several regions of the country.

national magazines *(Ch. 14)* Magazines that are distributed throughout a country.

national rate *(Ch. 14)* A newspaper advertising rate that is higher, attributed to the added costs of serving national advertisers.

needs *(Ch. 4)* The basic, often instinctive, human forces that motivate us to do something.

need-satisfying objectives *(Ch. 7)* A marketing objective that shifts management's view of the organization from a producer of products or services to a satisfier of target market needs.

negatively originated motives *(Ch. 4)* Consumer purchase and usage based on problem removal or problem avoidance. To relieve such feelings, consumers actively seek a new or replacement product.

network marketing *(Ch. 5)* A method of direct distribution in which individuals act as independent distributors for a manufacturer or private-label marketer.

networks *(Ch. 15)* Any of the national television or radio broadcasting chains or companies such as ABC, CBS, NBC, or Fox. Networks offer the large advertiser convenience and efficiency because the message can be broadcast simultaneously throughout the country.

news/information headline *(Ch. 12)* A type of headline that includes many of the "how-to" headlines as well as headlines that seek to gain identification for their sponsors by announcing some news or providing some promise of information.

Newspaper Association of America (NAA) *(Ch. 14)* The promotional arm of the American Newspaper Publishers Association and the nation's newspaper industry.

Newspaper Space Bank (NSB) *(Ch. 14)* An online database service through which advertisers can buy canceled, unsold, or remnant space in major market newspapers at deeply discounted rates after normal closings.

news release *(Ch. 10)* A typewritten sheet of information (usually 8 1/2 by 11 inches) issued to print and broadcast outlets to generate publicity or shed light on a subject of interest. Also called *press release.*

NLEA *(Ch. 2)* See *Nutritional Labeling and Education Act.*

noise *(Ch. 1)* The sender's advertising message competing daily with hundreds of other commercial and noncommercial messages.

noncommercial advertising *(Ch. 1)* Advertising sponsored by or for a charitable institution, civic group, religious order, political organization, or some other nonprofit group to stimulate donations, persuade people to vote one way or another, or bring attention to social causes.

nonpersonal communication *(Ch. 5)* Marketing activities that use some medium as an intermediary for communication, including advertising, direct marketing, public relations, collateral materials, and sales promotion.

nonpersonal influences *(Ch. 4)* Factors influencing the consumer decision-making process that are often out of the consumer's control, such as time, place, and environment.

nonpersonal selling *(Ch. 5)* All selling activities that use some medium as an intermediary for communication, including advertising, public relations, sales promotion, and collateral materials.

nonprobability samples *(Ch. 6)* Research samples that do not provide every unit in the population with an equal chance of being included. As a result, there is no guarantee that the sample will be representative.

nonproduct advertising *(Ch. 1)* Advertising designed to sell ideas or a philosophy rather than products or services.

nonproduct facts *(Ch. 2)* Product claims not about the brand but about the consumer or the social context in which the consumer uses the brand.

nonpromotional strategy *(Ch. 3)* For local businesses, reliance on word-of-mouth and return customers as opposed to advertising and related types of promotion.

nonverbal *(Ch. 11)* Communication other than through the use of words, normally visual.

Nutritional Labeling and Education Act (NLEA) *(Ch. 2)* A 1994 congressional law setting stringent legal definitions for terms such as fresh, light, low fat, and reduced calorie; setting standard serving sizes; and requiring labels to show food value for one serving alongside the total recommended daily value as established by the National Research Council.

objectives *(Ch. 7)* See *marketing objectives.*

objective/task method *(Ch. 7)* A method of determining advertising allocations, also referred to as the *budget-buildup method,* that defines objectives and how advertising is to be used to accomplish them. It has three steps: defining the objectives, determining strategy, and estimating the cost.

observation method *(Ch. 6)* A method of research used when researchers actually monitor people's actions.

off-network syndication *(Ch. 15)* The availability of programs that originally appeared on networks to individual stations for re-broadcast.

on-camera *(Ch. 12)* Actually seen by the camera, as an announcer, a spokesperson, or actor playing out a scene.

100 showing *(Ch. 17)* The basic unit of sale for billboards or posters is 100 gross rating points daily. One rating point equals 1 percent of a particular market's population.

online catalogs *(Ch. 14)* A form of the new digital interactive media where direct markets use the Internet to advertise their products.

on-sale date *(Ch. 14)* The date a magazine is actually issued.

open rate (*Ch. 14*) The highest rate for a one-time insertion in a newspaper.

opinion leader (*Ch. 4*) Someone whose beliefs or attitudes are respected by people who share an interest in some specific activity.

opinion sampling (*Ch. 10*) A form of public relations research in which consumers provide feedback via interviews, toll-free phone lines, focus groups, and similar methods.

opportunities to see (OTS) (*Ch. 8*) A possible exposure of an advertising message to one audience member. Also called an *advertising impression*. Effective frequency is considered to be three or more opportunities-to-see over a four-week period; but no magic number works for every commercial and every product.

organizational buyers (*Ch. 4*) People who purchase products and services for use in business and government.

orthographic film (*Ch. 13*) A high-contrast photographic film yielding only black-and-white images, no gray tones.

outdoor advertising (*Ch. 3*) An out-of-home medium in the form of billboards.

out-of-home media (*Ch. 17*) Media such as outdoor advertising (billboards) and transit advertising (bus and car cards) that reach prospects outside their homes.

outside posters (*Ch. 17*) The variety of transit advertisements appearing on the outside of buses, including king size, queen size, traveling display, rear of bus, and front of bus.

overlay (*Ch. 13*) On a pasteup, a piece of clear plastic containing a second image from which a second printing plate can be made for color printing.

packaging (*Ch. 17*) The container for a product—encompassing the physical appearance of the container and including the design, color, shape, labeling, and materials used.

paid circulation (*Ch. 14*) The total number of copies of an average issue of a newspaper or magazine that is distributed through subscriptions and newsstand sales.

PANTONE Matching System® (PMS) (*Ch. 13*) A collection of colors that are premixed according to a formula and given a specific color number. PANTONE® swatch books feature over 100 colors in solid and screened blocks printed on different paper finishes.

participation basis (*Ch. 15*) The basis on which most network television advertising is sold, with advertisers buying 30- or 60-second segments within the program. This allows the advertiser to spread out the budget and makes it easier to get in and out of a program without a long-term commitment.

pass-along readership (*Ch. 14*) Readers of a publication in addition to the purchaser or subscriber.

pasteup (*Ch. 12*) See *mechanical*.

patent (*Ch. 2*) A grant made by the government that confers upon the creator of an invention the sole right to make, use, and sell that invention for a set period of time.

people-based service (*Ch. 5*) A service that relies on the talents and skills of individuals rather than on highly technical or specialized equipment.

percentage-of-sales method (*Ch. 7*) A method of advertising budget allocation based on a percentage of the previous year's sales, the anticipated sales for the next year, or a combination of the two.

perceptible differences (*Ch. 5*) Differences between products that are visibly apparent to the consumer.

perception (*Ch. 4*) Our personalized way of sensing and comprehending stimuli.

perceptual screens (*Ch. 4*) The physiological or psychological perceptual filters that messages must pass through.

perfect information (*Ch. 2*) One of the four basic premises of free market economics. The principle is that access by buyers and sellers to all information at all times about what products are available, at what quality, and at what prices leads to greater competition and lower prices for all.

peripheral route to persuasion (*Ch. 4*) One of two ways researchers Petty, Cacioppo, and Schumann theorize that marketers can persuade consumers. People who have low involvement with the product or message have little or no reason to pay attention to it or to comprehend the central message of the ad. However, these consumers might attend to some peripheral aspects of an ad or commercial for their entertainment value. Whatever they feel or think about these peripheral, nonproduct aspects might integrate into a positive attitude toward the ad. At some later date, these ad-related meanings could be activated to form some brand attitude or purchase intention. Typical of advertising for many everyday low-involvement purchases such as many consumer packaged goods: soap, cereal, toothpaste, and chewing gum. See also *elaboration likelihood model*.

persona (*Ch. 1*) A real or imaginary spokesperson who lends some voice or tone to an advertisement or commercial.

personal audience venue (*Ch. 13*) A category of digital media based on audience size; where one person in front of a personal computer can receive multimedia information.

personal communication (*Ch. 5*) Marketing activities that include all person-to-person contact with customers.

personal processes (*Ch. 4*) The three internal, human operations—perception, learning, and motivation—which govern the way consumers discern raw data (stimuli) and translate them into feelings, thoughts, beliefs, and actions.

personal selling (*Ch. 5, 9*) A sales method based on person-to-person contact, such as by a salesperson at a retail establishment or by a telephone solicitor.

personal value system (*Ch. 2*) A level of ethics that is an individual's attitudes, feelings, and beliefs.

persuasion (*Ch. 4*) A change in thought process or behavior that occurs when the change in belief, attitude, or behavioral intention is caused by promotion communication (such as advertising or personal selling).

philanthropy (*Ch. 10*) Support for a cause without any commercial incentive.

photographers (*Ch. 12*) The artists who use cameras to create visuals for advertisements.

physiological screens (*Ch. 4*) The perceptual screens which use the five senses—sight, hearing, touch, taste, and smell—to detect incoming data and measure the dimension and intensity of the physical stimulus.

picture-caption copy (*Ch. 12*) A type of body copy in which the story is told through a series of illustrations and captions rather than through the use of a copy block alone.

picture window layout (*Ch. 12*) Layout that employs a single, dominant visual that occupies between 60 and 70 percent of an advertisement's total area. Also known as *poster-style format* or *Ayer No.1*.

platform licensing *(Ch. 13)* A fee paid to original software developers for the special key codes that access multimedia programs on certain computer networks.

point *(Ch. 3, 13)* In retailing, the place of business. In typography, the measurement of the size and height of a text character. There are 72 points to an inch.

point-of-purchase (P-O-P) advertising *(Ch. 9)* Materials set up at a retail location to build traffic, advertise the product, and promote impulse buying. Materials may include window displays, counter displays, floor and wall displays, streamers, and posters.

polybagging *(Ch. 9)* Samples are delivered in plastic bags with the daily newspaper or a monthly magazine.

pop-up ad *(Ch. 14)* A three-dimensional magazine ad.

positioning *(Ch. 5)* The way in which a product is ranked in the consumer's mind by the benefits it offers, by the way it is classified or differentiated from the competition, or by its relationship to certain target markets.

positioning era *(Ch. 1)* The 1970s, when marketers focused on how their product ranked against the competition in the consumer's mind.

positively originated motives *(Ch. 4)* Consumer's motivation to purchase and use a product based on a positive bonus that the product promises, such as sensory gratification, intellectual stimulation, or social approval.

postcards *(Ch. 16)* Cards sent by advertisers to announce sales, offer discounts, or otherwise generate consumer traffic.

posters *(Ch. 10)* For public relations purposes, signs that impart product information or other news of interest to consumers, or that are aimed at employee behavior, such as safety, courtesy, or waste reduction.

poster-style format *(Ch. 12)* Layout that employs a single, dominant visual that occupies between 60 and 70 percent of an advertisement's total area. Also known as *picture-window layout* and *Ayer No.1.*

postproduction *(Ch. 13)* The finishing phase in commercial production—the period after recording and shooting when a radio or TV commercial is edited and sweetened with music and sound effects.

postpurchase dissonance *(Ch. 4)* See *theory of cognitive dissonance.*

postpurchase evaluation *(Ch. 4)* Determining whether a purchase has been a satisfactory or unsatisfactory one.

posttesting *(Ch. 6)* Testing the effectiveness of an advertisement after it has been run.

preemption rates *(Ch. 15)* Lower TV advertising rate that stations charge when the advertiser agrees to allow the station to sell its time to another advertiser willing to pay a higher rate.

preferred position rate *(Ch. 14)* A choice position for a newspaper or magazine ad for which a higher rate is charged.

preindustrial age *(Ch. 1)* Period of time between the beginning of written history and roughly the start of the 19th century, during which the invention of paper and the printing press and increased literacy gave rise to the first forms of written advertising.

premium *(Ch. 9, 17)* An item offered free or at a bargain price to encourage the consumer to buy an advertised product.

prepress phase *(Ch. 13)* The process of converting page art and visuals into materials (generally film negatives and color separation) needed for printing.

preprinted inserts *(Ch. 14)* Newspaper advertisements printed in advance by the advertiser and then delivered to the newspaper plant to be inserted into a specific edition. Preprints are inserted into the fold of the newspaper and look like a separate, smaller section of the paper.

preproduction *(Ch. 13)* The period of time before the actual recording or shooting of a commercial—the planning phase in commercial production.

prerelationship stage *(Ch. 3)* The initial stage in the client-agency relationship before they officially do business.

presenter commercial *(Ch. 12)* A commercial format in which one person or character presents the product and sales message.

press agentry *(Ch. 10)* The planning of activities and the staging of events to attract attention to new products or services and to generate publicity about the company or organization that will be of interest to the media.

press kit *(Ch. 10)* A package of publicity materials used to give information to the press at staged events such as press conferences or open houses. Also, a package of sales material promoting a specific media vehicle. Also called a *media kit.*

press release *(Ch. 10)* See *news release.*

pretesting *(Ch. 6)* Testing the effectiveness of an advertisement for gaps or flaws in message content before recommending it to clients, often conducted through focus groups.

price element *(Ch. 5)* In the marketing mix, the amount charged for the good or service—including deals, discounts, terms, warranties, and so on. The factors affecting price are market demand, cost of production and distribution, competition, and corporate objectives.

primary circulation *(Ch. 14)* The number of people who receive a publication, whether through direct purchase or subscription.

primary data *(Ch. 6)* Research information gained directly from the marketplace.

primary demand *(Ch. 5)* Consumer demand for a whole product category.

primary demand trend *(Ch. 5)* The projection of future consumer demand for a whole product category based on past demand and other market influences.

primary rules *(Ch. 2)* Ethical behavior's two interrelated components of the traditional actions taken by people in a society or community and the philosophical rules it establishes to justify past actions and decree future actions.

prime time *(Ch. 15)* Highest level of TV viewing (8 P.M. to 11 P.M. EST).

printer *(Ch. 3)* Business that employs or contracts with highly trained specialists who prepare artwork for reproduction, operate digital scanning machines to make color separations and plates, operate presses and collating machines, and run binderies.

print media *(Ch. 3)* Any commercially published, printed medium, such as newspapers and magazines, that sells advertising space to a variety of advertisers.

print production manager *(Ch. 13)* Manager who oversees the entire production process, including reproduction of visuals in full color, shooting and editing of scenes, precise specification and placement of type, and the checking, approving, duplicating, and shipping of final art, negatives, tape, or film to the communication media.

print production process *(Ch. 13)* The systematic process a layout for an ad or a brochure goes through from concept to final printing. The four major phases are preproduction, production, prepress, and printing and distribution.

privacy rights *(Ch. 2)* Of or pertaining to an individual's right to prohibit personal information from being divulged to the public.

private audience venue *(Ch. 13)* A category of digital media based on audience size; where meetings, conferences, and seminars use computer-driven multimedia presentations to inform, persuade, remind, and entertain people.

private labels *(Ch. 5)* Personalized brands applied by distributors or dealers to products supplied by manufacturers. Private brands are typically sold at lower prices in large retail chain stores.

process *(Ch. 1)* A planned series of actions or methods that take place sequentially, such as developing products, pricing them strategically, making them available to customers through a distribution network, and promoting them through sales and advertising activities.

producer *(Ch. 13)* For electronic media, the person responsible for keeping the project moving smoothly and under budget, while maintaining the required level of quality through every step of the production process.

product *(Ch. 1)* The particular good or service a company sells. See also *product concept.*

product advertising *(Ch. 1, 3)* Advertising intended to promote goods and services; also a functional classification of advertising.

product concept *(Ch. 5, 11)* The consumer's perception of a product as a "bundle" of utilitarian and symbolic values that satisfy functional, social, psychological, and other wants and needs. Also, as an element of the creative mix used by advertisers to develop advertising strategy, it is the bundle of product values the advertiser presents to the consumer.

product element *(Ch. 5)* The most important element of the marketing mix: the good or service being offered and the values associated with it—including the way the product is designed and classified, positioned, branded, and packaged.

production *(Ch. 13)* An element of creative strategy. The whole physical process of producing ads and commercials; also the particular phase in the process when the recording and shooting of commercials is done.

production manager *(Ch. 13)* For print media, the person responsible for keeping the project moving smoothly and under budget, while maintaining the required level of quality through every step of the production process.

production phase *(Ch. 13)* The phase of advertising production that involves setting up the artwork and typesetting, completing ancillary functions such as illustration or photography, and melding the components into a final form for the printer or publisher.

product life cycle *(Ch. 5)* Progressive stages in the life of a product—including introduction, growth, maturity, and decline—that affect the way a product is marketed and advertised.

product placement *(Ch. 17)* Paying a fee to have a product included in a movie.

product shaping *(Ch. 4)* Designing products, through manufacturing, repackaging, or advertising, to more fully satisfy the customer's needs and wants.

professional advertising *(Ch. 1)* Advertising directed at individuals who are normally licensed to operate under a code of ethics or set of professional standards.

program-length advertisement (PLA) *(Ch. 15)* A long-form television commercial that may run as long as an hour; also called an *infomercial.*

programming format *(Ch. 15)* The genre of music or other programming style that characterizes and differentiates radio stations from each other (i.e. contemporary hit radio, country, rock, etc.).

program rating *(Ch. 15)* The percentage of TV households in an area that are tuned in to a specific program.

projective techniques *(Ch. 6)* In marketing research, asking indirect questions or otherwise involving consumers in a situation where they can express feelings about the problem or product. The purpose is to get an understanding of people's underlying or subconscious feelings, attitudes, opinions, needs, and motives.

promotion element *(Ch. 7)* The aspect of the marketing mix that consists of marketing communications between seller and buyer.

proof copy *(Ch. 14)* A copy of the completed advertisement that is used to check for final errors and corrections.

prospective customers *(Ch. 4)* People who are about to make an exchange or are considering it.

provocative headline *(Ch. 12)* A type of headline written to provoke the reader's curiosity so that, to learn more, the reader will read the body copy.

psychographics *(Ch. 5)* The grouping of consumers into market segments on the basis of psychological makeup—values, attitudes, personality, and lifestyle.

psychographic segmentation *(Ch. 5)* Method of defining consumer markets based on psychological variables including values, attitudes, personality, and lifestyle.

psychological screens *(Ch. 4)* The perceptual screens consumers use to evaluate, filter, and personalize information according to subjective standards, primarily emotions and personality.

public affairs *(Ch. 10)* All activities related to the community citizenship of an organization, including dealing with community officials and working with regulatory bodies and legislative groups.

publicity *(Ch. 5, 10)* The generation of news about a person, product, or service that appears in broadcast or print media.

public notices *(Ch. 14)* For a nominal fee, newspapers carry these legal changes in business, personal relationships, public governmental reports, notices by private citizens and organizations, and financial reports.

public relations *(Ch. 10)* The management function that focuses on the relationships and communications that individuals and organizations have with other groups (called publics) for the purpose of creating mutual goodwill. The primary role of public relations is to manage a company's reputation and help build public consent for its enterprises.

public relations activities *(Ch. 1)* Publicity, press agentry, sponsorships, special events, and public relations advertising used to create public awareness and credibility—at low cost—for the firm.

public relations advertising *(Ch. 10)* Advertising that attempts to improve a company's relationship with its publics (labor, government, customers, suppliers, etc.).

publics *(Ch. 10)* In PR terminology, employees, customers, stockholders, competitors, suppliers, or general population of customers are all considered one of the organization's publics.

public service announcements (PSAs) *(Ch. 3)* The time and space of ads on TV, radio, newspapers, magazines, and outdoor and transit media that are donated by the media as a public service.

puffery *(Ch. 9)* Exaggerated, subjective claims that can't be proven true or false such as "the best," "premier," or "the only way to fly."

pull strategy *(Ch. 5, 9)* Marketing, advertising, and sales promotion activities aimed at inducing trial purchase and repurchase by consumers.

pulsing *(Ch. 8)* Mixing continuity and flighting strategies in media scheduling.

purchase occasion *(Ch. 5)* A method of segmenting markets on the basis of *when* consumers buy and use a good or service.

push money (PM) *(Ch. 9)* A monetary inducement for retail salespeople to push the sale of particular products. Also called *spiffs*.

push strategy *(Ch. 5, 9)* Marketing, advertising, and sales promotion activities aimed at getting products into the dealer pipeline and accelerating sales by offering inducements to dealers, retailers, and salespeople. Inducements might include introductory price allowances, distribution allowances, and advertising dollar allowances to stock the product and set up displays.

push technology *(Ch. 16)* Information and news services, which are automatically updated over time, that are transmitted by request to a computer user. The service is often provided for free because it is accompanied by advertising.

qualitative research *(Ch. 6)* Research which tries to determine market variables according to unquantifiable criteria such as attitudes, beliefs, and lifestyle.

quantitative research *(Ch. 6)* Research which tries to determine market variables according to reliable, hard statistics about specific market conditions or situations.

question headline *(Ch. 12)* A type of headline that asks the reader a question.

radio personality *(Ch. 12)* A disc jockey or talk show host.

random probability samples *(Ch. 6)* A sampling method in which every unit in the population universe is given an equal chance of being selected for the research.

rate base *(Ch. 14)* With magazines, the circulation figure on which the publisher bases its rates.

rate card *(Ch. 14)* A printed information form listing a publication's advertising rates, mechanical and copy requirements, advertising deadlines, and other information the advertiser needs to know before placing an order.

rating *(Ch. 8)* The percentage of homes or individuals exposed to an advertising medium.

rating services *(Ch. 15)* These services measure the program audiences of TV and radio stations for advertisers and broadcasters by picking a representative sample of the market and furnishing data on the size and characteristics of the viewers or listeners.

rational appeal *(Ch. 11)* Marketing appeals that are directed at the consumer's practical, functional need for the product or service.

reach *(Ch. 8)* The total number of *different* people or households exposed to an advertising schedule during a given time, usually four weeks. Reach measures the *unduplicated* extent of audience exposure to a media vehicle and may be expressed either as a percentage of the total market or as a raw number.

readers per copy (RPC) *(Ch. 8)* Variable used to determine the total reach of a given print medium. RPC is multiplied by the number of vendor and subscription sales to determine the total audience size.

reading notice *(Ch. 14)* A variation of a display ad designed to look like editorial matter. It is sometimes charged at a higher space rate than normal display advertising, and the law requires that the word *advertisement* appear at the top.

rebates *(Ch. 9)* Larger cash refunds on items from cars to household appliances.

recall tests *(Ch. 6)* Posttesting methods used to determine the extent to which an advertisement and its message have been noticed, read, or watched.

receiver *(Ch. 1)* In oral communication, this party decodes the message to understand it and responds by formulating a new idea, encodes it, and sends it back.

recency planning *(Ch. 8)* Erwin Ephron's theory that most advertising works by influencing the brand choice of consumers who are ready to buy, suggesting that continuity of advertising is most important.

recruitment advertising *(Ch. 10)* A special type of advertising, most frequently found in the classified sections of daily newspapers and typically the responsibility of a personnel department aimed at attracting employment applications.

reference groups *(Ch. 4)* People we try to emulate or whose approval concerns us.

refunds *(Ch. 15)* Offers from companies in the form of cash or coupons that can be applied to future purchases of the product.

regional advertiser *(Ch. 3)* Companies that operate in one part of the country and market exclusively to that region.

regional advertising *(Ch. 1, 3)* Advertising used by companies that market their products, goods, or services in a limited geographic region.

regional agency *(Ch. 3)* Advertising agency that focuses on the production and placement of advertising suitable for regional campaigns.

regional publications *(Ch. 14)* Magazines targeted to a specific area of the country, such as the West or the South.

regular price-line advertising *(Ch. 1, 3)* A type of retail advertising designed to inform consumers about the services available or the wide selection and quality of merchandise offered at regular prices.

relationship marketing *(Ch. 7, 9)* Creating, maintaining, and enhancing long-term relationships with customers and other stakeholders that result in exchanges of information and other things of mutual value.

reliability *(Ch. 6)* An important characteristic of research test results. For a test to be reliable, it must be repeatable, producing the same result each time it is administered.

reputation management *(Ch. 10)* In public relations, the name of the long-term strategic process to manage the standing of the firm with various publics.

reseller markets *(Ch. 1, 4, 5)* Individuals or companies that buy products for the purpose of reselling them.

residual fee *(Ch. 13)* Payment to the talent if the commercial is extended beyond its initially contracted run.

retail advertising *(Ch. 1)* Advertising sponsored by retail stores and businesses.

retainer method *(Ch. 3)* See *straight-fee method.*

reverse knockout *(Ch. 13)* Area within a field of printed color on a page that is free of ink and allows the paper's surface to show.

RFM formula *(Ch. 9)* The RFM formula is a mathematical model that provides marketers with a method to determine the most reliable customers in a company's database, according to Recency, Frequency, and Monetary variables.

roadblocking *(Ch. 8)* Buying simultaneous air time on all four television networks.

ROP advertising rates *(Ch. 14)* Run of paper. A term referring to a newspaper's normal discretionary right to place a given ad on any page or in any position it desires—in other words, where space permits. Most newspapers make an effort to place an ad in the position requested by the advertiser.

rough *(Ch. 12)* Penciled sketch of a proposed design or layout.

run of paper *(Ch. 14)* See *ROP advertising rates.*

run of station (ROS) *(Ch. 15)* Leaving placement of radio spots up to the station in order to achieve a lower ad rate.

sale advertising *(Ch. 3)* A type of retail advertising designed to stimulate the movement of particular merchandise or generally increase store traffic by placing the emphasis on special reduced prices.

sales letters *(Ch. 16)* The most common form of direct mail. Sales letters may be typewritten, typeset and printed, printed with a computer insert (such as your name), or fully computer typed.

sales promotion *(Ch. 1, 5, 9)* A direct inducement offering extra incentives all along the marketing route—from manufacturers through distribution channels to customers—to accelerate the movement of the product from the producer to the consumer.

sales promotion department *(Ch. 3)* In larger agencies, a staff to produce dealer ads, window posters, point-of-purchase displays, and dealer sales material.

sales-target objectives *(Ch. 7)* Marketing objectives that relate to a company's sales. They should be specific as to product and market, quantified as to time and amount, and realistic. They may be expressed in terms of total sales volume; sales by product, market segment, or customer type; market share; growth rate of sales volume; or gross profit.

sales test *(Ch. 6)* A useful measure of advertising effectiveness when advertising is the dominant element, or the only variable, in the company's marketing plan. Sales tests are more suited for gauging the effectiveness of campaigns than of individual ads or components of ads.

sample *(Ch. 6)* A portion of the population selected by market researchers to represent the appropriate targeted population. Also, a free trial of a product.

sample unit *(Ch. 6)* The actual individuals chosen to be surveyed or studied.

sampling *(Ch. 9)* Offering consumers a free trial of the product, hoping to convert them to habitual use.

sans serif *(Ch. 13)* A type group that is characterized by a lack of serifs.

SAU *(Ch. 14)* See *standard advertising unit.*

scale *(Ch. 13)* The regular charge for talent and music agreed to in the union contract.

script *(Ch. 13)* Format for radio and television copywriting resembling a two-column list showing dialog and/or visuals.

seal *(Ch. 12)* A type of certification mark offered by such organizations as the Good Housekeeping Institute and Underwriters' Laboratories when a product meets standards established by these institutions. Seals provide an independent, valued endorsement for the advertised product.

search engine *(Ch. 16)* Web sites that are devoted to finding and retrieving requested information from the World Wide Web. Because search engines are the gatekeepers to information on the Internet they are extremely popular with advertisers.

secondary data *(Ch. 6)* Information that has previously been collected or published.

secondary (pass-along) readership *(Ch. 14)* The number of people who read a publication in addition to the primary purchasers.

selective demand *(Ch. 5)* Consumer demand for the particular advantages of one brand over another.

selective distribution *(Ch. 5)* Strategy of limiting the distribution of a product to select outlets in order to reduce distribution and promotion costs.

selective perception *(Ch. 4)* The ability of humans to select from the many sensations bombarding their central processing unit those sensations that fit well with their current or previous experiences, needs, desires, attitudes, and beliefs, focusing attention on some things and ignoring others.

self-concept *(Ch. 4)* The images we carry in our minds of the type of person we are and who we desire to be.

self-interest *(Ch. 1, 2)* One of the four basic premises of free-market economics. People and organizations tend to act in their own self interest. They always want more—for less. Therefore, open competition between self-interested sellers advertising to self-interested buyers naturally leads to greater product availability at more competitive prices.

self-mailer *(Ch. 16)* Any type of direct-mail piece that can travel by mail without an envelope. Usually folded and secured by a staple or a seal, self-mailers have a special blank space for the prospect's name and address.

serif *(Ch. 13)* The most popular type group that is distinguished by smaller lines or tails called serifs that finish the ends of the main character strokes and by variations in the thickness of the strokes.

service provider *(Ch. 16)* One way of gaining access to the Internet is by signing on directly with a basic service provider.

services *(Ch. 1, 5)* A bundle of benefits that may or may not be physical, that are temporary in nature, and that come from the completion of a task.

session *(Ch. 13)* The time when the recording and mixing of a radio commercial takes place.

share-of-market/share-of-voice method *(Ch. 7)* A method of allocating advertising funds based on determining the firm's goals for a certain share of the market and then applying a slightly higher percentage of industry advertising dollars to the firm's budget.

shoppers *(Ch. 3)* Weekly local ad vehicles that may or may not contain editorial matter. They can be segmented into highly selected market areas.

short rate *(Ch. 14)* The rate charged to advertisers who, during the year, fail to fulfill the amount of space for which they have contracted. This is computed by determining the difference between the standard rate for the lines run and the discount rate contracted.

short-term manipulative arguments *(Ch. 2)* Criticisms of advertising that focus on the style of advertising (e.g., that it is manipulative or deceptive).

showing *(Ch. 17)* A traditional term referring to the relative number of outdoor posters used during a contract period, indicating the intensity of market coverage. For example, a 100 showing provides an even and thorough coverage of the entire market.

SIC codes *(Ch. 5)* See *Standard Industrial Classification codes.*

signature cut *(Ch. 12)* See *logotype.*

Simmons Market Research Bureau (SMRB) *(Ch. 14)* A syndicated research organization that publishes magazine readership studies.

singular ethical concepts *(Ch. 2)* A level of ethics such as duty, integrity, truth, empathy, good, bad, right, wrong.

situation analysis *(Ch. 7)* A factual statement of the organization's current situation and how it got there. It includes relevant facts about the company's history, growth, products and services, sales volume, share of market, competitive status, market served, distribution system, past advertising programs, results of market research studies, company capabilities, and strengths and weaknesses.

slice-of-life *(Ch. 12)* A type of commercial consisting of a dramatization of a real-life situation in which the product is tried and becomes the solution to a problem.

slogan *(Ch. 12)* A standard company statement (also called a *tag line* or a *theme line*) for advertisements, salespeople, and company employees. Slogans have two basic purposes: to provide continuity for a campaign and to reduce a key theme or idea to a brief, memorable positioning statement.

slotting allowances *(Ch. 9)* Fees that manufacturers pay to retailers for the privilege of obtaining shelf or floor space for a new product.

smart cards *(Ch. 9)* Frequent-shopper cards, issued by supermarkets and retail chains, that are used for electronic couponing and other purposes.

social classes *(Ch. 4)* Traditional divisions in societies by sociologists—upper, upper-middle, lower-middle, and so on—who believed that people in the same social class tended toward similar attitudes, status symbols, and spending patterns.

social responsibility *(Ch. 2)* Acting in accordance to what society views as best for the welfare of people in general or for a specific community of people.

source *(Ch. 1)* In oral communication, this party formulates the idea, encodes it as a message, and sends it via some channel to the receiver.

special effects *(Ch. 13)* Unusual visual effects created for commercials.

special events *(Ch. 5, 10)* Scheduled meetings, parties, and demonstrations aimed at creating awareness and understanding for a product or company.

specialty items *(Ch. 17)* An advertising, sales promotion, and motivational communication medium that employs useful articles of merchandise imprinted with the advertiser's name, message, or logo.

spectaculars *(Ch. 17)* Giant electronic signs that usually incorporate movement, color, and flashy graphics to grab the attention of viewers in high-traffic areas.

speculative presentation *(Ch. 3)* An agency's presentation of the advertisement it proposes using in the event it is hired. It is usually made at the request of a prospective client and is often not paid for by the client.

speechwriting *(Ch. 10)* Function of a public relations practitioner to write speeches for stockholder meetings, conferences, conventions, etc.

spiff *(Ch. 9)* See *push money.*

spillover media *(Ch. 8)* Foreign media aimed at a national population that are inadvertently received by a substantial number of the consumers in a neighboring country.

split runs *(Ch. 14)* A feature of many newspapers (and magazines) that allows advertisers to test the comparative effectiveness of two different advertising approaches by running two different ads of identical size, but different content, in the same or different press runs on the same day.

sponsor *(Ch. 1)* The company or organization ultimately responsible for the message and distribution of an advertisement. Although the sponsor is often not the author, the sponsor typically pays for the creation of the ad and its distribution.

sponsorial consumers *(Ch. 1)* A group of decision makers at the sponsor's company or organization who decide if an ad will run or not, typically composed of executives and managers who have the responsibility for approving and funding a campaign.

sponsorship *(Ch. 1, 10, 15, 16)* The presentation of a radio or TV program, or an event, or even a Web site by a sole advertiser. The advertiser is often responsible for the program content and the cost of production as well as the advertising. This is generally so costly that single sponsorships are usually limited to TV specials.

spot announcements *(Ch. 13, 15)* An individual commercial message run between programs but having no relationship to either. Spots may be sold nationally or locally. They must be purchased by contacting individual stations directly.

spot radio *(Ch. 15)* National advertisers' purchase of airtime on individual stations. Buying spot radio affords advertisers great flexibility in their choice of markets, stations, airtime, and copy.

SRDS *(Ch. 14)* See *Standard Rate and Data Service.*

stakeholders *(Ch. 7)* In relationship marketing, customers, employees, centers of influence, stockholders, the financial community, and the press. Different stakeholders require different types of relationships.

standard advertising unit (SAU) *(Ch. 14)* A system of standardized newspaper advertisement sizes that can be accepted by all standard-sized newspapers without consideration of their precise format or page size. This system allows advertisers to prepare one advertisement in a particular size or SAU and place it in various newspapers regardless of the format.

Standard Industrial Classification (SIC) codes *(Ch. 5)* Method used by the U.S. Department of Commerce to classify all businesses. The SIC codes are based on broad industry groups, which are then subdivided into major groups, subgroups, and detailed groups of firms in similar lines of business.

standardized outdoor advertising *(Ch. 17)* Specialized system of outdoor advertising structures located scientifically to deliver an advertiser's message to an entire market.

Standard Rate and Data Service (SRDS) *(Ch. 14)* A publisher of media information directories that eliminate the necessity for advertisers and their agencies to obtain rate cards for every publication.

standard-size newspaper *(Ch. 14)* The standard newspaper size, measuring approximately 22 inches deep and 13 inches wide and is divided into six columns.

statement stuffers *(Ch. 16)* Advertisements enclosed in the monthly customer statements mailed by department stores, banks, utilities, or oil companies.

stimulus *(Ch. 4)* Physical data that can be received through the senses.

stock posters *(Ch. 17)* A type of outdoor advertising consisting of ready-made 30-sheet posters, available in any quantity and often featuring the work of first-class artists and lithographers.

storyboard *(Ch. 12)* A sheet preprinted with a series of 8 to 20 blank frames in the shape of TV screens, which includes text of the commercial, sound effects, and camera views.

storyboard roughs *(Ch. 12)* A rough layout of a television commercial in storyboard form.

straight announcement *(Ch. 12)* The oldest type of radio or television commercial, in which an announcer delivers a sales message directly into the microphone or on-camera or does so off-screen while a slide or film is shown on-screen.

straight-fee (retainer) method *(Ch. 3)* A method of compensation for ad agency services in which a straight fee, or *retainer,* is based on a cost-plus-fixed-fees formula. Under this system, the agency estimates the amount of personnel time required by the client, determines the cost of that personnel, and multiples by some factor.

straight-sell copy *(Ch. 12)* A type of body copy in which the text immediately explains or develops the headline and visual in a straight-forward attempt to sell the product.

stripping *(Ch. 13)* Assembling line and halftone negatives into one single negative, which is then used to produce a combination plate.

subculture *(Ch. 4)* A segment within a culture that shares a set of meanings, values, or activities that differ in certain respects from those of the overall culture.

subhead *(Ch. 12)* Secondary headline in advertisements that may appear above or below the headline or in the text of the ad. Subheads are usually set in a type size smaller than the headline but larger than the body copy or text type size. They may also appear in boldface type or in a different ink color.

subliminal advertising *(Ch. 2)* Advertisements with messages (often sexual) supposedly embedded in illustrations just below the threshold of perception.

substantiation *(Ch. 2)* Evidence that backs up cited survey findings or scientific studies that the FTC may request from a suspected advertising violator.

Sunday supplement *(Ch. 14)* A newspaper-distributed Sunday magazine. Sunday supplements are distinct from other sections of the newspaper since they are printed by rotogravure on smoother paper stock.

supers *(Ch. 13)* Words superimposed on the picture in a television commercial.

superstations *(Ch. 15)* Local TV stations that broadcast to the rest of the country via satellite and carry national advertising.

suppliers *(Ch. 3)* People and organizations that assist both advertisers and agencies in the preparation of advertising materials, such as photography, illustration, printing, and production.

survey *(Ch. 6)* A basic method of quantitative research. To get people's opinions, surveys may be conducted in person, by mail, on the telephone, or via the Internet.

sweepstakes *(Ch. 9)* A sales promotion activity in which prizes are offered based on a chance drawing of entrants' names. The purpose is to encourage consumption of the product by creating consumer involvement.

SWOT analysis *(Ch. 7)* An acronym for internal *strengths* and *weaknesses* and external *opportunities* and *threats,* which represent the four categories used by advertising managers when reviewing a marketing plan. The SWOT analysis briefly restates the company's current situation, reviews the target market segments, itemizes the long- and short-term marketing objectives, and cites decisions regarding market positioning and the marketing mix.

syndicated research services *(Ch. 6)* Companies that continuously monitor and publish information on subjects of interest to marketers, such as the reach and effectiveness of media vehicles.

syndication *(Ch. 15)* See *barter syndication, first-run syndication, off-network syndication.*

synergy *(Ch. 8)* An effect achieved when the sum of the parts is greater than that expected from simply adding together the individual components.

tabloid newspaper *(Ch. 14)* A newspaper size generally about half as deep as a standard-sized newspaper; it is usually about 14 inches deep and 11 inches wide.

tactics *(Ch. 7)* The precise details of a company's marketing strategy that determine the specific short-term actions that will be used to achieve its marketing objectives.

tagline *(Ch. 12)* See *slogan.*

take-ones *(Ch. 17)* In transit advertising, pads of business reply cards or coupons, affixed to interior advertisements for an extra charge, that allow passengers to request more detailed information, send in application blanks, or receive some other product benefit.

talent *(Ch. 13)* The actors in commercials.

target audience *(Ch. 1, 7)* The specific group of individuals to whom the advertising message is directed.

target market *(Ch. 5)* The market segment or group within the market segment toward which all marketing activities will be directed.

target marketing process *(Ch. 5)* The sequence of activities aimed at assessing various market segments, designating certain ones as the focus of marketing activities, and designing marketing mixes to communicate with and make sales to these targets.

taxicab exteriors *(Ch. 17)* In transit advertising, internally illuminated, two-sided posters positioned on the roofs of taxis. Some advertising also appears on the doors or rear.

tearsheets *(Ch. 14)* The printed ad cut out and sent by the publisher to the advertiser as a proof of the ad's print quality and that it was published.

technical *(Ch. 11)* One of the three components of message strategy, it refers to the preferred execution approach and mechanical outcome including budget and scheduling limitations

telemarketing *(Ch. 5, 9)* Selling products and services by using the telephone to contact prospective customers.

telephone sales *(Ch. 5, 9)* See *telemarketing*.

teleprompter *(Ch. 13)* A two-way mirror mounted on the front of a studio video camera that reflects moving text to be read by the speaker being taped.

television households (TVHH) *(Ch. 8)* Households with TV sets.

terminal posters *(Ch. 17)* One-sheet, two-sheet, and three-sheet posters in many bus, subway, and commuter train stations as well as in major train and airline terminals. They are usually custom designed and include such attention getters as floor displays, island showcases, illuminated signs, dioramas (three-dimensional scenes), and clocks with special lighting and moving messages.

termination stage *(Ch. 3)* The ending of a client-agency relationship.

testimonial *(Ch. 2, 12)* The use of satisfied customers and celebrities to endorse a product in advertising.

test market *(Ch. 6)* An isolated geographic area used to introduce and test the effectiveness of a product, ad campaign, or promotional campaign, prior to a national rollout.

text *(Ch. 12)* See *body copy*.

text paper *(Ch. 13)* Range of less expensive papers that are lightweight. More porous versions are used in printing newspapers and finer, glossier versions are used for quality printed materials like magazines and brochures.

text type *(Ch. 12)* The smaller type used in the body copy of an advertisement.

theme line *(Ch. 12)* See *slogan*.

theory of cognitive dissonance *(Ch. 4)* The theory that people try to justify their behavior by reducing the degree to which their impressions or beliefs are inconsistent with reality.

30-sheet poster panel *(Ch. 17)* The basic outdoor advertising structure; it consists of blank panels with a standardized size and border. Its message is first printed on large sheets of paper and then mounted by hand on the panel.

3-D ads *(Ch. 14)* Magazine ads requiring the use of 3-D glasses.

thumbnail *(Ch. 12)* A rough, rapidly produced pencil sketch that is used for trying out ideas.

top-down marketing plan *(Ch. 7)* The traditional planning process with four main elements: situation analysis, marketing objectives, marketing strategy, and tactics or action programs.

total audience *(Ch. 15)* The total number of homes reached by some portion of a TV program. This figure is normally broken down to determine the distribution of audience into demographic categories.

total audience plan (TAP) *(Ch. 15)* A radio advertising package rate that guarantees a certain percentage of spots in the better dayparts.

total bus *(Ch. 17)* A special transit advertising buy that covers the entire exterior of a bus, including the front, rear, sides, and top.

total market coverage (TMC) *(Ch. 3)* A free advertising vehicle delivered weekly to 100 percent of residents in a newspaper's market area.

trade advertising *(Ch. 1)* The advertising of goods and services to middlemen to stimulate wholesalers and retailers to buy goods for resale to their customers or for use in their own businesses.

trade concentration *(Ch. 9)* More products being sold by fewer retailers.

trade deals *(Ch. 9)* Short-term dealer discounts on the cost of a product or other dollar inducements to sell a product.

trademark *(Ch. 2)* Any word, name, symbol, device, or any combination thereof adopted and used by manufacturers or merchants to identify their goods and distinguish them from those manufactured or sold by others.

trade promotions *(Ch. 9)* See *push strategy*.

trade shows *(Ch. 17)* Exhibitions where manufacturers, dealers, and buyers of an industry's products can get together for demonstrations and discussion; expose new products, literature, and samples to customers; and meet potential new dealers for their products.

transformational motives *(Ch. 4, 11)* Positively originated motives that promise to "transform" the consumer through sensory gratification, intellectual stimulation, and social approval. Also called *reward motives*.

transit advertising *(Ch. 3, 17)* An out-of-home medium that actually includes three separate media forms: inside cards; outside posters; and station, platform, and terminal posters.

transit shelter advertising *(Ch. 17)* A newer form of out-of-home media, where advertisers can buy space on bus shelters and on the backs of bus-stop seats.

transnational markets *(Ch. 4)* Consumer, business, and government markets located in foreign countries.

trap *(Ch. 13)* Where, in the printing process, one color overlays the edge of another to keep the paper from showing through.

trial close *(Ch. 12)* In ad copy, requests for the order that are made before the close in the ad.

TV households (TVHH) *(Ch. 15)* The number of households in a market area that own television sets.

type families *(Ch. 13)* Related typefaces in which the basic design remains the same but in which variations occur in the proportion, weight, and slant of the characters. Variations commonly include light, medium, bold, extra bold, condensed, extended, and italic.

typography *(Ch. 13)* The art of selecting, setting, and arranging type.

UHF (ultrahigh frequency) *(Ch. 15)* Television channels 14 through 83; about half of the U.S. commercial TV stations are UHF.

unfair advertising *(Ch. 2)* According to the FTC, advertising that causes a consumer to be "unjustifiably injured" or that violates public policy.

Universal Product Code (UPC) *(Ch. 6)* An identifying series of vertical bars with a 12-digit number that adorns every consumer packaged good.

universe *(Ch. 6)* An entire target population.

usage rates *(Ch. 5)* The extent to which consumers use a product: light, medium, or heavy.

user status *(Ch. 5)* Six categories into which consumers can be placed, which reflect varying degrees of loyalties to certain brands and products. The categories are *sole users, semisole users, discount users, aware nontriers, trial/rejectors,* and *repertoire users.*

USP *(Ch. 1)* The unique selling proposition, or the differentiating features, of every product advertised; a concept developed by Rosser Reeves of the Ted Bates advertising agency.

U.S. Patent and Trademark Office *(Ch. 2)* Bureau within the U.S. Department of Commerce that registers and protects patents and trademarks.

utility *(Ch. 4)* A product's ability to provide both symbolic or psychological want satisfaction and functional satisfaction. A product's problem-solving potential may include form, time, place, or possession utility.

validity *(Ch. 6)* An important characteristic of a research test. For a test to be valid, it must reflect the true status of the market.

value-based thinking *(Ch. 11)* A style of thinking where decisions are based on intuition, values, and ethical judgments.

Values and Lifestyles™ (VALS) *(Ch. 5)* A psychographic typology for segmenting U.S. consumers and predicting their purchase behavior.

venue marketing *(Ch. 10)* A form of sponsorship that links a sponsor to a physical site such as a stadium, arena, auditorium, or racetrack..

verbal *(Ch. 11)* Words, written or spoken.

vertical cooperative advertising *(Ch. 3)* Co-op advertising in which the manufacturer provides the ad and pays a percentage of the cost of placement.

vertical marketing system (VMS) *(Ch. 5)* A centrally programmed and managed system that supplies or otherwise serves a group of stores or other businesses.

vertical publications *(Ch. 14)* Business publications aimed at people within a specific industry; for example, Restaurants & Institutions.

VHF (very high frequency) *(Ch. 15)* Television channels 2 through 13; about half of the U.S. commercial TV stations are VHF.

video brochure *(Ch. 17)* A type of video advertising which advertises the product and is mailed to customers and prospects.

video news release (VNR) *(Ch. 10)* A news or feature story prepared in video form and offered free to TV stations.

visualization *(Ch. 11)* The creative point in advertising where the search for the "big idea" takes place. It includes the task of analyzing the problem, assembling any and all pertinent information, and developing some verbal or visual concept of how to communicate what needs to be said.

visuals *(Ch. 12)* All of the picture elements that are placed into an advertisement.

voice-over *(Ch. 12)* In television advertising, the spoken copy or dialog delivered by an announcer who is not seen but whose voice is heard.

volume discount *(Ch. 14)* Discounts given to advertisers for purchasing print space or broadcast time in bulk quantities.

volume segmentation *(Ch. 5)* Defining consumers as light, medium, or heavy users of products.

wants *(Ch. 4)* Needs learned during a person's lifetime.

warrior role *(Ch. 11)* A role in the creative process that overcomes excuses, idea killers, setbacks, and obstacles to bring a creative concept to realization.

Web browser *(Ch. 16)* Computer program that provides computer users with a graphical interface to the Internet.

Web design house *(Ch. 3)* Art/computer studios that employ specialists who understand the intricacies of HTML and Java programming languages and can design ads and Internet Web pages that are both effective and cost efficient.

Web page *(Ch. 16)* A single page out of an online publication of the World Wide Web, known as a Web site. Web sites are made up of one or more Web pages and allow individuals or companies to provide information and services with the public through the Internet.

Web site *(Ch. 16)* On the Internet, a place where a company or organization is located.

WebTV *(Ch. 16)* A developing technology which allows users to browse the World Wide Web through a television set.

weekly newspapers *(Ch. 14)* Newspapers that are published once a week and characteristically serve readers in small urban or suburban areas or farm communities with exclusive emphasis on local news and advertising.

word-count method *(Ch. 13)* A method of copy casting in which all the words in the copy are counted and then divided by the number of words per square inch that can be set in a particular type style and size, as given in a standard table.

work print *(Ch. 13)* The first visual portion of a filmed commercial assembled without the extra effects or dissolves, titles, or supers. At this time, scenes may be substituted, music and sound effects added, or other changes made.

World Wide Web (WWW) *(Ch. 16)* One section of the Internet where advertisers use online services as an advertising medium.

writing paper *(Ch. 13)* Form of plain, lightweight paper commonly used for printing fliers and for letterhead.

End **Notes**

Chapter One

1. Adapted with permission from Catherine Merlo, *Heritage of Gold: The First 100 Years of Sunkist Growers, Inc., 1893–1993* (Sherman Oaks, CA: Sunkist Growers, Inc., 1993), pp. 3–58.

2. John McDonough, "FCB: From One-Man Fiefdom to Global Powerhouse," *Advertising Age,* Commemorative Section: "FCB at 120," December 13, 1993, p. F-4.

3. Communication process adapted from J. Paul Peter and Jerry C. Olsen, *Understanding Consumer Behavior* (Burr Ridge, IL: Richard D. Irwin, 1994), p. 184.

4. Barbara B. Stern, "A Revised Communication Model for Advertising: Multiple Dimensions of the Source, the Message, and the Recipient," *Journal of Advertising,* June 1994, pp. 5–15.

5. Adapted from American Marketing Association definition of marketing; see "AMA Board Approves New Marketing Definition," *Marketing News,* March 1, 1985, p. 1.

6. Tom Duncan and Sandra Moriarty, *Driving Brand Value* (New York: McGraw-Hill, 1997), pp. 69–94.

7. William O'Barr, address to the Council on Advertising History, Duke University, March 12, 1993, reported in *Advertising in America: Using Its Past, Enriching Its Future* (Washington, DC: Center for Advertising History of the National Museum of American History, 1994), p. 6.

8. Russell L. Hanlin, president, Sunkist Growers, Inc., "View from the Client Side," *Advertising Age,* Commemorative Section: "FCB at 120," December 13, 1993, p. F-10.

9. Ibid.

10. Helen Berman, "The Advertising/Trade Show Partnership," *Folio: The Magazine for Magazine Management,* May 1, 1995, pp. 44–47.

11. Some material in this section has been adapted from Hugh M. Cannon, *Course Packet for Advertising Management,* Fall 1996, Wayne State University.

12. John McDonough, "FCB: From One-Man Fiefdom to Global Powerhouse," pp. F-4–F-5.

13. Leonard L. Bartlett, "Three Giants—Leo Burnett, David Ogilvy, William Bernbach: An Exploration of the Impact of the Founders' Written Communications on the Destinies of Their Advertising Agencies," paper presented to the annual meeting of the Association for Education in Journalism and Mass Communication, Kansas City, August 13, 1993.

14. Marcel Bleustein-Blanchet, *La Rage de Convaincre* (Paris: Editions Robert Laffont, 1970), pp. 307–10, 375; Jean-Marc Schwarz, "A Brief History of Ad Time," *Adweek,* February 14, 1994, p. 46.

15. Jean-Marc Schwarz, "A Brief History of Ad Time."

16. Ibid.

17. Ibid.

18. Ibid.

19. Hugh M. Cannon, *Course Packet for Advertising Management.*

20. Warren Berger, "Chaos on Madison Avenue," *Los Angeles Times Magazine,* June 5, 1994, p. 14.

21. William F. Arens and Jack J. Whidden, "La Publicité aux Etats-Unis: Les Symptômes et les Stratégies d'une Industrie Surpeuplée," *L'Industrie de la Publicité au Québec* (Montreal: Le Publicité Club de Montréal, 1992), pp. 383–84.

22. Warren Berger, "Chaos on Madison Avenue," pp. 12, 14.

23. Debra Goldman, "Study: Advertisers Aren't Talking to Consumers," *Adweek,* August 27, 1990, p. 25.

24. Hank Seiden, *Advertising Pure and Simple, The New Edition* (New York: AMACOM, 1990), pp. 23, 47, 57.

25. R. Craig Endicott, "100 Leading National Advertisers: Brand Building Revs Up Ad Spending by 5.2% to Record $137.9 Billion," *Advertising Age,* September 28, 1994, pp. 2–3; "National Ad Spending by Media," *Advertising Age,* September 28, 1994, p. 72; Robert Coen, McCann-Erickson, 1995.

26. Tom Cuniff, "The Second Creative Revolution," *Advertising Age,* December 6, 1993, p. 22.

27. Kevin Goldman, "U.S. Ad Spending Is Expected to Jump," *The Wall Street Journal,* June 14, 1995, p.B16.

28. M. H. Moore, "Global Ad Trends Set Stage for '94," *Adweek,* January 3, 1994, p. 13.

29. John McManus, "Cable Proves It's Media's Live Wire," *Advertising Age,* November 26, 1990, p. S6; "Media & Measurement Technologies (Part 1)," *Direct Marketing,* March 1991, pp. 21–27, 79.

30. Clinton Wilder, "Interactive Ads," *Information Week,* October 3, 1994, p. 25.

31. Tom Cuniff, "The Second Creative Revolution."

32. Brad Lynch, address to the Council on Advertising History, Duke University, March 12, 1993, reported in *Advertising in America: Using Its Past, Enriching Its Future,* p. 3.

Chapter Two

1. Maya Stowe, "Say It with Sex: Calvin Klein's Advertising Campaigns Are Art," *The College Hill Independent,* November 16, 1995.

2. Kevin Goldman, "Klein Halts Jeans Ad Campaign," *The Wall Street Journal,* August 25, 1995, p. B5.

3. Carolyn Christenson, "Calvin Klein Ads: Art or Pornography?" *The Bucknellian Online,* September 14, 1995.

4. John O'Toole, *The Trouble with Advertising* (New York: Times Books, 1985), pp. 7–14.

5. Marcel Bleustein-Blanchet, *La Rage de Convaincre* (Paris: Editions Robert Laffont, 1970), p. 25.

6. Ernest Dichter, *Handbook of Consumer Motivations* (New York: McGraw-Hill, 1964), pp. 6, 422–31.

7. Richard E. Kihlstrom and Michael H. Riordan, "Advertising as a Signal," *Journal of Political Economy,* June 1984, pp. 427–50.

8. Ivan Preston, *The Tangled Web They Weave* (Madison, WI: University of Wisconsin Press, 1994), pp. 94–95.

9. John Kenneth Galbraith, "Economics and Advertising: Exercise in Denial," *Advertising Age,* November 9, 1988, pp. 80–84.

10. Fabiana Giacomotti, "European Marketers Keep Up Ad Budgets," *Adweek,* January 24, 1994, pp. 16–17.

11. Michael Schudson, *Advertising, The Uneasy Persuasion: Its Dubious Impact on American Society* (New York: Basic Books, 1984).

12. Ivan Preston, "A New Conception of Deceptiveness," paper presented to the Advertising Division of the Association for Education in Journalism and Mass Communication, August 12, 1993.

13. Ibid.

14. Ivan Preston, *The Tangled Web They Weave,* pp. 185–98.

15. Stuart C. Rogers, "Subliminal Advertising: Grand Scam of the 20th Century," paper presented to the Annual Conference of the American Academy of Advertising, April 10, 1994.

16. Ibid.; Martha Rogers and Kirk H. Smith, "Public Perceptions of Subliminal Advertising," *Journal of Advertising Research,* March/April 1993, p. 10.

17. Andrew Jaffe, "Advertiser, Regulate Thyself," *Adweek,* August 2, 1993, p. 38.

18. Ibid.

19. Ivan Preston, *The Tangled Web They Weave,* p. 164.

20. Kevin Goldman, "TV Promotional Clutter Irks Ad Industry," *The Wall Street Journal,* February 11, 1994, p. B6.

21. "French May Get Second Break," *Advertising Age International,* October 11, 1993, p. I–6.

22. Laurie Freeman, "Ad Group Balks at Rule Change," *Advertising Age International,* October 11, 1993, p. I–6.

23. Steven W. Coldford, "FCC Raises Ad Limit Specter," *Advertising Age,* October 4, 1993, p. 8.

24. Shelly Garcia, "What's Wrong with Being Politically Correct?" *Adweek,* November 15, 1993, p. 62.

25. Adrienne Ward, "What Role Do Ads Play in Racial Tension?" *Advertising Age,* August 10, 1992, pp. 1, 35.

26. Michael L. Klassen, Cynthia R. Jasper, and Anne M. Schwartz, "Men and Women: Images of Their Relationships in Magazine Advertisements," *Journal of Advertising Research,* March/April 1993, pp. 30–39.

27. U.S. Census Bureau, "Employment Status of the Civilian Noninstitutional Population 16 Years and Over by Sex, 1963 to date," 1998 (http://ferret.bls.census.gov/macro/171996/empearn/2_000.htm)

28. John B. Ford and Michael S. LaTour, "Differing Reactions to Female Role Portrayals in Advertising," *Journal of Advertising Research,* September/October 1993, pp. 43–52.

29. Michael L. Klassen, Cynthia R. Jasper, and Anne M. Schwartz, "Men and Women: Images," p. 38.

30. Mark Schone, "Rubbered Out," *Adweek,* July 18, 1994, p. 22.

31. Laurel Wentz and Geoffrey Lee Martin, "Cheaply Made Gore Scores," *Advertising Age,* July 4, 1994, p. 38.

32. Gary Levin, "More Nudity, but Less Sex," *Advertising Age,* November 8, 1993, p. 37.

33. Caity Olson, "Ad Boycott Concern Is Real," *Advertising Age,* June 13, 1994, p. 3.

34. "Dear Mr. President (American Advertising Federation advocacy ad)," *Time,* March 9, 1992, p. 54a.

35. Ivan Preston, *The Tangled Web They Weave,* pp. 94, 127–31.

36. Judith D. Schwartz, "Wal-Mart's 'Green' Campaign to Emphasize Recycling Next," *Adweek's Marketing Week,* February 12, 1990, p. 61.

37. James Maxeiner and Peter Schotthoffer, eds., *Advertising Law in Europe and North America* (Deventer, the Netherlands: Kluwer Law and Taxation Publishers, 1992), pp. 39, 41, p. v; Rein Rijkens, *European Advertising Strategies* (London, Eng.: Cassell, 1992), pp. 201–2.

38. "Last Minute News: U.K. Eyes TV Ban on Tobacco-Sponsored Events," *Advertising Age,* July 11, 1994, p. 44.

39. Karly Preslmayer, "Austria," in James Maxeiner and Peter Schotthoffer, eds., *Advertising Law in Europe and North America.*

40. Peter Schotthoffer, "European Community," in James Maxeiner and Peter Schotthoffer, eds., *Advertising Law in Europe and North America,* p. 89.

41. "Last Minute News: Singapore Condemns Ads with Harmful Values," *Advertising Age,* August 29, 1994, p. 42.

42. "Regulation Briefs: Costa Rica May Soften Pre-clearance Rules," *Advertising Age International,* April 18, 1994, p. I–4.

43. "Last Minute News: China Accepts Taiwanese Ads, after 45-Year Ban," *Advertising Age,* September 5, 1994, p. 38; Sally D. Goll, "Chinese Officials Attempt to Ban False Ad Claims," *The Wall Street Journal,* February 25, 1995, pp. B1, B9.

44. James R. Maxeiner, "United States," in James Maxeiner and Peter Schotthoffer, eds., *Advertising Law in Europe and North America,* p. 321; see also *Virginia State Board of Pharmacy v. Virginia Citizens Consumer Council,* 425 U.S. 748 (1976).

45. Ellen Joan Pollock, "'I Love My Lawyers' Ads May Spread to More States," *The Wall Street Journal,* December 7, 1990, p. B1.

46. See *Central Hudson Gas & Electric Corp. v. Public Service Commission of New York,* 447 U.S. 557 (1980).

47. Kartik Pashupati, "The Camel Controversy: Same Beast, Different Viewpoints," paper presented to the annual conference of the Association for Education in Journalism and Mass Communication, Kansas City, MO, August 11, 1993; James R. Maxeiner, "United States," pp. 321–22.

48. Steven W. Colford, "Big Win for Commercial Speech," *Advertising Age,* March 29, 1993, pp. 1, 47.

49. Steven A. Meyerowitz, "The Developing Law of Comparative Advertising," *Business Marketing,* August 1985, p. 81; *Consumer Reports,* November 1992, p. 687.

50. Eric Gross and Susan Vogt, "Canada," in James Maxeiner and Peter Schotthoffer, eds., *Advertising Law in Europe and North America.*

51. Federal Trade Commission, "Vision, Mission, and Goals," 1997.

52. Minette E. Drumwright, "Ethical Issues in Advertising and Sales Promotion," in N. Craig Smith and John A. Quelch, eds., *Ethics in Marketing* (Burr Ridge, IL: Richard D. Irwin, 1993), p. 610.

53. Daniel S. Levine, "FTC Sues Jenny Craig over Ad Claims," *Adweek,* October 4, 1993, p. 44.

54. Steven W. Colford, "Weight Watchers Plans to Fight FTC Ad Charges," *Advertising Age,* October 4, 1993, p. 2; Jeanne Saddler, "Three Diet Firms Settle False-Ad Case; Two Others Vow to Fight FTC Charges," *The Wall Street Journal,* October 1, 1993, p. B8.

55. John E. Calfee, "FTC's Hidden Weight-Loss Agenda," *Advertising Age,* October 25, 1993, p. 29.

56. "FTC Reaches Settlement with Jenny Craig to End Diet Program Advertising Litigation," FTC News Release, May 29, 1997.

57. "Exxon Settles FTC Charges; Groundbreaking Educational Ad Campaign Ordered," FTC News Release, June 24, 1997.

58. David Riggle, "Say What You Mean, Mean What You Say," *In Business,* May/June 1990, pp. 50–51.

59. Dean Keith Fueroghne, "But the People in Legal Said . . . ," (Burr Ridge, IL: Irwin Professional Publishing, 1989), p. 14.

60. Christy Fisher, "How Congress Broke Unfair Ad Impasse," *Advertising Age,* August 22, 1994, p. 34.

61. "Editorial: A Fair FTC Pact?" *Advertising Age,* March 21, 1994, p. 22.

62. "Crackdown on Testimonials," *The Wall Street Journal,* July 13, 1993, p. B7.

63. Minette E. Drumwright, "Ethical Issues in Advertising and Sales Promotion," pp. 615–16.

64. "Exxon Settles FTC Charges," June 24, 1997.

65. Gross and Vogt, "Canada," pp. 50, 67.

66. "The Food and Drug Administration: An Overview," http://www.fda.gov, September 1997.

67. "The Growing Brouhaha over Drug Advertisements," *New York Times,* May 14, 1989, p. F8.

68. "FDA to Review Standards for All Direct-to-Consumer Rx Drug Promotion," FDA News Release, August 8, 1997.

69. Steven W. Colford, "Labels Lose the Fat," *Advertising Age,* June 10, 1991, pp. 3, 54; Steven W. Colford and Julie Liesse, "FDA Label Plans under Attack," *Advertising Age,* February 24, 1992, pp. 1, 50; John E.

Calfee, "FDA's Ugly Package: Proposed Label Rules Call for Vast Changes," *Advertising Age,* March 16, 1992, p. 25; Pauline M. Ippolito and Alan D. Mathios, "New Food Labeling Regulations and the Flow of Nutrition Information to Consumers," *Journal of Public Policy & Marketing,* Fall 1993, pp. 188–205.

70. John Carey, "The FDA Is Swinging a Sufficiently Large Two-by-Four," *Business Week,* May 27, 1991, p. 44; Steven W. Colford, "FDA Getting Tougher: Seizure of Citrus Hill Is Signal to Marketers," *Advertising Age,* April 29, 1991, pp. 1, 53.

71. Joe Mandese, "Regulation," *Advertising Age,* November 30, 1992, p. 23.

72. "The Experts Speak Out," *TV Guide,* August 22, 1992, p. 19.

73. U.S. Constitution, Article 1, Section 8.

74. U.S. Copyright Office, Library of Congress, 1997.

75. Wayne E. Green, "Lawyers Give Deceptive Trade-Statutes New Day in Court, Wider Interpretations," *The Wall Street Journal,* January 24, 1990, p. B1.

76. Howard Schlossberg, "Marketers Say State Laws Hurt Their 'Green' Efforts," *Marketing News,* November 11, 1991, pp. 8–9.

77. E. J. Gong, "Fraud Complaints on the Rise, Reports D.A.," *Los Angeles Times,* February 13, 1994, p. B1.

78. John O'Dell, "Montgomery Ward to Pay $310,000 in False Ad Suit," *Los Angeles Times,* February 1, 1994, p. D6.

79. James R. Maxeiner, "United States," p. 321.

80. Ibid.

81. Felix H. Kent, "Control of Ads by Private Sector," *New York Law Journal,* December 27, 1985; reprinted in Kent and Stone, eds., *Legal and Business Aspects of the Advertising Industry,* 1986, pp. 20–79.

82. Caleb Solomon, "Gasoline Ads Canceled: Lack of Truth Cited," *The Wall Street Journal,* July 21, 1994, p. B1.

83. James R. Maxeiner, "United States," p. 321; NAD Case Report, National Advertising Division, Council of Better Business Bureaus, January 21, 1991.

84. Public Relations Department, KLBJ, Austin, TX, 1991.

85. Public Relations Department, KDWB, Minneapolis/St. Paul, MN, 1991.

86. Public Relations Department, KSDO, San Diego, CA, 1991.

87. Kevin Goldman, "From Witches to Anorexics, Critical Eyes Scrutinize Ads for Political Correctness," *The Wall Street Journal,* May 19, 1994, p. B1.

88. Shelly Garcia, "What's Wrong with Being Politically Correct?" p. 62.

89. Ibid.

90. Andrew Jaffe, "Advertiser, Regulate Thyself," p. 38.

91. Federal Trade Commission, 1991.

Chapter Three

1. Billie Sutherland, "Rubio's Plans Expansion with Venture Funds," *San Diego Business Journal,* February 27, 1995, pp. 1, 35; personal interview with Ralph Rubio, April 1995.

2. Jim Rowe, "Integrated Marketing Tips? Study Retail Trade," *Advertising Age,* April 4, 1994, p. 32.

3. Henry A. Laskey, J. A. F. Nicholls, and Sydney Roslow, "The Enigma of Cooperative Advertising," *Journal of Business and Industrial Marketing* 8, no. 2, 1993, pp. 70–79.

4. Riccardo A. Davis, "Retailers Open Doors Wide for Co-op," *Advertising Age,* August 1, 1994, p. 30.

5. Bradley Johnson, "Intel Co-op Boost Is Boon for TV, Radio," *Advertising Age,* April 3, 1995, p. 3.

6. "100 Leading National Advertisers: How Top 100 Advertisers Rank—From P&G to Delta," *Advertising Age,* September 28, 1994, p. 54; "100 Leading National Advertisers," *Advertising Age,* September 29, 1997, p. S48.

7. Ibid.

8. William O. Bearden, Thomas N. Ingram, and Raymond W. LaForge, *Marketing Principles & Perspectives* (Burr Ridge, IL; Richard D. Irwin, 1995), p. 96.

9. Bill Saporito, "Behind the Tumult at P&G," *Fortune,* March 7, 1994, pp. 74–82; *Hoover's Handbook Database,* 1994; "100 Leading National Advertisers," *Advertising Age,* September 29, 1997, p. S56.

10. "100 Leading National Advertisers," p. S56.

11. Alan Mitchell, "P&G Drops Old Job Tags in Rejig," *Marketing* (UK), October 14, 1993, p. 4.

12. Aelita G. B. Martinsons and Maris G. Martinsons, "In Search of Structural Excellence," *Leadership & Organization Development Journal,* 15, no. 2, 1994, pp. 24–28.

13. Jennifer Lawrence, "Thinning Ranks at P&G," *Advertising Age,* September 13, 1993, p. 2.

14. William D. Perreault, Jr., and E. Jerome McCarthy, *Basic Marketing,* 12th ed. (Burr Ridge, IL: Irwin/McGraw-Hill, 1996), p. 615.

15. "U.S. Firms with the Biggest Foreign Revenues," *Forbes,* July 23, 1990, p. 362.

16. Eric N. Berkowitz, Roger A. Kerin, Steven W. Hartley, and William Rudelius, *Marketing,* 5th ed. (Burr Ridge, IL: Irwin/McGraw-Hill, 1997), p. 130.

17. Anne Cooper, "Cosmetics: Changing Looks for Changing Attitudes," *Adweek,* February 22, 1993, pp. 30–36.

18. James E. Ellis, "Why Overseas? 'Cause That's Where the Sales Are," *Business Week,* January 10, 1994, p. 63; "How CAA Bottled Coca-Cola," *Fortune,* November 15, 1993, p. 156; Deborah Hauss, "Global Communications Come of Age," *Public Relations Journal,* August 1993, pp. 22–23; Sally Solo, "How to Listen to Consumers," *Fortune,* January 11, 1993, pp. 77–78; Jennifer Lawrence, "Delta Gears Up for Global Fight," *Advertising Age,* August 19, 1991, pp. 3, 44; Charles Hennessy, "Globaldegook," *BusinessLondon,* March 1990, p. 131; Raymond Serafin, "W. B. Doner Hits a Gusher," *Advertising Age,* June 6, 1988, p. 43.

19. Jim Patterson, "Viewpoint: Global Communication Requires a Global Understanding," *Adweek,* October 31, 1994, p. 46; "Efficacy of Global Ad Prospects Is Questioned in Firm's Survey," *The Wall Street Journal,* September 13, 1984, p. 29.

20. Patterson, "Viewpoint: Global Communication Requires a Global Understanding."

21. Aelita G. B. Martinsons and Maris G. Martinsons, "In Search of Structural Excellence."

22. Frederick R. Gamble, *What Advertising Agencies Are—What They Do and How They Do It,* 7th ed. (New York: American Association of Advertising Agencies, 1970), p. 4.

23. "Brands on Trial," *Adweek,* May 24, 1993, pp. 24–31.

24. Melanie Wells, "The Interactive Edge—Part II: Desperately Seeking the Super Highway," *Advertising Age,* August 22, 1994, pp. 14–19.

25. Daniel S. Levine, "Bigger Is Not Always Better, Some in San Francisco Learn," *Adweek,* August 16, 1993, p. 2; Debra Goldman, "Adweek Feature: Think Small," *Adweek,* November 15, 1993, pp. 36–40; "JWT Cranks Up 'Engine Room' Concept," *Adweek,* April 18, 1994, pp. 1, 5; Greg Farrell, "Think Small," *Adweek,* May 9, 1994, p. 20.

26. Bob Garfield, "Coke Ads Great but Not Always," *Advertising Age,* February 15, 1993, pp. 1, 60.

27. Kevin Goldman and Thomas R. King, "Interpublic to Acquire Media Buying Firm," *The Wall Street Journal,* October 31, 1994, p. B8.

28. *Inside the AAAA,* American Association of Advertising Agencies, 1994, p. 5.

29. Ibid., pp. 40–41.

30. Larry Weisberg and Brett Robbs, "Forum: Why Best and Brightest Shun Account Exec Role," *Advertising Age,* June 6, 1994, p. 28.

31. Daniel S. Levine, "For Goodby, Waiting Was the Hardest Part," *Adweek,* Western edition, March 22, 1993, p. 4.

32. Kevin Goldman, "IBM—Account Fight Lifts Planner Profile," *The Wall Street Journal,* October 26, 1993, p. B8.

33. Debra Goldman, "Origin of the Species: Has the Planner Finally Evolved into the Agency's Most Potent Creature?" *Adweek,* April 10, 1995, pp. 28–38; Douglas Atkin, Wells Rich Green, New York, personal interview, June 1995.

34. Betsy Sharkey, "Going Virtual," *Adweek,* May 16, 1994, pp. 29–35.

35. Sally Goll Beatty, "Leo Burnett Group to Decentralize U.S. Operations," *The Wall Street Journal,* September 17, 1997, p. B10; Sally Goll Beatty, "Leo Burnett to Offer Small-Agency Style," *The Wall Street Journal,* September 18, 1997, p. B4; Dottie Enrico, "Ad Agency Ready for a New Day," *USA Today,* September 19, 1997, p. 5B.

36. Alison Fahey, "Agencies Look to Shape Up, Slim Down," *Adweek,* August 16, 1993, p. 4.

37. William F. Arens and Jack J. Whidden, "La Publicité aux Etats-Unis: Les Symptómes et les Stratégies d'une Industrie Surpeuplée," *L'Industrie de la Publicité au Québec* (Montreal: Le Publicité-Club de Montréal, 1992), pp. 383–84.

38. Jon Lafayette and Cleveland Horton, "Shops to Clients: Pay Up—4A's Members Call for an End to Free Services," *Advertising Age,* March 19, 1990, pp. 1, 66.

39. Andrew Jaffe, "Has Leo Burnett Come to the End of the 'Free Overservice' Era?" *Adweek,* December 6, 1993, p. 46; Melanie Wells and Laurel Wentz, "Coke Trims Commissions," *Advertising Age,* January 31, 1994, p. 2.

40. John Micklethwait, "Cut the Ribbon," *The Economist,* June 9, 1990, pp. S16–S17; Tom Eisenhart, "Guaranteed Results' Plan May Suit Business Marketers," *Business Marketing,* July 1990, p. 32; Jim Kirk, "Miller Sets Free Rates," *Adweek,* January 24, 1994, p. 4.

41. "Benetton's Toscani May Quit amid Feud over Creative Control," *The Wall Street Journal,* April 20, 1994, p. B6.

42. James R. Willis, Jr., "Winning New Business: An Analysis of Advertising Agency Activities," *Journal of Advertising Research,* September/October 1992, pp. 10–16.

43. Andrew Jaffe, "The Fine Art of Keeping Clients Happy while Chasing New Business," *Adweek,* May 9, 1994, p. 38.

44. Melanie Wells, "Courtship by Consultant," *Advertising Age,* January 31, 1994, pp. 10–11.

45. Kevin Goldman, "Self-Employed: Agency Puts Ads on TV," *The Wall Street Journal,* November 16, 1993, p. B10.

46. Thorolf Helgesen, "Advertising Awards and Advertising Agency Performance," *Journal of Advertising Research,* July/August 1994, pp. 43–53.

47. Daniel B. Wackman, Charles T. Salmon, and Caryn C. Salmon, "Developing an Advertising Agency/Client Relationship," *Journal of Advertising Research,* December 1986/January 1987, pp. 21–28.

48. Kevin Goldman, "FCB Bumps Ayer as AT&T's Top Agency," *The Wall Street Journal,* November 22, 1994, p. B8.

49. Kevin Goldman, "Ties That Bind Agency, Client Unravel," *The Wall Street Journal,* November 16, 1994, p. B6.

50. Yumiko Ono, "Apple Picks TBWA," *The Wall Street Journal,* August 11, 1997 p. B3.

51. Paul C. Katz, "Getting the Most of Your Advertising Dollars: How to Select and Evaluate an Ad Agency," *Bottomline,* March 1987, pp. 35–38.

52. Steven Raye, "Agencies, Clients: It's Mutual Contribution for Mutual Gain," *Brandweek,* September 12, 1994, p. 20; Ed Moser, "Inside Information," *Adweek,* January 24, 1994, p. 22: Mat Toor, "Fear and Favour in Adland," *Marketing* (UK), November 15, 1990, pp. 30–32.

53. Paul C. N. Mitchell, Harold Cataquet, and Stephen Hague, "Establishing the Causes of Disaffection in Agency/Client Relations," *Journal of Advertising Research,* March/April 1992, pp. 41–48.

54. Isabelle T. D. Szmigin, "Managing Quality in Business-to-Business Services," *European Journal of Marketing,* 27, no. 1, 1993, pp. 5–21.

55. Ron Jackson, "If You Hire a Vendor, You Get a Vendor Mindset," *Marketing News,* April 25, 1991, pp. 13–14.

56. Steven A. Meyerowitz, "Ad Agency Conflicts: The Law and Common Sense," *Business Marketing,* June 1987, p. 16.

57. Andrew Jaffe, "For Agencies, Conflict Taboo Seems Strong as Ever," *Adweek,* January 24, 1994, p. 46.

58. Betsy Sharkey, "New Suit," *Adweek,* June 20, 1994, p. 20.

59. "Good News, Bad News," *Editor & Publisher,* May 3, 1997, p. 18; "Community Papers Circulation Up," *Editor & Publisher,* December 12, 1997 (www.mediainfo.com).

60. Kevin Goldman, "New York Times Campaign Stars Odd Trio," *The Wall Street Journal,* November 28, 1994, p. B7.

61. U.S. Bureau of the Census, *Statistical Abstract of the United States: 1993,* 113th ed. (Washington, DC: U.S. Department of Commerce, 1993), p. 567.

62. Ibid.

63. Sean Savage, "For Firms on Network, Net Gains Can Be Great," *ComputerLink,* Knight-Ridder News Service, November 29, 1994, pp. 3–4.

64. Amy Dockser Marcus, "Advertising Breezes Along the Nile River with Signs for Sails," *The Wall Street Journal,* July 18, 1997, p. A1.

Chapter Four

1. David Lynch, "A $1.2 Billion Debacle: How Prodigy Fell from Envy to Near-Ruin," *USA Today,* May 30, 1996, p. 1B (www.elibrary.com).

2. Ibid.

3. Ibid.

4. Marc Gunther, "The Internet Is Mr. Case's Neighborhood: Techies Hate It, but in Cyberspace America Online Is the Only Brand That Counts," *Fortune,* March 30, 1998 (www.pathfinder.com/fortune/1998).

5. Lynch, "A $1.2 Billion Debacle: How Prodigy Fell from Envy to Near-Ruin," p. 1B.

6. Julie Pitta, "The Cutting Edge: Prodigy Sold to Group Headed by CEO for $200 Million; Online Services: Company's Fortunes Have Slipped in Battle for Members with Competitors AOL and CompuServe," *Los Angeles Times,* May 13, 1996, business section, p. 1 (www.elibrary.com).

7. William D. Perreault, Jr., and E. Jerome McCarthy, *Basic Marketing,* 12th ed. (Burr Ridge, IL: Irwin/McGraw-Hill, 1996), pp. 5–6; Eric N. Berkowitz, Roger A. Kerin, Steven W. Hartley, and William Rudelius, *Marketing,* 5th ed. (Burr Ridge, IL: IrwinMcGraw-Hill, 1997), p. 24.

8. Lisa Brownlee, "'Murphy Brown' Sponsor," *The Wall Street Journal,* October 23, 1997, p. B2.

9. James J. Kellaris, Anthony D. Cox, and Dena Cox, "The Effect of Background Music on Ad Processing: A Contingency Explanation," *Journal of Marketing,* October 1993, pp. 114–25.

10. William O. Bearden, Thomas N. Ingram, Raymond W. LaForge, *Marketing Principles and Perspectives,* 2nd ed. (Burr Ridge, IL: Irwin/McGraw-Hill, 1997), p. 49.

11. "Real Gross Domestic Product," Bureau of Economic Analysis, U.S. Department of Commerce, September 26, 1997.

12. Ibid., p. 127.

13. Eric N. Berkowitz, Roger A. Kerin, Steven W. Hartley, and William Rudelius, *Marketing,* 5th ed. (Burr Ridge, IL: Irwin/McGraw-Hill, 1997), pp. 180–181.

14. Bearden et al., *Marketing Principles and Perspectives,* p. 99.

15. S. Kent Stephan and Barry L. Tannenholz, "The Real Reason for Brand Switching," *Advertising Age,* June 13, 1994, p. 31.

16. "Amazing Numbers," *Personal Selling Power,* September 1994, p. 50.

17. James J. Kellaris, Anthony D. Cox, and Dena Cox, "The Effect of Background Music on Ad Processing," p. 123.

18. Kevin Goldman, "Nestlé Chases Skirts at the Chocolate Bar," *The Wall Street Journal,* April 8, 1993, p. B6.

19. Michael J. McCarthy, "Mind Probe—What Makes an Ad Memorable? Recent Brain Research Yields Surprising Answers," *The Wall Street Journal,* March 22, 1991, p. B3.

20. Al Ries and Jack Trout, *Positioning: The Battle for Your Mind,* rev. ed. (New York: McGraw-Hill, 1986), pp. 30–32.

21. S. Kent Stephan and Barry L. Tannenholz, "The Real Reason for Brand Switching."

22. J. Paul Peter and Jerry C. Olson, *Consumer Behavior and Marketing Strategy,* 4th ed. (Burr Ridge, IL: Richard D. Irwin, 1996), p. 554.

23. R. E. Petty, J. T. Cacioppo, and D. Schumann, "Central and Peripheral Routes to Advertising Effectiveness: The Moderating Role of Involvement," *Journal of Consumer Research* 10, no. 10 (1983), pp. 135–46.

24. This section and the model are adapted from J. Paul Peter and Jerry C. Olson, *Consumer Behavior and Marketing Strategy,* 4th ed., pp. 554–55.

25. Ibid, pp. 556–57.

26. Laura Bird, "Grey Poupon Tones Down Its Tony Image," *The Wall Street Journal,* July 22, 1994, p. B5.

27. Karen A. Machleit, Chris T. Allen, and Thomas J. Madden, "The Mature Brand and Brand Interest: An Alternative Consequence of Ad-Evoked Effect," *Journal of Marketing,* October 1993, pp. 72–82.

28. Ibid.

29. J. Paul Peter and Jerry C. Olson, *Consumer Behavior and Marketing Strategy,* 4th ed., p. 513.

30. Ken Dychtwald and Greg Gable, "Portrait of a Changing Consumer," *Business Horizons,* January/February 1990, pp. 62–74; Larry Light, "Trust Marketing: The Brand Relationship Marketing Mandate for the 90s," address to the American Association of Advertising Agencies annual meeting, Laguna Niguel, CA, April 23, 1993.

31. Colin McDonald, "Point of View: The Key Is to Understand Consumer Response," *Journal of Advertising Research,* September/October 1993, pp. 63–69.

32. William D. Perreault, Jr., and E. Jerome McCarthy, *Basic Marketing,* p. 216.

33. John R. Rossiter and Larry Percy, *Advertising Communications and Promotion Management,* 2nd ed. (New York: McGraw-Hill, 1997), pp. 120–22.

34. Ibid., p. 121.

35. Laura Zinn, "Move Over, Boomers, the Busters Are Here . . . And They're Angry," *Business Week,* December 14, 1992, pp. 74–82; "The Yankelovich Monitor 1992," pp. 20–23; Jeffrey Zaslow, "Children's Search for Values Leading to Shopping Malls," *The Wall Street Journal,* March 13, 1987.

36. "The Worth of the Cool: Asking Teenagers to Identify the Coolest Brands," *Adweek,* May 9, 1994, p. 18.

37. Greg Farrell, "Star Search," *Adweek,* December 6, 1993, p. 26.

38. William D. Perreault, Jr., and E. Jerome McCarthy, *Basic Marketing,* pp. 138–140; J. Paul Peter and Jerry C. Olson, *Consumer Behavior and Marketing Strategy,* p. 368.

39. Carolyn A. Lin, "Cultural Differences in Message Strategies: A Comparison between American and Japanese TV Commercials," *Journal of Advertising Research,* July/August 1993, pp. 40–48.

40. Ibid.

41. Ibid.

42. J. Paul Peter and Jerry C. Olson, *Consumer Behavior and Marketing Strategy,* 4th ed., p. 413.

43. Thomas G. Exter, "Blacks to 2010," *American Demographics,* December 1992, p. 63; John Wall, "Minorities Slice the Advertising Pie," *Insight,* March 9, 1987, pp. 46–47; U.S. Census Bureau, 1991.

44. Betty Parker, "Hispanic-American Consumer Behavior: A Marketing Update," paper delivered to the annual conference of the Association for Education in Journalism and Mass Communication, Kansas City, MO, August 14, 1993.

45. Rebecca Purto, "Global Psychographics," *American Demographics,* December 1990, p. 8.

46. The classic studies on cognitive dissonance were initiated by Leon Festinger, *A Theory of Cognitive Dissonance* (Evanston, IL: Row, Peterson, 1957), p. 83; for more recent views, see Hugh Murray, "Advertising's Effect on Sales—Proven or Just Assumed?" *International Journal of Advertising* (U.K.) 5, no. 1, 1986, pp. 15–36; Hawkins, Best, and Coney, *Consumer Behavior,* pp. 663–65; and Ronald E. Milliman and Phillip J. Decker, "The Use of Post-Purchase Communication to Reduce Dissonance and Improve Direct Marketing Effectiveness," *Journal of Business Communication,* Spring 1990, pp. 159–70.

47. Larry Light, "Advertising's Role in Building Brand Equity," speech to annual meeting of the American Association of Advertising Agencies, April 21, 1993.

Chapter 5

1. Adapted with permission from *Everyone Knows His First Name,* Levi Strauss & Co., 1993; G. Paschal Zachary, "Exporting Rights: Levi Tries to Make Sure Contract Plants in Asia Treat Workers Well," *The Wall Street Journal,* July 28, 1994, pp. A1, A5.

2. S. Kent Stephan and Barry L. Tannenholz, "The Real Reason for Brand Switching," *Advertising Age,* June 13, 1994, p. 31, and "Six Categories That Hold Elusive Consumers," *Advertising Age,* June 20, 1994, p. 32.

3. Values and Lifestyles Program, Descriptive Materials for the VALS2 Segmentation System (Menlo Park, CA: SRI International, 1989).

4. Nancy Ten Kate, "Squeaky Clean Teens," *American Demographics,* January 1995, pp. 42–43.

5. "Weather or Not to Sell," *Personal Selling Power,* September 1994, p. 79.

6. James H. Leigh and Terrance G. Gabel, "Symbolic Interactionism: Its Effects on Consumer Behavior and Implications for Marketing Strategy," *Journal of Consumer Marketing,* Winter 1992, pp. 27–38.

7. Joel S. Dubow, "Occasion-Based vs. User-Based Benefit Segmentation: A Case Study," *Journal of Advertising Research,* March/April 1992, pp. 11–18.

8. Glen Fest, "Suits: Speaking the Language," *Adweek,* October 27, 1997, pp. 25–30; Christy Fisher, "Hispanic Media See Siesta Ending," *Advertising Age,* January 24, 1994, p. S1; Leon E. Wynter, "Minorities Play the Hero in More TV Ads as Clients Discover Multicultural Sells," *The Wall Street Journal,* November 24, 1993, pp. B1, B6; Betty Parker, "Hispanic-American Consumer Behavior: A Marketing Update," paper presented to the annual meeting of the Association for Education in Journalism and Mass Communication, Kansas City, MO, August 14, 1993, p. 8.

9. Leon E. Wynter, "Business and Race: JCPenney Launches Diahann Carroll Line," *The Wall Street Journal,* July 2, 1997, p. B1.

10. Jennifer Foote, "Shhh, It's a Secret: Buick Discovers Untapped Market of Mature Singles," *Chicago Tribune,* May 5, 1994, sec. 6, p. 4.

11. Kathleen Barnes, "Changing Demographics: Middle Class," *Advertising Age International,* October 17, 1994, pp. I–11, I–16.

12. Kevin Goldman, "U.S. Brands Trail Japanese in China Study," *The Wall Street Journal,* February 16, 1995, p. B8.

13. Barnes, "Changing Demographics."

14. Henry Assael and David F. Poltrack, "Can Demographic Profiles of Heavy Users Serve as a Surrogate for Purchase Behavior in Selecting TV Programs?" *Journal of Advertising Research,* January/February 1994, p. 11.

15. Emanuel H. Demby, "Psychographics Revisited: The Birth of a Technique," *Marketing Research: A Magazine of Management & Applications,* Spring 1994, pp. 26–29.

16. Values and Lifestyles Program, Descriptive Materials for the VALS2 Segmentation System.

17. Judith Waldrop, "Markets with Attitude," *American Demographics,* July 1994, pp. 22–32.

18. Lewis C. Winters, "International Psychographics," *Marketing Research: A Magazine of Management & Applications,* September 1992, pp. 48–49; John Garrett, SRI International, personal correspondence, June 1995.

19. For an excellent discussion of major psychographic studies used around the world, see Marieke De Mooij, *Advertising Worldwide,* 2nd ed. (Hertfordshire, UK: Prentice Hall International (UK) Ltd., 1994), pp. 165–90.

20. Winters, "International Psychographics."

21. William D. Perreault, Jr. and E. Jerome McCarthy, *Basic Marketing,* 12th ed. (Burr Ridge, IL: Richard D. Irwin, 1996), pp. 242–68.

22. James Hutton, "A Theoretical Framework for the Study of Brand Equity and a Test of Brand Sensitivity in an Organizational Buying Context," dissertation, University of Texas, Austin, 1993.

23. William D. Perreault, Jr. and E. Jerome McCarthy, *Basic Marketing,* 12th ed., p. 261.

24. U.S. Bureau of the Census, *Statistical Abstract of the United States: 1993,* 113th ed. (Washington, DC: U.S. Department of Commerce, 1993), p. 742.

25. Michael Schrage, "Think Big," *Adweek,* October 11, 1993, p. 25.

26. Perreault and McCarthy, *Basic Marketing,* pp. 48–49, 91–112.

27. Walter van Waterschoot and Christophe Van den Bulte, "The 4P Classification of the Marketing Mix Revisited," *Journal of Marketing,* October 1992, pp. 83–93.

28. The now widely popularized conceptual model of the 4Ps was developed by E. J. McCarthy, *Basic Marketing* (Homewood, IL: Richard D. Irwin, 1960); the usage of the marketing mix derived from Neil H. Borden, "The Concept of the Marketing Mix," *Journal of Advertising Research,* June 1964, pp. 27.

29. Perreault and McCarthy, *Basic Marketing,* pp. 310–21.

30. Gerald Schoenfeld, "Brands Can Flourish—with Lots of Care," *Advertising Age,* October 25, 1993, p. 29.

31. Kevin Goldman, "Stride Rite Puts Keds Account in Review," *The Wall Street Journal,* January 19, 1994, p. B12.

32. Laura Loro, "L'Eggs: Trend Troubles Category and Creates Snag for Leader," *Advertising Age,* October 3, 1994, p. S-14.

33. Adapted from William O. Bearden, Thomas N. Ingram, and Raymond W. LaForge, *Marketing: Principles & Perspectives* (Burr Ridge, IL: Richard D. Irwin, 1995), pp. 211–13, and from Philip Kotler and Gary Armstrong, *Principles of Marketing* (Englewood Cliffs, NJ: Prentice Hall, 1994), pp. 640–43.

34. Hank Seiden, *Advertising Pure and Simple,* new edition (New York: AMACOM, 1990), p. 11.

35. Rance Crain, "What Trout, Ries Have Wrought," *Advertising Age,* June 13, 1994, p. 30.

36. Kevin Goldman, "Xerox Touts Array of Products to Broaden Image Beyond Copiers," *The Wall Street Journal,* April 4, 1994, p. B5.

37. Pat Sabena, "Tough Market for New Products Requires Partnership," *Marketing Review,* June 1996, pp. 12–13.

38. Adrienne Ward Fawcett, "In Glut of New Products, 'Different' Becomes Key," *Advertising Age,* December 13, 1993, p. 28.

39. Hank Seiden, *Advertising Pure and Simple,* pp. 23–30; Robert Pritikin, *Pritikin's Testament* (Englewood Cliffs, NJ: Prentice Hall, 1991), pp. 25–33.

40. Kevin Goldman, "Ads Seek to Make Iced Tea the Hot Drink," *The Wall Street Journal,* August 17, 1994, p. B8.

41. Haim Oren, "Branding Financial Services Helps Consumers Find Order in Chaos," *Marketing News,* March 29, 1993, p. 6.

42. Julie Liesse, "Private Labels Appear Less Omnipresent in GMA Study," *Advertising Age,* April 25, 1994, p. 8.

43. Keith J. Kelly, "Coca-Cola Shows That Top-Brand Fizz," *Advertising Age,* July 11, 1994, p. 3.

44. Kyle Pope, "Computers: They're No Commodity," *The Wall Street Journal,* October 15, 1993, p. 31.

45. C. Manly Molpus, "Brands Follow New Shopping Patterns," *Advertising Age,* February 14, 1994, p. 22.

46. S. Kent Stephan and Barry L. Tannenholz, "The Real Reason for Brand Switching," p. 31.

47. Larry Light, "Brand Loyalty Marketing Key to Enduring Growth," *Advertising Age,* October 3, 1994, p. 20.

48. "Loyalty Just Isn't What It Used to Be—But Then Again, Neither Is Disloyalty," *Adweek,* September 6, 1993, p. 17.

49. Andrew Jaffe, "A Compass Point Out of Dead Calm: 'Brand Stewardship,'" *Adweek,* February 7, 1994, p. 38.

50. Linda Trent, "Color Can Affect Success of Products," *Marketing News,* July 5, 1993, p. 4.

51. Shlomo Kalish, "A New Product Adoption Model with Price, Advertising, and Uncertainty," *Management Science,* December 1985, pp. 1569–85.

52. Raymond Serafin, "Brands in Demand—BMW: From Yuppie-Mobile to Smart Car of the '90s," *Advertising Age,* October 3, 1994, p. S2.

53. Perreault and McCarthy, *Basic Marketing,* p. 16.

54. U.S. Bureau of the Census.

55. Janean Hube, "Franchise Forecast," *Entrepreneur,* January 1993, p. 75.

56. Stephanie Barlow, "Substantial Success," *Entrepreneur,* January 1993, p. 125.

57. Donald L. Baron, "A European Vocation: New Franchising Opportunities in the Old Country," *Entrepreneur,* January 1993, pp. 117–22.

58. Jim Emerson, "Levi Strauss in the Early Stages of Shift to Database Marketing," *DM News,* December 7, 1992, pp. 1–2; Lisa Benenson, "Bull's-Eye Marketing," *Success,* January/February 1993, pp. 43–48.

59. Walter van Waterschoot and Christophe Van den Bulte, "The 4P Classification of the Marketing Mix Revisited," p. 89.

60. *The 16th Annual Survey of Promotional Practices,* Donnelley Marketing Inc., 1994; Doug McClellan, "Desktop Counterfeiting," *Technology Review,* February/March 1995, pp. 32–40.

61. Walter van Waterschoot and Christophe Van den Bulte, "The 4P Classification of the Marketing Mix Revisited," pp. 89–90.

Chapter Six

1. John Martin, "Playing for Keeps: How to Build a Lasting Partnership," *Agency,* Summer 1997, pp. 16–18.

2. Beth Rilee-Kelley, personal interview, November 1997.

3. Martin, "Playing for Keeps," p. 18; Rilee-Kelley interview.

4. Chad Rubel, "Some Cute Super Spots Now Just a Memory," *Marketing News,* March 13, 1995, p. 15.

5. William D. Perreault, Jr., and E. Jerome McCarthy, *Basic Marketing,* 12th ed. (Burr Ridge, IL: Richard D. Irwin, 1996) p. 155.

6. Jack Honomichl, "Honomichl Global 25: Top 25 Global Firms Earn $6.1 Billion in Revenue," *Marketing News,* August 18, 1997, p. H2.

7. David G. Bakken, "Measure for Measure," *Marketing Tools,* premier issue, 1994, p. 14.

8. Brian Ottum, "Focus Groups and New Product Development," *Marketing News,* June 3, 1996, p. H26.

9. Ibid., pp. 14–15.

10. Don Peppers and Martha Rogers, "Welcome to the 1:1 Future," *Marketing Tools,* premier issue, 1994, p. 4.

11. Bakken, "Measure for Measure," p. 15.

12. Rilee-Kelley interview.

13. Jerry W. Thomas, "Media Advertising Is an Unfulfilled Promise," *Marketing News,* September 23, 1996, p. 28.

14. Ibid.

15. Cathy Taylor, "Brand Asset Valuator Turned toward Media," *Adweek,* July 11, 1994, p. 14.

16. Kevin Goldman, "New David Ogilvy Award Takes Research Out of Hiding," *The Wall Street Journal,* April 13, 1994, p. B6.

17. Pat Sloan, "DDB Boosts Planning by Hiring Brit Expert," *Advertising Age,* September 21, 1992, pp. 3, 53.

18. Rilee-Kelley interview.

19. "Quick Reliable Test Marketing Is a Virtual Reality," *Marketing Tools,* premier issue, 1994, p. 22.

20. Jerry W. Thomas, "Media Advertising Is an Unfulfilled Promise," pp. 28, 32.

21. Perreault and McCarthy, *Basic Marketing,* p. 153.

22. Jack Honomichl, "Research Cultures Are Different in Mexico, Canada," *Marketing News,* May 10, 1993, pp. 12, 13.

23. Paul Conner, "Defining the 'Decision Purpose' of Research," *Marketing News,* September 23, 1996, p. 18.

24. Michael L. Garee and Thomas R. Schori, "Focus Groups Illuminate Quantitative Research," *Marketing News,* September 23, 1996, p. 41.

25. Robert West, Schering Canada, personal interview, May 17, 1993.

26. William Weylock, "Focus: Hocus Pocus?" *Marketing Tools,* July/August 1994, pp. 12–16; Thomas L. Greenbaum, "Focus Groups Can Play a Part in Evaluating Ad Copy," *Marketing News,* September 13, 1993, pp. 24–25.

27. Pat Sloan and Julie Liesse, "New Agency Weapon to Win Clients: Research," *Advertising Age,* August 30, 1993, p. 37.

28. Gloria F. Mazzella, "Show-and-Tell Focus Groups Reveal Core Boomer Values," *Marketing News,* September 23, 1996, p. 9.

29. Honomichl, "The Honomichl 50," p. H2; Don E. Schultz, Stanley I. Tannenbaum, and Robert F. Lauterborn, *Integrated Marketing Communications: Putting It Together and Making It Work* (Lincolnwood, IL: NTC Business Books, 1993), pp. 149–50.

30. Richard Gibson, "Marketers' Mantra: Reap More with Less," *The Wall Street Journal,* March 22, 1991, p. B1.

31. Leah Rickard, "Helping Put Data in Focus," *Advertising Age,* July 11, 1994, p. 18.

32. Pamela L. Alreck and Robert B. Settle, *The Survey Research Handbook,* 2nd ed. (Burr Ridge, IL: Richard D. Irwin, 1995), pp. 56–59.

33. Ibid., pp. 37–40.

34. Ibid., p. 40.

35. Perreault and McCarthy, *Basic Marketing,* p. 173.

36. Pamela L. Alreck and Robert B. Settle, *The Survey Research Handbook,* pp. 88–90.

37. MINITAB software for IBM-PC, for Microsoft Windows, and for academic use in an inexpensive student edition through Addison-Wesley Publishing Co., Reading, MA.

38. George S. Fabian, panelist, "Globalization: Challenges for Marketing and Research," *Marketing Review,* February 1993, p. 23.

39. Maureen R. Marston, panelist, "Globalization: Challenges for Marketing and Research," pp. 20–21.

40. Michael Brizz, "How to Learn What Japanese Buyers Really Want," *Business Marketing,* January 1987, p. 72.

41. Simon Chadwick, panelist, "Globalization: Challenges for Marketing and Research," p. 18.

42. Thomas L. Greenbaum, "Understanding Focus Group Research Abroad," *Marketing News,* June 3, 1996, pp. H14, H36.

43. Marston, "Globalization: Challenges for Marketing and Research," p. 24.

44. Ibid.

45. John B. Elmer, "Travel the High-Speed Road to Global Market Research," *Marketing News,* September 23, 1996, p. 44.

46. Kevin Goldman, "Minorities Get the Leading Role in More Television Commercials," *The Wall Street Journal,* November 24, 1993, pp. B1, B6.

47. François Descarie, director, Impact Research, personal interview, May 17, 1993.

48. Gibson, "Marketers' Mantra."

49. Karen A. Machleit, Chris T. Allen, and Thomas J. Madden, "The Mature Brand and Brand Interest: An Alternative Consequence of Ad-Evoked Affect," *Journal of Marketing,* October 1993, pp. 72–82.

Chapter Seven

1. S. C. Gwynne, "The Right Stuff," *Time,* October 29, 1990, pp. 74–84; Raymond Serafin, "The Saturn Story," *Advertising Age,* November 16, 1992, pp. 1, 13, 16.

2. Alice Z. Cuneo and Raymond Serafin, "Agency of the Year: With Saturn, Riney Rings Up a Winner," *Advertising Age,* April 14, 1993, pp. 2–3.

3. William O. Bearden, Thomas N. Ingram, Raymond W. LaForge, *Marketing Principles & Perspectives,* 2nd ed. (Burr Ridge, IL: Richard D. Irwin, 1998), pp. 75–76.

4. Gwynne, "The Right Stuff," pp. 74–75.

5. Raymond Serafin, "The Saturn Story," p. 13.

6. William D. Perreault, Jr., and E. Jerome McCarthy, *Basic Marketing,* 12th ed. (Burr Ridge, IL: Richard D. Irwin, 1996), p. 119.

7. Saturn internal figures.

8. "Saturn SC1 and the Young, College-Educated Import Intenders," 1993 Case Study, NSAC: AAF College World Series of Advertising, pp. 2, 11, 23.

9. David Ogilvy, *Ogilvy on Advertising* (New York: Random House, 1985), p. 12.

10. R. Craig Endicott, "100 Leading National Advertisers," *Advertising Age,* September 29, 1997, p. S60; Laurie Freeman, "P&G Pushes Back against Unilever in Soap," *Advertising Age,* September 28, 1994, p. 21.

11. "Smale on Saturn—Don't Change What's Working," *Advertising Age,* March 28, 1994, p. S-24.

12. Daniel Rosenberg, "Pork Is Tasty, Say National Ads That Shift Focus from Nutrition," *The Wall Street Journal,* August 13, 1997, p. B5.

13. David Woodruff, "What's This—Car Dealers with Soul?" *Business Week,* April 6, 1992, pp. 66–67; David Woodruff, "Saturn," *Business Week,* August 17, 1992, pp. 86–91.

14. Adapted from Al Ries and Jack Trout, *Bottom-Up Marketing* (New York: McGraw-Hill, 1989), p. 8.

15. Frederick E. Webster, Jr., "Executing the New Marketing Concept," *Marketing Management* 3, no. 1, 1994, pp. 8–16.

16. Philip Kotler and Gary Armstrong, *Principles of Marketing* (Englewood Cliffs, NJ: Prentice Hall, 1994), p. 560; Don E. Schultz, Stanley I.

Tannenbaum, and Robert F. Lauterborn, *Integrated Marketing Communications: Putting It Together & Making It Work* (Lincolnwood, IL: NTC Business Books, 1993), p. 52.

17. Frederick E. Webster, Jr., "Defining the New Marketing Concept (Part I)," *Marketing Management* 2, no. 4, 1994, pp. 22–31.

18. Frederick E. Webster, Jr., "The Changing Role of Marketing in the Corporation," *Journal of Marketing,* October 1992, pp. 1–17, 22–31.

19. Ibid.

20. Ibid.

21. Kotler and Armstrong, *Principles of Marketing,* p. 559.

22. Ibid., p. 560.

23. Stan Rapp and Thomas L. Collins, "Nestlé Banks on Databases," *Advertising Age,* October 25, 1993, pp. 16, S-7.

24. Denison Hatch, "The Media Mix: How to Reach the Right Person with the Right Message in the Right Environment," *Target Marketing,* July 1994, pp. 8–10; Kenneth Wylie, "Direct Response: Database Development Shows Strong Growth as Shops Gain 16.9% in U.S.," *Advertising Age,* July 12, 1993, p. S-8.

25. Gary Levin, "Wunderman: 'Personalized' Marketing Will Gain Dominance," *Advertising Age,* October 25, 1993, p. S-1.

26. Kotler and Armstrong, *Principles of Marketing,* p. 560.

27. Glen Nowak and Joseph Phelps, "Conceptualizing the Integrated Marketing Communications Phenomenon: An Examination of Its Impact on Advertising Practices and Its Implications for Advertising Research," *Journal of Current Issues and Research in Advertising,* Spring 1994, pp. 49–66.

28. Thomas R. Duncan and Sandra E. Moriarty, *Driving Brand Value: Using Integrated Marketing to Manage Stakeholder Relationships* (New York: McGraw-Hill, 1997), p. 42.

29. Adapted from Kotler and Armstrong, *Principles of Marketing,* pp. 560–61.

30. Arthur M. Hughes, "Can This Relationship Work?" *Marketing Tools,* July/August 1994, p. 4.

31. Kotler and Armstrong, *Principles of Marketing,* p. 561.

32. Schultz, Tannenbaum, and Lauterborn, *Integrated Marketing Communications: Putting It Together & Making It Work,* p. 52.

33. Lou Wolter, "Superficiality, Ambiguity Threaten IMC's Implementation and Future," *Marketing News,* September 13, 1993, p. 21.

34. Regis McKenna, "Marketing Is Everything," *Harvard Business Review,* January/February 1991, p. 65.

35. Tom Duncan, "Integrated Marketing? It's Synergy," *Advertising Age,* March 8, 1993, p. 22.

36. Duncan and Moriarty, *Driving Brand Value: Using Integrated Marketing to Manage Stakeholder Relationships,* pp. 3–6.

37. Karlene Lukovitz, "Get Ready for One-on-One Marketing," *Folio: The Magazine for Magazine Management,* October 1, 1991, pp. 64–70.

38. Don E. Schultz, "Four Basic Rules Lay Groundwork for Integration," *Marketing News,* August 16, 1993, p. 5.

39. Ibid.

40. William F. Arens and Jack J. Whidden, "La Publicité aux Etats-Unis, 1992; Les Symptomes et les Stratégies d'une Industrie Surpeuplée," *L'industrie de la Publicité au Québec 1991–1992* (Montreal: Le Publicité-Club de Montréal, October 1992), pp. 365–99.

41. Regis McKenna, "Marketing in an Age of Diversity," *Harvard Business Review,* September/October 1988, p. 88; Schultz, Tannenbaum, and Lauterborn, *Integrated Marketing Communications: Putting It Together & Making It Work,* p. 21.

42. Duncan and Moriarty, *Driving Brand Value: Using Integrated Marketing to Manage Stakeholder Relationships,* pp. 78–90.

43. Ibid., p. 90.

44. Adapted from Tom Duncan, "A Macro Model of Integrated Marketing Communication," paper presented to the annual conference of the American Academy of Advertising, Norfolk, VA, March 23–24, 1995, pp. 7–10.

45. Don E. Schultz, "The Next Step in IMC?" *Marketing News,* August 15, 1994, pp. 8–9.

46. Rapp and Collins, "Nestlé Banks on Databases," pp. 16, S-7.

47. Don E. Schultz, "Trying to Determine ROI for IMC," *Marketing News,* January 3, 1994, p. 18; Don E. Schultz, "Spreadsheet Approach to Measuring ROI for IMC," *Marketing News,* February 28, 1994, p. 12; Matthew P. Gonring, "Putting Integrated Marketing Communications to Work Today," *Public Relations Quarterly,* Fall 1994, p. 45.

48. Don E. Schultz, "Integration Helps You Plan Communications from Outside-In," *Marketing News,* March 15, 1993, p. 12.

49. Regis McKenna, "Marketing Is Everything," p. 65

50. Schultz, Tannenbaum, and Lauterborn, *Integrated Marketing Communications: Putting It Together & Making It Work,* pp. 55–56.

51. Paul Wang and Don E. Schultz, "Measuring the Return on Investment for Advertising and Other Forms of Marketing Communications Using an Integrated Marketing Communications Planning Approach," paper presented at the annual conference of the Association for Education in Journalism and Mass Communication, Kansas City, August 13,1993.

52. Schultz, Tannenbaum, and Lauterborn, *Integrated Marketing Communications: Putting It Together & Making It Work,* p. 58.

53. Scott Hume, "Integrated Marketing: Who's in Charge Here?" *Advertising Age,* March 23, 1993, pp. 3, 52.

54. Cyndee Miller, "Everyone Loves 'IMC,' but . . . ," *Marketing News,* August 16, 1993, pp. 1, 6.

55. Don E. Schultz and Paul Wang, "Real World Results," *Marketing Tools,* premier issue, May 1994, pp. 40–47.

56. Ibid.

57. Don E. Schultz, "Integrated Marketing Communications: A Competitive Weapon in Today's Marketplace," *Marketing Review,* July 1993, pp. 10–11, 29.

58. Ned Anschuetz, "Point of View: Building Brand Popularity: The Myth of Segmenting to Brand Success," *Journal of Advertising Research,* January/February 1997, pp. 63–66.

59. Chung K. Kim and Kenneth R. Lord, "A New FCB Grid and Its Strategic Implications for Advertising," in *Proceedings of the Annual Conference of the Administrative Sciences Association of Canada* (Marketing), Tony Schellinck, ed. (Niagara Falls, Ontario: Administrative Sciences Association of Canada, 1991), pp. 51–60.

60. Johan C. Yssel and Mark W. Walchle, "Using the FCB Grid to Write Advertising Strategy," paper presented to the Annual Conference of the Association for Education in Journalism and Mass Communication, 1992.

61. Raymond Serafin, "Riney Media Strategy Gets High Marks," *Advertising Age,* November 16, 1992, p. 15.

62. Raymond Serafin, "The Saturn Story," p. 13.

63. Robert D. Buzzell and Frederick D. Wiersema, "Successful Share-Building Strategies," *Harvard Business Review,* January/February 1981, p. 135; Siva K. Balasubramanian and V. Kumar, "Analyzing Variations in Advertising and Promotional Expenditures: Key Correlated in Consumer, Industrial, and Service Markets," *Journal of Marketing,* April 1990, pp. 57–68.

64. Lacy Glenn Thomas, "Advertising in Consumer Goods Industries: Durability, Economies of Scale, Heterogeneity," *Journal of Law & Economics,* April 1989, pp. 163–93; James C. Schroer, "Ad Spending: Growing Market Share," *Harvard Business Review,* January/February 1990, pp. 44–48.

65. Bernard Ryan, Jr., *Advertising in a Recession: The Best Defense Is a Good Offense* (New York: American Association of Advertising Agencies,

1991), pp. 13–29; Priscilla C. Brown, "Surviving with a Splash," *Business Marketing,* January 1991, p. 14; Edmund O. Lawler, "A Window of Opportunity," Business Marketing, January 1991, p. 16; Rebecca Colwell Quarles, "Marketing Research Turns Recession into Business Opportunity," *Marketing News,* January 7, 1991, pp. 27, 29.

66. Fabiana Giacomotti, "European Marketers Keep Up Ad Budgets," *Adweek,* January 24, 1994, pp. 16–17.

67. Leo Bogart, *Strategy in Advertising,* 2nd ed. (Chicago: Crain Books, 1984), pp. 45–47.

68. John Philip Jones, "Ad Spending: Maintaining Market Share," *Harvard Business Review,* January/February 1990, pp. 38–42; and James C. Schroer, "Ad Spending: Growing Market Share," *Harvard Business Review,* January/February 1990, pp. 44–49.

69. Adrienne Ward Fawcett, "Brand Forecast: Interactive Looms Large in Budgets," *Advertising Age,* October 3, 1994, pp. S-1, S-16.

70. Richard Vaughn, "How Advertising Works: A Planning Model Revisited," *Journal of Advertising Research,* February/March 1986, pp. 57–66.

71. Amiya K. Basu and Rajeev Barta, "ADSPLIT: A Multi-Brand Advertising Budget Allocation Model," *Journal of Advertising,* 17, no. 2, 1988, pp. 44–51; Peter Doyle and John Saunders, "Multiproduct Advertising Budgeting," *Marketing Science,* Spring 1990, pp. 97–113; Glen L. Urban, John R. Hauser, and John H. Roberts, "Prelaunch Forecasting of New Automobiles," *Marketing Science,* April 1990, pp. 401–21; Bay Arinze, "Market Planning with Computer Models: A Case Study in the Software Industry," *Industrial Marketing Management,* May 1990, pp. 117–29.

72. Ahmet Aykac, Marcel Corstjens, David Gautschi, and Ira Horowitz, "Estimation Uncertainty and Optimal Advertising Decisions," *Management Science,* January 1989, pp. 42–50.

Chapter Eight

1. Daniel McQuillen, "A Promo Blitz for Windows '95," *Incentive,* November 1995, p. 16.

2. Bradley Johnson, "Windows '95 Opens with Omnimedia Blast," *Advertising Age,* August 28, 1995, pp. 1, 32.

3. "Microsoft Outlines Its Windows Strategy of 'Continuous Reinvention'," Microsoft News Release, July 23, 1997.

4. Laurie Freeman, "Experience Worth More than Byte," *Advertising Age,* July 23, 1996, p. S15.

5. Julie Liesse, "Inside Burnett's Vaunted Buying Machine," *Advertising Age,* July 25, 1994, p. S6.

6. Yumiko Ono, "Cordiant Puts Hamilton in Key U.S. Post," *Advertising Age,* July 18, 1997, p. B2.

7. Marilyn Rauch and Charlie Rutman, "Complex Consolidation for Coke a Delicate Maneuver," *Advertising Age,* September 15, 1997, p. S7; Joe Mandese, "Reinventing Services for Involved Clients," *Advertising Age,* September 11, 1995, pp. C44–45.

8. Jane Hodges, "Say Hello to a New Breed of Planner," *Advertising Age,* July 24, 1995, p. S12.

9. Jon Lafayette, "Agency Media Staffs Gain Clout," *Advertising Age,* March 4, 1991, p. 12; Peter J. Danaher and Roland T. Rust, "Determining the Optimal Level of Media Spending," *Journal of Advertising Research,* January/February 1994, p. 28.

10. "Business: Hi Ho, Hi Ho, Down the Data Mine We Go," *The Economist,* August 23, 1997, pp. 47–48.

11. Tom Duncan and Sandra Moriarty, *Driving Brand Value* (New York: McGraw-Hill, 1997), p. 100.

12. "VS&A Communications Industry Forecast," Veronis, Suhler & Associates, Inc., 1997, pp. 34–35.

13. "Business: Hi Ho, Hi Ho, Down the Data Mine We Go," p. 47.

14. Danaher and Rust, "Determining the Optimal Level of Media Spending," p. 33.

15. Gene Willhoft, "Is 'Added Value' Valuable?" *Advertising Age,* March 1, 1993, p. 16.

16. Joe Mullich, "The Voodoo of Value-Added," *Business Marketing,* October 26, 1992, pp. B20–B22.

17. Rick Klein and Jeff Jensen, "GM's Huge Pact Raises Olympics Bar," *Advertising Age,* August 4, 1997, p. 6.

18. Dorothy Giobbe, "Newspapers Urged to Be More Creative," *Editor & Publisher,* July 2, 1994, p. 38.

19. Scott Donaton, "Computer-Savvy Directors Muscle Way to Forefront," *Advertising Age,* July 20, 1993, p. S6.

20. Craig Reiss, "Agency Media People Come into Their Own," *Adweek,* March 14, 1994, p. 46.

21. Marilyn Rauch, "Media Buying & Planning: Intensive Courting Puts Indies in Spotlight," *Advertising Age,* August 4, 1997, p. S10; Joe Mandese, "Boost for Media Buyers," *Advertising Age,* March 7, 1994, p. 47.

22. Liesse, "Inside Burnett's Vaunted Buying Machine," p. S6.

23. Don E. Schultz, Stanley I. Tannenbaum, and Robert F. Lauterborn, *Integrated Marketing Communications: Putting It Together & Making It Work* (Lincolnwood, IL: NTC Business Books, 1993), pp. 81–82, 108.

24. Adapted from Donald W. Jugenheimer, Arnold M. Barban, and Peter B. Turk, *Advertising Media: Strategy and Tactics* (Dubuque, IA: Brown & Benchmark, 1992), p. 131.

25. Ibid., pp. 131–33.

26. Ibid., p. 132.

27. Ibid., p. 133.

28. Jim Surmanek, *Introduction to Advertising Media: Research, Planning, and Buying* (Chicago: NTC Business Books, 1993), p. 54.

29. Danaher and Rust, "Determining the Optimal Level of Media Spending," pp. 28–34.

30. Adapted from Surmanek, *Introduction to Advertising Media: Research, Planning, and Buying,* p. 106.

31. Jugenheimer, Barban, and Turk, *Advertising Media: Strategy and Tactics,* p. 135.

32. Joe Mandese, "Revisiting Ad Reach, Frequency," *Advertising Age,* November 27, 1995, p. 46.

33. George B. Murray and John G. Jenkins, "The Concept of 'Effective Reach' in Advertising," *Journal of Advertising Research* 32, no. 3, 1992, pp. 34–44.

34. John Philip Jones, *When Ads Work: New Proof That Advertising Triggers Sales* (New York: Simon & Schuster/Lexington Books, 1995); Colin McDonald, "From 'Frequency' to 'Continuity'—Is It a New Dawn?" *Journal of Advertising Research,* July/August 1997, p. 21.

35. Hugh M. Cannon and Edward A. Riordan, "Effective Reach and Frequency: Does It Really Make Sense?" *Journal of Advertising Research,* March/April 1994, pp. 19–28.

36. Ibid., pp. 27–28; John Philip Jones, "What Does Effective Frequency Mean in 1997?" *Journal of Advertising Research,* July/August 1997, pp. 14–20.

37. Kenneth A. Longman. "If Not Effective Frequency, Then What?" *Journal of Advertising Research,* July/August 1997, pp. 44–50; Hugh M. Cannon, John D. Leckenby, and Avery Abernethy, "Overcoming the Media Planning Paradox: From (In)Effective to Optimal Reach and Frequency," *Proceedings of the 1996 Conference of the American Academy of Advertising,* pp. 34–39.

38. Erwin Ephron, "Recency Planning," *Journal of Advertising Research,* July/August 1997, pp. 61–64.

39. Laurie Freeman, "Added Theories Drive Need for Client Solutions," *Advertising Age,* August 4, 1997, p. S18.

40. Schultz, Tannenbaum, and Lauterborn, *Integrated Marketing Communications: Putting It Together & Making It Work*, pp. 116–22, 132–33; and Julie Liesse, "Buying by the Numbers? Hardly," *Advertising Age*, July 25, 1994, p. S16.

41. Schultz, Tannenbaum, and Lauterborn, *Integrated Marketing Communications: Putting It Together & Making It Work*, p. 132.

42. Liesse, "Inside Burnett's Vaunted Buying Machine," p. S6; Don E. Schultz, "Integration and the Media: Maybe Your Approach Is Wrong," *Marketing News*, June 5, 1993, p. 15.

43. Laurel Wentz, "Media Buying Adds Creativity," *Advertising Age International*, July 19, 1993, p. I-15.

44. Derek Suchard, "Station Riles Dutch Government," *Advertising Age International*, July 19, 1993, p. I-6.

45. Joe Mandese, "Satellite TV Networks from U.S. Turn On Latin American Viewers," *Advertising Age International*, January 16, 1995, p. I-26.

46. Rein Rijkens, *European Advertising Strategies* (London, Eng.: Cassell, 1992), pp. 200–201.

47. Erdener Kaynak, *The Management of International Advertising* (Westport, CT: Quorum Books, 1989), pp. 70, 148; Nancy Giges and Joe Mandese, "Pan-Latin Study Could Open Global Floodgates," *Advertising Age International*, December 12, 1994, p. I-14.

48. Joe Mandese, "Cultures Clash as 'Optimizers' Sort Out U.S. Media," *Advertising Age*, August 4, 1997, p. S2.

49. Rijkens, *European Advertising Strategies*, pp. 86–87.

50. Jack Z. Sissors and Lincoln Bumba, *Advertising Media Planning*, 4th ed. (Lincolnwood, IL: NTC Business Books, 1993), pp. 135–48.

51. Mary Huhn, "Karen Ritchie, 1993 Media All-Stars," *Mediaweek*, December 6, 1993, p. M-16.

52. Todd Pruzan, "Global Media: Distribution Slows, but Rates Climb," *Advertising Age International*, January 16, 1995, p. I-19.

53. Neil Kelliher, "Magazine Media Planning for 'Effectiveness': Getting the People Back into the Process," *Journal of Consumer Marketing*, Summer 1990, pp. 47–55.

54. Stephen P. Phelps, "Media Planning: The Measurement Gap," *Marketing & Media Decisions*, July 1986, p. 151.

55. Taeyong Kim and Xinshu Zhao, "The Effect of Serial Position on TV Advertisement Recall: Evidence from Two Years of Super Bowl Advertising Data," paper presented to the Advertising Division, Association for Education in Journalism and Mass Communication conference, Kansas City, MO, August 1993.

56. Kenneth Longman, *Advertising* (New York: Harcourt Brace Jovanovich, 1971), pp. 211–12.

57. Kevin Goldman, "With Vietnam Embargo Lifted, Agencies Gear Up for Business," *The Wall Street Journal*, February 7, 1994, p. B8.

58. "The Power of Partnership," NBC Marketing Supplement, *Advertising Age*, November 16, 1992, p. 13.

59. Kevin Goldman, "Digital Warms Couch Potatoes with Only-on-Sunday TV Ads," *The Wall Street Journal*, November 22, 1994, p. B8.

60. Lambeth Hochwald, "SRDS Offers Media-Planning Software," *Folio: The Magazine for Magazine Management*, October 1, 1992, p. 28.

61. John Adams, "Grappling with Ad Schedules by Computer," *Marketing Computers*, September 1991, p. 16.

62. Danaher and Rust, "Determining the Optimal Level of Media Spending," p. 32; Heejin Kim and John D. Leckenby, "A Modified Dirichlet Model for Advertising Media Schedules," *Proceedings of the 1994 Conference of the American Academy of Advertising*, pp. 129–33.

63. Enrique Bigne, "Advertising Media Planning in Spain: Models and Current Usage," *International Journal of Advertising*, Summer 1990, pp. 205–19.

Chapter Nine

1. Mollie Neal, "Andersen Takes Great 'Panes' to Build Relationships," *Direct Marketing*, April 1993, pp. 28–30. Reprinted with permission, *Direct Marketing Magazine*, 224 Seventh St., Garden City, NY 11530, (516) 746-6700; Justin Martin, "Are You as Good as You Think You Are?" *Fortune*, September 30, 1996, pp. 142–44.

2. "Economic Impact: U.S. Direct Marketing Today," The WEFA Group and The Direct Marketing Association, 1997.

3. Lisa Benenson, "Bull's-Eye Marketing," *Success*, January/February 1993, p. 44.

4. Joan Throckmorton, "We Are Interactive—Repeat—We Are Interactive," *Direct*, November 1997.

5. Ray Schultz, "Wunderman at 75," *Direct*, February 15, 1996.

6. Bob Stone, *Successful Direct Marketing Methods*, 4th ed. (Chicago: NTC Business Books, 1988), p. 3.

7. U.S. Census Bureau, "Employment Status of the Civilian Noninstitutional Population 16 Years and Over by Sex, 1963 to Date," 1998 (http://ferret.bls.census.gov/macro/171996/empearn/2_000.htm)

8. "Economic Impact: U.S. Direct Marketing Today," 1997.

9. David Short, Peter Matthews, and David Carman, "Powerful Persuader Comes of Age," *The European*, April 4, 1996, p. 12.

10. Ibid.

11. Peppers and Rogers Group, *Marketing 1 to 1* (www.m1to1.com/success_stories).

12. Nicholas G. Poulos, "Customer Loyalty and the Marketing Database," *Direct Marketing*, July 1996, pp. 33–34.

13. Rob Jackson, "Database Doctor," *Direct*, January 9, 1996 (www.mediacentral.com).

14. Bob Stone, *Successful Direct Marketing Methods*, 4th ed., pp. 29–33.

15. Rob Jackson, "Database Doctor."

16. Thomas E. Caruso, "Kotler: Future Marketers Will Focus on Customer Data Base to Compete Globally," *Marketing News*, June 8, 1992, pp. 21–22.

17. Robert Kastenbaum, "Today's Challenges," *Journal of Direct Marketing*, Summer 1994, pp. 2, 3.

18. Seth Godin, "Guest Columnist: Permission Key to Successful Marketing," *Advertising Age*, November 1997 (http://adage.com).

19. Poulos, "Customer Loyalty and the Marketing Database," pp. 32–35.

20. Mollie Neal, "Marketers Looking Ahead in Chicago," *Direct Marketing*, March 1993, pp. 9–11.

21. Robert A. Peterson and Thomas R. Wotruba, "What Is Direct Selling?—Definition, Perspectives, and Research Agenda," *Journal of Personal Selling and Sales Management* 16, no. 4 (Fall 1996), pp. 1–16.

22. "Economic Impact: U.S. Direct Marketing Today," 1997.

23. Cyndee Miller, "Telemarketing Cited as Chief Form of Direct Marketing," *Marketing News*, p. 6.

24. Ted Belton, "Renewal Time for Insurers," *Canadian Banker*, November 1995, p. 30.

25. "Economic Impact: U.S. Direct Marketing Today," 1997.

26. Ibid.

27. Rama Ramaswami, "Computer Mailers Dominate this Year's Catalog Age 100 List," *Catalog Age* (www.mediacentral.com/Magazines/Catalog Age/100/96/intro.htm).

28. Laura Bird, "Beyond Mail Order: Catalogs Now Sell Image, Advice," *The Wall Street Journal,* July 29, 1997, pp. B1, 2.

29. Pat Sloan, "Avon Looks beyond Direct Sales," *Advertising Age,* February 22, 1993, p. 32.

30. "Losing Pitcher," *Entertainment Weekly,* May 21, 1993, p. 6.

31. Nancy Colton Webster, "Radio Tuning in to Direct Response," *Advertising Age,* October 10, 1994, pp. S14, S15.

32. Donna Petrozzello, "Interactive Ads May Be on Rise," *Broadcasting & Cable,* October 17, 1994, p. 52.

33. Murray Raphel, "Meet One of America's Top Salespeople," *Direct Marketing,* March 1994, p. 31.

34. Adapted from Barton A. Weitz, Stephen B. Castleberry, and John F. Tanner, Jr., *Selling: Building Partnerships* (Burr Ridge, IL: Richard D. Irwin, Inc., 1992), p. 5.

35. Edwin Klewer, Robert Shaffer, Bonnie Binnig, "Sales Is an Investment, Attrition an Expense," *Journal of Health Care Marketing,* September 1995, p. 12.

36. "Excerpt: Under the Radar," *Brandweek,* December 8, 1997 (http://members.adweek.com/archive/adweek/current/brandweek).

37. "Special Promotional Practice Report," *Direct Marketing,* July 1994, p. 40; Scott Hume, "Trade Promotion $ Share Dips in 92," *Advertising Age,* April 5, 1993, pp. 3, 43.

38. Larry Light, "Trustmarketing: The Brand Relationship Marketing Mandate for the 90s," address to American Association of Advertising Agencies annual meeting, Laguna Niguel, CA, April 23, 1993.

39. Magid M. Abraham and Leonard M. Lodish, "Getting the Most Out of Advertising and Promotion," *Harvard Business Review,* May/June 1990, p. 51.

40. Light, "Trustmarketing: The Brand Relationship Marketing Mandate for the 90s."

41. Larry Light, "At the Center of It All Is the Brand," *Advertising Age,* March 29, 1993, p. 22.

42. Donald S. Clark, Secretary, Federal Trade Commission, "The Robinson-Patman Act: Annual Update," April 2, 1998.

43. Emily DeNitto, "No Ad Bonanza in Heinz Strategy," *Advertising Age,* July 11, 1994, p. 4.

44. *The Point of Purchase Advertising Industry Fact Book,* 1997, p. 51.

45. Kelly Shermach, "Study: Most Shoppers Notice P-O-P Material," *Marketing News,* January 1995, p. 27.

46. *The Point of Purchase Advertising Industry Fact Book,* p. 39.

47. Kelly Shermach, "Great Strides Made in P-O-P Technology," *Marketing News,* January 2, 1995, pp. 8–9.

48. "Out of the Box: Alternate Delivery," *Brandweek Online,* Novermbr 18, 1996 (http://members.adweek.com/archive/adweek/brandweek/1992-1996/00038826.asp).

49. The 16th Annual Survey of Promotional Practices, Donnelley Marketing Inc., 1994.

50. Kate Fitzgerald, "Paper Coupons Losing Lure in High-Tech Store," *Advertising Age,* March 21, 1994, p. S14.

51. Ted Jackson, "Electronic Marketing and Retail's Future," *Advertising Age,* September 12, 1994, p. 36.

52. Larry Armstrong, "Coupon Clippers, Save Your Scissors," *Business Week,* June 20, 1994, p. 164.

53. Bruce Crumley, "Multipoints Adds Up for Quick Burger," *Advertising Age,* November 29, 1993, p. 14.

54. Daniel Seligman, "The Rebate Debate," *Fortune,* December 12, 1994, p. 255.

55. Lorraine Calvacca, "Polybagging Products to Pick Up Customers," *Folio: The Magazine for Magazine Management,* January 1993, p. 26.

Chapter Ten

1. "Intel's Chip of Worms?" *The Economist,* December 17, 1994, p. 65; Richard A. Shaffer, "Intel as Conquistador," *Forbes,* February 27, 1995, p. 130.

2. G. Christian Hill, "Despite Furor, Most Keep Their Pentium Chips," *The Wall Street Journal,* April 13, 1995, pp. B1–B4; Shaffer, "Intel as Conquistador," p. 130.

3. John Roberts and Steven Burke, "Intel Faces Steep Price to Recall Pentium Chip," *Computer Reseller News,* January 2, 1995, pp. 1, 123; David Kirkpatrick, "The Fallout from Intel's Pentium Bug," *Fortune,* January 16, 1995, p. 15.

4. Alex Stanton, "Pentium Brouhaha a Marketing Lesson," *Advertising Age,* February 20, 1995, p. 18.

5. Robert Faletra, "Oh No, Intel Is Inside!" *Computer Reseller News,* December 12, 1994, p. 14; David Kirkpatrick, "Intel's Tainted Tylenol?" *Fortune,* December 26, 1994, pp. 23–24.

6. Kirkpatrick, "Intel's Tainted Tylenol?" pp. 23–24; Robin Raskin, "Pentium Means Having to Say You're Sorry," *PC Magazine,* February 7, 1995, p. 30.

7. Hill, "Despite Furor, Most Keep Their Pentium Chips," p. B4.

8. Stanton, "Pentium Brouhaha a Marketing Lesson," p. 18.

9. Kirkpatrick, "Intel's Tainted Tylenol?" pp. 23–24; Bill Laberis, "Unsafe at Any Speed," *Computerworld,* December 5, 1994, p. 34; Robin Raskin, "Pentium Means Having to Say You're Sorry," p. 30; Sebastian Rupley, "When Good Chips Go Bad" and "The Pentium Papers: Where to Go On-line," *PC Magazine,* February 7, 1995, p. 32.

10. Thayer C. Taylor, "New Era, Same Old Mistake," *Sales & Marketing Management,* February 1995, p. 14.

11. Stanton, "Pentium Brouhaha a Marketing Lesson," p. 18.

12. Hill, "Despite Furor, Most Keep Their Pentium Chips," p. B4; Laberis, "Unsafe at Any Speed," p. 34.

13. Hill, "Despite Furor, Most Keep Their Pentium Chips," p. B4.

14. Jim Osborne, "Getting Full Value from Public Relations," *Public Relations Journal,* October/November 1994, p. 64.

15. Sandra Moriarty, "PR and IMC: The Benefits of Integration," *Public Relations Quarterly,* Fall 1994, pp. 38–44.

16. Jan Jaben, "Economics Drive Marketing Mix: PR Provides the Best Return," *Advertising Age,* September 5, 1994, p. B6.

17. Ibid.

18. Publisher's Statement, *Inside PR,* March 1993, p. 3.

19. Thomas L. Harris, "PR Gets Personal," *Direct Marketing,* April 1994, pp. 29–32.

20. Jane Weaver, "Perrier: Fighting Crisis with Laughter," *Adweek,* March 19, 1990, p. 12.

21. Bill Patterson, "Crisis Impact on Reputation Management," *Public Relations Journal,* November 1993, p. 48.

22. Dennis L. Wilcox, *Public Relations Strategies and Tactics* (New York: HarperCollins, 1994), p. 381.

23. Lloyd B. Dennis, "Public Affairs: Deja Vu All over Again," *Public Relations Journal,* April 1990, pp. 14–17.

24. "What's Your Best Marketing Tool?" *Public Relations Journal,* February 1994, p. 12.

25. Adapted from Stephanie Gruner, "Event Marketing: Making the Most of Sponsorship Dollars," *Inc.,* August 1996, p. 88.

26. IEG FAQ: "What is sponsorship?" IEG Network 1998 (www.sponsorship.com).

27. Ibid.

28. Ibid.

29. "Telco Ericsson Calls on James Bond, Volleyball," *Advertising Age,* June 1997 (www.adage.com).

30. "Let Sponsors Do Their Thing," *Advertising Age,* May 23, 1996 (www.adage.com).

31. "Impact of Sponsored Events Cited," *Advertising Age,* December 9, 1997 (www.adage.com).

32. Thomas R. Duncan and Sandra E. Moriarty, *Driving Brand Value: Using Integrated Marketing to Manage Stakeholder Relationships* (New York: McGraw-Hill, 1997), p. 203.

33. Ibid.

34. Ibid.; Terry G. Vavra, *Aftermarketing: How to Keep Customers for Life through Relationship Marketing* (Burr Ridge, IL: Irwin Professional Publishing, 1992), p. 190.

35. Terry G. Vavra, *Aftermarketing,* p. 192.

36. Lesa Ukman, "Assertions," *IEG Sponsorship Report* (www.sponsorship.com).

37. Vavra, *Aftermarketing,* p. 192.

38. "Corporate Sponsor Bucks," *USA Today,* February 16, 1998, p. 1B.

39. Bruce Horowitz, "The Sponsorship Game," *Los Angeles Times,* January 4, 1994, pp. D1, D6.

40. Jonathan Bond and Richard Kirshenbaum, *Under the Radar: Talking to Today's Cynical Consumers* (New York: John Wiley and Sons, 1998), p. 63.

41. Melanie Wells, "Going for Nagano Gold; Nagano's Remoteness Challenges Marketers," *USA Today,* February 6, 1998, p. 1B.

42. Stefan Fatsis, "Nike Kicks in Millions to Sponsor Soccer in U.S.," *The Wall Street Journal,* October 22, 1997, pp. B1, B8.

43. Charles P. Wallace, "Adidas," *Fortune,* August 18, 1997.

44. Junu Bryan Kim, "Most Sponsorships.Waste Money: Exec," *Advertising Age,* June 21, 1993, pp. S2, S4.

45. "ESPN Signs X Games Sponsors," *Advertising Age,* October 1997 (www.adage.com).

46. Ukman, "Assertions," *IEG Sponsorship Report,* February 23, 1998 (www.sponsorship.com).

47. "Soccer Sponsorship Grows Rapidly in Argentina," *Advertising Age,* September 9, 1997 (www.adage.com).

48. "Get Ready for the Bangalore Braves," *Advertising Age,* December 3, 1997 (www.adage.com).

49. Ukman, "Assertions," *IEG Sponsorship Report,* February 23, 1998 (www.sponsorship.com).

50. Ukman, "Assertions," *IEG Sponsorship Report,* November 3, 1997 (www.sponsorship.com).

51. Wilcox, *Public Relations Strategies and Tactics,* p. 384.

52. Ukman, "Assertions," *IEG Sponsorship Report,* November 3, 1997 (www.sponsorship.com).

53. David Lister and Colin Brown, "Arts World Takes Sides with Tobacco Kings," *Independent* (UK), June 30, 1997, p. 3.

54. Edward Robinson, "It's Where You Play That Counts," *Fortune,* July 21, 1997.

55. Paul Stanley, "'Sponsownership'": Sponsorships Will Become Standard for Events," *Potentials in Marketing,* June 1990, p. 64.

56. Ukman, "Assertions," *IEG Sponsorship Report,* November 17, 1997 (www.sponsorship.com).

57. Ukman, "Assertions," *IEG Sponsorship Report,* January 26, 1998 (www.sponsorship.com).

58. Vavra, *Aftermarketing,* p. 191.

59. "Corporate Advertising/Phase II, An Expanded Study of Corporate Advertising Effectiveness," conducted for *Time* magazine by Yankelovich, Skelly & White, undated.

Chapter Eleven

1. Gary Levin, "VitroRobertson Lets Success Do the Talking," *Advertising Age,* August 29, 1994, p. 29; Ken Mendelbaum, "I Wish I'd Done That Ad," for Magazine Publishers of America, *Adweek,* September 19, 1994, p. 29; private correspondence and interviews with Taylor Guitar and VitroRobertson, February 1995.

2. Adapted from interviews and private correspondence with Hugh G. Cannon, Wayne State University, 1997.

3. Adapted from Bruce Bendinger, *The Copy Workshop Workbook* (Chicago: The Copy Workshop, 1993), pp. 128–47.

4. Hank Seiden, *Advertising Pure and Simple* (New York: AMACOM, 1990), pp. 23–340.

5. Nancy A. Mitchell, Diane M. Badzinski, and Donna R. Pawlowski, "The Use of Metaphors as Vivid Stimuli to Enhance Comprehension and Recall of Print Advertisements," in Karen Whitehill King, ed., *Proceedings of the 1994 Conference of the American Academy of Advertising* (Athens, GA: Henry W. Grady College of Journalism and Mass Communication, the University of Georgia, 1994), p. 199.

6. Ibid.

7. Sandra Moriarty and Shay Sayre, "An Interpretive Study of Visual Cues in Advertising," paper presented to the annual convention of the Association for Education in Journalism and Mass Communication, Montreal, August 1992, p. 5.

8. Sal Randazzo, *The Mythmakers: How Advertisers Apply the Power of Classic Myths and Symbols to Create Modern Day Legends* (Chicago: Probus Publishing, 1995), pp. 28–51.

9. Barry A. Hollander, "Infomation Graphics and the Bandwagon Effect: Does the Visual Display of Opinion Aid in Persuasion?" paper presented to the annual convention of the Association for Education in Journalism and Mass Communication, Montreal, August 1992, p. 21.

10. Kevin Goldman, "Nike, H-P Gamble on New Sales Pitches," *The Wall Street Journal,* April 8, 1994, p. B8.

11. J. P. Guilford, "Traits of Personality," in *Creativity and Its Cultivation* (New York: Harper, 1959).

12. Allen F. Harrison and Robert M. Bramson, *The Art of Thinking* (New York: Berkley Books, 1984), pp. 5–18, 182.

13. Roger von Oech, *A Whack on the Side of the Head* (New York: Warner Books, 1990), pp. 35–37.

14. Anthony Alessandra, James Cathcart, and Phillip Wexler, *Selling by Objectives* (Englewood Cliffs, NJ: Prentice Hall, 1988), pp. 31–56.

15. Harrison and Bramson, *The Art of Thinking,* pp. 26, 34, 181.

16. Ibid.

17. Kevin Goldman, "Nike, H-P Gamble on New Sales Pitches," p. B5.

18. Roger von Oech, *A Kick in the Seat of the Pants* (New York: Harper-Perennial, 1986), p. 12.

19. Adapted with permission from Roger von Oech, *A Kick in the Seat of the Pants*, pp. 24–53.
20. John O'Toole, *The Trouble with Advertising*, 2nd ed. (New York: Random House, 1985), p. 132; Fred Danzig, "The Big Idea," *Advertising Age*, November 9, 1988, pp. 16, 138–40.
21. O'Toole, *The Trouble with Advertising*, pp. 132–33.
22. Adapted with permission from Roger Von Oech, *A Kick in the Seat of the Pants*, pp. 55–87.
23. Bob Garfield, "Lovestruck Praying Mantis Is Hooked on Fila," *Advertising Age*, February 13, 1995, p. 3.
24. Von Oech, *A Whack on the Side of the Head*, p. 6.
25. Ibid., pp. 108–43.
26. Kevin Goldman, "Leap Partnership Touts All-Creative Shop," *The Wall Street Journal*, December 23, 1993, p. B3.
27. William D. Perreault, Jr., and E. Jerome McCarthy, *Basic Marketing*, 12th ed. (Burr Ridge, IL: Richard D. Irwin, 1996), p. 492.
28. Adapted with permission from Roger von Oech, *A Kick in the Seat of the Pants*, pp. 89–111.
29. Kevin Goldman, "The Message, Clever as It May Be, Is Lost in a Number of High-Profile Campaigns," *The Wall Street Journal*, July 27, 1993, pp. B1, B8.
30. Adapted with permission from Roger von Oech, *A Kick in the Seat of the Pants*, pp. 15–16.
31. Bruce Bendinger, *The Copy Workshop Workbook*, pp. 170–74.
32. David Ogilvy, *Ogilvy on Advertising* (New York: Random House, 1985), pp. 17–18.

Chapter Twelve

1. Adapted from Sharon Edelson, "Elemental Considerations: Making Idyllic Images under Less than Ideal Circumstances," *American Photographer*, November 1989, pp. 18, 19, 22; Peter Kolonia, "The Complete Photographer: Eric Meola," *Popular Photography*, July 1993, pp. 22–28.
2. Elaine Wagner, Joel Geske, and Clay Conway, "Computer Use by Art Directors and Implications for Advertising and Visual Communication Educators," paper presented to the annual conference of the Association for Education in Journalism and Mass Communication, Kansas City, MO, August 1993.
3. Murray Raphel, "Ad Techniques—Off with the Head," *Bank Marketing*, February 1988, pp. 54–55.
4. Glenn Mohrman and Jeffrey E. Scott, "Truth(s) in Advertising? Part II," *Medical Marketing & Media*, October 1, 1988, pp. 28–32.
5. A. Jerome Jeweler and Bonnie L. Drewniany, *Creative Strategy in Advertising* (Belmont, CA: Wadsworth Publishing, 1998), p. 139.
6. Roy Paul Nelson, *The Design of Advertising* (Dubuque, IA: Brown & Benchmark, 1994), p. 107; J. Douglas Johnson, *Advertising Today* (Chicago: Science Research Associates, 1978).
7. John O'Toole, *The Trouble with Advertising*, 2nd ed. (New York: Random House, 1985), p. 149.
8. Axel Andersson and Denison Hatch, "How to Create Headlines That Get Results," *Target Marketing*, March 1994, pp. 28–35.
9. Murray Raphel and Neil Raphel, "A New Look at Newspaper Ads," *Progressive Grocer*, November 1993, pp. 13–14; David Ogilvy, *Ogilvy on Advertising* (New York: Random House, 1985), pp. 88–89.
10. Philip Ward Burton, *Advertising Copywriting*, 6th ed. (Lincolnwood, IL: NTC Business Books, 1991), pp. 65–66, 70.
11. Nelson, *The Design of Advertising*, p. 91.
12. Jeweler and Drewniany, *Creative Strategy in Advertising*, p. 115; Burton, *Advertising Copywriting*, p. 188; Julia M. Collins, "Image and Advertising," *Harvard Business Review*, January/February 1989, pp. 93–97.
13. Neil Raphel and Murray Raphel, "Rules to Advertise By," *Progressive Grocer*, December 1993, pp. 13–14; Murray Raphel, "How to Get A-Head in Direct Mail," *Direct Marketing*, January 1990, pp. 30–32, 52.
14. Jay Conrad Levinson, *Guerrilla Advertising* (Boston: Houghton Mifflin, 1994), p. 168.
15. Ogilvy, *Ogilvy on Advertising*, p. 71.
16. Raphel and Raphel, "A New Look at Newspaper Ads," pp. 13–14.
17. James H. Leigh, "The Use of Figures of Speech in Print Ad Headlines," *Journal of Advertising Research*, June 1994, pp. 17–33.
18. Ogilvy, *Ogilvy on Advertising*, pp. 10–11.
19. Andersson and Hatch, "How to Create Headlines That Get Results," *Target Marketing*, March 1994, pp. 28–35.
20. Burton, *Advertising Copywriting*, p. 54; Arthur J. Kover and William J. James, "When Do Advertising 'Power Words' Work? An Examination of Congruence and Satiation," *Journal of Advertising Research*, July/August 1993, pp. 32–38.
21. Burton, *Advertising Copywriting*, p. 58.
22. Raphel and Raphel, "A New Look at Newspaper Ads," pp. 13–14.
23. Burton, *Advertising Copywriting*, p. 54.
24. Ibid., p. 65; Andersson and Hatch, "How to Create Headlines That Get Results," pp. 28–35.
25. Kevin Goldman, "Ocean Spray Begins Youthful Campaign," *The Wall Street Journal*, March 7, 1994, p. B6.
26. Bruce Bendinger, *The Copy Workshop Workbook* (Chicago: The Copy Workshop, 1993), p. 177.
27. Burton, *Advertising Copywriting*, p. 12.
28. Raphel and Raphel, "Rules to Advertise By," pp. 13–14.
29. Bendinger, *The Copy Workshop Workbook*, p. 192.
30. Burton, *Advertising Copywriting*, p. 74.
31. Ogilvy, *Ogilvy on Advertising*, p. 119.
32. Burton, *Advertising Copywriting*, p. 79.
33. Leigh, "The Use of Figures of Speech in Print Ad Headlines," pp. 17–33.
34. Burton, *Advertising Copywriting*, p. 90; Marjorie Zieff-Finn, "It's No Laughing Matter," *Direct Marketing*, September 1992, pp. 38–40.
35. O'Toole, *The Trouble with Advertising*, p. 149.
36. Joanne Lipman, "It's It and That's a Shame: Why Are Some Slogans Losers?" *The Wall Street Journal*, July 16, 1993, pp. A1, A4.
37. Levinson, *Guerrilla Advertising*, p. 203; Burton, *Advertising Copywriting*, pp. 221–22.
38. Herschell Gordon Lewis, "Radio Copywriting—Not as Easy as You May Think," *Direct Marketing*, July 1992, pp. 17–18.
39. Adapted with permission from Bob Garfield, "The Best Ad Missed the Boat to Cannes," *Advertising Age*, June 23, 1997, p. 29.
40. Ogilvy, *Ogilvy on Advertising*, p. 109.
41. Ibid., pp. 103–13.
42. Bendinger, *The Copy Workshop Workbook*, p. 284.
43. Ibid., p. 250.
44. Terry Kattelman, "Future Shop," *Advertising Age*, January 7, 1991, p. S18.
45. Richard N. Weltz, "How Do You Say, 'Ooops!'" *Business Marketing*, October 1990, pp. 52–53.
46. Lennie Copeland, "Foreign Markets: Not for the Amateur," *Business Marketing*, July 1984, pp. 112–18.
47. John Freiralds, "Navigating the Minefields of Multilingual Marketing," *Pharmaceutical Executive*, September 1994, pp. 74–78.

Chapter Thirteen

1. Saatchi & Saatchi Los Angeles and Toyota Motor Sales, personal correspondence and interviews, March 1998.
2. Susan and Gregory Pyros, "Success Depends on Organization & Planning," *Computer Pictures,* January/February 1994, p. 31.
3. Personal interview, Charlene Washburn, Saatchi & Saatchi Los Angeles, March 1998.
4. "Argentinian Ad Industry Rocked by New 10.5% Tax," *Advertising Age,* August 1996 (www.adage.com).
5. Wayne Robinson, *How'd They Design and Print That?* (Cincinnati, OH: North Light Books, 1991), p. 6.
6. "Paper Costs Rise," *American Printer,* February 1995, p. 11.
7. "1996 Television Production Cost Survey," The American Association of Advertising Agencies, 1997.
8. Cleveland Horton, "Spots: Cheaper Is More Effective," *Advertising Age,* July 4, 1994, p. 6.
9. Kenneth Roman and Jane Maas, *How to Advertise* (New York: St. Martin's Press, 1992), pp. 26–28; Miner Raymond, "How to Cut Commercial Production Costs without Anyone Knowing You've Done It," *Sales & Marketing Management in Canada,* December 1987, pp. 20–22; "Marketing Guide 19: Advertising Production," *Marketing* (UK), February 7, 1991, pp. 21–24.
10. "Multimedia on Wheels," *Multimedia Today* II, no. 4 (1994), pp. 44–49.
11. Joe McGarvey, "Reach Out and Touch Some Information: Video Kiosks," *Inter@ctive Week,* January 30, 1995, p. 24.
12. Richard Wiggins, "Publishing on the World Wide Web," *New Media,* February 1995, p. 51.
13. Personal interview, Dean Van Eimeren, Saatchi & Saatchi Los Angeles, March 1998.
14. PANTONE® is a registered trademark of PANTONE, Inc.
15. Kathleen Lewis, "Printing: Teach Your Boss a Lesson," *In-House Graphics,* February 1990, p. 89.
16. Dave Zwang, "Proof of What? (New Technologies in Proofing Operations)," *American Printer,* October 1, 1996, pp. 40–44.
17. Jonathan Bond and Richard Kirshenbaum, *Under the Radar: Talking to Today's Cynical Consumer* (New York: John Wiley & Sons, 1998), p. 154.
18. Andrew Olds, "Creativity-Production: The Generalists," *Advertising Age,* January 1, 1990, pp. S26–S29, S31.
19. Adapted from Greg Hofman, "Splash Graphics That Say 'Gotcha,'" *Step-by-Step Graphics,* May/June 1991, p. 40.
20. David Ogilvy, *Ogilvy on Advertising* (New York: Random House, 1985), pp. 113–16.
21. Tom Cuniff, "The Second Creative Revolution," *Advertising Age,* December 6, 1993, p. 22.
22. Kate Fitzgerald, "Budget, New Media Issues on Front Burner," *Advertising Age,* April 4, 1994, p. 26.

Chapter Fourteen

1. National Institutes of Health.
2. "Milk Mustache Campaign Moves into Second Phase," *DQA Quest,* August 1996.
3. Laura Bird, "'Custom' Magazines Stir Credibility Issues," *The Wall Street Journal,* February 14, 1994, p. B10.
4. Ira Teinowitz, "Magazine Skips Film in Printing," *Advertising Age,* February 27, 1995, p. 36.
5. "Magazines," *Advertising Age,* October 14, 1997.
6. Patrick M. Reilly and Ernest Beck, "Publishers Often Pad Circulation Figures," *The Wall Street Journal,* September 30, 1997, p. B12.
7. Shu-Fen Li, John C. Schweitzer, and Benjamin J. Bates, "Effectiveness of Trade Magazine Advertising," paper presented to the annual conference of the Association for Education in Journalism and Mass Communication, Montreal, Quebec, August 1992.
8. Gene Willhoft, "Is 'Added Value' Valuable?" *Advertising Age,* March 1, 1993, p. 18.
9. Stephen M. Blacker, "Magazines' Role in Promotion," *Advertising Age,* June 30, 1994, p. 32.
10. Answers: *Car & Driver* is $59.15 CPM, *Road & Track* is $79.62 CPM; Carolyn A. Fisher, ed., *Gale Directory of Publications & Broadcast Media,* 130th ed. (Detroit: Gale Research, 1997).
11. Lisa I. Fried, "New Rules Liven Up the Rate-Card Game," *Advertising Age,* October 24, 1994, p. S-8.
12. Joyce Rutter Kaye, *Print Casebooks 10/The Best in Advertising,* 1994–95 ed. (Rockville, MD: RC Publications, 1994), pp. 63-65; Tony Case, "Getting Personal," *Editor & Publisher,* February 1, 1992, pp. 16, 31; Ann Cooper, "Creatives: Magazines—Believers in the Power of Print," *Adweek* (Eastern ed.), April 12, 1993, pp. 34–39.
13. Robert J. Coen, "Coen: Ad Spending Tops $175 Billion during Robust '96," *Advertising Age,* May 12, 1997, p. 20.
14. Robert S. Lazich, *Market Share Reporter 1998* (Detroit: Gale Research, 1997); "Community Papers' Circulation Up: Weeklies & Shoppers Guides Expand Reach," *Editor & Publisher,* December 12, 1997.
15. Coen, "Coen: Ad Spending Tops $175 Billion during Robust '96," p. 20.
16. Ronald Redfern, "What Readers Want from Newspapers," *Advertising Age,* January 23, 1995, p. 25.
17. "Circulation of U.S. Daily Newspapers by Circulation Groups," *Editor & Publisher International Yearbook* (New York: Editor & Publisher Co., 1997).
18. Ibid.
19. *Gale Directory of Publications & Broadcast Media* (Detroit: Gale Research, 1997).
20. Newspaper Association of America, *Facts about Newspapers 1994.*
21. *Newspaper Rate Differentials* (New York: American Association of Advertising Agencies, 1990); Christy Fisher, "NAA Readies National Ad-Buy Plan," *Advertising Age,* March 1, 1993, p. 12.
22. Christy Fisher, "Newspapers Are Far from Giddy over Rising Ad Prospects," *Advertising Age,* May 2, 1994, pp. 4, 50.
23. John Flinn, "State of the National Buy," *Adweek,* June 26, 1995, p. 56.
24. Christy Fisher, "Chrysler's One-Stop Ad Buys Boost Ailing Newspapers," *Advertising Age,* March 7, 1994, p. 49.
25. Dorothy Giobbe, "One Order/One Bill System Gets a Dress Rehearsal," *Editor & Publisher,* March 12, 1994, pp. 26, 46.
26. Fisher, "Chrysler's One-Stop Ad Buys Boost Ailing Newspapers," p. 49; Giobbe, "One Order/One Bill System Gets a Dress Rehearsal," pp. 26, 46.
27. Joe Mandese and Scott Donaton, "Wells Rich Tests 4A's Liability Clause," *Advertising Age,* April 22, 1991, pp. 1, 40; Willie Vogt, "Defining Payment Liability," *AgriMarketing,* May 1992, pp. 42–43.
28. Sally D. Goll, "Ignoring the Masses, Avenue Magazine Launches an Edition for China's Elite," *The Wall Street Journal,* September 28, 1994, p. B1.
29. Tom Eisenhart, "Opportunities Ripening for U.S. Business Publishers in Eastern Europe," *Business Marketing,* October 1990, p. 42.
30. Hanna Liebman, "Running Out of Time," *Adweek,* September 13, 1993, pp. 52–53.
31. Stephen Barr, "Moving Ahead," *Adweek,* January 31, 1994, p. 26.

Chapter Fifteen

1. Paula Mergenhagen. "How 'Got Milk?' Got Sales," *American Demographics,* September 1996.

2. Ibid.

3. Robert J. Coen, "Coen: Ad Spending Tops $175 Billion during Robust '96," *Advertising Age,* May 12, 1997, p. 20.

4. R. Craig Endicott, "100 Leading National Advertisers," *Advertising Age,* September 29, 1997, p. S63.

5. National Association of Broadcasters, 1997 (www.nab.org); Joseph R. Mullie, "The United States and Canada: There Is a Difference," Address to the Canada First! Seminar, Montreal, April 19, 1993.

6. *Cable Table, Fall 97,* Mediamark Research, Inc., 1997. (www.mediamark. com/pages/ct_f97a.htm); "CAB 1996 Cable TV Facts," *1996 CAB Factbook.*

7. Brian Jacobs, ed., *The Leo Burnett Worldwide Advertising and Media Factbook* (Chicago: Triumph Books, 1994).

8. Michael Burgi, "Welcome to the 500 Club," *Adweek,* September 13, 1993, pp. 44–45.

9. "Primetime 97/98: A Daily Guide to National Television Network Primetime Programming," compiled by the Cabletelevision Advertising Bureau, supplement to *Advertising Age,* September 23, 1997, p. A6.

10. *TV Basics 1990–91* (New York: Television Bureau of Advertising, 1991), p. 3; "Television vs. Other Media," *The Power of Spot TV,* supplement to *Advertising Age,* September 23, 1992, p. T15.

11. TV Dimensions '96, from *Media Fact Book,* Radio Advertising Bureau, 1997 (www.RAB.com); Don Tapscott, "Opinion: The Rise of the Net-Generation," *Advertising Age,* October 14, 1996.

12. "Basic Cable—Biggest Gains," *Cable Advertising,* CableSCAN, a division of Tapscan, Inc., December 1997 (www.cableads.com); *Marketer's Guide to Media,* Fall/Winter 1992–93, p. 50.

13. Michael Burgi, "Cable TV: New Investor Opens Them Pearly Gates," *Adweek,* September 8, 1997.

14. Regina Matthews, "U.S. Media Spending Up," *Media Central* (www. mediacentral.com), December 11, 1997.

15. Thomas R. Duncan and Sandra E. Moriarty, *Driving Brand Value: Using Integrated Marketing to Manage Stakeholder Relationships* (New York: McGraw-Hill, 1997), pp. 101–2.

16. Ibid.

17. Eric Schmuckler, "Betting on a Sure Thing," *MediaWeek,* January 23, 1995, pp. 18–20; Steve Coe, "UPN Beats . . . Everybody," *Broadcasting & Cable,* January 23, 1995, pp. 4, 10; T. L. Stanley, "Network Branding," *Brandweek,* January 9, 1995, pp. 30–32; Ronald Grover, "Are Paramount and Warner Looney Tunes?" *Business Week,* January 9, 1995, p. 46; David Tobenkin, "New Players Get Ready to Roll," *Broadcasting & Cable,* January 2, 1995, pp. 30–33.

18. Michael Freeman, "Lucie Salhany," *Mediaweek,* January 23, 1995, pp. 34–35; Eric Schmuckler, "New Network Ready to Roll," *MediaWeek,* October 10, 1994, p. 3; Eric Schmuckler, "Media Outlook '95: Network TV," *Adweek,* September 19, 1994, pp. S8–S12.

19. "Primetime 97/98: A Daily Guide to National Television Network Primetime Programming," p. A3.

20. Eric Schmuckler, "P&G Gets with the Programs," *MediaWeek,* March 6, 1995, p. 3.

21. Kathy Haley, "Spot TV Is Power Tool," *The Power of Spot TV,* supplement to *Advertising Age,* September 29, 1993, p. T3.

22. National Sales Reps Are Key to the Spot TV Mix," *The Power of Spot TV,* supplement to *Advertising Age,* September 23, 1992, pp. T10, T12.

23. Haley, "Spot TV Is Power Tool," p. T3; Kathy Haley, "Reps Zero In on Advertiser Goals," *The Power of Spot TV,* supplement to *Advertising Age,* September 29, 1993, p. T6.

24. Joe Mandese, "High-Tech Leap for Spot TV Buys," *Advertising Age,* March 14, 1994, p. 40.

25. Michael Burgi, "Welcome to the 500 Club," p. 45; Christopher Stern, "Advertisers Hear Promise of Smooth Spot Cable Buys," *Broadcasting & Cable,* April 26, 1993, pp. 56, 58.

26. "The Power of Programming," *1997 Guide to Advertiser-Supported Syndication,* supplement to *Advertising Age,* April 21, 1997, p. A6.

27. Ibid., p. A10.

28. "What Is Syndication?" *1994 Guide to Advertiser-Supported Syndication,* supplement to *Advertising Age* (New York: Advertiser Syndicated Television Association, 1994), p. A6; David Tobenkin, "Action Escalates for Syndicators," *Broadcasting & Cable,* August 29, 1994, pp. 29–35.

29. "Syndication Showcase," *Broadcasting & Cable,* January 24, 1994, pp. 82–86.

30. Kathy Haley, "The Infomercial Begins a New Era as a Marketing Tool for Top Brands," *Advertising Age,* January 25, 1993, p. M3.

31. Nancy Coltun Webster, "Marketers Look to Cable for Direct-Response Ads," *Advertising Age Special Report: Cable TV,* December 8, 1997, p. S8.

32. Jim Cooper, "Long-Form Ad Used in Contract Dispute," *Broadcasting & Cable,* May 24, 1993, p. 71.

33. Kevin Goldman, "CBS to Push Videotaping of Infomercials," *The Wall Street Journal,* November 15, 1993, p. B7.

34. Ibid.; Tom Burke, "Program-Length Commercials Can Bring These Six Benefits to a Major Brand Campaign," *Advertising Age,* January 25, 1993, p. M5.

35. Webster, "Marketers Look to Cable for Direct-Response Ads."

36. Robert J. Coen, McCann-Erickson Worldwide, 1996.

37. Jack Honomichl, "Top 25 Global Firms Earn $6.1 Billion in Revenue," *Marketing News,* August 18, 1997, p. H2; Nielsen Media Research, 1997 (www.cognizantcorp.com).

38. Bill Carter, "Television: A Monopoly Once More, Nielsen Is Still Unloved," *The New York Times,* September 7, 1992, p. 19; Jim Cooper, "Arbitron Exit Sparks Concern about Lack of Competition," *Broadcasting & Cable,* October 25, 1993, p. 45.

39. Jane Hall, "Company Town: Networks Give Nielsen a Low Rating; Television: Calling the Firm's Method Inaccurate and Antiquated, NBC, CBS and ABC Are Investing in the Test of an Alternate System," home edition, *Los Angeles Times,* May 24, 1996, p. D4.

40. Tracey M. Dooms, "Nielsen Comes under Fire; TV Networks Say Research Firm Hasn't Kept Pace with Today's Viewers," *Indianapolis Business Journal,* March 3, 1997, p. 17A (2).

41. Ibid.; Steve McClellan, "TV Networks Take Ratings into Own Hands," *Broadcasting & Cable,* February 7, 1994, p. 8.

42. Will Workman, "ADcom's Cable Meter: A Revolution in the Making," *Cable World,* March 17, 1997 (www.mediacentral.com).

43. Ibid.

44. Kevin Goldman, "CBS Pays Price for Losing Bet on Ratings," *The Wall Street Journal,* November 30, 1993, p. B4; Kevin Goldman, "CBS Again Must Offer Make-Good Ads," *The Wall Street Journal,* October 27, 1994, p. B6; Kevin Goldman, "'Scarlett' Make-Goods," *The Wall Street Journal,* November 21, 1994, p. B8.

45. Kevin Goldman, "Cable-TV Ads Fight Satellite Dish Threat," *The Wall Street Journal,* February 6, 1995, p. B8.

46. Joanne Lipman, "Video Renters Watch the Ads, Zapping Conventional Wisdom," *The Wall Street Journal,* April 28, 1989, p. B1.

47. Wei-Na Lee and Helen Katz, "New Media, New Messages: An Initial Inquiry into Audience Reactions to Advertising on Videocassettes," *Journal of Advertising Research,* January/February 1993, pp. 74–85.

48. "Welcome to Radio," *1997 Radio Marketing Guide and Fact Book for Advertisers,* Radio Advertising Bureau, 1997 (www.RAB.com).

49. "Radio Is Cost-Effective," *1997 Radio Marketing Guide and Fact Book for Advertisers.*

50. "Radio's Personalities Help Find Snapple's Sales Targets," *The Power of Radio,* special advertising supplement to *Advertising Age,* October 18, 1993, p. R3.

51. "Media Comparisons," *1997 Radio Marketing Guide and Fact Book for Advertisers; Imagery Transfer Study,* Network Radio Association, 1993.

52. Ibid.; *Media Facts: The Complete Guide to Maximizing Your Advertising* (New York: Radio Advertising Bureau, 1994), pp. 8–9.

53. "Maximize Your Marketing Message with Radio," *1997 Radio Marketing Guide and Fact Book for Advertisers; Radio Marketing Guide and Factbook for Advertisers: 1993–1994,* pp. 29–33.

54. "There's a Radio Format for Everybody," *1997 Radio Marketing Guide and Fact Book for Advertisers.*

55. *Network Radio: Targeting the National Consumer,* supplement to *Advertising Age,* September 6, 1993, pp. R2, R4; *Marketer's Guide to Media,* Fall/Winter 1992–93, pp. 69–70.

56. "Radio Enjoys Banner Year: December 1996 Continues Record-Breaking Growth Pattern," *RAB Press Release* (www.RAB.com).

57. Ibid.

Chapter Sixteen

1. Chad Steelberg, personal correspondence and interviews, January 1998.

2. Thom Forbes, "Ads in Cyberspace: Light Your Beacon, but Don't Get Flamed," *Agency,* Winter 1995, p. 32.

3. Frank Beacham, "Reinhard Tells Agencies to Get with It," *Advertising Age,* October 11, 1993, p. 40.

4. Direct Marketing Association, 1997 (www.the-dma.org).

5. "Forrester Predicts E-Commerce to Hit $327 Billion by Year 2002," *Advertising Age,* July 31, 1997 (www.adage.com/interactive/daily/).

6. Kevin Goldman, "Shopping Comes to Cyberspace with Launch of On-Line Catalogs," *The Wall Street Journal,* November 18, 1994, p. B7.

7. Reid Kanaly, "What Links Coffeepots, O. J., and the Louvre?" *San Diego Union-Tribune,* April 11, 1995, pp. 1, 6.

8. Internet Domain Survey, July 1997, Network Wizards (www.nw.com).

9. "Top 25 Websites for October Announced," Relevant Knowledge, 1997 (www.relevantknowledge.com).

10. "Intelliquest: Internet Audience Grows to 51 Million Adults," *Advertising Age,* September 1997 (www.adage.com).

11. Jared Sandberg, "MCI to Unveil Ambitious Plan to Link Consumers, Businesses to the Internet," *The Wall Street Journal,* November 21, 1994, p. B6; "45 Million Kids Could Be On-line by 2002, Study Says," *Advertising Age,* October 1997 (www.adage.com).

12. Mary Kuntz, "Burma Shave Signs on the I-Way," *Business Week* via America Online, April 17, 1995.

13. Ibid.

14. "IAB Advertising ABC's," Internet Advertising Bureau, 1997 (www.iab.net).

15. Georgia Institute of Technology, Graphics, Visualization & Usability Center (GVU), 1997.

16. Walter S. Mossberg, "The Marriage of TV and Home Computer May Last This Time," *The Wall Street Journal,* August 7, 1997, p. B1.

17. Netlingo Dictionary, 1997 (www.netlingo.com).

18. "Web Becomes a Viable Channel," *Advertising Age,* December 22, 1997 (www.adage.com).

19. Charles Waltner, "Going Beyond the Banner with Web Ads," *Advertising Age,* March 4, 1996, p. 22.

20. "An Old Friend in a New Medium," *WebTrack Advertising Monthly,* Jupiter Communications, June 1997, p. 5.

21. "Berkeley Systems Finds Interstitials Beat Other Ads," *Advertising Age,* August 12, 1997 (www.adage.com).

22. "'Intermercials,' Sponsorships Will Emerge as New On-line Ad Models," *Advertising Age,* June 27, 1997 (www.adage.com).

23. Michael Krantz, "Style in America: Modemocracy in Action," *Adweek,* November 7, 1994, pp. 28–31.

24. "Metrics and Methodology," The Media Measurement Task Force, Internet Advertising Bureau, September 15, 1997.

25. Kate Maddox, "ANA Study Finds Marketers Triple 'Net Ad Budgets," *Advertising Age,* May 1998 (www.adage.com).

26. Debra Aho, "Ad Industry Looks for Interactive Dollars," *Advertising Age,* May 16, 1994, pp. 20, 22.

27. Kevin Goldman, "Shopping Comes to Cyberspace with Launch of On-line Catalogs," p. B7.

28. Alicia Orr, "The Lowdown on High Tech," *Target Marketing,* January 1995, pp. 8–10.

29. Kate Maddox, "Don't Push It, Say Users and Web Marketers," *Advertising Age,* November 10, 1997 (www.adage.com).

30. "European On-line Ad Market: Lagging behind the U.S., but Growing," Jupiter Communications, 1997 (www.jup.com).

31. Ibid.

32. Ibid.

33. Alicia Orr, "The Lowdown on High Tech," *Target Marketing,* January 1995, pp. 8–10.

34. Ibid.

35. "Kiosks Bring Out the Vote," *New Media,* August 1994, p. 32.

36. "New Media Envision Multimedia Awards," *New Media,* August 1994, pp. S16, S19.

37. Orr, "The Lowdown on High Tech," pp. 8–10.

38. Information received from Interactive Network, July 1995.

39. Larry Riggs, "Get Ready for the Mail Boom: Ad Audit Services Predicts Triple-Digit Spending Growth by 2001," *Direct,* October 15, 1996 (www.mediacentral.com/Magazines/Direct); Richard H. Levey, "Coen: Direct Mail Gets Its Share of National Ad Dollars," *Direct,* June 18, 1997 (www.mediacentral.com/Magazines/DirectNewsline).

40. Laura Christiana-Beaudry, "Editor's Page," *Catalog Age,* August 1996 (www.mediacentral.com/Magazines/CatalogAge/9608/edit21.htm); Dom Del Prete, "Catalog Companies Cope with Higher Paper Costs," *Marketing News,* February 1996; Mari Yamaguchi, "Japanese Consumers Shun Local Catalogs to Buy American," *Marketing News,* December 1996.

41. Gary Levin, "JCPenney Tops List of Catalog Spenders," *Advertising Age,* October 10, 1994, p. S2.

42. Robert H. Hallowell III, "The Selling Points of Direct Mail," *Trusts & Estates,* December 1994, pp. 39–41.

Chapter Seventeen

1. Mary Yeung, *Print Casebooks 9: The Best in Advertising* (Rockville, MD: R. C. Publications, 1991), pp. 19–20.

2. "Industry Snapshot," Outdoor Advertising Association of America, 1997 (www.oaaa.org).

3. "Out of Home Media," Outdoor Advertising Association of America, 1997 (www.oaaa.org).

4. *Billboard Basics* (New York: Outdoor Advertising Association of America, 1994), p. 5.

5. "Industry Snapshot," Outdoor Advertising Association of America, 1997.

6. Mary Jo Haskey, "The Last Mass Medium," *Mediaweek,* December 6, 1993, p. 17.

7. Ibid., pp. 11, 21; Kevin Goldman, "Billboards Gain Respect as Spending Increases," *The Wall Street Journal,* June 27, 1994, p. B5.

8. Riccardo A. Davis, "Apparel, Movies Orchestrate an Outdoor Rebirth," *Advertising Age,* November 22, 1993, p. S2.

9. Press release, Institute of Outdoor Advertising, 1991.

10. "Industry Snapshot," Outdoor Advertising Association of America, 1997.

11. "Technology Standards," Outdoor Advertising Association of America, 1997 (www.oaaa.org/Tech).

12. Ibid.

13. Cyndee Miller, "Outdoor Advertising Weathers Repeated Attempts to Kill It," *Marketing News,* March 16, 1992, pp. 1, 9; *Billboard Basics,* pp. 15–16.

14. "Surveys Show Americans Like Their Billboards," Outdoor Advertising Association of America, 1997 (www.oaaa.org).

15. Davis, "Apparel, Movies Orchestrate an Outdoor Rebirth," p. S1.

16. Joan Brightman, "Signs of the Times," *Marketing Tools,* July/August 1995; Riccardo A. Davis, "Patrick Media Eyes Hispanics," *Advertising Age,* January 17, 1994, p. 27.

17. Riccardo A. Davis, "Retailers Open Doors Wide for Co-op," *Advertising Age,* August 1, 1994, p. 30.

18. "Advertising That Imitates Art," *Adweek,* June 20, 1994, p. 18.

19. Fara Warner, "DKNY Takes Upscale Ads Underground," *The Wall Street Journal,* October 6, 1994, p. B4.

20. James Ferrier, "Spotlight on Technology—Telecite," *Advertising Age,* November 22, 1993, p. SS10.

21. *The Point of Purchase Advertising Industry Fact Book* (Englewood, NJ: Point of Purchase Advertising Institute, 1992), p. 51.

22. "Industry Relations; Westpack '97: The World's Fair of Packaging National Manufacturing Week," Material Handling Equipment Distributors Online, 1997 (www.mheda.org).

23. W. Wossen Kassaye and Dharmendra Verma, "Balancing Traditional Packaging Functions with the New 'Green' Packaging Concerns," *SAM Advanced Management Journal,* Autumn 1992, pp. 15–23.

24. Ibid.

25. Ibid.

26. Chris Baum, "10th Annual Packaging Consumer Survey 1994: Consumers Want It All—And Now," *Packaging,* August 1994, pp. 40–43.

27. Wayne Robinson, *How'd They Design and Print That?* (Cincinnati, OH: North Light Books, 1991), pp. 74–75.

28. Kassaye and Verma, "Balancing Traditional Packaging Functions with the New 'Green' Packaging Concerns."

29. Susan A. Friedmann, *Exhibiting at Trade Shows* (Menlo Park, CA: Crisp Publications, 1992), p. V.

30. Ibid. p. 16.

31. Helen Berman, "The Advertising/Trade Show Partnership," *Folio: The Magazine for Magazine Management,* May 1, 1995, pp. 44–47.

32. Friedmann, *Exhibiting at Trade Shows,* p. 24.

33. Ibid., pp. 34–39.

34. Ibid., p. 44.

35. Ibid., pp. 70–71.

36. Ibid., p. 90.

37. "Promotional Products Fact Sheet," Promotional Products Association International, Irving, TX, 1995.

38. "1993 Estimate of Promotional Products Distributor Sales," Promotional Products Association International, Irving, TX, 1994.

39. *Promote Customer Referrals with Promotional Products* (Irving, TX: Promotional Products Association International, 1994).

40. *How Specialty Advertising Affects Goodwill* (Irving, TX: Specialty Advertising Association International, 1993).

41. Avraham Shama and Jack K. Thompson, "Promotion Gifts: Help or Hindrance?" *Mortgage Banking,* February 1989, pp. 49–51.

42. *Yellow Pages Industry Facts Booklet,* 1994–95 edition (Troy, MI: Yellow Pages Publishers Association, 1994), p. 32.

43. "Yellow Pages Revenue Picture Brightens," *Link,* April 1994, pp. 26–27; *Yellow Pages Industry Facts Booklet,* 1994–95 edition, pp. 1, 4, 25, 26.

44. Jaime Trapp, "Small-Business Aftershock Felt," *Advertising Age,* September 27, 1993, p. 28.

45. *Yellow Pages Industry Facts Booklet,* 1994–95 edition, p. 3.

46. Randall Crosby, "Is Ride-Along the Right Track?" *Link,* February 1995, pp. 17–23.

47. Kevin Goldman, "Capital Cities Builds New Media Sales Unit," *The Wall Street Journal,* January 24, 1994, p. B7.

The Epilogue

1. Chris Reidy, "This Is a Car Ad? What Else Are They Selling?" *Boston Sunday Globe,* September 28, 1997, pp. D1, D7.

2. Evelyn Kanter, "Toyota's New Deal," *Brandweek,* October 20, 1997, pp. 34–36.

3. Ibid.

4. Ibid., p. 36.

5. Ibid.

6. Ibid.

7. Ibid.

8. Michael Bevan, personal interview, April 1998.

9. "'Toyota/Everyday' Launched as Core Strategy in All-New Brand Advertising Campaign," Toyota news release, September 12, 1997.

10. Joe McDonagh, personal interview, April 1998.

11. Emily Weiss, personal interview, April 1998.

12. Howard Luck Gossage, *Is There Any Hope for Advertising?* Kim Rotzoll, Jarlath Graham, and Barrows Mussey, eds. (Urbana, IL: University of Illinois Press, 1986), p. xv.

13. "'Toyota/Everyday' Launched as Core Strategy."

14. Dottie Enrico, "Toyota Ads Dote on Family, Appeal to 'Everyday People,'" *USA Today,* February 16, 1998.

15. David Kiley, "Brandbuilders: Sienna College," *Brandweek,* December 1, 1997, p. 21.

16. "Saatchi Breaks Ads for $40 Mil Intro," *Advertising Age,* October 21, 1997, p. 4.

17. Dean Van Eimeren, personal interview, April 1998.

Credits and
Acknowledgments

Part One

p. 3 Eastpak backpack/piranhas: Courtesy Eastpak.

Chapter One

Photos/Ads

p. 5 Sunkist Web site: Courtesy of Sunkist Growers/Foote, Cone & Belding. **p. 7 Got Milk?:** California Fluid Milk Processor Advisory Board; photo by Hunter Freeman. **p. 9 BMW Web site:** Courtesy of BMW of North America. **p. 14 Northrop Grumman ad:** Courtesy of Northrop Grumman Corporation. **p. 15 Mannington Mills flooring ad:** Courtesy of Mannington Mills. **p. 16 Zithromax ad:** Courtesy Pfizer, Inc. **p. 17 Goodyear tires German ad:** Courtesy of Goodyear Tire & Rubber Co. **p. 20 Sunkist logo:** Courtesy of Sunkist Growers/Foote, Cone & Belding. **pp. 21–24 Portfolio Review: A History of Sunkist Advertising:** All ads Courtesy of Sunkist Growers/Foote, Cone & Belding. **p. 25 Early advertising tailor's sign:** Colonial Williamsburg Foundation. **p. 26 Early newspaper ad:** Library Company of Philadelphia. **p. 27 Scientific American old page:** Stock Montage, Inc. **p. 27 Ayer/Uneeda Biscuit ad:** Courtesy NW Ayer Agency. **p. 31 Early Coca-Cola ad:** Stock Montage, Inc. **p.32 VW Beetle ad:** This ad has been copyrighted by and is reproduced with the permission of Volkswagen of America, Inc. **p. 33 American Lung Association ad:** This public awareness billboard campaign is made possible through the American Lung Association of Los Angeles County and the donated services of the following individuals and businesses: Vince Aamodt, the art director who conceived and produced the idea along with the Santa Monica, CA-based advertising agency Rubin Postaer & Associates; Julie Nakagama; Jim Kroll; Annie Ross; Gerry Rubin and Larry Postaer; Gary McGuire and his staff who photographed the model, Juni B. Banico, photographer; Los Angeles County Museum of Natural History; the San Diego Zoological Society; and Graphic Services for retouching services. **p. 33 Long Fong ad:** Courtesy Bates Delvico. **p. 35 Pepsi TV storyboard:** Courtesy The Pepsi Cola Company. **p. 35 Coke Bear photo:** Courtesy The Coca-Cola Company. **p. 36 Discovery Channel Web site:** Courtesy of Discovery Channel. **p. 39 Boy Scout ad:** Courtesy DDB Needham/Dallas.

Exhibits/Checklists/Ad Labs

Ad Lab 1–A What Kills Bugs Dead: Reprinted with permission from *Ad Age*, December 13, 1993. Copyright, Crain Communications, Inc., All rights reserved. **Ad Lab 1–B** Wildwood Days: Courtesy Greater Wildwood. Midas sponge brake pedal: Courtesy Midas Corporation. Norwegian Cruise Line ad: Courtesy Norwegian Cruise Lines. **Exhibit 1–2** Advertising communications model: "A Revised Communication Model for Advertising," *Journal of Advertising*, vol. XXIII, no. 2, pp. 1–15. **Exhibit 1–6** Top 10 international advertisers: Reprinted with permission from the November 10, 1997 issue of *Advertising Age*. Copyright, Crain Communications, Inc. 1997.

Chapter Two

Photos/Ads

p. 43 Calvin Klein billboard: Courtesy France Presse Agency. **p. 44 Benetton ad:** Concept: O. Toscani; Courtesy of United Colors of Benetton. **p. 48 Nike/Jackie Joyner:** Courtesy of Nike, Inc. **p. 49 CPA ad:** Courtesy AICPA. **p. 50 BMW fence ad:** Courtesy Mullen Advertising. **p. 50 Edsel historic ad:** Stock Montage, Inc. **p. 52 Daffy shirt ad:** Courtesy Devito Verdi. **p. 53 Copper Mountain ad:** Courtesy of Copper Mountain; Citron Haligman Bedecarre; Marc Muench/photographer. **p. 54 Dresden Library of Congress ad:** Courtesy of Adworks, Inc. **p. 55 Buick LeSabre ad:** Courtesy Buick Motor Division. **p. 56 Australian shark ad:** Courtesy Kadu Surfwear: Paul Bennell; copywriter: Ben Nott; photographer: Simon Howsant; client: Richard Cram. **p. 57 School ad:** Courtesy of Friends of Public Education. **p. 58 Chevron ad:** Provided courtesy of Chevron Corporation. **p. 61 Finnish outhouse ad:** Courtesy BBDO Helsinki. **p. 63 Gilbert Tobin Web site:** © Gilbert & Tobin, Australia 1996–98. **p. 64 Dy-Dee Wash ad:** Courtesy Meyer & Wallis. **p. 65 GM service parts ad (English):** Courtesy General Motors. **p. 65 GM service parts ad (French):** Courtesy General Motors. **p. 66 Le Clerc ad:** Courtesy CLM/BBDO Paris. **p. 67 Transderm Scop:** Courtesy Grey Advertising. **p. 69 Coca-Cola trademarks:** Courtesy of The Coca-Cola Company. **p. 74 Radio Shack/Good Housekeeping seal:** Courtesy Radio Shack. **p. 76 Ketchum ad:** Courtesy Ketchum Communications Worldwide.

Exhibits/Checklists/Ad Labs

Exhibit 2–4 AAAA policies: © American Association of Advertising Agencies, Inc. **Exhibit 2–5** Advertising principles: Courtesy the American Advertising Federation.

Chapter Three

Photos/Ads

p. 81 Honda ad: Courtesy Honda North America; agency: Muse Cordero Chen. **p. 83 Rubio's ad:** Courtesy Johnson/Ukropina Creative Marketing. **p. 83 Embarcadero Center:** Client: Embarcadero Center; agency: Goldberg Moser O'Neill; creative director: Dave Woodside; art director: Russlyn Seiler; copywriter: Michael McKay; photographer: Paul Franz-Moore. **p. 85 Bronx Bagel Bar ad:** Courtesy Patterson Graham Design Grp. **p. 87 Sunshine Cafe ad:** Courtesy Pearson Crahan Fletcher. **p. 89 Hewlett Packard ad:** Courtesy Hewlett Packard. **p. 92 Pepsi Slam ad:** Courtesy Abbot Mead Vickers. **p. 93 Fallon McElligott Web site:** Courtesy Fallon McElligott. **p. 96 PC World ad:** Reprinted with permission of PC World Communications, Inc. **p. 98 Eagle River Interactive ad:** Courtesy Eagle River Interactive. **p. 100 Honda dealer kit:** Courtesy Honda North America; agency: Muse Cordero Chen; photo by John Thoeming. **p. 103 Photo agency office:** Courtesy TBWA Chiat/Day, Venice, California. **p. 104 Benetton ad:** Concept: O. Toscani; Courtesy of

United Colors of Benetton. **p. 106 Fallon McElligott ad:** Courtesy of Fallon McElligott. **p. 109 Levi's for Women:** Courtesy of Levi Strauss & Co. **p. 112 Citibank ad:** Courtesy Young & Rubicam/Sydney. **p. 113 Sunglass Hut ad:** Client: Sunglass Hut International; agency: Crispin Porter & Bogusky Advertising Miami, Florida; creative director: Alex Bogusky; art director: Diane Durban; copywriter: T. Grand. **p. 114 IBM Santa ad:** Courtesy Ogilvy & Mather/Paris.

Exhibits/Checklists/Ad Labs

Exhibit 3–3 Top advertisers in the U.S. in 1998: Reprinted with permission from the September 29, 1997 issue of *Advertising Age*. Copyright, Crain Communications, Inc. 1997. **Exhibit 3–4** Top advertisers in the U.S. in 1996 by total U.S. ad spending: Reprinted with permission from the September 29, 1997 issue of *Advertising Age*. Copyright, Crain Communications, Inc. 1997. **Checklist** Agency review: Adapted with permission from the March 30, 1981, issue of *Crain's Chicago Business*. © 1981 by Crain Communications, Inc. **Checklist** Better client: Adapted from Kenneth Roman and Jane Maas, *How to Advertise* (New York: St. Martin's Press, Macmillan & Co., Ltd., 1976), pp. 151–56. **Exhibit 3–10** Top U.S. media companies: Reprinted with permission from the August 18, 1997 issue of *Advertising Age*. Copyright, Crain Communications, Inc. 1997. **Exhibit 3–11** Top media companies by TV revenue: Reprinted with permission from the August 18, 1997 issue of *Advertising Age*. Copyright, Crain Communications, Inc. 1997.

Part Two

p. 118 Nike apparel ad: Courtesy Nike, Inc.

Chapter Four

Photos/Ads

p. 121 Prodigy Web site: Used with permission of Prodigy Services Corporation. Trademarks and Copyright 1998 Prodigy Services Corporation in the United States and other countries. **p. 124 Schwinn bike ad:** Courtesy Schwinn Bicycle. **p. 125 Alba Yamaha jetski ad:** Courtesy Big Bang Idea Engineering. **p. 125 Rolling Stone ad:** By Fallon McElligott/Rolling Stone. **p. 126 Ford ad:** Courtesy Ford Motor Company. **p. 127 Stein Mart ad:** Courtesy DeVito/Verdi. **p. 129 Daewoo car ad:** Courtesy The Campaign Palace. **p. 131 Bermuda Tourism ad:** Courtesy Bermuda Department of Tourism. **p. 132** Honda Civic ad: Courtesy of Honda North America, Inc. **p. 134 FMC ad:** Courtesy The Martin Agency. **p. 135 Edy's Ice Cream:** Dryer's Grand Ice Cream, Inc. is marketed and distributed as Edy's Grand Ice Cream in states east of the Rocky Mountains. **p. 137 Mercedes Benz ad:** Courtesy Mercedes Benz of North America. **p. 139 St. Patrick's Church:** Courtesy of BDDP-GGT Advertising, London. **p. 140 Shimano ad:** Courtesy Shimano American Corporation. **p. 141 Aston Martin ad:** Courtesy of Aston Martin of New England. **p. 142 Asian Foot Massage ad:** Ogilvy & Mather/Singapore. **p. 143 Army Reserves ad:** Army Reserve materials courtesy of the U.S. Government, as represented by the Secretary of the Army.

Exhibits/Checklists/Ad Labs

Exhibit 4–5 Source: Rossiter and Percy, *Advertising Communications and Promotion Management. Second Edition:* Reprinted with permission from the McGraw-Hill Companies. **Exhibit 4–6** Contemporary social classes: Equifax National Decision Systems. **AL4–B** Polaroid photo: Courtesy Leonard/Monahan, Providence.

Chapter Five

Photos/Ads

p. 149 Levi Strauss historical ad: Courtesy Levi Strauss & Co. **p. 150 Levi's Loose Fit ad:** Courtesy Levi Strauss & Co. **p. 151 Hunan Garden ad:** Courtesy David Yang. **p. 151 Guess ad:** Client: Guess, Inc.; Agency: Lambesis, Inc. Del Mar, CA.; creative director: Paul Marciano; art director: Chad Farmer; photo: Michele Clement. **p. 152 Columbia Sportswear ad:** Courtesy Columbia Sportswear. **p. 153 Audi ad:** Advertiser: Volkswagen Asia-Pacific; agency: DDB Needham Worldwide Ltd.; creative director: Christen Monge, Philip Morley, Richard Kramer; copywriter: Philip Morley; art director: Kelvin Tillinghast. **p. 155 Dr. Martens ad:** Courtesy Dr. Martens. **p. 157 Esab welding ad:** Client: Esab Welding; agency: Sawyer Riley Compton; photography by Doubilet Photography. **p. 158 Hewlett Packard ad:** Courtesy Herring/Newman Advertising, Inc. **p. 162 BMW ad:** Courtesy Fallon McElligott. **p. 164 Thermoscan ad:** Courtesy Braun, Inc. **p. 165 MicroTalk display:** Made by Telestar Interactive Corporation, Cincinnati, OH. **p. 167 Hummer ad:** Courtesy of AM General Corporation; agency: Pyro. **p. 168 Procter & Gamble products:** M. Hruby. **p. 169 Iomega package:** Courtesy Iomega Corporation. **p. 170 Smith Optics ad:** Courtesy Smith Eyewear. **p. 171 Volvo ad:** Courtesy Veritas Advertising. **p. 174 Haggar Stuff ad:** Courtesy Haggar Corporation. **p. 175 Computer Renaissance:** Courtesy Computer Renaissance. **p. 177 BMW ads:** Courtesy BMW of North America, Inc. **p. 178 Catalina Checkout coupon ad:** Courtesy Catalina Marketing Network.

Exhibits/Checklists/Ad Labs

Exhibit 5–1 Usage rates: Adapted from Dik Warren Twedt, "How Important to Marketing Strategy Is the 'Heavy User?'" *Journal of Marketing*, January 1964, p. 72. **Exhibit 5–2** U.S. Hispanic ad market: From *Hispanic Business*, December 1998, Santa Barbara, CA. **Exhibit 5–3** Heavy usage patterns: MediaMark Research, Inc. **Exhibit 5–4** VALS2™: Used with permission © SRI International. **Exhibit 5–5** SIC codes: Adapted from E. Jerome McCarthy and William D. Perreault, Jr. *Essentials of Marketing*, 5th ed. (Burr Ridge, IL: Richard D. Irwin, 1991), p. 156. **Exhibit 5–6** Proportional map: Adapted from U.S. Department of Commerce, Bureau of the Census, Census of Manufacturers, Area Statistics (Washington DC: Government Printing Office, 1995). **Exhibit 5–7** MicroVision system: Courtesy Equifax National Decision Systems, 1993. **Exhibit 5–8** Product life cycle: Adapted from Ben M. Ennis, *Marketing Principles* (Santa Monica, CA: Goodyear Publishing, 1980), p.351. **Exhibit 5–10** Reprinted with permission from the March 13, 1994 issue of *Advertising Age*. Copyright, Crain Communications, Inc. 1994. **Exhibit 5–12** Demand/supply versus price: Adapted from Elwood S. Buffa and Barbara A. Pletcher, *Understanding Business Today* (Burr Ridge, IL: Richard D. Irwin, 1980), p. 37.

Chapter Six

Photos/Ads

p. 183 Healthtex ad: Courtesy Healthtex/The Martin Agency. **p. 184 A. C. Nielsen ad:** Courtesy A. C. Nielsen. **p. 185 Healthtex ad:** Courtesy Healthtex/The Martin Agency. **p. 187 Healthtex ad:** Courtesy Healthtex/The Martin Agency. **p. 189 AT&T TV:** Client: AT&T-Baskingridge, NJ; product: corp. brand; agency: Ayer New York; chief creative officer: Patrick Cunningham; director creative services: Keith Gould; creative director: Mark Ryan; art director: Nick Scordato; copywriter: Gordon Hasse; executive producer: Gaston Braun; director: David Fincher; production company: Propaganda Films/LA; editors: Jim Haygood, Glenn Scantlebury Superior Assembly/LA;

music Elias Associates. **p. 190 Claritin TV:** Courtesy Cossette Communication-Marketing. **p. 193 Electric Library Web site:** Electric Library is a registered trademark of Infonautics, Inc. or its subsidiaries. The Electric Library Service is Copyright 1998 Infonautics Corporation. All rights reserved. **p. 196 Focus group photo:** Courtesy Nordhaus Research, Inc.: Southfield, Michigan, focus group facility. **p. 197 Envirosell video frame:** From Bearden et al: Marketing Principles & Perspectives Video Library © 1994 Richard D. Irwin, Times Mirror Higher Education Company. **p. 206 Tabasco TV spot:** TABASCO®, the TABASCO® diamond logo, and the TABASCO® bottle design are trademarks exclusively of McIlhenny Co., Avery Island, LA 70513. **p. 207 Hanes ad:** Courtesy Roper Starch Worldwide, Inc.; courtesy Sarah Lee Corporation.

Exhibits/Checklists/Ad Labs

Exhibit 6–1 Top research companies: Reprinted with permission from *Marketing News*, June 5, 1995, page 44, by permission of the American Marketing Association. **Exhibit 6–2** Research categories: Adapted from Edmund W.J. Faison, *Advertising: A Behavioral Approach for Mangers* (New York: John Wiley & Sons, 1980), p. 664. **Exhibit 6–4** Qualitative and quantitative research: *Marketing Tools* magazine, © 1994. Reprinted with permission. **Exhibit 6–5** Data collection methods: *The Survey Research Handbook*, by Pamela Alreck and Robert Settle, p. 57, © 1995 by Richard D. Irwin, Inc. **Exhibit 6–8** Reliability/validity diagram: *The Survey Research Handbook*, by Pamela Alreck and Robert Settle, "Comparison of Data Collection Methods," p. 32. © 1995 by Richard D. Irwin, Inc. **Exhibit 6–9** Professional research costs: The Professional Research Group. **Checklist** Effective questionnaire: From Don E. Schultz and Dennis G. Martin, *Strategic Advertising Campaigns* (Chicago: Crain Books, 1979).

Chapter Seven

Photos/Ads

p. 211 Saturn ad: © Saturn Corporation, used with permission. **p. 213 Saturn ad:** © Saturn Corporation, used with permission. **p. 214 Vince the Mover ad:** Courtesy of Vince the Mover. **p. 216 Hong Kong Bank ad:** Courtesy Clemenger Harvie. **p. 217 Siplast ad:** Agency: The Richards Group; art director: Jim Baldwin; writer: Mike Renfro. **p. 218 Hilton HHonors ad:** Courtesy Hilton Hotels. **p. 220 Saturn ad:** © Saturn Corporation, used with permission. **p. 222 De Beers ad:** Courtesy J. Walter Thompson. **p. 224 Benetton ad:** Concept: O. Toscani. Courtesy of United Colors of Benetton. **p. 226 BMW ad:** Courtesy Fallon McElligott. **p. 228 Oneida ad:** Courtesy of Oneida Ltd. **p. 230 U.S. Post Office ad:** Courtesy of United States Postal Service. **p. 231 Seattle Chocolates ad:** Courtesy of Seattle Chocolates Company. **p. 232 Kelsey Seybold Clinic ad:** Agency: Stan & Lou/Houston, TX. **pp. 232–35 Portfolio Review:** Strategic Use of the Creative Mix: **Digital ad:** Courtesy of Digital Equipment Corporation 1998; advertising agency: DDB Needham New York. **Apple ad:** Courtesy Apple Computer, Inc. **Sega ad:** Courtesy Sega of America. **Huet ad:** John Huet Photography; agency: Core, St. Louis Agency; art directors: John Dames & Wade Paschall. **Altoid Mints ad:** Courtesy Leo Burnett U.S.A. **Southwestern Bell radio spot:** Courtesy SBC Communications, Inc. **Isuzu ad:** Courtesy Goodby Silverstein & Partners.

Exhibits/Checklists/Ad Labs

Exhibit 7–7 IMC planning process: *Integrated Marketing Communications* by Don E. Schultz, Stanley Tannenbaum, and Robert Lauterborn (Lincolnwood, IL; NTC Business Books), 1993. Used by permission. **Exhibit 7–8** Factors influencing strategies: Reprinted by permission from *Advertising Age*, March 23, 1993. Copyright, Crain Communications, Inc. **Exhibit 7–10**

Message channels: *Marketing Tools* magazine, © 1994. Reprinted with permission. **Exhibit 7–12** Kim-Lord grid: Chung K. Kim and Kenneth R. Lord, "A New FCB Grid and Its Strategic Implications for Advertising," in *Proceedings of the Annual Conference of the Administrative Sciences Association of Canada (Marketing)*, Tony Schellinck, ed. (Niagara Falls, Ontario: Administrative Sciences Association of Canada, 1991), pp. 51–60. **Ad Lab 7–B** Economists view ad effects: Adapted from William J. Baumol and Alan S. Blinder, *Economics: Principles and Policy*, 3rd ed. (New York: Harcourt Brace Jovanovich, 1985), p. 386. **Exhibit 7–11** *Journal of Advertising Research*, figure entitled "Greater Popularity Occurs at Each Level of Frequency," p. 84. **Exhibit 7–13** Advertising expenditures: Reprinted with permission from *Advertising Age*, September 28, 1994. Copyright, Crain Communications, Inc. All rights Reserved.

Chapter Eight

Photos/Ads

p. 243 Microsoft Windows 95: Copyright Microsoft Corporation. **p. 245 Bill Gates and Windows 95 team:** Bettmann. **p. 246 Superbowl Web site:** Copyright NFL Enterprises. **p. 249 GM/Olympics sponsorship ad:** Courtesy of General Motors Archives. **p. 254 *Men's Health* magazine:** Client: *Men's Health* Magazine; Agency: The Martin Agency; art director: Sean Riley; photographer: Per Breichagen. **p. 260 Kinko's ad:** Courtesy Kinko's, Inc. **p. 261 MBC Arab TV ad:** The Advertising Practice, London. **p. 263 Fujitsu ad:** Courtesy Fujitsu Computer Products of America, Inc. **p. 264 Godiva ad:** Courtesy Godiva Chocolatier, Inc. **p. 267 All Media planning Suite:** Courtesy Telmar Information. **p. 269 E*Trade ad:** Courtesy E*TRADE Group, Inc. **p. 269 Eugenio Fabozzi:** Agency: Reggio del Bravo Pubblicita, Rome; art director: Agostino Reggio; copywriter: Pado del Bravo; illustrator: Daniele Melani. **p. 272 Media Planning system:** Courtesy SRDS. **p. 273 Media Plan flowchart:** Courtesy Media Plan, Inc.

Exhibits/Checklists/Ad Labs

Exhibit 8–2 Hours using media: Veronis, Suhler & Associates, Inc., 350 Park Avenue, New York, NY. **Exhibit 8–3** Value-added options: Reprinted with permission from *Advertising Age*, October 26, 1992. Copyright, Crain Communications, Inc. **Exhibit 8–4** Top accounts: Reprinted with permission from *Advertising Age*, July 26, 1994. Copyright, Crain Communications, Inc. All rights reserved. **AL8–A** *San Diego Union Tribune:* **Cartoon painted truck:** Agency: Mires Design Incorporated; Park Bench: Tracy Sabin; illustrator: Jose Serrano, designer. **Comic strip:** Courtesy Woody Wilson, Tony DiPreta, Mort Walker, Dean Young Stan Drake; illustrators: Jose Serrano, designer. **Exhibit 8–5** Top 20 independent media services: Reprinted with permission from the August 4, 1997 issue of *Advertising Age*. Copyright © Crain Communications, Inc. 1997. **Exhibit 8–6** Media planning activities: Adapted from Jack Z. Sissors and E. Reynolds Petray, *Advertising Media Planning* (Chicago: Crain Books, 1976); and Jack Z. Sissors and Lincoln Bumba, *Advertising Media Planning*, 4th ed. (Lincolnwood, IL: NTC Business Books, a division of NTC Publishing Group, 1993), p. 9. **Exhibit 8–13** Advertising response curves: Jack Z. Sissors and Lincoln Bumba, *Advertising Media Planning*, 4th ed. (Lincolnwood, IL: NTC Business Books, 1993), pp. 108–9. **Exhibit 8–14** BDI/CDI matrix: Adapted from Jack A. Sissors and Lincoln Bumba, *Advertising Media Planning*, 4th ed. (Lincolnwood, IL: NTC Books, 1993), p. 175. **Exhibit 8–15** Big 12: Reprinted with permission from *Advertising Age*, April 21, 1997. Copyright, Crain Communications, Inc. 1997. **Exhibit 8–16** Global media distribution: Reprinted with permission from *Advertising Age*, January 16, 1995. Copyright, Crain Communications, Inc. All rights Reserved. **Checklist** International media planning: Courtesy Directories International, Inc. **Exhibit 8–17** Readership scores: Adapted from *Cahners Advertising Research*.

Part Three

p. 277 Gateway ad: Courtesy Gateway 2000.

Chapter 9

Photos/Ads

p. 279 Andersen Windows ad: Courtesy of Andersen Windows, Inc. **p. 280 Andersen Windows brochure:** Courtesy of Andersen Windows, Inc. **p. 281 Target ad:** Courtesy of Target Stores. **p. 282 www.webmonkey ad:** Courtesy HotWired. **p. 284 American Airlines ad:** Client: American Airlines; agency: Temerlin McClain; illustrator: Michael Schwab; photographer: Dennis Murphy. **p. 287 Junk mail photo:** M. Hruby. **p. 288 Telemarketers photo:** Bruce Aryes; Tony Stone Images. **p. 289 Lands' End ad:** Permission granted by Land's End, Inc. **p. 291 Wit Capital ad:** Courtesy of Wit Capital. **p. 292 Pharmaceutical salesperson:** David J. Sams/Tony Stone Images. **p. 294 Saturn ad:** © Saturn Corporation, used with permission. **p. 295 America Online:** Courtesy America Online. **p. 296 Snapple ad:** Courtesy Tri-Arc Beverage Group. **p. 298 Kleenex ad:** Courtesy Kimberly-Clark Corporation as published in 1994. **p. 299 DeWalt store:** Ziggy Kluzny/Gamma Liaison. **p. 301 Nokia display:** Courtesy Nokia Americas. **p. 302 Taster's Choice:** © 1995 Nestle USA, Inc. **p. 302 Pic N' Save VIP station:** Photo by John Saller. **p. 304 Epson ad:** American Photo.

Exhibits/Checklists/Ad Labs

Exhibit 9–1 Reprinted with permission from the July 21, 1997 issue of *Advertising Age.* Copyright © Crain Communications, Inc. 1997. **Exhibit 9–2** RFM analysis of accounts, December 1998. Successful Direct Marketing Methods, pp. 30–31. **Exhibit 9–3** The top 10 catalog companies: www. mediacentral.com/magazines/CatalogAge, "The Big Players." The Catalog Age 100. **Exhibit 9–5** The Direct Marketing Association, (www.the-dma. org). "How Consumers Are Using Interactive Media to Shop." **Exhibit 9–6** Consumer promotion scorecard: Donnelley Marketing, Inc. 16th Annual Survey for Promotional Practices, "Type of Consumer Promotions Used," Chart 12. **Exhibit 9–7** Premiums: "Study: Some Promotions Change Consumer Behavior," *Marketing News,* October 15, 1990, p.12.

Chapter Ten

Photos/Ads

p. 309 Intel chip: © Chuck O'Rear/Westlight. **p. 311 Crain's New York Business ad:** Courtesy Crain's New York Business; agency: Goldsmith/ Jeffrey, Inc. **p. 312 Texaco ad:** Used with permission of Texaco, Inc. **p. 314 UPS ad:** Courtesy of United Parcel Service of America, Inc. **p. 317 Medicins Sans Frontieres ad:** Courtesy McCann-Erickson/London. **p. 319 Kinko's press release:** Courtesy of Kinko's, Inc. **p. 321 Excite/Quicken Web site:** Excite, Excite Search, and the Excite Logo are trademarks of Excite, Inc. and may be registered in various jurisdictions. Excite screen display copyright 1995–1998 Excite, Inc. **p. 323 VF Corporation:** Courtesy The Martin Agency. **p. 325 San Diego Opera ad:** Courtesy of San Diego Opera. **p. 326 Qualcomm Stadium:** H. How-Allsport. **p. 328 Andersen Consulting ad:** Reprinted with permission: Andersen Consulting. **pp. 330–33 Portfolio Review:** Corporate Advertising: **Augustine Land & Development:** Client: Augustine Land Development, Inc.; agency: Lyons & Sucher Advertising. **American Airlines:** Client: American Airlines; Agency: Temerlin McClain; Illustrator: Michael Schwab; Photographer: Dennis Murphy. **Mercedes Benz ad:** Courtesy Mercedes Benz of North America. **Specialized Bicycles ad:** Courtesy Specialized Bicycle Company, Inc. **Motorola ad:** Reproduced with permission from Motorola, Inc. **Kelly-**

Springfield Tires: Courtesy of The Kelly-Springfield Tire Company. **Sony ad:** Client: Sony Electronics Inc.; Agency: Lowe & Partners/SMS. **p. 334 Mobil ad:** Copyright of Mobil Oil Corporation. **p. 334 Imation ad:** Courtesy of Imation Corp.

Exhibits/Checklists/Ad Labs

Ad Lab 10–A Green advertising: Steven W. Colford, "Ad Groups Appeal Calif. Green Law," *Advertising Age,* September 12, 1994a, p. 13; Steven W. Colford, "Fade-out for Green?" Advertising Age, December 5, 1994b, pp. 1, 8; Joel J. Davis, "Environmental Advertising: Norms and Levels of Advertiser Trust," *Journalism Quarterly,* Summer 1994, pp. 330–45; Christy Fisher, "Green Seal Tries to Take Root," *Advertising Age,* April 18, 1994, p. 36; Keith J. Kelly, "Magazines Seek Green-Gold Formula," *Advertising Age,* April 18, 1994, p. 36; Robert Rehak, "Green Marketing Awash in Third Wave," *Advertising Age,* November 22, 1993, p. 22; Raymond Serafin, "Carmakers Paint Their Causes Green," *Advertising Age,* February 13, 1995, p. 33; and Charles Siler, "Body Shop Marches to Its Own Drummer," *Advertising Age,* October 10, 1994, p. 4. **Exhibit 10–1** Copyright 1998 *USA Today.* Reprinted with permission. **Ad Lab 10–B** David Ogilvy: Judann Dagnoll, "Ogilvy at 80," *Advertising Age,* November 4, 1991, pp. 1, 53; David Ogilvy, *Ogilvy on Advertising* (New York: Crown Publishers, 1985), pp. 117–26; and David Ogilvy, "We Sell. Or Else," *A.N.A./The Advertiser,* Summer 1992, pp. 21–25.

Part Four

p. 339 Royal Velvet ad: Courtesy McKinney & Silver.

Chapter Eleven

Photos/Ads

p. 341 Taylor Guitar ad: Agency: Franklin Stoorza; Creative Directors: John Vitro, John Robertson; Art Director: John Vitro; Copywriter: John Robertson; Photographers: Art Wolfe, Marshall Harrington. **p. 343 Land Rover ad:** Client: Land Rover; agency: Race & Rothschild Advertising. **p. 344 Taylor Guitar ad:** Agency: Frank Stoorza; creative directors: John Vitro, John Robertson; art director: John Vitro; copywriter: John Robertson; photographer: Art Wolfe. **p. 345 Motorcycle Safety Center ad:** Courtesy Martin/Williams Advertising. **p. 348 Mercedes SLK ad:** Art director: Mark Tutssel; copywriter: Nick Bell; creative director: Gerald Stamp; Photographer: Russell Porcas; Agency: Leo Burnett-London; Client: Mercedes Benz. **p. 349 Nike/Australia ad:** Courtesy Nike, Inc. **p. 351 Jeep ad:** Courtesy of Jeep. **p. 352 Nike ad:** Courtesy of Nike, Inc. **p. 354 Royal Life Life Insurance:** Courtesy Leo Burnett-Madrid. **p. 354 Red Chip Review ad:** Client: Red Chip Review; creative: Moffatt/Rosenthal Agency; illustration: Gary Houland. **p. 357 Taylor Guitar ad:** Agency: Franklin Stoorza; creative directors: John Vitro, John Robertson; art director: John Vitro; copywriter: John Robertson; photographers: Art Wolfe, Marshall Harrington. **p. 358 Tabasco ad:** Courtesy McIlhenny Company. **p. 359 Honda manual ad:** Courtesy Rubin Postaer & Associates; photography: Gary Hush Photography. **p. 357 Lexus ad:** Photography by Brett Froomer; agency: Team One Advertising.

Exhibits/Checklists/Ad Labs

AL11–B Shore's Lures: Courtesy Shore's Lures; agency: Birdsall Voss & Kloppenburg; creative director/copywriter: Gary Mueller; art director: Scott Krahn; photographer: Dick Baker. **AL11–C** The Creative Gymnasium: Exercises adapted from *A Kick in the Seat of the Pants* by Roger von Oech and George Willett. Copyright © 1986 by Roger von Oech. Reprinted by permission of HarperCollins Publishers, Inc.

Chapter Twelve

Photos/Ads

p. 371 Timberland ad: Courtesy of The Timberland Company. **p. 373 Pacific Bell/Willie Mays:** Copyright Pacific Bell. **p. 375 Muse Cordero Chen layouts:** Agency: Muse Cordero Chen, Inc./Los Angeles; creative director: Mike Whittlow; art director: Alfonso Covarrubias; copywriters: Chase Conerly, Jo Muse; production: Wilky Lau. **p. 378 Wallis ad:** Copyright Wallis. **p. 379 Stren fishing ad:** Mitch Sondreal/Ripsaw Inc. Photography. **p. 381 Yale New Haven:** Client: Hale New Haven Health System; agency: Katsin/Loeb Advertising, Inc. **p. 382 Allstate ad:** Courtesy The Allstate Insurance Company. **p. 383 Galaxy Army & Navy Stores:** Courtesy of Galaxy Army & Navy Stores. **p. 385 Bell Sport:** Courtesy of Goodby/Berlin & Silverstein. **pp. 386–89 Portfolio Review:** The Creative Director's Greatest Ads: **Norfolk Southern ad:** Courtesy of Norfolk Southern Corporation. **Shimano reels ad:** Courtesy of Shimano American Corporation. **Oneida ad:** Courtesy of Oneida Silversmiths. **Philips Petroleum ad:** Courtesy of Philips Petroleum Company. **Ricoh ad:** Permission granted by Ricoh Corporation. **Allen Edmonds ad:** Courtesy of Allen Edmonds. **Wrangler ad:** Courtesy of The Martin Agency. **p. 390 Nike ad:** Courtesy Nike, Inc. **p. 391 United Nations radio script:** Courtesy McCann-Erickson Worldwide. **p. 394 Ford Cool Planet:** Courtesy Ford Motor Company. **p. 396 Adidas soccer TV:** From concept through production of a magazine ad and television commercial: all visuals courtesy of Adidas; agency: Team One Advertising. **p. 397 Sprite TV spot:** Courtesy of The Coca-Cola Company. **p. 399 Korean Air (English):** Courtesy Korean Air; agency: Ogilvy & Mather/Los Angeles. **p. 399 Korean Air (Chinese):** Courtesy Korean Air: agency Ogilvy & Mather/Hong Kong. **p. 400 Schiesser ad:** Courtesy of RG Wiesmeier.

Exhibits/Checklists/Ad Labs

Checklist Writing effective copy: David L. Malickson and John W. Nason, excerpted from page 74 *Advertising: How to Write the Kind That Works.* © 1982 David L. Malickson and John W. Nason. Reprinted with permission of Charles Scribner's Sons; Jay Conrad Levinson, *Guerilla Advertising,* (New York: Houghton Mifflin, 1994), pp. 174–75; Neil Raphel and Murray Raphel, "Rules to Advertise By," *Progressive Grocer,* December 1993, pp. 13–14; William H. Motes, Chadwick B. Hilton, and John S. Fielden, "Language, Sentence, and Structural Variations in Print Advertising," *Journal of Advertising Research,* September/October 1992, pp. 63–77; and "Copy Chaser Criteria," *Business Marketing,* January 1991, p. 33. **Checklist** Creating effective radio commercials: Peter Hochstein, "Ten Rules for Making Better Radio Commercials," *Viewpoint III,* 1981. **Checklist** Creating effective TV commercials: Bruce Bendinger, *The Copy Workshop* (Chicago: The Copy Workshop, 1993), pp. 286–92; and David Ogilvy, *Ogilvy on Advertising* (New York: Random House, 1985), pp.103–13. **Ad Lab 12–B** Creative ways to sell on radio: Adapted from Wallace A. Ross and Bob Landers, "Commercial Categories," in *Radio Plays the Plaza* (New York: Radio Advertising Bureau, 1969). **Exhibit 12–4** Execution Spectrum: Courtesy Hank Seiden.

Chapter Thirteen

Photos/Ads

p. 405 Toyota 4Runner with kayak: Photographer Harry Vamos. **p. 407 Toyota ad:** 4Runner by Brian Trebelcock; Mountain/lake photo: Kathleen Norris Cook. **p. 410 www.excite Web site:** Excite, Excite Search, and the Excite Logo are trademarks of Excite, Inc. and may be registered in various jurisdictions. Excite screen display copyright 1995–1998 Excite, Inc.. **pp. 414–18 Portfolio Review:** Creative Department: From Concept through Production of a Magazine Ad and TV Commercial: **Toyota print production schedule:** Courtesy Saatchi & Saatchi/Los Angeles. **Toyota stock photo with retouching:** Courtesy Saatchi & Saatchi/Los Angeles. **Toyota**

4Runner photo: Courtesy Saatchi & Saatchi/Los Angeles. **Toyota approval form:** Courtesy Saatchi & Saatchi/Los Angeles. **Toyota mechanical:** Courtesy Saatchi & Saatchi/Los Angeles. **Toyota ad yellow:** Courtesy Saatchi & Saatchi/Los Angeles. **Toyota ad magenta:** Courtesy Saatchi & Saatchi/Los Angeles **Toyota ad cyan:** Courtesy Saatchi & Saatchi/Los Angeles. **Toyota ad black:** Courtesy Saatchi & Saatchi/Los Angeles. **Toyota ad CMYK:** Courtesy Saatchi & Saatchi/Los Angeles. **Toyota final approval:** Courtesy Saatchi & Saatchi/Los Angeles. **Toyota commercial script:** Courtesy Saatchi & Saatchi/Los Angeles. **Toyota Epiphany storyboard:** Courtesy Saatchi & Saatchi/Los Angeles. **Toyota Epiphany TV commercial:** Courtesy Saatchi & Saatchi/Los Angeles. **p. 420 Designer at computer:** John Thoeming. **p. 420 Designer at drawing board:** John Thoeming. **p. 421 Elena Ramirez:** Courtesy Elena Ramirez. **p. 421 Halftone screens:** John Patsch/Nawrocki Stock. **p. 426 Woman at audio console:** © Scott Wanner/Nawrocki Stock Photos. **p. 428 Sketch of car and man:** Courtesy: Saatchi & Saatchi/Los Angeles. **p. 428 Sketch of street scene:** Courtesy Saatchi & Saatchi/Los Angeles. **p. 430 Pepsi TV storyboard:** Courtesy Pepsi-Cola Company. **p. 433 Filming talk show photo:** Ron Sherman/Tony Stone Images. **p. 434 Toyota 4Runner TV:** Courtesy Toyota Motor Sales, U.S.A., Inc.; agency: Saatchi & Saatchi/Los Angeles. **p. 434 Gotcha commercial:** Courtesy Salisbury Communications. **p. 435 Toyota Web site:** Courtesy Toyota Motor Sales, U.S.A., Inc. **p. 436 www.hotwired Web site:** Courtesy HotWired

Exhibits/Checklists/AD Labs

Exhibit 13–2 TV commercial costs: Reprinted with permission from *Ad Age,* August 1, 1994. Copyright, Crain Communications, Inc. All rights reserved. **Exhibit 13–4** Background colors for Toyota ads: Courtesy Saatchi & Saatchi/Los Angeles. **Exhibit 13–6** Radio commercial production: Adapted with permission of Macmillan Publishing Co., Inc. from *Advertising,* by William M. Wellbacher, p. 273. Copyright 1962 by the Free Press.

Part Five

Photos/Ads

p. 441 Excite ad: Courtesy Ordiorne Wilde Narraway & Partners.

Chapter Fourteen

Photos/Ads

p. 443 Milk ad: Courtesy National Fluid Milk Processor Promotion board; agency: Bozell Worldwide, Inc. **p. 449 *Chicago* magazine cover:** Courtesy *Chicago* magazine. **pp. 450–53 Portfolio Review:** Outstanding Magazine Ads: **Nikon ad:** Courtesy Fallon McElligott. **Delta Blues Museum:** Client: Delta Blues Museum; agency: Lawler Ballard Van Durand, Birmingham, AL; writer: Steve Saari; art director: Chris Coles; photographers: Marion Post Wolcott (Library of Congress), John Dieter, John Rockwood. **Mongoose ad:** Agency: Riddell Advertising & Design; creative director/copywriter: Jim Hagar; art director: Jimmy Bonner; photographer: Dave Epperson. **Pioneer Electronics ad:** Image: Road Kill Diaries; photographer: Lars Topelmann; agency: BBDO West; client: Pioneer Electronics U.S.A. Inc. **Nissan ad:** © Nissan Motor Corporation South Africa. **Coleman ad:** Client: Coleman; agency: Martin/Williams. **Grand Canyon Trust ad:** Courtesy of Grand Canyon Trust. **p. 455 *Advertising Age* cover:** Courtesy *Advertising Age.* **p. 458 *Village Voice* ad:** Writer: Mikal Reich; art directors: Carol Holsinger, Gina Fortunato, David Cook; creative directors: Nick Cohen, David Cook; agency: Mad Dogs & Englishman. **p. 459 *USA Today* front page:** Copyright 1998, *USA Today.* Reprinted with permission. **p. 463 *Dallas Morning News* rate card:** Reprinted from May 1995, Newspaper Rates & Data, published by SRDS. **p. 465 Insertion order:** Courtesy of Newspaper Association of America. **p. 466 *Der Spiegel* cover:** © Der Spiegel. **p. 469 NAA Web site:** Courtesy Newspaper Association of America.

Exhibits/Checklists/Ad Labs

Exhibit 14–1 Top 10 U.S. magazine advertisers: Reprinted with permission from the September, 1997 issue of *Advertising Age International.* Copyright, Crain Communications, Inc. 1997. **Exhibit 14–2** Ad page position: Adapted from "Magazine Newsletter of Research," Magazine Publishers Association, vol. 8, no. 1. **Exhibit 14–3** Regional edition map: Courtesy the Reader's Digest Association. **Exhibit 14–4** Selected consumer magazine circulation and cost: Standard Rate and Data Service, May 1998. **Ad Lab 14–B** Innovations in magazine advertising. **HFC direct mail:** Courtesy of Intervisual Communications, Inc.

Chapter Fifteen

Photos/Ads

p. 473 Got milk? TV storyboard: Courtesy California Fluid Milk Processor Advisory Board. **p. 478 Nissan TV Storyboard:** All Nissan material used will be properly identified and credited as follows: "Copyright, Nissan (1997). Nissan and the Nissan logo are registered trademarks of Nissan." **p. 479 Campbell Soup:** Courtesy Campbell Soup Company, Camden, NJ. **p. 483 Lotto TV storyboard:** Courtesy Washington State Lottery. **p. 484 Infomercial:** Courtesy The Tyee Group. **p. 493 Got milk? radio spot:** Courtesy California Fluid Milk Processor Advisory Board. **p. 495 Radio Saigon poster:** BDDP, Mancebo, Kaye. **p. 499 Utah Transit Authority radio spot:** Courtesy of FJCNW&R Advertising.

Exhibits/Checklists/Ad Labs

Exhibit 15–3 TV influential medium: Reprinted with permission from *Ad Age,* September 23, 1992. Copyright, Crain Communications, Inc. All rights reserved. **Checklist** Broadcast TV advertising: Barry Monush, ed., *International Television and Video Almanac,* 40th ed. (New York: Quigley Publishing, 1995); Kevin Goldman, "Hollywood Is Expected to Seek Part of Networks' Ad Revenues," *The Wall Street Journal,* November 30, 1994, p. B8; and Kevin Goldman, "Cable-TV Ads Fight Satellite-Dish Threat," *The Wall Street Journal,* February 6, 1995, p. B8. **Exhibit 15–5** Top 10 cable TV network advertisers: Reprinted with permission from *Advertising Age,* September 29, 1993. Copyright, Crain Communications, Inc. All rights reserved. **Exhibit 15–6** Where money goes: Television Bureau of Advertising from data reported by CMR's MediaWatch service, April 1995. **Checklist** Cable TV advertising: "1991 Advertisers Guide to Cable," p. 21; David Samuel Barr, *Advertising on Cable: A Practical Guide for Users* (Englewood Cliffs, NJ: Prentice Hall, 1985), p. 71; and Judan Dagnoli, "Cable Test Hot-Wired to Consumer Preferences," *Advertising Age,* December 1, 1986, p. S10.

Ad Lab 15–A Nielsen people meter photo: Reprinted courtesy of Nielsen Media Research. TV ratings: Jack Z. Sissors and Lincoln Bumba, *Advertising Media Planning* (Lincolnwood, IL: NTC Business Books, 1993); Scott Hume, "Nielsen vs. IRI: Battle of the Research Titans," *Advertising Age,* October 12,1 992; and Jeanne Whalen, "Nielsen's Pricing Gets Look from Justice Dept.," *Advertising Age,* January 23, 1995, p. 38. **Exhibit 15–9** Source: Nielsen Media Research, Copyright 1997. **Exhibit 15–10** Market data from Nielsen Media Research: Reprinted courtesy of Nielsen Media Research. **Exhibit 15–11** Daily/weekly radio reach: Adapted from Radio Advertising Bureau data. **Exhibit 15–12** Imagery transfer: The Radio Network Association. **Exhibit 15–13** Radio station programming: "Percentage of Total Station Programming Each Format Type," *M Street Journal,* February 1993. **Exhibit 15–14** Mininetworks: Reprinted with permission from *Advertising Age,* 1995. Copyright, Crain Communications, Inc. All rights reserved. **Exhibit 15–15** Radio's top 10 national advertisers: Competitive Media Research. *Radio Marketing Guide and Fact Book for Advertisers:* 1993–1994, Radio Advertising Bureau.

Chapter Sixteen

Photos/Ads

p. 503 Ad Force Web site: Courtesy Imgis. **p. 504 amazon.com Web site:** Courtesy amazon.com. **p. 506–9 Portfolio Review:** Hot Web sites: **Playsite Web site:** © 1998 go2 Net, Inc. **jCrew Web site:** Courtesy jCrew. **Dow Web site:** Copyright 1997 The Dow Chemical Company. Used with permission. **New York Times Web site:** © 1998 The New York Times Company. Reprinted by permission. **Beatrice's Web site:** Courtesy Women.com Network. **UPS Web site:** Courtesy of United Parcel Service of America, Inc. **Dell Computer Web site:** Copyright 1998 Dell Computer Corporation. **MSNBC Web site:** Courtesy MSNBC on the Internet. **p. 511 Animal Planet Web site:** Courtesy Discovery Channel. **p. 511 Yahoo Web site:** Text and artwork copyright © 1998 by Yahoo! Inc. All rights reserved. Yahoo! and the Yahoo! logo are trademarks of Yahoo! Inc. **p. 512 PointCast Web site:** Courtesy of PointCast. **p. 515 Web TV® brochure:** Courtesy of Web TV® Networks. **p. 516 Banners:** Praco, Ltd. Advertising & Public Relations, Colorado Springs, CO. Praco Communications. **p. 519 Media Metrix Web site:** Courtesy Media Metrix. **p. 524 Excite French Web site:** Courtesy Excite, Inc. **p. 525 Kiosk:** Robert Daemmrich/Tony Stone Images. **p. 527 Webster Design campaign:** Courtesy Webster Design Associates; photo by Jack Whidden and Mary Zimmer.

Exhibits/Checklists/Ad Labs

Exhibit 16–1 Total online advertising and direct marketing revenues, 1996–2002: Jupiter Communications, Inc. **Exhibit 16–4** Activities people take time from to spend on the computer: Forrester Research, Inc. **Exhibit 16–5** Adoption curves for various media: Morgan Stanley Group, Inc. **Exhibit 16–6** The Direct Marketing Web Site (www.the-dma.org), Advertising expenditures by market, p. 1 of 2. **Exhibit 16–8** Internet advertising by top 50 advertisers: Forrester Research, Inc. **Exhibit 16–9** Top Web advertisers: Jupiter Communications, Inc. **Exhibit 16–11** Leading non-U.S. online ad markets in 1996: Jupiter Communications, Inc. **Exhibit 16–12** Total estimated world online ad revenue, 1997–2000: Jupiter Communications, Inc. **Exhibit 16–14** Top 10 mail order product categories: *The United States Mail Order Industry* by Maxwell Sroge, 2nd edition, 1994, published by NTC Business Books. **Exhibit 16–15** Doubleday Book Club: Direct Mail List Rates and Data (Consumer Lists), published by SRDS. **Ad Lab 16–B** Bistro cooking montage: Courtesy Air France USA; agency: Wunderman Cato Johnson.

Chapter Seventeen

Photos/Ads

p. 535 Garcia's Irish Pub billboard: Client: Garcia's Irish Pub; agency: Crowley/Webb & Associates; account executive: Joseph Crowley, Bart Tschamler; copywriter/creative director: Paul Cotter; art director: Jean Schweikhard; media director: Richard Spears. **p. 537 Louisville Zoo:** Courtesy of Doe-Anderson Advertising & Public Relations. **p. 538–41 Portfolio Review:** Out-of-Home Advertising: **Vauxhall:** Courtesy Lowe Howard-Spinks. **United Airlines ad:** Courtesy of Leo Burnett/London. **Pacific Science Center:** Courtesy Bozell Worldwide. **Mutual Community:** Courtesy Clemenger, Adelaide. **Antismoking billboard:** Courtesy of California Department of Health Services. **McDonald's billboard:** Courtesy DDB Needham/Sydney. **Brian Bohr Karate:** Courtesy of David Yang. **Guardian ad:** Courtesy of Leagas Delaney Partnership Ltd./London. **p. 544 Hong Kong night:** Nawrocki Stock Photos. **p. 548 Volvo billboard:** Courtesy of Veritas Advertising. **p. 549 DKNY ad:** Courtesy of Outdoor Systems Advertising. **p. 551 Shiseido packaging:** Courtesy of Shiseido Cosmetics (America) Ltd. **p. 552 Digital packaging:** Art directors: Bill Capers (Digital) and Robert Wood (Fitch Inc.); designers: Bill Capers, Weinda

O'Neill, Mary Bolsvert, Joe Pozerycki all from Digital, Robert Wood and Tammie Hunt from Fitch Inc.; studios: Digital (Industrial & Graphic Design Group) and Fitch Inc.; client: Digital Equipment Corporation. **p. 553 Reebok/Planet Reebok interior shots:** Courtesy of Reebok. **p. 555 Fossil watches with packaging:** Courtesy of Authentic Fossil. **p. 557 BMW roadster:** Courtesy of MGM/United Artists. **p. 557 ATM machine:** Poulides/Thatcher/Tony Stone Images.

Exhibits/Checklists/Ad Labs

Exhibit 17–1 Out-of-home media: Outdoor Services, Division of Western Media, New York, NY. **Exhibit 17–2** Outdoor ad expenditures: *Competitive Media Reporting*, presented by the Outdoor Advertising Association of America, Inc. **Checklist** Outdoor advertising: *Guide to Out-of-Home*, Gannett Outdoor Network, U.S.A., 1992, p. 21; and *Yellow Pages Industry Fact Book, 1994–1995 Edition* (Troy, MI: Yellow Pages Publishers Association, 1994), p. 16. **Ad Lab 17–A** Type and color in outdoor advertising: Outdoor Advertising Association of America, 1995. **Exhibit 17–3** Billboard locations: Courtesy Gannett Outdoor of Southern California. **Exhibit 17–4** Poster rates: Gannett Outdoor Network, U.S.A., *1995 Ratebook & Almanac*. **Exhibit 17–5** Packaging developments: W. Wossen Kassaye and Dharmendra Verma, "Balancing Traditional Packaging Functions with the New Green Packaging Concerns," *SAM Advanced Management Journal,* Autumn 1992, pp. 15–23. **Exhibit 17–6** Trade shows: Trade Show Bureau, Denver, Colorado. **Exhibit 17–7** Visitor waiting for sales rep: Allen Konopacki Incomm Research. **Exhibit 17–8** Yellow pages reach: Reprinted with permission of Yellow Pages Publishers Association (YPPA).

The Epilogue

p. 560 Toyota Portraits storyboard: Courtesy Toyota Motor Sales, U.S.A, Inc.; agency: Saatchi & Saatchi/Los Angeles. **p. 561 Toyota Camry ad:** Vic Huber Photography. **p. 563 Toyota ad:** Adventure Photo. **p. 565 Toyota RAV4 ad:** Todd Johnson. **p. 566 Toyota Affirmations ad:** Jeff Sedlik. **p. 567 Toyota Corolla TV storyboard:** Courtesy Toyota Motor Sales, U.S.A., Inc.; agency: Saatchi & Saatchi/Los Angeles. **p. 568 Toyota brand logos:** Courtesy Toyota Motor Sales, U.S.A., Inc.; agency: Saatchi & Saatchi/Los Angeles. **p. 568 Toyota.com Web site:** Courtesy Toyota Motor Sales, U.S.A., Inc. **p. 569 Toyota Sienna ad:** Sienna photo by Peter Rodger; Baby by American Stock Photo.

Reference Library

RL 1–2 Pioneers in advertising: "50 Who Made a Difference," 50 Years of TV Advertising, *Advertising Age Special Collector's Edition*, Spring 1995, p. 45. **RL 2–3** FTC complaint procedure: Gary Armstrong and Julie Ozanne, "An Evaluation of NAD/NARB Purpose and Performance," *Journal of Advertising* 12, no. 3 (1983), p. 24. Reprinted with permission. **RL 2–1** Advertising regulations in Europe: James Maxeiner and Peter Schoffhofer, eds., *Advertising Law in Europe and North America* (Deventer, The Netherlands: Kluwer Law and Taxation Publishers, 1992). **RL 6–1** Vitamin product marketing research: Adapted from Natalie Goldber, "How to Use External Data in Marketing Research," *Marketing Communication*, March 1980, pp. 76–82. **RL 7–1** Situation analysis: Adapted from Russel H. Colley, *Defining Advertising Goals for Measured Advertising Results* (New York: Association of National Advertisers, 1961), pp. 62–68. **RL 7–2** IMC builds relationships: Bill Davis, "Future Lies in Integrated Marketing, Not Communications," *Marketing News*, August 16, 1993, p. 2; Model adapted from Tom Duncan, "A Macro Model of Integrated Marketing Communication," paper presented to the Annual Conference of the American Academy of Advertising, Norfolk, VA, March 23–24, 1995, pp. 7–11; Tom Duncan, "Integrated Marketing? It's Synergy," *Advertising Age*, March 8, 1993, p. 22; Sandra Moriarty, "PR and IMC: The Benefits of Integrations," *Public Relations Quarterly*, Fall 1994, pp. 39–41; and Don E. Schultz, "How Communications Dis-Integrate," *Marketing News*, June 20, 1994, p. 12. **RL 8–2** Evaluation of advertising media: Adapted from Donald W. Jugenheimer and Peter B. Turk, *Advertising Media* (Columbia, OH: Grid Publishing, 1980), p. 90. **RL12–1** Motel 6 ad: Courtesy Motel 6. 3M ad: Courtesy 3M. **RL 13–1** Best printing method: From *How'd They Design and Print That?* copyright © 1991 by Wayne Robinson. Used with permission of North Light Books. **RL13–2** Heidelberg press: Courtesy Heidelberg. **RL 15–1** SRDS for radio station: *Spot Radio Rates & Data*, September 1, 1991, issued: published by Standard Rate & Data Service (SRDS). **RL 15–2** Arbitron listening rates: Courtesy The Arbitron Company. **RL 15–3** FCB spot commercial instructions: Courtesy Foote Cone & Belding, 1993. **RL 16–1** U.S. postal system: *Basic Product Information*, pamphlet printed by the United States Postal Service, 1995. **RL 17–1** Transit art sizes: Courtesy The Transit Advertising Association, Inc. **RL 17–3** Trade show budgeting checklist: Susan A. Friedmann, *Exhibiting at Trade Shows*, Crisp Publications, Inc., 1200 Hamilton Court, Menlo Park, California 94025; 800-442-7477.

Appendix D

Exhibit D–1 Careers in advertising: Updates based on data from *Advertising Age*, December 5, 1994, pp. S1-S12; and *Wall Street Journal National Business Employment Weekly—Jobs Rated Almanac*, 3rd ed. (New York: John Wiley & Sons, 1995).

Name Index

Company and Brand Index

Subject Index